IN THE RING

WITH

JACK DEMPSEY

Part II: 1919 - 1923

Adam J. Pollack

WIN BY
KO

Win By KO Publications

IOWA CITY

In the Ring With Jack Dempsey
Part II: 1919-1923

Adam J. Pollack

(ISBN-13): 978-1-949783-07-0

(hardcover: 50# acid-free alkaline paper)

Includes footnotes and index.

Cover design by Adam J. Pollack and Gwyneth Flowers ©

Cover photo colorizations by Gregory Speciale ©

Manufactured in the United States of America.

Win By KO Publications
Iowa City, Iowa
winbykopublications.com

CONTENTS

Life as the Champion

On July 4, 1919 in Toledo, Ohio, under a hot 95-degree-Fahrenheit sun, in one of the most vicious and exciting beatings anyone ever saw, 24-year-old Jack Dempsey won the world heavyweight championship from Jess Willard, who retired following the end of the 3rd round. Willard had been decked seven times in the 1st round, only being saved by the bell (which almost no one heard), out cold on the canvas at the round's conclusion, but gamely recuperated between rounds with the assistance of smelling salts (and possibly some extra recovery time, for Dempsey had left the ring, thinking that Willard had been counted out). Willard tried to fight back and survive, even landing some solid punches, but endured two more rounds of brutal blows before deciding that he had enough.

Dempsey's speed, two-fisted explosive power, fast feet in both circling and attacking relentlessly, and his head movement to elude blows, had inspired awe in those who had witnessed the carnage against a man who outweighed him by about 50 pounds. It was the first time in his career that Jess Willard ever had been down, including against the great Jack Johnson.

Not counting Dempsey's unofficial exhibitions, his official record included at least twenty 1st round knockouts in his career up to that point. He had knocked out experienced big men and strong punchers like Carl Morris, Gunboat Smith, Arthur Pelkey, Fred Fulton, and now Willard. Hence, at that point, many saw him as invincible, and already were comparing him favorably with past champions.

Following the victory, Dempsey's manager Jack Kearns struggled to haul the new champion through the admiring throngs that they encountered everywhere. Dempsey talked to everyone around him, and shook every hand thrust toward him. H. C. Hamilton said, "He is endearing himself more and more to Toledoans, the longer he stays. He will endear himself to people everywhere because that is his nature."

Dempsey was interested in fighting Georges Carpentier and Billy Miske, for there was money in those bouts, "and he never has shown any inclination to pass up money."[1]

---

[1] *Lincoln Star*, July 6, 1919.

As other former champions had, Dempsey and Kearns planned to capitalize on the championship with exhibitions and vaudeville, touring the country earning easy money by allowing folks to see him.

On July 6, 1919 at Chester Park in Cincinnati, Ohio, just two days after the fight, "Jack the Giant Killer" sparred 3 vigorous rounds with 230-pound Bill Tate, landing fearful stomach blows and frequently using his famous shift, left uppercut to the chin, and right to the heart. In the 2nd round, he decked Tate with an "inadvertent" blow to the chin.

Tate called Dempsey's punches "Big Berthas," for they were like the German Big Bertha naval artillery cannon that was used in the world war.

After the exhibition, films of Dempsey's training camp were shown. Folks in Ohio also could pay to see the films of the championship fight.

Jack said he would donate to the Toledo Salvation Army the 5-ounce gloves he wore for the big fight, even though he had been offered $1,000 for them.

DEMPSEY SHOWS BOYS HOW HE BEAT JESS

Jack Dempsey, telling group at Cincinnati how he dropped Willard.

Dempsey would perform in two exhibitions a day, for 15 minutes each, earning $1,000 a day for his work in Cincinnati that week.

Kearns accepted Otto Floto's $10,000 offer to Dempsey for a one-week contract to appear with his Sells-Floto Circus in August.

Kearns/Dempsey also planned to negotiate and sign a moving-picture contract once they arrived in Los Angeles.

Kearns received a $125,000 offer from promoter Cochran in Paris for a Dempsey fight against the winner of the contest between Georges Carpentier and Joe Beckett. Kearns said an international fight between Dempsey and Carpentier or Beckett would be an immense drawing card.

On July 9 in Cincinnati, in their 3 rounds, a vicious Dempsey swing to the chin decked Bill Tate, who finished the 3rd round on his feet. Tate had taken some stinging punishment.

Trainer Jimmy De Forest was going back home to Long Branch, New Jersey. He had tutored the champ for the past year, and believed he was entitled to some rest. It was said that De Forest had improved Dempsey and taught him the shift and other moves and blows.

De Forest said, "I am tired of training fighters. I have plenty to keep me the rest of my days. I have numerous other offers which I can accept, and after the engagement here this week I will return east, where I will rest awhile before taking up other work." He previously had been the athletic director at the Newark Progress Athletic Club, and had been asked to return. Jimmy did not say whether he would train Dempsey again, but his tone was in the negative. Reading between the lines, Kearns would have to offer him sufficient financial inducements to do so.

Dempsey was said to be very popular with women. He was asked to judge a bathing suit contest on July 11, and chose the winner.[2]

Moving picture magnates from the Pacific coast were making several offers to Dempsey.[3]

Jack appeared in ads for nuxated iron supplements, claiming it helped him win the championship. The ads ran in newspapers all over the country.

The *Cincinnati Enquirer* said although Willie Meehan had shaded Dempsey in 4 rounds, he would be a 10 to 1 shot in a championship battle against Dempsey, who in his present form would whip him as handily as he did Willard. Carpentier needed time to get sharp again after his military service.[4]

Henry E. Dougherty of the *Los Angeles Evening Express* predicted that Dempsey would be the most popular champion ever. He already was the idol of fight followers with his knockout wallop, and was a regular fellow with a smile and a warm handshake that generated enthusiasm among all with whom he mixed and mingled.

Dempsey was coming to Los Angeles as the most sought-after fighter in ring history. Bundles of offers were being shoved at him daily, according to his manager and pal Jack Kearns. "He has placed boxing back on the high pedestal that was once its portion."

The new champion was willing to fight, but planned to clean up a lot of coin in the process. He could realize on his title in multiple ways, including the movies, vaudeville, exhibitions, lectures, books, plays, and advertisements. Dougherty humorously said Jack also could be a bodyguard for millionaires, because not a burglar on earth would take a chance when he was around. Willard was lucky to get out of that fight alive.

Otto Floto said Dempsey had the best disposition of all champions. He would be as popular as or even more so than John L. Sullivan once was. Dempsey had a sunny disposition, whereas the Boston Strong Boy was gruff and surly with folks unless they were close or friendly to him. Dempsey could laugh, and was quite genial. He was level-headed. He did not hide his past, but was proud of his former hobo existence.

Dempsey planned to build his mother a comfortable home. "If I never do anything else I am going to put my mother beyond the pangs of want. It's the first big money I ever got my hands on, and it's going to be spent for a good cause."[5]

---

[2] *Cincinnati Enquirer*, July 7 - 12, 1919; *Brooklyn Daily Times*, June 30, 1919. Kearns allegedly had managed Jimmy Britt and Abe Attell at one time or another. Dempsey's final Cincinnati exhibition was on the 12th.
[3] *Dayton Herald*, July 18, 1919.
[4] *Cincinnati Enquirer*, July 13, 1919.
[5] *Los Angeles Evening Express*, July 16, 1919.

On July 17, Dempsey arrived in Los Angeles. Bellboys at the Van Nuys hotel found frequent occasion for trips to the 3rd floor, and many others were calling for that floor as well, for the hotel register had Jack Dempsey and Jack Kearns in rooms 304 and 305.[6]

Dempsey had asked the black porter to see to it that he not be disturbed or awakened. Many sportsmen wanted to go knock on his door, but the porter said, "Jest a minute, sah, don't do that. Mr. Dempsa left ordahs that he was not to be disturbed." "Oh, let us get him out." "No, sah, Mr. Dempsa ordahs are ordahs. If ah spoil his sleep and wake him ah go to sleep. Get away."

Former champion Jack McAuliffe said Dempsey hit like John L. Sullivan and Terry McGovern. He predicted a 10-year reign if he remained sharp and in top shape.[7]

Tex Rickard said, "There isn't a man in the world who can beat Jack Dempsey in a fight, no matter what the duration." No one had even the slightest chance against him. "I think he's the greatest of them all."[8]

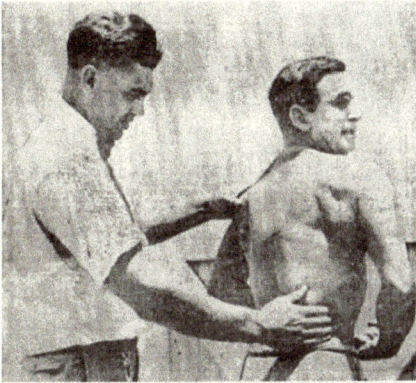

Dempsey examines movie star Douglas Fairbanks' back

Dempsey and Kearns visited movie star Douglas Fairbanks' movie studio. There was talk of Dempsey closing a deal to do a film with Charlie Chaplin and Fairbanks. (They eventually did a short together.) Early on, Jack enjoyed hobnobbing with movie stars and celebrities, which he would do often as champion.

Top to bottom: Dempsey, Douglas Fairbanks, and Charlie Chaplin

Kearns said they would fight Meehan if enough money was raised to warrant the match.

Kearns said Willard was the best man that Jack had met. Willard was prepared and in good shape, and would have beaten anyone else, including Billy Miske, but went up against the greatest two-handed fighter

[6] *Los Angeles Evening Express, Los Angeles Times,* July 17, 1919.
[7] *Dayton Herald,* July 17, 1919.
[8] *Brooklyn Daily Times,* July 18, 1919.

ever. "There isn't a man in the business today that would have a chance against Dempsey."

A reporter said there was a rumor going around that Dempsey was given cocaine before he entered the ring for a fight. Kearns replied, "I'd just like to have hold of the man that started that story. Why, it's nonsense. Dempsey is a clean-living young fellow with no bad habits. He doesn't drink, smoke, or chew. The dope story I brand as a malicious lie."

Jack loved to swim, and took a splash in the surf at 5 a.m. Kearns said Jack was a great big kid and as gentle as a lamb in all things but pugilism. "He loves to play with children and simply worships his mother."[9]

Former old-time fighter Jack Skelly said Dempsey and John L. Sullivan would have been evenly matched in 1888. "Dempsey is faster than Jim Corbett was when he defeated John L. Sullivan, and he is also a heavier hitter than was Bob Fitzsimmons."

The *Los Angeles Express*' Ring Cider said Dempsey liked to josh and fool around. He had a soft and sympathetic heart. He had no bad habits. He loved his art and wanted to be a fighting champion.

Ring Cider also reported that Dempsey said he had drawn the color line and would not meet a negro while champion. He would not jeopardize the crown to a black man while he reigned.[10]

On July 18, Dempsey arrived in San Francisco. That evening, at a boxing show at the Dreamland Pavilion, after being called upon to give a speech, Jack spoke to the crowd and received an ovation from the fans.

> Well, fellows, I'm mighty glad to be back here once more – back in the city where I began in the 4-round game. Everywhere I go I am asked, 'How does it feel to be champion?' I'll frankly say that I feel just the same as I used to when I fought in this same arena. Life isn't a bit different for me than it was before. I'm glad to be here, and I hope to be able to box here again for you.

Al C. Joy said, "As an orator Champion Jack Dempsey will never figure in the silver-tongue class. Yet he can stand right up in public and slam away with the king's English without leaving himself too wide open. His words are few and his sentences short, but in the little he has to say he manages to slip across a punch that scores a genuine knockout." Jack smiled and shook every hand he could reach. He struck one as being extremely human, natural, and likeable. Jack watched some bouts and then left.

In an interview, Dempsey admitted that he was not in a hurry to fight again, for he had fought all comers on the way up, and was going to make money out of the championship. "Why should I fight right away? This movie contract has been offered me, and in addition I have an offer of eight weeks in vaudeville and with a circus at $10,000 a week. No promoter of a fight would be able to show me any such money as that. I

[9] *Los Angeles Times*, July 18, 1919.
[10] *Los Angeles Express*, July 18, 19, 1919.

think I am entitled to get it while I can." Still, Dempsey also said, "I will fight anybody in the world any time the public demands." Meaning, if enough money was offered, greater than what he could earn at other endeavors, he would fight.

When asked what about Meehan, Kearns answered,

> Now, listen: Willie Meehan is well known here and is popular, and there is no question of his being a good fighter. But he doesn't stand so well in the East. He didn't make such a great showing there, and he isn't taken seriously as a contender. Mind you, we bar nobody. We'll be glad to take on Meehan, when it looks as though it would be a profitable match. But I think Willie should go out and win a couple of good matches first before he figures to be considered as a challenger.

Kearns noted that Meehan had lost to Miske and Greb (and Fulton as well), so he would be a tough sell to the public, particularly in the East. The 4-round game was too short for a championship, so there could not be a championship fight in California, where Meehan was popular, unless the law was changed.

Kearns said Carpentier appeared to be the most lucrative fight. He said Dempsey would be a popular champion because he would fight whomever the public demanded.

Kearns claimed that the movie industry was offering hundreds of thousands of dollars for Dempsey to star in movies with Chaplin and Fairbanks. Dempsey also had been offered $10,000 a week for a 40-week vaudeville show.[11]

While in town, Dempsey ate more food in one day, including steaks, than he did in three months back when he used to live in San Francisco.

Cleveland's Matt Hinkel (or Hinkle) was offering a $65,000 total purse for a 10-round Harry Greb vs. Dempsey fight on Labor Day. Cincinnati promoter Jimmy Shelvin also was trying to make a 15-round bout between them on the same date.[12]

The fight that would be the most lucrative, and therefore the one that Kearns/Dempsey most wanted, was against French and European champion Georges Carpentier. Carp was only a year and a half older than Dempsey. Yet, he was the far more experienced man, having started boxing as a 13-year-old, competing as an amateur featherweight even though he only weighed about 100 pounds. He began competing in 20-round professional contests as a 14-year-old. He won his pro debut in November 1908 via 13th round disqualification over Ed Salmon, but 29 days later, lost a rematch to Salmon via LTKOby18. Just imagine a 14-year-old today fighting 13 rounds in his pro debut and then 18 rounds in another fight less than a month later! In January 1909, just two days before his 15th birthday, Carpentier won a 15-round decision over Charles

[11] *San Francisco Examiner, San Francisco Chronicle,* July 19, 1919.
[12] *Pittsburgh Daily Post,* July 21, 1919.

Legrand, whom he fought to a 20-round draw the next month. To say that Carpentier was tough, talented, courageous, and willing is an understatement. He was fighting as a flyweight and bantamweight in 1909, including against grown men with far more experience. He was a lightweight in 1910.

In 1911, as a welterweight, American black Dixie Kid (56-23-14) stopped a 17-year-old Carpentier in the 5th round. Later that year, Georges won the European welterweight crown with a TKO10 over Young Joseph (86-14-20). He also had a 1911 W20 over Harry Lewis (101-35-25). Again, how many 17-year-olds today would or could fight 20-round bouts against grown men with over 100 fights of pro experience?

In 1912, Carpentier won the European middleweight championship with a KO2 Jim Sullivan (53-12-5), and also made a claim to the world middleweight championship. He even won a 20-round decision over highly respected American Willie Lewis (84-23-10).

In his next 1912 fight, although world middleweight champion Frank Klaus (61-12-13) weighed in 3 pounds over the middleweight limit, 18-year-old Carpentier fought him anyway, but was disqualified in the 19th round when his manager Francois Descamps entered the ring to protest what he claimed were fouls, though most thought it was done to save his fighter. Also in 1912, young middleweight Carpentier suffered an 18th round TKO loss to former world middleweight champion Billy Papke. Carp had been cut over his right eye in the 17th round, the blood rushing down his face, and his manager retired him in the corner at the bell to start the 18th round. That was his last stoppage loss. Carp had not been stopped since 1912, when he was an 18-year-old middleweight fighting world-class championship-level fighters.

A growing and maturing Carpentier moved up to light heavyweight and found even greater success, scoring a 1913 TKO8 Marcel Moreau (45-9) and KO2 Bandsman Dick Rice (32-6-4) to win the European and vacant IBU world light heavy crown.

Also in 1913, 19-year-old Carpentier won the European heavyweight title with a KO4 Bombardier Billy Wells (19-3), won a 20-round decision over very tough American Jeff Smith (33-8-1), and scored a KO1 over Wells in a rematch, despite a 17-pound weight disparity (Carpentier 172, Wells 189). He followed up with a KO2 Pat O'Keefe (74-23-7).

In 1914, 20-year-old 168 ½-pound Carpentier fought 184 ½-pound black Joe Jeannette (79-20-14), one of the world's best heavyweights, who had multiple fights with, and even some victories over, Sam Langford, Sam McVey, and Jack Johnson, and whom most top white heavyweights refused to fight. Although the courageous Carpentier lost a close and competitive 15-round decision, he managed to deck Jeannette in the 1st round, and showed that even with a weight, age, and quality experience disparity, he could compete against the world's best heavyweights. It was Carpentier's last loss up to the present (1919).

Also in 1914, 170-pound Carpentier won via 6th round disqualification over Gunboat Smith (48-9-5), who had victories over Frank Moran, Jess Willard, Jim Flynn, Carl Morris, Tony Ross, Sam Langford, and Arthur Pelkey. Carpentier danced in and out and drove in lightning-fast lefts to the face, and decked Smith in the 4th round with a body blow. In the 6th round, Carp missed a blow and went down, though some claimed he had been clipped on the jaw. Smith flagrantly hit Carpentier while he was down, and was disqualified.

Carpentier's last fight before entering the French military was a July 26, 1914 WDQ4 Kid Jackson, who was disqualified for hitting low.

Although during the Great World War he had boxed in the military and participated in many exhibitions, Carpentier had not competed in a formal pro fight in five years. He needed time to get sharp again.

On July 19, 1919 in Paris, France, still a young man at only age 25, weighing 171 ½ pounds, war veteran Georges Carpentier (76-11-5) had his first official comeback fight, knocking out former English champion 174-pound Dick Smith in the 8th round, outclassing him throughout to win the European heavyweight title and IBU light heavy title.[13]

Fight manager Leo P. Flynn claimed that Dempsey would fight Bill Brennan for around $50,000, in part to clear up things with John 'the Barber' Reisler, who would promote the match and then provide Jack with a quit-claim to his services, thus wiping out the controversy between them.[14]

Jack Skelly advised Dempsey not to take long layoffs, for remaining out of the ring too long had been one of the principal reasons for the downfall of many champions. He advised that three fights a year would be enough to keep a fighter sharp. However, economics and various other issues had kept many heavyweight champions out of the ring for great periods of time.

Bat Masterson said Dempsey would be the victim of pests. He would be pestered so often that he might begin to wish he had lost the title fight instead of winning it. Men, women, boys and girls all rushed him, grabbed him, hugged and kissed him.[15]

On July 21, Dempsey arrived in Salt Lake City, accompanied by Kearns. His chief purpose was to visit his mother, Mary Priscilla (a.k.a. Celia or Cecelia) Dempsey. He checked into the hotel Utah, then took a taxi to his mother's home, which he purchased for her about a year ago.

Jack said he would rather fight than anything else, but they were considering several lucrative motion picture and vaudeville propositions.

---

[13] Dick Smith had a 1918 W20 over Joe Beckett. A note about records herein, which primarily are taken from Boxrec.com. The website is a fantastic resource, but its records are in a constant state of flux owing to ongoing research. Fights can be added and/or subtracted, and results sometimes changed. The records herein are meant to give the reader a general sense of a fighter's experience.

[14] *San Francisco Examiner*, July 20, 1919.

[15] *Salt Lake Telegram*, July 19, 1919.

Still, they would entertain any fight offers from promoters. "Show me enough money and I'll fight anybody at any time." He said he wanted to be a fighting champion like John L. Sullivan. "I will fight any man who shows his head above the rest of the fighters." He most wanted to fight Carpentier, because big money was being offered for that fight. They already had received a $125,000 offer. Every morning they were flooded with new offers of every kind. When asked about the reports that he was matched to fight Bill Brennan for John the Barber, Dempsey laughed and said he had heard nothing about it.

At his mom's home at 3572 South State street, Dempsey played with a bulldog and two other dogs. The new champion said, "I expect to be the same Jack that I always was, and I haven't become swelled on myself one bit." However, he noted that he had found it necessary to "hide out" frequently to avoid all those who would pester him.

One visitor was Hardy K. Downing, the promoter who gave Jack his first fight. A friend asked, "Would you be willing to pay $2.50 for Jack's services now?" Downing responded, "That first $2.50 which Jack earned in his first fight for me has developed into a whole lot of dough since that time, hasn't it, Jack?"[16]

Jack McAuliffe, former lightweight champion, who used to travel with John L. Sullivan back in his day, said, "Jack Dempsey is the greatest heavyweight the world ever saw, with one exception – John L. Sullivan. Sullivan would have beaten Dempsey when John L. was at his best. The others would have been set-ups, virtually, for the new champion." McAuliffe said the perception of Sullivan as flat-footed was all wrong. Furthermore,

> Sullivan could hit with the same speed and snap as the youngster who defeated Willard, and he could punch with his right as well as his left. Dempsey can't.

> Sullivan didn't take care of himself. But while he was a fighter, there was no one who could stand before him. Dempsey would have given him a great fight, but he would have been beaten, for he would have run afoul of Sullivan's right hand. Then it would have been 'Home, James.'

> Dempsey's best hand is his left, and he pulls it from far back. Sullivan could stand flat-footed and knock the best man in the world down with a punch of six inches. No discredit to Dempsey here. He can beat any other man I ever saw. Corbett would have had no chance with him. He would have stopped Fitzsimmons or Jeffries or Johnson.[17]

Some criticized Dempsey's lack of war participation, saying he was unpatriotic. Dempsey replied,

[16] *Deseret News, Salt Lake Telegram*, July 21, 1919; *Salt Lake Tribune, Salt Lake Herald-Republican*, July 22, 1919.
[17] *Deseret Evening News*, July 22, 1919.

I tried to enlist in the navy, but was rejected because my left ear drum had been broke in a fight, and my right ear is also defective. I was placed in Class 4 by the draft board on this account, and since the country needed shipyard workers, I took a position in charge of employment of men at the Chester shipyard. Later I was reclassified in Class 2D, and was ready to join the colors any time Uncle Sam called.

He also noted that he raised money for the Red Cross, generating thousands of dollars in donations from his fights. Two of his brothers were in the service, and he was the main support for the family, including an invalid brother.[18]

THIS $20,000 home at 270 Center street was bought last week by Champion Jack Dempsey, and presented by him to his mother.

Dempsey purchased another Salt Lake City home for his mother, Celia Dempsey, for $20,000. Located at 270 Center street, the residence had eight rooms, was two stories in height, and three years old. It was equipped with a gymnasium, billiard room, shower baths, and a garage.[19]

On Friday July 25, 1919 in Salt Lake City, Utah, folks turned out en masse in the afternoon for "Dempsey day" at the baseball park, for the benefit of the Salvation Army drive. Jack helped raise over $1,000. There was wild applause when Dempsey and Kearns walked upon the field. Jack was introduced as Salt Lake's own, and both the town and he were proud of it. Jack gave a short speech in support of the Salvation Army, and then went into the crowd collecting

donations, accompanied by other donation collectors.[20]

Former champion James J. Jeffries said,

Despite all the men who have gone before him, Jack Dempsey is in line to make pugilistic history that will live forever. The record he has made in the last four years, with his sleep-producing punches, is one of the marvels of the prize ring and stamps him as a pugilist with hitting powers such as few champions have possessed.

[18] *Dayton Daily News*, July 22, 1919.
[19] *Salt Lake Telegram*, July 25, 1919; *Salt Lake Tribune*, July 27, 1919.
[20] *Salt Lake Telegram*, July 25, 26, 1919.

Many said Bob Fitzsimmons was the hardest puncher ever. Jeff said that as good as Fitzsimmons' record was, his list of knockouts was not as long as that which Dempsey had compiled in four short years.[21]

After taxes, Willard only earned $68,590 from the big fight. The Dempsey camp received $23,970.[22]

Former boxing champion Jimmy Britt rated Dempsey above all former heavyweight champions. Britt thought Jack was a wonderful fighter, and above all, he was a decent, likable fellow. But Jimmy also was friends with Corbett and Jeffries. Dempsey was a terrific puncher, had great speed, a peculiar crouching defense, and was capable of withstanding punches that would send an ordinary fighter into dreamland. He was the type of fighter produced only once in a century. Jim Corbett might outbox Jack in a limited-round contest, but in a long one, Dempsey would emerge victorious. Britt gave Dempsey the slight edge against Jeffries, owing to his superior speed. Dempsey was bigger and stronger than Fitz, at the very least his equal in power, but faster and set a better pace than Bob. Britt never saw Sullivan. "As for Johnson, I candidly believe that Dempsey would have beaten him down by sheer speed and punching ability combined with his indomitable do-or-die spirit."

Britt said it was a foregone conclusion that Dempsey would be a popular champion. "He is the style of battler the public likes – a battler who likes to battle." Because he was not a really big man like Jeffries and Willard, the public would give him even more credit for his achievements. "Aside from all this, Dempsey has a very pleasing and magnetic personality. He lets you know he is glad to meet you as soon as you shake hands with him. He bears his honors modestly and way down deep he is just a big good natured boy."[23]

On July 28, Dempsey and Kearns arrived in Chicago.

Jack wanted to have his nose operated upon. He had been bothered by incorrect breathing for many months. This explained why he often breathed through his mouth during fights, for he was unable to do so properly through his nose.

Dempsey was besieged with multiple offers, including $225,000 for 15 weeks as a stage actor, which was $15,000 per week. Already it was obvious that he would make a greater profit out of the title than any champion ever. Everyone wanted his services. Dempsey and Kearns agreed to the stage-work offer, which would begin on August 17.[24]

Serious race issues remained omnipresent, and likely percolated into the world of boxing, at least at its highest levels. During the summer of 1919, dozens of race riots erupted throughout the United States, in both the North and the South, making it become known as the Red Summer; for its hundreds of bloody deaths and massive property damage. Riots occurred in cities such as Bisbee, AZ, Charleston, SC, Chicago, IL, Elaine,

[21] *Deseret Evening News*, July 26, 1919.
[22] *Salt Lake Telegram*, July 28, 1919.
[23] *Salt Lake Telegram*, July 29, 1919.
[24] *Salt Lake Tribune*, July 29, 1919; *Chicago Tribune*, July 29-31, 1919; *San Francisco Chronicle*, August 3, 1919.

AR, Knoxville, TN, Longview, TX, Norfolk, VA, Omaha, NE, Washington, D.C., and many others, in states like Alabama, Arizona, Connecticut, Georgia, Illinois, Louisiana, Maryland, Mississippi, New York, Pennsylvania, South Carolina, Tennessee, Texas, and Virginia. In 1919, the revived Ku Klux Klan in the South committed at least 83 known lynchings.

One of the most serious race riots of the nearly 25 that that took place that summer occurred in the North, in Chicago's South Side, starting on July 27, 1919 and continuing until August 3. The National Guard eventually had to be called in. Well over 500 people were injured, 2/3 of the injured being black. 1,000 to 2,000, mostly black folk, lost their homes in fires. 38 people died, 23 black and 15 white.

It was part of a wave of intertwined racial- and labor-related violence caused by white anger at competition from black labor which had migrated in large numbers to the North from the South, as well as increased presence of blacks in or near white neighborhoods. White soldiers returning home from war did not appreciate the competition for their jobs and for homes. Blacks who had fought for the country wanted equal rights and treatment. The tensions eventually boiled over.

On July 27, Eugene Williams, a 17-year-old black youth, inadvertently drifted into a white swimming area at an informally/de facto segregated beach. One indignant white beachgoer threw rocks at him, one striking him, and preventing him from coming to shore, which caused him to drown. When blacks complained, and police refused to arrest the perpetrator, but instead arrested a black person, violence erupted between the two groups.

White gangs went into the "Black Belt," the negro district, attacked and shot at blacks, and started fires. The Chicago police turned a blind eye. The mayor refused to ask the governor for help for four days.

After the riots, even greater segregation resulted. Racial tension and segregation, whether de jure or de facto, was an omnipresent reality in both the North and South. Many private landowners in Northern towns had racial covenants in their deeds mandating racial segregation, which at that time was perfectly legal and enforceable.

Arriving in Benton Harbor, Michigan on July 30, Jack Dempsey told promoter Floyd Fitzsimmons that he would be ready to fight for him after his 4-month stage contract was over. "Fitzsimmons once did Dempsey a good turn and the champion wants to do something to square accounts." Jack enjoyed bathing in the Benton Harbor mineral baths.

On August 1 in South Bend, Indiana, Dempsey went to see a circus with Fitzsimmons. On August 3 in Michigan City, Indiana, Jack tossed the first ball at a baseball game, and after he threw a fast one over the plate, the spectators roared their approval.[25]

[25] *Benton Harbor News-Palladium*, July 31, August 2, 4, 6, 8, 1919; *Chicago Tribune*, August 1, 1919.

Chicago's *Collyer's Eye* said, "Jack may never fight a negro – he says he won't – but if he does this Wills person is just the one he'll have to beat."[26] Harry Wills had been the best black heavyweight for the past few years, but immediately after winning the title, Dempsey had drawn the color-line, just as Jess Willard had done. On July 4, 1919 in St. Louis, 30-year-old Wills had won an 8-round no decision over 33-year-old Sam Langford, decking him in the 3rd round with a left hook to the body.

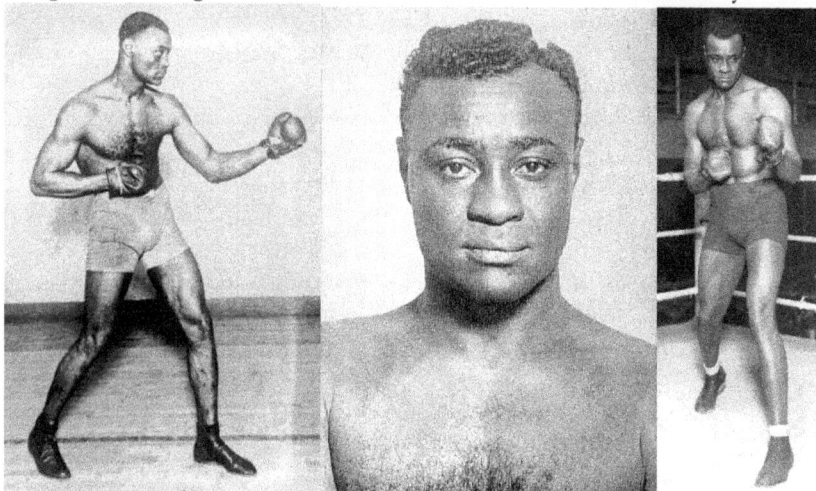

Sergeant Hank Gowdy, of 1914 World Series fame, noted that to equal Dempsey's future estimated profits from the heavyweight championship, a soldier would have to work for over 567 years.[27]

On August 9, 1919 in Grand Rapids, Michigan, Dempsey boxed with Denver Jack Geyer (28-17-6) in his debut with the Sells-Floto circus, a scheduled one-week appearance throughout Michigan and Indiana in which he would spar 3 or 4 exhibition rounds. He appeared in places like Kalamazoo on the 14th, Benton Harbor on the 15th, and Gary, Indiana on the 16th.

For the past week, the champ had been suffering from pain in his right ear, the result of an ulcer there, but he performed anyhow. Afterwards, he went to the hospital, where a doctor operated on it. Dempsey refused to take opiates for the pain.[28]

On August 10, 1919 in Nuevo Laredo, Mexico, 41-year-old former champion Jack Johnson won a 15-round decision over Tom Cowler (44-22-2), whom Miske and Fulton had stopped.

[26] *Collyer's Eye*, August 2, 1919.
[27] *Detroit Free Press*, August 10, 1919.
[28] *St. Joseph Herald-Press*, August 8, 1919; *Port Huron Times-Herald*, August 11, 1919.

On August 13, 1919 in Oakland, William LaRue dashed Willie Meehan's championship dreams, clearly beating Meehan from start to finish, boxing rings around him in all 4 rounds of their bout, hitting Willie with everything and receiving few in return, winning the decision.[29]

Although in the past year Meehan had beaten Jack Dempsey, Sam Langford, and Jeff Clark in 4-round bouts, he had lost to Fred Fulton, Harry Greb, Billy Miske, and now Bill LaRue.

Clay Turner said he had sparred with Dempsey so much that he believed he knew his every move. "Dempsey is a terrible hitter, I'll agree, but let me tell you more or less of a secret: Keep moving with Dempsey and he can't hurt you. If you don't get out of his way he'll crush you. His smashing rush is impossible to withstand." Turner advised - never allow Dempsey to get set for a punch, for the only way to beat him was to outstep him.

However, John Wray noted that Battling Levinsky had very fast footwork, faster than Turner, and yet he could not keep away from Dempsey. Meehan and Miske had survived by clinching, as well as moving, but no one thought they were better fighters than Dempsey.[30]

FOREST PARK **HIGHLANDS**

All This Week Each Afternoon and Eve.
The Mightiest Gladiator of All Ages

JACK DEMPSEY

World's Heavyweight Champion, and
His Manager, JACK KEARNS

with a de luxe entertainment of song, melody and mirth by world-renowned artists.

Prices—ONE DOLLAR. Special Ladies Matinee Every Day. Nights, $1, $1.50 and $2.

Admission to the Park FREE to 6 P. M. Night Admission, 10c

Seats now selling at Kieselhorst's, 1007 Olive St.; Stanley's, Eighteenth and Washington Ave.; Wolff-Wilson's, Seventh and Washington Ave.; Stanley's, 703 Olive St. Also at Forest Park Highlands.

Tour Direction:
Linick-Jacoby-Lichtenstein.

On August 17, 1919, Dempsey formally began a 15-week vaudeville career with the opening of a week's engagement at Forest Park, Highlands, in the St. Louis, Missouri area. Tickets were $1, $1.50, and $2. He exhibited in both the afternoon and evening, sparring 2 or 3 rounds each with Marty Cutler of Chicago and One Round Garrison of St. Louis. After Garrison tried to land a few stiff punches, Dempsey decked him with a blow to the jaw, but then helped him to his feet.

Crowds blocked the street, trailing Dempsey wherever he went.[31]

After a week in the St. Louis area, Jack planned to go to Detroit, Chicago, and Philadelphia, remaining on an eastern circuit. He would talk to the audience, introduce Kearns, and give an exhibition of boxing and shadow boxing.

On August 18, 1919 in Syracuse, New York, 30-year-old 205-pound Harry Wills (49-6-6) stopped 190-pound Jeff Clark (123-26-19) in the 4th round to retain his colored heavyweight crown. Wills decked Clark in the 1st round with a right uppercut to the head and left hook to the body, and thrice more in the 4th, until his seconds threw up the sponge. Wills utilized his terrible body punches, wicked right uppercut, left jabs, right hook, and punishing rabbit punches to outclass and batter the mostly covering-up Clark into submission.[32]

[29] *San Francisco Chronicle, San Francisco Examiner*, August 14, 1919.
[30] *St. Louis Post-Dispatch*, August 17, 1919.
[31] *St. Louis Star, St. Louis Daily Globe-Democrat, St. Louis Post-Dispatch*, August 18, 1919.
[32] *Syracuse Post-Standard, Syracuse Herald, Buffalo Commercial*, August 19, 1919.

In an interview with John Wray, Dempsey said,

> Meehan is just nothing at all. He has no punch, he is not a clever guy. He covers up like that One-Round Garrison did Sunday night. He doesn't fight, he slaps – he's a joke. Since he came East he has been shown up by Harry Greb and Billy Miske. Miske 'saved' him for Billy Gibson, or Meehan might have been knocked dizzy. Of course, I don't care if they match me with Meehan. The coin looks good to me. But it will be an awfully disappointing match and might hurt the game. Meehan is not a fighter and will not give a good exhibition.

Dempsey noted that he had a swollen hand going into their last bout. "Kearns had to promise Meehan that I would not knock him out before he would consent to the show." Jack still decked Meehan, but his hand went dead, and he eased up. "I didn't want to hurt him, anyhow."

When asked about Billy Miske, Dempsey said,

> Miske is a rugged fellow. He's hard to get at because he follows each lead with a clinch. He's tough, too. But he's not dangerous, and knocking him out would be just a question of how long before I could find an opening. They can't duck away from it forever – no man can stay away from me for 20 rounds without giving me a good opening.

Dempsey said Fulton could not think fast enough, though he didn't show enough in their short bout to let him know what he had. "From what I saw when I met him, he's a shining mark for a fast man with a punch."

The champ was not worried about the French/European champion either. "Carpentier, although a big money attraction, doesn't appear to be anything but a clever guy. American middleweights beat him. Gunboat Smith knocked him down." Jack said it was only a matter of time before he would get to him. "If they'll swap punches with me, that's what I want. I don't believe in delaying things any, although the further the fight goes the better I like it."

Kearns said Dempsey had both speed and cleverness. Many thought the fast, shifty, skillful Levinsky, with his fast feet and hands, would outbox Dempsey, as he had with so many others, but he could not do so.[33]

Grantland Rice said well-known heavyweights respected Dempsey's punch, and were not anxious to get into the ring with him. One told Rice confidentially that he could not stay away from Dempsey for even 15 seconds if Jack wanted to knock him out, and "neither could anyone else." Fred Fulton told intimate friends that he thought someone hit him with a crowbar, Dempsey hit so hard. Battling Levinsky said he didn't know what happened. "When I came to they were helping me out of the

[33] *St. Louis Post-Dispatch*, August 19, 1919.

ring. He must have hit me with a hammer. I'm supposed to be pretty fast, but he hit me so fast that I couldn't even see the punch start." Levinsky said although Dempsey appeared to be hittable, in order to hit Dempsey, one had to get close enough to hit him, but then Jack was in range to hit his foe too, and, "You know if he hits you once the fight is over. Feeling that way about it, there is no use stepping in unless you can hit him hard enough to knock him out, for if you step in and don't knock him out, you'll never know what happened until they carry you out of the ring." Dempsey hit so hard and fast that even really big men like Morris, Fulton, and Willard could not handle his power.[34]

On August 20, 1919 in Seattle, Washington, Willie Meehan and Ole Anderson boxed to a 4-round split draw, one judge voting for Meehan, one for Anderson, and another a draw. Local *Seattle Star* writer Leo Lassen believed that Anderson had the shade. "More than one fan at the ringside last night got a big giggle out of the thought of Meehan fighting Dempsey over a long route." Meehan was fast and his blows made a lot of noise, but Anderson said they didn't hurt at all. "How Meehan ever won from Dempsey in those two four-round fights is a riddle to me. Jack must have felt sorry for Willie because Meehan was so short and fat or else it must have been a pair of those San Francisco decisions after all." The *Vancouver Daily World* called Meehan a joke, and said Anderson won.[35]

Word from the West Coast about Meehan's clear defeat by Bill LaRue (and subsequent draw with Ole Anderson) proved that Dempsey was right about "Slapper" Willie. Dempsey called Meehan a "cheese fighter" who did not amount to anything. "He can't hit or box, and all he can do is cover, clinch and stall." Jack thought they would make a bad match, but if the money was right, and Kearns said the word, he would fight anyone.[36]

Heavyweight Bill Brennan and middleweight Harry Greb had fought three times, and were about to fight for a fourth time.

Of their February 10, 1919 bout in Syracuse, most reports said Greb won the 10-round no decision by outworking Brennan, while a minority of reports said Brennan won with his harder punches - heavy right uppercuts and body blows.

Of their March 17, 1919 10-round no decision rematch in Pittsburgh, Pennsylvania, Greb's hometown, Jim Jab said the local Greb was a shade winner by jumping, lunging, plunging, and throwing his fists here, there, and everywhere. Brennan hit harder, and was not affected by the blows, timing Greb's leads and landing rights and lefts, but Bill slowed his pace as the bout progressed.

Harry Keck said Greb tore in and outworked him in every round, winning decisively, though Brennan used his height, reach, weight, and strength to land straight punches better than any boxer Greb had met in a long time, as well as an occasional uppercut. However, Greb had a chin,

[34] *St. Louis Star*, August 20, 1919.
[35] *Seattle Star, Sacramento Star, Vancouver Daily World Victoria Daily Times*, August 21, 1919.
[36] *St. Louis Post-Dispatch*, August 24, 1919.

unstoppable attack, and great endurance, landing many more blows. No one could maintain his grueling pace. "He beat a heavyweight who, next to Dempsey, probably is the best man in his class in the country today."

Richard Guy said Greb beat Brennan to the punch most of the time with his speed, and never let up. Brennan landed some hard smashes, but Greb was on top of him all the time.

In their third fight, on July 4, 1919 in Tulsa, Oklahoma, the same day that Dempsey beat Willard, Greb won a 15-round decision over Brennan.

The *Tulsa Democrat* said Greb's jumping-jack slapping tactics earned him the points necessary to win decisions, but his hit-and-move style, with little punching power, failed to enthuse the spectators. "He is an expert tangoist and uses up much energy without netting results … For a victor he aroused about as little enthusiasm as any visitor ever shown here."

The *Tulsa Daily World* said Greb slashed, slapped, chopped, smashed, and slammed his way to victory with his speed. He moved continually and utilized a jumping-jack attack to outbox Brennan.[37]

On August 23, 1919 in Pittsburgh, 168-pound Harry Greb (133-10-14) beat 194-pound Bill Brennan (40-11-7) in a "sluggish" 10-round no decision bout.

The *Pittsburgh Post*'s "Gibby" scored it 6-2-2 for Greb, who piled up points with his left hand to the stomach and jaw, and an occasional solid right. Brennan staggered Greb in the 3rd round, and won the 6th, but tired in the latter part of the bout. Brennan was big,

Greb on left, Brennan on right

strong, and clever, had a nice left and heavy right, but he was not aggressive enough, though he was rugged and willing. Some thought Greb was affected by the heat and Brennan's size. Still, he did enough to earn a clear victory.

Jim Jab of the *Pittsburg Press* said Greb fought, while Brennan assimilated many smacks without return or even attempted block. Some wondered whether Brennan was stalling.

Harry Keck of the *Pittsburgh Gazette Times* said Greb won 9 rounds, and the other was even. Brennan had a stiff jab and hard right to the body, but Greb outpunched him by a wide margin.[38]

Jack Dempsey didn't relish speaking to crowds. He preferred to box. "I don't like this show stuff. I have stage fright every time I go to the front. I'd rather face a beating than that crowd."[39]

On August 24, 1919, Dempsey's vaudeville exhibition tour company was in Detroit, at the local opera house. His sparring partners included Canadian expeditionary heavyweight champ Jack Burke and Jack Doyle.

[37] *Buffalo Enquirer, Buffalo Commercial, Pittsburg Press, Elmira Star-Gazette*, February 11, 1919; *Pittsburg Press, Pittsburgh Post, Pittsburgh Gazette Times*, March 18, 1919; *Tulsa Democrat, Tulsa Daily World*, July 5, 1919.
[38] *Pittsburgh Post, Pittsburg Press Pittsburgh Gazette Times*, August 24, 1919. Greb was coming off a W15 Terry Keller just twelve days prior.
[39] *St. Louis Post-Dispatch*, August 24, 1919.

Kearns received a $175,000 offer for a Carpentier fight.

A $60,000 offer was made for Dempsey to fight Meehan in a 20-round bout in Reno.[40]

METROPOLITAN Opera House
Broad and Poplar Streets
Week Com. Mon. Evg., Sept. 8
Twice Daily Thereafter, 2.30 and 8.30
LINICK, JACOBY, LICHTENSTEIN present
J A C K
DEMPSEY
(HIMSELF)
WORLD'S HEAVYWEIGHT CHAMPION
7 SUPREMELY **Vaudeville Acts** 7
GOOD
NIGHTS, 50c to $1.50
MATINEES, 50c to $1.00
SEATS NOW SELLING

On September 8, the vaudeville show opened for a week in Philadelphia at the Metropolitan Opera House. Thousands saw Dempsey spar 3 rounds with Bill Tate.[41]

On September 9, 1919 in Oakland, Carl Morris scored a 2nd round knockout over Bill LaRue, the man who recently beat Meehan.

Dempsey temporarily ended his tour after only three weeks, some saying the ticket sales were disappointing, for the prices were too high and fans wanted to see him score knockouts, not engage in tame exhibitions. However, the real reason might have physical more than financial.[42]

On September 15, 1919 in Philadelphia, Dempsey underwent a nose operation. An injury received in a contest a year ago had been causing difficulty with his breathing. He was hoping to remedy it.

A $150,000 offer was made for Dempsey to fight English champ Joe Beckett, but Kearns said he first wanted to see what happened in the upcoming fight between Beckett and Carpentier. Beckett's representatives were presuming that he would beat Georges. The 24-year-old Beckett was a strong 190 pounds and fought like Dempsey. He was a rushing, tigerish, hard hitter. They did not think the smaller Carpentier could handle his power.[43]

The *Buffalo Commercial* reported that Dempsey's nose operation would put "the Toledo Terror" out of action for four months in order to heal, according to the doctor's orders. Jack said, "That operation he put me through was tougher to bear than any punishment to which I have been subjected in the ring. If the fight game was as hard as that I'd quit it mighty quick."[44]

Former champ James J. Corbett said Meehan's performance against LaRue put him out of the running, particularly since LaRue was stopped by Morris. Jim said the two men most qualified to battle Dempsey were Billy Miske and Bill Brennan, who put up the best fights against Dempsey since his re-ascendance in 1917. Miske had a baffling style, and Dempsey had been unable to knock him out. Dempsey stopped Brennan in 6 rounds, but Bill gave him a tough fight. Dempsey claimed he received more punishment from Brennan than he received in any five fights in the last two years. Brennan lasted longer than Fulton, Morris, and Willard combined, which gave him a lot of consideration. "At the present time

---

[40] *Chicago Tribune*, September 2, 6, 1919; *Reno Evening Gazette*, September 5, 1919. Dempsey was engaged for a two-day Milwaukee exhibition.
[41] *Philadelphia Evening Public Ledger*, September 9, 1919.
[42] *Philadelphia Public Ledger*, September 15, 1919; *Buffalo Commercial*, September 20, 1919.
[43] *New York Daily News*, *New York Herald*, September 16, 1919; *Brooklyn Daily Times*, September 23, 1919. Dempsey allegedly claimed that he could fight three men at once, Fulton, Carpentier, and Beckett, all in the same ring, and whip them simultaneously.
[44] *Buffalo Commercial*, September 24, 1919.

there are a number in the ranks of possibility, such as Beckett, Carpentier, Brennan, Miske, Willard, Moran, and Greb."[45]

When asked whether Dempsey could have beaten John L. Sullivan, Jim Corbett said there was no way to tell. "Dempsey is a wonderful fellow. He's the hardest hitter I think I ever saw, but he hasn't fought enough to give us a good line on him." It remained to be seen how good he was. He might lack something, or he might be the greatest heavyweight ever. "Sullivan in his day was a big, hard man. He was as tough as they came. He could take them on the chin or in the body and just hunger for more, and he could hit too. He hit like Dempsey."[46]

Robert Edgren said despite the fact that Carpentier was lightning-fast, flashy, clever, and a knockout puncher, the French war hero would be no match for Dempsey. The men against whom Carpentier had made his reputation would have been slaughtered by Dempsey. Georges still was only 170 pounds. The inactivity of the war years could not have helped him, despite his army exhibitions. He had declined to meet Jack Johnson back in 1914. The Dempsey whom Edgren saw at Toledo would have whipped Johnson in 2 or 3 rounds. Edgren said Dempsey-Carpentier would be cruel and senseless, and would end in a round if Dempsey went after him the way he did Willard.[47]

On September 29, 1919 in Spain, 172-pound Georges Carpentier knocked out 180 ¾-pound Jean Croissilles in the 2nd round.

Heading into the upcoming Wills-Langford fight, the *Ithaca Journal* said Wills had a record claimed to be as good as Dempsey's, and more than a few believed he could "take Dempsey's measure if they come together. One thing is certain and that is that Dempsey drew the color line."[48]

On September 30, 1919 in Syracuse, New York, Harry Wills (50-6-6) fought a 10-round no decision against Sam Langford (142-26-38).

The *Syracuse Journal* said Wills retained his crown on points, "but his margin of victory was not so very great as Sam displayed his usual science in the ring." "Wills tried everything that he had on Sam from uppercuts to smashes on the back of the head but old Sam never backed away from the man who towered a head over him." Only in the 6th round did Sam wobble, when Harry hit him with a wicked smash on the chin which drove him back to the ropes and forced him to hang on. Langford tried to overcome the height, reach, and weight advantages by parrying blows and sneaking in close to hammer away. "But Wills was stronger than Langford" and Sam had a hard time inflicting any punishment. This author did not believe Langford ever again would stop Wills, whereas Sam might be put away by "one of Harry's wicked blows." Langford said that after 17 years of fighting, he planned to retire soon. Weight estimates were Wills 215-220 and Langford around 195 pounds.

[45] *Binghamton Press*, September 25, 1919.
[46] *Ithaca Daily News*, September 30, 1919.
[47] *Pittsburgh Press*, September 28, 1919.
[48] *Ithaca Journal*, September 29, 1919.

The *Syracuse Herald*'s The Judge was not impressed. "Perhaps the world is wrong when they say Wills could give Jack Dempsey an argument. ... It isn't important whether Wills won or Langford won or it was a draw, or what. ... Tham's eye was closed and his mouth was cut. Wills suffered nothing more serious than a slightly damaged reputation."

Most dispatches said it was a disappointing draw. The *Ithaca Daily News* reported, "Wills was the master when he got a chance at long range, but Sam kept boring in and gave his taller and rangier opponent little opportunity to whale him effectively. At close quarters Langford gave about as good as he received."

The *Buffalo Evening News* said there was a time when it was claimed that Dempsey drew the color line because he was afraid of Wills. "Last night at Syracuse the best Wills could do with poor old Tham Langford was a draw in ten rounds. There must be some other reason for Dempsey's drawing the line." Others suspected that Wills had carried Sam, given that no white men would box him.[49]

From September 30, 1919 through October 1, 1919, Hoop Spur, Phillips County, near Elaine, Arkansas, was the site of one of the worst race riots ever, by far the deadliest racial confrontation in Arkansas history, and perhaps the bloodiest racial conflict in U.S. history. It much later became known as the Elaine Massacre.

Black sharecroppers were attempting to unionize and obtain from white plantation owners better pay for their cotton crops. They even hired a white lawyer to help them. Whites, fearful of what might happen if blacks organized, took violent action and began firing indiscriminately at and into the church where the meeting was taking place. Black veterans of World War I began firing back in self-defense, killing one white man.

False rumors of a black insurrection and plot to kill all whites spread quickly. White folk began shooting at every black person in the town: men, women, and children. Law enforcement was complicit and joined in. Federal troops were brought in at the request of Governor Charles Brough to put down the "Negro uprising" and "insurrection," and the troops slaughtered black folk with machine guns, including some who came out from hiding, thinking the troops were there to save them. Estimates of the number of blacks killed ranged from 100 to over 200, with only 5 whites (allegedly) losing their lives, with some whites being killed mistakenly by fellow white attackers in the posse. Many of the black folk who were captured were beaten, robbed, and tortured.

Over 100 blacks were prosecuted for various crimes associated with the riot. Newspapers published inflammatory articles. The subsequent trials, which featured all-white juries, confessions obtained by torture, and little to no legal representation or opportunity to present any defenses, testimony, or witnesses, in a lynch-mob atmosphere, quickly led to several convictions, 12 being sentenced to death, while the rest pled out, fearing

[49] *Syracuse Journal, Syracuse Herald, Ithaca Daily News, New York Herald, Binghamton Press, Buffalo Evening News*, October 1, 1919.

the death penalty or life in prison. Subsequent efforts were made to spread a false narrative and suppress the truth about the massacre, blaming the victims, and downplaying the number of deaths.

In February 1923, in *Moore v. Dempsey* (the keeper of the state penitentiary), 261 U.S. 86 (1923), the U.S. Supreme Court would overturn several of the Elaine convictions for the utter lack of procedural due process, including the use of confessions obtained via the use of torture, and trials held under mob domination.

One of the two dissenting justices was well-known for his bigotry; Justice James McReynolds, who back in 1913 had been the U.S. Attorney General under President Woodrow Wilson at the time that Jack Johnson was prosecuted federally under the White Slave Traffic Act. McReynolds had requested that Johnson be sent to the maximum-security Leavenworth penitentiary instead of the usual Joliet institution, a "special designation" for that case only, a request which Judge Carpenter granted.

On October 3, 1919, Jack Dempsey was in Chicago to attend a World Series game, won by the Chicago White Sox 3-0, winning their first game of the series after losing the first two games in Cincinnati to the Reds.[50]

The underdog Reds would go up 4 games to 1 in the best-of-9-game series, and ultimately win the World Series 5 games to 3 in an upset.

After the series was over on October 9, many, including Hugh Fullerton, suspected that the White Sox had thrown games and the series. Such stories had been circulated even during the series. Fullerton said the world series should be called off in the future. "Today's game in all probability is the last that ever will be played in any world's series. If the club owners and those who have the interests of the game at heart have listened during this series they will call off the annual inter-league contests. If they value the good name of the sport they will do so beyond doubt."[51]

Jack Dempsey arrived in Fort Worth, Texas on October 5, for he had re-joined the Sells-Floto circus, scheduled to begin in Ballinger, Texas on October 6 for a five-week engagement, despite the fact that he recently had nose surgery and only recovered for a few weeks.[52]

The Sells-Floto circus would tour the South - throughout Texas, Louisiana, Mississippi, Georgia, Alabama, Arkansas, etc. Jack would exhibit and demonstrate the punches he used to win the championship.

Dempsey said he expected his next fight to be with the winner of Carpentier-Beckett, given that it was between the French and English champions. "I never saw either man. Carpentier served in the French army. He was an aviator. ... I have been guaranteed $175,000."

Jack said surgeons had removed a handful of broken bones from his nasal appendage, which had been smashed in various contests. The nose damage had interfered with his breathing, which is why he often fought

[50] *Chicago Tribune*, October 4, 1919.
[51] *Atlanta Constitution*, October 10, 1919.
[52] *Chicago Tribune*, October 2, 1919.

with his mouth open. "I could not breath through my nose. The obstruction finally became serious and surgeons insisted that I must have the broken bones removed."[53]

When speaking with Vincent Treanor, Dempsey asked about an up-and-coming light heavyweight who had won the U.S. military championship, named Gene Tunney.

> He seemed very much interested in the reports about Gene Tunney, who came back from the war with the A. E. F. heavyweight championship hanging on his belt. He wanted to know if Tunney was a good fighter, and expressed a desire to have him down at Long Branch at his training quarters. We told him that Tunney might lick him in a year or so and rob him of his championship, to which Jack promptly replied that he didn't care as long as Gene happened to be a good American soldier. Tunney, by the way, is the most logical successor to Dempsey in the country at the present time.[54]

JACK DEMPSEY, NEW WORLD'S HEAVYWEIGHT CHAMPION, IS FOND OF PETS OF ALL KINDS

Dempsey with Otto Floto

Dempsey's circus contract called for an alleged total of eight weeks of work at $2,000 or $4,000 per week (depending on the source). He would not fight again until 1920. "Dempsey's promise of lots of activity in the heavyweight class seems to have been forgotten." However, others noted that he was on his way to becoming the richest boxer ever.

Kearns said the circus season ended in early November, after which Jack would go to the West coast to figure in two Pathe movie pictures.[55]

Charles Mathison said Harry Wills was the ablest negro boxer since the days of Peter Jackson. He was splendidly proportioned, had flexible muscles, and was one of the world's most scientific boxers. Although Langford and Jeannette were past their primes, they still were formidable fighters, so any victories over them were and would be significant.

Many conceded Wills a chance against Dempsey, and possibly even superiority. "The writer does not share that opinion, believing that Dempsey's speed and hitting would more than offset the boxing skill and long reach of Wills." However, Jack Kearns had "drawn the color line," in conformity with precedent, so there was no prospect of the two meeting.[56]

On October 20, 1919 at the Armory in Jersey City, New Jersey, 209-pound Harry Wills won an 8-round no decision over 204-pound Joe

[53] *Fort Worth Record*, October 6, 1919.
[54] *Tacoma News Tribune*, October 15, 1919.
[55] *Wilkes-Barre Times-Leader, Sioux City Journal*, October 15, 1919; *St. Louis Post-Dispatch*, October 16, 1919.
[56] *New York Herald*, October 19, 1919; *Buffalo Courier*, October 23, 1919.

Jeannette (118-25-19), outfighting him in every round. Joe was inclined to hold on throughout, which made the contest relatively dull. In the 2nd round, when they were coming out of a clinch, Wills decked Joe with a blow to the chin for a nine-count. Jeannette again went down in the 8th, though he rose quickly. Wills pummeled him with terrific stomach blows at close quarters.

On that same card, 196-pound Bill Brennan won an 8-round no decision over 171 or 173-pound Dan O'Dowd, handing him a bad beating and nearly stopping him.[57]

Len Wooster of the *Brooklyn Daily Times* wrote that there were not more than three or four fighters considered to have any chance with Dempsey: Joe Beckett, Fred Fulton, Harry Wills, and possibly Willie Meehan. This writer called Bill Brennan a "newspaper-made champion."

> By comparison with Wills, Brennan is a joke. The negro could pack a ring with the Brennan kind and pick them off one after the other with his skill and punch. Wills is the cleverest heavyweight we know anything about. He is greater than Dempsey in that respect and superior to Fulton in all around ability. The wallop of Dempsey and Fulton might flatten him if it landed but the pair of them would have a merry old time of it to drop it on the scientific black. Wills, however, is not accepted as a heavyweight contender. Because of his color it is presumed Dempsey will have nothing to do with Wills except as a sparring partner. ... Dempsey doubtless will follow the policy of his predecessors.[58]

The *Buffalo Courier* agreed, "Wills is a great fighter and would be a worthy foe for Jack Dempsey, if Dempsey would meet him."[59]

One New York fistic authority said Wills' recent performance in beating Jeannette in Jersey City proved why it was that the white heavyweights gave him a wide berth. "The crowd hooted and hissed the efforts of Wills only because he allowed Jeanette to stay the eight rounds and in doing so won some antagonism, but he surely showed that he towers above any other man in the ring as far as scientific boxing is concerned." Wills had a very good defense, cleverness, as well as every punch. "Dempsey has drawn the color line and refuses to have anything to do with Wills. From what was observed at this fight it is just as well that Dempsey bothers only with white heavyweights."[60]

Kearns said Dempsey was in wonderful condition. "He is boxing with Bill Tate and a couple of other big, husky sparring partners, twice daily, and is ready to fight on ten days' notice." Kearns would consider all offers.[61]

Otto Floto said Dempsey was too good for the sparring partners he met in his circus act. It was hard for him to go easy. When he first joined

[57] *Long Branch Daily Record, Paterson Evening News, New York Herald, New York Daily News, Brooklyn Daily Times*, October 21, 1919.
[58] *Brooklyn Daily Times*, October 23, 1919.
[59] *Buffalo Courier*, October 23, 1919.
[60] *El Paso Herald*, October 31, 1919.
[61] *Dayton Daily News*, October 24, 1919.

the show, they used 8-ounce gym gloves, but there were too many knockouts to keep a supply of partners. Now he was wearing 24-ounce gloves specially constructed for him. "And Big Bill Tate, the Alabama negro…is the only man we can find tough enough to give Jack an argument even when he is armed with these pillows." Floto said Dempsey was "proving a tremendous attraction."[62]

Dempsey told Will Hamilton in New Orleans that he was eager to fight again. "I will not care who my opponent is or how long the fight is to be." He wanted a rest from the circus life, for it was wearing on him. "Irregular eating and sleeping do not make a hit with me. Otherwise it's all right for a while."

Dempsey did not have the roughness or gruffness that characterized the speech and manner of Jeffries, nor the evasiveness of Willard. "He's a straighter and better talker than was either of his last two predecessors. And when he gets on a subject he likes he is buoyant, enthusiastic." He was not conceited or a braggart. Jack was 190 pounds of solid muscle.[63]

While the champ was in Atlanta, Floto predicted that Dempsey would fight sometime before April 1920. His contract called for another 33 weeks with the circus beginning on April 5, 1920. Hence, he likely would fight sometime in the first four months of 1920, after he concluded his circus tour in November and his motion picture work. "And Jack is eager to fight. … The title holder is a clean liver, a hard worker, and a natural-born athlete. Did you know that Dempsey is a corking-good football and baseball player and a fast sprinter?" He likely would fight Joe Beckett, for whom an offer of $150,000 had been made by Dominick Tortorich of New Orleans.

Kearns said, "Money is the thing we're after. … If they'll pay the price, Dempsey will take the chance. That's fair enough, isn't it?"[64]

While in Jackson, Mississippi, Dempsey said he was signed to fight Joe Beckett on March 17, 1920 in New Orleans for a 20-round contest for $125,000, if Joe beat Carpentier in December. If Beckett lost, Kearns would try to sign a fight with Carpentier instead. Jack said, "I believe in going after these fellows while I can trim them or while I think I can trim them."

Dempsey said he had improved greatly as a fighter, in part by watching others and studying their styles and methods. "I don't reckon there ever was a bigger boob in the boxing game than I was when I started out. I could always hit hard but I didn't know the slightest thing about defense and I was just a punching bag for everybody." Jack said he took a great punch. "I've stopped some stingers with my chin, but I never feel a blow. That is, I never feel the hurt of one."

[62] *Birmingham News*, October 28, 1919.
[63] *Arkansas Democrat*, October 29, 1919.
[64] *Atlanta Constitution, Arkansas Democrat*, October 31, 1919.

Regarding his manager, Dempsey said, "Kearns and I have been the closest of friends for several years. We understand each other, and 'Doc' (that's what I call him) is surely some manager. The fight world knows that." (Dempsey called Kearns 'Doc' because he was so smart it was like he had a doctorate in boxing. He was the fight doctor.)

Dempsey said he was born on a farm in Colorado about 40 miles from Denver. His folks lived in Salt Lake City now. "I've got a wonderful mother and father, you know." Jack did not smoke or drink, and never cared for either. He got along well with the 700 employees and members of the circus. "We have great times. It's like being one of a big, happy family." He liked the elephants. "I often ride in the parade, made up as a clown. ... Of course, nobody recognizes me in chalk face." Jack sparred twice a day with Bill Tate, which kept him fit. "Tate can take them."[65]

On November 5, 1919 in Tulsa, Oklahoma, Harry Wills won a 15-round decision over Sam Langford in a contest for the world negro heavyweight title. The *Tulsa Daily World's* Larry Dailey scored it 8-1-6. Wills won the 1st through 3rd, 7th through 10th, and 14th. Langford only won the 5th, while the rest were even. "Langford fought with all the cunning and craft of his long career but it was unavailing against the cleverness and accurate hitting powers of Wills." Youth won over age. "Wills, just at his prime, combined all necessary requisites for a champion, size, hitting power, cleverness, and stamina." He also had the longer reach and a slight weight advantage. Harry hurt Sam in the 8th round, but Langford covered and held well to survive the round, the only time that a knockout seemed on the horizon.[66]

John Wray said Dempsey's initial theatrical tour had closed after only three weeks. It had not been as profitable as expected, but nevertheless, drew about $15,000 per week. The circus tour had done much better. Floto claimed that Dempsey was paid $4,000 per week. It was estimated that Jack had earned about $27,500 from his fight purse with Willard, $45,000 in theatrical guarantees, and $32,000 with the circus. Even splitting those amounts 50-50 with Jack Kearns, he still was earning a lot of money. He could have earned $25,000 for an 8-round bout at Newark with Meehan, and there were several other offers for $25,000 and $50,000 for fights, but Kearns passed them all up, wanting to earn the easy money before accepting a big payday fight with the winner of Beckett-Carpentier.[67]

Henry Loesch of the *Arkansas Gazette* said Dempsey looked like a young fullback on a college football team. He was hungry to fight again, and did not enjoy the wait between bouts. He was very confident, but had a pleasing personality. He was easy to meet and a good entertainer. He preferred not to talk about himself.

Dempsey was a little fellow compared with the giant he toppled. At 212 pounds, his size did not impress one, and probably there were a half-

[65] *Jackson Daily News*, November 6, 1919.
[66] *Tulsa Daily World*, November 6, 1919.
[67] *St. Louis Post-Dispatch*, November 12, 1919.

dozen men in the hotel lobby who were bigger than he. When Jack went home after winning the crown, his father looked him over and remarked, "Somehow you don't look like a champion to me, but I guess you are." The general public had the same notion about him unless and until they saw him perform in the ring. "It is that terrible kick he carries in both hands that makes him look big."

Jack's ankle or foot had been injured when one of the portable circus rings gave way and an iron post crashed down on top of his leg, gashing it, requiring three stitches. He was limping slightly, but would recover.[68]

Dempsey stopped off at Salt Lake City on November 16 to spend a few days with his mother. He was on his way to Los Angeles, where he would fulfill a lucrative $100,000 movie contract until the spring, when he planned to fight again.[69]

On November 20, 1919 in San Francisco, Harry Wills stopped K.O. Kruvosky in the 1st round, a right to the jaw doing the trick. "Willis is so good that it will be difficult to dig up a man who can give him even a tryout. The big negro shapes up about 100 per cent better than he did when he was here five years ago."

Perhaps of some significance, Kruvosky was the first white fighter to take on Wills in five years, since October 1914 (also in San Francisco).[70]

Dempsey stopped off at Provo, Utah, where he was greeted by a number of the boys with whom he used to box. Otto Olsen, one of his earliest managers, was among those who greeted him.[71]

On November 25, Dempsey and Kearns arrived in Los Angeles. At a boxing show in Vernon that evening, Dempsey was introduced, along with Jim Jeffries, Jim Corbett, Kid McCoy, Jack Kearns, Leach Cross, and Charlie Eyton, and all received roof-raising bursts of applause.[72]

On December 1, 1919 in New Orleans, Bill Brennan knocked out 87-fight veteran Tom McMahon in 2 rounds. Back in 1914, McMahon had won a 12-round no decision over Jess Willard.

John Dempsey, the champ's brother, and Jerry Timmons, Jack's brother-in-law, visited Jack. They were going to Fort Worth to look over 1,200 acres which Kearns and Dempsey had purchased. Apparently, oil had been discovered there.[73]

On December 4, 1919 in London, England, 169-pound French champion Georges Carpentier (78-11-5) once again firmly established his European heavyweight championship by knocking out the British champ, 184-pound Joe Beckett (35-8), in 74 seconds of the 1st round, with a right to the jaw.

The larger Beckett was similar in size to Dempsey, 15 pounds bigger than Georges, had been active during the war years, and had impressive recent results, including 1919 TKO5 Harry Reeve (56-17-8), KO5

---

[68] *Arkansas Gazette*, November 13, 1919. Jack left Little Rock on the 13th to head to Kansas City.
[69] *Salt Lake Telegram, Salt Lake Tribune*, November 17, 1919. Dempsey and Kearns planned to go on a bear-hunting trip on the 20th. *Deseret News*, November 19, 1919.
[70] *San Francisco Examiner, San Francisco Chronicle*, November 21, 1919.
[71] *Deseret News*, November 22, 1919.
[72] *Los Angeles Times*, November 26, 1919.
[73] *Los Angeles Evening Express*, December 2, 1919.

Bombardier Billy Wells (39-6), and KO17 Eddie McGoorty (88-17-15), but it did not matter. The talented Carpentier was too fast and powerful.

Georges Carpentier had a mighty crack, and was very fast on his feet, dancing in and out with lightning swiftness. The impressive victory further enhanced the international desire to see him in the ring with Dempsey.

Carpentier, New Champ

Dempsey said of Carpentier, "I am ready for him or any other fighter in the world. They all look alike to me. I whipped the biggest man that has entered the ring in many years when I beat Willard, and therefore I don't think I would have much trouble in defeating Carpentier. I would rather fight than eat." Jack said his movie contract expired on March 1, and he wanted to fight soon thereafter, perhaps in April.[74]

Also on December 4, in San Francisco, Harry Wills stopped Ole Anderson in the 3rd round, pummeling his body unmercifully, and then rocking him to the jaw, until the referee stopped it. Anderson recently had fought Meehan to a draw.[75]

Harry Greb, who was coming off of 10-round no decision victories over 174-pound Clay Turner (Greb 167) and 162-pound Mike McTigue (Greb 162), said he seldom weighed over 170 pounds even when not in training, and would post a $2,500 forfeit to make 160 pounds at ringside for a world middleweight championship fight with champion Mike O'Dowd.

Clay Turner said Greb was a dauntless, untiring fighter with greater skill than most credited him, and was hard to hurt. "Too bad Harry hasn't twenty more pounds of beef and the strength that would naturally go with it. He would be a much better match for Dempsey than Carpentier." Only Greb's naturally small size held him back.[76]

Dempsey said that according to the reports, Carpentier showed all of his old-time speed and boxing ability against Beckett. He didn't have to show condition, but supposedly he went 20 rounds in training without trouble. "I suppose they will fix up a fight between Carpentier and myself sometime. I haven't the least idea when. I've noticed in the past that fights are more easily talked about than arranged." Jack expected to win, but was

[74] *Los Angeles Times*, December 5, 1919.
[75] *San Francisco Examiner, San Francisco Chronicle*, December 5, 1919.
[76] *Binghamton Press, Buffalo Express, Buffalo Courier*, December 13, 1919; *Buffalo Courier*, December 12, 1919.

not underestimating him, or any opponent. "I suppose that some day a big young fellow will come along and topple me over. I'm only human and it happens to all of them sooner or later. Judging from the way I feel these days I rather think it will be later in my case." Jack thought he could reign for a decade.[77]

Robert Edgren believed that soft living could have an adverse effect on Dempsey's career. Such a lifestyle came with rapidly acquired wealth. He advised Jack to be careful to take care of himself and not lay off for too long.[78]

The shooting of Dempsey's 15-episode western serial was set to begin in mid-December at the Brunton studios. He allegedly would receive $185,000. He would work with former fighter Al Kaufman in the episodes, amongst many others.[79]

Kearns believed Dempsey would earn at least $300,000 for a Carpentier fight. Georges had been offered $150,000. Promoter DeCoin in Paris was offering $250,000.[80]

On December 16, 1919 in Jersey City, in his first bout in the U.S. since returning from overseas military duty, 175-pound Gene Tunney (19-0-2) decisively won an 8-round no decision over 170-pound Dan O'Dowd. The *Brooklyn Daily Times* said, "The ex-soldier displayed wonderful speed and hitting ability and if properly handled, may make the topnotchers hustle to beat him." O'Dowd "could not penetrate the almost perfect defense of the Greenwich Village lad. Tunney jabbed with his left in a manner that would do credit to a McCoy, and his right-cross had the force of a Jeffries." The *New York Evening World* said Tunney had all the earmarks of a comer. "Tunney has everything but experience in finishing an opponent."[81]

New York native Tunney had been boxing since about 1915 (age 18), with the New York papers noting a July 21, 1916 10-round newspaper draw with KO Jaffe.[82] His military-service boxing-bouts included 1918 D10 Tommy Gavigan; and 1919 W4 Bob Martin and W10 KO Sullivan. On April 26, 1919 in Paris, France, Tunney had made a name for himself by winning the light heavyweight championship of the American Expeditionary Forces (A.E.F.) with a 10-round decision over Ted Jamieson; a fight that was filmed. The films show that at one point, Tunney scored a flash knockdown with his right, in a scrappy and entertaining fight.

On December 21, 1919 at Washington Park in Los Angeles, in a big benefit for orphans, Jack Dempsey refereed a wrestling bout.[83]

On December 22, 1919 in Philadelphia, Harry Greb won a 6-round no decision over light heavy Clay Turner in what was called a relatively tame bout. "If Greb possessed a really powerful wallop he should have

[77] *Los Angeles Evening Express*, December 12, 1919.
[78] *Los Angeles Evening Express*, December 13, 1919.
[79] *Los Angeles Times*, December 14, 1919.
[80] *Los Angeles Evening Express*, December 15, 1919; *New York Evening World*, December 17, 1919.
[81] *Brooklyn Daily Times, New York Evening World, Jersey Journal*, December 17, 1919.
[82] *Brooklyn Daily Eagle*, July 22, 1916.
[83] *Los Angeles Times*, December 22, 1919. Babe Ruth played in a baseball game, but no home run.

knocked Turner out of the ring as he hit him enough times to kill a fellow. As it was there was not even a knock down." Greb was fast, and danced in, out, and around, but the press criticized that he didn't have the necessary punch.[84]

Harry Greb had gone 45-0 in 1919 (including newspaper decisions), a very impressive feat, but only scored 5 knockouts. The 5'8" or 5'8 ½" middleweight was very fast and busy with both feet and hands, could fight on the inside or outside, was very relaxed, in great shape, very experienced, took a good punch, and recovered well when hurt, but he was not a puncher or finisher. Still, with his speed and high punch volume, he could outpoint even top heavyweights. Yet, because of his small middleweight size, relative lack of height and reach, and lack of knockout power, despite his impressive record, there was not a great push for him as a challenger to heavyweight Dempsey. However, he was mentioned occasionally as a man who possibly could give anyone, including Dempsey, troubles. His results proved that he could be very challenging for anyone to beat.

Greb said he wanted to fight Dempsey, despite the 25-pound weight disparity. "That doesn't bother me. I've fought other big fellows – truly not the calibre of the champion – but big tough fellows, and I always managed to hold my own with them."[85]

Jack Dempsey said, "I want to finish with the [motion] picture as soon as possible, so I can look after Mr. Carpentier and a few of the other boys who are crying for attention."[86]

From the movie studio, while getting his wax nose molded on, Dempsey said to Francis Perrett,

> This talk about my hesitating to enter the ring with Fulton and Meehan and these other so-called challengers is mostly bunk. ... It's true I'm not anxious to climb into the ring with any of them unless I'm paid for it, because it means a lot of work to get into condition for a scrap and there's always a certain amount of risk involved. ...
>
> You've seen my gymnasium at the other end of the lot...and you've seen me box several times with Al Kaufman and Harry Wills and some of the other boys. I'm sure they'd be glad to obtain a layoff any day and if Fred Fulton or anyone else wants to try me out at my gymnasium I'll gladly accommodate them. Of course, there wouldn't be any money in it for them but if one of them hooked one onto my chin and knocked me for a goal they'd have a lot of glory coming to them.[87]

Joe Jeannette said Carpentier was a formidable foe for Dempsey, for he was a great fighter, and would be the most difficult proposition Jack ever tackled. "Georges is fast, clever and strong, has a shrewd fighting

[84] *Philadelphia Inquirer*, December 23, 1919.
[85] *Reading Times*, December 24, 1919.
[86] *Los Angeles Evening Express*, December 24, 1919.
[87] *Los Angeles Evening Express*, December 26, 1919. Had Dempsey sparred Harry Wills? Did he mean Bill Tate?

head and is a good ring general. He is courageous and cool in the pinches. Jack has never met as worthy a rival." Joe said Carp would have little trouble hitting Dempsey, and was capable of decking him with his snappy punch. Still, Joe wasn't necessarily picking Carpentier to win. "Dempsey has such an annihilating attack that even as clever a boxer and sharp hitter as Carpentier might not be able to stop him." But the experienced Georges would be a tough nut to crack.[88]

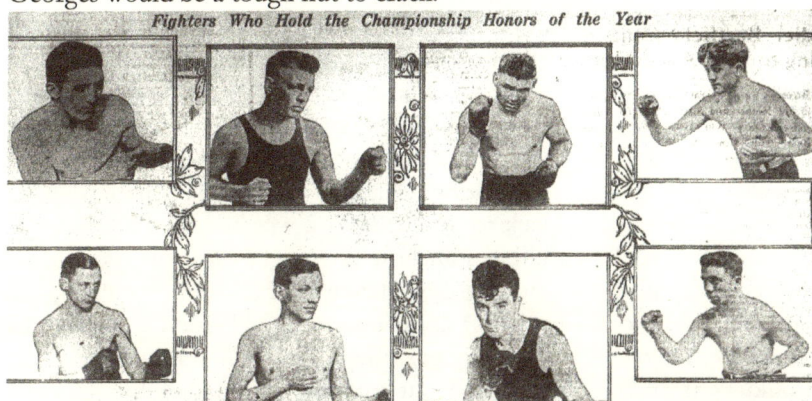

Fighters Who Hold the Championship Honors of the Year

Top - Georges Carpentier, European heavyweight champion, Mike O'Dowd, middleweight champion, Jack Dempsey, heavyweight champion, Johnny Kilbane, featherweight champion. Bottom – Benny Leonard, lightweight champion, Jimmy Wilde, flyweight champion, Jack Britton, welterweight champion, Pete Herman, bantamweight champion

Kearns said Dempsey would fight anyone if sufficient cash inducements were offered, but promoters knew that very few opponents would garner sufficient interest. Jim Coffroth did not think fights with Fulton (who was on a 10-fight win streak after losing to Dempsey, including wins over Meehan and Langford) or Meehan would draw. The big money fight was Carpentier. Every promoter wanted that fight.

Discussion about various offers for the Dempsey-Carpentier fight was omnipresent in the newspapers. Larger and larger amounts were being offered all the time, and the newspapers put it all in print.[89]

On January 1, 1920 in San Francisco, the colored contest between Harry Wills and Jack Thompson was stopped after the 3rd round and essentially declared a no contest when referee Eddie Hanlon ruled that Wills was hippodroming, not trying, and carrying Thompson. The bout was called a fiasco. The crowd hissed and groaned at Wills. "On the whole, it was a burlesque affair for which Wills isn't going to be forgiven or forgotten by local sports."[90]

Jack Kearns said Dempsey worked in a movie studio every day, but did not neglect his training. He was boxing with Bill Tate and Al Kaufman.[91]

On January 5, 1920, it was announced that Boston Red Sox owner Harry Frazee had sold 26-year-old Babe Ruth's contract to the New York

[88] *Evening Star*, December 31, 1919.
[89] *Los Angeles Evening Express*, January 1, 1920.
[90] *San Francisco Chronicle*, January 2, 1920.
[91] *Brooklyn Standard Union*, January 4, 1920.

Yankees for an alleged $125,000 (some said $110,000 - a combination of cash up front plus installment payments with interest), and, according to some, $300,000 in loans (the Yankee's owner would hold a mortgage on Boston's Fenway Park as collateral). Ruth helped the Yankees become baseball's dominant team for years to come.

In 1919, Ty Cobb was the highest paid player in baseball, making $20,000 per year. Ruth's annual salary in 1919 had been $10,000, but after threatening to retire if not paid $20,000 per year, Frazee sold his contract, and the Yankees agreed to pay him $20,000 in 1920. Jack Dempsey had made more than that just during his vaudeville/theatrical/circus tour, and was earning a whole lot more making movies.

Dempsey took a trip to Jim Jeffries' Burbank ranch, in the Los Angeles area, to meet the former champion. Jeff asked him what he weighed at Toledo, and Jack replied, "184 ½. I weighed over 200 a couple of weeks before the fight, but somehow the weight came off every day. I expected to put on some weight the last couple of days, but the drying out made me lose more. I couldn't put on a pound." Jack said he didn't drink or smoke. He went to bed early every night and was up at daylight. He would fight anyone they picked out for him. "I'd rather box than do anything else. I like it. I know a boxer's time is short and I want to make the most of it and be a real champion. … I'm taking just as good care of myself now as I did when I didn't have a dollar and nobody knew me." Jeff told him he ought to be champion for a long time.[92]

On January 7, 1920 in Kenosha, Wisconsin, Bill Brennan won a 10-round newspaper decision over Bartley Madden (23-13-5).[93]

In Los Angeles, Dempsey was working for the Pathe film company, filming *Daredevil Jack*, a 15-chapter/episode silent film serial; short subjects in which he appeared as a lead actor/hero.[94]

Kearns claimed that he and Dempsey would earn $500,000 as their share for the *Daredevil Jack* serial. For a heavyweight champion, boxing paid far better than baseball, but films paid much more than boxing.[95]

The movies could earn Dempsey a tremendous amount of money, which he was earning because he was the world's heavyweight champion. For Kearns, from an economic perspective, defending the title became less important, unless they were offered really good money, because defending the title always carried some risk, and the movies made them more money, which Dempsey only would earn while he remained champion. Still, Dempsey wanted to fight, and to remain at his best, he needed to be active.

[92] *Los Angeles Evening Express*, January 6, 1920.
[93] *Kenosha Evening News*, January 8, 1920.
[94] He also was filmed in *Daredevil Durant. Billings Gazette*, January 11, 1920; *Akron Beacon Journal*, March 31, 1920.
[95] *Lima Daily News*, February 2, 1920.

JACK'S GOING TO BE A RUINED BOY unless some one rescues him from the films. This is Jack Dempsey, world's heavyweight champion, who is taking the leading part in a new thriller entitled "Dare-Devil Jack," which is being filmed in Los Angeles. It is apparent the title holder doesn't devote all of his time to his work. Oh, Boy!

Dempsey with movie stars Rosemary Theby and Ruth Roland.

In Los Angeles, Dempsey with Lieutenant Ormer Locklear, ace pilot and premier aerial daredevil, and Viola Dana, movie star (Locklear's girlfriend), about to fly off in Locklear's plane. Locklear had performed aerial stunts in Toledo on July 4, 1919, above the arena, prior to Dempsey's winning the championship. The 28-year-old Locklear starred in *The Great Air Robbery* (1919), but would die on August 2, 1920 in a plane crash while performing nighttime aerial stunts for the film *The Skywayman*. The scene remained in the movie.

CHAPTER 2

Trouble

Jack Dempsey was enjoying the benefits of fame, but soon would experience several of its drawbacks.

On January 9, 1920, the American Legion post of Denver adopted a resolution branding Jack Dempsey as a "slacker," and declared opposition to holding the Carpentier fight in Colorado. Copies of its resolution would be sent to all American Legion posts throughout the U.S., with requests that similar action be taken by each. They wanted Dempsey barred from boxing. They criticized his lack of patriotism for failing to enlist in the war effort.

Reports about Dempsey's life as champion and the vast sums of money he was earning likely irked those who had risked their lives for the country for pennies. Reading daily reports about record sums of money being offered to Dempsey to fight Carpentier most certainly did not help.

A number of American Legion posts throughout the country started calling the new heavyweight champion a slacker.

Harry Grayson said Carpentier, though very popular, possibly more popular than Dempsey as a result of his war record, did not have much of a chance against the champion. As a fighter, Dempsey was a wonder, for he could hit harder than anyone since Sullivan, was as fast as a middleweight, and very dangerous, punching hard from any angle. Carpentier had to have lost something by not having a formal fight for four years.[96]

On January 10, 1920 in Bordeaux, France, 172-pound Georges Carpentier scored a 2nd round knockout over 180 ¾-pound Blink McCloskey, a 126-fight veteran who had lasted 6 rounds with Jack Johnson in 1918 before retiring with a hand injury.

On January 12, 1920 in Tulsa, in a rematch, Harry Wills won a 15-round decision over Jack Thompson (18-12-4) to defend his colored heavyweight title claim. Wills showed punching power and defense, winning 12 of the rounds. Thompson was aggressive and tough, recovering well after being hurt. He tried, and landed some good wallops, but could not get through Wills' defense on a consistent basis.

Still, Thompson scored a knockdown of Wills in the 6th round. Harry had a tendency to get decked on occasion in various fights, even when he won. Thompson had fought Langford to a couple 1919 15-round draws.[97]

Also on January 12, in Newark, New Jersey, 214-pound Fred Fulton clearly won an 8-round newspaper decision over former two-time title

[96] *Los Angeles Evening Express*, January 9, 1920.
[97] *Tulsa Tribune, Tulsa Daily World*, January 13, 1920.

36

challenger 194-pound Frank Moran. "The battle, however, showed convincingly that Fulton would have little chance with Jack Dempsey."[98]

Harry Grayson noted that there was a movement developing against Dempsey throughout the U.S., a feeling against him which was apt to alter his future plans and possibly even force him to fight Carpentier in France. Several American Legion posts had openly branded him as a slacker (while commending Carpentier for fighting for his country). "The legion is absolutely correct in its stand. Although Dempsey saw service in the shipyards, he did not step to the front during the war as did every red-blooded American. He is now reaping his just deserts."

The next day, it was reported that the "American Legion objects to Jack Dempsey as the defender of the prowess of America."[99]

The president of the New Jersey Athletic Commission said Dempsey would not be permitted to box in that state; a decision made in response to the American Legion's branding of him as a slacker. He said, "All red-blooded Americans should blush with shame when Dempsey's war record is mentioned." Heavyweight championship boxing always was intertwined with politics.

Jack Kearns defended Dempsey against the charges that he was a "draft dodger" and "slacker," eloquently stating that such charges could not be supported with facts.

> When the draft call came in 1917, Jack Dempsey was placed in class 4-A. This was because he was a married man, and, in addition was supporting a mother, an invalid brother and sister. Dempsey at the time made no claims for exemption, merely stating the true facts in his own case when filling out his questionnaire.
>
> Sometime later the draft board, readjusting the classifications, placed Dempsey in Class A-1, but almost immediately afterward put him in Class 2-B. He remained there during the rest of the war and was subject any day to call for war duty. ...
>
> During the course of the war Jack Dempsey was employed as a riveter and as a recruit in the Sun Shipbuilding plant of Philadelphia, and also in one of the shipyards in Seattle. And when he was not doing that he was appearing in fistic contests at the benefits for the different war charities. By this means, approximately $100,000 was raised for the various war funds.
>
> Dempsey not merely fought without a cent remuneration, but paid all of his traveling expenses to and from each battleground and each cantonment. He frequently was 'broke' as a consequence.
>
> Dempsey fought Willie Meehan in San Francisco for the benefit of the war charities fund. The fight drew about $27,000 and the money was equally divided between the soldiers and sailors. At least

---

[98] *Long Branch Daily Record*, January 13, 1920.
[99] *Los Angeles Evening Express*, January 12, 13, 1920.

$15,000 was added to the 'gate' in Brooklyn at the benefit affair staged by the Knights of Columbus because Dempsey willingly agreed to appear there in an exhibition bout. ... Dempsey...also appeared twice in New York, Denver, and nearly a score of smaller cities, and also in many of the cantonments and naval training stations.

Those who are charging Dempsey with being a 'slacker' because he worked in the shipyard – and helped to raise nearly $100,000 for the various war charities – apparently have overreached themselves in their charges, for by that contention they are smudging the reputation of every other exempted man who served the nation in the army at home – and served it so nobly – by working night and day in the essential industries, so that the war could be brought to a speedy and successful conclusion.[100]

Regardless of the solid defense, the *Los Angeles Evening Express* noted that the movement against Dempsey was growing by leaps and bounds.

Boxing promoter James W. Coffroth defended Dempsey, noting that Jack helped raise $25,000 for the cause by boxing Meehan for free.

I also wish to say that when I was acting as national chairman, division of boxing of the United War Work drive in November 1918, Dempsey came to New York to box for the cause in a show conducted in Madison Square Garden. That brought in $108,000. Jack Dempsey was always at call for any charity work during the war.

Kearns said, "Jack Dempsey is not ashamed of his war record. He has no reason to be and has no fear of public sentiment switching against him on this account. Jack did more good during the war than any fighter who did not actually enlist."

Kearns opined that the attacks started because of the numerous huge offers they had received for the Carpentier bout. He noted that the public seemed to forget the large amounts they had paid and would pay in income and war taxes. They were not the hogs that some charged.

He also noted that it was Carpentier challenging Dempsey, not the other way around. "Much of the censure being fired at Jack is because of Carpentier's remarkable war record and both Jack and I admire him for it. We will box him because the public demands it."

However, the *Los Angeles Evening Express* said that despite Kearns' statements, the matter could become serious for Dempsey. It was not out of the question or farfetched that he might be barred from fighting in the U.S.[101]

Jack's "charming" sister Elsie Dempsey and his mother Celia Dempsey came to town to spend the winter with him. They were there to take charge of his home at 7021 Franklin avenue, Hollywood. Jack said his

[100] *Los Angeles Evening Express*, January 14, 1920; *Dayton Herald, San Francisco Chronicle*, January 15, 1920.
[101] *Los Angeles Evening Express, Los Angeles Times*, January 15, 1920.

sister was the one person for whom he would take a fall. "I am quite sure she will get just about whatever she wants, as far as I am concerned. She is a mighty fine girl and I guess with mother to back her she will come pretty close to being the boss of the house."

Elsie said, "I never saw Jack fight. I don't think that I would care to see him in the ring. But I have seen him act in the movies and I really believe that he is a good actor." She said Jack was one to go about things with all his heart, which enthusiasm made him a success.[102]

The *San Francisco Chronicle* said world's champion Dempsey now was at the "center of a storm of agitation started by American Legion posts, who pointed to the fact that he did not enlist for active service."[103]

John S. Hogan, a San Francisco attorney who headed the exemption board in San Francisco, which had handled Dempsey's case, said Dempsey was not a slacker or draft dodger. Hogan had investigated Dempsey's exemption claims thoroughly, and after establishing and verifying the truth of his claim that he had dependents, placed him in class 4-A. Jack was exempt as a result of the fact that he was a married man, supporting his wife, parents, invalid brother, and sister, in addition to making payments on a ranch for his parents.[104] Hogan further said,

> If Jack Dempsey is a slacker, then I am a slacker, and the man in the first line trench was a slacker. Jack Dempsey is no slacker. As chairman of the local board which passed upon his exemption claims and placed him in deferred classification, I am in a position to make this unqualified statement. It is equally true that Dempsey at no time impressed me as a man who would willingly shirk his military duty.

> I was satisfied with Dempsey's claim of exemption and at the time I had no hesitancy at placing him in class 4-A, nor have I since been convinced that his classification was wrong or that his claim for exemption was to be disregarded any more than the thousands of others that came under my jurisdiction as an exemption board chairman.[105]

Jack Kearns said a Dempsey-Carpentier fight would not last more than 6 rounds, for both men would come to win by knockout.[106]

[102] *Los Angeles Evening Express*, January 15, 1920.
[103] *San Francisco Chronicle*, January 15, 1920.
[104] *Los Angeles Times*, January 16, 1920.
[105] *San Francisco Examiner*, January 16, 1920.
[106] *Los Angeles Evening Express*, January 16, 1920.

On January 17, 1920, the 18th Amendment to the U.S. Constitution went into effect, making the manufacture, sale, and transportation of intoxicating liquors illegal. It was the start of legal prohibition throughout the United States, and some later argued the birth of national organized crime. The amendment would not be repealed until 1933.

Making matters worse for the champ, Dempsey's former spouse Maxine, perhaps seeing her ex-husband under fire, and jealous of his fame, success, and money, seized upon the situation, and propelled and supported the slacker charges, trying to harm him. The divorced Mrs. Maxine Dempsey said Jack not only was a slacker, but had not actually worked in the shipyards, and had not supported her as he claimed.

On January 22, 1920, from Wells, Nevada, where she was living, Maxine Dempsey wrote the *San Francisco Examiner* and *San Francisco Chronicle*,

> I read the statement of John S. Hogan in the *San Francisco Chronicle*, where he claimed that if Jack Dempsey was a slacker then he (Hogan) is a slacker, too. I do not know Hogan, but I do know that Jack Dempsey never supported me, and that I had to sign papers, under threats, to say that he did, when, to tell the truth, I had to support him.

> Ask Dempsey to show you proofs where he worked in the shipyards. He wasn't even a shipyard slacker, because he didn't even work in one. But he went to the shipyards in Philadelphia, had his picture taken in a workman's uniform to fool the public.

> I have positive proofs of a letter in his own handwriting, naming his manager, Jack Kearns, and two others, and telling me how they succeeded in having him put in class 4A.

> Now, I hope you will publish this letter, so as to give Dempsey a chance to deny the same and try and prove that my assertions are not true. Then I will produce the facts in his own handwriting at any time before the proper authorities.

> Respectfully yours, Maxine Dempsey, divorced wife of Jack Dempsey.

Dempsey responded to her allegations, "Not one word of truth in it. … This woman is probably jealous of me and sore at herself. She is simply joining the pack in trying to hurt me. She hasn't proof to her name. I challenge her to produce any evidence that will support her name."

Jack Kearns said, "Absolutely ridiculous. Simply the ravings of a silly woman who wants to see her name in print and wants to hurt her divorced husband."[107]

Kearns said Maxine's claims were absurd. Dempsey had divorced her nearly a year ago. When Jack filled out the draft questionnaire, his wife

---

[107] *San Francisco Examiner*, January 24, 1920; *San Francisco Chronicle*, February 13, 1920.

signed it as well. She was living at that time with Jack's parents and supported by him. She signed a legal document saying he supported her. She never made such allegations before, including in the divorce suit, which she never defended in court. He challenged her to produce proof. Kearns indicated that it all was a scheme, and furthermore, she didn't even write the letter she allegedly wrote making the claims against Dempsey.[108]

Fred Bebergall, state secretary of the American Legion in California, said no American Legion post should condemn Dempsey prior to fully investigating the offense charged. Local state officials in San Francisco said Dempsey was placed in Class 4-A after his claims for deferred classification on the grounds of dependency had been investigated and approved.

During the war, Dempsey and Kearns appeared before the Thirteenth District Board in San Francisco. John S. Hogan was the chairman. Supporting a wife alone entitled him to be class 4-A. He also was supporting his parents, and had a widowed sister dependent upon him, she having two children. "The evidence presented to the board showed that Mr. Dempsey was supporting all of these people."

The Secretary also noted that some Legion posts had made Carpentier an honorary member, despite the fact that the Legion constitution expressly prohibited any honorary memberships.[109]

Maxine Cates (a.k.a. Maxine Dempsey) told the *Salt Lake Telegram's* F. E. Becker that she was compelled by threats to sign an affidavit that Jack was her support during the war, when in fact he was not. Later he compelled her by threats to sign the divorce papers so he could obtain a divorce. Cates was living in Wells, Nevada, a town with 300 people and a "two-berth roundhouse." She was a slender, dark-haired woman with flashing eyes.

Cates said she could prove her allegations with letters in Jack's own hand, which she had kept. She said the letters were locked in a vault, and the reporter could not see them at the moment. She claimed that she would at some point release them to the world. She said Dempsey was a slacker and not a patriot. She even declared that the letters would bring out unsavory things about others connected with Dempsey's anti-draft negotiations. To the best of her knowledge, Dempsey had not worked in a shipyard. He did put on overalls long enough to have a picture taken.

When asked why she had waited so long to bring up all of this, she responded,

> I didn't pay much attention to all the fight talk until the American legion took up the slacker charge. Then I thought I would help them out, because he was a slacker and I can prove it. I am not jealous or simply angry. In fact, there is no regard left, after the way he treated me. I only wish to show him to the world as what he was

[108] *St. Louis Star, San Antonio Evening News,* January 23, 1920.
[109] *San Francisco Examiner,* January 15, 1920.

when his country needed him. I don't want any money, not even from newspapers which want my story. I don't want a dime. My real motive is to show him in his own colors – not true colors. He did engage in boxing and some of the proceeds were turned over to war purposes, but boxing was vastly different from taking a chance with a bullet. Supposing every American had been like him, the Germans might have been over here. He and his manager, Jack Kearns, are trying to pull a big bluff on the public, and I am going to call their bluff.

Maxine said they were married in Salt Lake City on October 19, 1916, and divorced in February 1919. Maxine claimed that the divorce action was instituted at the instigation of Jack Kearns, "who did not like to have his fighter around women." She had received no money from Jack since then.

As a result of all the negative publicity, the U. S. Department of Justice began an investigation of Dempsey's divorced wife's slacker charges.[110]

On February 2, 1920 in Newark, New Jersey, 22-year-old 175-pound Gene Tunney (24-0-2) knocked out 174-pound Al Roberts (8-2) with a right or right hook to the jaw in the 8th round. Tunney had scored a knockdown in the 1st, and two or three knockdowns in the 7th, but Roberts had attacked gamely and fought hard throughout, in exciting give-and-take fashion.[111]

During early February 1920, the U.S. government's investigation of claims against Dempsey was proceeding.

Bud Ridley swore that Jack had worked in a Seattle shipyard. Shortly after June 15, 1917, Dempsey was employed as a ship-fitter's helper in the shipyards of the Seattle Construction Company, and he worked there for at least two weeks before leaving as a result of the sudden death of his brother in Salt Lake City.[112]

Many noted that photos of Dempsey as a riveter failed to hide the fancy cloth-top/patent-leather shoes he wore. Rumor had it that he allegedly told friends that the hardest work he did at the shipyards was to sign the payroll. The suggestion was that the job was obtained for him so he could apply for the exemption class, but essentially it was a sham to avoid the work-or-fight law which required one to work for the war effort to avoid being drafted. Photos of Dempsey as a riveter were staged, but the pictures made the fatal error of depicting him wearing brand new clean overalls (clearly not used) which were not quite long enough, revealing that he was wearing inappropriate beautiful cloth-top shoes, which no riveter would wear. Allegedly, Kearns helped set things up so that his fighter could avoid having to fight in the war, for such would derail or retard Dempsey's boxing career.[113]

[110] *Salt Lake Telegram*, January 26, 1920.
[111] *New York Tribune, Jersey Journal*, February 3, 1920. Al Roberts' record included: 1919 WND8 and LND8 Charley Weinert, WND8 Dan O'Dowd, and LTKOby2 Al Reich.
[112] *San Francisco Chronicle*, February 1, 1920.
[113] *San Francisco Chronicle*, February 2, 1920.

IN ANSWER to the question: Did Jack Dempsey actually work in a shipyard during the war? it safely can be said that he DID. In this picture you will see the handsome heavyweight champion sweating over a riveter in the yards of the Sun Ship Company, of Chester, Pa. You will note the working garb, neatly starched new overalls, patent leather shoes with pearl buttons and yellow kid uppers. (By Ledger P. S.)

Some said Maxine was under the influence of a negro woman named Lola Taylor, who was the "brains of the combination." The claim was that it was a blackmail scheme by the women, hoping that Kearns and Dempsey would pay them off.[114]

Soon thereafter, it was reported that Cates was repudiating her statements and charges previously made. Now she wrote and told a different story, stating in a sworn affidavit,

> Jack Dempsey is not a slacker and at no time did he try to avoid the draft for the war by intimidating me or otherwise. I voluntarily signed his questionnaire and with equal willingness signed his exemption when he sent it to me so that he could go to the war. ...
>
> On two different occasions I know to my own knowledge that Jack Dempsey tried to enlist in the military service of the United States and he talked with me about it and I begged him not to, because he had his father, mother and me to support. I further know that Jack Dempsey worked in the shipyards at Seattle as a shipbuilder. ...
>
> If I ever said that Jack Dempsey was a slacker, or signed anything to that effect, I did so because I was jealous of Dempsey and had been made mad at him at the time by his enemies continually ribbing me.

---

[114] *San Francisco Examiner*, February 3, 1920.

She also said Jack indeed had supported her while they were married, as he did his mother and father. She did not have any letters supporting her prior statements, and never did. It was signed Maxine Dempsey.

DIVORCED WIFE WITHDRAWS DEMPSEY SLACKER CHARGES

Left to Right—Jack Kearns, manager of Jack Dempsey; Mrs. Maxine Dempsey and Jack Dempsey, heavyweight champion. Mrs. Maxine Dempsey, of Wells, Nevada, divorced wife of Jack Dempsey, has withdrawn charges against her former husband of evading military service during the war. In his draft questionnaire Dempsey claimed he was the sole support of his wife. This she now declares to be true. Mrs. Dempsey is now a dance hall girl in Wells, a small town near the Nevada-Utah border.

Photo likely taken sometime in 1917, possibly 1918

So, Maxine had signed two letters which directly contradicted one another. When asked why she had written her prior allegations, Maxine said,

MRS. MAXINE DEMPSEY, NOW IN SAN Francisco, who says her charges against Jack Dempsey were untrue. She has "taken back" everything she said and adds that she's sorry.

Well, if you must know, it was the ribbing. I was sore at Jack and wanted to get even. Just a year ago in February, Dempsey and I were divorced. Later I was told that Tommy (Mrs. Wilson), proprietress of the dance hall at Wells, had gone East with Jack Dempsey, that she had given him $600. In the dance hall they urged me to get even with Dempsey. They kept me continually stirred up and nagged me until I wrote the letter. I found out later there was no truth to the story about this woman and then I was sorry.

She was sorry that she had caused him so much trouble. "Jack was a wonderful man and husband, so far as I know him."

44

Maxine had been brought into San Francisco on February 3. She had been hiding out at the Hotel Grand, registered as Lina Clark, and not available to the press until after the first leg of the federal investigation. She was on-call to the federal authorities.

Jack Kearns, who was in San Francisco, said he had not attempted to speak with Maxine, and did not propose to do so.[115]

On February 4, 1920 in Oakland, Gunboat Smith won a 4-round decision over Willie Meehan, decking him in the 2nd round.[116]

Making current matters even worse for the champion, Dempsey's character was called into question regarding his potential conduct in throwing the February 1917 Jim Flynn fight. There had been frequent hints that he had flopped and taken a dive.

Marion Salazar wrote that it came as no surprise to him to read that Maxine Dempsey had joined the movement to discredit her ex-husband as a slacker. Back in 1917, she had told Salazar that Dempsey had thrown the Flynn fight.:

> The Mrs. Dempsey that was is just as hard a fighter, in her way, as is the man she once loved but never honored or obeyed. She it is who, three or four years ago, gave the public the story, through the *Bulletin*, that Dempsey, for the sum of $500, permitted himself to be knocked out by Fireman Jim Flynn.

> Dempsey, who had come to San Francisco under the management of Fred Winsor, quarreled with Winsor and disappeared, leaving Mrs. Dempsey in a local hotel with but $30.

> Mrs. Dempsey, thinking herself a woman spurned, came to the *Bulletin* office with her story of desertion, and when Dempsey could not be located she told of the fake with Flynn, stating that she held the $500 paid Dempsey to "flop" and that she hid the money under a bathtub while Jack went "to take his punch on the chin."

> "And that stuff about Flynn breaking Dempsey's jaw was all wrong," said Mrs. Dempsey. "When Jack came back after taking the punch I had a chicken dinner for him and he chewed up the bones."

> Then came some unexpected developments. Dempsey, after an absence of four or five days, returned to San Francisco.

> Mrs. Dempsey, hearing of his return, telephoned to me, who had written the story, to look out for Dempsey; that he was ugly and might take a punch at me.

> A short time later, about 10 o'clock in the morning, Dempsey appeared at the *Bulletin* office and approached my desk. "I came to see you about that story," he said. "What about it?" I asked. "My

115 *San Francisco Examiner, San Francisco Chronicle,* February 5, 1920.
116 Kearns had been quoted as saying that Dempsey would fight Meehan if he beat Smith, but once again, Meehan's results failed to garner momentum and justification for a title shot.

wife says it isn't so," stated Dempsey; "that you made it all up, and she didn't say a word of it." "The thing to do," I suggested, "is to see Mrs. Dempsey and have her tell me so." "All right," said Dempsey, "we'll see her this afternoon." "We'll do nothing of the kind," I said. "We'll see her now or we won't bother about seeing her at all." "But she isn't up," protested Dempsey. "Then we'll go over to the hotel and wait till she does get up," I said. "We'll not wait until you intimidate her." Dempsey, unable to do as he wished, agreed to go to the hotel, where we waited for Mrs. Dempsey in the lobby.

The greetings, on the part of Dempsey, at least, were rather effusive. "Now tell him, dearie," said Dempsey – "tell him what you told me." "What did I tell you?" asked Mrs. Dempsey. "That what he put in the paper wasn't so; that you didn't tell him that stuff." "I'll do nothing of the kind," said Mrs. Dempsey. "And why won't you?" Dempsey demanded. "Because," said Mrs. Dempsey, "I did tell him."

I will say to the credit of Dempsey that he did not lose his temper or make any kind of a scene. "But why did you tell him?" he asked quietly. "Because," she explained, "I was sore. You went away and left me. I wasn't going to let you get away with that." "I didn't leave you," Dempsey declared. "You did, too," said Mrs. Dempsey; "you know you did."

I arose to go. "Looks like a family quarrel," I remarked, "and you had better settle it between yourselves – alone."

"What I told you was the truth," said Mrs. Dempsey, "and I want you to understand that I am not going to take anything back now or any other time." "You don't care for me," said Dempsey. "If you had cared for me you wouldn't have left me the way you did," shot back Mrs. Dempsey. "I didn't leave you," said Dempsey. "I had to go to attend to some business." "Must be rather peculiar business that takes you out of town several days without telling your wife," said Mrs. Dempsey.

I never saw a man so thoroughly whipped by a woman as Dempsey was that day.

Mrs. Dempsey is a tall, willowy, stunning brunette, and her black eyes snapped challenges at the world's champion-to-be to start something that she could finish. But Jack wouldn't start. He just sat there silently and took his licking.

When I arose to go he followed me out. "I hope you are not going to put anything more in the paper?" he said. "But," I added, "I'll have to say something about your return." "Well," he said, "don't say anything more about what my wife says. You can see for yourself that she's only a foolish woman."

Which may have been so. The fact that she married Jack when she had no idea that he'd ever amount to anything as a fighter would indicate that she was foolish. But she was a fighter, and, judging from what she's doing to Jack now in the way of offering proofs that he is a slacker, she is still a fighter.[117]

On February 11, 1920 in San Francisco, pursuant to a subpoena, Maxine Dempsey testified before the federal grand jury. Apparently, she testified to her original charges, and said that she falsely swore to an affidavit clearing Dempsey of her original charges. Allegedly, she had some letters in a safe deposit box in Wells, Nevada.[118]

ROYAL
Premier Showing
Sunday, Feb. 15th

JACK DEMPSEY
The Best Known Man in the World in
'DAREDEVIL JACK'
The Million Dollar Pathe Serial
— 15—15—15 —
Episodes of Breathless Interest
Episodes of Rousing Adventure
Episodes of Thrilling Action
See the First Episode and You'll Come Back Anxious for the Fourteen More

In mid-February 1920, the first episode of the *Daredevil Jack* moving-picture serial started showing in theaters. It would be exhibited all over the country.[119]

On February 18, it was reported that the U.S. authorities had secured Maxine's alleged slacker letters.

Maxine claimed to have been coerced into falsely swearing to an affidavit stating that Dempsey was innocent and supporting her at the time he applied for an exemption from service. She claimed that as a matter of fact, *she* supported *him*.[120]

Speaking about the Dempsey family, Jack's sister Florence said there had been ten children in all, but three were dead. The living men included brother Bernard, age 42, a silver miner, she thought, but possibly also copper, who lived in Eureka, Utah; Joe, who was 29, drove a taxi in Salt Lake City and had been sickly a fair amount; Johnnie, 25, called "Little Jack"; and William Harrison, 24, a.k.a. Jack Dempsey, whom the family called "Big Jack." Of the women, there was Effie, who had been Mrs. Clark but now was Mrs. William Barrow, who lived on a little farm four miles east of Salt Lake, which Jack gave to his mother after the Fulton fight; then Florence, who, like Effie, had been born in Logan county, West Virginia; and finally Elsie, the youngest girl, who had been born in Manassa, Colorado, like Jack. Joe and Johnnie also were born in Manassa. Of the boys, only Bernard was born in West Virginia. Of the three who had died, two were girls, and all three were young except Stella, who had died when she was about 20.

Florence said rumors that Jack was Jewish were incorrect. Florence said she was a Catholic, but the rest of the family did not belong to any church that she knew of; at least not now.

[117] *Enid Daily Eagle*, quoting *San Francisco Bulletin*, February 8, 1920.
[118] *San Francisco Examiner*, February 11, 1920.
[119] *St. Louis Post-Dispatch*, February 14, 1920.
[120] *San Francisco Examiner*, February 18, 1920.

She said both parents were very happy when their son won the world championship. After the Willard fight, Jack had bought his mother a large home at 270 Center street in Salt Lake City.

The family was worried about the maneuvers of the champ's divorced wife, Maxine Cates, fearing that any stranger might be an agent of hers.[121]

On February 21, 1920 in France, Georges Carpentier scored a KO2 over Georges Grundhoven (24-9).

In late February, Dempsey and Kearns were informed that true bills would be returned by the federal grand jury indicting them in draft obstruction charges. Dempsey said it was a trumped-up case to injure him because he had reached the top. Kearns said the charges were absurd.

On February 27, 1920, two indictments containing four counts were returned against the fighter and his manager. Warrants for their arrest were issued, and it was said that the two would turn themselves in voluntarily and post bail ($2,000 for Dempsey; $1,000 for Kearns). Dempsey was charged with attempt to evade the selective service by presenting falsehoods to the local board No. 13 at San Francisco - a claim for deferred classification on the ground of dependency, in that he had a wife and other dependents. He also was charged with filing an additional false statement relative to his dependency on June 14, 1918. Kearns was charged with having willfully and knowingly assisted in his conspiracy to evade military service.

The selective service act went into effect on May 18, 1917. On January 19, 1918, Dempsey was subject to registration under that act.

Allegedly, Dempsey wrote a letter on June 14, 1918, to Maxine, saying, "Say, dear, if I ask you, would you if I wanted you to, swear to an affidavit that I was supporting you."

On June 21, 1918, Dempsey wrote to John S. Hogan, chair of the local Board No. 13, asking for two weeks to file the fighter's questionnaire, on the ground that his wife and other dependents at Salt Lake would have to sign supportive affidavits. The indictment alleged as false his claims that he supported his wife, father, mother, widowed sister and her two children, they were fully dependent upon his labor and support, he had contributed $20 per month for the past 12 months preceding January 19, 1918, and no other person had contributed anything to their support.

It was alleged that Dempsey did not contribute to the full support of all of the alleged dependents, and they all knew it. If convicted of conspiracy, a felony, the penalty was imprisonment for up to two years and a fine of $2,000, for each count. The draft evasion charge, a misdemeanor, carried up to one year in jail.[122]

Making the situation worse still, Utah fight promoter Hardy Downing claimed that the first Dempsey vs. Jim Flynn fight was fixed, supporting Maxine Dempsey's claims. The fight was for the benefit of the Murray fireman's fund. Before the fight, Downing got the tip that the contest was

[121] *New York Daily News*, February 20, 1920.
[122] *San Francisco Chronicle*, February 25, 27, 28, 1920; *San Francisco Examiner*, February 27, 28, 1920.

on the queer, and he went to the sheriff's office in Salt Lake and told them, "If this fight turns out crooked it'll make a lot of scandal and hurt the whole game around here, and I want it stopped." The sheriff said he could not do anything, though he warned the folks who were hosting the show. Nevertheless, the fight went on. Hardy said when the fight started, Jack went into a shell, lowering his head and hunched over, but dropped his left, received a blow, put his right glove against his cheek and "did a little flopping." Downing called it an "artistic flop."

Sometime later, Dempsey asked Downing to make a rematch with Flynn. "I'll fight for you for nothing. I want to square myself here. You know I always had to figure on money for the folks, and probably I done things I ought not to done. But when they needed money I figured I had to get it some way." But Dempsey went to San Francisco, and then back East. Downing said, "I guess everybody makes bad, blind mistakes one time or another in life. I have. And he was young and had a hard row to hoe."

Downing had alluded to the Flynn fight being fixed in an another interview the week before, stating that Dempsey had been good to his family ever since he came up. "He takes care of his folks. Even that bunch he threw down at the Flynn fight out at Murray will say that. And believe me, the family had it hard. Why, as I remember it, even the old lady worked downtown sometimes." Not only was he alluding to the Flynn fight being fixed, but perhaps also that Jack's wife was a prostitute.[123]

Al Auerbach, Dempsey's early manager, also told about the Flynn fiasco, but he too highlighted mitigating circumstances. He was Jack's third manager, and also co-promoter of the Flynn vs. Dempsey fight at Murray. He did not know it was going to be queer. But he confirmed that Hardy Downing indeed had warned him in advance that the fight would be queer. Auerbach said Jack was his own trainer, but worked hard, and was out on the road every morning at 5 a.m. Hence, it appeared to him like he was training to fight to win.

Regarding Dempsey's motivation to throw the Flynn fight, Auerbach explained,

> Jack had dependents a-plenty. Jack paid the bills always. He'd be training hard between those early fights and then maybe get $25 or $40, and next day he'd be broke from paying mother's grocery bill. Now you take the Flynn fight and all the grief it caused. That was the result of driving need, I tell you. Of course, the boy had never seen $500 of which he or the family hadn't owed most. Jack spoke to me about these things once. He said, "I tell you, Al, if I had my life to live over I'd never do that thing again."

Auerbach confirmed that he had a contract with Jack, but it wasn't worth the paper upon which it was printed. Jack paid him back what he owed, and also sponsored Auerbach's attendance at the Toledo fight.

---

[123] *Chicago Tribune*, February 23, 24, 1920; *New York Daily News*, February 27, 1920, March 1, 1920.

"Why, my hotel bill alone was $360.70!" Auerbach further said, "As a rule a prize fighter's got no heart or soul, but with this fellow it was different. No sooner got to Salt Lake than it was a home for the family – not much of a one, but it was the best he could do."[124]

The problem with the revelations made by Downing and Auerbach regarding the Flynn fight is that their statements bolstered Maxine's credibility, and impugned Dempsey's integrity. However, it also served to show that Dempsey had been poor, supported his family financially, and was willing to do whatever it took to help and support them if necessary; even if it meant fixing a fight.

John C. Derks, a sporting editor for the *Salt Lake Tribune*, talked about Dempsey with Eye Witness, sports writer for the *Chicago Tribune*. Derks said Dempsey abhorred vaudeville, disliked circus life, and was bored by the motion picture game. Jack told Derks, "I'm a fighter, and I want to fight. I don't want to act. I'm no actor. The quicker we get through with this picture making and get back in the ring where I belong, the better pleased I'll be." Derks said Dempsey hit hard enough to knock down a wall. "Dempsey would rather fight than eat." He said Jack had a wonderful fighting heart and a total absence of fear, or mercy.

To illustrate Dempsey's lack of fear of punishment, Derks discussed the Flynn fight, which he attended.

> In the first round, indeed, at the second blow, Flynn landed a terrific punch on Dempsey's jaw. Flynn has a reputation for putting tremendous force into his blows, and there is no gainsaying that the blow which he delivered to Dempsey's jaw was terrific. It developed later that the fight was a frame, and that to distinguish it from other frames it was agreed to end it quickly. Now, if there is any fear in the makeup of a man who will deliberately stick out his jaw to permit Jim Flynn to hit it, then I do not know what is meant by fear.

Jack never drank much to excess. But he had few, if any, refining influences, and no moral restraints. He fell in with bad associates, which could have led him down the path to being a nobody.

Derks said Dempsey was pleasant, obliging, and good-natured. In the early years, he was rather diffident (modest or shy because of a lack of self-confidence). Yet, he was not brash after his great success. He was not a cursing or flashy type. He used to be bashful in the presence of persons of larger mental attainments. However, lately he had lost a lot of his backwardness. Being financially secure and gradually becoming accustomed to rubbing elbows with folks of a higher walk, Jack had come to the conclusion that he was as good as any of them, "a conviction perhaps strengthened by the knowledge that physically he is the superior of any of 'em. When he was last with me he talked in the language of a man of substance." Dempsey believed it would be at least three years

[124] *Chicago Tribune*, February 26, 1920; *New York Daily News*, March 3, 1920.

before anyone could be developed who could give him any kind of a challenge.

Regarding Dempsey's family, Derks said Maxine was "the bad actress." Jack's affection for his mother was genuine. When asked about Jack's father Hiram, Derks made a zero with his index finger and thumb, meaning Hiram was a big zero, or nothing.[125]

Dempsey and Kearns

Dempsey said his great-grandmother on his mother's side was half-Cherokee Indian of the Virginia mountains, back when there wasn't any West Virginia. His grandfather, his father's father, was a captain in the Confederacy. In slavery times, his father's uncles owned colored folk.

Jack said he never used racial epithets. The reporter noted that Jack did not use the word "nigger" even when Bill Tate was not around, whereas many supposedly gently bred persons used the spiteful word even when colored folk were present, even though they knew it hurt like a lash. Jack tried to be a decent gentleman.

His father's folks were from Kildare, Ireland. His mother was Scotch-Irish. Her name was Celia Smoot. Her father died before she was born. Her mother married a man named Ellis. Her family were farmers in West Virginia. Jack's father had brothers there too, farmers and coal miners.

The champ's parents came to Colorado 30 years ago to find a fortune and a farm. "They didn't." His sister Florence told him that his father always had farmed for a living. "Well, he hasn't, unless shoveling snow in the streets of Salt Lake City is a kind of farming." Wow. His father was well into his 60s now. He was up against it most of his life. Local Salt Lakers described Hiram as a tall, thin, wiry man who did not do much, and liked his booze.

Dempsey said he was born on June 23, 1895, not June 24. He had lived in Manassa and Montrose, Colorado, Provo, Utah, Logan county, West Virginia, Salt Lake City, New York City, San Francisco, Chicago, and recently Toledo. He was named after President William Harrison.

Jack married Maxine in 1916 in Farmington Utah, and it turned out bad. "I think she takes something; I can't explain it any other way – how one day in the newspaper interviews I'm the candy with her and the next day a crook. That's the way it runs – about 50-50."

Supposedly, Jack fought his first prizefight in Montrose. He said it was in Montrose when he was about 16 years old. "I fought Freddie Woods. It was three rounds. I knocked him out."[126]

---

125 *Chicago Tribune*, February 29, 1920; *New York Daily News*, March 6, 1920.
126 *Pittsburgh Daily Post*, February 29, 1920; *New York Daily News*, March 5, 1920.

Thereafter, Dempsey either was working or fighting. Mostly mining, but sometimes a job washing dishes, or driving a wagon – he took any job in the Montrose, Provo, Salt Lake days.

After Montrose came Provo. They lived there for a couple of years.

He and his family spent about a year at Logan, West Virginia. He worked in the coal mines. He would drive a coal wagon, mix concrete, and every now and then pick up a fight. At home, he washed dishes and mopped the floor while his mother and brothers were out at other work.

In 1914, they came to Salt Lake City and made it home. In 1918 and 1919, Jack lived in Chicago for a year and a half on West Madison street, around the 4800s, with a nice old Irish lady, Mrs. Sheehy, who was like a mother to him.[127]

On March 5, 1920 in Saginaw, Michigan, 203-pound Bill Brennan fought 190-pound Captain Bob Roper to a 10-round no decision in which the local writer said and most dispatches reported was a draw, though some reported that Roper had a shade. The local *Saginaw News Courier* said, "To call it anything other than a good draw would be an injustice to either man. Brennan seemed the hardest puncher, but Roper was the more clever and got in many more clean blows." Brennan had a slight edge in the infighting, but Roper fought back all the way. Brennan won the 1st and 9th, Roper the 4th and 10th, with the others even. Hence, 2-2-6. Roper allowed Brennan to lead so he could counter him coming in. Bill played for the stomach. His right to the jaw in the 9th rocked Roper, but Bob eventually recovered and fought back. Roper landed many more blows in the 10th. Roper had a split lip, while Brennan's nose bled during the contest.[128]

Also on March 5, 1920, in Los Angeles, at Jack Doyle's pavilion, before a record house, Jack Dempsey boxed 3 exhibition rounds with former foe Terry Kellar/Keller. Jack's quickness of hand and foot and his stiff punches made a hit with the fans, and he was cheered to the echo. He hardly was breathing at the end.[129]

That same day, Maxine Dempsey answered the door of her room at the Lincoln Hotel in Seattle to be interviewed by a reporter. She was wearing a pink silk negligee. She was tall, slender, and black haired, with a smile that belied her reputation as more than a match for her former husband. She had been visiting her mother in Yakima, Washington. Maxine planned to leave Seattle for "Tia Juana," where she would attend the races.

Speaking of Dempsey, Maxine said, "Jack is a wonderful man, but I cannot hand him much as a husband. He's just a kid, a happy go-lucky kid. We had quarrels, every married couple has them, but none of them was very serious. I blacked his eye once, but I didn't really mean to." If

---

[127] *New York Daily News*, March 5, 1920.
[128] *Saginaw News Courier*; *Muskegon Chronicle, Chicago Tribune, Battle Creek Enquirer*, March 6, 1920. The *Muncie Evening Press* and *Chicago Tribune* reported that Roper shaded Brennan, landing repeatedly with lefts, though Brennan excelled at infighting. Roper's record included: 1919 L10 Jack Johnson (Roper's 7th pro bout) and WND10 Frank Moran; and 1920 LND10 Harry Greb.
[129] *Los Angeles Times*, March 6, 1920. World lightweight champ Benny Leonard exhibited as well.

called to testify at his trial, she would, and "I am going to tell the truth." When asked about her prediction of the trial's result, she said, "They've got the letters that Jack wrote to me, and they have indicted him. It looks as though they must have some evidence." When asked whether Jack worked in a shipyard during the war, she asked, "What shipyard?" When asked what work he did during the war, Maxine responded to the question with a question: "What work did he do during the war, that's what I'd like to know?" Upon being questioned about the report that she had changed her testimony regarding Jack since the investigation began, Maxine replied, "Since I was subpoenaed I have told absolutely nothing but the truth."[130]

Dempsey said he had raised money for war charities in patriotic exhibition bouts, including $40,000 in Brooklyn, $80,000 in New York, $26,000 in San Francisco, and $70,000 for the Salvation Army Affair in Chicago that did not come off but still was a benefit because those who had purchased tickets did not take their money back.

Upon seeing the photos of him in new overalls and patent leather shoes at the shipyard, the public felt that it had been swindled. Dempsey explained that some military personnel, including Lieutenant Kennedy, told him that the money he could raise in exhibitions would do more good for the war effort than his working in the shipyards. However, Dempsey was asked to help recruit labor for the military, which would be valuable, and to take photos for that purpose. "We want the pictures for advertising purposes for recruits," Dempsey was told. So he obliged them and they took the famous photos. He and Kearns were given a 60-day labor recruiting card. Jack said, "I never claimed to be working in the Sun shipyards on the strength of the pictures. They were an advertising stunt for recruiting labor." He did it at the request of military personnel, in order to help the military. He did what the military requested of him. His bout with Meehan earned between $28,000 and $30,000 for the cause. After that, Lieutenant Kennedy wired the San Francisco draft board to release Mr. Dempsey, which it did. Still, he went to New York for another patriotic show. Soon thereafter, the armistice was signed and all enlistments stopped.[131]

Jack said his favorite amusements were baseball, football, swimming, jumping, running, tennis, basketball, handball, and golf. He liked all kinds of animals, but dogs were his favorite. He also liked to play with kids.

Speaking of the color line, Jack Kearns said, "I won't let Jack fight a colored man, for then he'd have to fight 'em all."[132]

On Tuesday March 9 in Tijuana, Julius E. "Bert" Gardner, an alleged Dempsey friend, was arrested as an alleged conspirator. Special agent O. O. Orr of the Department of Justice believed that he had frustrated Gardner's attempt to spirit Mrs. Maxine "Wayne," Maxine Dempsey's current name, from the jurisdiction of the U. S. courts. She was not

[130] *Los Angeles Times*, March 6, 1920.
[131] *New York Daily News*, March 9, 11, 1920.
[132] *New York Daily News*, March 12, 13, 1920.

arrested, but accompanied Orr to Los Angeles voluntarily, after which he would accompany her to San Francisco. Gardner was jailed on charges of threatening, intimidating, influencing, and corrupting a witness. The allegation was that Gardner persuaded Maxine to leave her mother's home in Yakima, Washington, and go to Tijuana, Mexico. Maxine arrived in Mexico on Sunday the 7th. Gardner also allegedly attempted to force her to sign letters which could be used for the defense.[133]

Another report said Maxine had Gardner arrested, and the arrest took place in San Diego. She had warned federal authorities that attempts were made to bribe her. Gardner invited her to go to "Tia Juana" to play the races. Other communications allegedly received led her to believe that not only were offers made to bribe her, but also threats made to intimidate her. Acting on advice, she accepted Gardner's invitation to go to Tia Juana. The Grand Jury had investigated Gardner regarding his alleged actions at Wells, Nevada when she first made the charges against the champion. No indictment was returned.[134]

Mrs. Jack Dempsey and Federal Agents.
The man in the rear is Special Agent O. O. Orr of San Francisco. At Mrs. Dempsey's left is Special Agent Cooksey of this city.

There were fears and concerns that Kearns, or Dempsey, or both, or others acting on their behalf, conspired, or might conspire to have Maxine Wayne sent out of the country to avoid her giving testimony. Hence, federal agents were guarding her closely.[135]

The press noted that Jack Dempsey was generous to his family. He purchased a 537-acre ranch for $53,000 and gave it to his father. He gave his mother a $48,000 home in Salt Lake City, and also gave her $50,000. He set up his brother John Dempsey in the oil business in Texas, gave him $1,000 cash, and established his brother Jim in an automobile accessory business in Oregon.[136]

Fooling around to entertain Marines, in their short film, famous silent film comedian Charlie Chaplin knocks out Jack Dempsey, with film star Douglas Fairbanks refereeing.

[133] *San Francisco Chronicle*, March 12, 13, 1920.
[134] *San Francisco Examiner*, March 12, 1920.
[135] *Los Angeles Times*, March 13, 1920; *San Francisco Examiner*, March 20, 1920.
[136] *Winnipeg Tribune*, March 13, 1920.

On March 21, 1920 in San Francisco, Dempsey and Kearns pled not guilty to willfully violating the selective service draft (by allegedly making false statements to local draft board No. 13), and Kearns plead not guilty to the charge of entering into a conspiracy to assist Dempsey in evading military duty and to defeat the selective service law. Jack rapidly chewed gum with his hands in his pockets, seeming unconcerned. Kearns seemed worried and nervous.[137]

Trial was set for April (though it would be continued). The *San Francisco Examiner* noted that Dempsey had a slight advantage in that he could assert a marital privilege, which meant that all communications which took place between Jack and Maxine while they were married were privileged and could not be used against him.[138]

On March 23, 1920, Georges Carpentier arrived in New York with his pretty 17-year-old bride and retinue. He looked more like a bank clerk on vacation than a pugilist. He spoke through an interpreter/translator, for he spoke little to no English. "I am anxious to box Jack Dempsey for the world's heavyweight championship as soon as the match can be arranged." Georges said he was weighing 176 pounds and stood 5'10".

[137] *Los Angeles Times*, March 21, 1920.
[138] *San Francisco Examiner*, April 5, 1920.

55

Some claimed that Carpentier told the press that he would whip Dempsey within 6 rounds. Carpentier knew that Dempsey was a rushing fighter, but Georges said he was better at beating that kind than any other. His footwork enabled him to side step and counter with power.[139]

Dempsey wired a greeting to Georges via telegram, saying, "A sincere welcome to America. Good luck and best wishes. Jack Dempsey."

Georges and his manager Francois Deschamps/Descamps met with Tex Rickard. Descamps said Carpentier would not box Dempsey until Jack's "military affairs" had been cleared up. Kearns agreed that Dempsey would need to be cleared of the draft evasion charge before any title fight could take place.[140]

Harry Greb manager Red Mason claimed that Greb was matched to fight Dempsey in Buffalo on May 31. However, the claim appeared to be an attempt at publicity and to stir up talk. Kearns said he knew nothing about it. "Dempsey has not been offered any match by any Buffalo promoter…and the story undoubtedly was put out simply to get some cheap publicity."

Bat Masterson, veteran writer for the *New York Morning Telegraph*, said Dempsey was not likely to fight until after the federal courts got through with him. "The idea of pitting Harry Greb against Jack Dempsey is such a ridiculous proposition that it's doubtful if a promoter anywhere in this country outside of Buffalo could be found who had the effrontery to even entertain such a proposition."[141]

However, Jimmy Bronson, Bob Martin's manager, said he believed Greb could outpoint Dempsey in a 10-round contest, with his great energy and freakish style.[142]

By a 30 to 19 vote, the New York senate passed the Walker boxing bill, which would legalize 15-round matches in New York. The bill was progressing through the required processes to become law.[143]

Allegedly, New York State Senator James J. Walker had been informed that former servicemen in the assembly would defeat the bill legalizing boxing if he did not make certain that Jack Dempsey could not fight under its provisions in New York. Walker said he was willing to accept an amendment which stated that no man convicted of evading the draft would be allowed to box in New York. Governor Al Smith would have to approve the law as well.[144]

On March 24, at her hotel in San Francisco, Maxine told the story of a woman scorned. She was anxious to testify against her former husband. While Jack Dempsey had been posing for the movie cameras in Los Angeles before the admiring gaze of movie queens, Maxine had been

[139] *New York Daily News*, March 24, 26, 1920.
[140] *San Francisco Examiner*, March 24, 1920; *New York Daily News*, March 25, 1920.
[141] *Pittsburgh Press*, March 22, 1920; *Buffalo Enquirer*, April 3, 1920. In late January, it had been reported that Buffalo's Queensberry club had offered Dempsey $50,000 and Greb $15,000 to fight there on Memorial Day, May 30. However, it appeared that Kearns was then holding out for a more lucrative fight with Carpentier. *Pittsburgh Gazette Times*, January 20, 1920; *Des Moines Tribune*, January 23, 1920.
[142] *Pittsburgh Gazette Times*, March 30, 1920.
[143] *New York Daily News*, March 25, 1920.
[144] *San Francisco Chronicle*, March 28, 1920.

playing a piano in Wells, Nevada, a freight division point with 200 inhabitants. Maxine said,

> Those who criticize me for telling the truth about Jack should picture me sitting in the town of Wells neglected, while Jack got easy money and fame. I had assisted Jack while he was a 'ham and egg' fighter. He lived off my money. Then, when he knew he was about to whip Willard, he divorced me. Did I get automobiles and pretty clothes? No! I was playing a piano for the amusement of freight-handlers and miners.

She said she did nothing until the American Legion posts all over the country began attacking Jack's war record.

> I knew they didn't have the goods on Jack, and that I did, but I didn't do anything. Then one day, about a week after the American Legion got busy, I got a package from Los Angeles. What do you suppose was in that package? It was Jack's photograph. He sent it with 'love.' Jack was afraid I would testify against him, and he thought he would win me back to him that easy. I sat down and wrote a letter to a newspaper saying I had the goods on Jack and that he was a slacker. That started things. Jack tried to phone me. Men began to arrive in Wells to see me. I wouldn't phone Jack and the men had no luck.

Maxine said life as the wife of a fighter had its drawbacks. For days before a fight, Jack would be sullen and savage. She admitted though that she once had blackened his eye. "It was after he had a bad fight with Willie Meehan. Meehan had cut his eye open. Jack and I were quarreling. He pushed me. I struck at his bad eye, but missed it and hit the other. Oh, what an eye I gave him."

She paid Jack Kearns the tribute of being the only man who could handle Dempsey.

Jack had divorced her on February 1, 1919. They had been married for about 2 years, 4 months. He had won the championship five months after their divorce. Maxine had not heard from him again directly until after the American Legion attacked his record, she said.

The *Arkansas Democrat* said Maxine clearly had a deep and bitter hatred for Dempsey. "She is so bent on revenge for some wrong, real or imagined, that she is willing to sacrifice those ideals of loyalty which commonly govern the actions of men and women, even after their love dreams are shattered, keeping them from the revelation of secrets which were the confidences of their former lives together." Although Jack Dempsey had a deadly punch, "we are inclined to the belief that the former Mrs. Dempsey has the 'deadlier' punch of the two." Everyone knew that Dempsey's former spouse was trying to hound him into the federal penitentiary on draft evasion charges. But now she was going further still, tipping off Carpentier as to the best way to beat him.

Maxine claimed that Dempsey not only had a weak back but was addicted to the use of strychnine (which was a deadly poison, but in low doses could be used as a cardiac/respiratory/muscle stimulant). "Jack goes strong at first, but he has a bad back, which weakens in the fourth. If Carpentier can hold out until that stage, he should win. When Jack gets past the fifth round and is filled up with strychnine, he is a hard man to beat."[145]

Maxine also accused Dempsey of using sniff/cocaine. She said he used dope before his fights, which helped his strength and courage, and helped him remain on his feet after being hit with hard blows. In her rage against him, trying to send him to prison in disgrace, she not only was branding him a slacker who hid behind her skirts to evade service during the war, but she impugned his integrity as a fighter as well. Maxine said,

> I advise Carpentier or any other fighters to stay away from Jack for the first three rounds, and then go in and play for Jack's stomach and the region around his heart. It is not known but Jack has his 'snort of snow' before he steps out for the first round. For three rounds he is unbeatable and Carpentier, with hypnotic eye and all that, had better keep away from him for the first three sessions. After the third round, if he has a hard fight, the effect of the 'snort' wears away and Jack gets nervous and his weak back begins to hurt him. If Carpentier plays for Jack's heart and stomach then he will lick him before the end of the fifth round. Before Jack goes out for the sixth round he receives an injection of strychnine and he regains his courage, but a good blow about the heart is liable to kill him then.[146]

So, Maxine had accused Dempsey of throwing the Flynn fight, conspiring to dodge the draft, and using cocaine and strychnine to win fights.

Marion Salazar said Jack Dempsey was "picked for a sucker in Oakland years ago and that's the real story of his start." Al Norton had beaten several men, and there was no one in sight for him, so they got Dempsey to be the opponent after he had been stopped in one round by Flynn, thinking that he would be another Norton victim. But Dempsey fooled them, proving that he was a real fighter.[147]

Jack Kearns said Dempsey's jealous former wife, Mrs. Maxine Wayne, perjured herself before the grand jury. "Federal investigators hold written receipts of telegraph money orders Dempsey sent his wife during the war to support her."

Kearns said Jack currently was working hard on the coast with the Pathe film company, and was not concerned, for his wife's affidavit was false.[148]

---

[145] *Arkansas Democrat, Enid Daily Eagle, Wichita Eagle*, March 25, 1920; *Regina Morning Leader*, March 26, 1920; *Lawton Constitution*, March 26, 1920, claimed the article was written by Dan Beebee, United Press Staff Correspondent.
[146] *Collyer's Eye*, March 27, 1920.
[147] *Anaconda Standard*, March 27, 1920.
[148] *Salt Lake Herald-Republican*, March 26, 1920.

Promoter Tex Rickard said the Dempsey-Carpentier fight likely would not take place until 1921.[149]

On March 30, 1920 in Aurora, Illinois, Bill Brennan won a 10-round no decision over Bob Devere.[150]

On April 5, 1920 in Newark, New Jersey, 175-pound Gene Tunney knocked out 170-pound KO Sullivan in the 1st round with a short right to the chin. Tunney previously had won a 10-round decision over Sullivan in April 1919 in Paris, in a military service bout.[151]

--TOMORROW--
The Heavyweight Champion of
the World

JACK DEMPSEY
IN
"DAREDEVIL JACK"

Despite his legal troubles, *Daredevil Jack* still was playing all over the country.

On April 13, 1920 in Oakland, Jack Dempsey was arrested for speeding, traveling at 32 miles per hour. Jack said he was 6'1", 200 pounds, and resided at 214 Sunnyside Avenue in Oakland.[152]

More and more, Dempsey was being treated like, and his life mirroring, that of Jack Johnson's. Like Johnson, he was arrested for speeding, had an ex-lover/wife trying to destroy him, the government was coming after him, and various jurisdictions indicated that he was not wanted there and/or would not be allowed to fight. Clearing up the draft dodging accusations was of paramount importance to his life and ability to carry on with his boxing career.

In late April, Kearns allegedly came to terms for Dempsey to fight for promoter Floyd Fitzsimmons of Benton Harbor, Michigan, for a bout to be held there on July 5. The promoter was in discussions to obtain either Fred Fulton, Billy Miske, or Bill Brennan as the opponent. Such plans appeared to be very tentative and dependent upon the timing and result of the upcoming trial.[153]

In somewhat of a surprise, it was revealed that Maxine Dempsey had been married and divorced prior to her marriage to Jack Dempsey. The government argued that the marital privilege did not apply, because Mrs. Dempsey got married too soon after her previous divorce, and hence her marriage to Jack Dempsey was invalid. Apparently, there was a 6-month wait period required before a person could remarry after getting divorced, and it had not been fulfilled. She had been divorced for only 4 days (another source said 13 days) before marrying Dempsey. Hence, the government argued that she never was his legal wife.

Jack Dempsey had not been made aware of Maxine Wayne's former marriage, and she made every effort to conceal the fact. She had been married to George Glasshoff, a brakeman, and received an interlocutory

[149] *San Francisco Examiner*, March 27, 1920.
[150] In 1918, Dempsey had stopped Devere in the 1st round. Devere had a 1917 WND10 Jim Flynn; 1916 WND10 Sam Langford; and 1917 LND10 Langford. The *Montreal Gazette*, December 30, 1916, said Devere had a slight edge on Langford. The *Montreal Star* said Langford received a "bad drubbing." "Devere is a pretty hard hitter, displays a good defence, and appears to be able to take punishment."
[151] *Binghamton Press, New York Tribune, New York Herald, Brooklyn Daily Eagle*, April 6, 1920. Some later claimed that Sullivan either decked or hurt Tunney in their 10-round service bout, but there is no verification for such claims.
[152] *San Francisco Examiner*, April 14, 1920.
[153] *Los Angeles Evening Express, Los Angeles Times*, April 22, 1920. At that time, Kearns and Dempsey were in Salt Lake City.

decree for divorce on September 26, 1916. She married Dempsey 13 days later, on October 9 (perhaps only 4 days after the divorce was finalized).[154]

State of Washington marriage records showed that on February 27, 1915, 18-year-old Maxine Cates, a housekeeper, married George Glasshof, age 27, a clerk. Glasshof of Kennewick, Washington, was listed as being from Wisconsin originally, and Cates, of Pendleton, Washington, as being from Oregon. Cates had been married to Glasshof for just over a year and a half before the divorce and immediately marrying Dempsey.

On April 23, 1920 in Denver, Colorado, Harry Wills won a 15-round referee's decision over Sam Langford. For the *Denver Post*, Rick Ricketson said Wills dropped Langford four times in the 1st round, but couldn't stop him. "Wills can't lead. His lack of aggressiveness cost him a knockout." The fight looked like a "Giant and a midget. Wills was much stronger. He was able to wrestle Langford over the ring." He was heavier and faster. Harry gave Sam a terrific body walloping. Still, "Wills did not come up to his advance notices. He would last about a round with Dempsey and maybe five with Fulton. To compare him with Jack Johnson is a joke."

For Denver's *Rocky Mountain News*, Abe Pollock said that despite being decked four times with wicked rights in the 1st round and practically out, and hurt again in the 5th, Langford managed to keep in close, clinch, and survive the distance. "How he stayed on his feet under the terrific punching of Wills was a mystery to the ringside fans. Never once did he weaken, but kept trying continually to put over his famous haymaker." However, Wills was younger and bigger, and youth was served.[155]

On May 2, 1920, Negro National League baseball began, also known as the Negro Leagues. Since major league teams would not allow any blacks to play, blacks players started their own league, led by Andrew "Rube" Foster (a.k.a. Rube Foster). America's number one team sport, baseball, which was rivaled in popularity only by the sport of boxing, was segregated, and would remain so until 1947.

Professional football had at least one black player, Fred (Fritz) Pollard, who once had played halfback for Brown University, and played pro

---

[154] *New York Daily News*, April 27, 1920; *San Francisco Chronicle*, April 26, 1920; *Daily Arkansas Gazette*, April 28, 1920.
[155] *Denver Post, Rocky Mountain News*, April 24, 1920. The next day, Langford's lips were swollen to twice their size, one eye was almost closed, a large cut was in his forehead, and his nose looked as if it were pushed out of shape. Langford said he did not remember anything until the 9th round. Sam called Wills one of the best two-handed fighters in the ring at present. *Rocky Mountain News*, April 25, 1920.

football in the 1919 season. "Fritz played professional football last fall [1919] with Akron, O., and in five games is said to have pulled down the munificent sum of $1,200." At the time, pro football was considered to be a minor pro sport, with a small following, while amateur college football was considered to be much more important.[156]

The *New York Age* said men like Pollard showed what Negro youths could accomplish when given an equal opportunity with their white brethren. Yet, men like Pollard "have all been pointed to by the white man and called exceptions."[157]

Pollard would lead the Akron Pros to the APFA (later known as the NFL) championship in 1920. In 1921, he became the co-head coach of the team while still playing as a running back, making him the first black head coach in pro football.

By 1926, there would be less than ten black football players in the entire league. However, all either left or were removed from the league at the end of the season, never to return. By the end of 1933, the league once again became fully segregated, based on a silent agreement amongst the owners, a movement led by Redskins owner George Marshall. No black player was allowed into the league again until 1946.

On May 6, 1920 in Boston, Italian southpaw Johnny Wilson won the world middleweight championship from Mike O'Dowd, winning a 12-round referee's decision.

On that same date, in Rochester, New York, 195-pound Bill Brennan administered a severe beating to win a clear 10-round newspaper decision over 186 ½-pound Ole Anderson.[158]

On May 15, 1920 in Pittsburgh, 166-pound Tommy Gibbons (49-0-4) won a clear 10-round no decision over 165-pound Harry Greb (153-10-14). The *Pittsburgh Gazette Times'* Harry Keck said Gibbons gave middleweight Greb a decisive beating, completely outboxing and outfighting him, badly punishing Greb throughout, winning every round by a wide margin, except the 1st, which was even. The battered Greb was tired and weak at the finish, holding on to survive, left eye closed, face puffed, body red, and a number of front teeth missing.

The *Pittsburgh Post's* Florent Gibson said Gibbons solved and foiled Greb's attack, and at the same time found Greb's defense easy to penetrate. Gibbons carried the fight to Greb at all stages and held the lead from the start, giving him the licking of his life, winning 7-2-1.

The *Pittsburg Press'* Jim Jab said Gibbons was an easy winner, never letting up, winning 9-0-1. Greb was unable to check his onslaughts.

Gibbons had won a clear 1915 10-round no decision over Greb as well, making him 2-0 against Greb.[159]

[156] *Winona Daily News*, January 2, 1920.

[157] *New York Age*, March 20, 1920.

[158] *Rochester Democrat and Chronicle*, May 7, 1920. Anderson had fought Meehan to a 4-round draw that many thought Anderson won. Anderson also had a 1919 W4 Jim Flynn and W6 Carl Morris, but had been stopped by Harry Wills in the 3rd round.

[159] *Pittsburgh Gazette Times, Pittsburgh Post, Pittsburg Press*, May 16, 1920. Regarding their prior November 16, 1915 contest in St. Paul, Minnesota, the next-day *Minneapolis Morning Tribune's* Fred Coburn said Gibbons "clearly outpointed" Greb, 6-1-3, staggering him in the 9th. The *Minneapolis Journal* said Gibbons clearly won the fight 6-1-3, winning the last 5 rounds after it was even, 1-

On May 19, 1920 in Philadelphia, 190-pound Bill Brennan won a 6-round no decision over 196-pound Willie Meehan, further putting Meehan out of the running for any title-shot consideration, and enhancing Brennan's reputation. Meehan had "comical windmill swings," while Brennan "showed lots of class and proved he is a man to be feared. Brennan got the decision and Meehan got the laughs."[160]

Jack Dempsey was filming movies in Los Angeles. He said he would make no fight plans until his trial was over and the verdict returned.[161] The truth, though, was that he had no choice. No jurisdiction was going to allow him to fight and defend the world title with the cloud of the criminal prosecution hanging over his head. Politicians would step in to prevent a Dempsey contest. Regardless, few promoters would want to take the risk, given the potential public outrage.

The trial was continued several times, until eventually set for June 8.

On May 24, 1920, New York Governor Al Smith signed into law the Walker boxing bill, permitting 15-round bouts with a formal decision, restoring boxing to full legal status in New York.

> Boxing was placed under the jurisdiction of a state athletic commission by the Frawley law in 1911, but the commission was abolished when the law was repealed in 1917. This law limited contests to ten rounds, without decisions. Before the Frawley law became effective, twenty-round bouts were permitted under the Horton law.[162]

On June 4, 1920 in Bayonne, New Jersey, Bill Brennan and Bartley Madden, "two of the best of the heavyweight crop," fought to what the *New York Evening World, New York Tribune,* and *Jersey Journal* called a 12-round newspaper draw, though the *Brooklyn Daily Times* said Brennan won by a shade. It was nip and tuck throughout. Brennan was the aggressor most of the way, but Madden scored many blows too. Earlier that year, Brennan had won a clear 10-round no decision over Madden.[163]

Also on June 4, 1920, in Boston, Massachusetts, Governor Calvin Coolidge signed a new state law legalizing 10-round bouts, allowing decisions by two judges, with the referee to act as the tiebreaker if necessary. Participants had to be licensed, and a 5% tax of the gross receipts would be levied.[164]

Hence, recently, two major states, New York and Massachusetts, had loosened the legal reigns on boxing. Still, at that time, boxing was legal in less than half of the country. Boxing was a sport that always did have a tenuous existence under the law; and politicians always could abolish or limit it in some way, or legalize it, at their discretion. This was something of which boxing's participants, including promoters, remained cognizant.

1-3, after the first 5. Although tough and awkwardly clever, Greb bled freely from several cuts and was punished heavily toward the end. Gibbons "apparently would have won by a knockout in a longer battle."
[160] *Philadelphia Inquirer, Philadelphia Evening Public Ledger,* May 20, 1920.
[161] *San Francisco Chronicle,* May 4, 1920.
[162] *Rochester Democrat and Chronicle,* May 25, 1920.
[163] *New York Evening World, Brooklyn Daily Times, New York Tribune, Jersey Journal,* June 5, 1920.
[164] *Boston Post, Pittsburgh Post, Los Angeles Evening Express,* June 5, 1920.

CHAPTER 3

The United States vs. William Harrison Dempsey

On June 7, 1920, a federal judge denied Jack Dempsey's lawyer's request to inspect prior to the trial the letters allegedly written by his client to Maxine Dempsey, as well as the draft questionnaire he signed. The defense had not seen the evidence.[165]

On June 8, 1920 in San Francisco, the federal criminal trial against William Harrison Dempsey, otherwise known as Jack Dempsey, began. The trial would last about a week. Crowds thronged to see the proceedings. The champ and Jack Kearns both wore dark blue suits. Dempsey entered wearing a straw hat. His mother and father were present. His mother, a modest woman, wore black. His father had a black cane. The 200-seat courtroom was crowded to capacity.

The jury mostly was comprised of business men, only one of whom had seen a prize fight. None knew anything about the Dempsey case. Two were dismissed for cause, because they had developed opinions about the case as a result of having read about it in the newspapers. Only two prospective jurors admitted to having seen Dempsey in action. One later was challenged by the government. One man who said he saw the Dempsey-Meehan fight and admired Dempsey as a fighter was allowed on the jury.

The judge was Maurice T. Dooling. Dempsey's lawyers were John W. Preston and Gavin McNab. Representing the government were Colonel C. W. Thomas, R. B. McMillan, and Annette A. Adams. Nearly 100 witnesses were expected to testify.

The counts charged Dempsey with evading the draft, attempting to evade the draft, and conspiracy to evade the draft. The charges alleged that on Dempsey's questionnaire signed in Chicago on January 19, 1918, he swore that his wife, mother, father, and his widowed sister and her two children were dependent on him for support. He contributed $80 a month to them. He swore that he had been living with his wife for 18 months prior to the signing of the questionnaire. The questionnaire listed his employer as Jack Kearns, and declared his profession to be boxing. Jack originally had registered for the draft in San Francisco on May 31, 1917. He then listed his employment as carpenter.

The government claimed it would call witnesses to the stand to show that neither his mother, father, nor his sister were dependent upon Dempsey for support. The government alleged that in fact, his father had

[165] *San Francisco Chronicle*, June 8, 1920. They didn't have the pre-trial disclosure discovery rules back then that we have today.

been earning around $300 per year at odd jobs. Seven witnesses would tell how his family worked for their support.

The defense planned to show that Dempsey made $300,000 for the Red Cross in various boxing exhibitions, doing his part for the war effort, and he indeed supported his family.

The testimony showed that other members of the Dempsey family besides Jack were contributing to the family support during 1917. However, the statute required them to be "mainly dependent," which was open to interpretation. It did not say "solely dependent." Hence there was an argument that even if others provided support, his answers were not necessarily deceptive.

The government introduced into evidence Dempsey's questionnaire, registration, and classification cards. Miss Margaret O'Keefe, deputy registrar of voters, testified.

John S. Hogan, chairman of local board No. 13, testified that to the best of his belief, Dempsey was classified correctly when placed in Class 4A.

Rudolph Goodman, a Chicago notary who witnessed Dempsey's signature to the questionnaire, testified that he went over the January 19, 1918 questionnaire questions and answers with Dempsey, and that Jack approved certain additions made in filling out incomplete portions. When asked who supplied the additional information, he said, "Jack Kearns answered the questions, and Dempsey said his answers were correct." Kearns did the talking for Dempsey. Dempsey described himself as a boxer employed by Kearns. He stated that, if called to service, he preferred aviation. He said that he had worked at the trade of carpenter, and was an expert miner as well as boxer. He told Goodman that he had earned $2,500 during the preceding year (1917); that his wife was "sickly" and never had been employed, and that dependent upon him were his wife, parents, and widowed sister and her two children, contributing about $20 each (about $80 total) a month to their support.

Seeking to refute Dempsey's declaration in the questionnaire that Hiram Dempsey had earned only $300 at odd jobs during the previous year, H. S. McCann, Salt Lake auditor, produced the local payrolls, which showed that Hiram had been paid $472.38 for laborer services for work on the streets.

Freda Gibson, owner of the house in Salt Lake City where the Dempseys lived, said Hiram earned the money, gave it to Mrs. Dempsey, and she paid the $12 monthly rent.

A. J. Auerbach said Jack's sister Effie Clarkson/Effie Barrows worked for his hair goods establishment from 1916 until recently. She was paid from $10 to $12 per week. But he admitted on cross examination that she was ill and only able to work about half of the time during 1917.

E. H. Butts, a Huntington, West Virginia attorney, stated that during 1917, he was conducting a lawsuit in Mrs. Dempsey's interests (Jack's mom) regarding a claim to an acre of land near Huntington, West Virginia, which resulted in her receiving about $700. However, the defense brought out that she did not settle or receive this money until the spring of 1918, well after Jack's questionnaire was filled out, and she was obliged to spend a large portion of it for expenses during the suit.[166]

The next day, Helen Goodrich, Maxine's associate in the "night life," was asked at what Maxine was "working" in 1917. She answered that Maxine was a member of the underworld, practicing prostitution. Dempsey's attorney Gavin McNab sprang to his feet and exclaimed, "This is the first time in the history of jurisprudence that vice has been declared to be work. The United States Government has prosecuted that sort of work. Is it now to be upheld by Government prosecutors?" Continuing, he eloquently thundered, "Since Moses brought down that great commandment from Mt. Sinai, 'thou shalt not commit adultery,' this is the first time in all history that vice has been called work." "If the United States Government calls that work, and hopes to convict this defendant on that definition, it is a violation of Scriptural injunction and the first recognition of adultery as a legitimate enterprise."

Judge Dooling overruled the objection, as well as the request to strike the testimony, saying that the question was not whether or not the work in which she was engaged was proper or not, but whether she was working at anything or dependent on Dempsey for support, and whether he knew that his wife was doing this.

Attorney Preston rose to his feet and said, "Every sin committed by this wife was over the protest of her husband. Dempsey did not know where she was and could not find her. This we will show by abundant proof." Attorney McNab declared, "We will show that Jack Dempsey protested vigorously against Maxine's living that life."

Continuing, Goodrich testified that she and Maxine Dempsey traveled to various cities practicing prostitution. They traveled from Waco to Spokane, St. Louis, and finally Cairo, Illinois. In Cairo, Maxine went by the name of Bobby Stewart, and became an inmate of a disorderly house (of prostitution) run by Mrs. Nannie Coffey. Goodrich said Maxine received no money from Jack during their travels. Maxine did receive a letter from him at Cairo, but Goodrich did not know what it said.

So, apparently, sometime after Jack and Maxine separated in 1917, she had traveled the country practicing prostitution.

Nannie Coffey took the stand. She spoke strongly, in contrast with Goodrich, who had spoken in a low voice, evidently suffering as a result

166 San Francisco Examiner, San Francisco Chronicle, June 9, 1920.

of being forced to display "her own past shame" to public curiosity. Goodrich had shyly and quietly admitted that she had been working in the same manner that Maxine Dempsey was.

Coffey was more aggressive. She admitted that she kept a house of ill-fame in Cairo. She didn't care who knew it, or at least such was her attitude. Coffey said Maxine was then known as Bobbie Stewart, and was an "inmate" at her house. "Said she was separated from her husband. Went away and left a lot of unpaid bills." "Did she pay you?" "She did."

What was established was that Maxine Dempsey was a woman of the underworld, traveling about the country in the company of women who "pass in the night," even after she married Jack.

The matter was ended when the defense admitted that Maxine received no money or supplies from Dempsey while she was an inmate of any house of ill-fame. McNab added that during most of this time, Jack did not know where his wife was.

Charles Goff's testimony was ruled out as inadmissible. He was the head of the San Francisco morals squad in 1917, and would have been asked about the reputation of the Gibson hotel, where Maxine lived, as a house of ill-fame.

John D. Ellis, half-brother of Jack's mother, Mrs. Hiram Dempsey, testified that Jack's mother was said to have been paid about $700 on some property, but his testimony didn't add much.

Dr. Joseph Fife told about being called to the Gibson Hotel, where Maxine lived in San Francisco, in May 1917, to attend to a woman who was suffering from a dislocated jaw, which she said she received in a fall downstairs. It was not a paper jaw syndrome, but a nuxation of the inferior maxillary. The prosecution was trying to imply that it was the result of domestic violence at the hands of Jack. The government used the same tactics against Jack Johnson at his trial, which appellate courts later said was improper.

Next up would be Maxine Dempsey. However, outside the presence of the jury, legal arguments ensued. Dempsey's lawyers argued that marital privilege prevented her from testifying to conversations or communications she had with Dempsey while they were married. The prosecution showed that she had been married to George Glassoff, and divorced from him via interlocutory decree on October 5, 1916, marrying Dempsey only four days later, on October 9, 1916. They contended that the marriage to Dempsey was void because she had not received a final decree of divorce, and therefore she was not legally married to Dempsey, and hence the marital privilege did not apply.

However, the government received a solar plexus blow. The judge ruled that the marriage certificate and the divorce decree were the best evidence that Jack and Maxine were legally married at the time that Jack Dempsey signed the draft questionnaire. They were married on October 9, 1916 in Farmington, Utah. On February 4, 1919, a Utah court granted Jack a divorce from Maxine, reciting that the two had been and were husband and wife. The Utah divorce decree established that a marriage relation had existed. Hence, the marital privilege applied to their communications while married, and communications between Jack and his wife while they were married were barred and excluded from the trial as confidential, including any letters he allegedly sent to his then wife. As a result, 35 letters Jack wrote to Maxine Dempsey, purportedly asking her to sign an affidavit that he was supporting her and therefore eligible for deferred draft classification, were ruled inadmissible. Divorce did not remove the barrier to testimony concerning such communications while they were married.

Nevertheless, the judge also ruled that Maxine Dempsey could testify to matters that did not involve communications between her and Jack, and could testify to acts for which she did not obtain knowledge via the confidential relationship.

THE "WOMAN SCORNED"

The next day, on June 10, Maxine Dempsey took the witness stand. She testified that she had lived under half a dozen aliases. She also had used the names Maxine Cates and Maxine Glesshof (or Glasshoff), for she had been married to George Glesshof and then divorced.

She told her story of "underworld life," sometimes "sordid," sometimes humorous, but always certain. She never hesitated under direct examination by Colonel Thomas. She spoke without emotion, telling of "her life of scarlet" with no more reluctance than as though it were a mere nursery rhyme.

The government wanted to ask her whether or not during her travels about the country she had, according to the testimony of her associates, been an inmate of various houses of ill-fame (meaning she had been a prostitute in whorehouses), whether she had received money or clothing from Jack, and what her relations with Jack were when she first met him (perhaps implying that she was a prostitute even then). Objections and argument outside the presence of the jury followed. According to government witnesses and Maxine Dempsey's own admissions, she had an interesting past life. Like Jack Johnson, Jack Dempsey had been married to a woman who engaged in prostitution.

The judge ruled most questions to be irrelevant to the charges at hand, saying,

The only question is whether or not Dempsey evaded the draft, not whether he violated the white slave law or any other question of morals. Because Jack Dempsey happens to be a prizefighter and because the newspapers have played up his case he is not going to get any different sort of a trial than if he were plain John Doe, charged with the same offense. ... We are here to try this man on the question of whether he evaded the draft; not as a moral slacker. We shall not try him because he is a prize fighter and has a big crowd at his back.[167]

Judge Dooling ruled that Maxine could testify regarding how much money she received from Jack, for the sending of money was not a communication.

According to Maxine, she traveled from place to place from February 1, 1917 on, and that even for the short time she was living with Jack, they constantly were on the move. Their sojourns in various cities would last from a few days to a few weeks, often multiple residences even in the same city.

After one of his early prize fights, Jack purchased a diamond ring for her, and a diamond pin for himself. Later, he had the pin made into a ring for her, but when they decided to leave Salt Lake City and come to San Francisco, he took the rings from her and sold them to pay for the railroad tickets. (That actually contradicted the story she told in 1917, claiming that Dempsey took her rings when he suddenly disappeared in San Francisco.)

Maxine claimed that the dislocated jaw for which she was treated at the Gibson hotel in San Francisco resulted from a blow struck by Jack. "I hadn't made any money that night, and Dempsey struck me and knocked me down."

In the spring of 1917, she left San Francisco to go to Pasco, Washington to enter a life of prostitution. She had only 50 cents and no clothes except what she could get into a small handbag.

Dempsey joined her in Pasco, and went with her as far as Seattle. After a short time, she eventually went to Cairo, Illinois on her own. From the spring of 1917 to November 1917, she received from Dempsey only $50, in sums of $10, $25, and $15. He also sent her a ticket to come to Salt Lake City. She left Cairo in November 1917.

One report claimed she testified that up until the time she signed Dempsey's questionnaire on January 25, 1918, she had received in all about $900 from him during their married life, including sums for clothing. Another report claimed she said that Jack sent her $900 between January 25, 1918, when she signed the supporting affidavit for his questionnaire confirming that she was dependent upon him, and November 1918, when they finally separated. After she signed his questionnaire in January 1918, he began sending her money.

[167] *San Francisco Chronicle, San Francisco Examiner,* June 10, 1920.

As her last dig on the witness stand, Maxine told a story, that Tommy Fitzgerald, a Salt Lake City café man, had called on her in Wells to say that Jack Kearns had asked him to call on her and get her to shut up. He offered her a diamond ring if she would go to Los Angeles and see Jack. She told Tommy all that had happened, and he changed his mind about her. She denied telling Fitzgerald that she had enough letters to hang Jack or send him up (to prison) for white slavery.

She told her story with apparent enjoyment. She actually seemed eager to dwell on the sordid details of her life in one city after another. It was unmistakably clear that when she and Jack had drifted apart, after just months of life together, she had made a bee-line for the underworld, where apparently she was most at home.

When the defense attacked her on cross examination, Maxine became a woman at bay, alert, sparring, fighting every inch. Her brown eyes sparkled, and her slightly pale face set into lines like a tigress. Her profession had taught her a primeval self-defense against man. Time and again, Maxine played for time when asked questions, apparently failing to hear the question, and often fell back on the statement that she did not remember. Whenever she did answer, she answered cautiously, and avoided direct statements. Her knowledge of English grammar was hazy, but her wits were keen.

Under cross examination, she admitted that the amount she claimed Dempsey provided her was a guess; that she "guessed" it was about $900. She could not remember specific amounts or dates, but somehow, she brought the total to $900. Maxine was unable to remember various sums of money the defense sought to show that she had received from Jack.

Maxine reluctantly admitted under cross examination that during those months when she and Jack were together, he paid the bills.

The defense claimed Maxine actually received at least $1,800 in support from him. Three Western Union men from Salt Lake City were allowed to testify by permission so that they could return to duty. They testified that Maxine Dempsey received many remittances by wire from Jack, so many that they noted her as a frequent visitor to the office. Both Maxine and Jack's mother Celia received money, but Maxine came more often than his mother. "After the date of the Fulton fight [July 1918] Maxine Dempsey got $200. I remember, because she said that Fulton must have hit Jack hard to jar him loose from $200." A night manager of the Western Union office during 1918 testified that Maxine had spoken to him about Jack's remittances, and had said, "Jack always sends plenty of money when he has it." Once, she received money two nights in succession, and when he remarked on that fact, she said, "I needed it. I lost the first lot shooting craps."

The long-awaited letters made their first appearance in court, but nobody read them except the judge and the attorneys, outside the presence of the jury. Judge Dooling refused to allow Maxine to testify to anything contained in the letters sent to her by Jack, particularly the one concerning the draft. "I will not permit Maxine Dempsey to testify to anything regarding that letter." But the lawyers did cross examine her about what she did with the letters that Jack sent her.

The defense attorneys grilled her regarding her motives, why she kept certain letters but destroyed others, why she made her charges public through certain newspapers before reporting them to the government, why she entrusted to Beulah Taylor, a negress piano player at the Wells, Nevada house of ill repute, of which Maxine was an inmate, the letters that the government later obtained from the safe deposit box where Beulah stored them. She said she gave the letters to Taylor because she was afraid someone would get them from her. She admitted that the letters were selected from a number of letters that Jack had written to her, and she had destroyed the others.

McNab asked whether she had told Beulah and Peggy Murray at Wells that she had read in the newspapers that Dempsey would get $250,000 for the Carpentier fight, and she was going to have $40,000 of it or else she would drag Jack down to the same level as herself. "I did not. That was suggested by Beulah Taylor after a talk with another woman, but I did not assent to it." "There was a discussion, but I didn't say that. I didn't pay any attention to it; I knew Jack would never part with $40,000." McNab asked whether her purpose in saving the letters was that she was thinking of his rapid rise to fame and comparative fortune, and what she might get out of it. "If Jack had given you $40,000 would you have given him the letters?" "I didn't think Jack would give $40,000 for anything. At the time I destroyed the other letters; I never dreamed Jack would ever have $40,000." This brought laughter from the crowded courtroom. The Judge warned those in the back that he was "not running a show."

When McNab cross-examined Maxine about an attempt to extort money out of Jack by using the letters to blackmail him, Maxine often would reply, "I don't remember. I'm not swearing to anything." She denied participation in any blackmail scheme. She claimed that she only wanted to help the government. Her story was notable principally for the portions she failed to remember. Her jaunty air had left her, not smiling with the same carefree assurance as earlier. She was sullen and smoldering.

Maxine admitted that Taylor actually had written the letter which appeared in the *San Francisco Chronicle* on January 23, 1920, in which Maxine first disclosed her willingness to give evidence against Dempsey, stating she had letters to show. Taylor's literary style was better than hers, so she composed the letter and Maxine signed it.

She was asked why she waited so long to make her charges public, and why she did it in early 1920. "We hadn't written to each other for a long time, and then he sent me a photograph of himself, and it made me mad. I didn't care what I did."

To demonstrate that she was not an unwilling convert to and participant in the ranks of prostitution, McNab introduced a letter written by Maxine from Elko, Nevada to a woman friend whom she addressed as

"Tommy," saying, "Well, here I am right side up. It certainly seems good to be sporting again [meaning engaged in prostitution]. You know, when you've been at it for seven years it's hard to get away from it." Holy cow. 7 years! That meant she had been engaged in prostitution well before she met Dempsey, even before she had been married the first time, likely since the age of 15 or 16, possibly even younger, depending on when she wrote that letter (which might have been written as early as 1917). Remember, she was 18 years old as of her first marriage in early 1915. In anticipation of a potential objection, McNab noted, "This is not a privileged communication. It's a letter from one prostitute to another." Hence, Maxine seemed to be happy to be a prostitute again after leaving or being separated or divorced from Dempsey, just as she had been prior to meeting Dempsey.

Maxine was asked if she knew that Jack had donned the overalls and had his picture taken at the behest of the government, to boost enlistments for shipyard work. She claimed that she knew nothing about Jack's work for war relief except what she had read in the newspapers. "Didn't you know that when Jack Dempsey went to work in the Philadelphia shipyards and was photographed in his overalls it was with Government approval as a move to advertise the yards and attract labor?" "I didn't know it, and I do not know it now."

She admitted that since February 1920, the government had detained her in San Francisco, and was paying her $3 a day.

At the end of her cross-examination came a significant statement. Maxine admitted that on October 25, 1918, she signed a waiver of her claims as a dependent, so that Jack Dempsey could apply for enlistment to join the Marine Corps. He was just completing his enlistment, the defense asserted, when the armistice interfered.

On redirect, Maxine claimed that while living at the Gibson Hotel in San Francisco in 1917, she and Jack occupied the same room, but she was practicing prostitution to earn a living. Wow.[168]

The government rested its case.

The next day, the defense put on its case.

Tommy Fitzgerald testified that he knew Maxine when she worked in his café in Salt Lake City. Kearns recently had asked him to call on her in Wells, Nevada. Fitzgerald went to ask Maxine what the trouble was. She said Jack had not treated her right, and she wanted to "hang him." He advised her to get a lawyer, and she said she already had a lawyer. She called in Beulah Taylor, and said, "Here is my lawyer." He replied, "Well, I buy a drink on that." He asked what the idea was, and Maxine replied, "The idea is five figures." She said this meant $40,000. She told Fitzgerald that she would give up the letters for that amount.

Fitzgerald called Kearns the next day and said a party there wanted $40,000, if agreeable.

[168] *San Francisco Chronicle, San Francisco Examiner,* June 11, 12, 1920.

71

Fitzgerald testified that he then telephoned and told Dempsey that Maxine demanded $40,000 on threat of giving out the letters. Dempsey replied, "Whatever they've got they can give to the government or anybody else and go to hell."

Peggy Murray corroborated Fitzgerald's statement regarding the $40,000 and Maxine's expressed desire to get it from Jack. They told of several conversations in Wells in which Maxine made it clear that it was money she was after, and did not care a whit about the government.

Murray was an inmate at the house in Wells. She said Maxine had shown her a letter which Beulah Taylor had written to the *San Francisco Chronicle*, and Maxine said Beulah had declared that the letter would start the ball rolling so she could get $40,000. Beulah asked, "Don't you think I'm a good lawyer?" Maxine replied, "You bet your life."

Mrs. Tommy Wilson, the madam of the house, corroborated Tommy Fitzgerald's story about his visit to Wells.

Jack's mother, Priscilla Dempsey, known as Cilla or Celia Dempsey, testified last that day. She said her boy was a good boy. He had worked hard since he was 14 years old, and since age 18 or 1915 or thereabouts, he practically had been her entire support and the support of the other members of the family. Even before 1917, in May 1916, Jack had sent her four checks totaling $125. She could not have managed in 1917 or 1918 without Jack's support. The family had hard luck in the years before Jack fought his way to fame and fortune. Husband Hiram was crippled with rheumatism and inclined to times of absent-mindedness and melancholy. He had been physically and mentally unable and unfit to support the family. Celia had been ill for many months. Effie, his sister, also had been ill and had undergone operations. She was too weak to gain a livelihood. Johnny, the younger brother, suffered three operations, and both he and Joseph, another brother, were in such poor health that they were given limited service by the draft boards. In 1917, 16-year-old Bruce, the baby of the family, was murdered.

She said Jack was the only help. Two other brothers were married and taking care of families of their own. So the burden of caring for others fell on Jack's shoulders. She described a boy who used to bring home what he earned and say, "Here, mother, do what you like with it, but be sure you buy yourself some clothes." After a fight in Milwaukee, he sent her $150 with a clipping about his victory. He deprived himself of his winnings to give them to his mother. After a Meehan fight, he sent her money, as he did after other fights as well.

By that time, Maxine was in Wells, tired of the slow life of respectability. She preferred to be with others of her kind. Maxine was restless for a long time, feeling that life in Salt Lake was too slow. "I'd rather go back to my old life and smoke hop than stay in any slow place like this," she allegedly said. Maxine would complain that her hands were a little rough from helping Celia. She didn't like that. Celia tried to persuade her to stay, that Jack would buy her a nice house once he won the championship, but she could not be persuaded, was not interested in the domestic life, and left.

His mom further said that Jack sent her many sums of money in 1917 and 1918. In those two years, she received about $37,000 from him, including two houses he purchased for her. After the July 1918 Fulton fight, he bought her a $4,500 home in Salt Lake City.

Celia said Jack wanted to go into the service, and wanted to go to war. She declared that Jack was the sole and only support of the family, and just as soon as he got them in a financial position so that he could leave, he enlisted, or tried to do so.

After the Willard fight, he bought her a $20,000 home in Salt Lake City. Prior to that, she had lived in a three-room cottage, wherein seven members of her family resided.

Cross examination brought out no new facts and was unable to shake her. The *San Francisco Chronicle* said the ugly picture painted of the champion had been reversed by his white-haired mother's testimony.[169]

An interesting side-development occurred when stories were circulated that Otto Orr, an agent and chief investigator for the Department of Justice, who had obtained evidence for the government in the case, had been suspended on charges of "undue friendliness" with Maxine Dempsey. Hence, he was not called to testify. The government would not confirm the report, but they did not deny it either.

Orr supposedly had secured from Maxine in Wells, Nevada the alleged "slacker" letters. Later, when she went to Tijuana and Los Angeles, Orr procured the federal grand jury indictment of Bert Gardner, who allegedly had attempted to spirit Maxine across the Mexican border.

On Monday June 14, 1920, Lieutenant John F. Kennedy of the battleship Mississippi testified that he knew Dempsey when stationed at the Great Lakes station. In 1918, Dempsey came to him and said he didn't feel right about seeing boys in uniform. Jack said if he knew his family would be fixed, he wanted to enlist. He wanted to obtain a release to be able to enlist. He was told to write the draft board for his release, which he did. When it arrived, it was arranged for him to go to Philadelphia to enlist, but while on the way there, the armistice ending the fighting was signed. Kennedy said there was no talk of an end to the war when they spoke, so the interest was not feigned.

A. J. Auerbach of Salt Lake City, a proprietor of a hair-dressing establishment, who was dabbling in real estate and boxing on the side, testified that in 1916 he discovered and picked up Dempsey. Jack was a raw youth from the farms and mines. Auerbach made Dempsey quit work, and he paid him a $25 weekly salary. A. J. wanted Jack to focus on his training exclusively. Jack gave most of this money to his family, who were living in poverty. Auerbach also employed Jack's sister to help out.

Members of Jack's family often borrowed money from Auerbach, and Jack always paid it back. He testified to the excellent reputation borne by

169 *San Francisco Examiner, San Francisco Chronicle,* June 12, 1920.

Dempsey for his continual care for his family. Auerbach advanced Dempsey money each week so he could support the family.

Jack was a nice boy, easy to handle, and well liked. Auerbach gave him suits, but he wouldn't wear them, preferring to go about in shabby clothes.

After the Willard fight, Jack had settled his account in full, when he gave Auerbach a check for $2,124. Auerbach testified that he could be credited with Jack's success, starting him out and financing him. A. J. gave up what could have been a fortune, because his daughters did not want him to be connected with prize fighting.

Effie Barrows, Jack's sister, testified that he had supported her and her children for years, and without his aid she would have been in hard straits. She was married in June 1918 to William Barrows, a soldier, who had undergone much hospital treatment as a result of war injuries. Jack paid the medical bills. Through some clerical error, the military had sent her only $52 in allotment money in 1919, received after the war was over.

Other witnesses who testified included Frank G. Menke, a newspaper man who corroborated the story of the demand for $40,000 and Dempsey's reply. Theodore Hayes confirmed that he was taking Jack's draft release to him when the armistice was signed. Henry Marquard of the Adena Hotel testified that Jack paid the bills when he and Maxine stayed there. Soren Christensen, San Francisco attorney, formerly of Salt Lake City, appeared as a character witness. H. H. Stolurow told of helping Dempsey fill out the draft questionnaire. L. Lichtenstein, a chief of the American Legion at Chicago, corroborated testimony concerning the questionnaire. Henry Kersten, clerk at the Gibson Hotel, gave further testimony concerning the dislocated jaw, which Maxine claimed to him had been the result of an accident (not assault). Thomas Simpson of the West Oakland Athletic Club discussed certain bouts in which Dempsey appeared.

As the trial's final witness, Jack Dempsey took the witness stand in his own defense. According to the *San Francisco Examiner*, he testified for nearly two hours, telling a simple, unadorned story, giving as good an account of himself as a witness as he had in the prize ring. Jack wore a well-fitting blue suit. The day's theme, and impression given, was that he was a country boy who came to fame through a hairdresser's belief in him (Auerbach), and he loved an unworthy woman.

Dempsey started his story by going back to the days when he worked on a farm in Colorado. He had been the principal support of the large family almost from the time he had been able to work. He began bringing in money at the age of 14, and worked on the farm before and after school. In about 1915, he began boxing, and also at various times was working as a farmer, concrete mixer, carpenter, miner, mechanic, and dish washer.

In 1916 and 1917 he earned $3,800 at boxing. He recalled his fights and their purses. The largest amount he earned during that time was from the Flynn fight on February 13, 1917, in which he got a purse of $1,500. He gave $1,000 of it to his mother.

In 1918, he engaged in numerous exhibitions that took him all over the country. For war charities and war relief organizations, he helped generate a total of more than $331,500. Not a penny went into his own pocket. He paid his own expenses, receiving at most only transportation. The Dan Ketchell fight gathered up $3,500 for the Salvation Army. The Clay Turner exhibition generated up to $26,000 for the Knights of Columbus. A tournament at Madison Square Garden yielded $180,000 for the Army and Navy War Activities. Another scheduled exhibition that was not held still netted $70,000 for the Salvation Army in advance sales. The final Meehan fight in San Francisco resulted in $17,000 for the Army and Navy War Activities. He donated other smaller sums as a result of other exhibitions. He thought he was doing his country some good by helping to raise money for these funds and relief efforts. He wanted to box Willard at Chicago for a war charity, but Jess wanted to be paid.

Dempsey showed the jury two watches and letters of appreciation from charitable organizations and army officers, attesting to the esteem he had won for his war charity activities.

When asked whether he was willing to fight and die for his country, Jack replied, "I love my country and felt out of place when I saw men in uniform. As soon as I found out I could provide for my family I tried to enlist." Dempsey was on his way to Philadelphia to enlist as an artisan in the navy when enlistment was stopped.

Jack told of taking Maxine into his mother's home so she could live there and absorb knowledge about home life, but she left to become a prostitute while he was at Long Branch, New Jersey, which eventually led to him divorcing her. He wanted a good wife who could raise a family.

Discussing the incident at the Gibson Hotel in San Francisco, where Maxine suffered a dislocated jaw, Jack said it was an accident resulting from "too much beer." Dempsey said he awoke from a sleep one night to find Maxine on the floor of their room with her jaw injured. She told him that she had tripped over a raised door sill and had fallen, striking her chin. She had stumbled while going to the bathroom. "I called a doctor." So, his version was she fell down in a drunken state and struck her chin. He denied striking her at all. "I never struck a lady in my life." In fact, even the doctor testified that she had informed him that she had fallen.

Jack once had left Maxine in San Francisco when he went to Salt Lake City, when they were at the Adena Hotel. He claimed that he gave her $150 before leaving. When he returned two weeks later, she had disappeared, and he spent three weeks looking for her. He eventually learned that in his absence, Maxine had circulated stories charging that he had "laid down" in the Flynn fight. "I tried to get fights here, as I was about broke, but all the promoters told me I wasn't worth thirty cents, after what my wife had told."

When asked if hypothetically Maxine had behaved herself and not returned to her old life, would he have stayed with her, Jack replied, "Yes I would. She would have more than she has today. I told her I couldn't buy the kind of a home I wanted to give her until I made some more money; but just as soon as I could I wanted to buy her a nice house and everything I could get for her."

His plan when he married her was to have a good wife and family. Knowing what her life had been, he had dreams of leading her into something better. So he took her to his mother's house to live, but she complained that life there was slow, and she left to go to Wells and the old familiar life. "I figured that she might learn better if she stayed with my mother. I never did anything in my life to degrade her or send her back into the kind of life she had been living." Continuing, Jack said, "I did everything Maxine wanted me to do and gave her everything she wanted. If she had stayed with me she would have more than she has today. She would have a fine home and everything." He would have clung to his wife had she behaved herself and kept away from her old life.

Jack denied that she ever had practiced prostitution while living with him. (At least, not to his knowledge.)

Dempsey denied that he ever had failed to support his wife when he had money and knew where she was. He told of many instances of sums given to her, which she usually used to buy clothing. He denied Maxine's story that he had taken back and pawned diamond rings he gave her after the Flynn fight early in 1917 in order to raise money for their trip to San Francisco. "Anything she wanted she could have if I could get it for her."

After their trip to Seattle, when she went on to Yakima, Washington to visit her mother, she failed to return. He was unable to find out where she was until he heard from her mother that she was in Cairo, Illinois, again at her customary occupation. Jack was "pretty disgusted." "She was my wife, and I loved her, and it made me feel pretty bad to think she could do a thing like that."

The questionnaire was discussed. At the time he filled it out, Dempsey said he had not been at home for some time, and did not know exactly how much his father had made, but answered as best as he could. He had no desire or intent to misrepresent.

Regarding the alleged demand for $40,000 on threat of publication of alleged letters, Dempsey said he had refused to be frightened. "I told them I wasn't afraid of anything they might have; that I wouldn't give them any money, and for them to go ahead and shoot."

Working under orders of the Department of Labor, Dempsey recruited between 300 and 400 laborers for the Pennsylvania shipyards.

Dempsey spoke with Lieutenant Kennedy about his anxiety to get into the service. Jack had come to the station to help with athletic instruction. Kennedy spoke to him about enlisting in September 1918. Jack said he wanted to enlist if there was a way to have his people looked out for. Kennedy helped Jack take steps to be able to enlist. The release papers had been received, and he was on his way to Philadelphia when the Secretary of the Navy ordered enlistments to cease, and the armistice was signed.

Jack paid many doctors' bills, for his brother Joe, who had heart trouble, and sister Effie. He put up $3,500 to start his brother in the taxi business.

The *Chronicle* said Jack testified simply and unaffectedly, with an earnestness that lent additional emphasis to his statements. He had worked at anything he could find to do, sent home all the money he could spare for the support of a large and helpless family, earned at least $331,500 for various war relief enterprises, and as soon as he had provided for the support of his family and been assured that he might allow them a share of his pay, he sought to enter the service.[170]

The judge instructed the jury that the only question the jury had to decide was whether or not Jack Dempsey sought to evade military service by falsely answering certain points in the questionnaire, and whether or not, if false statements were made, they were made willfully and knowingly. Regarding the statement in the questionnaire that his wife had not been employed, Judge Dooling said, "Proof that Maxine Dempsey had been engaged in practicing prostitution is not to be regarded as proof that she was working. Prostitution is not to be classed as work." The judge also emphasized the necessity for a careful interpretation of the words "mainly dependent" in considering the support afforded by Dempsey to his family.

The case was given to the jury on June 15, 1920, and after only ten minutes of deliberation, they quickly returned a verdict: "Not guilty." The case allegedly had cost the government $80,000.

Jack Dempsey's Father and Mother Aid Him in Trial for Draft Evasion; Heavyweight Champ Is Acquitted

Nearly every person in the courtroom waited to congratulate Dempsey on his victory.

The defense would request a dismissal of the conspiracy indictment against Jack Kearns, whose trial was scheduled to follow that of the pugilist. Kearns said, "There wasn't anything else to do. It was a clear case for Jack." Kearns also said it was a clear case of blackmail and an attempt to shake down Dempsey for money, and they were glad to have the opportunity to show-up these people. John Hogan, who gave Dempsey the deferred classification, felt that the verdict vindicated him and his classification.

---

[170] *San Francisco Examiner*, June 15, 1920; *San Francisco Chronicle*, June 15, 16, 1920.

Indications were that the government was inclined to dismiss against Kearns, given the results of Dempsey's case.

Maxine said she intended to publish the letters which were barred from admission. Dempsey's defense attorneys said they actually had no objection to the admission of the letters, once they finally were allowed to read them. The government had refused to produce them to the defense prior to the trial. The defense had raised the marital privilege prior to and without having been given the opportunity to review the letters.

Maxine said she was heading to North Yakima, Washington, to live with her mother, Mrs. Adeline Cates. She never did publish the letters.

Although Jack's parents had joined forces to support him during his trial, all was not well between them. On July 9, 1920, Mary Dempsey, Jack's mother, was granted a divorce from Jack's father Hyrum Dempsey on grounds of nonsupport. She said it was her son Jack who supported her.[171]

[171] *Oregon Daily Journal*, July 10, 1920.

CHAPTER 4

The Future

On June 11, 1920 at Nicollet Park in Minneapolis, Minnesota, before a crowd of 2,500, in his first fight in nearly a year, in a workmanlike manner, 188-pound Billy Miske (51-11-15) scored a technical knockout over Jack Moran in the 2nd round. The Chicago heavyweight went down four times in the 1st round, and when he was down again in the 2nd round, on the floor in a helpless state, the referee stopped it.

E. R. Hosking said, "Miske looks as though he had never retired from active ring work." He severely punished Moran and hit "hard enough to knock out almost any heavyweight."

Leo Sullivan said Miske, challenger for Dempsey's crown, proved that he was not through. He went at Moran with tiger-like ferocity, decking him with a fusillade of blows five times in the 1st round, and several more in the 2nd.

On the undercard, Georges Carpentier boxed 3 flashy rounds in an exhibition with his Belgian heavyweight champion sparring partner (likely Paul Journee), decking him in the 2nd round. Observers were impressed, calling him a dangerous contender. Those who previously were dubious as to his chances with Dempsey now were certain that he was a tough opponent. Local writer Charles Johnson said, "Look out, Mr. Dempsey!" "Carpentier has the punch, and in both hands, he has the dazzling speed; he has the ring generalship and craftiness of a veteran; he is a boxer from A to Z; his footwork is brilliant and he's a regular honest-to-goodness fighter." He didn't speak much English, but made up for it with his snappy fighting, never stalling. "He is up and at 'em at all times." A wicked left sent his sparring partner to the floor. Georges would be no set-up for Dempsey. "The Frenchman seems to have all the attributes of a champion and it's a good gamble that he will make the American go plenty fast to win."

E. R. Hosking said the French champion fully came up to advance notices of his prowess. He proved to be "the fastest heavyweight in the world." He was faster than Fred Fulton, "and he hits hard, too." He boxed "like a master of the art."

Edward Walker said Carpentier unquestionably was a worthy rival for Dempsey's title, for he displayed wonderful speed and hitting power, decking his sparring partner in the 2nd round with a right. "Carpentier is every inch a fighter." He had an ideal build, and appeared to be a wonderful ring general with excellent footwork. "His blows are like bolts of lightning." He always was ready to deliver a blow, and his defense was good, riding with and going away from the majority of blows.

When called upon to give a speech, Georges said, "Ladees and gintlemen: I no speake the Anglish language, but I thank you for the great reciption."

Leo Sullivan said Carpentier displayed cleverness, speed, and hitting power. He was rugged, a real fighter, and made a great hit with the fans.[172]

In late June 1920, Jack Kearns was in negotiations for a Dempsey vs. Billy Miske championship bout to be held on Labor Day. Dempsey was offered $50,000 guaranteed, but with the privilege of taking 50% of the gate if said amount was larger than the guarantee. That sounded like a good deal to Kearns, who believed the fight would draw quite well and likely earn them much more than the guarantee.[173]

Folks liked the potential match because the power-punching Dempsey had not stopped or dropped Miske in two fights (10 and 6 rounds), and Billy had been competitive in both. 26-year-old Miske was young, yet experienced, scientific, game, with very good speed and solid power, and had excellent durability, never having been dropped or stopped in nearly 80 contests. He had suffered a recent illness, which had kept him out of the ring for a while. Yet, he had recovered (or was in remission), and looked good in his recent bout.

The *Fayetteville Observer* said Dempsey's acquittal was received with general satisfaction, for the fistic public generally believed that Jack was framed and the victim of jealousy.

Potential future opponents for the champion were said to include Tommy Gibbons, Martin Burke, Bill Brennan, Gene Tunney, Billy Miske, Battling Levinsky, Bob Martin, Fred Fulton, and Georges Carpentier. Gibbons was one of the cleverest boxers in the business, could hit with both hands, and had grown into a light heavy. Fans were sad that Carpentier would be returning to France without having engaged in a fight in the U.S.[174]

On June 26, 1920 in Cleveland, Ohio, Bill Brennan knocked out Ole Anderson in the 8th round.

Just two days later, on June 28, 1920 in Jersey City, New Jersey, 176-pound Gene Tunney stopped the same 183-pound Ole Anderson in the 3rd round, when the referee terminated the contest. Anderson had been decked with rights twice in the 2nd round.[175]

Kearns said Dempsey was ready to take them all on as fast as they come. Carpentier had been offered first chance, but now that he passed it up, others would be considered. "All we ask is that the challenger provide a promoter, a purse, and the battleground." There was discussion of potential matches with Miske, Brennan, or Meehan, the only men who made any kind of a showing with Dempsey when he was on his way up.[176]

While in Wichita looking over oil fields, Kearns said, "Jack should never have been brought to trial. All charges have been dismissed against

[172] *Minneapolis Morning Tribune, St. Paul Dispatch, Minneapolis Journal, St. Paul Pioneer Press,* June 12, 1920.
[173] *Wichita Daily Eagle, Davenport Democrat and Leader,* June 21, 1920; *Elmira Star-Gazette,* June 22, 1920.
[174] *Fayetteville Observer,* June 25, 1920.
[175] *New York Tribune, Sun and New York Herald, New York Times,* June 29, 1920.
[176] *Washington Times (Washington, D.C.),* June 28, 1920.

Dempsey now, and we are ready to take on all comers. … Billy Miske will be his first opponent." Yet, no formal announcement had been made yet. Kearns said he would bet all of his money that Dempsey would beat Carpentier.[177]

On July 2, 1920 at the Stockyards Stadium in Denver, Colorado, before a crowd of 3,000, Dempsey boxed in exhibition bouts. The *Rocky Mountain News'* Abe Pollock said 170-pound K.O. Brown of Salt Lake was decked three times and was bleeding from the mouth, even from "little taps," and had enough after 2 rounds. 220-pound 6'3" Jack Smith was decked by the first two punches, and wanted no more.

The *Denver Post* said Dempsey carried K.O. Brown through 2 rounds. A man named Davis only lasted a round, for he was badly bleeding and dazed, and Dempsey had to hold him up. 220-pound Jack Smith lasted less than a minute. A straight left to the jaw sent him down with a thud, and it was over.[178]

On July 5, 1920 in Benton Harbor, Michigan, at Floyd Fitzsimmons' newly constructed fistic arena on Fair avenue, before a crowd of 12,000, world lightweight champion Benny Leonard successfully defended his title, knocking out Charley White in the 9th round.

In attendance and introduced was Jack Kearns, who announced from the ring that Jack Dempsey would defend his title there on Labor Day against anyone the local management chose to put against him.[179]

Former champ James J. Corbett wrote that Billy Miske's return to the ring would stir up interest in the heavyweight division. His impressive victory over Jack Moran demonstrated that he was far from being through. He had suffered a back strain about a year ago, which took time to heal. Many heavies wanted a Dempsey fight so they could earn the loser's end, but Miske had a real chance to be competitive, for he was the only one who withstood Dempsey's onslaughts for 10 rounds, and again for 6 rounds. Miske had beaten a prime Jack Dillon, as well as Willie Meehan. He had the agility of a panther, and a quick brain. He boxed a 10-round draw with Fred Fulton when Fred was the top contender, and had a 1919 W15 and DND8 against Bill Brennan, one of Dempsey's most persistent challengers.[180]

Discussions regarding a potential Dempsey-Carpentier match were ongoing. However, it seemed that Carpentier was not quite ready to sign. Some felt that Carpentier still needed more time to regain his pre-war form, for if he fought Dempsey too soon, he would be a chopping block.

Hence, in early July, Kearns made a tentative agreement for Dempsey to fight Irish Chicago heavyweight Bill Brennan after Miske. Brennan had lasted 6 rounds with Dempsey in an entertaining war, and had obtained a great deal of experience since then. Kearns said, "Brennan will be the best card against the champion."[181]

177 *Wichita Daily Eagle*, June 29, 1920.
178 *Rocky Mountain News, Denver Post, El Paso Herald, Oregon Daily Journal,* July 3, 1920.
179 *Benton Harbor News-Palladium*, July 6, 1920.
180 *Binghamton Press*, July 8, 1920.
181 *Brooklyn Citizen, Muncie Evening Press*, July 9, 1920.; *San Francisco Chronicle*, July 25, 1920.

BILL
BRENNAN

The *San Francisco Chronicle* said if Dempsey really wanted to fight the worthiest opponent, he would fight Harry Wills, who "stands out far ahead of any of the white heavies."[182]

The press reported that Dempsey had reversed his attitude on the color line, which he was erasing, and announced that he was willing to fight Harry Wills or anyone else, in part because he needed the money.

The *Pittsburgh Gazette Times* said, "This is different from the note struck by his manager, Jack Kearns, some time after Dempsey won the title. Kearns drew the color line and started talking about purses of $250,000 and then raised the ante to $500,000, all of which got Dempsey into a peck of trouble." The argument was that Kearns initially showed his true feelings and intentions, then was over-demanding and outpricing a potential Wills fight so it couldn't be made. Or perhaps, like others had done, he simply demanded a really stiff price for risking the valuable title to the most dangerous man out there.[183]

Dempsey said,

> As for the colored boxers, you can say for me, and make it as strong as you like, that I have absolutely no scruples whatsoever about boxing them. After I won the championship, Jack Kearns, my manager, contended that mixed bouts are injurious to the sport, and for that reason would not consider any for me. It is different now. If the press, public, or promoters want me to box a negro, I'll gladly take the match. That goes for Harry Wills and the rest of his ilk. To be quite frank about it, I need the money.
>
> When Wills and Fulton meet in Newark, I'll be right down there at the ringside. … When boxing opens up in New York I hope to be one of the busiest champions around here. … I am ready to give my attention to boxing again. And the sooner I get into the action, the better pleased I will be.[184]

Jack Kearns was quoted as saying,

> While I have doubts as to the advisability of mixed contests and would not match Dempsey with a negro in opposition to public sentiment, still I will say that the champion will not take refuge behind any excuse in order to avoid a bout with any logical opponents. If Harry Wills is regarded by the public as a fit opponent for Dempsey and the compensation is satisfactory, I

---

[182] *San Francisco Chronicle,* July 18, 1920.
[183] *Pittsburgh Gazette Times,* July 20, 1920.
[184] *Montreal Gazette,* July 21, 1920.

would not hesitate to make the match. In substance, Dempsey has no reason to avoid a match with any man in the world.[185]

Hyatt Daab said the fastest route back into the heart of America was by getting back into the ring. Dempsey said he would meet any man, black or white, and was not drawing the color line. "For which he deserves unstinted praise." Fighting would restore his faded prestige.

> There is no reason under the setting sun why Dempsey or any other pugilist should draw the color line. It is at best a spineless subterfuge, used purely as a shelter from formidable negro fighters. There is swiftly growing sentiment against such discrimination, and by matching Fulton and Wills the International Sporting Club probably has erased the color line – in New York state at least.

Daab further said there was no reason for Dempsey to draw the color line against Wills, for

> Dempsey unquestionably is superior to Wills, or any other negro pugilist for that matter. He probably would decapitate them as quickly as he beheaded Willard or the other victims of his chopping block. ... If the champion desires again to win the respect of the nation let him meet all comers and fight his way back to public esteem.[186]

Over five years after he lost his heavyweight title to Jess Willard, on July 20, 1920, 42-year-old Jack Johnson surrendered to U.S. federal agents at the Mexican border and was taken into custody, where he would remain until his resentencing hearing. Johnson claimed that he could whip Jack Dempsey with ease. "Nothing to it."[187]

Also on July 20, at the Van Kelton Stadium, an airdome in Manhattan, New York, at 57th street and 8th avenue, in front of a packed crowd of spectators, Jack Dempsey trained, as he would every afternoon there. He did pulley exercises, hit the punching ball with great vigor, shadow boxed, and sparred 3 rounds with big Bill Tate, showing all of his wonderful speed and activity. Tate remarked that his life insurance had run out, and asked Dempsey to be a little careful until a new policy had been obtained.

The *New York Herald's* Charles Mathison said Dempsey's work as an actor had not caused him to lose his physical vigor, as some feared.[188]

[185] *Sacramento Star*, July 21, 1920.
[186] *Buffalo Commercial*, quoting the *New York Telegram*, July 23, 1920.
[187] *Los Angeles Times*, July 21, 1920; *San Francisco Chronicle*, July 26, 1920.
[188] *New York Herald*, July 21, 1920.

JACK DEMPSEY PUTS ON THE GLOVES.
Contrary to report that his rapid pace as film actor had reduced his physical vigor the champion is making a splendid showing in his first days of training in New York city.—Copyright, Keystone View company.

Dempsey told the *New York Evening Journal's* lady reporter, Winifred Van Duzer, that boxing as exercise developed the mind and body, for both men and women. "He told with delight that University of California women now are instructed in boxing as part of their curriculum." He said a sound body and sound mind travel together. "I believe the time is coming when every American woman will go to a gymnasium two or three times each week to practice boxing."[189]

Dempsey hoped to box under the Walker law, in New York, where the biggest purses would be available. He was residing at the Beechhurst Country Club at Whitestone, and training at the Manhattan airdome.

On July 24, 1920 at the airdome, Dempsey boxed 20 rounds with men of all weights, including welter champ Jack Britton, Joe Benjamin, Joe Welling, Jim/Jack Montgomery, bantam Joe Lynch, Bill Tate, Babe Sullivan – Britton's sparring partner, and one or two others. At the conclusion, he did not appear to be the least bit fatigued.

When asked who gave him his toughest fight, Dempsey said Willard, who shook him up several times. Jack said it was up to the public whether he drew the color line or not. He would fight any man, regardless of color, if the public demanded it.[190]

Dempsey wrote that he wanted to fight again soon, and the tougher the man, the more it would please him. "In hurling this defi I want to state that I am not drawing any color line. It has always been my feeling that the man who is acclaimed the greatest fighter of his time must be one who can whip every other formidable rival. Otherwise, how could he, in all fairness, claim to be champion?"

Dempsey said many declared that Harry Wills was the greatest of all challengers. Wills had an upcoming late-July bout with Fred Fulton. "Right here and now I want to say personally I am willing to meet the

---

[189] *New York Evening Journal, Buffalo Courier,* July 24, 1920.
[190] *Brooklyn Daily Eagle,* July 25, 1920.

winner of that bout." If Wills beat Fulton in spectacular fashion, and as a result there was sufficient public demand for them to fight, and therefore a promoter made a fair offer, he would fight him.

Dempsey noted that Billy Miske twice had stayed the limit with him, and that entitled him to another chance. "But Billy has been sick during the past year and reports have it that he is far removed from the condition of two years ago."

Bill Brennan gave Jack a hard fight before he was stopped. The press said he was game and had a splendid record. Hence, he too was on tap.

The man Dempsey most wanted to fight was Carpentier, for that bout would be the biggest money-maker.[191]

Harry Wills was so good that the New York press noted that "white heavyweights have fought shy of him." He was fast and rangy and had a kick to his punch.

Fred Fulton, 60-7-1, believed that beating Wills could garner him momentum for a rematch with Dempsey, who had knocked him out within the first 30 seconds of the 1st round in July 1918. Since that loss, Fulton had gone undefeated in his last 19 bouts, with victories such as: 1918 W4 Willie Meehan and W4 Sam Langford; 1919 W4 Meehan; and 1920 WND8 Frank Moran, TKO3 Tom Cowler, KO8 John Lester Johnson, KO4 Porky Flynn, WND6 Bartley Madden, KO2 Gunboat Smith, and TKO6 Jack Thompson. In order to overcome the bad impression from the Dempsey loss, Fulton needed a really big win.

Wills and Fulton were fighting for a $35,000 purse, of which Fulton would earn $25,000, win or lose.[192]

On July 26, 1920 in Newark, New Jersey, in a scheduled 12-round bout at the First Regiment Armory, before a crowd of 7,937, which paid from $3.30 up to $16.50 per ticket, generating nearly $75,000 (though later reports said $97,212.50 was generated), 204-pound Harry Wills scored a 3rd round knockout over 210-pound Fred Fulton. The first two rounds had been somewhat competitive, but in the 3rd round, Wills hurt him with a left hook to the body, and Fulton clinched tightly. After breaking, Harry kept hitting the body. In close, a Wills right uppercut to the heart and then another right uppercut to the chin sent Fulton down and out.

The *Brooklyn Standard Union* said Wills was too fast for Fulton, outboxing, outslugging, outgeneraling, and outclassing him. "Wills was like lightning. He crumpled Fulton up with body smashes; he was in and out like a bantam." Fulton barely landed, and what he did land the colored man practically ignored.

After the fight, Wills came over to the side of the ring where Jack Dempsey was sitting in the front row with Jack Kearns, extended his gloved hand over the ropes, and Dempsey shook it and wished him luck.

Dempsey, who had received a tremendous ovation from the crowd when introduced before the fight, said he was sorry that Fulton was

---

[191] *Pittsburgh Press*, July 26, 1920.
[192] *New York Evening Journal*, *New York Morning Telegraph*, July 26, 1920.

knocked out, for he wanted to meet him again, although he had thought that Wills would win. Jack said, "Fulton had two weak spots," and, tapping his own heart and chin, continued, "Wills found both of them."

Dempsey told the *New York Evening World*, "Fulton has every qualification that goes to make a great fighter except one thing, and really that's the most essential thing of all. He's not there with the courage." Jack said Fulton did not have a strong jaw, his heart was weak, and he did not like rough going. Before the fight, Jack had advised his friend Al Jolson, who was sitting with him, not to bet on Fulton.

Dempsey was not impressed with Wills either. "Wills showed me nothing. Those taps he landed on Fulton I don't think would have made a fellow like Frank Moran slow up a bit. Wills is as slow as he can be. He may be able to punch fairly well, but he is so slow that I wouldn't have any trouble whipping over one on his jaw and sending him to oblivion." Jack would bet that Moran could beat him, especially in a 15-round bout. "There's nothing about him to worry me."

> If the public demands that I fight a negro I will do so, but I don't think it for the best interest of sport, as it arouses too much race antagonism. But if there is a clamor for such a match I'll be Johnny-on-the-spot. I fear no man. Anybody that could take that giant Willard that was considered invincible and practically stop him in a round need not fear any slow-moving fighter as is Wills.

Another reported that when asked if he would fight Wills, Jack replied, "It makes no difference to me. I'm willing. It is up to Kearns." He also was quoted as saying, "If people think I ought to fight Wills I'll be mighty glad to do it, and I will knock him kicking, too. I don't think it will take me as long to finish Wills as it took Wills to finish Fulton. He is a fellow that comes in, and that makes things easy for me."

Jack Kearns said, "Dempsey will fight any man in the world. That goes. Dempsey is a public servant, and if the public wants him to fight Wills then he'll fight him." Another quoted him as saying,

> It all depends on public opinion. If the public wants Jack to defend his title against Wills he will do so. There has been sentiment both for and against such a mixed bout. We'll watch and see what the newspapers, which reflect public opinion, have to say. If their verdict is in favor of the bout, why Wills will be given his chance.

His understanding was that the public most wanted to see Dempsey fight Carpentier.

In an article written by him, Dempsey agreed that Wills was one of the world's best heavyweights. "I do think so. But whether he is entitled to an immediate crack at the heavyweight crown is a question that will be left to my manager." He understood that the public demanded that he fight Carpentier. He knew that Wills would beat Fulton, particularly when he saw Harry attack, hit the body, and engage in infighting, which was the way to beat Fulton, as he already had proven (in less than 30 seconds). Jack said Harry was too clever, strong, and aggressive for Fred.[193]

The *New York Evening Telegram*'s George Underwood (a former Olympic track athlete) said Wills was Dempsey's foremost challenger and about the only one worthy of truly testing the champion and having a chance to beat him. "A clever, lightning fast, hard-hitting big man, capable of both giving and taking severe punishment, Wills undoubtedly will give the great Dempsey the sternest test of his ring career."

The *Brooklyn Daily Times* said Wills proved conclusively by his performance against Fulton that he was Dempsey's logical challenger and strongest contender. He had the makings of a champion. Fulton never had a chance, and was bullied from the start. Some believed that Dempsey/Kearns would draw the color line, for they would be taking a big chance with Wills.

The *Brooklyn Citizen* said, "For years, it has been known that Harry Wills, the giant New Orleans negro, was one of the greatest fighting machines ever developed. But the white heavies were always careful to steer clear of Wills so that the negro was forced to confine his battling to bouts with other members of the colored brethren." Fulton took a chance, and it cost him. Wills' manager Paddy Mullins was confident that Wills could knock out Dempsey. Many were of the opinion that "Dempsey would have his hands full in a battle with the giant black."

The *Brooklyn Daily Eagle's* Thomas Rice said the 6'3" Wills was sturdy and clever, and showed ring sense and persistence. He dashed in, infought, held a lot, and held and hit, but in 99 out of 100 bouts, no American referee would disqualify such an offender. "Boxing rules seem to be made for the special purpose of being forgotten by the boxers and ignored by the referees." He suggested that Wills held and hit to knock out Fulton.

Rice said the knockout of Fulton brought back again the color question in boxing. Rice predicted that the color question would be a powerful and conclusive factor in preventing a mixed-race heavyweight championship fight, regardless of Wills' good personal habits and character.[194]

Not everyone agreed that Harry Wills had proven himself ready for Dempsey. The *New York Evening Journal* said Wills did not class with the champion, for although he polished off Fulton in a business-like manner, "close followers of boxing do not believe that he showed enough to give him much of a look in with Jack Dempsey, should the champion finally decide to take on a colored man." Wills was a good fighter, but old-timers said he was not in Dempsey's class. "The champion is too strong, has youth in his favor and hits too hard for Wills, is the general opinion."

[193] *Pittsburg Press*, July 27, 1920.
[194] *New York Evening Journal, New York Evening Telegram, New York Morning Telegraph, New York Evening World, Brooklyn Daily Times, Brooklyn Standard Union, Brooklyn Citizen, Brooklyn Daily Eagle, Pittsburg Press*, July 27, 1920; *New York World*, July 28, 1920; *New York Evening Telegram*, July 29, 1920; *New York World*, July 30, 1920. On an undercard bout, Frank Moran won a 10-round no decision over Wild Burt Kenny, who once lost a 10-round no decision to Dempsey.

Others said Dempsey would have to endure a bombardment of heavy punishment both to the body and head before he could drop Wills, who was a better man than Willard ever was.

Dempsey said he would fight whomever the public most demanded. He wanted whatever fight made him the most money. However, "the impression is that a Dempsey-Wills bout will not draw any too well." Conversely, a fight with Carpentier would be a very big gate draw.[195]

George Underwood agreed that the time was not ripe for a Dempsey-Wills contest. He said Wills first needed to show his ability against a give-and-take fighter. "Before experts hazard any guesses regarding Wills' ability to defeat Dempsey they want to see his mettle tested against a fighter who can stand up and take it and give it. And all the skill, strength and science in the world will avail an opponent little against Dempsey unless the challenger has the true fighting heart to back it up." (What then, were Sam Langford, Sam McVey, and Joe Jeannette?)

Underwood said Bill Brennan, who already practically had been matched to fight Dempsey, "will offer a fitting test for the champion." Underwood did not believe Miske was in proper physical condition to extend the champ.[196]

Tom O'Rourke, who managed Fulton, said Wills was so good that he would back him if he fought Dempsey. "I think he hits too hard and comes too fast for any man in the world. It is all right for Dempsey to be in there knocking over someone who is not hitting him back, but Wills will be doing that, and for that reason I think he can beat Dempsey." Dempsey's wide-open style of fighting would leave him vulnerable to Harry's wallops. "If, however, Dempsey can hit as hard with either hand as I've been told he can he might catch Wills coming in and drop him for the count, but, unless he could do that he would be quite apt to get whipped. The negro hits straight with both hands and has an unusually good defense."[197]

William "Bat" Masterson reported that a London promoter, C. B. Cochran, had offered Dempsey 50,000 pounds, which was almost equivalent to $200,000, to fight Carpentier in London. Europeans loved Carpentier. "Carpentier is more than a prizering champion with the allied nations that crushed the despicable Hun. He is a war hero with all who fought the Kaiser's forces, besides being the foremost ring man of Europe." Masterson said such were distinctions of which Dempsey could not boast.[198]

Jack Kearns wrote that he had received telegrams from all over the country:

> Some asked if I would consent to a match between Dempsey and Wills, while others advised against agreeing to any such match, citing the race difficulties that arose over Johnson's victory over

[195] *New York Evening Journal*, July 28, 1920.
[196] *New York Evening Telegram*, July 28, 1920.
[197] *New York World*, July 28, 1920; *New York Morning Telegraph*, August 1, 1920.
[198] *New York Morning Telegraph*, July 27, 1920.

Jeffries. It is true that was a very unpleasant affair. Personally, and likewise speaking for Dempsey, I wish to say that we consider Wills pretty soft picking. He is a very good man, but he does not class with Dempsey. ... I candidly believe that Dempsey can take every heavyweight of prominence now before the public, both in this country and abroad, five nights running, and stop them all in short time.

I am not going to do anything that will injure the great game of boxing. Dempsey is a fighting champion, the best of all time, to my way of thinking. If the public and the press demand that Dempsey meet Wills he will do so. ... However, we would much prefer not to meet Wills for the good of the sport, for should Dempsey settle the colored boy in quick fashion, which is practically a foregone conclusion, it would arouse race-feeling just the same. Dempsey is not picking his opponents. We are anxious to meet the best in the business, one after another.

Kearns said there was a possibility of taking Jack overseas to fight Carpentier. He had closed contracts for Dempsey to appear in more movie films as well. Contrary to rumors, Jack was training and remaining in top shape. He maintained his speed by boxing with bantamweights, and could step into the ring on a moment's notice against anyone.[199]

BILLY MISKE

The day after Wills-Fulton, on July 27, it was announced that Jack Dempsey would be fighting Billy Miske 10 rounds in a championship bout in an open-air arena at Benton Harbor, Michigan on Labor Day, September 6, for Promoter Floyd Fitzsimmons, for $50,000 guaranteed, with the privilege of accepting a percentage of the receipts (allegedly 50%) if it yielded an amount larger than the guarantee. Miske was guaranteed a $25,000 flat fee.

Representatives signed articles of agreement that day in Chicago. Allegedly, a decision would be rendered at the end of the contest if the Michigan commission would permit one. Manager Jack Reddy posted a $1,000 forfeit guaranteeing Miske's performance. Promoter Floyd Fitzsimmons put up $2,000. Miske promised to establish training quarters in Benton Harbor a month in advance of the contest, and to call off two scheduled matches.

Promoter Fitzsimmons regarded Miske as a good and logical opponent given that he twice went the distance with Dempsey in competitive contests, the general impression being that the first was a shade to

[199] *Brooklyn Standard Union*, July 28, 1920.

Dempsey or a draw, and the second clearly going to Dempsey. Miske claimed that he won both fights, having outpointed Dempsey. He said he had grown heavier, was stronger now, and hitting harder, weighing 192 pounds. Miske was a highly respected, experienced, skillful, and durable veteran who had the speed and ability to test the champion.

Although it was said that Miske had been ill for several months, his illness had resolved, and he had regained his strength, recently scoring a knockout victory.

Others said Miske's present condition was doubtful, given his recent recovery from a long and serious illness. One said he had suffered from hip and kidney trouble. Hence, some thought he was seeking a loser's end. Even in his old form, the most he could hope for was to stay the limit.[200]

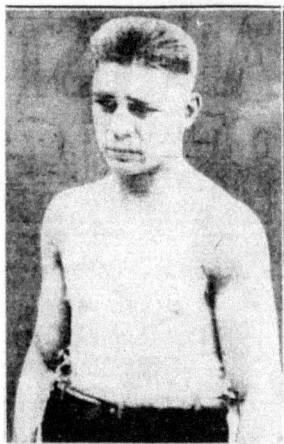

JACK DEMPSEY
2 P. M. (HIMSELF) 2 P. M.
NOW TRAINING
Von Kelton Stadium,
57th St. and 8th Av.
LADIES INVITED.

That same day, on Tuesday July 27, 1920 in New York, at the big Van Kelton Stadium open-air training quarters at Broadway and 57th street, Jack Dempsey boxed 4 hard rounds with middleweight Harry Greb, who was preparing for another bout with Tommy Gibbons, scheduled to be held in four days. The arena was packed with 2,000 fans who paid 50 cents each to see the workout.

Greb had asked the champ to spar and help him prepare for the Gibbons fight. Greb would work with Dempsey on the 28th and 29th as well, before leaving for Pittsburgh for the fight, which would be held on the 31st. Gibbons had beaten Greb twice before.[201]

The next day, on July 28, seat prices were raised to $1, yet the open-air arena was sold out. Kearns was "so taken by the way Greb showed against Dempsey that he at once made arrangements with Manager Mason to bring Greb to Chicago to work for Dempsey's Labor Day fight." Kearns thought Greb could help Dempsey prepare for Miske, who also was fast. "Dempsey told Tex Rickard, who kept time while Greb and the champion were boxing, that Greb was the first fellow who ever gave him a real workout." Rickard had signed a lease for Madison Square Garden, and said he would make every effort to get middleweight champion Johnny Wilson to fight Greb.[202]

Greb's hometown *Pittsburg Press* reported, "Dempsey is said to have given [Greb] a number of helpful pointers."[203]

---

[200] *New York Evening Telegram*, July 27, 1920; *Rochester Democrat and Chronicle, Chicago Tribune, New York Tribune, Elmira Star-Gazette, Oneonta Daily Star, San Francisco Examiner*, July 28, 1920; *Boston Globe*, July 30, 1920; *Pittsburg Press*, July 31, 1920.

[201] Despite weighing only 165 pounds, the "Pittsburgh Windmill" Greb held decision/no decision victories over Meehan (1917 WND6, 1919 WND10), Miske (1915 DND6, 1918 LND10 - close, 1919 WND10 - clear), and Brennan (1919 WND10, WND10, W15, WND10). Although not known as a puncher, winning most fights by decision, he was known to throw a lot of punches, generally outhustling his foes. He was very fast with his hands and feet. He could dance around, sticking and moving, or he could lunge in, clinch, grab, smother, maul, and work on the inside. He had an excellent ability to take it.

[202] *Pittsburgh Gazette Times*, July 28, 29, 1920; *Pittsburg Post*, July 28, 1920.

[203] *Pittsburg Press*, July 29, 1920.

On July 28, 1920 in Charleston, South Carolina, Bill Brennan (59-13-8) knocked out George Ashe (53-46-12) in the 2nd round.

Regarding their sparring on Thursday July 29 (their third day in a row), the *Pittsburgh Post* claimed that local Pittsburgh hero Greb cut Dempsey.

> A big surprise was sprung on those present by the way Greb tore into the champion and in the middle of the second round time had to be called when the Pittsburgher landed a hard right on Dempsey's left eye and split it open. After a few seconds Dempsey told his handlers he would try it again. But after a few exchanges he told them he would have to call it off for the day. ... Greb looked as strong as a young bull.

Everyone said Greb would beat Gibbons.

Dempsey then posed for photographs with Douglas Fairbanks, who was present.

However, George Underwood in the local *New York Evening Telegram* said Greb *butted* Dempsey over the left eye and caused a "shiner" and "mouse" to form as big as an egg, not a cut. Jack then sparred Douglas Fairbanks, the motion picture actor, who did not attempt any "billy goat tactics." Underwood did say that if Greb beat Gibbons, he likely would be matched with Dempsey.

The *New York Morning Telegraph*'s Sam Taub said Dempsey had a *bump* over the eye from the "friendly" set-to with Greb.

The *Boston Post* reported that Greb only gave Dempsey a *black eye* on the 29th, landing a left hook under Jack's right eye. They sparred 3 2-minute rounds. The injury was not serious, and did not interfere with Jack's boxing 3 1-minute rounds with Douglas Fairbanks afterwards.

Footage of Dempsey's sparring with Fairbanks shows him to have a puffy right eye. Jack just played defense with Doug, quickly moving around and ducking.

The *Pittsburg Press* said Dempsey had been "much enamored of Harry's ring methods."

The *Des Moines Tribune* noted that Jack the movie star was starring in a 15-reel serial entitled "Dead or Alive," based on his life. "And, oh, girls, isn't he good looking?"[204]

The *Scranton Republican* said Dempsey deserved a great deal of credit for not hiding behind the color line, saying he would fight Wills if the public demanded it. "Ring followers have grown tired of champions who

[204] *Pittsburgh Post, New York Evening Telegram*, July 30, 1920; *Boston Post, Pittsburg Press, New York Morning Telegraph, Des Moines Tribune*, July 31, 1920.

look for excuses. Everyone knows that if the negro heavyweights were easy marks little would be heard about a color line in the ring." Still, many thought that Dempsey was "only bluffing" and that when the time came, he would manage to sidestep Wills. Others thought it was a matter of economics and risk. He wanted Fulton to beat Wills, because he would have earned the same money for a Fulton contest as one with Wills, and Wills was the tougher proposition. Some said he was considering a Wills fight because he wanted a big payday, and if that was the one fight that would deliver, he would take it. "If Dempsey were outclassed by the negro, as little Tommy Burns was outclassed by Johnson, the match would be a bad one for both Dempsey and the promoter. But Dempsey figures to win after a hard fought battle, so that there is no reason to fear the outcome."

Since beating the gigantic Willard, Dempsey had been called "the greatest champion the ring has ever seen." Of course, nearly every champion was called the greatest after their title-winning effort was fresh in mind. Even Willard was called a superman after beating Johnson. "But Dempsey's calibre is vouched for by many of the old time followers of the ring, all of whom are conservative when it comes to comparing the present day ring warriors with their old favorites."

This writer said if Dempsey really was a great fighter, beating Wills would be a way to prove it. "Not that Wills is so great himself that a victory over him would stamp Dempsey as the marvel of the ages. Wills is not a wonder, but he is good enough to put Dempsey to a real test, and the sporting public always wants to see a great horse or a great fighter extended at least once during his career."[205]

The *San Francisco Examiner* wrote that the "dark man" loomed as Dempsey's real foe. Only the "smoky menace of the mighty Harry Wills" had a chance against him. The opinion was that no white man had any chance with Dempsey, including Carpentier or Miske. "But Wills could unquestionably give Dempsey a fight. It is even within the bounds of possibility that he would defeat Dempsey, which leads one to hope that they never meet." The recollections of Jack Johnson, who currently was in prison, were not to be forgotten. "Nobody wants another epidemic of African assertiveness such as spread then."

Many demands would be heard for Dempsey and Wills to fight. Dempsey declared that he would fight Wills as long as a satisfactory purse was offered.

> But there would be general disapproval of such a match and its drawing power would be extremely doubtful. Wills has a reputation as a faker. Besides, the general public does not believe a white champion should risk his title in a bout with a negro. So it is a fairly safe prediction that there will be no pell-mell rush of promoters

[205] *Scranton Republican*, July 30, 1920.

offering king's ransoms in the way of purses for a Wills-Dempsey match.[206]

Despite Billy Miske's sick spell last year, the world was being notified that he was in better shape than ever, and was even bigger since his 1919 draw result with Battling Levinsky (though some said Miske lost). The *Examiner* predicted that Dempsey would dispose of Miske, as well as other whites, until he reached the point where the only one left to conquer would be Wills. This writer believed that eventually some promoter would take a chance and put up a sizable enough purse that would overcome even the scruples of Jack Kearns against a white vs. black contest.[207]

The press said Tom Gibbons had whipped Harry Greb decisively in both of their two prior contests, giving him an "artistic lacing." They wondered whether he could make it three in a row.[208]

On Saturday July 31, 1920 at Forbes Field in Pittsburgh, before a crowd of 10,000 or nearly 12,000, 160 ½-pound Harry Greb of Pittsburgh fought a 10-round no decision against Tommy Gibbons (who did not weigh in at 10 a.m. as Greb did to make the contracted 163-pound weight limit, and as a result forfeited $250 for failing to weigh in at all, but likely weighed 165-170 pounds). Two of the three local Pittsburgh papers awarded the 10-round no decision to the local man Greb.

The *Pittsburgh Gazette Times'* Harry Keck said Gibbons threw harder, but could not keep up with the pace that the well-conditioned Greb set. Gibbons stung Greb in the 7th, dropping him to one knee for a flash knockdown, but Greb rose quickly and only attacked and fought harder. The last four rounds were fought in a heavy downpour. Keck said Greb won 7 of the 10 rounds, reversing his prior defeat to Tommy back in May.

However, Jim Jab for the *Pittsburg Press* said Gibbons shaded Greb, for he landed the more effective blows, while Harry's holding tactics counted against him. "The writer believes Gibbons took most tricks, piling up points of continued aggressiveness, cleanest hitting in the open and a rare if any desire to tie up the tussle by resort to hugging." Yet, this writer acknowledged that Greb battled so speedily and grandly at intervals that many believed he had won clearly. When they met last, "Gibbons showed marked superiority." This fight was much closer.

The *Pittsburgh Post's* Florent Gibson agreed with Keck, saying Greb won 7 of the 10 rounds, giving Gibbons a good thumping in a furious fight. Gibbons was dangerous, fighting a rugged, hard, slashing battle, but could not follow the pace that the "jumpingjack" cut out. Gibbons stung Greb in the 7th, but only provoked a harder attack. Harry finished strong, mauling Tom at the bell. It was a different Greb than the one who had been ineffective against Gibbons in May. He landed more this time.[209]

---

206 The allusion to Wills being a faker likely was referencing his January 1920 bout with Jack Thompson in San Francisco, which was stopped after the 3rd round and declared a no contest, for neither one was doing much, and the referee believed the fighters were stalling and had hippodromed, working with one another. Their purses were withheld.
207 *San Francisco Examiner,* July 29, 1920.
208 *Pittsburg Press,* July 24, 1920; *Scranton Republican,* July 30, 1920.
209 *Pittsburgh Post, Pittsburgh Gazette Times, Pittsburg Press,* August 1, 1920.

Greb and Gibbons

Greb, Gibbons

Greb, Gibbons

Gibbons, Greb

Lobbying for a Dempsey-Wills contest, the *New York Evening Telegram* wrote,

> The attempt to create the impression that Dempsey would not be justified in making a match with Wills does not appear to have a foundation of reason or logic. Athletes who are afraid to meet opponents because of a difference in color of the skin do not amount to much. There is not the slightest reason to doubt that Dempsey is willing to meet Wills, and the only reason for not doing so would be a pressure of adverse public opinion. College and other amateur athletes have competed with negro opponents for years without any racial outbreaks, and many a boxing title has been held by negroes. No riots followed victories by Dixon, Gans, Walcott, Peter Jackson and other great boxers, and all these men were well behaved. Because Jack Johnson has not conducted himself as he should is no reason for barring all colored men from competition for pugilistic titles.

The *Evening Telegram*'s George Underwood ran an article asking the public whether Dempsey should defend his title against Wills. In response to Kearns' statement that the Wills fight would take place if the public demanded it, Underwood asked readers to vote and send their thoughts on the potential mixed match, which views would be published. However, Underwood also said that nothing disrespectful or discourteous regarding either fighter, or prejudicial remarks regarding the black or white races, tending to incite racial feelings, would be published. He asked whether race or color should factor into Dempsey's choice of title defenses, and whether bouts between blacks and whites were in the best interest of the sport. Responses were printed daily for two weeks, and included:

For Dempsey-Wills

"I am a Southerner by birth, yet am of the opinion that a bout of this sort...would not harm the sport. ... I believe, in view of the shortage of good heavyweights and the period of broadmindedness through which we are living, a Wills-Dempsey bout would aid in the uplift of the sport. Public prejudice which swept the country as a result of the arrest and conviction of Jack Johnson is a thing of the past." Mixed bouts were staged regularly in the military, and anything good enough for Uncle Sam's fighters should be good enough for private citizens.

"Is the color line drawn in college sports? Do not negroes meet whites in football, baseball and track and field? Are there not several negroes on the American Olympic team?"

"Hoping to have the distinguished pleasure to know in the near future, between Dempsey and Wills, which one of the two is worthy of the championship belt."

Several noted that there was no color line in the world war, for blacks as well as whites fought for the U.S.A. (although neglecting to mention that units were segregated and separated based on race): "We forgot about the color line on the blood-stained fields of France, so forget about it here in America." "There was no color line drawn when Uncle Sam called his men to defend the Stars and Stripes in the world war." "I think if the colored men were good enough to fight for this country, then why not for the championship?" "If [Wills] is good enough to fight for Uncle Sam, why shouldn't he be good enough to fight Dempsey?" "Did we draw the color line in our last war? Wills is the only man who stands out to make Dempsey extend himself." One man said the "negro element" constituted a large part of the army that won the war overseas, and therefore deserved to be treated as full citizens.

"By all means let them fight. ... Wills is a very good hearted, game, wonderful fighter. I know him personally and can say he is one fine chap."

"As a lover of liberty I say, 'Down with the color line!'"

"I feel that a champion in all cases should defend his title against any challenger who has won the right to challenge him. Now, Mr. Wills has done more than just win the right to challenge the champion. He is the leading challenger and most eligible contender for a championship bout in the world today."

Some noted the fact that Wills was a gentleman and family man [and married to black woman, not a white woman], and there was no reason to believe he would prove less a credit to the profession than numerous other negro fighters. Furthermore,

"The suggestion that such a mixed bout will arouse racial antagonism is unlikely. Boxing fans the country over desire above all else to see the best man on top. If the game is to prosper there must be no fake champions. Pride, of course, makes it very agreeable to have the best fighter in the world a white champion, but our sense of justice makes us disgusted with the champion who will not prove his claim to the title. … Let some promoter sign them and watch the way the tickets go. There is no arena in the country large enough to hold the many who would try to see the bout."

"That a Dempsey-Wills contest is undesirable from a 'race feeling' point of view is undeniable, but from another point of view… [t]o call oneself the world's best fighter and yet bar a possibly better fighter because of his color sounds silly."

"For Dempsey to draw the color line as some other pugilists have done would certainly injure his reputation…"

"I have never had any use for a man that draws the color-line. In my estimation any man, white or black, that draws that line is yellow."

"They are both good fighters, and a match between two good fighters always draws well."

"I think Wills is just as good a fighter as Dempsey. Give him a chance."

"For the benefit of the 'knockers' who think Wills can't fight, I would like to inform them…that Wills knocked Sam Langford out twice, and he (Langford) is a better man than Dempsey ever beat."

"We want to see a fight when we pay our money. Dempsey is rated to be one of the greatest, if not the greatest, champion of all time. We want to see him defend the title against all comers."

"If Harry Wills was Benny Leonard's weight and size, Leonard would not beat around the stump and ask questions. Leonard would be an undisputed champion or none. Unless Dempsey fights Wills, his title will read, Dempsey, champion of the White Race."

"Wills is a wonderful fighter, regardless of his color. Dempsey is said to be even more wonderful. Let them fight, and may the best man win."

"The only way to decide who is the better is to let them come together. The sooner the better."

"I can't see that this is a question of color at all. Jack Johnson may not have been a very moral man, but neither are some of our white fighters. … [C]olor has nothing to do with the inside of the man. By all means let us have the fight."

"[A] champion who draws the color line and uses that bunk is not worthy of being called champion. … I think today a match between Dempsey and Wills will fill the Garden."

One man said the only white fighter who could beat Wills was Dempsey, who would polish him off. Dempsey was duty-bound to "give this powerful slow moving giant his medicine."

"Before the Fulton-Wills fight took place, it was published in all the papers that Dempsey would meet the winner. He did not make any condition as he does now, saying that he would meet Wills if the public demands it. It seems as if he did not intend to meet the winner in the first place, especially after his refusal of Wills' challenge."

"This talk about Jack Johnson and race riots is just a screen and a dodge. It does not necessarily require a boxing match to start a riot. Suppose that George Dixon or Joe Gans had drawn a race line, and refused to fight an Irishman or an Englishman; what kind of champions would they have been?"

"I never knew a fighter who barred a colored boxer if he thought he was easy."

"If the 'Jamaica Kid' [and Bill Tate] [were] not too black for Dempsey to fight daily in preparation for the Willard fight, why in the name of heaven should there be any discussion as to the propriety of his meeting Wills?"

"How could the champion of the world draw the color line? It is a paradoxical absurdity. … Such a policy is a reflection upon the courage of the dominant white race. … In this age of self-determination and individual worth, the American public cannot afford to harbor a 'cheese' champion, excuse or defend a slacker in the prize ring, no less than it could condone the conduct of one on the field of battle."

"That a record-breaking crowd would attend a Dempsey-Wills fight can be clearly shown by the thousands of fight fans who turned out to see the Fulton-Wills affair. I'm sure that all those who saw Wills in action will agree with me that he is the logical opponent for Dempsey."

"Dempsey isn't champion of the white race, but champion of the world. Down with the 'color line.' We were all created equal. Dempsey will batter Wills, but give the negro a chance."

"I think the white race should rise or fall on its own merits."

"It is my opinion that Mr. Dempsey fears Wills. I think Dempsey is a four-flusher."

"I dare say if Wills won the heavyweight title, which I doubt he could do, and I hope he cannot, because I want the title retained by a white man, I'm sure it will be in the hands of a man who will not disgrace the game as did Jack Johnson."

"Wills through half a dozen years of boxing has proven his ability against real tough battlers, and I think has fully qualified for a test with Dempsey."

"By all means let us have a Dempsey-Wills match and prove to the rest of the world that we have democratic ideals."

"People seem to think because one colored man disgraced an exalted position all are the same. Apparently the whole race is judged by the offense of one man."

"I am acquainted with persons who know Wills well and speak of him in nothing but the highest terms. He is a credit to his race and a gentleman through and through."

"The true sportsmen of the world want a champion who fears no one."

"Little credit is due Wills for putting a man out like Fulton, so get it over, Dempsey, as quick as you can. It won't take long."

"It is not traditionally American to restrict the progress of a people because of the culpable acts of an individual."

"What seems to ail our Mr. Dempsey? Is he also developing a case of nerves, a la Fred Fulton, and trying to hide the true state of affairs behind the sham of public sentiment? ... If he wins, more power to Dempsey, and if Wills be victorious it would add new interest to the game by developing a new crop of 'white hopes.'"

"One good blow by Dempsey will send Wills spinning like a top. Give Wills a chance. We all know he won't win anyhow, but let them fight and may the better man win."

Against Dempsey-Wills:

"As a ring fan for many years following, I protest against any Dempsey-Wills match, especially at the present time here in New York. After being starved for years, we are about to have boxing on a plane the sport never has enjoyed. Why jeopardize the game here with any mixed matches? Let the blacks mingle with the blacks and the whites with white."

"Why match Wills with Dempsey? Who has Wills whipped? Let Mr. Wills go out and mow down all rivals, as did Dempsey before he secured his match with Willard."

"I do not think a match between Dempsey and Wills would invigorate the game. While I feel satisfied Jack would knock Wills kicking, sometimes a lucky punch is put over, in which event when I remember Johnson as champion of the world and his tactics during such time, it would certainly prove detrimental and disastrous to the sport to have another such, as Wills might turn out to be. Let's not take a chance of the 'lucky punch.'"

One man said if a Wills-Dempsey contest would cause a repetition of the same spirit shown by whites when Johnson fought Jeffries and Willard, then it should not take place. "I suggest Dempsey should conquer as many white challengers as possible first before tackling this colored gentleman."

"Why match Wills to box Dempsey when there are more good white heavyweights who can give Dempsey more fighting than Mr. Harry Wills can?"

"I think in Brennan and Miske, New York fans would see a much better fight than a Dempsey-Wills match, and in order to give boxing a chance in this State, why should it start mixed bouts in this class."

One man said it was too soon, that Wills first should prove himself against men like Miske, Levinsky, and Brennan, just as Dempsey had done.

"John L. Sullivan would never fight a colored man. Why should Jack Dempsey?" – 500 members of the Shipmasters' Club of New York.

"I feel that [Wills] would have no chance with Dempsey, who would make short work of the negro fighter."

"A fight fan who has the interests of boxing at heart says keep the game alive by preventing a Wills-Dempsey bout. Why the sudden propaganda? Who is Wills that we are asked to start a campaign that will force Dempsey into a match with him? We have had enough scandal in boxing. Let us avoid further trouble."

"I think Jack Dempsey could lick any boxer living. I do not think Dempsey should be called upon to fight Wills, as in the event Wills should win he might do what Jack Johnson did after losing his world's title to Jess Willard – say he faked the bout."

"With Jack Johnson in prison, reiterating his statement of months ago that he had faked his bout with Jess Willard, I think it very untimely for your fine paper...even to suggest consideration of a proposed Wills-Dempsey match. Johnson, as the standard bearer of his race, threw his people down when he committed grave crimes against our laws, and I think it very untimely to even think of his possible successor. Let Wills box among his own people."

"Have we not had enough scandal in the Johnson case without taking any more chances? Even if the question of mixed bouts is eliminated, by what right does Wills come in line as the second best heavyweight? Avoid ill feeling throughout the country by preventing a Dempsey-Wills fight."

"In regard to the proposed Dempsey-Wills match I do not think it will help boxing any. We must not forget what happened before Willard won the title. It is not a case of the individual, but the public. In the event of Wills winning things will happen that will cause the game to be frowned upon and open the way for professional reformers to ruin the sport. I am not writing out of prejudice, but prevention is better than cure, and while boxing is healthy let it remain so."

"To my mind the game suffers when a black man wins the belt. The fans go to the fights then not to see a good, clean fight but to see the negro champion beaten. This leads unscrupulous managers and promoters to match the champion with third rate 'white hopes' and the fan pays first rate prices to see the match. It is easy to stall and dodge dangerous matches while adding to the bank account. ... Baseball, the national game, bars the negroes and is successful. Why should not boxing follow suit? Who questions the title 'world's champs' in baseball?'"

"We had one black heavyweight champion. Suffice it to say we don't want another one. ... Let the negroes fight among themselves, as they have done for the last five years or more."

More Ambiguous

"If the purpose of having these bouts is to find out who is the best boxer of his class, then the Dempsey-Wills fight ought to take place. If, on the other hand, boxing is a money making gamble at which the white want to see only whites, then by all means do not have the bout take place."[210]

Hyatt Daab of the *New York Evening Telegram* noted that in the wake of the war, there had been a widespread expansion of professional sport, and it had become big business. Millions were being spent on the erection of stadiums and other structures to entertain the sport-mad populace.

Tex Rickard had taken out a 10-year lease on Madison Square Garden to conduct activities there, with emphasis on boxing. Big financial interests were backing him, which showed they realized the tremendous money-making possibilities of professional sport.

The desirability of a Dempsey-Wills match could be debated, but Daab said the fact remained that Wills was the only rival worthy of a shot at the crown who had any chance to win. Everyone knew that Dempsey would beat men like Miske and Brennan. "The question of the color line will ever remain a problem." The fear was that a mixed-race bout would incite racial animus and result in renewed political crackdowns on the sport. However, Daab called the color line a spineless subterfuge as a means of shelter against formidable challengers.[211]

George Underwood said Dempsey was taking on all-comers in his training camp, but needed real sparring partners, for he had to pull his punches when sparring novices and smaller men, which slowed him up

[210] *New York Evening Telegram*, July 29 - 31, 1920, August 1 - 14, 1920.
[211] *New York Evening Telegram*, August 2, 1920.

and was of no benefit to him. He was good-natured and obliging, so he sparred with almost everyone who wanted to know what it was like to box with him. Friends, actors/performers/moving picture stars (including Al Jolson), Wall Street men, politicians, and even clergymen all had the gloves on with him. They loved the publicity. Jack either played defense or just slapped and cuffed them, being exceedingly careful to pat them gently. He was so powerful naturally though, that even slightly thrusting his paw to the face often resulted in his opponent going down. Sometimes he even allowed them to hit him, not seeming to mind at all. It was like a grown man playing with children. His training quarters was a fan Mecca.

Jack Dempsey (left) and Al Jolson.   Champion Jack Dempsey Going Three Fast Rounds with Al Jolson, Celebrated Comedian.

When Dempsey took on regular sparring partners like Bill Tate, Jack found it difficult to stop his play, which was not good, for Bill hit him more than he used to do. Hence, Underwood believed the champ needed to get down to serious business. The Miske contest was one month away.

Dempsey was a diligent trainer, waking up bright and early at his Long Island training quarters. He took a long walk and went swimming before breakfast. Then he did road work, 5- or 10-mile jogs, mixed with walking and running, racing from 200 to 400 yards at a fast clip, slowing down to a walk, and then uncorking another sustained dash. This helped him prepare for sustained, short, rapid bursts in the ring. In the afternoon, he went to the Van Kelton Stadium. He usually was in bed by 11 p.m.[212]

Underwood said Dempsey wanted to meet Wills. Many were misinformed, feeling that he feared Wills. "At no time has Dempsey declared he would not meet the colored challenger or shown any fear of Harry. The champion, in fact, is eager and anxious to get into the ring against the negro. ... But Dempsey is under contract to Jack Kearns, believes in his manager and abides by his every decision."

Kearns understood the feeling against mixed bouts in some quarters, and did not wish to be accused of jeopardizing the game just as it was blossoming again. Hence, he wanted to ascertain just how strongly the public felt about it. Kearns welcomed the opportunity the *Evening Telegram*

[212] *New York Evening Telegram*, August 3, 1920.

offered to learn about public sentiment. The indications were that they would fight, but not until both had engaged in other contests.

Kearns said that if the public really wanted a Dempsey-Wills contest, it could have it. However, Kearns wanted a chance to recuperate their fortunes first. What money they made in the Willard fight was burned up in fighting the court case. Kearns recognized that Wills had a dangerous wallop, and a lucky punch could prove disastrous. "It isn't right for anyone to ask us to take the chance against Wills until we get a little better on our feet financially. Once we get back a little of the money we spent I gladly will let Jack meet Wills, provided public sentiment is in favor of it." Hence, Kearns recognized that Wills at least posed a risk.[213]

George Underwood said Kearns should be convinced, for 86 2/3% of fans who wrote in to the *New York Evening Telegram* overwhelmingly wanted the Dempsey-Wills fight. "For every two persons registering opposition against the bringing together of Dempsey and Wills, thirteen persons have declared themselves in favor of it." 349 letters had been received. A number were from black folk, but the majority were from whites. Therefore, argued Underwood, given the overwhelming public desire to see the fight, the two likely would fight at some point in the future. Dempsey had bouts scheduled with Miske and likely Brennan, while Wills had a bout scheduled with McVey.[214]

190-pound Miske claimed he was fully recovered from his illness and was ready. He recently had knocked out Jack Moran in short order, and critics declared his form to be as good as ever.[215]

WORLD'S CHAMPION WHO BOXES BILLY MISKE LABOR DAY

On August 11, 1920 in New York, Jack Dempsey and Bill Brennan, along with their managers, Jack Kearns and Leo Flynn, met and signed articles of agreement to fight in New York sometime later that year. Promoters would be allowed to bid to host the match.[216]

[213] *New York Evening Telegram*, August 6, 1920.
[214] *New York Evening Telegram*, August 9, 1920.
[215] *Benton Harbor News-Palladium*, August 9, 1920.
[216] *New York Daily News*, August 12, 1920.

Jack Dempsey, Jack Kearns, Leo Flynn, and Bill Brennan sign to fight.

The *Lansing State Journal* said any claims that Dempsey's gloves were loaded was fistic fiction. There were rumors that he had plaster of Paris or horseshoes in his gloves even *before* the Willard fight. The day before that fight, Dempsey had said, "They say that I have lead weights in my gloves. All that I ever pack in the gloves are these," raising his two brown fists. "If I get the chance, you'll see him tipped over. I haven't hit one right yet that didn't fall."

Some writers said the way Willard was cut up indicated that Dempsey must have hardened his fists in some way. This writer said Willard was not cut badly at all. He had a puffy black eye, and a cut mouth, but it was not ripped, and such was understandable given the number of hard blows he had taken. "Willard looked exactly as did Jim Jeffries after the fight with Johnson. He was just beaten up a bit, but not slashed. Any glove can do what was done to Jeff and Willard without being doped."[217]

On August 12, Dempsey left New York to head to Benton Harbor, Michigan to prepare for the Miske fight. "The champion was laughing like a boy as he stepped on the train. Jack is in wonderful condition and could step into the ring against any man in the world this afternoon."[218]

Some wondered whether Dempsey had softened up over the past year, owing to the easy life, with the white lights of the moving picture studio. Female reporter Jane Dixon said Dempsey looked as good as ever, packing the same wallop he did against Willard one year ago. She saw him at the open-air arena adjoining the West Side Y.M.C.A., where "Jack Dempsey, himself no more than an overgrown boy with a boy's heart and a boy's love of prowess, was showing a mob of hard-fisted young metropolitan 'newsies' how to grow up into regular man-sized men. It is difficult to say who was enjoying the carnival more, Jack or his howling guests."

Dempsey had a happy smile, with boyish freckles peppered across his tip-tilted nose, with brown-black eyes, and dark hair.

---

[217] *Lansing State Journal*, August 12, 1920.
[218] *New York Evening Telegram*, August 12, 1920.

He has grown easier in manner. His inherent shyness, a pleasing part of his personality, remains, but its owner has this trait a trifle more under control. He is just as direct in speech and look, as unspoiled, as free from pose as in those days when he tracked the Nevada trails, a boy-wanderer seeking the fortune of the open road.

Jack said he preferred the ring to the movies. "I am a boxer, not an actor. I began to chaff under the inactivity, though goodness knows I was active enough in a way. But not my way, which is in the ring." They usually started filming at 7 a.m. and went until 5 or 6 p.m., sometimes later. He still worked out in the evenings, sometimes every night, but never less than three or four days a week.

When asked if he would beat Miske, Jack replied, "Don't know. A bout is a good deal like a horse race. You never can tell until the horses start running which one is going to come under the wire a winner. I'll be able to tell you more about the Labor Day performance when we get inside the ropes and start going."

Dempsey said he did not know much about Carpentier, and had not seen him fight. He heard he was a great boxer. The lady reporter said, "He looks so much smaller than you." Jack replied, "Maybe, but so did I look a lot smaller than Willard." Bill Brennan had fought Dempsey at top speed, and was better now in every way, scientifically and physically, so Jack anticipated a tough fight with him. He hoped that New Yorkers would see them fight, "to be convinced that boxing is a real man's sport."

When asked if he would fight Harry Wills, Jack replied,

> If the public wants me to box Wills I will do so. However, I am far from convinced the public desires such a meeting. I am not sure it would be wise. There has been entirely too much race disturbance lately. A bout between representatives of the two races might only kindle smouldering fires to blaze. I believe the authorities would frown on a match between Wills and myself. We have succeeded in placing boxing on a plane above any it heretofore has held. Why not keep it there?

Jack said he was in a peculiar position, having achieved his goal.

> All my life I wanted just one thing – to be the world's champion boxer. Now that I have won the honor I can go no further. The best I can do is to hold my own, with the fear of going back always before me. That means I must progress in some other direction or be without ambition, which would be deadly.

The champ also said New York was the greatest city on earth, making all other cities look like mining camps by comparison.

On August 14, the *New York Evening Telegram* reported that only 35 out of 750 letters it received were opposed to mixed-race bouts. 95% favored a bout with Wills. Since Kearns publicly had announced that he would stand by the opinion of the *Telegram's* readers, it was up to him to make good. Paddy Mullins, Wills' manager, was well-pleased with the results, and declared that in view of the public demand, he would trail Dempsey and Kearns until the match was clinched. The International Sporting Club, which promoted Fulton-Wills, said it would try to make the match. It also was trying to host the Dempsey-Brennan contest.

George Underwood said the sporting world would understand Dempsey defending against Miske, Brennan, and then Carpentier, and possibly even a rematch with Willard, but after that, he would be expected to face Wills. Thereafter, a new man would need to be found. The younger generation, which needed time to develop properly, included Martin Burke, John Burke, Bob Martin, and Gene Tunney. "Unless Tunney and Martin Burke pick up weight they are scarcely likely to develop into boxing material worthy of testing the great Dempsey. It looks as if it would be either John Burke or Bob Martin who stands the best chance of development."[219]

Harry Greb

Edward Tranter said Harry Greb followers declared that he would have a chance against Dempsey because he was much faster than him. "Personally, I believe Dempsey would annihilate Greb at this time." Greb was scheduled to spar with Dempsey to help Jack prepare for Miske, returning the favor that Jack did for him in helping Harry prepare for Gibbons.[220]

Dempsey and film star Ruth Roland on Santa Monica beach

[219] New York Evening Telegram, August 13 - 15, 1920.
[220] Buffalo Enquirer, August 21, 1920.

CHAPTER 5

Billy Miske

In mid-August 1920, after seeing Miske training in Chicago, the *Chicago Tribune's* Ray Pearson said a new and improved Billy Miske would be facing Jack Dempsey. He had the chin, the defense, a solid punch, and the speed and skill to score an upset. Dempsey had improved since they last met, too, but would have to be at his best to handle a man like Miske. Nearly a year ago, Miske suffered a hip condition which threatened his career. He had been fighting too often (with 9 fights in 1919; 16 in 1918). Resting for a while actually had improved him physically. He healed up and no longer was overworked.[221]

The *Lansing State Journal* said there had been several stories afloat that Miske had been ill. His manager Jack Reddy said the stories were false, and Miske was in great shape. He would train in public for all to see his form, and those who saw him would be impressed.[222]

Having seen Billy in training recently, Mike Gibbons gave Miske a good chance to win. "I don't know what has kept Miske out of the ring for nearly a year, but I do know that I have never seen him looking better or boxing better than he is right now." Gibbons said Miske was stronger and putting more snap into his punches than ever before. He had seen Miske in action three times against his brother Tommy Gibbons. Miske had gone the distance with Dempsey on two occasions, so Billy was familiar with Jack and would have confidence. Miske was a better boxer than Dempsey, though he could not hit as hard. But Miske was not a light hitter by any means. Hitting Miske would not be as easy as hitting Willard, for he was quite shifty. He potentially could outbox the champ.

Miske said,

> I have twice met Dempsey, and don't figure that he had anything on me in either of our bouts. I have not done much battling for a year, but the champion has done none at all. I know I am stronger and that I hit harder than ever before in my boxing career. I also am boxing better than ever before. If I was good enough to hold Jack even two years ago, and I have greatly improved since then, why shouldn't I beat him, especially as I don't think Jack has improved since he beat Willard? Jack has spent a lot of time on the Pacific coast in the film world since he won the title, and the moving picture business does not tend to improve a boxer's condition.

---

[221] *Chicago Tribune*, August 15, 1920.
[222] *Lansing State Journal*, August 16, 1920.

Miske further said that although he and Jack were friendly with one another, Dempsey had done his best to knock him out in their prior bouts, because he was trying to establish himself as the logical contender to Willard, yet could not do it. Miske said he would not simply try to last 10 rounds, but would fight to win the title and knock out Dempsey if he could.[223]

26-year-old Miske's 78-fight record (53-11-14), which began in 1913, included: 1914 LND10 Tommy Gibbons; 1915 DND6 Harry Greb, WND10 Mike O'Dowd, and LND10 Tommy Gibbons; 1916 WND10, LND10, and WND10 (twice) Jack Dillon, WND10 (twice) Battling Levinsky, and WND10 Bob Moha; 1917 WND10 (twice) Charley Weinert, WND10 Jack Dillon, LND10 Levinsky, KO1 Joe Bonds, WND10 Carl Morris, and L12 Kid Norfolk; 1918 DND10 Fred Fulton, WND10 Gus Christie, TKO7 Tom Cowler, W10 Gunboat Smith, L/DND10 Jack Dempsey (slight majority said Dempsey won), D4 Willie Meehan, W4 KO Kruvosky, WND10 Gunboat Smith, WND8 Bartley Madden, WND10 Harry Greb[224], WND6 Tom McMahon, LND6 Dempsey, KO2 Jim Flynn, and TKO10 Gus Christie; 1919 WND6 and KO4 Tom Cowler (a 210-pounder), LND10 Harry Greb[225], W15 Bill Brennan (close fight)[226], WND10 Willie Meehan (giving Meehan a bad beating, decking him in the 9th and nearly stopping the last man to defeat Dempsey), LND10 Kid Norfolk, DND10 Tommy Gibbons (Miske 177, Gibbons 167)[227], DND8 Bill Brennan (local newspaper said both fighters

[223] *Saint Joseph Herald-Press*, August 16, 1920. St. Joseph, Michigan was just a few miles from Benton Harbor.
[224] Regarding the September 21, 1918 Miske-Greb fight, the *Pittsburg Press'* Jim Jab said 159-pound Greb was beaten, and 174-pound Miske dominated the last 4 rounds, almost putting him out.

The *Pittsburgh Gazette Times'* Richard Guy said 190-pound Miske outpunched Greb. The local middleweight had a lead up to the 6th, when Miske opened up an attack of solid right wallops. "So terrific was the onslaught of the big boy from the Northwest that he overcame a lead which the Pittsburgher had, mainly through superior speed, and speed alone, that he not only beat down the advantage but almost caused Greb to succumb to his hard right hand punches. Greb was well-nigh all in at the end of the fight. … Miske was unscathed. It was the worst beating Greb has experienced…"

The *Pittsburg Dispatch's* Sporting Editor William Peet said Miske outpointed Greb by a slight margin in a furious encounter. The aggressive, rushing Harry had the clear lead through the 8th round with his fast pace, but weakened and was groggy in the final two rounds. A vicious right opened up a cut over Greb's eye. It was a good big man beating a good little man, for 174-pound Miske used his weight on the 159-pound Greb in the clinches. Yet, the round-by-round account scored it clear for Miske, 5-1-4. 1-E, 2-M, 3-E, 4-M, 5-G, 6-M, 7-E, 8-E, 9-M, 10-M. Former champion Abe Attell agreed, saying, "The Dispatch was justified in giving the decision to Miske, for he earned it during the last two rounds."

The *Pittsburgh Daily Post's* Florent Gibson said Miske opened a cut over Harry's eye, turning the tide late and giving Greb his hardest battle. Greb barely held the advantage, 5 rounds to 3, with 2 even. Miske landed the sensational blows, but Greb's early lead with his volume gave him a slim advantage at the end.

Harry Keck scored it 6 Greb, 3 Miske, and 1 even. Greb threw and landed more, but Miske landed cleaner, harder, and more effectively, giving Greb a beating in the last two rounds, cutting his eye. He came close to evening up the affair with his finish, but it was Greb's fight by a shade on his good early lead.
[225] Regarding the March 31, 1919 Greb-Miske contest, Harry Keck scored it 8-1-1 for the aggressive Greb with his unorthodox frequency of attacks. Neither one ever was in distress, though Miske's face was puffed in the grueling contest.

Richard Guy said Greb won clearly 7-1-2, and was faster, though Miske occasionally landed telling blows.

Jim Jab said Miske stalled and punched only intermittently. Greb, though lighter and shorter, was all over him, raining blows upon Miske, who only once in a while flashed his punching ability, particularly to the body. Miske mostly played defense, riding, tugging, tussling, and stalling. *Pittsburgh Post, Pittsburgh Gazette Times, Pittsburg Press*, April 1, 1919.
[226] The *Tulsa Daily World's* Charles Brill said Miske's sensational rally in the 14th round, showering blows upon Brennan, won it for him, but Brennan put up a game battle, drawing even in the 13th after being outclassed early on. Brill scored it close, 6-4-5 for Miske.

The *Tulsa Morning Times'* Lou Duffy said although the referee awarded Miske the contest, Brennan deserved to win, 7-4-4. *Tulsa Morning Times, Tulsa Daily World*, April 29, 1919.
[227] Regarding the June 19, 1919 Miske-Gibbons contest, Referee George Barton said Miske was entitled to no less than a draw, and actually had a shade on points as a result of his aggressiveness. Miske was stronger, and came on better at the end. Another reported that Referee George Barton said he would have called it a good draw, had he been empowered to render a decision.

The *St. Paul Pioneer Press* said Gibbons-Miske was a draw, 4-4-2. Miske did more fighting, but Gibbons showed more class as a boxer. Miske's aggressiveness offset Gibbons' superior skill. Scored as a boxing match, Gibbons won a slight shade over Miske, but Billy evened up the score by his aggressiveness and willingness to make it a battle worth the money paid, so a

were capable of winning the title), L/DND12 Battling Levinsky (dull/cautious boxing match); and 1920 TKO2 Jack Moran.

The local *Benton Harbor News-Palladium* estimated that Miske weighed about 215 pounds in street clothes, and would be 196 stripped on fight night. The *Chicago Tribune*'s Ray Pearson estimated that Miske weighed 192 pounds.[228]

When asked about potential matches, Dempsey said everything was up to Kearns. "Say, now, listen. I don't have anything to do or say about the technicalities of any of my matches. I leave all that to Jack Kearns. He's got the noodle for this corporation. And anything he signs for goes."

Regarding the upcoming fight, Dempsey said, "I don't think Miske has improved any since I last met him and I know I have. Billy is in great condition again, they say. I sincerely hope he is. Naturally I expect to win, but I do devoutly hope for one thing, and that is for Billy to give me a good, hard, tough battle. I need one."[229]

Miske's sparring partners included 6'4" 226-pound Walter 'Farmer' Lodge.[230]

Dempsey would be trained by Chicago's Ben Smith, as well as Kearns. He would spar with black fighters Bill Tate and Panama Joe Gans. Middleweight Harry Greb, who had fought Miske three times (1-1-1), also was expected to work with him. Dempsey said, "Too many champions have suffered defeat because they thought they could not be beaten and refused to take their training seriously. I, for one, do not intend to follow in their footsteps."[231]

The Benton Harbor, Michigan arena was being enlarged to fit more than 20,000 people. Promoter Floyd Fitzsimmons was anticipating a capacity Labor Day crowd. Many from Miske's hometown of St. Paul, Minnesota were expected to come. Ringside seats were $30, with others available at $20, $10, and $5, plus the 10% war tax on each ticket.[232]

---

draw verdict did neither an injustice. There was a lot of clinching and much dancing, mostly by Gibbons. 1-G, 2-G, 3-M, 4-G, 5-G, 6-E, 7-M, 8-M, 9-M, 10-E.

The *Minneapolis Tribune's* Fred Coburn said, "The fight was a draw and nothing else. Miske was the better man on aggressiveness and Gibbons landed the cleaner punches and did the snappier work." Tom showed no desire to stand and mix. Miske tore in, but Tommy was elusive, dancing, dodging, and side-stepping. Yet, Coburn's round-by-round scoring had it 5-4-1 for Miske. 1-E, 2-M, 3-G, 4-G, 5-G, 6-M, 7-G, 8-M, 9-M, 10-M.

The *St. Paul Daily News'* Empty Caine said Gibbons barely outpointed Miske by a scant shade margin, slightly outboxing him, though Miske was the aggressor, rushing him about the ring. However, Tommy's dancing and elusiveness prevented Miske from landing, while Miske landed a bit more than Billy did. Both also covered and wrestled often.

The *Minneapolis Journal's* Ed Walker said Gibbons won by a shade, 4-2-4. Miske was the aggressor, while Gibbons "was content to dance and jab his way to a hairline decision. ... Miske was 10 pounds heavier, bulled Tom round the ring, but could not catch Gibbons to land many solid blows." 1-G, 2-G, 3-E, 4-G, 5-G, 6-E, 7-E, 8-M, 9-M, 10-M.

[228] *Benton Harbor News-Palladium*, August 17, 1920; *Chicago Tribune*, August 19, 1920.
[229] *Richmond Item*, August 17, 1920.
[230] *Ironwood Daily Globe*, August 18, 1920.
[231] *Saint Joseph Herald-Press*, August 18, 1920.
[232] *Lansing State Journal*, August 21, 1920; *St. Joseph Herald-Press*, September 4, 1920.

On August 22 at Eastman Springs, Benton Harbor, after sparring 3 rounds with Miske, getting decked by a straight right in the 1st and nearly knocked out in the 3rd round, Chicago heavyweight Jack Heinen said Miske had Stanley Ketchel's shift and a punch equal to that of Jess Willard and Jack Johnson. Heinen was in a position to judge. "I have boxed Jack Johnson and Jess Willard in training when those boys were at their best and I want to truthfully say neither could hit any better than did Miske in our first workout here." Heinen said Miske actually hurt him more than Willard did. Miske's speed and power were surprising. Billy could get in and out rapidly and effectively, and actually fought a lot like Dempsey. "I firmly believe Miske is in better shape than Dempsey."

The pleasantly-surprised 500 fans at ringside believed Miske would give Dempsey a much tougher fight than many previously had realized. The performance convinced fans that he was a worthy foe to meet the champion. "Billy Miske has been greatly underestimated," and was "far from being down and out." He possessed an accurate, powerful punch, a shift, and wonderful ring generalship.

Billy actually had been training steadily for the past five months in St. Paul, Milwaukee, and Chicago, and his condition was marvelous. He was being trained by Ike Bernstein, who had trained world lightweight champion Benny Leonard for his July 5 fight with Charley White.

Dempsey was training less than a mile away, just outside Floyd Fitzsimmons' athletic field, working in a temporary ring constructed on the baseball diamond.

On Sunday the 22nd, after doing morning road work, in the afternoon, for 2 rounds each, Dempsey punched the bag, skipped rope, and shadow boxed. Dempsey also sparred 4 rounds, 2 each with Bill Tate and welter/middleweight Panama Joe Gans (44-12-5). Jack displayed flashes of the form that won him the championship. "His wind was good, his legs strong and after the first round brush, his speed and judgment of distance picked up much after the fashion of a racing car just released from traffic." Fans who saw the "Utah mauler" were convinced that he was the same old Jack, and had lost nothing by his year-long layoff.

Dempsey said,

> [B]oxing the next two weeks will improve my speed and judgment of distance. ... I do not anticipate any trouble getting down to the form I was in when I met Willard. I have only a few extra pounds to remove now. At Toledo I was in and out of form during that long training siege several times. I have kept in shape by doing light road work for several months, boxing exhibitions and the like, and my work here to date has done me a lot of good.

Harry Greb was scheduled to arrive soon. Kearns said,

> Greb is fast, a clever boxer and although light, should give Jack the chance to develop speed. Gans is a fast man, too, and while small, provides the right kind of opposition. Tate is the biggest of the

three and an excellent defensive fighter. Those piston-like arms of his make him hard to hit. He's big enough, too, to take a considerable amount of punishment, and they must all stand a little battering when they get in there with the champion.[233]

The 26-year-old Miske was a likeable chap. He had been boxing for eight years, and held his own against every man he had boxed. Speaking of his prior contests with Dempsey, Miske said, "I gave a good account of myself in both of those fights. … I was stung a few times, it is true, but I was always able to fight back." Some even thought he won or earned a draw. He had suffered from "illness" the past year, but he underwent an operation which "corrected a curvature in his spine." He then knocked out Jack Moran.

After 5 miles of roadwork in the morning, Miske said,

> I came through our first two bouts nicely and am confident that I can do even better this time. I will be in the best shape of my career…certainly in better condition than I was back in 1918 when I fought him. … I cannot see how Dempsey can be as good as the day he beat Willard. … He will have had a 14 months' layoff. While I have boxed only once myself…I have kept in good shape. My training since my discharge from the hospital six months ago has all been with a Dempsey bout in view. … Don't be surprised if I deliver the goods… I know I can box with any man in the world and hold my own. I have done this twice before with Dempsey. When we meet for the third time I will have new health, new punching power and new confidence at my command. … I will be in better condition.

On the 23rd, Miske sparred with Jack Heinen, Billy Burke (or Jack Burke), and Jim Delaney. Miske pounded upon them so severely with terrific wallops that they all were well used up after 2 rounds each.

Those who originally thought Miske would not have the ghost of a chance against the heavy-punching Dempsey were changing their minds. The form and punch he was exhibiting in his public training caused observers to take notice.

Jack Reddy said Miske carried a kick in both hands and would not be soft picking, as their prior two fights proved. Dempsey had been "able to march through a lot of slow moving fighters of the truck horse variety."

That same day, Dempsey sparred 6 rounds, 3 each with his black sparring partners, 230-pound Bill Tate and fast welterweight Panama Joe Gans.

> Dempsey showed the fans that his shift is working to perfection and that his left hand is apparently as good as the day he defeated Willard. His footwork was lightning fast, while his dodging, which makes him the hardest champion to hit the ring has ever seen, kept

[233] *Saint Joseph Herald-Press, Benton Harbor News-Palladium*, August 22, 1920.

both Gans and Tate puzzled throughout the workout. His entire body seems to be employed in every punch.

On the 24th, Miske floored Heinen three times in the 1st round with left hooks, and lifted him out of the ring in the 2nd round with a straight right to the jaw. Jim Delaney fared a little better because of his speed and cleverness, but Billy still drew blood from his nose.

Dempsey sparred 6 rounds total. Panama Gans was as fast as a flash on his feet, with quick jabs, and Jack had to chase him around for 3 rounds. Against the bigger, stronger, but slower-moving Tate, Jack tore in with both hands. Late in the 3rd round, Tate shot a hard left to the midsection, but it only riled Dempsey, who fired his left to the jaw and stomach in rapid fashion. Tate continually held on for dear life thereafter, and Dempsey only occasionally broke free from his clasp.[234]

14 months out of the ring seemed to have done Dempsey no harm.[235]

Jack was taking Billy seriously, saying that he regarded him as a better fighter than Willard.

> I am frank to say that I think Miske is a stiffer puncher than Willard and certainly is much faster, and he can stand up under severe punishment. I even failed to knock him down, although I put every ounce of strength behind my punches. Miske is as big as I am and perhaps will slightly outweigh me. … I figure to go into the ring under the 190 pound notch. I hope to be at the same weight as I was when I fought Willard. 187 pounds.[236]

There were rumors that Dempsey had been injured in an auto crash. Kearns denied it and said it was a fake newspaper story. Dempsey was notified of his injuries after completing his road work. He gave Gans and Tate a hard mauling in sparring, proving that the story was untrue.[237]

Marty Farrell (16-4-6), Pacific coast middleweight, joined Dempsey's sparring crew, and boxed him 2 rounds on August 26.[238]

Also on August 26, 1920, the 19th Amendment to the U.S. Constitution was ratified (by the final state vote necessary), making its inclusion into the U.S. Constitution official. Women finally had a constitutional right to vote. No longer could there be voter discrimination on the basis of sex.

Jack Dempsey said he was more confident as champion. He felt better than he did against Willard.[239]

On the 27th, Miske sparred 3 rounds with Jack Heinen, 1 round with Carl Davis, and 2 rounds with Johnny Tillman (who was scheduled to fight Jack Britton for the world welterweight crown), walloping them all with stiff rights to the jaw.

---

[234] *Saint Joseph, Herald-Press*, August 24, 25, 1920.
[235] *Escanaba Morning Press* (Michigan), August 25, 1920.
[236] *Lansing State Journal*, August 26, 1920.
[237] *Lansing State Journal*, August 27, 1920.
[238] *Port Huron Times-Herald*, August 27, 1920.
[239] *Buffalo Times*, August 28, 1920.

That day, Dempsey sparred Bill Tate, Panama Joe Gans, and middleweight Marty Farrell, pounding them all in the body.

At that point, wagering had Dempsey as only a slight 10 to 8 favorite. Jim Pugh, who owned Eastman Springs, bet $2,500 at even odds that Miske would last the full 10 rounds.

Miske said he was very happy, for his life's dream was about to be realized. He was confident that he would win, but not overconfident or cocky. "I know that I am going to battle one of the greatest fighting men of history – if not the greatest – but nevertheless, I have tested him and I know that I stand a first class chance of beating him."

> I was at the ringside when Dempsey lifted the title from Jess Willard. Jack put up a wonderful battle and I was one of the first to congratulate him. … Dempsey thanked me for my sportsmanship and declared that I was the toughest man he ever fought. He promised that I would be given the first chance at the title and he has lived up to his word.

> I am in better condition today than I have ever been before in my life. It is true that I was out of the game for a time with illness, but I recovered several months ago and have been training steadily since early last spring.

Miske felt great in his victory over Jack Moran, boxing better and hitting harder than ever. He had worked harder during the past year than Dempsey had.

> I am stronger, taller, and heavier than I was a year ago. While it may sound unbelievable, I have grown more than a quarter of an inch the past 12 months. When I fought Dempsey in St. Paul and Philadelphia I weighed 179 pounds. When I resumed training last spring I weighed 210 pounds. I took off some weight for the Moran contest, but I will enter the ring weighing around 190 pounds when I swap punches with the champion on Labor Day.[240]

Those who saw Miske in training said Dempsey would have no cinch on his hands. Miske might not win, but he was certain to make things interesting.[241]

Robert Edgren wrote that the scarcity of opponents might compel Dempsey to cross the color line, although such would not be in the sport's best interests. While there was no great demand for a mixed-race heavyweight championship, Harry Wills' recent victories might rouse or compel the champ to fight him, for others were not eager to do so. "There's little doubt that Dempsey could polish Wills off. Yet there is just a shade, and the world isn't anxious to risk a repetition of the disorders attending the short reign of Jack Johnson that began in Australia and ended at Havana." True, Dempsey-Wills would be a great fight.

---

[240] *St. Joseph Herald-Press*, August 28, 1920.
[241] *Detroit Free Press*, August 29, 1920.

[Y]et it is a fight no reputable promoter is going to look for. Another world's heavyweight championship bout between champions white and black would arouse national opposition, and perhaps cause adverse legislation. Boxing is doing very well now because hundreds of thousands of boys in our armies during the great war became skilled boxers, and their influence has helped to pass liberal boxing laws in several states. No matter how interesting a bout between Dempsey and Wills might be, as a contest between two splendid and well-matched athletes, no promoter with any interest in the sport would put it on.

Still, if Wills kept knocking out potential Dempsey foes, Jack might have to fight him. The champ was in awe of no living man.

Edgren said Billy Miske was a splendid boxer, lion-hearted, and able enough, so it looked like a great fight on paper, but Dempsey still would be too much for him.[242]

On Saturday August 28, in front of a crowd of 2,000 or 5,000 at Springbrook park, South Bend, Indiana (about 38 miles south of Benton Harbor), Billy Miske boxed 3 rounds each with Jack Heinen and welter Johnny Tillman. He decked Heinen three times with left hooks, and showed speed and defense with Tillman.

Miske's snappy exhibition drew rounds of applause. Billy appeared to be in the pink of condition, his skin brown from his outdoor road work, and he radiated confidence.

The *South Bend Tribune* said those who saw 194-pound Miske (weight taken after the workout) were convinced that he was classy, and would give Dempsey a tough fight. "Miske works faster than Dempsey, uses his head in placing punches and is much shiftier. And he demonstrated here that he has the kick necessary to enable him to win a championship."

Miske said, "On Monday, September 6, I expect to win the world's heavyweight boxing championship." He had done what no other man had done recently – gone the distance in 10- and 6-round bouts with

[242] *Buffalo Times*, August 29, 1920.

Dempsey, and never was off his feet. "Willie Meehan has boxed Dempsey several times, always four rounds, and by his peculiar methods lasted. Outside of that, every other heavyweight in America that has climbed through the ropes with him has been knocked out." Miske had beaten Meehan soundly; the last man to beat Dempsey.

Regarding his first contest with Dempsey, Miske said, "I did not run for cover. I fought him. He shook me up in the second round with a fearful left, yet I fought him off his feet and drove him into the corner before that same round ended. He cracked me another big punch in the seventh round and I shook it off and came back and made him break ground..." Billy claimed to be ill in both fights, very ill the second time, yet some newsmen gave him the decisions or said the bouts were even. "Now I am well, am bigger, heavier and much stronger than ever before in my life. My chances of beating him are much better."

Miske explained that up until six months ago, he had not been well for several years. "I have had trouble with my hip which caused a pressure on the nerves in my back and as a result my back was weak. I suffered pains similar to those of neuritis. I could not train properly, was unable to do road work, as my legs and back would ache." The pressed nerves caused bladder trouble. He claimed to have had this condition when he fought Dempsey twice, as well as Gibbons, Levinsky, and others. He also had a fever and boils when he fought Gibbons.

Given that he was feeling great now, he was quite confident, having stopped Jack Moran nicely in his last contest. He was a new man. "I would not meet Dempsey if I did not think I had a very good chance of beating him."

Miske noted that Dempsey was heralded as a superman, the greatest fighter of all times, and the greatest puncher ever. Yet, Billy never was off his feet against him, so he had confidence in his ability to take his blows. Miske also fought hard punchers like Fulton, Morris, Gunboat Smith, Cowler, Weinert, and Jack Dillon "when he was the real Dillon. In nearly 150 fights I have never been off my feet and do not expect to get toppled off my pins on Labor day." When Dillon was at his best, he hit nearly as hard as Dempsey.

Miske said although Willard was big, game, and could hit, he needed time to deliver a punch, and had no defense (other than his height and reach). Billy believed that he matched up better with Dempsey than did Jess. He had defense, could take it, and could hit back. He claimed to have hit Dempsey so hard in their first fight that Jack had a big lump on his jaw afterwards and could not eat steak for a week.

> I can outbox him and I can hit him. I hit him in both our battles.
> ... I am not going to let Dempsey back me around letting loose
> those terrible hooks of his. He is a hook puncher, swaying his body
> with his punches and hooking with fierce force with either hand.
> He has his body, from the toes up, behind his punches. I will box
> him at times, block off some of his hooks and bob down, if he

shoots over me, I will come up in close and batter at him. It worked before; now that I am punching better I expect to shake him up when I hit him. … If you stand still with Dempsey and lead at him he counters with hooks. He hurts when he lands, he is bound to land some, but this time I am also going to land.

On August 28, Dempsey worked on his boxing rather than attempting to punish Tate, Gans, or Farrell. Tate's left drew some blood from Jack's nose, the first time in this training camp that had happened.

Dean Snyder said Dempsey's 14-month layoff had made no difference in his ability. "No boxer ever got more actual enjoyment out of fighting than the present champion. The only trouble with Dempsey is that he has to be held back from over-doing. He tears into his sparring partners like it was a real fight." It was hard for him to pull his punches. Rumors that he had grown fat and soft were false, for he was 192-193 pounds, with no apparent superfluous flesh on his muscular body.

Dempsey said he liked to be in the ring regularly, for that kept a fighter's eye quick, though he felt stronger than when he won the title. "Miske is a strong, tough fellow. They say he is heavier and in better health than when I boxed him at both St. Paul and Philadelphia two years ago. I hope he fights me, for those are the kind of birds I like best."

Dempsey's camp was pitched within 100 yards of the battle arena. He and his retinue all were staying at promoter Floyd Fitzsimmons' cottage. Jack liked drinking the local mineral water, which he pumped fresh from the rear of the cottage.

Dempsey started the day with a 5-mile run, accompanied by his colored sparring partners. He rose at 6:30 a.m., ate a light breakfast, and was on the road at 8 a.m. After the road work, Ben Smith gave him a rubdown. Then Jack would have time on his own, and often would be perched on a plum tree limb. Local children were his confidants. They liked the plums that Jack shook down for them. They liked him too. "He has always had a great way of attracting children to him." A light lunch at noon, reading the papers, a game of solitaire, sometimes a nap, and perhaps a spin to the downtown headquarters in Fitzsimmons' big red roadster filled the time.

His training ring was just in front of the ball park grandstand. He boxed at 3:30 p.m. daily. Miske worked out at 2:30 p.m. at Ike Bernstein's quarters, about ¾ of a mile up the road from Dempsey's training location. Hence, crowds could see both men train daily, getting the inside dope.

Dempsey always rushed everything. First, he hit the punching bag, then his sparring partners, then the 250-pound leather-covered sand bag. He sparred 3 rounds each with Tate and Gans. He used Tate to work on body blows, but also took some pretty stiff smacks from Tate's powerful swings. He liked how it toughened him up. The 148-pound Gans kept Dempsey working on his speed.[243]

[243] *Chicago Tribune, Fort Wayne Journal-Gazette, South Bend News-Times*, August 29, 1920; *Brooklyn Daily Eagle*, August 28, 1920; *South Bend Tribune*, August 30, 1920; *Lansing State Journal, St. Joseph Herald-Press, Buffalo Times, Buffalo Express*, September 1, 1920.

Special trains would take fans to the arena. Benton Harbor's mayor had fixed the prices of food, so there could be no exploitation.[244]

Benton Harbor was ideally situated because it could tap into fans from all over Michigan, Indiana, and Illinois.

On the 29th, Dempsey trained in the rain. He boxed 2 rounds each with Tate, Gans, and Farrell, hammering and punishing them, and also worked a bit with newcomer Al Greenwood.

That day, Miske pounded on two new arrivals from Chicago, Joe Wagner and black "Rough House" Wilson, in exciting and rough fashion. It looked like Billy was preparing to pull and haul and fight hard. However, in the 4th round, an accidental Wilson head butt caused a small slight cut over Miske's left eye and drew some blood. The cut was not deep though.[245]

Miske felt that he had fought Dempsey evenly in two bouts when he was 178 and 176 ½ pounds respectively, had learned a few things from those fights and about boxing since then (with 12 more bouts since he last fought Jack), and was bigger and stronger now. Dempsey had not fought since July 1919, whereas Billy had fought in July 1919 and also had a recent tune-up bout in June, so he believed he actually would be sharper than Dempsey.[246]

[244] *Lansing State Journal*, August 30, 1920.
[245] *St. Joseph Herald-Press*, August 30 1920. Another newcomer at the camp, Thunderbolt Smith, would have followed Wilson had it not been for the bum eye.
[246] *Benton Harbor News-Palladium*, *Port Huron Times Herald*, August 30, 1920.

DEMPSEY.		MISKE.
25	Age	26
190	Weight	193½
6 ft. 1¼ in.	Height	6 ft. 1 in.
78	Reach	77
39	Chest (normal)	39
44	Chest (expanded)	44
17	Neck	17¼
20½	Shoulders	20½
32	Waist	33
15	Biceps	15 1-5
14¼	Forearm	13½
8	Wrist	7¾
21	Thigh	22½
14½	Calf	15½
8½	Ankle	9

Dempsey with trainer Ben Smith

Physically, they were evenly matched. They weighed about the same. Miske was only one year older at 26 to Dempsey's 25. They were about the same height as well, with the 6' 1 ½" Dempsey about a quarter-inch taller.

Dempsey was very relaxed and not nervous at all. He enjoyed playing cards with Tate. He said he weighed 189 ½ pounds after his last workout. "My day's layoff will add a little poundage, but from now on I will speed up in my boxing as never before."

165-pound Harry Greb, who on August 20 in Kalamazoo won a 10-round newspaper decision over Chuck Wiggins, and on August 28 in Grand Rapids fought a 10-round bout against Ted Jamieson (Greb was decked by a left hook to the jaw in the 1st round, but came back to draw or earn a shade newspaper win), was en route to train with Dempsey.[247] He was set to fight Wiggins again on the Labor Day card.

Jack Kearns said,

> Whatever it is about Miske that makes him hard for Jack to fight is something that I cannot understand. Of course he'll be in shape – better than he was when he fought him before. We expect to win, but it's beyond me to figure out just when we will be able to cop. Jack's shift and the old left hand that has sent the others into

---

[247] *La Crosse Tribune, Lansing State Journal*, August 29, 1920. Jamieson had lost a 10-round decision to Gene Tunney the previous year.

dreamland is in working order and I fully expect that Miske will fall like the rest.

Kearns said they had bouts in sight with Brennan and Carpentier, which would make Dempsey more money than any heavyweight champion ever earned before.

The *Chicago Evening Post's* Dean Snyder said Miske wasn't doing the holding, pulling, and hauling that Dempsey anticipated he would do. He planned to fight to win, not just survive. Nevertheless, Miske was confident that he would stay the full 10 rounds.

> Miske's new-found health is the chief buzz of conversation. … Miske makes a good appearance in his workouts. Wearing a padded headgear he bounces into the ring like a lightweight and begins to sock. If he fights that way on Labor day Dempsey is going to be both surprised and pleased. … Miske is the picture of health now.

Jack Reddy said now that Billy's back problems were alleviated, he actually stood an inch taller. The wound over his eye was healing nicely.[248]

Three tiers accommodating 3,000 seats had been added around the arena, while bleacher seats would provide for 5,000 more, so that 20,000 could be accommodated. The arena previously had been used for the Benny Leonard vs. Charlie White contest.

It was perhaps the most novel arena in the country. Instead of being built from the land up, it had been built down into the ground, 15 feet below sea level. Its highest point was only five feet above ground. The arena was built of hard sand, wetted and rolled until it was baked almost as hard as concrete. The center of the ring was only 115 feet from the last row of seats. The various sections were fenced off with wire netting. The arena was located on the eastern outskirts of Benton Harbor, within a block of Dempsey's training camp.

Dempsey sometimes walked over to the arena and offered to help the workers, picking up a hammer, saying, "This is nothing new for me. I'd been glad many a time to get $2 a day for this kind of work."[249]

On August 31, Dempsey boxed 8 rounds, 2 with each man. Despite the fact that he was wearing 10-ounce sparring gloves, in their 2nd round, a short Dempsey left hook to the jaw badly dazed and de facto knocked out Army boxing instructor Soldier Jack Riley of Chicago. Riley was out on his feet, and began to fall, but Jack caught him under the armpits and held him up until he shook the cobwebs from his dizzy brain. The soldier had started socking away in earnest, which forced Jack to open up more.

Bill Tate asked Jack to lay off his jaw, so he obliged and hit the body. Panama Joe Gans followed. Jack liked to work with Gans for speed. The last foe was middleweight Marty Farrell, who was fast on his feet and clever with his hands, hitting from any angle for his 2 rounds.[250]

---

[248] *St. Joseph Herald-Press, Chicago Evening Post, Buffalo Courier*, August 31, 1920. Homer Smith arrived in camp. Miske would spar Jack Heinen, Billy Burke, black George Wilson, light heavy Joe Wagner, Carl Davis, black Cyclone Smith, and Homer Smith.
[249] *Lansing State Journal*, September 1, 1920.
[250] *New York Times, St. Louis Post-Dispatch*, September 1, 1920.

Ray Pearson said Dempsey was in a fighting mood. At the end of the sparring session, Jack said to "Doc" Kearns, "Gosh, Doc, I wish the fight was tomorrow. I feel great. The way I feel right now I could whip two Miskes in as many minutes."

That day, 195-pound Miske sparred with Roughhouse Wilson, Joe Wagner, and Homer Smith. Roughhouse was given considerable rough treatment for 2 rounds. Wagner took a lacing, and Smith was out on his feet at the end of 1 round. Another paper said Miske boxed 5 rounds, 2 apiece with George Wilson and Johnny Tillman, and 1 with Homer Smith.

Jack Kearns told reporter Harry Hochstadter, "Dempsey is the greatest heavyweight fighter ever developed because he fights faster and hits harder than any we ever had before. ... Dempsey wants to fight as often as I can dig up opponents. We don't underestimate any man in the world, but I think Dempsey is the greatest ever."

Hochstadter said Dempsey trusted Kearns. "Dempsey admits that he owes all he has in the pugilistic world to Kearns." Kearns took chances with Dempsey and went into debt to carry him through the early stages. "Today he sits back and calmly turns down offers for $50,000 purses."

Kearns first wrote to Hochstadter about Dempsey in 1917, calling him the Submarine. When Dempsey first came to Chicago, the writer's January 5, 1918 column said Kearns was challenging Willard, and any agreement would suit them. Respected men like Jimmy Coffroth, Eddie Graney, and Spider Kelly all saw Dempsey in action on the west coast and were ready to back him to the limit any time he got a crack at the title.[251]

Jack Dempsey (right) sparring with Big Bill Tate at Benton Harbor. (NEWS photo)

[251] *Chicago Tribune, St. Joseph Herald-Press, Chicago Evening Post*, September 1, 1920. Eugene Kessler, sporting editor for the *South Bend Tribune*, visited both camps on the 1st.

Another pose of Miske at Benton Harbor.

Billy Miske, who challenges Jack Dempsey.

Sam Hall reported that Kearns/Dempsey would not risk the title on a decision bout. Miske was hoping for a decision victory, but Kearns balked at an official decision verdict. Decisions were permissible in Michigan if the commission authorized it. "But the custom has been to run all shows no decision style, and that situation probably will prevail next Monday." Reddy/Miske were confident that they could win a decision, but Kearns was not inclined to gamble on a decision in a short fight, which the writer said was understandable.[252] Still, some took that to mean Kearns suspected Miske might last the distance, and at least had a chance to outpoint Dempsey.

Jack Reddy said Billy was far better now than in either of the prior Dempsey fights. After boxing Levinsky a year ago last July, 1919, Miske sought the advice of a specialist, and learned that he was suffering from spinal trouble and a kidney ailment that dragged him down physically. Rest and treatment had cured and improved him.[253]

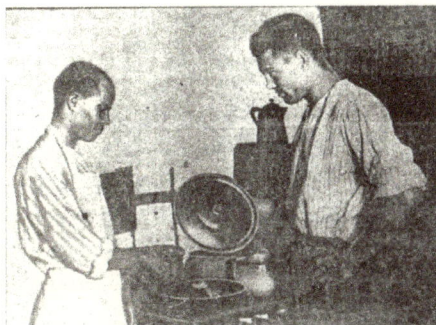

Dempsey with his cook, waiting for his steak.

On Wednesday September 1, 1920, for the first time in this camp, Harry Greb sparred Dempsey. Their fights were just five days away.

Early that morning, Dempsey did his usual road work, which typically was 5 miles. In the afternoon, prior to boxing, Jack worked a couple of rounds with the sandbag and pulleys. He smiled when he heard of Miske's boast that he would outbox him.

According to the nearby *St. Joseph Herald-Press*, Dempsey sped up his work that day. He boxed 8 total rounds with only 30 seconds of rest between each round. He sparred Bill Tate, Harry Greb, and Marty Farrell, in that order. He sparred Tate first, for 2 rounds, hammering Bill's body.

After the 30 seconds of rest, next up was 165-pound Harry Greb, the past master at the art of scoring points, who was in, out, under, around, and on top of the champion for 3 rounds. They traded punches, though Jack refrained from using his full strength, and the melee was interesting.

While Dempsey was shifting about the ring in the 1st round, Greb landed a good left uppercut and two good rights to the chin. The 2nd round saw Greb use his bouncing tactics and the ropes to good advantage. He got close enough once to land three lightning lefts to the face. Some newsmen believed that Greb rocked the champ with a right to the chin in the 3rd round.

Clever Marty Farrell was up last, and gave Dempsey 3 more interesting rounds, all with 30 seconds of rest between rounds.

[252] *Chicago Herald and Examiner*, September 1, 1920.
[253] *Ironwood Daily Globe, Lansing State Journal*, September 2, 1920.

South Bend Tribune sporting editor Eugene Kessler, who was on scene, said Harry Greb rushed the champion about the ring and even jarred him a little. Greb displayed a flash of speed and made the gloves fly so fast at the champ's face that several got home. A right to the chin in the 3rd round made Dempsey put the brakes on his rush and stop long enough to shake off the jolt. "But this workout showed fans that the champion is a hard fellow for the cleverest to knock out. He was also able to get in a few hard punches and could have sent the easterner to the canvas." Jack held back, for he was working with the smaller man.

Kessler expected Dempsey to stop Miske in about 5 rounds, though it would be a terrific fight while it lasted. Both were in top form and condition. Miske was fast on his feet and drove home lightning-fast haymakers. He was faster than Dempsey, and cleverer. However, Dempsey was shiftier, had a perfect head roll, could take a punch, and had a knockout blow that could stop anyone in the world.

Yet, Miske also had a knockout wallop and a chin. His straight right to Roughhouse Wilson's jaw in the 2nd round caused Wilson to stop work for the day. Heinen was pounded on for 2 rounds as well.

Ed W. Smith wrote that Greb's speed awoke Dempsey in a lively sparring bout. Greb injected a lot of ginger into the work of the previously lethargic champion. Greb, the human rubber ball, was just what Dempsey needed. Harry got him out of his sluggish ways and pasted him enough to make Dempsey wake up for the first time during his training camp and show some fine work. Jack clearly believed that fast boxing was necessary for the upcoming encounter, and he worked on his speed (and not punching power). Greb did not know what fatigue meant, and he showed it against Dempsey, going at him. Although "we all know that there was more or less of a 'Barney' about it, we can assure you, dear reader, that this Greb person staggered Dempsey a couple of times during the engagement, which lasted only three rounds." Greb's staggering of Dempsey "isn't any commentary on the champ. We believe that Greb, in his wonderful style, can do that to any man that lives, and this includes the mighty Dempsey, at one time or another." The bout was so good that it brought forth applause.

Despite how well Greb had done, folks still came away from the encounter and workout believing that Dempsey was invincible in a real fight and would crush Miske. "Naturally, this thing between Dempsey and Greb was not in the nature of a real fight of any kind. It was merely a training workout and was understood to be such, but there was a lot of vigor and snap to it that doesn't generally apply to things of this sort."

P. T. Knox for the *Pittsburgh Gazette Times* reported that despite being 25 pounds lighter and 4 inches shorter, Greb gave the champ a real battle. Dempsey had not seen so many gloves in a long time. Greb was all over him and kept forcing him around the ring. Dempsey could do little with the speedy man, while Greb seemed able to hit him almost at will. Greb made the champ miss time and again, and countered with heavy swings to the head and hooks to the body. He was a veritable whirlwind, and made the champ step very lively. When Dempsey stood up straight, Harry had to jump off the floor in order to hit his head.

However, Knox acknowledged that Dempsey was not hitting as straight as he did in Toledo. "He can hit straight when he wants to and when he does his blows carry a wealth of power behind them, for the champion knows how to put his powerful shoulders behind his punches… It may be that Dempsey does not care to hit straight from the shoulder, fearing to punish his partners too severely."

The *Pittsburgh Post* reported that Greb tore into him like a hurricane, piling up points with his rapid, erratic style, and eluding retaliatory efforts with ease. He was throwing a mess of assorted but not too well-directed punches from all angles, though without doing any appreciable damage. Still, he gave Jack a stiff workout.

Ray Pearson said Dempsey was ready, for he proved his condition by going 8 rounds with three different men with only 30 seconds rest between each round. Each of the 8 rounds was a "screamer," but his 3 rounds with Greb were worth the price of admission and more, for it was a real battle. There was nothing easy about the going for either man, and when it was over, the crowd shouted wildly.

Sam Hall said Greb gave the champ all he could handle, and they mixed it to the crowd's delight. Their 3 rounds were corkers, and the crowd frequently applauded. Jack went 2 with Tate, 3 with Greb, and 3 with Farrell.

> Dempsey and Greb cut loose and it looked like a real fight in spots. They exchanged mighty wallops and seemed to like the heavy going. Some of the fans thought Greb was outscrapping Dempsey. Perhaps he did on points, but Jack, you know, had to pull back with his best wallops. They wound up with a red spot on Dempsey's right cheek and Greb crimsoned about the mouth and nostrils. Their setto was well worth the price of admission.

Afterwards, Red (Reddy) Mason, Greb's manager, said Dempsey was the most even-tempered fighter he ever saw, for no matter how hard Greb happened to hit him, Jack never batted an eye, got mad, or tried to knock out his fighter. Dempsey was a great fighter with a punch, but held it back against Greb. "Mason considers the champion the best heavyweight he ever looked at."

The *Chicago Daily News* reported that Dempsey the boxer, not the fighter, was on display, showing fans that he would box Miske, giving a clever exhibition of ring work. Some told Jack that Billy intended to outbox him. Jack replied, "He may do that, but after I plant a couple I'll have him swinging. Then I'll finish it." Whatever his battle plan, Dempsey took to boxing that day rather than attacking.

Frank Menke, Universal Service Staff Correspondent, who also was there, wrote,

Jack Dempsey doffed the role of slugger today and donned that of a boxer and startled the assemblage by his remarkable skill in the new role. Dempsey was a revelation – and so different from the Dempsey that the fight world knows that it didn't seem as if the same man was performing.

The champion was a phantom – when he chose to be. The speediest of his sparring partners, invited to "knock my head off if you can," made the most violent efforts to reach him – and failed.

The king of pugilists ducked, side-stepped, shifted, swirled in and out in a way that was bewildering. The "man without a defense" showed this afternoon that whenever he elects he can defend as well as any gladiator in the ring game. In several flurries with his partners he simply stood still, let them swing their mightiest blows – and simply fended them off.

The clash with Harry Greb, light heavyweight and perhaps the cleverest of American ring men, had the crowd wild with delight. Every minute of the three rounds was filled with famous action.

Greb boxed and slugged, Dempsey merely boxed. He never unlimbered his heavy artillery and confined himself to jabbing and short wild hooks. Greb was a whirlwind in action, but Dempsey, despite his greater bulk, kept a pace with the great Pittsburgher.

And the "champion without a jab" demonstrated the fallacy of that title. For Dempsey, affecting the orthodox style of fighting and totally abandoning at times his familiar crouch, jabbed away with the speed and skill of a Jack Britton. He made no real effort to drive home with knockout force, but simply displayed the fact that if he wants he can jab in an amazing way. But every jab that he sent home jarred his partner. … For Dempsey of the brawny arm and the mighty hands jabs with power equal to an ordinary heavyweight's "haymaker."

Dempsey also demonstrated his trick shift - lead rights often followed by left crosses after stepping through with his right. "And even though the punch was mild and covered by 14-ounce padding, these blows shook up the boy." It was hard to tell just what Dempsey would do at any moment. "And Dempsey hits so swiftly that one second of confusion on the part of the other fighter, one second of hesitancy as to which way he should twist to avoid a Dempsey blow, may prove fatal to his hopes for victory."

That same day, Miske sparred 4 rounds, giving clever Chicago negro heavy Roughhouse Wilson a harder pounding than usual for 2 rounds. Miske discarded his headgear in the 2nd round of his bout with Jack Heinen, and gave him a pounding as well. Billy was breathing easily and seemed to be in good spirits.

Jack Reddy said Dempsey was in for the hardest fight of his career. "Miske will not be knocked out. You can bank on that." Reddy said he never saw a fighter good enough to stop Miske. They wanted a formal decision, and noted that it was the other camp that did not want a decision, refusing to take a chance, which to him showed who had the real confidence. Kearns was not about to risk a formal decision against his man. Reddy was betting on Billy to last the distance.

E. R. Hosking said Miske's morale was great, and his stock was rising. He was full of life and pep and in good spirits. Two weeks ago, it was easy to get bets that Miske would not last 5 rounds, but now it was difficult to get even money that Dempsey would win by a knockout. Bigger and stronger than he was two years ago, Billy's admirers believed he had a real chance to win if he could weather the first 4 to 5 rounds, figuring the champ would tire himself out.

Jack Kearns insisted that Dempsey had improved 40% since he won the title.

Floyd Fitzsimmons announced that the advance seat sale had exceeded $50,000 already. He was anticipating a house of at least $125,000.

Harry Hochstadter said a crowd followed the champ wherever he went. He was idolized.

The confident Dempsey told his best friends that he was not worried about the fight's outcome, but when speaking for the general public, he admitted that Billy was a strong, rugged fellow who could stand the gaff with the best of them.[254]

Dempsey and Greb

A 17-year-old high school gal named Lola Wallin traveled to Benton Harbor from Rockford, Illinois to see the fight. She thought the tickets would not cost any more than a movie, and was shocked to learn that the

[254] *Salt Lake Telegram*, September 1, 1920.; *St. Joseph Herald-Press* (Michigan), *South Bend Tribune*, *South Bend News-Times*, *St. Louis Star*, *Elmira Star-Gazette*, *Pittsburgh Gazette Times*, *Racine Journal Times*, *Butte Miner*, *St. Louis Post-Dispatch*, *Pittsburgh Post*, *Chicago Tribune*, *St. Paul Dispatch*, *Minneapolis Journal*, *Chicago Daily News*, *Chicago Evening Post*, *Chicago Herald and Examiner*, *San Diego Union*, *Kansas City Post*, September 2, 1920.

cheapest ticket was a whopping $5.50, including tax. She didn't have the money, so she went to work at an ice cream parlor to make up the deficit. One night, Dempsey and Promoter Floyd Fitzsimmons wandered into the parlor to cool off. She recognized Dempsey from his photos and gave them two heaped up dishes of cream, which made a big hit with the champ. Jack asked, "How'd you like to see me fight?" She then told him her story. As a result, Jack gave her a $30 ticket to the fight.[255]

Lola Wallin of Rockford, Ill., thanking Jack Dempsey for giving her a $30 ticket to see him fight Billy Miske on Labor Day.

Daredevil Jack was showing in Benton Harbor and around the country. Folks could see Jack in the ring, or on film, or both.

There was no hotel space left in Benton Harbor, for all were totally booked. Folks would have to rent private rooms or stay in a nearby town.

Miske sparring partner Jack Heinen said Miske would win by knockout, for he hit harder than Willard and was faster than Johnson.

However, Bill Tate said, "This boy Dempsey is ringing all them there bells he used to ring in Toledo, when he hit – and a few more, too. I always thought that boy sort a reached the top of his punching power just before he fought that there Willard but I made a mistake. This boy is hitting harder than he ever did." 230-pound Tate was the only one to experience Dempsey's real power, for he was the only one big enough to absorb the blows. Jack had to hold back against everyone else.[256]

Frank Menke noted that some were offering 4 to 1 and 5 to 1 odds on Miske, the underdog, and could find no takers. Menke said Miske could not hurt the champ; so he could not knock him out. There was only a slim chance of Miske outpointing Dempsey, though Menke did not think he could do it. Menke said Dempsey won both of their prior fights by wide margins. "Miske never really won a round in either of those fights. He was outclassed from beginning to end." Miske had improved, and was taller, faster, heavier, and more experienced since then, but Dempsey had improved as well.[257]

---

[255] *Benton Harbor News-Palladium*, September 3, 1920.
[256] *Olean Times Herald*, September 2, 1920.
[257] *Buffalo Courier*, September 2, 1920.

Dempsey insisted that the fight would not go the full 10 rounds.[258]

The fight would take place in the outdoor arena on time, rain or shine.

The *Benton Harbor News-Palladium* said because no hotel space was left, the Chamber of Commerce was doing its best to encourage locals to rent rooms. Next-door neighbor St. Joseph had about 1,000 rooms available.

On Thursday September 2, before a crowd that packed the grandstand at Fitz's ball park, just four days before the fight, Dempsey sparred 3 rounds with Harry Greb and 3 more with Marty Farrell, both middleweights. It was the largest audience that attended an afternoon workout since the champ pitched his camp a few weeks ago, estimated conservatively at 1,500. The crowd size was due largely to the publicity given to Dempsey's brief encounter with Greb the previous day.

According to the local *St. Joseph Herald-Press* version, this time, Dempsey added a little more steam to his blows and injected more speed into his footwork, and as a result, Greb was more cautious than he was the day before. Both used 8-ounce gloves. The champ was somewhat peeved over a statement some scribes sent out to the effect that Greb shook him with one of his punches the previous day, and he tore into the Pittsburgh lad from the start, more than he had previously, wanting to show that he had been taking it easy on Greb the prior day.

Dempsey worked on Greb's body with rights and lefts, both in close and at long range, and also planted his noted left hook on the ex-navy champ's chin throughout the 3 rounds. Greb managed to elude many hooks by his footwork, but could not dodge the body blows when they came to close quarters. Greb got in some mighty hard wallops at the start, but seemed to slow down considerably before the finish. They mixed savagely in many instances. Dempsey boxed the last round and a half with blood trickling from his mouth, the result of a collision with Greb's head, which cut the champ's tongue. Harry apologized. When they finished, the crowd shouted, "More, more." The 3 rounds pleased everyone.

Dempsey then sparred 3 more fast rounds with Marty Farrell.

Dempsey was working on speed more than power. Some wondered whether that would affect his punch adversely and therefore Miske might last the distance. Others said Dempsey had the power but had to hold it back or he might knock out his smaller sparring partners; instead working on his speed and boxing skill, for he respected the same in Miske.

Ray Pearson said Dempsey and Greb's 3 hard rounds had plenty of punching. "Greb isn't the sort of a scrapper to take things easy and shot a lot and took a lot of hard wallops." Farrell then stepped 3 fast rounds as well. The champ appeared to be prime.

Pearson said Dempsey wasn't throwing with the force that he put behind his wallops at Toledo, but his sparring partners weren't as big. Working with smaller men, he was holding back his power, working for speed. His sparring partners gave him interesting work though, and made him extend himself.

[258] *Brooklyn Daily Eagle*, September 2, 1920.

The *South Bend Tribune's* Eugene Kessler said Dempsey showed 2,000 fans that he was ready for Miske, sparring 6 fast rounds total with Greb and Farrell, who gave him a good workout. He demonstrated that he was a boxer as well as a fighter. "Jack was compelled to take advantage of his long reaching straight right to keep away from the terrific, bouncing Greb and emerged from the exchanges of gloves with a trickle of blood coming from his mouth as the result of the light heavy accidentally butting him in the second." The fans cheered roundly, as the two furnished them with plenty of action. The champ displayed a greater ability to dodge the fast ones and did not receive the blows he withstood the previous day. Jack's speed had improved.

Afterwards, Dempsey said, "I know I'm ready to step the full ten rounds at top speed, but I don't think it will go that long."

Frank Menke's version said Dempsey concluded sparring with a sliced tongue as a result of a savage Greb head butt in a clinch. Greb seemed quite relieved when the 3rd round was over, for he took quite a socking in the stomach in the last round, which caused him to believe all that he had heard about Dempsey's terrible power. In that last round, Jack finally took off the "wraps," sailed in, and showed his real ability.

Dempsey started off boxing, and through the 1st round, more than held his own with one of the shiftiest fighters in the business. In the 2nd, Greb landed a crashing right flush on the chin, which annoyed Dempsey. Soon thereafter, in a clinch, Greb butted, broke loose, and popped away at Dempsey as the bell rang. In the 3rd, Dempsey, perhaps having in mind the butt and the punch to the jaw, looked for revenge, and proceeded after Greb. He was kind enough to refrain from driving for the jaw, but he hammered a few into his stomach. "Two of them lifted Greb clear off his feet and sent him spinning backward." Greb tried to retaliate, but Dempsey blocked, ducked or side-stepped every punch, hit the speedy Greb where he willed, and made Greb look slow in comparison, startling as that may seem. The crowd cheered Dempsey, who by his performance proved that he had been holding a lot back previously.

Ed Shave, *St. Paul Daily News* sporting editor, who was on scene, said nearly 2,000 people were at the baseball park to watch the champ box two really good middleweights, Harry Greb and Marty Farrell.

> Greb again gave Dempsey a great workout. He landed a lot of blows, but Dempsey had speeded up from yesterday, and with that terrible left hook of his at times nearly lifted Greb off his feet.

> Greb ducked, bobbed and leaped around, making Dempsey do considerable missing, although not as much as on Wednesday. Dempsey would come in closer and placed his hooks more for the body. He did not use his right much.

> Greb drew blood from Dempsey's mouth with some left swings, and in the third round he accidentally butted the champion…cutting Dempsey's lip.

Dempsey then boxed with the speedy and clever Farrell, who was fast on his feet, quick at slipping punches, and had a neat left. Dempsey mostly worked on his defense, blocking and trying some left leads.

Shave noted that Dempsey was working with superior sparring partners to what Miske had.

Allegedly, both Miske and Dempsey scaled 189 pounds before their workouts, with Dempsey perhaps a half-pound heavier.

The *Chicago Evening Post's* Harry Hochstadter said Dempsey went 3 fast and furious rounds with 165-pound Greb and 3 more with Farrell. It was a corking good workout, for Greb made the champ step at a lively pace. "Greb made the sad mistake of butting Dempsey in the mouth in the second round, and after blood ran, William Harrison kept piling in murderous body blows. At the end of the three rounds Greb was tired and leg weary." It was "very encouraging to the Dempsey followers to see the way the champion handled himself." Bill Tate said he knew those body shots and their effects quite well.

Dempsey told Hochstadter that he was more pleased with his present training camp than the one in Toledo. He was not the least bit worried about the outcome.

Greb on left sparring Dempsey

The *Chicago Herald and Examiner's* Sam Hall said Greb went 3 wicked rounds with Dempsey. Harry's jabbing and butting cut the champ's tongue. Some said if Greb was 20 pounds bigger, he would be the man to fight Dempsey, and have a chance to win.

This time, Dempsey took on Greb first, instead of second. The publicity about their sparring the day prior caused the grandstand to be packed. Their 3 rounds were more like a real fight. Dempsey boxed the last round and a half with a trickle of blood coming from his mouth from an accidental head butt in the 2nd round which cut Jack's tongue. Harry apologized, and Jack said it was all right. However, Greb had boxed Dempsey while Harry was training for the Gibbons fight in New York, and butted him there too. Also, "On that occasion he hit Jack between the eyes and blackened them up for a whole week."

Using 8-ounce gloves, the sound of their smacks could be heard all over. "Harry bounces around so much that it is hard to tell where he is coming from…" They had one or two furious rallies in which it looked as though somebody might get hurt. Greb landed well at the start, but was slowing down toward the finish, for Dempsey worked viciously on Greb's body. Greb evaded the left hook to the head, but could not avoid the body wallops from both quarters, "and it was with these punches that Dempsey finished fairly well in front on the actual fighting done." Manager Jack Kearns twice had to caution Dempsey to slow down, while Manager Reddy Mason kept telling Greb to be careful.

Dempsey boxed 3 more rounds with Farrell, preferring the speedy work that the smaller men gave him.

Red Mason could see nothing but Dempsey in the upcoming fight.

Greb, who had fought Miske a few times (1915 DND6, 1918 LND10, 1919 WND10), thought more highly of Billy's chances, saying he had a lot of speed, which could cause some trouble. He would need it, though.

That day, in front of a crowd of nearly 1,000 people, 190-pound Miske boxed 6 rounds with Rough House Wilson, Joe Wagner, and Jack Heinen, looking great, with his lightning left hook to the head and body. He gave them such a rough thumping and had them in such bad shape that he had to back off, pull his punches, and work on defense. Overall, Miske timed his stinging punches well and made them count.

Harry Hochstadter said, "Miske appears to be fit and ready. To all outward appearances, he looks like a husky, tough bird." Still, his workouts were not as impressive as Dempsey's.

Ed Shave said Billy looked great, moving at high speed.

One man wagered $5,000 at even odds that Miske would stay the limit. One wagered $10,000 to $8,000 that Dempsey would win.

A *Chicago Tribune* staff correspondent noted that in Miske's 9-year career, he never had been knocked off his feet. George Barton, who refereed the first Dempsey-Miske fight, said it was on the level, and both threw as hard as they could, but Miske was too tough to go down.

That day, Dempsey and Miske briefly met at a downtown barber shop. Coincidentally, Dempsey was in the chair when Miske came in. They shook hands, and then Miske left until Dempsey was through. Jack later commented on the fact that Miske looked larger and stronger than ever.

A few weeks ago, Dempsey was the 3 to 1 favorite, but the odds had dropped to 2 to 1, and then 10 to 8, so the odds had been steadily tightening up as a result of Miske's good form in training.

At night, Hochstadter said he played cards with Dempsey, his crew, and another newsman. Everything was peace and contentment in Jack's camp. Ben Smith attended to the training, while Teddy Hayes, under the direction of Kearns, supervised the work.

Miske had a wife and two children. He said the money he earned would go to his family, and help him to get along in the automobile business back home.[259]

Frank Menke said Dempsey was showing far more brilliancy as a boxer than in the past. His wonderful skill amazed him day after day. Nothing illustrated it better than his clashes with Greb, the Pittsburgh rubber ball. Greb was one of the shiftiest men ever, a phantom, a whirlwind puncher, with vast experience, and dazzled them all. They could not hit him, nor avoid being hit by him. But Dempsey outboxed Greb on two occasions clearly. At first Dempsey was a little mystified by his style, and had trouble stemming the attack. But then he solved it, and from then on caught all of Greb's leads in the air and beat him practically to every punch. What made it more impressive was the fact that he had not put all of his steam into any of the punches, and focused mostly on the body, not wanting to hurt Greb.[260]

The champ was the 10 to 8 favorite to end the fight within 10 rounds. It was even money that he would win within 8 rounds. Given that Dempsey was boxing more and focusing on speed, not power, seeming less vicious than usual, many folks thought he was anticipating that he might have to go the distance and be able to handle a fast and shifty boxer.[261]

Dempsey said folks had nothing to worry about. It was true that he had not been tearing into his sparring partners with all of his viciousness or punishing them half as severely, but he had his reasons. He was training differently for Miske than Willard. He was working on his speed and skill more than his power. Miske was not as easy to hit solidly as Willard, for Billy never was still, always moving, shifting, and whirling. To catch him, Jack needed speed and footwork. Some thought that by using speed, skill, footwork, and boxing, working on tricks and moves, he was fooling around and not taking matters seriously, but they were wrong. He also did not like to use his heaviest blows on his sparring partners, because if he did, he would be minus a camp of sparring partners the next day. That is why he held back, even refraining from hitting Tate on the jaw, at Bill's request. He was even more careful against the smaller Gans and Farrell, never letting out even half his power, for fear of hurting them. He said he could throw even faster and harder if he wanted, which he would do in the actual fight.[262]

Dempsey wrote that he intended to be a fighting champion, and wanted to take on every formidable opponent in due course. His hope was to drop Miske for the first time. "I am going into the battle with the sole thought of knocking out Miske in a hurry."

[259] *St. Joseph Herald-Press, Chicago Tribune, South Bend Tribune, Benton Harbor News-Palladium, St. Paul Daily News, Minneapolis Journal, San Francisco Chronicle, NY Tribune, El Paso Times, Brooklyn Standard Union, Chicago Daily News, Chicago Evening Post, Chicago Herald and Examiner, San Francisco Examiner*, September 3, 1920. The card was scheduled to commence at 3 p.m.
[260] *Olean Times Herald*, September 3, 1920.
[261] *Saint Joseph Herald-Press*, September 3, 1920.
[262] *San Francisco Examiner*, September 3, 1920.

His next fight would be against Knockout Bill Brennan, a rough, tough, slam-bang man. "I hit that bird for six rounds with everything but the roof girders before I could win the fight from him. He is a mighty dangerous athlete because he has a knockout punch in either fist and is proven by the fact that he has scored 60 victories via the knockout route."

Jack liked to work hard and fight often. He once fought three times in one week, and thought nothing of it to fight every week or two. "In fact, the oftener I fought the better I seemed to get."

Others who were seeking a match and dickering with Kearns were Carpentier, Fulton, Moran, Tunney, Levinsky, Meehan, and Bob Martin.

> And then there's Harry Wills, the negro, who whipped Fred Fulton. I saw that baby at work on Fulton – and I think I've got a pretty fair line on what he could do against me – and what I could do to him. Sort of like to take him on very early. Haven't the slightest personal objection to meeting him – if the public really demands that I fight him.

Dempsey said he was willing to fight anyone and everyone whom Kearns told him to fight.[263]

Harry Greb believed that he was the real light heavyweight champ, given that he had defeated Battling Levinsky in six consecutive bouts. He felt that he was the logical man to battle Carpentier.[264]

Regarding their work on September 3, P.T. Knox of the *Pittsburgh Gazette Times* said Dempsey and Greb's sparring was rather tame, given that the fight was so close - only three days away - and that Dempsey had cut his tongue the previous day. They mostly feinted and worked on footwork for 2 rounds, with few exchanges. Farrell also boxed lightly for 2 rounds with the champ.[265]

Ed Shave noted that fans paid 50 cents at each camp to watch the champion and challenger work out.

Dempsey was fit, but not as fit as he was in Toledo. He did not tear and slug as he used to do. On the 3rd, against Greb and Farrell, he was moving around more, trying to improve his boxing, making them miss, slipping punches and blocking. He sparred 2 rounds with Greb and then 2 with Farrell. "Greb tore loose and kept Dempsey busy, although the champion looked far better with Greb than he did two days ago." Greb gave Dempsey more action in one round than Miske got all afternoon.

A respectful Dempsey said Miske was one of the toughest men he ever faced, and the only one he never had been able to put off his feet. He anticipated a great fight.

Reddy Mason, Greb's manager, told Sam Hall that Dempsey was a great fighter. He believed that Dempsey was better prepared for a grueling milling than was Miske. "Dempsey has trained harder, though not as long

[263] *Buffalo Times*, September 3, 1920.
[264] *Akron Beacon Journal*, September 3, 1920.
[265] *Pittsburgh Gazette Times*, September 4, 1920.

as Miske, and has had much better help in the way of sparring partners. … I doubt if Miske goes the limit, though admitting he's pretty tough."

Regarding the Greb-Dempsey sparring on the 3rd, Sam Hall said, "Greb tore after Dempsey, and Jack allowed him to take the play, seldom retaliating. Manager Kearns had given Dempsey the hunch to take care of his fighting tools, meaning hands. Greb was not quite so frisky as usual and did not land as often, because Dempsey moved around more, but it was a swell workout at that." Jack also pulled his punches against Farrell.

Robert Maxwell, *Philadelphia Evening Public Ledger* sports editor, said he saw Dempsey spar on the 3rd with Greb for 2 rounds, "and he looked good." Maxwell said in his opinion, Greb "is a better man than Miske. Jack tore into the Pittsburgher, landed many hard slams and punches better and with more accuracy than at any time in Toledo. Greb was helpless against the terrific attack, and the only thing which saved him from taking the high dive was the heavy gloves."

Dempsey said, "I expect to stop Miske as soon as I can. If an opening comes, I will knock him stiff. He would do the same to me, and I am not taking any chances."

Frank Menke saw matters similarly to Maxwell. He said the champion, heretofore merciful and careful not to inject any steam into his drives, shifted tactics. He slugged, "and oh, what a pasting Greb and Farrell had to take! … It was the old time Dempsey who flashed around in the ring this afternoon – the rushing, tearing fighter of swishing arms and whirling fists - the same man who has been acclaimed the surest, safest and at the same time the hardest puncher that lives and breathes." No longer were folks wondering whether he was as great as he was a year ago.

> He proved that when he wants to put steam into his drives he can shoot them home as speedily and with as unerring accuracy as ever – if not a little better. Dempsey danced around the ring with a speed that at times even eclipsed that of his lighter opponents. On his toes, springing here, bouncing there, dodging to this side, then to the other, now boring in – but ever and ever in a position to hit. That was Jack Dempsey this afternoon.

That day, Miske sparred with Roughhouse George Wilson, Jack Heinen, and Joe Wagner, battering and buffeting them around.

Both Miske and Dempsey did some work for the movie men.

The advance seat sale was up to $70,000. Fitz predicted a gathering of not less than 15,000 would be on hand, and a $150,000 gate.

On September 3, 1920 in Cleveland, Ohio, world welterweight champion Jack Britton decisively won a 10-round newspaper decision over Miske sparring partner Johnny Tillman (57-25-14) of St. Paul.

It was confirmed that the big fight was scheduled for 10 rounds, with no decision to be rendered if there was no knockout. Jack Kearns refused to allow a formal decision. He did not want to risk losing the title on a decision in only 10 rounds (the longest distance Michigan would allow). Some took this as fear that Miske might outpoint Dempsey.

According to the *Lansing State Journal*, shortly after Miske-Levinsky in 1919, Miske took to bed, attacked by Bright's disease (a kidney disorder). He was very ill for a long time. Clean living and careful diet overcame his ailment. He was bigger and stronger than ever before, but the question was whether he could handle the champ's crushing blows.

Dempsey felt that he was fit to go 50 rounds. Before his workout on Friday September 4, 1920, he stepped on the scales at 189 pounds.

Harry Hochstadter believed that Miske would last as long as Dempsey allowed him to last, though the type of style Miske employed also could determine matters. Few were willing to wager that Miske would win, but many were wagering that he would last the full 10 rounds.

Dempsey's work with Harry Greb and Marty Farrell, two fast men, "has convinced every one he is as good as ever, has regained his eye and can measure the other fellow to the fraction of a second." He was ready.

Hochstadter believed that Miske would be crumpled up in a heap within 7 rounds, even if he fought to last and survive. If Miske fought back, trying to win, he would be gone quickly. Then again, if Dempsey tore at him in his old-time manner, it could be curtains in a hurry, regardless of what Miske did.

Dempsey meant business. He was getting grouchier as the battle approached.

Special trains and boats would take patrons from all over to the fight, including from Chicago. Advance seat sales were brisk.[266]

The *Brooklyn Daily Eagle* said Dempsey was a 4 to 5 favorite, and it was even money that Miske would stay the limit.

George Barton, the *Minneapolis Daily News* sporting editor, who refereed the first Dempsey-Miske fight in May 1918, said the fight was a draw (though the majority of sports writers present said Dempsey won).

> Those who gave the fight to Dempsey based their decision on the seventh round in which Jack hit Billy on the chin with a terrific right uppercut. If the blow had floored Miske or if he had been forced to run or clinch to save himself, the sporting writers might have been justified in awarding the contest to Dempsey. However Miske was not forced to run or clinch in order to save himself. Instead he came right back with a rush and drove Dempsey all over the ring. I figured that Miske's spurt after receiving such a vicious blow evened up matters. Miske held his own in the other nine rounds and clearly was entitled to a draw.[267]

Dempsey and Miske had become friends after their first encounter. They were photographed together at Neptune Beach in June 1918. That didn't stop them from fighting again later that year.

Since the hotels were full, rooms in private houses were going for a whopping $8 a day and up.[268]

Jack Dempsey and Billy Miske Taking a Dip at Neptune Beach, San Francisco, When Fighting Was Far From Their Minds.

Dempsey said, "I hear Miske plans to carry the fight to me. Great news. That'll make it easy for me. Nothing I'd like better than to mix it toe-to-toe with the St. Paul boy. If he gives me just a round or two of it that's about all I'll need. But if he starts the old runaway stuff, victory may be delayed for a little while – until I catch him. But I'll catch him."

Frank Menke said Miske had no chance if he tore in, despite looking awfully good, better than ever before. Miske was amazingly fast, displayed marvelous cleverness, and was whaling his sparring partners with considerable vigor. When one saw only Miske, the impression was that he would be a winner.

---

[266] *St. Paul Daily News, Lansing State Journal, Chicago Evening Post, Chicago Herald and Examiner, Philadelphia Evening Public Ledger, San Francisco Examiner,* September 4, 1920.
[267] *Brooklyn Daily Eagle,* September 3, 1920.
[268] *Ithaca Journal,* September 4, 1920.

However, the disillusionment came when one saw the mighty Dempsey in action. "Dempsey always was fast – but he's faster today than ever before. Except when he permits his sparring partners to smash him so that he can toughen himself against attack, Dempsey is more or less of a phantom." He could box as well as slug. "But despite Dempsey's great boxing improvement, the fact is indisputable that Miske is his superior. But as an offset, Dempsey is the most crushing puncher of all time – and Miske never could flatten anybody with a fairly stout jaw. And Dempsey's is like concrete."

Menke predicted that whenever Dempsey landed, the fight would be over soon thereafter. If Miske fought toe-to-toe, the fight would be over quickly. If he ran, it only would delay matters, not change the result. Menke said Miske could not decision Dempsey either, because even though their prior two engagements went the distance, Billy never won, and only "desperate holding tactics saved the St. Paul youth from being dropped for the count. And Dempsey is a better man today than he was in that period of his career."[269]

Edward Walker said few gave Miske a real chance to win, despite his apparently excellent physical condition. Although it was even money that Miske would stay the 10 rounds, Walker predicted that Dempsey would win by knockout. Despite Billy's great outward appearance, Walker had to consider that Miske had been ill a year ago with kidney trouble, which he and his manager now claimed was a curved spine. Regardless, "it is doubtful if he will be able to stand up under the sledgehammer blows of Dempsey."

Miske said, "I think I have an excellent chance of going home to St. Paul with the championship. I feel like a new man and expect…to give the titleholder the hardest fight of his career."

Dempsey, while admitting that his long layoff was not for the best, said his punch still was there, and that was what won fights. He expected to win by knockout.

The town was situated on Lake Michigan. The arena was one mile from the center of town. Dempsey's training quarters, formerly a private home, were about 300 yards away from the arena.

Miske was at Eastman Springs, about a half mile from the arena, in the House of David section. His manager was willing to wager hard cash that Miske would stay the limit. Billy was the second twin-city boxer to face a heavyweight champion. Patsy Cardiff of Minneapolis once fought John L. Sullivan to a 6-round draw.

About 100 newspapermen from all over the country were on hand. Although most were impressed with Miske's work and appearance, they remembered Dempsey's long list of knockouts. Still, many said Dempsey did not have the same rip-tearing attitude as he did before the Willard fight. The question was whether the layoff, strain of court proceedings, and the circus life had robbed him of some of his pep. Miske supporters

[269] *Collyer's Eye*, September 4, 1920.

claimed that Dempsey was quite tired at the end of 3 rounds against Willard, and believed if Miske could weather the early rounds, he could win.

Ed Walker's opinion was that Miske did not punch as hard as Willard, nor would he be as difficult to hit. Dempsey could take whatever he offered, for Jack had taken several Willard punches flush to the jaw.[270]

Sam Hall said the champion was a great fighter who had no weaknesses, though the challenger might put up a great battle. Dempsey not only could punch hard, but move fast as well. He would be able to outpunch and/or outbox Miske.

Still, Hall was not sure whether Dempsey would win by knockout. "Miske is about as dangerous as anybody they could dig up to fight the champion." Regardless, Hall did not think *anyone* could whip Dempsey. If Miske lasted, he likely would be mussed up terribly.

> Dempsey is not like some of our hard hitters. He has everything else as well as the punch in both mitts. Jack can box, and don't let anybody tell you he can't. He's a clever fellow. His speed is the greatest for a heavyweight since Jim Corbett's day, and he hits much harder than did Gentleman Jim in his prime. He has the Corbett speed with the Fitzsimmons punch, and that's some combination, one must admit.

Hall said Miske was fast, but Dempsey faster. Kearns said Dempsey could box with smaller fellows and outscore them even using light punches. "We don't doubt it."

Hall believed Miske would have to hurt Dempsey to have a chance, but that was doubtful. Dempsey started fast and maintained such a fast pace that few had time to figure out what to do with him. Miske was tough and had a proven ability to take it, but "Dempsey will knock down any man he hits right."

Miske would have to be careful of Dempsey's left, for it shot out like a flash to either the head or body. His right was powerful too, though not quite as fast or as versatile as the left. "Jack pegs it awfully hard for the body. His usual attack is that right for the midsection, followed by his swinging left hooks to the chin. The right starts 'em on their way and the left puts 'em to sleep."

No one was certain how to fight Dempsey. He could fight it out up close or quickly track down a mover. "He hits so hard, so fast and so often that it's murder either way."

After Michigan state boxing commission chairman Tom Bigger said that Philadelphia's James Dougherty could not referee because he was not licensed in Michigan, Kearns asked the commission to license him. Initially, the commission refused to license Dougherty, for he was said to be friends with Dempsey. Kearns declared that there would be no fight unless Dougherty refereed. The two parties had agreed upon him as the referee several weeks ago.

Dougherty was said to have fixed up Dempsey with some sort of a job in the shipyards years ago, and also refereed the Philadelphia fight between Miske and Dempsey.

After a conference between Fitzsimmons, Kearns, Reddy, and state commission chairman Bigger, the commission eventually relented and gave Dougherty a license, for he was well known as one of the most capable referees.[271]

Miske said he would box for 6 or 7 rounds at a fast pace, and then, after tiring Jack out, he would slug with him in the hope of bringing him down.[272]

Frank Menke said that during the past few days, Dempsey had shown that he could punch with his old-time power, rapidity, and unerring accuracy. "Whenever he has elected to hit, the bull's eye has been smashed. And mind you, Dempsey has been doing that with sparring partners like Harry Greb and Marty Farrell – men infinitely faster than Miske."[273]

The *St. Joseph Herald-Press* believed that Dempsey would win, owing to his punching power. Most believed that if he landed one of his hooks; it would be curtains. Miske was confident though, and declared that his wounded eye was healed completely.[274]

Eugene Kessler said at least 700 fans from South Bend would attend the fight, according to the advance sale of tickets in that area. Anticipation was that the 20,000-seat arena would be filled to the brim, and Dempsey would earn a lot more than his $50,000 guarantee.

Kessler called Kearns a crafty manager by seeing to it that it would be a no-decision affair. The feeling was that Dempsey could not be stopped.

Jack Reddy said he saw Willard shake Dempsey with a left, so he could be stung. Miske had a kick in both hands and would not be anything like the soft-picking Kansan was. Reddy said Dempsey had marched through a lot of slow-moving fighters.

Dempsey had only a one-inch reach advantage – 78 vs. 77 inches. Miske had a year more of experience, had taken on tougher foes, and had more fights, but Dempsey had a higher knockout percentage. They weighed about the same, give or take a few pounds.[275]

JACK KEARNS

Miske told Ray Pearson, "This is going to be a fight, and make no mistake about that. I'm going in there to beat the champion. That's what I'm here for." Pearson said Billy was in fine condition, but that did not mean he would win.

[271] *Chicago Herald and Examiner, New York Tribune*, September 5, 1920.
[272] *Buffalo Courier*, September 6, 1920.
[273] *San Francisco Examiner*, September 5, 1920.
[274] *St. Joseph Herald-Press*, September 4, 1920. Newspaper scribes from New York and San Francisco had arrived.
[275] *South Bend Tribune*, September 4, 1920.

The impression Pearson got from speaking with Dempsey was that he treated them all alike.[276]

In other news, on September 4, 1920, Babe Ruth hit his 46th home run of the season, breaking the home run record previously held by Perry Werden set in 1895.[277]

Ray Pearson said thousands of fans were cluttering up the twin cities of Benton Harbor and St. Joseph, on the eastern shore of Lake Michigan. The great majority hailed from Chicago. However, folks were arriving from Minneapolis, St. Paul - Miske's home, Milwaukee, Indianapolis, Detroit, and even New York.

Both men were in shape, proven by their training. Pearson picked Dempsey because of his knockout power. Miske's best chance was to box cautiously.

Ed Shave said everyone in Dempsey's camp, Kearns, secretary Hayes, trainer Smith, and Greb, were predicting a Dempsey victory. They were willing to give 2 to 1 odds and bet Dempsey would win by knockout.

Shave said the question of the fight was not so much whether Miske could win, but whether he could last 10 rounds against "the most ferocious, most terrible hitter that the world of fistiana has ever known." One terrific smash from the "superman" could spell a knockout. Shave did not think Miske would be able to stand the kind of body punches that Dempsey could let loose.

George Barton was firmly convinced that the championship would not change hands. "Dempsey can outpunch, outrough and outlast Miske." If anyone scored a knockout, one could bet the family jewels that Dempsey would be the one to land it. Miske looked great, but Barton did not believe he would be able to withstand the champ's terrific punches. "Against any heavyweight other than Dempsey, Miske probably would win, but opposed to a murderous walloper like the champion I fear the St. Paul lad's chances are hopeless." Barton noted, "Dempsey is one of the hardest punching heavyweights the ring ever produced." He was far more powerful than Miske, and had knocked out better men than Miske had.

Miske had plenty of courage and ruggedness, but he was not a big puncher, and "a fighter has to be able to punch hard to whip a battler of Dempsey's class." Miske had wonderful faith in himself, but it took more than confidence to beat Dempsey. Barton would have liked to have seen Miske take more than one tune-up bout, and utilize better sparring mates.

Dempsey had only about five weeks of real training. Still, he showed improvement in his work on the 3rd, demonstrating "more speed and pep, punched harder, timed his blows better and proved a more elusive target for Harry Greb and Martin Farrell, the two speed boys who boxed with him."

[276] *Chicago Tribune*, September 4, 1920.
[277] *Brooklyn Standard Union*, September 5, 1920.

At left, Dempsey with 6-year-old Floyd Fitzsimmons, Jr., the promoter's son.
At right, Dempsey loved playing with the many children that flocked to his camp.

The Champ and the Contender

MISKE HAS TRAINED HARD FOR GREAT BATTLE OF HIS LIFE

Dempsey admitted,

> I know I should have taken at least two months of training…but this bout came up so suddenly that I was forced to get into condition as quickly as possible. I know the long layoff I took after the Willard fight was bad for me, and I never will go again for such a long period without engaging in a fight. I am feeling good, however, and am sure of beating Miske. From now on I am going to fight just as often as possible. There is only one way to keep in shape, and that is by fighting regularly. …

> Boxing is my profession, and it behooves me to keep in condition. I owe this much to the public, which pays to see me perform and bets money that I will win.

Barton noted that Dempsey still was the same big, quiet, likable kid. Dempsey further said,

> I am in splendid condition and expect to knock out Miske in less than 7 rounds. I will flatten him in one punch if I can, but Billy is a tough boy and may give me some trouble in the early rounds. I am not underestimating him at all. He is a rugged, aggressive fighter who can punish, but I am sure I can outlast him and knock him for a goal.

Dempsey also said that in order to last the 10 rounds, Miske would have to be better than he was when they met before, back in 1918.

Two days before the fight, on the 4th, Miske sparred 2 rounds with Heinen, twice having to hold him up after blows almost decked him.

Miske said, "I am in wonderful condition and really expect to win. I am rarin' to go and will give Dempsey all the fighting he will want for one day. I have fought Dempsey 16 rounds already in two bouts and his hardest punches didn't bother in either contest. I am bigger and stronger now and I am sure he cannot stop me." He also said,

> I know Dempsey's style well and just how hard he can hit, and I have prepared myself especially to meet him. I never felt more confident in my life of being able to win. If I don't knock him out I expect at least to satisfy the newspaper critics that I am the better boxer of the two. This is the great opportunity of my career and fans who know me may rest assured that I intend to make the most of it.

E. R. Hosking opined that Miske lacked the lithe freedom of movement that Dempsey had, and was nowhere near as fast or as light on his feet. Plus, Dempsey had a deadly wallop. Miske would not be as wide open a target as Willard was, and Dempsey might not connect solidly enough to stop him in only 10 rounds, but a Miske victory was unlikely.[278]

---

[278] *Chicago Tribune, St. Paul Daily News, St. Paul Pioneer Press*, September 5, 1920.

The *New York Herald's* Charles Mathison said Miske was apt to give Dempsey much trouble. Even back when Miske weighed only 174 pounds and was conceding 40 or more pounds, he made it interesting for men like Morris and Fulton. So at 190 pounds, he likely would be quite difficult to subdue. Still, chances were that Dempsey eventually would win by knockout at some point, for he was the greatest champion since the days of Jeffries, Corbett, and Fitzsimmons.

The only white heavyweight currently generally conceded to have a chance to defeat Dempsey was Carpentier, who was clever, fast, and hard-punching. This opinion was shared by Jack McAuliffe and Willie Lewis. However, Mathison disagreed, feeling that no white man had any chance.:

> They apparently forget that Dempsey in the matter of speed and hitting never had a superior and that in addition he is rugged enough to take a punch and still go on fighting. On the other hand, Carpentier has demonstrated that he cannot stand up under punishment. It goes without saying that when Dempsey and Carpentier meet in the ring Dempsey will hit the Frenchman at least once, and that will be sufficient. Looking over the entire field, there is but one man who would be conceded a real chance with the champion, and that is Harry Wills.[279]

Dempsey was confident that he would win by knockout, but admitted that Miske previously gave him "pretty stiff battles" and would be a challenge. "I'm in better shape than when I fought Willard."

> I shall try to win as quickly as possible. I have not made the mistake of believing that I am going to have a picnic. Miske is tough, can take and give punishment and is a dangerous hitter. I fought him twice and was shaken to my heels both times. I have worked as hard for this fight as I did for Willard and will take no chances of losing the title.[280]

Miske said, "I've fought Dempsey twice, and, though he hurt me badly, I held my own. I am better and stronger now and Dempsey will have little chance of beating me by tearing as he did with Willard. I'll be ready for him."

Ray Pearson said Dempsey was a "fighting devil," probably the greatest heavyweight of all time. Miske was a very good fighter meeting a superior one. Billy got the fight because he was the only one whom Dempsey had failed to deck, had a solid record against the best, and was well-regarded as a real fighter. A great fight was anticipated. Pearson believed Dempsey would win by knockout, and the only question was when.

Boxing chairman Tom Bigger insisted that there be no holding that would require the referee to pry them apart. The kidney punch was barred. The fighters could not hold and hit. They had to break clean at the

---

[279] *New York Herald*, September 5, 1920.
[280] *Chicago Daily News*, September 6, 1920.

referee's command, but also had to protect themselves at all times. A large gong/hammer and bell would be on hand to ensure there was no repetition of what happened in Toledo.

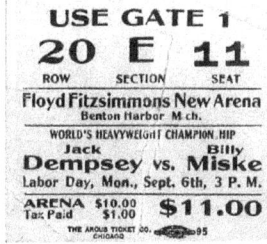

USE GATE 1
20 E 11
ROW   SECTION   SEAT
Floyd Fitzsimmons New Arena
Benton Harbor M.ch.
WORLD'S HEAVYWEIGHT CHAMPION. HIP
Jack   Billy
Dempsey vs. Miske
Labor Day, Mon., Sept. 6th, 3 P. M.
ARENA $10.00 $11.00
Tax Paid $1.00
THE AKOUS TICKET 00. 95
CHICAGO

The night before the fight, Dempsey played rummy with his sparring partners. Miske took in a movie show.[281]

Harry Keck of the *Pittsburgh Gazette Times* told readers to look out for a potential Greb-Dempsey fight in the near future. Pittsburgh's Greb had made a big impression with his willingness to tear in and razzle-dazzle the champion with his peculiar attack, and all the critics had been singing his praises. Greb had been matched with Dempsey for a potential bout in Buffalo last Memorial Day, but the champion was mixed up in his court mess and the battle fell through. Greb lost to Gibbons, but after sparring with Dempsey, who helped him prepare, he won the return engagement. Dempsey was so impressed with Greb's speed and ability that he asked Harry to return the favor for the Miske contest. Red Mason noted that Jeffries was a Corbett sparring partner prior to beating him later on.[282]

On Labor Day, Monday September 6, 1920, in Benton Harbor, Michigan, at the Floyd Fitzsimmons arena, 25-year-old Jack Dempsey (52-4-9) defended his world heavyweight championship for the first time, against 26-year-old Billy Miske (53-11-14). It had been 14 months since he won the title.

The day of the fight, Ed Shave said the city was packed with a mass of humanity. "There is something magnetic about a heavyweight title bout. It draws as no other title match does."

Ed Walker said the odds were 3 to 1 that Dempsey would retain the title, but only even money that it would be by knockout.

Miske was smiling, calm, and confident as ever. He expected to do no worse than earn the newspaper decision.[283] Billy said,

> Dempsey couldn't knock me out in our previous engagements and I feel certain he won't be able to turn the trick to-day. This is the chance I have been waiting for. I am bigger, carry more weight and am a better fighter than I was when I met Dempsey two years ago and will carry the fight to him. But I won't be careless. I am not going to predict that I am going to knock Dempsey out, but I am going to give him the greatest fight he ever had. Dempsey is a terrific hitter, but my previous engagements have convinced me that I can hit him.[284]

---

281 *Detroit Free Press, Chicago Tribune,* September 6, 1920.
282 *Pittsburgh Gazette Times,* September 6, 1920.
283 *Minneapolis Journal,* September 6, 1920.
284 *Chicago Daily News,* September 6, 1920.

The show was scheduled to start at 3 p.m. local time.

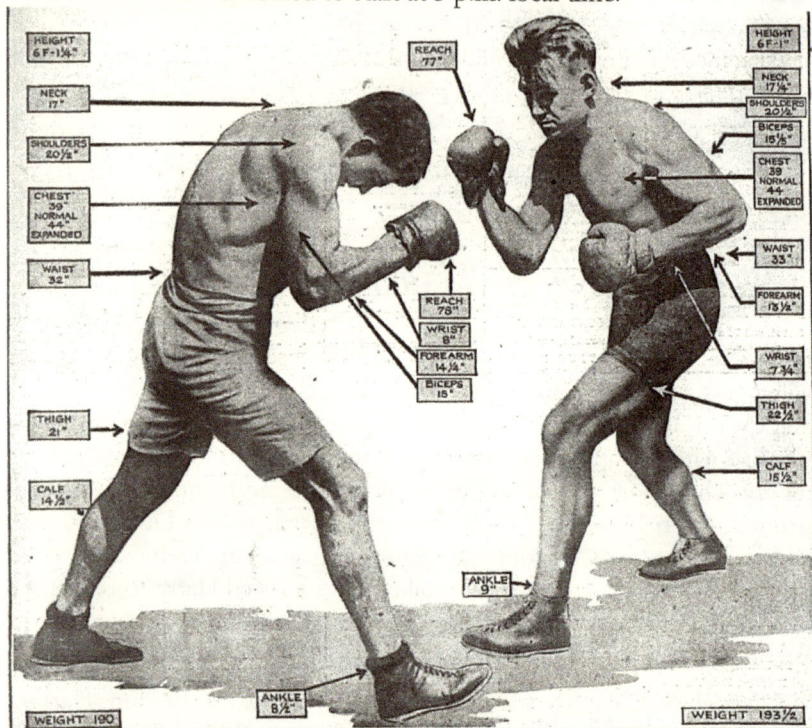

Champion Jack Dempsey.   Challenger Billy Miske.

Local reporters said the fight attracted the greatest throng of spectators in the state's history. As usual, reports of crowd size widely varied, estimates including 11,348, 11,500, 12,000, 15,000, 16,000, 17,000, 18,000, 19,000, to nearly 20,000, running the total gate receipts to $134,904, more than $150,000, $160,000, $170,000, or close to $200,000, depending on the source. Based on the photos, the arena appeared to be packed, the capacity being 20,000.

Promoter Floyd Fitzsimmons estimated the receipts to be about $175,000. He claimed the arena was sold out. If true, and Dempsey had the privilege of a 50% share, then he and Kearns would have earned $87,500. Some said the total receipts were $134,904 (announced before the first fight began), including the state and war tax. Such numbers seem low in light of local reports that the arena was full or nearly full, and Floyd Fitzsimmons' representations. Plus, the tickets weren't cheap ($30, $20, $10, $5). So, the question is whether the lower numbers were accurate, or deflated in order to reduce the tax bill. Even the lower amount would mean Dempsey would earn $67,452. The way Dempsey acted towards Fitzsimmons thereafter strongly suggests that he was paid very well and was quite happy. Most said Miske earned a flat guarantee of $25,000. One said Miske's share was 25%, and he earned $33,726.

One of the special trains from Chicago jumped the track, leaving a small block of seats unoccupied. However, those seats still had been sold and paid for, so the revenue was realized. 10,000 folks were standing outside the arena just waiting to hear the returns.

The arena was built into the sand, with the top row of seats only a few feet above the ground level. It was an immense, sun-swept, sand-pit, punch-bowl-shaped arena on the outskirts of Benton Harbor. The day was nice. The dark and rain-laden clouds of the early morning parted at about 10 a.m. and the sun broke through. The high temperature that day was 68 degrees Fahrenheit, with a low of 57.

At 1:56 p.m., the moving picture machines were being placed. By 2:30, many movie cameras were scattered throughout the arena. One was placed in the ring to take a panorama of the arena.

Folks on the bleachers purchased peanuts and soda. The crowd was one of the most orderly ever. By 3 p.m., almost every seat was filled. Some even stood in the aisles. Many women wore bright clothing and carried gaily colored parasols and brilliant corsage bouquets. Men soon peeled off their coats, for the sun was shining brightly. Telegraph keys in the press row clicked above the sound of babbling voices, while the movie- and camera-men hustled themselves with getting pictures.

The preliminaries began nearly an hour late, at 3:52 p.m. 230-pound Big Bill Tate, Dempsey's sparring partner, clearly outfought and outpointed 194-pound Sam Langford in their 6-round no decision bout. Tate was so long and rangy that Langford could not get to him. Langford was aggressive but ran into everything. His age showed up plainly.

160 ½-pound Harry Greb (162-11-13) fought 164-pound Chuck Wiggins (33-11-9) to a very entertaining 6-round no decision full of fast and furious action. The local Benton Harbor News-Palladium called it a good draw. Several other observers called it a draw. Many said Greb shaded him by a small margin. One said Greb clearly won by forcing the fighting, landing more often and with more steam. Another said Greb could fight at a fast clip, faster than the average bantam, swinging wildly, but was so fast, aggressive, and busy that Wiggins was unable to dodge all of the blows, and many went home. Wiggins was cut over the left eye, which he claimed was from a head butt. Frank Menke said Tate outpointed Langford over 6 and Wiggins and Greb fought a 6-round draw.

Delayed special trains held back the main fight and caused a long wait.

The movie camera was placed in the ring, taking shots of the arena, which was completely filled. Some were standing in the aisles and on the fence.

Miske was first to enter the ring, at 4:57 p.m., smiling from ear to ear. His white fighting togs bore his initials, BM, elaborately embroidered in silk on his left leg. He was attired in a blue and yellow striped bathrobe, and wore a light cream cap. A battery of photographers swarmed into the ring. Billy posed while the cameras clicked away at him. He appeared to be in good condition, large and muscular. His father (a Minneapolis policeman) and Billy's wife were present in the crowd.

Miske was seconded by welterweight contender/friend/sparring partner Johnny Tillman, Jack Heinen, manager Jack Reddy, trainer Ike Bernstein, Jack Britton, and Jim Delaney.

Referee James Dougherty followed Miske into the ring, which was filled with celebrities of the game, including boxers and promoters.

Dempsey kept Miske waiting for quite a while, and in the meantime, Billy chatted and joshed with the ringside press, sitting on his stool. He waved to the crowd and seemed to be having a good time.

Various folks were introduced, including boxer Charley White, who wanted to fight Benny Leonard again, promoter Floyd Fitzsimmons, boxing commissioner Tom Bigger, former Indianapolis fighter Jack Dillon (who received the best hand), etc.

About 15 minutes after Miske appeared, at 5:13 p.m., Jack Dempsey entered ring, wearing the same old bright red or maroon sweater that he wore for the Willard fight, loose-fitting white silk trunks, and red, white, and blue belt around his trunks. Unlike Miske, he had no bathrobe, and also unlike Miske, seemed very serious. Harry Hochstadter said Dempsey had not shaved in three days, and actually appeared two shades darker than Bill Tate, he was so tan. He was followed by his seconds, Teddy Hayes, trainer Ben Smith, Marty Farrell, Harry Greb, Panama Joe Gans, Bill Tate, and Jack Kearns. The champion posed for the photographers.

One writer said Dempsey did not receive many shouts of enthusiasm, which was strange for a champion. He had been seared by many slanderous tongues. He had proven not to be a slacker, but simply had not gone to war. The omission was no reason not to cheer. Perhaps though, it simply was a reserved crowd.

Jack looked a little drawn physically. The cameramen photographed him as he shuffled his feet in the resin. They finally got him to stand still long enough to get a good photo of him. He looked like a lithe young panther with ferocity written all over his unshaven face. He did not acknowledge those in the crowd who called out to him.

The fighters, referee, promoter, and chairman Tom Bigger all posed together for the photographers. The combatants did not exchange greetings until asked to pose for the picture men. As they shook their already-wrapped hands, Jack looked at the cameraman, but Billy looked at Jack. Floyd Fitzsimmons congratulated the boxers on their fine condition and offered them his best wishes for success. Through it all, Dempsey seemed impatient and somewhat annoyed, wanting to get on with it.

Their 5-ounce gloves were put on inside the ring.

The fighters' managers, Jack Reddy and Jack Kearns, were introduced.

Miske's weight was announced as 187 pounds, while Dempsey's was announced as 188 pounds. (Tom Andrews reported that Dempsey weighed 187 five hours before the fight, and Miske 189.)

At 5:17 p.m., the state troopers cleared the 18-foot ring.

A couple minutes later, Referee Jack Dougherty called them to ring center to receive final instructions. They shook hands and returned to their corners.

At 5:20 p.m., the gong started the battle.

1st round

Despite Miske's prior claims that he would box for 5 rounds, instead he tore right into Dempsey and landed the first blow, a left hook to the head. It was a hard blow that carried great steam, but did not harm the champ any, for Jack partially blocked it calmly and they clinched. After breaking, Miske kept firing his left jab and left hook.

Dempsey fought cautiously at first, showing his craftiness, dancing and weaving around and feeling for an opening. He was not impetuous. One almost wondered if Dempsey was allowing Billy to gain a little false confidence in order to make it easier to land a big blow with his 5-ounce gloves. Except for the fact that he was slower in starting, the champ's tactics practically were the same as in Toledo. They measured one another with a cautious tattoo of lefts and rights to the head. Some in the crowd even yelled at Dempsey to speed it up, and Miske smiled.

Dempsey interspersed his movement by eventually firing hard rights and lefts to the body, followed by a left hook to the head, the first really hard blow of the round, though Billy took it well. Usually when Dempsey fired, the careful Miske effectively blocked and/or clinched. Still, Dempsey time and again smashed his terrific wallops through his guard, landing rights and lefts to the head and body. Miske's wonderful defense and ability to take it enabled him to remain on his feet and fire back, landing some lefts to the head and stomach.

A right under Miske's heart fairly boomed with its solid impact and left a red mark. Miske backed away and covered up, though without showing signs of real distress. Dempsey feinted a left to the body and followed with a right to the head. In close, Dempsey landed several short hooks to the head and body. Miske landed a right to the head. They were clinched at the bell.

Miske was a very adept, skillful boxer, making a better showing in the 1st round than Willard did. However, all of the on-scene reporters agreed that Dempsey clearly won the round, landing more, harder, and more effectively. Still, Miske was game and not afraid to mix it here and there. One reporter said that when Miske landed his blows, they only spurned Dempsey on and made him more ferocious. Like a swarm of bees, once a stick is thrust into the hive, trouble is stirred up.

Dempsey on left as Miske on right opens with an attack

Miske at left, Dempsey on right in his crouch, dipping to the right.

Miske attacks!

2ⁿᵈ round

They measured each other for a bit. Miske grew ambitious and took some chances, swapping blows. There were a series of exchanges and clinches. The referee had difficulty in parting them from the clinches. Dempsey's footwork was pleasing to watch as he stepped in and shot a right to the body. He also landed a right to the cheek, and Miske clinched. Dempsey landed a terrific left hook and right cross, both to the chin, jolting Miske's head. Each time there was an exchange there was a clinch. Feeling the power, Miske grew a bit more cautious and broke ground. Sensing that Billy might be hurt, Jack kept on top of him.

Dempsey stepped in and fired a terrific, very powerful right jolt to the body under the heart, and Miske went down to the floor on his haunches. One writer said it was one of the hardest body blows ever delivered. Another said it was the hardest punch he ever saw land. The sound of the blow could be heard all over the arena. It literally lifted Miske off his feet, landing on the floor five feet away, half sitting, half laying on his side. He sat on the canvas with a look of pain on his face. Reports varied regarding whether it was a straight right, right hook, or right uppercut. One said it was two rights to the kidneys. Most said it was under the heart. It was the first knockdown Miske had suffered in his entire 9-year, 78-fight career.

Miske remained down for about three to five seconds, rising relatively quickly, refusing to take the full benefit of the count, despite the shouts of his handlers to take all the rest he could. However, he clearly was stung. His body showed a crimson bruise as big as a baseball. "The only wonder is that Miske was able to continue fighting."

Billy tried to back away, but Dempsey was right on top of him quickly, plugging away. Miske clinched as best he could, but Dempsey was good at working himself free and punching. In the clinches, Jack landed a few lefts to the jaw and several rights to the body. Dempsey landed a high right on top of the head. He also landed a left to the jaw and right to the heart.

Miske's gameness and courage still remained, though. He actually began fighting the champion toe-to-toe, perhaps figuring that moving, clinching and fighting cautiously was not working, so he might as well swap blows to try to turn the tide of events. "Perhaps he thought that if Dempsey could deal that sort of treatment despite watchfulness he might get along better by going out and fighting the champion." Miske shot a fair left hook to the champ's jaw and landed a good right to the head.

Dempsey smothered a body blow, and missed a right swing. He rushed Miske to the corner and hooked a left to the body and right to the chin. He also hooked a left to the chin. Billy fought back gamely, landing some lefts, but was being outpunched. Dempsey landed two lefts to the body and four or five lefts to the face. He was trying to measure Miske, working in on him fast and furiously, landing one left hook to the face and a right to the head. They were sparring at the bell.

All reporters agreed that once again this was a clear Dempsey round. The body-shot knockdown appeared to be the beginning of the end.

Dempsey waiting for Miske to reach his feet after the first knockdown. A second after this photograph had been snapped the champion was on his opponent like a tiger.

Miske realized that he was beaten unless he landed a blow to change the tide, so he took the initiative and decided to fight it out. This brought a cheer and applause from the crowd. There was a rapid exchange. Miske landed a left to the jaw, right to the body, and right to the head. In a clinch, Bill scraped his glove upward across Jack's nose. This only seemed to arouse the champ's ire and viciousness.

An annoyed Dempsey scowled and coolly worked in. The champ landed a hard right to the body, then a couple solid lefts to the jaw. Miske retaliated with a left to the chin and right high on the head. However, Dempsey's blows carried far more power, for he was a "punching devil." Miske went back to the defensive, for he had been punished severely in the exchange.

Dempsey quickly found an opening and landed a left hook to the jaw and/or right to the jaw and Miske crumpled to the canvas for the second time in the contest. One reporter said it was a left to the stomach that did the trick. Three observers said it was a hard right. Others said it was a left hook to the chin. Yet another said it was a left and right to the jaw.

Badly dazed, Miske got to his knees in a few seconds, and waited in that position, taking the count and trying to get as much recovery time as possible.

Just as he struggled to rise at nine, wobbly, the dark-skinned Dempsey rushed up, carefully measured his distance and drove his right hook or cross upward through his defense, squarely onto his jaw, and Miske crumpled down like a log onto his face or side as if shot, thoroughly out cold. He was lying partly under the ropes, near his own corner. Dempsey stood over him.

The referee slowly tolled off the ten seconds, giving him every chance to rise, but he was out. When the count concluded, Jack helped lift up Billy in his arms and placed him onto his chair, which Miske's seconds had shoved into the ring. Manager Jack Reddy's eyes were filled with tears as he came to his fighter's aide. Miske remained there for about a minute and a half, until he came to after a liberal amount of cold water had been poured onto his head. Dempsey shook his hand, then hopped through the ropes and away. Miske was heartbroken, and left the ring in tears, for he had hoped to stay the limit.

Detroit radio station 8MK, later known as WWJ, operating from the *Detroit News* Building, broadcast the fight's progress via wireless radiophone, the first time the results of a boxing match were communicated via radio. The fight returns/results were sent to approximately 300 wireless stations by the *News* radiophone.

Miske down in 3rd round, before the final knockdown

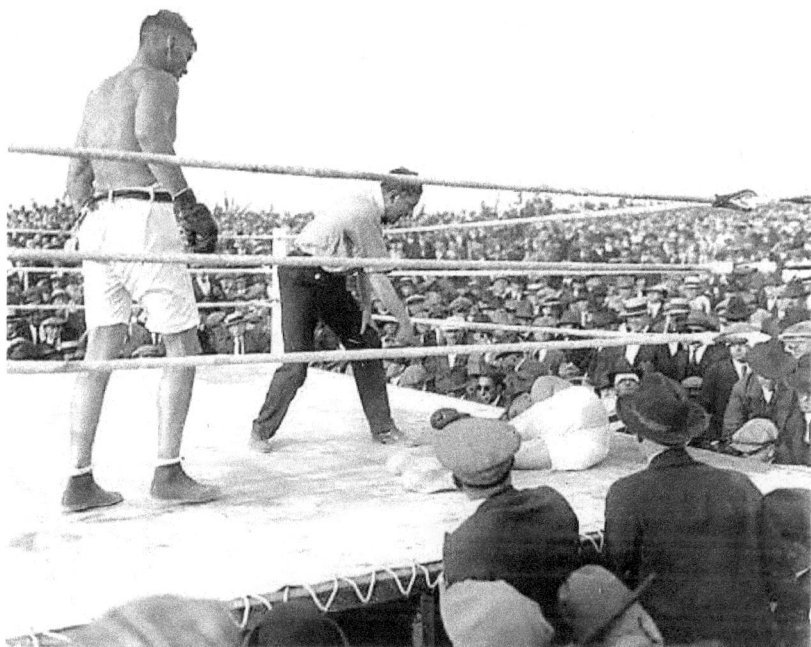
Miske counted out

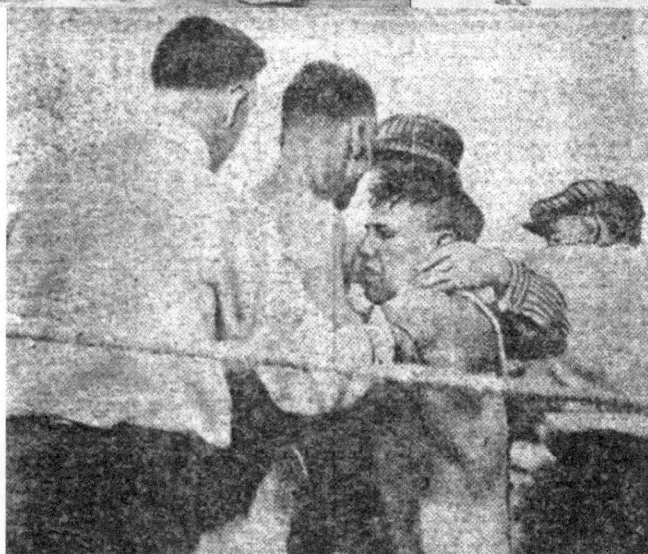

Afterwards, Miske said,

> Dempsey is a better man than I am. That fellow hits too hard. The punch that floored me in the second round all but caved in my ribs. I never was hit so hard in my life. The blow took all of the steam out of me and I had not recovered from its effects when the third round opened. I think Dempsey is unbeatable. There isn't a heavyweight living that can stand up under his punches. I fought the best battle I could but was whipped before I really got started.

Billy also said, "I for one am convinced that Jack Dempsey is a great fighter. What else can I say? I thought I had a chance to win the championship. And then I got that one under the heart. But my ribs were not broken."

Another quoted Miske as saying of Dempsey, "He is the greatest man in the ring, and I bow to his superior ability." The "Dempsey of today is so much better than the man of two years ago that there is no comparison." Jack had improved skill and bewildering speed. "I have no alibis. I was beaten by a great fighter – certainly the greatest of this day, and probably the greatest of all time."

Dempsey said he never had any doubt.

> Miske is tough and I trained and fought him with as much caution as I would fight any heavyweight. He did not hit me hard enough to seriously hurt. The punch that started him on his way was a smash to the stomach in the second round. I felt my fist sink into his ribs and knew he was hurt. After that I was confident I could end it whenever I wanted to, but I fought carefully and took no chances. The finish came before I could get warmed up.

Another quoted Dempsey as saying,

> I am very glad to learn that Miske's ribs were not broken. I was somewhat anxious to show the public that I still was able to fight, and I was afraid that in my anxiety I had harmed my opponent. Miske fought gamely and I can only speak my admiration for the way he tried. I am feeling very fit and looking forward already to my next bout.

The local *Benton Harbor News Palladium* said Dempsey licked Miske all the way. Kearns said Dempsey would meet Carpentier whenever Georges wanted the fight.

The nearby *Saint Joseph Herald-Press* said Dempsey had little trouble in beating Miske into submission, knocking him out with a series of fatal body blows, showing his true class in stopping a man who twice before had gone the distance with him, and who never before had been decked or stopped.

It took just 7 minutes, 13 seconds of actual fighting time for Dempsey to prove that he was a master of his art, a human fighting machine, one that would take years to wreck. 1 minute 13 seconds into the 3rd round,

Miske lay on the canvas, a crumpled mass. Dempsey fought wonderfully. He was cool, cautious, and careful, playing his game to perfection and satisfying the crowd.

From the start, Miske had no chance. Dempsey was an overwhelming force, his attack too much to be avoided. His punches were murderous, his footwork lightning, and his guarding clever. He scored points so rapidly and at such close quarters that it was difficult to keep track of the blows. Many thought he could have done in the 1st round what he did in the 2nd and 3rd, but was a bit slow to cut loose.

This was a different Dempsey than Miske had fought before. The author came to this realization early in the 1st round, when Dempsey landed two rights to the head that shook the challenger from head to toe. Miske fought gamely, but his blows had no effect other than to spur on Dempsey to greater effort.

Harry Bullion for the *Detroit Free Press* said a knockdown blow to the heart in the 2nd round made it merely a question of how long the fight could last. A knockdown in the 3rd round was from a wicked left that dropped Miske like a log for a nine-count. The final knockdown blow was a measured right. Miske did not recover for five minutes.

The *Glens Falls Post-Star* had a reporter at ringside. Despite 14 months of inactivity, Dempsey had the same frown, danced about the ring with his old-time light-footedness, and he still had his big punch. In the 2nd, Miske was down for a five-count. In the 3rd, he took nine, after being decked by a rain of lefts and rights to the stomach and chin. When he just regained his feet, Dempsey landed a hard right to the chin to end it.

The *Chicago Tribune's* Ray Pearson said Dempsey was the world's most wonderful heavyweight, playing the game carefully, coolly, and grimly. No man could endure those murderous punches and retain the ability to think. In the 3rd round, after being knocked down by a left hook, Miske rose at about nine, wobbly. Immediately after he rose, Dempsey took three steps forward and shot a right hook to the jaw with all his force, and Miske went down and out at 1 minute 13 seconds into the round (fighting time, not including the final 10-count). There was no need to count, but Jim Dougherty counted to ten.

It was a great fight while it lasted. Billy got through the 1st round safely, although he was outpointed. He tried to mix it up, to no avail. Miske's attempts to play defense were worthless. He landed only a few solid punches throughout the contest, and while some of them carried a lot of force, no damage was done to the champion.

The *Chicago Tribune's* Harvey Woodruff said Dempsey fought like a champion. Some said the champ was cautious in the 1st round, but it was not caution, but rather craftiness backed by superb confidence, weaving around and feeling for a decisive opening. He actually had done the same to Willard, upsetting him by the suddenness of his attack, which baffled Jess. Miske knew what to expect, so there was no reason for an impetuous attack. One even wondered whether Dempsey was luring him into a false sense of confidence in order to make it easier to land the sledge-hammer blow. Still, even in the 1st round, in the clinches, Dempsey was jolting his short lefts to the chin. He worked hard rights and lefts to the body which would cause Miske to bring down his guard to open the route for the ultimate left hook.

A straight right to the body in the 2nd round decked and ended Miske's chances of staying the full 10 rounds. It was one of the hardest body blows ever delivered in an American ring for the distance it traveled. Miske rose unsteadily and clinched. He lasted the round by battling purely defensively for self-protection. Dempsey did not force sufficiently enough to end it, though he might have ended matters if he had attacked like a wild man. Instead, he was the same cool, crafty Dempsey, going about his task methodically. In the clinches, he shook up Miske with short hooks and uppercuts.

In the 3rd round, Miske tried to fight it out to change the tide, which drew cheers, but Dempsey was too good, too powerful, and too impervious. After a rapid exchange in which Jack's blows carried far more power, Miske went back to his defensive tactics.

Eventually, Dempsey landed his left hook to the jaw, and Miske's head went sideways from the force as he fell. He rose at nine, while Dempsey paced impatiently behind the referee.

Billy's hands were only partially up as he rose, and Dempsey rushed up, drove his right through, and Miske fell on his face, thoroughly out in his own corner. As soon as Dougherty tolled off the ten seconds, Jack helped lift Billy onto his chair.

Percy Hammond, also for the *Chicago Tribune*, said Miske turned out to be only a comma, a slight punctuation to the great Dempsey epic.

Hammond was a Carpentier fan, partial to the man who went to war. Though Dempsey was prudent and had his reasons for not going overseas, because Carpentier had been a solider, Hammond did not want to see Dempsey knock him out, as he suspected would be the case.

Sam Langford said of Dempsey, "He sure can hit. There is no fighter living today who can beat him."

When asked whether Dempsey would be permitted to fight Jack Johnson, Kearns said, "We'll fight anyone if the proper inducements are offered. Jack Johnson, Harry Wills, or any of the other colored fighters are not barred. ... We are ready to meet any man the public demands that Jack should fight." Kearns said Brennan was next, then likely Carpentier.

The *Chicago Herald and Examiner's* Sam Hall said Miske never had a chance, and nobody else did either. The champion possibly could have accomplished the knockout in the 1st round had he so chosen. "Dempsey was so fast and was hitting so hard that Bill might as well have been trying to lick a freight train."

In the 1st round, Dempsey landed blows hard enough to hurt, but still had not lit the fuse to his real dynamite.

In the 2nd round, a right to the kidney decked Miske. "A lot of fellows are going to say that said right hand was struck under the heart but we were right close to them and saw Jack's Mary Ann go home. It landed way back over the kidney and hurt Bill like he never was hurt before." Dempsey's blows were hard enough to break bones.

Nevertheless, Billy rose quickly. He tried to make a fight of it, "bucking right into the greatest fighting machine we ever looked at, and having seen a lot of them we believe we know what we are talking about." Dempsey tried to measure him, but could not land the clean finisher.

In the 3rd, a left hook to the chin decked Miske again. He got to his knees, but turned his back to Dempsey while Referee Dougherty counted to nine. When he arose, Dempsey was behind him. Jack just shifted over a little bit and nailed him with the right to the jaw that ended matters. Dougherty counted slowly and gave Miske every chance, but he was stiff and could not rise. "It's the first time we ever saw Dempsey wind up a fight with the right paw. Jack is a left-hander naturally, but his right is a pip, we'll say." Jack Dempsey was a natural lefty/southpaw, even though he fought in the right-handed stance, just like Jim Jeffries.

After picking up Miske and placing him on his stool, Dempsey left the ring immediately, but Miske sat in his corner for several minutes. "Being hit by Dempsey is like butting your head against the old stone wall."

Summarizing, Hall said, "Dempsey was a great fighter this afternoon. He had everything. He was fast on his feet, boxed well, guarded himself cleverly and hit like the mule kicks. It's an old gag about the mule kick, but that's just the way Dempsey was clouting."

Bob McAuliffe, at ringside for the *South Bend News-Times,* said Dempsey dispelled all doubt as to his ring capabilities. He still was the same terrific slugger that cut down Willard. The pile driver to the stomach in the 2nd round actually won the fight. Distressed upon rising, Miske danced away and clinched. In the 3rd, Dempsey floored him with a right hook over the heart. Billy rose groggily at nine. Jack landed a straight right to the chin that would have knocked the head off an ordinary man. Miske stayed down, sprawled out on his stomach in his own corner, his head resting on his right arm.

After Miske was revived with water, he put his hand to his jaw and rubbed it, and then opened his mouth and worked his lower jaw to make sure it wasn't broken.

The *South Bend Tribune's* Eugene Kessler said Dempsey stopped Miske sooner than expected. The world now thought even more of Dempsey. Everyone who saw the fight agreed that America had the champion of all champions. It would be difficult to find an opponent worthy of him.

Dempsey showed his power in the 1st round, landing a couple jarring left hooks to the chin, but also showed that he could box. In the second half of the round, Miske clinched continually. Even at the grappling game, Dempsey showed his ability to land blows at a very short range.

In the 2nd round, the champ stepped around Miske and landed a right to the body. Miske clinched. After the break, Dempsey shot across two fast rights to the body, the second landing squarely on the left side just below the heart and knocking Miske off his feet. Billy rose at five, and fought gamely. Dempsey was trying to measure off a sleep producer.

In the 3rd, Miske rallied, landing a right cross to the jaw. The champ covered up and landed a right to the heart. Miske got through Jack's guard, landing a left hook to the face. Dempsey sent a right to the body. Following a clinch, a left hook to Miske's chin sent him to the floor for the second time in the fight.

Billy got to his knees, then rose at 9. Dempsey, like a flash, rushed across with a right to the chin that sent him sprawling in his own corner for the 10-count.

Summarizing, Kessler said, "Miske was a game boy. He demonstrated the fact that he is clever. He shot across the ring opening the bout with a left hook to the face and then hooked a right to the neck." It was evident that Miske was trying to land a big one early. He might have tried to stay away. He didn't try to outbox Jack, but instead chose to slug with him, but at that game Dempsey had no equal.

Early on, "Dempsey played a safe game and covered up good." He waited for Miske to open up and give him an opportunity to land his big blows. He was patient, and took no chances. "His footwork and shoulder roll was perfect and aided him in keeping at a safe distance from Miske's punches. He also put a damper on the whisper that he can only hit and not box. Dempsey outboxed his opponent at all stages of the game. In clinches, he took advantage and hurt Miske with a short uppercut." The champion showed everything, and didn't even appear to be giving him the full steam of his punches. "As a whole it was a better scrap than the Willard affair and not so murderous." Dempsey "demonstrated that he is a two handed, superhuman hitter who can stand a lot of punishment."

Tom Andrews said that when Dempsey won the title, he was a wild-swinging, tearing-in fighter of the rough and ready variety, with a knockout punch in either hand. Yesterday, Dempsey was a cool, collected, and deliberate fighter with a touch of finish that was refreshing. Most of the fans expected him to rush pell-mell into the battle, but instead, he fought carefully, using excellent judgment. His work was a revelation.

Andrews had seen John L. Sullivan fight.

> [I] do not hesitate to say while Sullivan was a wonderfully hard hitter and an accurate one, he did not carry a more powerful blow from a short distance than Jack Dempsey. John L. had tremendous power back of his right-hand punches, but Dempsey hits equally hard with left or right. To my mind, Jack is more deliberate and sure of his blows than was Sullivan, and for that reason just as dangerous as ever John L. was.

Andrews believed Dempsey was playing possum in the 1st round, yet still won it. Miske landed snappy blows to start the round, but Jack started a series of rights and lefts to the face and body that caused Miske to become more defensive. The blows hurt, yet Jack still did not put his full steam behind them.

As the gong sounded to start the 2nd round, someone shouted to Dempsey, "Say, Jack, don't play with him! Remember what happened at Toledo. Take no chances." Dempsey grew more serious, uppercut the body and sent his left to the jaw, followed by a right cross to the cheek. Dempsey stepped back an instant, and then let go a short right to the body that doubled up Miske like a jack knife as he went down for a five-count. Miske was driven about the ring thereafter, until saved by the bell.

In the 3rd, Miske tried to rally, but it merely was a flash. The champ landed two rights to the body and a left to the jaw, followed by a right, and Billy went down. He arose semi-conscious, and Jack shot over his famous right cross and it was all over. Dougherty finished counting ten at 1 minute 22 seconds of the round. Dempsey was far too clever and strong for the game St. Paul boy.

W. O. McGeehan said Dempsey's mastery was plain to see. He used his left to the body and jaw almost as he wished, and seemed very confident.

> There is no doubt but that Dempsey is as good, or even better, than he ever was. He was not quite so furious as in other fights, but he was perhaps more calculating in working Miske into a condition where he was easy prey for his mighty right. ... He was fast as a cat and as accurate as a sharpshooter and handled the bull-like Miske with the greatest ease.

McGeehan believed that Dempsey could have knocked out Miske in the 1st round, or earlier than he did, had he so chosen. Jack landed a hard right to the body in the 1st round, and some thought it might be over soon, but instead of finishing, he played with him.

In the 2nd round, a right to the body dropped Miske for a five-count. In the 3rd, a left hook to the jaw followed by a right to the jaw decked him again. Miske rose at nine, Dempsey shot over his right, and it was over.

The *Chicago Evening Post's* Harry Hochstadter said the way Dempsey toppled the blond Norseman indicated that suitable opponents would be few and far between, for he would slaughter most everyone.

The next day, the spot under Miske's heart was red and sore, a punch which Miske admitted really sent him toward defeat. His ribs were bruised, and his jaw was sore. Dempsey did not bear a mark.

Hochstadter opined that Dempsey was a great two-fisted fighter and would remain unbeaten for many a day to come. "He is just as good as, if not better than, the day he uncrowned Jess Willard."

Miske took his beating and went down fighting hard. Dempsey's murderous wallops hit the vital points, and though they did not bruise as much as they did with Willard, their effect was clear. Dempsey was a ring master, fast as a cat, and as accurate as a sharpshooter. He used his left to the body and jaw almost at will, and appeared certain of his movements.

Referee Jim Dougherty said no one but Dempsey could have whipped or knocked out Miske. Dougherty said Miske was very game to have taken those terrible blows. A solar plexus punch in the 2nd round turned the tide. Dempsey knocked him clear across the ring into his own corner, where he took a count of three. It was a right over the heart.

Miske trainer Ike Bernstein said Dempsey still was the great fighter he was in Toledo, with greater effectiveness and no loss of punching power.

Edward W. Smith said fans saw the best battling man of this and perhaps any other time. Miske gave his best, but Dempsey was all of the adjectives used about him – awful, terrible, terrific, murderous, superman, and more. Some even believed that Dempsey was fighting under wraps and putting on the brakes, not wanting to win so quickly.

The *New York Evening World*'s Vincent Treanor said the knockdown right to the body in the 2nd round was the most paralyzing right drive to the body the writer ever saw. Miske proved his stamina, toughness, and gameness in rising from it and recovering enough to fight back. No "sick man" could have risen. James J. Corbett and Fred Fulton had been hit with such blows, but failed to rise. At the end of the round, it looked like a painted red mark where the blow landed, right on the solar plexus. Billy had a lump on his left cheekbone as well.

Nevertheless, Miske took the aggressive in the 3rd round, landing an uppercut to the chin, but Dempsey appeared to take no notice of it. Billy plunged in with a left to the jaw, but again Dempsey paid no attention. Dempsey maneuvered around until he got Billy where he wanted him, and decked him a with a left hook and right, both to the jaw and chin.

A less game man than Miske would have stayed down, with no apologies to make. Yet, Miske rose again. Dempsey, moving from behind the referee, where he had stood during the count, waited until Billy had turned toward him, and then shot a long overhand right to finish it. It took about ten minutes before Miske was revived fully.

Dempsey proved that "he is probably the deadliest sharpshooting hitter pugilism ever knew."

When asked whether Miske ever hurt him with any of his punches, Dempsey replied, "Hurt me? Why, he never hit me." The writer reminded Dempsey that Miske indeed had landed several times, including the first punch, and many times thereafter. "Well, if he did, I never felt them; but that's how a lot of fellows like that get licked. They keep on jabbing out with their lefts. I let them do that until I get them into position to let my punch go." Still, he complimented Miske. "Billy is a good fighter, and he'll take 'em. Others won't. Yes, he's game."

Treanor said the fight proved that Miske indeed was physically rejuvenated. At 187 pounds, he was bigger, stronger, and more active. If Miske had a kidney ailment, as had been diagnosed, it was in remission. He fought well, but went up against an all-time great.

Frank Menke said Dempsey was the master throughout, and never in danger, battering the challenger into submission. Miske hardly laid a glove on him, whereas Dempsey gave Billy a terrible body punishing. It was a super fighter against one who was outclassed.

If Dempsey had gone out to slug in the 1st round instead of boxing with him, he possibly could have won in that round. He flashed his boxing ability and defensive trickery, which did not hearten Carpentier followers. He beat Miske at his own style, outspeeding him and running circles around him. His speed was bewildering. Though Miske fired a score of his famous jabbing leads, Dempsey either brushed them away, ducked, or side-stepped.

One round of boxing was sufficient to convince Dempsey that he could show boxing skill when he wanted, but he was ready to rush forth with this slugger style, intent on crushing him. In the 2nd round, he fought coolly and carefully, yet with a fury, tearing in. He never swung until reasonably certain that he could hit his mark. Miske made desperate efforts to cover, but Dempsey was not to be denied. He whipped short rights to the body to slow up Miske, maneuvered him into position, and then like a flash sent his right to the body. Miske had expected a left hook and raised his guard, but the right crashed straight through, under his heart, and he went down on his side.

When Miske rose after a short count, instead of charging in furiously, Dempsey circled around to find another opening. Miske was hurt, and leapt into a clinch. It required strenuous efforts by the referee to tear him loose. To survive, Billy clinched again and again.

In the 3rd round, Dempsey circled a couple of times to prevent Miske from clinching. Jack bluffed a rush and stopped as Miske came in. At once, the left flashed into the body, followed by a right. Miske's face took on a look of intense pain. Dempsey hooked a short left to the jaw and followed with a short right. Miske backed away, and Dempsey tore at him, flashed out with the famous right hook, and Miske sank to the floor.

Dempsey walked away six or eight feet while Referee Dougherty counted. By a herculean effort and rare display of gameness, Miske somehow got to his feet at nine.

Dempsey simply walked over and shot the right to the jaw, and Billy fell in a helpless heap in his own corner to be counted out. After a brief handshake, Dempsey ran across the ring, picked up his old red sweater, threw it around his shoulders, climbed out, and ran to his training quarters. Jack never was one to linger afterwards. "Once more Jack Dempsey had proved to the world that he is the greatest fistic gladiator."

Dempsey told Menke,

> Well, my first battle in defense of the title is over – and I won a whole lot easier than I expected. I figured that I probably would have to take a little punishment from Billy before I brought him down. But, as far as I can recall, he never socked me with anything but short lefts or rights in the clinches.

> He was pretty soft, but I certainly did have to wallop the boy before I could end the show. That body smash I landed under his heart in

the second was about as hard a blow as I ever hit anybody. But Billy got up and continued the battle – a happening which did surprise me quite a little. But never, from the end of the first minute of the fighting in the first round, did I have any other belief than that I would get him – and do it before we had traveled very far.

One of my ambitions, ever since I won the title, has been to improve in boxing. Throughout the past year I schooled myself in it. I came to believe that I could box fairly well. And I determined to put myself to a test in that first round with Billy.

Dempsey said he boxed in the 1st round as practice for when he would meet Carpentier. "They tell me that he's the greatest boxer in the world." Hence, he had been practicing his boxing in training, and boxed during the 1st round. He thought he did fairly well as a boxer. "Any way, I didn't let Billy hit me – and although I simply boxed it with him in the first, I had no trouble hooking or jabbing him almost at will."

In the 2nd round, "I shed the boxing togs, and went out to get Billy in the way that I've gotten Willard, Fulton, Morris, and the rest." He walked around with the intent of finding an opening before wading in to slug, and once he did, he let loose.

Miske was tough, "don't make any mistake about that," and "could take an awful socking." So Jack tried to chop him down gradually rather than with one terrific blow, and then finish him at the right moment.

Though Miske was cagey, Jack found a right lead that went straight through to the body under the heart, and Billy went down.

Miske rose after a five-count. Jack tried to finish him, but Billy had a lot of sense left. He clinched as much as possible, turning the round into a wrestling affair. Still, Jack missed no chance in the clinches to keep him groggy and wear him down.

In the 3rd round, Dempsey started by carefully avoiding Miske, who he knew wanted to clinch, whereas Jack wanted to hit him in the open. Billy had slowed up a lot, so Jack had little trouble keeping out of his way or hitting him. Every short lead was a hit, whether for the head or body. "I hooked a short left into Miske's stomach – and when he winced and seemed to sag I knew that I had him. So I tore in then, tricked him into letting down his guard by faking a punch for the stomach – and then I shot a right hook with all my power." It landed on the jaw, and Jack knew it was over. Miske sank down onto his side, his face writhing in pain. Dempsey doubted he would rise, and stepped away.

Miske beat the count, "something that I don't think any other fighter in America, so badly hurt, could duplicate." Jack knew he was gone though, so he walked over, took careful aim, hit his jaw once more, and it was over.

And now, if they'll bring on the rest of the heavyweights in this country – and elsewhere – I'll be glad to oblige them. I needed this first fight to tune up. I've had it. I'm ready – and ready to fight every week if necessary. I used to do it before I became champion and I certainly ought to be able to do it now.

The *Los Angeles Record's* Darsie L. Darsie said no living man could hold his own with the champion. Miske, despite being the cleverest of the heavyweight contenders, was not in the same class as the champion, who crushed him. Dempsey was a wonder.

Jack carefully felt him out in the 1st round, decked him with a right to the ribs in the 2nd, and in the 3rd, a vicious right to the chin dropped Miske again. As he rose slowly at nine, Dempsey stood behind him. Miske turned to renew the battle, and as he turned, Jack struck with all his power and Miske fell, rolled over onto his face, and lay there motionless.

Bill Brennan, supposedly his next challenger, was said to be a heavier hitter than Miske, though Billy was thought to be cleverer. French ace Carpentier was said to be exceptionally clever and fast on his feet.

> If [Carpentier] is fast enough to keep away from Jack, he should have been placed on the French Olympic team. Dempsey will get him, too, and from all the available data, should batter him to the mat in record time. One man of importance remains, and that is big Harry Wills. ... He is clever, strong, and rugged, but he has not displayed anything in the way of a defense that would lead one to believe he could withstand the sledge hammer blows Dempsey makes a habit of delivering.

For the *Minneapolis Journal*, Ed Walker said Miske was hopelessly outclassed, despite his game efforts. Yet, Miske's performance compared creditably with those of Fulton and Willard. "It is doubtful if any man living could have stood up before the sledgehammer blows of the champion, who deals out punishment with either hand, blows calculated to make any opponent wince with pain."

The impact of Dempsey's body blow that decked Miske in the 2nd could be heard throughout the arena. In the corner, Miske was administered smelling salts, but he seemed to be in pain.

Miske tried to give it everything he had in the 3rd, but Dempsey would not be denied. A terrific left to the jaw dropped him for a second time, sprawling along the ropes. Miske barely rose at nine, hands at his sides, eyes glassy. The champion, as cool as an iceberg, watched.

Miske had his back to his rival when he rose. As soon as he turned around, Dempsey fired his murderous right, landed squarely on the chin, and down he went for the full count, stretched out, laying on his side.

It was five minutes before Miske was able to leave the ring, and he still swayed from side to side. He was very much downhearted, but the fans, who appreciated that he did his best, gave him a round of applause.

Walker believed it would be a long time before a white man would be found who had a ghost of a chance with Dempsey, for he looked unbeatable. If Carpentier knew what was good for him, he would avoid Dempsey. "About the only boxer in the limelight of today who has a ghost of a chance is Harry Wills, the negro.... Even Wills, a giant physically, probably would wilt under Dempsey's blows."

Dempsey told Walker, "I knew I would win, but I did not expect to turn the trick so soon. ... I am glad to know I have not lost any of the fighting stuff I displayed when I beat Willard. I am now ready to meet any heavyweight in the world and naturally prefer Carpentier."

Miske said, "I confidently expected to go to the 10th round at least. That punch under my heart in the 2nd round was the beginning of my finish. ... That blow certainly hurt, although the short jolts he landed in the 1st round were not love taps. He is a great fighter and I know of no one who can beat him."

St. Paul's E. R. Hosking said the fans agreed that the title holder was a marvel. Billy was not slow, but Jack simply was a whirlwind, and far superior to all others. He might even be the champion of all champions.

Hosking believed that if Dempsey had thrown caution to the winds and given it his all, he probably could have stopped Miske in the 1st round. But he fought cautiously, as befits a champion who should not take unnecessary chances. Even in the 1st round, Dempsey's snappy and punishing left and right hooks cut through Billy's guard and sapped much of his strength.

Even after decking Miske in the 2nd, Dempsey preferred to exercise some caution. That body punch left a bright red welt under Miske's heart, which by the end of the fight had changed in color to a greenish blue. He also had green spots on both cheeks.

Hosking said Miske put up the best fight he could, as good as anyone else could with the present title holder. Some might say that Miske had not recovered from the effects of his illness, but it could be "safely stated" that in Dempsey's current form, "Miske never saw the day that he could have lasted longer than he did yesterday." Dempsey was so far superior to all others that his fights were mere exhibitions. Miske failed at a task in which no other contender could succeed. The "superman" had "immeasurable superiority over any other fighting man now before the public." Miske took more punishment than most others could survive. Few would have risen from the first knockdown.

A heart-broken Miske left the ring in tears, for he had hoped and expected to stay the limit. His father and wife had seen him lose. "I did my best and I am very sorry that I did not make a better showing for St. Paul. Dempsey is a wonder. He hit me harder than he did in either of the other fights, and there is no one in the world who has any chance at all with him."

St. Paul's Ed Shave said the swarthy-faced, dark-haired champion proved that he still was the world's mightiest fighter. The relentless champion's crushing, pile-driving smash was not to be denied.

The 1st round was very fast. Miske did not cover and run, but fought, leading at the champ as much as the champ led at him. Still, Dempsey won the round, for when he led, he usually landed solidly and hard.

The body blow that Dempsey landed in the 2nd round would have scored a clean knockout over many other heavies.

Although Miske spurted at the start of the 3rd, and landed with considerable force, Dempsey shook off the hard blows as if they had not landed at all. Jack hooked a left to the stomach, they clinched, broke, and Dempsey hooked two lefts and a right. He then shot a terrific left hook into the stomach and right cross to the jaw and Billy collapsed on his face. It looked like it was over, but he rose at nine. He hardly was up to his feet, hands down, when Dempsey, who was standing right over him, drove home one more right, and he crumpled down and out on his side.

Shave criticized Referee Dougherty's performance. When Miske was decked for the nine-count, "Dougherty did not keep Dempsey away, he did not send the champion back at all, but allowed him to remain right on top of Miske, and the punch which put Bill into oblivion came as Miske arose before he had his hands up."

Shave did not believe Miske was the Miske of old, but even if he had been, the result would have been nearly the same, for Dempsey's mighty punches could subdue any man in the world, in about the same amount of time. "There is none can stand up and exchange punches with this champion." Shave did not think anyone could give Dempsey a real battle. The clever, fleet-footed Carpentier might be able to keep away for a few more rounds, but if he took a punch like Miske did in the 2nd, he too would lose much of his speed and go under. Dempsey rightfully could be called a "superman." "He's one of the greatest champions, if not the greatest of all time." Miske went down, but so had all the others, and he went down fighting gamely, which was all anyone could ask.

The *Lansing State Journal* said Dempsey, though exonerated of the draft evasion charges, still had a name to clear with the fight-loving public, and the only way to do that was to mop up his challengers. He appeared to better advantage against Miske than against Willard, by far. He did not rush in as much, but was cool, deliberate, and workmanlike. Miske landed but two or three clean punches, which only served to urge Dempsey to a faster pace. In the clinches, Dempsey was the master every time. He hurt Miske as much with the infighting as at long range.

Floyd Fitzsimmons declared that the show was a success in every way. "The house was virtually sold out. I believe that the few vacant seats that were in the one section were sold in Chicago and that the tickets were held by some of those who were unable to arrive on time due to an accident on the railroad."

Many patrons were victims of pickpockets, including a state boxing commissioner, who lost $180 at ringside.

That evening, Dempsey had dinner with promoter Fitzsimmons and friends, and danced at a summer pavilion in St. Joseph.[285]

---

[285] *Benton Harbor News Palladium*, September 6, 1920; *Saint Joseph Herald-Press* (Michigan), *Detroit Free Press, Detroit News, Lansing State Journal, Glens Falls Post-Star, South Bend News-Times, South Bend Tribune, San Francisco Examiner, Los Angeles Record, Chicago Daily News, Chicago Herald and Examiner, Chicago Evening Post, Buffalo Enquirer, Brooklyn Standard Union, Minneapolis Journal, St. Paul Dispatch, St. Paul Pioneer Press, St. Paul Daily News*, September 7, 1920; *Chicago Tribune*, September 7, 8, 1920; *St. Louis Star*, September 6, 7, 1920.

Before leaving for Chicago, Dempsey gave his big yellow car, worth $6,500, an Owen Magnetic, to promoter Floyd Fitzsimmons' wife, Mrs. Irene O'Brien Fitzsimmons. Clearly, Dempsey was very happy with Floyd Fitzsimmons.[286]

The next day, Edward Walker said Miske's defeat was not the end of his career. Miske intended to continue fighting, and hoped to be back in the ring again soon. Billy called Dempsey the greatest heavyweight ever.

Walker did not believe Carpentier had any chance with Dempsey, and might not last as long as Miske did. "Right now Bill Brennan and Harry Wills look the best attractions, and it is very, very doubtful if either of these two maulers will be there to hear the tap of the gong to start the 5th round."[287]

Word was that Dempsey was going to fight Gunboat Smith in Boston on September 18 or 25, and then Bill Brennan in October in New York.

The morning after the fight, Dempsey was as happy and funny as a kitten. He woke up the camp at 6 a.m. by playing a victrola, and pulled everyone out of bed.

Dempsey said he wanted to fight again as soon as possible. He expected to fight Smith soon, then Brennan, and possibly Frank Moran.

> If anybody wants to match us he can have it. The same thing goes for the highly touted Gene Tunney. And, in due course of time, I'm going to take on Georges Carpentier – and also Harry Wills, if the public wants the latter match. It's my ambition to knock out – not merely outpoint – every fighter in the heavyweight ranks today – or in the near future.

Miske said the body shot that decked him in the 2nd round was the hardest he ever received. That evening, he had a terrific headache, but it disappeared by the morning, though a large lump was on his jaw.[288]

Despite knocking him out, Dempsey and Miske remained friends. When both were in Chicago the day after the fight, Dempsey visited Miske and his wife, who were having lunch at the Morrison. Both praised the other. Dempsey encouraged Miske not to retire, telling him that he could beat all of the other heavyweights. Billy said he had no intention of retiring. Mrs. Miske said, "Mr. Dempsey, I want to thank you for helping my husband to his corner after he had been knocked out." The champ replied that he hated to have to take the second punch at Bill in the 3rd round. Mrs. Miske said she did not care to see another fight.

Dempsey and the reporters were right about how good Miske was. Billy went on a win streak thereafter, winning his next 17 fights from 1921 to 1922, defeating several world-class heavyweights. Over the course of 23 fights from 1921 to 1923, Miske would lose only once (a decision) and draw once. The only fighter ever to drop or stop Billy Miske (officially) in his entire 101-fight career was Jack Dempsey.

[286] *Benton Harbor News Palladium*, September 7, 1920.
[287] *Minneapolis Journal*, September 8, 1920.
[288] *Chicago Herald and Examiner*, September 8, 1920.

Dempsey and Kearns hopped on a train bound for New York.[289]

Two days after the championship fight, on September 8, 1920 in Philadelphia, 205-pound Harry Wills and 211-pound Sam McVey (76-18-12) fought a 6-round no decision, but the referee stopped the bout during the final round, essentially declaring it a no contest, claiming that the two were stalling and not giving best efforts in the tame bout. He had warned them throughout, but they mostly held, pulled, and tugged.

The *Philadelphia Public Ledger* said it looked as if Wills was trying, and McVey was the chief offender, but still, "the alleged contender for Jack Dempsey's crown failed to do anything that resembled boxing. While McVey held on and refused to box, Wills also did some hugging, tugging, pulling and jerking around."

The *Philadelphia Inquirer* said, "McVey wouldn't fight and Wills didn't show any disposition to fight..." "Wills, the fellow who knocked off Fulton with a punch, and who is really a capable fighter, missed as many blows as a dub batsman in a big league ball game. McVey...just stalled along very gently and so neither man was hurt and the crowd booed." Neither one was paid. The police banned the two from boxing again in Philadelphia.[290]

Discussing potential title challengers, the *Lansing State Journal* said Fulton quit when hurt, everyone beat Frank Moran now, Meehan was too fat (and was beaten by Miske, Fulton, Smith, and Brennan), Levinsky already was beaten badly by Dempsey, and Tunney and Martin were not yet ripe. Carpentier was a great boxer, with speed and power. Yet, his own manager was confident in Carpentier against everyone *except* Dempsey. That left Harry Wills and Jack Johnson. "Wills, like Fulton, quits when he is hurt. Dempsey never fought anyone whom he didn't hurt." (Yet, Wills had not been stopped since 1917; a retirement owing to injury – a broken wrist, which was avenged, and his last prior stoppage loss was in 1916 in the 19th round to Langford, also avenged.) Johnson was old, in jail, and had not taken care of himself, yet could be the strongest contender, for the "colored boxer has a longer life than the white man." Dempsey had a tiger's fierceness, a lion's heart, and a mule's kick in either glove. He likely would be champion for a long time.[291]

Robert Edgren said most champions did not flop until they were old, fat, or weakened and dissipated by luxurious living (and inactivity). The current champion was not likely to be upset anytime soon.[292]

Dempsey wanted to fight often. "Feeling fine and ready for business. Guess Kearns will keep me on the jump for ten months or so. The more the merrier. I'm out to fight them as fast as they come along."[293]

Harry Greb told the *Pittsburgh Gazette Times* that he was interested in fighting Dempsey if the opportunity presented itself, feeling confident, though he wasn't pushing for it.

[289] *Chicago Tribune*, September 9, 1920.
[290] *Philadelphia Evening Public Ledger*, *Philadelphia Inquirer*, September 9, 10, 1920; *Pittsburg Press*, September 11, 1920.
[291] *Lansing State Journal*, September 9, 1920.
[292] *New York Evening World*, September 11, 1920.
[293] *Brooklyn Daily Times*, September 11, 1920.

Dempsey couldn't do anything with me in the gym, and he was trying. We used eight-ounce gloves and not the big pillows a lot of people seem to think. I just kept him busy moving around and scored at will. They took movies of Jack working out every day, but they never took any of my bouts with him, because he didn't show to any particular advantage when I speeded up and used the old footwork and threw a barrage of gloves. However, I don't think Jack would want to box with me in a regular fight just now. We got to be pretty good chums while we were together, and unless business demands, there is no reason why we should quit enjoying our friendship to go through a bout. Nevertheless, I am confident from my showings with Jack that he can't do anything with me, because he can't reach me to hit me.[294]

Word was that Dempsey-Brennan would be held on October 1.[295]

W. O. McGeehan said Dempsey demonstrated quite clearly at Benton Harbor that "there is no man in the world who would have a chance with him under Queensberry rules." He could have won by knockout even sooner if he had attacked as ferociously as he did against Willard. This time, he wasted not a move, every punch landed, and he finished Miske with the precision of a trained marksman. "As a ringman Dempsey of to-day is the greatest of them all, past or present. His punches

THE FIGHT IN PICTURES.—When THE NEWS' cameraman called on Jack Dempsey at his suite in the Hotel Belmont yesterday, the heavyweight champion was looking over the pictorial record of his Labor Day fight with Billy Miske as exclusively presented in THE NEWS of Wednesday morning. "You guys certainly hustled to get those pictures here," Jack said.   (NEWS photo)

have the precision and the swiftness of the striking of a gorilla." Carpentier knew all the tricks of the trade, and was a good, fast boxer with a punch, but regardless, Dempsey still could dispose of him with ease. The champion had the instincts of a conqueror and the strength of an ape, and Carpentier's mind would carry him only so far.[296]

The proposed Gunboat Smith contest was dropped, for most believed he simply was not a good enough opponent to make any kind of a contest, and therefore attendance would be poor.[297]

A week after the fight, the *Elmira Star-Gazette* reported that H. C. Walker, *Detroit Times* sporting editor, took quite a slam at Dempsey, calling him a bad sport, though a great fighter. "As a fighter he is one of the best the pugilistic game has developed. I think Dempsey can hit harder than any other fighter who ever got into a ring. ... It is my belief that Jack Dempsey is the Babe Ruth of the prize ring." Pound-for-pound,

[294] *Pittsburgh Gazette Times*, September 11, 1920.
[295] *Brooklyn Daily Times*, September 12, 1920.
[296] *New York Tribune*, September 13, 1920.
[297] *New York Herald*, September 13, 1920. In 1920, Gunboat Smith had losses to Bill Tate, Fred Fulton, Lee Anderson, and Chuck Wiggins.

lightweight champ Benny Leonard probably could hit harder, proportionately for his size, than Dempsey, and if he could go up to 195, would beat Dempsey, but in terms of sheer force generated, "I think Dempsey is the hardest hitter the game has yet produced."

However, Walker said Dempsey was a "bum sport," without sand.

> He got behind helpless Billy Miske the other day and knocked him cold when Billy wasn't looking, and, furthermore, when Dempsey didn't have any right to hit him.
>
> The knockout blow that put Billy Miske to sleep was one of the most cowardly blows I have ever seen. And it doesn't lessen the offense that Jack Dempsey's personal referee didn't know enough to or didn't want to prevent the blow.
>
> Dempsey sneaked up on Miske, hit him from behind and knocked him out, and 19,999 other men saw him do it. And the rules of boxing under which the men were fighting were supposed to protect the befuddled Miske at the time the shameful smash landed on his jaw. ...
>
> But, contrary to the rules under which that match and all others in this country are held, Dempsey was standing over him, ready to knock him down as soon as both knees were off the floor. And Dempsey did, despite the fact that he had no right to do it. The Marquis of Queensberry rules say: "If either man fall through weakness or otherwise, he must get up unassisted, ten seconds to be allowed him to do so, the other man meanwhile to return to his corner." ... But Dempsey violated the rules and hovered over Miske, BEHIND THE HELPLESS FIGHTER, and hit him as soon as both knees were off the floor. The bully needn't have done it, for he could have licked Miske squarely quite as easily. Only he didn't.

Another criticism of Dempsey was that he made Miske and 20,000 fans wait for more than 15 minutes, although the time already was an hour later than the fight was scheduled to be held. "There was no excuse for Dempsey's delay, save one. He wanted to get Miske's goat. It didn't matter to him that he also got the goats of 20,000. Miske kept his appointment like a white man and Dempsey didn't. He not only wasted 15 minutes of Miske's time; but he wasted 15 minutes of the time of the other 20,000."

Walker said Dempsey whined until he got his own referee, and insulted the Michigan Boxing Commission by inferring that a referee picked by the commission would job him. He then proceeded to fight foully, which was totally unnecessary. He was a brute. "Yet he is a wonderful fighter. But the crowd will yell with glee when some good guy puts a sleep wallop on his jaw."[298]

---

[298] *Elmira Star-Gazette*, September 15, 1920.

CHAPTER 6

Build-Up and Forced Delay

On September 13, 1920, Georges Carpentier arrived in the U.S., scheduled for a world light heavyweight championship contest with Battling Levinsky (161-38-34), whom no one had stopped other than Dempsey. Carpentier said he would not sidestep Dempsey, and would be pleased to meet him in the ring after his fight with Levinsky. He always spoke through interpreters, for he spoke rather poor, broken English.

Carpentier would prepare for the Levinsky fight at Summit, New Jersey, sparring with Joe Jeannette, French welter Marcel Thomas, and English light heavy Jack Blumfield.[299]

On September 14, 1920 in Chicago, at Jack Johnson's re-sentencing hearing, for violation of the White Slave Traffic Act, otherwise known as the Mann Act, for paying for the transportation of a woman across state lines for immoral sexual purposes, even though the Court of Appeals had overturned all of his prostitution convictions, Judge George A. Carpenter once again sentenced Johnson to serve a one-year-and-a-day prison sentence at Leavenworth Prison and pay a $1,000 fine.

On September 15, 1920 in Atlanta, Georgia, before a crowd of 2,000, Harry Wills stopped black Jack Clark (not Jeff) in the 4th round, when his seconds tossed in the towel, feeling that he had suffered enough punishment. The *Atlanta Constitution*'s Gene Hinton wrote, "Wills did not show the killing punch last night, however, that would place him on anything like a par with Dempsey." Harry had to be given some credit for stopping Fulton, but then again, Fred was known for having a "glass jaw."[300]

On September 17, 1920 at Madison Square Garden, in a Tex Rickard promotion, the first boxing show in New York under the new Walker law under Governor Al Smith took place. "It will be the first decision contest in the Garden since Jim Corbett and Kid McCoy boxed in the famous arena twenty years ago last month." Finally, formal decisions would be allowed again, and up to 15 rather than 10 rounds. All fighters and clubs would have to be licensed. There would be two judges, and the referee would act as a tiebreaker if they disagreed. Chairman Joseph Johnson warned that crooked work would not be tolerated, and "we shall try to see

---

[299] *New York Tribune*, September 14, 1920.
[300] *Atlanta Constitution*, September 15, 16, 1920.

that they do not ruin boxing again." Jack Dempsey was the first fighter to be granted a boxer's license.

Both Dempsey and Carpentier were guests at the show, and introduced from the ring. They climbed into the ring, shook hands, and patted each other on the back.[301]

The New York Boxing Commission refused to authorize a Dempsey-Brennan bout at that time, wanting to delay matters until a bit later. They claimed that they wanted to wait until the game was thoroughly organized and the machinery of the new law in good working order before permitting a big fight, whatever that meant.

Dempsey decided to remain at Long Branch and continue training there so he would be ready to defend the title on short notice.[302]

The Boston boxing commission refused to sanction a Dempsey vs. Frank Moran fight, but gave no reasons.[303]

James J. Corbett said Dempsey was the perfect fighting machine. He was a great hitter who also had science, fast footwork, and could take a punch. He had the fighter's heart, and loved fighting. "As a hitter, I don't think any man ever lived who was in Dempsey's class." He could score knockouts with either hand, at any angle, or any distance, to the stomach or jaw. "His punch is practically irresistible in its power." This comparison included Sullivan and Fitzsimmons. "Dempsey is fast – amazingly fast." He even showed that he could box against Miske. "And so we have Dempsey, a great boxer, a slugging marvel, the fastest heavyweight afoot, a man with a fighting heart and of proven ability to take punishment. What more is needed to answer the title of 'super-fighter'?"

On September 22, 1920 in Milwaukee, in a rematch, Harry Greb badly punished Ted Jamieson, who retired after the 6th round owing to a broken right thumb.[304]

There was some discussion of a Dempsey-Willard rematch having been signed. However, Willard denied it.[305]

[301] *Brooklyn Daily Times*, September 17, 1920; *Daily News, Buffalo Times*, September 18, 1920. In the main event, lightweight Joe Welling won a 15-round decision over Johnny Dundee. The first formal decision rendered under the new law was on the undercard, a bantamweight fight: Sammy Nable W6 Bobby Hansen.
[302] *New York Times*, September 19, 1920.
[303] *New York World*, September 20, 1920; *New York Tribune*, September 21, 1920.
[304] *Binghamton Press*, September 21, 1920. *Oshkosh Northwestern, Racine Journal-News, Chicago Tribune*, September 23, 1920.
[305] *New York Daily News, New York World*, September 27, 1920; *Brooklyn Standard Union, New York Daily News*, September 28, 1920.

During September 1920, a grand jury began investigating the 1919 World Series, for there were strong suspicions and rumors that the Chicago White Sox had fixed and thrown the series to the Cincinnati Reds. On September 28, Eddie Cicotte confessed to his participation in the scheme, having received $10,000. "Shoeless" Joe Jackson admitted that he received $5,000, but had been promised $15,000 more. Both later would recant, and their signed confessions went missing (but many years later were found in the possession of the lawyer for White Sox owner Charles Comiskey).

On September 29, 1920, the grand jury indicted eight Chicago White Sox players, and eventually on October 22, five gamblers as well, in a conspiracy to fix the 1919 World Series. It was a huge scandal.[306]

Gambler Arnold Rothstein, known as "The Brain," was implicated, but prosecutors could not obtain sufficient evidence to indict or prosecute him. He possibly won money gambling on inside knowledge, but it was not provable whether he was part of or had generated the conspiracy.

Former world featherweight boxing champion Abe Attell was reported to be in on the scheme as well, as an intermediary between Rothstein and the players. Interestingly, Attell had worked Jim Jeffries' corner for the 1910 Jack Johnson fight. Jeffries subsequently claimed that he had been doped. Attell claimed that Johnson had agreed to throw the fight, but double-crossed Jeffries. Jeff branded that claim a lie. Could Attell have drugged Jeffries?

In order to save baseball and rehabilitate its public image, in late 1920, former federal Judge Kenesaw Mountain Landis was appointed as baseball's first commissioner and given broad authority. Landis had been involved in the Mann Act case against Jack Johnson, setting his bail at a whopping $30,000, but refused to accept cash. Landis placed the accused Chicago White Sox players and anyone allegedly involved in (or knew about but did not report) the fixing of the 1919 World Series on an "ineligible" list. They would not be allowed to play baseball again.

As commissioner, Landis was a staunch color-line advocate, never allowing a black player to enter the major leagues during his tenure. Apparently, he believed that segregation was for the good of the sport.

Writers loved to discuss heavyweight contenders and rank them. One Eastern writer considered Wills the number one contender.

However, the writer also opined that the columns of matter written about the color problem in boxing were so voluminous that they could stretch from New York to San Francisco and back again, which could be a problem in terms of getting an interracial heavyweight championship match made. "Tex Rickard...is reported to have made the statement that he would not match a negro and a white man for exhibition purposes in his establishment." Some thought he might change his mind if enough money was in it. However, Rickard was fully cognizant of all the problems

[306] *Chicago Tribune, Boston Globe*, September 29, 1920.

associated with and the aftermath of Johnson-Jeffries, which he had promoted, and likely did not want to risk a repeat.

As far as the public is concerned, there are many persons who are opposed to the meeting of the black and the white man, but it is equally true that there as many, if not more, who believe that a fighter is a fighter, irrespective of his color, and if a negro behaves himself, and comports himself according to Hoyle, he has as much right to make his living as the white man.

A "great prejudice was aroused when Johnson was the champion, but many who have analyzed the feeling express the opinion that this feeling was more against Johnson himself and his escapades than against his color." Many felt that sooner or later, Dempsey and Wills had to face each other in the ring, for amongst the contenders, "Wills seems to be by far the best."[307]

An eastern boxing critic rates the heavyweights, famous and otherwise, in the game today as follows:
1—Jack Dempsey.
2—Harry Wills.
3—Jess Willard.
4—Fred Fulton.
5—Georges Carpentier.
6—Bill Brennan.
7—Bartley Madden.
8—Billy Miske.
9—Bob Martin.
10—Gene Tunney.
11—Willie Meehan.
12—Battling Levinsky.
13—Charlie Weinert.
14—Frank Moran.
15—Tom Cowler.
16—Martin Burke.
17—Joe Beckett.
18—Bob Roper.
19—Gunboat Smith.
20—Al Reich.

The *Glens Falls Post-Star* responded to an eastern boxing critic's high ranking of Wills by saying,

Nobody will question the selection of Jack Dempsey for the top of the list. But why he puts Harry Wills, the negro boxer, ahead of Jess Willard is beyond me. Wills is the best of the colored heavies and his victory over the weak-hearted Fred Fulton and other heavies has shown him to be a good man. But there is no reason to believe he could lick Jess Willard.... Willard would kill Wills in thirty seconds if they ever met. Wills is not as husky or as tough as Dempsey.... There is no record on which to compute Carpentier's merits. I believe Billy Miske ought to rank above Fulton. Believe Billy could lick the plasterer. As for the tail-end of the list, it's a case of shaking a lot of second-raters up in a bag and drawing them out blindfolded. There can be little choice in the array of cheese.[308]

Leo Flynn managed both Bill Brennan and black fighter Panama Joe Gans, who helped Dempsey train for the Miske fight. Gans told Tad Dorgan that he spent two miserable weeks with Dempsey, who suspected that he was a spy for Leo Flynn and Brennan.:

The second day I boxed he hit me on the ribs under the heart. Say, that's two weeks ago and I ain't slept on that side since. He ain't no man, but a bear. ... This Dempsey man is a killer. I explained to him after that punch that I was no spy for Brennan, no matter what anybody says. He laughed at me and says, BOSH, but I never got near enough to him for him to hit me with a rock after that. In my heart I thought he'd kill me. Let that Bill Brennan go in there, but with lots of caution.[309]

[307] *Santa Ana Register*, October 1, 1920.
[308] *Glens Falls Post-Star*, September 29, 1920.
[309] *Buffalo Commercial*, September 29, 1920.

Jim Corbett said Harry Wills was gathering some publicity by taking a crack at Dempsey and his manager, saying, "Dempsey is afraid to fight me – at least Jack Kearns, his manager, is afraid that I will whip the champion – and that's the same thing." Wills believed,

> I can whip Dempsey – and Kearns knows it. Kearns has been saying that he will give me a fight with Dempsey if the public demands it. But, that doesn't mean anything. He hasn't stated positively that he will give me a fight and he hasn't said positively that he won't. But I know he won't because he has got it all figured out that I am the boy that can take away the championship from Dempsey any time we get together.

Harry pointed out that none of the top white fighters would give him a chance because of his color. He even asserted that some folks had offered him money to "lay down" to white fighters, including $12,000 to throw the Fulton fight. However, he would not say who made the offer "in a roundabout way."

Corbett said Wills scored the 3rd round knockout over Fulton "very largely because of tactics in clinches which many persons figured were akin to fouling. It took Jack Dempsey just 14 seconds to dispose of the same Fulton." Many complained that Wills liked to hold and hit.

Continuing, Wills said,

> The reason I think I can beat Dempsey is because I figure that he was made to order for me. He is a wide open fighter – and that is the kind of a man I like to fight. Any fellow who comes at me rushing and without a guard is going to be hit. And when I hit, the man that is on the other end of it isn't going to stand on his feet. Anybody that I ever fought or anybody that ever saw me fight will tell you the same thing.

> I know that Dempsey is a hard hitter. But before he can drop anybody he has got to hit him. And Dempsey isn't fast enough and shifty enough to land on me.

> Dempsey's weakness is getting a bit rattled when the other fellow comes at him. He can always win a fight when his opponent is going away. But I'm not afraid of Dempsey. I would go right in and keep right on him until I dropped him. By carrying the fight to him and making it fast I would have Dempsey in a bad way in a couple of rounds because he doesn't know how to protect himself – especially if he is being rushed by his opponent.

> Right now I want to say that if I ever get a chance at Jack Dempsey I will whip him sure. But I am afraid that the chance to fight Dempsey is never going to be mine because Jack Kearns is too smart to give me a crack at the man I can beat.[310]

---

310 *Binghamton Press*, September 30, 1920.

Another newspaper quoted 31-year-old Wills as saying,

> Kearns knows that I can beat his meal ticket, so he is not going to take a chance. He pretends he is willing for Dempsey to meet me, but he doesn't mean what he says. He talks of making the match as soon as the public demands that Dempsey fight me. That is all bunk. He doesn't care anything about what the public thinks. I am not going around challenging Dempsey when I know he doesn't want to fight. I am just waiting until people get tired of seeing him knock over the set-ups. Then they are going to ask why he doesn't fight Harry Wills. It's so hard for me to get fights that I have to work at the docks sometimes although I can beat any man in the world.[311]

Charles Mathison noted that the New York commission had refused to sanction Carpentier-Levinsky, which had to be moved to New Jersey. Apparently, word was that the commission did not want to handle any big boxing matches until after the upcoming election. Politics and boxing always were intertwined.[312]

Carpentier had been described as a "tiger," with "swift dancing feet."

However, Robert Edgren said that when sparring with Joe Jeannette in Summit, New Jersey, Georges always was attacking. Yet, he didn't step in or rush in, but slid forward smoothly. When he saw his opening, he struck like a flash, straight to the mark with his body behind the blow. He pulled away from punches and avoided them by inches, and always was ready to counter. He obviously was holding back a lot in reserve. He seemed very concentrated, and could flash suddenly with blinding brilliance. His upcoming fight was somewhat of a tryout, to show the American public whether he had a real chance against Dempsey.

Georges was starring in a film called *The Wonder Man*, which didn't hurt his popularity.[313]

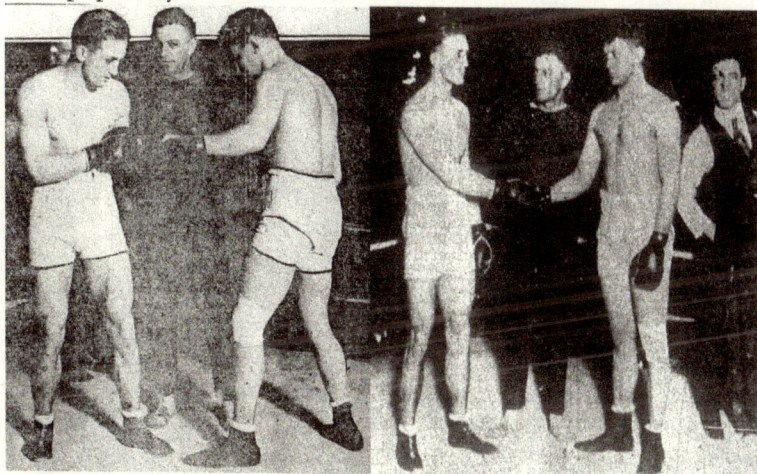

---

[311] *El Paso Times*, October 1, 1920.
[312] *New York Herald*, October 26, 1920.
[313] *New York Evening World*, September 30, 1920; *Elizabeth City Independent*, October 1, 1920.

On October 12, 1920 in Jersey City, New Jersey, before a crowd of about 15,000 - 20,000, in a fight for the world light heavyweight championship, 170 ½-pound Georges Carpentier knocked out 175-pound veteran Battling Levinsky for the 10-count in the 4th round. In the 2nd round, Carpentier decked Levinsky twice, with a flock of rights and lefts. The knockout blows in the 4th round were a right smash to the jaw followed quickly by a sharp left uppercut.

In over 230 fights, including against Miske and Brennan, the only man to have stopped Battling Levinsky other than Carpentier was Jack Dempsey, who in 1918 did so in the 3rd round. Since his last loss, which was over a year prior, a September 1919 LND10 Harry Greb, Levinsky had gone 10-0-3, including victories over Bartley Madden, Clay Turner, and Bert Kenny. Georges Carpentier had shown not only that he was clever, but had a mighty wallop in either hand.

Afterwards, Levinsky said Carpentier hit even harder than Dempsey. He knew what he was talking about, having fought both. "Why, when that Frenchman knocked me down with that right hand wallop in the second round, I thought a building had fallen on me. ... That boy can sure wallop, I'm telling the world, and he ought to make Dempsey hustle to beat him."

Jack Kearns said Carpentier "is one of the greatest punchers in the world. Of all the present-day fighters he is the one who could give Jack Dempsey a stiff battle."

Louis De Casanova said Carpentier had a pleasing personality, a hard punch with both hands, a rough and tumble method of boxing, and a fairly nimble pair of legs. Yet, it was a question whether he could stand up before half a dozen recognized heavyweights, let alone Dempsey, the kingpin of them all.

Charles Mathison said Carpentier impressed the great throng with his skill and punching power. He had earned a match with Dempsey. Yet, nine out of ten believed that Dempsey would settle him in jig time.[314]

The *New York Daily News* asked whether Carpentier could cope with Dempsey, and responded that experts generally believed that he should avoid Jack. Fans conceded that Carpentier was a great fighter, with skill, speed, and a wonderful wallop, but they were not prepared to say he was big enough to tackle such a tough proposition. Some said he was a wide-open fighter, at times wild with his swings, and that Dempsey would hit him. No one could grow lax with Dempsey even for a moment and get away with it.

However, Carpentier had a legion of supporters who insisted that he had everything that made up a great fighter, and they wanted to see him fight Dempsey. Robert Edgren called Carpentier brilliant and dashing, easily the king of his class. The *New York Journal*'s Bill Hicks said Carpentier's slamming of Levinsky all over the ring, knocking him out in

[314] *New York Daily News, Brooklyn Daily Times, Brooklyn Citizen, Brooklyn Daily Eagle, New York Herald,* October 13, 1920.

the 4th round, showed him to be a wonderful two-handed fighter with a kick that could finish anyone.

The general view of experts was that Carpentier was the world's best light heavyweight, but that going out of his division to meet such a great puncher and ring general as Dempsey would prove to be too much. Many said it would be a great fight, but Dempsey simply was too powerful and would outclass him, for he was the greatest champion ever.

Tex Rickard said, "Carpentier is a very good fighter… There is one thing certain, he can punch. I don't care to say how I think he would class with Dempsey."

Welterweight champ Jack Britton said of Carpentier, "I must admit that he is a very good fighter, an aggressive fellow, a heavy hitter and one anxious to fight. I think he can give Dempsey a good fight."

Benny Leonard said a good little man usually loses to a good big man. Carpentier was a classy fighter, but Dempsey's superiority in weight and hitting would make him too much.

Tom O'Rourke said Carpentier was confident, tricky, and slippery, with a knockout punch. Levinsky did not extend him even slightly.[315]

The *New York Herald's* Daniel wanted Carpentier to prove his fitness for a Dempsey bout by fighting Harry Wills. "If Carpentier really wants to fight Dempsey let him meet Wills first. That's fair."[316]

Chester Gumpert, a New York stock broker, got into a physical altercation with his pretty young wife Louise, which left both of them well marked up. Gumpert was charged with wife-beating.

Gumpert, of 15 Broad street, claimed that Jack Dempsey was the cause of their trouble, for Jack had visited his pretty young wife the previous night (and on other occasions) at her apartment at 226 West 70th street. (For whatever reason, the Gumperts were not living together.) Gumpert claimed that his wife threatened to have Dempsey beat him up.

However, Mrs. Gumpert denied knowing Dempsey, except by sight. She brought a separation suit, charging that her husband beat her.[317]

Chester Gumpert claimed the champ frequently called on his wife Louise Gumpert

The *Buffalo Times* (possibly Edgren) said the trouble with Dempsey was that he was too good. Promoters and the public were concerned that they would not get a good run for their money. Dempsey was too honest of a

[315] *New York Daily News, New York Evening World,* October 14, 1920.
[316] *New York Herald,* October 16, 1920.
[317] *New York Daily News,* October 15, 16, 1920.

fighter for his own good, by failing to pull and hold back in his fights and make them competitive. Years before, Abe Attell had scored early knockouts, but discovered that he could earn more money by holding back a bit, which he did. Johnny Kilbane did the same. "Jack Johnson was a natural born framer." Johnson boxed to draws, carried opponents, and got purses he would not have obtained if he had done his best in every round. Was that advice to Dempsey?[318]

Jim Corbett claimed the New York Athletic Commission feared that Dempsey might slaughter Brennan and cause the reformers to rise up and condemn the political administration that backed the boxing law in New York. Hence, they wanted to postpone Dempsey-Brennan until after the election, just in case.

The Boston commission had refused to sanction Dempsey bouts with Gunboat Smith and Frank Moran, likely for the same reasons. They feared that Dempsey was entirely too formidable.

Corbett said it was an injustice to Dempsey to prevent him from fighting and earning a living.

Jack Curley said Carpentier had more than an even chance to beat Dempsey. He had multiple styles of fighting at his disposal. He could fight and he could box. He was fast, could punch hard, and was clever. He could take the offensive or defensive. He knew how to feint and take advantage of openings in lightning fashion. He knew every trick. Some claimed he was too open against Levinsky, but they forgot to mention that he started the fight tightly covered, and not until he took his measure and weakened Levinsky did Georges venture forth with his open style.[319]

The *New York Daily News* reported that a Dempsey-Carpentier fight was a certainty. According to those in the know, they practically were matched to fight for Tex Rickard, and only a few legal obstacles stood in the way. Others wanted to fight Carpentier, including Mike O'Dowd, Tommy Gibbons, and Harry Greb, but it appeared that the lucrative heavyweight championship fight was going to be clinched soon.[320]

The *New York Herald's* Daniel asked why Dempsey was indifferent about Wills. For whatever reason, Wills was not getting as much of a boost that his victory over Fulton should have given his position.

> We note a strange apathy in the Dempsey camp whenever the name of Wills comes up. Can it be possible that the world's champion is afraid of the negro? Before Wills met Fulton Dempsey let it be announced that he would meet the winner. He also let it be announced that he had abandoned the color line. ... Now Dempsey's manager says that the champion will meet the black only if the public shows that it wants such a match.

[318] *Buffalo Times*, October 17, 1920.
[319] *Binghamton Press, Buffalo Commercial*, October 18, 1920.
[320] *New York Daily News*, October 19, 1920.

Daniel said that at the moment, the two men who stood out as worthy of a match with Dempsey were Brennan and Wills.[321]

Edward Tranter said many conceded Wills to be the logical candidate for the title. "The fact that Wills is a negro has prevented him from getting many contests, most of the heavyweight battlers of the Caucasian race respectfully declining the issue on the plea of drawing the color line."[322]

Grantland Rice said Carpentier was a fast, well-trained boxer with a punch, and would have a chance to beat Dempsey. Both carried dynamite in their gloves, so the fight might be short and abrupt, but exciting for as long as it lasted.[323]

On October 20, 1920, in Media, Pennsylvania, Jack Dempsey attended the opening of the Rose Tree Hunt Club's race meet. Admirers mobbed the champ so much that it was necessary to call out more than a dozen reserve officers. Dempsey met world's champion sculler Jack Kelly, as well as famous racing horse Man o'

THREE WORLD CHAMPIONS.—Three absolute monarchs of their own fields are shown at the Rose Tree Hunt Club's race meet at Media, Pa. From left to right are Jack Kelly, world's champion sculler; Man o' War and Jack Dempsey.

War, who many to this day consider the greatest race horse ever, winning 20 of 21 career races. His only loss was in 1919, to a colt named Upset.[324]

On October 21, 1920 in South Bend, Indiana, 2,000 people saw Pittsburgh's "Rubber Ball," 165-pound Harry Greb, knock out 175- or 177-pound Gunboat Smith in the 1st round.

Eugene Kessler said Greb completely outclassed him.

> Harry showed superb speed, dancing around Smith like a flash and landing ten clean blows within a few seconds. A right body jab doubled the Gunner up, six or eight short right and left hooks made him clinch and hang on and a right hook over the eye dropped him in a semi-conscious condition.

Smith's right eye was in very bad condition. (Smith later claimed that he was thumbed in the eye.)

M. F. Scully said Greb's first blow blinded the Gunner. "A few seconds of sparring, a long lunging left to the eye by Greb, a clinch and E. Smith's count of ten over the prostrate form of Gunboat Smith" was all there was to it. After being hit in the eye, following a clinch and break,

[321] New York Herald, October 19, 1920.
[322] Buffalo Enquirer, October 20, 1920. Paddy Mullins, who managed Wills and former middleweight champion Mike O'Dowd, was willing to send either one into the ring with Carpentier.
[323] Glens Falls Post-Star, October 20, 1920.
[324] New York Herald, Brooklyn Daily Eagle, October 21, 1920. Likely incorrect legend has it that Upset's defeat of Man o' War generated the famous term when an underdog wins: an "upset." Man O'War defeated Upset 4 out of the 5 times they raced.

Smith reeled and fell down, and Referee Ed Smith counted him out. Some cried fake. Yet, Smith was in acute pain, for his right eye was driven completely back from its socket. A couple minutes after it was over, the right side of his face became swollen.

Scully believed that Greb had earned a match with Carpentier for the light heavyweight championship.

Kessler reported that Promoter Floyd Fitzsimmons offered Greb, via his manager James Mason, a match with Dempsey. Mason agreed to come to Benton Harbor the following week to sign articles.[325]

Larney Lichtenstein subsequently claimed that Greb jammed his thumb into Gunboat Smith's eye, blinding him temporarily, which set up the knockout blow. "My observation of Greb's record convinces me that he resorts whenever he can to such tactics."

Greb retorted, "I didn't jam my thumb into Smith's eye at all. I hit him in the eye with everything I had – then I hit in a few other places. Smith went down and was counted out." Greb further said if it did happen, it was an accident.

However, "Examination by physicians forced the conviction that a punch could hardly have caused the injury – that only a jamming of a finger of a gloved thumb into the eye could have brought about such a condition." Lichtenstein further said, "The sporting world undoubtedly was surprised when it read that Greb, ordinarily a light hitter, could stop so tough a man as Smith in one round. And it's no wonder that it is puzzled." He said Greb could not score a knockout using fair tactics.[326]

On October 22, it was reported that sources had learned that the previously delayed Jack Dempsey vs. Bill Brennan contest would take place on November 26 at Madison Square Garden; 15 rounds for the world's championship.[327]

Ted Hooks of the black-owned *New York Age* said Harry Wills had the heavyweights too frightened to fight him, including Jack Dempsey. Hooks said it had to be frustrating to know you were the greatest fighter in the world, and have all the sane sporting writers and boxers know it, yet none of them be willing to admit your greatness to the public. That was Harry Wills' predicament. Such had been his situation for so long that he was accustomed to it. Inside dope was that Wills had agreed to lay down to Fulton, and that was why Dempsey had announced his willingness to meet the winner. Yet, Wills had pulled a double cross and fought to win. Now Dempsey and his manager were again hiding behind the color line.

> This despite the fact that some of the dailies threw their columns open to the public to state their opinions as to whether Dempsey should meet a colored man. Despite the overwhelming majority in letters to the paper favored and in some instances begged the champion to come out of his shell. Meanwhile Wills goes without

[325] *South Bend Tribune, South Bend News-Times,* October 22, 1920. In 1920, Gunboat Smith had losses to Bill Tate, Fred Fulton, Lee Anderson, and Chuck Wiggins, though he was coming off a WND10 Bob Roper.
[326] *Binghamton Press,* November 26, 1920.
[327] *New York Daily News,* October 22, 1920.

engagements. Dempsey claims that there is no one to meet him, and Carpentier [is] skillfully steered clear of the Negro. ... Wills has all the other heavies too scared to fight and few of them are as frightened as Jack Dempsey, who saw the rib crushing blow that ended Fred Fulton's aspirations.[328]

Robert Edgren said Carpentier was the best fighter from overseas since Charley Mitchell. "He is all he was said to be in skill, hitting power and splendid self-confidence." Carpentier carried the fight to Levinsky, showing amazing speed. At times he intentionally left himself open in order to get Levinsky to punch, so he could counter. He thought and acted in a flash. However, Dempsey was much stronger and sturdier, fully as skillful and fast, just as smart, and very accurate and efficient.[329]

The *New York Daily News* said Dempsey needed a real opponent, or else he would find himself in the same position that Sam Langford was in several years ago – having to carry his opponents. One suggestion was a tournament to develop an opponent.[330]

The *New York Herald's* Charles Mathison said the French, including French Canadians, would not acknowledge Dempsey as the true world champion unless and until he beat the European champ, Carpentier. One man said Carpentier was more agile, scientific, and faster, hit harder, and was smarter than Dempsey. Mathison said Dempsey was the undisputed champion because he beat Willard, who beat Johnson, who beat Burns and Jeffries.[331]

Kid McCoy advanced the idea that state boxing commissions should rate each fighter, so matchmakers would have something to guide them. The *Reading Times* printed its or McCoy's list of top 20 heavyweights.[332]

1—Jack Dempsey.
2—Harry Wills.
3—Jess Willard.
4—Fred Fulton.
5—Georges Carpentier.
6—Bill Brennan.
7—Bartley Madden.
8—Billy Miske.
9—Bob Martin.
10—Gene Tunney.
11—Willie Meehan.
12—Battling Levinsky.
13—Charlie Weinert.
14—Frank Moran.
15—Tom Cowler.
16—Martin Burke.
17—Jot Beckett.
18—Bob Boyer.
19—Gunboat Smith.
20—Al Reich.

On October 25, 1920 in Paterson, New Jersey, 174-pound Gene Tunney won a 10-round no decision over 172-pound Paul "Sampson" Koerner (13-5-2), doing most of the leading. The *Paterson Evening News'* Caesar wrote that the less said about the exhibition the better, for even Carpentier, who gave an exhibition earlier on the card, left his seat "in disgust" during the 7th round. Tunney failed to live up to his reputation as a "leading contender for the heavyweight title." Every time Sampson opened up, came out of his shell and attacked, Tunney retreated. "But for the fact that Sampson spent the greater part of the time in a clam-like defense, he would have copped the honors."

There was very little action, though in the 4th round, Tunney whipped in a right to the chin which sent Sampson to the canvas. Other than that, Tunney was a most "peaceful" man, and the crowd booed and hooted. They finally mixed it a bit in the 9th. In the 10th round, Sampson attacked,

[328] *New York Age*, October 23, 1920.
[329] *New York World*, October 23, 1920.
[330] *New York Daily News*, October 23, 1920.
[331] *New York Herald*, October 24, 1920.
[332] *Reading Times*, October 25, 1920.

backing Tunney around the ring, landing rights and lefts which drew blood from Gene's nose and mouth. Tunney fought back though, and was plastering him hard when the bell sounded. "The honors went to Tunney by a slim margin."

In sparring with Italian Joe Gans and Marcel Thomas earlier on the card, Georges Carpentier, "the million dollar idol of France," showed a couple thousand fans that "he can break almost every American heavyweight who might be pitted against him." He had a wonderful left jab and right cross. "If Gene Tunney's work last night is a criterion, it may be stated here that it would be the height of folly to send him against Carpentier, because Georges would annihilate him." Afterward, while smoking a cigarette, Carp signed autographs for a bunch of boys.

The *Paterson Morning Call* said, "Carpentier is all that has been said of him. He is one of the cleverest, if not the cleverest heavyweight that ever appeared here. He is as fast on his feet as a bantamweight and how he can hit when he wants to." The fans gave him a fine reception.

Tunney-Sampson did not come up to expectations, for although Tunney was willing to mix, Sampson had a wholesome respect for his right, and did little fighting, continually covering up. Tunney decked him in the 4th, though Sampson jumped right up before the referee began a count.

The *Hackensack Evening Record*'s R. H. Wynkoop said Tunney won because Sampson mostly covered up, only fighting on rare occasions. Half the fans left before the fight was over.[333]

Daniel noted that Dempsey did not attend Carpentier-Levinsky, and never had seen Carpentier fight. Conversely, Carpentier had been studying motion pictures of Dempsey-Willard. Georges said that in order to prepare for him, he had seen that film more than 50 times, and had taken careful note of Dempsey's way of doing things. Clearly, the films had been transported, either across state lines or overseas.

On October 26, the Dempsey and Carpentier parties (managers Jack Kearns and Francois Descamps) met with promoters and agreed to fight, with the formal articles scheduled to be signed the next day. The fight would take place sometime between Feb. 1 and July 15, 1921, in a bout between 10 and 15 rounds. Each fighter would receive 25% of the moving picture receipts, and the other 50% went to the promoters - Tex Rickard, London's Charles Cochran, and William A. Brady, Cochran's representative. Robert Edgren said the combination of promoters was hard to beat. John Ringling was a silent partner as well.

They would clash for a $500,000 purse, $300,000 to Dempsey and $200,000 to Carpentier, the largest purse ever by far, exceeding the $127,500 total paid for Dempsey-Willard.[334]

Dempsey still was scheduled to fight Bill Brennan in a 15-round bout at Madison Square Garden on November 26.[335]

[333] *Paterson Evening News, Paterson Morning Call, Hackensack Evening Record,* October 26, 1920. The *New York World* called it a draw.
[334] *Brooklyn Daily Eagle,* October 26, 1920; *New York Daily News, New York Tribune,* October 27, 1920.
[335] *Yonkers Herald,* October 27, 1920; *New York Daily News,* October 28, 1920.

When the parties, including the fighters, met on the 27th, Kearns did not want to sign the contract, because he (or his lawyer) found some terms to be objectionable, particularly concerning the forfeit money. The final details needed to be fleshed out.

When they met, Georges commented on Dempsey's "meelyon dollah smile." Jack replied, "You got a pretty good one yourself."[336]

Dempsey went to Montreal for some exhibition work with Bill Tate. On November 2, he allegedly announced that he had agreed to fight Willard again on March 17. However, a denial soon followed.[337]

On November 5, 1920 at the Hotel Claridge in Manhattan, New York, Dempsey and Carpentier signed a contract binding them to meet either in March or between May 29 and July 4. The bout would be from 10 to 15 rounds, date and location to be determined by January 21. By November 20, the promoters had to post/deposit $100,000 forfeit money with a trust company as a guarantee, and the contestants each had to post $50,000 forfeits as their performance guarantees. Dempsey would earn a guaranteed $300,000 and Carpentier $200,000. The *New York Evening World*'s Robert Edgren would be the stakeholder.[338]

l to r, standing: Jack Kearns, Senator William Lyons, Robert Edgren, Harry Heckheimer, Nathan Vidaver, Captain Moffat; seated: Jack Dempsey, William A. Brady, Charles Cochran, Tex Rickard, Georges Carpentier, and Francois Descamps.

Vincent Treanor said that as he signed, Dempsey appeared to be the least interested of all in the proceedings. Yet, he was friendly. "Like the old-fashioned ward politician, Dempsey had a word for nearly everybody, and a pat on the shoulder. He has a remarkable memory for faces and names,

---

[336] *New York Daily News*, October 27, 28, 1920; *Brooklyn Daily Times*, October 28, 1920.

[337] *New York Herald, Brooklyn Standard Union*, November 3, 1920.

[338] *New York Daily News*, November 6, 1920. The contract stipulated that notice would be given on January 1 if the promoters wanted the contest to take place in March, and if so, the fighters would not engage in any other bout until then. If the promoters selected any day between May 29 and July 4, 1921, either contestant could engage in any contest up to May 21, but not thereafter.

too." He laughed and talked to the groups which surrounded him. Jack said he had been doing some training every day and playing golf.

The *Brooklyn Daily Eagle's* Louis De Casanova noted that although the motion pictures of Dempsey-Carpentier could not be shown in the U.S. (other than in the state where they were taken), they could be shown overseas, where a fortune could be generated.

Physically, it looked as if Dempsey could break Carpentier in two. Of course, that was the impression one got when Willard stood next to Dempsey, too. One observer said a man with a punch always was dangerous, and Carpentier had a punch powerful enough to win.

The *New York Herald's* Daniel said Dempsey stood alone as the world's best fighter, and there was no second. "But he must make more money, and Carpentier is the only man in the world who can give him a chance to make it in large wads."[339]

The next day, Carpentier set sail back to France.[340]

Carpentier and Descamps

Former lightweight champion Jack McAuliffe said Dempsey would find it easy to hit Carpentier, and he had more power behind his punch. McAuliffe said he had boxed with both men, so his opinion was based on his experience in the ring with each. The Dempsey-McAuliffe sparring was filmed, and it shows Dempsey lightly bouncing around, playing defense, moving his head, and tapping McAuliffe.

> I like Dempsey's style of boxing and I don't like the form of Carpentier. Dempsey slides in and glides around like a panther. I have never boxed with a man so hard to hit. He has a clever knack of twisting his head that makes even the best directed shot just a glancing blow. On the other hand, Carpentier comes in straight and rushes in a crouched position. This style of fighting would be pie for the champion. Another thing. I don't like Carpentier's overhand punching. He leaves himself wide open and gets himself off his balance. … [Dempsey] rocked me several times with short blows that didn't come more than an inch or two and yet he insisted that he was drawing them. Both are punchers, but Dempsey has more behind them. … I don't believe anyone's defense is strong enough to withstand the kick that the champion puts in a blow.

[339] *Brooklyn Daily Eagle*, November 5, 6, 1920; *New York World*, *New York Herald*, November 6, 1920.
[340] *New York World*, November 6, 1920; *Brooklyn Daily Times*, November 7, 1920.

Although Jack Curley said Carpentier had 57 styles of fighting, one for every kind of fighter, McAuliffe said he would need all of them to keep from getting pickled by one of Dempsey's blows. Carp had great confidence, but that would not stop a railroad express train from running a man over, and it would not stop Dempsey.[341]

James J. Corbett said Dempsey would be meeting the fastest man of his career when he entered the ring with Carpentier. Dempsey admirers claimed that he could take more punishment than any man in the game, could hit harder, and was speedier with both hands and feet. Corbett said never had Jack been tested the way Carpentier would test him, for Georges was very fast and powerful, with both hands and feet. Dempsey showed his speed against Miske, who also was known for being very fast.

Corbett noted that boxing had come back in New York, for wildly enthusiastic throngs had turned out for every fistic clash since the new law became operative. Madison Square Garden's seating capacity had been expanded to nearly 15,000, and yet there still were not enough seats. The only other club that had been operating was the Commonwealth Sporting club, which was small in comparison, but still packed every fight night. Boxing once again was a major sport in Gotham. However, there had not yet been a championship contest.[342]

The *Buffalo Commercial* noted that with the election over, the first heavyweight match to be held in New York likely (or hopefully) would be Dempsey vs. Brennan.[343]

A November 18, 1915 check for $50 was produced, endorsed by Dempsey, the amount he was paid for a fight in Cripple Creek, Colorado with George Coplen, which he won in the 6th round. Ed Gaylord refereed. The champ would earn 6,000 times that amount to fight Carpentier.[344]

Some asked whether Dempsey could take Carpentier's punch. Dempsey could punch, but could he take it and return the compliment, was what fight fans were asking. Kearns replied, "You bet your life he can take it." Even when Dempsey was green, when he fought Gunboat Smith, the Gunner landed a big punch flush on Jack's jaw that could have laid out anyone. Jack not only took it but got the Gunboat into a corner and whaled on him. Between rounds, Jack didn't appear to hear or understand a word of advice Kearns gave him, but nevertheless he came out crowding the old sailor with his short punches and mixed it up, toe to toe. When the 4th round was over, the referee awarded Dempsey the decision. Afterwards, in the dressing room, Jack asked Kearns, "Who won the fight? How did we make out?" "That boy Dempsey was virtually out from the time that Gunner landed the wallop…but the old fighting instinct within him kept him going and landed him the winner, just as it does every time that he is stung." Smith later told Kearns that he put

[341] *Brooklyn Daily Times*, November 6, 1920.
[342] *Binghamton Press*, November 6, 1920.
[343] *Buffalo Commercial*, November 6, 1920. Dempsey had been in Montreal, giving exhibitions with Bill Tate. There was talk of Tate fighting Harry Wills.
[344] *Buffalo Times*, November 7, 1920.

everything he had into the punch that he landed on Dempsey, and when he saw the latter plunge right back at him, he lost heart and was satisfied that Dempsey could not be beaten.[345]

Jim Corbett said Kearns had done much to boost the fight game in the U.S. His managerial genius had brought Dempsey from obscurity to fame and the championship. Countless columns of publicity brought reawakened interest in boxing, generating thousands of new enthusiasts, and restored pugilism to life from the comatose condition it had known for years. Corbett said no man other than Dempsey could have beaten Willard. If not for that victory, the heavyweight division would be as dead today as it had been for several years.

Dempsey started off as a mining-camp battler, powerful but crude, inaccurate with his punches, with little defense, and he took a lot of pounding. He became disgruntled with the game, and in early 1917 decided he had enough of it. He got a job in a shipbuilding plant. But then Kearns dug him up. He saw his potential, and worked with Dempsey on his defense, punching techniques, and accuracy. Kearns told him that he could be developed into a champion. Dempsey took his advice and improved. Kearns skillfully managed and developed him. With the publicity he obtained as a result of his performances, interest in boxing revived. Folks were excited again.

Dempsey's overwhelming victory over Willard, and Carpentier's impressive victory over Joe Beckett, led to a natural international matchup. Once more, prominent men in the sporting world started agitation for restoration of the boxing game in the Empire state, clamoring for a fight law, until their plea finally was answered. "But no one has tossed the well-earned bouquets at Jack Kearns for the mighty part he played in it. For, if it hadn't been for Jack Kearns of California, Dempsey today might be a ship builder, Willard would be champion – and interest in boxing would be at an ebb even lower than it was before Kearns restored it to life."[346]

The *New York Tribune's* W. O. McGeehan noted that there was a lot of worry about boxing's future in New York. Politics always was involved in the sport and the making of big fights, and the promoters were anxious to hear from new governor-elect Nathan Miller, for they did not know how he would regard Dempsey-Carpentier. Tex Rickard once had invested a lot of money into building an arena for Johnson-Jeffries, after the governor told him the fight would be allowed in California, but then, after the arena was half-built, the governor reversed course and said neither that fight nor any boxing would be allowed in California. Rickard made the shift to Reno, but it cost him many a gray hair, as well as a lot of money. Hence, before building any new arena in New York, Rickard wanted assurances. New Jersey might allow the bout, but its laws authorized only 12-round no decision contests (no points decisions).[347]

[345] *New York Daily News*, November 8, 1920.
[346] *Binghamton Press*, November 10, 1920.
[347] *New York Tribune*, November 11, 1920.

Carpentier's manager Francois Descamps said, "Americans have remembered that Carpentier was beaten by Klaus [1912 LDQ19], Papke [1912 LTKOby18] and Jeannette [1914 L15], forgetting that he was only 18 years old when he met Klaus, that he trained down too fine in order to make the weight for the Papke battle [at middleweight] and that the referee erred in the Jeannette decision." Klaus had 86 fights of experience, and Papke 56. The March 1914 decision loss to Jeannette, a man who had over 100 fights of experience, when Georges was only 20 years old, was the last time that Carpentier had lost a fight. He was older, more mature and experienced now, and did not have to worry about his weight at all.[348]

On November 12, it was reported that Dempsey likely would defend his title against Bill Brennan in early December. The bout had been scheduled to be held in early October, then November 24 or 26, but owing to the state boxing commission's continued reluctance to issue a license for a heavyweight championship fight, the match was postponed yet again. Tex Rickard was promoting the contest.[349]

Carpentier said the winner of his fight with Dempsey would be the one who landed the first heavy blow. They would feel each other out carefully, then attempt to land the weakening blow that would spell the beginning of the end. Both of them could punch with knockout force, so likely the one who landed the first big blow would win. He would endeavor to be first, and avoid Dempsey's terrific punches. He was not underrating Dempsey. He did not think the fight would last more than 8 rounds.

Carpentier said Dempsey was an amiable gentleman. They got along well. They even played golf together. Georges claimed he beat Jack at a game of golf (though he later claimed the opposite). When he set sail back to France, Dempsey sent him a wireless message wishing him Godspeed.[350]

Word was that the New York boxing commission soon would let down the bars and allow Dempsey-Brennan. "Brennan is no star of the first magnitude, but he is a good, willing scrapper and for a while at least will be in there battling the champion."

Kearns/Dempsey were considering going to California to film another serial. *Daredevil Jack* already had netted the champ over $100,000.[351]

Some fighters liked to watch and scout other fighters to study their methods, strengths, and weaknesses. Yet, Dempsey had not seen Carpentier fight, and did not bother to see him against Levinsky. "I'll find out all I want to find out about him when I meet him in the ring."[352]

In mid-November 1920, Jim Corbett said the New York commission seemed to frown on heavyweight clashes. It had refrained from authorizing any heavyweight contest thus far. If they were concerned

[348] *New York Daily News*, November 11, 1920.
[349] *Buffalo Courier*, November 13, 1920.
[350] *New York Daily News, Buffalo Courier, Brooklyn Daily Times*, November 15, 1920.
[351] *Brooklyn Daily Times*, November 15, 1920. Kearns was looking to match Bill Tate with Harry Wills.
[352] *New York Tribune*, November 15, 1920.

about excessive brutality, they were mistaken. Lightweight bouts often were even more brutal.[353]

On November 17, the *New York Daily News* reported that an authoritative source informed it that Dempsey-Brennan would be held at Madison Square Garden on December 14. It would be the first heavyweight contest since the Walker law went into effect.[354]

The head of the International Reform Bureau asked for a repeal of the boxing law and for the prevention of Dempsey-Carpentier in New York. He said boxing had become thoroughly commercialized, and in the interest of true, clean sport, the Walker law should be repealed. Vigorous action would be taken to prevent Dempsey-Carpentier. "It is impossible to have true sport when the money element is injected into it." He called the sport brutal and immoral.[355]

The *Brooklyn Daily Times* alerted readers that multiplying signs indicated that Dempsey-Carpentier would not take place in New York. Republican leaders said Republican Governor-elect Nathan Miller would step in if an attempt was made to hold the fight in New York. "Their statement is not to be taken lightly. Up-State Republican politicians know invariably what they are talking about." Miller would cater to those elements which supported him, who were opposed to boxing, particularly any fight that involved so much money. Rather than hurt boxing as a whole and risk repeal of the boxing law, it would be best to hold the big fight elsewhere. Hence, chances were poor for Dempsey-Carpentier to be held in New York.[356]

[353] *Binghamton Press*, November 15, 1920.
[354] *New York Daily News*, November 17, 1920.
[355] *New York Tribune*, November 17, 1920.
[356] *Brooklyn Daily Times*, November 17, 1920.

CHAPTER 7

Bill Brennan

After several delays and uncertainty regarding whether or when it would be authorized, on November 18, 1920, the New York boxing board sanctioned the 15-round Jack Dempsey vs. Bill Brennan heavyweight championship fight, to be held on December 14 at Madison Square Garden, promoted by Tex Rickard. It would be the first heavyweight contest under the Walker law. They would fight to an official decision. The commissioners declared that a point had been reached in the operation of the new boxing law wherein they felt justified in permitting heavyweight boxing contests. Hence, their self-created ban on heavyweight contests was lifted. Others said it was because the election season was over, and heavyweight fights always garnered the greatest publicity and therefore concomitant political pressures. The Garden management would charge no more than $25 for the best seats.[357]

27-year-old "K. O." Bill Brennan had over 80 fights of experience under his belt, with a 60-13-8 known record. Also known as Bill Shanks or Wilhelm Schenck, he was born on June 23, 1893 in Ireland, and was a couple years older than Dempsey. He stood 6'1" and was about 10 pounds bigger than Dempsey, typically weighing around 200 pounds. He was known for his toughness, skill, and solid punch. His first fight with Dempsey was considered highly entertaining, for Brennan showed rare gameness, absorbing punishing blows, getting knocked down, but rising and fighting back hard throughout, landing some heavy blows of his own until stopped in the 6th round, lasting longer than anyone since 1918 other than Miske (10, 6, and 3) or Carl Morris (4, 6, and 1).[358]

Since being stopped by Dempsey in 1918, major bouts on Brennan's record included: 1918 DND10 Tom McMahon, DND8 Bartley Madden, and TKO3 Joe Bonds; 1919 LND10 (thrice) Harry Greb, L15 and DND8 Billy Miske (the local paper said both were capable of winning the title), L15 Greb, KO2 Tom McMahon, and WND6 Sailor Ed Petroskey; 1920 WND10 and D/WND12 Bartley Madden[359], D/LND10 Bob Roper, WND10 Bob Devere, WND6 Willie Meehan, and KO8 Ole Anderson. Bill had 31 more fights of experience since the loss to Dempsey. In 1920 alone, Brennan had gone 13-0-2, with 8 KOs. Dempsey had been the only man ever to stop the durable Brennan in his entire 7-year career.

---

[357] *Buffalo Express*, *New York Daily News*, November 19, 1920.
[358] Prior to fighting Dempsey the first time, Brennan had victories that included KO7 and TKO3 George Rodel, KO8 Tony Ross, WND10 Terry Kellar, KO3 Joe Cox, WND10 Homer Smith, KO2 Joe Bonds, WND10 Bob Devere, WND10 Bartley Madden, W12 Battling Levinsky, and WND10 Tom McMahon. He also had a 10-round newspaper draw with Jim Coffey, which some thought Brennan won.
[359] *Brooklyn Daily Times* reported that Brennan shaded Madden over 12 rounds. *New York Evening World* said they boxed to a hard draw in a nip and tuck battle all the way. Brennan was the aggressor. *New York Tribune* and *Jersey Journal* reported a draw. June 5, 1920.

"BILL" BRENNAN

Dempsey, who already had been training for a couple months in anticipation of a potential fight, trained on an old 1807 U.S. military man-of-war battleship which now served as a training ship, called the U.S.S. Granite or Granite State, anchored in the Hudson River (also called the North River) at the foot of 96ᵗʰ street in Manhattan, New York. Others said it was located in the Riverside Drive section of New York, at the foot of W. 97ᵗʰ street and Broadway, which was the headquarters of the First Battalion, Naval Militia. James J. Corbett said Dempsey trained for an hour daily. With government consent, Dempsey used the unobstructed second deck as a gym. On the spacious upper deck, a ring had been erected. A variety of muscle-building devices were there as well.[360]

On Monday afternoon, November 22, at the 22ⁿᵈ Regiment Armory, Dempsey fired the starting gun to begin a bicycle race. About 10,000 participated.[361]

Photo at the left shows the start of the International six-day bicycle race in the Twenty-second armory, New York. Jack Dempsey, heavyweight champion (left) is about to fire the gun which will put the contestants into action.

That same day, Dempsey sparred 3 2-minute rounds with lightweight Joe Welling (52-26-12), who was preparing to fight lightweight champ Benny Leonard in four days.[362]

---

[360] *New York Daily News*, November 20, 1920; *Binghamton Press*, November 22, 1920. *Brooklyn Daily Eagle*, December 5, 1920.
[361] *New York Daily News*, November 22, 1920.
[362] *Brooklyn Citizen*, November 23, 1920.

Bill Brennan was training at Joe Thomas' farm near Providence, Rhode Island. The big Chicago-based fighter was said to be in great shape, confident that he would surprise and extend the champ.

In Salt Lake City, Dempsey's sister Effie charged her husband, William Barrow, age 24, with assault and battery. Barrow defended himself, essentially claiming self-defense, saying, "My wife is the sister of Jack Dempsey, heavyweight champion of the world, and she can't forget she has fighting blood in her veins." Barrow was released when the complaining witness - his wife Effie, declined to appear against him.

In the *Buffalo Evening News*, Karpe's Comment said the man that Dempsey should meet next was Harry Greb. Karpe believed that Carpentier should have fought Greb to prove himself to the American public, not the shopworn Levinsky.

> I think that Greb's peculiar in and out tactics and galloping footwork would likely bother the champion considerably. If Jack should get in one of his sockdolagers, of course it would be all off, but Greb is not very easy to hit. Greb points out that he has beaten Levinsky 12 times and Bill Brennan four times. He also declared that Dempsey is trying to engage him as a sparring partner to avoid being challenged.[363]

On November 25, Dempsey was in Hackensack, New Jersey. He spoke with local high school football players, watched them in a game, and signed hundreds of souvenirs. "A great man is this bashful champion who makes multitudes of friends wherever he goes."[364]

On November 25, 1920 in Philadelphia, 175-pound Gene Tunney won a 6-round no decision over 173-pound Leo Houck (134-36-25), his most experienced foe to that point.[365]

Dempsey took to the Broadway Theatre stage briefly as a guest to assist Jack McAuliffe in his vaudeville monologue.[366]

Henry Farrell said Dempsey was a new type of champ. He went to bed every night at 10 p.m., and he hated to talk for publication. Success had not turned his head, and he had not been felled by temptation. "He's the same big affable boy with the same pleasant smile that won him friends by the legion in Toledo." He was a clean-living athlete, and unlike other champs, had not succumbed to the "bright lights." Other champs found training a bore once they became champion, and lived the fast-paced life that ruined their boxing careers.

Dempsey said he woke at 6 a.m. and ran through Central Park. After breakfast and an hour rest, he took a long walk. After lunch, he went to his training quarters and put in two or three hours, working with the rope, the bells, medicine ball, shadow boxing, and a few rounds of sparring with

[363] *New York Daily News, Brooklyn Daily Times, Buffalo Evening News*, November 24, 1920.
[364] *Hackensack Evening Record*, November 26, 1920.
[365] *Philadelphia Evening Public Ledger, St. Louis Post-Dispatch*, November 26, 1920.
[366] *New York World*, November 27, 1920.

Bill Tate, Ray Smith, and various others who came around. He mixed in golf when he got the chance.

Jack enjoyed watching boxing, but did not like to stay up late, and did not like smoke-filled arenas, which did more harm than good, so he did not attend many fights.

Farrell said,

> Dempsey has a lot of personality. He has that happy faculty of meeting people well and remembering them the second time. He never 'high-brows.' He's accessible at all times and he'll dig in his pocket for any cause.
>
> Talk with him for an hour and he will scarcely ever speak in the first person. He's no master of English but he's grammatical and he isn't handicapped with a lot of vulgar parlance of the ring.
>
> It's a hard task to get him to talk about any of his conquests. He always refers to one of his vanquished opponents as a 'mighty good boy.'

Dempsey never made predictions, and did not presume victory over Carpentier or anyone else. Jack said, "Carpentier is a great boy. He's bound to be a fighter with the experience he's had. I never pick a winner in advance of anything."[367]

On November 26, 1920 at Madison Square Garden, Dempsey and Kearns saw Benny Leonard pummel Joe Welling until the bout was stopped in the 14th round. The gate was at least $100,000, possibly the biggest ever drawn by lightweights. Gans-Nelson at Goldfield drew around $70,000. Arnold Rothstein, "who has received a little more publicity lately than he cares for," was present.[368]

New York Daily News writer Harry Newman said one never could take anything for granted in boxing, for wild or lucky punches had changed outcomes in boxing before, and Bill Brennan was big, strong, tough, and could punch.[369]

Floyd Fitzsimmons was negotiating with Kearns for a potential 10-round bout between Harry Greb and Dempsey. "Greb has been trying to get into the ring with Dempsey for several months." He particularly wanted to fight Dempsey after beating Gunboat Smith.[370]

On the U.S.S. Granite State, 118-pound bantamweight Jackie Sharkey was sparring with Dempsey that week in preparation for Sharkey's upcoming contest with Joe

Dempsey Down to Bantam Class With Sharkey

[367] *Buffalo Times, Buffalo Evening News*, November 27, 1920.
[368] *Buffalo Courier*, November 27, 1920. 150-pound Panama Joe Gans knocked out 158-pound George Christian in the 3rd round (for the colored middleweight crown). In 1916, Dempsey had stopped Christian in the 1st round.
[369] *New York Daily News*, November 29, 1920.
[370] *New York Daily News, New York Herald*, November 30, 1920.

Lynch. Little Sharkey said, "Dempsey gives me a swell workout together with advising and teaching me all the tricks which he has mastered."

There was talk of and negotiations for a potential Willard-Dempsey rematch to be held on March 17, 1921. Some reported/claimed that Willard had signed a contract with Rickard.[371]

James J. Corbett noted that although Dempsey had won their prior bout via technical knockout, he had not floored Brennan for the count. Dempsey had improved considerably since then. He hit straighter, truer, and harder, and was bigger. Still, so long as Brennan was on his feet, he would be dangerous. He carried dynamite in his right hand, having knocked out more than 50 opponents in a few years. He too had improved, with far more bouts than Dempsey since their contest.

Ultimately though, Corbett predicted a Dempsey win by knockout, for he had the advantage of speed, hitting power, and boxing ability. He had better defense, was one of the fastest big men ever, and crushed his foes when he landed solidly. The fight would give New Yorkers a chance to see in action the man ranked with the greatest fighters who ever lived.[372]

Harry Greb claimed to have the best right to meet Dempsey. Greb pointed out that he had victories over Brennan, Levinsky, Meehan, Madden, the Gibbons brothers, Dillon, and others. Greb was at least 1-1-1 against Miske, beating Billy clearly the last time they fought, 2-0 against Meehan, and 4-0 against Brennan.

Greb intimated very strongly that Dempsey was afraid to box him. He said Jack ran out of a proposed match at Milwaukee in which he could have earned $60,000 for a 10-round bout. However, newsmen said even Dempsey's worst enemies would admit that he was not afraid of anyone. The *Ithaca Journal* wrote, "Almost everyone except Harry and his manager, Reddy Mason, will admit Greb wouldn't have a chance against the champion." Furthermore, Dempsey would earn more than that for the Brennan fight. It later was revealed that Rickard was going to pay Dempsey $100,000 to fight Brennan. Dempsey earned more than $67,000 for the Miske contest, possibly around $87,500. Hence, his price appeared to be going up with each contest.

Greb remarked that Kearns and Dempsey were trying to line him up as a sparring partner in order to establish an amicable understanding so that Greb would be out of consideration when it came to picking opponents. He said training with Dempsey when Jack was preparing for Miske only gave him confidence, for he knew all about the champion. He didn't want to spar with Dempsey; he wanted to fight him.[373]

Right or wrong, the perception by most was that the 5'8" 160-165-pound middleweight simply was too small and not a hard enough puncher to have any real chance against Dempsey, who was much bigger, and a

[371] *Buffalo Commercial*, November 26, 1920; *New York Daily News*, December 1, 1920; *New York Herald*, December 4, 1920.
[372] *Binghamton Press*, December 1, 1920.
[373] *Ithaca Journal*, December 1, 1920.

tremendous puncher with speed and relentlessness. In addition to all of his size deficiencies, Greb rarely won by knockout. Most thought he did not have the punching power to keep Dempsey off him or the physical frame to withstand Dempsey's brand of power. The hard-punching Brennan was close to 200 pounds, and Dempsey about 190, so the matchup was an easier sell to the public. Even the fast, skillful, and famously durable Miske at 187 pounds could not get out of the 3rd round with the champion.

Of course, that did not mean Greb would not provide a challenging or interesting match, with his speed, punch volume, footwork, defense, versatility – ability to fight on the inside or outside, conditioning, toughness, and experience. Still, there was not a great push from the press for a Greb contest, nor was a really big purse offered, at least not one that was bigger than what Dempsey would earn for fighting others. The question for Kearns was how much money such a match would make for him and Dempsey versus the proposed purses for other potential matches.

Henry Farrell said New York Governor-elect Nathan Miller neither affirmed nor denied the reports that he was going to scrap the Walker bill, which made boxing promoters uneasy, including Tex Rickard, who was trying to decide where to hold Dempsey-Carpentier.[374]

Bill Brennan had been training for three months at Joe Thomas' gym in Providence, Rhode Island. He then moved his training to Stillman's gym in Harlem, but after two days, shifted to Billy Grupp's, also in Harlem. Jim Cullen trained him.

Dempsey had been training hard as well, for he respected Brennan. He said, "Nothing is ever absolutely sure in boxing."[375]

The *Brooklyn Citizen* opined, "Harry Wills will never get a shot at the title until Dempsey has played all white contenders off the boards again, just to prove he didn't win the title on a fluke."

Gordon Williams of the *Binghamton Press* thought Jess Willard was foolish to consider fighting Dempsey again. Some writers believed such a fight might kill boxing in New York, for Dempsey would brutalize him again. Willard was claiming that he did not train faithfully for the Dempsey fight, underestimating him. However,

> Jess moves too slowly and Dempsey can hit him from all angles. Giants are pie for Dempsey. It is the little fellows who give him trouble, although he disposed of Billy Miske without much trouble. It is the fact that Carpentier is just as fast as Dempsey and can hit just as hard that is convincing experts that the Frenchman has a chance with the world's champion.

Still, a Dempsey-Willard rematch would draw a large crowd, which Rickard knew. Money talked.[376]

---

[374] *Buffalo Times*, December 1, 1920.
[375] On December 1, Dempsey boxed 3 light rounds with bantam Jack Sharkey, who was set to fight the next day. On the 2nd, 117-pound Joe Lynch knocked out 118-pound Sharkey in the 15th round.

Harry Newman reported that on December 2, Dempsey sparred Bill Tate at a furious clip, but the big and shifty Tate gave Jack several hard wallops in return over the course of 4 very fast rounds. Dempsey took no rest between rounds, but instead worked on his footwork, prancing about the ring.

In the 1st round against Joe Roberts, "a dark spot from Boston," a sweeping Dempsey right sent the "spade" into the first row of spectators. He asked to be excused from further participation.

Dempsey also waded into white Dan O'Dowd without letup. O'Dowd's record included: 1919 LND8 Bill Brennan and LND8 Gene Tunney; and 1920 W10 Eddie McGoorty.

Good-natured Jack smiled a lot and did not mean to hurt his sparring partners. When he did, he apologized, "Excuse me, excuse me."

Jack said, "Brennan is a tough fellow, and I'll be in shape for him." "I always expect trouble from my opponents and have never yet neglected to prepare accordingly. Brennan is a big, shifty fellow and he gave me a great fight the last time we met."

A good sleeper, Dempsey went to bed at around 9 p.m., rose at 7 a.m., and went for a brisk walk. Breakfast consisted of toast, eggs, and fruit. At around 9 a.m., Dempsey walked or jogged 6-7 miles through Central Park or along the roads adjacent to Riverside Drive, where he found "the harbor air very beneficial." He then read a newspaper, magazine, or book. He kept up with current events. Jack enjoyed classy, jazzy music. At noon, trainer Ben Smith gave him a rubdown. He then had lunch. He was not a heavy eater, preferring vegetables, potatoes, and beans. But he also would have a nice juicy steak, or some chops.

In the afternoon at the gym (around 2 p.m.), Dempsey usually worked with chief sparring partner Bill Tate, who was big enough to stand up under the pretty rough milling. Tate was the only one who stood the gaff and consistently came back after Jack occasionally cut loose. Few sparring partners lasted very long. Most avoided Dempsey or quit quickly. Jack did not mean to be so rough but was so enthusiastic about everything that sometimes he got a little carried away.

When asked about the agitation against the sport of boxing, Jack said, "I can't see any reason for suppressing boxing. It may have its elements of danger, but when I was at school and played football, I suffered more injuries than I ever got in the prize ring." Ultimately, "The people of the country know what they want and will have it."[377]

Black fighters Kid Norfolk and Panama Joe Gans (a previous Dempsey sparring partner) were sparring with Brennan, who "appears to be in better shape at present than at any time in his ring career."[378]

The *Buffalo Commercial* noted that when Dempsey fought Brennan at Milwaukee, he hit Bill so hard that he broke Bill's ankle. For the rematch,

[376] *New York Daily News, New York Times, New York Herald, Buffalo Enquirer*, November 30, 1920; *Brooklyn Citizen, Buffalo Commercial, Binghamton Press*, December 2, 1920.
[377] *New York Herald*, December 3, 1920; *New York Daily News*, December 3, 4, 1920; *Brooklyn Daily Eagle*, December 5, 1920.
[378] *Buffalo Commercial*, December 2, 1920; *New York Daily News*, December 4, 1920.

"chances are Dempsey will clip Brennan on the chin and break his toes."[379]

After the Brennan fight, Dempsey planned to return to Los Angeles to appear in more moving pictures.[380]

The *Philadelphia Inquirer's* Joe Vila said Professor James De Forest, who had trained Dempsey for Willard, a week before the fight had predicted a 1st or 2nd round knockout for Dempsey over Willard.

> De Forest last summer told me at the Aqueduct race track that he had wound Dempsey's hands with adhesive tape, the kind he used to put on Kid McCoy's 'mawleys' in the old days. Perhaps the wise men knew something about the adhesive tape, which, it was said, enabled Dempsey to cut Willard's face into ribbons. De Forest, by the way, wasn't guilty of sharp practice, for Willard would have examined Dempsey's bandages minutely if he hadn't been overconfident.[381]

Regardless, their agreement allowed for tape and soft bandages.

De Forest later said the bandages he used on Dempsey were perfectly legal, and denied any claims that the bandages were doctored in any way.

The *Brooklyn Daily Eagle's* Ed Hughes said Dempsey was the lord of the ring, shattering the lofty aspirations of his antagonists in a few hurricane rushes punctuated with bone-crushing blows.

Dempsey lived like an aristocrat. He occupied a furnished 10-room apartment at 97th street, just off Broadway, in the 2 B Suite. It featured an elevator, phone, and maid service. The hallway was carpeted. "A Nubian elevator pilot rips the steel cage back with a crash." Jack inquired about the stability of the "market," meaning stock market.[382]

On December 4, Dempsey sparred 8 fast rounds with 230-pound Bill Tate, 210-pound "Adonis" Al Reich (28-11-1), Dan O'Dowd, Frankie Farrell, and Irish lightweight Patsy Kline, and at the end wasn't even puffing.

Tate had an almost impregnable defense, but Jack still rocked him with quick, stunning punches. At the conclusion of their 2 rounds, Tate exclaimed that he was sure there was a bell manufacturing concern in the vicinity. "At any rate, there's an awful clanging of 'em around heah somewhere. I heahs 'em every afternoon, jes' like I did at Toledah. Wish we could sometime find a trainin' spot where dey ain't a makin' dem bells all the time," he moaned.

Boston's Dan O'Dowd mixed it, and just before the end of the round, Dempsey let one go for real, Dan reeled into Referee Harry Neary's arms, and a halt was called. O'Dowd survived another round, though.

Frankie Farrell, another Bostonian, was hammered for a round.

---

[379] *Buffalo Commercial*, December 3, 1920.
[380] *New York Times*, December 4, 1920. Teddy Hayes was in Los Angeles already, planning for Dempsey's arrival.
[381] *Philadelphia Inquirer*, December 4, 1920.
[382] *Brooklyn Daily Eagle*, December 5, 1920.

Big Al Reich, who was next, was respectful, particularly after he sampled a few blows. Dempsey weaved about in his puzzling manner, bobbing his head and body and striking viciously from every angle, which had Reich perceptibly worried.

Walter Monaghan, who trained Willard for Dempsey, was an interested observer. He said,

> Jack looks as good to me today as he did at Toledo. The coordination of mind and muscle in his boxing is really astounding. … In all his boxing I have never once seen him telegraph a blow. … Added to this singular process of mental and muscular co-ordination is his unerring timing and precision. He rarely misses the mark. His is the most natural, original and dangerous style I have ever seen in any fighter.

Kearns said everything necessary for Dempsey's comfort was kept at the apartment, so there was no need for reveling in the bright-light district of Broadway for his pleasures.

> As a matter of fact, Jack's not at all inclined that way. He's always at home here evenings, playing cards with his friends, enjoying his player-piano or victrola, or drawing on our fine library of books. He's the cleanest living champion the ring ever had. In fact, Jack likes the bright lights of literature and music more than those along Times Square. I don't claim Jack is a book worm; but he's been reading a lot here lately.

Dempsey was enjoying *Les Misérables*. For music, he liked "The Bell-Hop Blues" and the Grand March from Aida.[383]

Harry Newman said Dempsey cuffed the dickens out of his various sparring partners. Outside the ring, he was ever-smiling. "Dempsey is just a big boy who loves to see everybody happy, but is a veritable lion when unleashed in the ring with opponents."

When asked about his training and whether it was hard on him at times, Dempsey said, "No, I live a sort of methodical life, and the work just about enters into my everyday idea of living."

He had trouble retaining sparring partners. "You see, I sometimes forget that it is only a training stunt and frequently cut loose. Some boys don't like being mussed up, and the next day they forget to come back."

Jack never worried the night before a fight. "Not on your life. I haven't any time for worry. … I can imagine that worry has beaten many a good man, but if it ever comes along my way, I am going to get out of the game."[384]

---

[383] *Brooklyn Daily Eagle*, December 5, 1920. Al Reich's record included: 1915 LND10 and D10 Jim Flynn, TKO3 Arthur Pelkey, LND10 Porky Flynn, KO2 Al Norton, and LND10 Gunboat Smith; 1916 L12 Battling Levinsky, WND10 Porky Flynn, and LTKOby9 Fred Fulton; 1917 TKO5 Terry Kellar and LND10 Charley Weinert; 1919 TKO4 Porky Flynn; and 1920 WND6 Dan O'Dowd, KO11 Ole Anderson, and L15 Martin Burke. After the sparring, Dempsey reclined on the floor at full length and then pulled himself up to a sitting position, touching his toes, doing this about 50 times. Ten minutes of work at the wrist machines, a shower, and rubdown, and the day's work was complete. World bantam champ Pete Herman also was training with Dempsey on the Granite State. *Brooklyn Standard Union*, December 5, 1920.
[384] *Buffalo Express*, December 5, 1920.

Dean Snyder for the *Buffalo Times* said Brennan had been in hard training for three months in anticipation of the fight, making the most of his opportunity. In their first fight, Brennan sprained his ankle in one of his falls, and he claimed that hampered his performance thereafter.

DEMPSEY		BRENNAN
25	Age	27
188¼	Weight	197
6 ft. 1½ in.	Height	6 ft. 1½ in.
8 in.	Wrist	8 in.
8½ in.	Ankle	8 in.
17 in.	Neck	17 in.
15 in.	Biceps	15 in.
37 in.	Chest Normal	38 in.
41¼ in.	Chest Expanded	42¼ in.
29 in.	Waist	30½ in.
78 in.	Reach	77 in.
23 in.	Thigh	23 in.
18 in.	Calf	18 in.

The Brennan fight would be Dempsey's first in New York since winning the title. Although prior to becoming champion, Jack had fought in Buffalo, New York in 1918, as well as Harrison, New Jersey, he had not fought in the New York City area since 1916, when he was a relatively green nobody and fought in the Bronx and Harlem.

> The field of heavies is scarce pickin's at best. Harry Wills and Tate are about the two most formidable fellows they could stack up against Jack. But both are colored. Tate, of course, being a sparring partner, is out of the question just now and Wills will never get a shot at the title until Dempsey has played all white contenders off the boards...[385]

BILL BRENNAN

As a display of strength Brennan lifts a 300-pound dummy.   He's faster than Dempsey at this.

Brennan lifts 300 pounds overhead.

Brennan appeared to be in great shape, better than ever before. The Chicagoan told Harry Newman of New York City's *Daily News*,

[385] *Buffalo Times*, December 5, 1920.

I am going to beat Jack Dempsey. I never was more confident of anything else in my life. I have been waiting for two years for this chance and I'll take the champion just as sure as fate. He's just the kind of a bird that I like – his style of tearing in suits me to a T and you can look for a new heavyweight boss on Dec. 14.

HEIGHT 6' 1½" REACH 77" HEIGHT 6' 1½"
NECK 17" WRIST 8" NECK 17"
BICEPS 15"
CHEST
NORMAL 42"
EXPANDED 45" CHEST
NORMAL 39"
EXPANDED 44"
BICEPS 15"
WAIST 30½"
WRISTS 8"
WAIST 29"
THIGH 23" REACH 78"
THIGH 23"
CALF 18" CALF 18"
ANKLE 8½" ANKLE 8½"
WEIGHT 190" BRENNAN DEMPSEY WEIGHT 189"

Brennan believed that he matched up very well with Dempsey. "There may be heavyweights that can beat me, but Jack Dempsey is not among them." Most of the fellows Bill had beaten fought like Dempsey. He predicted that their upcoming fight would be a humdinger, and Dempsey would not floor or knock him out. "Dempsey's style of rushing in wide open is cherry pie for me." Newman said he could not help but admire Brennan's confidence.

Bill claimed that when he went to the floor in the 2nd round of the prior 1918 Dempsey fight, it was the result of twisting and breaking his ankle, not because of a blow. He had been holding his own up until then. Even in his handicapped state, he still gave Jack the toughest fight he ever had. In the 4th round, he had Dempsey so hurt that Jack started to go to the neutral corner after the round ended. Bill stuck it out for as long as he could on one leg, until the referee stopped it in the 6th, with Brennan still on his feet. Bill always felt that Dempsey was made to order for him, and badly wanted a rematch for a long time.

Brennan enlisted in the Navy and served for 14 months during the war. Upon his release from the military, he set about gunning for Dempsey. That fight always had rankled him, and now that he had the opportunity, he was going to make the most of it. He was in wonderful condition already. He was sparring with three black fighters: Black Thunderbolt Kid Norfolk (75-17-6), Panama Joe Gans, and Bob Armstrong, all of whom gave him lively work. He loved boxing, and was happiest when wearing a pair of gloves. Like Dempsey, he did his 6 miles of roadwork through Central Park.

Brennan also loved baseball, and had played in a semi-pro league when he was younger. His flattened nose came not from boxing, but baseball. There had been a "slight misunderstanding" during a game; everybody got to swinging bats, and someone swung a bat into his face.[386]

Ticket prices were $5, $10, $15, $20, and $25 ringside. Promoter Tex Rickard was anticipating a $200,000 house.[387]

On December 6, 189-pound Dempsey boxed with Bill Tate, Dan O'Dowd, and Marty Farrell, whaling away in his usual brisk manner, to the great delight of a large gallery of observers.[388]

The *New York Tribune*'s W. O. McGeehan said the fight likely would pack the Garden, even though Dempsey probably would stop Brennan. Although folks were saying that Brennan never looked better, the same was said of Miske, who also looked great in training. Brennan intended to fight it out, which caused some to think it would end quickly. Still, both men were very tough, strong, and could take a punch. The fans just wanted to see a fight between two men who came to win and give it their all, which both would do. Hence, folks wanted to see the fight.[389]

The *New York Herald's* Daniel said the feeling was that Dempsey stopped Brennan once and would do it again. If he was not dead certain of Dempsey's ability to take care of Brennan, Jack Kearns would not have made the match and risked the more valuable Carpentier fight. Still, "At the same time, Brennan, next to Harry Wills, is the most able opponent who could be selected for Dempsey. He has size and weight and a punch, and he can take it. The last item, perhaps, is the most important." He was no set-up, and it would be a real fight for as long as it lasted.[390]

Many who saw Brennan spar with Kid Norfolk and Panama Joe Gans declared that he would go the limit against the champ. Kid Norfolk agreed. Bill appeared to be in splendid shape.[391]

Dempsey finally had gotten rid of an annoying cold. On the 7th, he sparred Bill Tate, Marty Farrell, Joe Farren, Dan O'Dowd, Joe Jeannette, and Al Reich.[392]

[386] *New York Daily News*, December 4, 6, 7, 1920; *Brooklyn Citizen*, December 6, 1920; *Binghamton Press*, December 13, 1920. Kid Norfolk's record included: 1916 KO2 Gunboat Smith, W20 Bill Tate, W20 Jeff Clark, and KO13 Arthur Pelkey; 1917 KO13 Pelkey, WND10 Gunboat Smith (twice), W12 Billy Miske, and LKOby2 Sam Langford; 1918 TKO7 Bill Tate, and LND8 (twice) Joe Jeannette; 1919 W12 Billy Miske, W15 John Lester Johnson, and WND10 Clark; and 1920 KO1 John Lester Johnson, and W15 and TKO2 Clark.
[387] *Binghamton Press*, December 6, 1920; *New York Herald*, December 4, 1920; *New York Times*, December 7, 1920.
[388] *New York Daily News*, December 7, 1920.
[389] *New York Tribune*, December 8, 1920.
[390] *New York Herald*, December 8, 1920.
[391] *Brooklyn Standard Union*, December 10, 1920. *New York Daily News*, December 9, 1920.
[392] *New York Herald*, *New York Daily News*, *Brooklyn Daily Times*, *Brooklyn Citizen*, December 8, 1920. Dempsey's sparring partner Tate would be fighting Brennan's sparring partner Norfolk on the Tuesday fight undercard. Featherweight Packy O'Gatty also was training with Dempsey on the Granite State. *Brooklyn Standard Union*, December 9, 1920.

Sparring Bill Tate on the U.S.S. Granite State

On December 7, 1920 in Jersey City, New Jersey, 175-pound Gene Tunney won a 10-round no decision over 180-pound Leo Houck (134-37-26), who primarily covered up his face with his gloves and was very cautious, though Tunney found it difficult to penetrate the armor. According to the *New York Evening World*, in the 7th round, Tunney decked Houck with a right swing that landed high, and Houck took a nine-count. Houck recovered and gave Tunney a "shiner" in the 8th. In the 10th round, Tunney mauled and punished him, but Houck lasted the distance. Gene's manager, Frank Bagley, revealed that Tunney broke his left hand in the 4th round. The injury would cause the cancellation of fights, and ultimately put Gene out of action for over six months.

The *Hackensack Evening Record* said Tunney made a "poor" and "deplorable" showing against the clumsy Houck.

> Gene won handily over the prescribed route of ten rounds, but he worked like an elephant. Fans at the ringside accused him of pulling his punches, but the truth of the matter was that Houck was really a hard man to hit and Gene found it almost impossible to gauge his jaw. At any rate Leo mussed Gene up quite some, raising a 'mouse' under his right eye in the sixth round, but he was hopelessly outclassed.

Despite the clear victory, the *Brooklyn Standard Union* called Tunney's performance a "decided disappointment." The *Brooklyn Daily Eagle* agreed that Tunney's "prestige as a heavyweight possibility was sadly tarnished." The *Paterson Evening News*, while agreeing that Tunney won on points, also said, "It was a deplorable exhibition on the part of Tunney."[393]

Walter Monahan believed it was a chance blow under Willard's heart that paralyzed him and led to his defeat. He believed Dempsey could not repeat it. Monahan said Willard could take it like no other man in history, and his uppercut was powerful enough to reclaim the championship.

> Mind you, I'm not trying to belittle Dempsey's ability. I think that he is one of the most remarkable fighters that ever lived. I have seen the best of them through many years, but I never knew a man of Dempsey's size who could hit with the same terrific power, who was as fast, or who had a fighting brain like Dempsey's. He is an amazing warrior.[394]

When asked which hand carried Dempsey's strongest punch, Bill Tate said, "They're both the same. I got one from his right one day and went to sleep without an effort. The next day it was Jack's left that made the bell ring. They tried smellin' salts but I didn't know it until that night."

The 25-year-old Dempsey was "everything from a tigerish scrapper to a very, very likable sort of chap, who plays pinochle and pedals a playerpiano." He was vicious in the ring, combining science, speed, cunning, power, and ferocity, but outside the ring he was affable and kindly.

---

[393] *New York Evening World, Hackensack Evening Record, Brooklyn Standard Union, Brooklyn Daily Eagle, New York Tribune, Paterson Evening News,* December 8, 1920.
[394] *Binghamton Press,* December 9, 1920.

When asked if he expected to beat Brennan, Dempsey simply smiled. Although things looked bright for Dempsey, "his opponent is a tough man to handle." Brennan could hit and take it, and such a man always had a chance. The boys in Dempsey's camp, including bantamweight champion Pete Herman and Midget Smith, were of the opinion that Dempsey would be champion for some time to come.[395]

On December 9, after Brennan donned a headgear and sparred a few rounds with Kid Norfolk, Bill's manager Leo P. Flynn said, "He looks great. Do you notice how he steps. Watch him while he is skipping the rope. You never saw a heavyweight skip that gracefully, did you?"

Flynn said Brennan's flattened nose was not from boxing. He used to be an iron worker, and one day fell from the roof of a building and landed on his nose, breaking it. Bill was far too clever a boxer to allow anyone to do that to him with their fists. "Ah, yes, Bill is very clever." Of course, that contradicted Bill's story that a baseball bat did it.

Brennan declared, "I'll be there on my feet at the end of

The contender for the pugilistic crown exchanges blows with Kid Norfolk.

"KNOCKOUT" BILL BRENNAN,

the 15th round. … I know how to take this guy, and you watch me do it." Regarding his ankle injury in their prior fight, Brennan said, "I was on the floor and I was trying to get up in a hurry and I turned my left ankle." He did not explain what he was doing on the floor at the time. "Perhaps he had just sat down a few seconds to rest or to meditate." Hs explanation contradicted the prior impression that a crack on the jaw from Dempsey broke his ankle as he was falling.

Bob Armstrong was not overly impressed by Dempsey or Brennan, saying, "There was only one heavyweight. Ah has seen them all and Ah knows that there was only one. That was that Jim Jeffries!" Armstrong had fought Jeffries (L10) and had been a sparring partner for him, as well as Bob Fitzsimmons.[396]

[395] *Buffalo Courier*, December 10, 1920.
[396] *New York Tribune*, December 10, 1920.

Grantland Rice said in order of comparative chances to win against Dempsey, the remainder of the heavyweights were Jess Willard, Georges Carpentier, and Harry Wills. Dempsey believed that Carpentier would have a better chance than the others, because he was the only one who could match his speed. The champion remarked, "Carpentier is a fast, skillful boxer with a punch. That's all any one needs. The others are too slow." Yet, many still believed that a well-trained Willard would have the best chance.[397]

145-pound entertainer Al Jolson said that some months ago he had sparred with Dempsey, who forgot to pull one of his punches, hit him on the nose, dropped him, and left a scar.[398]

Dempsey sparred on Friday, December 10, four days before the fight.[399]

W. O. McGeehan claimed that Big Bill Tate and Sam McVey/McVea had been working out with Dempsey daily until very recently. Heavyweight Al Reich usually inevitably found a soft spot on the mat.

Dempsey also played a game of 2-on-2 basketball. Jack said, "It's great for the wind and it helps the speed."

The champ said he was ready and eager to fight. He had trained as hard or harder for this fight than he had for Willard and Miske.

Kearns said Dempsey was a bit peeved at Brennan's ravings and would make him pay.

That same day, the 10th, Brennan and Kid Norfolk went at it hard for 5 rounds. Bill landed two cracking rights on the Kid's chin. Panama Joe

---

[397] *New York Tribune*, December 10, 1920.
[398] *Buffalo Commercial*, December 11, 1920.
[399] One said he boxed 4 rounds each with Tate and O'Dowd. The *Tribune*'s W. O. McGeehan said Jack sparred with lightweight Irish Patsy Cline and middleweight Marty Farrell, just working on his speed, restraining himself from hitting hard. The *Brooklyn Citizen* and *New York Times* said he roughed it with Bill Tate, Marty Farrell, Al Reich, and Dan O'Dowd in succession, and then several embryo champion youngsters. December 11, 1920.

Gans also took a thrashing. Gans previously had been a Dempsey sparring partner, and he told Bill all about Dempsey's various tricks.[400]

Also on December 10, 1920, in London, England, Frank Moran knocked out Joe Beckett in the 2nd round. Joe had been doing well, landing the greater number of blows, until a Moran right wobbled him, and another right decked and finished him.[401]

Georges Carpentier said Dempsey was his pal and friend and would be until the bell rang. He called Jack a charming "garcon," or gentleman. Jack was very juvenile in appearance and manner, which was to be expected, given that Dempsey was a year and a half younger than he. "I played a game of golf with him, but he is much too good on the links for me. I hope he has not the same superiority when it comes to boxing."

Georges never had seen Dempsey fight live, but had studied him on film. "I would say he is very strong and powerful, a rushing and tearing sort of a man, a fighter to a degree. When I meet him I must call on my reserve of coolness so as to weather the storm."[402]

Jack Skelly said game ring battlers always had been fan favorites. Fans wildly cheered gallant gladiators who displayed great courage and fighting spirit. That's what made Jack Dempsey so popular. He was all of that.[403]

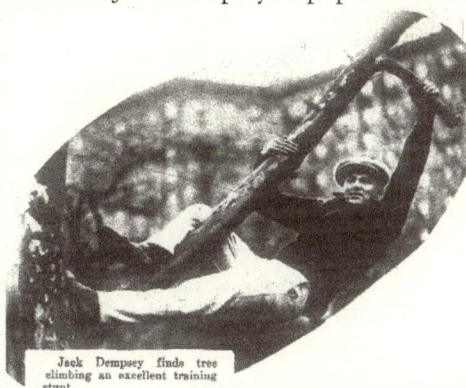

Jack Dempsey finds tree climbing an excellent training stunt.

The *New York World's* Vincent Treanor said Dempsey was on the move all the time. Jack hopped out of bed at around 6 a.m., went for a short walk, then ate breakfast. Patsy, the colored maid, always seemed to know what he wanted. He read some, then did his road work, a combination of walk and run. He spoke with the youngsters at the local parochial school. He got a light rubdown. Pinochle, his favorite game, and music with the piano or victrola with campmate Max Caplan passed the time. Jack said, "Max is a good fellow to have around. He's always livening up the place with the piano or the victrola, and they both sound good."

Treanor saw Dempsey eat three big meals, including vegetables, lamb chops, tomatoes, corn, steaks, carrots, lima beans, potatoes, green peas, jelly, and a pear.

Jack said, "I'd rather stay indoors. It's just like home here. And if I went out I would not be able to get half a block away until I'd be

[400] *Brooklyn Citizen*, December 11, 1920.
[401] *New York Daily News, New York Tribune, New York Herald*, December 11, 1920.
[402] *Brooklyn Standard Union*, December 11, 1920.
[403] *Yonkers Herald*, December 11, 1920.

surrounded by people." Even when he just went to get a shave, a crowd formed outside which blocked traffic so much that police reserves had to be called. Walking home, the police surrounded him. "I was afraid some people would think I had been arrested." He also feared going to shows or cabarets. Once in a while he went to the movies when it was dark. "Downtown I'd meet a lot of people who would be telling me what a great champion I am, and I'd have to talk my head off. No; I duck all that stuff if I can." Folks constantly wanted him to put in various appearances. "You have no idea of what a champion is asked to do these days."

Dempsey said he owned six suits which cost about $200 apiece. His chest was 42 inches, and waist only 29 inches. He had large calves, shoulders, and arms.

Jack told of a recent operation on his nose, which bothered him for some time. A piece of cartilage had been cut out. He said he was liable to colds.

At the Granite State, there were at least 1,000 people waiting for his arrival. The ship was two and a half blocks from his apartment. Throngs followed him. Both women and men looked at him. Kids held his arms and clutched at his coattails.

On the ship, he played with the weights. For sparring, he wore a head protector. "I don't like these things, but they tell me they're good to wear to prevent last minute cuts and bruises which might be reopened in the ring."

Jack boxed with three big huskies, and, although he tried to soften his punches by using 18-ounce gloves, the sparring partners still went through an awful ordeal. He fired blows to the body and head and exhibited fast footwork. "He has a habit of crouching low, with both hands ready to strike as he moves his body from the waist up to either side. This makes him a sort of pendulum target and at the same time puts him into a position to strike and strike hard with either hand."

One sparring partner told Treanor that he had boxed with nearly every heavyweight in the world, and none of them ever hit him so hard. What made it more impressive was that Dempsey was not trying to hurt them and was wearing big gloves.

Jack said his right was as good as his left, and it all depended on the openings he saw. He expected Brennan to give him a good battle.[404]

The *Brooklyn Citizen* reported that Dempsey was 25 years old to Brennan's 27. Both stood about 6' 1 ½ ". A referee and two judges would decide the championship. They would weigh in at 2 p.m. on the day of the fight, pursuant to the commission's rules. Dempsey allegedly would receive $100,000 and Brennan $35,000.[405]

The *Brooklyn Daily Eagle* said Brennan was built like a sturdy oak, could take a punch without flinching, and dish it out as well. Dempsey was the only one ever to have stopped him. Brennan usually won by knockout,

[404] *New York Evening World*, December 11, 1920.
[405] *Brooklyn Citizen*, December 12, 1920; *New York Daily News*, December 14, 1920.

though he also could go the route and win on points. He had a worthwhile record, one of the best of the present crop of heavyweights.

Dempsey was a topnotch champion, and like Sullivan and Fitzsimmons, a bone-crushing, first-class knockout artist, a man of quick action who generally won his battles quickly.[406]

There was some talk of a potential Dempsey vs. Tom Gibbons contest in Toledo, for on December 6, Gibbons had won a 12-round no decision over Chuck Wiggins (33-12-9) there, impressing observers.

Most thought Dempsey would win the upcoming contest, but the question was whether it would be via knockout or not, and if so, how quickly. The general belief was that Dempsey would win within 6 rounds. Still, others conceded Brennan a chance to go the distance.

According to the *Binghamton Press*, those in the know said Brennan had improved a million per cent since their prior encounter, was punching harder than ever, and appeared to be a new man. "Dempsey fears Brennan more than he does Carpentier or Harry Wills. The prediction of sporting men in New York is that while the fight lasts it will be the greatest ever fought."

Brennan noted that any man could be knocked down. He had scored 50 knockouts and saw no reason why he could not hit and hurt Dempsey, who rushed in wide open.

> I gave Dempsey the toughest fight he ever had. He'll admit that frankly. I hit him and damaged him considerably. I had him mightily worried in a couple of rounds. He landed on me with his famous left and equally famous right and he couldn't put me away. That shows I can take about everything that Dempsey can pass out.

Bill noted that the referee stopped it on a technical knockout, and he only was in a bad way because of his ankle, which hampered his footwork.

Brennan had improved a great deal since then. "I hit straighter and harder. I have been toughened up a lot and can take more punishment than ever before. Everyone tells me I am faster and display more ring science." He believed that overall, he had the edge on the champion.[407]

The challenger told the *New York World's* Alex Sullivan that he had been training for five months and was bent on winning. He never before had trained so hard or for so long.

> When I get in the ring with Dempsey I know the sort of fighter I'm getting in the ring with. That man-killer stuff hasn't got me frightened. It's what has got most of his opponents scared. They're beaten before they start. He's a good puncher, but I think I can punch as well — and another thing, I think I am faster than he is right now.

Bill's body looked rock solid. He had been sparring with fast and clever colored fighters in Norfolk and Gans, who were instructed to give

[406] *Brooklyn Daily Eagle*, December 12, 1920.
[407] *Binghamton Press*, December 13, 1920.

him all they had. Bill took every blow without flinching, returned fire, and had them backing up. "I feel sure that I will enter the ring in better condition for a hard fight than will Dempsey. Of course, Jack will look fit to fight a great fight, but he hasn't had the training I've had. He has nobody boxing with him but fellows who are afraid of him."

Brennan noted that even with a broken ankle suffered in the 2nd round, Dempsey still could not finish him off. The referee stopped it in the 6th round; but he still was on his feet, willing to fight on. "So you can see why I don't fear him."

Brennan claimed it was *he* who sent Miske into temporary retirement. "I hit him so hard and often that he wasn't any good again, and only a shell of his old self when Jack Dempsey fought him…." Bill said he had done better against Meehan than Dempsey. "Four months ago in Philadelphia I fought Willie Meehan, who has been credited with whipping Dempsey a couple of times on the Coast. Willie was pie for me. I floored him in both the 2nd and 5th rounds, and it was only because he clinched and ran that he stayed the distance."

Bill realized that it meant a million dollars to him to win. "You'll see I'll give him the fight of his life. If he stops me inside of 15 rounds I'll acknowledge that he's in a class by himself."

The *Brooklyn Daily Times* said it was the greatest card since the Horton Law days, and Madison Square Garden likely would be packed from floor to roof with humanity.

Frank Menke said although Brennan had improved vastly, so too had Dempsey. Even if Brennan landed a lucky swing and decked him, chances were that Jack simply would rise up fighting mad. Since their prior bout, Brennan was somewhat shiftier, punched with greater speed and accuracy, and perfected a fair defense. But Dempsey's improvement in the two years since they fought eclipsed Brennan's by a dozen miles. At first, Dempsey was a rough, tough, slam-bang youth who could give and take awful beatings. But he lacked technique, finesse, and scientific knowledge regarding punching, attack, and defense. That no longer was the case. He was gifted in every branch of the profession, seemed unhurtable, and crushed whomever he hit solidly, either to the body or head. He had a great heart blow. "The fight game never produced a man who can hit to the body with such dynamic fury as Dempsey." His punches crumbled and paralyzed foes.[408]

The *New York Daily News* asked whether Dempsey ever would defend the title against the next best man in the division, Harry Wills. "Will Dempsey Meet the Smoke?" Back in the day, John L. Sullivan refused to fight Peter Jackson. "Peter was not invited to the party because Mr. Sullivan had his doubts. Peter could not have been knocked out…and John saved the white world by discretion." Dempsey had a preference for men he had defeated once before, but appeared willing to fight all but one: Harry Wills. "We know that the good white man can lick all other

[408] *New York World, Brooklyn Daily Times, Buffalo Times,* December 13, 1920.

white men not so good; but can the good white man lick a good black man?" After he disposed of whites and "the Frog, as we hope he doesn't but know he will," this writer wanted to see Dempsey take on Wills to "see just how far the white race can go against the residual gorilla formations in a Negro fighter." If Dempsey happened to be knocked out by Wills, "as he probably would be, it would prove that as man develops his intellect his bone structure weakens. We think Mr. Dempsey ought to make the experiment in the interest of science." Kearns had been prudent in making matches, and "we do not blame him for taking care of his meal ticket," but after he had cleaned up enough money to retire, he should take a chance with Wills.[409]

On the day of the championship fight, the *New York Herald* said most believed that Dempsey would knock out Brennan within the limit, giving 3 to 1 odds on that proposition.

The *Herald's* "Daniel" said Brennan was a more able antagonist than Miske, but Miske was known for his chin and durability, and even he went out quickly. Hence, Brennan likely would be knocked out quickly as well. That seemed to be the general opinion. Brennan had more experience than Dempsey. But upsets were rare.

As a precaution against funny business, the referee and judges would not be named until 7 p.m. on the evening of the fight.[410]

Fair Play wrote that Dempsey was the sort of man who upon seeing a crowd at one corner would go through ten back streets to avoid it. He was as bashful as a boy and had "all sorts of qualities that indicate an attractive nature." He had no "front." He was apt to invite visitors to play pinochle. He was "considerate, kindly, lovable." He had the heart of a boy, and greeted crowds of kids as though he were a boy himself. He was not boastful, recognizing that Brennan was tough and would put up a hard fight, but said Bill would get his just as the rest have.

In addition to the reported $100,000 win or lose to Dempsey, and $35,000 to Brennan, Rickard also would award a $2,500 championship belt to the winner.[411]

Dempsey denied that he would carry Brennan. "Some persons have connected with the idea that to furnish a little entertainment for the crowd I might stall around for a while and not get under way until the 2nd or 3rd round." Jack said he would finish him as soon as he could, for Bill was not one with whom to trifle. Yet, the champ recognized that Brennan was one of the world's toughest fighters.

> He'll be in the ring for the purpose of knocking me out and if I don't watch my step there is always a possibility of his doing it. I always like to give the crowd a run for its money, but never have I done so at a risk to myself. I can't afford to do it. My business is fighting. My fighting program calls for putting away an opponent as

[409] *New York Daily News*, December 14, 1920.
[410] *New York Herald*, December 14, 1920.
[411] *Buffalo Evening News*, December 14, 1920.

soon as it is humanly possible for me to do so. I have never deviated from this course since my ring comeback – and I never will.

Dempsey had stopped Fulton, Morris, and Willard as fast as he could. He sparred a little in the 1st round against Miske to try out his boxing ability, and then ended matters quickly thereafter. His ability to stop men quickly is what lifted him up and got him a title shot. Hence, he was not going to carry Brennan. He hoped to win quickly. "If I can't I am going to batter away at Bill until either he goes out – or he gets me."[412]

On Tuesday December 14, 1920 at Madison Square Garden in New York City, New York, 25-year-old Jack Dempsey defended his world heavyweight championship crown for the second time, against 27-year-old Bill Brennan (60-13-8).[413]

At 2 p.m. on the day of the fight, Dempsey officially weighed in at 188 ¼ pounds (some said 188 ½), while Brennan tipped the beams at 197 pounds. Both looked very fit.

Fight fans flooded the spacious Garden to see the year's biggest fight. As usual, reports varied regarding attendance, including 10,875, 11,956, 12,000, 13,000, fully 14,000, and 15,000, including women, who jammed the Garden to its capacity, filling every seat. One said there were 11,956 seats, but that did not take into account about 1,000 temporary bleacher seats and 2,000 persons who obtained standing room. Hence, there were nearly 15,000 spectators present. The ticket prices were $5, $7, $10, $15, $20, and $25. Outside, 25 men were arrested as ticket speculators, who were called sport-killing parasites.

Inside the arena, quiet and order prevailed. The well-handled, well-behaved crowd represented a stratum of the metropolis. Evening clothes were much in evidence. Many notables were present, including Theodore Roosevelt, Jr., Anne Morgan - daughter of the late J. P. Morgan, Pennsylvania Governor William Sproul, and Harry Payne Whitney.

Brilliant rays of light shone from the lights installed for motion picture filming purposes. The fight was filmed in its entirety. Some portions of the films still exist, but they are far from complete.

In the preliminaries, Dempsey's sparring partner, 155-pound middleweight Marty Farrell, won a 6-round decision over 157 ½-pound Frank McGuire.

The *Brooklyn Daily Times* reported that Dan Hickey originally was to have refereed the main event, but after Johnny Haukap/Haukop had refereed the Farrell bout, which was first on the card, Boxing Commission Chairman Joseph Johnson approached him and whispered in Haukap's ear, informing him that he would referee the main event. There was no explanation for the shift in arbiters.

---

[412] *Buffalo Times*, December 14, 1920.
[413] The following fight discussion and analysis is taken from the *New York Daily News, New York Evening World, Brooklyn Daily Eagle, New York Tribune, Brooklyn Daily Times, Brooklyn Standard Union, New York Herald, New York Times, Buffalo Times, Buffalo Evening News, Buffalo Commercial, Buffalo Courier, Chicago Tribune, Boston Post*, December 15, 16, 1920.

185-pound heavyweight Charley Weinert won a 10-round decision over 181 ¾-pound Bartley Madden.

Brennan's sparring partner, 182 ¼-pound Kid Norfolk, won a clear 10-round decision over Dempsey's sparring partner, 234 ¾-pound Bill Tate, in a bout that was filmed. Based on the existing films, the much shorter and smaller Norfolk was able to get in quickly with a quick-step or leap-in and fire fast punches either on the way in or once inside. He could slide, bounce, feint, or dip, and not allow Tate to time him on the way in. Tate played a defensive waiting game and mostly tied up and held while Norfolk tried to attack and work. Norfolk was good at dipping down off to the side and eluding Tate's blows and countering them quickly. Tate had the clear height, reach, and weight advantages, but simply was not active, quick, or accurate enough. One might even say he suffered from sparring-partner-syndrome from too much work with Dempsey. He had become too comfortable with and used-to survival-mode boxing.

After the preliminaries concluded, fresh rosin was sprinkled around the canvas-covered ring. New gloves were brought in for the main event. Cameramen positioned themselves pursuant to announcer Joe Humphries' suggestions. Joe carried a big black box containing the championship belt, which was to be presented to the winner.

At about 10:25 p.m., Bill Brennan came to the ring, grinning. He wore green trunks and a maroon sweater. He was with manager Leo P. Flynn and trainer Jim Cullen. He hopped over the ropes and took the stool just vacated by Kid Norfolk. He sat there, smiling, while the motion picture men got busy. Bill's hands were bandaged already.

A couple minutes later, Dempsey followed, with a scowl and sneering look. The champion was unshaven, with at least a day's growth on his chin. He wore white trunks, with a red, white, and blue belt. Jack did not bother wearing the customary bathrobe, but had a towel around his shoulders. He entered through the same corner as Brennan, shook his hand warmly, briefly examined Bill's tape and bandages, and extended out his own hands for inspection. Leo Flynn examined Dempsey's hand bandages. Jack then took the other corner, appearing very confident.

With Dempsey were Jack Kearns, Marty Farrell, and a couple others. Kearns adjusted Dempsey's gloves. "Pete the Goat" did the same for Brennan.

The ring was cluttered with a small army of photographers.

Pete Herman

Famous announcer Joe Humphries introduced Pete Herman, bantam champ, and Joe Lynch, the principals for the following week's card there.

Humphries then introduced as the heavyweight champion and most wonderful, hardest-hitting puncher the game has ever known: Jack Dempsey. He got up and bowed simply, with a faint smile, to applause.

Humphries presented the intrepid challenger, and champion of the middle west: Bill Brennan. One reporter said he received a bigger applause than the champion. Another said he received a faint cheer.

Dempsey was announced as weighing 188 ¼ pounds to Brennan's 197.

Brennan sat in his corner; his shoulders covered with his red sweater. He smilingly spoke with his seconds, seeming calm and relaxed.

Dempsey sat as well, looking out over the crowd, smiling occasionally. He listened to Jack Kearns' advice. Others said he had a scowl on his face.

Humphries displayed the diamond-studded belt presented by Tex Rickard, which the winner would receive. Humphries asked the crowd to please refrain from smoking.

Photographs were taken at ring center. One said Dempsey scowled at Brennan. Another said he did not even look at Bill. One said Bill looked down. Leo Flynn stood beside Brennan and joked with him. The fighters shook hands, and the impatient crowd, calling out to the brigade of cameramen, yelled, "Get out of there."

The men returned to their corners and the photographers were cleared out of the ring.

Referee Johnny Haukap of Brooklyn was introduced. He hailed the fighters back to ring center. After a brief discussion of the rules, he slapped both on the shoulder blades and said, "Back to your corners."

Humphries read a telegram from Jess Willard challenging the winner, which the crowd hooted.

After briefly returning to their corners, at about 10:35 p.m., with what looked like a little gold hammer, Bob Stoll struck the bell, and the sound of the gong went off, resounding all over the building. The house was as quiet as a wake. The following is an amalgamation of the summaries of the writers who were there at ringside and provided next-day accounts.

1st round

Instead of sparring for an opening, Brennan went to work right away, as if to gamble early on. The crowd gasped at his temerity. Brennan used his left jab and right from range, and closed in and used his right uppercut in close. They punched, mixed, and clinched. Dempsey crouched and landed short rights and left hooks to the chin in the clinches, and also smashed in some short, hard body blows. Bill planted left and right to the head, as well as several short punches to the stomach. They both pummeled and plugged away earnestly.

Dempsey smashed a right hook over the heart, and Brennan retreated under fire. Dempsey crowded in, but Bill kept him off with a long left. One said Jack was shifting and swaying continually, ducking, turning, and weaving for defense. Another said he seemed a bit careless defensively. Inside, Jack fired several uppercuts to the jaw. Brennan uppercut with his right several times as well. The bell sounded with them clinched and working at close quarters. The crowd roared and cheered, having enjoyed the combat.

Harry Newman said they were fighting hard. Dempsey had a slight advantage. Brennan's right eye was cut slightly.

Vincent Treanor said there was no serious damage done in the round. Brennan went to his corner smiling. It was Dempsey's round, but with little to choose between them.

W. O. McGeehan said they mixed it up gamely, both landing to the body and head.

The *New York Times* said the round featured leads and clinching by both. Dempsey boxed cautiously but forced the fighting steadily.

The *Brooklyn Standard Union* said it was a tame round, with no really hard punches landed by either. Jack was smiling as he took his rest. His handler waved two large green fans to cool him off. Brennan was cool, and seemed anxious for the next round to start.

2nd round

They kept punching and clinching, indulging in short, snappy blows and cuffs to the body and head. The crouching Dempsey landed a couple uppercuts to the mouth, but Bill retaliated with lefts and a right to the jaw. Jack hit the body. Bill jabbed the mouth, and they exchanged to the body.

Brennan's right eye bled slightly from one of Dempsey's inside blows. A left hook drew a trace of blood from Bill's mouth as well.

Dempsey forced the fast pace, landing a right uppercut to the body. Brennan landed some rights. Jack landed a right on the jaw, then left, and then whipped it down to the body. Instead of dropping, as others had, Brennan went right after him and forced matters. He was full of fight.

Brennan outfought the champ at long distance with his long left and swinging right.

Brennan swung a heavy, wicked right to the jaw, as well as a left, and the crowd was in an uproar as the champion retreated from the follow-up blows, some saying he was rocked. Another version said Bill held Jack's left glove, then shot in a smashing right to the jaw that worried the champ. Yet another said Jack missed a right and Bill caught him with a hard counter left to the jaw.

Dempsey sought to retaliate with left and right to the head, but was wild, and they clinched. Shortly thereafter, Brennan's hard right uppercut drove Jack's head back. Although bothered, nevertheless Dempsey rushed in close. In a clinch, he chopped Bill's jaw on both sides, and landed a hard left to the body. A slight fleck of blood appeared in Bill's nose.

At the bell, the crowd cheered Brennan to the echo. He was giving the champ a real fight.

Harry Newman claimed it was an even round. He also said the round found Brennan working a series of uppercuts to the head. When he mixed it in furious fashion, the great crowd was in an uproar.

Others said Brennan had landed the hardest, most significant blow or blows of the round, several claiming that Dempsey either was hurt, momentarily stunned, or at least affected by some of the punches.

3rd round

Brennan was quite aggressive, landing hard blows, including a left hook to the body, right to the jaw, and a left as well. He was making Dempsey miss. Dempsey hooked the body, but his blows only made Bill fight harder. Two hard right smashes to the jaw drove Dempsey back to the ropes. The crowd yelled and cheered wildly at every one of Bill's punches. Brennan cut a small gash on the bridge of Jack's nose.

Dempsey came back, plunged forward and attacked the body and head at close quarters, crouching. He landed a left to the chin and wicked right to the heart that sent Bill reeling along the ropes and clinching. The crowd was in an uproar.

Bill landed a couple good right uppercuts. Dempsey crossed a right to the jaw, but looked surprised when Bill sent two rights to his face. Dempsey hit a trifle low and Haukap mumbled a warning.

Dempsey frequently was half turning and walking away from Brennan, who took advantage of one of the turns and smashed his jaw. Brennan crowded Jack to the ropes and landed a stiff left and right to the head. The crowd gave Bill a great hand.

Dempsey slowed up for a moment, but recovered quickly and began forcing again. He smashed in several short jolts on the inside. They were fighting at a furious pace.

Harry Newman said Brennan's mouth was bleeding, but he had surprised the spectators with his aggressiveness. Honors were even.

Vincent Treanor said it was an even fight thus far. Brennan gave as much as he took. Kearns looked worried, while Brennan's side of the ring looked confident and hopeful.

W. O. McGeehan said, "Once more it was Brennan's round." In his corner, Dempsey seemed irritated.

Damon Runyon said Brennan looked tired as he returned to his corner. Dempsey had a cut on the bridge of his nose.

4th round

Brennan began aggressively. Dempsey came out dancing and shot a left to the stomach. They clinched. Dempsey followed with two smashing shots to the body. Jack ducked a right and dug his own right into the ribs, then cuffed Bill around the ears as they came to close quarters. Another clinch. Brennan uppercut twice before they broke. Jack danced away; with his body weaving to either side, but Bill struck a clean left onto his chin. Crouching low, Dempsey rushed; they clinched, and worked on the inside. Coming out of the clinch, Brennan landed a left to the jaw. Brennan again smashed a hard right to the jaw. Jack crowded in and another scrimmage followed.

Brennan worked well in the clinches, landing some good blows. At long range, he smashed Dempsey twice on the jaw with right and left punches. Dempsey hooked a left to the jaw. Brennan connected with a left jab to the chin, sending Jack's head back. The champ blocked a right.

By mid-round, Vincent Treanor said some folks were beginning to think Dempsey was not so wonderful after all.

W. O. McGeehan said Brennan was trying to keep close, play for the body and fire uppercuts. The pace slowed greatly.

Damon Runyon said Brennan was landing several rights to the head and jaw, as well as body blows. Dempsey dug his left into the body.

However, at one point in the round, all agreed that the tide started to turn. Dempsey crowded in and pounded the stomach. He forced the fighting. Brennan's attacks mostly were blocked.

Dempsey landed a left hook to the jaw and Brennan's legs shook. Dempsey forced him back. Another short left and right to the jaw staggered Bill. He tried to jab and keep him away, but Jack persisted, jostling and cuffing him with left and right hooks at the bell. Brennan was wobbling a bit.

Between rounds, Dempsey received a good sponging, and sucked on an orange. Brennan took a mouthwash of water as his seconds worked over him.

Summarizing, Newman said hard smashes to the jaw had rendered Brennan groggy. The champ now was getting his range, and Brennan appeared tired at the bell. Dempsey round.

Treanor said Brennan was beginning to show signs of distress, hurt by several blows, which caused him to lose some of his aggressiveness.

McGeehan said Dempsey drove Brennan back, for the blows hurt, and Bill wearily returned to his corner.

Runyon said Jack had sped up, landing left hooks to the face and rights to the body.

5th round

Brennan started with awe and respect on his face. They mauled each other around, clinching and infighting. Dempsey kept ripping in body blows, worrying Brennan. A right under the heart made Bill wince. He tried to clinch, cover, and return the blows, but his efforts were fruitless. Dempsey was the clear master, working confidently, trying to wear him down. He was giving him an awful body beating. Short uppercuts seemed to hurt Bill.

Dempsey roughed it on the inside, really asserting himself. He even shoved Brennan away with his right. The referee cautioned him, and he offered his hand in apology. Another author said Jack had hit on the break, and apologized and shook Bill's hand. At times, Bill tried to keep in close to hold and/or smother the blows.

Dempsey was hitting Brennan almost every time he led, and he had him backing up. Still, Bill occasionally would land his hard straight right, which could be heard from far away.

Dempsey followed him around the ring, trying to land a finishing haymaker. He paid little attention to Brennan's efforts.

A Brennan right grazed the jaw/face, and the crowd yelled, for they were with him, but Jack quickly returned the fire with a short right.

Harry Newman said the round ended with Dempsey calm and collected, while Brennan appeared to be growing weaker. It was Dempsey's round.

W. O. McGeehan said Brennan seemed weary when he returned to his corner.

According to the *Brooklyn Standard Union*, between rounds, Brennan took a whiff of the smelling salts, received a good rubbing about the head, and was fanned by his second.

Vincent Treanor disagreed, saying Brennan did not seem to need much attention. Kearns sponged Dempsey. Treanor also said it was unclear whether Dempsey was playing with Brennan to prolong the battle, but he coasted a bit and did not use the same force in his blows.

6th round

Dempsey danced around, circling, feinting his left, seeking openings, finally jabbing, then landing a short right that jolted Bill's head. He rushed Brennan to the ropes and worked the stomach at close quarters. Brennan's blows mostly missed or fell short. A jab sent the champ's head back, but Jack countered with a right to the stomach. They kept alternating punches with clinches. Bill fired rights, uppercuts, and held. Jack landed a right to the jaw and left to the stomach. The champ sent four lefts to the face. Bill's straight left sent Jack's head bobbing. Dempsey sent his right to the body. On the inside, Dempsey worried Brennan with short, choppy punches to the head and body.

Dempsey's mouth was bleeding from the close-quarter jolts. In close, Jack kept working in his short hooking blows.

The *Brooklyn Standard Union* said that after the round concluded, Dempsey was spitting blood. Both seemed a trifle tired.

Runyon said Dempsey was not fighting like he did against Willard.

McGeehan said Brennan spat a little blood as he went to his corner.

Treanor said Dempsey's heretofore vaunted punch had not shown itself. Some thought he was under wraps, for he missed several inside uppercuts that should have hit their mark.

Newman said Brennan was tired at the bell, but smiling as he went to his corner. Dempsey's round.

The writer known as Daniel said the round had a lot of weak sparring, and it was only a shade for Dempsey. The crowd was wondering.

7th round

Dempsey crouched, sparred, and sent Bill's head back with a left jab. He forced the fighting, backing Brennan about the ring with lefts. Jack alternately danced and moved about, always seeking an opening before attacking. In the clinches, he pounded the stomach. Jack attacked and ducked and countered to the body. He landed two hard lefts. They worked in the clinches, exchanging blows. Dempsey drove his right to the ribs and left uppercut to the jaw. Brennan occasionally fired a hard one to deter Dempsey momentarily, and then either moved away a bit or closed in for a clinch. The crowd encouraged Brennan, cheering his blows.

Dempsey landed a hard right hook and left hook to the jaw that jolted and wobbled Brennan momentarily. Bill's right eye was swollen. Yet, he still came back and swapped punches.

Harry Newman said it was a rough round for Brennan. Dempsey was taking it easily.

Treanor said Dempsey moved around livelier than usual in this round. It had been a hard fight. He could not tell whether Dempsey was trying or simply showing badly from the effects of overtraining. The fight was proving his ability to take it, for Brennan had hit him with several good blows. Between rounds, Dempsey was told to go get him.

Runyon said Dempsey appeared riled by Bill's showing.

Daniel said Dempsey finally cut loose and landed hard rights to the jaw and followed with lefts to the body and right to the heart. Yet, in the final minute, Brennan landed two rights to the head. Just before the gong, Dempsey elbowed his man and was hissed. It was Dempsey's round.

8th round

As the round started, one of the large lights over the ring went out. As usual, Dempsey was the aggressor, but Brennan was willing to swap punches. The champ stepped around and circled, then attacked. He landed two left and right uppercuts to the stomach and ribs, a hard left to the jaw, and a right near the heart. He tied up Bill's hands when they came close. Brennan scored a right uppercut. Jack smashed him on the jaw with a right wallop, but Brennan worked in close and brought a stinging left up to the face.

Jack feinted with his right and instead whipped his stiff left hook across to the jaw and knocked Bill back ten feet. Jack then drove a right to the stomach and clipped him on the face with the same hand. Dempsey shot in a right uppercut, then pushed Bill away for a good crack at his jaw. Brennan seemed weary, but still was fighting back.

Dempsey moved in and staggered Brennan with a long right to the chin followed by left hooks and short rights to the jaw. Brennan was groggy and tried to hold. Jack's hard stomach blows shook him off. The champ smashed a hard right to the jaw, but Bill stayed up.

In spite of the punishment, Brennan fought back gamely. Bill was short with two lefts but landed a right, forcing the champ back to a corner at the bell.

Harry Newman said the round was slightly in Dempsey's favor. The crowd gave Bill a great cheer for his clever work. Jack's mouth was cut, and required special attention from his seconds in the corner.

Vincent Treanor said Brennan began to look a sorry sight. He was taking a lot of punishment, and Dempsey's superiority began to assert itself. It was beginning to look like the real thing now, and it seemed only a question, barring accidents, of when Bill finally would topple. He plainly was weak in his corner.

Runyon said Brennan appeared tired.

The *New York Times* and *Brooklyn Standard Union* said Brennan had been shaky and staggering in the round. The *Times* said that early in the round, Brennan rocked under the force of the body blows, but was far from being on the verge of a knockout. He made Dempsey give ground by cutting loose a vicious right that landed on the back of Jack's neck. He still was strong. After some equal infighting, Dempsey landed only a glancing blow on the jaw, yet Brennan appeared somewhat groggy. He clinched and recovered. By the end of the round, he was fighting hard.

Daniel said Dempsey really got going in the 8th, working his right hard, with telling effect. Yet, Brennan, his face crimson, took everything without flinching.

9th round

They again mixed it up, exchanging and landing hard blows, particularly at close quarters. Dempsey used his nifty dance step before moving in. Brennan smashed hard rights to the jaw, as well as jabs, much to the crowd's surprise and delight. Jack paid no attention to the blows, and landed left hooks to the jaw. He also focused on the body on the way in and during the inevitable clinches that followed leads.

Bill danced around. Jack slipped under a left lead and landed his famous hard right to the heart, which weakened Brennan. He followed Bill around, landing a right to the chin and left hook to the body. They clinched and exchanged. Dempsey put his left arm on Bill's left shoulder while pummeling his face with his right.

Brennan landed a hard uppercut to the jaw, which hurt and made Jack appear worried. They worked on the inside before breaking. Brennan fired his jab and right, and Dempsey sidestepped and hooked his right to the ear. Bill kept working his uppercut to the face, and followed with a left hook to the jaw and right smash that made Dempsey retreat for a bit, while Brennan attacked the face and body at close quarters.

Harry Newman said it was Brennan's round.

Runyon said Dempsey's mouth was bleeding at the bell.

The *New York Times* said Brennan's right eye was puffed badly. Yet, his right drew blood from Dempsey's nose. Although Brennan at times seemed tired, at various moments he would liven up, attack, and land well. His comeback surprised Dempsey, who backed away and gave ground. Bill attacked and they engaged in infighting.

Daniel said Brennan got the crowd cheering when he landed a right cross to the jaw and finished the round with a splendid rally, landing rights. Dempsey looked worried. Bill was at least even in that round.

10th round

Dempsey was forcing the fighting, stepping livelier than ever, circling about and then attacking. At close quarters he worked continually. He worked whatever hand was free. Brennan was trying hard to keep in close and smother and grab. In a clinch, Dempsey landed a right and short left to the stomach, then hooked his left to the jaw. Bill held Jack's right glove. Treanor thought Brennan was ripe for the finish, but wondered whether Dempsey was holding back, for he did not show his well-known power, and missed several blows. The referee was forced to pull them apart from the clinches.

Brennan soaked a right to the jaw and several short lefts to the face. Jack rocked him with a short left uppercut in a clinch, and Bill returned with a light left to the face. Bill's hard left to the jaw slightly staggered Jack.

Dempsey sent home several hard smashes, including a hard straight right flush to the chin and left hooks to the stomach and jaw, and it looked like a staggered Brennan soon would be counted out, for he was in a bad way, seeming about to topple.

However, Bill recovered and came back with left to the mouth and right smash to the left ear, drawing blood. He had an excellent ability to recuperate and fight back whenever he seemed on the verge of defeat.

Both were tired and bleeding at the mouth. Dempsey's left ear was bleeding freely, the blood running down onto his chest and smearing his white trunks with crimson.

In the clinches, Dempsey kept shooting lefts to the mid-section. Holding Bill with his left, Jack shot in two rights to the head, and the crowd hissed and booed what they considered unfair practice. Both were fighting hard at the bell. The crowd cheered.

Newman said the round was even.

The *Times* said Brennan was groggy and wilting. Dempsey landed some hard right and left hooks to the jaw, causing the blood to spurt from Brennan's split lips. A Brennan right to the left ear cut the champ's ear. Some said it was from a collision of heads. It was not clear. Either way, the blood was gushing down. Dempsey had been stung and was fighting mad. He rushed and drove in a series of short body blows. Brennan's knees sagged and he pitched forward into a clinch.

The *Brooklyn Standard Union* said Brennan seemed unconcerned.

Treanor said Dempsey's seconds paid a lot of attention to his cut ear, plastering it up.

Daniel said there was more hissing for Dempsey, but it only spurred him on. After a couple of minutes, Dempsey crossed his right to the jaw and followed with a left uppercut. Brennan staggered, and might have been put out had Dempsey gone after him instead of walking away, and then the bell rang.

11th round

Dempsey danced about with the blood flowing from his ear and covering his chest. He was scowling savagely. They mixed it up. Jack seemed anxious. He was getting busy now, trying desperately to land effectively.

A series of Brennan jabs cut Dempsey's lip. A right further opened up the cut on Jack's ear. Blood was flowing from the champ's lips and ear.

Dempsey smashed left and right to the jaw, while Brennan uppercut him. Jack hit the stomach. Bill returned with hard right to the jaw.

Treanor said Dempsey landed a right to the stomach and then hooking right to the chin. Three times thereafter he did something he had not done thus far, which was to stab Bill with a left to the face, then hit him on the jaw with a right hard enough to make the water spray from his sodden glove.

Newman said Brennan stepped in with two hard smashes which shook up the champ.

Treanor said after Brennan landed an inside right hook, Jack walked into Bill with a right on the chin and dug his left deep into the body. Again he whipped his right to the jaw. Bill swung his right to Jack's bleeding ear. Both seemed to be tiring. Jack was content to cuff in his punches at close quarters rather than strike out at long range. Brennan's gameness was surprising everyone.

Newman called the round even. He opined that Dempsey's punches seemed to have lost their sting, for Bill was back at Jack after every lead. Dempsey was bleeding from his ear and mouth and looked sorry. The round was furious, and the stand that Brennan made led many to believe that he would weather the complete journey.

McGeehan agreed that whenever Dempsey hit him, Brennan came back strong and banged away with rights and lefts. A Dempsey left knocked Bill's head back. Brennan kept pressing in close and trying for the body. Dempsey bombarded the stomach with choppy rights, but received several jabs.

Runyon said it was Dempsey's round.

The *New York Times* said Dempsey kept up the attack, sending Brennan back. Bill pounded the bleeding left ear with his right. In the clinches, Dempsey kept peppering the face and body. Brennan suddenly forced the fighting and landed to the head with both hands, making the crowd yell. In the clinches, Dempsey severely pounded the stomach. At the bell, the champ bled from his ear and mouth. Brennan seemed weary and tired.

At another point, the *Times* said Brennan came back strong in the round, but his blows lacked steam. His defense held up and prevented Jack from finishing him.

The *Brooklyn Standard Union* said Brennan was as tough as nails.

Daniel said at the start of the round, Dempsey's left ear was bleeding. At that point, it was evident that the champion was trying his utmost, but could not get to his man. Toward the end of the round, he landed a terrific right to the jaw, but Brennan weathered that storm too. At the close, Dempsey was holding and hitting.

12th round

Dempsey was serious and plunged in with a left to the nose and fired the same hand to the waistline. He was firing rights and lefts to the body, while Brennan primarily hit the head. The crowd was admiring the great battle that Brennan was putting up, so his inside uppercut to the chin drew forth the cheers which the underdog receives when he is doing well or better than expected.

Brennan landed a hard right to the head. Dempsey jabbed twice but Bill came right back with two lefts to the face. Bill shook Jack with a hard left to the mouth. Jack's white trunks were red from his own blood; his mouth and ear bleeding considerably. He returned with a hard left and right. Brennan worked his right uppercut.

Each local writer had his own version of the end. The general consensus was that Dempsey landed several hard body blows that doubled over Brennan, followed by a right to the head, and Brennan went down.:

Harry Newman – The round had progressed nearly two minutes when Dempsey feinted and then quick as a flash drove his hard left jolt to the stomach and in the same motion brought his right around with a sweeping blow, landing flush on his jaw, and Brennan crumpled to the floor in a heap, where Referee Johnny Haukap counted him out. Dempsey stood back a few paces, watching the count.

Vincent Treanor - Dempsey drove a hard right squarely over the heart. He followed with a left and right. He repeated both doses, and as Brennan leaned doubled over like a man with a stomach ache, Jack fired a downward cleaver-like smashing chop onto the neck of his bent-over foe, and Bill went to the floor. Referee Haukop counted him out. Bill was assisted back to his corner, with Dempsey helping and guiding him.

W. O. McGeehan - Dempsey hit the pit of the stomach, and Brennan sent another left to the head. Dempsey stepped in with left and right to the wind, drove another hard right over the heart, and ripped a left hook to the stomach on the other side. Brennan sagged, crumpled, and almost doubled up, floundering forward, and as he tottered towards the floor, Dempsey sent him sprawling down onto the mat with a right smash down onto the base of his skull. Brennan rolled over once, and then struggled painfully to his knees. Dempsey hovered nearby, and the referee pressed him back as he counted. He reached ten with Brennan still on his knees. Time of the end was 1:57 of the 12th round.

Damon Runyon - At close quarters, Dempsey shot two hard lefts to the body. Brennan landed a left to the head, but Dempsey stepped in with left and right to the wind. He then then drove a hard right near the heart, sinking into the stomach, and immediately followed with a left hook to the stomach so fast that the two blows almost seemed to be one punch. That right was "for all the world as if Dempsey had stooped, picked up a stone and let fly with it." His fist seemed to disappear into the stomach.

Brennan, with glazed eyes and red, puffy cheeks, winced and crumpled from the middle of his body, almost doubled over from the effects, as if the smashes had broken him in two. As Bill bent over, a scowling Dempsey, with his dark eyes glaring, swung again with his right, which landed on the back of the already tottering Brennan's head and was the finishing touch. Brennan went sprawling down. The blow over the heart had done its work.

Referee Haukop, his white trousers flecked with blood, began counting. The crowd rose, screaming; the high, shrill voices of women mingling with the men. Dempsey hovered over Brennan.

Brennan tried his utmost to regain his feet, but only rolled about on the floor while Referee Haukop counted off the ten seconds. After

Haukop reached ten, Brennan, who was crawling aimlessly about the floor like a drunken man, lifted himself up. Haukop's arm went under him to prevent Bill from falling as he staggered against the ropes. Leo Flynn and Brennan's handlers entered the ring to assist him. Dempsey walked over, put his arm on Bill's shoulders, said something, and walked back to his corner.

New York Times - Dempsey fired powerful swings. Bill scored a right to the ear. Jack retaliated with a left to face, and a clinch followed. Jack sunk his right into the body under the heart. Bill's legs sagged at the knees and his body bent over. A left to the ribs sent Brennan down on his hands and knees. The house was in an uproar.

Just as the referee finished the count, Brennan staggered to his feet in a corner. Dempsey leaped in to resume, but the referee waved him aside, for Brennan had been counted out at 1 minute 57 seconds into the round.

Brooklyn Standard Union - Dempsey shot a wicked short right hook to the heart and a left to the stomach. As Brennan doubled up and slowly fell to his knees, Dempsey landed a right on the top of Bill's head as he was leaning over and falling.

On his knees, Brennan groaned and wiggled about, groping around the floor to grasp something in order to pull himself up. Referee Haukop tolled off the ten count before Bill rose in the corner.

Although very weak, Brennan tried to put up his hands to continue to fight, but he had been counted out. He hardly could stand. The referee and Dempsey assisted him to his corner.

W. C. Vreeland - Slightly battered and torn, with lips and left ear trickling blood, Dempsey ended it with three punches, a left hook to the solar plexus, a straight right to the mouth, and a right chop behind the ear. Brennan's knee sagged with the blow that landed in the stomach, his head dropped and his body bent. Dempsey drove a right to the mouth that caused him to totter. While doubled up, Dempsey threw a right chop behind the left ear and it was over. He fell on his knees.

Brennan staggered to his feet, fell toward the ropes, grasped the top strand as though it were a life raft, and pulled himself along the edge of the ring in his effort to keep on his feet. Half the time, he had his back to Dempsey. Brennan was on his feet at 10, but he was a pitiable wreck of a fighting man, could not lift his hands, and was coughing and gasping, trying to fill his lungs with air, unable to resume at the count of 10. Brennan said he thought he beat the count, but the referee told him he had not, and directed him to return to his corner. The solar plexus blow was the one that really won it, for the others simply finished him off.

Daniel - The devastating punch was a smashing right over the heart. Brennan gasped and tried to hold, but a left hook to the body followed and he doubled over. He attempted to hold again and reeled. As he sagged at the knees, Dempsey threw his right over the left ear, Bill fell over on his side, and was counted out.

Jack Dempsey had scored a 12th round knockout, successfully defending his championship for the second time.

As usual, reports regarding the financial numbers varied, some saying the show was a financial success, and others saying it operated at a loss for Rickard.

The *World* claimed that the $145,935 gate failed to cover the $147,000 in purses ($135,000 main event, $12,000 undercard). Tex had other additional miscellaneous expenses, including a $7,296.75 state tax. Rickard allegedly lost nearly $30,000. However, Rickard could earn a healthy profit with his 1/3 share of the motion picture proceeds from the film exhibitions throughout New York State. Each fighter's camp owned a 1/3 share of the moving picture proceeds as well. The fight had been exciting and competitive enough that folks would pay to see the films.

Vincent Treanor agreed that Rickard lost heavily on the gate, but his interest in the moving pictures could earn him very good money in New York, particularly since it was a good contest.

The *Chicago Tribune* estimated the expenses to be $165,000.

Others reported the gate as $209,852.50. Dempsey-Willard had generated $452,522 at the gate, the sport's record. Still, the Dempsey-Brennan house set a record for New York City. The previous local record was Willard-Moran at $151,524, also promoted by Rickard. Minus the 10% government tax of around $21,000, 5% state tax of about $10,500, the fighters' purses, and miscellaneous expenses, the estimated profit for the promoter would be $13,374.63 on the gate, plus the valuable motion picture revenues.

For the *New York Daily News*, Harry Newman was at ringside. He said Dempsey's face was smeared with crimson, flowing from cuts over his ear and from wounds on his face.

Surprising fans with his ability, Brennan had been holding his own and putting up a great fight all the way up to the moment that Dempsey landed the two awful blows that ended matters. While Dempsey was the aggressor throughout the greater part of the contest, Brennan surprised everyone by stepping along with the champ every inch of the way, even up to the moment that he received the final crushing blows. At that point, it had looked as if he would go the distance.

Brennan surprised Dempsey from the start, wading in with relish. Jack tried his famous shift, but Bill retorted with well-timed left smashes which shook him up.

It was even in the 3rd, but after that frame, Dempsey started to draw away and had a slight advantage in most of the other rounds. Several times though, Brennan shook him up with stinging right uppercuts, but the champ would not be denied and kept shuffling into his heavier opponent with the object of landing a finishing blow. In about the 8th round, Dempsey's punches had lost their sting, but it turned out that he was conserving energy.

The challenger was in no way disgraced. He received cheers for his gameness.

The *New York Evening World* reported that Dempsey admitted that Brennan gave him one of the hardest bouts of his career. Dempsey's lower left lip was cut and bleeding, as well as his left ear. Some caustic was applied in the dressing room, and the slight bleeding stopped.

For some reason, the fans booed the champion as he left the ring. "There cannot be any legitimate reason, because Dempsey has fought a man's fight and won." Many lost money betting on the fight, having wagered that Dempsey would knock out Brennan quickly, which in part might explain some anger towards Dempsey, despite it being an exciting and entertaining contest terminating with a clean knockout. Dempsey apparently informed his friends that he intended to stop Brennan inside of 4 rounds. It was said that Dempsey himself bet heavily that he would win inside of 6 rounds. Hence, allegedly, many thousands were lost by friends who relied on his assurances.

WINNING BLOWS OF FIGHT - - - - **By Thornton Fisher**

New York Evening World, December 15, 1920

Evening World writer Vincent Treanor said it had been a ripping battle. For the first 4 rounds, under the moving picture lights, Brennan fought with a fury which seemed ill-advised, and he actually had the better of the 2nd round, but after that round, the going favored Dempsey in nearly every round. Dempsey didn't begin turning loose his real power until the 5th round, and after that it was just a case of when he would put over the real crusher. Still, Dempsey only fought in spots from the 5th round on.

In the 7th round, Dempsey showed like an in-and-outer. One minute he would look like a real champion, and the next recede to looking ordinary. The crowd plainly was puzzled by the differences he exhibited at intervals.

In the 12th, Dempsey doubled up Brennan with rights and lefts to the body, which started the finish, then dealt him a cleaver like punch on the back of the neck which sent him down helpless onto his hands and knees. It was a rabbit blow, barred in England and Australia, but not universally barred in the U.S.

The referee counted to ten. Brennan thought he beat the count, but in attempting to do so, fell again into the ropes.

Brennan proved a big surprise, and Dempsey showed that he could go the route if necessary. At times it looked so one-sided that it appeared that Dempsey was holding back. Perhaps he was pacing himself.

The result was surprising, because 9 out of 10 men thought it would end early. Hence they left both pleased and disappointed. Pleased because they got a run for their money, and yet disappointed at the more methodical contest, without the sensational repetition of Dempsey's string of quick knockouts. He didn't fight like a superman.

Now, some were suggesting that Dempsey was overrated, and might have been beaten by fighters of yesteryear like Tom Sharkey, Kid McCoy, or Jim Corbett. Still, his relative struggle compared to his quick knockout victories might make the Carpentier fight more intriguing and marketable. Yet, Carpentier still was only a light heavyweight. Brennan was bigger than Dempsey, and his heft and sheer physical strength, durability, and ruggedness helped keep him in the contest longer. It was only his second stoppage loss in 81 contests, and both times, Jack Dempsey had turned the trick.

The *New York Times* said Dempsey withstood his foe's heavy blows. Brennan fought with no fear. True, he was cautious, but that was necessary given Dempsey's power. He was content to jab with his left and wait for openings to crash in a right cross or right uppercut. He landed several times, and Dempsey was forced to clinch and hold to protect himself. The crowd cheered Brennan's efforts. Dempsey frequently missed his punches.

Brennan started strong, having Dempsey wobbling in the 2nd round. Bill gave a good account of himself early on, but quickly showed traces of the punishment.

In the early rounds, Dempsey paid particular attention to the midsection. Several times he made Brennan gasp from the impact of his powerful body punches. Bill was rocked by heavy swings and hooks as well. The punishing blows gradually weakened Brennan, who was weary after the 4th round, and only fought in flashes.

It wasn't until the 5th round that Dempsey showed his true or usual form. Up to then, he had been slow on his feet and had not stepped around his opponent with his usual agility. He came out dancing in and out and around, trying to feint him into a position for a big blow. But Brennan was not about to be led into a mistake. He maintained his defense, covering his jaw well, fighting in a crouching position.

Brennan fought him to a standstill in the 6th and 7th rounds. This writer believed that up to the 8th round, Brennan had given slightly more than he had received. Dempsey started hurting him more often thereafter, but Brennan clinched, recovered, and kept coming back strong, surprising Dempsey and everyone else. Brennan still made a good showing in the 9th round. Yet, Dempsey had the decided edge in most rounds. The champ's terrific body punching, coupled with the jolting short-arm blows in close, wore down Brennan.

The body blows mostly were what sapped Brennan's strength. Several times, Dempsey had him groggy and shaky, but Brennan held his feet and fought back gamely. In the 12th, the body punches finally ended it.

The *Brooklyn Daily Eagle's* W. C. Vreeland said Dempsey's prestige hung in the balance until the knockout. He retained the title, but not impressively. Most were surprised it had gone so long, expecting an early knockout, within 3, 6, or 10 rounds. Scarcely a bet was made that it would last 10 rounds or more. Another surprise was that the champ had suffered a battering himself; not to a pitiable or frayed condition, but tired, with his lips swollen and bleeding and the lobe of his left ear torn and trickling blood. His new white fighting trunks, with belt of the national colors, was sprinkled and flecked with crimson stains. On his shoulders, chest, and arms, there were blood stains as well. Brennan had been bleeding from the mouth. He was not afraid, and tried to win. He fought hard to the end. Some thought he might make it the distance.

There were many changes and shifts in the bout. Four times, in the 4th, 7th, 8th, and 10th rounds, Dempsey drove his right and left into the pit of Brennan's stomach and followed with punches to the face that made him groggy. But each time, Bill recuperated quickly and came back with punches that cut and bruised, fighting himself out of trouble.

This writer believed that as the bout progressed, Brennan gained strength, while Dempsey became weaker. Bill stung the champ with long rights to the face and several uppercuts. Brennan's supporters' hopes grew in the 9th round, when with three straight rights he knocked Jack back onto the ropes and pinned him there. That flash caused the crowd to roar. It was a fine and unexpected rally. But Dempsey worked in close, which saved him.

At infighting, Dempsey was a masterful artist, very effective. Brennan would have done better if he had kept away and fought at long range. Dempsey's short jolts to the stomach carried terrific force and robbed Brennan of much of his strength, weakening and helping to bring him down at the end. Jack seemed to know this was the weak spot, and he played for it nearly to the exclusion of the face. He used his left to the stomach more often than the right to the chin.

Vreeland said if he had failed to win by knockout, Dempsey would have lost much of his prestige. Even at that, many said he was not a real knockout artist like Sullivan or Fitzsimmons. The performance made many believe that Carpentier could beat him. Others believed he was stalling to give the fans a run for their money, or the moving picture men a better film, because films were worth more when they were longer and the fight was not a quick blowout. Some thought it possibly was done to make the Carpentier fight more marketable. Dempsey denied it all though. Still, many believed otherwise. Boxing folks could be quite suspicious.

The *New York Tribune's* W. O. McGeehan said the bout was dramatic. Brennan started with a rush and held an early lead. Brennan carried the fight to the champ and made a melodrama out of what was anticipated to be a farce. Dempsey suffered some "humiliation," and the fight lowered his estimation in the minds of many, for he had been punished. His ear had been torn open in the 10th round, dripping red blood, and he was scowling furiously. Brennan was open-mouthed and gasping from the effect of an accumulation of body blows throughout. It had been a sensational fight.

Brennan earned the respect of the fans. More than once he had hurt Dempsey, and worse still, he hurt the champion's pride. He was leading on points after 5 rounds. There was a gasp when after the 10th round, Dempsey flopped back into his corner with his ear battered and a stream of blood pouring from it.

From the start, to everyone's surprise, Brennan carried the fight to the champion. Bill kept forcing the fighting gallantly. He made a real drama out of it. He pressed in close, and more than once sent the champ's head bobbing backward.

But all the time, Dempsey was playing for Brennan's body. The accumulation of the body blows was wearing Bill down. Brennan would go to his corner with his mouth open. He gradually sagged at his knees. Bill occasionally spurted with some effective blows, and got the gallery hopeful and cheerful, but Dempsey just kept plugging away, breaking him down gradually. However, in the 10th round, Brennan again jarred and jolted Dempsey. But he was weary, and it was his last stand. In the 11th, Bill still was fighting, but the champ's choppy blows were telling cruelly. Those who saw Brennan's face could tell that the end was coming soon, and it did, as a result of the hard body blows in the 12th. Still, Dempsey's pride was hurt, and he likely would have a cauliflower ear from the battle against a man whom many previously regarded as second rate.

The *New York Tribune's* Grantland Rice said the Chicago boxer surprised the fans with his fine stand. The champion finally won, but lost four-fifths of his glamor. He was bleeding profusely from the mouth, nose, and right ear. Brennan became weary after the 10th round, and finally fell from a right and left to the body.

Dempsey won, but Brennan was the hero of the event. He carried the champion longer than anyone ever had. He proved that he could take it, "and he had also proved that just a good, ordinary heavyweight could hit Dempsey almost at will."

Brennan put up an astonishing battle, standing toe to toe, and, in a series of savage slugging fests, frequently drove Dempsey back to the ropes. Bill never was afraid of the "man-eater." Early in the fight, Brennan had Dempsey half-groggy on at least two occasions.

The first gasp of astonishment came in the 2nd round, when Brenan whipped back Dempsey's head at least six inches, and for a few seconds Jack had a half-groggy, worried appearance, holding on.

Brennan actually had the lead on points after 3 rounds, crossing Dempsey with right and left jabs that brought forth a look of startled surprise to the champ's battered face. When Dempsey tore in, Brennan took all he had to give, and would knock Dempsey's head back with a stinging uppercut.

Often when Brennan was in a bad way, he suddenly would show new fighting spirit and draw more blood from the champ's face.

Brennan began weakening in the 8th and 9th rounds. Dempsey seemed a bit weary as well. His nose and mouth were bleeding badly, and his ear looked like a cross between a veal cutlet and a sponge dipped in gore.

By the end of the 11th round, Brennan was all in. Dempsey was tired, but still keen to end the scrap.

In the 12th, the champ rushed and slugged, until finally a right and left to the body dropped Brennan. Bill attempted to rise just as he was counted out. His final collapse came as much from sheer exhaustion as from anything else.

Dempsey took more punishment than ever before. He shed as much or more gore than Brennan, who soaked up many a lusty wallop before he finally buckled up and sank slowly to the floor for the fight's only knockdown.

For those who had looked for an early knockout, Dempsey's performance was a big disappointment. But he had met a man who was not afraid to trade, and he could take it too. It had been a great battle.

Dempsey proved his condition, for at no time did he lose the sting in his walloping power, although he did not carry quite the knockout crash which he had featured in most of his other fights. Rather, it was his long series of pounding blows that finally wore down Brennan.

Damon Runyon said Brennan had Dempsey worried in the early rounds, but gradually was cut down and put away. The champion was careless at times, but wicked at the finish. Brennan gave the spectators a tremendous thrill. He held his ground, and at times even outfought the champ, wading in grimly under showers of blows, risking everything.

For the greater part of the fight, Brennan had the crowd on its feet cheering for him. There were one or two fleeting moments when it looked as if the title might change hands. The champ was bleeding from a cut behind his ear, and from his mouth. His white silk trunks were smeared with red. Most had expected a quick collapse of the Chicago man within 3 rounds. After all, few had lasted longer in recent years.

Yet, with his brown gloves, the champion was cutting down Brennan in the clinches, hitting either side of his jaw with short blows that shook Bill down to his toes. These punches were not so apparent at a distance, but they were doing their deadly work, and eventually Brennan went down and out, though the end came suddenly.

The *Brooklyn Daily Times'* Len Wooster said Dempsey's victory was not impressive, for he was slow and sluggish, while Brennan surprised everyone. He was a tough man to batter down, giving as good an exhibition of gameness as ever seen. A left to the body doubled him up. Quick as a flash Dempsey shot a right behind the ear and it was over.

Dempsey won, but was not great in victory. He had been hailed as one of the greatest heavyweights of all time, but his vaunted speed never was in evidence. Against Miske, he was as fast as a flash, but against Brennan, he was slow and sluggish, measured distance poorly, and missed often. Many said if that was his best, then neither Carpentier nor Wills need fear him. When Frank Moran recently knocked out Joe Beckett in the 2nd round, many said the result did not make Carpentier's chances against Dempsey look good. However, Dempsey's performance against Brennan robbed Jack of some luster. Brennan was slow and not overly scientific. Yet he got to Dempsey and punished him severely at times.

> Now if Brennan can do these things it cannot be denied that Carpentier can do the same. The Frenchman is a magnificent boxer, cool and calculating, has a much better head than Dempsey and punches hard. If it had been Carpentier that was facing Dempsey and he had got in that right uppercut to the jaw that shook Dempsey to his heels in the second round there would have been a follow up that might have caused the championship to change hands right there. But the slow methodical Brennan did not take advantage of his opportunity and in a few seconds Dempsey's head had cleared and he went viciously after the Chicagoan to offset the damage he had done.

Dempsey's pride had been hurt, for the longer Brennan stuck around, the more the experts wondered whether they had not overestimated his ability. "Jack the Giant Killer" was having all kinds of troubles with a "so-called second rater." It appeared that he was doing his best to terminate the bout with a knockout. But he was slow on his feet and only a fair judge of distance. He did not follow-up advantages. He frequently pulled his punches.

Some thought he was carrying him and willing to allow Brennan to last. Others said he was trying, or else he would not have taken such punishment. "For punishment he received lots of it." Brennan cut him behind the left ear in the 10th and opened his lip in the 11th. It was a severe test.

Dempsey wore him down with his infighting. Close-range work was the one redeeming feature of the champion's efforts. His short, snappy punches ultimately brought Brennan to the point where he was ripe for the finishing wallop.

Yet, Brennan took all he had and looked for more. Bill carried the fight to him frequently. He was a willing, game, and persistent plodder. He battled remarkably well and tried to win. His aggression was a surprise, taking it to the champion. The 2nd round was his best, rocking Dempsey with a right uppercut to the jaw.

Brennan again was aggressive in the 3rd, but Dempsey's infighting was beginning to tell. Yet, Bill took all the punishment handed out without flinching. It looked like the end was near in the 4th, as the champ fought systematically and seemed to be wearing him down. In the 5th, Brennan was weak from short rights to the stomach. The 6th saw Brennan weary, and at times wobbly, but the hardest blows from the champion could not sink him. The fight progressed like that until the 10th, when two hard rights over the heart made it appear that Brennan was ripe for the finish. Yet, he pulled himself together and connected with a right hook that cut Dempsey's ear. The fans rooted lustily. Brennan's courage was renewed, and in the 11th he hit the damaged ear, landing his stinging left and right in succession in a valiant effort to turn the tide.

In the 12th, Brennan was just as willing as ever, but it was evident that he was tiring, and after taking some hard knocks at close range, Dempsey whipped a left to the body, followed by a right to the ear, and Brennan went down. At ten he was about to rise, but did not make it on time.

The *Brooklyn Standard Union* said Brennan left the ring about 25 seconds after the knockout. Dempsey was presented with the championship belt, stood at ring center, waved both arms to the crowd, and smiled though his battered features. "The fight leads one to believe that Carpentier may have a chance with Dempsey." However, "The one thing that stood out above all other things in the contest was Dempsey's confidence. When he was being pummeled most severely he never lost that air of confidence." He seemed to believe that he would land the knockout blow at some point, and it was only a question of when. He was proven correct.

Henry Farrell wrote that Brennan cut up the champion, who was a sorry-looking sight the next day. Dempsey's left ear was mashed and torn, his lips were puffed out and cut, jaw swollen, and eyes puffy and red. Brennan made him work harder and take more than he ever had taken before. Nevertheless, in the 12th round, two vicious stomach punches and a smashing right to the head folded Brennan up and he fell on his head and elbows for the count. The steady pounding on his heart and stomach had sapped his endurance.

The fight was a surprise because most expected to go home early, but it turned out to be really hotly contested, and the gallery gods up in the smoke clouds were in a violent uproar of excitement, thinking that there was a possibility that they might see a championship change hands.

From the start, Brennan carried the fight to the champ and landed several hard blows, even rocking Dempsey twice with rights in the 2nd round. That aroused Dempsey's scowl. The crowd wondered about the result up to the 8th, when the tide began to turn. Brennan had won the first 5 rounds and was even up to the 8th, when Dempsey landed crushing blows to his stomach. Brennan winced with pain and went to his corner with his mouth open. From then on, Dempsey won. He had more endurance and more steam in his punches.

Daniel said it was the hardest battle of Dempsey's career. Brennan fought an aggressive, courageous fight and generated the highest admiration from the fans.

When it was over, after being assisted to his corner in a daze, eventually Bill walked over to Dempsey to congratulate him. He shook his head and seemed to be fighting back a sob. As he walked back to his dressing room, Brennan received a thunderous cheer and ovation for his game efforts. Many hissed Dempsey.

To the astonishment of the onlookers, Brennan carried the fight to the champion throughout. Even when he was weakened, Bill fought with desperate energy. He received terrific punishment in nearly every round, proving his ability to take it. But he also inflicted more damage on the champion than any other foe had given him.

Dempsey staggered Brennan several times. The Chicagoan seemed on the verge of a knockout on two or three occasions, but with dogged courage, he weathered the storm of blows, and while wobbly at the close of several rounds, managed to respond for the next bell with praiseworthy aggressiveness.

Brennan received a closed right eye, a few cuts about the face, and $35,000. Dempsey got a cut on the nose, a slash on the left ear, and $100,000. He also would receive valuable motion picture royalties.

Many wondered why Brennan was able to last double the time he did in 1918, when Dempsey stopped him in the 6th round. Some said either Dempsey was overrated, or he was a hipppodromer and motion picture actor. If the bout had ended early, the motion pictures would be worth little. But a film containing 12 rounds of action would carry great financial weight on the picture market. Whether merited or not, many began to wonder and harbor suspicions. However, it was possible that Dempsey had gone back, or that Brennan had improved and simply was that tough.

Daniel said both men held and hit, though the champion received the hisses. Dempsey once even elbowed him, which brought more hisses.

Dempsey kept cuffing with his left while his right hung idle at his side, or crooked closely to his chest. There were rumbles of wonderment, suspicion, amazement, and doubt.

Victory finally came in the 12th round. Hence, judges Joe Ruddy and Thomas Shortell were not needed. The finish was sensational. It was a lightning-fast right to the heart, the same that landed on Fred Fulton. Jack had landed that same punch on Willard, which convinced him to throw in the towel. Brennan gasped and tried to hold, but a left hook to the body doubled him up. As he sagged at the knees, Dempsey hit him with right over the left ear, and Brennan fell.

"Karpe" said the fight proved that Dempsey could go a route and take considerable punishment, yet still have a knockout punch at his command. Dempsey was slow to get going. The final blows were a right to the heart and left to the stomach, and then a right crack on the ear as Brennan was going down, which finished the job.

Karpe did not agree with those who said Dempsey had gone back. A man who can find a knockout body punch in either mitt in the 12th round has not lost much of his hitting ability or stamina. No one else had stopped Brennan, who proved that he was a 100% improved fighter. Dan Morgan had declared that Dempsey would find Brennan a hard man to beat, and he was.

Early on, Dempsey found it difficult to land on the jaw. Brennan defended himself well and carried the battle to Dempsey. He even had the better of the 3rd, and a couple of other rounds were even.

Jack settled down to a campaign of infighting, terrible close-up jolts to the head and body, which punished Brennan cruelly, and it was a wonder how he stood up to it and came back cheerfully for more.

Some who watched Dempsey's slow opening rounds and Brennan's "apparent slight advantage" scoffingly said those rounds were for the benefit of the motion picture men. Karpe disagreed. It seemed that Dempsey realized he had a tough man in front of him, conserved his strength, and fought a wearing-down battle. By the end of the 7th round, this treatment was having its effect.

At the start of each round, Brennan would come out apparently reinvigorated, and sometimes sent Jack's head back with stiff leads. But even though he was staggered once or twice, Dempsey never was in serious trouble, and all the time kept up that deadly and ceaseless short-arm punishment.

Brennan really began to weaken in the 8th round, when for the first time he hung on and covered. His pressure was diminishing, though he fought back valiantly at all times, bringing the crowd to cheers even if the blows he threw were blocked on Dempsey's elbows; the usual underdog sympathy stuff.

Even when Bill landed on the chin, he did not faze Jack. He could not hurt him with his best blows. Dempsey took some punishment, but was administering more, until finally in the 12th round, Brennan sank to his knees, gradually flattened out on his stomach, rolled partly over, and tried to rise. He had just managed a stooping posture at ten, and declared out. Dempsey assisted him to his corner.

Bill was cut badly about the face. Dempsey had blood coming from his left ear and a trickle from his mouth, but otherwise scarcely was marked. "It was Dempsey's hardest fight, but he won it impressively."

Brennan's stock got a substantial boost on account of his gallant attack and fine gameness.

Many said Carpentier would have had a much tougher and longer fight with Brennan had Bill been in there instead of Levinsky. Bill could take it.

"Fair Play" said it remained an unanswered question regarding what Dempsey could do against a clever boxer. Dempsey's showing raised the hopes of Georges Carpentier's followers.

Sport followers and fans were divided over the champion's showing. Dempsey's reputation had been that of a quick knockout artist. Few had any idea that Brennan would last more than 5 rounds. As round after round progressed, with Bill sticking and doing a lot of hitting, amazement grew. Some said that owing to motion picture concerns, Dempsey allowed him to recuperate from blows when he might have finished him. The writer doubted it. Brennan was a big, strong, tough man who was able to take punishment, and had a dangerous wallop himself. Dempsey could not afford to take chances with such a man. The sooner he could get him out the better. Brennan put up a game and skillful battle. Still, many thought Dempsey was holding back his full power, fighting under wraps.

Every time that Brennan would receive fearful punishment, he would come back and fight Dempsey to a standstill. The crowd stood up and cheered wildly. Then Dempsey would come back strong and have Bill holding on to save himself. Yet, Brennan kept recovering.

However, the body blows that Dempsey had rained upon him throughout the fight and the short-arm jolts to the jaw had taken their toll. Brennan still fought hard, but eventually Dempsey caught him under the heart with a left hook that came like lightning. Brennan slumped in the middle. The champ hit the body with the right. As Bill slid to the floor, Jack cracked him behind the ear, and he fell on his knees.

Dempsey watched the count from about 12 feet away. Brennan rose, pitching toward the ropes, seizing them in a dazed state. The referee threw up his hands. Dempsey came over, took Bill's arm, and helped him to his corner.

Overall, Dempsey seemed pale and a little drawn. His judgment of his blows, especially his right, was bad. Time after time he missed, and he did not shine defensively. Brennan landed several solid socks.

The question was what Dempsey would do against a clever man who could keep him off with jabs, like Carpentier, and avoid his punches. However, the question also was whether Carpentier could stand the fearful effect of the blows that he would receive from Dempsey. Brennan surely proved that he could take a punch.

It was a clean, fair battle. Once Dempsey struck him with his elbow, but immediately held out his hand to apologize, which Brennan accepted with a nod.

C. J. Murray said Dempsey was on the verge of a knockout in the 2nd round, but showed the cleverness of a lightweight in fending off Brennan's attack. It had been a grueling fight.

The end came in the 12th, when Dempsey landed a terrific right hook under Brennan's short ribs, near the heart, instantly followed by a left clip to the chin. Bill doubled up, tottered, and went down from a finishing right hand wallop that landed squarely on the back of his neck, sending him down to the canvas head first. Bill's forehead hit the floor first.

Brennan slowly raised himself to his knees, and got off the canvas at eight, but with his back to Dempsey, and he staggered like a drunken man towards the ropes. Dempsey advanced, but there was no more fight left in Brennan. As Bill slowly turned around, Dempsey drew back ready to fire a finisher, but the referee mercifully stepped between them, and caught the swaying Brennan under the arms, saving him from dropping again. Dempsey closed in and the pair helped Bill to his corner. His seconds shoved a stool underneath him. Jack patted him on the back and muttered between his bloody lips, "Good, game fight you gave me, Bill. Better luck next time." Brennan sat down, and his seconds poured water over him to revive him.

Brennan eventually got up, crossed the ring to Dempsey's corner and said to Jack, "I thought I was the next champion in the second round but I couldn't quite make it. Maybe we'll meet again, Jack. You are a great fighter. Put it there," and they shook hands warmly.

Murray said Dempsey won, but it was a tough fight, and Brennan was the toughest man he ever faced. Dempsey was near defeat in the 2nd round. He definitively answered in the affirmative the question whether he could take a punch. "Yes, Dempsey can take a punch, and a nerve-shattering, pile-driving punch, too, right on the chin and come back."

Brennan was as strong as a bull and hit terrifically with his right, soaking him squarely on the point of the chin in the 2nd round. It stung and shook the champion, who went back on his heels. Brennan swung away, attempting to finish him. Dempsey seemed dazed and in bad shape. Yet, he closed in and bluffed it out, mauling and fussing around. Still, Bill fought like a fiend, and forced Dempsey to show the cleverness few realized he had. Jack was not strong enough at that moment to stand and slug, so he glided in and out and demonstrated marvelous scientific boxing. He actually made Brennan miss by a lot, and lasted out the round.

Between rounds, smelling salts were administered to Dempsey, whose seconds worked over him like wild men, rubbing his legs and arms. Brennan waved for his seconds to get out of the way so he could have a peep at Dempsey, sprawled out on his stool.

At the bell for the 3rd round, Brennan rushed in and made a furious attempt to grab the title. Dempsey again fell back on his cleverness and outboxed Brennan ten to one, making him look foolish. Some ringsiders shouted that Dempsey had been kidding. But he wasn't kidding in the 2nd round. He had to call forth all the tricks of the trade. He did not dare allow Brennan to get too close, for he had a mighty smash.

Dempsey had to come back gradually to be himself again. He turned the trick, showing himself to be a master fighter.

Brennan put forth six rounds of effort in that 3rd round, but got nowhere in particular. He was more tired than Dempsey when the bell ended the round, for he had wasted his strength and speed, while the champion had conserved his.

The 4th round found Dempsey his old self again. Brennan's chance had passed, and from then on, he took a thorough licking, though never flinching and always fighting. Yet, he gradually was slipping downhill, by degrees bowing to the champion.

In the 8th round, "Dempsey literally crucified Brennan, batting Bill from side to side with stiff, heart breaking short jolts that must have rattled Bill's teeth." Watching Brennan suffer under the pounding, one had to gaze and wonder what on earth prevented him from collapsing.

Yet, in the 9th round, Brennan came out full of fight. While he was slipping fast and taking an awful punching, his heart still was in the right place, and he swung many a haymaker. But it was no use. Dempsey's terrific body smashes and jolts to the chin had sapped Brennan's stamina, and he was well licked.

In the 10th and 11th rounds, Dempsey was absolute master of the situation, fighting wonderfully well. He was deliberate in his attack and guarded with extra caution, for though Brennan was wobbly, he still was dangerous with his right haymakers.

Brennan looked better coming out for the 12th than he had in a while, but Dempsey's punches had undermined him, and he collapsed from a punch that did not appear to be any harder than any one of dozens he took earlier in the fight and shook off.

Summarizing, Murray said Brennan was as game as any man who ever entered a ring, and fought until he had nothing left.

Dempsey did not look like the superman who slaughtered Willard. His rugged appearance had faded some, and he seemed thin and drawn. He wore a tired, though serious look. His muscles were less prominent than they had been at Toledo. He did not have the same snap and wicked attack. "There was not the same terrible effect to his punches and he did not have the old sharp shooter's judgment of distance that marked his winning fight against Willard." He was more uncertain, and hesitated often. Against Carl Morris in Buffalo in 1918, he tore in, disregarded danger, and battered away, never hesitating. "Dempsey says this is due to lack of outdoor exercise in the whirlwind of New York life." For whatever reason, he did not look or fight like the same man-eater seen on several prior occasions.

Murray thought Dempsey should leave New York City and get back to the country and the simple life. He still was a marvelous fighter, but not as great as he had been.

Of course, Brennan deserved some of the credit. He was far better prepared than Willard was, and fought a vastly different fight. He bothered Dempsey with flashes of speed and cleverness. Regardless, the champ had to "brush himself up or he is going to have an awful time whipping Carpentier." And yet, Murray said that whether stale or faded, Dempsey proved he could take it, and also was something more than just a rough and tumble slugger. "He demonstrated that he is clever, very clever."

It had been a great fight and wonderful evening for the fans.

Despite the record gate, Rickard did not make much, for he had paid so much to the fighters.

The *Boston Post* wrote that there was nothing to Dempsey's performance that would serve to make him a top-heavy favorite over Carpentier. Both Harry Wills and Kid Norfolk "would have done even better" than Brennan, and this writer opined that the champion could not have stopped either one of them.

Frank Smith said a powerful right to the stomach, a more powerful left to the midsection, and a right clip on the jaw sent Brennan down for the count.

The remaining existing footage of the fight shows a somewhat different story than told by many of the newsmen, highlighting why both written and visual records are so important, because quite often they differ. Of course, the same way written accounts sometimes have omissions and inaccuracies, so too do many old films have great portions of the bout missing due to deterioration. Only select portions of several rounds are available, even assuming the rounds claimed indeed are the rounds represented. Several versions claim the same footage from a particular round is the footage from a different round, and they cannot both be right. Such is a common problem with old fight films. They often are incomplete and/or out of order.

The films reflect that Dempsey constantly applied pressure, digging short uppercuts, body shots, and hooks. It wasn't flashy or obvious, but over the course of many rounds, such work would take its toll. It proved that Dempsey could pace himself and win by using a methodical method, grinding a man down gradually over the long haul. He was not just a fast-starting, explosive, short-burst fighter who had to knock out a foe quickly in order to get a knockout. He could pace himself for a lengthier fight too. From that perspective, it proved Dempsey's versatility, condition, durability, and adaptability.

It is clear that Brennan put up a good fight. He looked quick, strong, sturdy, and willing, and was at his best when throwing jabs and rights from a distance, though he did not do that very often, perhaps in part because of Dempsey's relentless pressure. It mostly was an inside fight, and Brennan seemed quite content and able to fight there, not really moving very much. It was a grueling, grinding fight, with both men keeping a good pace, whether throwing on the outside and stepping in, or working consistently with single shots on the inside, to the head and body. They clinched, but also punched frequently and consistently in the clinches. Both had a full arsenal of blows, punching and countering back and forth.

Dempsey was quite at home on the inside. He generally was the aggressor and initiator throughout, while Brennan mostly seemed content to fight in a reactionary manner, countering when Dempsey stepped inside, though Bill also took the initiative on plenty of occasions, and was not shy about attacking at times.

Brennan looked sharp, landing nice, single, quick, powerful leads or countershots, particularly with snappy but heavy rights and right uppercuts, sometimes setting them up with some jabs, putting up a competitive fight. However, his punches did not really seem to faze Dempsey, who took it well, but also dipped, turned, and rolled his head to the side to take some of the sting off many of the blows, and nevertheless, Jack maintained a consistent, almost nonstop pace, digging many punches on the inside.

Dempsey appeared to dictate the fight. He didn't always move in, but sometimes moved back or off to the side. He can be seen lightly bouncing or moving about, or occasionally turning and walking off to the right, setting up his attack and making it difficult for Brennan to time him on the way in.

To get inside, Dempsey often would dip to the right to avoid incoming blows and step in quickly with a jab or lead right, under or over.

Dempsey imposed his will on the bout, getting to the inside relatively easily, making it the type of fight which was to his liking. He kept a fast pace, on the inside digging multiple single nonstop punches consisting of uppercuts, hooks, and body shots, often with the same hand, then switching to the other, over, under, around, wide, centered, anywhere he could find or create an opening. He was adept at firing off short left hooks, uppercuts, and body blows, cuffing right hooks, and digging right uppercuts to the body. Sometimes he fired under with one hand and over with the other, and vice versa.

The scrappy Brennan kept up the pace as well, content to fight at any range, landing some solid blows here and there, and he kept it competitive and entertaining, but Dempsey really set the tempo, was more consistent with his punches, and was the effective aggressor. Brennan was more of the quick, explosive puncher, but less often, while Dempsey had the heavier, thudding, more compact, less flashy, but more metronome, short-snap, consistent attack. Both men clearly could take a punch quite well.

Dempsey had the ability to work well on the inside, avoiding being held for too long. The ability to avoid the clinch or work himself free from the clinch with a free hand, consistently working on the inside, was something he had demonstrated against Willard as well. Brennan sometimes held with his left and fired off a good right uppercut.

What was most impressive about Dempsey was not only the mix of crisp punches, head movement, and footwork, but how relaxed, calm, and poised he was even at a relatively fast pace for heavyweights. He did not mind getting into range and remaining there, and was not rattled by his opponents' blows. He had an assassin's confidence, calm and certain, never overreacting.

From the limited existing footage, it appears that Dempsey was in control, gradually wearing Brennan down over time with consistent pressure and heavy digging blows all over, like water on a rock in a war of attrition. It showed that Dempsey could fight in a consistent manner at a good clip over a long period of time. Although not as ferocious, fast, and explosive as he was against Willard, he was more relaxed and methodical, less wild, his punches more compact, and yet still able to work at and maintain a relatively fast, peppy clip.

Dempsey's attack really was flowing in the 10th round, and he was landing quite often, even seeming to stun Brennan slightly with a lead right to the jaw. Nevertheless, Bill kept fighting, landing jabs and right uppercuts, and clinching, putting up a good scuffle. But one could tell that Dempsey was coming on. The pace still was quite brisk.

In the 11th round, Dempsey was jabbing more often, standing straighter, and had a bit more pep in his step, though he still was doing his usual good inside work with short uppercuts and hooks to the body and head.

In the 12th round, they kept up the fast pace, punching and clinching. Dempsey was firing a right to the body and left hook to the head in combination.

The knockout sequence is of poor quality, and there is missing footage, but it appears that Dempsey landed a jolting left uppercut to the jaw of an already leaning-over Brennan (who likely already had been hit with the body blows), wide right to the body (perhaps side or kidney), followed by a right to the side of the head as Bill was leaning over even further, and he went down face-first on his hands and knees.

The referee counted, but it is unclear whether Brennan beat the count. It seemed to be a slightly fast count, though film replay projection rates can vary and be misleading. It does appear that if going by the referee's arm moving up and down, at the tenth downward swing, Brennan's glove or gloves still were on the canvas as he was in the process of rising.

Regardless, when he rose, Brennan still was crouched over in pain, he staggered forward a bit into the ropes or corner, his back turned away from the referee and Dempsey, and when he turned around, with Dempsey right there, he did not seem ready or able to continue, still crouched/doubled over, clearly cringing in pain, with his hands down. He would have been a sitting duck for pulverizing blows at that point had it been allowed to continue. Dempsey shook Bill's hand, and, along with the referee, assisted Bill back to his corner, where he sat down on a stool.

Brennan subsequently walked to Dempsey's corner, shook his hand, returned to his own corner, and exited the ring. Dempsey stood up, walked to ring center, and raised his arms up in the air, to which apparently he received a rousing cheer and ovation. Shortly thereafter, he left the ring through Brennan's corner.

Overall, the footage demonstrates an impressive performance, even if not a spectacular one, a lot better than the next-day critics opined. Their criticisms were a bit harsh and unfair. There are more positives to take away than negatives. It seems that because it was not an overwhelming, explosive, quick knockout, and Brennan was more competitive than expected, and because Dempsey had been so greatly hyped as a superman and all-time great, there was a bit of a backlash as a result of the high expectations. As boxing history has shown, not everyone is going to be easily subdued. Bill Brennan was an experienced, rugged, tough, strong competitor, who came to win. He was in shape, had skills, tried his best, could take a punch, and simply was durable. Not everyone is going to be knocked out quickly. Nevertheless, Dempsey fought to break him down, and he did, stopping a man whom no one else had stopped up to that point.

It should be noted that Dempsey was the first to knock out several foes in his career, including Levinsky, Willard, Miske, and Brennan, all of whom had a lot of high-quality experience and were noted for their durability. What also is impressive about Dempsey is that his tactics, methods, and skills are easily translatable and useful to the modern fighter. His effectiveness has a timeless quality to it.

Another thing to consider is that often the fighters who are explosive, fast knockout artists tend to fatigue as bouts progress. There is a risk of fatigue when investing so much energy into the early rounds. Against some fighters, it is necessary to pace oneself and be more efficient and methodical, rather than fruitlessly expend too much energy. Dempsey appeared to sense that he needed such a style and methodology with this version of Bill Brennan. Hence, he showed his versatility.

Benny Leonard was allowed to enter Dempsey's dressing room, and he said, "What a fight! What a fight! I wouldn't take one of your punches for all the money in the world. Gee, Jack, you sure are a wonderful champion. A real honest to goodness heavyweight boss. Congratulations, old man. You are a wonder." Dempsey blushed and said, "Thank you."

In article he wrote, Dempsey, a great sport, declared that Brennan gave him the hardest battle of his career.

> Oh, what a tough bird Bill Brennan turned out to be! It took me twelve rounds to finish him, the longest, toughest fight of my career. Brennan's power to stand up under punishment through the fast eleven rounds was amazing, and it's a perpetual testimony to his superb gameness – his almost uncanny power to take punishment and come for more and get more. Brennan's showing surprised me somewhat. It surprises the sporting world still more – that's because the rank and file of fans underestimated Brennan. I didn't. I knew he was tough, that he was a marvel in taking punishment, as well as handing it back, and he proved it tonight.

> The fight tonight made it possible for me to prove one thing. And that is there is within me the power to take on a formidable foeman, travel a distance, do it with all my speed, take punishment,

and still go on to knockout victory. Yes, I did take punishment, for Bill hit me on the body, let me have terrific lefts and rights to the jaw and opened my left ear with a solid right hand hook. He hit me oftener tonight than all the men I have faced in three years hit me altogether.

My main thought was to get that right hander planted against Bill's heart. ... A dozen times through the other rounds I landed the right to the body but I didn't hit the bull's eye. ... But the 12th – well, I accomplished my purpose then. A few opening bangs to the head seemed to unsteady Bill a bit. Then I feinted with the left, pulled up his guard and opportunity was mine. I rammed the old right hander home and felt Bill sort of give way with the force of the punch. I knew Bill was through. A left to the body, another right to the head – and Bill began to sink to the floor. One final tap – more a shove than a blow – and Bill was down and being counted out. Referee Billy Haukop chanted "ten' over Bill as he partly kneeled on the floor with his face almost on the canvas.

But, hardly had the count finished when Bill, groggy, bewildered, got to his feet, the splendid fighting instinct still directing him. Bill got up and faced me, staggering and a little bent over – but still willing to go on. That's courage and Bill Brennan demonstrated it a hundred times over tonight. Bill didn't know he had been counted out but then Haukop pushed him back and told him what had happened. I helped Bill back to his corner and the fight was over.

My marksmanship tonight was little bit off, or was some of my missing due to Bill's clear [clever] ducking? I'll leave the answer to the sport experts, but the fact is indisputable that I failed to find the target with quite a few of my hardest swings. Maybe it was because I was a little too impatient to score a knockout and didn't time my punches as perfectly as I should have. Brennan surely fought fiercely, courageously, cleanly. The way he'd take smashes to the jaw, pile driver rights and lefts to the pit of the stomach might have been discouraging if it hadn't been for the confidence I had that I was Bill's master and that I would get him before the 15th.

But memories of that fight will remain. I guess those who saw it will concede that there was plenty of action in it, that there was excitement of some sort or other in every round of it, and I'll remember that part, too, remember it for a long time, for the battle which Brennan gave me tonight was the hardest I have ever had to wage, and my hat is off to Bill Brennan.

According to the *New York Times* and Daniel, Dempsey said, "Brennan was tougher than I expected. He stood up under my blows longer than I thought he could. Brennan's blows didn't hurt me at any time during the bout, but I found him a hard man to hit properly and a tough man for taking punishment. I thought I could finish him earlier than I did, but he surprised me."

W. C. Vreeland quoted Dempsey as saying that Brennan was tough to knock out.

> I realized he would be hard to drop early in the bout. That is why I saved my punches. I tried to wear him out, to sap his strength, by planting blows in the pit of the stomach. When I thought he was ripe for the knockout I sent it over. No, I did not fight for the movies. I did not delay the knockout to suit the pictures or give the crowd a run for its money. I fought with but one object – to knock out Brennan – and my line of attack was all the line to accomplish it, no matter how long it took. I did not delay the K.O for anything or anybody.

Jack Kearns said, "Dempsey was a bit overtrained and slow." The champ did not have a surplus ounce, and was drawn too fine. It took him 5 rounds to get warmed up and going before showing anything like his real form. Kearns admitted that Dempsey missed frequently, his timing slow, and eye off.

Nevertheless, Kearns said Dempsey always was the master of the situation, and took his time. Despite the fact that his lower lip was cut badly and left ear split, Dempsey never was hurt to any great extent.

Brennan was tough and rugged, and Dempsey had to beat him into submission, hitting the heart and stomach to do it. Also, Brennan hung on and held at every chance, which affected the bout.

Kearns noted that because Dempsey had won so many fights so quickly, and fans had come to expect a quick knockout victory in a punch or two, or within a few rounds, with such high expectations, now that he took so long to stop a hard, strong fighter, some thought the champion was vulnerable to defeat and that someone was going to get him. They were wrong.

Kearns said they expected to fight Willard in a rematch on St. Patrick's Day, March 17, 1921.

Henry Farrell said Kearns declared that Dempsey was overtrained, scarcely willing to give Brennan credit for his splendid performance.

After the mob faded from the building, C. J. Murray sat down with Dempsey, who asked, "Did I look good or rotten?" Murray said he did not fight as impressively as he did in Toledo. Dempsey replied, "I know it, felt it all the time, but do you know what was wrong? I overtrained. I worked too long for this match. I felt stale all week. I'm going to California, in to the mountains for two months. When I start the next time I'll be right."

In an interview in the cab ride home with reporter Richard Freyer, Dempsey said,

> I was boxing a tough man. I fought him before and I knew what I was up against. I just took things easy for a while and wore Brennan

down. I'm sort of glad the fight went twelve rounds, because it showed me, as well as the general public, that I can travel a distance and win by a knockout. Brennan made the fight hard for me because he did not lead once that I know of. I started him toward the knockout with a hard blow to the stomach and finished him with a right hand smash in back of the neck. ... It was one of the hardest fights I ever engaged in, even though I do not believe I received one real hard damaging blow.

Jack's left ear was bleeding a bit and his lower lip was swollen. Jack said the injuries were the result of head butts in the clinches, though unintentional.

Evening World writer Robert Boyd interviewed Brennan. Bill said Dempsey was the hardest man he ever stood up against.

Dempsey is the greatest fighter in the world. I only wish that the referee had not been so hasty in stopping the fight. I arose at what I thought was the count of nine, although later they informed me it was ten. I was a bit dazed from the head and body punching Dempsey had been sending at me all through the fight. In the twelfth round he got his left into the pit of my stomach. It doubled me up and I fell forward. My head was down. Suddenly Dempsey shot a short overhand right on the back of my left ear. I was near Dempsey's corner and the sharp jolt in the head sent me to the canvas, my knees hitting the floor first, and then I fell on my hands. Yes, I was dazed and the Garden was in a noisy turmoil. When the referee reached what I thought was nine, I got up and backed into a neutral corner ready to continue. Just then the referee raised his arm and waved Dempsey back, ending the fight. I was fairly beaten. ... No I have no alibi to offer. He is the toughest man I ever fought. His punching was harder than anything I have ever stood up against in my career as a fighter, but I want the public to know that I went down fighting.

Bill said he was not afraid of Dempsey, and fooled all those who predicted that he would be lucky to last a round. Brennan's right eye was badly bruised, damaged by a straight left, but he said it did not affect him much.

When asked if Dempsey had improved, Bill said,

Oh yes; more than 100 per cent. He has always been a tough man to fight, but now he is much tougher. He seems to have the speed of a lightweight now, and in our last fight he did not display the fast footwork which he evidenced tonight. He hits from any angle, and although from the spectator's viewpoint his blows do not look to be hard, yet they are snappy and they sting.

Still, Brennan wanted to fight him again, for

I think in several stages of the fight I outgeneraled Dempsey. At least, I thought so. I know I outboxed him for the first few rounds, and in the second round I had him groggy from a left to the head and a right cross to the jaw. After that Dempsey seemed to put a little more power behind his punches, and his blows had more effect on me.

The *New York Times* said Brennan felt vindicated by his performance. "I fought longer against Dempsey than any other man." He wanted another fight. "I know I had him going in the second round, but I could not follow up the advantage. His blows did not hurt me except the punches to the stomach, which carried plenty of steam. In the twelfth round a right to the stomach and a left which followed quickly were the hardest blows I felt." He was not satisfied with the result, naturally. "I just forgot to get out of the way of one of Dempsey's rights." "I thought I had beaten the referee's count."

Leo Flynn said Brennan was the world's second-best heavyweight. Bill gave Dempsey the fight of his life, and had the champ going in the 2nd round.

Vreeland quoted Brennan as saying a solar plexus blow did it. "I was going strong until that blow in the solar plexus." It paralyzed him, and he could not breath. "Up to that time Dempsey hadn't hurt me. I had walloped him good and plenty. He felt my punches." Bill was willing to fight him again, any time and place.

Daniel quoted Brennan as saying, "I am not satisfied that Dempsey is my superior." Still, Dempsey had stopped him in both of their fights.

John McGarvey and John Bell of the Motor Square Boxing Club in Pittsburgh offered Dempsey $50,000, some saying with a privilege of 50% of the gross receipts if more than the guarantee, to defend his title against Harry Greb in a 10-round bout. However, Dempsey had made $100,000 guaranteed against Brennan, double that offer. He was scheduled to face Carpentier for $300,000 guaranteed. The *Buffalo Times* called the offer to meet Greb a relatively paltry amount.

Supposedly, Jess Willard was set to meet Dempsey on March 17, but no definite announcement had been made.

The next day, at breakfast, Dempsey allegedly told a reporter,

No use in a man kidding himself. I wasn't on edge last night. ... I know I was bad, very bad, and I don't blame you for saying it looks like I've slipped a little bit. ... I'll tell you the truth. I was stale, dead stale. ... I knew it days before the fight. And knew what I had to face, but when I left the dressing room I said to myself, 'Jack old boy, slug it out, slug it out, get him in a punch if you can, but if the storm breaks, make him travel a pace to get you.' I wasn't in my stride until the fifth round. Didn't I look good after the fifth? .... I could feel it. I began to limber up. I could feel my muscles working easier and I was hitting harder. I had a better range, too, and didn't miss so often. … I had him going in the tenth and I was a sure thing to win in the eleventh. But Brennan is tough, golly, he's tough.

Jack said he left his fight in the gymnasium. The fight was on and off again several times, and the continual postponements and preparing over and over again caused him to overtrain. It left him sluggish. He couldn't even toss Bill Tate around like he usually did.

He knew Brennan was no set-up like some folks said, but a darned good fighter and tough man. Even if Jack had been at his best, he could not punch Bill out in 1 round like many were expecting. So, given the expectations, that he knew Bill was better than people said, and that he did not feel at his best, it was like carrying a ton of bricks into the ring.

Jack admitted that he was hurt in the 2nd round. "You've got it right when you say he clipped me a wicked punch in the second. I know it. I was actually groggy. Good thing I had sense enough to step around." He thought perhaps to slug it out, but realized Bill was too strong at that point.

I gave him the old waltz and I nursed myself along carefully until after the fourth round. Then all my strength came back in a flash and I knew I was once more old Jack Dempsey… and I knew it would take a better man than Brennan to floor me. … The old valves seemed to open up and I was alive with ginger or pep.

Jack wanted to train the next time in the mountains in the open air, not in the city, where the air was stuffy.[414]

The *New York Tribune's* Grantland Rice said Dempsey was no maneater, and his next foe would enter the ring with confidence. Brennan had been looked upon as a setup, having been outpointed by Levinsky. Yet, he gave and took well, and had the champ bleeding freely from the mouth, nose, and ear, extended to the limit. Instead of blasting him out in a few rounds like Willard and Miske, in the 2nd round it was Dempsey who was clinching to protect himself.

Rice believed the fight proved that a good heavyweight could take Dempsey's punch and keep going, that the champ could be hit, and that Dempsey could take quite a beating himself and keep fighting at top speed. Hence, any top heavyweight with speed and power would have a chance against him. This writer believed that Dempsey did even better against big, slow, clumsy, easily hit big men, or smaller men who were afraid to mix. Brennan was bigger than him, but not so big as to be clumsy. He had skill and power, and wasn't afraid to step in and exchange.

Though perhaps Dempsey was a bit overrated, he still stood out as a fast, hard hitter. "But he has shown that he is no wonderful boxer against a fairly fast man with a fairly good defense, and that his own defensive qualities are none too strong." Brennan punished him badly, even though

[414] *Buffalo Commercial, Buffalo Times*, December 16, 1920.

Bill never was known as a maneater. "This engagement will at least tend to make Dempsey's next battle even more interesting."

Hence, seeming vulnerable increased the marketability and interest in other fights. It could encourage opponents, and perhaps affect Dempsey's confidence. "It will also prove that a fast, hard hitter – such as Carpentier is – will have a better chance, and that a man like Wills will have a first class chance to get away with a winning blow."

Tad Dorgan said Dempsey was not himself. Jack Kearns remarked that the poor showing would make the odds on upcoming fights better. Former Willard manager Tom Jones said Willard would have beaten the Dempsey that fought Brennan. Folks were saying Jack did not have the same steam to his punches, and he lacked timing and direction. Tad believed that Jack would be himself the next time he fought - the slugging, fearless, pitiless caveman he had been previously.

The *World's* Vincent Treanor said abuse instead of deserved praise was being heaped on Dempsey. Yet, he had proven that he wasn't just the short distance fighter that critics said he was, and although his reputation as a quick finisher was lost or diminished, it would or should do him good. All the criticism was because he didn't quickly knock out a strong, hulking foe, with more ring experience, who had trained better and harder than in all his life, and whom only Dempsey had stopped. The press was unfair, for Dempsey had shown poise, toughness, condition, and the ability to wear down his foe and still carry a knockout punch late into a fight. It was the old story of failing to give credit where credit was due.

Tex Rickard estimated his profit on the gate would be about $15,000. Brennan received $25,000, not the previously reported $35,000. They all would earn much more from the motion picture proceeds, for the films could be shown throughout the state of New York and overseas.

W. C. Vreeland said many suspected that Dempsey "pulled" in the Brennan fight in order to hide his true form and to influence the odds and interest in the prospective Carpentier bout, or he played to the motion pictures to make more money. He did not fight in his usual impetuous fashion. Others thought he stalled to help friends who had wagered that Brennan would last more than 8 rounds. (As usual, speculation was rampant in boxing, without any evidence. They used to say the same things about Jack Johnson.)[415]

W. O. McGeehan said the Brennan fight had boosted the stock of Dempsey-Carpentier. Before the former, sentiment was that Dempsey was such a hard hitter that the Carpentier fight might be a fiasco. But after Brennan, many began giving the Frenchman a real chance.

McGeehan said the punches that dropped Willard were not in evidence. "This strengthens the theory that Dempsey had his bandages reinforced at Toledo. There Willard did not examine the bandages of Dempsey and his seconds were more or less amateurs. ... Did Dempsey

[415] New York Tribune, Buffalo Enquirer, Evening World, New York Times, Brooklyn Daily Eagle, December 16, 1920.

have something in his glove at Toledo which he did not wear at Madison Square Garden? It looked that way." McGeehan was an agitator.

Daniel noted that folks went from saying Dempsey was the greatest champion of all time to saying that because he struggled somewhat with Brennan that he would have been beaten by all of the past champions, including Sullivan, Corbett, Fitzsimmons, and Jeffries. Dempsey still was a great fighter. Just because he won a tough fight did not change that. "Dempsey may not rank high in defense, but he is a remarkable fighter on attack. When he wants to keep going he keeps going, and he showed against Brennan that he can go quite a way at a pretty fast pace."

Still, the fight caused the French joy, and their belief had grown stronger that Carpentier would stop him.

> And it might not be a wise thing for Dempsey to tackle Harry Wills. Weinert and Greb would be more in Jack's line just now. He had better get several additional fights under his belt before he takes on the Frenchman. Dempsey is of the type which requires action all the time, and even a short lay off is bound to make him rusty.

The chair of the New York boxing license committee was not pleased with the fight. "In my opinion, it was the poorest heavyweight combat I ever saw, especially one in which the class title was at stake. Neither Dempsey nor Brennan showed the slightest form, and I am confident I could have dug up two longshoremen who would have put up as good if not a better fight." He was disappointed in Dempsey. "If that was the best he can do I fear he will not hold the title much longer."

The chairman also did not like all of the publicity given to the large purses that the fighters received, which he thought was bad for the sport, though without saying why. He also was against motion pictures, which he believed were not conducive to good performances. He was in favor of prohibiting them.

Jess Willard said he wanted a rematch with Dempsey to prove to the public that he was not himself at Toledo.

Harry Wills was scheduled to fight Bill Tate next, even though Tate lost to Norfolk. "Wills is without question the best of the colored heavyweights. A great many shrewd critics claim Wills is a better man than Dempsey." Paddy Mullins, who managed Wills, "has not pressed Wills's claim for a crack at Dempsey, simply because Mullens [sic] realizes that the time is not ripe for Wills to step into the picture and force Dempsey into a fight."

Kearns said he had no intention of accepting the offer for Dempsey to fight Harry Greb, for Dempsey could make a lot more than the $50,000 offered, particularly given that he just made $100,000 for fighting Brennan. They were going home to spend the holidays with family.[416]

The champion visited several ear specialists, hoping to prevent cauliflower ear. He was concerned about the damage done to his ear.

[416] New York Tribune, New York Herald, Buffalo Commercial, New York Evening World, December 17, 1920.

Dempsey was upset that folks were not giving him enough credit for his performance, or Brennan for that matter. He said it was not easy to subdue a tough, strong, skillful, experienced man.

> If I had knocked him out in two rounds they would have said I was a rough slugger. Then when I didn't knock him out until the 12th, they say I've gone back and that I let him stay so as to make good moving pictures. I'm blamed either way. I'm heavyweight champion, and I expect to fight my fights in the manner I think best.[417]

The *Binghamton Press* quoted Dempsey as saying, "Seems like I got all the panning and Brennan didn't get a bit of credit for the fine showing he made. Brennan is an awful hard boy to beat, and because I didn't finish him in a couple of rounds they say I've gone back." Jack said he had trained too long and was somewhat stale. Still, he was the only fighter who could say that he had knocked out Bill Brennan.[418]

Damon Runyon interviewed Brennan. Bill insisted that the right-hand punch to the belly in the 12th round did not bother him.

> I hear a lot of talk about it, but the sock that finished me was a short left chop to my floating ribs on my right side. I ought to know. I was the one that got it. It was delivered after the punch to the stomach. It paralyzed my legs. ... I've also heard much talk about the lick Dempsey hit me on the back of the head, some people calling it the rabbit punch. I remember that very well. It didn't phase me. My legs had already quit working under me, and the smash to the ribs did the business.

Brennan believed that Dempsey was dazed and tired, made a final dying effort to get him, and succeeded. Gans and Norfolk had warned him against many of Dempsey's moves, but that one finally got him. He thought he was up at nine, but was told that he was not.

Ever since their early 1918 fight at Milwaukee, Brennan believed that he had a good chance to beat Dempsey.

> I hit him so hard then that I knew no man could ever forget it. When we were weighing in the other afternoon I said to him: "Well, I soaked you pretty hard at Milwaukee and it looks as if I'm going to finish you up tonight." He turned on me like a fellow who suddenly decides to take a punch at a man and then suddenly changes his mind.

Brennan claimed to have seen Dempsey's legs shaking before the fight, which gave him even more confidence. He had worked hard for seven years, and it was his first chance at the title and some real money. His motivation and confidence were sky high.

---

[417] *Brooklyn Daily Eagle*, December 18, 1920.
[418] *Binghamton Press*, December 18, 1920.

After the 1st round, Bill felt that he was going to win. He said to his manager, "Leo, I'm the unluckiest fellow in the world if I don't win. I've got him. I can nail him any time I want to with my left, and I think I'll try with my right for his belly." He and Flynn agreed that Dempsey was not fighting his fight at all, but like a mug. After the 4th round, Brennan commented to Flynn that he could not hit him with the right because Dempsey always was turning and running away from him. After the 9th, he believed that Dempsey was more tired than he was. After being knocked out, he said to Leo, "I'm an unlucky fellow." Brennan was surprised and offended that he did not get more credit from the press for his showing, especially in view of the fact that Dempsey was the only man to knock him out, and he gave Jack the best fight he ever had.[419]

The *Tribune's* W. O. McGeehan claimed that Jimmy De Forest, Dempsey's trainer at Toledo, allegedly had made some interesting claims about Dempsey's power. "De Forest declared some time after the Toledo fight that Dempsey had used tape bandages which hardened immediately after they had been placed on his hands. That made his fists as formidable as the cestus used by the ancient boxers." Jack's blows did a great deal of damage to the cheek, jaw, and ribs. Yet, against Brennan, his blows did not do the same. "One must infer that Dempsey has gone back to an incredible extent or that his fists were reinforced as De Forest claimed for the Toledo fight." It would have been easy to do, for Willard acted as his own manager and trainer, and did not carefully examine Dempsey's hands in the way a shrewd professional second would have done. The feeling was that Dempsey would not do such a thing against Brennan, because Leo Flynn was experienced and knew all the tricks.[420]

The *Philadelphia Inquirer* also said,

> The wearing of bandages around the knuckles is a practice that has been abused by many boxers. At first thin gauze was twisted around the hands to prevent injuries, but in time boxers used adhesive tape, which, becoming hardened, enabled them to inflict harmful injuries.
>
> Jimmy De Forest, who trained Jack Dempsey for the battle with Jess Willard in Toledo, wound the present champion's 'maulers' with adhesive bandages, which hardened as soon as the gloves were drawn on. The terrific punishment which Willard received has been attributed to the condition of Dempsey's hands.

Against Brennan, Dempsey wore gauze bandages, not tape bandages. Jess Willard believed he could make a better showing if Dempsey was made to wear only soft bandages and no tape.[421]

These viewpoints overlooked the fact that Dempsey for several years had been knocking out top contenders, most of them quickly, even before Willard. He also had knocked out Miske, another very tough man who,

[419] *El Paso Times*, December 18, 1920.
[420] *New York Tribune*, December 19, 1920.
[421] *Philadelphia Inquirer*, December 20, 1920.

like Brennan, no one had stopped other than Dempsey. Every great fighter has some tough fights, and not everyone is easy to knock out, especially a man like Bill Brennan.

Essentially, use of gauze was seen as allowing or facilitating less powerful punches than a combination of tape and gauze, which is what Dempsey had in Toledo. Of course, today, applying tape over gauze bandages is standard practice, but back then, there was some uncertainty and debate about the use of tape and its potential impact on punching power. Even James J. Jeffries claimed that Bob Fitzsimmons' use of hand wraps (gauze and/or tape) had enabled him to cut him up.

The *New York Herald's* Charles Mathison said Dempsey was not overrated. "It is a reasonable proposition that a champion's status is established by his performance against the best boxers of the period in which he holds the title. Judged on that basis, Dempsey must be conceded to possess remarkable ability, for he has shown overwhelming superiority over the best heavyweights of the time." Mathison said Brennan was underrated. Still, there also was a feeling that either Dempsey was not the same fighter he was when he beat Brennan the first time, or was not making a genuine effort to beat him as soon as he might have done. Of course, it might have been a better version of Brennan too.

Regarding hypothetical matchups, Mathison said, "Jack Johnson at his best would have made it interesting for Dempsey, for the negro was a wonderful boxer. ... Johnson at his best would have given a hard battle to Dempsey at his best." He also said Jeffries vs. Dempsey at their best would have been a great contest in which endurance would have won.[422]

In an interview with W. C. Vreeland, Referee John Haukop said it was the left hook to the solar plexus that gave Dempsey the victory.

> Some of the men who saw the bout…thought the knockout punch was the one behind the ear…. They assumed because it was the last blow struck that it was the knockout punch. The knockout punch really was the one beneath the heart. It was a left hook to the solar plexus. It was a terrific punch. I don't know that I ever saw a harder blow struck at such short range. It caused Brennan to choke and gasp as though he had been kicked by a mule. His legs sagged under him and he was helpless.

> Brennan told me in his dressing room 20 minutes after the bout that he did not know that he had been hit in the mouth and struck behind the ear after the blow in the solar plexus. … He never felt those punches. I don't believe he realized that I was counting time on him. The wind was fairly knocked out of him and he was so busy trying to catch his breath that all other thoughts were submerged. Like a drowning man, his one thought was air. … In all my experience as a referee I never felt so sorry for a man as I did for Brennan. … His face was distorted with pain.

[422] *New York Herald*, December 19, 1920.

When asked whether he thought Dempsey fought to make the moving pictures worthwhile and didn't try to knock out Brennan as quickly as he could have, Haukop did not believe such was the case. "You must remember that Brennan was the first man who has ever walked close to Dempsey and handed him a real battle. Brennan was not afraid of him."

Others, including Willard, had moved away from Dempsey, which simply gave him more forward momentum as he attacked. Brennan anticipated his attack and beat him to it, punching hard and often, stepping in and crowding him. His punches checked Jack's attacks, disconcerted him, and made him cautious. Still, at no time was Dempsey on the verge of losing his title. He never was hurt, and though somewhat tired, he was not weak.

In the dressing room, while his lips and torn left ear were being patched up, Dempsey said Brennan had butted him in the lips and ear. However, Haukop said he saw no foul blows struck by either man. Brennan did the damage with left and right smashes. Dempsey was mistaken.

Brennan was confident from start to finish. He did not believe Dempsey could knock him out.

Haukop said Dempsey could not hit quite as hard as Fitzsimmons at long range, but he could hit harder at close quarters. "No man can hit as hard as Jack at close quarters. That is why he makes a specialty of in fighting." Not even in his prime was Sam Langford "able to send over a punch that measured up in force with one of Dempsey's short arm jolts."

Dempsey used Fitz's inside shifts and moves. He worked in and outside of the zone of attack much like Fitz. Like Bob, he also had a peculiar way of using his left shoulder to block a punch aimed for his chin.

Not many men could have stood up to Dempsey's terrific short-arm punches for as long as Brennan did. Referee Haukop's version was that Brennan simply was that tough, as opposed to Dempsey not hitting as hard as advertised.

Dempsey was very nervous and anxious both before the bout and early on, but it wore off. "While the photographers were in the ring taking his picture he was on edge to such an extent that he fairly shook. He was eager to get on the job and have it over." Jack was not anxious about the result, but anxious to finish the job.

Dempsey was not a big man, not as muscular as Brennan and many others, probably not as physically strong, but he had great nervous force. At times he was overanxious and missed the head, overeager to land a knockout blow sooner than he had the last time they fought. He was too eager to make a good impression and please the New York fans, and failed to measure the distance correctly. But after he had failed to land a number of punches to the face, he confined his attack to the stomach, and he never missed the mark there.

No man can stand up before Dempsey when he gets in close. His short arm punches carry too much force. He will knock out any man that he can reach, whether it is a hook to the stomach or a right cross to the chin. I believe his hooks carry more force than his straight punches. He also uses a sort of chop – a hammerlike blow with the heel of his fist – to good effect. Whenever Dempsey and Brennan were at close quarters Brennan was the first to stop the milling and either hold Dempsey's glove or move out of the zone of attack. Brennan was no match for Dempsey at infighting.

Haukop said Brennan was a real fighter, very tough and could stand up under severe punishment, fearless in the endeavor, which made him a first-class fighting man. He had a good straight right that he crashed into Dempsey a number of times. "Dempsey did not lose his prestige with me because he took twelve rounds to whip Brennan. I don't know of another man that could have whipped Brennan in thirty rounds. ... All Dempsey has to do to beat Carpentier or any other man is to get near him. His short punches will finish the job." "I know of no man that can stand up under his short-arm punches."[423]

The Dempsey-Brennan fight was said to have given boxing a big boost. The *Buffalo Commercial* said casting aside suspicions and extraneous theories, viewing matters dispassionately, the bout was helpful to the sport because it was a well-matched, competitive, entertaining battle. Brennan was a pleasant surprise. Although Dempsey's performance was below his usual standard, he still fought a most meritorious fight. As Dempsey said, "Every man has two hands. Brennan made good use of his. I cannot belittle him. He blocked me repeatedly when I thought I was set to end it." Brennan gave almost as good as he received. He effectively used jabs and uppercuts to make a spectacular showing. He was courageous. He landed many left jabs to the face at long range; breaking up Dempsey's charges with his jabs, and at close quarters punished the champion with uppercuts. The contest created demand for other fights.[424]

Many were saying that if Carpentier had been in the ring with Dempsey, there would have been a new champion. However, others said Carpentier was "not built to take such gaff" that Brennan took. He could bounce around and dart in and out in a faster and livelier fashion than Brennan, but when it came to the roughhouse stuff and ability to take it, the *Evening World's* Vincent Treanor was not so sure Carpentier could match Brennan in that department.

Since the war, Carpentier had knocked out Levinsky in 4 rounds and Joe Beckett in 2 rounds, without really being hit himself. It took him 8 rounds to stop Dick Smith, a mediocre third-rate English fighter. Frank Moran stopped Beckett in 2 rounds as well. Dempsey had beaten far superior opponents, "the greatest living heavies in the world to-day, men who stand out head and shoulders over the inferior opponents the French

[423] *Brooklyn Daily Eagle*, December 20, 1920.
[424] *Buffalo Commercial*, December 20, 1920.

fighter has beaten." Anyone who saw Dempsey against Willard (or Miske) would say that it was not the same Dempsey against Brennan. He would be much better prepared for Carpentier.[425]

Daniel noted that Ty Cobb would get a $30,000 salary next season for both managing the Tigers and playing center field. Babe Ruth was earning $20,000 a season. Yet, Dempsey just earned $100,000 for one fight. A college president was fortunate if he earned $10,000 a year. The President of the United States earned an annual salary of $75,000. Dempsey earned more than that for less than 40 minutes of work.[426]

Dempsey was en route to Los Angeles, but on the 19th, he arrived in Salt Lake City to visit family for the holidays.

As a guest of honor at a Rotary club luncheon, Dempsey said, "To be sociable, I will fight any one in the room," which drew laughter.[427]

Jack Kearns allegedly sent a letter to John Bell, manager of the Motor Square Boxing Club in Pittsburgh, stating that Dempsey was willing to box the winner of the Harry Greb vs. Jeff Smith bout scheduled for Christmas day. Kearns was willing to negotiate terms.[428]

On December 21, 1920 in Boston, before a crowd of nearly 8,000, Harry Greb clearly won a 10-round decision over Bob Roper (16-14-4) (who usually weighed 180-185 pounds). Doc Almy said Greb fought like a wild cat from bell to bell throughout, firing in a shower of blows from all angles, keeping Roper on the defensive. "Had Greb any punch, which he has not because of his dancing, tip-toe style of running in and his round-arm punching, he would have scored a knockout early in the bout."

Regarding their hand bandages, "Both men wore soft, cotton bandages instead of the yards of electric tape which the average fighter twines and retwines about his hands, one of the main reasons why they do so much slapping instead of clean hitting."

Daniel Saunders said Greb landed at will, was too fast, and Roper saw more gloves flying at him than ever before. While having no great force behind his blows, they stung. "He kept dancing in and out all through the contest, and it was remarkable how he could keep up such speed on a padded floor." Greb puzzled him. A Roper right to the heart made Greb

[425] *New York Evening World*, December 20, 1920.
[426] *New York Herald*, December 20, 1920.
[427] *Buffalo Times*, December 20, 1920; *Binghamton Press*, December 22, 1920.
[428] *Olean Times Herald, Binghamton Press*, December 21, 1920.

wince, and a right to the jaw shook him up for a few seconds, but in general, whenever Harry was hit, he would dance in and send a fusillade of blows to the body and head. The bout was a "big boost for Greb in the latter's efforts to get a match with Dempsey."[429]

James J. Corbett said fans booed Dempsey when he deserved cheers and thunderous applause. "Nothing is more difficult to understand than the average fight fan." Jack was late in landing the knockout blows, but he did land them, and he gave the crowd a great run for its money. He worked incessantly, honestly, cleanly, earnestly, and sincerely, aggressively forcing the pace all the way. He might have lacked his usual dash and snap, but under such circumstances, showed wisdom and brains in determining to chop Brennan down gradually, and indeed he broke Brennan, then finished him with a solid right to the heart and left to the short ribs. He was utterly fearless. He didn't cover, or back away, but always was on top of his foe, taking punches just for the opportunity to drive in his own to vital spots. He shook off Brennan from the clinches. He would not countenance stalling. Dempsey was there to fight, and fought and forced his opponent to do likewise. He was wonderfully aggressive and entertaining, workmanlike, and scored a clean knockout. And for that, the crowd inexplicably booed and hissed him. If he had scored a 1st round knockout, they would have said he beat a set-up.[430]

Corbett subsequently said that grilling Dempsey because it took him a dozen rounds to dispose of Brennan was an absurdity and injustice to both fighters. Brennan was one of the game's toughest heavyweights. No other man ever had floored or stopped him. Dempsey went in to knock him out, and he did. Bill was not one to be put out with ease. Every former champion on occasion found a foe or two who was difficult to subdue. Sullivan had Mitchell. Jeffries had Sharkey. Several men went many rounds with Johnson and lasted longer than expected. Dempsey had not slipped, nor was he overrated. He was off form from overtraining and met a mighty tough customer.

Ben Smith, who had trained Dempsey for Miske and Brennan, had handled more than 500 fighters at various times, including Attell, Flynn, Ferguson, Brennan, Wolgast, and Gunboat Smith. He said some fighters were so enthusiastic that there was a danger that they might overtrain, always wanting to do more. Dempsey was like that. Another kind was lazy and overconfident, who thought they knew more than a man with experience. One had to be held back a bit, and the other driven. "If he is inclined to over train you can talk gently and kindly to him. If he is lazy and doesn't want to work, it is necessary to spank him in a verbal way."[431]

The *Brooklyn Daily Eagle's* Thomas Rice watched the fight films and said the movie failed to settle arguments. Three cameras had captured the fight. Two were at a much greater distance, and one was close to the ring. Two of the cameras failed to show the knockout properly, and one did

[429] *Boston Post, Boston Globe*, December 22, 1920.
[430] *Binghamton Press*, December 24, 1920.
[431] *Binghamton Press*, December 27, 1920.

not show it at all. One had a mishap just as the right-hand punch landed, and, while the blow was registered, the flash, or whatever it was that followed immediately, spoiled the picture.

Rice said moving pictures made it more difficult to discern the power of the blows. It also was not as clear which punches landed and which were blocked. "Even men in the ringside press seats frequently disagree as to the effectiveness of a particular blow or blows."

Some believed that in order to give the crowd a run for its money (or to make the films more valuable), Dempsey was not trying his best in the first six rounds. He missed far more leads in the first six rounds than he did in the last six. "In the second half of the bout he was a quite different Dempsey. Whether that was due to Dempsey trying harder, or whether it was due to the fact that, although he missed a number of leads in the first six rounds, he had got home enough punches to reduce Brennan's stamina, is a question."

The films showed that in the second half of the fight, Dempsey hit harder and with more accuracy. In the 7th or 8th round, Dempsey landed a full right swing to the body that was the beginning of the end. In the last three rounds, Brennan plainly was being worn down. Brennan was game and persistent though, fighting hard throughout. Although Bill still was rushing and firing, he was far from the Brennan of the 2nd round, in which he actually had Dempsey going. He seldom broke ground for most of the fight, but in the last three rounds, Brennan seemed to be breaking ground because he was weary.

Those who saw the bout said Brennan finally went down from a left to the body, right to the head, and an overhand chop to the neck as he was falling. In the pictures, the left was not apparent, but its result was, for Brennan crumpled, which left him open to the right to the body that "finished the former Bill Shanks. The overhand chop to the neck may have been plain to some, but we failed to see it."

Brennan pulled himself up by the ropes, and was on his feet at 10, but was entirely helpless, even if up. His leg control was not there, and he could not breath. He was wobbling, and his hands were on his midriff, registering pain, when the referee declared Dempsey the winner, which no one could question.

The most astonishing feature was Brennan's improvement from past performances. He appeared to have improved both in his attack and defense, making tremendous strides.[432]

When hyping the upcoming Wills-Tate fight set to be held in Buffalo, the *Buffalo Courier* said there was keen interest in seeing Wills, "the only man who has an even chance to beat Jack Dempsey, if he ever gets the chance to fight him." Wills was content to wait until the public demanded a match between he and Dempsey. While he was waiting, he was working

[432] *Brooklyn Daily Eagle*, December 24, 1920.

hard. "Wills has the speed of Leonard, the cleverness of Griffo, and can hit as hard as Dempsey."[433]

On December 25, 1920 in Pittsburgh, Harry Greb won a 10-round no decision over middleweight Jeff Smith (88-21-3). Greb kept Smith on the defensive, winning 6-2-2, according to Florent Gibson. Jim Jab said Smith was outworked. "Jeff didn't like Greb's favorite trick. Harry has a habit of sticking his left mitt in a foe's face, then socking him with his right on the jaw." Neither man ever was wobbled.[434]

The *New York Tribune's* W. O. McGeehan again said that Dempsey's poor showing against Brennan "lends color to the story that Dempsey wore 'iron bandages' in Toledo when he beat down Willard."[435]

McGeehan said Jack Johnson would be out of prison soon, and some wondered how he would do with Dempsey. However, it was not likely that Kearns would risk putting Dempsey in with anyone, other than a set-up, until the Carpentier fight, for fear of blowing the big payday.

McGeehan said Dempsey was not going to fight Johnson, regardless, because such a fight would put the sport of boxing in peril, risking banishment or further legal jeopardy.

> It was because of Johnson that the Federal law prohibiting interstate traffic in moving pictures of prizefights was passed. Jack's eccentricities and mode of living when he was champion made a great many people wonder if the game that was responsible for Jack Johnson was worth preserving. If Johnson appears in the ring again it certainly will be the signal for another campaign against professional boxing.[436]

At year-end 1920, the world champions were:

BOXING — Heavyweight champion, Jack Dempsey; light-heavy-weight champion, Georges Carpentier, American champion, Battling Levinsky; middleweight champion, Johnny Wilson; welter-weight champion, Jack Britton; lightweight champion, Benny Leonard; featherweight champion, Johnny Kilbane; bantam-weight champion, Joe Lynch; flyweight champion, Jimmy Wilde; American champion, Johnny Ruff.

[433] *Buffalo Courier*, December 24, 1920.
[434] *Pittsburgh Daily Post, Pittsburg Press*, December 26, 1920.
[435] *New York Tribune*, December 26, 1920.
[436] *New York Tribune*, December 27, 1920.

CHAPTER 8

On the Shelf

Several writers criticized the high dollar amounts Jack Kearns required to put Jack Dempsey in a fight. They thought it ridiculous. One wondered how Dempsey would feel about fighting Carpentier in France for hundreds of thousands of dollars when thousands of American soldiers were content to fight there for $30 a month and the flag, sacrificing their lives.[437]

In early January 1921, Dempsey and Kearns were in Los Angeles. Training quarters were being built for Dempsey at the Brunton Studio, where he was making a film serial.[438]

Noted was the fact that lightweight champ Benny Leonard, after seeing Dempsey-Brennan, said he would not take one of Jack's punches for all the money in the world, so Dempsey's punches had to have real power, and he wasn't pulling much, if at all.[439]

Jim Corbett said if Dempsey beat Willard and Carpentier, only Wills stood out as a probable contender for the title. "Dempsey never has taken the attitude that he wouldn't fight Wills, nor has he stated positively that he would give the dusky warrior a chance. But those who know Dempsey intimately are certain that if the time comes when insistent public voice asks him to fight Wills, he will not back away from it." Dempsey was confident that he could whip anyone, white or black.

> There is a thought in some quarters that Wills should be denied the chance with Dempsey simply because he is a negro. It is pointed out that Jack Johnson disgraced the fistic game while he was king of the sport and there are some folks who think that Wills might do likewise. But this is a grievous injustice to Wills and to the negro race as a whole. Just because one negro discredited himself and brought criticism upon his profession is no reason to believe that every negro will do so. ...
>
> Personally, I believe that if Dempsey ever took on Wills, the champion would win without excessive effort. Wills is one of those slow-moving fellows of the type seemingly made to order for Dempsey. ...
>
> Wills' conduct in or out of the ring so far has been above criticism. He is a quiet, clean living, home loving negro. ... He is modest, quiet and unassuming. Wills' habits are good. Wills has made a

---

[437] *New York Tribune*, January 2, 1921.
[438] *Ithaca Journal*, January 3, 1921; *Pasadena Post*, January 4, 1921.
[439] *Los Angeles Record*, January 4, 1921.

good record as a fighter. Perhaps he isn't in Dempsey's class. But if the time comes when Dempsey wants a fight and he has knocked over the Willard and Carpentier opposition, Wills should not be denied a chance simply because he was born a negro.[440]

Henry Farrell said the recent setting of price limits on tickets would prevent Dempsey from fighting in New York. Although New York typically was the one state where a championship affair could be held with the least financial risk, the commission's recent edict that ticket prices for ordinary bout cards could be no more than $10, and for championship affairs, $15, removed New York from consideration for major fights. Higher prices would be necessary to fulfill large contracts.[441]

Dan McKetrick, who had managed fighters for more than 25 years, believed Carpentier would give Dempsey the toughest fight of his career. If Dempsey made one mistake, he could be in a perilous position.

> I was handling Joe Jeannette back in 1914 when he took on Carpentier. The Frenchman was outweighed…, was the smaller man in every way, yet he put up a phenomenal battle. He floored Jeannette early in the fight – the first and only white man that ever knocked him down. I was amazed at the showing of Carpentier then and in later battles my opinion of him has increased.

In Carpentier, Dempsey would be meeting "one of the toughest, fastest, hardest-hitting and quickest thinking heavyweights that ever stepped into a ring. He has an uncanny brain for boxing." He was both fast and powerful. If he was just one or the other, he would stand no chance, but he was both fast as lightning and had a mule's kick. He also had fast feet and good instincts. If Carpentier did not knock him out early, he still had a chance to outpoint Dempsey nevertheless.

Regardless, McKetrick respected Dempsey's power.

> I belong to that legion of fistic fans who appreciate the dynamic power of Dempsey's punch. I doubt whether a man lives who can take a smash to the heart from Dempsey's right hand and still hold to his feet. If he lands that blow against the Frenchman, Carpentier will probably do as all the others have done – crumple and go down and out.

But in Carpentier, Jack would be boxing a phantom, not a punching bag. And Dempsey would have to be careful. "If he grows tired or makes one false move, there may be a new champion."[442]

Most who saw Jack Johnson exhibit at Leavenworth federal penitentiary said he still was a formidable man, powerful and dangerous, with his skill and vast experience, but questioned his ability at age 42 to stand up against Dempsey. The *New York Age* said, "It is not likely that he will get another crack at the championship – it is generally understood

[440] *Binghamton Press*, January 4, 1920.
[441] *Buffalo Times*, January 5, 1921.
[442] *Binghamton Press*, January 7, 1921.

Dempsey has drawn the color line." Opinion was that at this point, Harry Wills would knock Johnson out cold.[443]

Joe Vila said Harry Wills ranked close to Dempsey and would be a real foe. Kearns had said that he would match Dempsey with Wills if he could be convinced that there was genuine public demand for such a match. "That there now is such a demand cannot be questioned. The public now realizes in view of his showing in his bout with Bill Brennan that Dempsey is not by any means a superman." Prior to that fight, no one believed that *any* heavyweight could stand before Dempsey for more than 1 or 2 rounds. Some even opposed the Brennan fight, feeling that Bill would be slaughtered unmercifully, which would be a blow to boxing in New York.

Now, there was increased interest in seeing Dempsey fight others. "Of these, none deserves higher ranking than the New Orleans negro." Fears that Wills would be another Johnson were groundless. He enjoyed the respect of white followers of the game. "Not only Dempsey, but all the other heavyweights, shun him, so far as meeting him in the ring is concerned, though his personal popularity among them is greater than that of the other champion." Wills was modest. He insisted that Dempsey was a splendid fighter, but not a superman. Vila said black champions in the lighter weight classes had conducted themselves well after winning championships. "Johnson was the only one who ran amuck. It seems unfair to make Wills suffer for the faults of the conqueror of Jeffries."[444]

Suspicion continued that Dempsey did not give it his all to stop Brennan quickly, as a result of wanting to make the moving pictures more valuable. "The pictures, to be of any value for presentation before the public, must necessarily be long enough to fill in a period of time that will retain the interest of the patrons of the movie houses." Most of the public was not aware beforehand that motion pictures would be taken, and had they known, would not have wagered on Dempsey to win so quickly.[445]

Coming Mon.--Tues. Jan. 17-18	O. S. HATHAWAY'S Lyceum--Mon.-Tues.--Jan. 17-18
Matinee and Evening. Tex Ricard Presents the Only Official Moving Pictures of the **JACK DEMPSEY—BILL BRENNAN** Boxing contest for the Heavy Weight Championship of the World. Every blow shown in detail, including the famous knockout, on which most of the sporting writers disagreed. These Pictures will positively not be shown at any picture house in this city.	Four Shows Daily—2:15, 3:30, 7:15, 8:30. TEX RICKARD PRESENTS THE OFFICIAL MOTION PICTURES OF THE **Jack Dempsey vs. Bill Brennan** CHAMPIONSHIP BOXING CONTEST AT MADISON SQ. GARDEN, NEW YORK —NOTICE— Every detail of the wonderful battle shown in clear photography. It shows the much disputed and famous knock-out punch. Every sport fan and lover of athletics will see it!!! **All Seats 50c—Plus the Tax**

On or about January 11, 1921, at John's chophouse, a restaurant at 6754 Hollywood boulevard, in Hollywood, California, shortly after midnight, Jack Kearns and his two companions – Teddy Hayes (Kearns' secretary), age 30, and Joseph Benjamin (lightweight boxer), age 22, were arrested on a charge of disturbing the peace. The three were creating a

---

[443] *New York Age*, January 8, 1921.
[444] *Buffalo Courier*, January 11, 1921.
[445] *New York World*, January 11, 1921.

disturbance in the restaurant, and one hurled an overcoat in the waiter's face. They were released on $100 bail each. The waiter subsequently sued all three, claiming he had been assaulted and beaten.[446]

Kearns said Dempsey was frozen out of New York, for the Boxing Commission had fixed a $15 maximum on ticket prices, which made a planned March 17 Willard or subsequent Carpentier fight economically unfeasible. Hence, big fights would not be able to take place in New York. As a result, Kearns was expecting to hear from Rickard that the Willard rematch was off. Dempsey instead expected to begin work on a film production, a drama showing his rise to the championship.[447]

Bill Tate said he had not fought much over the past year because he was making good money as Dempsey's sparring partner. He had an upcoming Wills bout. When asked if anyone had a chance to beat Dempsey, Tate laughed and said, "No, sir. No one's going to beat that boy for some years to come." Bill said Dempsey worked too hard and too long for Brennan. Nevertheless, he was like "dynamite," a "copperhead for poison," and boxing with him was like being attacked by a flock of wildcats. Both arms were like triphammers, and no one ever could hit as hard. Dempsey only would lose when he slipped as a result of age.[448]

On January 17, 1921 in Buffalo, New York, 210-pound Harry Wills knocked out 230-pound Bill Tate in the 2nd round, landing a sleep producer coming out of a clinch. The 1st round was relatively uneventful and even. In the 2nd, Tate began landing well, rushing and sending Harry to the ropes, and Wills clinched. Almost at the same time that the referee commanded a break, Wills shot in a half-overhand right to the head and Tate went down and out. Some said Tate had been hit on the break.

The *Buffalo Evening News* said, "It cannot be said that Wills' showing was particularly impressive. The general impression seemed to be that either one of them would be easy dark meat for Jack Dempsey. Wills is faster than Tate, which is not saying many volumes, but Dempsey is much speedier than Wills as he shaped up last night."

Karpe's Comments noted that folks were dissatisfied when Dempsey took so long to thump Brennan into oblivion, but also were disappointed when Wills stopped Tate so quickly. The fans never were satisfied.

Regardless of the quick knockout of Tate,

> If Harry Wills showed the best he had in his few moments of ring action last night, Jack Dempsey need have no fear of this dusky Hercules. If Harry in a ring with Dempsey should for one instant leave himself as wide open as he did in attacking Tate last night, it would be all over but the twinkling lights and the tinkling bells for him before the lapse of one round.

[446] *Los Angeles Evening Express*, January 11, 12, 14, 1921.
[447] *Los Angeles Evening Express, New York Daily News*, January 14, 1921. This was another example of how bureaucratic meddlers actually can impede the sport and the economy.
[448] *Buffalo Courier*, January 14, 1921.

Billy Kelly for the *Buffalo Courier* said a short right hook to Tate's chin just after or at the tail end of the break did it.

> The knockout came after the men had split out of a clinch and Referee Dick Nugent had stepped back away from them. Tate's arms were still half extended, but not in position of defense, when Wills leaped in and bent that wicked right with all his force and weight. … The sudden termination came just at a time when Tate seemed to be winning.

In the 1st round, Wills had shown speed and punching power, while Tate showed all of the cleverness claimed for him, blocking and knocking aside punches with ease. In the 2nd round, "Tate let go with a straight right and Wills was jolted right down to his heels and fell into a clinch. Tate sensed he had hurt him, and tried to throw him off, but Harry held until Nugent split them out." They fought a bit more, until there was another clinch. The referee separated them, and as he stepped back, Wills nailed Tate with the right that knocked him out.

Afterward, Tate said he was stepping out of a clinch and had not expected the lunge. "That man beat Dempsey; why, I can beat that bird myself, and I was doing it."

Kelly said Wills showed speed and a punch, "but nothing that would indicate that he is an even-money chance with Dempsey." Many noted that Tate was fighting a winning battle and hurt Wills just before he received the quietus.

The *Buffalo Enquirer* said Wills knocked out Tate after Bill had stung him with a right cross. Wills let go a short right jolt to the jaw, and Tate stiffened out and crashed to the floor. Few saw the punch. Tate defended well in the 1st round. In the 2nd, Tate landed a straight right that sent Harry's head back. Wills clinched and wrestled, and then broke. He backed away, with Tate after him. They clinched again. Coming out of the clinch, or going back into it, Wills let his short right jolt fly a short distance and Tate went down and out. The crowd did not like it, in part because it happened so suddenly and unexpectedly.[449]

The *New York Age* said Wills "is considered by pugilistic authorities to be the only fighter with ability equal to the champion."[450]

The *Los Angeles Record* said fans were wondering when Wills would be matched to fight Dempsey.

Dempsey said Jess Willard underestimated him in their first fight, and therefore would prepare better for a rematch. Jack was taking Carpentier seriously, and would not underrate him like Willard did with him. Carpentier was known to be smart and fast, and could hit, which made him dangerous. Nevertheless, Jack expected to win by knockout. "I never was as good as I am and as I expect to be when I meet Carpentier. …That slipping talk is the bunk!"[451]

---

449 *Buffalo Evening News, Buffalo Courier, Buffalo Enquirer,* January 18, 1921.
450 *New York Age,* January 22, 1921.
451 *Los Angeles Record,* January 19, 1921.

Tex Rickard.

There were some issues concerning the failure to post required deposits for the Dempsey-Carpentier contest, tentatively scheduled for July 2. William Brady withdrew from the promotion. Tex Rickard said he would take over sole control. The $500,000 fight still was on. Tex was trying to secure the best location for the fight.[452]

The *Binghamton Press* said the films, which were playing locally, showed that Brennan gave Dempsey a rough, tough, hard battle.

STONE Tonight
IF YOU MISS IT TODAY COME THURSDAY
4—Shows Daily—2:30, 3:45, 7:15, 8:30

TEX RICKARD
Presents the Official
Moving Pictures.

JACK
DEMPSEY
—vs.—
BILL
BRENNAN
For Heavyweight
Championship of the
world at Madison
Square Garden, N. Y.

ADMISSION—50c. ALL SHOWS, PLUS TAX

> For 10 rounds, Brennan stood up and swapped punches with Dempsey and on many occasions he had the better of the milling. Dempsey was a target for Brennan's left hand in the early rounds and Bill seemed to have no difficulty landing his right uppercut. But the strain began to tell on Brennan about the tenth and from then it was a question when Dempsey would land the final blow. Dempsey missed with his famed right many times and his killing left hook did not find the mark early in the bout. Brennan's style appeared to puzzle the champion.
>
> It was noticeable all through the fight that Dempsey was watching for an opening to land his right to the body and in the twelfth he caught Brennan under the heart with a straight right and the fight was over.[453]

On January 21, 1921, despite the prison parole board's unanimous recommendation that he be paroled, the Justice Department, at the behest of U.S. Attorney General A. Mitchell Palmer, denied Jack Johnson parole, and he was required to serve his full one-year and a day prison term, less any required credits for time previously served. Palmer was the attorney general who in response to strikes, race riots, and fear of communism and anarchism had created the General Intelligence Unit, which would be led by J. Edgar Hoover.

Sports editors of New York papers declared that the Dempsey-Brennan films (which were showing throughout New York state) refuted

452 *New York Daily News*, January 20, 1921.
453 *Binghamton Press*, January 20, 1921.

the story that Dempsey held his man up because of the pictures. Five cameras shot the fight from every angle. Three cameras caught the knockout. Brennan seemed to get to his feet at ten, though he was doubled up. The referee said although Bill did not beat the count, he would have stopped the fight anyhow, even if he had.[454]

The *Buffalo Times* said the films showed that Brennan made a splendid showing, proving that he was good enough to tackle anyone.

The *Buffalo Enquirer* and *Buffalo Courier* said the films clearly showed how Dempsey stopped Brennan – with a left to the stomach and right cross to the jaw.[455]

Dempsey told "Hek" that he hoped the belief that he was going back would help make more fights marketable. He said such belief was in error.

> Bill is a better man than they give him credit for being. Believe me, he took plenty before I nailed him. Naturally I stopped a few myself. … I must have been pretty strong to go 12 rounds and then slip over a clean knockout.
>
> I am not bothered by the criticism. I won my fight and that is what I was in the ring for. Then, too, I showed a lot of wise birds that I could go a route and still have the sleep-producing punch. …
>
> The beating Willard got in Toledo isn't going to do him any good. He has waited so long that he has probably forgotten what a trimming he received. He's game and all that, but when we get in there that old Toledo thing is going to ease its way into his mind and he isn't going to be as calm as he is right now. …..
>
> Personally I like Carpentier very much. He is a regular fellow, but I'll go in to stop him just as I would any other fellow. I think it will be some scrap while it lasts.[456]

Jess Willard said he was weighing 247 pounds, and was eager to rematch Dempsey. "It was because I underrated him in our last match that I let him paste me – and the first blow was a heavy one that sent my brain going like a merry-go-round. I'll know better now and intend to do the socking myself."

In another interview, Willard said, "I lost to Dempsey by accident. He hit me when I broke clean in a clinch." Willard claimed that the agreement was for clean breaks, and he stepped away clean, but Dempsey did not, and instead let one go while he was unprotected, and after that blow on the chin, he never was the same. "I'm not crying. It is all part of the game, but I do want another chance…"[457]

On January 26, 1921 in Portland, Oregon, at the Milwaukie arena, which charged $5.50, $3.30, and $2.20 for seats, Jack Dempsey engaged in a 6-round exhibition (each round being 2 minutes) with former foe Terry

---

[454] *Buffalo Times*, January 23, 1921. Norfolk vs. Tate was filmed and shown as well.
[455] *Buffalo Times, Buffalo Enquirer, Buffalo Courier*, January 24, 1921.
[456] *Long Beach Daily Telegram*, January 24, 1921.
[457] *Oregon Daily Journal, New York Daily News*, January 26, 1921; *Los Angeles Times*, January 30, 1921.

Keller, mauling him around for the enjoyment of 4,000 spectators. Though he tried to hold back his punches with 14-ounce gloves, Jack rocked Terry repeatedly. At the conclusion, Dempsey was not even puffing hard. "Throughout the six rounds, Dempsey displayed great cleverness. He showed that he could hit from any angle and was always in a position to land." It was estimated that he would earn over $10,000 for the exhibition.[458]

The *Brooklyn Daily Times* said Wills was willing to fight Jack Johnson.

It may be argued that a victory over Johnson would strengthen the claim of Wills to recognition by Jack Dempsey. This is doubtful. Dempsey will have no part of Wills without being forced by public opinion to fight him. The field of white heavies is easier to wade through unless Georges Carpentier is capable of affording the champion rough going.[459]

Carpentier with film star Charlie Chaplin, who in late January 1921 released *The Kid*, which would earn $5,450,000 at the box office.

On February 3, 1921, it was announced that the Dempsey – Carpentier fight would take place on July 2. Also, the Willard fight would be delayed until Labor Day. Hence, the March 17 date was declared off.

Tex Rickard said,

For various reasons I have decided to postpone the Dempsey-Willard match until Labor Day, Sept. 5. …. I have decided that the contest can better be staged in the open air following the Dempsey-Carpentier contest on July 2. The surprising demand for tickets for

[458] *Oregon Daily Journal*, January 26, 27, 1921. The show featured a scheduled 38 rounds of boxing.
[459] *Brooklyn Daily Times*, January 28, 1921.

the Willard-Dempsey bout clearly indicates that Madison Square Garden would accommodate but a fraction of those who desire to see the bout.[460]

JACK DEMPSEY HELD UP!—Not at the point of a gun, or with the aid of a blackjack, but on the stalwart shoulder of Doug Fairbanks. Doug even smiled as he performed the feat. (By Wide World)

Former lightweight champ Jack McAuliffe, who had sparred with both Dempsey and Carpentier, said Jack was a sure winner. Although Carpentier was an extraordinarily clever boxer who could deliver a knockout blow, Dempsey was more of a natural fighter, bigger, had a punch like the kick of a mule, and his rushing tactics would sweep Carpentier off his feet in short order.

McAuliffe believed Dempsey was as good as ever, and took as long as he did with Brennan because he decided to box with him to give the crowd a good run for its money. He was not a boxer, and it was like holding back a harness horse and causing it to lose its stride.

McAuliffe believed Willard would be little more than a punching bag for Dempsey.

---

[460] *New York Daily News, Los Angeles Times, Brooklyn Daily Eagle,* February 3, 1921.

McAuliffe also said, "I was always a great admirer of John L. Sullivan and I think he was one of the greatest." With Dempsey's "tiger-like fighting methods, he and Sullivan would have made a great fight could they have met."[461]

On Sunday February 6, 1921 in Los Angeles, at the Rogers air field, in a benefit for disabled war veterans, before 22,000 people, Dempsey boxed an exhibition with his sparring partner Bull Montana.[462]

Pursuant to the contract with Rickard, Dempsey only was allowed to engage in exhibitions until the Carpentier fight.[463]

Jack Kearns claimed he was anxious to get Dempsey into action, and was a bit peeved by the long delay. "We cannot afford to lay idle much longer. There are any number of promoters anxious to have Jack go along and box for them." Yet, he also said, "I have absolute faith in Tex Rickard."[464]

On February 11, 1921 at the Fourth Regiment Armory in Baltimore, Maryland, Harry Wills stopped black Jeff Clark (124-34-20) (who likely weighed 180-185 pounds) with ease in the 2nd round. The *Baltimore Sun* said, "The match was a joke. Clarke never had a chance and is too old to apply his trade any more." Clark did not land a blow, and was knocked down, pushed down, or fell down nearly a dozen times.[465]

D. Scott Chisolm of the *Los Angeles Express* said he played golf with Dempsey at the Pasadena course, along with Bob Edgren and others. When Dempsey sunk a 40-foot putt, he joyously patted Chisolm on the back, but what Jack considered a gentle tap was sufficient to send the 195-pound Chisolm rolling into the sand trap.

> Jack Dempsey is a splendid fellow, a thorough gentleman, a true sportsman and he acts just like a big, overgrown schoolboy. Never in a year's travels would you know from him that he was ever in a prize ring. I particularly liked him for that. He is void of all vanity and when I put him down for a five at the eighteenth hole he protested and changed the score card himself to a six.[466]

Dempsey told Frank Menke that he wasn't happy as champion, frustrated by his lack of fighting activity.

> The happier days for me were those when I was an obscure bloke fighting anybody, anywhere, any time, drawing no color line – fighting for only a few bucks – but getting real joy out of life.
>
> Maybe, if I had known a few years ago that being a champion means being a prima donna and being coddled and nursed, and being forced to loaf instead of being turned loose every week or so against the toughest of the tough – well, maybe I wouldn't have

461 *Olean Times Herald*, February 4, 1921.
462 *Los Angeles Evening Express, Los Angeles Times*, February 7, 1921.
463 *Brooklyn Citizen*, February 5, 1921. A scheduled European tour eventually was canceled or delayed.
464 *Los Angeles Times*, February 11, 1921.
465 *Baltimore Sun*, February 12, 1921.
466 *Los Angeles Express*, February 14, 1921.

been so anxious to get a crack at Jess Willard. Maybe I'd just let that bird keep his championship.

I became a fighter not because of the money in it, but because I love to fight – always have, ever since I was a kid. ...

I quit the ring early in 1917 after dubbing around in it for a couple of years, and went to work in a shipyard. Decided I was all through with fighting – that I was going to settle down and learn a trade. But the love of fighting was too strong to kill off like that.

Even after briefly deciding to give up boxing, Dempsey still hung around and worked out in gyms. One day, he sparred in Jack Kearns' gym in Oakland, helping a fighter to prepare for a contest. Kearns told Dempsey, "You'll be a champion some day if you'll correct a few faults – and learn a few tricks." Well, "That sounded good. Jack's praise made me forget that I was through with boxing. And Jack, right away, began to teach me a few tricks. I saw how they helped me." He got interested in fighting again. Soon thereafter, he signed a managerial contract with Kearns. He fought whenever and wherever he could, taking some fights with only 2 days advance notice. "Fought three fights in a week and was peeved because I couldn't get a fourth."

After winning the championship,

I've been just as wildly anxious to fight anybody, anywhere, anytime since then as before. But I've fought only twice in nearly two years. And it will be four to six months before I'm sic'ced on to someone else. Rough stuff – that's what it is! And I'm getting rusty and losing my temper... Being champion – that's a great thing in the minds of a lot of people. Used to be in mine. But no more. I'd be happier – a whole lot happier – if I was battling all comers every other night or so...

Dempsey was learning how the big business of championship boxing (as well as politics) often slowed down a fighter's activity.[467]

Another paper noted that Dempsey's idea of a good time was being in the ring punching rivals from post to post. Jack said,

I hate this long gap between bouts. I had the time of my life when I was fighting my way up to the Willard match. ... I like to have these big fellows tear at me and then drive them back. That's my idea of sport. It's fun to have them coming diving in, then hook 'em and see them stop. You know a fellow gets rusty loafing. If I could have a bout every month I'd be better off. It's not the money I'm thinking about, because Kearns takes care of that end, but it's the thrills I get when I go into action. ... As it is now I have to dilly-dally and wait for bouts.[468]

[467] *Binghamton Press*, February 14, 1921.
[468] *Buffalo Commercial*, February 23, 1921.

On February 18, 1921 in New York's Madison Square Garden, 193 ¼-pound Bill Brennan won a 15-round decision over highly touted 184 ¼-pound Bob Martin (29-5). Since the Dempsey fight, Brennan had been fighting frequently, going 6-0 with 4 KOs, including a KO2 over English fighter Bandsman Dick Rice (65-18-6) in Buffalo.[469]

Edward Tranter said word on the street was that Kearns was arrogant and cheap, not paying or treating various sparring partners and trainers properly, including Ben Smith, Billy McCarney, Bill Tate, Jamaica Kid, and Panama Joe Gans (who worked with Dempsey for Miske but then helped Brennan). Jimmy De Forest's name was not mentioned, though it was odd that he had worked with Dempsey successfully for several fights, including Willard, but had not worked with Dempsey since. Frank Spellman, a moving picture man who claimed to have helped Dempsey/Kearns when they had their government troubles, was suing them. Tranter said although Dempsey was quiet, unassuming, and likeable, Kearns' diminishing reputation in handling his affairs might hurt the champ.[470]

Kearns said Dempsey was 26 years old and in love, but wasn't sure whether he would marry the gal he was seeing.[471]

Rickard had taken over sole control of the Dempsey-Carpentier promotion, so both Brady and Cochran were out. Kearns said, "Jack and I are prepared to string along with Tex. He has treated us fairly and we will gamble with him."[472]

On February 25, 1921 in Boston, Harry Greb won a 10-round judge's decision over fellow middleweight Jeff Smith. The *Boston Globe* agreed, saying Greb won 7 of the 10 rounds.

However, the *Boston Post's* Doc Almy disagreed with the decision, saying Greb's flashy work blinded the judges to Smith's effective fighting. Greb was willing to mix, and his dancing and bulling tactics also counted. "The writer, however, also many close to the ropes, credited Smith for his wonderful blocking, countering and cleaner hitting, and it appeared that he had a majority of the rounds in his favor." In the later rounds, both men did too much holding.

Almy subsequently said Greb was good with aggressive action and well-delivered partial blows, but almost nil in clean hits. Smith successfully blocked, made Greb miss often, and showed plenty of balance and readiness to counter-attack with cleanly landed blows.[473]

[469] *New York World, New York Tribune, New York Daily News*, February 19, 1921. On January 27, 1919 in Paris, in a military service bout, Martin had lost a 4-round decision to Gene Tunney. Martin's bouts included: 1919 TKO11 Joe Bonds and KO3 Arthur Pelkey; 1920 TKO6 Ted Jamieson, KO5 Tom McMahon, LND12, WND10, and L10 Bob Roper, and KO1 Larry Williams; and 1921 TKO5 Martin Burke.
[470] *Buffalo Enquirer*, February 22, 1921.
[471] *Los Angeles Record*, February 22, 1921.
[472] *New York Tribune*, February 25, 1921.
[473] *Boston Globe, Boston Post*, February 26, 1921; *Boston Post*, February 28, 1921.

John Reisler said of Dempsey, "I saw that guy fight when he came to New York in 1916. He looked like a sure champion to me even then. I signed him up a contract that was to run five years. Then he got homesick or something and lit out for the West. Next thing I heard Jack Kearns was managing him." Reisler had sued Dempsey about 20 times in about a dozen cities. "So far [Reisler] has lost to the legal tilt." He still insisted that the contract was good and that Dempsey owed him $134,000 in damages. Dempsey's lawyers claimed the contract wasn't equitable and therefore not binding, pointing to an unbroken string of legal victories to back them up. Reisler wanted his son, who was a featherweight, to grow and take on Dempsey. "And then – oh, then, I will have the joy of seeing my own flesh and blood crush and crumple Jack Kearns' meal ticket."[474]

The *Brooklyn Daily Eagle's* Ed Hughes said Harry Wills had a hard time obtaining matches. Therefore, he worked on the docks on the waterfront between bouts as a longshoreman. Wills was the greatest black fighter since Peter Jackson, regarded as the one man who could furnish a real test of Dempsey's fighting ability. "But oddly enough there is little talk of the fight, and Wills himself has little hope of ever getting a chance at the title. In fact, Harry has great difficulty getting matches of any description, let alone a titular affair."

Hughes said Wills was not another Jack Johnson. He was modest and decent, and "has none of the revolting characteristics which made Johnson a felon and the most generally disliked champion the game ever had." Johnson was a "disgrace to his race and to the fight game."

Drawing the color line could have deprived the boxing world of some great champions like Dixon, Gans, and Walcott. "Walcott…knew his place in society. He made it a rule never to sit at a training table with white fighters unless extended an invitation." Langford was modest and quiet-mannered. "He wouldn't have disgraced the office of champion had he won it. But Johnson, a man of his own color, refused him the opportunity to gain this distinction." Jeannette also was a gentleman. "No, all colored fighters aren't Jack Johnsons – not by a long shot."[475]

On March 7, 1921 in St. Paul, Minnesota, Jack Dempsey refereed the Billy Miske vs. Farmer Lodge fight, which 184 ½-pound Miske won by 4th round knockout over 225-pound Lodge.[476]

Dempsey was displaying his skills on a vaudeville boxing exhibition tour that week at the local Minneapolis Pantages theater, starting on the 6th. Dempsey's exhibition contract would carry him throughout the entire Pantages circuit.

---

[474] *Binghamton Press*, February 26, 1921.
[475] *Brooklyn Daily Eagle*, March 6, 1921.
[476] Miske was coming off a February 9, 1921 W10 over black Lee Anderson, who one fight previously had held Sam Langford to a 12-round draw.

They even would exhibit in Canada. Bull Montana was one of his sparring partners. If he could not fight, Jack would exhibit on tour, earn money that way, and continue to realize from the Brennan moving pictures.[477]

When asked about potential title challengers, Dempsey said, "Many are tough, but few are dangerous." He considered Brennan to be the best of the bunch, and Willard the gamest.[478]

Although the Dempsey-Brennan fight films only could be transported and shown legally in New York state within the U.S., they could be transported to foreign countries, including Canada. After a viewing at the Dominion Theater in Winnipeg, Manitoba, Canada, the local *Winnipeg Tribune* said the films showed that Dempsey did not use the rabbit punch to win. Few writers had

Dominion THEATRE
Week Commencing **Mar. 14**

Jack Dempsey
WORLD'S CHAMPION
In the Fight of His Life

Jack Dempsey vs. Bill Brennan
12 Rounds to a Knockout
3 Cameras Show the Knockout 3 Times

Admission 50c

gotten it right, until they saw the films, which showed body blows followed by a trip-hammer right to the side of the head ending it.

Willie Lewis, who had trained Carpentier and taught him everything he knew, after seeing the Dempsey-Brennan films, opined that Carpentier would beat Dempsey with ease.

The *Winnipeg Tribune* subsequently said it was a good thing that Tex Rickard braved any criticism sent his way for making Dempsey-Brennan and had films taken of it. The fight pictures showed that although the champion was a great fighter, he took punishment from Brennan, and was not invincible. Carpentier had a chance. Dempsey was in bad shape in the 2nd round, and had to use all of his abilities and strength to win. Those who said he allowed Brennan to stay needed an excuse after having built up a house of cards which came tottering down. Also, Brennan was not put away with a rabbit punch, and the ravings of the experts who made such a claim faded into whispers when they saw the pictures.

Dempsey arrived in Winnipeg on March 14. While there, Jack watched the Brennan fight films, smiling at various times. "The pictures show that Brennan put up a remarkable fight against the titleholder and forced the fighting on a good many occasions."

When asked about his ideal woman, Dempsey said he liked two parts domesticity – the love of and ability to keep a home and care for children, one part learning, one part good health, one part old fashioned virtue, with the whole slightly flavored with pep and charm. He liked pretty girls rather than plain, neither tall nor short, and preferred light hair to dark. He liked girls who could talk sensibly.[479]

---

[477] *Minneapolis Morning Tribune, Minnesota Daily Star*, March 6, 8, 1921; *Los Angeles Record*, March 22, 1921. The Dempsey Pantages Northwest vaudeville circuit tour consisted of a comedy wrestling match between Marty Cutler and Jack Dribbs, Kearns gave a talk about boxing, Dempsey boxed 3 rounds, and then demonstrated his famous knockout punches.
[478] *Buffalo Commercial*, March 16, 1921.
[479] *Winnipeg Tribune*, March 11, 14, 15, 19, 1921.

Without disclosing his source, Henry Farrell said Rickard would stage Dempsey-Carpentier in New Jersey.[480]

Jack Skelly believed there were almost no really dangerous contenders for Dempsey except probably Harry Wills, "the dusky and husky fighter, who is barred by the champion on account of his color." Carpentier was the only really scientific, brilliant mitt artist who had a chance. All others either were annihilated already or unworthy of him.[481]

Dempsey purchased 18 acres on the Grand Terrace, west of Redlands, on the road to Riverside, California. There were orange trees and good farming land. Jack Price, Dempsey's friend, was in charge. The champ allegedly would train there and build a home for his mother and "invalid" brother. Alfalfa would be grown there.[482]

Various towns and syndicates were competing to host the Carpentier fight, offering increasingly large numbers. Fallon and Broken Hills, Nevada guaranteed $800,000 for the fight.[483]

New York Governor Nathan Miller frowned upon the Dempsey-Carpentier bout, and wanted to prevent it being held in his state. He was not opposed to boxing, but wanted the sport freed of commercialism. He essentially wanted to take the prize out of prizefighting. Ugh. Certainly, if he was not going to authorize Dempsey-Carpentier, then he was not going to authorize a Dempsey-Wills fight either.[484]

Word was that Jersey City, New Jersey had been selected as the fight site, though no formal announcement would be made for another week.[485]

Carpentier forwarded his $50,000 forfeit to the U.S., to be held by official stakeholder Robert Edgren.[486]

On April 8, 1921 in St. Louis, Missouri, 210-pound Harry Wills won an 8-round newspaper decision over black 207-pound Jack Thompson (19-16-6), administering a beating throughout, though failing to deck him. Despite the battering, Thompson sneered at Wills during the fight, saying, "Jack Dempsey sho' needn't be worried about you. ... You look like an almost-champion to me." Thompson finished with a bleeding gash under his eye, a split ear, and slight mouth and nose cuts.[487]

---

[480] *Brooklyn Citizen*, March 9, 1921. The parties allegedly agreed to an amendment in which the fighters would earn 60% of the proceeds, with the winner taking 60% of that and the loser 40%. Another said Dempsey would receive 36% of the proceeds and Carpentier 24%. However, either such claims were not true, or it shifted back to a flat fee. *Los Angeles Times*, March 22, 1921; *New York Daily News, Ithaca Journal, New York World*, March 24, 1921.
[481] *Yonkers Herald*, March 25, 1921.
[482] *Los Angeles Times*, March 27, 1921.
[483] *New York Daily News, New York Tribune*, March 29, 1921. Dempsey was in Spokane doing vaudeville daily. *New York Daily News*, March 31, 1921.
[484] *New York Tribune*, April 1, 1921.
[485] *New York Daily News*, April 2, 1921.
[486] *New York Daily News*, April 8, 1921.
[487] *St. Louis Post-Dispatch*, April 9, 1921.

CHAPTER 9

The Road to Dempsey-Carpentier

On April 9, 1921, it was formally announced that the Dempsey-Carpentier fight would be held in New Jersey, most likely Jersey City. A huge octagonal arena would be constructed. Ticket prices would range from $5 up to $50, in $5 and/or $10 increments. Jersey City was across the river from New York, close to New York City. Tex Rickard wanted to tap into the big New York market, for it was the most populous state in the nation and the most economically successful state, but he also wanted no price limitations on tickets. Unlike New York, New Jersey wasn't going to price fix and limit the fight's earning potential, nor was there political opposition. Carpentier had fought Levinsky in New Jersey, so they were familiar with his prowess and wanted to see him again. New Jersey's governor was a boxing fan, as was the Jersey City mayor.

The fight likely would yield the largest gate ever, some predicting that over one million dollars would be generated for the first time ever, more than doubling the record of $452,522 set by Dempsey-Willard, and the $270,755 of Johnson-Jeffries.

New Jersey Governor Edward Edwards let it be known that he would not try to stop Dempsey-Carpentier, and had no objection to boxing conducted according to the law. 12-round no decision bouts were allowed at that point (unless the law was amended). Hence, Carpentier only could win the title officially if he won by knockout. Many believed his best chance was to win on points. Of course, even without a formal decision, if most agreed he had won, he would be recognized as the real champion, and/or there would need to be a rematch.[488]

European champion Carpentier had started boxing as a young teenager, turning pro around age 14 as a flyweight. He became one of the few fighters who could claim to have fought in every weight division, from flyweight all the way up to heavyweight. He became white world heavyweight champion with his victory against Gunboat Smith. He even refereed and decided Jack Johnson vs. Frank Moran in 1914, which could give him the unique distinction of having refereed a world heavyweight championship fight before fighting in a heavyweight championship fight. He already was a big name in boxing prior to the war, knocking out most foes in Europe. After fighting valiantly in the World War, he came back an even bigger hero. Plus, he was handsome, with blond hair, blue eyes, and movie star features, which didn't hurt with the female fans. His war record provided a contrast with Dempsey. Plus, there was the international angle to the fight.

[488] *New York Daily News*, April 9, 1921; *New York Tribune, New York Herald, Brooklyn Standard Union*, April 10, 1921.

276

For the past five weeks, Dempsey had been touring the northwest giving exhibitions in connection with a vaudeville act. After his show on April 9, Dempsey quit the stage and headed east.[489]

On April 11, 1921 in Toronto, Ontario, Canada, 168 ½-pound Harry Greb, despite being decked in the 2nd round by a right to the body, knocked down 175-pound Soldier Jones several times in the 3rd and 4th rounds to earn the knockout victory.[490]

Tommy Gibbons, who "is now the talk in pugilistic circles as being a formidable contender for Jack Dempsey's title," was in New York. Gibbons had won his last eight fights, including WND12 and WND10 Chuck Wiggins, KO1 219-pound Al Reich (overcoming a 37-pound weight disparity), and TKO2 Paul Samson Koerner (Koerner's first knockout loss; he had lost a 1920 10-round no decision to Tunney).

On April 12, 1921 in New York City, 175-pound Tommy Gibbons stopped 181-pound Larry Williams in the 4th round, decking him multiple times throughout.[491]

Bill Brennan picked Dempsey to finish Carpentier in 4 rounds.

> Carpentier is fast enough to keep away from Dempsey for about three rounds, but he'll get it no later than the fourth. The Frenchman is a wonderful boxer but he's not rugged enough to take the wallops that Dempsey is bound to get over on him. Carpentier is not a lot heavier now than when he was taking a lacing from all the American middleweights.

> Yes, Carpentier can punch, but I don't believe he can hit a whole lot harder than I can. In our last fight I hit Dempsey square on the jaw three times with every ounce of strength I had and he didn't go down. I had him groggy…but he came right back. Dempsey's recuperative power is remarkable and Carpentier can't help but lose heart when he puts over one of his famous shots and the champion takes it.

Brennan said Dempsey stopped him with a stomach blow, not the rabbit punch.[492]

Frank Farley, sporting editor for Denver, Colorado's *Rocky Mountain News*, said Dempsey would knock out Carpentier in 6 rounds. He said Willard was entitled to a return match. When asked whether a world's champion should defend his title against a negro, Farley answered, "No." Farley said one referee should decide a fight, not two judges and a referee. Champions should be compelled to defend their titles at least once every six months. When asked to name a suitable challenger, and whether Gibbons was one, Farley answered, "Harry Greb. Gibbons isn't rugged enough."[493]

---

[489] *Buffalo Commercial*, April 13, 1921.
[490] *Montreal Gazette, Pittsburgh Post*, April 12, 1921.
[491] *New York World*, April 13, 1921; *New York Daily News*, April 11, 13, 1921.
[492] *Brooklyn Citizen*, April 12, 1921.
[493] *El Paso Herald*, April 13, 1921. The *Buffalo Commercial*, on April 20, 1921, noted that Greb had earned $18,172 total for his last seven fights under George Engel's management, averaging just under $2,600 per fight.

On April 15, Dempsey arrived in New York, but intended to go to the Freddy Welsh Health Farm near Summit, New Jersey for two or three weeks of rest, hiking, golfing, and fun.

Jack said, "I feel fine except for the fact that I am tired and need a rest. I've been doing vaudeville for some time, and that business is worse than fighting." He had managed to do a little training each day while he was running around the country. "I boxed several rounds daily."[494]

Dempsey said he would be as good or better than he was against Willard for the Carpentier fight. He realized Carpentier was a good man, with speed and power, and although folks said Jack would hurt Georges when he hit him, he knew that he had to catch him first. Although he would go in to win by knockout, he never was overconfident, and one never could tell what might happen in the ring.

Jack said he couldn't get going in the Brennan fight for quite a while, and felt he must have been stale and overtrained. "I worked on and off five months for that fight, and instead of getting better I got worse as the time wore on."

On his recent tour, Dempsey knocked out a local man in Winnipeg who kept challenging him, stopping him in the 2nd round.

"Doc" Kearns said that after Carpentier, Dempsey would accommodate men like Willard, Gibbons, Greb, and the rest. "All they have to do is show up [with] a promoter who will pay."[495]

World welterweight champ Jack Britton thought Dempsey would beat Carpentier within 10 rounds. "Dempsey is the strongest, a terrific hitter and a wonderful fighter. ... I expect to see the Frenchman put up a fast, game fight, however."[496]

Tex Rickard said Dempsey was a real champion. "You make him an offer to fight, and he agrees right away. Other champions interpose a hundred 'ifs' and 'buts' before they will pin themselves down to a contract. All Dempsey wants is an opportunity to fight, and he signs up. Details don't bother him at all." Of course, when the offer was for the kind of money Rickard was offering, quick assent was understandable.[497]

On April 17, at a late-night party held after midnight on the roof of the Ziegfeld Frolic in New York, Jack Dempsey met baseball great, King of Swat, Babe Ruth. The Babe had just hit his first home run of the season that day. Jack wished him luck in setting a new home run record and earning pennant money. Babe told Jack he hoped the championship would stay in America. Dempsey replied, "There's nothing to it. It will."

Initial Wall Street wagering favored Dempsey over Carpentier at 3 to 2 odds.[498]

[494] *Brooklyn Daily Times*, April 15, 1921; *New York Daily News*, April 16, 1921.
[495] *New York Evening World*, April 16, 1921. *Buffalo Courier*, April 17, 1921.
[496] *Brooklyn Standard Union*, April 17, 1921.
[497] *New York Evening World*, April 18, 1921.
[498] *New York Daily News*, *Buffalo Express*, April 18, 1921.

On the 18th, Dempsey moved to Freddy Welsh's farm. He planned to ride horseback, play golf, swim, play handball, and a little baseball. With him were John O'Reilly, Teddy Hayes, and Joe Benjamin.[499]

At Summit, N.J., Dempsey is with Mrs. Lane of Boston and Mr. and Mrs. Freddy Welsh.

From Paris, 173-pound Carpentier allegedly said, "Jack's got nothing on me. I, too, expect to win before the 12th round."[500]

On April 19, 1921 in Newark, New Jersey, Tommy Gibbons stopped Dan "Porky" Flynn in the 11th round, giving him a terrific lacing, having him bleeding badly from the nose and mouth throughout. Flynn took terrific right smashes to the jaw and a bad body pounding, until he was broken down.[501]

Frank Menke said if Carpentier slugged, Dempsey, who was bigger, stronger, longer, and more powerful, would stop him very quickly. Carpentier could box and try to outpoint him, but if Dempsey was as good as he was against the clever, shifty Miske, despite Carpentier's speed, Dempsey was too quick and panther-like in his movement, and likely still would stop Carpentier within 3 rounds.[502]

Edward "Gunboat" Smith, who had fought both men, said Dempsey was much stronger physically than Carpentier. "One thing I will say in Carpentier's favor, he has the hardest straight punch I ever encountered. He is as fast as lightning and exceptionally tricky." Dempsey would have to be careful. Carpentier could appear to be out of range, but could step in quickly like a tiger with his snappy, deadly blows. He had a peculiar style of ducking that could cause Jack some trouble. He could duck and

---

[499] *New York Daily News, New York Tribune*, April 19, 1921.
[500] *Brooklyn Daily Times*, April 19, 1921. Carp planned to come to America in early May.
[501] *New York Herald*, April 20, 1921.
[502] *Binghamton Press*, April 20, 1921.

sway from the hips, and also bend his legs, so it appeared as if he was about to touch the canvas, but he could spring up with a straight punch. "If it ever connects Dempsey will know he has been hit." However, Dempsey could take a hard punch. "He is a glutton for assimilating punishment, although he has never been compelled to take what you would call a real hard pummeling in any of his bouts. The harder he is hit the harder he will fight back." Dempsey took more punishment in training for Willard than most would care to receive in an actual fight. "That is proof enough that he can take all that comes his way and refuse to back away. He is a human tiger of the constantly boring-in type. His aggressiveness and stamina are remarkable." "Dempsey is as strong as an ox and the longer he goes the better he gets."

Smith said Dempsey took Brennan too lightly and was not the Dempsey that fought Willard. He did not train as hard. Regardless, the one solid blow he landed in the entire fight spelled curtains for Brennan. Dempsey would take Carpentier much more seriously.

Although Carpentier had been training and fighting since his return from the military, beating Battling Levinsky in 4 rounds, Georges Grundhoven and Blink MacCloskey in 2 rounds, Joe Beckett in 1 round, Jean Croissilles in 2, and Dick Smith in 8 rounds, going 6-0 with 6 KOs since mid-1919, the five years out of the ring had to have some negative impact. Since his return, he had beaten men with ease, and did not have to extend himself, suffering no rough usage.

Smith believed that he would have beaten Carpentier had he not been disqualified (1914 LDQ6). He also noted that in 1912, middleweight champ Frank Klaus won via DQ19 (Carpentier hurt and his manager entered the ring). Middleweight Papke, whom Ketchel beat, stopped an 18-year-old Carpentier in 18 rounds (his manager retired him). Of course, Carp still was just a kid. Carpentier won a 20-round decision over Jeff Smith in 1913, which was impressive, but Smith was not a champion. "[Jeff] Smith would last one round with Dempsey." The Gunboat said Carpentier could not handle Dempsey's body attack, as his losses proved.

Still, in 1913 a 19-year-old Carpentier had knocked out 189-pound Bombardier Billy Wells twice, in 4 rounds and 1 round respectively, to win the European Heavyweight title. He started his pro career in 1908, when he was only 14 years old. From January 1913 through 1914, Carpentier had gone 18-1 with 14 KOs, the one loss a close 1914 15-round decision to 184 ½-pound Joe Jeannette (flooring Joe in the 1st round in the process). Some even thought Carpentier won. Georges Carpentier was fighting one of the world's best heavyweights in 1914, at age 20, before Jack Dempsey had even started his pro career. Georges still was only 27 years of age, so he was young and fresh and still in his physical prime.

Smith granted, "I will say that the Frenchman is a more deadly puncher than Dempsey, but I have the height of confidence in Jack's ability to keep out of the danger zone. Both are good scientific men."

Ultimately, Smith concluded, "Dempsey is the greatest heavyweight ever developed in this country." Jack had improved greatly. In their first meeting in 1917, Dempsey "was exceptionally slow at the time and I nearly knocked him out." Yet, in their rematch, Dempsey "was as fast as a bantamweight and I had trouble in seeing him, he set such a fast pace."

Although Smith believed Dempsey would win by knockout within 6 rounds, "I want to say that there is a possible chance of Carpentier winning by a knockout. A man with a good punch, such as Carpentier carries, is dangerous at all times. Very few fighters have it. As a single puncher, Carpentier has it on Dempsey. Still, I do not expect him to win."[503]

Carpentier said he did not think the fight would last more than 4 rounds, no matter who won. Georges asked Joe Jeannette to be his chief sparring partner and adviser.[504]

Vincent Treanor said Dempsey would profit by training away from the city. He had worked on and off again for so many months for the Brennan fight, with all its delays, that training became a bore for him. As a result, he fought with little of his usual speed and aggressiveness. He was not the bruising, rushing, cyclonic fighting machine. Dempsey had a tough time getting going in that fight, but his inherent ability and class finally came through. Brennan put up a stubborn battle, even having the best of it for part of the way, but eventually succumbed to a right hand which seemed to go into his stomach and come out of his back.

Carpentier was a different kind of challenge. He was lithe, active, clever, catlike, and stealthy, flashy in attack, with power. Many said the Dempsey of the Brennan fight might lose to him. Kearns said they were taking Carpentier seriously.

Grantland Rice said many shrewd judges who picked Dempsey to beat Willard now were picking Carpentier to beat Dempsey. They liked Carpentier's combination of speed, skill, and hitting power. He would not be slow-moving, overconfident, or a fixed target like Willard, which enabled Dempsey to plant himself and put everything he had into his wallops. Carp was shifty and fast moving. Even Brennan was able to avoid many of Dempsey's blows, few landing with solid effect. Bill was able to ride, duck, or block to diminish the sting of most blows. Carpentier was faster than Brennan, and supposedly a better boxer. Brennan hit Dempsey, and Jack could not afford to take too many risks against such a hitter as Carpentier.

Dempsey received boos at Madison Square Garden after beating Brennan, and Carpentier would be an even bigger public favorite, which would not be uplifting to Dempsey. Many members of the public could not forget that Carpentier served in the war and Dempsey did not. Such difference of opinion about the men and the fight would boost the gate receipts.[505]

[503] *Brooklyn Daily Eagle*, April 20, 1921.
[504] *Buffalo Enquirer, New York Herald*, April 22, 1921.
[505] *New York World, New York Tribune*, April 23, 1921.

Kearns made Kid Norfolk, Harry Wills, and the Jamaica Kid "flattering offers" to spar with the champion. "Irrespective of his attitude on other occasions, Dempsey does not propose to draw the color line in training." The best whites were welcome, too. Dempsey was willing to spar with anyone.[506]

The Scene of the Big Fight

Tex Rickard announced that the fight site was Boyle's "Thirty Acres," also known as the Montgomery Oval, in Jersey City, near the Grove street and Summit avenue stations of the Hudson tubes and ferry landings, owned by John Boyle and representatives of the Browning estate. Rickard leased the grounds, and was having a large arena built. The legal authorities had assured him of protection and cooperation.[507]

Dempsey was resting, eating, and having a good time. He jogged a couple miles with Freddy Welsh, Joe Benjamin, and Teddy Hayes. Breakfast was ham, eggs, and fresh milk. Lunch was lettuce salad, tenderloin steak, milk, and tea. Pinochle games, nickel tossing, and a wrestling match followed. He also was taking walks, and playing a little handball, tennis, or golf. He enjoyed playing with Welsh's children. He was like a big boy at play. He wasn't going to do real work until they got to their Atlantic City training camp.

DEMPSEY IN NEW JERSEY—THE HEAVYWEIGHT CHAMPION IS PICTURED HERE AT FREDDY WELSH'S REST FARM AT SUMMIT, FROLICKING WITH WELSH'S TWO CHILDREN AND PLAYING THE PIANO. MORE STRENUOUS WORK COMES LATER.

[506] New York Tribune, April 24, 1921.
[507] New York Herald, April 20, 1921; New York Daily News, April 20, 26, 27, 1921.

Dempsey at the Freddy Welsh health farm, doing road work, sparring playfully, playing tennis and golf, doing rope skipping and farm work, etc.

Dempsey said,

> I'm feeling as good as I ever did and I can get in shape with six weeks' work. I overtrained for Bill Brennan, and I'm not going to make the same mistake this time. Yes, I have been dancing a little bit, and I went up to a midnight show last week with Babe Ruth. I know I was criticized for doing it, but a fellow's got to have a little amusement once in a while.

Jack had been playing handball as well. He tried pocket billiards, but was not very good.

Regarding the details of the upcoming fight, Jack said, "I don't care. Doc will take care of those things." He didn't care who refereed. "As long as he knows how to count."

Fred Winsor, a former Dempsey manager, said, "Dempsey will win in 4 rounds. Carpentier cannot withstand the attack of the champion. Dempsey is a cruel punisher. He doesn't have to inflict his damage at long range. He'll start Carpentier on his way in the clinches with short punishment dealing blows."[508]

Dempsey told Harry Newman, "Never felt better in my life. I am taking things easy for the present ... All the hard work will come later. I'm on a vacation now, trying to get even with myself for the many hours

---

508 *Brooklyn Standard Union*, April 28, 1921.

I lost flopping around the country." Working too long for Brennan caused him to go stale. "I couldn't get started in that bout with Brennan…but I guess the finish was satisfactory enough to my friends."

Regarding the upcoming fight, Jack said, "I am not given to making predictions. This boy Carpentier is a great fighter. His record speaks for itself. … Of course I expect to win. … Tell them that I will be ready when the time comes, and that I will never stop trying from the clang until the whistle blows ending the contest."[509]

Some New Jersey ministers protested the bout, calling it a shameful humiliation to the city, for six boxing deaths had resulted from "these brutal encounters during the three years the law has been in existence." The religious/ministerial/anti-boxing lobby always remained a threat to the sport. Some politicians occasionally caved to such pressure.[510]

Dempsey, who confessed to weighing 200 pounds, said he hadn't had a hard fight in five years. He had been extended here and there, but the hardest fights had been when he first took up boxing. He took some terrible whalings on an empty stomach. "Why, the quarrels I have had since I won the title were picnics compared to some of those jams in the lovable periods when I was trying to convince myself that I was a fighter."[511]

Charles Murray, matchmaker for the Queensberry Athletic Club in Buffalo, remembered how Ed W. Smith, sports editor for the *Chicago American*, recommended Dempsey to fight Carl Morris, so the match was made. However, Morris was 250 pounds, and Dempsey did not appear to weigh more than 180. Murray wanted to call it off, thinking the weight disparity would be too much; fearing he might give the sport a black eye. Dempsey replied, "This is one bird that I want to fight. Morris is rated a great fighter in the East. They don't know me. I'll knock him out and that will give me a start. For the love of Mike, don't ditch this fight!" Dempsey pleaded so hard and earnestly, with such conviction that he would lick Morris, that Murray decided to allow it. Jack even said, "If I don't make a great showing with Morris, if I don't satisfy you, take the $750 I'll have coming and give it to the Red Cross."

When the match took place, "I nearly fell off my seat when I saw Dempsey, graceful as a dancing master, dead sure of his moves, panther-like in action, dead shot with either fist." Morris fouled, hitting low incessantly, but Dempsey begged for Morris *not* to be disqualified, for he wanted to knock him out cold. Afterwards, Murray said, "You're a fighter, you son-of-a-gun." "And a fighter he proved to be, a marvelous fighter, the greatest I ever saw in action." After that fight, Murray knew that Dempsey would beat Willard and become the next champion.[512]

On May 3, 1921 in Summit, New Jersey, Dempsey refereed the Freddy Welsh vs. Willie Jackson lightweight contest, won by Welsh via KO8. At

[509] *New York Daily News*, May 1, 1921.
[510] *Buffalo Courier*, May 1, 1921.
[511] *New York Herald*, *New York Daily News*, May 4, 1921.
[512] *Buffalo Labor Journal*, May 5, 1921.

one point, after they failed to listen the first time, Dempsey sternly ordered them to break. Afterwards, Jack said, "I always obey the referee's orders when I am boxing, and I want boxers to do what I say when I am the third man in the ring."

On May 4 at Welsh's farm, Dempsey boxed 3 rounds each with Pacific coast lightweight Joe Benjamin, rugged Scranton welterweight Pete Latzo, and then Oregon welter/middleweight Alex Trambitas, for 9 total rounds. Jack worked on his speed, holding back his power, practicing his counterpunches. He demonstrated his defensive skill, ducking, side-stepping, parrying, and blocking.[513]

Carpentier didn't mind exuding confidence, and was brasher and more boastful than Jack. He said, "That fellow Jack Dempsey was made to order for me and I honestly believe that I will floor him for the count inside of three rounds."[514]

When asked to respond to Carpentier's statement that he would knock out him out within 3 rounds, Dempsey replied, "Maybe he will. I prefer to do my fighting in the ring."[515]

Frank Menke said a story trickled over the wires purportedly quoting Dempsey as saying, "I'll never defend my title against a negro." Menke said that did not sound like Dempsey. "Dempsey fears no living man. ... Left to his own devices, Dempsey by this time would have fought and whipped every man in the heavyweight division – or lost his title trying." Menke believed Dempsey when he said he wanted to fight all the time, against the toughest men. Not long ago, Dempsey had commented on the color line, saying,

> As far as I'm concerned I'll fight anybody in the world and color doesn't make any difference. I fought Negroes when I was coming along and I didn't find any of them very hard to whip except John Lester Johnson who caught me in 1916 before Jack Kearns taught me ring trickery. Personally, I'm not barring anybody. If there's a public demand for a match with a Negro, and Jack Kearns wants me to go ahead with it, I'll report for work on fight night and guarantee that no Negro will win the championship from me.

Menke said the color line was a white fighter's alibi to avoid meeting a dangerous negro, and essentially was a confession of fear. Just because Jack Johnson disgraced his race was no reason to bar a clean-living black fighter from a crack at the title. Men like George Dixon, Joe Gans, Joe Walcott, Peter Jackson, Joe Jeannette, Bob Armstrong, Sam Langford, and Sam McVey had been good for the profession.

Lots of top fighters and champions never drew the color line, including Frank Erne, Benny Leonard, Young Corbett, Abe Attell, and Gunboat Smith. Menke believed that after Dempsey beat Carpentier and

[513] *New York Herald*, May 5, 1921.
[514] *New York Daily News*, May 5, 1921. Carpentier was getting ready to travel to the U.S from Paris.
[515] *Brooklyn Daily Times*, May 5, 1921.

some other outstanding white challengers, if the public wanted him to fight Wills, he would do it.[516]

Marian Hale was pleased to be able to interview Dempsey at Welsh's, for women normally were tabooed. Dempsey played golf and piano and frolicked with Welsh's two children. Hale asked Jack, "What do you think of women, Mr. Dempsey?" Jack replied, "I ain't married, and I haven't got a girl, and when the big fight comes off, and the women take their places with the men on the other side of the ring, one won't make my heart beat faster than another." Also, "Put me down as saying that men are men, a fight is a fight, but that women are dolls." Jack said he did not care for drama or literature (contrary to reports that claimed he was a reader). "I am just a fighting guy. Sometimes I wish I had gone beyond the grammar school, but there is no use whimpering now."[517]

On May 6, 1921, Dempsey transferred to Atlantic City. He would train formally at the Airport Airdome, which was under construction.

The level of coverage that newsmen gave the Carpentier fight, for two months leading up to the contest, with daily training reports, predictions, and analysis, was on par with or even exceeding past huge contests, including Jeffries-Johnson. Nothing like it exists in boxing today.

Dempsey meets Atlantic City Mayor Edward L. Bader

Atlantic City Mayor Edward L. Bader presented Dempsey with the keys to the city. Jack even was made an honorary member of the police force. New Jersey Governor Edward Edwards had invited U.S. President Warren G. Harding to the big fight.[518]

On May 7, Carpentier set sail for America from Le Havre, France. Georges said,

Well, I'm off today for America and I'm leaving with the greatest confidence and eagerness that I never felt before a contest.

I know my fight against Jack Dempsey will be the greatest of my career and I'm going into it in better condition than I have ever been before in my life.

Through my contest with Joe Beckett and by the training that I have engaged in since then, I know that I have overcome any physical relapses that might have resulted from my four years in the army.

[516] *Binghamton Press*, May 6, 1921.
[517] *Brooklyn Citizen*, May 9, 1921.
[518] *New York Times*, May 6, 1921; *New York Daily News*, May 5-7, 1921.

I am in real fighting trim and have in addition superior strength and endurance.

I realize that I will face the hardest adversary I have ever confronted. Perhaps that is the reason I am in such fine spirits, because difficulty has always stimulated me. ...

I consider it a great honor to compete for the world's title with an opponent of the character of Jack Dempsey. ... I have the greatest respect for American sportsmanship, courtesy and hospitality, and I am glad to be going back to the Americans again. Next to fighting in my own country, I prefer America.

Regarding the result of the contest – well, the better man will win.[519]

Carpentier called Dempsey one of the greatest champions ever – strong, agile, aggressive, scientific, and cunning, a skillful ring general who knew how to take instant advantage of openings. Dempsey also had a surprising resilience and a wonderful capacity for taking punishment. Georges was not underestimating him. He had seen the films.

Yet, Carpentier's attitude also was, "Come right on, Jack, and the faster and more furious the better I will like it." Georges said throughout his entire career he had knocked out bigger and stronger men, and some of his finest victories had been won in the face of "certain defeat," as the dopesters said before the contest. Even as a kid, he was knocking out full grown men. He was not intimidated.[520]

Unlike Carpentier, Dempsey usually did not watch films of or attend opponents' fights. He simply liked to do what he did and make adjustments in the ring.[521]

Harry Newman said the dopesters were up in the air about the likely result. Though most thought Dempsey figured to win, many were inclined to give the Frenchman more than a chance, saying it was a tough fight to pick. One man said, "I honestly think that if Carpentier stays four rounds with Dempsey it's a five-to-one shot that he will cut the champion to pieces...and yet it seems like a five-to-one shot that Frenchman won't be around there for the four rounds. The longer the fight goes the better it will be for Carpentier."[522]

Francois Descamps believed the fight would not last more than 6 rounds. Both men would seek relatively quick knockouts. He believed whomever landed the first real blow would win, for they both had a punch heavy enough to end it with one blow. What Carpentier lacked in raw physical strength and size he made up for with superior knowledge of how and where to hit. Both men would expend more energy and force in their blows in 6 rounds than old timers expended in four or five times that length of time. Hence, it seemed that all of the principals were

[519] *Binghamton Press*, May 7, 1921.
[520] *Trenton Evening Times*, May 9, 1921.
[521] *New York Daily News*, May 8, 1921.
[522] *New York Daily News*, May 9, 1921.

expecting an explosive, fast-paced, hard-punching contest, which is what the fans wanted to see.[523]

Jack sent his mother a bouquet of flowers on Mother's Day, along with a message saying he was going to train so she would not be disappointed on July 2. She responded, "Dear Boy – I just knew you wouldn't forget your mother. We know what to expect in Jersey City. Mother." Jack exclaimed, "Some girl! Confidence is a great thing, not only when you have it yourself, but when it is shown by your best girl."[524]

Harry Newman reported that Dempsey was the betting favorite at 1 to 2 odds.

Dempsey climbs a water tower

Dempsey had spent a couple days in Atlantic City shaking hands, receiving various delegates, playing golf, enjoying the beach, etc. He stayed at a hotel on the Boardwalk. He transferred to his training quarters, where he would stay out of sight behind a high board fence.[525]

The champ would live in a two-story frame house, located on a plot formerly used as an aviation field. Teddy Hayes, Jack's secretary, dealt with the barrage of daily letters.

As a slap at Dempsey's lack of a war record, the Atlantic City Post of the American Legion invited Carpentier but not Dempsey to train at their resort. The Post insisted that a man who had served his country during the war was entitled to more consideration than a man they regarded as a slacker.

However, on May 10, the local Atlantic City Rotary Club honored Dempsey. Jim Corbett gave a speech complimenting Jack's devotion to his family.[526]

Rickard insured the upcoming big fight with Lloyd's of London with a $100,000 policy. The fighters were insured against injury, accident, or any cause that might keep either from fighting.

[523] *Camden Post-Telegram*, May 9, 1921.
[524] *New York Tribune*, May 9, 1921.
[525] *New York Tribune, Daily News*, May 10, 1921
[526] *New Brunswick Daily Home News, New York Herald, Paterson Evening News*, May 11, 1921; *New York Daily News*, May 12, 1921.

On the 11th, Mayor Bader paced Dempsey on his morning run, accompanying him on horseback.[527]

Former bantamweight champ Johnny Coulon said Carpentier had a good chance to beat Dempsey.

> I have seen enough of Carpentier to form a very good opinion of him. In some ways he is better than any boxer in the world... Carpentier has more science than any living fighter and has innumerable little tricks that no other boxer possesses. Carpentier also packs a terrific punch that will knock out any living man if he lands it.

Georges lived cleanly, always was in shape, and had a wonderful temperament.[528]

Charles Mathison said Carpentier's victims were not great; many overrated. The skilled men did not have a punch (Levinsky), and the punchers lacked either the skill or the ability to take it (Wells, Beckett). Mathison questioned Carpentier's ability to take hard knocks, for he had been stopped several times, though mostly early in his career when he was a still growing kid fighting grown men with superior experience. (Judging Carpentier for losses at a young age would be like judging young Dempsey for his losses to Jack Downey, Jim Flynn, or Willie Meehan, as well as his several early draws.) Mathison granted that Carpentier had quality victories, including W20 Willie Lewis, decking Lewis in the 8th, W20 Harry Lewis, and W20 Jeff Smith.

It was true that Carpentier was very active on his feet, could box with skill, and could punch. But ultimately, Dempsey was a battering ram. He was larger, stronger, quite as speedy, better able to take punishment and remain on his feet, and he hit harder.[529]

New York Governor Nathan Miller signed the Simpson-Brundage bill, which amended the Walker boxing law. The new law provided for the appointment of a three-member volunteer commission. They were empowered to appoint deputies, who would be paid $4,000 per year.

On May 14, New Jersey Governor Edward Edwards invited Dempsey to lunch with Mayor Edward Bader and others, which Jack accepted.

Governor Edwards responded to the criticism lodged by ministers of him and the big fight. He noted that boxing matches were not London rules prize fights, but gloved contests with humane rules; exhibitions of skill. The law authorized boxing exhibitions. "If the ministers do not like the laws of the State of New Jersey, why do they not leave the State and dwell elsewhere?" No one was forced to participate, nor did they have to watch the fights.

> During the war an important part of the government's welfare work among soldiers in cantonment and overseas consisted of boxing

[527] *New York Herald*, May 12, 1921.
[528] *Brooklyn Citizen*, May 14, 1921.
[529] *New York Herald*, May 15, 1921.

instruction. Many of the teachers were professional pugilists, and the highest military authorities testify to the splendid results of their instruction. … I do not recall that the clergymen who now criticize me entered any protest against American soldiers being taught the art of self-defense by professional boxers. These teachers performed a real service during the war, but it seems that now that the war is ended they are not entitled to derive any benefit from the exercise of their skill. Dempsey and Carpentier represent in themselves the highest quality of the boxing skill that the Government strove to impart to American soldiers during the war.[530]

Dempsey had no idea how Carpentier would fight, and would be prepared for anything. He would decide what to do based on what he saw in the ring. "I want the championship to remain in America. Carpentier is a very fine fellow and as much as we love France, I love America, first, best and all the time."[531]

From prison in Leavenworth, Kansas, Jack Johnson predicted that Dempsey would lick the Frenchman. "That lad will knock Carpentier out in eight or ten rounds. The Frenchman is a nice boxer – but Dempsey is a hitter." Jack said Carpentier was clever, but not clever enough to offset the champion's rushes. It would take a strong defense to beat Dempsey. Johnson later said that Carpentier was "not capable of swapping punches with Dempsey." Johnson had sparred Carpentier in France.[532]

As good a milkman as he is a fighter, said his watchers yesterday.

Kearns concluded a $50,000 deal with a motion picture corporation for a one-reel picture entitled, "A Day With Jack Dempsey."[533]

On the evening of May 15, Georges Carpentier arrived in the U.S., but did not disembark from the ship until May 16. He was weighing 175 pounds, and expected to weigh about 173 for the fight.

Decamps said Carpentier studied boxing and Dempsey like a student. Georges had about 100 fights of experience, more than Dempsey (who had around 70 fights). Dempsey was scientific, but not as scientific and smart as Carpentier.[534]

---

[530] *New York Herald*, May 15, 1921.
[531] *New York Daily News*, May 15, 1921.
[532] *Ogden Standard Examiner*, May 15, 1921; *Yonkers Herald*, May 16, 1921. Johnson said his prison job had been to give athletic instruction to other prisoners.
[533] *Brooklyn Standard Union*, May 15, 1921.
[534] *Binghamton Press*, May 16, 1921; *New York Daily News*, May 17, 1921.

"I have never felt better."

The challenger and 'Flip' salute the Statue of Liberty.

The *New York Tribune's* W. J. Macbeth said the principals owed Bill Brennan a debt of gratitude. Following the victory over Willard, Dempsey was hailed as an unbeatable superman, the greatest champion ever, and the Carpentier fight was seen as a mismatch. However, Dempsey's performance against Brennan caused many to believe that Carpentier had a real chance, which made the upcoming fight more marketable. Some skeptics believed Jack was under a pull, but if that were so, he carried the comedy to dangerous lengths. Champions as a rule did not trifle so far with anything as dear as the heavyweight crown.[535]

This time, Carpentier had left his wife behind to attend to their baby Jacqueline, who was born last November. Georges said he already was in top shape, the best of his life, and never felt better. His training quarters would be at Manhasset, Long Island, New York. Georges said the odds were even in France. "I am going to win this fight. I will win no matter how long it lasts, but I hope it will be short."[536]

Carpentier preferred to do his training in private. He was with 190-pound 23-year-old Paul Journee, Gus Wilson, and Battling Marcot, and planned to spar with Joe Jeannette as well.

When told that Dempsey would weigh about 190 and have nearly 20 pounds weight advantage, Descamps replied, "Eet is nothing."[537]

—Underwood Photo

Georges Carpentier brought with him as training partners, Paul Journee and Battling Harry Marcot.

[535] *New York Tribune*, May 16, 1921.

[536] *New York Evening World*, *Brooklyn Standard Union*, May 16, 1921.

[537] *Buffalo Enquirer*, *New York Daily News*, *New York Evening World*, *New York Herald*, *New York Tribune*, May 17, 1921. Tad Dorgan picked Dempsey to win within 6 rounds.

Carpentier was the idol of France, and the fight was said to be the most important in French history.

Jack Curley said, "Carpentier will win the championship. His speed and skill will counteract what weight and strength advantages Dempsey will have over him. Carpentier has as much punch as Dempsey and can hit more accurately. The fight may not be long. The more rounds it goes the easier it will be for Carpentier."[538]

Jim Corbett visited Dempsey's camp on Tuesday, May 17. Corbett said, "The champion is hard as nails and rough as granite. His wind is great and he is feeling like a colt." "My, what a rough young man Dempsey is. He expended enough energy to win several heavyweight championships in nine rounds of boxing with three sparring partners."

Corbett saw Dempsey spar with Jack Renault (17-4-1), a big, rough Canadian heavyweight, who was decked by a head blow in the 3rd round, Leo Houck (134-37-26), a capable battler who could take it, but was thankful that the champ was wearing big gloves, and then Alex Trambitas (26-9-24), Pacific coast welter, who wore a head gear. In their 3rd round, Jack landed an uppercut to the chin that lifted Alex clear through the ropes and out of the ring, landing on his head. Luckily, the headgear saved Trambitas. Dempsey showed no signs of fatigue, despite the fact that he ran 6 miles in the morning as well.[539]

In Manhasset, New York, Carpentier's camp would be barricaded with barbed wire, not open to the public, and open to the press only on certain occasions. Corbett noted that Georges worked in private for the Beckett fight, so this was nothing new.

Films of Dempsey's training were shown to the public in New Jersey, generating additional revenue.

ARENA

Three Days, Commencing Tomorrow.

JACK DEMPSEY in Training

THREE SHOWS DAILY,

2:30, 7 and 9.

1,000-Foot Reel, Showing the Champion in Preparation for His Coming Bout With Georges Carpentier.

OTHER GREAT FEATURES.

Mats., 25c; Evenings, 25c., 50c.

---

[538] *Brooklyn Standard Union*, May 17, 1921.
[539] *Buffalo Enquirer, New York Tribune*, May 18, 1921.

Corbett noted that a lot of women were interested in the upcoming fight and wanted to see it.[540]

On May 19 in Atlantic City, Harry Newman said Dempsey forced his sparring partners to beg for mercy, ripping and tearing into them with viciousness. Veteran Leo Houck got the worst cuffing of them all, and several times had to appeal to the champ to ease up, but Jack paid no attention, and Leo had to bear it.

Jack Clifford, another giant heavy, got the same pasting. He mixed it quite often, and Jack urged him on. Occasionally it looked like a real fight. Clifford wore a head gear, but was reeling several times and on the verge of a knockout.

Jack Renault was punished severely, particularly for "getting too gay" in the clinches. The champion never rested between bouts, and kept on the move every minute.[541]

Also on May 19, 1921, U.S. President Warren G. Harding signed into law the Emergency Quota Act, also known as the Immigration Restriction Act. It was designed to limit the influx of Southern and Eastern European immigrants by setting quotas based on their national origins.

Tad Dorgan noted that Dempsey enjoyed the company of his two Belgian police dogs. He worked out at an indoor gym at the aerodrome.

Jack Renault

He was a smiling, boyish chap outside the ring, but inside, a serious fighting man, all business. For recreation, Jack liked to play baseball with the local newspaper boys.

On the 20th, Dempsey tore right into Jack Renault, knocking him all over the ring and staggering him with a left hook to the chin. They engaged in fierce slugging. Renault said, "That fellow sure is socking them today." Dempsey closed Jack Clifford's right eye with a rasping left hook. Leo Houck was bounced around the ring like a rubber ball, receiving the worst of it. Each man only lasted 1 round.[542]

---

[540] *Buffalo Enquirer*, May 19, 1921.
[541] *New York Daily News*, May 20, 1921.

Light-heavyweight Leo Houck turned pro in 1904, and amongst his 200 fights, his more recent record included: 1917 W/DND6 Willie Meehan; 1918 WND6 (twice) Chuck Wiggins, W12 and L12 Johnny Wilson, WND6 Clay Turner, WND6 Gunboat Smith, DND6 Jeff Smith, and LND6 Battling Levinsky; 1919 L12, LND6, and LND10 Harry Greb, LND8 Mike Gibbons, WND8 and WND6 Bert Kenny; and 1920 LND6 and LND10 Gene Tunney.

Heavyweight Jack Clifford's record included: 1917 LND10 (twice) Jamaica Kid, LND10 Gunboat Smith, LND10 Jack Dillon, and LKOby4 Bill Brennan; 1918 LND8 Clay Turner; 1919 LND10 Jim Coffey; and 1920 LKOby2 Charley Weinert, LND6 Farmer Lodge, LND10 (twice) Ted Jamieson, and LKOby3 Gene Tunney.

Heavyweight Jack Renault had a 28-fight record that included: 1920 L12 Dan Porky Flynn and DND12 Battling Levinsky; 1921 LND10 (twice) Harry Greb, and W10 Ted Jamieson.

[542] *New York Daily News, New York Herald, Buffalo Enquirer*, May 21, 1921.

Also on May 20, 1921, in New Orleans, 165-pound Harry Greb and 161 ½-pound Jeff Smith fought to an official 15-round draw decision.

The local *Times-Picayune's* William Keefe disagreed, feeling that Smith won, for he had landed the clean, hard punches, and fought in sportsmanlike fashion, while Greb's fighting was quite the opposite. "Greb continually held while trying to make it seem Smith was holding…. Our tab of the fight by rounds gave Smith a big majority." Greb landed several wild swings and locked up Smith effectively in the clinches. Greb held around the neck, tried to choke Smith, and also butted him, opening up a wicked gash. Greb proved that he could take a punch, for he took body blows that would have sent others to the mat. Greb's jaw though, was a bobbing, elusive target. The only clean punches that Greb could land were right crosses to the jaw. Most other blows were blocked. Despite this writer feeling strongly that Smith won, he acknowledged, "Referee Wambsgans [draw] decision seemed to be a popular one."[543]

Jim Jeffries said Dempsey would find it a lot more challenging to land his hard punches on a fast, clever man. Jeff struggled to hit Jim Corbett, and if Carpentier was as fast and clever, with the same good footwork, it would not be so easy to land cleanly. Carpentier had plenty of experience, more than Dempsey, with nearly 100 fights.[544]

FOOTSURE.— One of the first acts of Georges Carpentier, heavyweight challenger, on his arrival here was to test the canvas floor of his training ring.

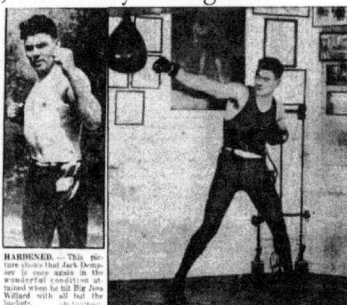

HARDENED.— This picture shows that Jack Dempsey is once again in the wonderful condition attained when he hit Big Jess Willard with all but the buckets.

PROTECTION. — Carpentier is determined not to be killed by kindness and wherever he goes around his training camp he is escorted by his trainers to ward off speeches of welcome, loving cup committees, and just plain pests.

A female admirer wrote of Georges, "He has a record of which he can be more proud than can our champion, Jack Dempsey, of his. Carpentier is a modest and unassuming man and I, for one, hope this 'orchid', as 'Whit' calls him, will surprise a few of his belittlers by knocking Dempsey cold." – Mona Traell, Boonton, N.J.[545]

543 *Times-Picayune*, May 21, 1921.
544 *New York Evening World*, May 21, 1921.
545 *New York Daily News*, May 22, 1921.

In their sparring on the 21st, Dempsey had Clifford groggy and bleeding from the mouth, and a left hook to the chin sent him reeling into the ropes. Clifford left camp after only six days, saying Dempsey had been too rough. He had been knocked out once and badly bruised on other occasions.[546]

On May 23, Georges was snappy in his work and in fine form. "If you can forget about Dempsey; Carpentier certainly looks mighty good." One called him, phonetically, "Koppenteer."

The *New York Tribune*'s C. F. Fitzgerald said 172 ½-pound (verified weight) Carpentier worked 40 minutes at top speed. He clearly was fit, with not an ounce of fat on his body. He had every blow at his disposal, and all were impressive. He was adept at side-stepping. He could move and prance left or right, but also rush or leap in, panther-like.

On the 23rd, several hundred, including women, paid 50 cents each to watch Dempsey train. Dempsey wrote, "The fair sex, judging from their applause, seemed to enjoy the bag punching more than they did the real bouts."

In sparring that day, Jack primarily worked on defense. He said the Pacific coast's Babe Herman was a flashy featherweight and one of the fastest men he ever saw in action. Herman boxed 2 fast rounds, and the Babe was in and out and all around him. After Portland welterweight Alex Trambitas went 2 rounds, Leo Houck was last. "I cut loose with Leo and had to hold him up in the second round a little to let him recover. Some of those punches I was sending in were pretty heavy."[547]

Jack White, comedian, puts up dukes to Dempsey.

Georges tries some Lewis stuff.

Carpentier in training costume.

Jack whistling jazz to his German police dog.

BALANCE. — Georges is not impersonating the Statue of Liberty, he is resting on a ring post to demonstrate that he still has the sense of equilibrium so necessary to a champion. (NEWS photo)

Boxing manager Dan Morgan picked Carpentier to win. "The Frenchman hits faster than Dempsey and he hits equally hard with both hands. He is the better boxer and has the best thinking head." Georges would punish Dempsey badly enough in the first few rounds to make the

[546] *New York Daily News, Brooklyn Daily Eagle*, May 22, 1921; *New York Evening World*, May 23, 1921.
[547] *Buffalo Times, New York Tribune*, May 24, 1921.

champion careful, and Carp would outgeneral him thereafter. "His lightning fast defensive work will also make Dempsey miss many of his punches, and will finally keep the champion busy defending himself until the finish." After 4 rounds, Dempsey's greater weight would slow him down. "Willie Meehan and Harry Greb had no trouble hitting him, and they both claim Dempsey is always ready to clinch when the mixing gets hot. ... Big men are easy to hit."

A HOT WEATHER SMILE.
—It must be funny weather in France. Despite the heat, Georges was done up like an Eskimo, but he managed to keep good natured just the same.

NICE AND COOL HERE.—Jack Dempsey took things easy at Atlantic City yesterday and after a light work out retired to a cool spot in his bathrobe to read his favorite paper.

HURDLING.—Carpentier took on a new trainer yesterday. Kid Coogan is the new pacemaker's fighting cognomen, but to screen fans he is better known as "The Kid." Jackie gave Georges a stiff workout and now wishes to be a fight champ.

Billy Miske said, "Carpentier is fast, smart, a good ducker and blocker. I have seen Carpentier fight, and with his remarkable skill in ducking and bobbing he will make it extremely difficult for Dempsey to land any really telling blows." Georges also was an accurate puncher. That said, "I do not mean to reflect upon the first-class fighting ability of Jack Dempsey. He is a great fighter, and has my respect."

Pete Herman said Dempsey was a sure winner. He would force matters and score a knockout quickly, for Carpentier would not be able to withstand or elude his terrible power. Jack would drive the fight and break him with body punching. Despite the fact that Carpentier was dangerous, fast, clever, and confident, Dempsey would hurt him badly.

In one article, Mike Gibbons conceded Carpentier a chance, saying,

> I know that I am not alone in my contention that Carpentier is the type of boxer best suited to give Dempsey a real row. The big fellows move so slowly that Jack can keep out of their way and at the same time he can pound them to pieces. Dempsey must fight differently against a fast opponent. Dempsey is not a hard man to hit. Therefore, a good boxer who can make the most of openings should do very well – so long as he is conscious.

In another article, Mike Gibbons said Dempsey would win within 5 rounds, because he was too rugged and too hard a puncher. Dempsey was a game fighting cock who loved the battle. He was gamer than Carpentier, whose European style was inferior to the American style. "If Dempsey fights his tearing, slashing, tiger-like battle, he is sure to win."

Tommy Gibbons said Dempsey would win within 6 rounds or less. Carpentier was a great fighter, but could not take the punishment that Dempsey would hand out. Furthermore, no pugilist in history ever retired for four years and then came back as good as the day he quit. Carp's war years had to leave him worse off (despite the 2-year, 6-fight comeback).

On May 23, 1921, in Canton, Ohio, Tommy Gibbons knocked out former Jess Willard sparring partner Jack Heinen in the 1st round. Heinen was decked six times.

The *Buffalo Times* said Carpentier had dazzling speed, fast feet, a hard punch, and the cunning necessary to beat Dempsey.[548]

The *New York Herald* noted that not many men were eager to spar with Dempsey. Jack would spar anyone, black or white, but few wanted to absorb the punishment he was apt to hand out to anyone who actually tried to test him. He played defense against smaller men, but anyone near his size would have to take some heavy blows.[549]

On May 24, U.S. Attorney General Harry M. Daugherty, a boxing fan, arrived, having announced his intention to visit Dempsey's headquarters at the Air Port to see him train. Daugherty shook Dempsey's hand and wished him luck. He told Jack that if he ever ran out of sparring partners, he could call on him.

That morning, Jack covered 7 miles on the road. In the afternoon, Dempsey sparred a tempestuous round with Bridgeport's 180-pound Larry Williams (48-40-14). After Larry landed several solid punches

---

[548] *New York Herald*, May 23, 1921; *Buffalo Courier, Buffalo Times, New York Tribune*, May 24, 1921.
[549] *New York Herald*, May 24, 1921.

to the head and body, including an uppercut to the chin, Dempsey danced about and under the blows, came at him, and it looked like Jack was going to stop him. After 1 round, Williams asked to be excused for the remainder of the day.

Jack Renault, wearing a head guard, took a hammering for 2 rounds. Leo Houck had quit, so the champ took on welter Alex Trambitas for 2 rounds and feather Babe Herman for 1 round, holding back his punches, showing his science. Renault then went another round.

The Attorney General called Dempsey's agility wonderful.[550]

Dempsey with the son and daughter of an Atlantic City building inspector.

Carpentier and Dempsey were different in temperament. Carpentier preferred solitude. Dempsey was more affable and friendly with a crowd.[551]

Dempsey did not show up to court in Philadelphia, where he was being sued by Dr. H. M. Goddard, who claimed a $500 balance was due on a $1,000 bill for a submucous recession operation on the champion's nose on September 17, 1919. Allegedly, the jury ruled in Dr. Goddard's favor for the $500.[552]

Tad Dorgan said there would be nothing to it but Dempsey if it were a fight to the finish or a 25-round bout, but Carpentier had a bright chance in a shorter contest. History proved that clever men had the advantage over punchers and huskier men over only 12 rounds. Jack never had faced a fast-moving target as fast as the French marvel. With only a 12-round bout, Jim Corbett would have beaten Fitzsimmons and Jeffries. Philadelphia Jack O'Brien was another boxer tough to beat in limited rounds bouts. Kid McCoy could make many men look silly for 10 rounds. However, Dempsey was fast too, and if he landed one, that might be all that was needed. Gunboat Smith and Bombardier Wells had made Carpentier kiss the canvas. Dempsey probably could as well. Yet, Carp was a fighter, for he had risen and won. However, "With Dempsey it will be a bit different. His opponents may get up, but they're never the same after taking one of his wallops on the kisser."[553]

Jack Kearns said they were not drawing the color line. Dempsey's next engagement would depend upon the trend of public clamor. If the public demanded he fight a negro (including Kid Norfolk), and a promoter was found who would guarantee the sum necessary, Kearns would be ready on

[550] *New York Tribune, New York Herald, New York Daily News,* May 25, 1921. Larry Williams' career included: 1915 LKOby5 Joe Jeannette; 1916 LND10 Bill Brennan, LND6 Willie Meehan, LKOby3 John Lester Johnson, and LND6 Billy Miske; 1917 D12 Bert Kenny; 1918 LND8 Clay Turner; 1919 WND8 Turner, LND10 Tommy Gibbons, DND8 and LKOby1 Kid Norfolk, W8 Kenny; 1920 L12 Turner, LND10 Harry Greb (6-3-1), L12 and TKO3 Turner; 1920 L12 Turner, LND10 Greb (8-1-1), L12 Turner, LND10 Greb, LND10 Norfolk, and LKOby1 Bob Martin; and 1921 LTKOby4 Tommy Gibbons and L15 Joe Cox.
    Renault had returned following his 1ˢᵗ round knockout victory over Frankie Britton in Trenton on Monday May 23.
[551] *New York Daily News,* May 25, 1921. Carp would be sparring with Paul Journee and Henri Marcot.
[552] *New York Herald,* May 25, 1921.
[553] *Yonkers Herald,* May 25, 1921.

behalf of Dempsey to eliminate the color line. "Dempsey is a free-for-all champion. He has the ambition to be pronounced the greatest heavyweight of all time. I believe that consideration is coming to him and I think that on July 2 he will make the verdict unanimous."[554]

Sam McVey said,

> Georges is too fast for Dempsey, I think. He's the speediest boxer I've ever seen, and, in addition, is one of the cleverest and brainiest men in the ring. I think he'll beat Dempsey and surprise everybody. Jack's a heavy hitter, there's no getting away from that. When he hits, they fall. But he has no speed or cleverness and doesn't compare with Carpentier in these departments.[555]

Carpentier liked to wear his lucky white silk bathrobe decorated with Gila monsters.

Dempsey did not understand why Carpentier trained in seclusion. "It's a good thing to get used to a crowd." They would fight in front of a crowd, so Jack liked to get accustomed to the cheers, hollers, boos, and outside-the-ring fights between spectators.

Those who saw Carpentier work said Jack would not find an easy target. Georges was quite fast. Some said Carpentier would outpoint Dempsey. Others said Dempsey was too powerful for him. According to the *Daily News*, at 78 inches, Dempsey had a 9-inch reach advantage, or 4.5 inches with each arm. Others said Jack only had a 1-inch reach advantage.[556]

Dempsey had received a gift of an English bull terrier. He loved dogs.

Jack often was followed around by a curious crowd. Yet, he seldom was still. He would stop and chat for a few seconds, but then swing off somewhere else, walking at a rapid gait. It was amusing to see folks try to keep up with him.

	Dempsey.	Carpentier.
Age.	26.	27.
Height.	6 feet 1 in.	5 feet 11½ in
Weight.	197 pounds.	172 pounds.
Reach.	74 inches.	73 inches.
Neck.	16½ inches.	16¾ inches.
Biceps.	16¼ inches.	14½ inches.
Forearm.	14¼ inches.	13 inches.
Wrist.	9¼ inches.	7¼ inches.
Chest (nor)	42 inches.	41 inches.
Chest (exp.)	46 inches.	43½ inches.
Waist.	33 inches.	31 inches.
Thigh.	23 inches.	23 inches.
Calf.	15¼ inches.	16¾ inches.
Ankle.	9 inches.	8½ inches.

Carpentier was twice decorated in the war, having enlisted in the aviation branch. During the war years, he gave many boxing exhibitions for French and American troops, which kept him fit.[557]

When some named Tommy Gibbons as the next best heavyweight in the ring outside of the champion, Dempsey said Tommy would get his turn if the clamor for the battle was sufficient.[558]

[554] *Brooklyn Daily Eagle*, May 25, 1921; *New York Age*, June 4, 1921.
[555] *New York Evening World*, May 26, 1921.
[556] *New York Daily News*, May 26, 1921.
[557] *Buffalo Times*, May 26, 1921. Jack planned to wrestle with Bull Montana, who had just arrived.
[558] *New York Tribune*, May 26, 1921.

Tad Dorgan said Jack Curley was the first man whom he ever heard boost Dempsey. In 1918, Curley had seen Dempsey beat the huge Carl Morris in Buffalo, a fighter whom he represented. Curley then told Tad, "You never saw a fighter like him in your life. You can't stop him and he can hit the way dynamite bucks. He took my Carl Morris and almost killed him. Morris didn't budge him and he hit Dempsey with everything he had." Curley predicted that Dempsey would knock out Fulton, whom Tad believed in greatly at that time. They wagered $15 on a potential Dempsey-Fulton contest, and Tad lost.

Yet, despite Curley's admiration for Dempsey, this time he was predicting that Carpentier would beat him and startle the world.

William Brady, who once managed Corbett and Jeffries, and picked Dempsey against Willard, also was predicting a Carpentier victory. Brady said Dempsey had been too inactive, with only two fights in the past two years, and that was not enough to keep him in top form. "He has slowed up considerably." Against Brennan, he did not show 1/3 the speed that he had against Willard. "He has never met a really good man and never faced one the equal of Carpentier. The Frenchman will beat him just as Corbett beat Sullivan. He's too fast and knows much more about fighting than the heavy hitting Dempsey. Carpentier is the greatest glove man since the days of Corbett."

With the fight still more than a month away, the advance ticket sales, at $525,000, already assured a world's record gate. The gate for Johnson-Jeffries was $270,755, exceeded by Dempsey-Willard at $452,522. Tex Rickard had promoted all three of the biggest box-office fights ever.

Jack Johnson would miss the fight. He still was in prison, and not scheduled to be released until a week after it took place.[559]

Harry Newman said many pretty women came to watch Dempsey train and paste his sparring partners.

On May 26, before a crowd of more than 1,000 paying, cheering customers, Dempsey sparred 8 rounds total, 2 each with four sparring partners, traveling at a fast pace. Dempsey pummeled Larry Williams with stiff thumps all over, giving him the worst mauling, but it was his own fault, for in the 2nd round, Larry landed a good right, which riled the champ. The short, ripping body shots had Williams badly winded. One writer said a left to the eye cut open a 2-inch gash on Williams.

Montreal's Big Jack Renault, wearing a headgear, was a good hitter and fairly clever boxer. Dempsey rapped him hard, but Renault took the blows and tried his best to fight back against a fierce body attack. Despite wearing the biggest gloves that could be found, the champ's power still was felt, and he was not good at pulling his punches. When Dempsey hit him with an especially hard right and Renault reeled back, a woman spectator let out a shrill scream, and the crowd smiled as she hid behind her escort, embarrassed. Renault almost went down under a shower of

[559] *Camden Daily Courier, Buffalo Commercial, Buffalo American*, May 26, 1921.

short punches. Dempsey rattled his teeth with a stiff left, and the crimson flowed. The crowd cheered Renault for taking a bad beating.

Against Portland welter Alex/Alec Trambitas and Kearns' lightweight Joe Benjamin, who wore a leather headgear (Jack once had broken his nose), Dempsey mostly practiced defense, dodging about.

The champ usually woke up at 7 a.m. and did roadwork (walking and/or running) with his oldest brother Bernie Dempsey, who was set to take over as chief trainer. Friend Mike Trant, a Chicago police officer, was at the camp serving as general supervisor. Dempsey later said Trant was a detective-sergeant in Chicago, and was with him at Toledo and Benton Harbor as well.[560]

Dempsey said he couldn't get the best results in his preparation when he pulled his punches so often in his training bouts. He needed to hit hard to get his correct timing. As a result, Jack Clifford and Leo Houck had left, and Larry Williams was about to leave.

Jack said he could not take it easy when his opponent started to warm up and get going. When Larry Williams began pumping them in, he forgot about his good intentions to box easily, and started after him. "I soon had him lying across the ropes with right and left hooks to the body and jaw." He allowed him to recover, but soon went after him again. Lightweight Joe Benjamin was very fast, but Jack found no difficulty in keeping right on top of him. Alex Trambitas gave him a fast, hard bout, and could take quite a punishing without a whimper. Jack Renault gave him a hard infighting battle. Dempsey did not even sit down between rounds, and "at the end I felt just as fresh as could be."

Dempsey said he had strong hands. "My hands have never given me any trouble, though I've landed punches with all I had behind them on the heads of some of the toughest birds in the world. I have no fear of breaking my hands and therefore have no need to pull my punches."

During a fight, he never worried about his condition. "All that I have to do is think of just how I'm going to carry the battle to the other man."

Kearns told reporter Sid Mercer that they did not bar anybody from sparring with Dempsey, and the more the merrier. The report that Greb was coming to spar was news to him. Kearns wished Greb *would* come.[561]

Jack Reddy, Miske's manager, said Carpentier was clever, a quick thinker, one of the fastest men he ever had seen, and had a number of puzzling blows. However, Dempsey also was fast, and had a wallop that would wear down the Frenchman, likely within 6 rounds. As soon as Dempsey hit him solidly a couple of times, Georges would be through and en route to defeat. Still, Reddy believed it would be a great fight while it lasted.[562]

On the 26th, in private, Carpentier sparred Joe Jeannette for 2 rounds, and 2 more with Italian Joe Gans of Brooklyn.

---

[560] *New York Tribune, New York Daily News*, May 27, 1921. Babe Herman did not spar because he had a fight scheduled for the next day. 200-pound tough red-headed cauliflower-eared Martin Burke had arrived, and soon would work with the champ.
[561] *Yonkers Herald*, May 27, 1921. Dempsey did not wrestle with Bull Montana that day, for the Bull had lost a wrestling contest the prior night. Jack liked wrestling with him, for it helped strengthen him for the clinches.
[562] *New York Daily News, Camden Morning Post, Buffalo Times*, May 27, 1921.

Jeannette said Carpentier was faster and in much better condition than he was for his bout with Levinsky.

Georges obtained a permit to use firearms at his training quarters, so he could have some target practice.[563]

J. P. McEvoy said his name was pronounced Car-pen-tee-ay. He mostly spoke French. He called his manager Deschamps a "smart guy." Georges said, "I am sure I will knock Dempsey's block off."

Jack Renault in headgear sparring with Dempsey

Bantam champ Joe Lynch said Dempsey would win in 6 rounds, for his aggressiveness and bulldog tactics would break down the Frenchman's defense. Jack's first good wallop would be the beginning of the end.

Featherweight Andy Chaney said although Carpentier was remarkably clever, Dempsey had too much class, and his great offensive drive ultimately would prove too much.

Midget Smith picked Dempsey in 7 rounds, for he was too rugged and strong, just as fast as Carpentier, and had a knockout punch in either hand. However, it would be a tough fight for Dempsey while it lasted, for Carp knew the game and would be no punching bag.

Boxing manager Eddie Meade said Dempsey would win in 5 rounds, though if Carpentier could last longer than that, he had an even chance, for a good straight puncher was the type who could beat a hooking puncher like Dempsey. Still, Dempsey was the best puncher who ever lived, and he had great courage, so likely his terrible punching ability, which took out Fulton, Willard, Miske, Brennan, and many others, would break down even the Frenchman's wonderful defense.[564]

A prominent bookmaker told Tad that he was offering 10 to 1 that Dempsey would not win in 1 round, 8 to 1 not in 2, 6 to 1 not in 3, 4 to 1 not in 4, 2 to 1 not in 5, and even money that Dempsey would not win within 6 rounds.[565]

On the 27th, Dempsey sparred 2 rounds each with Jack Renault and Leo Houck (who had returned), the latter almost getting knocked out with a hook in the 1st round, and, sagging at the knees, Dempsey had to grab and steady him on the ropes. Dempsey then wrestled for 10 minutes with

[563] *New York Daily News, New York Tribune, New York Herald,* May 27, 1921.
[564] *Buffalo Courier,* May 27, 1921.
[565] *Buffalo Enquirer,* May 28, 1921.

Bull Montana, the screen actor and wrestler. When Jack held his head and rushed him into the ropes, bumping the Bull's head on the ring post, the wrestler cried out that Jack was too rough, and refused to continue.

Harry Newman said Dempsey had thumped his ring mates roughly, knocking them from pillar to post with his one-two. He started the day with a 5-mile walk. He played a game of cribbage with Teddy Hayes. He also played a baseball game with the scribes, the latter team winning, and a game of soccer, which Jack played in his usual rough style, several players being knocked down.

That day, wearing 8-ounce gloves, Carpentier boxed 2 fast rounds with 155-pound Italian Joe Gans and 1 round with Henri Marcot, wrestled with Gans for 5 minutes, and also did 35 minutes of gym work, and 10 miles of road work, running and walking, that took over two hours. After the workout, Carpentier weighed 171 ½ pounds.

Ray Pearson of the *Daily News* said, "Carpentier is fast, make no mistake about that. He is the fastest foot worker we've looked at since the days of Jim Corbett."[566]

On May 27, 1921 in Brooklyn, New York, 211-pound Harry Wills knocked out 213 ½-pound black Kid Arthur Johnson in the 1st round, battering him from the start and decking him three times.

William Granger said Wills convinced the crowd "that the big negro would make a mighty dangerous opponent for Champion Jack Dempsey." The *Brooklyn Standard Union* said, "The manner in which Wills went to work against his opponent and the tremendous punching ability he disclosed proved to the satisfaction of the fans that he is deserving of all the praise that has been directed his way." Wills was "one of the most popular of the colored heavyweights ever to appear in the ring," and the fans gave him a great hand.

Wills said, "Every time I hear or read of Jack Dempsey being called the heavyweight champion of the world it gives me a pain. Mr. Dempsey is only the white champion and I am the best of the negro heavies. My life's ambition is to fight Dempsey for the world's title."[567]

Some said that one had to pull for Dempsey against Carpentier, because he represented America, so it was a matter of patriotism.

On the 28th, Carpentier boxed 2 rounds with 200-pound Paul Journee and 1 round with Italian Joe Gans. Carpentier worked on speed, footwork, defense, crouching, shifting, firing uppercuts and overhand rights, lunging or leaping in at times, and firing from different angles.[568]

On May 28, in front of 278 women and 946 men, Dempsey took it easy on Larry Williams for 2 rounds, for

Paul Journee

[566] *New York Daily News, Buffalo Courier, Brooklyn Daily Eagle,* May 28, 1921.
[567] *Brooklyn Citizen, Brooklyn Daily Eagle, Brooklyn Standard Union, Brooklyn Daily Times,* May 28, 1921.
[568] *New York Daily News, Buffalo Courier,* May 29, 1921.
  Paul Journee's record included: 1920 D15 Bandsman Dick Rice, LKOby13 Bombardier Billy Wells, LKOby2 Frank Moran, LTKOby16 Wells, and LRTD5 Tom Cowler; 1921 TKO1 Bert Kenny, and LTKOby10 Marcel Niles.
  Italian Joe Gans' record included: 1917 LND10 (twice) Mike O'Dowd, LND10 Ted Kid Lewis, DND10 and LND10 Soldier Bartfield; and 1920 L15 and D15 Bartfield.

in the 1st round, a left jab or hook opened Larry's eye again, and thereafter Jack avoided hitting there.

Dempsey had 2 slam-bang rounds with Jack Renault, but unfortunately, a collision of heads opened up a cut on the champ. Dempsey had driven Renault into a corner in a furious mix, and after Dempsey missed a hard right swing, Renault in ducking accidentally butted him, opening up a half-inch cut over the champ's left eye. Kearns wanted to stop the sparring, but Dempsey insisted it was not serious, and they finished up.

Another reporter said the wound was over the *right* eye as a result of a clinching match in a corner. The wound was slight and cut only skin deep.

Dempsey slugged for 1 more fast round with Houck, allowing Leo to pummel away at his midsection to harden him up.

Franklin Grant said Dempsey at 198 pounds seemed bigger and stronger than he was when he went up against Brennan.

Harry Wills said Dempsey would whip Carpentier, for his strength would offset Carpentier's speed and cleverness. "The Frenchman has speed, but speed doesn't count for everything. Dempsey has the greater strength and weight and will wear down the Frenchman. ... Meanwhile I think I can whip either of the boys – if they ever decide to give me a chance. Which, I'm afraid, they won't." Harry believed that he was the only fighter in the world who could beat Dempsey.

FOR SPEED.—Carpentier yesterday continued his sparring before small and select audiences. Italian Joe Gans is a welterweight calculated to develop the champion's speed, and he is here shown ducking one of Georges's fast ones during a mixup. What if it landed?

IN A CORNER.—Work is scarce and jobs are few, but any one would hesitate about looking for a job as the French champ's partner. This picture shows Gans defending himself from a rush.

MIXING IT.—Jack Renault, one of Dempsey's punching bags, mixes it a little more roughly with the champ than the other partners. Here he is wearing a headgear, the reason he is less afraid.

WEIGHTS. — Crowds jammed Dempsey's training quarters and the champion entertained them with the weights, developing muscle to carry the gate receipts to the bank.

ON THE MIDRIFF.—Alex. Trambitas, the Portland, Ore., welterweight, got one on a vital spot. But the gloves are big and soft—and that's a lucky thing—for Alex.

Some thought it astonishing that nearly two-million dollars potentially could be generated for a no decision bout. According to the promoter's figures, the huge arena would accommodate 104,752 spectators.

Many believed Carpentier's best chance to win was by decision, but since it was a no decision bout, he could not win officially without a knockout or disqualification. Some gamblers would settle their wagers based on the majority of newspaper reports, or certain newsmen they agreed were good and honest judges, if it went the distance.

One writer said this would be the greatest sporting event in history. More people knew who Dempsey was than the U.S. President. Likewise, Carpentier was the best-known foreigner. In the wake of the war, folks were turning with relief to sports. "The Dempsey-Carpentier fight not only draws on our deepest and oldest instinct but it draws on others almost as venerable, especially the instinct of race and the sentiment of nationality." The eyes of the world were focused upon it. "No contest in the ring ever drew on so many elements of interest and partisanship."[569]

C. F. Fitzgerald said, "Carpentier is in infinitely better physical shape to-day than Dempsey." Georges seemed more serious about upholding the honor of France. However, the fight still was a month away.

The belief at the Dempsey camp was that Jack would be prepared to travel at top speed from the start and try to finish Georges early. If he could not do so, he would be sturdy enough to take punishment for a few rounds and come back late in the fight to stop him, just as he did with Brennan.

Fitzgerald said Carpentier was fast, and tore into his sparring partners. He never relaxed, but dodged and struck back earnestly. He could crouch and engage in shifty footwork. Carpentier was an accurate hitter, and the combined force of several of his blows would counterbalance Dempsey's superior one-punch power.

Dempsey took things comparatively easy, and appeared to take more blows than he administered. Still, there was "no doubt that Dempsey can hit much harder than Carpentier," and therefore Georges would have to be careful.

Despite the small cut suffered the prior day, on May 29 in Atlantic City, Dempsey sparred. After getting hit with a right to the chin in the 2nd round, Dempsey tore in and cut loose, and 180-pound Larry Williams was near being knocked out at the end of 2 rounds, dizzy and sagging at the knees. Jack had ripped in some awful left hooks to the body and a right jolt to the chin, though Williams managed to land many a good soak on the champ in return. The crowd applauded the work.

Dempsey also took on for 2 rounds each Leo Houck (who wore a headgear for the first time) and Irish Patsy Cline, a lightweight. The champ eased up on Houck, but roughly handled Cline, knocked him flat with a right to the jaw in the 1st round, and pummeled him more in the 2nd.

[569] New York Times, Buffalo Times, Brooklyn Daily Eagle, New York Daily News, Buffalo Courier, May 29, 1921.

The sparring partners were cautioned not to hit Dempsey's damaged right eye. One writer said they avoided it. Another claimed Williams landed a straight left and reopened it.

Old-timer Young Griffo watched him train, and believed Dempsey was the best heavyweight of all time; picking him to win in 3 rounds.

Featherweight champ Johnny Kilbane said Dempsey was a sure thing.

However, Willie Lewis (who in 1912 had lost a 20-round decision to Carpentier) said, "I can't see how Dempsey can withstand Georges beyond the 8th round. … Georges will cut Jack to pieces if the latter starts rushing. If Jack attempts to mix, he's gone."

Eddie Kane, Tommy Gibbons' manager, thought Dempsey would stop Carpentier in 4 rounds. "If it were not for the fact that eight-ounce gloves are to be used, with nothing but soft bandages to bind the hands, Dempsey would win sooner." Nevertheless, he would break Carpentier early on with heavy body punches. No one had pressed or tested Carpentier the way Dempsey would, certainly not in the last 7 years.

Sam Goldman, Pete Herman's manager, said although Dempsey would be forced to take punishment as a result of his aggressive methods, Jack would break him down over time, until Carpentier's speed waned and the champion stopped him with a powerful onslaught that no man could absorb, in about the 9th round.

Martin Burke said, "Jack is a better boxer than the experts think." Those who thought Carpentier had more of a chance the longer it went were wrong, because Dempsey could wear him down as well, even if he did not get him quickly.

Many said Carpentier simply was too light, Dempsey would tear into his body, and he'd be lucky to last 3 rounds.

However, Sparrow McGann said weight was an overrated factor. Speed, power, and endurance would be the deciding factors, particularly in a mere 12-round fight. Dempsey never fought someone as fast or as scientific. Carpentier had speed and power in abundance, would hit and get away, trying to make a fool of Dempsey like Corbett did with Sullivan and Jeffries. The fight might come down to who could hit the hardest and take the most punishment, because both could hit.

Dempsey and Mayor Bader officially opened a new Atlantic City amusement park, and they got the first thrill of the rides and amusements.

Harry Ertle allegedly had been selected as the referee. He had been officiating in New Jersey and New York for several years, and was thought of as a capable official.[570]

On Decoration Day, also known as Memorial Day, May 30, 1921 at Ebbets Field in Brooklyn, New York, 7,000 or 10,000 fans saw 168-pound Tommy Gibbons stop former Dempsey sparring partner 180-pound Jack Clifford in the 3rd round. In the 2nd round, Gibbons floored him thrice, and in the 3rd round, after a straight right to the chin decked him yet again, the referee stopped it.

---

[570] *New York Tribune, Buffalo Courier, New York Evening World, New York Daily News*, May 30, 1921.

Just after Tommy Gibbons knocked out Jack Clifford in the third round.

Carpentier was in attendance, and when the announcer introduced him to the audience, he smiled as he received a big round of applause. Harry Wills also was introduced and given a big hand, as was Frank Moran.

Gibbons impressed the *Brooklyn Citizen's* William Granger as "the only good-looking heavyweight in sight." "Gibbons showed he could hit, and what was more to the purpose gave evidence that his marksmanship was away better than that usually found in heavyweights." Another said Gibbons was "America's leading contender for the heavyweight championship of the world." Even Carpentier said, "Tommy is the best fighter I have seen in America. He moves so beautifully and he can punch so very well." Another quoted Georges as saying Gibbons was "exquisite."

That same day, in New York, in honor of Decoration Day, Carpentier visited and placed a floral wreath upon the grave of former U.S. President Theodore Roosevelt, which Americans found touching and ingratiating.

ON THE NOSE!—Carpentier yesterday was treating his nose with tenderness after stopping one of Journee's ham-like fists. This picture shows the clout as it landed. (NEWS photo)

RIGHT AT IT!—Aleck Trambitas, a Dempsey partner, was yesterday receiving congratulations for the fearlessness he has shown with the champion. This picture shows him earning his fee. (By Atlantic)

LIKE DEMPSEY?—Fight fans were yesterday discussing points of similarity in Journee's fighting tactics with those of the American champion. Here the French heavyweight is rushing Georges. (NEWS photo)

ABDOMINAL EXERCISE.—Jack Dempsey's food capacity is commented on by all visitors entertained at his training table. But the perfect physique of the champion never indicates it. Yesterday he was demonstrating how to keep his stomach muscles in trim. (By Underwood)

AN ARMY of carpenters is working industriously in Jersey City rushing to completion the big arena that will witness the biggest international boxing contest in history on July 2. Yesterday crowds flocked to inspect the progress of the work and to try out the board benches that fight fans are paying such fabulous prices for. Promoter Tex Rickard is still buried under applications for tickets. (NEWS photo)

On May 30 in Atlantic City, Dempsey covered 6 miles that morning with his three dogs. A passing motorist struck one of the dogs, though it was not seriously injured.

That day, a large crowd of about 1,500, including several hundred women, jammed the champ's open-air arena, paying from 50 cents up to two dollars apiece to watch Dempsey train and spar 6 rounds with three sparring partners, 2 rounds each.

180-pound Larry Williams received another battering. Renault and Houck followed, and they mostly retreated. In their 1st round, Jack sent Houck to his haunches with a straight left.

The champ wore a strip of white court plaster over his right eye to protect it. The wound was healing nicely.

Freddy Welsh, former lightweight champ, said 195-pound Dempsey ought to win, but only after the hardest bout of his career, for the Frenchman was a skillful and tough bird with a great clout. Dempsey was not as slow as some thought. Regardless, he was too strong.[571]

A HELPING HAND.—Guests at Dempsey's camp were yesterday praising the special Memorial Day dinner of Mrs. Hutchinson, Jack's cook. The champion is showing his appreciation by hanging out the wash.

RECOVERED.—Sophie Ginsberg, Jack Dempsey's Belgian police dog pet, was fully recovered yesterday from her recent injury. This shows Jack as a veterinarian dressing the cut.

The American champion entertained a festive crowd at the Airport yesterday. Pinochle is his favorite diversion while resting, and he plays a good game. John O'Reilly is his partner.

EXERCISE.—This feather mattress brought from the attic of the training farm to serve as a rowing machine yesterday.

—A batch of new records for Carpentier's phonograph arrived yesterday. Georges doesn't care much for American records, but dressed in his lucky bathrobe he is trying to appear entertained.

This shows Carpentier as he appears today, spite his mild program of exercise he appears trained to the minute, and a careful study will show the absence of surplus flesh.

[571] Brooklyn Citizen, New York Tribune, New York Daily News, Brooklyn Standard Union, Camden Post-Telegram, Buffalo Evening News, May 31, 1921. Fearful that he might overtrain, Kearns did not want Dempsey getting his edge too soon before the fight, so he wanted Jack to rest that week, or at least not spar. He was weighing around 195 pounds. Kearns wanted Jack to get to 200 before the final stretch of training.

In other news, as of May 30, 1921, the segregated Greenwood section of Tulsa, Oklahoma, a district known as Black Wall Street owing to its wealthy and prosperous black community, was one of the most successful, flourishing black neighborhoods in the country. However, on that date, an incident occurred between a white 17-year-old female elevator operator named Sarah Page and black 19-year-old shoeshiner Dick Rowland. The local *Tulsa Tribune* on May 31 published an inflammatory story, saying a white female claimed that black "Diamond" Dick attacked her, scratching her hands and face and tearing her clothes. Her screams brought a clerk to her assistance and Rowland fled. Prior to the attack, he allegedly had looked up and down the hallway to see if anyone was in sight. Rowland denied trying to harm her, but admitted he put his hand on her arm.[572]

Rowland was taken into custody. Word quickly spread that a white lynch mob intended to take the law into its own hands and kill Rowland. A group of black men, including veterans of the World War, assembled outside the jail to protect Rowland from the approaching lynch mob, wanting him to have a fair trial, trying prevent a lawless lynching. Whites attempted to disarm the blacks, a shot was fired, and violence erupted.

Whites who were jealous of black success in the area, wanting to assert white supremacy, used this incident as an excuse to rampage into the Greenwood district and loot, shoot, kill, destroy, and burn down the neighborhood, including black-owned businesses, barber shops, the newspaper buildings of the black-owned *Oklahoma Sun* and *Tulsa Star* (black newspapers often were the target of white rioters), homes, churches, grocery stores, restaurants, movie theaters, a hospital, bank, post office, libraries, schools, law offices, airplanes, and buses. The white mob even used airplanes to launch gasoline and dynamite bombs from the sky. The mob, led in part by members of the Ku Klux Klan, which included policemen, killed black men, women, and children, shooting and burning them. It was a massacre. Whites wanted to wipe out "Little Africa" with the torch. The mob prevented firemen from doing their duties. It was a systematic destruction of the negro section of the town. Many blacks fought to protect their neighborhood, shooting back and killing several members of the mob, but they were overwhelmed.

By the time troops were deployed the next day, the town virtually had been obliterated. Instead of arresting whites, the troops arrested thousands of blacks and held them in custody for several days before releasing them. No whites ever were arrested or charged.

Over 600 successful black businesses were ruined. Although the official death toll claimed 26 black deaths and 13 whites (even though the *Tulsa Tribune* on June 1, 1921 claimed 9 whites and 68 blacks *already* had been slain), the American Red Cross estimated over 300 deaths (many of whom were buried in mass graves), which is closer to the truth, 8,624 people in need of assistance, and over 1,000 homes and businesses

---

[572] The article later was torn out of the *Tribune's* existing archived edition, prior to being microfilmed, though the June 1 state edition still exists.

destroyed. At least 35 square blocks had been torched. It was the worst incident of racial terrorism in the United States up to that point.

Not a War Zone in France: Race Riot

The June 3, 1921 *Black Dispatch*, out of Oklahoma City, summed it all up: "THIS IS A WHITE MAN'S COUNTRY." It was the job of certain elements to thrust that fact down the throats of the Tulsa black population.

It quoted the *Tulsa World*, which reported that the only possible assault Rowland made was when he grabbed Page's arm, so said the chief of detectives. Her story was, "When he grabbed my arm, I screamed and he fled," which was substantially the same as told by Rowland himself [likely as a result of losing balance either as a result of tripping when entering the elevator that had not been stopped flush, or when the elevator stopped abruptly]. The riot in part had been the result of yellow journalism. The police were not certain whether the case even warranted a charge, and only took Rowland into custody for his own protection after the false story was published.

The case once again highlights why due process and a fair trial are such important rights; because the press often gets it wrong, sometimes intentionally so, with ulterior motives.

The *Black Dispatch* lamented that true justice would exist if there were arrests of the white newspaper editor who allowed a false story to be published, the white hoodlums who tried to lynch Rowland, the white rioters, the officers who knew about the preparations to burn up the negro section but did nothing, the policemen who turned machine guns on blacks but not on the white mob, and the police who did nothing to stop it all.

Instead, the police had "laid down," failed to do their duty, and $2.5 million in negro property had been destroyed. "Nothing remains." The Stratford Hotel, Red Wing Hotel, Dreamland Theatre, Dixie Theatre, *Tulsa Star*, *Oklahoma Sun*, A.M.E. Church, the new $485,000 Second Baptist Church, Welcome Grocery Store, Elliott and Hookers Clothing, and others, everything on North Greenwood, together with the entire residential section, a square mile, was in ruins. In an organized effort, fires were started simultaneously in at least 50 places, beginning at Boston and Archer. The whole of the Negro district, including Boston, Exeter, Easton, Greenwood, Hartford, and the North Addition, was laid waste.

The *Black Dispatch* lamented that as a result of propaganda, every white woman who saw a negro thought he wanted to rape her. Word was, even from whites in the know, that Rowland had tripped upon entering the elevator and stepped on Page's foot. She struck him as a result, and after he apologized and she tried to strike him again, he grabbed her arm. She was not bruised, nor was her clothing disarranged in any way.[573]

The June 18, 1921 *Chicago Broad Ax* reported that a member of the NAACP, Walter White, investigated and said between 150 and 200 negroes were killed, including men, women, and children, many burned alive, and at least 50 white persons. 44 square blocks of business and residential property valued at $1.5 million were destroyed. "Mr. White declared that the riot was largely due to a misuse of the word 'attack' and 'assault,' the impression being given that a colored man had attempted rape upon a white girl, whereas he had merely stumbled in an elevator and in attempting to recover his balance stepped upon her foot."

Many whites blamed the riot on negro "radicalism," but when asked what that was, "I found invariably that it consisted of demands by Negroes that the federal Constitution be enforced and that lynching, peonage, disfranchisement and Jim Crowism be abolished." In the opinion of Tulsa citizens, investigation would "amount to nothing." The riot convinced him that "the only hope of averting repetitions of it lies in federal interference."

Eventually, on September 28, 1921, the charges against Rowland were dismissed and he was released from prison. The report that had spread through the city that Page had accused him of assault was untrue. The *Black Dispatch* wrote, "It was brought out in the investigation that he was entirely innocent, the girl never having complained that such were the facts as published in a local WHITE PAPER. Sarah Page has vanished and has never been apprehended since the day she made a statement refuting the charges alleged against Rowland." She never actually entered a charge against him. Another paper wrote, "It was later learned that this report was false, and that the girl had made no such accusation. Shortly following the riot Sarah Page made a statement that Rowland was entirely

[573] *Black Dispatch*, June 10, 17, 1921.

innocent of any wrongdoing. She disappeared immediately, and has not been seen since." Dick Rowland, an innocent man, had been held in jail for 4 months without any evidence of criminal wrongdoing.[574]

Charred Debris Is All That Remains of Tulsa's Negro Quarter.

Joe Choynski told Tad Dorgan that Georges Carpentier had a good chance to beat Jack Dempsey. It appeared to be an even fight, for either one could win with one punch, depending on who landed it first. Both were knockout swingers, but Carpentier was faster and could throw two blows to Dempsey's one. Neither one was overly scientific or fought a measured, studied battle. The first one to land solidly likely would win.

Jim Corbett said Carpentier had met and defeated bigger men, so size alone was no handicap to him. He had floored Wells, Smith, Beckett, and Jeannette. Joe Jeannette was much bigger, vastly more experienced against the best in the game - having fought Johnson, McVey, and Langford multiple times, very clever, had a cool head, and a solid punch. Yet, even a very young, much less experienced, and smaller Carpentier held his own with Jeannette in 1914 and managed to floor him, losing a close 15-round decision. Corbett said anyone good enough to stand off Joe Jeannette for 15 rounds as far back as 1914 had to have something, for at that time Joe was a fine boxer and a strong hitter. Georges had learned from that contest and improved since then, his last loss.[575]

Tex Rickard strongly denied that the tickets were in the hands of seat speculators.[576]

Len Wooster of the *Brooklyn Daily Times* said a series of matches between top men could develop the champ's next most deserving

[574] *Black Dispatch*, September 29, 1921; *Topeka Plaindealer*, October 7, 1921; *Coshocton Tribune*, October 9, 1921; *Chicago Whip*, October 15, 1921; *Oklahoma City Times*, June 1, 1921; *Pittsburgh Press*, June 12, 1921; *Topeka Plaindealer*, June 17, 1921.
[575] *Buffalo Enquirer*, June 1, 9, 1921. *New York Tribune*, June 9, 1921.
[576] *New York Times*, *Daily News*, June 1, 1921. Sam McVey was available to spar with Carpentier, as well as Italian Joe Gans, Marcot, Journee, and Jeannette.

challenger. Many wanted to see a rematch with Willard, for "there is a lingering suspicion in the minds of thousands that Willard can beat Dempsey properly conditioned. As a drawing card Dempsey and Willard are best." Other top men included Wills, Norfolk, Gibbons, and Moran. Wooster wanted the winners between the blacks to fight the winners between the whites. The question was whether Dempsey would agree to fight the winner if it was a black man. "Despite the report that Dempsey has wiped out the color line, there is a deep-rooted suspicion that Dempsey never will fight a black man, least of all Wills."

Tex Rickard mentioned Gibbons as a potential next challenger for the winner of the upcoming championship.

Jack Kearns resented the talk that Dempsey was slow in comparison with Carpentier. He said Jack was plenty fast. "The champ is the fastest big man in the ring and he'll show Carpentier a few things about stepping around when he gets in the ring. Maybe Carpentier can run but he can't run a long ways in that ring. We'll be right on top of him because we are pretty good runners ourselves."

Tad said many believed size would not matter in the upcoming battle. Corbett and Fitzsimmons had beaten bigger men. Jem Mace did it in the bareknuckle days. Choynski and Sharkey gave Jeffries some of his toughest fights. Joe Walcott and Sam Langford beat bigger men. Carpentier had the speed, skill, and power to do the same.

Heywood Broun said Dempsey did not look like a fighter. He had splendid big white teeth, all present and in line. He could pass for a university fullback.

When it was noted that fighters never admitted when they were all through, Dempsey replied that fighters didn't like to admit it because no one wants to see a fighter when he's through. When asked if he ever would admit it when he was, he replied, "It'll all depend upon how I'm fixed."

C. F. Fitzgerald said Carpentier had a deadly leaping knockout blow. He even could lead with his right.

Philadelphia Jack O'Brien said Georges was training for speed.[577]

Dempsey enjoyed listening to music on the phonograph, which kept him in good humor. He read, but usually not more than half an hour. When he went to get a haircut at a barber shop, everyone who could get in crowded into the shop, while the street outside was crowded with people. "I never had so many questions shot at me in all my life, and the worst of the lot was the barber himself. The next time I get a haircut I'm going to bring a barber out to the camp."

Kearns was in New York settling up a million details about the fight. The champ said, "It may seem strange but it's a fact that Kearns and I are rarely ever together except when I am working out or talking business. I think that is one of the reasons we get along so well together. He has his friends and I have mine and everything is always congenial between us."

---

[577] *Brooklyn Daily Times, Olean Times Herald, New York Tribune,* June 1, 1921.

Jack heard that Harry Ertle of Jersey City would be the referee, and that suited him, for Ertle knew the game well.

> I often wonder if the fight fans realize how important a referee is in making a battle good, bad or indifferent. A good one can do more to make it a real treat than most people imagine. On the other hand I have seen incompetent referees ball everything up when both the fighters were doing their best, and if left alone would have put up a real fracas.[578]

Dempsey had an affection for kids. He enjoyed reading letters from kids from all over the nation wishing him good luck, which often included good-luck pennies.[579]

Dempsey was called a playful grownup boy. He amused himself by engaging in target practice with a pistol.[580]

Where Dempsey Is Training For Big Bout

BARBED WIRE ENTANGLEMENTS SURROUND CARPENTIER'S QUARTERS

On June 1 at Manhasset, Carpentier sparred Joe Jeannette and Panamanian middleweight Jack Goldberg, 2 rounds apiece.

C. F. Fitzgerald said Carpentier had a great right from the outside, but also was clever at close range and able to slam in short left jolts to the body or jaw with piston-rod precision. He kept a very fast pace. He often apologized to Jeannette for solid rights. 220-pound Jeannette absorbed some choice blows as he crowded in. Carpentier fought him from a crouching position, getting under Joe's guard and hitting his stomach with both hands. He also came out of clinches and hit the side of Joe's head with his quick left. One left in the 2nd round shook Joe quite a bit. Georges immediately apologized. Joe smiled and replied, "All right; it's all right. Come on. I'm here for 'em. They're good for you." Georges repeatedly shot lefts to the head so fast it was difficult to keep count, and he followed with a sortie of body punches. He eluded Jeannette's long swings with gracefulness and countered accurately.

Georges intentionally allowed Goldberg to hit his body, as if to get used to the punches. In the 2nd round, as Goldberg hit Carp's body with several hooks, Carpentier shot a terrific right to the jaw that knocked

---

578 *Buffalo Times*, June 1, 1921. Such still holds true today.
579 *Buffalo Times*, June 1, 1921.
580 *New York Daily News*, June 2, 1921.

Goldberg off balance, and he shivered and staggered as if about to fall, but Georges kindly held him up.

Goldberg commented, "He's got a sweet right hand. But I don't think much of his left. I ain't afraid of that. But he's got a right that will fool any of them. It comes from nowhere." "You never know when it is coming and if you do there is no escape. And as for speed, Carpentier has the Twentieth Century Limited looking like a farm tractor."

Sam McVey agreed, and predicted that Dempsey would experience unconsciousness on July 2. "That French boy can hit. It's just a question who gets there first. He's got a bad right hand. If Misto Dempsey thinks he's goin' to have a cinch he better get that notion out of his head right away."

Veteran manager Tom O'Rourke said, "This Carpentier is good. ... He is very fast, dead game, and can hit. Dempsey must be good on the defensive, because if he gives the Frenchman an opening he is going to feel it."

Retired lightweight champ Jack McAuliffe said Carp's best punch was his right. His left was good too, but he staked everything on his snappy right, which he fired with lightning speed. He was fast on his feet and a great boxer, but not the most graceful.

Jack Veiock said Carpentier was in shape, calm and confident. Reports of his speed and hitting power were not exaggerated. He was fast, shifty, and agile, with one of the best rights ever. His footwork was one of his greatest assets. He could hit from any position. Jeannette crowded him at all times, and Georges let go some vicious blows. He let up against Goldberg, for he would have knocked him out had he not.

When asked if he would knock out Carpentier, Dempsey replied, "I have a hunch that I will, and if I'm feeling good that day the fight will be over inside of four rounds." Some wondered whether he was overconfident.

Jack denied reports that he was studying French so he could confuse Carpentier. "That's the bunk. ... A good stiff punch means the same in all languages."[581]

Speaking of the Gunboat Smith fight, Carp said he had decked Smith in the 4th round, but the bell saved him. In the 6th round, Carp said he missed a right and went down. Smith then hit him in the back of the head while he was down. He was not knocked down.[582]

McAuliffe said Carpentier needed more sparring partners, for the ones he had were too slow. Also, Jeannette had been pulling his punches. Georges needed to take a few, too. "He's going to face a murderous body hitter and he ought to get ready for it."[583]

Jim Corbett said Dempsey might not be a scientific wizard, but the fact that he bore no marks indicated that he was able to take care of himself. He was a rushing, punishing type whose offense in many ways

[581] *Elmira Star-Gazette, New York Tribune, Brooklyn Standard Union, Hackensack Evening Record,* June 2, 1921.
[582] *Buffalo Enquirer,* June 2, 1921.
[583] *Brooklyn Standard Union,* June 3, 1921.

was his best defense. He was two-fisted, as strong as a bull, and enjoyed fighting. He was at his best when he rushed and got right into action with his nervous tension. He could not make his best fight in any other way, as the Brennan fight proved.[584]

Will Jack break through this guard?   What does this confident expression mean?

Jack Kearns.

Francois Descamps.

[584] *Buffalo Enquirer*, June 3, 1921.

THE VICTIM IS LARRY WILLIAMS

Paul Journee (left) spars Carpentier

On June 2, over Kearns' objections, Dempsey participated in a baseball game with sparring partners, newsmen, and theatrical stars. Kearns feared an injury would occur.

That evening, Dempsey attended a film called *The Wonder Man*, featuring Carpentier as the hero. Wherever Jack went, neatly dressed, looking like a business man on vacation, he caused a blockade, but paid no attention to the crowds.[585]

Jack McAuliffe said Carpentier was clever, on his toes all the time, could hit from every angle, was very coordinated, and could take advantage of openings with tremendous speed. "I have no doubt that he will land on Dempsey, but I'm not so sure that he will be able to stop the 'big train.'" Carpentier was hittable with the left, though he might be allowing those blows to land in order to set up counters.[586]

On June 3, after mixing in lively fashion, 220-pound Paul Journee clinched Carpentier to avoid punishment, gave him a hard shove, Georges stumbled, and both fell while clinched, with Carpentier on the bottom. Carp ordered destroyed all photo plates that showed him on the canvas. The newsmen agreed not to use any such photos, for they would be misleading. Journee's face and body wore abundant marks of the punishment he had been receiving, including bruises, a lump over his left eye, and a cut over the eye.[587]

Dempsey said his nose and breathing still bothered him. The operation he had received last year in Philadelphia was unsuccessful. He recently had seen a specialist and planned to have another nose operation after the fight. He still could fight with it, but it caused him discomfort. "Sometimes I wish I had the doctor who performed the operation in the ring with me for a few minutes, with or without gloves."

Teddy Hayes, his trainer, had brought a pair of rubber linings to put inside Jack's gloves to cushion the blows and help prevent Dempsey's sparring partners from being too hurt by his punches.

That day, Jack shot his gun at targets (with Trant), rode a horse a few miles along the shore, and played the phonograph.

---

[585] *Buffalo Courier, New York Herald, Paterson News*, June 3, 1921. Billy Roche picked Carpentier to win.
[586] *Brooklyn Daily Times*, June 4, 1921.
[587] *New York Tribune*, June 4, 1921.

Jack said that in his early days, he had a few fights in which he did not use any hand bandages at all. He was lucky not to have broken his hands.

> Nowadays I use a lighter bandage than most boxers, just enough of smooth cotton wrapped around the knuckles to fit comfortably and a foot or two of adhesive tape to keep it in place is all I need. I usually bandage my own hands while training but for a big fight my manager, Jack Kearns, attends to the job.[588]

Explaining why their camp generally was not open to the public, Descamps said Carpentier was in the U.S. to fight and beat Dempsey, not to give exhibitions.

One report claimed that Dempsey was training in secret, unobserved in the hangar at the back of his camp, and then sparring for the public for money.[589]

217-pound Sam McVey said Carpentier would make a scientific fight of it at long-range, for it would be foolish to mix it up with the heavier Dempsey in close. McVey was helping to train Carpentier.

Criticizing Harry Wills, McVey said, "He wants to hang on with one hand and hit with the other. That is the only way he will fight."[590]

Jack Kearns said he believed that Wills merely was seeking a bit of cheap publicity by offering to attempt to knock out Dempsey for free in sparring. Kearns had offered him $5,000 if he could knock out the champ in the sparring ring. Kearns noted that Wills had been invited to spar with Dempsey for the Willard camp, but declined the invitation.[591]

On June 3, 1921 in Syracuse, New York, Harry Wills knocked out colored heavyweight Battling Jim McCreary in the 7th round with a right to the heart, having decked him previously in the 1st round as well.[592]

On June 4, after four days of rest from sparring, Dempsey sparred 6 rounds, 2 each with Martin Burke (17-7-2) of New Orleans, Jack Renault, and Larry Williams, and (possibly) a round of defense with Alec Trambitas.

The 6'3" Burke was faster than Williams or Renault, and a clever boxer. Burke was tall, lanky, rangy, a sharp hitter, and aggressive. He was quick on his feet, dancing in and out, landing some stinging blows. However, it was a good thing that Burke was wearing a head guard, for when Dempsey landed his blows, "it sounded like the thud made by a strong man beating rugs."

Renault, also wearing a head guard, was strong, rugged, a heavy puncher, and could stand up under punishment. He slammed heavy swings at the champ and did not back away in the mixing for his 2 rounds.

Williams was next. Dempsey employed his famous shift against Renault and Williams, feinting them into left-hand leads and then landing solid left hooks to the body and head. Dempsey also displayed clever

[588] *Buffalo Times*, June 4, 1921.
[589] *New York Evening World*, June 4, 1921.
[590] *New York Age*, June 4, 1921.
[591] *New York Times*, June 4, 1921.
[592] *Boston Globe, Pittsburgh Daily Post*, June 4, 1921.

straight right-hand hitting, countering left jabs with his whipping right. One left hook flush on Williams' chin necessitated the champion's holding him up for a few seconds so that Williams could clear the cobwebs out of his dizzy brain.

After watching him work, Philadelphia Jack O'Brien said, "He looks every inch of a champion – a super fighting man."

Dempsey was confident, more confident than before he became champion. "Of course I have more confidence now. A champion must have confidence or he'll get licked." However, Dempsey also said, "I am not going off half cocked with the notion that Carpentier will be easy. I am going to tune myself up for a 12-round fight. Carpentier is a smart, tricky fighter, from all I can gather, and I will get myself into the best possible condition."[593]

DEMPSEY AS HE LOOKED PREVIOUS TO DEFEATING WILLARD.
PHOTO BY INTERNATIONAL.

PHOTO BY UNDERWOOD & UNDERWOOD

DEMPSEY'S APPEARANCE WHEN HE BEGAN TRAINING FOR CARPENTIER FIGHT

Harry Newman said Carpentier had one of the best right hands he ever saw, which he could whip in from any angle, without telegraphing it, coming from nowhere, fired as fast as if from a gun; it landed true and could drop an ox. Folks simply could not see it coming. He had great legs, and wonderful conditioning. However, Newman questioned Carp's defense, feeling that he was hit too often and too solidly. Journee

Carpentier spars Marcot

[593] *New York Tribune, Herald, Daily News*, June 5, 1921. Houck had left again, saying he could not stand the punching.

Martin Burke's record included: 1919 W15 Terry Keller, TKO10 Dick O'Brien, and LTKOby10 George Chip; 1920 W15 Al Reich, W15 Willie Meehan, and LND12 Bartley Madden; and 1921 LTKOby5 Bob Martin, W15 Bob Roper, and L15 Madden.

hit Carpentier a fair amount, and if his defense was not better, it might prove disastrous with Dempsey. "It hardly seems fair to ask him to concede twenty pounds to such a fighter as Dempsey, but that right hand kick might furnish the surprise of the century."[594]

On June 4, 1921 at Long Island City, New York, one night after stopping McCreary, 210-pound Harry Wills knocked out 208 ¼-pound black Ray Bennett in the 1st round, primarily with body blows.[595]

Robert Edgren noted that Carpentier (82-11-5), had far more experience than Dempsey. Although Georges looked like a movie hero, he was born to fight. He had been into acrobatics, savate (kickboxing), fencing, football, and boxing as early as 10 years of age. At age 12, he won the French savate championship of Northern France in the featherweight class, beating 20 full grown men. A year later, he won the national championship, beating 16 men. He was an all-

Carpentier's wife and daughter

around athlete. In the French army games, he was a champion at sprinting and high jumping. He had catlike footwork. He even studied jiu-jitsu in the army. It all came naturally to him. He was fighting grown men as a pro as early as age 13. Despite some losses, he kept growing and learning, improving his strength over time. He twice had been decorated for heroic exploits in the war. He had no scars except where a German machine gun bullet grazed his instep. He had no fear, and would meet Dempsey's attack with his own blows. He was boxing the greatest heavyweight in many years, and although it was only an outside chance, he had a chance to win, for both men could punch.

James J. Jeffries knew how good Dempsey was, but no man ever got to the top as Carpentier had without having the goods, so he had a chance, and Dempsey knew it. Hence, he was preparing for a hard fight.

Dempsey was a 2 to 1 favorite in New York. Carpentier was the 5 to 7 and 4 to 5 favorite in France.[596]

Heywood Broun said Carpentier's right-hand power was sufficient to bring down Dempsey, yet the champion was the heavy favorite. Dempsey rushed against Willard, but was overly cautious and tried to box with Brennan, which was not his strong suit. In that fight, he only tore in when stung hard. Dempsey was the more durable of the two. Carpentier had good footwork and hit with great precision and speed, but his blocking was ordinary. Some thought Carpentier might try to stay away, box, and win an unofficial decision. "The title, of course, would not change hands in such a battle, but a newspaper decision in favor of Carpentier would be almost as good as a victory." Others thought Carpentier would try to set up and gamble on a clean and clear knockout victory.

[594] *New York Daily News*, June 4, 5, 1921.
[595] *Brooklyn Standard Union, New York Herald*, June 5, 1921.
[596] *Buffalo Times*, June 5, 1921.

C. F. Fitzgerald said Carpentier failed to show class on the defensive, and his public exhibitions indicated that he would take the fight to Dempsey with a rush.

One observer said Carpentier proved he could take a hard punch, for he took some heavy blows from 220-pound Journee, a man bigger than Dempsey.

Some said Carpentier varied his defense, depending on what his opponent showed; sometimes allowing them to land so he could counter. Regardless, his flashes of speed and power in sparring Paul Journee and Henri Marcot was a "beautiful thing to look upon."[597]

On June 5, 1,000 people came to the inlet of the Curtiss Aeroplane Company's Airport to see Dempsey spar 6 rounds with Martin Burke, Jack Renault, and Larry Williams. Dempsey wore a plaster patch over his left eye while boxing. An old cut, the one the Jamaica Kid inflicted at Toledo, was reopened 8 days ago by Renault, and had been slow to heal.

Dempsey spars Martin Burke with left eye bandaged.

After Burke went 2 rounds, he said Dempsey had improved since he saw him last at Toledo and sparred with him in 1919 exhibitions prior to that fight. "He is in great shape right now and punches hard and accurately." He had improved as a boxer, and paced himself better.

In the 2nd round with Renault, after being clouted with three merry blows, in retaliation, Dempsey ripped into Renault and all but knocked him out. A wicked left hook flush on the chin stiffened Renault's legs, his arms flew up over his head as if he had touched a live wire, he swayed into the ropes, knocked stiff, and slid into the arms of trainer Teddy Hayes, who was acting as referee. After that, Dempsey only hit the body, while Renault clinched.

Like Renault, Williams paid for it ten-fold whenever he landed well. Further, "Trying to clinch with Dempsey invites a salvo of jolts and body blows that annoy like a plague."

However, Dempsey's eye was reopened in the 1st round with Williams. The champ missed a right, and Williams, trying awkwardly to evade, butted Dempsey over the eye. A thin stream of blood gushed from the wound. Another said Williams opened it with a right swing. Some first-aid

---

[597] *New York Tribune*, June 5, 1921.

was applied, and the champ boxed the 6th round with a bloody smear across his forehead and face. Dempsey nearly dropped Williams twice during the last round.

Another claimed that it was Renault who first struck the eye, causing some blood to ooze from it, loosening the plaster, but Williams put on the finishing touches with a punch.

Kearns said Dempsey likely would not spar again for four or five days, so as to give the wound a chance to heal. A stitch was taken to close it.[598]

On June 6, in the 1st round of sparring with Joe Jeanette, Carpentier's right hand scored a knockdown. The blow landed as Joe was walking in, and he was sent down backwards, landing with a thud at full length. Jeannette rose slowly but continued, mixing things as briskly as he had done before the knockdown. After that round, Journee was up, and he was ferocious, rushing Carpentier about the ring. Georges showed pretty footwork and speed, only toying with him. Jeannette then sparred one more round.

Charles Mathison said, "It was noticeable that Carpentier had none the better of Jeannete in the exchanges at close quarters, but when sparring at long range the Frenchman outboxed his opponents and got in some telling jolts," including the clean knockdown of Jeannette. Joe had fired a lead left, but Carp countered and beat him to the punch with astonishing speed. Joe's left did not land, but the blow to his jaw toppled Jeannette onto his back.

Descamps informed the photographers that they must not take or use pictures of the knockdown. Carpentier was a bit more careful thereafter. Georges was one to apologize, saying "Pardon," after landing with unwanted force. Journee tried hard to land heavy blows, but missed. Toward the end of the round, Carp punished him. In his second round with Georges, Jeannette confined himself to the inside, in close, giving as good as he received. They both clinched a great deal.

Afterwards, Jeannette said, "Carpentier should win because he has a terrible right that will put any man down. He is fast enough and gets it over so snappy that I'm sure he will be able to get to Dempsey with it. When he does the champion is going down. Carpentier looks open, but he's hard to hit."

Jack McAuliffe said Carpentier's right was powerful enough to win the title. "He has about as much force in his right as any heavyweight I have ever seen. He put it over on Joe Jeannette yesterday, and the big colored fellow went down. Of course, we know that Jeannette is through and all that, but it takes some strength to put down a 220-pound man with a short blow."

[598] *Buffalo Courier, New York Tribune, New York Herald, New York Daily News*, June 6, 1921.

Sam Hall said, "The Frenchman was much more impressive than on the other occasions we have seen him box. He can fight and hit all right, but it will take a terrible man to lace Jack Dempsey."

Harry Greb, who saw Carpentier train, said, "Dempsey is my choice for every cent I've got."

Billy Gibson, Benny Leonard's manager, said Carpentier was dangerous, particularly if he landed his right before getting stung himself by Dempsey. He was no cinch.

> While I like Dempsey's chances better, I realize that Georges is a great fighter and as dangerous as any man Dempsey can meet, because he can sock. He has hit some tough fellows and everybody he has hit has been hurt. There is no question but that he can punch hard enough to do some real damage to Dempsey. He's a fast starter, too, and may beat Dempsey to the punch. If he does, the short-enders may collect.

Although Gibson figured Dempsey would win, he was no huge favorite the way the odds had him, for the Frenchman was tricky, wily, game, without fear, and would do his best to win. "I want to predict right now that it will be a wonderful fight while it lasts and I look for a short fight."[599]

Descamps said Carpentier would train in front of the newsmen only two days a week; the rest of the time in private.[600]

Sid Mercer said 160-pound Teddy Hayes held the 60-pound stuffed felt bag while Dempsey hit it, and the blows often drove Hayes and the bag back four or five feet.

Johnny Kilbane said Dempsey was in splendid shape, hitting harder than ever. He had sped up his punch and footwork greatly. He was the same boyish, plain, rough-and-ready fighter he always had been. "He doesn't like to bother much about the technical side of fighting. What he wants to do is 'just fight.' ... The effect of the coat of scientific veneer that has been applied to the champ by his manager, Jack Kearns, is noticeable, however." Dempsey was boxing far more cleverly than in the past. Still, he preferred to fight and punch than box. His punches were wicked, and he shifted and slid around with ease and speed. The punches which earned him the name of "man-killer" were much in evidence. He could punch without drawing back his arm, with an amazing amount of steam in short blows. In sparring, he rarely missed an opening.

Robert Edgren said Dempsey looked better than he did before the Brennan fight. In sparring, whenever he was about to topple over his foes, he would allow them to clinch and recover.

Brother Bernard Dempsey said, "The boy's there. When Jack begins that shifting an' punching from all sides he's feelin' fit."

---

[599] *Buffalo Courier*, June 7, 1921.
[600] *New York Tribune, Daily News, Buffalo Courier, New York Herald*, June 7, 1921.

The champ's Atlantic City training quarters were ideal. He had a well-furnished house. His staff lived next door.

Jack did not like meeting the crowds of visitors, slipping away whenever he could do so politely. "They ask me the same old questions over and over, and some ask the most foolish things. I get tired of answering them."

Dempsey had not seen any of the old-timers box. He said the first real heavyweight fight he remembered seeing was in 1916 in New York, between Barney Williams and George Ashe. "No, I never had any of them to copy from. When I started fighting I just went in to knock the other fellow over or get knocked over myself."

CHAMPION JACK DEMPSEY ILLUSTRATING BY POSTED PHO-TOGRAPHS TO JOHNNY KILRANE THE FIRST, SECOND AND THIRD MOVEMENTS OF DEMPSEY'S "SWITCH SWING" WITH WHICH HE EXPECTS TO KAYO CARPENTIER AND WHICH KILRANE DESCRIBES TODAY.

The champ rated his career foes. He said the hardest fight of his life was against Johnny Sudenberg. Jack was better, but took a pounding and actually looked worse than Johnny afterwards. "Meehan was the hardest fellow to hit I ever fought. He had a way of sliding in and out." Bob McAllister was the cleverest. "I beat him the night we met but it was like shooting a ghost." Willard hit him the hardest, with a right to the chin, and he had to grab on. Gunboat Smith also hit him with a "beut" in San Francisco. He was dizzy thereafter, but won.

Jack said he did not talk to his foes in the ring.

He had met Carpentier and said, "George, I'm glad to see you." Carp replied, "I thank you. I come to fight this time; no movie pitch." Jack laughed and said, "I'm glad to hear that, George: I need the money."[601]

New York Governor Nathan Miller named William Muldoon, former champion wrestler, who once had trained John L. Sullivan for the Kilrain fight (and was a known racial separatist), as the chairman of the New York State Athletic Commission. His term would last until January 1, 1924.[602]

Grantland Rice said France was convinced that Carpentier would win. He was their "man of destiny." The fight meant a lot to the French, much more than the Americans. "If Carpentier wins, France will go into a more violent convulsion of joy than she did at the close of a victorious war. If Carpentier is beaten, knocked out, France will go into unbelievable

[601] New York Tribune, Daily News, Buffalo Courier, New York Evening World, Yonkers Herald, Brooklyn Citizen, June 7, 1921.
[602] Brooklyn Standard Union, New York Tribune, June 7, 1921.

mourning. … And if Dempsey loses the national pulse of Uncle Sam won't even quiver."

On June 7, the 200 spectators who paid $1 each were astonished by Dempsey's power, gasping as he ripped terrific hooks into the bags, just as he did on the 6th.

Odds on the fight fluctuated, with Dempsey a 9 to 5 favorite, then 2 to 1 and 2 ½ to 1.[603]

Mrs. Cecelia Dempsey, the champ's 61-year-old mother, never had seen a fight, and had no desire to see her son in action, but she read about fights for years, and actually knew more about boxing history than any member of the family. 42-year-old Bernard Dempsey, the champ's brother, who was with him, revealed that fact. When Jack won the championship, she sat in a Salt Lake City newspaper office and listened to the battle's progress. Johnny Dempsey, the champ's other brother, age 28, was there as well.[604]

A Congressman in the U.S. House of Representatives called Dempsey "a big bum who dodged the draft." He proposed a resolution to prohibit the upcoming Carpentier fight until real war fighters were rewarded. One man retorted,

Dempsey's Mother Won't See Him Perform in Championship Bout.

Mrs. Cecelia Dempsey

> Read an article in your paper referring to Mr. Jack Dempsey stating that he would have the good will of the people if he had been in France with our boys and not at the ship yards. Allow me to recall the money which Mr. Dempsey made for the Red Cross. Jack Dempsey was not a slacker but a true born American and loyal to Uncle Sam.[605]

Robert Edgren was impressed with Dempsey's "supreme concentration. He has this quality to a degree unequalled by any other boxer I ever saw." He was a focused worker. He never noticed anything going on outside the ring. "If the whole camp got up and walked out, Jack probably wouldn't notice it." He shadow boxed without slowing up; turning, twisting, ducking, sidestepping, pulling away, plunging in and punching the air, all with a scowl. In sparring, he moved swiftly in an endless attack, driving in blows, blocking counters, and taking instant advantage of openings.

Jack told Edgren that when a fight began, it was not thrilling or exciting, but matter of fact to him. All he thought was,

[603] New York Tribune, Paterson Morning Call, New York Herald, June 8, 1921.
[604] Ithaca Journal, June 8, 1921.
[605] New York Daily News, Elmira Star-Gazette, June 8, 1921.

There he is – go get him. ... I may step aside to draw him on or stand and wait a moment for him to come to me, or go straight after him, the way it seems best. But the only thought I really have in my mind is to look for an opening and then drive through it. ...

When I'm hit I never know it. It doesn't make any impression on my mind. Unless it hurts, of course, and I just have a sort of a side thought that I mustn't let another punch like that come through.

I don't see anything outside of the ring, or hear anything.[606]

On June 8, Carpentier sparred 2 rounds each with Paul Journee, Dave Rosenberg - a former amateur champion of the Metro district who recently lost a 12-round decision to Mike Gibbons, and Italian Joe Gans. The skillful Carp did not allow his partners to land a solid blow.

The *New York Times* reported that Georges worked at top speed and employed his left jab more than usual. He danced in and about, ducking, sidestepping, countering cleverly, and then drawing back out of range. Carp worked on his body-attack-defense against Gans, encouraging him to attack him on the inside.

Jack McAuliffe said Carpentier put more into his work in private than he did on "newspaper days."[607]

On the 8th, Dempsey wanted to spar, but Kearns refused to allow it, wanting his eye to heal further. Dempsey argued, "I tell you they will never reach that eye. They can't hit me unless I let them do it. Think I can't keep away from these fellows? I've got to work. The fight is less than four weeks off. You make a guy feel like a loafer."

One elderly woman ran up to the champ, grasped his hand, and said, "I'm for you, Mr. Dempsey. I hope you knock him out." Jack told Kearns, "She reminds me of my mother. Please give her a complimentary ticket to the camp."

Ray Pearson said there were a lot of fellows who would rather miss a meal than fail to see Dempsey train. Regulars watched his every move. Tongues began to buzz when they saw him hitting the bags. The way he punched was far from ordinary.

Jack said he never fought a man towards whom he had more kindly personal feelings. He and Georges liked one another. Still, "I've got to knock Koppenter out; that's final." Jack wasn't sure how to pronounce his name, pronouncing it both "Koppenter" and "Koppentier." He turned to a newsman and asked, "How the deuce do you say that fellow anyway?"

When asked if he would retire after the fight, Dempsey responded, "Quit the game? Me quit the ring? Now, not on your life! I've got a lot of scrapping still left under my belt and some of the big fellows are talking too much. I'll shut them up one at a time."[608]

---

[606] *Minneapolis Journal*, June 8, 1921.
[607] *Yonkers Herald, New York Tribune, Brooklyn Daily Times, New York Times*, June 9, 1921.
[608] *New York Tribune, Buffalo Enquirer, New York Daily News*, June 9, 1921.

WHY?—Manager Descamps, without explaining, yesterday clamped down the padlock on Georges's camp. Is this bout with Journee, when the challenger fell to the floor, the answer?

SOME BULL!—Bull Montana may not make a good sparring partner for Jack, but he gives the champion some real exercise when they have their wrestling bouts. (C. & U.)

FRENCH SYMPATHY.—Dempsey supporters are enthusiastic over the reported popularity of the American champion in France. Another indication of French sympathy is in the presentation of a loving cup to the fighter by Countess de Montebng of Paris. (A. P.)

THOSE LEGS!—Here is a close-up of the famous underpinning that is expected to bring Carpentier the championship. By this exercise the Frenchman is also strengthening his stomach muscles. (News photo)

PUBLIC.—Rope skipping is a favorite exercise of Carpentier, and he does it right before visitors. But yesterday Georges trained privately. Did he do more than skip rope? (News photo)

SECRETS!—Handshakers who tried to see Dempsey yesterday did not get far, for the good nature of the champion has been too long imposed on. However, when Winifred Westover, movie star, wanted to give Jack advice, it was another matter.

327

On June 8, 1921, in St. Paul, Minnesota, at the Lexington baseball park, 180-pound Billy Miske narrowly won a very close and competitive 10-round newspaper decision over 198-pound Bill Brennan. Three local papers gave it to Miske, one to Brennan, while one called it a draw.

The *Minneapolis Morning Tribune's* Earl Arnold said, "Billy wasn't given a chance before the battle, but while his margin was not great, he won without a doubt." He boxed cleverly, dancing and shooting, and when they did mix it up, his stinging blows made Brennan back away from the exchanges, while Brennan found him hard to hit. Arnold scored it 4-2-4 for Miske.

The *St. Paul Pioneer Press'* Carlton Hanton said Miske outpointed Brennan in a close battle, 3-2-5. Brennan not only failed to make good his boast that he would stop Miske, but lost another decision to him. Still, Brennan showed how he went so many rounds with Dempsey, because he took Miske's blows to the head and body quite well. "Miske outboxed Brennan throughout, but Bill proved that he is tough by taking everything the St. Paul boy sent in without any sign of being injured. Both men were in excellent condition and fought at top speed all the way."

The *St. Paul Daily News'* Ed Shave said Miske surprised everyone with a clean-cut victory over Brennan, 4-3-3. Miske "cleanly defeated" Brennan in 10 fast rounds. Miske won rounds 1, 3, 6, and 7, Brennan won rounds 4, 9, and 10, with rounds 2, 5, and 8 even. "Brennan will never be a champion. He can't hit. He is a fairly good boxer for a big man, has a good defense, but if he cannot sock any harder than he did last night he will never knock out any one that amounts to anything."

Yet, the *Minneapolis Journal's* Edward G. Walker said Brennan won, coasting to victory, doing enough damage to win the honors by a slight shade. "Brennan had Miske on the run most of the time, a very wise plan of attack for Miske to follow. At times, when Brennan would ease up, Miske would tear in, but 7 out of every 10 blows landed on the New Yorker's arms or gloves." Miske's spurts looked spectacular from the grandstand, for when he attacked, Brennan gave ground, but from ringside, it could be seen that none did any real damage. Brennan's blows were harder and had more effect, making Miske wince. Miske was cut by a head butt in the 5th round.

The *Minneapolis Daily Star's* Charles Johnson called it a draw at 4-4-2, and yet he also said Brennan's performance was a disappointment, missing and clinching often, while "Miske looked so good." Brennan emerged unmarked, while Miske's left eye was badly cut and his lip bleeding continuously.[609]

By arrangement between Tex Rickard and the Radio Corporation of America, the upcoming fight's details would be transmitted instantly to 100 cities within a 200-mile radius of Jersey City. The General Electric Company would install a most powerful sounding apparatus. The

---

[609] *Minneapolis Morning Tribune, Minneapolis Daily Star, Minneapolis Journal, St. Paul Pioneer Press, St. Paul Daily News, Chicago Tribune, Wisconsin State Journal,* June 9, 1921. Most national dispatches reported that the majority of newsmen present said Miske had shaded Brennan. The *Chicago Tribune* reported that Miske had won 7 of 10 rounds.

Magnavox and amplifier would be attached to the wireless telephone, making it possible to hear the shouting of the fans in the arena.[610]

George Engel told Robert Edgren that Carpentier did not resign from the 1912 Papke bout. The cut he suffered from a head butt looked so bad to the crowd that they made the referee stop the fight. Carp was far from beaten. He was forced to make 160 pounds just before the fight and had to half kill himself to do it. He did not eat or drink for 17 hours before he entered the ring, and was dried out to the limit, utterly weight drained. Yet, he fought well in the later rounds. A head butt caused a cut clear across, blinding him. Eventually, the referee stopped it at the start of the 18th round. "There's no quit in him." He was stronger as a heavyweight, because he never had to worry about making any particular weight. He just weighed what he weighed.

Edgren said there were great differences between Dempsey and Carpentier. Jack's nose was dented, his lips thickened, and there were battle scars along his eyebrows. He didn't mind being hit. He actually suffered more punishment in training than in his fights, encouraging his sparring partners to hit him as hard and often as they could. In actual fights he rarely suffered injury, because he attacked so ferociously and kept his foes so defensive that they did not have time to do much accurate hitting. He was asking for more sparring partners who could maul and stand a mauling.

Dempsey's workouts attracted a great many visitors who flocked to see him. Men, women, and children appeared, and the "fair sex in particular made a strong showing."

Carpentier was unscarred. He used all his skill to find openings and hit without being hit. He was as elusive in a real fight as in practice bouts, avoiding real punishment, and "even Dempsey is going to have trouble finding him. Not that Carpentier runs away. He doesn't." He moved in or out no more than necessary, was well balanced and light on his feet, always near enough to deliver a blow if he saw an opening, but far enough away to escape danger.

Noted was the fact that government taxes on the fighters' purses would be quite substantial. Taxes on Dempsey's $300,000 purse would amount to $161,270. Carpentier's taxes on his $200,000, after exemptions for wife and child were subtracted, would total $93,334. Rickard's profits would be taxed as well. The average American citizen paid tax on an annual income between $5,000 and $6,000. Uncle Sam would get close to $500,000 out of the big fight. The government would benefit more overall from the fight than any one participant. New Jersey had taxes too.[611]

On June 9, 1921 in Columbus, Ohio, Martin Burke knocked out Joe Downey in the 11th round.

Burke had sparred with Dempsey recently. He said Jack's six-inch blows to the back of the neck in the clinches were quite damaging, for

[610] New Brunswick Daily Home News, June 10, 1921.
[611] Minneapolis Journal, Paterson Morning Call, New York Daily News, New York World, June 10, 1921.

they stunned him. "If you will watch him, you'll see that he is always in position to punch from any angle and that his heels rarely touch the ground."[612]

Several reporters said Carpentier's real training was done in secret. He did not show his true form in his public sparring. Some thought his manager did not want scouts to be able to pick up useful information to give to Dempsey's camp. Others reported that his manager said a fighter might be inclined to show off for a crowd rather than get all he can out of his exercises. Carpentier was not afraid of crowds, for he had been performing in front of them all of his life.

C. F. Fitzgerald said Dempsey tore into punching bags as if he had a grudge against them. "No man living can take a smash from either of Jack Dempsey's paws and hope to stand up thereafter. The champ hits like a cyclone, either straight out or off the hip." He possessed "the most powerful swing imaginable. The only way to appreciate the kick in Dempsey's punches is to witness them."

Jack Curley humorously called himself a "spy from Manhasset." Dempsey told him, "I wish you would take a few pointers back to Manhasset. Tell Carpentier anything you see and don't think I'll have a grudge against you for it. My camp is wide open and I'd like to have Georges come down and look the place over."

When asked about Harry Greb's prediction that he would win decisively, Jack said, "Harry ought to be a good judge of the way things will go in Jersey City. Greb is a classy Pittsburgher. If he says I'll win I guess he knows what he is talking about."[613]

Featherweight champ Johnny Kilbane said, "Georges is the fastest heavyweight I ever have seen." Although his right was his favorite blow, he had a wonderful left, and was lightning fast with jabs and hooks. He had flying punches as well, veritably throwing himself through the air at his opponent with every ounce of steam and strength behind the blows. His foes usually crumpled up when he hit the chin, regardless of size. He could dance in and out with jabs, circling, setting up a big blow. The plan was to stay out of a mix, use long-range stinging jabs, and watch for an opening for his big blows. He was training in a 12-foot ring so that he would be able to elude the attack even more adeptly in a larger ring.

Dempsey said his trainer was Teddy Hayes, along with Jack Kearns. Hayes had trained Gus Christie and Jack Dillon, and had been a boxing instructor at the Great Lakes Naval Training Station.

Jack said he would be in the best shape of his career for this fight. His cut would be healed soon, so he could resume sparring. "I'll welcome that. Whether these walloping partners of mine will – well, that's another matter."

In response to the debate regarding how good Carpentier was or was not, Dempsey noted, "He knocks 'em when he hits 'em." Jack was doing

[612] *Elmira Star-Gazette*, June 10, 1921.
[613] *New York Tribune, New York Herald*, June 10, 1921.

the same before the Willard fight, and many claimed that his record was phony and the men he licked were no good, predicting that Willard would beat him. They said the same about Willard before he beat Johnson. Hence, he was taking Carpentier seriously.

Although Dempsey asked others about Carpentier's methods, he was not worried or stressed. "If I can hit him I can lick him."[614]

Sam Harris said Dempsey was another Terry McGovern, whom he had managed. He called McGovern the greatest little fighter who ever lived. Dempsey was the best big man he ever had seen, and he saw them all from Sullivan on. He had picked Willard to beat him, for he did not believe Dempsey was big enough or strong enough, but Jack proved him wrong. Harris said Dempsey's form was even better now than it was in Toledo. "He is so much faster than I thought. And he can hit – phew." He always was eager, with nervous energy. "I believe he is the hardest hitting big fighter we've ever had and one of the shiftiest." Dempsey was faster than Sullivan, stronger than Corbett, faster on his feet than Jeffries, and more rugged than Fitzsimmons. "Don't forget that Dempsey has never been off his feet for a count with the exception of the time he took it all with Jim Flynn and I understand that affair was a barney." Harris said to take a look at his nose and the scars over his eyes. "Someone has hit him in the past and hit him good and hard." Dempsey had proven that he could take a punch. "Don't let anyone tell you [Willard] didn't sock Dempsey pretty good in the second round at Toledo. The fact that Dempsey came on after getting that smash convinces me that Jack can take it." Jack Johnson was the greatest defensive boxer ever, but not a finisher. He took things easy and seldom was offensive.

One observer was so impressed with Dempsey's left-hand punches that he asserted that Jack was left-handed. However, others said Jack was right handed, and his facility with his left was due to development of it. No one was quite sure.

TEX RICKARD AND THE MODEL OF HIS PRIZE ARENA.

Frank J. Bartley, former pro boxer and now an engineer, designed and built a model for a ring for the big fight in which the ropes were held far from the corner posts by adjustable turnbuckles, and the canvas was laced to the frame by canvas lashings. Corner seats and rimmed shelves for water buckets were fixed to swing on bars hinged to the corner posts so they could be pushed in and out of the ring. The canvas was backed with felt, and there as a vacuum between the

[614] *Buffalo Times, Buffalo Courier,* June 10, 1921.

layers, which kept it taught and created a suction that prevented slipping and made for fast footwork. A ladder on the side allowed them to climb into the ring. There was no tack, screw, or nail in the entire apparatus, and it could be assembled and taken down quickly.

Dempsey said it would suit him just fine if all he heard about Carpentier's vaunted tricky punches was true, for he liked it when his foes came at him with blows. "The greatest trouble I've always experienced in my battles is to get the other fellow to come to me. I usually have to chase 'em. When they come in at me it isn't half so hard to sock 'em as it is when they are going away."

Billy Roche predicted a Carpentier victory in 6 or 7 rounds, for he was fast and could hit. Dempsey wasn't the man he once was, for hanging around movie stars did not keep him in good form. Brennan hit him with ease, so Carpentier would as well. It would be a great punching fight.

Jack McAuliffe said Carpentier was the most accurate puncher he ever saw. He rarely missed the point of the jaw, and could hit from any angle or position. Most believed that he would hit Dempsey first. He was fast and shifty on his feet, a moving target hard to hit, unlike the ponderous Willard. He had the speed of a flyweight and punch of a heavyweight. Yet, McAuliffe still thought Dempsey would win, but he needed to be in top shape.

Willie Meehan, who currently was running a grocery store in San Francisco, said, "Jack will knock Carpentier for a row of brick flats on July 2. … I'm the only guy that knows how to lick Dempsey. He's a pip puncher. He can lick big fellows, but he can't get at me." Speaking of their last fight, "He dropped me with a left hook to the chin in the 2nd round, but I got up and won the decision."

Still, Meehan had lost so many times since then; there was no clamor for another contest. Since his last 1918 controversial 4-round decision victory over Dempsey, 195-pound Meehan had lost decisions to Fulton, Greb, Miske, Gunboat Smith, and Brennan,

WILLIE MEEHAN. — Soda dispenser who can boast of two decisions over Jack Dempsey.

amongst many others. His only victories of any significance were 1919 4-round decisions over Sam Langford and Jeff Clark.[615]

The entire French press was picking Carpentier to win.

The *Chicago Tribune* had acquired Carpentier's official war record, obtained from his dossier at French Aviation Headquarters, and it revealed that he actually had spent 18 months at the front, flying a two-seater observation airplane, and he received decorations of the Croix de Guerre and the Medaille Militaire. He first served as a chauffeur to the

[615] *Buffalo Times, Brooklyn Standard Union, Buffalo Enquirer,* June 11, 1921.

Second Aeronautic Division at the outbreak of the war in 1914, until he received a pilot's license on May 24, 1915. He was sent with a squadron to the front for a few months.

On August 28, 1915, Carpentier injured a leg in an airplane accident, but recovered quickly and was back to the front in two weeks, on September 11, 1915, for reconnaissance work for an ill-fated French offensive at Champagne which began September 25, 1915. Carpentier was commended for his work on September 25, for he did not hesitate to fly in mist and rain, less than 200 yards above enemy lines. He never returned until his mission was accomplished, often with his machine riddled with bullets and shell splinters.

On April 19, 1916, Carpentier took part in the Crown Prince's attack on Verdun, when French aviators massed in that sector.

On November 5, 1916, Carpentier received a medal for heroic action on October 26, during the French counterattack. The citation stated, "Sergeant Pilot Carpentier as a clever aviator impresses every one with bravery, executing daily perilous missions. He distinguished himself during the attack October 26, flying over the enemy lines at a low altitude for four hours, despite unfavorable weather and even in contempt of danger."

In December 1916, Carpentier became ill and was hospitalized. He never returned to the front. Two months convalescence leave was granted to him on January 15, 1917. On February 16, he obtained permission to visit the U.S. and give exhibitions, which never took place.

On May 16, 1917, Carpentier was assigned to the escadrille stationed at Algeria, but after obtaining an extension of the convalescent leave, he had himself declared unfit to continue as a pilot, and became a physical instructor at the Joinville school of the French Army, five miles outside Paris. He remained a French Army boxing instructor in the summer of 1917, touring the French, Belgian, British, and American fronts, giving boxing exhibitions, and also boxing at base hospitals all over France for wounded soldiers. Six months after the armistice, Carpentier was switched back to aviation and demobilized.

Many American war veterans were rooting for Carpentier.

175-pound black heavyweight Battling Ghee had joined the Dempsey camp. Jack Renault tested him out. Ghee told him, "White boy, you all ain't goin' to hit me at all." His words were pretty nearly true. Ghee was a fast ducker, with fast footwork, having Renault missing often, winking at spectators. They were convinced that he would give Dempsey the work he needed.

On June 10, Carpentier boxed 6 rounds, 2 each with Paul Journee, Joe Jeannette, and Italian Joe Gans. The Frenchman took thumps without blinking, and returned them with interest. He worked his inside game with Jeannette, and his body blows had Joe puffing hard.[616]

[616] *Yonkers Herald, New York Evening World, New York Herald,* June 11, 1921.

George Engel said Carpentier's best strategy would be to box cautiously for 4 or 5 rounds before trying to put over any heavy punches. However, "I doubt that he will do it. His inclination is always to go in and try to put his man down. He is like Dempsey in that. ... I look to see him jump in like a flash and take a crack at Jack's chin the first time he sees an opening." Engel believed that Carpentier was too game for his own good. Georges had no fear. Carp told him, "After what I have seen in the war, meeting Dempsey is nothing."[617]

Most of the wagering, which had been light, had Dempsey the 3 to 1 favorite to win and 2 to 1 favorite to win by knockout. Gamblers on Wall Street were offering 20 to 1 odds that Carpentier could not stop Dempsey. It was even money that Carpentier would not answer the bell for the 6th round.

Joe Jeannette told Jack Veiock, "I know a fighter when I see one, and believe me, this Carpentier is a fighter." Joe said no one ever hit him harder than Carpentier did, which was a high compliment coming from a man who had fought Jack Johnson, Sam Langford, and Sam McVey.

> Georges will fool Dempsey. Mark what I tell you. He is a fast, snappy puncher. He can hit and he can take it, too. Dempsey will not find him the easy mark to hit he found Fulton, Morris, Willard, and the rest. And after he has uncorked a few, only to find that Georges isn't there to receive them, he'll get wild. That's where Georges will start. See if I'm right.

Johnny Coulon predicted a great scrap. Some thought Carp was a delicate dancer, but they were wrong. Coulon had seen Carpentier in fights and exhibitions in Europe. "The Frenchman boxed and trained hard all the time he was on that tour. He's in great shape, and Jack will find him a hard man to beat." Carpentier hit hard enough to knock out anyone, including Dempsey. He was the fastest puncher Coulon ever saw.

Coulon also said some thought the champion was a slow, lumbering elephant, but they were wrong about him too. Dempsey had speed and finish. It was anybody's fight, for either one could score a knockout at any moment, and both could move in lively fashion.[618]

On the 11th, Jack's brother Johnny Dempsey boxed lightweight Joe Benjamin, but Joe knew too much, and the younger Dempsey quit at the end of 2 rounds. He failed to respond to the champion's coaching.

One writer said when Dempsey dropped Willard, he loomed up as the hardest hitter ever. It seemed as if he was carrying Miske, until he decided to end it, which he could have done at any time. Many were puzzled by the Brennan bout. Brennan did much better than expected, landing fairly often, and Dempsey started slowly. Despite all of that, anyone who watched closely could see that eventually Dempsey would stop him. "Dempsey was playing methodically to the body. One or two of these

[617] *Elmira Star Gazette*, June 11, 1921.
[618] *New York Daily News, Buffalo Times, Brooklyn Standard Union*, June 12, 1921.

punches landed in every round and the accumulated punishment was wearing Brennan down." The body punches ended him. The Dempsey who met Carpentier would be as close as he could be to the one who met Willard.[619]

Larry Williams said the champion was clever. Some thought he was just a puncher, but the best persons to opine as to his cleverness were those who had been in the ring with him. "Jack is clever, very clever. ... I think Renault and Burke and myself ought to know, and we are all agreed on that." When sparring, Dempsey kept them working hard, and "I don't know of any man who can hit surer." Jack did not deliver useless blows.

Charles Mathison said, "Without the slightest doubt, Dempsey, the quickest, hardest hitting and most aggressive heavyweight in the history of the ring, will reach Carpentier at least once." Once possibly would be enough. Carp's ruggedness or lack thereof would be proven.[620]

Jim Corbett said that despite comparisons, Carpentier was not the type of boxer that he was. Georges was more aggressive, slugging with very good judgment, with quick, snappy blows.

A prominent sporting man told Tad that against Brennan, Dempsey appeared to be through, burnt out, a wreck, and had gone far back. He was lucky that Carpentier was not in the ring that night. "The stage stuff, those big purses, those parties – that's what set that fellow back. He was just a shell. Didn't you notice them giving him strychnine tablets between rounds, and rubbing him around his heart?" No one could train successfully for a fight on Broadway the way he did, and therefore he got the scare of his life. That fight frightened him into doing real work for Carpentier.[621]

OFF AGAIN.—The cut over Jack Dempsey's left eye is said to be entirely healed and he is now ready to resume sparring. Marty Burke is here trying to clinch to save himself punishment. (By A.I. Times)

ROCKING.—This shows Journee, the French heavyweight sparring partner of Carpentier recovering from a hard jolt. The figure in the cap is Descamps, Georges's wily manager. (NEWS photo)

[619] New York Tribune, June 12, 1921; Brooklyn Citizen, New York Tribune, June 15, 1921.
[620] New York Daily News, June 14, 1921.
[621] Buffalo Enquirer, June 13, 1921.

Dempsey and Robert Edgren

Carpentier spars Battling Marcot

On June 12, a throng of more than 1,000 spectators gasped in amazement as Dempsey hit the various bags. They wondered how long Carpentier could stand up under such a terrific bombardment.[622]

Johnny Kilbane believed that Dempsey would attack the body and try to inflict sufficient punishment to loosen Carpentier's guard so that he could break through with a left to the chin. Carpentier, who was speedier and shiftier than Dempsey, would play for Jack's chin. The outcome might depend upon who landed the first big blow.

Dempsey said he would knock out Carpentier as fast as he could and keep the title in America. Rumors that he would stall around for a few rounds for the movies were false. He had no film interests, for Kearns already sold them for a flat sum. "I regard Carpentier as a dangerous

[622] Brooklyn Daily Times, New York Daily News, June 13, 1921.

foeman. Any opponent who is fast and clever and who can hit with knockout force is a menace to me until he is on the floor and out. I am not going to take any chances with that Frenchman. I'm out to win from him the first minute that I can."[623]

Martin Burke said, "Dempsey'll win in a hurry. Why, he's chain lightning. I never dreamed he was as fast as he is."

Carpentier intended to drop Dempsey if he made one single mistake. Georges said he had been decked several times by Bombardier Billy Wells, but always believed in himself throughout the fight. Once the opening came, he took it, and the fight was over. Hence, no matter what Dempsey did, Georges only needed that one opening. Regardless, he expected to land the first hard punch of the fight.

Georges said his chief workouts were being done in the morning, privately. He did some public work to satisfy the newspaper men, but that wasn't his real work. He was in perfect condition, weighing 174 pounds. He was 170 for Levinsky and 171 for Beckett.

On the 13th, Carpentier sparred 5 rounds total with French welter Marcel Denys or Denis, 200-pound Paul Journee, and Italian Joe Gans.

Georges was a strong favorite with the ladies and the upper classes, who believed he would win the "battle of the century." "Georges is especially strong with the smart set and the women folks are unanimous in their opinion that Jack Dempsey hasn't got a ghost of a chance against the handsome blond fighter."

Jess Willard said Dempsey beat him with a lucky punch. After he was clipped on the jaw in the 1st round, he was out of it for the rest of the contest. Although he was 39 years old, he wasn't past it, because he didn't start boxing until he was 25. He still had several good fights left in him. He believed Dempsey would not be as lucky in a return match.[624]

Dempsey wrote that he stepped on the scales on the 14th in front of two newspaper men and registered 196 pounds, within 6 pounds of what he intended to weigh for the fight. Jack said he was ready, and did not want to go stale, which explained why he was laying off for a few days. He learned his lesson from the Brennan fight. That day, Jack McAuliffe played pinochle with him. The champion was not nervous at all.[625]

On the 15th, Dempsey said loafing around was harder for him than training. Kearns wanted him to wait to spar until his eye was healed. "But I've boxed often with an eye far worse than that of mine which, by the way, is about all healed. So I've got a young hunch that Jack is using the cut over the eyes as the excuse for laying me off training. He always thinks I train too strenuously anyway…. So he's laid me off."[626]

William Brady called Carpentier the greatest boxer since Corbett. He was scientific, quick, and powerful. Carp would beat with ease all of the men that Dempsey had beaten. The champion was up against the smartest

[623] *New York Tribune, Brooklyn Citizen, New York Evening World, Buffalo Times,* June 13, 1921.
[624] *Elmira Star-Gazette, Brooklyn Citizen, New York Tribune, New York Evening World, New York Daily News, Yonkers Herald,* June 14, 1921. Burke no longer would spar, owing to a cauliflower ear which required an operation. But he would be Dempsey's guest.
[625] *Buffalo Times, Brooklyn Standard Union, New York Herald,* June 14, 1921.
[626] *Binghamton Press, Buffalo Times,* June 15, 1921; *New York Tribune, Buffalo Times, New York Evening World,* June 16, 1921.

fighter of his entire career. "When those big fellows clash you'll find that Carpentier's clever defensive tactics will offset Dempsey's rushes and heavy blows."[627]

Both Carpentier and Dempsy Start From Crouch

When Carpentier "Wades in" He Loses His Debonair Manner

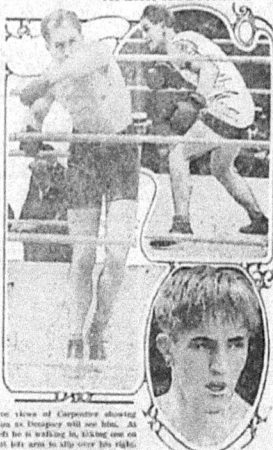

Three views of Carpentier showing him as Dempsey will see him. At left he is walking in, ticking out on his left arm to slip over his right. At right he is crouched, ready to spring and land his left. Below is a closeup of his fighting face.

TWO KINDS OF FIGHTERS.—Richard Croker, champion of many political fights in New York City, posed for this picture when he visited Jack at Airport. At Dempsey's left is Abe Erlanger, theatrical magnate. (By Al. Fate)

Wouldst Prefer Light or Dark in Fistic Embellishment?

Carpentier spars Italian Joe Gans

[627] Brooklyn Citizen, Buffalo American, June 16, 1921.

On June 16, Dempsey sparred for the first time since June 5, eleven days prior. He boxed 4 rounds, 2 each with 150-pound Irish Patsy Cline and featherweight Babe Herman, working on his speed, primarily using his left hand, which "travels so swiftly that it is hard to follow it."

Jack Lawrence said, "Dempsey appeared lightning fast this afternoon." "His defense seemed perfect." Jack was wearing a heavy leather head guard, with white gauze wedged between the leather and his left eyebrow.

Ray Pearson said those who were sweet on Carpentier's chances were figuring that he could travel at such a fast pace that Dempsey would not be able to catch him in 12 rounds. However, the speed and fast-stepping that Dempsey showed that day was a revelation. "No, brother, after watching these steppings today, don't send in the bankroll that the dimpled Georges is going to work the dogs at a pace too fast for Jack Dempsey to keep up."

Jack McAuliffe believed Dempsey was in better condition now than he was at Toledo two years ago. "Dempsey is a worker. That is one of his greatest assets." He had improved a lot since he won the title. He wasn't a boxer, but a seeker, and was sticking to it. His footwork had improved. He could glide in and out, and stepped to the side much better.

On the 16th at Sherry Park in Manhasset, NY, for the official pictures, movie camera men filmed Carpentier training. He walked, sprinted, shadow-boxed, performed acrobatics and floor exercises, sparred, bag punched, and rope skipped. He moved with cat-like quickness.

Quite a fair sprinkling of the "fair sex" was present. "One pretty young woman from Chicago expressed horror at the thought at such a cute boy as Georges Carpentier is to be tossed into the ring with such a rude person as Jack Dempsey." She was assured that Georges was a tough guy himself.

Fred Hawthorne said Carpentier sparred with four men: Marcel Denys, Paul Journee, Joe Jeannette, Italian Joe Gans, and then Journee again, for 5 rounds. Carpentier put on quite a show, buffeting them about in a fast workout, looking better than on any prior occasion. "We watched the French hero when he knocked out Battling Levinsky last October, but he did not show nearly as well on that occasion as he did to-day." He blocked and smothered the hardest blows, and rolled his head and came up smiling. Whatever punches landed on him he took well. He ripped in jarring blows to the head and body. His one-two was so swift the eye scarcely could follow the gloves. He and Jeannette roughed and bullied each other about, doing a lot of infighting. Carp's breathing always was under perfect control.

Bill Brennan said Carpentier was in splendid condition, a neat boxer, fast on his feet, and packed a good punch. However, all that said, he still did not have much of a chance with Dempsey, who likely would get him within 5 rounds. "If the world's champion lands one of his left hooks in Carpentier's stomach it will settle the fight then and there. From

Carpentier's boxing style I would say he is not a hard man to hit, and any one that Dempsey lands solidly on is going to drop."

A. J. Auerbach, who was on hand, said even if Dempsey was within 60% of his form in Toledo, he would win handily. One man retorted that Jack would lose if he was in his Brennan form.

Gus Wilson, Carp's trainer, said, "George will win because he knows too much for Dempsey. Carpentier's experience, skill, and condition will win for him."

Willie Lewis said Carpentier held back his power in training, not wanting to hurt his sparring partners. He was picking Carp to win in 6.

Eddie Foy said Dempsey went in with head down to draw a lead from his foe. "He can take a blow on the head for the sake of getting in a counter, and when he lands the other fellow is done for." The Frenchman was fast and clever, but "Dempsey carries too heavy guns for him."

Carpentier wrote that any referee the New Jersey board selected would satisfy him.

Atlantic City Mayor Edward Bader ordered the police to use more than ordinary vigilance in their annual "clean-up" of the town, given the fear that boxing attracted more of the criminal element.[628]

On the 17th, Dempsey sparred 6 vicious rounds, 2 each with three men. His partners all wore head guards, as did Dempsey, to protect his eye. Jack tore into Renault, who stopped so many lefts and rights to the body that he was glad when his 2 rounds were over. There was a lot of infighting, and Dempsey worked his left continually.

Dempsey then had a spectacular bout with cocky black 175- or 185-pound Battling Ghee of Memphis, who was shorter and stockier than Carpentier, who claimed he had beaten Langford (actually 1920 LKOby2) and Kid Norfolk (actually 1920 D8 and 1921 L8), and also claimed that Dempsey would not be able to hit him, and could not punch hard enough to hurt him.

In the 1st round, Ghee, showing no fear, landed some mighty hard punches on the champ, attempting to show him up with his fast left, but Dempsey was there with the comeback every time, particularly with his fast left jab and hook, and knocked Ghee flat onto the canvas. On another occasion, Ghee went down so hard and violently, on his face, which was cut up, and his mouth bleeding, that it looked as though he would stay down, but he gamely continued.

In the 2nd round, Ghee still showed no respect, but after 40 seconds, a piston-rod left caught Ghee and he sank to his knees. Dempsey caught and lifted him up in his arms and they stalled about in a clinch. Another said Dempsey nailed him with a right that would have caused a knockdown, but Jack caught and held him up as he fell, keeping him up on his feet. Just before the end of the round, Dempsey landed a right to the body and short stabbing left to the jaw and Ghee went down again.

[628] New York Tribune, Brooklyn Daily Times, New York Herald, New York Evening World, Buffalo Evening News, New York Daily News, June 17, 1921; Brooklyn Daily Times, June 18, 1921.

The final 2 rounds were with Larry Williams.

Dempsey decks Battling Ghee

Dempsey said that against Ghee, he faked a left and popped him on the chin with a right, and Ghee went to his knees. They wrestled for a while, and went back at it. The round ended with Ghee on the floor upon his stomach, the result of another right to the chin. He recovered and boxed the 2nd round. After 30 seconds of mixing, Jack broke loose from a clinch, feinted a blow, then hit him with a short right to the jaw, and down he went once more. After that, Jack eased up on him, practicing his jab. Dempsey wore 12-ounce gloves. "The old socker seems to be working nicely."

This is a new headgear which Jack wears frequently to protect a cut he received recently over his left eye.

Jack Lawrence said Dempsey gave his three sparring partners severe lacings. When they left the ring, each one was reeling. Ghee was bleeding from the mouth and nose and decidedly groggy at the end of his 2 rounds, with a Willardesque look in his eyes.[629]

Afterwards, Ghee said, "If any man had told me I could get cut up and knocked flat with 12-ounce gloves I'd thought he was crazy. Mercy be, how that boy does hit. ... Dempsey can whip a roomful of Ghees and Norfolks. I won't be right for many days." Another quoted him as saying, "Believe me, brothers, that Dempsey can sure hit." That was with big gloves and holding back a bit, "so you can suppose yourself what he can do with little gloves on when he ain't pullin' 'em."

Former Dempsey manager Al J. Auerbach said he bet $12,000 on the champ. "Dempsey looks 40% better than he did at Toledo. He's bigger and stronger and has learned a lot since then." Some said Auerbach had wagered at even odds that Carpentier would not make it to the 6th round.

When some newsmen told Jack they were aching for him to cut loose on his sparring partners and knock them out, Dempsey replied, "Knock 'em out? Why, those lads are my pals. I wouldn't hurt them for the world." Even taking it easy, Jack still pummeled them aplenty.

Dempsey told Jim Corbett he intended to win as quickly as possible.

> My plan, as you know, has always been to carry it to the other fellow and carry it fast. I've found it successful. ... I believe a sharp attack serves also as a fine defense and I try to nail my man before he gets a chance to nail me. They tell me Carpentier is very clever. Well, maybe he is. But I don't expect to change my system against

---

629 *New York Daily News*, June 18, 1921.

him. The way I look at it, the better he is, the better a victory for me will be if I win, and I expect to. You know, Jim, they'll all fall if you hit 'em hard enough.

In a divorce suit in Pawhuska, Oklahoma, F. R. Boulanger, an Osage Indian, was divorcing his wife Lilly. He charged that his wife had been carrying on a correspondence with Dempsey, and claimed to have letters written by Dempsey to her.

Dempsey thought it was a joke. "I never heard of the people mentioned in the Pawhuska story. I never heard of the town until now and do not know the woman. Someone is pulling a big joke. It gives me the best laugh I have had in a year."[630]

Mrs. Lillian Boulanger said, "I didn't write to Jack Dempsey, although I've known him since we were children. We went to school together. The insinuations made by my husband are absurd." She insisted they were but childhood friends, nothing more. Another claimed the Dempsey letters were written when they were children. They were "childhood sweethearts" in Colorado as kids, but nothing more.[631]

The *Daily News'* Ray Pearson said he never saw a man hit so hard as Dempsey. He was a fighter, and liked to make his foes fight him. He hit so hard that he only needed to land once, and it could land anywhere and the fight would be over. Dempsey knew about Carpentier's right, his clever boxing, and his wonderful foot speed. "But to Dempsey that means nothing." Dempsey could speed across the canvas and land rib-crushing blows. He didn't really care what his foe did. He simply said, "We'll fight."

Heywood Broun said Dempsey was a man of Cain, not Abel. Carpentier apologized if he landed too hard. Dempsey said nothing, scowled and cuffed away as if he was paying off old grudges. Even when he shadow boxed, he seemed to be riled about something, and slashed at the air as if it had better not get in his way.

On the 18th, Dempsey sparred 2 rounds each with welterweight Irish Patsy Cline, lightweight Joe Benjamin, and middleweight Eddie O'Hara. He worked on his defense, pulled his punches and worked more on his speed with the smaller men, but still punished them a bit, drawing blood, making faces puffy, almost knocking them over, doubling them up, etc.

[630] *Brooklyn Citizen, Elmira Star-Gazette, Buffalo Times, New York Tribune, New York World, Buffalo Enquirer, New York Herald, Brooklyn Citizen, New York Daily News,* June 18, 1921.
[631] *New York Daily News, New York Tribune,* June 19, 1921.

"In spite of the fact that Dempsey does not satisfy the eye as much as Carpentier, it seems to us that he deserves his position as favorite. He is a little less speedy, but far more rugged."

Bill Brennan said, "The Frenchman isn't going to find it easy to hit Dempsey. That weaving business of his makes it hard to land on him solidly. Carpentier may keep away from him for awhile, but in 12 rounds Dempsey's sure to tag him."

Dempsey wrote that Bill Brennan told him that he would win, and then should give him another match. "I'm willing. Bill certainly gave me the toughest fight of my career. ... But I like the tough ones. That's why I told Bill that if any matchmaker wanted to toss us into another ring together he'd find me ready." Jack regarded no man as soft until he was down and out.[632]

Jack Kearns said he would refuse to allow Dempsey to box if the New Jersey commission named a referee who did not meet his approval.

> I have a million-dollar asset in Dempsey. I am not going to stick him into the ring on July 2 with Carpentier unless assured the referee is unprejudiced, will let the men fight it out fairly and will be capable. Dempsey can take care of himself. But when I turn him loose I want him to fight one man, not two.[633]

On June 19, Dempsey sparred a round each with four different sparring partners while motion picture cameras filmed his training.

First up was former amateur middleweight champ Eddie O'Hara or O'Hare. The fast-moving, fast-punching New Yorker showed that Dempsey could be hit, particularly with a fast jab. Several experts said he would be a mark for Jack Johnson's jab back in the day.

Next up was 43-year-old Philadelphia Jack O'Brien, former world light heavyweight champ. According to Harry Newman, the lively O'Brien actually attacked and landed a looping right smash to the face, but was repaid for his rashness. It resembled a real fight, and Dempsey had O'Brien on the verge of a knockout just before time was called for their 1 round.

With a bloody mouth, O'Brien said, "He's too tough for me." O'Brien declared that Dempsey was the sharpest and most accurate puncher he

---

[632] New York New York Daily News, New York Tribune, Rochester Democrat and Chronicle, June 19, 1921.
[633] Buffalo Courier, New York Daily News, Brooklyn Daily Eagle, June 19, 1921.

ever had faced. "When he lets fly with a punch to your chin it's going to land on your chin – not your cheek or high up on the face." In another interview, O'Brien said that despite wearing large 14-16-ounce gloves, "he made me feel as though a mule kicked me." He had fought Fitzsimmons, Burns, Ketchel, Johnson, Hart, Choynski, Maher, Ryan, and many others, but "none hit as hard as Dempsey does when in so close. They say that Ketchel could hit, but he had to swing to be effective." Dempsey had equally powerful short rights and lefts in close. Plus, he kept a fast pace.

A fellow doesn't get a chance to think when he's in there with Dempsey. He's on top of you all the time and hits so hard and often that there's no chance to use your wits. I hit him with a left hand a couple of times and he crossed me with a right as pretty as you please, following it up with a left hook that knocked me silly for a few seconds.

Next, Jack belted Larry Williams with rights to the head and left rips to the stomach, forcing him to break ground, move, hold, and cover.

Jack Renault got knocked back several feet by a right, and stayed away thereafter, refraining from mixing. [634]

O'Brien then re-entered the ring and did a tugging stunt with the champ. They pushed and heaved at each other, but O'Brien was driven back. At times, Dempsey fairly lifted him from the floor, and O'Brien went so far backward that he toppled in a heap on the canvas.

Dempsey wrestles and pushes with Philadelphia Jack O'Brien.

Next, Dempsey skipped rope. It was a good thing it was not a rope-skipping championship, for Carpentier was far superior at that endeavor. The champ finished with some floor calisthenics. Photos and movies were taken of his shadow boxing and pulley weight exercises as well.

Writing for the *Buffalo Times*, Dempsey said rope skipping was not usually a part of his training, but he did it for the moving picture folks. "I guess everybody was willing to admit that Georges Carpentier has it all over me in the matter of skipping."

---

[634] *Buffalo Courier, Buffalo Commercial, New York Daily News*, June 20, 1921. Heywood Broun said the order was O'Hare, Larry Williams, Renault, and then O'Brien. Another said it was O'Brien, O'Hara, Williams, then Renault. Dempsey said it was O'Hara, O'Brien, Williams, and Renault.

Dempsey said Philadelphia Jack O'Brien appeared to be within 10 pounds of his prime weight when he was world light heavyweight champion. At first, the champ wasn't sure whether to go after him or take it easy. However, "The old timer whirled into me with the speed of a cyclone and in about three seconds the air became full of flying gloves." Dempsey was impressed. "That fellow surely is a wonder yet and I can easily appreciate now why he was a terror in the days of his real greatness. He showed a splendid defense, a very tricky attack, and whenever I reached out in the early part of a round for a smack at his nose, he ducked or sidestepped or fell into a saving clinch." They went at it merrily, and Dempsey was just beginning to solve his method when time was called. He wished O'Brien was younger and more active, for he could provide wonderful help as a regular sparring partner. After sparring two others, he and O'Brien engaged in a shoving contest, "and I guess I earned what you would call the popular decision."

Jack McAuliffe predicted that Carpentier would hit the hittable Dempsey first, but would not and could not topple him. "The champion has no defense – but strange as it may sound he has the best defense, a perfect offense." He tore in with fists flying so fast that he did not need to know about blocking, because his foe didn't get a chance to counter. McAuliffe granted that Dempsey had a knack for moving his head swiftly, and many blows would land on shoulders or the side of his head. He also could crouch and bend his body at close quarters.

Martin Burke said Dempsey would win because he was the hardest hitter the ring ever had known. Burke said he ought to know, for he had sparred and exhibited with him several times. "Dempsey has improved 100% since he won the championship. They say Carpentier is the fastest boxer in the world. He needs to be, for just as soon as Jack gets to him it will be all over."[635]

Descamps said Georges would make Dempsey look foolish as he nimbly side-stepped the furious rushes and countered him.

Henry Farrell noted that Dempsey was modest. He had a generous regard for other ring men, including his opponents. He did not like to be told how good he was. "Dempsey never boasts of his conquests. He credits most of his successes to his luck in getting over the punch." When folks liked to denigrate Carpentier in order to ingratiate themselves with him, Dempsey told them that they were wrong, for Carpentier had a fine record of victories, and he had to have the goods to have such results. After Brennan visited him, Dempsey said, "Bill Brennan is a fine fellow and he's a tough boy. Just a little bit more and he'd be a champion. I always like to hold the friendship of all the boys I meet. When they come back to see me it makes me feel like I can't be such a bad fellow. I know that Carpentier and I will be the same way after the fight."[636]

[635] *Brooklyn Citizen*, June 20, 1921.
[636] *Buffalo Enquirer, New York Tribune, New York Herald, Buffalo Times, Brooklyn Standard Union, New York Evening World*, June 20, 1921.

Carpentier allegedly said he had fought and knocked out men of Dempsey's size before. "I am the better boxer, both offensively and defensively. I believe I can hit harder than Jack and if I hit him right he will go down – and he won't get up, either."

However, in another article, Carpentier wrote that he was annoyed by fake interviews. "I have never declared that I would knock out Dempsey, and insist that any one who wants me to talk about the fight shall wait until July 3." Meaning, don't always believe what you read in the newspapers.

The prevailing odds had Dempsey as the 3 to 1 favorite.

Women loved Carpentier. Even though Dempsey was a handsome man, the ladies thought Carpentier was so good looking; his frown was more attractive than Jack's smile.

Percy Hammond said Carpentier was too nice a person to be successful against the homicidal Dempsey, who was grim, cold, sneering, and cruel. Carpentier was innocent, sympathetic, smiling, and kind. "Two men more unlike never before came together." Dempsey had an ominous appearance in the ring; he was dark, with three days growth of whiskers, a venomous glitter in his beady eyes, appearing mean and muscular.

On the 20th, Dempsey boxed New York middleweight Eddie O'Hare, Battling Ghee, Larry Williams, and Jack Renault, 2 rounds each, for 8 total rounds.

Heywood Broun said in the 2nd round with O'Hare, a Dempsey left brought a trickle of blood, and Jack apologized. (So he apologized too!) Damon Runyon said Dempsey cuffed O'Hare about in sprightly fashion and boxed and stepped better than the previous day, motivated by having read some reports that O'Hare had outboxed him.

Dempsey spars Larry Williams

Dempsey said that against fast and clever O'Hare, he did defensive work, ducking, side-stepping, and blocking. Many said O'Hare's moves and tricks were like the Frenchman's, for they both were trained by Willie Lewis at one point. Eddie was hard to hit, for he shifted, turned, and whirled, but after a while, Jack solved him, and at the end was finding him successfully.

Broun said one left swing to the stomach sent the moving Ghee down to the floor. Runyon said Ghee "streaked it from start to finish," meaning he ran away, wanting no part of the champ, taking three steps to the champ's one. Dempsey said Battling Ghee was shy this time, trying to protect his teeth, which Jack had loosened.

The writers said Dempsey slugged Larry Williams to his knees. Dempsey said Williams was very game, a second Joe Grim, willingly mixing it toe-to-toe every so often. One left hook slammed Larry back to the ropes, and another to the jaw lifted him off his feet, sprawling onto the ropes and down. He rose and came back at Jack.

Shifty Renault boxed with speed and caution. Jack said he got plenty of punching and boxing, as well as work in the clinches.

Broun said Dempsey looked better because he fought more and boxed less. He ducked and blocked well, but he was a much better fighter than boxer. His best defense was his rushing, smashing attack.

Jack McAuliffe said Dempsey's fighting instinct was his greatest asset. He loved to fight, and was a great two-handed fighter. His blows knocked foes off balance and drove them back, which helped him avoid the danger of counters. "He has wonderful footwork. He covers more ground with less effort than any heavyweight since the days of Sullivan." He glided in and out and always was set to punch or go back with one. He was a marvelous infighter. He also was dead game, calmly absorbing punishment, taking one and giving it right back. He had confidence and was absolutely cool under fire. "His cleverness and brain in the ring are underestimated." He forced opponents to mix with him, and had the speed to keep up with anyone.

Dempsey said, "I never even think of losing a fight. ... I never care what the other fellow has. The only thought in my mind is to get close enough to him to sock." He found openings, hit fast, and kept hitting until they dropped.

The referee issue was bothering Kearns, but Dempsey was not concerned at all. He attended to the fighting, and let Kearns worry about everything else. Kearns feared that the Carpentier side would try to win on a false claim of foul. Georges had won via foul three times before, and that concerned Kearns. He wanted a capable referee who knew the difference between a fair punch and a foul one. Dempsey said, "It won't make any difference to me who referees, as long as he can count up to ten." He did say that to get to a fast man, he needed to hit the body, and would be careful not to allow them to pull a trick on him regarding an alleged foul. "I never use any tricks and I don't think Georges would either because he's a good sport." "But I string with Kearns. He started with me when I was working by the day and hardly getting enough to keep my family from starving and he got me the matches that made me champion." The champ did whatever Kearns told him to do, and trusted his judgment.

Edgren said Dempsey was in an "unfortunate position." Thousands who did not know the facts of the case still harped on the "slacker" charge. It should have been enough that he was tried and acquitted, that the charges were proven to have originated in a blackmail attempt, and to have been bolstered with forged letters. Dempsey was a clean, decent fellow who supported his mother and family since he was a boy. Still, the feeling against him in many quarters was strong.

Edgren was concerned by the fact that he noticed that Jack largely had eliminated his natural swaying defense, standing straighter and boxing more like others, which he believed would be a serious mistake against Carpentier. His natural shifty style was superior to any other champion's style that Edgren ever saw, and "the most effective fighting method ever developed in the ring. Dempsey should stick to it."

Carpentier's training on the 20th included 2 rounds of sparring with Marcel Denys and 3 rounds with Jeannette.

Carpentier wrote that he was taking it easy, just doing some work to please the sporting writers. He was ready to fight.

On June 20, 1921 at Ebbets Field in Brooklyn, 185-pound Charley Weinert stopped Carpentier's sparring partner, 198-pound Paul Journee, in the 5th round. 155-pound Augie Ratner stopped 156-pound Carpentier sparring partner Italian Joe Gans in the 10th round.[637]

On the 21st, although Eddie O'Hare was very fast, Dempsey was right up and at him at all times for 2 rounds.

According to Harry Newman, in the 1st round against Larry Williams, a Dempsey left hook to the body followed by a looping right put Williams to sleep. One writer said the body blow to the ribs was so loud that you could hear it half a block away. Jack followed with a one-two and down Williams went. Larry was picked up and set right. They resumed, and the same punches dropped him again, this time on his hands and face, all out. Bernie Dempsey and Teddy Hayes picked him up and lugged Larry to a corner. "Being paid for standing before this fellow's punches is like being reimbursed for testing the electric chair with one's own flesh and blood. Nothing can live before the Dempsey smash, so far as man is concerned. He is a freak of nature..." Dempsey said he meant no harm to Williams, and had not struck in anger.

[637] *New York Daily News, Brooklyn Citizen, Buffalo Courier, Buffalo Times, New York Tribune, New York Evening World,* June 21, 1921.

Jack Renault went 1 round as well. Battling Ghee had left, saying that Dempsey was too rough. After the sparring, Dempsey engaged in some rough and tumble wrestling with Bull Montana.

Kearns said, "Jack is better than he was at Toledo. He is a little bigger and he is just as fast, in spite of reports. He knows more about boxing. Maybe he has changed his style a little, and maybe he doesn't weave the way he used to, but he's there, and when he faces the Frenchman you'll see the greatest world champion that ever stepped in a shoe."

Edgren said rumors that Dempsey was wild and living the night life were false, which Mayor Bader confirmed. "Dempsey is one of the most generally knocked champions we've ever had, and one of the cleanest men that ever held the title."

Jack O'Brien told Edgren that Dempsey hit cleanly and accurately on the chin, and was so fast, one could not duck. "There's no getting away from his punches when you're in close. I thought I could fool him with some old-time stuff, but that baby knows everything, take it from me."

Willie Ritchie, former lightweight champ, said he was betting on Carpentier. "Brennan couldn't box as Carpentier can," and after Dempsey missed his blows, he would lose his confidence, not be as aggressive, and get outpointed or even dropped. Carp was game and had more experience, having been boxing for 12 years. In a short 12-round bout, speed mattered more than weight.

Hugh Fullerton believed that Carpentier was in better shape than Dempsey. Jack was "heavier than he should be," weighing about 195 pounds. Claims that he would weigh much less were "bunk." Yet, Dempsey's wind was good, and he hit just as fast and freely as ever, and seemingly just as hard. Dempsey was the least worried of anyone around his camp. "His mental attitude is that it doesn't make any difference what the other fellow does and that it is no use to think about it." He would be ready for anything. It was said that he was getting more cross, surly, and rough in camp, but outside of camp, he had the same easy smile and style.

Charles Mathison said the champ possessed all his speed, and was hitting with uncontrollable force, fit to put up the battle of his career. The last vestige of the "pallid, nervous and clumsy chap" who fought Brennan had disappeared. He now closely resembled the vigorous, speedy, "superb animal" who battered Willard into submission. The training Mathison saw Dempsey do for the Brennan fight was far inferior. He had recaptured his speed of foot and hand. This writer could not see how Carpentier could withstand the champ's panther-like rushes and savage blows.

Discussing his weaknesses, which he said were not serious, Jack McAuliffe opined that Dempsey needed a lot of wind for his high-speed offense, focusing on stopping foes quickly, which could sap his energy and burn him out too quickly. At times he led with his right, which was dangerous, for he left himself open to counters. His defense was nonexistent, for he was wide open with a poor guard, and he would be hit by anyone fast enough to beat him to the punch. His left eye had a tendency to cut.[638]

WINIFRED WESTOVER PUTS ON THE GLOVES WITH JACK DEMPSEY
The Selznick star visits the Champion at Atlantic City. In the friendly bout the odds are in favor of Miss Westover, for surely Jack will never hit a lady.

Dean Snyder said both Jack and Georges applied the bandages and tape to their own hands. Carpentier bandaged his hands more loosely than Dempsey, who wrapped pretty tight. Most fighters did not like them too tight, for fear of cutting off the circulation.

Willard believed Dempsey had a rock mixed up in the tape on his hands at Toledo. "I didn't see Dempsey put the tape on his hands. He had them all fixed up when he came into the ring. I had a feeling that everything wasn't just right, but I couldn't make a scene in the ring. After the fight I wasn't able to investigate his bandages." Of course, if he thought something was wrong, he easily could have raised an objection after shaking Dempsey's wrapped hands.

Dempsey laughed at Willard's notions. "I tape my fists so well that I could hit a brick wall and never hurt 'em." He soaked his hands in beef brine for a short time every day, and also rubbed it on his face.

Tom Andrews said Dempsey was better-liked by the reporters because he was more accessible and held his training open to them and the public. Carpentier was loathe to train in public or for the reporters, and only met with them because Rickard said he had to do it.

---

[638] *New York Daily News, Elmira Star-Gazette, New York Evening World, Brooklyn Daily Times, Yonkers Herald, New York Herald, Brooklyn Standard Union, New York Tribune*, June 22, 1921.

McAuliffe said Carpentier's greatest asset was his speed of both hand and foot, combined with great coordination, able to accept the slightest opening. He was a fine boxer, with long experience, and knew every trick. He was efficient and knew how to hit; a great sharpshooter with a knockout punch. He was better at a distance than at close range.

Georges took a look at the arena where the fight would be held, and exclaimed, "Marvelous!" He wanted to study the lighting conditions at the time of the fight. As he was leaving, Georges met New Jersey Governor Ed Edwards and they shook hands.

A Carpentier advisor went to watch Dempsey train on the 22nd, so as to report back what he saw. Dempsey said anyone was welcome, for he had nothing to hide.

Jack said he needed huskier sparring partners who could take it. The ones he had were splendid in that they gave him wonderful practice in speed, clever defensive work, and other scientific features. But he wanted someone who could step in, mix it, and permit him to let loose with what he really had, so he could get in real punching practice. Kearns would pay well, and sent out many invitations, but so far no one had arrived. Instead, Dempsey sparred 2 rounds with bantam Babe Herman and 3 with shifty lightweight Joe Benjamin. Jack was eager for the fight to arrive. "I'm getting a bit savage because of waiting."

HARRY ERTLE.

Word was that Harry Ertle would referee the fight. Ertle had refereed Carpentier-Levinsky. Kearns said Ertle suited him, for he was known as capable and his integrity beyond dispute.[639]

On June 22, 1921 in Cleveland, Ohio, Tommy Gibbons stopped Willie Meehan in the 1st round, the referee terminating the contest after Meehan had been floored three times. Although the usually durable Meehan had several decision losses over the years, not one top fighter had managed to stop him, including Wills, Dempsey, Fulton, Brennan, or Miske, so the manner in which Gibbons had won was impressive and unique. Edward Tranter said if Gibbons could stop Meehan in 1 round, a man who once beat Dempsey, then "he must be credited with being a worthy challenger for the heavyweight crown."

On June 23, in what was advertised as his final public workout, Carpentier pummeled four opponents. He sparred 1 round each with several men, decking each one with his right to the chin, including middleweight Dave Rose (recent name-change to Danny Ross), former amateur welter champ Dave Rosenberg, and middleweight/light heavy Chris Arnold, who was groggy and bleeding from his nose and mouth. Joe Jeannette was the only one who did not go down, for they mostly clinched, pushed, pulled, and hit lightly, with a bit of infighting.

The fight would be in an 18-square-foot ring, which favored Dempsey.

[639] *Brooklyn Citizen, New York Daily News, Buffalo Commercial, Buffalo Times, New York Evening World,* June 23, 1921.

Thomas Rice believed that Dempsey could win either quickly or by wearing him down over time with body punishment. "He has extraordinary force in his short blows." Dempsey was great at crowding in, as proved by the way he moved in on the taller Fulton and Willard. Rice did not see how Georges could resist his onslaughts. Even if Carpentier happened to deck him, Dempsey would get up and continue pouring it on.

On June 24, Jack Dempsey celebrated his 26th birthday. He received hundreds of telegrams and well-wishes. He took a layoff day.

Carpentier sent birthday greetings to Dempsey via telegram. Jack said, "Georges is a nice fellow." Heywood Broun noted that another tradition had been smashed. In the old days, fighters rarely spoke of each other without curses and dire threats. Conversely, these two once had played golf together. They would pick and smell flowers, and romp around with kids. Dempsey only shaved twice a week, but still did not look ferocious. He had a good-humored grin. He answered questions, "Yes, sir," or "No, sir."

Yet, despite being mild and unassuming outside the ring, inside the ring, they both were ferocious. When boxing, Dempsey did not smile or say anything. Billy Miske was one of his best friends, but that did not stop him from knocking him out. He had nothing against Larry Williams, but he knocked him out regularly. Sometimes he said he was sorry, but only while he was picking up the prostrate man.

Odds still favored Dempsey at 3 to 1 and 4 to 1, hovering back and forth amongst those numbers.[640]

Carpentier was not worried about Dempsey's strength. "Beckett was strong. Very strong. Strong as Dempsey and me put together."

Corbett said the man who landed the first big punch might win by knockout, because both had knockout force. Carpentier was fast, shifty, and tricky, feinting his foe into a lead so he could counter. He had faster feet than the champ. Dempsey was a mighty hard hitter, essentially knocking out in the 1st round Willard, Fulton, Morris, and others. He could knock out any man he hit, just like Jeffries, Fitzsimmons, and Sullivan. "Dempsey hits harder than most of the hard-hitting heavies in ring history."

McAuliffe predicted that Carpentier would land but lose heart when Dempsey proved he could take it, and then Jack would batter his body with terrific lefts and stop him. Some thought the Frenchman might run away in the early rounds, but McAuliffe thought he had too much pride to do that, so he would mix, and that would lead to his demise. Carp was too frail to take the type of body punching that a driver like Dempsey would hand out. Carpentier fought too high, and was off balance when he

---

[640] New York Tribune, Brooklyn Daily Eagle, Buffalo Times, Brooklyn Daily Times, New York Herald, New York Daily News, Buffalo Evening News, June 24, 1921. Dr. Herbert Goddard had obtained a $500 judgment against Dempsey for a nose operation he performed in Philadelphia, and was going to attempt to attach Jack's auto unless paid.

missed. He seemed to be open to a left hand, and Dempsey had the best left since the original Jack Dempsey.[641]

Dempsey with Carmen E. Pantages

Dempsey sparring with Williams, Renault, and Williams again

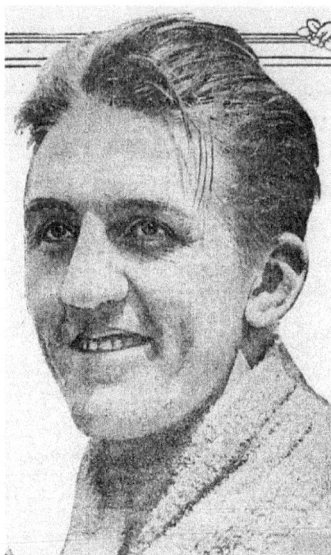

The arena was the largest ever constructed, covering 300,000 square feet. It would hold at least 91,613 people, and was constructed at a cost of $250,000. It required 2,250,000 feet of lumber.

Fred Hawthorne said Carpentier had a good chance to win, for he had a knockout punch, speed, endurance, gameness, brains, and experience, but Dempsey was the logical favorite, with his greater strength and ruggedness. Hawthorne had seen Dempsey knock out Fred Fulton, and that fight left no doubt in his mind that Jack was a deadly body puncher. "I do not believe the man lives who can stand up for more than two or three rounds if he allows Dempsey to get home those terrible deadening punches to the body." It was almost impossible to keep away from Dempsey as he kept crowding in to close quarters, ripping in with a vicious, savage intensity. He could attack with a suddenness that caught his foes off guard.

[641] *Paterson Evening News, New York Tribune, Buffalo Enquirer, Brooklyn Citizen, Binghamton Press, Asbury Park Evening Press, New York Daily News, New York Herald,* June 25, 1921.

Charles Mathison said, "Beyond all question, the Dempsey-Carpentier match has aroused more public interest than any similar event in history." Carpentier was clever, crafty, and experienced, a master of defense and attack, and a hard, accurate, effective puncher. His adherents claimed he had marked superiority in science to Dempsey, "but it is more apparent than real." Dempsey was not as showy, but his system nevertheless was very effective, both in defense and attack. Most believed Carpentier was faster of foot and hand than Dempsey, but Mathison believed such was in error as well. Dempsey was faster, employing startling speed on the attack. As hard as Carpentier hit, Dempsey hit with double the force. He also had superior powers of punch assimilation and resistance. Dempsey took Willard's and Brennan's hardest thumps without being deterred. Carpentier had been decked, hurt, or stopped more times, though most occasions were when he was younger, smaller, and less experienced. Ultimately, Mathison believed that Dempsey's superior weight, size, hitting power, ruggedness, and speed would lead to his knockout victory.

Tom Andrews said Dempsey had the punch, but also was fast, and his peculiar style of swaying back and forth was puzzling to opponents. He could hit from any angle with either hand. There was no bar against the rabbit punch in New Jersey, and Jack knew how to use it perfectly. True, Fitzsimmons at the same size as Carpentier could knock out men as big or bigger than Dempsey, so size did not always matter. Both men could put others to sleep, but Dempsey had the greatest powers of resistance. Both likely would try to win by early knockout.

On June 25, 1,500 watched Dempsey work for 45 minutes under the broiling hot sun. He sparred 6 rounds, 2 each with Eddie O'Hare, Larry Williams, and Jack Renault, cuffing all three about the ring. He also wrestled for a round with Bull Montana.

Dempsey spoke with international correspondents. Benny Bettison of the *London Daily Telegraph* said, "Dempsey is a charming fellow. We talked about everything except the fight."

Jack said he was ready, in better shape than he was for Willard.

> I am aware that Carpentier is a shifty, clever boxer and a hard hitter, and that is a combination not easily overcome. I hope to win and thus keep the title in America, but if I am defeated I will be the first to congratulate the victor. Win or lose I will continue to fight in the ring as often as there is a demand for my services.

Dempsey was eager to enter the ring, for he could not cut loose with his sparring partners. He had to pull his punches, and if he rocked one of the boys with a blow, he dared not follow up, but backed off until they steadied a bit. "Boy! Oh, Boy! How I wish that somebody would hop into the camp and let me slug away at him with everything I've got."

A sergeant-at-arms of the district court was trying to serve Dempsey with a court summons regarding the $500 physician's lawsuit regarding his nose surgery, but Dempsey told the grounds guardians, "Don't let that man in!" They bolted the gate.

On the 25th, Carpentier sparred 5 rounds with Journee and Buffalo light heavy Chris Arnold. Descamps told Georges that he would be the next world champion. It seemed that Carp's strategy was to play defense and keep away until he could connect with his right.

172 ½-pound Georges said, "I feel confident that I shall win, although I expect a hard battle from Dempsey. … Win or lose, I shall never forget the welcome that has been extended to me by the American people."

Lady reporter Harriette Underhill said of the 27-year-old Carpentier, "How he can move!" She had seen him spar Marcel Denys, Italian Joe Gans, Paul Journee, and "last of all, a very dark, enormous man named Joe Jeannette," who hit Georges in the body on the inside, but afterwards, Carpentier laughed and smiled. He then jumped rope for 10 minutes without missing. She said he had wonderful eyes, a sweet disposition, and would do well in the movies. The ladies wanted him to win.

On June 26, Gunboat Smith watched Carpentier spar 2 fast rounds with Marcel Denys and 3 more with Joe Jeannette. Smith said Carpentier could both hit and take a punch. "He's no egg!"

> Don't fool yourself into thinking that guy can't take a punch. Bombardier Wells couldn't hurt him, and believe me, the Bombardier can hit. I don't think he's rugged enough for Dempsey, but he is certainly a good 3 to 1 shot, because he carries a punch and can take one in return. If he tries to stay in close during the fight, Dempsey will play The Star Spangled Banner on his ribs.

When someone commented on Carpentier's intelligence, the Gunner replied, "In order to be a great fighter you have to be 99% dumb. As soon as I became educated I was through."

Grantland Rice said it was the most amazing drama in the history of sports. Yet, it was somewhat inexplicable, because the vast majority considered it to be as close to a cinch as one could have, with odds as big as 4 to 1 on the champ. Regardless, over 1 million dollars would be generated, the most ever. The international aspect added a flash of color. Carpentier was the best European heavyweight in 30 years. He had class, good looks, a nice personality, and was a decorated war veteran. Despite Carpentier's fistic abilities, which were significant, Rice still believed Dempsey would knock him out within 6 rounds. Yet, it was not the probability but the possibility that was attracting so many. Georges appeared to have all of the qualities necessary - skill, speed, power, footwork, and experience - to give Dempsey a real test, no matter how long it lasted. What made the champ the heavy favorite wasn't that Georges wasn't good, but that Dempsey was so very good. He also had speed and skill, with greater hitting power, good legs, and the ability to absorb punishment and dish it continually throughout the contest.

Harry Newman predicted that Dempsey would knock out Carpentier in 4 rounds, but conceded Carp a chance, for he packed the greatest right ever known. It snapped from any angle and was powerful enough to hurt anyone. Georges was a fast, shrewd, cunning trickster. He likely would try to trap Dempsey with a big right early in the contest. If he hurt him, he knew how to finish. Conversely, Dempsey would try to drive a left hook clean through his body. Dempsey was "without doubt the greatest hitter in the history of the game, and right now in the best shape of his life."

> [It is] hard to conceive of the handsome, comparatively frail Frenchman standing up under the cruel smashes of the rough looking and unshaven American. Dempsey, in my opinion, is too big for Carpentier. He will smash through George's guard and nail the foreigner after a round or two. … Incidentally the champion is very fast for a big man and his supporters do not give Carpentier a look-in.

Carpentier sparring Marcot and Gans

Percy Hammond said Jack Kearns was the most abused and hated man in pugilism. He was blamed for any of the champ's perceived errors. "Dempsey has been caught in questionable contests. It was Kearns's fault. Dempsey's domestic life has not possessed the fragrant tranquilities which distinguish the matrimonies of public men. Kearns is responsible. Dempsey did not go to war. Kearns kept him out." Kearns bore it all on his back with fortitude, saying,

> Here is the way I think about it. I've come up from nothing much. I've helped to make a champion. I have money, and I'm good to my mother and the folks. I'd feel fine if I wasn't knocked so much, but they tell me that every man who has done well is abused by the old friends who haven't. I'll forget all my troubles next Saturday, after Dempsey does the job.

Kearns defended Dempsey's war record with documents, figures, and eloquence. He said the champ was patriotic, and the victim of circumstance. "We've all done wrong, I guess. I know I have, and so has Jack, but not more than the average man. Jack wasn't in the war, though he wanted to be. We have proved it, but a lot of people won't believe us; so what's the use. We go along, knowing that we are all right with ourselves."

The *Brooklyn Citizen* said Dempsey's favorite hobbies were dogs and children.

Nothing suited him better than to have children call on him at his camp. He had four dogs; his fancy in particular being Belgian police dogs.

Dempsey and Joe Benjamin

Johnny Kilbane said if Dempsey won, his next title defense likely would be against either Willard or Tommy Gibbons. That was the inside dope. They "loom up as the logical men for him to meet next." Willard had been claiming that he would train much harder for a rematch. Gibbons "has been paving the way for this scrap by laying a dozen good boys low." His recent impressive knockout of Willie Meehan had boosted him further. "Gibbons deserves a chance with the titleholder."[642]

It was confirmed that the fighters would be paid a guaranteed flat fee rather than percentage, with Dempsey receiving $300,000 and Carpentier $200,000, win or lose for both. Despite the fact that they would have to pay taxes, expenses, and their managers, both fighters would earn more from this fight than any boxer ever had earned for any contest.

Ray Pearson said Carpentier was "meeting the greatest fighter of all time." Georges might possibly have a slight shade on the champ in boxing ability, for he was faster on his feet than any man since Corbett. But when it came to hitting, there was no comparison. Dempsey hit harder; and with both hands. No fighter ever was more aggressive than him, and there was "nothing about Carpentier that indicates that he is built to stand punishment. … One smash on the head or jaw might send Georges down and out." He might be equal to Dempsey in generalship, but not better.[643]

---

[642] *New York Daily News, New York Tribune, New York Times, New York Herald, Brooklyn Daily Eagle, Buffalo Express, Buffalo Times, Brooklyn Citizen,* June 26, 1921.
[643] *New York Daily News,* June 26, 1921.

On June 26, in the morning, Dempsey ran 6 miles. In the afternoon, before a crowd of 2,500, Dempsey sparred 6 or 7 rounds with Eddie O'Hare, Baltimore wrestler-fighter 200-pound Herman Miller, Larry Williams, and Jack Renault, and he also wrestled with Bull Montana. Dempsey hit them hard and often, giving them a good pasting. Renault nearly collapsed from a hard stomach blow. Jack said, "My orders to them were to let loose with everything they had and not to spare me the slightest."

Objecting to his rough treatment of them, Dempsey's sparring mates threatened a strike unless Jack eased up. He even slammed Bull Montana on the chin with his bare hand during their wrestling match.

Dempsey was called a caveman who depended on superior strength, brawn, and ferocity to win. Carpentier was called a debonair gentleman, "the orchid of the ring," who depended on his intelligent ring craft, game plan, and speed to win.

Battling Nelson said Dempsey had improved since he won the championship. "Dempsey is more polished and better developed."

Kearns said Dempsey never was in better condition. "He is bigger and stronger than he was when he defeated Willard at Toledo and I am convinced that he is even a greater fighter."

One of Carpentier's sparring partners said, "Georges has shown me more ring tricks in three minutes than I have learned in five years."

Georges was receiving hundreds of letters daily from war veterans and other Americans wishing him well. "They want me to win."

A very confident Descamps told Rickard that after Carpentier beat Dempsey, they wanted a match with Tom Gibbons or Bill Brennan on Labor Day.

James J. Jeffries said, "Jack Dempsey has yet to prove that he is a real heavyweight champion." Those who figured he had a walkover with Carpentier "are crazy." Carpentier would be no cinch.

> Dempsey by no means has shown that he classed with such men as Corbett and Fitz. There are no men fighting today in a class with the heavyweights I have mentioned unless Dempsey can prove he is by decisively whipping the Frenchman. Carpentier is the first fast heavy man that Dempsey ever stacked up against. I would say that if Jack beats him, and beats him without any question of doubt, that he can take rank as a great heavyweight champion.

Jim Corbett believed that each man had the power to win by knockout with a single blow. Carpentier was faster, but Dempsey was more rugged, and had more power in his left than Georges.

A pastor who spoke out against the fight said it was typical of the brutality and greed of the times, two of the strongest factors that threw the world into the World War. "A prizefight eclipses even a great scandal in public interest." Folks preferred the manly art to every other matter of interest. Ten years ago, a woman at ringside was rare, but now, even some leading society women patronized boxing.

Tex Rickard posted a half million dollars with Robert Edgren, stakeholder for the fight. The fighters' money was guaranteed.[644]

Dempsey with Winifred Westover, movie star (above), who came to visit him, and "Mother" Lizzie Hutchinson, who cooked and kept house for the champ.

On June 27, in private, Dempsey worked for 55 minutes, with only 30 seconds rest between rounds, maintaining his speed at a terrific pace. He sparred 2 rounds each with O'Hare and Williams. Jack also took a 4-mile morning jaunt under the blistering-hot sun.

Carpentier sparred 6 rounds, 2 each with Buffalo light heavy Chris Arnold, Joe Jeannette, and 200-pound Harlem heavyweight Paul Samson Koerner. Georges said, "I could easily have gone another six rounds."

Speaking of Dempsey, Georges said, "He has never been really hurt. How do we know that he can take punishment when he has never been put to the test?" Carp said he hit hard and quickly, without exertion.

Robert Edgren believed that Dempsey's record outclassed anything Carpentier had done, with a majority of Jack's bouts against fairly good men. Even the best of them were stopped in a round or so. The strongest force he would contend against would not be Carpentier's fists, but the hostility of many at ringside. That hostility had reached him in letters, telegrams, and published criticism. Dempsey's only retort was, "I'll answer them in the 1st round."

Frank Menke said Dempsey's ring brains were underrated. He was the greatest natural fighter who ever lived, who fought with infallible instincts. "No warrior lived who ever has shown fistic braininess beyond the champion." As a young man, he fought men who were taller and heavier, with more experience and cleverness. One by one he battered them down en route to the championship.

Menke noted that Dempsey knew how to adapt and fight differently based on the opponent, using the method best suited to the particular contest. He did not panic, but fought to win and knock out his foe when the opportunity presented itself, in the manner most effective for the occasion. That showed his intelligence.

Instinct told him to attack Fulton like a whirlwind with a rushing attack, that Fulton was a slow starter. Against Willard, who expected him to rush, he started cautiously, moved about, lured him in, and then suddenly attacked. He wasn't quite himself against Brennan, who was a

[644] *New York Daily News, New York Tribune, Binghamton Press, Brooklyn Citizen, Trenton Evening Times, Buffalo Courier, Buffalo Times, Buffalo Enquirer,* June 27, 1921.

whole lot tougher than imagined, but he did not panic or begin a wild, furious attack, but instead beat him down gradually and methodically, as the occasion dictated. He worked the body in the clinches and softened him up. He was a winner.

Jim Jeffries recalled how the quick and clever Jim Corbett had him worried up until the 23rd round, many saying he was being outpointed. This was despite the fact that Jeffries was bigger and stronger, just like Dempsey. Carpentier was fast and clever as well, and he only had to keep Dempsey off for 12 rounds.

However, Jim Corbett had noted that he and Carpentier were different. Carpentier was not as big, tall, and long as he was, and Georges was less cautious and more aggressive than Corbett, though he hit harder.

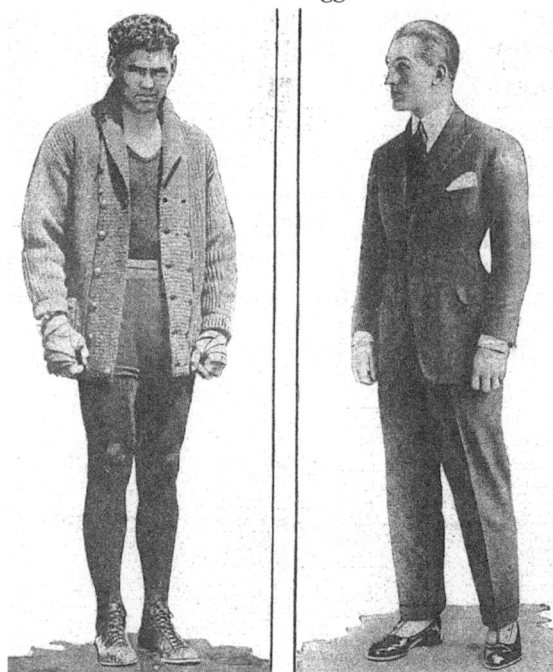

James Hopper said the soldier-hero's war record made him civilization's emissary. Many folks had secret preferences, even if illogical. To him, it was Carpentier who represented America, not Dempsey.

True, there was a certain unfairness and cruelty to the criticism of Dempsey. He was likeable and a hard worker. Yet, one U.S. Senator had called him a lazy bum. Some said he lacked courage, but that was silly.

Dempsey had not evaded the draft, but merely took advantage of some of the draft provisions. He had not committed a crime, but omission. "He lacked the vision which sent so many of the young men of his age to sacrifice." He had not been like Carpentier, who in 1914 volunteered without even being called to duty. Carp's commendations said, "Never returned without having accomplished his mission."

Dempsey said he wanted to enlist with the marines, but his unnamed manager (obviously Kearns) guilted him, telling him, "I've spent my time and my money on you and now I've given up all my business. And now, just as I'm getting a chance to get even, just as I stand to get back a little wad, you want to get out and leave me cold." Dempsey acknowledged, "That was true, what he said. He had spent money on me and kept me fed when I wasn't making much." The manager asked him to wait at least until he was called by the draft. "Well, I didn't go, and I've been sorry for it ever since." But he felt obligated out of loyalty to his friend and manager, who had risked all on him.

Although the writer was sympathetic to Dempsey's reasons, the fact remained that Dempsey did not fight, and Carpentier did, which was why the champ did not represent America. "For every Frenchman that fought, in fighting for France, was also fighting for America. Just as every American soldier that fought, in fighting for America, was also fighting for France." Carpentier represented civilization, but it was unclear what Dempsey represented.

Charles Mathison noted that reformers restricted their attack to title bouts only. Thousands of fights had been held under the law and thousands of dollars had gone into the state treasury, yet the International Reform Bureau never entered a protest or asked for an injunction before. "The bureau apparently holds the idea that all boxing contests are legal unless the opponents are title holders." Fortunately for the fight, the New Jersey officials, from the governor on down, seemed to be impervious to the publicity-seeking efforts. Eventually, three courts refused to enjoin the fight. Rickard said the troublemakers were done.

Still, such efforts were a nuisance which promoters had to deal with and endure. There always was fear and concern from Rickard when making any big fight that the politicians might buckle under to political pressure and prevent a fight. Hence, he always wanted political assurances beforehand, behind-the-scenes, prior to signing any big fight.

The Public Service Commission wanted to take no chances of a fire in the pine arena, and banned any potential combustibles. That included newspapers, which some used to shield themselves from the sun. No cigars or cigarettes either. No hot food, including hot dogs. Folks would have to rely on cold ham, cheese, or chicken sandwiches.

The artist Ripley warned Dempsey to be careful. He noted that when Georges was just a young middleweight, he fought the great Joe Jeannette 15 rounds and dropped him for a nine-count. Old Jim Flynn knocked out Dempsey in a round, although "Jack explains this as a joke." Willie Meehan handed Dempsey two defeats 3 to 4 years ago, and Jack didn't look so terrible then. He didn't look like a man-killer after the Brennan fight. Brennan found Dempsey easy to hit, and "Carpentier can hit!" Underdogs like Corbett, Fitzsimmons, Jeffries, Johnson, Willard, and Dempsey all had won the title despite the odds, so it was not out of the question for Carpentier to pull off an upset.[645]

[645] *New York Daily News, Brooklyn Citizen, Elmira Star-Gazette, New York Tribune, New York Evening World, Binghamton Press, Brooklyn Daily Eagle, Ithaca Journal, New York Herald,* June 28, 1921.

On June 28, 1921 in Philadelphia, a vehicle valued at $15,000 belonging to Jack Dempsey was seized outside a hotel to satisfy a judgment obtained against him by Dr. Herbert Goddard for an unpaid $500 balance for Dempsey's nose operation. The fighter had paid one-half, declaring that to be sufficient, but the doctor sued and won a judgment. James Dougherty, the champ's friend, had driven the car there on an errand for the champion.[646]

Dempsey strenuously denied rumors that he had split with manager Kearns. He said there was no truth to it, for they never had been on the outs. However, there were reports that Kearns had left the camp, that Dempsey had been ignoring him, and that quarrels had resulted in a wide breach between them. "Not a word of truth in it. Not one word." "There hasn't been any row between Kearns and myself, and what is more there is not likely to be any."

Jack said he was ready. He did not care what Carpentier did. He just would go in there and bang away.

Dempsey denied false rumors swirling around that he was going to lay down to Carpentier and was betting on Georges to win. Any reporter who printed such falsehoods would not be allowed in any of his camps. "Not as long as there is one ounce of energy within my body will I surrender the heavyweight championship of the world. I wouldn't sell out for all the money that exists today. I treasure my title more than anything in life."

On the 28th, four days before the fight, Dempsey sparred only 1 round each with Eddie O'Hare and Larry Williams. It was a short day.

Jack said, "I'll be glad to have this thing over with. You have no idea of the hardships of a long training grind. It is terrible. If I was offered $500,000 for a fight a month from now I would not go through all this again. I am tired of training. I want to take a rest." After the fight, he planned to go home to Salt Lake City, and then west for a vacation.

On the day before the fight, Jack would abstain from eating certain foods and only drink water. He weighed 193 pounds.

Grantland Rice said Dempsey lacked the sprightliness of Toledo two years ago. He still was a relentless, destructive engine, but his Maumee Bay boyishness and buoyancy had been crushed by worry and time. He no longer was carefree. He had only a bare nod for Harry Greb. His expression was that of a half frown. Dempsey had discovered that being champion was no dream life. He endured a multitude of people turned against him, an ever-extended reach for his waning bank roll, and knowledge that it was much more fun climbing to the top than holding on after arriving.

Dempsey still had jolting power, but it was more like a jolting prod than a whip-like flash that traveled faster than the eye could follow. He did not have the same muscular freedom and suppleness, a condition which he showed against Brennan, although he still was quick enough at hitting to reach any man in the ring, and the old thud still was there. "He

---

[646] *Evening World*, June 28, 1921.

may not hit Carpentier as quickly and as easily as he would have hit him two years ago, but he is fast enough to hit him, and when he does, something is bound to bend, if not to break." There had been a slight falling off in the snap of his punches, but the crushing effect remained. Rice predicted a Dempsey victory in 4 to 6 rounds.

Fred Hawthorne claimed that a reliable source told him that Tom Gibbons had sparred Carpentier in secret on the 25th and 26th, and their sparring had all the trimmings of a genuine fight.

However, Robert Edgren said stories of Carpentier sparring Gibbons were false. Georges was sparring with Jeannette, a Harlem heavy named Samson, and his French mates. "He has done little hard hitting. Both men have taped their hands carefully this week and have avoided all chance of injury. Dempsey's cut eyebrow has healed entirely, only a narrow white scar showing the location of the injury." Carp had a slightly bruised eye a few days ago, but was all right again.

Gibbons' manager Eddie Kane subsequently emphatically denied that Gibbons had boxed Carpentier.

Jack Johnson was denied parole to see the fight. Efforts to obtain a pardon for him were thwarted as well. His full prison term did not expire until July 9, 1921, when the 43-year-old would be released.

Jim Corbett told Tad Dorgan that a lawyer could take either side of the fight question and convince you to bet on it. The pro-Dempsey argument was that Carpentier was too small, couldn't beat top American middleweights like Dixie Kid, Frank Klaus, and Billy Papke, and Dempsey was a terrific hitter and a bulldog in the ring.

The pro-Carpentier advocates said no man could stand up to Carpentier's right to the chin, for he proved he could hit and hurt anyone. Dempsey, who lost to Meehan, whom Gibbons knocked out in 1 round, was hittable, for even sparring partners hit Jack on the chin repeatedly, and Carpentier would land at least once, which was all he needed.

A poll of fighters, managers, and promoters had it 23 for Jack and 6 for Georges, while the fans and general public were in doubt.

FAC-SIMILE OF GENUINE TICKET

Special trains would take New Yorkers to the fight grounds.

New Jersey Governor Edward Edwards' brothers had built the stadium at a cost of $250,000. That's business and politics for you. Grading cost $40,000. Two million feet of lumber, enough to fill 133 freight cars, had cost $95,000. Grading began April 27, carpentry work began May 11, and was finished by June 25.

35 tons of nails had been used. The supporting posts were cross-braced. The arena had a carrying capacity of 1,000 pounds per square foot. A 12-foot-high fence surrounded the arena, with strands of barbed wire at the top.

The arena was inclined, to give everyone a good view. The first 100 feet had an upward pitch of 12 inches to every 10 feet, the second hundred feet was 20 inches to every 10 feet, and for the last 100 feet, the pitch was 24 inches to every 10 feet.

The octagonal arena's diameter was 600 feet. The first row was 2 feet from the edge of the ring. The last row was 288 feet from the ring, and was 34 feet above the ground. Standing up in the last row, one would be 1.5 city blocks from the ring. The arena's circumference was 2,016 feet, each section being 252 feet wide at the outer edge. It was nearly half a mile around it.

Ringside and box seats would be folding chairs with backs. All others, including those costing $40 or less, would be of the circus seat type – planks two inches thick and 9.5 inches across. Each seating space was 16.5 inches wide.

There were 7,500 ringside and box seats. There were two rows of boxes, each containing six chairs, 256 boxes in all. The boxes were at the outer edge of the ringside seats, just in front of the $40 seats. The rear railing of the boxes was 130 feet from the ring.

There were 18 entrances and two additional emergency exits. Four of the entrances were for ringside ticket holders.

8 concession booths would be available. 75,000 bottles of pop would be ready. A railroad yard had been set aside for parking Pullman cars, so special train parties would not require hotel accommodation. 1,200 police would be at the arena, 600 inside. Several hundred firemen would be on duty. More than 250 detectives from other cities and 100 Jersey City detectives would deal with pickpockets and anyone who attempted to pass fraudulent tickets or gain illegal entry.

Safety precautions had been taken. A high-pressure water main and a mile of pipe had been laid, with 17 fire plugs inside the arena. The flooring would be doused with water as a precaution against fire.

Also on June 28, 1921, at the Pioneer Club in New York, 186-pound Gene Tunney of Greenwich Village, A.E.F. light heavyweight champion, knocked out 175-pound Johnny Ambrose of Brooklyn after 2 minutes 45 seconds of the 1st round of a scheduled 12. Tunney used a strong left jab with good effect, and shifted to the body. A left hook to the body and right to the jaw finished him. It was Gene's first fight in seven months, after suffering a broken hand in his last bout against Leo Houck. Tunney was scheduled to fight on the undercard of the big fight just four days later.[647]

[647] *Olean Times Herald, Brooklyn Citizen, New York Tribune, Buffalo Enquirer, New York Daily News, Buffalo Times, Buffalo Courier, New York Evening World,* June 29, 1921.

On June 29, three days before the fight, wearing a head gear and gauze padding over his eye, Dempsey sparred 3 rounds with Larry Williams. "His speed in footwork and cleverness in blocking convinced the experts that Carpentier will not have an easy task hitting him."

Dempsey said he could not understand why the fans booed him. "Why do they do that to me? I've always done my best, and I've made good." He noted that his people were among the earliest settlers in Virginia, and he even had Indian blood in his veins, making him more American than most. "Well, I know a lot of my friends are with me, and I'm not going to worry about the rest."

On the 29th, Carpentier did a 45-minute workout. He boxed four different sparring partners 1 round each.

On the 30th, Georges said, "I received 45 telegrams yesterday from different American Legion posts wishing me good luck and success. The total from these posts is about 500."

Walter Kelly said Dempsey was too fast, powerful, and hard to hit, and would win inside of 3 rounds. He loved to fight, and would not be affected by the fact that 200 million people around the world would be on the wires following the fight's progress and awaiting its result.

Jack Dillon said Dempsey would win in 5 rounds if he could get to Carpentier. If Georges could stay away for 5 rounds, he could make Dempsey lick himself by getting tired by chasing, throwing, and missing, and then Carpentier would have a good chance to win. "I have my doubts, however, that the challenger has speed enough to keep the champion off him in a small ring."

The champion's brothers made their predictions. Johnny Dempsey said 5 rounds, Bernie said 3, and Bill Timmons, Jack's brother-in-law, said the fight would last from 1 to 6 rounds. Naturally, all picked Jack to win.

Carpentier's sparring partners all said Dempsey would not hit Georges, who would outbox him, and eventually his paralyzing right would stop him.

Carpentier told Jim Corbett that the Brennan fight increased his confidence. Georges said, "I look on the Brennan fight with very much satisfaction. It proved some things to me. ... Dempsey can be hit, and by a boxer who is comparatively slow. If Brennan could hit the champion, why not I? And I believe if I can hit him he will go down." Carpentier said the reports that Dempsey was not in shape for the Brennan fight were false. If he was not in good condition, he could not have taken quite a beating from Brennan in the first 6 rounds and then come back in the final rounds to knock out his man. "I'm quite sure he was not as bad off as has been claimed." He also noted that Gibbons, who was about his size, had knocked out Meehan, something Dempsey failed to do. "Now then, is this fellow such a man-killer after all?" If Carpentier won, he gladly would give Gibbons a fight on Labor Day.

Predicting a Dempsey victory in 5 rounds, Jack Veiock said Dempsey was a terrific punisher who carried concentrated dynamite in either hand. The clever Carpentier would be hard-pressed. Dempsey might not be as fast on his feet as the Frenchman, but he was the "wickedest two-handed fighter in modern heavyweight history and his cyclonic attack is a great defense in itself." Dempsey was no freight train in speed, and his offense counterbalanced any advantages Carpentier might have in cleverness. Jack had an uncanny way of moving his head or moving aside and not getting hit in vital spots. Carpentier had impressive victories, but top American heavies, including Gibbons, could beat Beckett, Wells, and Levinsky to a frazzle as well.

Dempsey's auto was released. His attorney posted bond appealing for a new trial on the suit decided against the pugilist. Dempsey said it wasn't the money, but the point, for he felt that he had been overcharged.

The New Jersey Commission preferred 8-ounce gloves to 6-ounce gloves, so that was what would be used. New Jersey rules required a ring of not less than 18 nor more than 22 feet on each side.

Descamps planned to examine Dempsey's bandages, "because he has heard the charge made by Willard at Toledo regarding the unnatural hardness of Dempsey's bandages." Willard claimed that Jimmy De Forest used powdered plaster of Paris or tinfoil between the strips of adhesive tape that bound Jack's bandages. De Forest denied that there was anything wrong with the bandages.

Celebrities from all over the world planned to attend the fight, including Theodore Roosevelt, Jr., Kermit Roosevelt, Governor Edwards, Attorney General Daugherty, J. P. Morgan, Henry Ford, Harry Whitney, Harry Guggenheim, Percy Rockefeller, Vincent Astor, and Russel Colt.[648]

Over 700 newspaper men, authors, and novelists would tell the world about the big fight with the aid of 200 telegraph wires at ringside. 500 million people all over the world were looking forward to the results.[649]

[648] *New York Daily News, Brooklyn Standard Union, Buffalo Times, New York Tribune, Buffalo Courier, Buffalo Enquirer, New York Evening World, Yonkers Herald, Glens Falls Post-Star, New York Herald*, June 30, 1921.
[649] *New Brunswick Daily Home News*, July 1, 1921.

On the 30th, when asked how long he would let Carp last, Dempsey replied, "Wait for 48 hours more and I'll tell you. I'll be an expert on the fight then myself. See all these guys sitting up here? They think they are experts." Jack frequently smiled, laughed, and slapped with a friendly whack on the back anyone who happened to be sitting next to him.

Dempsey said he was in better shape for this fight than he was for the Willard fight. He was confident that he would win by knockout, but could not say how long it would take. He wanted to win by knockout or lose by knockout.

He heard different theories regarding how Carp would fight. "I'm not worrying so much about what Georges Carpentier is going to do. What concerns me mostly is what I'm going to do."

William Brady said Carpentier was the fastest, brainiest, trickiest, hardest-hitting boxer Dempsey ever met. Dempsey faced the fight of his life. At 3 or 4 to 1 odds, Brady was wagering on Carpentier, even though he had bet on Dempsey to beat Willard within 4 rounds.

Brady said Carpentier decked Gunboat Smith in the early rounds. Later, Carpentier slipped, and was not knocked down. Smith deliberately struck him while he was down on his knees, and was disqualified.

Carp could change his style from moment to moment. "He is as quick on his feet as Jim Corbett ever was and hits a ton harder." He wasn't slow-moving or slow-thinking like Fulton, Willard, or Morris. Carp was far better than Brennan, "and if he hits Dempsey as easily as Brennan did it will be all over but the shouting." Dempsey was in shape for the Brennan fight, for it lasted 12 rounds and he won by a knockout. Dempsey simply was easy to hit. Even Willard proved that, landing on him often in the 2nd and 3rd rounds of their fight, notwithstanding the beating that Jess took in the 1st round. Miske twice had gone the distance with Jack and held his own. Their recent bout "should not be counted, as Miske had been in a hospital nearly a year." Meehan had decisioned him. Jack was not invincible. Hence, Dempsey would have to prove himself further for Brady to be convinced about him. His glory was from beating big men who hardly could get out of the way. A smaller, craftier, quicker man like Carpentier was much harder to hit.

Brady believed that Carpentier was very confident, and had the psychological edge. When the articles of agreement were signed in Brady's office, Carp insisted on Dempsey signing personally, as opposed to just Kearns. He waited for Dempsey to arrive. When he did, Carp sprang to his feet, looked over Dempsey, and even felt his muscles all over his body, laughed, and said "magnifique," "tremendous," "superb," "wonderful," "Mons. Jacque." Dempsey stood speechless at the impudence, and said nothing. The next day, they played 18 holes of golf.

Ultimately, Brady was not predicting a Dempsey loss, but he liked the odds, and felt that if a knockout came in the early rounds, Carpentier would be the one to score it, and if it came down to endurance and ability to take a beating, Dempsey would win.

Len Wooster said Carpentier had a royal chance, for he was cool, skillful, and resourceful. Both were wallopers and fast on their feet. Carpentier was more scientific though, a better ring general, and a quicker thinker. Carp had prepared himself for Dempsey's hooking style. Dempsey could be hit. "It ought to be even money and take your pick."

One reported that the odds had shifted to 2 to 1. Hence, Carpentier money was coming in. Some reported that bets were scarce, for too many folks were uncertain.

Edgren said the age of the 24-foot ring had been dying out. New Jersey called for a ring of 18 to 20 feet, and the 18-foot ring was what Rickard always used. Once Carpentier saw the ring, he withdrew any objection to its size.

Although fighters were used to 5- and 6-ounce gloves, Edgren believed that a few more ounces (8 ounces required by New Jersey rules) would not have a significant impact, and a knockout was just as likely. Some felt that a boxer could punch even harder with the greater hand protection. There might be less danger of a cut or bruise with 8-ounce gloves. Both fighters preferred smaller gloves, but had to bow to the commission's decision.

Edgren said some of the many rumors in circulation were funny. One was that Jimmy De Forest, who trained Dempsey for Willard, said that Jack had an iron bar in each glove. What he actually said was that Dempsey's hands were like iron, pickled by rubbing with brine. He didn't have any iron bars.

> As for the 'iron bar' stuff, both Dempsey and Willard entered the ring with hands soft-taped, and tape and gloves were carefully inspected by the referee, who inspected and supervised the putting on of the gloves, assisted in each case by men from the opposite corner. The only thing in Dempsey's gloves was a set of big, hard knuckles. Small-time boxers sometimes try to push the padding back from the knuckles, but every first-class boxer knows this is likely to cause a broken hand, and that a more effective blow can be struck with the padded knucks than with a bare fist.

Edgren said betting was light. The public liked Carpentier, but the probabilities favored Dempsey. His long list of 1st round knockouts was imposing. The English heavyweights whom Carpentier had beaten also had been beaten by Americans, like Frank Moran, "who is so far from being in Dempsey's class that a Dempsey-Moran match would be laughed at in this country."

Edgren believed, however, that although Dempsey was bigger than he was at Toledo, "he is undeniably slower." He was better when he had ring engagements nearly every week, plain food, much hard work, and little luxury. He had two years of soft living, punctuated only by two bouts. "Still, Dempsey is a great fighter, and as for soft living, I haven't seen Georges Carpentier doing much work with a pick and shovel either."

Disabled veterans hissed Dempsey's name, and various American Legions telegraphed good luck and well wishes to Carpentier, their comrade in arms.

One man wrote in Dempsey's defense, "Jack Dempsey is an American to the core, and we are proud to have him our champion. … and yet some people are unwilling to allow him to wear the flag of his country in the ring. He was entirely acquitted of the charge of 'slacker,' even though it takes and is taking a lot of prejudiced people some time to assimilate the fact."

Jack McAuliffe, who had known him at Toledo, boxed with him for Brennan, and spent 10 days with him in Atlantic City, said Dempsey was not worrying at all. If he was hissed or booed, it would not affect him. Inside the ropes, Jack turned into a savage.

Henry Farrell predicted Carpentier would be finished within 5 rounds, as soon as Dempsey hit him with his left. Still, Carp's stock had jumped in the last two days, owing to some tales of worry and anxiety that Dempsey was going through, which might have been due to false rumors which were designed to affect the odds.

Dempsey's mother said,

> I know Jack is in good training, as he keeps in touch with me and he has taken good care of himself and hasn't wasted his strength. I am not going to watch the returns from the fight. It would make me nervous. I am going to spend Saturday working and I know that Jack will let me know the result as soon as the fight is over. He always does.
>
> He always has been a wonderful son to me. He built me a wonderful home, but goodness gracious it was so big I didn't know what to do in it, so I moved back into the old home in a few weeks.
>
> I am proud of Jack. As a boy he was always dutiful and I never had to punish him.
>
> He always loved to box and I believe in a man doing the things he loves best and can do best.

Ed Smith of the *Chicago American* said if Carpentier could get out of the 1st round he had a good chance to win, and if it went into the 3rd round, "Carpentier is almost sure to win the title."

The Chief of Police said no airplanes would be allowed to fly over the arena while the big fight was in progress.

Nearly 1,000 policemen and firemen went through final drills for the handling of the patrons and fans.

On July 1, the *Brooklyn Daily Times* said, "From the sporting point of view, no greater event has taken place in the United States in decades …." Not since the days of Charlie Mitchell had there been such a serious European contender.

Several agencies would attempt to be the first to deliver the fight films to Europe. They would fly the films to ships that already had left, heading to Europe, drop off the films on the boats, and then fly back.

Every room in every hotel within a 50-mile radius was jammed-packed and full, sold out. Some even had to use army cots. Folks were in town from all over the country and world, including as far away as Japan, Australia, France, England, Spain, and South America.[650]

Dempsey said he had trained faithfully, and if he lost, would have no excuses. He planned to keep the championship in America, where it belonged.[651]

The evening before the fight, Dempsey had steak for dinner. At 9:10 p.m., he went to the arena to inspect the conglomerated mass of white pine boards. At 10:10 p.m., he returned to where he was staying temporarily, at the home of General William C. Heppenheimer, about 1.5 miles from the arena. Jack went to sleep at 10:35 p.m.

Fight predictions included:

Bill Brennan: "As soon as Jack reaches his body it will be over. 3 or 4 rounds is the most the Frenchman can last." "I ought to know."

Johnny Buff, American fly champ: Dempsey in less than 6.

Martin Burke: "Carpentier may be the fastest boxer in the world, but he will need to be, for just as soon as Jack gets to him with one of his healthy wallops it will be all over."

James J. Corbett: Dempsey by knockout, for he is as strong as a bull and as quick as a cat. A good big man beats a good little man. Still, Carp's speed might win the day.

Johnny Coulon, former bantam champ: "It's a toss-up." vs. "Both men are great fighters. Jack Dempsey is the bigger and heavier, and will win."

Jack Curley: Carpentier will win, for he hits just as hard and has the speed and skill. The longer it goes the better it will be for him.

Robert H. Davis: Carpentier will win, for he is the "most perfect fighting machine that has ever been seen in this country."

Floyd Fitzsimmons: Dempsey in 4.

Mike Gibbons: Carpentier has a good chance. Dempsey is not hard to hit.

Jack Gleason, former promoter: Dempsey in 4, for the Frenchman is not strong enough to keep Jack away from him.

Percy Hammond: "Hurl but a stone, and the giant dies."

Joe Jeannette: Carpentier's terrible right will win it for him, for it can deck any man. "Carpentier looks open but is hard to hit."

[650] *New York Herald, New York Tribune, Brooklyn Standard Union, Buffalo Enquirer, Brooklyn Daily Times, Buffalo Times, New York Daily News, New York Evening World, Yonkers Herald,* July 1, 1921.
[651] *New York Daily News,* July 2, 1921.

Jack Johnson: Dempsey between rounds 8 and 10. "He is much stronger and a faster puncher."

Johnny Kilbane: The Frenchman is in prime physical condition, but not big enough to withstand Dempsey's ferocious attacks.

Frank Klaus: "Dempsey should win with a K.O. in four or five rounds. Carpentier will be too busy dodging the champion's shifty wallops to set himself for a dangerous punch. He has improved his defense since I fought him, but isn't rugged enough to take Jack's body punches."

Benny Leonard: Dempsey by the end of the 4th round.

Battling Levinsky: "Carpentier is the harder hitter, and he is harder to hit. If he fights a waiting game he will have better than an even chance."

Joe Lynch, world bantam champ: Dempsey by knockout in 6 or 7. Carpentier will not be able to elude the body blows and will be cracked in two by those that land.

Charles Mathison: Dempsey is larger, speedier, and carries the more crushing wallop.

Willie Meehan: "Jack will break the Frenchman in half before the fight has gone 2 rounds."

Harry Newman: If Carp misses his right, Jack will drive a hole clear through his body. Dempsey within 4 rounds.

Philadelphia Jack O'Brien: Dempsey will have to be at his best to keep his crown, for Carpentier is like a shadow and carries a knockout blow; the best man Dempsey ever has met.

Tom O'Rourke: Carpentier is fast, dead game, and can hit. "Jack will have to watch his guard, because if he gives Georges an opening, he will feel it." If Dempsey does not end it in the 1st round, it will be a great battle. "Dempsey should win if he does not elect to box the Frenchman. In my opinion Carpentier will not answer the bell for the 5th round."

Billy Papke: "Nothing to it. Dempsey will win as soon as he lands a hard one …. I hit Carpentier whenever I wanted to, and I wasn't any Dempsey."

Jack Reddy, Miske's manager: Dempsey within 6 rounds. "Carpentier is clever and one of the fastest men I have seen, but Jack also is fast and carries a wallop that will wear the Frenchman down."

Willie Ritchie, former lightweight champ: Carpentier has a chance, for he is faster than Brennan, who gave Dempsey troubles. "Carpentier will give Dempsey a hard fight, but nine times out of ten you win when you pick the American."

Billy Roche: Carpentier is large enough and fast enough to win. Dempsey is not the man he was at Toledo.

Babe Ruth: Dempsey, because the big wallop wins in every sport.

Tommy Ryan: "The Frenchman has more experience, is a better boxer, has a better head, can hit just as hard, is faster, and has all the stuff of the best old timers." Dempsey could beat the big men like Willard, but a man like Carpentier would trim him and surprise the world.

Tom Sharkey: "Nothing to it but Dempsey. He's got a good old Irish name and he fights like I used to. He'll put the Frenchie out in a punch."

George Bernard Shaw: Carpentier should be the heavy favorite, and will knock out Dempsey.

James Sinnott: "I cannot conceive of Carpentier eluding the relentless, tireless, hard punching champion for very long."

Midget Smith, bantam: Dempsey in 7.

Philadelphia lightweight Lew Tendler: "If Carpentier lasts beyond the 3rd round I'll be the most surprised man in the arena."

Dominick Tortorich, promoter: Dempsey in 10. Carpentier is underrated.

Bombardier Wells: "I think the winner will be the one who gets in the first effective punch. I favor Dempsey…within seven rounds."

George Underwood: Carp might last the full 12 rounds if he fights at long range.

Freddy Welsh, former lightweight champ: Dempsey, for he is too strong, but only after the hardest bout of his career.

Johnny Wilson, middleweight champ: Dempsey inside of 4 rounds.

Tom Gibbons and Fred Fulton both picked Dempsey to beat Carpentier in short order.

The day of the fight, Tad Dorgan picked Dempsey to win by knockout before the 6th round. Dempsey was a good boxer, could take a punch and give a punch, and was in excellent shape. He had beaten top heavyweights and practically cleaned out the division. People called his foes second raters *after* he knocked them out, but that wasn't what was said before the contests. He tore in and had no fear of what the other fellow had to offer. Carpentier never had seen anything like him. Jeannette fought Carp, but was not as aggressive or as powerful as Dempsey. Dempsey was the most aggressive man since John L. Sullivan; a snarling bulldog. Carpentier "will have to be the most wonderful boxer that ever laced a pair of shoes if he wins today, because he is meeting one of the most wonderful heavies we've ever seen." Tad said it would be a miracle if Carpentier won.[652]

Tex Rickard said the fight already was the most successful that he ever promoted, in every respect. It was the largest arena ever built for a boxing contest. The advance seat sale was the largest paid attendance ever, a new record.

652 *Hackensack Record*, July 2, 1921.

The bout itself has created greater interest, both national and international, than any other ring contest at any weight. After the promotion of the Johnson-Jeffries match at Reno in 1910 I thought that no future bout could equal that battle in general interest, but a short span of eleven years has produced another heavyweight title bout greater in every respect.

Tex had received a greater number of applications for press seats than ever before, and virtually every country in the world would be represented in one manner or another at ringside. Aside from the usual and trifling annoyances attendant to a promotion of such magnitude, everything had moved smoothly. Both managers had been easy and reasonable to deal with from a business standpoint. He hoped the bout would prove interesting to watch, a benefit to the sport, and without unpleasant aftermath.

Dempsey said,

> I am in the best shape of my career. ... I expect to win, and win as quickly as possible. ... But regardless of how long the fight goes, the public can depend upon me to do my level best every second of the way. I am proud to represent America against the European challenger, and this pride will cause me to make what I feel will be the greatest fight of my life.

> I never was more anxious to win a fight than this one. Of course, I know that Carpentier is a great hitter, but I feel confident that I will be able to successfully defend my title. ... I put in ten weeks of work – six weeks of real hard training. I am ready.

Dempsey also said, "I hope to send Georges along on the roughest journey he ever traveled in a ring. I am not going in there with the idea that I am going to have an easy time."

Jack Kearns said,

> We expect to win over Georges Carpentier in 3 or 4 rounds. I will not be surprised if Dempsey stops him in the 1st round. This, of course, depends upon the style adopted by Carpentier.

> The Dempsey who will defend his title as world's champion is the fastest, hardest-hitting, gamest heavyweight who ever stepped inside of a ring. After the fight is over I think everyone who saw it will agree with me.

> Dempsey is in better condition than he has ever been. ... I never felt more confident of winning a fight. ... The champion is bigger and stronger and even a greater fighter than when he defeated Willard two years ago.

Carpentier said, "When I go into the ring against Jack Dempsey I will be prepared to make the supreme effort of my fighting career." "I am confident and ready."

Trainer Gus Wilson said Carp would bring his 14 years of experience to bear. If Dempsey beat him, he could claim to be a real champion, for "Georges Carpentier is a great fighter, and to beat him will indeed be an accomplishment. We have no excuses to make, and we believe victory will be ours."

Francois Descamps/Deschamps was confident that Carpentier would win inside of 5 rounds. Georges was in the best condition of his life. He was ready for anything, and supremely confident.[653]

The weather forecast was for the thermometer to reach 80 to 85 degrees Fahrenheit for the fight. Though it might be cloudy, rain was not forecasted.

Lawson Robertson did not believe Carp could withstand Dempsey's sledgehammer punches. "Jack has tremendous power in his blows. I cannot see how Carpentier is going to ward them off long. While Dempsey lacks the litheness and speed that were so noticeable when he broke through Willard, he still possesses his driving power." He hit so hard that even Willard's arms were a mess of bruises. Carp, much lighter, would need to depend on speed rather than blocking, but his speed, agility, and craftiness would not be enough in an 18-foot ring against a man who packed such stunning blows. Even if Carpentier landed his vaunted punch, "Dempsey is a horse for punishment. It seems to me as if a pile driver would be necessary to put him to sleep." Dempsey was an unstoppable relentless force, and although not quite as fast as he once was, it would not matter.

Charles Mathison said, "Dempsey is the personification of rugged, powerful manhood, coupled with agility, combativeness and a forcefulness of attack seldom combined in any other heavyweight boxer, past or present." His "catapultic attack" had swept everyone off their feet, usually to speedy defeat. His victims had crumpled under his crushing blows. It would be fatal to risk a mix-up with him. Dempsey hit with such pile-driving force and attacked so tornadically that it would require the speed of a flash of lightning to avoid being hit. Hence, the smartest plan would be for Carp to stay away and try to tire him. That was his only hope, and it was a remote one. "Dempsey has disposed of nearly every heavyweight in America in quick time, the only exceptions being Wills, the negro, and the rotund Meehan. There is not a shadow of doubt that Dempsey as he stands to-day could make short work of either."

Mathison concluded that with the addition of confidence and experience, Dempsey was a better man than at Toledo. Carp might avoid danger with his feet for a while, but whenever he got aggressive, he would be met with a counter-attack that would spell defeat.[654]

The last effort of reformers to stop the fight had failed. A Hudson County Grand Jury in Jersey City declined to return indictments against the promoters, managers, or fighters.[655]

[653] *New York Tribune*, July 2, 1921.
[654] *New York Herald*, *New York Daily News*, July 2, 1921.
[655] *New York Daily News*, July 2, 1921.

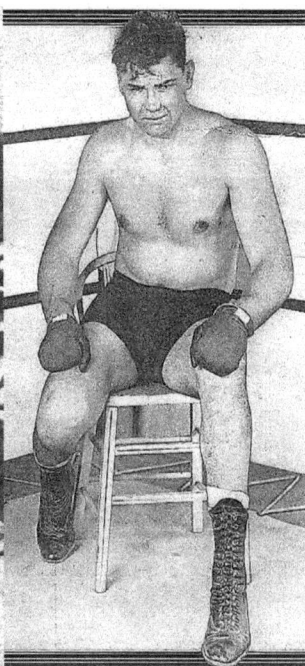

6'1"—HEIGHT—5'11½"
192—WEIGHT—173·
74"—REACH—73"
16½"—NECK—16¾"
16¼"—BICEPS
14¼"—FOREARM
9¼"—WRIST

CHEST
42"—NORMAL—41"
46"—EXPANDED—43¼"

BICEPS—14½"
FOREARM—14½"
WRIST—7¼"

32"—WAIST—31"

22"—THIGH—25"

15¼"—CALF—16¾"

9"—ANKLE—8½"

JACK DEMPSEY, AGE 26 YEARS   CARPENTIER, AGE 27 YEARS

CHAPTER 10

The Battle of the Century

On Saturday July 2, 1921 at Boyles' Thirty Acres in Jersey City, New Jersey, 26-year-old Jack Dempsey defended his world heavyweight championship for the third time, against 27-year-old French and European heavyweight champion and world light heavyweight champion Georges Carpentier.[656]

At the Jersey City home of millionaire bank president and sportsman William C. Heppenheimer, where he spent the previous night, Dempsey awoke at 6:00 a.m. He bathed and got rubbed down. At 6:40 a.m., for breakfast, he had two boiled eggs, toast, and a pot of tea.

Jack said, "Never felt better in my life." He tried to go for a walk with trainer Teddy Hayes, but a large crowd of hero worshippers congregated, which forced him to return to the house.

Kearns said Dempsey was the greatest defensive fighter because he was so offensive. He could box if he wanted. He was full of movement, even when aggressive, always ducking and wiggling around, making him hard to hit cleanly. He could make featherweights miss.

Carpentier woke up at 6:30 a.m., full of pep and in high spirits. He took a shower, dressed, and had breakfast at 7 a.m. At 8:30 a.m., Carp took a walk. He said, "I never felt better in my life. … I had eight hours solid sleep last night." "I will win. My right hand will make me champion of the world."

Carp planned to leave Manhasset at 11 a.m. by yacht, and after arriving at Jersey City, would remain on the yacht until 2:30 p.m., the time that Rickard expected him to appear in the arena.

---

[656] The following fight descriptions and analysis are an amalgamation of: *Ithaca Journal-News, Buffalo Evening News, Binghamton Press, New York World, Olean Times Herald, Brooklyn Standard Union, Passaic Herald-News,* July 2, 1921; *New York Daily News, Brooklyn Daily Eagle, Buffalo Times, Buffalo Courier, New York Daily Tribune, Brooklyn Standard Union, New York Times, Buffalo Illustrated Express, Chicago Tribune, Boston Post, Buffalo Enquirer, St. Louis Globe-Democrat,* July 3, 1921; *Buffalo Times,* July 5, 1921.

Many fans spent the night outdoors outside the arena, wanting to get in first to obtain choice vantage points in the stands. One man who was first in line for the $5.50 seats arrived at 8 p.m. the prior evening.

The only bit of color to relieve the monotony of the dull, rain-soaked brown arena were American and French flags over the entrances and hanging all around the arena, dropping down and remaining still from lack of a breeze.

At 8:15 a.m., there were about 10,000 people already wanting to enter. Cars rapidly were filling up parking spaces a mile away from the arena.

There were leaden gray skies, though the threatening weather did not keep any fight fans away. A light, misty rain fell at 9 a.m., but ceased by 9:25 a.m.

The arena gates were opened at 9:45 a.m. The gallery gods entered first, having camped out all night for the privilege of paying $5.50 for the worst seats. One carried a telescope under his arm. The fans kept coming right up until the hour set for the big battle.

It was a huge saucer of yellow pine. It filled up from the brim down.

It was advertised as "the battle of the century."

There was constant threat of rain, as there were clouds covering the sun. Neither the sun nor the rain came, but it still was hot.

Telegraph instruments were set up around the ring.

Hundreds of ushers in red caps, and food vendors in white coats, bustled busily.

Buses charged $2 to transport passengers to the arena gates. Taxicabs charged $5.

Some were arrested for having snuck in without tickets. Several folks tried to enter the arena by claiming that they were Tex Rickard.

From ringside, Jim Corbett wrote that "of all the battles I have seen, I was never more uncertain of what to expect."

Towering more than 50 feet away and 20 feet above the ring was a steel framed crow's nest platform for motion picture operators. The stand was held up by a slim steel girder that appeared not to hinder the views.

Two airplanes appeared shortly before 10 a.m., circling the arena like buzzards at a good altitude, but did not pass directly over the stadium. They eventually turned back toward New York.

At 10:45 a.m., Tex Rickard appeared at ringside. "The weather is just what I wanted. The crowd is coming fine. I think I'll have a million and a half house." Tex said the main-event would start at 3 p.m., rain or shine.

The ring was snow white. The ring ropes were bound with white flannel tape. The canvas covering was pulled taut. New Jersey boxing officials felt the padding under the canvas, tugged at the ropes, and looked over the tape wrapped around the boundaries of the 18-foot ring.

At about 11:15 a.m., Jack's older brother John Dempsey was at ringside. "Everything's fine. Are we going to win? You know it."

Although there were clouds, the temperature continued rising, and fans shed their coats.

There were myriads of refreshment stands scattered about the arena disbursing soft drinks and food. Hawkers sold peanuts, buttons, opera glasses, and sandwiches. Vendors sold bottled drinks, sandwiches, and field glasses at $2 apiece. Raincoats sold for $1 each, for darkened clouds threatened rain.

More than 1,000 policemen were on hand.

Officials announced that more than 2.5 million words descriptive of Jack Dempsey's training campaign had been sent out of Atlantic City over the wires of the Western Union and Postal Telegraph companies. Nearly 3 million words had been sent by mail.

To help fans pass the time during the long wait, a brass band played.

With the fight only three hours away, Jack had steak, potatoes, string beans, and toast, with tea. The servant who waited on him said, "He's got a good appetite for a supposedly nervous man." Jack played pool with Atlantic City Mayor Ed Bader. Jersey City Mayor Frank Hague came to pay his respects as well.

Barry Faris, International News Service Staff Correspondent, said that from a spectacular standpoint, it was the greatest fight ever fought. The sight around ringside was one never to be forgotten. Millionaires and perhaps even some billionaires rubbed elbows with those who were willing to spend $50 for a ringside seat. All kinds of people from all walks of life were there: society women, shop girls, merchant princes, and clerks. Many had sunglasses and pillows. Women were scattered here and there throughout the crowd. The crowd was amazingly orderly.

Neal O'Hara said, "Artistically, socially and otherwise this match was one tremendous human spectacle. ... Everyone seemed to be there, from every pathway of endeavor." The rich and the poor were jumbled together; 90,000 people in an 8-sided bowl. "No such mobilization of American folk has ever been seen in the lengthy history of our athletics."

The *Buffalo Evening News* said folks from every corner of the world and country were on hand, the excitement was so great. "The bout unquestionably has excited the greatest interest ever aroused by a pugilistic encounter."

Prominent members of the crowd included Henry Ford, Percy Rockefeller, Vincent Astor, J. P. Morgan, Harry Frazee, William Brady, George M. Cohan, Flo Ziegfeld, Al Jolson, Theodore Roosevelt, Jr., Spanish Ambassador Don Juan Riano y Gayangos and his wife, Douglas Fairbanks, Jim Jeffries and his wife and daughter, Jim Corbett, Tom Mix (movie star), Tony Drexel Biddle, and many others.

Rickard started the first preliminary just after 12 p.m. Veteran announcer Joe Humphries (Humphreys) was on the job.

The prelims began before a perspiring crowd, for "it was humid as Hades... It was truly hot enough to fry an egg. ... Nobody cared much about the preliminary boys." There were neither cheers nor moans, for the crowd was listless. No thrills could be derived from anyone but the main eventers.

In the first fight, which began at 12:13 p.m., between 122-pound featherweights, Johnny Curtin outpointed Mickey Delmont over 8 rounds, but pursuant to New Jersey law, there was no formal decision.

Just before 1 p.m., at the home where he was staying, Jack Dempsey went upstairs for a one-hour nap. His mother sent him a telegram from Salt Lake City, expressing hope and confidence that he would keep the championship in America. Jack said, "That I will win I am certain. If one punch isn't enough, two or three will be."

The second bout was 129 ½-pound Packy O'Gatty vs. 125-pound Frankie Burns. Jimmy De Forest refereed this contest, which went the full 8 rounds. One writer said Burns won, while another said O'Gatty won.

124-pound Babe Herman stopped 128 ½-pound Joe Metranga in the 5th round, when Metranga was hanging helpless on the ropes, forcing the referee stoppage. Herman was a member of the Dempsey camp.

121-pound Dick Griffin stopped 120 ½-pound Benny Coster in 6th round, after Coster had been down twice in that round and was being further pummeled, helpless on the ropes, causing the referee to stop it.

Prior to leaving his yacht, Carpentier had a light lunch and an hour's nap. Motorcycle policemen escorted his auto from the yacht to the arena. Georges said, "I've had a good sleep and feel fine."

Carpentier arrived at the arena at 1:45 p.m. with Descamps, flanked by five mounted Jersey cops on either side, who cut a channel through the wild crowds. Carp entered the arena and went to his dressing room.

Greenwich Village's 185-pound Gene Tunney defeated Toronto's 175-pound Soldier Jones in the 7th round. The referee stopped it when Tunney had him pinioned on the ropes and was battering him into submission. James Dawson wrote, "The contest was unexciting and lacked anything of spectacular nature. Tunney appeared off form and unimpressive against Jones, who was a slow-moving, wild-swinging novice." Gene eluded almost every blow. Yet, Tunney also "was comparatively slow and wild. He weakened Jones with drives to the body and was on the road to a knockout when the bout was stopped."

Neal O'Hara, who was at ringside, said in the 2nd round, a Jones roundhouse right swing from the floor shook Tunney from his head to his heels, but he held his ground and fought back. Tunney hurt Jones in the 3rd with a right, and also landed several hard body smashes. However, thereafter, the bout slowed, and the crowd yelled to have them taken off, until the referee stopped it in the 7th and declared Tunney the winner.

Dempsey left the Heppenheimer home and headed to the arena.

In order to ensure that the main event would start on time, the final preliminary, Billy Miske vs. Jack Renault, was shifted to take place after the championship contest, as a walk-out bout.

A world's record crowd was on hand, some saying 91,600, others saying 105,000. 6,000 automobiles were on site. Several ticket holders were denied admission, in possession of forgeries or having been sold fraudulent tickets.

The heat of the people packed into the arena added to the great heat of the sun, which was veiled by the clouds. 5,000 women attended, and with few exceptions, would root for Carpentier. Some puffed on cigarettes. Makeup fared badly under the intense heat. The crowd was relatively quiet.

Historical weather data for July 2, 1921 for Jersey City indicates a high of 78 degrees Fahrenheit with .11 inches of precipitation. The humidity and densely packed humanity likely made it seem hotter.

After the preliminaries concluded, "a bevy of very beautiful dames circulated the whole crowd collecting for some New Jersey hospital."

A floral horseshoe with the word "Success" emblazoned upon it was placed inside the ring.

The champ entered the arena at 2:40 p.m. and went to his quarters.

At 2:56 p.m., Georges Carpentier entered the ring. A big roar received him. Accompanying him were Descamps, Gus Wilson, Paul Journee, and Joe Jeannette. Georges was all smiles. He wore a long, dark-gray, silk bath robe, bordered with black stripe edging at the sleeves and neck, with blue cuffs; a very somber-looking outfit.

Carpentier Greets the Crowd

Georges clasped his hands high in the air as if to shake with the entire crowd. He smiled and bowed like an actor taking an encore. Carp showed his pleasure at the mighty greeting. His blond golden hair was brushed back, pompadour fashion. His hair was cut shorter than usual, for his long silky locks had been shorn. He was clean shaven. He took a seat in the southeast corner. He watched the crowd, and at times looked up at the airplanes circling the arena overhead, machines like the ones he had flown on the battlefields in France.

Manager Descamps wore a cap and gray sweater. His face was red, and he was excited.

A couple minutes or six minutes later (depending on the source), a roar as big or even bigger in volume than that which greeted the Frenchman's arrival went up as Dempsey, led by a squad of police, and accompanied by his seconds, approached quickly and ran up the ring stairs. Dempsey was stolid and unemotional, but relaxed a trifle, and a suspicion of a smile made its appearance. Another said he looked determined, like a race horse ready to face the barrier.

Martin Green said that as they approached the ring steps, each man received a tremendous roar of applause, magnificent in volume, greater than any chorus of voices ever heard before.

Jack wore his customary white trunks, and had his shoulders covered by a maroon red sweater. He wore no bathrobe. His belt/silk sash was red, white, and blue. He was unshaven, with a three- to five-day growth of beard, and was dark browed.

Julia Harpman said Dempsey looked sullen and grim.

Sophie Treadwell said Dempsey had a frightening, tramp-like, threatening look, with a heavy stubble of beard, wearing a red sweater and a cap on the back of his head. But he also was smiling and his step was swinging and carefree.

Carp rose from his chair to greet Dempsey with a hand shake. Jack said, "Hello Georges." Cameramen snapped photos.

The big horseshoe made of flowers, sent by his admirers, was placed behind Dempsey, but he declined to be photographed with it, preferring instead to be photographed sitting down on his stool. "The chair was really a soda stool, such as fronts many a soda fountain."

Carp, looking like a lithe greyhound, smiled, appearing unconcerned and very confident. Dempsey, who looked like a ferocious, rugged bulldog, mostly scowled.

In the champ's corner were Jack Kearns, Joe Benjamin, Teddy Hayes, Mike Trant, and Bernard Dempsey, the champ's brother.

Jack jumped up to shake hands with Carp for picture taking purposes, allowing the cameramen to snap their photos. Carp smiled and looked at the champ, but Dempsey simply glowered and looked at the cameras, never glancing at the challenger. When that was concluded, Dempsey quickly returned to his corner.

Julia Harpman said, "Carpentier's leanness and his look of freshness appealed to my love of beauty and cleanliness. Dempsey's sullen, morose, one day unshaved visage repelled me. Not once did he look his challenger in the eye. Mere courtesy would demand that, thought I."

To Harpman, Dempsey seemed "fearfully nervous," while Carpentier was smiling, relaxed, and confident.

Back in his corner, Jack placed both hands on the upper ropes, and pranced up and down in limbering-up fashion.

Dempsey began bandaging and taping his own hands, watched by Carp's seconds, Descamps, and a boxing commissioner. An excited Descamps was voicing vigorous protest to Dempsey's methods of fixing up his knuckles, but his objections were futile, "as Jack was using nothing but linen taping prescribed by law. If it was the French manager's intention to get Jack's goat, he didn't succeed." His hand taping was "honest." Descamps finally was quieted down by those around the ring, and thereafter he stood silently, watching every move as Dempsey applied the tape. Another observer said three layers of white cotton bandages and gauze tape were all that was permitted and applied. Confident Kearns looked amused by Descamps' protestations.

Kearns went over to Carp's corner and chewed gum, observing while Carpentier applied bandages to his hands, also under the supervision of a commissioner, doing so much more slowly than Dempsey did.

While the bandaging was ongoing, announcer Joe Humphries introduced Bob Doherty, chair the New Jersey boxing commission.

Fred Fulton entered the ring and shook hands with both men.

Humphries introduced Jersey City Mayor Frank Hague, and he was cheered.

Introduced as "the best and gamest governor the people of New Jersey ever had," the Honorable Edward Edwards received a wonderful roar for his efforts to put on the fight despite the thunderings of the reformers. He received his cheers with a wave of recognition.

The governor walked over and shook Carp's hand. He subsequently took Jack's hand in both of his hands and gave it a vigorous shake. "How are you, Jack?" "Fine," replied the champ.

Tommy Gibbons and Bill Brennan (in a checked suit) entered the ring and were introduced. Both Gibbons and Brennan challenged the winner.

New pairs of 8-ounce gloves were brought in, reddish-brown mittens, tied with blue strings. They were larger than the usual 5-ounce gloves, but required by New Jersey law. They were removed from the boxes which had to be torn open. The principals had tried them on several days ago. The seconds began knocking the leather to make it more pliable.

Bernard Dempsey and Hayes completed the champ's hand bandaging as Descamps watched. Joe Benjamin watched Carpentier's taping.

Jack put on the left glove first. Kearns tied the gloves. Descamps evidently took stock in the report/claim that Dempsey's hands were full of some foreign element in Toledo, and did not return to his corner until after Dempsey's gloves had been laced up and the ends of the laces cut.

Carp had not yet finished taping up his hands. Eventually, Descamps laced the gloves on Georges, who watched the airplanes. He recognized a friend in the audience and smiled and bowed. He seemed quite confident.

Dempsey seemed annoyed, scowling fiercely. He generally liked to get on with matters, never liking to sit still for too long.

Harry Ertle, referee, was attired in white flannels, white canvas shoes, and a white shirt with a soft collar. After being introduced, he bowed, and then paced the center of the ring while the gloves were tied on the hands of each principal.

Joe Bannon of New York was introduced as the official timekeeper.

It was a quiet, dignified crowd.

Tex Rickard was introduced, and received a big hand from the crowd. He grabbed Dempsey's right glove, shook it and said, "Jack, may the best man win." "O.K.," Jack replied.

Tex then walked across the ring and did the same with the Frenchman.

Descamps patted Carp on the back as he put his toes into the rosin in his corner. An attendant massaged Carp's face and brushed his hair.

Carpentier wore a set of white jersey knit trunks with an inch-thick blue stripe running down.

Humphries introduced the world's champion, Jack Dempsey, which drew polite applause. Jack got up and did a jig step. One writer said he got a surprisingly good reception from the crowd. Another said Dempsey was given a tremendous ovation. "The hostility of the public toward him on account of his war record was expected to bring him perhaps the jeers and boos that he got when he beat Bill Brennan last winter." Still, the champ looked glum. Another said he received mild applause mixed with some hooting.

Humphries introduced Georges Carpentier as the pugilistic idol of the old world and a "soldier of France," which drew a tremendous, rousing cheer, one of the greatest ever. There was a significant flash in the Frenchman's eyes, enjoying the crowd's reception. He bowed and smiled and turned around in a circle. One said Carp's reception was three times as great as Dempsey's, while another said it was ten times bigger. Horace Lerch said Dempsey probably never would

forget the contrast in reception. A tremendous roar greeted Carpentier and shook the arena. Ray Pearson said the arena rocked from the cheers for Carpentier. He clearly was the crowd's favorite.

Kearns patted and tickled Dempsey on his tanned/sunburned back, scratched and rubbed the back of his neck, massaged his sides, spoke into his ear, and rubbed and smoothed his heavy eyebrows, likely with some Vaseline, which he took from his pocket.

Dempsey continued glowering, and put his feet into the pile of resin that had been dumped in front of his chair. He bounced up and down.

The telegraph instruments were jangling and humming. "You marvel that so much interest can possess the world for this single fight." Around 300 reporters were on scene.

Their weights were announced officially as Carpentier - 172 pounds, Dempsey - 188 pounds, though some believed Dempsey actually was 192 or more. When Dempsey's weight was announced, someone remarked, "They had a string on those scales." Johnny Dempsey winked. Ring Lardner said, "Dempsey's weight was given as 188 pounds, but I would hate to pay a dollar an ounce for all he was over that." Carpentier said he weighed 172, "and whatever he did weigh, I don't believe his Mrs. will ever make him give up potatoes." Carp looked thin, while Dempsey was more thickly built, particularly in his upper body. Carp had bigger legs. One claimed that Jack lost weight as a result of the drying-out process.

At ring center in the 18-foot-ring, Referee Harry Ertle gave them final instructions regarding the rules, clinches and breaks, etc. They both looked down as they faced one another. Odds of 2 to 1 prevailed inside the arena, with Dempsey the favorite.

After they returned to their respective corners, Dempsey danced in his corner, facing away from ring center. Carp stretched himself on the ropes.

Humphries exclaimed his famous "Let 'er go." Official timekeeper Joe Bannon rang the gong at 3:16 or 3:18 p.m., starting the "Battle of the Century." An excited man in the crowd tore the flowers from the hat of his lady companion and tossed them into the air.

1st round[657]

Carp immediately walked forward, leapt in with a quick left and clinched. Dempsey fired his short, quick right to the body and head. Referee Ertle broke them. Dempsey moved forward, but Carp was faster, firing off a blazing-fast right and right uppercut, then clinched. Dempsey pumped away with his close-in right to the head, twice to the body, and head, and body again, the head blows partially to the back of the head as Carp leaned and bulled forward. Break.

Dempsey moved in and Carp launched a quick jab, clinched, then landed a head-jolting right uppercut. They clinched and scuffled. Carp fired a hook over the top of a ducking Dempsey, but landed a left hook to the body in the clinch. Break. Carp's jab missed the ducking, advancing Dempsey and Georges clinched.

Dempsey fired four wide right hooks to the side/back of Carp's head, then after a Carp right uppercut, Jack dug the rights into the body. Break.

---

[657] As usual with old films, many versions have the rounds out of order, or parts of one round included in another round, or a different angle or closer-up view represented twice, sometimes in a different round, so as to make up for disintegration or missing/lost footage, so an accurate accounting can be tricky. But in an attempt to match the films with the written accounts, the following is what the films show.

Carp moved away, ducked, fired a right that landed on the back of a ducking Jack's head, and clinched. Dempsey worked short inside uppercuts with both hands to the head and body. Break.

Dempsey again moved in and Carp fired a left jab followed by a right (that Jack rolled) and clinched, followed by some left hooks to the head and body that Dempsey partially blocked or smothered, the body blows landing more cleanly. Inside scuffling.

Dempsey really dug in some hard right uppercuts to the body and head, as well as a rabbit punch. Carp clinched more tightly and bulled in. Break. Carp moved, jabbed (which Jack ducked), clinched, and Jack pumped away with his right to the body and head. Carp snuck in a right uppercut.

Jack kept pumping in heavy right uppercuts and right hooks in nonstop relentless fashion, particularly to the body, and then came over the top with a right as Carp was trying to get closer in the clinch. Jack followed up by landing a left uppercut to the head and his right uppercut to the body, then double right uppercut – down to the body and up to the head.

Carp moved and walked off to the side, circling to his right, and then timed Dempsey on the way in, landing a right (that Jack rolled slightly), then right uppercut in the clinch. Jack might have snuck in a left to the body. They broke away.

Carp backpedaled, fired a right that missed, and Jack missed a counter right uppercut. Clinch, and Dempsey snuck in several short left uppercuts to the head while holding with his right over Carp's shoulder onto his back. Break.

Carp moved, landed a quick jab, both fired quick rights at the same time, followed by a clinch, and Dempsey landed his right underneath to the body and over to the side of the head, and then dug in several nonstop lefts to the body, then a right to the body. Carp fired some inside body blows as well, but they were feeble in comparison with the power and effectiveness of Dempsey's thudding blows. Jack tried a couple smothered left uppercuts.

A leaning-forward Carp fired a right that missed or partially landed and he went down face first to the canvas, his right arm going through the ropes, but on the way down after missing he was hit in the head with a short counter right uppercut. It was more of a swing and fall-down as a result of being off balance, though he was struck and his head did jolt up prior to hitting the deck, so one technically could call it a knockdown. Carp had a habit of overthrowing his right and falling forward a bit off balance as a result of the great force he put into the blow.

Georges rose within 1 or 2 seconds, without a count, as Referee Ertle simply walked between them. Carp stepped left, then walked off to the right. Dempsey jabbed and Georges slipped under it and walked off to the right again.

As Dempsey advanced, Carpentier timed him and stepped in with a fast, jolting right to the head, though Dempsey did ever so slightly roll to the right to ride with the punch and take some of the sting out of it, as he usually did. Carp then moved in quickly with some short left hooks, and a right uppercut as Dempsey moved back and clinched, while Georges' momentum forced Jack back to the ropes in the corner momentarily.

Dempsey dipped under and dug his right uppercut into the body, bulling in. Ertle broke them. Bell.

Overall, Dempsey had been fairly relentless on the attack, rarely moving away, constantly applying pressure, wanting to keep a fast pace, not allowing Carpentier any rest. He dipped or rolled as blows came his way. Carp wanted to fire snappy, powerful blows, and then either move away or move in and clinch. His punches were faster and had more of an explosive quality, but Dempsey's were heavier, thudding blows, with great strength. Once inside, Jack was good at working consistently with nonstop single blows with little time in between, firing any punch and finding whatever opening was there to the head or body, wide or centered, working up and down, often with the same hand.

What the writers said:

Carpentier opened the fight with a lead left to the head. He also stepped in with a whipping right that started high and came down. He was carrying the fight to Dempsey in an aggressive manner, but also boxing and moving. He jabbed the face with his left, sticking and moving, or springing/leaping in with quick powerful blows.

Dempsey would not be driven back, but forged forward stolidly and grimly with his head lowered, getting inside and working both hands to the body in the clinches. Carp's left was stinging, but not as demolishing as his right. Carp landed a wicked right uppercut at short range, but it had no effect on Dempsey, who pummeled the body. Carp broke and moved around, then returned quickly with a right to the jaw.

Some said Carpentier's fast whipping blows would have knocked out anyone else, and some punches momentarily shocked, shook, or staggered Dempsey, but the champion quickly would recover and lunge forward, driving so hard at the body that Georges was forced to give ground. The blows came so fast that they hardly could be followed. Dempsey was punishing him unmercifully on the inside.

A blow drew blood from Carp's nose, cutting it. On the inside, some rights landed to the back of Carp's head. (The rabbit punch was legal.) Jack sometimes would hold with his left and hit with his right. Dempsey's blows, from either hand, body or head, were less flashy, but they hurt and shook Carpentier, leaving red marks, sometimes making his legs sag.

Most said Carpentier threw one right so hard that in missing he fell through the ropes.

Carpentier rose quickly and attacked again, landing several body blows. Carp landed another hard right that jolted Jack's head, but once again, Dempsey was not deterred, advancing while Carp retreated. The crowd was mad with excitement, cheering the round at its conclusion.

Most agreed that Dempsey had won the round. Between rounds, Carpentier's seconds worked on his cut nose and stopped the flow of blood.

Summarizing the 1st round, the *New York World's* Vincent Treanor said Carpentier's ribs and stomach were red from the vicious short punches, and his nose was cut. Both men landed several hard blows.

The *Olean Times Herald's* Jack Veiock said the round was even, though Dempsey looked to be too strong for Carpentier, taking his hard blows and chasing him around the ring.

The *New York Daily News'* Harry Newman said Dempsey did the better work inside, beating him unmercifully, and he smashed Carpentier all around the ring, forcing Georges to run away.

The *Brooklyn Daily Eagle's* Thomas Rice said Dempsey was the superior infighter, both offensively and defensively. The infighting was hurting Carpentier, demonstrated by his breaking and retreating. Georges still returned though and fired and his own hard blows.

Yet, Dempsey was much more skillful at pulling or rolling his head out of harm's way than was Carpentier. Carp had trouble landing flush on the jaw very often. He landed eight or ten head blows, but Dempsey tucked his jaw well behind his left shoulder and moved his head out of line enough to cause the blows to land high. Conversely, Dempsey's hard body blows had a weakening effect. Hence, Dempsey won the round with the more effective punches.

Robert Edgren said Carpentier would spring in with very hard blows. Dempsey would not retreat, but came in constantly, driving his punches at short range, mostly to the body. Dempsey's plan was to wear him down. Although twice in the round a Carpentier right shook Dempsey, Jack kept driving in and forcing Georges to retreat. Carpentier showed some effects from the body punishment he received. It was a great round. Carpentier was as advertised, and would be no cinch.

The *New York Tribune's* W. J. Macbeth said Dempsey was hit with very good blows at long range, so he charged in like an infuriated bull. At close quarters, the champ kept his two hands going like pistons. He fired short, crushing jolts to the ribs and wind. Carp was wilting under the terrific drubbing. A right hook landed flush on Carp's nose, staggering him and bringing blood.

On the outside, Carp again landed some wicked blows to the jaw. Whenever hit, Jack came back with heavy artillery, coming after him with ferocity. At short range, Dempsey showered a rain of crushing left and right jolts on the challenger's wind and ribs. George broke and moved unsteadily, clearly hurt, but he was game, landing a flush, powerful right to the jaw that snapped the champ's head back with a jerk. The crowd was thoroughly enjoying the combat.

Horace Lerch said Carpentier fought with astonishing vigor, putting up a brisk battle from the start, darting in with blows. Yet, Dempsey mussed him up considerably in the close-range battling. Jack jolted and hooked with short blows, with just a few inches of drive, but they bobbed Carp's head and battered his body. One left skimmed Carp's nose and drew blood. A furious exchange in close ended with Carpentier falling through the ropes. Georges gamely flew at Dempsey and they exchanged body blows. Carpentier's fleetness of foot saved him. He was trying hard, and was dangerous, using his open style, which found favor with the spectators. Dempsey's round.

Ray Pearson said Carpentier had the speed of a flash, showering Dempsey with an assortment of accurate lefts and rights. He led by a wide margin, until at the end of the round Dempsey began pummeling him. Jack obtained first blood from a right to the nose, splitting open a cut on it. Dempsey showed no marks, despite being punched badly.

Neal O'Hara said Carpentier made swift, darting lunges. He danced around, fell into clinches, and tried to land uppercuts. Dempsey landed a mean swipe under Carp's left eye, gashing the skin, and blood dripped. The mob roared. Carp missed several blows. Once he missed and was thrown off balance, falling to the canvas, half of his body draped on the ropes. Some thought he was knocked down, but he was not.

In the clinches, Jack delivered a blistering cuffing. The blows were short, but mighty, and really told. Just before the end of the round, the Frenchman sent a right to the jaw that staggered the champ for an instant. A lot of clinching followed.

Between rounds, Carp was breathing more heavily than his foe, with his body blazing red from the champ's terrific infighting. Jack looked composed, and much less nervous than before the fight started.

2nd round

On the films, Dempsey approached while crouching low, dipping to the right as Carp flitted about. Georges stepped in, grabbed and pushed a bit, then snuck in a left uppercut to the head. Break. Dempsey quickly stalked as Carp moved about.

Georges often liked to start with a left stiff-arm range-finder to set up his lightning right, which he fired and landed hard to the head as Dempsey rapidly advanced. Clinch, and each snuck in a right to the body. Break. Carp walked off to the right, and then to the left. He crouched low with his left extended as if getting ready to pounce, but then danced off to the side. Dempsey kept advancing and pressuring, but Carp moved away again, with Dempsey following him around. Carp jabbed his left into Dempsey's face, they clinched, then Carp snuck in a right uppercut to the jaw. Dempsey backed for a moment, then advanced again.

Carpentier nailed Dempsey with a hard 1-2 (jab-right) combination that Jack rolled slightly. Yet, it was Carp who clinched and wrestled thereafter to prevent counters. Dempsey tried to dig in some short shots in the scuffle, and was more of the aggressor, trying to work his right, a short left to the body, and partially smothered rights to the body and head, while Carp snuck in a hook to the head. Break. As usual, Carp walked away, moving backwards to the left, circling, with the relentless Dempsey stalking ahead.

Dempsey led with a right to the head, and they clinched. While holding his right around the back of Carp's head, Jack worked his left uppercut to the body and head several times in his usual nonstop fashion, one jolting Carp's head up, and then Jack snuck in a right the body. Carp broke free and danced away.

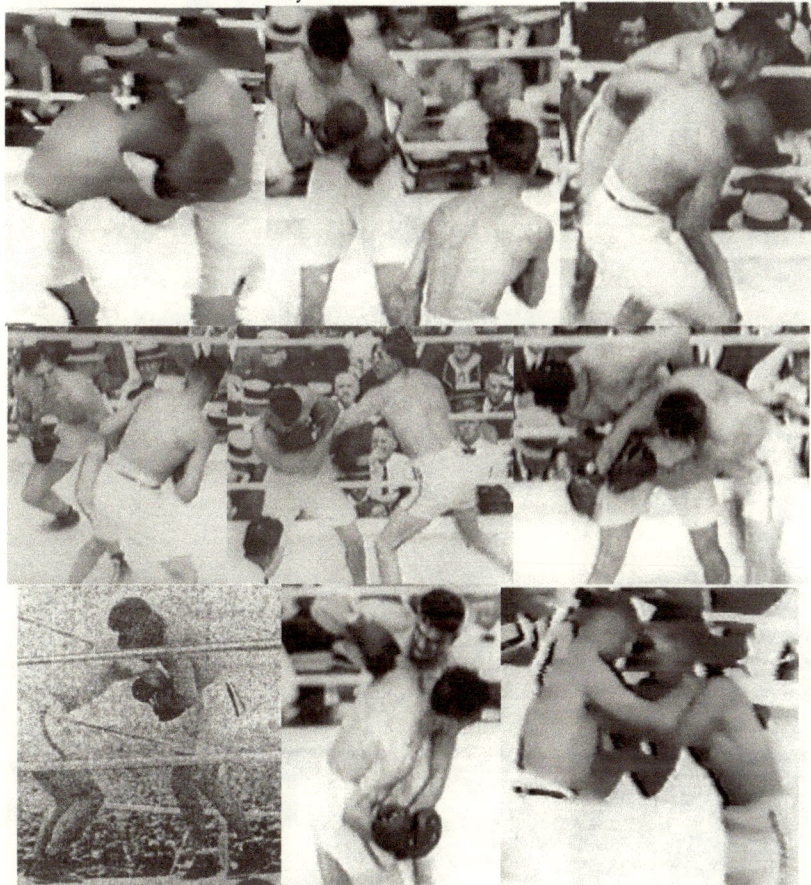

As Dempsey advanced into his range, Carpentier leapt in with his quick left jab/stiff-arm into his face, and then launched a powerful right that landed solidly high on the head and sent Dempsey dipping down to the right. A partial clinch, and Carpentier followed up with an explosive, blazing-fast combination of right to the jaw, left hook to the jaw, and right to the face, knocking Dempsey backwards off balance momentarily and leaning over to the right. He never touched the ropes (as some writers claimed) or canvas, but the crowd was in an uproar upon seeing him jolted back. Carp advanced and fired a right that landed to the back of the head of the ducking Dempsey. A hook followed, then right uppercut to the jaw as Dempsey was trying to bull forward and clinch. Carp stepped back and nailed him with a right to the jaw, and then another to the head that sent Jack back a step. Yet, Dempsey's legs seemed stable. He dipped and advanced slightly, which drew a third right in a row which missed as Dempsey quickly moved back away from it, then moved in and fired a right at the same time that Carp fired his right. A clinch followed, and Carp snuck in a head-jolting right uppercut to the jaw, and another as Jack pushed and bulled forward, clinching. Break.

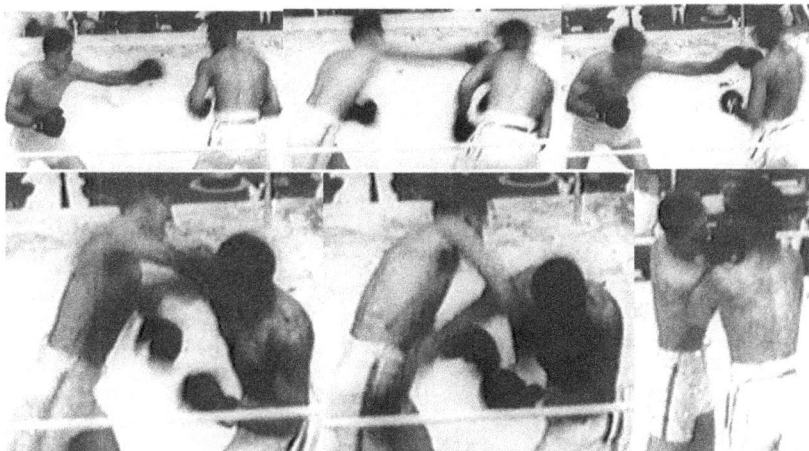

Carp peppered with his jab, and Dempsey stepped in with a right to the body and hook that missed around the head of the ducking Carp. Clinch and break. Dempsey moved in and ducked under a leaping jab. Clinch and break. Carp feinted a right, Dempsey missed a right, then advanced with a hook that missed as Carp danced away.

Carpentier again timed the advancing Dempsey with a 1-2 to the head or jaw. Jack held, and in the clinch that followed, he worked his left to the body and head, and then right to the head, body, and head, while Carp snuck in a right uppercut. Break.

Carp again nailed the advancing Dempsey with a head-jolting right to the jaw as Jack was firing a right uppercut down low. Yet, in the clinch that followed, Jack seemed unphased, trying to work and find an opening for his short inside shots as Carp was doing more of the holding. Break.

The Frenchman set him up with his outstretched left, peppering his jab a few times, and then fired an overhand right on the dipping Dempsey which landed on the back of his head. Carp grabbed Jack's left arm, but the champ snuck in a short right hook and right uppercut to the head while being held and smothered. Break.

Dempsey circled left and then stepped in firing a fast lead hook-right combination that missed as Carp moved away and stuck out his left arm. Georges kept retreating and circling away from the fast-advancing Dempsey, but stopped to nail him with a jab and clinch. Carp pushed off and broke away, then stepped in with a lead right, hook to the head, and then body as Jack bulled forward. In the clinch, Dempsey worked his double right – once to the body and then over the top to the head, possibly to the back of the head. Carp clinched more tightly. Break. Carp jabbed. Bell.

Dempsey's corner seemed a lot calmer than the written reports would have one believe, though it does appear that Kearns put something under Dempsey's nose, possibly smelling salts/ammonia. One man waved fans at Dempsey to cool him off. A cut can be seen under Carp's left eye.

It was a clear Carpentier round, for he landed several pulverizing rights to the head, some even knocking Dempsey back off balance momentarily.

However, each time he was nailed, Dempsey quickly collected himself and continued his attack, even landing some heavy blows of his own.

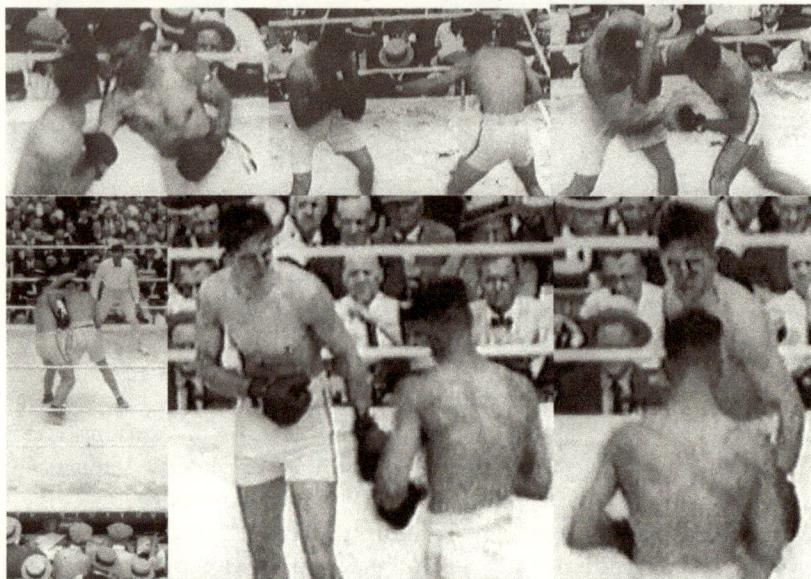

According to the writers, in the 2nd round, the semi-crouching Dempsey moved forward consistently in a business-like manner, forcing, chasing, or crowding Carp around the ring. Carpentier would fire and move, or fire and clinch. When Carp danced, his supporters roared their approval, feeling that he needed to stay away and fight at long range. Carp landed a hard right that had no effect, and he backed away. In a clinch, Jack hit the body. Dempsey hooked a right to the jaw, then followed him, and once inside, he beat Georges around the body and head with rights, rocking his skull.

Carpentier moved again, suddenly stopped, glided in and crashed a flush right on Dempsey's jaw, staggering him back a bit. Carp followed up with a combination of six furious, fast rights and lefts to the jaw with all his speed and strength, knocking Dempsey back on his heels, reeling. Jack grabbed on to save himself. Carp ripped in rights to the body, and a right uppercut.

However, the dogged and determined Dempsey soon came back, landing a right and/or left hook to the cheek, splitting the Frenchman's skin under the eye (some said left eye, some right). Blood flowed from the gash. Jack's blows caused Georges to wear a pained expression. They exchanged body punches in the clinch as the bell rang.

Carpentier had landed the best punches in the round, and yet his face was bruised and bleeding. The crowd cheered him wildly. His hard, fast, jolting blows aroused his followers' hopes, for they believed that Dempsey had been hurt. Everyone agreed that it was Carpentier's round.

In the corner, Jack's seconds worked on him furiously. Kearns was nervous, one claiming that his hand was trembling. Carpentier had a red lump under his eye, and his nose was slightly cut. Dempsey still was unmarked.

Jim Corbett said, "It was all Carp's round."

Harry Newman said the Frenchman was very crafty.

Thomas Rice said although Carpentier proved that he could hurt Dempsey with his right, Dempsey proved that he could take the very best that Carpentier could send his way and keep coming. Carp kept trying to land something big, but Dempsey just kept plugging away, trying to wear him down.

Robert Edgren said the way Dempsey came back after being clouted on the chin and hurt, still moving forward, left no doubt that he was a real champion. He could take punishment and fight. Carpentier had hit him harder than any man ever hit him before, and he weathered it. Carp tried another rally, but Dempsey met him blow for blow.

W. J. Macbeth said when Carpentier hit and moved and kept matters at long range, he was winning with ease and making Dempsey miss. Dempsey's best work was done on the inside. Clear Carpentier round.

R. L. Goldberg simply said Dempsey had Carpentier groggy early on, but Carp outboxed Dempsey while backing away, receiving the crowd's cheers. It was Carpentier's round.

Horace Lerch said Carpentier kept giving ground but stopping to fire or even leap in with blows as Dempsey kept coming in. Carp finally landed his beautiful right flush on the jaw. The great crowd sprang to its feet as Dempsey staggered back. Like a tiger, Carp piled in with a series of wicked ripping drives to the head, and Jack hung on coolly. Breaking out of a clinch, Carp lifted three beautiful rights to the jaw. Georges tried again and again to get a knockout, but it was not to be. It was Carpentier for a fleeting moment, but he could not drop him. Dempsey kept coming in. Carpentier's skinned, bleeding nose and the abrasion/cut under his left eye bore testimony to the weight of the champ's punch.

Ray Pearson said the round was full of thrills. Carp, who had gathered confidence by his success in the 1st round, got the knockout fever, and tried to knock him out. With speed, cleverness, and all the steam he could put into his right, he nailed Dempsey time and again, and Jack careened around the ring with shaky knees, holding when the opportunity presented, and blocking what he could. Some thought it looked curtains. Jack clearly lost the round.

Neal O'Hara said Dempsey went after him at first, but Georges belted him a lulu on the jaw that sent him reeling back. The crowd suddenly woke up to the fact that Carp was very much there. He followed it up. While the champ was thrown off his balance, Carp crashed in some telling work. Dempsey was groggy. Carp forced the fighting. However, in the last minute of the round, Dempsey started coming back. He whacked another blow under the eye, then got in some more close-in bangs.

Carpentier eluded a jab to the body by moving and walking away to the right, circling. He ducked and weaved under a left hook and stepped away to the right again. Dempsey approached in his crouch, dipping up and down to the right in anticipation of a potential blow on the way in, missed a jab, and then a right, missing over the top of the slippery, elusive Carp, who ducked and moved his head and feet, stepping off to the left this time.

Carp timed the advancing Dempsey with a fast 1-2, the right landing solidly, though Jack rolled/dipped his head slightly to the right to take a bit of the sting off. Carp clinched to prevent counters. Jack snuck in a right to the body before Ertle broke them.

Carpentier partially landed a jab as Dempsey parried, dipped, and jabbed. Carp dipped down and grazed a right on a head-turning/rolling Dempsey, who missed a counter right uppercut, and they clinched. Carp bulled forward, while Jack struck a right to the body.

Carp broke and backed away, then fired a fast right uppercut that missed the advancing Dempsey, but Georges then fired another which jolted Jack's head up, before more clinching. Break. Carp missed a right uppercut and they clinched.

Carpentier stepped away, walked off to the right, ducked and weaved under a Dempsey left, then countered with a right to the head and tried to hold, but Jack snapped his short left uppercut to the head, body, head, and body again, and then right uppercuts to head and body. Break.

The champ advanced and Carp nailed him with another lead right, but Dempsey was good at ever-so-slightly rolling and/or dipping his head with the blows, such that even though they were landing solidly, he took a bit of the sting out of them. Plus, Jack clearly had a hard head. Carp bulled in as Dempsey dug his right uppercut twice to the body, and then up to the head. Break.

Carpentier stepped off to the right and walked away, circling to the right. He stopped and tried to nail Jack with another lead right, but this time Dempsey sensed it was coming and rolled right and stepped away to make it miss. Jack moved in with a left jab, but Carp dipped under it and grabbed. The champ again worked his short shots – left hook to the head, left uppercuts to the head, and digging right uppercut to the body. Break.

Carp stepped in quickly with a jab and clinch, smothering. Dempsey worked his short uppercuts to the head with both hands to create some room, the final right uppercut jolting Carp's head up. Georges tried some body blows. Jack struck another right uppercut, but Carp countered with a fast right that missed as Dempsey pivoted off to the left and took a step back.

Carpentier dipped down on the ready, stuck out his left range-finder, and overthrew a big right that Dempsey rolled to elude and then came right back with a counter right hook underneath to the head, right uppercut to the body, then head, left uppercut, and a somewhat slapping/cuffing downward right to the head. They exchanged jabs.

Carp ducked down and posed, moved away, then jabbed, but Dempsey advanced with a harder angling left jab or hook that landed solidly.

Dempsey moved in, Carp moved back, but then asserted, dipped, and launched a right that Dempsey eluded with his subtle head roll. Carp followed with a fast left hook that landed and caused the champ to step back. Carp leapt in with a left hook that Jack may have blocked. In the clinch, Dempsey worked his rights to the body. Break.

Carpentier snapped in a left jab, then followed with a 1-2 that missed. The Dempsey roll was avoiding the right much better. Clinch and break. Jack moved in, Carp ducked down, then stepped right and walked away quickly.

The champion kept advancing, and Carpentier stepped in with a fast jab that Dempsey rolled and ducked, but Carp followed with a jolting right that landed high on the head. Jack clinched with his left around the neck, but Carp quickly fired away at his body in combination, bulling Dempsey into the ropes. Clinch and break.

Carp moved back, dipped down and landed a jolting right high on the head of the advancing Dempsey, but Jack may have ever-so-slightly dipped/rolled to ride it a bit and ensure that it did not land on the jaw.

Carpentier bulled in and they clinched, but Jack stepped back, and, while holding with his right, launched his left uppercut to the head three times, stepped away, and then stepped in with a glancing hook and a right in combination. Carp seemed a bit affected by all the blows, not clinching as usual, but rather covering and rolling. Jack followed with a right to the body. Carp launched a counter right that missed, and Dempsey countered his counter with a couple right uppercuts, then four fast, jolting left uppercuts, the last of which clearly lifted Georges' head up. Bell, and Ertle broke them.

Carp walked to his corner, seeming fine, not groggy or staggering as some writers claimed. His seconds fanned him as usual.

Between rounds, a gentleman can be seen entering the ring with a big placard with the number 4.

Both men were having their moments and employing their strategies. Carp was using his footwork and timing to set up big blows, landing well here and there, while Dempsey was using his consistent pressure and digging inside blows to wear him down. His defense was improving a bit.

The sportswriters said Dempsey began the 3rd round by crowding and coming in, while Carpentier ducked, backed away, and moved around the ring warily, landing jabs, watching keenly for an opening. Dempsey still was very strong, as strong as ever. Jack backed him to the ropes and landed a short right to the chin. Carp landed two body uppercuts in the clinch. Dempsey hit the body as well. Carp landed right uppercuts to the head and chin.

Dempsey missed a left and Carpentier got his right over to Dempsey's jaw. He was outboxing Jack on the outside. Georges reached his jaw with another long right smash. Dempsey was good at rolling or dipping just enough to take some of the sting off the blows, and he kept advancing. Owing the body pummeling he received when close, Carpentier was trying to remain on the outside. Dempsey kept pressing in.

Once Dempsey got inside again, he was outroughing and outpunching Carpentier with spiteful body punches, punishing him viciously. Jack rapped a left uppercut to the mouth. He also clubbed him with two rabbit punches with his right, and some short hooks to the jaw. Carp clinched as Dempsey cuffed him with his left.

Carpentier nearly fell when he missed a right. Dempsey sunk wicked lefts into his stomach. He also landed on the mouth, and Carp licked the blood from his lips. Georges was crouching on the inside to protect himself.

Carpentier circled around, waiting for another chance for his right, but he appeared to be weakened from Jack's inside body punches and short blows to the chin. The challenger's right was sliding off of Dempsey's shoulder. Dempsey kept pressing, chasing, and rushing until he got inside.

Dempsey battered him with terrible rights and lefts to the head and body, and Carp clung hard in a clinch, the bell saving him. Some said Carpentier seemed groggy or tired.

Between rounds, Descamps gave Carp a drink of brown fluid.

Treanor said it was Dempsey's round. Veiock agreed. Corbett said, "Dempsey is wearing a smaller man down. His weight is beginning to tell."

Thomas Rice said Carpentier was moving and whipping marvelously fast and accurate rights to the left side of Dempsey's head, but Jack was good at moving his head just enough that the blows landed on the head or upper jaw instead of chin or lower jaw. Many blows were grazing or deflected by the wrist or shoulder. Carpentier's punches stung but did not jar Dempsey, whereas Jack's blows were jarring. Many foes would have dropped from the challenger's punches, but Dempsey kept pressing in and engaging, forging ahead regardless of the blows launched at him, firing his own constant bombardment. Carpentier was fading rapidly, being jolted and worn down by the hooks to the jaw and the body punishment, as well as Dempsey's relentless attack and fast pace.

Robert Edgren said there was fast, hard fighting in the round. Carp moved swiftly, leaped in to attack, and then leaped away to safety, outboxing Dempsey, but he was weakening from the body attack. His offense came in spasmodic spurts of amazing speed and power, but it was not continuous like Dempsey's nonstop attack. Regardless, Edgren believed it still was anybody's fight when the bell rang.

Goldberg said Carpentier looked tired, but was boxing all the time. He was so fast that he made Dempsey look slow by comparison. Still, Dempsey was landing terrific blows.

According to Lerch, at the start of the round, Carpentier outboxed and outstepped Dempsey, using his left beautifully, hitting with great force with both hands, driving in some stiff rights and right uppercuts to the jaw. But Dempsey had recovered himself and kept forcing the close-range work, at which he excelled. He jolted Carp to the jaw and punished him badly on the body. Carpentier's attack weakened under Jack's wicked short-arm hits. It was evident that Carp was not taking the punches very well and that Dempsey's blows were weakening him. Ultimately, Carpentier's wicked drives to the jaw were without effect, and Dempsey had turned the tide of the fight.

Macbeth said Dempsey was beating him down with crushing body blows. Carp was trying to hang on, but did not have the strength to pinion Dempsey's arms, which flailed constantly into his body. A Dempsey right to the pit of the stomach made him wince. Carp tried to move and fire, but Dempsey took the blows well and kept attacking and staying on top of him as much as possible. Carp clinched to save himself, but was groggy from the unmerciful body beating. The bell was welcome relief.

Ray Pearson said Dempsey turned the tide, and he came into his own style. He took the aggressive and forced Carpentier to break ground continuously. Carp often was on the run. A wicked left opened a small cut under Carp's left eye. Dempsey got him against the ropes near a corner and punished him with hard body punches. Carp clinched to save himself. Dempsey had made up considerable lost ground. When they went to their corners, Jack was the stronger of the two by far. Georges gave evidence of being a trifle leg weary.

Neal O'Hara said Carpentier was the same little flitting flea, dancing around, backing, then swooping on sideways, always unbolting a crack or two. Jack was mad by now. He was starting to be less defensive, lessening his guard and wading in. Carp tried his big right slam, yet always missed his mark. Meanwhile, Dempsey was belting in some hooks with his long reach. The Frenchman's body now was as red as a lobster from all the body blows. By the end of the round, Carp showed signs of weakening. Between rounds, his breathing was heavy. Descamps gave him some mysterious brown fluid to drink.

4<u>th</u> round

Dempsey moved in and jabbed, but Carpentier moved back and turned off to the right, ducking down into the ropes, but quickly ran away and circled. Jack pressed in and fired a lead right, a straight left and a couple short, snappy left hooks to the head, and then, while Carp was holding his left arm, a heavy right uppercut to the body, short right hook to the head, and back underneath with another right uppercut to the body. Carp bulled in, attempting to smother, but Dempsey pulled his arm free and landed a head-jolting left uppercut and a right to the head that sent Carpentier back.

Dempsey advanced and got to the inside again. Carp launched a fast left hook and right to the head, and another hook. He grabbed Jack's left arm, so Dempsey pounded away with a heavy right uppercut to the body, a wide right to the body and then right to the side of the head. Carp clinched his right arm, and Jack followed by working the left uppercut up, down, and up to the head and body, back and forth, landing well.

Georges broke away and Dempsey fired a long right that missed, and Carp countered well with a right of his own. Clinch, and Jack worked a right to the body and several left uppercuts to the body. Carp clinched, bulled in, and smothered as Jack kept trying to work. Break.

Carp backed up, then stepped in and landed a jab, left hook, and right. Clinch. Jack grabbed Carp's right arm with his left and dug in a right uppercut to the body, let go and followed with a heavy right uppercut to the jaw. Carp backed away.

Dempsey stepped in and fired a very fast jab in a slight hooking/diagonal fashion to the jaw, instantly followed by a fast downward right to the jaw of the forward-ducking Carpentier, and Carp went straight down to the canvas, initially on his hands and knees, but then he collapsed down face first, with his head resting on his right arm and glove, the fight's first knockdown.

Carpentier appeared to be out of it and the fight over, but after the count of 9, suddenly and quickly Carp bolted up. Dempsey was right back at him with a right that went over the top of the face-first ducking-down Carpentier, possibly landing on the back of the neck. Dempsey followed with a wound-up right uppercut to the body, and possibly snuck in a very short left hook to the jaw (it is difficult to tell because of the angle and old footage), and Carp went down on his side.

Georges tried to move his arms and legs, raising them up in the air and down as if trying to get up, but the circuits were fairly frozen and he could not rise at all. He went back down on his side, his head touching the floor.

Once the ten-count was concluded, Dempsey, along with the referee, picked him up, Carpentier's cornermen came over and assisted as well, and they all walked/helped/carried him back to his corner. Law enforcement entered the ring to prevent pandemonium.

Dempsey returned to his corner, shook hands, and conferred with various folks. Carp was sitting on his stool recovering. Eventually,

Dempsey walked over wearing his open sweater and he met Carp, who got up and had just passed mid-ring, and they shook hands.

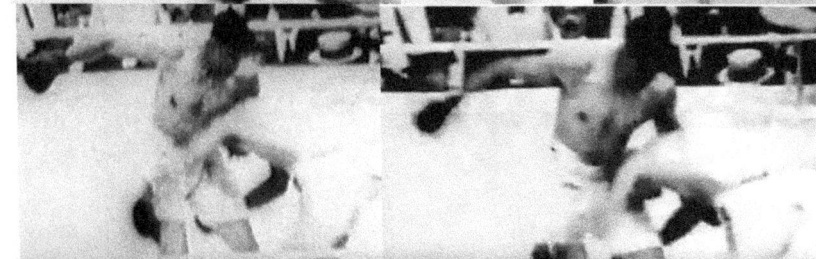

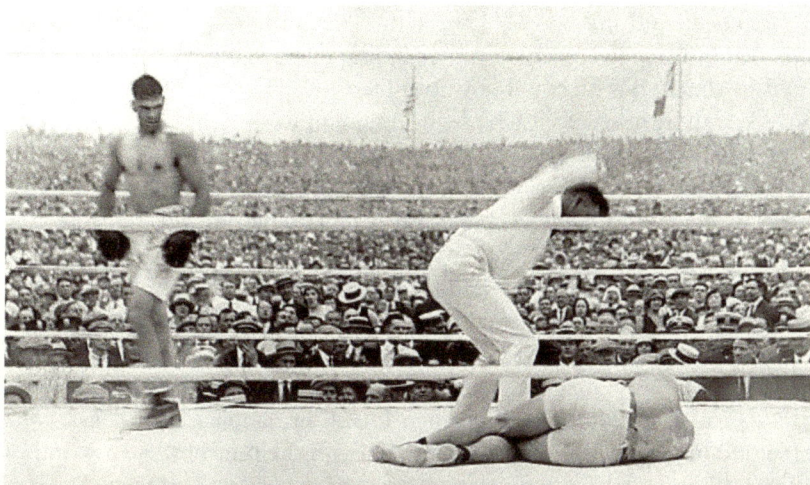

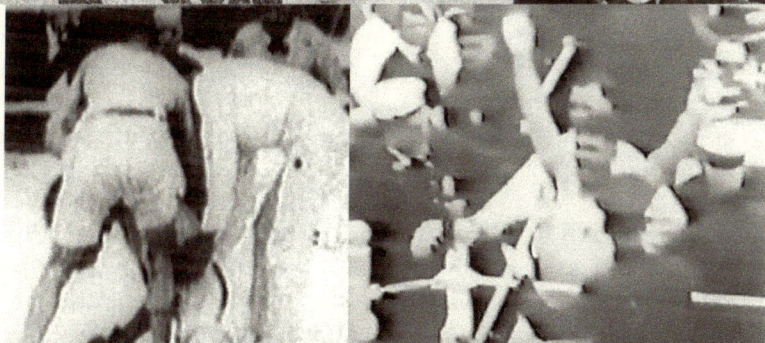

According to the writers, in the 4th round, without hesitation, Dempsey went right after Carpentier, pressing hard. Carp moved or walked away, shifty, foxy, alert. Carp leaped in to attack, but when his quick blows landed, they lacked the crushing force of the rounds before; the result of the body hammering he had received.

A right to the head drove Carp back. Dempsey got in close and punished him severely with terrific punches under the heart and jaw. Carp fought back a bit, but it was feeble compared with what he was taking. Dempsey practically ignored his blows.

Dempsey drove Carpentier half-way through the ropes with a left to the body. He also drove a terrific right smash to the heart. They were separated, but a short left to the jaw jarred Carp. Dempsey held Georges in the clinches and gave him an awful body lacing. Dempsey continually and relentlessly followed him around, sinking rights and lefts into his body.

Macbeth said the body beating had taken away Carpentier's legs, and the champ bounded after his prey, landing pile-driving body blows. Carp tried to clinch, but he could not hold Dempsey, who drubbed him with a tattoo of short hooks to the body, beating him to a pulp.

Lerch said Carp gave ground freely, but was boxing beautifully, fighting back hard. However, Dempsey was much the stronger of the two now, with superior stamina. He drove a terrific right to the body as they clinched, and Carpentier faded.

Ray Pearson said the champion was a vicious, ripping, tearing, merciless crusader. He came out of his corner like a catapult, and relentlessly tore after Carp, crouching, swaying, and more aggressive than he had been in the first few rounds. Carpentier gamely tried to fight back. He was fast, and hit more often than Dempsey, landing left hooks to the chin and hard rights to the jaw. But, although the punches had a world of sting to them, Jack never flinched.

When Dempsey hit the body, the thud of the impact could be heard for several rows back from the ring. Carpentier's face began to look sallow, and the speed of his feet diminished. The terrific bombardment continued. There were rapid exchanges of steamy blows. Dempsey's short left to the jaw had the power of a mule's kick.

Neal O'Hara said Dempsey started slugging. He took Carp's blows just so he could deliver the slam that he wanted, confident that with the proper treatment, Georges would cave in just like anyone else. The champion landed tremendous swats.

The writers varied regarding which punch or punches decked Carpentier, some saying a left hook to the jaw, or a right to the jaw, or a straight left to the jaw followed immediately by a whipping right. Carp went face first down to the canvas. The crowd roared and leapt up. Carp lay with forehead resting on his right side, on his folded arms, his knee bent. Most thought he was done for and all in. No one expected him to rise in time. Dempsey prowled around the ring, behind the referee. Carpentier lay there utterly motionless, but when Ertle said nine, Carp suddenly sprung to his feet with the speed of a tiger. That he rose at all was a tribute to his gameness.

Again, the writers had multiple different versions of the final sequence, including short right to the chin or head, ripping right to the heart, left hook to the stomach or chin, and Carpentier crumpled and collapsed in a heap with a thud at ring center, as if he had been shot. Carp was on his side, knees drawn up. He tried to rise, but could not, and fell back in a helpless heap on his side. At the count of ten, Carpentier still was folded up like a jack-knife. Time of the knockout was 1 minute 16 seconds into the 4th round.

Some said the crowd roared, while others said they were quiet when it was over. Others said the crowd roared for the first knockdown, but after the second, they were more reserved, like a funeral.

When the count concluded, Dempsey helped Gus Wilson, the French trainer with the English name, tenderly pick up the bleeding blond scrapper and carry him to his corner to sit on his stool. His seconds took charge of him – manager François Descamps, Marcel Denys, and Wilson.

Dempsey went to his corner to be met by Jack Kearns and brother Bernard Dempsey, who removed his gloves. Policemen excluded those who tried to rush in. The crowd gave Dempsey a big reception. He raised his hands in the air.

Carpentier recovered in about five minutes. As Dempsey walked over, Carp got up and approached him, they shook hands, and Georges smiled warmly. Supposedly, Dempsey said, "I'm sorry to have knocked out so good a man."

The ring was jammed with police, and Jack was kept busy shaking various hands.

Georges bowed to the crowd, showing gratitude for their great tribute.

In conclusion, overall, the films show that Carpentier was good at moving around and circling Dempsey, who constantly advanced almost without retreat to get close as soon as possible so he could work inside. Carpentier tried to time the advancing Dempsey on the way in. He either would stop and fire very fast, powerful blows, primarily rights and right uppercuts, but sometimes jabs and hooks too, or sometimes he would leap in on the attack. If Jack moved into the punches, the impact would be doubled, but if Carp also sprang forward to land on a forward-moving target at the same time, the powerful impact would be even greater.

Carp could walk, dance, run, circle, or slide, then stop instantly and fire a blazing-fast powerful right, sometimes off a lead jab or measuring left. He was good at suddenly stopping or changing direction/momentum and stepping forward with his blows, trying to maximize his speed and power with timing. Unlike a lot of movers, Carp was good at bending his legs and dipping too, getting a lot of leverage and power from his strong legs.

Carpentier was faster, more explosive, and snappier with his blows than Dempsey. Between punches, Carp would try to clinch, occasionally firing an inside blow, or he would move away. Carpentier used his clinching as a defensive method, for often after Georges threw, Dempsey would fire back right away in response. Carp's clinching also was an attempt to slow up Dempsey's inside attack, although it was not particularly effective.

However, it appears that Carpentier's punches required a lot more energy, so he did not throw quite as often. Carp's explosive power was the kind that requires more recovery between blows, particularly given his movement, while Dempsey's brand of calm, relaxed power had more of a consistency to it, requiring less of a breather, enabling him to maintain a nonstop pace. Dempsey's blows were more controlled and compact, whereas Carp shifted and torqued his entire body into his right with total abandon and full commitment, so much so that at times he overthrew and lost his balance if he missed.

Dempsey was physically stronger, and his blows were heavier, like thuds, but still snappy - a combination of heft, strength, and snap, whereas Carpentier's blows were sharp and stinging, with great velocity, the power coming from a speedy, explosive snap with everything he had on it.

Dempsey was much better at maintaining a consistent, rapid pace, which actually was very fast and relentless. Carpentier fought in bursts, whereas Dempsey kept plugging away whenever he was in range. Dempsey was much more relaxed, calm, methodical, and consistent, undeterred by anything Carpentier did, almost never relenting in his forward momentum.

Jack was much more comfortable and active when in close. He was strong enough and good at working his hands free from Carp's grasp in the clinches and firing away, or he would fire with the free hand when the other was being held. He was great at working at least one hand relentlessly.

Although not throwing combinations that often, each single Dempsey blow quickly was followed by another single blow, in nonstop fashion, with little time between blows, but not quite rapid enough to be deemed combination punches. He took whatever opening was there, and he wanted to keep plugging away as much as he could, particularly to the body.

Sometimes Dempsey would grab with one hand and keep Carpentier on the inside so he could dig away with inside punches. Dempsey primarily enjoyed firing uppercuts to the body and head on the inside. He occasionally fired a right over the top to the head, or a right hook to the side or back of the head, but he really focused on coming underneath in a nonstop, single-blow-at-a-time metronome method.

Carpentier threw both on the inside and outside, but he wanted to take more breaks in between punches by either moving or clinching. Georges liked to fire more often from the outside, where he had more snap and better defense than he did up close. He primarily sought to land a big right, his money punch.

Carpentier landed some very nice, snappy, powerful blows, including rights and right uppercuts, but Dempsey took them quite well, demonstrating his iron jaw. Everyone else Georges had hit like that had gone down. Dempsey was a tank.

Dempsey had fast feet, and did not stop too far away, but kept moving in with his chin tucked and head dipped down slightly off to the right side, with his guard somewhat low, his right arm close-in to his body, and left across his body or out slightly. Dempsey would dip or roll as the blows came at him, relying mostly on head movement for defense, to elude or ride and take the sting out of Carpentier's blazing-fast right, and then continue advancing, even when hit, or aggressively counterpunch off of his defense, constantly applying pressure, keeping the pace fast and forcing Carp to engage as often as possible, or at least keeping him working hard.

Overall, the outside was Carpentier's, but the inside was Dempsey's. Carp's work was flashier, but Dempsey's work was more compact and subtle, but clear to those who could see the up-close belting.

Dempsey could fire quick leads as he was advancing, or he would just move in without punching at all, allowing Carp to fire first so he could duck or roll and step in.

Dempsey's style was effective at wearing opponents down and making them eventually stop and fight, because he kept coming and was undeterred by their offense, confident in his ability to slip and counter. Once inside he was very good at avoiding being held and firing many short shots.

Dempsey seemed able to impose his will. Even though he kept a very good, consistent pace, he wasn't wild, but calmly and methodically went about his business, unphased by anything Carpentier did.

Some said that had Carpentier moved more, he could have done better. However, moving more might have worn out his legs and simply delayed the inevitable. Dempsey advanced so rapidly and consistently that it would be nearly impossible to keep moving that much or that fast on a consistent basis without taking some breaks. Carpentier tried to conserve energy by clinching and smothering. He tried to punch Dempsey so hard that it would deter his advance, but no matter how fast or powerful his blows, Dempsey simply would not be discouraged. No matter how fast Carp moved, Dempsey relentlessly came after him, such that moving more simply would have worn out Carp and reduced his offense. Hence, Dempsey essentially forced Carpentier to work on the inside more than he wanted, or else he would have to move so much it would sap his legs and his ability to punch.

In the 2nd round, Carpentier landed some flush, beautiful, powerful blows with both hands, his right, right uppercut, and left hook, which appeared to rock Dempsey back off balance for a moment. However, his legs did not buckle, nor was he wobbly. It was more like a flash stun and being hit so powerfully that he was knocked back. He quickly steadied himself and ducked and advanced again, took some, threw some, and clinched as well. He was momentarily stunned, but not to such a great extent that one might think he was on the verge of going out. The positive for Carpentier was that he demonstrated that he hit hard enough to rock Dempsey. The negative was that he hit him with his best blows, and still he did not deck Jack, who kept coming forward without fear.

Although Carpentier might have broken his right hand in the 2nd, as he claimed after the fight, and a doctor confirmed, he did not fight like he knew it, or cared. He still fired very powerful rights in both the 3rd and 4th rounds. He still had plenty of zip to his blows throughout. But Dempsey, in determined fashion, kept applying pressure and working as much as he could when in range and in close, methodically and gradually breaking him, unconcerned by what was coming at him, confidently advancing, dipping, and rolling with the blows sent his way.

True, Dempsey wore him down, but it wasn't as pronounced as one might think from reading the post-fight articles. There was no point in which it was obvious that Carpentier clearly was wilting or about to collapse. It was subtle. Georges still was trying and doing what he did – moving, firing, and clinching, etc. But he simply could not keep Dempsey off of him. He still occasionally landed some hard blows, but Dempsey was doing better at dipping or rolling with the punches, such that even when the rights did land, they were landing high on the head and not the chin. Dempsey was landing more as the bout progressed. Jack kept advancing and firing away in undeterred fashion, blasting the body and head, until Carp finally went down. The right uppercut that landed seconds before the left-right combination that decked Carpentier likely had a bigger effect than most realize.

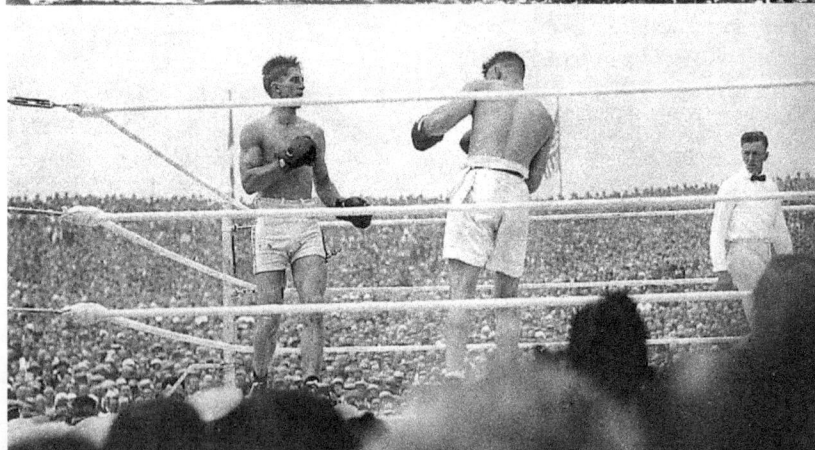

DEMPSEY PUNISHES IN CLINCH

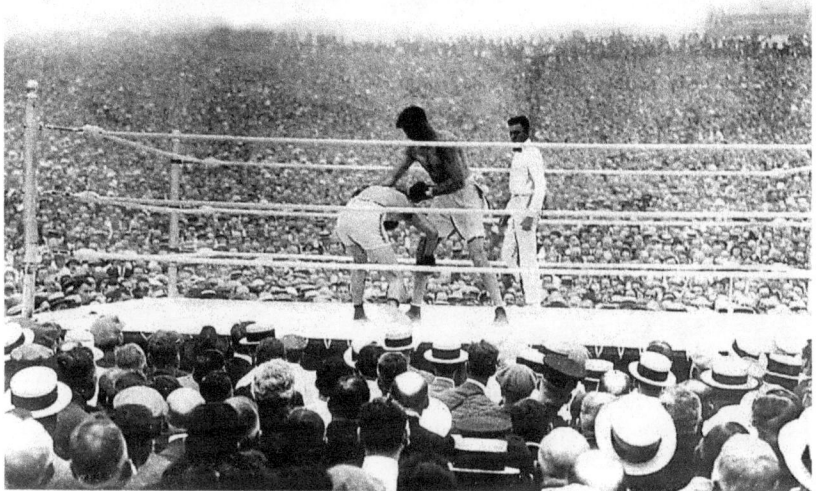

Before the fight, and——

After Carpentier's recovery from the knockout.

Dempsey smiling his pleasure at the plaudits of the crowd after the bout.

The champion, preceded by Manager Kearns, had to fight his way out.

How the biggest fight in history looked. A general view of the ring in the center of the monstrous arena. Dempsey hooking a right to the challenger's body—first round.

(NEWS photos)

FOLLOWING are the figures showing the receipts and purses in many of the great ring battles of the past:

	Boxers' share.	Total gate.
*Dempsey-Carpentier	..$500,000	†$1,600,000
*Dempsey-Willard	 127,500	600,000
*Dempsey-Brennan	 125,000	162,720
*Jeffries-Johnson	 121,000	270,775
*Willard-Moran	 77,250	152,000
*Leonard-Mitchell	 68,000	136,508
*Wilson-O'Dowd	 46,000	108,619
*Leonard-Welling	 38,000	99,750
Johnson-Burns	 55,000	97,000
*Lynch-Herman	 30,000	82,683
*Gans-Nelson	 22,000	69,715
*Willard-Johnson	 35,000	68,000
Jeffries-Sharkey	 36,465	66,300
Jeffries-Corbett	 43,648	63,340
Corbett-McCoy	 38,810	56,350
McGovern-Erne	 26,000	52,000

*Promoted by Tex Rickard.
†Estimated.

Toward the end of the first round Dempsey sent Carpentier half way through the ropes, but——

In the second the Frenchman rallied, and rose into the champion with fervor. Dempsey——

In the third Georges hung on in a clinch after those body blows, taking hard punches. And——

In the last round Dempsey landed his opponent like this for the count of nine, before the K. O.

The blow.

The collapse.

Down.

The count.

In the walk-off bout, Billy Miske won an 8-round no decision over Dempsey sparring partner Jack Renault. Since being knocked out by Dempsey, Miske had won five fights in a row, including a close, early June 1921 10-round no decision over Bill Brennan. Hence, attempts to reduce the significance of Dempsey's victory over Miske are not supported by the facts.

This final bout helped reduce traffic congestion; some leaving after Dempsey's victory, while others remained to see the last contest.

The gross gate receipts were reported to be more than $1,600,000, a world's record, the first million-dollar gate ever, though Rickard said it probably would be several days before a final and accurate accounting could be made. The paid admissions were in excess of 80,000, which, combined with the various free admissions, raised the total to a little more than 90,000. Many had paid speculators for tickets at a 400% to 500% mark-up.

Rice said Rickard made about $600,000 in profit. Dempsey's $300,000 was earned at a rate of $29,268 a minute. Even Carpentier's $200,000 was more than any fighter ever had earned before, champion or not. It was the largest purse in history. Jim Corbett said, "I was born too early." He had fought Peter Jackson for four hours in 1891 and only earned $2,500.

Carpentier took his defeat gamely and praised Dempsey as a great champion. "I staked my all to win in the second round. I hit him hard, but could not drop him. I tried again in the third but a right to my neck seemed to daze me. I do not know how he got through my guard in the fourth. America should be proud of Dempsey. He is a great champion." Georges said a clubbing right to the back of his neck in the 3rd round caused his downfall. He was not able to be effective after that.

Another quoted Carpentier as saying (through a translator),

This has been one of the best sporting matches in which I have engaged. I have no excuses to make or apologies to offer. Dempsey is the most powerful man I have ever met. He hits with terrific force and without a doubt proved himself a better man than I am. I did my best and have no fault to find. It was, however, my misfortune to fracture a small bone in my right thumb in the second round. The hardest blow I received, and which knocked me out, was the blow on the top of my head in the fourth round – a terrific smash.

Carpentier said he had confidence entering the ring, all the way through the 2nd round. "I kept my confidence of ultimate victory until the second round. Even when I felt Dempsey's hard blow, I felt I could beat him. In the second round I made my supreme effort, and know I had Dempsey breaking ground before me. But my hand cracked on that iron jaw and from then on, I knew I was through." He fought to stave off the inevitable. Still, he admitted that despite his injured hand, Dempsey was the better man. "He is the greatest champion that ever fought."

Carp's eye was swelling from the blow which broke open his left cheek. His nose was badly swollen. Purple marks from the body blows were present on his stomach and kidneys. His hand was badly swollen at the base of the thumb, to the size of a goose egg.

Carp said he wasn't using the hand as an excuse. "I am sensitive to such things, and do you know I was honestly a little bit sorry for Jack, whose own countrymen were favoring me."

In another interview, Carpentier said he staked his all in the 2nd round. He had hit him with everything he had in those blows, but the American could take it. Georges could do nothing more than try to fight him off. Somehow or other the American's blows had gotten past his guard, and they were the stiffest jolts he ever had encountered.

I lost, and I am sorry. Dempsey is the most powerful puncher I have ever met. In the second round I broke the lower joint of my thumb on the right hand. I had caught Dempsey twice on the jaw with a right and then a left, and then, as we were drawing away, I let the right go again. The punch landed high on Dempsey's head and I felt the bone in my thumb crack. After that I tried to hold him off with my left, but he was too strong for me. I have no excuse to offer. I decided to stake my all in the second round on that right-hand punch, and I thought that it staggered Dempsey. But he came right back with some terrific blows. I realized, as I saw Dempsey stand up after taking my best, that I was up against a harder proposition than I had counted on. In the third round I decided to make another big effort, and again I threw everything I had into a right, but again the champion stood up and hit harder than ever. He hit me a terrific punch on the neck, and that wilted me. I do not remember how he managed to pass my guard in the fourth. But he did.

Another paper quoted Carpentier as saying,

> Dempsey is a real champion. He hits terrible blows. Before the fight he looked worried, and I decided to go after him, instead of keeping away as I had first planned. But the fearful punches he landed in the clinches told me I had made a mistake.
>
> In the second round, however, I had the joy of seeing him back away after I had landed some of my rights to his head. Then, just as I swung to his head as he came into a clinch, I felt a sharp pain in my hand and I knew it was broken.
>
> I outboxed Dempsey in the third round, but he took my punches so he could hit me.
>
> In the fourth, a left and a right put me down. I got up at the count of six, but before I could land a blow he hit me under the heart again. I did not hear the count.

Descamps said, "It was a case of the greatest light heavyweight in the world against the greatest heavyweight. Dempsey was too heavy and too strong. It was like Stanley Ketchel trying to beat Jack Johnson."

After the fight, Dempsey "was the smiling, big-hearted, rollicking boy that he really is."

Dempsey said, "Well, it was a great fight. I guess everybody was satisfied. ... The Frenchman is a game fighter and deserves all the credit in the world." Another quoted Dempsey as saying,

> I want to hand it to Carpentier. He certainly was game. But I think I showed conclusively that I have it on him every which way. I beat him just as I thought I would. It was a fine battle and I believe the public is satisfied. I tried my hardest and finished the challenger as soon as I possibly could. ... There is one thing that puzzles me. They tell me that in the second round Carpentier hit me a terrific right on the jaw and staggered me. Well, if he staggered me, I did not know it. I do not remember getting that blow. I do not remember that Carpentier even hit me hard enough to shake me up at any time. I had that fight well in hand all the way. ... I knew that Carpentier could not hit me hard enough to hurt and I knew that I had everything on him – that I could batter him down early. He fought the best way he could have fought. It is likely that the blow which they say staggered me got me off my balance, but I certainly was not in danger then or at any other time. I might have knocked him out a little sooner, but I was not taking any chances. ... Carpentier is the heavyweight champion of Europe and I had my own title at stake and wanted to take no unnecessary chance of losing it.

One day after the fight, Dempsey told "Square" Eddie Forbes, "Georges is game and he made a good fight. He did his best and no man can be asked to do more. That is all that I did. He's clever. Cleverer than he has been given credit for." When asked about his punch, Jack said,

Georges can punch, but he does not know how to hit. His punches did not hurt me. I won't say they did not bother me, for then I would not be telling the truth. He did not sting me but he riled me. I cannot stand being hit. The best proof that he does not carry an effective punch is that I am not marked. I knew where I was every moment during the fight and I knew that it would be only a matter of minutes after the bout started when I would get him. The one thing I want emphasized is that Georges is game and moreover he is exceptionally clever. Can I say more?

Jack said he trained hard for the fight, and needed a rest. "It has been a strain and I want to get away from it all. Let's talk of something else."

Yet, in another newspaper, Dempsey praised Carpentier's power. Writing for the *Buffalo Times*, Dempsey said there was glory in defeat for the Frenchman. Europe sent its greatest ring battler developed in 40 years. Carpentier's blows were terrific, and he was game and clever, but he was a little too light and small to win the title, which remained in America. Georges put up a splendid fight and gave Jack a tough battle. He was very fast and clever, and could hit really hard. Twice Georges landed rights that shook him up, but Jack stayed on his feet, and it was then he knew that he could not lose. "I abandoned the early caution, for I had nothing more to fear and went out to cut him down in a hurry."

The Frenchman surprised him with the opening-bell rush. But Jack was prepared for the right swing.

I fought through that first round with more than usual caution. I had 12 rounds to finish him in and I wasn't going to take any foolish chances with wild rushes. I let him lead and was quite pleased whenever he came into a clinch. For I knew that in the clinches I could smash and batter away at his rather slim body. I didn't get in a really clear shot in the first because I didn't do much opening up. I was waiting for the opportunity to present itself. But no real one came into sight. So, the first ended with Georges wearing a red nose and a reddened body from clinch battering.

In the 2nd round, Carpentier showed what made him the idol of France and Europe. He kept coming in with his right. Several missed, but one landed, and like a flash he drove the same hit to the same spot. "And I'll confess with all honesty that he socked me just about as hard as anyone has hit me in years." Georges landed a glancing third right and the rush carried them into a clinch. Jack knew that he could stand up under some tough hammering. Carp kept rushing, but the crisis was over. Jack had taken all he had, and still was on his feet full of fight, which made him absolutely sure of victory.

Carpentier seemed weary in the 3rd round, and lacking the earlier fighting spirit. Jack decided to use that round to wear him down more. He kept looking for a good opening, but Carp either danced away or fell into clinches. But the clinches harmed Georges more than they helped, because Jack kept ripping into his body and lifting short uppercuts to the chin that weakened him more and more. At the bell, Jack knew that Georges could not weather another round. He was being rocked with lefts and rights at close quarters, and he was wobbly, no longer fighting back.

In the 4th round, Dempsey went after him. He faked a left to the head and then sent home a lifting right to the heart at short range with everything he had behind it. It was the same blow that had helped pave his way practically to every important victory. He felt Carp sag, but he did not go down, showing superb gameness. Georges backed away, and Jack was after him. Carp tried some sidesteps and ducks, and Jack tried to maneuver him into a position to hit him. Georges started a right but Jack let loose a left hook that caught him flush on the chin. As he staggered, a fraction of a second later, Jack landed a right hook and Georges crumpled to the floor.

Carpentier seemed utterly beaten, but gamely rose at nine. Jack measured him with his left and fired a right and Georges toppled to the floor on his right side. He tried to rise at six, but the power was gone from him. After Harry Ertle counted ten, Jack picked him up off the floor. He commended Georges for being a fine, warm, game man of courage, who fought until the last ounce of strength was gone, "and no man can do more."

Another paper quoted Dempsey as saying,

> I found Georges Carpentier one of the toughest men I ever faced, and no one can tell me he isn't game. He has a mightier good right hand and I know it. But I'm mighty glad that he landed it, because I think it demonstrated pretty well that I can take a real punch on the chin and then come in and do something myself. I tried to win right off the bat, but Carpentier was in mighty good shape, too, and I had to work to get him. That was a fine rally he staged in the second but after that was over, I knew I had him. ... I consider Carpentier a game fighter, a clever boxer, and a good fellow. I honestly enjoyed my tussle with him. ... he surely won my fighting admiration for the fierceness and technique he combined in the second round onslaught on me.

Dempsey said it was a blow over the heart that really finished Carpentier.

Jack told Joe Benjamin, "You've got to hand it to Carpentier, he was surely game."

Jack Kearns said,

> It happened just as I expected. The Frenchman is a game fighter and gave Jack a hard battle, especially in the second round, when he nailed the champion with left and right hand smashes, but I was satisfied when Dempsey came back to his corner at the end of that round that he would take the Frenchman in a few rounds more.

The only thing that surprises me is that the Frenchman was able to stay in there so long. He took an awful punching about the body from Jack and showed wonderful gameness in fighting back at the champion. The fight was surely but slowly going against him.

Kearns also said, "I think the public will believe me now, that Dempsey is a 100% more improved fighter than he was when he defeated Willard at Toledo. I never saw a cooler man in the ring than Jack was today. He handled himself wonderfully. He never lost his head and he timed his punches perfectly."

The same-day *Ithaca Journal-News* said Dempsey severely punished the French challenger, giving him an unmerciful beating. He opened up a cut under his eye and batted him viciously around the head with rights and lefts until Carp's face was swollen and bleeding. Georges fought back gamely, but was outclassed. In the 1st round he was half knocked and half pushed through the ropes, and he was knocked down twice in the 4th. Most of the time he was going away from the champ, who kept driving after him throughout. When it was over, Dempsey tenderly picked him up.

The same-day *Buffalo Evening News* said Dempsey was the greatest champion since John L. Sullivan, and one of the hardest hitters of all time. He had to be given credit, for Carpentier had been called a "Greek god," "Mystery man," "Gorgeous Georges," "Man of Destiny," and "Wonder Man," acclaimed as the "greatest heavyweight Europe has produced."

According to William Abbott, Kearns said neither he nor Dempsey had wagered a cent on the contest. Carpentier had bet $10,000 on himself.

The *New York World's* Vincent Treanor said the battle was furious from the start. The Frenchman worried Jack in the 1st and 2nd, but the bell saved the challenger in the 3rd, and in the 4th, Dempsey paid no attention to his blows, but waded in and finished him.

Carp returned to his dressing room through an admiring throng, beaten but not disgraced. He had put up a wonderful fight, and several times the championship seemed to be but one well-directed punch away.

Carpentier had tested the champion. "Dempsey proved that he could take it, and that's really why he won." Jack never lost his coolness, even in the 2nd round when he briefly appeared to be on the verge of being knocked out. Carp fought as if he was trying to win with a single blow. He landed cleanly several times, but each time, Dempsey shook off the effects and crowded into him. The great crowd acclaimed the winner, but expressed sympathy for the defeated man.

Robert Edgren noted that back in late 1919, he wrote that putting Carpentier into the ring with Dempsey would be cruel and senseless, and it would be over in a round if Jack went after him the way he did with Willard. Dempsey was 196 pounds when he stopped 200+-pound Fred Fulton within the first 30 seconds, and Carp would be too small to give him a fight.

Yet, Edgren said he never saw a greater fighter pound-for-pound than Carpentier. It was a thrilling battle. At times, Dempsey was bewildered by Carpentier's terrific punches. Carp was a master, with amazing speed and force. He was courageous and game. He could beat any other man. Dempsey was forced to the limit of his skill, and won though superior strength and stamina. Jack had no limit to his grit, courage, and determination, and physically there was no other man like him.

Edgren said it was the greatest crowd ever. Dempsey was cheered when introduced, but when Carpentier was introduced as "The idol of his people and a soldier of France," the applause was deafening. After the fight, Dempsey said, "Too bad, George. You gave me a great fight."

Before Dempsey left the ring, Referee Ertle removed his gloves, examined them and his bandages again, and found them to be all right.

It was rumored later that Carpentier broke his hand and wrist in the 2nd round, but if he did, he surely hit some wonderful blows with it thereafter.

The *New York Daily News'* Harry Newman reported that Dempsey retained his title in 4 short but grueling rounds. Dempsey's cruel punches were too much for his lighter opponent, though Carpentier fought back gamely. It briefly looked as if the Frenchman was going to defeat Dempsey, but the Yankee's crushing blows soon reduced the European to a condition which made him easy prey for the champ's vicious attacks.

Carpentier surprised everyone by stepping out in the first minute and trading punches. Dempsey rapped him with left and right hooks to the stomach, and it was apparent then that the Frenchman's weakness was in the body. No man of his build could weather those punches for long, and, realizing his only hope lay in driving home one of his right wallops, he kept using that member at every opportunity.

In the 2nd round, the Frenchman drove in a right with everything he had, and the blow landed on the jaw. The champ reeled, and when Georges followed it up with another to the face, Dempsey grabbed. While his head was clearing, Jack ripped hard body punches which had a terrific effect. The body blows weakened Georges and forced him to break ground continually. Finding it impossible to stay in close, he was compelled to retreat in circles to escape the terrible onslaught.

The 4th round found Dempsey crowding with every step. His vicious, wicked, murderous body blows finally left Georges vulnerable to the finishing punches, and Carpentier crumpled up and went down.

Carpentier left the ring staggering, but received almost as many cheers as the victor. It had been a great and entertaining exhibition.

Copies of the fight films were put on a ship to be taken to Europe, where big money could be made.

Carpentier said he broke his right thumb and sprained his wrist when he nailed Dempsey's cheekbone in the 2nd round.

Dr. Joseph Connolly examined him and verified that Carp was suffering from a compound fracture of the metacarpal bone of his right thumb, and he also had a slight wrist sprain. Carp's hand was swollen to three times its normal size.

Carpentier had fought more defensively in the 3rd and 4th rounds, but he did not noticeably avoid using his right in any way. When the opportunity arose, he fired it.

The *Brooklyn Daily Eagle's* Thomas Rice said science plus brute strength had prevailed. Carpentier was too frail to absorb Dempsey's blows. Every one of Dempsey's punches told, whereas only a few of Carpentier's made any impression on the champion. Dempsey could give more and take more.

Carpentier pumped his left, sought to follow with his right, and then either move away or clinch. But he also forced the fighting, wanting to land the harder blows first, before he received a weakening blow from Dempsey. He thought he could knock him out while he was fresh. He possibly could have been more cautious and clever and tried to wear him out gradually, but in doing so he also might have given Dempsey more opportunities to catch him. So, he tried to land big blows early on. Second-guessers were saying that he made a mistake by not playing a more defensive battle and trying to outpoint Dempsey over the 12-round limit. However, with such tactics, he could have received even more punishment too. He conducted a "sporting" battle that won him as much or more honor than if he had "tin-canned" and ran away. He took risks in order to win.

Despite reports that Carpentier had broken his right thumb and sprained his right wrist in the 2nd round, he still was firing very powerful blows in the 3rd round. Dempsey simply was unaffected, and fired away at the body to sap his strength. Carp boxed defensively, but was aggressive when he thought the opportunity offered.

Carpentier afterwards said a rabbit punch in the 3rd round dazed him, and he never recovered. Still, Carp threw several more rights to Dempsey's head even after the rabbit punch landed, fighting hard.

Carpentier entered the 4th round weakened from a hard left and right to the jaw in the 3rd, as well as the steady body punishment at close quarters which gradually had reduced his resistance.

Dempsey simply was too big and strong for him. He had more skill than some realized, as well as stamina and a resistance to shock that made him almost unbeatable. Jack's blows made Carp flinch. Blows that Carp landed, which would have brought to the floor any other heavyweight, were taken by Dempsey as if they were routine or ordinary.

U.S. President Warren Harding, when told of the result, simply asked reporters, "Was it a good fight?" They confirmed that it was.

W. C. Vreeland said Dempsey was stung when Carpentier was introduced as the "Soldier of France." The American's lack of a war record was an underlying stigma, and he had been maligned by inference as a slacker – a coward. When Humphries introduced Carp, a scowl passed over Dempsey's face. From that moment on, there was but one desire on his part – to crush Carpentier and prove that it was not fear that kept him out of the war.

Dempsey's stomach blows beat Carpentier. It was a battle between a grizzly bear and a bull terrier. Brute strength, courage, coolness, pugnacity, and tenacity wore down and smashed cleverness, speed, and courage. Dempsey had the strength to stand up under a crushing blow, throw it off, crash over thunderbolts at short range, and smother and beat down Carpentier's rapier-like thrusts.

At 3:16 p.m., Carp sprang out of his corner and landed the first blow, a long left to the chin. At 3:27, he was flattened out, prone on the canvas, the result of a crushing blow over the heart.

Dempsey proved his courage. If he had been a weakling, he would have crumpled onto the mat in the 2nd round, when he was hit flush on the chin with a long, straight right that would have knocked out cold anyone else. Jack did not even go down. Carp lost his chance to win in that round, when he failed to seize his opportunity adequately.

Carpentier was quick and clever and fought fast and furiously. His fury and strength carried him along at a fast pace in the first 2 rounds. After that, his fury and strength faded. He had no reserve force to call upon. He was battered in the 3rd and 4th rounds.

Dempsey was strong, perfectly coordinated, and his muscles were whipcords, as powerful and pliable as steel wire. He seemed somewhat tense, nervous, and eager before the fight. But when the bell rang, he never was nervous, and became a machine of crushing power, his shaggy eyebrows almost touching under the influence of his scowl. He watched carefully and never turned his back except when in the 2nd round Carp landed on the point of the chin and turned him sidewise.

Dempsey was stronger and could absorb punishment without wilting. He had wonderful vitality and power to deliver a blow like a battering ram at close range. The short punches sent with terrific force at less than a foot away, to the head and body, were what battered Carp down. "It was at in-fighting that Dempsey excelled. It was that kind of battling that won him his triumph." He tied up Carp's arms in a knot, pinned them, and then planted short blows to the stomach and ribs. Carp was not a good inside fighter. He seemed vulnerable to stomach blows, which appeared to affect and weaken him.

In the 1st round, Carp forced the fighting. At the bell, he tried to catch Dempsey unaware by sprinting out of his corner as if projected by a powerful spring. He took Dempsey by surprise, but Jack met the attack by bracing his feet, and he was able to stand the force. Carp carried the fight to Dempsey at long range. But after that round, Dempsey became the aggressor. Thereafter, Carp always was moving backward, twisting and turning to get away from the short punches and to sidestep fighting at close quarters.

Dempsey did not try to block, smother, or catch the blows. He depended more on twisting his head to one side as the punch came toward his face. He was good at dodging, and it was very effective, for the blows did no damage. When Carp missed, the momentum carried him into the zone of trouble, where Dempsey could hook him to the face, rip a stomach blow, or use an uppercut. So, his head movement served to bring Carpentier in close.

Their fortunes ebbed and flowed back and forth. Carpentier fought himself out in the first 2 rounds. His attack was so furious, his blows sent over so fast and with such force, that they sapped a great deal of his strength. Many times, his right missed and curved around Dempsey's head like the lash of a whip. He soon was panting from his own exertions. The cut on his nose and the gash under his left eye hurt him mentally more than physically. Each wound bled freely. Dempsey's face showed no marks at all.

The 18-foot ring helped as well, for it limited Carpentier's ability to escape, restricted his footwork, and enabled Dempsey to keep on top of him.

Dempsey had the better of the 1st round. Carp's long straight punches jarred Jack several times but did not hurt him. They merely served to check momentarily his boring-in style of attack.

The 2nd round was decidedly in Carp's favor. He crashed the right that caused a frenzy of excitement. But he failed to follow up his advantage. Opportunity never again came his way. It was unclear whether he was afraid to rush in for fear that Dempsey was playing possum, not really that hurt, or he failed to grasp fully his chance. But he let his chance slip away. (Perhaps it was because Dempsey kept coming forward and nailed him with some good blows.)

The 3rd round was the beginning of the end, for Dempsey got him at close quarters and shook Carpentier with heavy stomach blows and uppercuts to the chin. Dempsey sent in a shower of short punches to the face and body like a steady stream. Carp was unable to cover up or strike back. The punches were having their effect, and his legs were starting to sag when the bell rescued him. When he went to his corner, Carp seemed to be exhausted, in distress, gasping for breath through his mouth. His chest rose and fell with violence.

In the 4th round, Dempsey never gave him a second's rest. He was after him all the time, bent on crushing him to the canvas. A hard right under the heart staggered and doubled up Carpentier. Georges backed away and missed punches. Dempsey stepped in and sent over a left to the chin and short right to the chin and Carpentier crumpled to the mat. He rose at nine, dazed. Dempsey stepped in with a terrific right near the heart and knocked him out. Carpentier fell on his right side, his body doubled up. He tried to rise, but could not.

After Carp had recovered, they walked towards one another and shook hands. Carpentier told Dempsey, "You won fairly and squarely and I wish you the best of luck. You are a great fighter and possess a heavy punch. Oui, oui, it hurt – those punches. You are certainly a wonderful fighter."

Dempsey replied, "Good luck to you. You put up a fine battle. I'll say that you're the best man that I have ever faced in the ring. I hope you are not hurt. I wish you all the luck in the world."

Dempsey wrote his mother a telegram, "Mrs. C. Dempsey, 3572 S. State St., Salt Lake City, Utah. Dear Mother – Won in the fourth round. Received your wire. Will be home soon as possible. Love and kisses. JACK."

Victor Breyer, editor for the *Echo de Sports*, Paris, said,

> It was a wonderful fight, full of action and thrills from start to finish. The best man won, but everybody who was present will agree that Carpentier put up a wonderful fight. He might have done better yet, if his right hand…had not gone when he staggered Dempsey in the second round. … Carpentier proved he was the best boxer of the pair, but Dempsey proved the finest fighter. He is just the terror every one told me he was – one who is able to assimilate punishment and deliver same. He is, indeed, worthy of the title of World's Champion.

French writer M. Andre said Dempsey had too much power, strength, energy, endurance, and iron ruggedness. Carpentier fought a courageous battle, attacking ceaselessly, trying to impose himself, and in the 2nd round almost snatched victory from the fates, but he was pitted against a most powerful and admirable fighter, who although seeming to move slowly, moved all the time and always forward. Georges had the advantage when he boxed and moved, but in the infighting, was punished severely. After the 2nd round, the knockout seemed inevitable. Dempsey essentially was an impenetrable tank that kept moving forward and could not be discouraged.

B. Benneson of London's *Daily Telegraph* said, "It was a great and dramatic fight. The best man undoubtedly won. Dempsey is the best and strongest fighter for more years than I care to remember. … Carpentier, except in the second round, never looked like winning. Dempsey was too strong for him and he was faster than most Europeans thought him to be."

The *Excelsior's* Andre Glarner said Carpentier would remain a French idol. "He was beaten by a better, greater and more complete boxer." Still, he came close to being champion in the 2nd round, when he landed a perfect 1-2 to the jaw, the same that put out Wells, Beckett, and many others. When those punches failed even to put Dempsey down, "we all knew he wouldn't win."

Andre Fanger of *Progress de Lyon* said this Dempsey was much better than the one seen against Brennan. He showed more speed than expected. "You have the best in the world."

Jack Kelly said Dempsey was too strong and hit too hard. Carpentier outboxed him and often beat him to the punch, but Dempsey kept boring in, and once close, he hooked savagely to the jaw and pounded unmercifully to the body. It didn't take many punches to make Georges wilt. Dempsey won the fight with his terrific body punches.

Dempsey found out in the 1st round that he could take the vaunted right-hand punches, and he waded in, pounding away, disregarding his defense. He obviously was tearing him down. Within two minutes, the blood oozed from Carpentier's nose and lips.

Still, in the 2nd round, Carpentier brought the 91,000 fans to their feet, yelling like mad when he staggered Dempsey with overhand swings. He drove Dempsey before him with the fury of his attack and landed a right cross flush on the jaw. But he could not put Dempsey out, or even down, which likely discouraged him. It was Carpentier's final big effort.

In the 3rd, Dempsey bore in, and the challenger could not evade him despite running. Body blows and short hooks to the jaw weakened Carpentier, who used all his speed and science, and tried to retreat and box, attempting to win with one hard blow, but he was missing or not landing well enough, for Dempsey would move his head slightly to make the blows slide off. Dempsey caught and pummeled him with pile-driving body blows. Even when Carp landed flush rights, Jack took them like nothing and retaliated with cruel body blows. Georges was bleeding under his eye, which was closing rapidly, his mouth was open, and blood running from cut lips. It was apparent that he could not last much longer.

More body blows in the 4th round took all of Carp's power away. He still lunged at Dempsey, but made little impression. Kearns was yelling, "Go after him now, boy; you've got him." The sneering Dempsey bore in wide open, pounded the body, and put Carpentier down twice. At ten, Carpentier was on his right side with left leg in the air and left arm pawing at the air for help.

He was out of it for three minutes. Even when he left the ring ten minutes later, Carpentier still could not hold himself erect. It had been a great battle.

Dempsey said, "Carp is a fine boy and gave me a tough fight."

Several days later, Kelly said Carpentier could beat either Brennan or Gibbons, for his speed and straight hitting was enough to outpoint them if not knock them out. Neither Brennan nor Gibbons hit as hard or as relentlessly as the champion. Carpentier could beat any other man in the ring, barring Dempsey and Wills. No one hit as hard to the body as Dempsey, but Carp took it for as long as he could.

Kelly believed that Carp should have been more cautious. He was too gallant for his own good. But to his credit, he tried to win rather than merely survive. His gameness made him even more popular. He fought hard, and even tried to get up after being decked the second time, but could not.

The greatest crowd in the world's history saw the fight. It wasn't that Dempsey was unpopular, for they cheered for both, but Carpentier's popularity overshadowed his. Dempsey deserved a great deal of credit for his victory over such a great man.

To my mind, Dempsey will never receive full credit for the wonderful fight he put up, probably because he was expected to do just what he did. The champion fought a stubborn, cool battle. After the challenger reached his head and jaw in the first round, Dempsey elevated his left shoulder as a sort of shield for his jaw and with his arms partly extended walked grimly into the challenger. Once close to his man, Dempsey was a veritable demon. He hooked, slugged and slashed, and wherever he hit he must have hurt terribly.

Dempsey was wobbly and staggered in the 2nd round, although he denied it. It was fortunate for him that he was in top condition. "Now they are talking of a Dempsey-Willard fight. Well, if the champion doesn't fight Harry Wills, that [Dempsey-Willard] is about the only fight left for him, and that, if Dempsey is in good shape and trains like he did for Carpentier, should be a second Toledo."

Johnny Kilbane, featherweight champ, was not as generous, saying Carpentier was knocked out because he failed to use his brains. Kilbane said the next most logical opponent for Dempsey was the very skillful Tommy Gibbons, who would have put up a better fight than Carpentier did. Carp could have won by boxing and using his skill, but he was a fool. When he boxed, he was doing well. But he did not stay out of clinches, and that is where Dempsey did his damage and overcame Georges' greater speed and skill, wearing him out. Kilbane said brute strength beat skill. Still, Kilbane believed Carpentier had fought an even fight up until the 4th round.

Kilbane said Dempsey beat him in the 1st round with short uppercuts in the clinches, mostly lefts. Despite the fact that Carpentier was weakened by the punishment, he managed to have Dempsey groggy in the 2nd round, which unquestionably belonged to Carpentier. He was too fast and his boxing too good. Dempsey was missing and Carp landing worthwhile punches. The 3rd was a draw. Carp landed more blows, but Dempsey landed harder. On the whole, Carpentier landed more clean blows than Dempsey.

Kilbane felt that had Carpentier danced his way out of the deadly clinches, as he had done in the 2nd round, he might have won. "Carpentier didn't do the thing he could do better than Dempsey and he tried to do the thing that Dempsey could do better than he could. That was Carpentier's fatal mistake."

Kilbane failed to recognize the fact that Dempsey's relentless pressure forced Carpentier to clinch and fight on the inside. It was not easy keep away from this version of Dempsey.

The crowd truly enjoyed the fight, which was competitive throughout. The fans appreciated and admired both men. Never before did so many women attend a bout.

Overseas, Parisians were dumbfounded by the result, and at first refused to believe it. First news reached them at 8:32 p.m. Even French

President Millerand, Premier Briand, and other ministers received a series of bulletins.

The English were gloomy too, for Carpentier had been a popular favorite with them as well.

However, the real followers of pugilism had Dempsey the strong favorite. Even Beckett and Wells, who lost to Carpentier, picked Dempsey, although they said they would be pulling for Carp. They gave him a chance, but predicted a fierce but short duel.

The *New York Daily Tribune* contained several articles by different writers who were at the fight.

Jack Lawrence said a record crowd of 90,000 in a huge bowl-shaped arena at Boyle's Thirty Acres in Jersey City, New Jersey saw the historic bout. It was the greatest crowd ever to witness a sporting event. The huge throng was orderly, good-natured, and remarkably undemonstrative.

Only three times were there really spontaneous bursts of enthusiasm, once when Governor Edwards entered the arena, once when Carp rocked Dempsey to his heels with hard lefts and rights to the jaw in the 2nd round, and finally when the champion delivered short hooks that brought the battle of the century to a close. During the preliminaries, the fans were indifferent and bored. They were not there for appetizers.

Both fighters received ovations when they entered the ring, but it was rather formal. The champ drew the most applause during the march down the aisles. Carpentier, his blond hair brushed back and not looking like a prizefighter, drew great applause from the several thousand women present, who favored him, and they took his defeat the hardest. One woman wept copiously during the fight, and every time Dempsey landed a telling blow, she winced. When a crushing right hook to the jaw sent Carpentier down to defeat, she screamed and collapsed. Two firemen escorted her from the arena.

Bandages merely were white cotton, both fighters winding their own.

Dempsey earned about $487 per second to earn his $300,000 share, before taxes.

The *New York Tribune's* Heywood Broun said Carpentier was *too eager* when victory seemed near, but he went down with his fists flying. He bled and fought hard to the end.

In the 2nd, Carpentier was within a punch of the championship. His long straight right hit flush on the chin. Dempsey went back on his heels. He was swaying a little, and Carp was too eager to hit a moving target, rather than taking his time to set up a finisher.

During the rest of the fight, Dempsey was on top. He kept close, using his superior weight and strength, which told enormously. He was only 16 pounds heavier, but it seemed like much more. He could move his challenger about as he pleased and punched him severely whenever they came together.

Carpentier's gallantry was a handicap. He would not stay away and make a running fight. Even in the 3rd and 4th rounds, when his strength was being hammered away, he kept throwing punches.

Carp was smiling, but began bleeding in the 1st round, and suffered from the body punches. He kept coming in though.

Dempsey was methodical and efficient, like a guillotine. The champ fought fairly and squarely, even carrying Georges to his corner after the fight. He said, "He's a good tough boy!"

Perhaps Carpentier did not like being called the "orchid man," and wanted to show that he could keep close and trade punches. But that was not the wisest strategy. It became evident in the 3rd round that he was a beaten man. He was groggy from heavy, short hooks.

In the 4th round, a powerful right finished it. Carp could not rise until assisted by Dempsey, Deschamps, and Journee. Four or five minutes elapsed before he was revived. He came to ring center and he and Jack talked and shook hands.

When Carpentier entered the ring he smiled, whirled about, his hands high above his head, acknowledging the applause. It was heartier than that which Dempsey received.

In the fight's first clinch, Carp was punished severely and came out with a bloody nose. But he had much the better of it at long range. He landed often and had no trouble making Jack miss. But Dempsey constantly kept edging in, and instead of giving ground, Carp moved in too, and often rushed in and fought up close. It was ill advised. The blows that knocked out Beckett and Bombardier Wells could not drop Dempsey. Carpentier's will was broken against a great rock.

All of Paris was shrouded in gloom at the news of its hero's defeat. Georges' wife canceled her trip to the U.S., and said she would wait for him to return home. Thousands who received bulletins said, "It can't be true." They became sad and depressed, particularly when they read that Carpentier was completely outclassed and outfought.

Grantland Rice was at ringside. He said three blows shattered France's idol. Hooks to both sides of the jaw and then a crusher to the region of the heart caused his collapse. Dempsey nearly was knocked out himself, but proved that his jaw was like a granite wall, and he was the most destructive hitter ever to hold the championship. He took Carpentier's best punch in the 2nd round, but never went down.

At 3:16 p.m., Carpentier stood at ring center receiving one of the greatest ovations ever given a fighter. At 3:27 p.m., he lay stretched out on the resin. The lily of France was a broken blossom. His right thumb was broken in two places and his right wrist sprained and swollen from contact with Dempsey's cast-iron jaw.

Carpentier stood up to the crushing power of Dempsey's blows for 3 rounds plus 1 minute 16 seconds of the 4th, but that was all he could take. His face was cut to crimson ribbons and his frailer body almost broken in two by the hardest-hitting heavyweight ever. He buckled up and dropped before a mighty left and right hooked in lightning succession to each side of his jaw. At nine he rose, but a terrific right hook over the heart sent him into unconsciousness.

The knockout blows were only the finishing effects. It was the body-breaking infighting that broke him down. Even in the 1st round, one could see that the short, savage jolts made the Frenchman's body quiver and give way from the unbearable pain of the punishment. His lone moment came briefly in the 2nd round, but it passed. The two pile-driving rights to Dempsey's jaw hurt, and created a noisy thud. The champ reeled and faltered, but the punches were not enough to finish him.

The Frenchman was fast, skillful, and game. He had the kick of a mule in his blows. Only a fighter of remarkable stamina and unusual toughness could have taken what Dempsey took in that 2nd round and still have the ability to come back in as if he never had been hit. Other big men had been rendered unconscious from the same blows. Dempsey was impregnable, and Carpentier lost his steam. Dempsey kept boring in with heavy blows. Carp had deep gashes under either eye. He was dejected.

Some said Carpentier should have played a waiting game and stayed away. Dempsey hopelessly outclassed him on the inside. However, even when Carpentier did try to keep away, Dempsey quickly glided into reach with a speed that equaled Carp's own. Dempsey always was upon him, no matter where the challenger turned. He simply could not keep away. Jack's punches cut and jolted. Georges weathered the storm for as long as he could.

Dempsey proved his speed, power, and ability to take it. Carp's defense on the inside was not good enough. Jack had the speed to close in quickly, and too much power to be held in check. He landed two to one in the clinches, and had twice the power.

W. O. McGeehan was at ringside as well. He said Carpentier battered Dempsey groggy in the 2nd, but was battered and knocked down twice in the 4th, into a huddled inert heap. The Frenchman fought gallantly. He was confident, wearing a bright smile.

From the start, Dempsey tore at him savagely, ripping body blows in the clinches. Carp's nose bled. A glancing right opened a cut under his left eye. Carpentier gradually grew weaker from Dempsey's choppy body blows.

In the 2nd round, Carp shot Dempsey's head back and dazed him with left to the jaw. The same punch dropped Joe Beckett. Dempsey rocked and tottered but did not fall. He recovered in an instant and fired jolts to the body with both hands. The result was a still-erect Dempsey, a broken right thumb, and a sprained wrist. It was as though Carp's fist had been a last shell bursting against an impenetrable armor plate. The bleeding Carpentier essentially was beaten then, but he wore that same smile.

The 3rd round was futile. Carp threw, but his blows rolled off Dempsey's head, and he kept getting worn down.

In the 4th round, a left followed by a right crashed on the jaw and Carp dropped. He rose, Dempsey shot in a terrific right over the heart, and Georges crumpled and dropped on his side. There hardly was any cheering. The hush was like a funeral. Carpentier looked dead.

Dempsey showed that he could stand punishment as well as deliver it. The blows that Carp landed would have dropped many a heavyweight. They only rocked Dempsey. The end was inevitable. Carp could not withstand Dempsey's sheer power and strength. Few could.

It was only after dashing water on his face that Carp awoke. His nose was bleeding. There was a ragged gash under his left eye. He realized what had happened, shook Dempsey's hand, and congratulated him, smiling. Dempsey said, "I am sorry that I knocked out such a good man."

The moral of the bout was that the punch wins. Carpentier made a gallant effort. As for Dempsey, McGeehan concluded that no heavyweight could stand up against him for some time to come.

W. J. Macbeth said Carpentier lost but was not disgraced. He looked great in defeat. He was a speed marvel; a sharpshooter with a sting to his punches delivered with either hand. At long range he had Dempsey mystified and missing. But Georges was too ambitious and overestimated his ability to assimilate crushing blows. Carp was beaten down by brute force. He fought too much, and the body blows sapped his strength quickly. As early as the 3rd round it could be seen that he was done.

Sophie Treadwell said the fight was a bayonet charge going against heavy artillery. It was gallantry, beauty, courage, and skill going down under blows that were just too strong. Carp fought brilliantly and bravely. Dempsey was sure and powerful.

In the 2nd round, Carp's skill was thrilling, with his swift blows, sudden shifts of the body, his poise, and coordination. He fought with genius. He placed perfectly timed blows. But Dempsey was like fate; too strong. He was hit terrifically, but did not and would not go down. In the 3rd round, Carp's face was smeared with blood from a cut on the side of his nose and a cut on his cheek, but he still was smiling. Dempsey had a black face, the look of overwhelming, unbeatable brutality. The knockout was inevitable. The crowd screamed at the first fall, but were almost stilled at the second.

The *Brooklyn Standard Union*'s William Rafter said Carpentier shook and staggered Dempsey for a moment in *both* the 1st and 2nd rounds. Carpentier's blows, left and right, were delivered with the speed of a rifle bullet to Dempsey's chin. The lightning blows were hard to follow. The champ seemed amazed. The Frenchman was not afraid to leap at the American from the start. In the 2nd round, Dempsey was helpless for about four seconds. Yet, Dempsey rallied quickly, fought his way out of trouble, and administered fearful punishment to his plucky but helpless opponent. It was his fight from then on. The Frenchman had shot his bolt.

Dempsey proved his gameness and ability to assimilate punishment and come through with flying colors. He withstood an attack that would have knocked out anyone else. A right to the jaw in the 4th put Carpentier down. Another right chop to the jaw and down he went again.

James J. Corbett said history repeated itself, as a good big man licked a good little man. Dempsey won decisively, cutting him down, though Carpentier was far from disgraced, for he was game, courageous, and a real fighter.

> For his weight and inches, I have never seen such a quick and vicious hitter. His right hand was all that had been said of it, but the ruggedness of Dempsey enabled him to shake off the punches… Georges shot his bolt and lost. Dempsey won because he is bigger, stronger, and a terrific puncher. Carpentier fought like a tiger when he was able, but he tired after he had made his supreme effort.

A left and right decked Carpentier. A body blow finished him.

Corbett said it would take some man to defeat Dempsey. His punches were deadly and he could take a punch.

An attorney for the International Reform Bureaus demanded that the police arrest Dempsey for criminal assault and battery upon the person of Carpentier, but the police refused.

The *New York Times* said Dempsey forced Carpentier down with an incessant rain of terrific blows. The great throng gave a louder cheer for Georges at the start, but gave Dempsey his acclaim at the end.

> Dempsey was in many ways the most unpopular of white champions. Those who know him best say that this unpopularity is largely undeserved; but the fact remained that millions of people in Dempsey's own country were hoping that the foreign challenger could have beat him.

When it was over, they cheered Dempsey, who proved that whatever else may be said about him, he was no accidental champion. "He can fight." He steadily hammered the body, occasionally the face, with short but terrifically violent punches. Although Carpentier was better on the outside, fighting with incredible speed and power, Dempsey was not slow-moving, and he had great endurance, moving in and punching relentlessly. Although Georges stunned Dempsey in the 2nd round with a right, thereafter Jack was pretty good at ducking and rolling with that blow. Sooner or later he always got to close range, and, once clinched, Dempsey began that terrible punching that would break Carp down. "Carpentier lost because he could not keep Dempsey from hitting him and because he had not the strength to endure Dempsey's blows."

Ray Pearson said gameness was not enough for Carpentier to win. He landed, but Dempsey's jaw seemed to be made of iron. Carp took a terrific beating, as Jack rained short, powerful body punches in close. Dempsey had crunching blows that only he could propel. It was a great fight, great Dempsey, and great Carpentier, in a wonderful stadium. Thrills followed thrills like a machine gun. Carp fought a heroic battle. He would have been victorious against any man other than Dempsey.

Pearson said Dempsey did not really hit his stride and show his true form until the 3rd round. He was more of a boxer in the 1st round than a fighter. He did not use his shift. In the first 2 rounds, he was not hitting the way he can hit, but he opened up more starting in the 3rd round, and continuing in the 4th.

Dempsey's act of lifting Carpentier up and carrying him to his chair earned him applause, something sadly lacking when he entered the ring. It took Carpentier 5 minutes to recover.

Percy Hammond said the big fellow beat the little man to death. "A heavy, black, extensive, forbidding, cruel, painsgiving engine obliterated a weak and imprudent, though thrifty atom which lay in his track." Carp stood no chance against the inevitable American, who was as resistless and mean as all the bad diseases put together.

Eye Witness, in a special from ringside, said early on, Carp's face took on the aspect of an uncooked meal. His face was red. He was dancing with pain and anxiety. It was a dance of doom, for a bear whose shoulders were working with the drive of a catapult was closing in upon the serpent. Dempsey's infighting was astounding, bringing gasps from the audience. Dempsey's face was expressionless, but if there was any expression, it was intenseness. The end was thrilling and glorious, but also piteous. "But let us not sob the moments away." Never had the author seen a sight so grandiose.

A crowd outside the exit gates gave Jack a round of cheers as he drove away in a motor car with Kearns.

R. L. Goldberg said Carpentier had superb composure. He was smiling and confident, the most unconcerned man in the ring, and game to the core, but Dempsey was the world's most dangerous man. At times Carpentier outboxed Dempsey, but he also suffered a terrific mauling.

Horace Lerch said Carpentier was a pleasant-faced man, smiling and full of courage. He left a loser in fine grace, and a smile for his lamenting friends. Dempsey's face and attack were vicious.

This writer did not think Dempsey was as fast or as good as he was in the Willard fight, but he still was a tremendous figure. Carpentier was amazingly popular even in the loss.

Ertle was a capable referee, and the timer's gong was in good hands; no awful bungle like in Toledo.

The arena saucer was packed; an inspiring image. Arrangements were perfect. "No one ever saw such a fight crowd as that of today and possibly there will never be such another, although the big arena is to be kept intact for boxing of the immediate future."

Julia Harpman offered a woman's perspective. It was the first fight she ever saw. The world had come to a stop for this fight. It was a spectacle unlike anything ever witnessed – stupendous, appalling, and altogether beautiful. Several thousand women were present. Ironically, a reverend who was a sworn enemy of the sport attended. Early in the day, a slight drizzle turned to steam with the appearance of the burning sun. Spectators shed their coats and vests.

The first minute of the fight showed that Carpentier was no match for Dempsey, and a wave of pity was felt for him. Dempsey was too strong, too bull-like. "Dempsey hangs his head over his chest, and it swings from side to side while he slashes at his opponent." The graceful Frenchman was not like him. The inequality "was nauseating" and robbed the bout of its glory. Dempsey's blows upon Carpentier's bare body sounded like "the popping of rubber balloons." Carpentier's nose bled, his eye was swollen, and he fell against the ropes. He was punished tremendously.

Yet, Harpman marveled at Carpentier's tenacity when he came back in the 2nd round. George had astonishing pluck and gameness, and he had Dempsey groggy.

Again in the 3rd round, Carpentier accepted fearful blows, until he went down to his doom in the 4th.

Harpman was proud of the fact that an American as always was the greatest, but she was sorry for the Frenchman. "I would be more proud if Dempsey had found a challenger more of his own ilk." Some women wept when Carpentier fell. Yet, Carp smiled when he became conscious again, so Harpman followed suit.

Hiram/Hyrum Dempsey, the champ's father, said, "It's just as I expected. ... I expected Carpentier to have put up a stiffer fight."

Damon Runyon said Dempsey was like a bull terrier tearing up a French doll. Carpentier had been mauled by "Iron Mike," Dempsey's right hand.

Dempsey began the fight cautiously, his jaw tucked behind his shoulders. He skimmed the skin from Carp's nose with a smash. Carp was scurrying backward around the ring, one moment seeming like a scared rabbit, but then suddenly lashing out with a right like an infuriated leopard. Dempsey maintained a sinister expression. Inside, he chopped at Carp, trying to knock him down with the rabbit punch.

In the 2nd round, Carp landed the right, and everyone who had wagers on Dempsey went pale. The punch must have dizzied him for an instant. He closed in, chopping at Carp's body with short blows. The champ quickly shook off the smash's effects, but obviously had considerable respect for Carp's right. It was the punch that he had been advised to avoid, and it was all that ever had been said of it.

Carp was outweighed, meeting a more rugged and much stronger man. From the start, it was difficult to see how Carp could win, barring such a punch. Dempsey flung him around in the clinches as he pleased. A good little man usually loses to a good big man, but Carp had the spirit of a giant. This author did not think he would last a round, but he did.

After the 2nd, it was but a question of time. Dempsey kept chopping away at Carp's body and cracking the tip of his jaw with long-range blows, wearing him down.

In the 4th round, the dark and scowling Dempsey shot out his left in pawing fashion, his right hand went over with a vicious chopping motion, Carp's legs crumpled, and he fell in a heap. As Ertle counted, Dempsey turned and went toward his own corner. To everyone's amazement, Carp rose. Again Jack's left shot out, the right came down, and Carp fell almost in the center of the ring. He did not rise this time.

Women in the crowd squealed hysterically as Carp fell for the first time. Some were crying. The feminine sympathy largely was with Carpentier, the soldier of France. The hardened male fight followers had bet on Dempsey.

After the fight, the two talked for a full minute, Dempsey smiling for the first time. "What they said is not correctly reported save this, that Dempsey told Carpentier the indubitable truth – Carpentier is a great little fighter." Carp smiled and said Dempsey was a great fighter too.

After the fight, a police lieutenant who assisted in removing Carpentier's hand bandages said his right hand was badly swollen, and he even saw the bones sticking out through the flesh.

Bill Brennan credited Dempsey with the best fight of his career. He was cool, calm, and resourceful, a terrific hitter, and never made a real mistake. It never was a question of who would win, but how long the Frenchman could last. It was the terrible, merciless damage inflicted in the clinches that broke Carp's body and fighting spirit and made him easy for Jack to finish when he finally decided to open up with his big guns. Still, Carp fought a game, splendid fight, and deserved praise for his great showing against a powerful man. He shot over his right with wonderful speed and force. But Dempsey's jaw was much harder than those of Beckett, Levinsky, or Wells. "I hit that jaw just like the Frenchman did and I've got a suspicion he wears a few slabs of iron there instead of bone."

The two good socks on the chin that Carpentier landed in the 2nd awoke Jack and got him started. Up until that time he had held back and didn't do a great deal of offensive fighting. "Everything that Carpentier had was in those blows. They did not drop Jack, just jiggled him up a little." Jack's face seemed to have an expression as if to say, "This bird can not knock me out. Nothing more to worry about. Now I'll go out and get him." So he got under way and mauled Carp's body and chin the clinches through the rest of the round. He did the same in the 3rd, and at that point it was a cinch that Jack would win. "He was fresh and going great; the Frenchman was reeling and weak." In the 4th, a right smash to the body took Carp's last real strength away. He backed away and Jack tore at him, landed a 1-2 that dropped him, and repeated the dose to finish him.

Carp fought a great and game fight, with every natural advantage against him, opposed by one of the most powerful fighters in all of ring history. "He gave his best, but it was not good enough to whip the mauler from Utah."

Ring Lardner said when Carpentier hit Dempsey on the chin, he only made it stormy for himself. Most of those who bet against Dempsey, like George Bernard Shaw, never had seen him fight. That was like picking against the famous horse Man O' War without having seen it race.

Based on the 2nd round, "Two things become apparent. One of them was that Georges can sock and the other was that Jack can take it." Blows that Carp had used to knock others down and out only staggered Dempsey, and made him frown a little deeper. It had to be discouraging. Nevertheless, Carp was as game as they come throughout, and always had a right-hand chance, even if it was a long one.

Lardner identified the usual discrepancies about which blows led to the knockout. "But I can speak at more length about round four, because when theys a knockout in a fight like this, all we boys see it different even if we are experts." Lardner believed it was a terrific right to the heart. "You could hear the crack in the $25 seats." Jack immediately followed with a right hook to the jaw and Georges went down. When he rose, in another instant, Dempsey hit him again. "I don't know what the boys will say was the real knockout blow; it looked to me like another right hook to the chin, probably it was just a case of general debility." Carp fell, made a feeble effort to rise, and then turned over on his face, licked.

Afterwards, Dempsey said to Georges, "I'm sorry I had to do it to as good a man as you." Carp smiled. Lardner replied, "Personally, I was glad he didn't have to do it to as good a man as me." "All in all, Georges made a much better showing against this guy than Willard." However, Lardner made one final prediction: "Dempsey won't get no credit for doing what he done and the fight writers will get even less for telling you in advance that he was going to do it."

Neal O'Hara, at ringside for the *Boston Post*, said Carpentier put up a good fight, his fast footwork and speed making the champ look slow by comparison. Carpentier was even more dangerous than Willard. He put up a valorous battle and had Jack dizzy in the 2nd. "Carp took pleasure in outboxing Jack and making him look as slow as a boxcar by comparison."

However, in the middle of the 3rd round, "Dempsey discarded cautionary tactics and waded in to end it all. He looked like a human trouncing machine as he belted the lily savagely and true." By the end of the round, it looked like Carp would be finished. Between rounds, Descamps fed Carp some brown fluid from out of a bottle. No one knew what it contained, but it didn't help.

In the 4th, Dempsey sailed in with unbridled fury. He paid no attention to Carp's blows. He took punches in order that he might send in a telling or finishing blow. The strategy worked. A left and right to jaw sent him down. The crowd shrieked at first, but then 90,000 rose to their feet, cheered and roared so madly that one would have guessed it was unanimous for Dempsey. Georges rose at nine, but a right crash to the body and hook on the jaw sent him down supine and out, curled up like a half moon on the canvas.

Carpentier had given the champ a run for his money. "He gave a neat and impressive showing of boxing, landed a half-dozen walloping blows and at one time during the second round even stepped up and forced the fighting."

However, even those in the cheap seats could hear the sound of the raps when Dempsey whammed Carpentier's torso, a "trip-hammer crash." In the end, "Neither science nor strategics amount to much when Jack wades in to send his blow and bring his forearm down. He proved that much today conclusively. He can take a bunch of punishment, but deliver twice as much."

For less than 15 minutes, the entire world was focused sharply on 36 square yards of resined canvas. "No wonder 90,000 attended. This fray has been built up by a year and a half of publicity, constant and cumulative. The deft manipulations of press agents, coupled with the public's penchant for blood lust and an urging to be present, right in the swim, accounts for the record shattering attendance, and about $1,350,000 in gate receipts." At least 5,000 were women, ages 18 to 35. No prior fight had come close to the revenue generated by this fight.

Tex Rickard figured that $954,000 would cover expenses, and would leave him with about $400,000 in profit, minus income tax.

The films would have been worth more if Carp had won, for they would have sold like a prairie fire in Europe. Still, plenty of folks in New Jersey, Europe, and elsewhere would want to see them.

One felt sad for Carp, until considering that he earned $200,000 compensation. Dempsey got as much money for 10 minutes of work as the U.S. President did for his entire 4-year term: $300,000 vs. $75,000 a year x 4. "Jack should be glad that he wasn't born to be president."

Tex Rickard said, "I feel sure that today's boxing contest shows that the sport can be conducted in such a manner that will entitle boxing to a place on the same high plane with other professional sports, such as baseball and hockey. There was not the slightest trouble or disturbance at any time in the arena…" Tex thanked local officials. "I never saw a crowd better handled, and it was the greatest that ever gathered around a ring. … The whole affair should prove to those who try to prevent boxing contests that the game has reached a plane where it may be left alone." He wanted the attacks on the sport to stop, and for the politicians and laws to loosen up.

Regarding the fight, Rickard said, "Dempsey has proved himself to be the same wonderful fighter as previously. Carpentier showed he is one of the cleverest and best fighters I have seen. The Frenchman was game throughout the fight." There was honor for both men. "Jack was too big and strong for Carpentier, but the latter gave the crowd plenty of action and many thrills until Dempsey's powerful punches ended the bout."

Tex said Kearns told him that Dempsey would be available for a fight on September 5. Willard was being considered, if he wanted it.

Frank Spellman, president of the International Gypsum Co. and proprietor of Spellman's Motorized Circus, tied up Dempsey's $300,000 purse with a writ of attachment, claiming that commissions were due for getting the champ moving picture contracts and for personal services. Dempsey would have to deal with more legal issues.

On the same day as Dempsey-Carpentier, on the evening of July 2, 1921, at the Queensboro A.C. in Long Island City, New York, 214-pound Harry Wills stopped former Dempsey sparring partner 243 ¾-pound Bill Tate in the 6th round, with a right to the jaw.

However, Tex Rickard insisted that he would not match Dempsey with Harry Wills. "There is no chance that I will attempt to match Wills with Dempsey. I will not match a negro with a white man. There was too much trouble attendant to matching two white boys." Meaning, as much trouble as it was to hold a white vs. white fight, there would be even greater challenges and obstacles in bringing off an interracial world heavyweight championship fight.

VANQUISHED, BUT A HERO | THE WINNER | THE LOSER

JACK DEMPSEY | GEORGES CARPENTIER

In an interview conducted the day after the fight, Descamps said, "Jack Dempsey is the greatest heavyweight who ever lived. But I'll claim that my Georges comes next. Dempsey was too heavy and too powerful for Georges. We will not seek a return match." Descamps believed that Dempsey really was 194 pounds, not 188. Many agreed.

Descamps claimed that Carpentier actually had a hurt hand coming into the fight.

> It was, of course, an unfortunate thing that Carpentier broke his hand in that second round yesterday. He may have gone on and defeated the champion, but the chances are that the result would have been the same, only it would have come later in the fight.
>
> Georges suffered an injury to his hand two weeks ago while boxing with Joe Jeannette and it may have been this that caused it to snap yesterday. After the workout with Jeannette that day he told us he had hurt his hand, but asked us to keep it quiet. He said if the newspapermen learned of it people would say he was preparing an alibi. It was for this reason that he started secret training.

Carpentier cabled his wife after the fight, saying, "Have no fear. I am all right. I did my best."

Carpentier said that after the 1st round, he came back to his corner and told them that every one of Dempsey's blows hurt. "Then keep away from him," they told him. But he wanted to fight.

Carp said he had fractured his right hand slightly in a training bout with Joe Jeannette two weeks before. The hand mended nicely and was not troubling him when he started the fight. However, in the 2nd round, he hit Dempsey with right hooks and right uppercuts with all his power behind them, breaking the bones near the base of the right thumb.

Carpentier with trainer Gus Wilson, holding his injured hand

I put all my strength into those blows I landed on Dempsey's jaw in the second round, and when he didn't drop, and I felt the sharp pain in my hand, I knew I could not defeat him. There was nothing to do then but to go on fighting, trusting to luck that I could escape his hardest blows. ...

When I went at him in the third I felt the pain in my right hand and somehow I could not use it accurately or with power. I got it in several times, but I could tell that it had little effect. Then Dempsey's right hand caught me in the back of the neck just at the crest of the spinal column. My body was numb all over and I thought I was gone, but managed to last the round.

I felt a little fresher when the bell rang for the fourth, but at the outset Dempsey got to my body and the numb feeling returned so that I did not feel the blow that floored me. I gritted my teeth and managed to arise but the next blow, I believe it was a right to my chin, was the end. I kept saying to myself: "Georges, you must get up; you must go on and fight;" But I could not.

Dempsey fought cleanly and acted the gentleman all the time. There was not an untoward remark passed during the four rounds. It was an honor to have fought him, and believe me, I don't think it is a disgrace for any man to be defeated by him. He's a great fighter, the greatest I've ever met, and it is my prediction that he will be champion for many years to come.

Gus Wilson said that after the fight, Dempsey came to the corner and said, "You're a game fellow, Georges, and we'll be friends always." Carp responded, "You bet Jack, always." There was a two-inch cut under Carp's left eye.[658]

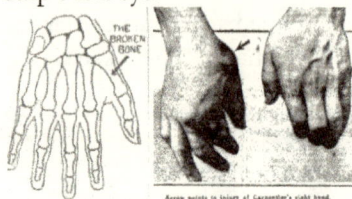

THE BROKEN BONE

Arrow points to injury of Carpentier's right hand.

Another writer said Descamps and Capt. Pierre Mallett, friend and adviser, admitted that ten days before the fight, Georges injured his thumb on Joe Jeannette's elbow. However, "it was nearly all right again when the time came for the fight. We nursed it along as carefully as we could."

Yet, they were not using the hand as an alibi. "Dempsey is the greatest fighter alive today. No man of any weight that I know of can even put him in danger." Carp said he was rocked by every blow that landed on him. "Every one of them hurt, but three that I got behind the head hurt the worst of all, much worse than the body blows. I was never unconscious. I heard the referee counting off the seconds very distinctly, and I tried to get up, but I was powerless. No man can hurt Dempsey."[659]

Trainer Lawson Robertson said the Frenchman did not follow the right game plan. Rather than play the waiting game, Carp took it to the champion, which proved to be a fatal mistake, though it also showed that Carp believed he could bring him down. He had the superior speed, and might have lasted longer had he been more cautious:

> He was out to win and we must credit him with a rare amount of courage in the fact that he made a great fight of it, all things considered. He was simply outclassed. ... On the whole it was better Carpentier lost as he did. Had he made a running fight of it by dodging Dempsey it would not have changed the outcome in any way, although it might have delayed his being knocked out for a few more rounds.

Carp didn't simply try to stall and last longer; he tried to win. As a result, everyone admired him for his plucky performance.

Many who had supported Carpentier shifted to cheering for Dempsey. Everyone liked a winner, particularly one who hit hard, came forward, and proved he could take it. "The crowd is a peculiar thing."

Dempsey's trainer Teddy Hayes said they had planned on a 4th round knockout. While they wanted him to win as soon as possible, they did not want Jack to rush the issue or take any chances and get careless. Carp did what they thought he would - try to nail Dempsey with the right. "He tried very hard, but he never bothered the champion much. Talk that Carpentier had Dempsey wabbly is pure nonsense." Dempsey was cool and collected at all times. He was a far better version of himself than the one that met Brennan.

Daniel said Harry Wills was most entitled to the next match. Charles Mathison agreed. "There is no question that Wills would extend

[658] *Buffalo Courier, New York Tribune*, July 4, 1921.
[659] *New York Herald*, July 4, 1921.

Dempsey, for the negro would have twenty pounds advantage in weight, has a longer reach, is a good boxer and a hard hitter and fairly fast." Dempsey still would be the favorite, though.

Some intimated that a rematch with Willard was next, but he was not active, while Dempsey was getting even better.

An Englishman said of Dempsey, "Gad, what a hitter. If we only could have a champion like that in England I believe we would even forgive him for not being in the war. If Dempsey were an Englishman Britain would go wild about him. He's the greatest yet."[660]

Ray Pearson quoted Carpentier and his manager as saying that they had no intention of fighting Dempsey ever again, but would fight anyone else. Descamps said, "Georges can't beat Jack so he won't fight him again." Carp said,

> I did my very best.... I fought Dempsey as hard as was humanly possible. I didn't box and I didn't exhibit because I want the world to know Georges is a fighter. He was too big for me and hits too hard. Oh, how does he hit!

> When I found out that it was not hard for me to hit Dempsey with my right in the first round I went out to win in the second round. In that round I shot three right hooks and three right uppercuts to Jack's jaw with all the power of my body behind those blows. I never hit any one as hard in my life. And when Dempsey didn't fall I knew that I couldn't whip him. In that session I must have broken a bone in my hand, for when I came out for the third round I felt a pain in the hand. From that time on to the finish I couldn't land with my right accurately and I couldn't put any steam in the blows.

> I knew then that it was simply a matter of how long I could last. But I came to America to fight, not to play the game of boxing and stall along for my own protection. So we fought along until – well that's an old story now.

Carp told Julia Harpman, "When I hit Dempsey with my right it was like striking a house. I knew then it was impossible to win."[661]

President Warren G. Harding's declaration that the World War was over officially, having signed a peace decree with Austria and Germany, was given very little press coverage in comparison with the fight. Newspapers had columns and columns of fight coverage.

It was the first million-dollar gate ever. Dempsey would go on to have five in his career. Joe Louis would have three, and up until 1971, there would be only nine total million-dollar gates. Hence, for the majority of the century, Jack Dempsey's fights represented most of the million-dollar gates. And he did it when the purchase power of the dollar was greater.

[660] *New York Herald*, July 4, 1921.
[661] *New York Daily News*, July 4, 1921.

Rickard estimated the gross gate receipts to be $1,623,380, but said those numbers were not final. That was a pretty specific estimate, though.[662]

A week later, it was reported that 75,328 paid to see the fight, and the receipts were $1,552,422.15, exclusive of the war tax. Those numbers did not include the 1,147 employees and 778 working press tickets. The tickets were $5.50, $10, $15, $20, $25, $30, $40, and $50. As usual, over time, the numbers tended either to become deflated or inflated, depending on the interest in doing so.[663]

Harry Greb said Carpentier was no match, but put up a wonderful battle nevertheless.

> Dempsey was too heavy and too rugged for the Frenchman. Carpentier hit him hard enough in the second round to knock out any ordinary good fighter, but he merely dazed Jack momentarily and when the latter was able to recover himself and take the lead again, Carpentier's chance to win was a forlorn one.

> Carpentier is a great fighter. Make no mistake about that. He has a wonderful right hand, courage, boxing skill and a knowledge of ring strategy such as can be gained only by experience.

> Georges knows more about boxing than Dempsey. His science stood out in bold relief throughout the bout. It was only because he was up against a marvelous fighting champion that he did not win. I thought Carpentier was wonderful at long range. Dempsey took all he had and then beat him down at close quarters. It was that terrific body pounding that sapped the strength of the brilliant and game French challenger to such an extent that he was unable to recuperate from the effects of the blows that rendered him helpless, but did not knock him unconscious.[664]

Tad Dorgan said Dempsey proved he was a great fighter. He had all the qualifications of a champion - physical build, courage, a punch, and he could take it. Dempsey was not simply bigger than Carpentier; he was better. Carp was a "great fighter," much better than most thought. "He has almost everything a heavyweight champion should want, but he can't take it." With his dynamite right, he had knocked out bigger men. He landed the same knockout blows on Dempsey, "but, instead of kissing the canvas, Dempsey staggered back a few feet, pulled himself together, absorbed another and another, and was still on his feet. Right there is where Dempsey proved himself the better man." Carp landed his best punches, his right and right uppercut, but could not stop him. A few moments later, Dempsey was himself again.

Many great fighters could deal it out, but could not take it. "Jim Jeffries never would have been a world's champion if it hadn't been for

[662] *Buffalo Times*, July 5, 1921.
[663] *Buffalo Enquirer*, July 13, 1921.
[664] *Pittsburgh Gazette Times*, July 3, 1921.

his ability to take it." In their second bout, Fitz nailed him and closed his eyes, but Jeff took it and knocked him out, insensible but unmarked. Boxing was a game of give and take, and the great ones could do both.

Pittsburgh Sun Sporting Editor James Long humorously said that one never would guess that a man named Dempsey had been mixed up in that little Jersey affair. "It's Carpentier this and Carpentier that, all about the idol of France and the gameness, speed and other things that he displayed." One might think he won and not Dempsey. There was entirely too much inclination to play to sentiment, and the result was Carp was given too much credit and Dempsey not enough. "If Carpentier is so great, it naturally follows that Dempsey must be greater." Folks loved that Carp fought hard and tried his best instead of stalling or running away. He owed the public his best efforts, given the massive purse. He showed gameness and courage, and covered himself in glory.

Yet, Dempsey did all that was asked of him. It was the fight that the public wanted, and he came through successfully. He "proved himself a greater champion than ever," because he proved he could "take it." He was an iron man. "Dempsey was not hurt as much as some reports made it appear. He was rocked, but he was far from being in distress, as shown by the way he came back and finished his man shortly afterward. As a matter of fact, Carpentier hurt himself more than he hurt Dempsey. He broke the thumb of his right hand and sprained his wrist," and his failure to deck Jack likely broke his own heart. If they had fought with 5-ounce gloves, Jack might have stopped him in 1 round.

Long said Harry Wills was the one man with a chance to beat Dempsey. Many were discussing challengers such as Gibbons, Brennan, Fulton, and the winner of Bob Martin-Frank Moran, strangely overlooking the only man with a real chance. "In the opinion of many, Wills is the best heavyweight in the world. He has the size, the strength, the skill, the hitting power, and the necessary ring knowledge and if given a fling at the title he would stand a mighty good chance of snatching it from its present holder." Harry's right broke Fulton's ribs, and a man who could hit that hard with his right would have a chance against Dempsey, who seemed to take rights.

Jim Coffroth said with the exception of Corbett and Johnson, most heavyweight champions were hittable, but they all proved they could take it – Sullivan, Fitzsimmons, Jeffries, and Willard, which in part made them champions. "Now we get down to Dempsey. He, too, has been hit in all his fights. But, then, he can take it. He doesn't seem to care about the other fellow at all. Jack wants to get in where he can hit the other fellow. He knows that when he lands he will bring the other fellow down and I think he's right."

Tex Rickard said he wanted to see boxing forge ahead. "I am not in boxing for today only. ... I like the game, and I want to see it prosper, because I can prosper with it. I will not arrange any matches in the future that might hurt the sport." He wanted to avoid any contests that might retard the sport's progress, and he wanted to keep fistiana from being saddled with any more burdens. Hence, he wasn't about a single payday, but the sport's long-term health. Implicit in that statement was that he would not promote another interracial heavyweight championship.

Henry Farrell complimented the New Jersey commission for refusing to allow Jack Johnson to box there, having "the interest of the whole sport at heart." There was a "desire to keep the game from carrying more burdens than it is saddled with now." Rickard was of the same mind. "Tex Rickard knows the public pulse better perhaps than anyone connected with the American boxing game and he was the first to say that a match with Johnson would not go."

Rickard said he needed to be convinced that Willard was in shape again before he would match him with Dempsey. Brennan already had been knocked out twice by Dempsey. "Tommy Gibbons, if he succeeds in beating Carpentier will be the one entitled to a bid for the title." That match would be made if Carp's hand healed sufficiently for a Columbus Day bout. "Gibbons in his present form ought to beat the Frenchman."

Farrell concluded, "Dempsey has been fighting only once a year and he can wait another year for a real contender instead of taking on second raters who have no chance against him." Farrell did not mention Wills.[665]

The *Pittsburgh Sun* reported that Kearns denied rumors that Dempsey contemplated leaving him, though he did not deny that their contract would expire soon. Still, he expected that their fruitful relationship would continue. "We have got along very well, and since I have managed him he has won the championship of the world and defended it successfully three times."

Kearns also denied rumors that Dempsey was about to get married again. The champ allegedly was dating motion picture film actress Sylvia Jocelyn. "Jack had one unfortunate matrimonial experience, and I don't think he cares to try that game again. It seems to me that it is time people let up on Dempsey and quit spreading stories about him." No other champion was as abused or misrepresented, and all he asked for was fair play. (Of course, Kearns was forgetting about Jack Johnson.)

Leo P. Flynn, manager of Bill Brennan, Kid Norfolk, Panama Gans, and others, said,

> Jack Dempsey is the greatest heavyweight, champion or otherwise, boxing ever has known. ... I have seen every titleholder from John L. Sullivan down to Dempsey. ... And I sincerely mean it when I

665 *Pittsburgh Sun*, July 5-7, 1921.

say that Jack Dempsey is the greatest of all time. They prate about the poor class of heavyweights of today. Get this: There are far better men boxing in Dempsey's division just now than ever, and Jack has whipped a bunch of men that…would have made suckers of Corbett, Jeffries and the rest of them.

Flynn said Dempsey had it all. He was fast, could punch really hard with both hands from any angle, kept up a terrific onslaught throughout a fight, and he could take it. There was no escaping him. No other heavyweight of the past could knock over such men as Willard, Miske, Morris, Fulton, Carpentier, and Levinsky, all within 4 rounds. Flynn said Dempsey could have beaten all of the past champions, including Jack Johnson.

Discussing Carpentier, Dempsey said,

He is a very dangerous fighter. He is liable to knock out anybody except yours truly. … I think I could have turned the trick before the fourth round had I elected to get a bit tougher. … I can be whole lot rougher than I was with Carpentier … Mind you, now, I am not knocking the Carpentier punch. His right is a pippin. But…he did not hurt me much. The first right hander stung all right and staggered me because I was off balance. There was nothing serious about the situation, however… I knew then that I had him. The chief criticism I can make of Carpentier as a fighter is that he is woefully weak at infighting. He did not seem to know much about how to work one arm free. I did a lot of execution in the clinches for that reason. He was easy to reach behind the ears and in the body, and I was hurting him in both places and hitting him often. The only other fault I noticed is that when he punches he gets up on his toes and when he misses is all scrambled up. A fighter with only two faults is a pretty fair fighter. Carpentier is a good fighter, a very dangerous fighter.

Dempsey said that while not predicting the outcome of such fights, Carpentier hit hard enough to knock out anyone, including Brennan or Gibbons. "Harry Greb would be the boy to bother Georges if he could hit, but he can't hit hard enough to accomplish anything with that fiery Frenchman."[666]

Carpentier saw the fight films in a Newark, New Jersey theater on July 7, and said, "They are great. They showed a good fight." Descamps said, "You see, even the picture shows Dempsey is much bigger than Georges." The 20 pounds difference told. According to the *New York Times*, the pictures were sharp and clear, despite the fact that the day was overcast (though still hot). "Carpentier is shown steadily in retreat from the champion's unrelenting offensive, the challenger occasionally stabbing out with straight left or crossing inaccurately with the right." Carpentier was half-pushed and half-wrestled down to dangle over the ring ropes in

---

[666] *Pittsburgh Sun*, July 7, 8, 1921.

the 1st round. In the 2nd, Carpentier lashed out with his terrific right and staggered Dempsey. The strength of the punch and Dempsey's reeling were pronounced. But subsequently, Carpentier gradually was beaten down. The action was so fast it barely could be followed.

Preceding the bout, episodes of their training were shown. When Dempsey's face appeared, the only person in the audience who clapped was Descamps. When Carpentier was shown, there was a thunderous applause, which caused Carp to laugh.

THE OFFICIAL
DEMPSEY-CARPENTIER FIGHT PICTURES

NOW
Towers Theatre
Broadway & Pine St.
CAMDEN, N. J.
11 A. M. TO 11 P. M.
Every Incident of the Big Contest.
These Pictures Cannot Be Shown Outside of the State of New Jersey

The *Buffalo Evening News'* Lawrence Perry also saw the films. The famous right that staggered the champion in the 2nd round was shown. It was a wonderful punch, fearful in its swift dynamic quality. It was thrown with everything Carpentier had behind it, and landed on the chin. The champ was knocked backward about four feet. The next instant, a right uppercut missed the jaw. Dempsey clinched and weathered the storm.

Between rounds, it appeared that Kearns administered smelling salts to Dempsey (not illegal then). Kearns appeared in the corner at Jack's left elbow. From a hip pocket he took a bottle and placed it to Jack's nose, and Jack inhaled.

Thereafter, Carpentier did not make as much use of his right, and usually did so in uppercuts.[667]

Discussing the recent fight, Carpentier said, "I thought I was strong enough to hold him in the clinches. Once in the first round I did get an uppercut over in a clinch but that ended it." Georges said he had trained for close fighting with Jeannette and Journee. "They are great big fellows and I thought they were about as strong as the champion. I had no trouble in holding their arms in the clinches but Dempsey just knocked my arms down and hit me at will." He also explained that he did not keep away from Dempsey because he could not do so. "In the third round I changed my tactics and tried to outspeed the champion but I couldn't do it. He is much faster than we had thought. He kept on me all the time. Twice in the third round I danced away from him but the third time he caught me against the rope and rocked me with one of his great left hand punches." Carp fought his own fight and tried everything he could. "I found out in the second round that I could not drop the champion. I realized that if Dempsey was to be beaten he would have to beat himself." Some told him that Dempsey burnt himself out after a few rounds, and if Georges stayed away for 5 or 6 rounds he would win. "I tried to do that after the second round but he was too fast for me."

Rickard paid the preliminary fighters $13,050 total, with Miske and Tunney the highest paid at $2,000 each. Frankie Burns got $1,800, Renault $1,500. All the rest drew $750, except Coster, who got $500. Referee

[667] *New York Times, Buffalo Evening News,* July 8, 1921.

Harry Ertle earned $1,000. Harry McCoy and Jimmy De Forest, referees for the preliminaries, each earned $50. One said the officials, including referees, and an alternate, received a total of $275.

Jim Jab did not believe Dempsey was the best ever, but rather the 4th best of all time. This writer ranked the heavyweights at their best as follows: 1. James J. Jeffries, 2. John L. Sullivan, 3. John Arthur Johnson, 4. Jack Dempsey, 5. Bob Fitzsimmons, 6. Peter Jackson, 7. Jess Willard.

Regardless, Jab called Dempsey "physical perfection" for a heavyweight. His legs were built for speed. "Dempsey sliding sharply without any lost motion cornered Carp when and wherever he pleased. No dancing, no prancing, all effective weaving in. This effort on the champion's part was an act of brilliancy overlooked by hundreds."[668]

George Underwood said Dempsey's "Iron Mike" of a right brought home the bacon, but it took his trusty left to unlock the door. Most champions had good left hands. "Dempsey's best punches are his left hooks to the head and body and his right smash to the heart, or rather just at the edge of the ribs under the heart. Like Fitzsimmons, Jack employs a shift, but it is better executed and more effective than was Bob's." He could step forward with either hand and thrust himself into shooting position. He had a pretty double left, down and up, modeled after the Nonpareil, though Dixon had the best double left. One weakness Dempsey had was that sometimes he drew his left back, which left him open for a right. Luckily for him, he had a granite jaw, like Jeffries.

John L. Sullivan had a "mighty good left" as well. "The belief that the Boston Strong Boy was solely a right-hand puncher is a fallacy." Experts who saw or fought him when he was at his best agreed on that. Mike Donovan said Sullivan had a lightning left jab and corking left hook, decking several men with his left. Many writers simply said a knockdown was from "'Sullivan's mighty right.' It made their yarn sound better." Jake Kilrain agreed that Sullivan did him the most damage with his left. However, it was true that there "were few, mighty few men, who could stand up under John L.'s right handers."

Corbett had a great left jab. Fitzsimmons had a great left hook, particularly to the body, which won him the heavyweight championship. Jeffries did most of his execution with his left. "His straight left probably was the most powerful the ring ever saw." It was quick, powerful, and well timed, and it was like running into a beam.

Underwood said Johnson was the greatest defensive champion ever. But he also could hit with the speed and power of a mule kick. He had a lightning jab, but his pet punches were his inside uppercuts.

James Long said all of the high-sounding superlatives and laudatory phrases used about the recent fight were misleading, for the reality was that Carpentier had been beaten into a helpless state in short order in a lopsided, uneven match in which Carp had no chance to win. He was only

[668] *Lincoln Star Journal*, Pittsburgh, *Press*, July 8, 1921; *Pittsburgh Gazette Times*, July 9, 1921.

a toy in Dempsey's hands, to be broken and tossed aside at will. Dempsey's jaw was so hard that when Carp nailed him with his vaunted right, all he did was hurt himself – breaking his own hand. That took his morale too, and boosted Dempsey's confidence. Long felt that reports of how hurt Dempsey was were exaggerated greatly. He was knocked off balance and momentarily staggered, but what he did to Georges in the 3rd and 4th rounds showed how far he was from being harmed. Long said it was a "queer world" that gave Carpentier so much credit and Dempsey so little for administering a beating.

Joe Choynski was not impressed by the Dempsey-Carpentier fight, and said it was by no means a great fight, despite what the public and press thought, although the fighting was hard and earnest.

> Neither Dempsey nor Carpentier showed me anything. Neither of them knows anything about the finer points of boxing. Carpentier has nothing but speed and a snappy right. He has absolutely no defense, and rushed in merely with the wild hope of slipping in a winning punch. As for Dempsey, he fought solely on the principle of going in and defying his opponent's blows, seemingly having adopted the policy of 'I'll take one of your punches and give you two in return for it.' … Can that be called a great fight or a fine exhibition of boxing?

Choynski also said a referee in a no decision bout was not a referee at all, but merely a "third man in the ring."[669]

Jim Corbett said Carpentier had the fastest right hand he ever saw, and was like a cat in his ability to seize openings and pounce. Unless his foe was as quick as a flash or had an iron jaw, Carp would give him a lot of trouble. But Jim also said Carp was not as clever as claimed; not as clever as Griffo, Dempsey the Nonpareil, Tommy Ryan, or Jack McAuliffe.

Corbett said Dempsey showed him no cleverness or speed, despite what the stories about the fight said. Still, he also gave him credit.:

> Dempsey is more like Jeffries than any other heavy I've ever seen. He is a big, strong fellow with a pile-driver punch and an iron jaw. They talk about matching him with Brennan or Gibbons; that would be murder. Right now there is not a man in the world who has a chance with him. He's too young and strong for them. His body blows will stop any of them in a few rounds.[670]

[669] *Pittsburgh Sun*, July 9, 1921.
[670] *Buffalo Enquirer*, July 13, 1921.

CHAPTER 11

Who and What is Next?

Jim Jab wanted to see Dempsey go against Gibbons next. "This writer is sweet on Tom Gibbons." He also liked Bill Brennan.[671]

Some discussed the possibility of Dempsey fighting Jack Johnson once he was released from prison. Dempsey was quoted as saying, "Sure, I'll fight Jack Johnson or anyone else. It's up to Jack Kearns, my manager." Kearns said, "The public can have a Dempsey-Johnson match if it wishes, but I believe there is no demand for the bout now or in the near future."[672]

However, on July 8, while passing through Omaha, Nebraska on a train en route to Salt Lake City, Dempsey said, "I refuse to fight any negro – not only Jack Johnson – but any negro, and the only thing that may make me change my mind is a positive public demand that I give some negro a chance at the heavyweight crown." Another quoted him as saying, "I will never fight a colored man. There is nothing to this talk of me meeting Jack Johnson. I am confident the public doesn't want this fight, and while I will govern myself to a large extent according to the public's wishes, I cannot see my way clear to fight Johnson or any other colored man." Still another quoted Dempsey as saying, "I will fight any man that the public demands, but the demand will have to be overwhelming before I will consent to enter the ring with Johnson or any other colored man." "The public is my boss. If it wants a Dempsey-Wills or Dempsey-Johnson bout then I will fight my dusky-hued rivals, but not until then." Jack also said there was no truth to the rumor that he was to be married.

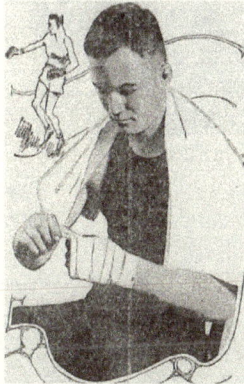

When asked who was his most worthy opponent, Jack said, "There are a lot of people talking about Tommy Gibbons. I've never seen him box, but I think he's too small to prove a very serious contender." Jack mentioned Brennan and Willard as well. Another quoted him: "Tommy Gibbons is a mighty good man, but he's too light." A third quote: "I will meet anyone that Kearns picks for me. Gibbons, I understand, is a good man, although I never have seen him work. As I have drawn the color line, I am free to say that I think Harry Wills is a great fighter, one who will whip the very best of them. You know as much about Johnson as I do. As for Willard – I'll fight him any time – and lick him, too." He

---

[671] *Pittsburgh Press*, July 8, 1921.
[672] *Muskogee Daily Phoenix*, July 7, 1921.

also was quoted as saying about Wills, "Oh, he's a pretty tough boy, but it took him 7 rounds to put away Bill Tate, and I know how good Bill Tate is – and then, Wills is a negro."

Regarding the Carpentier punch in the 2nd round, "Oh, I wasn't groggy. He landed a good hard punch. I guess it was the hardest punch I ever took, but I knew where I was and knew what I was doing. It knocked me out of balance, but I don't think it hurt me much." Jack said the 8-ounce gloves did not save him. The main difference between a 4 or 5-ounce and 8-ounce glove is the latter did not cut as much, but the power difference was slight.

Dempsey made all of these statements freely and on his own, for Jack Kearns was not with him, but was in New York.[673]

Robert Edgren said the opposition to inter-racial fights might keep Wills from a title chance. Wills was nearly as big as Fulton and a better boxer. Wills-Dempsey would draw a crowd and furnish a real battle. "If Wills were a white man nothing could keep him out of a chance to win the heavyweight title. He outclasses all the bunch except Dempsey. But when there is talk of championship bouts his name is discreetly forgotten."[674]

Pittsburgh Sun, July 9, 1921

James Long noted that Dempsey had defeated Fulton, Willard, Miske, Brennan, and Carpentier in 23 rounds total, just over an hour's worth of work. There was no heavyweight alive who had any chance with

[673] *Omaha Daily News, Omaha Evening World, Omaha Bee*, July 8, 1921; *San Francisco Examiner, Chicago Tribune*, July 9, 1921.
[674] *St. Louis Post-Dispatch*, July 8, 1921.

him other than Harry Wills. "Dempsey himself appears to share this opinion of the dangerous qualities of Wills, judging from his statement of last night in which he draws the color line." Long said that was unfortunate, for a real champion should be willing to fight any one.[675]

On July 9, 1921, 43-year-old Jack Johnson was released from federal prison after his white wife Lucille paid the $1,000 fine attached to his one-year-and-a-day prison sentence. Johnson said, "The ambition of my life is to get Jack Dempsey in the ring." Jack Kearns had taken a critical stance against Johnson's character. Johnson replied, "My character is just as good as Jack Kearns's."[676]

BACK FROM THE FIGHT —

One man who was so disturbed by Dempsey's lack of a war record offered to raise and give $250,000 to any former serviceman who could whip Dempsey for the title.[677]

Jack Kearns said he had not drawn the color line on behalf of the champion, but thought that Jack Johnson should fight Harry Wills or another leading negro boxer first before justifying a potential title shot. A Pasadena, Texas promoter offered Dempsey a $200,000 guarantee to fight Johnson on Labor Day.[678]

Most states, including the New Jersey and New York state athletic commissions, said Jack Johnson would not be permitted to box there. Of course, New York had not allowed Johnson to fight there even when he was champion, prior to his Mann Act conviction. In fact, after Johnson defeated Jeffries in 1910, almost no state would approve a Jack Johnson fight. In 1912, he had to fight in the remote locale of Las Vegas, New Mexico, which had just become a state earlier that year. Indeed, following his release from prison, it would turn out that no state would sanction a fight with Johnson as a participant, regardless of who he fought, black or white.[679]

The black-owned *Chicago Broad Ax* said Johnson was suffering on account of race prejudice and for beating Jeffries, the white man's hope. It said the white man's justice was a sham.[680]

Several writers were mentioning Tom Gibbons as a potential likely next best opponent for Dempsey. Harry Greb also was challenging Dempsey and under consideration for a title shot. "It looks now as if either one of those two boys will be selected." Neither Greb nor his manager George Engel could understand why Gibbons should be given any more consideration than he, given that Greb held a 1920 10-round no

[675] *Pittsburgh Sun*, July 9, 1921.
[676] *New York Daily News*, July 10, 1921.
[677] *San Francisco Examiner*, July 9, 1921.
[678] *Dallas Express*, July 9, 1921.
[679] *New York Age*, July 30, 1921.
[680] *Chicago Broad Ax*, July 9, 1921.

decision victory over Gibbons; although Gibbons held two prior 10-round no decision victories over Greb (1915 and 1920).[681]

Tom Gibbons.

He's a Dangerous Lad

Other than the one no-decision loss to Greb, in a career that began in 1911, Gibbons had been undefeated in 70 professional contests, with victories over Billy Miske, Battling Levinsky, Harry Greb, Porky Flynn, and Willie Meehan. In late June, Gibbons had scored a 1st round technical knockout over the usually very durable Meehan, who was floored three times, proving not only his skill but punching power. Gibbons was given credit for stopping the man whom no other top fighter had stopped, including Dempsey and Wills. It was the first time that Meehan had been stopped by punches (although in 1912 a young Meehan lost by TKO when as the result of wresting, he fell out of the ring and hit his head).

W. E. Clark of the *New York Age* said some claimed that Gibbons should be given a title fight next, owing to his long string of victories. Others wanted Brennan, whom only Dempsey had stopped. Some wanted Willard again. Rickard appeared to be planning for a potential Dempsey-Willard rematch on Labor Day. Several writers voiced sentiment that Harry Wills should be given a chance.

> In reply to this sentiment Dempsey states that he will give Wills a chance for the title if the public wants the fight. Whether he means that part of the public that is interested in boxing or the public in general, he does not say. But if he means the boxing fans, there will be no question about a fight between Dempsey and Wills, for they have on numerous occasions expressed a desire to see those fighters meet.

[681] *New York Daily News*, July 10, 1921.

Although the newspaper men as a whole do not like Dempsey and would like to see him defeated, many of them take the stand that a mixed bout for the championship would be against public policy as it would tend to increase race prejudice. For this reason few of them are advocating a Dempsey – Wills fight.

Clark further said the general opinion was that Dempsey could defeat all white contenders, and, although Wills might not get first chance at the title, eventually the boxing public would turn to Wills as the most formidable opponent for Dempsey.[682]

Jack Johnson said, "It doesn't make any difference what Dempsey says about drawing the color line; the public wants Dempsey whipped, and the public knows I am the one to do it."[683]

Ray Pearson said Carpentier proved that he could outbox and outfoot Dempsey, but he could not outfight him. Once Dempsey decided to tear in without fear, he changed the fight.[684]

Charles Mathison believed that Dempsey was the greatest heavyweight champion ever. Dempsey had many ring qualities that surpassed all of his predecessors. Folks who said he was not clever were wrong. He was no parlor boxer, but had an effective system of boxing both in defense and attack. He had superior effectiveness to Corbett, who relied on speed and defense, but was not a puncher and was vulnerable to being knocked out as soon as he lost his speed and condition. Hence, Dempsey eventually would have stopped Corbett. Dempsey's effective speed and power eventually would have enabled him to defeat all other heavyweights as well, including Sullivan, Jeffries, and Johnson, the latter of whom at his best would have given him a hard battle. "In substance, Dempsey combines in himself the speed of Corbett, heavier hitting than that of Fitz, and he closely approaches the ruggedness of Jeff. ... He can stand a punch, which Corbett could not do. He is so much faster than Fitz that it is difficult to hit him, and when he hits his man it is curtains. He is aggressive and combative, in which particular Jeff was utterly lacking."[685]

The *Buffalo Commercial* urged that Jack Johnson should not be allowed to put up his fists anywhere in the country. He already was seeking a bout with Wills or Dempsey. Tex Rickard stated that he would not promote a bout in which Johnson was a combatant. The New Jersey State Boxing Commission insisted that Johnson would not be allowed to fight under its jurisdiction. The *New York Mail* commended such positions. Johnson was 43 years old, and likely would be vulnerable to suffering a loss after serving a prison term, but,

> I have no desire to see this theory of mine that the negro is through as a boxer put to the test. Irrespective of whether he was largely the victim of circumstances or really at fault, the fact remains that Jack

[682] *New York Age*, July 9, 1921.
[683] *New York Tribune*, July 10, 1921.
[684] *Rochester Democrat and Chronicle*, July 10, 1921.
[685] *Buffalo Evening News*, July 11, 1921.

Johnson managed to give boxing a black eye that it took the game nearly ten years to recover from. ... The negro boxers should be the last to wish Johnson to return to the ring. His actions were largely responsible for the feeling against mixed bouts that still persists, and has made their living rather precarious.

Boxers like Langford, Wills, Jeannette, McVey, and Kid Norfolk, all of excellent personal character, "can lay their failure to secure recognition as championship contenders at Jack Johnson's door." This author said they should refuse to fight him, for he was a criminal and a confessed faker.[686]

Harry Newman said Dempsey was not likely to fight Johnson, for such a battle would hurt the sport. "Boxing at its best is skidding along on thin ice, what with those reform fellows running rampant, trying their derndest to wreck the sport. The thought of a Dempsey-Johnson contest would provide the blue law chaps with enough material to wreck the whole business." Even an attempt to match the two would wreak havoc with the boxing game, and "should it ever occur, you can go put the shutters up on the old game for a long time." That would cost everyone more money in the long run, even if in the short-term that particular fight made money.

Rickard announced that he would not have anything to do with a bout between Wills and Dempsey either, for the same reasons, "and that about excludes the colored scrapper as an opponent for the titleholder."[687]

No promoter in the U.S. was willing to put Jack Johnson on any of their cards. Many politicians made it clear that they would stop any fight with Johnson as a participant. Ultimately, Johnson would not fight at all until 1923. He would not fight in the United States again until 1926, his last U.S. bout prior to that being in 1912. In the meantime, the only fights Johnson would have would be in Cuba, Canada, and Mexico. No elite contender, black or white, would fight him.

On July 12, 1921 in the Bronx, New York, 185-pound Bob Martin, A.E.F. heavyweight champion, scored a 7th round knockout over 200-pound Frank Moran.

Copies of the Dempsey-Carpentier fight films had been smuggled out of New Jersey into New York, and the plan was to exhibit them there.

The motion pictures were advertised to be shown all day at a Broadway Theatre in New York City. A lot of folks wanted to see those films, and would pay for the privilege. A great deal of money could be made by all parties concerned. There simply was too much money to be made for them not to try. The feeling was, or so it was hoped, that since enough years had passed since Jack Johnson was champion, and because the combatants were white, the government might let it slide.

It was a violation of federal law to take fight films across state lines. However, the government would have to prove exactly who did it. The films still could be exhibited, because the exhibition was not illegal, but the *transportation* was. At least, that was what many argued.

[686] *Buffalo Commercial*, July 11, 1921.
[687] *New York Daily Mail*, July 11, 1921.

Certainly, the exhibition and fact that the films were in another state would be evidence of transport, but the government still would have to prove who did the transporting. The exhibitors potentially could be prosecuted if they were part of a conspiracy, or if they received the films via mail or government carrier. Proving it could be challenging.

F. C. Quinby/Quimby, who had an interest in the film rights and arranged for the exhibitions in New York, claimed that his attorneys had secured a ruling from Attorney General Daugherty that the film exhibition was permissible. Daugherty was a boxing fan and Dempsey admirer.

However, federal U.S. District Attorney William Haywood said that transportation was illegal. Haywood said the punishment for interstate transportation of fight films for exhibition purposes was a $1,000 fine or up to two years imprisonment (others said up to one year), or both. Haywood said Tex Rickard and all the officials connected with the fight would be summoned before a grand jury to tell what they knew about the transportation of the films.[688] (Of course, they all had a 5th amendment right against self-incrimination and could decline to testify.)

Text of Federal Law Bearing on Fight Films

THE text of the law approved July 31, 1912, dealing with prize fight pictures, follows:

"That it shall be unlawful for any person to deposit, or cause to be deposited in the United States mail for mailing or delivery, or to deposit or cause to be deposited with any express company or other common carrier for carriage, or to send or carry from one State or Territory of the United States or the District of Columbia to any other State or Territory of the United States or the District of Columbia, or to bring or cause to be brought into the United States from abroad, any film or other pictorial representation of any prize fight or encounter of pugilists, under whatever name, which is designed to be used or may be used for purposes of public exhibition.

"Section 2—That it shall be unlawful for any person to take or receive from the mails, or any express company or other common carrier, with intent to sell, distribute, circulate or exhibit any matter or thing herein forbidden to be deposited for mailing, delivery, or carriage in interstate commerce.

"Section 3—That any person violating any of the provisions of this act shall for each offence, upon conviction thereof, be fined not more than $1,000 or sentenced to imprisonment at hard labor for not more than one year, or both, at the discretion of the court."

In late July, in the federal district court at Manhattan, Tex Rickard and Fred Quimby, who produced the motion pictures, quickly admitted their part in the transportation of the fight films and immediately plead guilty (possibly cleverly cutting a plea deal with federal prosecutors behind the scenes) and were ordered to pay fines of $1,000 each for transporting the fight films into New York in violation of federal law. They would make many hundreds of times that amount (or more) in revenue from the film exhibitions, because it was the transport that was illegal under the law, not the exhibition, or so it was agreed by various district attorneys thereafter. From a purely economic standpoint, as long as they did not have to go to prison, violating the law made financial sense.

Judge William B. Sheppard, who levied the fines, criticized the law, and said, "The law was enacted to meet a peculiar situation and while it is probably constitutional, it looks to me like an unnecessary interference by Congress into the affairs of states where such encounters are allowed." The judge noted that the crowd at Jersey City contained a gathering of many thousands of people of refined tastes. The pictures had been shown

---

[688] *Buffalo Times, New York Herald,* July 23, 1921.

to wounded soldiers at a hospital on Staten Island after being brought over from New Jersey into New York, where boxing was legal as well.

The "peculiar situation" that the judge referenced as motivation for the law, which everyone knew by implication, was the fact of a black heavyweight champion and interracial prize-fights, for the law specifically was proposed and passed while Jack Johnson was champion, and its author specifically referenced the prevention of films of his fights being spread. Apparently, enough years had passed since Johnson was the champion, such that the judge took a more lenient view of matters, especially given that the current champion was white and the fight was not a mixed-race bout likely to engender ill-will or rioting. The judge also accurately stated that it was nonsensical to prohibit the transport of fight films into states where boxing bouts were legal.[689]

Certainly, promoters like Tex Rickard took note of the fact that he could earn a lot of money with lucrative fight films when the combatants were white, and that the law/judges appeared to and might take a more lenient view of law violations under such circumstances. Such likely would be different for an interracial heavyweight championship contest.

Rickard had no personal moral scruples against an interracial fight, for he had promoted several, including Jeffries-Johnson. But he was acutely aware of that fight's political, legal, and economic fallout and impact upon the entire sport. The political and legal reigns had been loosening up again in recent years, in the wake of Johnson's loss of the title.

The problem with violating the fight film law was that each time the films were transported across state lines into a different state, Rickard potentially would be subject to another federal prosecution, in a different jurisdiction, and one never knew when a judge might crack down and send them to jail/prison. The ultimate goal, long term, was to get the federal law repealed. Fight films were big business, and could generate far more revenue than the gates themselves.

However, in order to get the federal law repealed, sufficient support would need to be garnered from the Southern delegation, and to achieve that, promoters believed that they needed to avoid a mixed-race world heavyweight championship, at least for the foreseeable future. Rickard certainly was savvy enough to be cognizant of all of this.

But, for the time being, the thought clearly was to smuggle the films to select locations where the economics made sense and political climate might be more inclined to levy fines rather than seek imprisonment. Thankfully for us, economic value, copying the films so many times, and bringing them to so many locations facilitated greater film preservation.

Back on June 27, 1921, a criminal trial began. The government alleged that eight Chicago White Sox baseball players and others conspired to fix the 1919 World Series. Trial testimony started on July 18, 1921. On July 28, 1921, the jury acquitted all of the defendants, finding them not guilty.

[689] *Brooklyn Standard Union, Buffalo Commercial,* July 27, 1921; *Brooklyn Daily Eagle,* July 30, 1921.

Despite the acquittals, Baseball Commissioner Kenesaw Mountain Landis made it clear that those who had been indicted would not be allowed to play ever again, banning indefinitely all eight players allegedly involved in the fixing of the World Series, as well as anyone else who had knowledge but did nothing to stop it. Two others not tried were banned as well.

44TH ST. THEATRE, West of Broadway.
Continuous 11 A.M. to 11 P.M.
TEX RICKARD Presents

Dempsey-Carpentier

Official Ringside Motion Pictures

TEX RICKARD
PRESENTS

DEMPSEY-CARPENTIER

OFFICIAL RINGSIDE MOTION PICTURES

EVERY DETAIL IN MARVELOUS
CLOSE-UP VIEWS, SHOWN AS DETAILS
NEVER HAVE BEEN SHOWN BEFORE.

On July 30, 1921, the Dempsey-Carpentier films began exhibiting again at the 44th street theater in New York. The exhibitions would continue daily. Both the *New York Evening World* and *New York Daily News* advertised exhibitions of the fight films. Other theaters throughout New York state quickly followed.[690]

On August 4, 1921 in Manhattan, before a crowd of 6,000, 178-pound Gene Tunney won a 10-round decision over 175 ½-pound Martin Burke, a former Dempsey sparring partner, who clinched incessantly. The *Brooklyn Standard Union* said, "Tunney was not so good, but Burke was worse." The *New York Evening World's* John Pollock said Tunney could not show his class, owing to Burke's clinching. The *Brooklyn Daily Times* called it uninteresting and slow.[691]

TECK THEATER

Presented by Fred C. Quimby and
C. J. Murray.

ORIGINAL

DEMPSEY CARPENTIER

MOTION PICTURES

Reproduction in detail of the
big battle at Jersey City, showing knockout and all side features.
Picture runs one solid hour. Clear-
est and most thrilling fight picture
ever shown.

Week of August 8

Prices 50c, 75c and $1

Ten complete shows daily beginning at noon.

The *Buffalo Commercial's* C. J. Murray said the Dempsey-Carpentier films were the best reproduction of a prize fight ever filmed, even better than Jeffries vs. Johnson. Fred Quimby took films of the prefight training, as well as close ups, and scores of novelties. He captured the entire fight, and not one punch was missing. The 2nd round showed Carpentier slugging Dempsey hard, and had the champion rocking. The long overhand right is clear. The punch drove Dempsey's head back quite far. The Frenchman tore in and fired away in a whirlwind attack. The pictures also substantiated the stories that Dempsey crucified him with terrific body smashes. Throughout, the rapid-fire pile-driving blows were pumped into Carpentier's midsection. Carpentier was fleet-footed and tricky. But he could not dodge the always on-coming relentless champion who never took a backward step. There even was a slow-motion view of one of Dempsey's short uppercuts rocking Carpentier's head. The introduction of slow-motion photography enabled the audience to see every motion slowed down to one-eighth normal speed.[692]

Jack Kelly said the fight descriptions by so-called experts were shown-up by the films. Carpentier tried to rise from the second knockdown, with one leg and arm quivering spasmodically in the air as he tried to reach for

[690] *New York World, New York Daily News*, August 5, 1921; *Elmira Star-Gazette*, July 23, 1921.
[691] *New York Evening World, Brooklyn Standard Union, Brooklyn Daily Times*, August 5, 1921.
[692] *Buffalo Commercial*, August 8, 1921; *Brooklyn Daily Times*, August 7, 1921.

an invisible aid to help him to his feet. It was as if he was trying to regain control of his body and get up, but could not.[693]

More than 20 cameras were used to film the fight, including the slow-motion instrument.[694]

When reviewing the fight films, the *Brooklyn Daily Times* said Dempsey's powerful, punishing left hooks were shown clearly, as was Carpentier's daring fighting spirit. He took cruel body blows, one after another, but kept coming back until he received the last one. Dempsey let the invader carry the fight to him, but systematically wore him down with wicked heart and body punches.

The film version of the much discussed "Carpentier's chance" in the 2nd round showed him hitting the champ freely but "not much more than rocking him slightly with his volley of right-hand smashes against the iron jaw, and Dempsey simply coming back and continuing the march towards his goal with body blows." Carp took it to the champ, taking every chance he could, but he also took a crushing for as long as he could.

Another writer said the films clearly showed the American to be the Frenchman's master at every stage, but at the same time demonstrated Carpentier's gameness and aggressiveness. Carp stood the vicious body blows for as long as he could. The motion pictures gave two views of the fight, one from right on top of the fighters, and the other from 100 feet or so away. "At no time does either view show the champion in danger, and Carpentier's fusillade of rights in the second round scarcely threw the American off his balance more than a moment." Training scenes, road work, gym work, shadow boxing, sparring, their training quarters, the arena, the crowd, all were shown in the films.[695]

The *Brooklyn Citizen* said the films of the 1st round showed Dempsey on the defensive, with Carp being punished severely for taking the fight to the champ. The 2nd round showed Jack take the wallop on the jaw that nearly put him away. "It showed Dempsey staggering back against the ropes. But it was only for a second, as he quickly recovered himself and fought his way out of danger." The 3rd round was Jack's, though Carp fought gamely. In the 4th round, the pictures showed the knockout.

There was one surprise. "It was interesting to note that while there was applause when the picture of Carpentier was flashed upon the screen, the crowd was in an uproar when the smiling face of Dempsey appeared."[696]

On August 12, 1921 in Chicago, Dempsey clarified his prior statement regarding the color line by saying that he *was* willing to fight Jack Johnson or Harry Wills *if* the public demanded such a match. However, he said Johnson would have to beat Wills before he would be given a chance.[697]

Some thought there were so few potential opponents for Dempsey that he might consider fighting the winner of a Wills-Johnson bout. Of course, no jurisdiction seemed to be willing to allow such a contest. Jack

[693] *Buffalo Times*, August 8, 1921.
[694] *Brooklyn Standard Union, Brooklyn Daily Times*, August 8, 1921.
[695] *Brooklyn Daily Times*, August 9, 1921.
[696] *Brooklyn Citizen*, August 9, 1921.
[697] *Brooklyn Citizen, New York Evening World*, August 12, 1921.

Johnson simply was not wanted anywhere in the U.S., despite the fact that he had served his sentence.

The *Brooklyn Daily Times* claimed there was little public clamor for a third Brennan fight. "Bob Martin, Bob Roper, and Gene Tunney, developments of the war, will not do at present." There were others too, but they all needed further development and promotion to generate sufficient demand. The interest simply was not there at present.

This newspaper said the only one that would stand a chance of beating Dempsey was Harry Wills. And neither Dempsey nor promoter Rickard seemed eager to cross the color line to make such a match, particularly given the political opposition to a mixed-race heavyweight championship contest.[698]

Charles Mathison said Dempsey had no fight in sight, and the only prospect for a big fight, against an opponent the public would accept as worthy, "unfortunately" was a black man, so Jack would have to step over the color line and fight Harry Wills, who "would unquestionably give the champion a hard tussle." Wills never had done anything to bring himself disrepute.

Kearns said he had offered Wills the opportunity to beat Dempsey every day in sparring, offering him big money to spar with Dempsey before both the Willard and Carpentier fights, but he turned down the offers.

Notables of the World at 44th Street Theatre

The scene is "Boyle's Thirty Acres," and there are 90,000 spectators gathered together from all parts of the world to see the greatest sporting event in history.

A Standard Oil man has travelled all the way from Amoy, China, just to be present for fifteen minutes. The Spanish Ambassador and Senora Don Juan Riano; Prince Antonio Bibesco of Rumania; the Earl of Dundonald, who stopped over on his way to Peru; Prince de Walder and Count Francis de Baron-Kuhn of France; Senators and Representatives—all are there.

And Society, too. The Roosevelts, the Vincent Astors, the Craig Biddles, the Drapers of Boston and the Ogden Armours of Chicago.

And the world's greatest writers—Arthur Brisbane, Irvin Cobb, Heywood Broun, W. B. Masterson, Alfred W. McCann and more than one hundred others, equally well known.

And then Jack Dempsey and Georges Carpentier, exactly as they fought, blow by blow and round by round, with the slow-motion photography showing every detail of the great battle.

Tex Rickard presents the authentic ringside motion pictures of the Dempsey-Carpentier World's Championship Boxing Contest at the 44TH ST. THEATRE (just west of Broadway), EVERY DAY, INCLUDING SUNDAYS, CONTINUOUS FROM 11 A. M. TO 11 P. M.

Also being shown at the Shubert-Riviera Theatre, Broadway and 97th Street, and the Shubert-Crescent Theatre in Brooklyn.

Direction of Fred C. Quimby, Inc.

However, Wills did not want to fight Dempsey that way, in sparring, but wanted a real purse and a fight for the championship, which he deserved. Yet, if Wills had beaten, knocked out, or even knocked down Dempsey in sparring, that potentially could have created even greater demand for an actual fight.[699]

The Carpentier fight films were doing tremendous business in New York, showing daily throughout the day.

The *Brooklyn Citizen* said the film exhibitions brought to light the overwhelming sentiment in Carpentier's favor. Whenever he landed heavily, the vast crowd rose as one and rooted for him.

After crashing three solid rights to Jack's chin in the 2nd round, which caused the champ to flounder about, Carp misjudged another right, and

[698] *Brooklyn Daily Times*, August 15, 1921.
[699] *Buffalo Evening News*, August 15, 18, 1921.

permitted Dempsey to weather the storm by clinching. Carp proved his gameness, withstanding real punishment, particularly to the body.[700]

In late August, from Atlantic City, Dempsey said he would not fight Jack Johnson, because he did not want to do anything that could hurt the sport.

> I'll not meet him on any terms. The public doesn't want the match and as champion I will do nothing against public sentiment. If that match that certain people are calling for went through the boxing game would go back to where it was. I think boxing is now on a good plane. Why spoil it? I may be tempted to meet Johnson. They could of course tempt me with a big purse if I happened to be broke. But if the day ever comes when I'm broke, I'll go out and look for work before I'll consider any proposition that will hurt boxing. Why do they pick on me with this color line stuff? Why don't they go after the big colleges? Do you ever hear of those colleges entering their athletes against colored competitors? Of course you don't. Do you ever hear them knocked because they don't? Nix on the knock.[701]

The *Brooklyn Daily Times* said Dempsey was "playing with the color line game." One day he would be quoted as saying he was willing to fight a black fighter, but the next day he would refute the statement.

> It is not to be held against Dempsey that he refuses to fight Johnson. He is rendering boxing a service by giving him no consideration, but he cannot hurdle Wills as easily. Wills is the embodiment of all a professional boxer should be and eventually Dempsey will learn that the public far from opposing endangering the supremacy of the white race in boxing is eager to see him give Wills a crack at the title.[702]

Dempsey said he thought Carpentier could lick Fulton, and any light heavyweight, for he was a corking good boxer who sure could hit. However, he would not have a chance against Willard, who simply would have too many physical advantages in weight, height, reach, and durability.

> He'd hit Willard and hit him hard but he couldn't bring him down. It takes something more than punching to beat Willard. I gave him everything I had – every ounce of strength I had – trying to keep him down in the first round. I put everything I had into every punch and it took all of it. If I'd needed an ounce more I might not have beaten him. His strength and vitality were amazing. I didn't see how a man could get up after I'd hit him on the chin and over the heart half a hundred times – I must have hit him that many in the first round. Georges could hit Willard hard, but he wouldn't have that strength to throw into the fight the way I did. In the

---

[700] *Brooklyn Citizen*, August 21, 1921.
[701] *New York Herald*, August 21, 1921.
[702] *Brooklyn Daily Times*, August 22, 1921.

second round I was so tired, from giving everything I had, that I could hardly lift my arms, and I had to rest before I could try again. It wasn't that Willard was such a great fighter, but that he was so big and so strong that it took an awful lot of plain strength to beat hm.[703]

Bill Brennan wanted a $30,000 guarantee for another Dempsey fight. The Queensberry club offered him $25,000. If he did not accept; they would go after Harry Greb or Bob Martin, the "logical contenders." Either Greb or Martin would "hustle Dempsey" and extend him, which is what folks wanted to see.

However, it appeared that Dempsey (or his manager) preferred to take on Brennan or Martin rather than Greb. When Greb was suggested to Kearns, he remarked, "Dempsey would have to be in tiptop shape for Greb, as good as he was for Carpentier." When asked why, Kearns responded,

> Well, because Greb is a clown and Jack would have to go and get him. Greb is a jumping jack and a moving target is always hard to hit. Jack might have to chase him for six or eight rounds before he'd get a good sock at him. Brennan and Martin, slow moving, are easy for Dempsey to hit – and anybody Jack socks must fall. That's why.[704]

Walter Kelly said the four leading candidates, Bill Brennan, Bob Martin, Tommy Gibbons, and Harry Greb, should fight one another for the honor of meeting the Dempsey demon. Martin, by his recent 7th round knockout over Frank Moran, proved himself a highly promising contender. However, Martin had lost a 1921 15-round decision to Brennan (and a 1919 4-round decision to Tunney), amongst other losses. Many believed Gibbons to be the most formidable candidate, "owing to his wonderful skill, exceptional speed, and recently developed hitting power." Greb was a tough chap who could keep anyone busy for a time. He did not have a knockout punch, but was rugged, and always put up an interesting fight. He landed wallops from all angles, delivered plenty of punishment, and could take it too.[705]

Greb had proven that he could beat top heavyweights. However, the toughest issue with selling him to the public was that he was a middleweight in size, making 160 pounds on the afternoon of a fight with ease, rarely weighed over 165-170 even when just walking around, only stood 5'8", and rarely won by knockout. He would have greater size handicaps than Carpentier, and did not hit anywhere near as hard as Georges, though he threw more and seemed to take it better (although one never knew how one would absorb Dempsey's brand of power with the small gloves when he was going all out).

[703] *Buffalo Times*, August 22, 1921.
[704] *Buffalo Commercial*, August 25, 1921.
[705] *Buffalo Enquirer*, August 25, 1921.

There was occasional discussion of and references to an anticipated Dempsey tour of Europe. The tentative plan was to make easy money giving exhibitions in London and Paris.[706]

On August 29, 1921 in Pittsburgh, before a crowd of around 5,000, 161 ¼ or 162-pound local Harry Greb (180-11-17) and 178 ¾ or 179-pound black Kid Norfolk (88-18-6) fought to a very close 10-round newspaper decision draw, with several saying Norfolk won, and several saying Greb won. Norfolk scored a knockdown of Greb in the 3rd round with a hard right to the jaw, though Greb rose immediately. Greb lost most of the first half of the fight, but came on strong in the second half. The next-day *Pittsburgh Sun, Chronicle-Telegraph, Press,* and *Gazette Times* all had Norfolk winning, but the *Pittsburgh Post, Dispatch, Leader,* and the referee said Greb won.

The *Pittsburgh Gazette Times'* Harry Keck said Norfolk won 6-4. Greb was beaten clearly in the first 6 rounds, but won the last 4. "Norfolk was the winner, and that, on punishment inflicted, by a deal more than the proverbial shade."

The *Pittsburgh Press'* Jim Jab also said Norfolk won, though only by a shade.

The *Pittsburgh Sun* said Greb could not overcome Norfolk's early lead. "The Negro won six of the 10 rounds, and the other four were captured by Greb." In the 3rd round, Norfolk landed a ferocious right that sent Greb to the canvas. Harry was up in a flash, but took a hard left to the stomach. He was cautious thereafter. This paper said it was the first time Greb was decked in Pittsburgh since he was a novice against Joe Chip (1913 LKOby2). (Others had decked Greb too, including Joe Borrell in 1914, Whitey Wenzel and Al Rogers in 1915, Soldier Bartfield in 1918, Tom Gibbons and Ted Jamieson in 1920, and Soldier Jones in 1921, though Greb usually rose and fought even harder.) Norfolk won the first 6 rounds. Thereafter, Greb stood toe to toe and landed several telling blows, opening a cut in the 7th. Greb's aggressiveness in the 7th through 10th rounds "earned him a shade in these rounds," but Norfolk's early lead was "too big for him to overcome."

Conversely, the *Pittsburgh Post's* Regis Welsh scored it 6-4 for Greb, saying he won the last 6 rounds after having a rough time of it early on, getting decked by a right to the jaw in the 3rd.

The *Pittsburg Dispatch's* William Peet said Greb shaded Norfolk. The Kid ran up a big lead in the early rounds, but the local boy wound up in whirlwind fashion. Pittsburg's "best battler" won a "hair line decision." Greb had an "uncanny ability to come from behind after being hopelessly outpointed" during the first 4 rounds. "It was one of the closest battles I have been called upon to decide in years." Norfolk scored a knockdown in the 3rd. Harry was much smaller, and met a stronger and huskier fighter who also was fast, shifty on his feet, aggressive, and able to fight in the clinches. "I gave Norfolk the first four rounds. The fifth was a tossup, 50-

[706] *Elmira Star-Gazette,* August 27, 1921.

50, and Greb by winning the next five was entitled to the decision." Peet's written description had it 5-4-1 Greb, though his separate round-by-round narrative had it 6-3-1 Greb. Harry opened a cut over Norfolk's left eye, rushed him to the ropes, and piled up points galore. "The opinion among the fans was divided after the scrap."

The next day, the bout's referee, Yock Henninger, said that had he been allowed or asked to render a decision, it would have gone to Greb.[707]

The interesting aspect of newspaper decisions is that newspapers around the country could choose which version of the truth they would report, so some chose to report that Greb won by a shade, while others reported that Norfolk won, and yet others reported a draw.

That same day, it was reported that an agent of Tex Rickard's named Clarence Gray was arrested by federal authorities in Omaha, Nebraska and charged with transporting the Dempsey-Carpentier fight films from New Jersey. Gray posted a $1,000 bond and was released.

On September 26, 1921 at the Dyckman Oval in Manhattan, New York City, Gene Tunney won a 7-round decision over England's Herbert Crossley (24-5-6), outpointing him with ease. The fight was scheduled for 10, but cut to 7 so the main event would start on time.[708]

Dempsey and Kearns were involved in a civil suit with Frank Spellman, who alleged that he was due part of the proceeds from Dempsey's film career, including *Daredevil Jack*. Dempsey denied having any contract with Spellman, who claimed they had an oral agreement.

At the trial in Batavia, New York on October 5, the plaintiff's attorney tried to bring up Dempsey's lack of a war record, asking, "You did not serve your country in the World War, did you?" The court sustained an objection. Dempsey denied charges that he sent Spellman to Wells, Nevada to fix up things in connection with the war slacker charges. He denied ever having any conversation regarding Spellman's share of the motion picture returns. He admitted that he never had voted in any election, and said he was residing at the Hotel Belmont in New York. Jack objected to being called a prizefighter, and insisted that he was the champion *boxer* of the world. He was quite annoyed by the questioning, raised his voice, and answered defiantly to some of the questions asked.[709]

Ultimately, the jury was hung and could not agree. Dempsey said it was the second trial of the matter. "I have met my opponent twice in his own ring and he has failed to win."[710]

On October 7, 1921 in Buffalo, New York, 173 ¼-pound Tommy Gibbons, "recognized as the leading challenger for Jack Dempsey's title," knocked out 77-fight veteran 184 ¼-pound Clay Turner (a former Dempsey sparring partner) in the 1st round with a left hook to the jaw. Eddie Kane, Tommy's manager, said, "I think I have the greatest fighter in the world." They expected to face Dempsey within the next year.

[707] *Pittsburgh Post, Press, Gazette Times, Dispatch, Sun*, August 30, 1921; *Pittsburgh Post*, August 31, 1921.
[708] *New York Daily News, Buffalo Courier*, September 27, 1921.
[709] *Elmira Star-Gazette*, October 6, 1921.
[710] *Ithaca Journal*, October 7, 1921.

The *Buffalo Commercial* said, "If [Gibbons] ever gets a shot at Carpentier he will win in a few rounds." However, it also said that Gibbons, as good as he was, still was far from being a dangerous man for Dempsey.[711]

On October 10, 1921 in Havana, Cuba, before a crowd of 12,000, Harry Wills knocked out Gunboat Smith (82-45-12) in the 1st round with body shots, a right to the back of the neck, and a left uppercut to the chin. It was Smith's fourth knockout loss in a row. He never fought again.[712]

On October 14, 1921 at Madison Square Garden in New York, 178-pound Gene Tunney stopped 189 ½-pound Jack Burke (a former Dempsey sparring partner), who retired after the 2nd round with a deep gash over his left eye, the result of a powerful right smash.[713]

Yet another man accused Dempsey of stealing his wife. Al Seigel, songwriter and husband of vaudeville star Bee Palmer, claimed that Jack had stolen his wife, and he instituted an alienation of affection suit for $100,000 against the champ. Dempsey said, "I know Miss Palmer, but I have never been out with her. All this talk about taking her out to dinner in secluded restaurants is the bunk."

Palmer subsequently sued Seigel for divorce, charging cruelty.[714]

Dempsey later joked, "I'll wager a little that I know more process servers than any other guy in America. Any takers?" That was another way in which he was like Jack Johnson. Both had been sued quite often.[715]

Some claimed that Dempsey and Willard had agreed to fight again in July 1922.[716]

On October 24, 1921 in Buffalo, 166 ½-pound Harry Greb won a 10-round judge's decision over 161 ½-pound Jimmy Darcy, although Greb was dropped by a Darcy left hook to the jaw in the 4th round.[717]

A Minneapolis promoter was offering a $100,000 purse for a Dempsey-Gibbons fight.[718]

There were rumors that Willard had made a strike in one of his oil investments and would be so rich that he might not see the wisdom in getting struck again by Dempsey.[719]

In late October 1921, Dempsey agreed to a vaudeville tour across the continent. During the last week of October, he was at the Pantages in Minneapolis. On November 1, 1921 at the Pantages theater in Winnipeg, Dempsey sparred 3 rounds with his regular sparring partner, Larry Williams. He also engaged in repartee with Jack Kearns.[720]

Robert Edgren noted that when Dempsey won the title, he said he never would fall for the hero vaudeville stuff. However, now he was on a

[711] *Buffalo Enquirer*, September 28, 1921, October 8, 1921; *Buffalo Courier, Buffalo Commercial*, October 8, 1921. Kane said Gibbons could knock out Brennan as he did with Meehan, but Bill would not fight Tommy.
[712] *Buffalo Courier, New York Times*, October 11, 1921.
[713] *Brooklyn Daily Times, New York Herald, New York Daily News*, October 15, 1921.
[714] *Olean Times Herald*, October 17, 1921; *Buffalo Courier*, October 20, 1921.
[715] *Nashville Banner*, November 13, 1921.
[716] *New York Times*, October 22, 1921.
[717] *Buffalo Evening News, Commercial, Courier, Enquirer, Times*, October 25, 1921.
[718] *Buffalo Enquirer*, October 27, 1921.
[719] *Ithaca Journal*, November 11, 1921.
[720] *El Paso Herald*, October 24, 1921; *Minneapolis Tribune*, October 30, 1921; *Winnipeg Evening Tribune*, November 2, 1921.

30-week vaudeville tour. He had been bitten by the bug, and soon folks would hear about him doing a monologue. It was too much easy money to turn down.[721]

On November 4, 1921 in New York City, before a crowd of about 9,000, 163 ¾-pound Harry Greb won an official 15-round decision over 178 ¼-pound Charley Weinert (53-12-4), decking Weinert in the 1st round with a right and dominating thereafter. The aggressive Greb was on top of Weinert throughout, circling and sending in rapid blows from every angle, nullifying the size disparity.

The *New York Times* said whirlwind Greb's only weakness was his inability to measure a foe for a crushing punch, losing effectiveness through wildness and lack of clean, hard punches, which enabled Weinert to go the distance. However, the fury of the tornado's attack completely baffled Weinert and kept him defensive throughout.

The *New York Tribune's* Fred Hawthorne said, "Greb fought one of his typical battles, letting punches fly from every angle every second. His favorite trick was to rush in with both maulers flying and then pinion Weinert's arms in a clinch and keep on hitting with one hand."

The *New York Evening World's* Vincent Treanor said, "Greb is a remarkable fighter, good to look at. He is the next thing to perpetual motion, but he hasn't the real thing in socks."

Greb had agreed to fight Tommy Gibbons for Rickard. Greb's manager George Engel said, "I consider Gibbons a fine boxer and fighter, but I think Greb is still greater. I tried to get Carpentier into a match with Harry, but no chance."[722]

On November 16, 1921 in Windsor, Ontario, Canada, 173-pound Tommy Gibbons stopped 178-pound Soldier Jones in the 1st round, decking him three times. Jones had lasted 7 rounds with Gene Tunney in July. Gibbons had knocked out his last 17 opponents, including Clay Turner in 1 (who went the distance with Greb seven times), Dan O'Dowd in 3 (who went the distance with Tunney and Brennan), and Willie Meehan in 1 (who went the distance with Dempsey, Wills, Brennan, Miske, and Greb).[723]

On November 18, 1921 in Portland, Oregon, 210-pound Harry Wills (70-6-6) stopped 212-pound Denver Ed Martin (25-8-4) in the 1st round, decking him six times. The local *Oregon Daily Journal* said, "Martin offered no more resistance than would a chronic invalid."[724] Martin never fought again.

Wills said he would not chase after Dempsey. "I would like to meet Dempsey, but if he is sincere in his avowal to draw the color line I guess I will have to be content to go along without a crack at the title." Wills was not in favor of the campaign started by some New York fistic critics

[721] *Buffalo Times*, November 13, 1921.
[722] *Brooklyn Daily Eagle, Brooklyn Citizen, New York Daily News, Times, Herald, Tribune, Evening World,* November 5, 1921.
[723] *Brooklyn Daily Times, Brooklyn Standard Union*, November 17, 1921. Harry Greb's results against Soldier Jones included: 1919 KO5; and 1921 KO4 (Greb dropped for a flash knockdown in the 2nd round).
[724] *Oregon Daily Journal*, November 19, 1921.

panning Dempsey for drawing the colored line. "Those attacks on the champion have been made without consulting me, and I do not like them. Dempsey has a right to do whatever he desires in the matter."[725]

On November 25, 1921 in Newark, Harry Greb stopped Homer Smith (39-16-7) in the 5th round, when he quit, claiming a broken rib. In 1918, Dempsey had stopped Smith in the 1st round.

On that same date, in New Orleans, Tommy Gibbons stopped Dan O'Dowd in the 6th round. O'Dowd was coming off a November 2nd 12-round decision loss to Bill Brennan.

Ray Pearson wrote an interesting article for the *Chicago Tribune* (Dec. 4), announcing that on Saturday, December 3, 1921 in Saskatoon, Saskatchewan, Canada, Jack Dempsey had knocked out Jack Johnson in the 7th round of an exciting fight in which Dempsey was decked in the 5th round. The headline: "Dempsey Knocks Out Jack Johnson in Seven Rounds." Only at the very end of the lengthy, detailed article, which claimed that it was one of history's greatest battles, was the truth revealed: It didn't happen. The *Chicago Tribune* finally informed readers, "This is the first of a series of articles by Ray Pearson describing mythical battles between present day champions and those of a decade or more ago. The object of the articles is to show possible results of battles if each of the principals was in his prime today." That was an exciting and tantalizing way to start a series on fantasy matchups.

However, some, without reading to the end, took the article seriously, and erroneously thought it was an actual report. Some, when reprinting the story, intentionally left out the ending in which the truth was revealed. Sensational stories sell newspapers, even if not true. Some simply received the story without the editor's note and were fooled until they did further investigation.

On December 6, the *Chicago Tribune* said the story of a "mythical fight" between Dempsey and Johnson, "the first of a series of imaginary bouts," had caused many tongues and ears to wag. "So widespread did the belief become that there had really been a fight that President Harding's own newspaper, the Marion Star, today carried a story about it." The *Marion Star* noted, "Many local fans read part of THE TRIBUNE story or all save the short paragraph at the end which related the mythical part." As a result, the *Tribune's* phone operators were "kept busy informing the callers the fight didn't really take place, and that it was a mythical story telling what might have happened had the pair met when both were in their prime." 207 calls were answered by the *Tribune* regarding the story within two days.

The United News service announced that "considerable disturbance had been stirred" since many newspapers reprinted the mythical story in whole or in part, "but left off the explanatory paragraph of the nature of the article."[726]

[725] *Oregon Daily Journal, Racine Journal Times*, November 19, 1921.
[726] *Chicago Tribune*, December 4, 6, 1921.

Louis De Casanova for the *Brooklyn Daily Eagle* reported Pearson's story, with the headline, "Xtra! Xtra! Jack Dempsey Knocks Out Jack Johnson in a Great Fight at Saskatoon." He noted that the story came East "with no explanation of how the fight was arranged, the size of the purse or any incidental news regarding the contest. The authority for the tale is one Ray Pearson, a special writer for the Chicago Tribune. He was at the ringside and saw the fight." At the end of De Casanova's article reprinting the Pearson story, he noted,

> Unfortunately for the Chicago Tribune and its special ringside correspondent, neither Dempsey nor Johnson were in Saskatoon last Saturday. Note what the sporting editor of the Saskatoon Star has to say: … **No Dempsey-Johnson bout here. Dempsey on Coast. Has not been here yet. (Signed) Cameron, Saskatoon Star**. Anyway it was a corking good story and worth reprinting. Ray Pearson is losing time. He ought to be writing fiction.[727]

The *Butte Miner* noted, "Incidentally Dempsey was appearing in Seattle last Saturday night in the theatrical performance which was staged in Butte last month." So, Dempsey was in Seattle on December 3 on the theatrical stage, not Canada in a fight. "The Chicago paper is credited with running the greatest fake story in many years. The fight did not take place and the story is branded as a master falsehood by all concerned."[728]

The *New York Daily News* printed the story on December 11, using a fight date of December 10, but included the same *Tribune* editor's note about it being the first in a series of articles by Pearson describing possible results of mythical battles between fighters if they were in their primes.[729]

Even to this day, there are some who have been fooled or misled by attempts to claim that Dempsey and Johnson fought, or they try to do the fooling themselves. As someone once said, "When the legend becomes fact, print the legend." But the fact remains that it did not happen.

On December 8, 1921 in Denver, at the Stockyards stadium, Harry Wills won a 12-round decision over Bill Tate, punishing him in every round. The *Denver Post* said Tate was disappointing, for he would not fight, fearful of Wills' punches, holding at every opportunity. Had the kidney punch been barred, which Wills used on the inside, there would have been little entertainment. "Even with all his holding tactics Tate couldn't escape a beating and his body showed big welts where Wills had landed some heavy punches." The *Rocky Mountain News'* Abe Pollock said it was a lethargic contest. "It was Wills' fight from start to finish." Tate made no effort other than to stay the limit, clinching throughout, only firing back occasionally. Harry walloped Bill's body and kidneys, particularly with his hard right. Pollock scored it 8-0-4 for Wills.[730]

[727] *Brooklyn Daily Eagle*, December 7, 1921.
[728] *Butte Miner*, December 10, 1921.
[729] *New York Daily News*, December 11, 1921.
[730] *Denver Post, Rocky Mountain News, Colorado Springs Gazette*, December 9, 1921.

Jack Dempsey—Harry Wills

The *New York Daily News* asked whether Dempsey and Wills would meet, and if so, when. Harry Newman wrote, "There are days when one who is interested in boxing wonders whether or not a fight between a black man and a white man is ethical, sane and in accordance with the accepted idea of modern sportsmanship." At one time, it was not uncommon for mixed fights to be held, and several colored fighters held championships.

However, at present, all championships were held by white fighters, and it was not clear if or when another colored boxer would be given an opportunity to fight for a title, particularly given the legal and political impediments, as well as short- and long-term economic considerations. "There is no State in these United States which will authorize a mixed fight. Those who govern boxing hold that fights between white and black boxers are not to be permitted. No bodies which govern fights will countenance a scrap between the black and the white." Despite what some writers, members of the boxing fraternity, and even some members of the general public in the metropolitan melting-pot East hoped, those with political power were not in favor mixed-race championship fights.

Furthermore, no promoter was willing to offer a big purse and take a risk on a mixed-race fight. They declared that mixed fights were out of fashion, interest in such contests had waned, and the public would not pay to see such a battle. Rickard said he wanted nothing to do with a Wills-Dempsey bout. He said no state would stand for it, and such a fight might kill the game. The American people did not like the idea of a black man getting a chance to become heavyweight champion. One member of the New York State Athletic commission said there was not a chance in the world that such a fight would be authorized. Even if such a fight made money, in the long run it might cost everyone more money, because the politicians would clamp down on the sport again, and be less likely to repeal laws such as the one barring the interstate transport of fight films.

So, would Dempsey and Wills ever fight? "It is not likely, unless there is a marked change in the attitude of fight fans about mixed fights." Europe would need time to recover from the financial strain of the war, so European promoters likely would not be willing to put up a sufficient purse either.

Everyone agreed that Wills could give the champion a tough tussle. "In height and weight Wills has it on the champion. He is a clever fighter, rangy and shifty." He had floored many foes as well. There was no doubt that it would be a good scrap. He undeniably was entitled to a fight, and was the logical opponent, the next best man in the division, but it was unclear whether they ever would or could fight.[731]

Some cynics might theorize that for economic reasons, Rickard did not want to risk a Dempsey loss. Dempsey was a huge money generator.

---

[731] *New York Daily News*, December 18, 1921.

Johnson vs. Jeffries, the most lucrative fight ever as of 1910, had generated $270,755, which was astronomical for the time. Yet, two of Dempsey's fights already had far surpassed those amounts: Willard - $452,522, and Carpentier, $1,626,580. If Rickard could find other matches for Dempsey that would generate very good money, he would not have to deal with the potential political or legal hassles or fallout of a mixed-race heavyweight championship fight like he did both before and after Johnson-Jeffries (including loss of money from building a stadium and having the fight banned in California, the riots, fight films being banned, laws being passed to ban, limit, or clamp down on the sport, personal criticisms of him for promoting such a fight, etc.), and the money train was more likely to continue. Regardless of the reasoning, it was clear that Rickard, boxing's greatest and most successful promoter, was not eager to match Dempsey and Wills.

On December 19, 1921 in Grand Rapids, Michigan, Tommy Gibbons won a clear 10-round newspaper decision over Bartley Madden, who only lasted the distance by exhibiting great gameness. "Gibbons lived up to his reputation of being the greatest puncher of his weight and inches in the game today. Using everything in the repertoire of a high class boxer, Gibbons literally cut Madden to ribbons…" One of Madden's eyes was closed, and the other nearly closed. Madden barely managed to end Gibbons' 19-fight knockout win streak.[732]

Harry Wills said he would fight Dempsey or any man in the world, black or white, and would go anywhere in the world to do it.

> I never challenged Dempsey, fearing that the prejudice against mixed bouts which followed the actions of Jack Johnson when he defeated Jeffries for the championship was too severe for me to issue any challenges to Jack which might be misunderstood. I concluded that I would go along quietly until such time as the public might demand a battle between Dempsey and myself, or whoever else might be champion.

Harry Wills

Wills thought and hoped the prejudice against mixed bouts was waning, and soon the public would be clamoring to have them go at it. "I'm not making any claims, but I do not think that Dempsey can beat me. Remember, I am not saying that I can beat Mr. Dempsey, but if he should happen to beat me he will know full well that he has been in a quarrel." Harry said he had lived a clean life, and would set a good example for all fighters if he won the title.[733]

In letters to the editor of the New York Daily News, some said Dempsey should fight Wills or be considered to have forfeited his title, for the public wanted to see a real fight and get its money's worth. Another wrote that Wills would be the next champion if ever he was

[732] Benton Harbor News-Palladium, December 20, 1921.
[733] New York Daily News, December 21, 1921.

given the chance, and Jack knew it. Yet another said Dempsey was looking for soft ones.

Others said that neither Johnson nor Wills should get a title shot, and there should be separate champions for the black and white races. One wrote, "In my estimation Jack Dempsey would put Johnson away in the first round. Even if Johnson was at his best he would have no chance with the annihilating superman. Dempsey hits too hard for all of these so-called fighters." Wills recently went 12 rounds with Bill Tate, "who at his best couldn't work Dempsey up to a good sweat. ... Personally, I believe that Dempsey could take on both Johnson and Wills in one night and think nothing of it." Others said Wills would last about as long as Willard and Carpentier did.[734]

A Cuban promoter offered a $300,000 total purse for a Dempsey – Wills contest in Havana over 20 rounds.[735]

On December 22, 1921 in New York City, 175 ½-pound Gene Tunney, the "Pride of Greenwich Village," knocked out 167 ½-pound Eddie O'Hare (16-2-1) (a former Dempsey sparring partner) in the 6th round with a right uppercut, left hook, and straight right. O'Hare had been down in the 3rd round as well, from a left hook to the jaw. Tunney sustained a slight cut that bled. Vincent Treanor said Tunney demonstrated a combination of boxing and fighting rarely seen.[736]

Jack Dempsey was tiring quickly of vaudeville, and was negotiating with Alexander Pantages for a release from his theatrical contract.[737]

Denver promoter Jack Kanner offered a $100,000 purse for a 20-round Dempsey-Wills fight. He said Wills was the only man who could be classed as a worthy opponent for Dempsey.[738]

Bill Tate said, "Eventually Dempsey will have to fight one of us and I think he can whip Mr. Wills."[739]

The *Buffalo Express* humorously noted that although they say Dempsey will fight any man, if so, Harry Wills must be a bird, a fish, an insect, or a beast.[740]

Still, many papers continued to note that it was unlikely that a jurisdiction could be found which would authorize a mixed-race heavyweight championship contest and could financially support such a big fight. The bitter memory of Jack Johnson still lingered.

On January 2, 1922 in Portland, Oregon, Harry Wills was disqualified in the 1st round of his fight with Bill Tate, for after the referee's call to break, Tate dropped his hands to break, but Wills struck him and knocked Tate down. The men had agreed to break and step back cleanly at the referee's command.[741]

[734] *New York Daily News*, December 23, 25, 1921.
[735] *Yonkers Herald*, December 23, 1921.
[736] *New York Herald, New York Tribune, New York Evening World, New York Daily News*, December 23, 1921.
[737] *Binghamton Press*, December 28, 1921.
[738] *Brooklyn Standard Union*, January 1, 1922.
[739] *New York Daily News*, January 2, 1922.
[740] *Buffalo Express*, January 5, 1922.
[741] *Oregon Daily Journal*, January 3, 1922. Tate claimed the Colored Heavyweight Championship.

In order to satisfy the extremely disappointed fans, both fighters agreed to another fight, free of charge, four days later.

On January 6, 1922 in Portland, Oregon, Harry Wills and Bill Tate fought to a 10-round draw. George Bertz of the local Portland *Oregon Daily Journal* said, "As far as landing the cleanest and hardest punches, Tate had it over Wills, but Wills was entitled to the draw decision because he was the aggressor." Wills did most of the leading. He landed a lot of rights to the kidneys, but Tate never lost his smile.

However, in rounds scoring, Bertz seemed to have Tate winning. Tate showed to a big advantage in the 5th and 9th rounds, even dropping Wills to one knee in the 9th with a right to the head, and shaded several other rounds, including 1, 3, 6 (Wills' eye was cut by a terrific right uppercut and his knees sagged), and 10.

Bertz further said, "Jack Dempsey need have no fear about losing his crown." That was the opinion of the 5,000 on hand. "Against Dempsey, Wills' chances seem very slight because of his apparent lack of resourcefulness, his frequent wildness and his tendency to lose his head, in which case Dempsey would perhaps tear him to pieces."

Given the way Dempsey dominated Tate in sparring, Wills' performance did nothing to garner further momentum for a title challenge. It was "probable that Dempsey could batter his way through the defense of either one of these men in a few rounds."[742]

Some Mexican promoters wanted to arrange a Dempsey–Johnson fight. Dempsey said he was willing to discuss terms with them.[743]

On January 12, 1922 in London, England, 170-pound Georges Carpentier knocked out 189-pound Australian George Cook in the 4th round, with a left and two rapid rights to the chin.[744]

On January 13, 1922 in New York, 172 ½-pound Gene Tunney won the American light heavyweight championship with a clear 12-round decision over 176 ½-pound Battling Levinsky (168-42-35). The only men to have stopped Levinsky in over 300 fights were Dempsey and Carpentier.

The *Brooklyn Daily Eagle* said, "The principal criticism of Tunney at present is his lack of punch." Tunney was fast and clever, and could hit the body or head. Still, "Tunney did not show that

Gene Tunney.

he had the punch at long or short range to stop Carpentier, who is twice as fast with his feet and hands as Levinsky was last night." This writer said if Gene could beat Gibbons and Greb, then he would be ready for world light heavyweight champion Carpentier.

---

[742] *Oregon Daily Journal*, January 7, 1921. Bertz scored it: 1 – Tate by a shade, 2 – even but Wills doing the forcing, 3 – Tate by shade, 4 – Wills by shade, 5 – Tate big/wide margin, 6 – Tate by shade (Wills' eye is cut by terrific right uppercut and his knees sagged), 7 – even (or a shade to Wills), 8 – Wills by a shade, 9 – Tate, sending Wills to floor with right to head, 10 – Tate or even. Wills twice before had knocked out Tate, though he recently won a 12-round decision over him and lost by disqualification several days before.

[743] *Elmira Star-Gazette*, January 12, 1922.

[744] *Rochester Democrat and Chronicle, New York Daily News, New York Herald*, January 13, 1922.

Conversely, Charles Mathison said Tunney was young and vigorous, outclassing the veteran with his speed and power. "Tunney, showing the best form he has yet displayed in recent months, outboxed, outhit and outgeneraled the clever and resourceful Levinsky." Tunney several times had him in serious trouble. Tunney hit straight and hard with both hands, landing smashing blows to the body and head, drawing blood and puffing up the champ's nose and eyes. There was little doubt that he eventually would get a match with Carpentier.

Jack Lawrence said Levinsky fought a game battle, but was not able to withstand Tunney's aggressiveness and vigor. Tunney carried the fight to him all the way, and in several rounds had him in distress. "It was only the lack of power behind Tunney's drives that saved Levinsky from a knock-out."[745]

The *Binghamton Press* noted that Gene Tunney, born James J. Tunney, was the first A.E.F. champion to come through and win a title since the war. He easily defeated Levinsky for the American light-heavyweight championship. Tunney was a native of Greenwich Village, New York, only 23 years old (actually 24), and an army product. While serving in the Marines in France, he won the light-heavyweight A.E.F. championship, defeating Bob Martin in a special match in Paris. He was an excellent boxer, a good straight hitter, and undefeated. He might have a tough time with and lose to Greb and Gibbons, who would give him rough treatment. "However, they must get him quick, because he is improving very fast."[746]

On January 17, 1922 in Portland, Oregon, 208-pound Harry Wills won a 10-round decision over 190-pound Sam Langford, using his superior height, reach, and weight. The local *Oregon Daily Journal* wrote, "It was a fairly fast contest for big men, and it served one good purpose in that it demonstrated again, beyond all doubt, that Harry Wills is not in Jack Dempsey's class." Wills landed quite often at long range, both right and left, with unchecked power, but beyond temporary shakeup, the blows left the "ancient 'Tar Baby' little the worse for wear. One cannot imagine Dempsey hitting a man so often without disastrous results to the recipient." Langford showed no fear, often was the aggressor, and had his larger opponent backing into the ropes blocking fusillades of blows. Still, Wills clearly outboxed him at long range and deserved the decision.

Afterwards, Langford said, "There's your champion for you, just getting a decision over an old man like me. That fellow can't beat me, because he can't punch hard enough. With more time to train and in a longer fight, say of 20 rounds, I think I could put Wills out."[747]

When one expert proposed that Dempsey box Wills in London or some foreign county, the *Brooklyn Daily Eagle* responded, "Aren't there already too many dark clouds over the game?"[748]

[745] *New York Daily News, Tribune, Herald, Brooklyn Daily Eagle, Buffalo Express,* January 14, 1922. On that same card, Fred Fulton vs. Bartley Madden was called a 12-round draw.
[746] *Binghamton Press,* January 18, 1922.
[747] *Oregon Daily Journal,* January 18, 1922.
[748] *Brooklyn Daily Eagle,* January 19, 1922.

In a shocker, in New York, on January 21, 1922, Tex Rickard was arrested. Three girls, ages 11, 12, and 15, accused Tex Rickard of assault on the 15-year-old, Alice Ruck, who lived in Manhattan. The Children's Society complaint alleged that Rickard met Ruck at the Madison Square Garden swimming pool last summer. Rickard managed the Garden pool. The allegation was that Rickard enticed her into his "tower office" last summer, giving each witness $1.

The complaint stated that on December 18, 1921, George L. (Tex) Rickard, promoter and lessee of Madison Square Garden, took Alice Ruck and Anna Hess to an apartment at 21 W. 47th street in Manhattan, listed as occupied by a person named Walter Field. On another date, he took the same two girls to an apartment at 24 W. 27th street. On a later date, he carried them to the Madison Square Garden tower, where he promised them some wine. The alleged assault was said to have taken place there. There was some ambiguity regarding whether he had attempted assault on Ruck on prior occasions.

Rickard, a married man, denied the accusations.

> There is nothing to the charge. ... To a lot of kids around there I gave quarters and small coins and maybe she was one of them. I never took any of them to the tower and never knew there was such a place as the house on 47th street. At first I thought this was a frame-up by some enemies, but now I believe that these kids got into the hands of the society and told a wild story to get out of trouble. I don't think that any one who knows me will believe this yarn for a minute.

Rickard said Walter Field was employed at the Garden, but was not his secretary. He was a box office attendant. He did not know where Field lived, and he never had taken the girl to Field's home.[749]

Facing Rickard in court were (l to r): Anna Hess, age 11; Elvira Renzi, age 12, the Children's Society agent (witnesses), and Alice Ruck, age 15 (alleged victim)

[749] *Brooklyn Standard Union, Brooklyn Daily Eagle,* January 21, 1922; *New York Daily News, New York Times,* January 22, 1922.

When accuser/alleged victim Alice Ruck appeared in court on January 25, she "admitted a score or more of falsehoods on prior occasions." The girl's own mother defended Rickard, crying out to the magistrate, while her daughter was on the witness stand, "My little girl has been influenced by someone. She never had anything to do with Mr. Rickard." The *New York Daily News* noted, "The girl contradicted herself in several instances. She admitted telling many lies to the police and to Dr. McClure at Bellevue, whom she told of being chloroformed. Only when she and Anna Hess, her little friend, were separated and made to tell the detectives their story singly, did they break down, she admitted." Nevertheless, Ruck claimed Rickard had given her $38 total, sums ranging from $5 to $10. Hess always accompanied her. Hess always got $1 less than she did.

The complaint alleged that on December 18, Rickard criminally assaulted the Ruck girl, and that Hess was in the house at the time.

Ruck claimed that the prior Friday she rode to Bellevue Hospital and told a false tale of being kidnapped and having been chloroformed by a strange man.

Police detectives recognized Hess as a girl who had caused the arrest of another man she accused of attacking her on December 2, 1920, but he was discharged for lack of corroboration.

Under questioning by the detectives, the girls broke down and admitted they had told the kidnapping story because they had stayed out so late, were afraid to go home, and wanted a place to sleep. They then were sent to the dormitory of the Society for the Prevention of Cruelty to Children, which led to further investigation and their claims about Rickard. Ruck admitted to having carried a picture of Rickard for three months in the cuff of her overcoat.[750]

After Hess was questioned on the witness stand for 5 hours, corroborating Ruck's testimony, the judge refused to dismiss the case, sending it to the grand jury. Yet, "She acknowledged that she had fabricated many startling stories and that several times she had been a witness against men accused of offenses similar to that with which Rickard is charged."[751]

Making matters worse, another 15-year-old gal was found who also was making similar accusations, named Sarah Schoenfield.[752]

Frank Spellman's civil claim against William H. Dempsey and his manager Jack Kernan (Kearns) was going to be set for re-trial. A jury twice had failed to reach an agreed-upon verdict. Eventually, Dempsey and Spellman settled their lawsuit for an unspecified amount.[753]

In late January 1922, William Brady made a $200,000 offer for a Dempsey-Wills fight. The *New York Daily News* said, "Mr. Dempsey would prefer to refuse the proffered battle and keep the white world

[750] *New York Times*, January 22, 1922; *New York Daily News*, January 26, 1922.
[751] *New York Tribune*, February 4, 1922.
[752] *Brooklyn Daily Times*, February 3, 1922.
[753] *Rochester Democrat and Chronicle*, January 23, 1922; *Buffalo Enquirer*, January 28, 1922.

safe." There also was talk of a potential rematch with Carpentier in Europe, or a possible third fight with Bill Brennan.[754]

Dempsey paid $42,500 for a house in Los Angeles, where he planned to live.[755]

Kearns said he and Dempsey were not drawing the color line, but feared the many difficulties that might arise in making such a match. They were not convinced that there was a real public demand for such a fight.

The *New York Tribune* said that in Broadway boxing circles, the consensus of opinion was that while a Dempsey-Wills fight likely would be a financial success, there would be considerable difficulty in finding a place to hold it. There was no chance for it to be held in a city in or near New York, to take advantage of the population base and money there. Once the race prejudice angle was injected, anti-boxing reformers would come out in force and double the efforts they made to prevent matches between white fighters. That likely would cause politicians to make moves to prevent the contest.[756]

Robert Edgren was against a Dempsey-Wills fight. He wrote, "Boxing isn't on such a firm foundation that it can stand the pressure of criticism a Dempsey-Wills match would surely develop."[757]

The boxing fans and true sportsmen wanted the fight, knowing that Wills was the only one who could test Dempsey. However, the general public/non-boxing fans, and likely the politicians and police, were against it; not wanting to deal with the potential collateral consequences and fallout from such a contest.

New York boxing commission chairman William Muldoon said he would not authorize another Dempsey-Brennan fight. Muldoon did not believe that Brennan had defeated enough quality opponents since the last Dempsey fight to justify another title shot. He also criticized Kearns, Leo Flynn, and Rickard. "There has been plenty of time in the last six months for these men to convince boxing followers that Brennan is entitled to another match against Dempsey. They have not done so. Until they do, I will oppose whatever plans they entertain of rematching them here." Another quoted him as saying, "Dempsey is too much for Brennan. He has proven that on two occasions and I think that ought to be sufficient." One writer suggested that Muldoon wanted a series of elimination fights; for contenders to prove who was most entitled to fight Dempsey.

Rickard, Kearns, and Flynn had hoped for a March 17, 1922 St. Patrick's Day Dempsey-Brennan III fight in New York. Given how competitive their last fight had been, they believed a third fight would be even more successful financially. But Muldoon decided to meddle in matters. Plus, Rickard was dealing with serious criminal accusations, which likely would put his big promotions on hold for a while.

[754] *New York Daily News*, January 27, 28, 1922.
[755] *Rochester Democrat and Chronicle*, January 27, 1922.
[756] *New York Tribune*, January 28, 1922.
[757] *New York Evening World*, January 31, 1922.

Muldoon also was known to be opposed to a Dempsey-Wills contest based on "mixed bout" grounds. Muldoon coyly said "they were not discussing mixed matches just now, and would not consider that proposition at this moment." Hence, New York appeared to be out of the question for that fight as well.[758]

Most thought Muldoon was being unreasonable, for Brennan's performance against Dempsey had been noteworthy. Since his LKOby12 to Dempsey in December 1920, Brennan had gone 13-1 with 9 KOs, including victories over Bandsman Dick Rice (56-17-6), Bob Martin (29-5), and Texas Tate (21-9-6). His only loss was a very close newspaper decision to the well-regarded Billy Miske, who since his September 1920 loss to Dempsey had gone 8-0.

Several New York writers said they had not received objections to a Dempsey-Wills match. Most agreed that Wills was not like Johnson, and they were opposite types of men. He was clean-living, industrious, honest, and modest.

> One might almost say he knows his place like one of the old-time Southern darkies. He is a credit to the ring and to his race, and is as popular with white patrons of boxing as with negroes. ... Talk of race prejudice is rot, and is easily to be traced to its proper source. Johnson was not unpopular because of the color of his skin; his deeds outside the ring brought the wrath of the whites down on his head. If he had conducted himself properly Johnson would have been popular, for with all his personal habits he was a very likable fellow.[759]

Dempsey and Kearns said they were willing to sign to fight the winner of the upcoming Greb vs. Gibbons contest.[760]

The *New York Daily News* noted that when Dempsey came to New York, he said he was willing to fight anyone, including Wills. However, Kearns essentially had ignored William Brady's offer for the fight, saying that he had not heard any good offers.

Of course, Kearns likely believed the Dempsey-Wills fight was worth a lot more than the $200,000 purse Brady offered ($150,000 guaranteed to Dempsey). Dempsey had just fought for $300,000 guaranteed in a fight with a $500,000 purse, which generated over $1.6 million.

Given that for as long as he was champion, Dempsey could make very good, easy money in vaudeville exhibitions and films, Kearns likely was not going to risk the title against a tough man unless a very lucrative offer was made. This seemed to be the business model/pattern for most heavyweight champions; risking the valuable title, a highly lucrative economic asset, as little as possible, only against tough foes when very strong financial inducements were made. Kearns was willing and able to be very patient about making decisions and accepting offers. Yet, the

[758] *Brooklyn Standard Union, New York Daily News, Elmira Star Gazette*, February 1, 1922.
[759] *Brooklyn Daily Times*, February 7, 1922.
[760] *Brooklyn Standard Union, New York Evening World*, February 11, 1922.

ironic risk of that pattern always was that inactivity often left champions less sharp and more vulnerable to defeat.[761]

On February 16, 1922, a grand jury indicted Tex Rickard on separate charges of abduction and assault on Sarah Schoenfeld and Alice Ruck, each age 15. Rickard again strenuously denied the charges, insisting he did not know the girls other than in a passing manner.

Some questioned to what extent Rickard would be able to promote boxing shows while the charges were pending. They quickly got their answer. The following day, Rickard resigned as the matchmaker and president of the Madison Square Garden Sporting Club. Supposedly, the athletic commission had threatened to investigate whether his license should be revoked, but his announcement forestalled the inquiry.[762]

On February 20, 1922 in Cincinnati, Ohio, 164-pound Harry Greb fought 163-pound Jeff Smith (95-25-4) to a 10-round newspaper decision draw. The *Cincinnati Enquirer* said an even break was given to Greb for being the aggressor, but Smith inflicted the most punishment. Had Smith stepped on the gas and been more aggressive, he would have won. "Smith did not receive a mark, while Greb's left eye was closed and his face badly swollen. Smith made Greb's nose bleed early in the contest, and gave Harry the most severe beating he ever received in any bout in this city." Smith's blows were cleaner and harder, though Greb carried the fight to him throughout, which secured him the draw. "Smith displayed wonderful defensive tactics, while Greb was open and easy to hit." Greb's blows did no harm.[763]

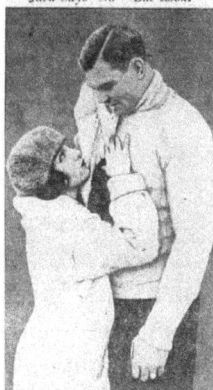

Jack Dempsey was dating actress Bebe Daniels, although he was shy about admitting it, saying there was nothing to the claims. "Miss Daniels is an extremely charming girl."[764]

The *Binghamton Press* said Dempsey did not fear Wills, who at 30 years old (actually 32) was not getting any better. "According to Jack Kearns he is going back. Kearns bases his argument on the fact that Wills has not been able to do much with Bill Tate in recent bouts. Tate, a former sparring partner of Dempsey, never was capable of extending the

[761] *New York Daily News*, February 16, 1922.
[762] *New York Daily News*, February 17, 1922; *New York Herald*, February 18, 1922.
[763] *Cincinnati Enquirer*, February 21, 1922.
[764] *New York Daily News*, February 22, 1922.

champion." Wills had stopped Tate a year ago, in January 1921, in 2 rounds so brutally that he was taken to the hospital, but had gone the distance with him of late, including a more recent draw.[765]

The general feeling was that as long as Dempsey had marketable white opponents, he would avoid Wills, but if there were no big paydays available, and he was getting low on cash, thought there was a big payday with Wills, and the legal authorities would allow it, then he probably would be willing to fight him.

Dempsey began another month-long theatrical exhibition engagement, at the Hippodrome in New York, called "Get Together." He would earn $1,400 a week for 30 minutes of work daily (15 minutes twice a day), for a little boxing with Larry Williams (and various others) and also making a few wise cracks. The Carpentier fight was exhibited as well.[766]

A man hired to paint the champion's training quarters in Los Angeles alleged that the champ's secretary Teddy Hayes and the champ's brother Joseph H. Dempsey had assaulted and beaten him up badly, ordering him to stop working and leave.[767]

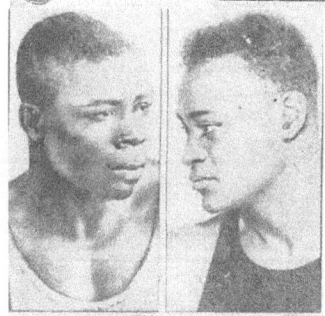

On March 2, 1922 at Madison Square Garden, New York, 211 ¾-pound Harry Wills scored a KO2 over well-respected 176-pound Kid Norfolk (91-19-6). A short, speedy right uppercut to the jaw ended matters. It was so short and fast that few saw it, leading some to call it a fake or frame-up. Nevertheless, Wills' stock jumped back up again, at least with some.

Grantland Rice said Wills proved to have the strength, speed, and power to knock a man down with a short

[765] *Binghamton Press*, February 27, 1922.
[766] *Brooklyn Citizen*, *Evening World*, February 28, 1922; *Brooklyn Daily Times*, March 3, 1922. Jack said his two-a-day performances with the gloves and a little morning road work kept him in condition. He admitted that he went out a little at night, and he liked dancing.
[767] *Oneonta Star*, March 1, 1922.

blow. "By the quick finish the dusky heavyweight steps forward as the most logical contender in the field for Dempsey's crown, provided any one can locate the battlefield that will stand for the entertainment."

Harry Newman agreed, "Harry Wills proved conclusively…that he is entitled to a chance at Jack Dempsey for the heavyweight championship of the world."

The *Brooklyn Standard Union* said Wills won so impressively that "his claims to a title match cannot longer be ignored."

One noted, "Dempsey has said that he would box Wills if the bout promised a house." Indications were that such a fight would draw a big house, for the gate for this show was $55,415.80. "The human decorations were strikingly black and white. There has not been so much interest among the colored population since the days when Arthur Johnson was king of his division and unacquainted with the interior color scheme of jails."

Wills said, "I think my victory…should entitle me to a match for the world's title." His manager Paddy Mullins said,

> I guess the boys will admit now that Harry deserves a shot at Dempsey's title. … He is a great fighter, and I think he will be champion of the world as soon as we can induce Dempsey to meet him in the ring. … I had a talk with Kearns not so long ago, and he told me he was willing provided a big enough purse was offered. Now that the public is convinced that Wills is a fit opponent for the champion, they will support such a match and make it possible for a promoter to offer a purse large enough to suit the champion.

New Jersey Governor Ed Edwards said he would permit a Wills-Dempsey championship provided that there was sufficient public demand; whatever that meant. Likely, he would have to analyze it politically before making a final decision.[768]

When asked if he would be willing to meet Wills, Dempsey replied, "Certainly. Boxing is my business and I will box any man the public is interested in seeing me box, whether he is yellow, green, white or black."

However, the *Brooklyn Daily Eagle*'s Thomas Rice said Wills had not yet proven himself to be a suitable rival for Dempsey, for it appeared to him as if Norfolk was looking for a way out of the contest.

> As a matter of fact, the affair proved nothing at all. It will be seized upon by the sensationalists who are determined to bring about a Dempsey-Wills scrap and do their utmost to kill the game in the United States, as a subject for propaganda, but Wills demonstrated nothing whatever to prove that he should be matched with Dempsey.

Rice said the man who would beat Dempsey had to have both a left jab and lots of footwork which could be used to set up a right cross. Wills

[768] *Buffalo Enquirer*, March 3, 1922.

did not have Tate's left jab, or the necessary footwork. "Dempsey could beat the Wills of last night with one hand tied behind him." Furthermore, "Wills lacks ring science. He has been played up by a certain element of newspaper writers as a marvel, but he is not, and the men who follow boxing know he is not. He does not hit cleanly." He could not hit Dempsey with the same blows without a comeback. "Dempsey would have crossed him to the jaw or have ripped a left or right to the body that would have made Wills see stars." Wills did not have the punch and cleverness that Jack Johnson had. Johnson would feint him, jab him, and hit him with rights whenever Wills started something. "Dempsey could and would do the same thing. He would not feint as scientifically as Johnson, but his two-handed leads would accomplish the same purpose of tying up Wills and the end would be the same."[769]

On March 3, 1922 in Grand Rapids, Michigan, 174-pound Gene Tunney won a 10-round no decision (7-0-3) over 170-pound Fay Keiser.[770]

Damon Runyon said Wills might not be good enough to beat Dempsey, but he was a great fighter nevertheless. Dempsey hit harder and was faster, but 6'3" (some said 6'2") Harry was big, tall, fast, and strong enough to give him a real fight.[771]

Boston Red Sox president Harry Frazee offered $350,000 to Dempsey for a Dempsey-Wills fight on September 2 in either New York, Boston, or Jersey City.[772]

Kearns said he would accept $350,000 as Dempsey's end for a Wills fight. "The terms are very satisfactory. Very satisfactory indeed." However, he wanted some form of a guarantee, with a substantial forfeit posted by Frazee to be paid to Dempsey if for whatever reason Frazee was not able to bring off the fight. They did not want to take the time required to train, and forgo other opportunities, only to have the bout canceled because of political opposition. Posted cash spoke louder than words. Kearns said, "I hope that nothing happens to the poor fellow [Frazee] until he gets a chance to sign the papers and post a forfeit."

Although New Jersey's governor did not oppose a Dempsey-Wills contest per se *if* the public wanted it, ultimately, he said that he was leaving the matter up to the boxing board. However, the New Jersey boxing commission opposed the mixed-race fight. Its chairman issued a statement expressing the belief that "the public generally were opposed to this match." There always seemed to be various political games and verbal pyrotechnics going on, indicating that the bout was not wanted by those in power. This theme would continue elsewhere.

The Massachusetts boxing commission also made it clear that it would not allow a Dempsey-Wills fight, so Boston was out of the question as well. "The commissioners have nothing personally against those fighters,

[769] *New York Herald, New York Evening World, Brooklyn Standard Union, Brooklyn Daily Eagle, New York Tribune*, March 3, 1922. On the same card, 186-pound Billy Miske stopped 183-pound Al Roberts (20-7-1) in the 2nd round.
[770] *Battle Creek Enquirer*, March 4, 1922.
[771] *Buffalo Courier*, March 5, 1922.
[772] *Brooklyn Daily Times*, March 5, 1922; *Brooklyn Standard Union*, March 6, 1922.

but they figure it would do the game such harm that the boxing law would be quickly repealed if such bouts were staged." Commissioner Buckley said, "Such a bout would hurt local boxing. The promoters want to hold the bout for the money they would get out of it, while the commissioners are against it for the sake of the sport here."

The *Boston Globe* noted that although Dempsey-Wills would draw a big crowd and generate a lot of money, "The opposition that would be stirred up against such a bout would be very strong. The commissioners do not want to stir up any protests."[773]

Such statements out of New Jersey and Boston likely had an impact on Harry Frazee, who would not want to post a large forfeit and spend money investing in the promotion of such a fight only to lose it all if he would not be able to bring off the contest owing to political opposition. Hence, ultimately there was not much follow-up from Frazee regarding the proposed Dempsey-Wills bout.[774]

HARRY GREB

According to the *Buffalo Times'* Robert Stedler, Tommy Gibbons, "prominently mentioned as the logical opponent for Champion Dempsey," would be given an acid test by Harry Greb in their upcoming contest. Gibbons "has proved that he packs a knockout punch." Conversely, "Greb has never established a reputation as a knockout artist. Rather he has won praise for his shiftiness. Few big men are faster on their feet than the Pittsburgh boy. He bounds around like a rubber ball and is a mighty hard man to hit, since he seldom is flatfooted."[775]

The *Seattle Star's* Seaburn Brown wrote, "Greb can hardly be considered as a championship possibility, even if he whips Gibbons. He weighs around 165, which is heavy enough for him to fight on fairly even terms with Gibbons, but far too light to rate him as a possible conqueror of the champion." Of course, this same writer said Harry Wills was not entitled to a Dempsey fight either.

On March 6, 1922, Babe Ruth signed a new contract for three years at $52,000 per year. It was the largest sum ever paid to a ballplayer up to that point, and it represented 40% of the team's total player payroll.

---

[773] *Boston Globe*, March 4, 5, 1922. Promoter Murray of Buffalo allegedly offered Dempsey $300,000 to fight the winner of the upcoming Tom Gibbons – Harry Greb battle. However, there was no local confirmation of the offer.
[774] *New York Herald, Olean Times Herald*, March 6, 1922.
[775] *Buffalo Times*, March 7, 1922.

At New York City's Hippodrome, Jack Dempsey was performing in "Get Together." In conjunction with the exhibition of the Carpentier fight films, the champ did some training stunts and sparred various men. For the week starting Monday March 6, Dempsey sparred bantamweight Johnny Buff (refereed by Harry Greb); featherweight Vincent (Pepper) Martin on Tuesday; bantam Sammy Nable, newsboy Harry London, and Young Jimmy Hussey on Wednesday the 8th (attended by 3,000 newsboys), and on March 9 and 10, 3 rounds with middleweight Mike McTigue (82-23-6).[776]

Unfortunately, the New Jersey legislature passed a bill that limited the price of ringside seats to $15, and on March 13, Governor Edwards signed the bill. That complicated matters in terms of a potential big fight being held there. Such a limit made any world heavyweight championship bout held in New Jersey less economically viable. Promoters did not want to make big financial guarantees and then have their ability to generate sufficient revenue to cover those guarantees be limited by law. That reduced the prospects of potential future Dempsey contests being held in New Jersey.

In light of the various statements by state athletic commissions, and the new law in New Jersey, the *Brooklyn Daily Times'* Nat Ferber wrote, "Certainly Mr. Frazee's offer of $350,000 to Dempsey doesn't go today. The Boston baseball man had visions of the $1,600,000 gate at the Dempsey-Carpentier fight when he made that offer." W. O. McGeehan concurred, saying that at present, the Dempsey-Wills bout looked like an "airy dream." Indeed, eventually, Harry Frazee withdrew his offer.[777]

Harry Wills shakes hands with schoolkids   Wills with his wife in their Harlem home

In its push to foster a Dempsey-Wills fight, the *New York Daily News* highlighted the fact that Wills was a likeable, upstanding citizen, and never did anything objectionable. He had a light-skinned colored wife

[776] *Seattle Star*, March 4, 1922; *Brooklyn Daily Times*, March 6, 9, 10, 1922; *New York Tribune, Brooklyn Standard Union*, March 10, 1922.
[777] *New York Herald*, March 7, 12, 15, 1922; *Brooklyn Daily Times*, March 9, 1922; *New York Times*, March 14, 1922.

(contrasting him with Jack Johnson, who married white women), and he enjoyed home life.

On Monday March 13, 1922 at Madison Square Garden in New York, before a crowd of 14,000, 163 ½-pound "Pittsburgh Windmill" Harry Greb won a 15-round decision over 171-pound Tommy Gibbons. Overall, Greb and Gibbons were 2-2 against each other, though Greb had won the last two, the most recent and longest of their contests, and the only formal, official decision. The fight generated $117,268 in ticket sales.

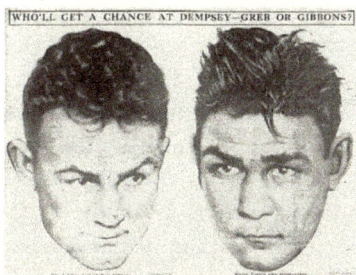

Jack Dempsey was present, and said it was the fastest fight he ever had seen. "Greb is so fast that he will give any big man some trouble. Would I fight either of them? Surely, or both. I will fight anybody they want me to fight." However, the general verdict amongst sportswriters was that Greb was not a viable opponent for Dempsey.

The *Brooklyn Standard Union* said although Greb won decisively, "the Pittsburg 'Windmill' can by no stretch of the imagination be considered a fit opponent for the world's titleholder. It is not a question of ability. Merely one of weight." Greb was a great fighter with untiring energy and willingness to fight, gaining victory over a "better boxer and a harder puncher" in Gibbons, who only weighed 7.5 pounds more. Harry outpunched and outsmarted him, keeping the harder-punching Gibbons mostly on the defensive. Gibbons had good defense, and landed the cleaner, harder blows, but he simply was not active enough to overcome Greb's superior punch volume. "But great a fighter as he proved himself to be, Greb is not heavy enough to combat Dempsey."

Greb said, "I kept him so busy blocking my punches that he had little time to do any damage of his own. He is a great fighter, though, and I had to be on my guard all the time. One punch might have changed the whole complexion of affairs. Dempsey? Ask my manager. Dempsey is only a fighter, and that is what I am."

Gibbons said, "Frankly, I think the judges gave me a bit the worst of it. I outboxed Greb in nearly every round and landed the cleaner punches. I blocked every punch that he threw at me. ... Aggressiveness is all right in its way, but what good is it if it is not effective?" However, all of the newsmen agreed with the decision. Another quoted Gibbons as saying, "I was not myself. I just couldn't get going. ... I can't account for it except that I was stale."

The *Brooklyn Daily Eagle*'s W. C. Vreeland quoted Greb as saying he had no desire to fight Dempsey, but would fight Tunney or Carpentier. When told that he had earned a match with Dempsey, Greb responded, "Yes, I know; one was offered me by Charley Murray of the Queensbury Club of Buffalo, but I don't think I'll accept it." When asked why not, Greb replied, "Because Dempsey is too heavy for me. I don't think I could concede him about 25 pounds. There was only about 8 pounds difference between Gibbons and me, and it took all my strength to overcome that handicap." He would readily fight Tunney or Carpentier, who were not much bigger than he was. His manager George Engel said the man they most wanted to fight was middleweight champion Johnny Wilson. "You mustn't overlook the fact that Greb is only a middleweight, and to fight Tunney or Carpentier he must concede pounds to each."

Vreeland said, "It will be seen from this conversation that Greb has no wild desire to fight Dempsey. Like a good fighter he knows his limitations."

Others quoted Greb as saying he was willing to fight Dempsey. Certainly though, he was not overly anxious or strongly pushing for such a bout, preferring to fight middleweights (which is what he was), or slightly larger light heavyweights.

Much of the press did not treat seriously a potential Dempsey-Greb bout, primarily owing to Greb's lack of size, weight, and punching power, particularly against a man of Dempsey's superior strength, size, and punching power combined with speed and relentlessness.

Thomas Rice said the judges' decision was absolutely correct, but "a lover of real boxing could not help feeling that the wrong man won." Greb was a "jumping jack" with "cleverness of a sort," but not the kind that would be of much use if "one's life were at stake." Gibbons was an orthodox boxer with a straight left and right cross. Greb was "absolutely unorthodox," employing no straight punches at all, and neither landing with precision nor force. Nevertheless, he won, just as he had been doing for years. "Greb won last night more because Gibbons acted as if afraid, or in a trance."

Gibbons did not live up to his reputation or show his punching power. He had ability, a punch, and command of scientific boxing, but refused to uncork it. Tom said he was stale and had overtrained.

Greb was on his toes constantly, dancing up and down, diving in quickly from unexpected angles, and he could hit from any possible direction. He had very fast hands. He hit high, low, and in between, and could change the original intention of a blow with astonishing swiftness, confusing his foes. "Greb's speed and endurance are phenomenal." He kept up an incessant attack, and had amazingly fast footwork, attacking from off to the side and then in. He also could move away from leads with his fast feet, and was good at ducking, though Gibbons was a good ducker as well.

Yet, despite all the energy Greb expended, his blows lacked steam, having "surprisingly little force." He could take a punch very well. He took a lot of heavy jolts from Gibbons, yet mostly seemed unaffected. The only time Greb seemed hurt was in the 14th round, when Gibbons staggered him with a right to the head but failed to follow up the advantage.

Rice said Greb likely would be matched with Tunney, and the winner would meet Carpentier.

For the *New York Tribune*, Grantland Rice said neither boxer loomed up as a real opponent for Dempsey.

The *New York Herald* said Gibbons failed to show the class of a coming champion.

W. O. McGeehan said, "This settles the question as to whether or not Gibbons is a suitable opponent for Jack Dempsey. He is not." Gibbons had the punch to do harm if he could connect, but Greb knew it too, and kept on the move.

McGeehan did not believe Greb was a suitable foe for Dempsey either. "As for Greb he is too light to even dream of getting a loser's end with the heavyweight champion." He was a middleweight, and if Johnny Wilson fought him, there would be a shifting of the world middleweight championship.

Kearns was melancholy after it was over, lamenting that the result did not develop a title challenger.

The *Brooklyn Citizen* said "the impression stood out all over that either one, or both, would be easy for Dempsey." Still, Greb at least would make it interesting for a while, for he was a perpetual motion machine who kept a fast pace. "Greb really is one of the marvels of the ring. ... He might be easy for Dempsey, but it's a sure thing that he would make it mighty lively for the champion while it lasted."

The *New York Times* said Gibbons was supposed to be Dempsey's next opponent, "now that the proposed Wills engagement has been placed under a temporary ban of public disapproval." Yet, he was a disappointment. Greb assimilated whatever Gibbons had to offer, and came boring in for more. "He danced in and about and around his opponent, darting in with body blows and then rushing into a clinch to avoid the uppercuts that Gibbons radioed were coming." Gibbons simply was too slow on this occasion, though many said he was stale, left his fight in the gym, and could do better than his performance showed, which he had done in the past.

HARRY GREB

When Jack Dempsey was asked how long it would take him to put either of them away, he only replied with a smile.

The *New York World*'s Vincent Treanor said Greb beat Gibbons, outslapping and outgaming him, but would be no match for Dempsey.

> Tom, judged on his last night's showing, is lacking in a mysterious something. He is of an odd type. He looks as if he could do things and then doesn't. At least that's how he appeared against Greb. As for Greb, he won alright, but in doing so really eliminated himself as a serious rival of Dempsey. Jack could beat both of them easily.

Greb prevented Gibbons from setting. He rushed in, clinched, and whaled away, keeping Tom defensive. Gibbons landed heavy body blows, but Greb took them and recovered well, even when they seemed to be about to affect him. When Gibbons landed solidly, he did not tear in to find out if he had hurt Greb, "as a Dempsey would have done." He seemed easily discouraged, not because of the damage Harry did, but merely because of Greb's sheer willingness to mix. Plus, Greb knew how to hold and hit, pinning Tom's arm and hitting with the other, or getting him in headlocks with his left and hitting him with his right.

The *Brooklyn Daily Times*' Nat Ferber said Greb slapped out a victory. He was a human fly climbing all over a man who towered over him. "If Jack Dempsey was at the ringside, his heart must have sunk within him. Certainly any chance of an opponent with big-purse possibilities that this bout might have developed was sent sky high." They both were better suited as opponents for Tunney than Dempsey. This writer believed both men could beat Tunney, but "beating Tunney won't mean anything." Still, it would be better for the one who did that to be looked upon as an eventual opponent for Dempsey.[778]

The *New York Daily News* (Harry Newman) said Harry Wills stood alone as the logical challenger, for the fight had put both Gibbons and Greb out of the picture. Greb won, "but he didn't quite show enough stuff to warrant a combat with the big heavyweight champion. … Greb is out of the question. The plain truth of the matter is that Harry can't hit a lick. He's a good, aggressive boy with a good fighting heart, but he is not ready for a man of Dempsey's proportions and probably never will be." Wills had the size and physique to stand up to Dempsey.

Karpe's Comment said, "Now that Greb has beaten Gibbons, an opponent for Jack Dempsey seems farther away than ever. It is hardly probable that any promoter will suggest a Greb-Dempsey match, though Dempsey, naturally enough says he is willing."

The *Buffalo Courier* noted that the plan was for Greb to meet Tunney in May, and if he won, hopefully Carpentier next.

A couple days after the fight, W. O. McGeehan again said, "If Greb were about twenty pounds heavier and four inches or so taller he might be able to cause Jack Dempsey an evening's annoyance. But Greb is a middleweight and that ends that. He is a nice boy, but he is no Bob Fitzsimmons."[779]

However, E. W. Dickerson said it was not an absolute cinch that Dempsey would beat Greb, even though he had many natural advantages and superior punching power.

> The champion is a wonderful puncher, but that does not get a fighter anything when opposed to a man so fast he cannot be reached.

[778] *New York World, New York Times, Brooklyn Citizen, Brooklyn Daily Eagle, New York Herald, Brooklyn Standard Union, New York Tribune, Brooklyn Daily Times,* March 14, 1922.
[779] *New York Daily News, Buffalo Evening News, Buffalo Courier, New York Herald,* March 15, 1922.

Dempsey and Kearns once said in the presence of the writer and several other sporting scribes they did not care to ever box Harry Greb, and frankly gave his speed and boxing cleverness as a reason for not desiring intimacy with the Pittsburgher. If the inducements are tempting enough, he will no doubt change his mind.[780]

In a nationwide poll taken by N.E.A. service newspapers, which ended before Greb-Gibbons, fans voted on who they wanted to see Dempsey fight. The results: Wills, 131,073; Gibbons, 125,167; Brennan, 52,179; Martin, 40,921; Roper, 29,613; Carpentier, 28,174; and Willard, 20,108. Billy Evans noted, "There is little likelihood Greb will be matched with the champ, as the difference in weight is too great." Greb was not even mentioned on the ballot, but neither were Carpentier and Willard, yet they each received over 20,000 write-in votes.[781]

Dempsey said he was perfectly willing to fight Greb. He told Harry to dig up someone to promote the fight. He doubted whether anyone thought well enough of Greb's chances against him to put up the necessary coin. Still, Jack recognized Greb's ability and class.

Dempsey said, "Sure, I'll mix it with Harry Greb! But who'll sign us up? What promoter has the idea that Greb and I are so evenly matched in fighting ability that he'll take the gamble of offering me a fair sized purse – and hang up another for Greb?" Dempsey acknowledged that no one had more self-confidence than Greb. However, Jack would outweigh him by nearly 30 pounds, and have great height and reach advantages as well. Regardless, if the money was right, Dempsey was willing to fight him.

The fight's result did not surprise Dempsey much.

> Greb was my sparring partner once. He was the fastest thing I ever saw in action. Hitting him is one of life's most difficult jobs, because he's never 'set' for a second, never comes at you the same way twice, never does anything in ring warfare which can be called orthodox. He's always doing the unexpected and because he does, he's one of those phantom targets which you hit more by luck than through the use of skill.

Dempsey thought Gibbons was overtrained, the same as Jack had been against Brennan. On that night, punches which Dempsey normally landed were missing, and punches which he ordinarily would duck or block were landing on him. Eventually Dempsey got going, but Gibbons could not.

Dempsey gave Greb credit, however, for he was such a whirlwind, he never let Tom get set. He crowded all the time. "I said I'd fight the winner of that mixup – if any promoter cared to pit me against him." Jack knew that Greb would fight anyone.

> Greatest wild cat the prize ring ever knew. Seems as if he can't be hurt, or dropped, and nothing can stop him from coming in. ...

---

[780] *Grand Rapids Herald*, March 14, 15, 1922.
[781] *Arizona Republican*, March 15, 1922.

Yep, I'll fight Greb – or anybody else whom the public demands I should tackle. ... Won't some nice kind promoter step forward and make noises like a match for me against Wills, Greb, Willard – anybody in the world?[782]

Despite the fact that Greb had beaten a lot of top fighters, including heavyweight contenders, most folks, particularly New York writers, and the general public, simply could not get over the fact that he was just a middleweight in size, stood only 5'8", and was not a big puncher or finisher, so they just couldn't picture him having any chance with Dempsey. Perception was important for marketing and economic reasons.

A week after Greb-Gibbons, the *Brooklyn Daily Times* said Greb was a great little fighter, but hardly more than a heavy middleweight. He probably would beat middleweight champ Johnny Wilson for the title if Wilson could be induced to fight him, and possibly Gene Tunney for the light heavy title, "but if he got Dempsey there could be nothing but another victim on the Manassa mauler's list."

Greb's friends claimed that he mussed up the champ considerably when sparring with him before the Brennan fight. "He may have bothered him then and he would annoy the champion for a while if they went into the ring now, but it would be only for a while. Against Gibbons, Greb showed that he can't hit a lick and no one is going to stand a chance with Dempsey who cannot hurt the big fellow."

Tommy Gibbons was clever and could punch, but Greb's style was all wrong for him. Harry was just too fast and busy for him. Hence, "it may be that judgment on Gibbons ought to be withheld until he has another chance with a first-class opponent." Still, to beat a Tunney or Carpentier, Gibbons would have to work harder, hit more accurately, and move around more quickly than he did with Greb.[783]

The *New York Sun's* Fred Keats said,

> That Harry Greb is too small and harmless a hitter to be worthy of a match with Jack Dempsey was the general opinion in local ring circles following the Pittsburgher's bout with Tom Gibbons, but that is not the opinion in Harry's home town. In Pittsburgh they think that Greb is good enough to beat any one regardless of weight, and they are demanding that he be matched with the champion.
>
> Buffalo is another town that would stand for a Dempsey-Greb affair if the Boxing Commission would consent. Charley Murray, the leading up-State promoter, long has held the opinion that little Greb would cause Dempsey more trouble than any of the big fellows would. For the last two years he has talked of putting on the match.

[782] *Pittsburgh Press*, March 19, 1922.
[783] *Brooklyn Daily Times*, March 22, 1922.

Keats admitted that perhaps Greb could give Dempsey trouble and hold his own. After all, fat Meehan, who also was not much of a puncher, did (although Meehan was 190-220 pounds). Ultimately, Keats noted,

> The champion would have a great deal to lose and nothing much to gain, because a Dempsey-Greb bout would not be a big money maker. To the average ring follower it looks altogether too uneven a match. It probably would be, but there is just a chance that Greb, with his clownish tactics, would prove a harder problem for Dempsey to solve than men who are much better fighters than the little fellow from Pittsburgh.[784]

For his hometown paper, Greb wrote that he was at his best at about 163 pounds, which forced him to give up weight to most of his foes. He wanted to win the middleweight title against southpaw Johnny Wilson, but believed Wilson was dodging him. Harry believed he was better than Tunney, too.

Greb also wanted to fight Jack Dempsey, and felt that his victory over Gibbons justified him to consideration, despite his size.

> What is more, I have better than an even chance to win the title. ... I am honest when I say that I feel that I can outbox Dempsey in a bout of 12 to 15 rounds. There would always be the chance of a knockout by Dempsey of course. ... There was always that chance in my bout with Gibbons. ... Of one thing I am positive, I would make a far better fight than did Carpentier.[785]

Freddie Welsh said Greb could throw more punches and put them together better than any other fighter, and no one could box as fast as he did. Savants said Dempsey might not be able to solve his whirling style, and if Jack did not win by knockout, he would be outpointed.[786]

The United Press said, "Neither Tom Gibbons nor Harry Greb are ready to be thrown in the cage with Jack Dempsey." That was "perfectly clear to all" who saw their recent contest. "Gibbons ought to make an opponent for Dempsey, but he lacks something. In the gym he looks like a million dollars. He has the size, he is clever and can punch." But against Greb, Tom seemed sluggish, slow, and wild. He usually was a sharpshooter, but had no idea of range that night.

Welterweight champion Jack Britton opined that Gibbons was stale against Greb and left his fight in the gym. The writer agreed. "It was strikingly apparent that Gibbons was off form for some reason or other." Judgment on him would be reserved. "If he ever gets Greb again, and there is small chance for it, he will be almost sure to beat him." Unfortunately, "the more the 'logical contenders' show themselves, the more supreme Dempsey looks in his class." Some believed that Dempsey would have to sit on the shelf for a long while to be beatable.[787]

---

[784] *New York Sun*, March 22, 1922.
[785] *Pittsburgh Press*, March 23, 24, 1922.
[786] *New York Tribune*, March 31, 1922.
[787] *Santa Rosa Republican*, April 1, 1922.

Regardless, there was some talk of a potential Dempsey fight with Greb. Harry's manager said he would put Greb in with Dempsey. While admitting that Greb could not hurt Jack, he thought Dempsey would struggle to land on or hurt Greb.

Kearns actually lobbied a bit for Greb, saying that he had a sneaking notion that Greb showed enough to entitle him to a fight with Dempsey.

> It strikes me rather forcibly that a lot of the fight fans have been overlooking that boy Greb. He's the busiest little fellow I have seen in many a moon. He works somewhat along the lines of Willie Meehan, tossing them in every direction at every step.

> Of course, we're not overlooking the idea that most of the folks would rather have a Harry Wills and Dempsey bout. I'm not going to bother about that right now until some of the promoting element decide that the time is opportune for such a contest.[788]

Robert Edgren echoed others in saying that Greb was "out of luck," and despite beating Gibbons, no heavyweight title bout was in sight for him. Greb was powerfully built, very fast, and full of grit and stamina, but he was too little.

However, when asked who would give him the most trouble, Dempsey said, "Greb. He's a busy bee. He's stinging all the time." Dempsey said giants were big and slow and easy to hit. It was the smaller, quicker men who gave him trouble. Greb had beaten the man who was being groomed for a chance at the champ. Tom Sharkey gave Jeffries his toughest fight, and he was much smaller than the champ. Size did not always matter. "Looks as if he deserves some sort of a chance to show what he can do." Yet, there was not a big push for a Greb-Dempsey fight.[789]

The *Daily News* mentioned another potential contender on the horizon, a South American from Argentina named Luis Angel Firpo, a big, strong, 6'3" 227-pound man with a heavy punch, who would be one to watch as he developed.

Having turned pro in 1917, Firpo had won the South American heavyweight championship in 1920 with a KO1 over Dave Mills, a KO1 feat he repeated that same year, twice avenging a prior 1919 15-round decision loss to 185-pound Mills, a former Jack Johnson sparring partner. In 1921, Firpo won a 12-round decision over Gunboat Smith, but in the rematch that same year, he scored a 12th round knockout over Smith.

[788] *New York Daily News*, March 21, 1922. Kearns said they were scheduled to leave for Europe on April 11.
[789] *Kansas City Star*, April 1, 1922. Harry Frazee allegedly was offering $350,000 for a Dempsey-Wills contest, but Kearns' only response to the offer was a polite smile. He wanted posted guarantees and a substantial forfeit.

Firpo was improving rapidly. He recently had come to the U.S., and in his first U.S. fight, on March 20, 1922 in Newark, New Jersey, he scored a KO7 over 197-pound Sailor Tom Maxted.[790]

Also on March 20, 1922, Tex Rickard's trial for abduction and assault on Sarah Schoenfeld began. A separate trial was planned to be held for the alleged assault on Alice Ruck.[791]

During the trial, the judge had Rickard held in jail.

15-year-old Sarah Schoenfeld said she visited Rickard at his invitation eight times, to rooms he maintained, at 24 W. 47th street and two doors east, at number 20, under the name of "Fields." She met five other girls there, including Anna Hess, Alice Ruck, and Elvira Rienzi. Rickard gave her wine, danced with her, and led her to a rear bedroom, alone. Rickard gave her $5 and warned her not to tell anybody. On each occasion that she visited Rickard, he gave her money, varying from $5 to $20. She repeatedly went to Rickard's office, and though she knew what Rickard was doing was wrong, she did so because she "wanted the money." A letter was introduced into evidence, penned by Rickard, addressed to her mother, referencing his efforts to obtain the release of Sarah's brother, who was serving a term for larceny in Wisconsin. Sarah had asked Rickard to help her brother.[792]

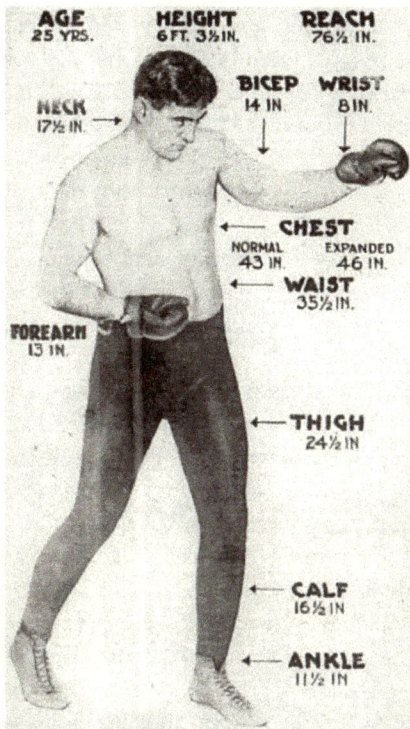

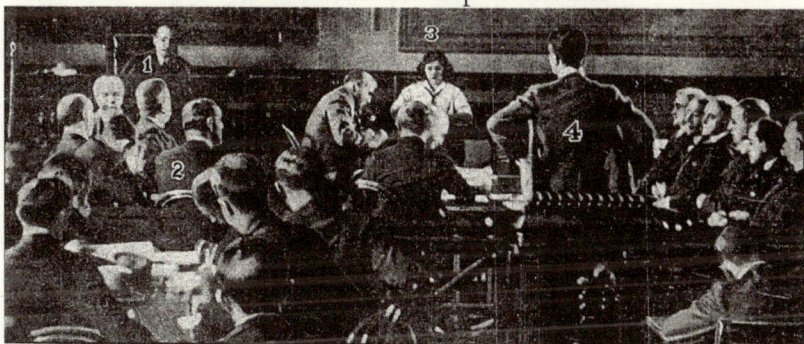

RICKARD ACCUSER UNSHAKEN.—Under a searching cross-examination yesterday by Max D. Steuer before Supreme Court Justice Wasservogel (1), Sarah Schoenfeld (3), fifteen, accusing Tex Rickard (2) of assault, held to the story she previously had told on the stand to Assistant District Attorney Pecora (4). Another girl, Nellie Gasko, thirteen, testified in corroboration of the Schoenfeld girl's story.

[790] *New York Daily News*, March 22, 1922. Firpo's only other loss was in his second pro bout, when he had been stopped in the 1st round by Angel Rodriguez, who was 25-2 at the time. Firpo improved thereafter, winning a 15-round decision over former Jack Johnson sparring partner 178-pound Calvin Respress.
[791] *New York Daily News*, March 20, 1922.
[792] *New York Daily News*, *New York Tribune*, *Brooklyn Daily Times*, March 22, 1922.

Another girl, 12-year-old Nellie Gasko, corroborated Schoenfeld's story, but admitted that she had forged checks and committed burglary upon a home to steal money. She admitted to stealing from a Jewish Relief Fund. She also admitted that she had used Schoenfeld as an instrument to get money from Rickard, that Sarah had stayed out at night with another boy, and Sarah had "admitted wrongdoing with the boy to her."[793]

Rickard's attorney said that on November 12, the day of the alleged assault, Rickard was at the Polo Grounds watching a football game. He never saw Gasko until she appeared in court. He met Schoenfeld when she was brought to Madison Square Garden by her mother, who appealed to him to assist her son, who was in prison.

Witnesses supported Rickard's alibi claim that he had been at the Polo Grounds that day. A doctor said he had been called to the promoter's home on the evening of November 12 to attend to Mrs. Rickard, and Tex and two other persons were there. Frank Flournoy, MSG matchmaker and Rickard's partner in Dempsey-Willard, said he dined with Rickard that night at Rickard's home. Rickard's wife Mary supported his alibi claim.

The judge excluded defense efforts to prove a $50,000 blackmail/extortion plot after Rickard was charged.

A janitor for the West 47th street apartments testified that Rickard warned him to keep quiet about his visits there.

A point brought out by Rickard's attorney in his endeavor to prove that the case was a frame-up was the fact that a superintendent for the Society for the Prevention of Cruelty to Children and one of the girls had spent 30 minutes in one of the apartments, observing closely all details of the furniture.[794]

On March 27, 52-year-old Rickard took the stand in his own defense. He was born in Kansas City, Kansas, and brought up in Texas, going to work at age 10. He later became a cowboy, following the cattle drives from Texas to Montana. He had been a pioneer gambler and miner in Alaska in 1895, where he cleaned up between $600,000 and $700,000 at the tables, only to lose it in the gold-mine fever. He had run gambling houses, both in Alaska and Goldfield, Nevada. He ran a couple of oil companies. He promoted Gans-Nelson and Jeffries-Johnson, both mixed-race fights, making a great deal of money.

He flatly denied the charges against him. He never asked the girls to meet him anywhere, and never met them anywhere in private, including at the residences discussed.

Rickard revealed that he wore a badge and carried a card as a secret member of a special service force which Police Commissioner Enright had assembled. He said Nellie Gasko had been driven away from MSG because she was begging for money at the door. Mrs. Schoenfeld had offered to work a year for Mrs. Rickard for nothing if her son was freed

[793] *New York Tribune, Brooklyn Daily Eagle,* March 23, 1922.
[794] *Buffalo Times, Buffalo Evening News,* March 24, 1922; *New York Herald,* March 25, 1922; *Brooklyn Daily Eagle,* March 27, 1922.

from prison, where he was serving a sentence for burglary. Sarah was with her mother when they visited his office.

Rickard admitted to having been arrested on three occasions – once for carrying a revolver in Chicago, and twice for transporting boxing films into New York State and Illinois.

Regarding the conversation with the janitor, Rickard said it was about a quantity of liquor he had stored there, and he had asked him to keep quiet about it.[795]

After 1 hour 20 minutes of deliberation, just after midnight on the morning of March 29, the jury found Tex Rickard not guilty.

Rickard said to the newsmen, "Thank you all. God bless you! You've been very good to me." "Boys, I was never so happy in my life. I once shot craps for $35,000 a throw, but the suspense of that was nothing [compared] to the last hour. That jury was made up of the greatest poker faces I've ever seen. They have my heartiest thanks."

Additional indictments against Rickard remained outstanding, and it was not certain whether they would be dismissed. But, given the acquittal, and fact that all of the gals had credibility issues, dismissal was likely.[796]

In the meantime, according to the *New York Daily News*, which consistently lobbied for a Dempsey-Wills fight, Dempsey allegedly said there was no use in talking about a Wills fight.

> The public, whatever that is, has no interest in it and would not pay to see it, he says. We think Mr. Dempsey underestimates public curiosity. A great many people would like to know whether he is heavyweight champion of the world or white heavyweight champion. We shall assume that he is white heavyweight champion until he gets into a ring with Wills and proves otherwise. P.S. – The reason Dempsey does not fight Wills is because he is afraid to do so – not physically afraid to exchange wallops, but afraid to take a chance with his title and the money he can make with it.[797]

Dempsey was scheduled to head to Europe in April, not to fight, but for fun, and possibly to make money in exhibitions.[798]

A poll conducted in Minneapolis to decide the public's choice of opponents for various champions ran for six weeks. Votes to box Dempsey included: Harry Wills – 37,300, Tom Gibbons, 30,100, and Bill Brennan, 19,400. To box Johnny Wilson: Mike Gibbons, 42,400, Harry Greb, 14,000. Of course, the Gibbons brothers were Minnesota natives.[799]

Hype Igoe believed that although Greb was fast enough to beat bigger men, and would outpoint Carpentier, he had no chance to beat Dempsey, even if beating Carpentier put him in a position to obtain the fight. Against Dempsey, "he will find himself facing one of the fastest, hardest hitting big men that ever held the title. One good punch would settle the

[795] *New York Daily News, New York Herald*, March 28, 1922.
[796] *New York Daily News, New York Herald, Yonkers Herald*, March 29, 1922.
[797] *New York Daily News*, March 23, 1922.
[798] *New York Daily News*, March 26, 1922.
[799] *Tampa Tribune*, April 1, 1922.

hash of a man of Greb's build." Greb would have no more chance to stand up against Dempsey's thundering fists than Stanley Ketchel had against Jack Johnson. Greb might have a chance to win on points in only 8 rounds, but in a 15-round contest, "hardly a chance." "Punch, weight, strength, height, reach and bulldog tenacity are the obstacles in the way of Harry Greb in his mad dream of whipping Jack Dempsey."[800]

There was some talk of Firpo and Wills being matched.

Jack Kearns said, "I realize that a Dempsey-Wills bout is the logical match, but I am afraid that it will take considerable time before the demand is keen enough over here or that some one is game enough to take the gamble and proceed with the promotion of a fight between Jack and a colored man." Kearns said he would see whether there was interest in such a promotion in England.[801]

On April 4, 1922 in Newark, New Jersey, Luis Angel Firpo stopped Joe McCann in 5 fierce rounds. McCann dropped Firpo in the 3rd round with two shots to the face. Yet, Firpo was "wonderfully strong" and shook off the effects without much trouble. Luis kept tearing in with a fearful fury. He even wrestled McCann to the floor. His rights shook up McCann every time they connected. McCann took an awful lacing in the 5th, and retired in the corner. Firpo clearly had strength and hitting ability.

Harry Newman said, "Firpo showed a lot of stuff during the brisk engagement. He must be considered seriously among the candidates who are begging a chance at Jack Dempsey." The crowd was excited by his style of firing hard punches. "With Dempsey it might be a different story, but Firpo isn't a mut by any means." He had a left, and varied his attack with heavy rights to the body.[802]

Dempsey said he was willing to fight former sparring partner Bill Tate, provided a promoter offered acceptable terms. "Bill would probably give me a better fight than Willard, Miske, or Carpentier did." Tate had proved his improvement in his recent 10-round draw with Wills.[803]

When asked whether he was willing to fight Wills, Dempsey replied, "For the thousandth time I would like to reiterate that I will fight him."[804]

Regis Welsh said given that Dempsey was about to travel abroad, a proposed Dempsey-Greb bout in Philadelphia was not likely to happen any time soon. Rumors were that Dempsey had been offered $100,000 and Greb $25,000.[805]

On April 10, 1922 in Pittsburgh, 176-pound Gene Tunney stopped 176-pound Jack Burke (10-3-1) in the 9th round, having decked him twice in the 8th round. Harry Keck said, "Tunney didn't show much last night, but he didn't have to." He was cautious, took no chances, and spared his hands, taking his time to break down Burke, fighting a "champion's fight." Tunney "proved a showy boxer and a clean, though not hard,

[800] *Detroit Free Press*, April 2, 1922.
[801] *New York Daily News*, April 5, 1922.
[802] *New York Daily News*, April 5, 1922.
[803] *Glens Falls Post-Star*, April 6, 1922.
[804] *New York Daily News*, April 8, 1922.
[805] *Pittsburgh Post*, April 9, 1922. Of course, it could be challenging to convince Dempsey/Kearns to fight for a third of the amount earned for his last fight, particularly since the Carpentier contest generated a very healthy profit for the promoter.

hitter." Still, some disgruntled spectators jeered, "You'd better stay away from Harry Greb!"

Regis Welsh said, "Gene cannot punch. He is not the best boxer in the world, and he lacks that classy look of any titleholder. … Harry Greb can give away 12 pounds and beat him so easily that it would be a joke."

Jim Jab said Tunney slaughtered Burke but did not quite know how to finish him off [even though he did]. Gene was not yet the finished product.[806]

The *Brooklyn Standard Union* said that upon his return from Europe, Dempsey might box Greb for 8 rounds in Philadelphia. "While at first hand this would look like a onesided match, not a few persons think that Harry, small as he is, can go over a limited round route with Dempsey. Greb is a mighty busy man while in the ring, and if he can use his feet as fast against Dempsey as he has against several other fighters he may be still there at the end of eight rounds."[807]

Jack Kearns said,

> Dempsey will probably return home in time to take on Harry Greb in an eight-round no-decision affair outdoors in Philadelphia. I am reliably told the public really wants the affair to be brought off, and we would like to see Harry make some money, even if he gets mussed up a bit in doing it, to convince him that the best middleweight isn't heavy enough for the big fellow in the game.

Tex Rickard said although Dempsey-Wills loomed as the most attractive ring prospect available, he insisted it carried "dangerous elements which would militate against successful promotion." It would be a difficult proposition to secure permission to hold the bout at any place in the country, and the financial difficulties would make it a hazardous undertaking, particularly given such insecurity. He would not associate himself with a mixed heavyweight championship unless given assurances that the public demanded it. Public demand meant that the politicians, who represented the people, had to be on board.[808]

On April 11, 1922, Jack Dempsey, Jack Kearns, Teddy Hayes, and Joe Benjamin set sail for Europe on the Aquitania. They were not going there to fight, but for a holiday, and perhaps some friendly exhibitions. However, they would consider any offers, if lucrative enough.

Jack Dempsey, Jack Kearns, Joe Benjamin, Teddy Hayes (left to right).

Before departing, Dempsey kissed several women, including Florence Walton, Mary Lewis, and Mary

---

[806] *Pittsburgh Gazette Times, Pittsburgh Post, Pittsburgh Press,* April 11, 1922. Tunney previously stopped Burke in 1921 when Burke declined to continue after the 2nd round as a result of a bad cut.
[807] *Brooklyn Standard Union,* April 12, 1922.
[808] *New York Times,* April 12, 1922.

Sherman. Lewis said, "Mr. Dempsey is one of the loveliest gentlemen I know. He is a great overgrown kid. He is not at all as people think. Really, you wouldn't expect a prizefighter to be like him, and I don't think in his heart of hearts he even wants to be a prizefighter."

Some of Those Who Bid Bon Voyage to Jack Dempsey

Flo Walton, actress, kisses Jack good-by.

When Dempsey sailed for Europe, Shirley Kellogg held on to him until Florence Walton, dancer and actress, finished kissing him goodbye.

The *New York Age* reported that Dempsey had no plans to fight while in Europe, but if a satisfactory purse was offered, he would be willing to meet anyone, including Wills. Dempsey "said he has no prejudice because of Wills' color, but that prejudice in America might make it best that such a match be held in Europe."[809]

William Harrison Dempsey's March 22, 1922 passport application said he was born at Manassa, Colorado on June 23, 1895, and he currently lived at 415 Western Avenue, Los Angeles, California. His father Hiram Dempsey lived in Salt Lake City.

On board the ship, Dempsey met famous filmmaker D. W. Griffith, who directed the controversial but popular 1915 film, *The Birth of a Nation*.[810]

While on the ship, on April 17, 1922, Dempsey sparred in friendly fashion with bantam George Mason, the Aquitania's boxing instructor. D. W. Griffith was Dempsey's chief second. They boxed 3 one-minute rounds in friendly fashion.

[809] *New York Daily News*, April 13, 1922; *New York Age*, April 15, 1922; *Binghamton Press*, April 17, 1922.
[810] *Buffalo Times*, June 1, 1922.

Tom Andrews said it generally was acknowledged that Wills was the most deserving contender, the best of the colored heavies, and better than any white contenders. A Dempsey-Wills match would have a great attendance, likely more than double that which would attend a fight with Willard.

Dempsey playfully spars with D. W. Griffith

Dempsey was confident that he could whip any living man, and "has not the slightest fear of the colored challenger, which is more than can be said for some of the champions of the past." Bill Tate, who had sparred Dempsey and fought Wills to a draw, "thinks that Dempsey is a certainty to beat the colored challenger [Wills]."

Yet, "There are many boxing fans who would prefer to have Dempsey ignore the challenge from Wills on account of the color line, fearing it will result in trouble for the game should the colored man win, as in the case of Jack Johnson when he defeated Jim Jeffries at Reno, Nev., in 1910."[811]

Jack McAuliffe said there was not enough money for boxing in Europe to make a Dempsey-Wills purse attractive, so it likely would not be held there.

McAuliffe believed that Rickard "would like to stage a bout between Dempsey and the big colored fighter if he had a place where he was sure he could do it." However, Tex also knew "it would be fine meat for the reformers to chew on." Boxing's legality constantly was under threat, and the race angle would put it in greater jeopardy. There was a thought that the longer they waited to make the match, the greater the public desire for it could be worked up, and thus potentially to stand for such a contest. "That is Rickard's game."

McAuliffe said Dempsey was talking about meeting Greb, but advised him to avoid such a fight, for he had nothing to win and ran a big chance of losing a lot of prestige. He would have a tough time getting to Greb for quite a while, and ultimately would get little credit for knocking out a middleweight, if he did.[812]

Jack Lawrence said New York fans had awakened to a very considerable interest in Luis Firpo, who was in line for a more severe test of his abilities. "Stalwart, game and capable of hitting with either hand, Firpo has bowled over his opponents with a regularity that has won him

[811] *Brooklyn Daily Eagle*, April 16, 1922.
[812] *Brooklyn Standard Union*, April 16, 1922.

the attention of the boxing world." Already there was talk of him being the next champion.[813]

After one week at sea, on April 18, 1922, Jack Dempsey and his pals/comrades arrived in Cherbourg, France. Members of the ship were surprised that Dempsey ate very little, drank even less - only three beers the entire journey, and did not smoke.

Dempsey traveled to Southampton, and then London, England. The champion was heralded with advance publicity that the London press had accorded only to two other Americans – President Woodrow Wilson and film star Charlie Chaplin. Jack was given a royal welcome, including by fighter Ted Kid Lewis.[814]

A SECRET?—Jack Dempsey (left), champion heavy-weight, and Ted Kid Lewis, holder of three titles, had a laugh as Jack arrived in England.

PALS.—The much defeated English champion, Joe Beck-ett, accompanied our tourist champion, Jack Dempsey (left), to Epsom to see the English racing classic.

On April 19 in London, accompanied by Joe Beckett, Dempsey attended the Epsom Downs horse races. King George V, Queen Mary, the Duke of York (the future King George VI), and other royals were in attendance. Although the champ did not actually meet the King and Queen, he saw them, and they saw him.[815]

Len Wooster said he admired undersized challengers like Greb, who was willing to fight Dempsey in Philadelphia on July 4, a contest which was being discussed. However, it seemed that Greb was "shooting at the moon." True he was game, fast, clever, and a good ring general, yet Carpentier had all of these qualities, was 10 pounds bigger, and in addition was a dangerous puncher, but all he could do was flash one rally, and was but a plaything in the champ's hands. "Greb will travel the route of Carpentier."

Harry Greb said if he fought Dempsey, he would sail right in at him just like he did with Gibbons. "I beat Bill Brennan twice. Brennan went 12 rounds with Dempsey. I have boxed with Dempsey in training many times and I know he can't catch up with me in 8 rounds. And I have boxed rings around all the big fellows and know how fast they move." He planned to weigh 163 pounds for a Dempsey fight.

[813] New York Tribune, April 18, 1922.
[814] New York World, April 18, 1922; Buffalo Express, New York Tribune, April 19, 1922.
[815] New York Daily News, Buffalo Courier, April 20, 1922.

Henry Farrell said, "Loud laughs no doubt would greet a serious prediction that Greb would have a chance with the champion." Yet, some believed he could last 8 rounds. "It is agreed that he would make things mighty interesting while he lasted." Greb believed he moved so fast that Dempsey would not be able to get set to land. Of course, "Dempsey wouldn't get any credit if he knocked out Greb. His reward would be a raspberry for picking on a little fellow."[816]

Regarding Greb, one writer said, "Harry is not so very good himself, but he has the faculty of making his opponents look cheap. No one ever gets anything but trouble fighting Greb. Even those who shade him obtain no credit, while the men he beats are made to look like third raters. Dempsey now is about to make the same mistake that Gibbons did." Jack was in a no-win situation. If Greb went the distance or outpointed him, which was a possibility, Dempsey would be called an overrated champion, or some would call it a fake. If he knocked out Greb, he would receive little or no credit for beating such a small man. Greb was a much smaller but faster edition of Willie Meehan. "Meehan was distinctly a second-rater and yet none of the top notchers could do anything with him. Rolling in fat, with no hitting ability, and a laughable style of boxing, he made his opponents look as bad as himself."[817]

There remained talk of a potential third Dempsey fight with Brennan, or one with Bob Martin if he could beat Brennan.

Dempsey dined with Carpentier at Carp's camp in London, where he was training to fight Ted Kid Lewis, whom Dempsey had met upon his arrival in England.

No fewer than 150 gals already had written to Dempsey, making marriage proposals. Many folks wrote him asking for assistance. He had received 3,000 letters total at the Savoy Hotel.[818]

Former champion Tommy Burns said, "The only fighter who has a real good chance to win the title from Jack Dempsey under 'protect yourself at all times' rules is Harry Wills." Burns had refereed Harry's fights against Langford and Jim Johnson. "Wills won both fairly easily." "Wills is as big as Jack Johnson and a better natural fighter than he ever was but not as good in defense."[819]

Bob Dorman wrote that Luis Firpo probably possessed the most colorful personality of any fighter. He was taller and heavier than Dempsey. He was trying hard to learn English. While in college in Buenos Aires, he saw Wills, Langford, and other Americans in exhibitions, and took up boxing. After graduating college, he became a pro boxer. Luis said, "I have been in some 30 fights in my own country, 20 of which I won by knockouts." He thought he would be ready to beat Dempsey in a year or two. In the meantime, he would try to work his way to the top. "I am half Italian, half Spanish."[820]

[816] *Brooklyn Daily Times, Harrisburg Evening News, St. Louis Star*, April 20, 1922.
[817] *Arizona Daily Star*, April 23, 1922.
[818] *New York Herald*, April 21, 1922.
[819] *Brooklyn Daily Times*, April 21, 1922.
[820] *Yonkers Statesman and News*, April 22, 1922.

On April 21, Dempsey was Lord Northcliffe's guest at his home in the fashionable Carlton Terrace.[821]

On April 22, Dempsey and Kearns reached Paris. Jack dodged a crowd of thousands, hailed a taxi, and was driven to his hotel.[822]

That evening, Dempsey was given a warm welcome on the stage at the opening night of the review at the Casino de Paris. American movie star Pearl White invited him to come up on the stage. He did, received cheers, and spoke a few words.

Dempsey subsequently said, "I'm tired of popularity and tired of crowds. I want to walk about by myself in Paris and see the things best worth seeing." He wanted to see educational things like the Louvre. When asked if he would drink the French wine, Jack said he did not like drinking. "If I liked the stuff, I would take it."[823]

From Paris, Floyd Gibbons wrote that the French women were going wild over the champion, who was sightseeing. Folks cheered, rushed to shake his hand, or pat him on the back, etc.[824]

On the 23rd in Paris, Dempsey visited the Longchamps racetrack. However, he received such an enthusiastic mobbing from admirers, the police eventually had to assist him out through the gates.[825]

Dempsey at Longchamps

[821] *New York Herald*, April 22, 1922. Dempsey planned to visit Paris, Berlin, and Vienna.
[822] *Buffalo Commercial*, April 22, 1922. Jack also planned a jaunt to Monte Carlo. Others said Dempsey's reception in France was not quite as warm as in England.
[823] *New York Times, Brooklyn Daily Eagle*, April 23, 1922.
[824] *New York Daily News*, April 24, 1922.
[825] *Elmira Star-Gazette*, April 24, 1922.

Dempsey and Kearns were discussing the possibility of a Wills contest with an English promoter, George McDonald. There also was some talk of a Carpentier rematch in England or France.[826]

On April 24, 1922 in Paris, Dempsey refereed the Billy Balzac vs. Maurice Purnier fight for the French middleweight championship, won on points by Balzac after 20 rounds.

Jack primarily was on vacation, sightseeing, going to races, the theater, having lunches and dinners, meeting various dignitaries, admirers, and fighters, and enjoying the company of various women. He visited the Louvre and Napoleon's tomb.[827]

Grantland Rice said Dempsey was champion because he had terrific punching power due to great strength, leverage, speed, and a whiplash snap, and he was catlike on his feet, had an iron jaw, his mind and muscle worked together in complete coordination, he had quick reactions, was a weaving, shifting target hard to hit, and perfectly built for speed and power.[828]

Billy Evans said Harry Greb would have an "outside chance" against Dempsey. Greb told him that he believed he would be able to outpoint Dempsey in a 12- or 15-round bout, "unless Jack should rock me to sleep before the finish." Of course, giving away 25 - 30 pounds, there always would be a danger of the big fellow putting over the knockout punch.

Evans said although Gibbons lost to Greb, he "might make a better showing than Greb. The style that Dempsey would use differs widely to that of Greb, and there would always be the chance for Gibbons to sweep over his dangerous right against the champion."[829]

The *Oklahoma City Times* said if Greb-Dempsey was arranged, "we hope…that Dempsey has promised to fight with one hand behind his back. If he uses both paws Greb will be lucky to leave the ring alive."[830]

There also was talk about a Greb vs. Tunney light-heavyweight contest, which I.N.S. writer Davis Walsh predicted Greb would win. Eventually, a match was set between them for late May.[831]

On April 29, Dempsey bid farewell to Paris and headed to Berlin. Jack said he enjoyed his stay in France and was treated wonderfully.[832]

Robert Edgren said Gene Tunney was another Gentleman Jim. He was modest, and Carpentier's most logical opponent. He boxed in the marines (having enlisted), winning a decision over Bob Martin in the A.E.F., as well as Ted Jamieson. He was born in Greenwich Village, New York City, 23 years ago. His real name was James J. Tunney, and two other men named James J. had won the heavyweight championship – Corbett and Jeffries; hence it was a good omen. A baby sister could not pronounce "Jim," and called him "Gene." The family humorously started

[826] *New York Herald*, April 24, 1922. In 1911, England had refused to allow Jack Johnson to defend his title there, concerned about the implications that a mixed-race heavyweight championship fight would have upon its colonial holdings.
[827] *New York Daily News, New York Herald*, April 25, 1922.
[828] *New York Tribune*, April 26, 1922.
[829] *Ogden Standard-Examiner*, April 25, 1922.
[830] *Oklahoma City Times*, April 27, 1922.
[831] *Yonkers Herald*, April 27, 1922.
[832] *New York Evening World*, April 29, 1922.

calling him Gene, and the name stuck. Before the war, Tunney was a clerk in a New York shipping firm. In his boxing career, he tended to have hand troubles. Tunney had beaten Dempsey sparring partners Martin Burke and Eddie O'Hare (who recently died from a broken neck in an accident jumping from a wharf and landing on ice).

Tunney did not tell off-color stories, never swore, and made no rough remarks. He was shy around women. "Gene is more of an intellectual type than any other title holder in years." He had speed and skill, and was unmarked, except for a slightly puffed ear from sparring with Willie Jackson. "If he ever becomes heavyweight champion he will be one of the most popular that ever held the title." However, he had a lot of hard fighting ahead to achieve that goal.[833]

On April 30, Dempsey arrived in Berlin, Germany, and received a royal welcome by an enormous crowd of thousands of men and women. The plan was to have an official reception and luncheon with the mayor the following day at City Hall.

Kearns said he had received a $500,000 offer from a French syndicate for another Carpentier bout. Dempsey would return to London in a few days to see the Carpentier-Lewis fight. "Jack is here on a pleasure trip and not for business." He wanted to see art galleries. However, he was willing to fight in Europe eventually against the winner of Carpentier-Lewis.[834]

The *New York Daily News* asked readers to vote for who they wanted Dempsey to fight next. Dempsey had claimed that he would fight whomever the public wanted him to fight. So, Harry Newman asked readers to mail in their votes. The results were updated continually.

As of April 30, the top mail-in results were Harry Wills, 4,005, Bill Brennan, 1,175, Jess Willard, 610, Harry Greb, 590, Georges Carpentier, 294, Jack Johnson, 205, and Gene Tunney, 198.

As of May 1, the poll results were: Harry Wills 4,835, Bill Brennan 1,320, Harry Greb 725, Jess Willard 700, Georges Carpentier 360, Jack Johnson 305, and Gene Tunney 298. Luis Firpo, who to that point had been seen only in two fights in the U.S., received 112 votes, Tom Gibbons 98, and Billy Miske 88. Humorously, lightweight champ Benny Leonard received 35 votes.[835]

On May 1 in Berlin, Dempsey visited a vaudeville house and

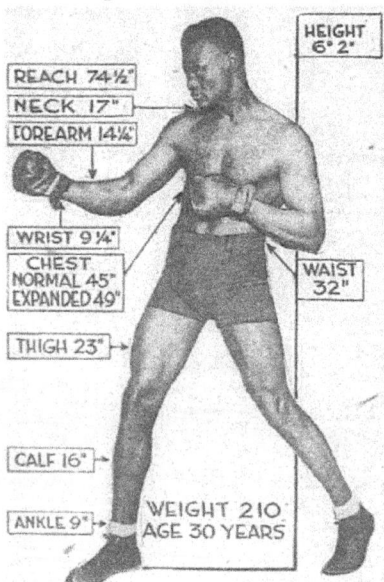

HEIGHT 6' 2"
REACH 74½"
NECK 17"
FOREARM 14¼"
WRIST 9¼"
CHEST NORMAL 45" EXPANDED 49"
WAIST 32"
THIGH 23"
CALF 16"
ANKLE 9"
WEIGHT 210 AGE 30 YEARS

Harry Wills, the real contender.

[833] *Buffalo Times*, April 30, 1922.
[834] *Brooklyn Daily Eagle, New York Evening World, Brooklyn Standard Union*, May 1, 1922.
[835] *New York Daily News*, April 30, 1922, May 1, 1922.

watched women boxers in 3-round bouts. He coached a middleweight blonde to victory. He purchased a police dog, jewelry, opera glasses, and other souvenirs. Some expressed awe at the size of his hands. "What an awful fist!" Jack said the pace of life set for him in Europe was wearing him out, and he was looking forward to returning home.[836]

On May 1, 1922 in New Orleans, 174-pound Tommy Gibbons stopped 176-pound Harry Foley (14-2-1) in the 6th round, when the referee stopped it after Foley had been down three times in the round.

The *Binghamton Press* said no one believed that European promoters could or would scrape up enough money to induce Kearns to permit Dempsey to meet Wills in Europe, for the fans there were far more interested in seeing Dempsey fight Carpentier again. Wills was somewhat of an unknown quantity to the average fan in Europe.[837]

Jess Willard re-took the lead over Harry Greb in the *Daily News* poll, at 980 to 950, but Harry Wills and Bill Brennan remained the clear #1 and #2 voters' choices.[838]

Dempsey left Berlin on the 2nd to head back to Paris.[839]

On May 2, 1922, the New Jersey boxing commission outlawed the rabbit punch and kidney blow.[840]

The *New York Daily News* poll as of May 3: Wills 6,420, Brennan, 1,985, Willard, 1,643, Greb, 1,143. Votes were coming in fast.

Charles Mathison said Dempsey likely would fight Willard in September at the Garden, and Wills the following year in England.

> The Garden management will not consider a Wills-Dempsey bout for this country, as it is believed the obstacles would be too great to overcome. Prejudice against a mixed match would be apt to imperil the financial feature of such a bout and for that reason no attempt will be made to bring Wills and Dempsey together in America.[841]

Lula Firpo.

Thomas Rice said Luis Firpo was a big and tall 210-pound man who could scrap, for he could dish it and take it, and had a long string of knockouts. His father was Italian, from Genoa. His mother was an Argentine native of Spanish descent. His family had been in Argentina for 50 years.[842]

Dempsey/Kearns said they were willing to fight anyone, including Willard, Carpentier, Brennan, Greb, or Wills, provided sufficient inducements were offered by a responsible promoter.

Dempsey would sail home on May 13, but first he would leave Paris for London to see Carpentier-

[836] *New York Herald, New York Tribune,* May 2, 1922.
[837] *Binghamton Press,* May 2, 1922.
[838] *New York Daily News,* May 2, 1922.
[839] *Brooklyn Daily Eagle,* May 2, 1922. Dempsey had been well received well everywhere he went. Women sent him marriage proposals. He met various political dignitaries and famous people in Europe.
[840] *New York Times,* May 3, 1922.
[841] *New York Herald,* May 4, 1922.
[842] *Brooklyn Daily Eagle,* May 4, 1922.

Lewis. Kearns said nothing was certain in the fight game. Ted Lewis was fast and shifty and might outspeed Carpentier for a time, "but I cannot see how he can withstand Carpentier's punches."

Kearns said that once Dempsey returned to New York on May 20, he would go west to fulfill a theatrical engagement. He did not have time to give any boxing exhibitions while in Europe.[843]

The plan was to open a theatrical engagement on the Pantages circuit, starting in Salt Lake City. Dempsey/Kearns had a contract with Alexander Pantages for a longer tour than they made the prior winter, and after Pantages threatened a suit, unwilling to cancel the contract, the champ and his manager decided that the easiest thing to do would be to complete the tour. Although the engagement was very profitable, Dempsey said he did not care for theatrical work.[844]

A group of French financiers offered a $400,000 purse, split 75% winner/25% loser for Dempsey-Carpentier II. Kearns also was negotiating with British promoters for the same match.

Dempsey said his offer to meet all comers included Harry Wills. "I have no desire to draw the color line. If the American public wants me to meet Wills I will do so. He is a much less dangerous opponent than Willard."[845]

As of May 8, Bill Brennan was closing in on Harry Wills in the *New York Daily News* poll, which had it Wills 8,110, Brennan 7,638. Inexplicably, mysteriously (perhaps as a joke or as an early form of trolling), making zero sense, Al Roberts, whom Miske had knocked out in New York in 2 rounds earlier that year (and had been knocked out by Bob Roper, Charley Weinert, Gene Tunney, and Al Reich), received 2,662 votes, even though he had done nothing to justify such, placing him in 3rd place. Was it because he was a Staten Island native? Other results included Jess Willard 2,068, Harry Greb 1,358, Luis Firpo 775, Georges Carpentier 725, and Jack Johnson 676. Tunney had 493 votes, and Gibbons 253.[846]

As of May 9, the *Daily News* poll had *Bill Brennan* in the lead, with 8,622 votes to Harry Wills' 8,351. No one else was close to those two.

Many felt that Europeans would not stand for another Carpentier-Dempsey match, not wanting to see their man defeated again.

Luis Firpo was training for an upcoming contest with Jack Herman. Young Bob Fitzsimmons, who was sparring with Luis, said, "This fellow Firpo has the heftiest wallop I ever experienced."[847]

Dempsey arrived in London on May 9. He wrote that he was in Europe because he had seen nothing of the world, and wanted to do so. "London goes down in my memory as the bright city of pretty, smiling girls."[848]

---

[843] *Buffalo Express, New York Times*, May 5, 1922.
[844] *Buffalo Courier*, May 6, 1922.
[845] *Buffalo Times*, May 7, 1922.
[846] *New York Daily News*, May 8, 1922.
[847] *Brooklyn Standard Union*, May 9, 1922.
[848] *Buffalo Express*, May 10, 1922; *Brooklyn Citizen*, May 11, 1922.

On May 11, 1922 in London, England, before a crowd of 17,000 that jammed the Olympic arena, world light heavyweight champion 175-pound Georges Carpentier scored a 1st round knockout over very experienced European middleweight champion (and former world welterweight champ) 154-pound (157 with clothes on) Ted 'Kid' Lewis (209-36-20). Just after breaking from a clinch, Carp stepped in quickly with his right to score the knockout. Dempsey was at ringside, and he met Prince Henry. Jack said the fight was no contest at all. Despite Lewis' tremendous, high-quality experience, Carpentier simply was too big and powerful for him.

Jack Kearns gave mixed statements regarding whether Dempsey would fight Harry Wills. "I believe that the people would rather see white men fight together and negroes fight together." However, "Of course if the public wants it and the proper inducements are forthcoming Dempsey will meet Wills."[849]

Harry Wills was back in the close lead over Bill Brennan in the *Daily News* poll, at 10,698 to 10,618.

On May 12, 1922 in Boston, 168-pound Harry Greb stopped 175-pound Al Roberts (23-8-1) in the 6th round, flooring him thrice in the 1st round, twice in the 4th, and twice more in the 6th round before the referee stopped the bout.[850]

Jess Willard said he was not interested in another Dempsey bout, and was too busy with his businesses. Willard often would vacillate, one moment claiming he wanted a Dempsey rematch, and another saying he did not.

As of May 13, Brennan was back in the lead in the *Daily News* poll, 11,103 to Wills' 11,044. The two would go back and forth daily, but no one else had even half of their vote counts.

On May 13, Dempsey departed London for home. Jack said he had a wonderful time, and when he returned, it would be for business.[851]

Also on May 13, 1922, at Ebbets Field in Brooklyn, New York, 211-pound Luis Firpo knocked out 184-pound Italian Jack Herman in the 5th round with a right uppercut to the chin. Herman was unconscious for a full eight minutes until he finally revived. Firpo had him on the floor in the 2nd and 3rd rounds as well, from a shower of overhand wallops to the head, chin, and back of the ear.

[849] *New York Daily News, Yonkers Herald, Buffalo Courier,* May 12, 1922.
[850] *Boston Globe,* May 13, 1922. They weighed in at 3 p.m. on the day of the fight.
[851] *Kingston Daily Freeman,* May 13, 1922.

Writers said Firpo was a very strong, primitive cave man, with enough speed and power to deck even Dempsey, but he needed to develop his boxing skills further. Jimmy De Forest currently was training him, and thought he had real potential. No one could deny that he was a very hard puncher.[852]

Westbrook Pegler said Carpentier's 1st round knockout of Ted Kid Lewis was a "fair indication" of what might happen in Dempsey-Greb.[853]

On May 16, 1922 at Madison Square Garden in New York, 195 ½-pound Bill Brennan knocked out 187-pound Jim Tracey in the 8th round, with a succession of left hooks followed by a right to the jaw. Tracey had been down in the 6th as well. Tracey had received 639 votes in the *Daily News* poll asking whom Dempsey should fight next.

Harry Greb said, "I want to get that fellow Carpentier after I settle with Mr. Tunney, and then for a shot at the champion, Dempsey." Regarding Dempsey, Greb said,

> I boxed with him about ten times and always held my own. I have beaten Bill Brennan five times and Bill stayed in with Dempsey for twelve rounds. ... The longer the fight went the better it would be for me. Dempsey tires early and is not good for a long distance. I feel I am the logical man among the white fighters to meet Dempsey and I hope to get it sooner or later.[854]

The *Daily News* noted that Dempsey said he would fight whomever the public selected, and in its poll's final standings, Harry Wills had received the most votes, with 12,177, although Bill Brennan was a very close second at 11,982. Al Roberts hilariously still was third at 4,590. Jess Willard was next at a very distant 2,568. Harry Greb was in fifth place at 1,535, and then Luis Firpo with 1,296. No one else broke 1,000 votes.[855]

In response to whether they would fight Wills, Jack Kearns replied, "We will fight anybody if we get enough money."

Reacting to Dempsey's statement that it had been his first chance to see Europe, one newspaper responded, "Funny thing about that, when so many others were given a chance in '17-'18." Some simply could not let go of the fact that Dempsey had not enlisted.[856]

Upon his arrival back in the U.S. on May 19, 1922, Dempsey claimed that he had been engaged for some time to a 19-year-old gal named Edith Rockwell of Denver, whom he had known since he was a boy. However, no one ever had heard of her, so some wondered whether Dempsey was playing a joke as revenge for all of the false reports about the various women with whom he may or may not have been involved. Kearns said, "We don't know Edith Rockwell. ... We never heard of her and never saw her. Dempsey is not figuring on getting married. It is just a fable."

[852] *New York Daily News, New York Tribune, New York Herald*, May 14, 1922.
[853] *Oregon Journal*, May 14, 1922.
[854] *New York Daily News, Brooklyn Daily Times, Rochester Democrat and Chronicle, New York Times, New York Tribune*, May 17, 1922.
[855] *New York Daily News*, May 19, 1922.
[856] *New York Herald, New York Daily News*, May 19, 1922.

This Photograph, Taken During the Recent Visit of Champion Jack Dempsey to Berlin, Gives Some Idea of the Enormous Crowds That Flocked Around Him Every Time He Ventured Out for a Walk. The X Indicates Dempsey. "I doubt," Writes Peggy Hopkins, Who Met the Champion Abroad, "whether the King of England could have drawn such a crowd—such a mob." The Insert Photograph of Jack Dempsey Holding Juliette Compton Was Taken Aboard the Aquitania Returning from Europe.

Say, fellers, pipe the glass eye!

Many women had been linked to Dempsey, including Bebe Daniels, who watched him train in Atlantic City for Carpentier, Sylvia Jocelyn, same, Florence Walton - who hugged and kissed him emphatically when he was leaving for Europe, Peggy Joyce, Bee Palmer - a vaudeville actress whose husband was suing him for alienation of affection, Helen Lee Worthing, the "Follies" beauty, and so on.

When informed of the *Daily News* poll results, Dempsey said, "Certainly I'll fight Harry Wills or any other man. Why not? If the fans want me to fight Wills, I'm ready. Now let us see what the promoters will do." "It's up to the promoters now."

Edward Tranter predicted that Dempsey would not fight Wills, because it did not make business sense to tackle the tough negro and risk his crown when he was receiving offers for hundreds of thousands of dollars to fight easier foes, such as Carpentier and others.

Kearns said Dempsey had theatrical and other engagements which would take up his time through the summer, so no bout could come before September 1922.[857]

---

[857] *New York Daily News*, May 20, 21, 1922; *Brooklyn Daily Times, Buffalo Enquirer, New York Herald*, May 20, 1922.

Dempsey subsequently admitted that he was kidding about Rockwell, playing a joke on the reporters.

> I've been married or reported married to every girl of public prominence with whom I have conversed since I became champion. … All that stuff put me in wrong with a certain girl for whom I have a deep respect. Never mind her name or where she lives. But when I was queried so persistently on whether I was to be married, I just thought I'd have a little fun.[858]

Harry Newman admitted that when the *Daily News* several months ago suggested that Dempsey had to fight Wills, "there were those who were inclined to scoff at the idea. Incidentally several promoters, including Tex Rickard, refusing to believe that any one could stage a match between the champion and the colored boxer." However, given the fan support for the fight, many promoters were seeing if there was a way to make it work. There was talk of Dempsey-Wills potentially being held in Canada.

Rickard and Fluornoy would talk with the participants. "Dempsey has just returned from a trip to Europe and he says he will fight Wills. We hope he is not trying to kid anybody, as he said he was when he tipped the newspaper boys off that he was going to be married to a Denver girl."

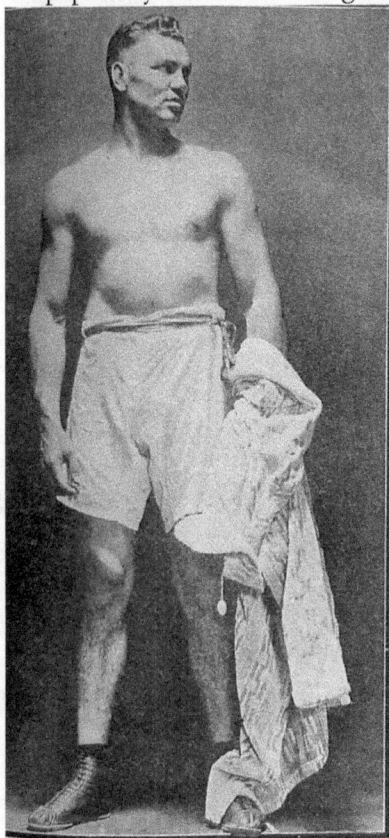

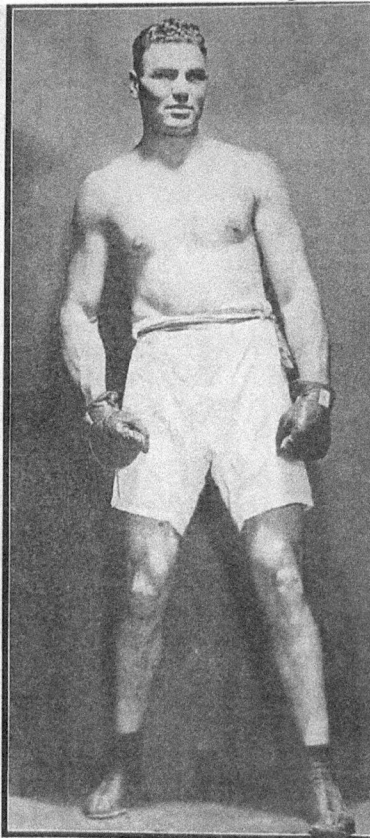

[858] *New York Times*, May 21, 1922.

The public wanted to see Dempsey in a real fight. "There has never been any question in the minds of the fans but that Wills was the logical candidate to meet Dempsey for the championship." Wills was a strong hitter and fast for his size. He had been thoroughly tested, and was very experienced. "Dempsey may put over the old crusher on the colored man, but we believe that he will know that he had been in a fight."[859]

Word was that there were no legitimate offers for a Wills fight, and any such talk was just publicity and ballyhoo. Floyd Fitzsimmons was negotiating with Kearns for a Labor Day Dempsey-Brennan contest.[860]

Dempsey said he likely would fight a rematch with Carpentier in London sometime in the next year, for there was great demand there for such a contest. Kearns echoed that they had an offer of 100,000 pounds, which was about $450,000, guaranteed. Continuing, the champ said, "Whether I will fight here before I return to England depends entirely on what may develop. I am booked for about 10 weeks of vaudeville, which was interrupted by my trip abroad. I expect to stay in Los Angeles for a few days to visit my mother, and after that I won't lose any time in returning to the stage." Regarding opponents, Dempsey said,

> I'll fight Wills or any body else. Why not? It doesn't make any difference whether it is Wills, Brennan, Willard or any heavyweight. Whoever the public thinks has the best chance against me will be the man selected. All I care about is a promoter who is willing to stage the bout guarantee what I want and find a place where it can be held.

However, *Pittsburgh Sun* sporting editor James Long said that forced by objection and protest to abandon his color-line stance, Dempsey now was trying to find another way to escape meeting Wills, which was to make his demands so high that promoters would not be interested. Allegedly, Kearns had turned down an offer of $350,000 to fight Wills in Montreal in July, demanding $500,000 for such a fight. Kearns figured that a Wills bout would draw well over a million dollars. However, Wills would require his share, and there would be additional overhead. That was a great risk for a promoter to take, particularly when there was fear of last-minute political interference. "The general opinion is that Kearns is deliberately fixing Dempsey's end at a prohibitive figure in order to get out of signing for the match." But was that a prohibitive figure?

Davis Walsh, International News Service Staff Correspondent, believed that Gene Tunney had neither the speed nor the punch to stop Harry Greb inside of 15 rounds, and all indications pointed to Greb outpointing any man of his weight or near his weight. Yet, Tunney's manager Frank 'Doc' Bagley was predicting a Tunney knockout. Damon Runyon thought Tunney was a good short-end bet. Yet, Walsh said, "Tunney never has shown any particular ability, even in winning the title

[859] *New York Daily News*, May 21, 1922.
[860] *Buffalo Courier*, May 22, 1922.

from the decrepit Bat Levinsky." He was fast and hit just well enough to gain respect, but nothing more.[861]

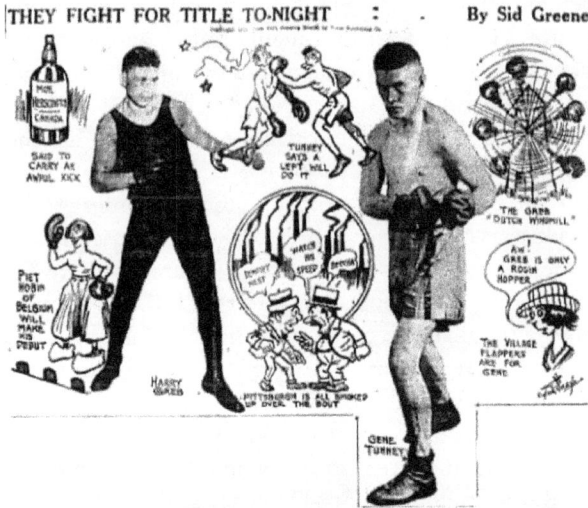

THEY FIGHT FOR TITLE TO-NIGHT : By Sid Greene

Vincent Treanor said Greb likely would outpoint Tunney in their upcoming bout, for Harry was very busy at all times and all over his foes. Tunney was bigger, stronger, and a harder puncher, but so too was Tommy Gibbons. Greb was a master at winning decisions with his activity, even if he rarely scored a knockout.[862]

Henry Farrell reported that Greb was favored to win the American light heavy title from Tunney, for his attack was too fast. Greb could go 15 rounds faster than any other man in the ring, and Tunney would see more gloves whirring around his head than ever before. Mike Gibbons said Greb was great at preventing his foes from getting set for a punch. Willie Lewis said Greb could go 15 rounds with Dempsey, and "nothing but a freak can beat him." Farrell concluded, "Tunney has never impressed anyone by his activity in the ring and he has shown himself puzzled several times by the sort of erratic attack that Greb advances." His chances of winning a decision over Greb were "mighty slim."

[861] Pittsburgh Sun, May 22, 1922.
[862] New York Evening World, May 23, 1922.

James Long said Greb ought to defeat Tunney without trouble, for he was too fast and experienced for him. Tunney had been winning, but not particularly impressively.[863]

On May 23, 1922 at Madison Square Garden in New York, before a crowd of 9,214 (paid admissions), 10,000, or up to 13,000, which generated $58,914.12 (tickets went from $2 up to $13.63), 162 ¼ or ½-pound Harry Greb (194-10-18) won a unanimous 15-round decision over previously undefeated 174 ½-pound Gene Tunney (47-0-2) to win the American light heavyweight title. Their weights were taken at 2 p.m. on the day of the fight. The judges were Tommy Shortem and Eddie Hurley, and the referee Billy 'Kid' McPartland.

Greb drew blood from Tunney's nose and mouth, and opened up cuts over both of Tunney's eyes (some saying it was the result of punches, others saying head butts, or a mix). Tunney showed courage and landed the harder blows, but Greb was more aggressive and landed more. The New York writers unanimously agreed with the decision, as did the crowd.

Harry Newman said Greb's speedy, whirlwind attack, which never eased up, was too much for the village pride. Greb threw more punches at Tunney than Gene ever experienced before. The fight was spirited, though at times not very scientific. Some hooted Greb for holding and using his head continually in the clinches.

Tunney had a slight edge in the first 5 rounds, landing rapid lefts and rights to the body. But in the 6th round, Tunney suffered a severe cut over his left eye from a right swing, and the steady stream of blood blinded him, proving too great a handicap. The aggressive Greb forced Tunney to the ropes continually throughout. In the last 2 rounds, Tunney tired. He tried to stave off defeat with a haymaker, but fell short. He took his beating gracefully and never whimpered.

Tunney (left) and Greb in a clinch.

Jack Lawrence said Greb defeated Tunney by a wide margin in a furious and stirring battle, winning the American light heavyweight

[863] *Pittsburgh Sun*, May 23, 1922.

championship and earning the right to fight for Carpentier's world title. Greb was a master at landing a dozen blows to the other fellow's one. Greb gave Tunney a far tougher lacing than he gave to Gibbons. Tunney had ragged gashes over each eye, which poured a crimson flow all over, his lips were swollen, and his nose battered.

Gene was game and had the crowd with him, but Greb maintained his terrific speed throughout, smothering all of Tunney's efforts with a deluge, tornado, hurricane of blows. Unable to land on Greb's face very often or with any effect, Gene focused on the body. Greb brought blood from Tunney's nose in the 1st round. The left eye was opened in the 5th with a vicious right, the right eye opened in the 8th, and the steady loss of blood weakened the ex-soldier. Greb won every round, though the 5th, 7th, and 10th could have been even. Nevertheless, Gene fought back desperately, and frequently landed punches that shook Greb to his heels, particularly the body blows. Greb was good at flitting out of range from Tunney's head punches.

Grantland Rice said Greb excelled Tunney both in speed and experience. Tunney fell into a hornets' nest and came near being stung to death. Gene bravely rode the storm under the whirlwind assault, leaving the ring as if he just emerged from a sausage mill. From the start, Greb swarmed all over him with a fusillade of blows. Tunney showed a stout heart, but like Gibbons, was badly baffled and bewildered by Greb's windmill, tidal-wave attack. Tunney had no chance to get set for his blows, and did not know how to meet a rushing offensive that came from so many different directions all at once.

Between rounds, Tunney's trainer was kept busy applying "new-skin" over fresh cuts. Neither man ever was rocked or badly jolted. Greb had no killing punch, and if Tunney had one, he never had a chance to plant it on the target which darted in and out, back and forth, up and under like a phantom. Still, they slugged and exchanged, though Greb ducked to safety with his greater speed and far greater ring craft. It was the master whipping the pupil, never tiring as he charged, stormed, and hustled. He had marvelous stamina. The victory justified a challenge to Carpentier.

> What a wonder he would be if he only had a punch. Even as it is his peculiar bewildering style will give him a great chance against any living man anywhere near his weight. He would have no chance against Dempsey, but against the French star he would be close to an even bet. For Greb can take his share of punishment as well as launch one of the fastest attacks ever seen in a ring.

Greb said, "I am faster than Gene, and just outspeeded him." Nevertheless, Harry said Tunney was game and deserved credit. "Carpentier, did you say? I'll fight him any time, any place. I've seen him fight and think I can lick him. I'd like to try anyhow."

Tunney said, "When our heads came together it was my eye that opened. It could have happened to Greb instead of to me, but luck was the other way. Greb is a wonderful fighter though. … I think I can reverse the verdict if given another chance."

Davis Walsh, INS correspondent (whose report was reproduced in the *Brooklyn Standard Union)*, said New Yorker Tunney was a bloody ruin and battered mass, smothered by the incessant stream of Greb's punches, his face cut into human hamburger, and he never had a chance after the early exchanges. Tunney's nose spurted blood in the first 30 seconds, his lips were raw and bleeding, his right eye dripped a constant crimson stream, and his left barely was discernible through the gushing blood. "Greb's attack, as always, was confined to speed alone. He packed no punch, [and] if Tunney had any, it failed to show because the Pittsburgh panther never gave him a chance to let one go." Greb flailed away at the same pace from first to last, only taking a breather in the 10th and 11th rounds. Otherwise, there was no letup in his advance.

Tunney had attempted to fight at Greb's pace, but was arm-weary before it was half over. The cut over Tunney's left eye, "the worst of all, had been opened by coming in contact with Greb's head." It affected his vision, and the sight was ghastly. Tunney had a 12-pound weight advantage, but a "mere dozen pounds

makes no particular difference, however, to a man who can hit you faster than the second hand can tick."

Vincent Treanor said Rickard offered Carpentier $150,000 to fight Greb, but if Georges had any regard for his good looks, he would turn it down. He might knock out Greb, but he'd have a real mussy time before he could turn the trick. Greb, the Pittsburgh Bear Cat, was a "fighting freak." He was tireless perpetual motion personified. He shot punches with no form or style, flailing about, sometimes from the shoulder, then from his knees, and over his head, wherever. It seemed as if even he did not know where the punches would land, nor did his opponent.

Tunney tried to avoid the blows and instill fear and respect with well-meant body drives, but found himself too busy trying to defend the puzzling attack. "He was unhurt but completely befuddled." Tunney landed hard on the body, sometimes slowed up Greb and caused him to hold, but whenever he seemed to have Harry hurt, Greb would liven up quickly and get busier than ever. From the 6th round on, Tunney was a sorry sight, full of blood.

Greb kept on top of him all the time, "and in doing so pulled many a trick not strictly according to rules." "He has no idea of boxing ethics, if there are any such things." Greb knew how to hold around the neck and pummel with his right. He got his head under Gene's chin and bucked upward while he flailed on the ribs and eyes with blows too fast and numerous to detail. He could hold around the waist one second as if seeking safety, and then let go with a fresh collection of punches.

Tunney tried for the body, but always found himself too smothered or pinioned to land a clean shot. He had to content himself with little clublike hits to the back of the neck while locked. Whenever Gene did land some solid blows to the head, Greb took it well, and soon was bobbing in and out and around again. Overall, Tunney was too busy defending himself to keep up his offense. "It must be said that few of Greb's punches were clean, while most of Tunney's were. Still it was apparent that the Pittsburgher's blows were doing all the ripping and tearing, landing haphazardly as they did throughout. If Greb could punch hard the fight wouldn't have gone the limit." Even though he lost, Tunney showed courage and gameness, and gained a lot in experience.

Thomas Rice said his opinion about Greb was unchanged. He was neither a boxer nor a fighter, falling into neither category, despite the fact that he won decisions constantly. "Greb does no real boxing, except footwork in keeping on the move and making it difficult for an ordinary opponent to reach him solidly. He does some blocking of free swings and he blocks effactually in the clinches." Because of Greb's windmill style of swinging from all angles, a foe could hit him in the body, which were Tunney's most effective blows. Greb averaged a minimum of 20 ineffective leads per round, and did not even average 3 clean punches per round. He often landed with open gloves, or the underside of the fist, or the forearm around the body, on the neck or arms, "merely haphazard blows – and were not punches."

Rice questioned Greb's skill, power, effectiveness, and ability to land cleanly and properly with the knuckles. "The secret of Greb's success with both Gibbons and Tunney was not so much that he fought as that his incessant, aimless slapping and pulling and hauling and switching punches kept the other fellow from fighting." Tunney's nose began bleeding in the 1st, and in the 6th his left eye was badly cut. Gene did well in the first 7 rounds, but thereafter tired.

Rice said that under modern judging, the decision was correct, but under old-school refereeing, he might have called it a draw. Tunney put up a better fight than Gibbons had, trying harder.

Rice predicted a Carpentier victory over Greb.

> We venture to predict that if they ever meet, Carpentier will knockout Greb. Carpentier is the fastest big man in the world, if not fastest big man the world has ever known, at shooting hard and accurately with either hand while on his toes or while flatfooted. ...
>
> Carpentier will be able to reach Greb. Make no mistake about that, and he will hurt him when he does reach. Greb is fast on his feet in a bouncing sort of way, but when it comes to being fast in the legitimate boxing sense of the word, that is, using speed of foot combined with speed, accuracy and force in hitting, Carpentier has it all over the new American champion. Certainly what the rather

inept Tunney could do as long as his nerve and strength lasted Carpentier, who could make Tunney look like an amateur, can do to Greb.

The *Brooklyn Daily Times* said Greb won by a safe margin, but Tunney proved to be a worthy foe, putting up stubborn opposition in a vicious bout. Greb punched and butted his way to victory with his tireless windmill style, but his butting with the top of his head helped him win, opening cuts and drawing blood.

Unlike Gibbons, Tunney made a real fight of it, tearing in and landing many staggering body blows, particularly through the first 7 rounds. "Tunney won the seventh round, when he landed heavy rights and left to the body, causing Greb to stoop to the mat. Harry was up in a flash fighting gamely, but was rushed to the ropes by the determined attack of his heavier opponent."

However, blinded by the blood, Tunney was handicapped, and Greb came on strong thereafter. Gene was game, but tired rapidly and his blows lost their force. Nevertheless, Tunney put up a great fight, doing better with Greb than most, and still had championship potential with more experience.

W. O. McGeehan said Greb won with his fast pace. He drew crimson from the nose, mouth, over the left eye, and then right eye. Blood spattered everywhere.

Greb could give Carpentier a "fairly reasonable fight," but not Dempsey. "If Greb weighed about twenty pounds better he certainly would give Dempsey some trouble, but as it stands he would have no chance."

Greb used few straight punches, but hooked and clawed away like a wildcat. Tunney could not land squarely on his whirling, twisting foe. Greb also held and hit. He bewildered Tunney, whose face was a crimson smear. "Tunney put up a braver show than Tom Gibbons, who seemed to have a chance with the Pittsburgher but lost it through sheer stupidity."

McGeehan said the dream of a having a world champion from the A.E.F. had vanished. Greb would win the world middleweight title, and could fight Carpentier for the world light heavy title.

The *New York Times* said there was no question as to the victor, and the crowd received the decision without a dissenting voice. The battered Tunney was a sorry sight, while Greb was unmarked. Greb proved himself a qualified rival for Carpentier's light heavy title. He was a human perpetual-motion machine. In the 1st round, he brought blood from Tunney's nose as a result of an overhand left hook. Blood poured from a nasty gash over Tunney's left eye, where an old cut was ripped open early on when their heads collided. Greb's fists cut open a gash over Tunney's right eye, and the champ's beaten nose was bleeding freely.

Greb never ceased his assault, and his persistent, unrelenting offense won it for him. He wasn't a damaging puncher, but he made up for his lack of power with ability to keep on the move and tear in at all times.

"Greb carried off twelve of the rounds beyond a question. Not a round went to Tunney." Tunney merely was even in the 3rd, 4th, and 7th, but was convincingly outpointed in every other round. Greb completely frustrated him with his windmill-like assault, even though it was aimless and without accurate direction, but it was consistent and active. Greb justified his 3 to 1 favorite status. Tunney tried, but could not offset Greb's remarkable activity, and could not defend the rain of blows.

Harry Keck of the *Pittsburgh Gazette Times* said Pittsburgh's greatest fighter beat the previously undefeated ex-soldier in a grueling bout. Greb now was Carpentier's logical foe for the world's light heavyweight championship. Tunney put up a great fight, landing solidly to the head and body with both hands, trying to catch Greb on the way in, but was not good enough to beat down the ever-rushing Greb, who when hit, only fought back harder. Keck said Gene put up a much better and faster fight than did Gibbons.

Jim Jab of the *Pittsburgh Press* said, "Tunney was outclassed, both on outside and inside battling." His nose bled in the 1st, lip in the 2nd, and in the 6th, he suffered a gash over his left eye. Gore blinded him, and kept his cornerman Doc Bagley working overtime.

Boxing commissioner Tom O'Rourke, sitting ringside, noted that it was a bad match for Tunney, whom he thought should take the lead more often instead of waiting. Greb was hard to hit, for he was shifty, moving all over like a floating ball in a shooting gallery. Greb used his speed and experience to defeat the relative novice.

The *Pittsburgh Post's* Regis Welsh said the local Pittsburg "hero" Greb, though outweighed, set a furious pace over 15 terrific rounds, never stopped fighting, and Tunney weakened toward the finish. Harry was quick, game, and aggressive. "Pittsburgh can well be proud of its newest hero." Tunney was game though, and fought back hard, moving faster, boxing better, and hitting harder than Gibbons had against Harry.

Afterward, Tex Rickard said, "If there ever was a champion there is one, and...I stand willing to give him a crack at the middleweight championship if I can get Wilson in the ring with him. Then it will be Carpentier in Jersey."

The *Pittsburgh Sun's* sporting editor James Long said Greb traded money for the chance at the title, content to take a comparatively small portion of the gate. The receipts were $58,014.12. Tunney got $22,387.20, while Greb earned $8,394.20 and the American championship.

In other news, the New Jersey State Boxing Commission, via its chairman Louis Messano, declared that the state would not tolerate a Dempsey-Wills championship fight, nor would Dempsey-Willard be allowed unless Jess could prove his condition. "No permit will be granted for a bout between Dempsey and Wills, because I do not think there is a public demand for such a bout." "No public demand" became the political mantra for: "We don't want it here."[864]

Upon his return to Pittsburgh, Harry Greb said, "I am glad to have won the championship after years of hard struggling. I'm glad to have won it for myself, and I'm glad to have won it for Pittsburgh. Nothing is too good for this old town and I'll always be proud to call it my home." He was glad to be back with his ill wife and daughter. Harry said he most wanted a match with Carpentier for the world light heavyweight championship. Rickard had offered Carp $150,000 for such a fight in the U.S. Greb thought Carpentier would be easier to beat than Weinert, Gibbons, or Tunney. "I really mean that. I actually believe that Carpentier will not be as hard to beat as any of my last three opponents."

Greb said he had heard no more about a proposed bout with Dempsey in Philadelphia since Jack's return from Europe. "They told us to wait until after the Tunney fight, and that was the last we heard from them. We accepted a flat sum to box Dempsey in Philadelphia, so the next move is up to the champion."[865]

Davis Walsh said Harry Wills had a pair of brittle hands, which would be a problem for him against Dempsey, who was like hitting concrete. Some said Dempsey's trips across the country and world were designed to avoid Wills. Others said Kearns wanted $600,000 for the fight, and was willing to wait until he got it. The other issue was finding a jurisdiction that would allow the fight and be able to generate a sufficient gate.

Fred Keats in the *New York Evening Sun* said Greb was in line to fight Carpentier, but if he attempted one-tenth of the rough stuff against Georges that he got away with against Tunney, nothing could stop Francois Descamps from hopping into the ring to argue with the referee.

> The new champion is about the roughest person that ever climbed into a local ring. He cares nothing at all about rules and regulations. He has two active hands that fly around in all sorts of weird motions, but the top of his head is his most dangerous weapon.
>
> Greb makes his own rules as he goes along. With him it is anything to disconcert his opponent. He butts, heels, wrestles and anything

[864] *New York Tribune, New York Daily News, Brooklyn Standard Union, New York Evening World, Brooklyn Daily Eagle, Brooklyn Daily Times, New York Herald, Brooklyn Citizen, New York Times, Pittsburgh Gazette Times, Pittsburgh Press, Pittsburgh Post, Pittsburgh Sun,* May 24, 1922.
[865] *Pittsburgh Sun,* May 25, 1922.

else he can think of that will prove annoying. If the rules of boxing were enforced strictly Greb would not be able to last a round without being disqualified. His whole system of fighting is based on clinching and hitting with one hand while holding with the other.

Greb's gameness, ruggedness and stamina are his only admirable qualities. … If all boxers followed his style of milling the sport soon would be legislated out of existence in a hurry and it would be a good riddance. … Greb would do well under London prize ring rules, but he does not fit in modern boxing.

Greb denied that he was rough, pointing out that it would be mighty difficult for a much shorter, smaller man to rough up a bigger man like Tunney, for when they went into a clinch, "my head was beneath his chin. It couldn't be any higher than that because he was so much taller than I. I didn't butt him or use any illegal tactics at all. … I am not a New Yorker, and if I was fighting unfairly in my bouts in that city, it is strange that the boxing commission would not take notice of it."

Ralph Davis wrote, "Greb doesn't need to worry much about the wails of the Gothamites. Harry is a 'provincial,' to the New York way of thinking and, of course, the haughty metropolitans don't like to accept him as a champion. But he owns the title."[866]

Damon Runyon said although fistic technicians called Greb a clown, and pointed out multiple flaws in his style, he had to have something if he could take on one larger man after another and win. He was a human pinwheel, and could maul, claw, whirl in, fire in all directions, push, shove, pull, and haul, using his head and elbows.

Greb is a veritable giant killer. He shows much better against a big man than against a chap his own size or smaller than himself. … Greb can slide around, and get under and on top of the big fellows. He never gives them a chance to uncoil. He blankets them. He would probably have more trouble with Benny Leonard than with Bob Martin. The big boys are his dish. …

Tunney is bigger and stronger than Greb, but aside from hanging himself on Harry's shoulders like a lump of lead, he did not employ his greater strength. He did not know how. Tunney let Harry do all the roughing in close. The Pittsburgher constantly smothered the Villager's blows. And Gene can have no alibi, because everybody knew in advance how Greb would fight.

It must be said for Tunney, however, that in losing he demonstrated he is a better fighter than many persons thought. He has not had enough experience against experienced men.[867]

Walter Trumbull said,

[866] *Pittsburgh Press*, May 26, 1922.
[867] *Washington Times*, May 26, 1922.

Greb is a great boxer. If he had a punch he could take any of them – and we are not excluding Dempsey. People don't always give Harry the credit due him. Before Gibbons fought Greb they said he was a wonder. Afterward they said he was a boob. Tunney was hailed as a clever, hard hitting fighter. Now they say he was overrated. That's the point. Greb is a man who can make good battlers look simple. Gibbons is a good fighter and so is Tunney – but not against Greb.

We don't think that Greb is the best man of his weight we ever saw. We believe that Fitz might have beaten him in a few rounds or that Ketchell might have stopped him. But he's faster than a wildcat and he's good – don't make any mistake about that.[868]

Tad Dorgan said Carpentier never had seen anything like Greb, who would test his generalship and gameness. "None of the American boxers seems to be able to figure out a way to offset Greb's peculiar tactics." Tom Gibbons was fast, clever, and a great hitter, but could not do much with the swarming Greb, who bewildered him. Tunney was another clever boxer with a wallop and game besides, but was "completely disconcerted by Greb's clawing tactics." "Gibbons might have won if he were gamer and Tunney might have won if he were more rugged." The referee for Greb-Carpentier would have his hands full.

Manager Descamps has an eagle eye for fouls when Georges is losing. He would kick up a tremendous row the moment Greb began to rough Georges as he did Tunney, and he would have some reason for complaint. If Greb is wise he will never go to Europe to fight Carpentier or anyone else. He would be thrown out of the ring in the first round.

Over here the idea is to give the crowd a run for its money regardless of the rules. If a boxer has a natural style that is foul he is allowed to get away with it just because it is his natural style. ... Greb butts, wrestles, holds and hits and breaks other rules in a way that no one else could do with impunity.

The fact that Greb usually is the smaller man is another reason why he escapes being disqualified. To see a little fellow roughing up a bigger man is more or less of a joke to the crowd, but if the bigger man were to use the same tactics it would be a decidedly different matter. ...

Perhaps Greb can fight fairly if he cares to do so, although he would not be half as effective.[869]

---

[868] *Shenandoah Evening Herald*, quoting *New York Herald*, May 27, 1922.
[869] *Washington Times*, May 27, 1922.

In an interview later that week, Tunney claimed that his nose was broken in the 1st round as a result of a Greb head butt, and as a result he bled internally and therefore was unable to do his best.

> I never was so sure of anything in my life as that I can get my title back if they will give me another chance at Greb. … I'm willing to take anything for my end to get a shot at the title, for I'm the better man. Greb fouled me all through the fight. He held on and butted. Also, he alone knows how nearly out I had him in the fifth.[870]

Tunney claimed that a second butt in the 6th round broke open an old cut suffered in his bout with the late Eddie O'Hare. "The cut was opened in training, and we had it patched and disguised as much as possible, but Greb's head found it."

Gene Tunney.

Doc Bagley said it was Tunney's first 15-round bout, and his 31st contest. "Greb should have been disqualified, and I entered a protest with the commissioners. He broke all the rules of boxing." Bagley complained that Greb held, wrestled, and held around the neck and hit.[871]

Tex Rickard said Dempsey wanted $500,000 for a Wills fight. Tex said the fight was not likely at that price.[872]

Writing for the Associated Negro Press, William Pickens noted that Dempsey said he was "willing to box Harry Wills, if ---." "But the whole procedure seems to stall at the 'if.' 'If' what? If Wills were white and as well qualified as he is, Dempsey would have to box him or get out." Pickens said in America, whites proved their superiority to negroes by never measuring their strength against theirs; and proved that a negro can't by never letting him try.[873]

Dempsey's mom, "Cecilia"

Dempsey said he had purchased a home in Los Angeles for his mother, and put his brother Joe in charge of it. He had provided for the rest of his family as well.[874]

On May 24, Dempsey arrived back in Los Angeles, at his Western avenue home. Commenting on the recent Greb-Tunney fight, the champ said that while he thought Greb was a "mighty good man," he was "out of the question as a heavyweight possibility, simply because he's too light."[875]

Jack Kearns sent a telegram to Dempsey indicating that he was making arrangements with promoter Floyd Fitzsimmons (who promoted the Dempsey-Miske title

---

[870] *New York Call*, May 28, 1922.
[871] *St. Louis Post-Dispatch, Wilkes-Barre Evening News*, May 25, 1922.
[872] *Brooklyn Daily Times*, May 24, 1922.
[873] *Buffalo American*, May 25, 1922.
[874] *Buffalo Times*, May 25, 1922.
[875] *Buffalo Express*, May 26, 1922.

fight) for Dempsey to fight on September 4, 1922 in Michigan City, Indiana, against either Bill Brennan (who was a very close 2nd in the *Daily News* poll regarding who Dempsey should fight) or Jess Willard.[876]

Kearns and Floyd Fitzsimmons   Dempsey sparring Lee Moore

On May 29 at Tommy McFarland's gym in Los Angeles, under the watchful eye of trainer Teddy Hayes, Dempsey worked out and sparred. One of his 2-round bouts was with lightweight Lee Moore, an old pal.[877]

The *Los Angeles Evening Express* said, "The greatness of Jack Dempsey is made evident every afternoon when he works out at pudgy Tommy McFarland's gymnasium."

Kearns confirmed that Dempsey would fight Bill Brennan on September 4 in Michigan City, Indiana.[878]

Harry Greb said Jeff Smith gave him his toughest fights. He preferred to fight taller foes. "I have been wondering if the fans will recognize me as an opponent for Dempsey, now that I have beaten Tunney. Dempsey will not show as good against a fast moving boxer like myself and I am anxious to meet him and prove it."[879]

Harry Grayson wrote that Dempsey had explicit confidence in Jack Kearns, with total loyalty towards him. He had made all the right moves in taking him to the championship, so he trusted his judgment. Kearns had obtained purses for Dempsey that were far beyond the imagination of the old school.[880]

Grayson had a point. Kearns brought Dempsey to the title within 2 years of working with him. Dempsey earned nearly as much as the challenger to Willard ($27,500) as champion Jack Johnson demanded for title *defenses* ($30,000). Dempsey had earned increasingly larger amounts for each title fight. He earned between $67,000 and $87,000 to fight Miske. He earned $100,000 for Brennan, and $300,000 for Carpentier. Plus, all the money from vaudeville, exhibitions, and films. From a financial perspective, Jack Kearns had been the best manager ever.

---

[876] *Los Angeles Express*, May 27, 1922.
[877] *Los Angeles Times*, May 30, 1922.
[878] *Los Angeles Evening Express*, May 31, 1922. On June 9 at the McFarland gym in Los Angeles, Dempsey worked out with One-Round Andrews, Young Abe Attell, and Sam Sherman. *Los Angeles Evening Express*, June 9, 1922.
[879] *Brooklyn Daily Eagle*, May 30, 1922.
[880] *Los Angeles Evening Express*, June 1, 1922.

Jess Willard said he would train longer and harder for a Dempsey rematch.

> He beat me with the first punch he landed. I never knew what happened after that. I underestimated Dempsey. He has bull-like strength and he has a good punch. I don't think he's a clever boxer, but he has all the speed in the world and a punch. He didn't need anything more. I thought it would be easy to beat Dempsey because he was so much smaller than I was, and I knew he couldn't match me in strength and that I was a better boxer. I was careless. I worked in the pictures until my training time was too short. It would have been long enough for any one but Dempsey, but, as I say, I underestimated him.[881]

W. O. McGeehan said, "I have it on fairly good authority that Dempsey is a bit weary of the boxing game. It has begun to bore him. He will not fight Wills for less than $300,000 for himself and what Kearns can get for Kearns." McGeehan said Dempsey should be honest about it and stop claiming that he would rather box than eat or act. "If Dempsey boxes at all it should be with Wills. He is the only heavyweight in sight likely to give him an argument."[882]

Harry Greb, the "giant killer," said he would fight anyone, regardless of size.

> I know it is going to make some people laugh, but I am positive I can defeat Dempsey in a 12 or 15-round decision bout. Of course I wouldn't expect to knock Dempsey out. My biggest thought would be to keep from getting knocked out. That is all I would have to do in order to win a decision bout with Dempsey, who is no harder to hit than Gibbons, and who, I feel sure, would have as much trouble reaching me as Gibbons did. I haven't the slightest fear of Dempsey, regardless of the fact that all the experts say he is much too big for me. … Dempsey is strong and can hit. If he reached me on the button it would be curtains. However, I feel that in a limited bout I would be able to stay away from him. In the meantime I would be doing so much execution that the judges would have to award me the decision.[883]

Harry Newman said Luis Firpo had the natural ability to make a great fighter. "How he can hit!" He had a savage attack. If he improved his boxing skills, he would make an awful lot of trouble for anyone.[884]

Henry Farrell doubted that Dempsey would agree to a Wills match. In early June, Kearns said Dempsey ought to get $300,000 to defend his title, "and the mere suggestion of a purse like that leaves every promoter out of the running with the exception of Rickard." Hence, "Dempsey at the present time is showing no great desire to meet the big colored fighter. …

[881] *New York Evening World*, June 3, 1922. Notice that Willard did not claim Dempsey had loaded gloves.
[882] *New York Herald*, June 4, 1922.
[883] *Buffalo Times*, June 4, 1922.
[884] *New York Daily News*, June 4, 1922.

Kearns possibly figures that he ought to get away with some easier bouts before he signs for the colored man."[885]

A well-known boxing critic of London, England, known as "Boxing Major," said England did not want a Dempsey-Wills contest. "Wills and Dempsey will not box together in this country, judging from the way the public feels about it."[886] England's Home Office had prevented Jack Johnson vs. Billy Wells in 1911, and would have the same racial concerns about Dempsey-Wills' potential impact upon the British Empire.

De Witt Van Court said Dempsey's crown appeared to be secure, for he already had beaten the best men, like Brennan, Miske, and Fulton. Before Carpentier was given a rematch, he needed to beat men like Tunney, Gibbons, and Greb.

Van Court said chances were that Dempsey would not take on Wills, even though Jack probably would beat him. "A match between Dempsey and Wills may possibly be a drawing card, but in my opinion, Jack is too game and too fierce a fighter to be beaten by Wills." Regardless, "A match between white and colored fighters is bad. Too much race prejudice for the good of the game. There are many boxing fans in this country who would like to see a fight at any cost regardless of the results or harm it may do the game."[887]

On June 11, 1922, Floyd Fitzsimmons announced that he had signed Dempsey to box Bill Brennan at Michigan City, Indiana on Labor Day.[888]

Kearns maintained that he would allow Dempsey to fight Wills if the public wanted it. The best evidence of public demand would be if a promoter offered Dempsey a $300,000 guarantee. After all, he had made that much to fight Carpentier.[889]

On June 13, 1922, Harry Wills, through his manager Paddy Mullins, issued a formal challenge to Dempsey, and asked the New York State Boxing Commission to force the fight, as it had done with some others. The challenge was backed with a $2,500 deposit/forfeit filed with the commission. However, "It must be remembered that the Boxing Commission never as yet has sanctioned a fight between a white man and a black man."

William Muldoon, chair of the New York commission, refused to comment publicly on what the commission would do with the challenge, nor would he commit himself as to the commission's position regarding mixed-race bouts.

However, some said that privately, Muldoon criticized non-fighting champions, including Dempsey, calling him a disgrace to the game. "Dempsey assured me in his dressing room in Toledo only a few minutes after he had become champion that he would be a fighting champion. What manner of a champion has he shown himself?" Muldoon allegedly also said he would try to use his power to force Dempsey to meet a

[885] *Brooklyn Daily Times*, June 5, 1922.
[886] *Brooklyn Daily Eagle*, June 6, 1922.
[887] *Los Angeles Times*, June 12, 1922.
[888] *New York Herald*, June 12, 1922.
[889] *Brooklyn Citizen*, June 13, 1922.

suitable opponent; describing Wills as about the only boxer capable of giving him a real match. "Jack Dempsey has not fought one real opponent and yet he is commercializing his title in a most disgraceful fashion." Willard was out of condition. Miske had undergone an operation. Dempsey already had knocked out Brennan once before. Carpentier was outweighed by more than 20 pounds. Now he was considering rematches with men he already had knocked out – Brennan, Willard, and Carpentier.

Muldoon also purportedly said a time limit would be placed on Dempsey's acceptance of the Wills challenge. If he refused, the commission was prepared to declare his title forfeited or his license revoked (the same threat which was issued to other champions who refused to defend often enough or against worthy challengers).[890]

Jack Kearns said they would make decisions based on what the public wanted and what a promoter could offer. "Dempsey does not fear Wills or any other fighter. At times there is agitation against mixed matches."

Los Angeles Evening Express writer Harry Grayson said it was well known that Kearns/Dempsey would fight Wills if conditions were satisfactory and they were certain that the authorities would not step in and prevent the match after big expenses had been incurred.

However, Tex Rickard realized that "there never was a match that did so much to hurt the boxing game as the [Jeffries-Johnson] bout at Reno. Indignation was aroused all over the country and it was years before bouts of any duration were permitted in many states." Rickard did not want a return to the time when the law and politicians were hard on the sport.[891]

Word was that Kearns had signed Dempsey to fight Brennan on Labor Day for Floyd Fitzsimmons for a flat guarantee of $200,000 for a 10-round no-decision contest.[892]

Dempsey again said, "I shall be only too glad to fight any man the public demands, Harry Wills not excepted. I have expressed my stand to this effect some time ago..."

Jess Willard did not approve of a Dempsey-Wills bout. "The Jeffries-Johnson affair at Reno in 1910 did more to hurt boxing than anything else in the last 50 years. ... A Wills-Dempsey fight would bring forth a lot of unfavorable talk. Those in charge of the boxing game should let well enough alone."[893]

The Fighting Willards

THEY even have to muzzle the dog at the Willard home. Here we have Big Jess, his two good-looking sons and the family Airedale, "Flip." Allen Willard, aged 3, is on the left; Jess, Jr., aged 8, on the right. The ex-champion is the proud father of five children, all attending school here.

[890] *Los Angeles Times, New York Evening World,* June 14, 1922; *New York Daily News,* June 15, 1922.
[891] *Los Angeles Evening Express,* June 14, 1922.
[892] *Brooklyn Daily Times,* June 14, 1922.
[893] *Los Angeles Evening Express,* June 15, 1922.

Tex Rickard said he was prepared to erect a new stadium in New York for a Dempsey-Wills contest. However, he reiterated that Dempsey/Kearns had to recede from their $500,000 demand. He also said it would be necessary for the state athletic commission (and the governor) to sanction such a bout formally and unequivocally. He did not want to invest a great deal of time and expense only to have the bout thwarted at the last moment.

The *Los Angeles Times* noted that some states definitely were against a Dempsey-Wills match. New York had not had *any* mixed match since the New York Boxing Commission began to function, so it was not clear that New York ultimately would authorize a mixed heavyweight championship contest.[894]

Some thought that prohibitive financial demands would be one way to dodge the Wills contest. Others thought the demands were reasonable given that Dempsey got $300,000 for Carpentier, a 3 to 1 underdog, the fight generated over five times that amount, and the Wills fight appeared to be even more competitive; the biggest fight in boxing. Kearns reasoned that if the public demand really was there, then a promoter should be able to back the fight with big money.

Such financial holdouts were nothing new in boxing. Tommy Burns had held out for what was then considered a big guarantee to fight Jack Johnson, and eventually got it. Johnson held out for similar guarantees to fight tough foes as well.

Bill Brennan said the body-beating that Dempsey gave him in their 1920 fight "was the worst ring experience I have ever gone through, and proved the toughest battle I have ever been in." It was one of the most grueling fights ever. Yet, Bill said he had Dempsey in distress too. "I had Jack floundering around, punch drunk from a volley of rights and lefts in the second round, and any human being would have been knocked out – but Jack." Thereafter, "Dempsey's body smashes began to weaken me and I was forced to do the hardest fighting of my career." He stood toe-to-toe for 12 rounds, swapping punches. "While I was hurt badly in almost every round, Dempsey did not really fease me until he knocked the wind out of my system in the twelfth with a right to the solar plexus, and I caved in. … I was unable to rid myself of the effects of that body blow. It was the hardest punch I have ever received."

Brennan said the critics gave Dempsey a lot of alibis, but did not give Bill enough credit for making Dempsey struggle. He had fought to stop Dempsey within 6 rounds, figuring that the champion could not take it as well as the public thought. Hence, Bill claimed that he was not prepared to go the long route; and had not paced himself for a long fight. He believed he knew how to beat Dempsey, and would be in even better shape for a third fight.[895]

---

[894] *Los Angeles Times, Brooklyn Citizen,* June 15, 1922.
[895] *Brooklyn Standard Union,* June 15, 1922.

On June 17, from Los Angeles, Dempsey allegedly announced the dismissal of his trainer, Teddy Hayes. Jack supposedly said, "Hayes is working for Kearns. In the future I'll select my own handlers." This gave rise to speculation that there were tensions between Dempsey and Kearns.[896]

ANOTHER POSSIBLE MRS. JACK DEMPSEY—Looks as though Jack and Doris Deane, movie star, might be sealing an engagement with a kiss, but then again it may have been just for the camera.

Dempsey rumored to be involved with film actress Doris Deane

Kearns said the reports were false, for Hayes simply was with him on a trip. Dempsey denied the reports as well. "Nothing to it."[897]

Dempsey's family was living at 24th street and Western avenue in Los Angeles. Jim Jeffries was living in Burbank, just outside Los Angeles.[898]

While in Chicago, en route to New York, Kearns reiterated that Dempsey had not drawn the color line, and if the public demand and financial inducements for Dempsey-Wills were sufficient, such a fight could be staged.[899]

The Lord of the Manor Mows His Own Hay.

Dempsey at his Los Angeles home.

Davis Walsh said public desire for Dempsey-Wills was not likely to be gratified within a year. Walsh believed that Floyd Fitzsimmons and Kearns were in an alliance, being one and the same. Brennan served the purpose of being a buffer between Dempsey and Wills. After him would be Willard and Greb. Hence, it would be a year or more before Kearns would consider Wills. His exorbitant demands for a Wills fight also would put it off. "The public undoubtedly wants to see Dempsey take on Wills, knock him as flat as a glass of stale beer and dispose of the matter once and for all."

From Los Angeles, Jack's father, "Pa" Dempsey, said he urged his boys to box when they were young:

---

[896] *New York Daily News*, June 18, 1922. Others said gossip was that Dempsey was disgusted with several brawls about the training quarters, one of which resulted in a damage suit by a carpenter who claimed to have been beaten up by Hayes and others. Word was that Lee Moore, Jack's friend, would replace Hayes.
[897] *Brooklyn Citizen, Yonkers Statesman and News*, June 19, 1922. Apparently, the opponent for the Floyd Fitzsimmons promotion had not yet been firmly set. Kearns was conferring with Fitzsimmons for a September 4 Labor Day battle featuring Dempsey against either Brennan, Willard, or Greb. Kearns seemed to prefer Willard.
[898] *Los Angeles Evening Express*, June 19, 1922.
[899] *Los Angeles Times, New York Times*, June 20, 1922.

I bought gloves for the lads and let them go to it in the back yard. Pretty soon all the boys in the neighborhood were eager to test punches with my youngsters, and we had a steady series of scraps every Sunday afternoon. In those days our Johnny could beat the tar out of Jack. In fact he gave his younger brother his first fistic lessons. Johnny was a pretty fair lightweight in his day.[900]

Kearns said he and Dempsey wanted to know what the New York State commission's official policy was regarding mixed-race bouts, for they would fight Wills just as soon as some promoter could guarantee a lucrative fight without any official interference. Kearns said of Dempsey,

> He is tired of making millions for others. Tex Rickard made a million and a half from the two big fights [Willard and Carpentier]. … From these two fights we got $327,500. We propose no longer to take the short end of it. It will have to be more than half the pot – or nothing doing. Heretofore we have been poor business men. It is the intention to correct that mistake.

Kearns said if a promoter could guarantee a suitable site where there would be no interference, they would gamble with that promoter on a percentage basis, "but we will name the percentage."[901]

Kearns said there was a potential Labor Day fight, though no formal final articles had been signed yet. He left it up to Floyd Fitzsimmons to choose the opponent. Promoter Fitzsimmons was considering men like Brennan, Willard, Gibbons, and Greb.[902]

On June 22, Kearns and Rickard met for two hours to discuss a potential Dempsey-Wills fight, and allegedly any difficulties between them were threshed out. However, the New York commission had been silent regarding whether it would sanction such a battle. Its chairman, William Muldoon, thus far had declined to say whether a Dempsey-Wills fight would be sanctioned.

Both Rickard and Kearns were concerned that without official political sanction, Dempsey-Wills ultimately would be derailed by politicians or regulators. James Crusinberry was not optimistic, for he wrote, "There seems to be little chance that the commission will sanction it."

There were doubts whether New Jersey would allow a mixed-race heavyweight championship either, given that its commissioner previously said that such a fight would not be sanctioned. "Politics plays an important part. A certain high official, who has much to say, is up for office this fall. A mixed fight might hurt his chances to be elected." Most politicians did not want to deal with the political fallout of a mixed-race championship fight, particularly in the heavyweight division.

Kearns had been convinced that there was demand for a Wills fight, and he and Rickard seemed interested in the fight if the political and legal

---

[900] *Olean Evening Times*, June 20, 1922. Pa Dempsey said the only man he feared had a chance with his son was Willard.
[901] *Binghamton Press*, June 22, 1922.
[902] *Brooklyn Daily Times*, June 22, 1922. Kearns also was arranging for Dempsey to go on tour giving exhibitions in various cities, such as Boston, Wichita, and Omaha, and cities in Canada.

authorities would agree to support it and not interfere. Kearns said he knew the only real fight was with Wills, and he knew the public wanted it. He and Dempsey wanted it too.

> Dempsey is ready now to fight Wills. I wish it could come off this summer. But the thing is hard to arrange, because it's a mixed bout. You see Tex Rickard had experience in the Jack Johnson-Jim Jeffries affair. He's afraid of them. If the New York commission would sanction it, all would be easy. ... But he don't want anything to happen that would hurt the boxing game here.

> Now, over in Jersey, it's tough just now because politics has entered into it. You see there's an election this fall and the big fellows who run things don't want any holler about a mixed fight. After the election is over things will be all right. ... There doesn't seem to be any other promoters or any other place where it would be worth holding.

Meanwhile, Kearns had promised to fight for Floyd Fitzsimmons at his Michigan City arena on Labor Day against either Brennan, Willard, Gibbons, or Greb, whomever Fitzsimmons selected.[903]

Before Kearns or Rickard would go forward with a Dempsey-Wills promotion, they wanted assurances from a potential locale's state governor, attorney general, athletic commission, the local mayor, and the local police commissioner that the fight would be allowed. They did not want to forgo other opportunities, take the time to train and incur all of the incidental expenses associated with training and promoting, building an arena, etc., only to have the fight thwarted by the authorities at the last minute.

The plan was for Dempsey to have one or two interim matches until assurances could be obtained that there would be no interference with a Wills contest.[904]

The *New York Age* quoted Kearns as saying his demands regarding a Wills contest were not unreasonable, given that Rickard had cleared a profit of $1,500,000 in two Dempsey fights. Dempsey had made far less, even though he was the attraction. They wanted a fair reward, given the risk, time and expense of training, and lost opportunities, etc.

Kearns said let the critics who want the Wills fight so badly go out and find a venue where it could take place. "But I don't intend to sign for a bout and thus tie myself up, and then have every Governor through the country come out and say the battle cannot be held in his particular State." The New York commission notified him of a challenge by Wills, but "the commission did not notify us that it would sanction such a match if I consented to sign for it." Kearns said they would sign for the match if the commission would authorize it.

---

[903] *New York Daily News, Brooklyn Daily Eagle,* June 23, 1922.
[904] *New York Evening World, New York Herald,* June 23, 1922.

While awaiting final decisions, Dempsey would be on an exhibition tour throughout New England, the Southwest, Middle West, and Canada. The tour was scheduled to start in Boston on June 29 or 30.[905]

The New York Commission did not specifically say that it would or would not sanction or interfere with a Dempsey-Wills fight, but did inform Dempsey that he had until July 10 to state whether he accepted or declined the Harry Wills challenge.

Kearns and Rickard wanted the commission to give the Dempsey-Wills fight its official, formal stamp of approval. "Looks now as if Dempsey and Kearns will accept Wills's challenge and then see what the comish will do about granting a sanction for the mixed bout."

Thomas Rice said the commission essentially had committed itself to sanctioning the Wills fight, or otherwise it had gotten itself in a peculiar position, given that it gave Dempsey a deadline to accept the challenge or declare his title open.[906]

On June 24, 1922, Jack Dempsey turned 27 years of age. He said, "I'll fight any man in the world, Wills or anybody, tomorrow or the next day, if that's what Kearns says. He's my manager and I stick to his orders."[907]

The *Brooklyn Daily Times'* Len Wooster suspected that Kearns' declarations about the Wills bout were not sincere, but rather talk and bluster, and the public regarded such claims with suspicion. Modern champions were reluctant to defend their crowns. "If they were really sincere they would stake their titles without being forced by boxing commissions."

The *Brooklyn Daily Eagle* also believed that Kearns would come up with any manner of subterfuge to avoid fighting Wills.[908]

The *Pittsburgh Gazette Times* reported that Dempsey and Greb might be fighting in Pittsburgh on Labor Day. At least that was the hope. The *Pittsburgh Press* said the purported offer was $100,000 for Dempsey, while Greb would earn $30,000, for a 10-round no-decision contest. Apparently, George Engel, Greb's manager, agreed. It was said that the offer had been communicated to Kearns over telephone, and allegedly he received it favorably.[909]

Greb said,

> Bill Brennan lasted 12 rounds with Dempsey, proving that Jack is not the most to be feared fighter in the ring. I figure from past experiences with Dempsey in his training camp at Benton Harbor that I can make the pace fast enough to offset his hardest punches and be there at the finish and will welcome the chance to get into the ring with him. I have fought bigger men than Dempsey and

[905] *New York Age*, July 1, 1922. Scheduled towns included Oklahoma City on July 3, Omaha on July 4, Wichita on the 5th, as well as five Canadian cities.
[906] *Brooklyn Daily Eagle*, June 24, 1922.
[907] *New York Daily News*, June 26, 1922.
[908] *Brooklyn Daily Times*, *Brooklyn Daily Eagle*, June 26, 1922. Yet, it also was reported that an agreement for a Dempsey-Wills fight to be held sometime before June 30, 1923 was to be signed by the fighters' managers and Rickard. *New York Daily News*, June 27, 1922.
[909] *Pittsburgh Press*, *Pittsburgh Gazette Times*, June 28, 1922.

beat every one of them and unless he connects with his knockout wallop early I may be able to tire him out.[910]

Kearns also was in negotiations for potential matches for Dempsey against Wills for Rickard, or Brennan or Willard for Fitzsimmons. Kearns wanted to make as much money as possible, patiently considering all offers, as he always did.

On June 28, 1922 in Providence, Rhode Island, at the Kingsley Avenue ball park, in a show sponsored by the Veterans of Foreign Wars to benefit disabled veterans; attended by 6,000 or 7,000 people, 195-pound Jack Dempsey made his first appearance in the ring in the East since his return from Europe, in a 4-round exhibition with Larry Williams. Dempsey was fast on his feet and pounded on Williams hard from start to finish. Although 10-ounce gloves were used, Williams was wobbly at the end. The defensive Williams had landed only two or three clean blows.[911]

On June 29, 1922, Dempsey and Kearns formally notified the New York State Athletic Commission that they accepted the Harry Wills challenge. They requested that a conference be held to set the date.[912]

New York Governor Nathan Miller claimed that he would maintain a hands-off policy regarding the Dempsey-Wills fight. He had no objection to a black man fighting a white, but left the matter up to the boxing commission. Yet, many were skeptical, feeling that ultimately, the fight would not be allowed to take place, and that the governor and/or the commission said one thing for public consumption while feeling another way privately. Henry Farrell wrote, "However, it is almost a safe bet that the fight will not be staged in this country." Politicians said one thing publicly so as not to offend one constituency, and spoke differently privately to thwart matters so as not to offend another constituency.

Tex Rickard said it would be impossible to promote such an important contest inside of six or eight months, so Dempsey-Wills could not be held until 1923, and likely was a year away.[913]

On June 30, 1922 in Trenton, New Jersey, 211-pound Harry Wills stopped 183-pound black Jeff Clark (126-37-22) in the 2nd round. Clark was floored three times in the 1st round and twice in the 2nd.[914]

Many prospective promoters were backing away from mixed-race fights "because of possible objections by reformers."[915]

The *New York Daily News* said that initially Dempsey ignored Wills, then he drew the color line, which really was the danger line. Then when newspaper pressure mounted, Dempsey said he would fight whomever the public wanted. Its poll had Wills the clear winner. Then when there was risk that his championship might be declared vacant for having failed to accept Wills' challenge, Dempsey said he was willing to fight Wills.

[910] *Pittsburgh Daily Post*, June 28, 1922. There also was talk of another Greb-Tunney contest.
[911] *Boston Globe, Bangor Daily News, Buffalo Commercial*, June 29, 1922. Dempsey left for Omaha, set to exhibit there on Monday July 3.
[912] *New York Evening World*, June 29, 1922.
[913] *Brooklyn Citizen, New York Herald, New York Times, Binghamton Press*, June 30, 1922.
[914] *New York Tribune, New York Evening World, Binghamton Press*, July 1, 1922. Kearns and Wills' manager Paddy Mullins were set to meet on July 8 to discuss the fight.
[915] *New York Daily News*, July 2, 1922.

Hence, this newspaper believed its campaign and the pressure exerted had worked.

Thomas Rice said Montreal, Canada's bid to host Dempsey-Wills was not convincing. There was great opposition to mixed-race bouts in Canada and by the British Empire, fearing the disturbing influence such a contest might have throughout the Empire (of which Canada was a part). "Since the war the racial and color problems [are] 10 times as acute, and there are 10 times as many reasons why fuel should not be added to the fire by a black vs. white bout for the heavyweight fighting championship of the world."[916]

It had been one year since the Dempsey-Carpentier fight.

On July 3, 1922 in Oklahoma City, Oklahoma, 190-pound Billy Miske knocked out 195-pound Willie Meehan in the 1st round, with a left to the body and right to the jaw.

On the undercard that same evening, Jack Dempsey boxed a 4-round exhibition with former foe Andre Anderson. In the 2nd round, a right cross to the jaw sent Anderson through the ropes. Jack picked him up and nursed him along to the finish.[917]

On July 4, 1922 in Ashland, Kentucky, Bill Brennan won a 12-round no decision over touted contender Bob Martin (42-8-1).[918]

On July 5, 1922 in Wichita, Kansas at the local Forum, before a crowd of a couple thousand, Dempsey, who was on an exhibition tour, boxed 6 rounds (3 each) with two men, Ed Warner - the local heavyweight who was Jack's old friend from Salt Lake City, and Andre Anderson.

Even wearing 16-ounce gloves, Dempsey decked Anderson with a short six-inch left sock to the jaw. The champ picked him up and carried him for the remainder of the time.

Supposedly, Ed Warner once fought Dempsey for $10 in Salt Lake. Warner said even then he knew that Jack had the makings of a champion. Dempsey hit him lightly for 3 rounds, and did not allow him to land. Overall, the impressed crowd enjoyed the champion's clever work.

Bob Armstrong, who was present, said Dempsey would beat Wills or any other boxer in the world.[919]

Kearns verified that he had received an offer for a 10-round Dempsey-Greb bout in Pittsburgh on Labor Day for $100,000 guaranteed, with a privilege of 50% of the receipts (others said the offer was 35%, but Kearns wanted 50%). Although the offer looked good to him, he was leaning toward the Fitzsimmons promotion, which would pay more.[920]

[916] New York Daily News, New York Evening World, Brooklyn Daily Eagle, July 3, 1922.
[917] Oklahoma City Times, Lincoln Star, July 4, 1922.
[918] Since his loss to Dempsey, Brennan had gone 16-1, his only loss being a close 1921 10-round no decision to Miske.
[919] Wichita Beacon, Wichita Daily Eagle, July 6, 1922.
[920] Chicago Tribune, July 7, 1922

Unfortunately, on July 7, Indiana Governor Warren T. McCray said someone needed to convince him that the pugilistic encounters scheduled for Indiana within the next few months were boxing exhibitions and not prize fights, and unless they could do so, the fight game was dead in his state. He said, "I don't think there will be any more fights in this state." As a result, things were not looking too good for a Labor Day Dempsey fight in Michigan City, Indiana.[921]

Also on July 7, 1922, in Rockaway Beach, Queens, New York, 174-pound Gene Tunney won in dominant fashion a 12-round judges' decision over 167- or 172-pound Fay Keiser (26-17-8).[922]

In ranking the contenders, Kearns placed Willard first, then Brennan, Greb, Carpentier, and Wills. He said no one would dictate what Jack Dempsey did or who he fought, including any boxing commission.

The *New York Daily News* noted that although Dempsey claimed he loved to fight, it appeared that he preferred the vaudeville stage and exhibition touring to real fighting.[923]

On July 8, Jack Kearns and Wills manager Paddy Mullins met, but nothing formal was signed. Mullins declined to sign an agreement that could put the date of the Dempsey-Wills fight off past 1922. The proposed contract stated that the contest would provide for bids by promoters whom the parties were satisfied were financially responsible, and the bids had to be sufficiently large and satisfactory to all.

Mullins did not like that the agreement did not bind Dempsey to any specified time limit in which to box Wills. He also wanted the bout simply to go to the highest bidder, regardless of the bid size. Kearns did not want to bind himself in that way, but said if sufficient inducements were offered, and a suitable location could be found, they would fight at any time. Basically, it was no agreement at all, but rather a vague, indefinite agreement to agree to fight, more symbolic than anything.

Kearns said he was considering the Greb offer. The bout at Michigan City appeared to be on the ropes, because Indiana Governor McCray recently said he did not believe in hosting prize fights in his state.[924]

However, John Bell, the Pittsburgh promoter, said Kearns had waited too long to accept his offer to fight Greb, and if Kearns had accepted his offer made nearly two weeks ago, for a $100,000 guarantee, with the privilege of 35% of the gross receipts if more (not 50% as reported, or as Kearns said he wanted), he could have arranged the bout for Labor Day, but the time was too short now to make preparations (even though that date still was two months away). So now that offer was off the table. However, Bell said his offer still stood for a potential later date.

Of course, if not on Labor Day, a Greb-Dempsey date in Pittsburgh likely would have to be for the spring or summer 1923, owing to the weather and necessity for a large enough outdoor arena. Big-money fights

[921] *Logansport Pharos-Tribune, Richmond Palladium*, July 7, 1922.
[922] *Brooklyn Daily Eagle, Buffalo Times*, July 8, 1922.
[923] *New York Daily News, Brooklyn Daily Times*, July 8, 1922.
[924] *New York Times, Buffalo Times, New York Tribune, New York Daily News*, July 9, 1922; *New York Times*, July 10, 1922.

rarely took place indoors, because the seating capacity for most such arenas was smaller. Hence, with some exceptions, big fights rarely took place in the winter because of the weather and need for a large arena.[925]

On July 10, 1922 in Philadelphia, before a crowd of 18,000 to 20,000 at Phillies Park, Philadelphia, 167-pound Harry Greb won a close and competitive 8-round no decision over 163 ½-pound Tommy Loughran (34-3-2). 6 newsmen had it for Greb, and 2 for Loughran.[926]

On July 11, 1922, Jack Kearns and Paddy Mullins signed a Dempsey-Wills agreement, even though it lacked any definiteness. No time or place for the fight was named, nor the financial terms. Mullins had withdrawn his objections as to when the fight would be held. The contract allowed both to take part in other bouts in the meantime as well.

AT LAST!—Yes, gentlemen, it has happened. Paddy Mullins (left), manager for Harry Wills, and Jack Kearns, Dempsey's boss (center), yesterday signed for title bout while Dan McKetrick, praise agent, looked on.

Jack Will "Warm Up" Before Tackling Wills

Dempsey agreed to box Wills for the heavyweight championship, but that was all. The time and place would need to be mutually agreed upon. Bids were to be submitted, and had to be satisfactory to all. So really it just was an agreement to agree at some future date when the terms were more definite. Some said the agreement meant practically nothing, and the fight was no closer to being made. The bout needed a

Dempsey training with Jerry Luvadis, his new trainer, at left, and Jack Renault, his sparring partner, at right, in Saranac Lake, New York.

[925] New York Tribune, Allentown Morning Call, July 11, 1922; Great Falls Tribune, July 13, 1922.
[926] Philadelphia Inquirer, Philadelphia Evening Public Ledger, July 11, 1922; New Castle Herald, July 12, 1922.

promoter, a location, a date, a purse amount, and agreed-upon split of the proceeds. Still, symbolically, it showed that the color line was not being drawn, and Kearns was open to a Wills fight.[927]

Tex Rickard said he probably would bid for the Dempsey-Wills fight, but not in the immediate future. Rickard did not foresee a Dempsey-Wills contest being held before July 1923. If it was held in New York, he would

Dempsey farming at Saranac Lake

have to build a new arena capable of holding the crowd, which would cost him a lot of money, nearly $200,000. "The promoter of such an event would be the only one to assume any risk and must proceed with caution."[928]

Jess Willard did not see why there would be any talk of a Dempsey-Wills contest. "I fought a colored man once, but the circumstances were different." The whole country wanted to see someone take the title away from Johnson. He accomplished that.

> The public never wanted me to cross the color line again, and Dempsey has no more reason to do it than I had. Mixed bouts never do boxing any good. …. I don't think the public wants mixed bouts, and I'll never take part in one. I beat the best colored boxer of them all and I won't have to beat any more to prove it can be done.

Jess said the only way he would cross the line was if Wills beat Dempsey, and then he would have to regain the championship as the 'white hope' once again. "But I don't consider that a possible condition. Wills has a weak jaw and he'd never stand up against Dempsey more than a few rounds."[929]

It is interesting that Willard thought Wills did not have the best chin. He had been stopped in 1912 in 2 rounds by George Kid Cotton, but had avenged the loss four times, all by knockout. Wills had been stopped twice by 190-pound Langford (1914 LKOby14 and 1916 LKOby19), but had avenged those losses several times as well, both with decisions and knockouts. The last time Wills had been stopped was in 1917, when he retired at the end of the 2nd round against Battling Jim Johnson as a result of a broken wrist. He avenged that loss with a 10-round no decision victory. That was the same year that Dempsey was stopped by Flynn, a loss he avenged a year later. So really, the last knockout loss Wills had was back in 1916 to Langford, and then only in the 19th round.

[927] *New York Tribune, New York Evening World,* July 12, 1922.
[928] *New York Herald,* July 12, 1922; *New York Daily News,* July 13, 1922.
[929] *Evening World,* July 13, 1922.

However, Wills had been decked several times, even when he won. Wills had been down in 1918 against McVey in the 11th round, but won a 20-round decision. In 1919, John Lester Johnson knocked him down, yet Harry rose to win that no decision contest. He also suffered a knockdown against Jack Thompson in 1920, though Harry won a 15-round decision. He was dropped again in 1922 against Bill Tate, fighting to a 10-round draw in that contest. In recent years, he generally got up and won.

But some saw the fact that Wills could be dropped that often as a sign that he would have trouble handling Jack Dempsey's brand of power. Some said that because Wills was game, attacked, and mixed it up, he would be vulnerable to a Dempsey blow. True, Wills was good at clinching, but Dempsey was a great in-fighter who knew how to get his hands free and work in the clinches. Regardless, when removing race from the equation, and all its implications, from a sporting perspective, most boxing fans wanted to see the fight. But, of course, the race angle indeed was a huge impediment in the 1920s.

One writer noted that bids for Dempsey-Wills were conspicuous by their absence. Race was the only reason such a fight would lack bids.[930]

On the afternoon of July 17 at the Exhibition Grounds in Sherbrooke, Canada, before a crowd of 2,000, Dempsey boxed 4 rounds with Sherbrooke native Jack Renault (22-6-1)(1922 LKOby13 Billy Miske).

That evening in Quebec, Dempsey boxed another 4 rounds with Bermondsey Billy Wells (30-3-3), claimant of the British and Canadian welterweight championship.

Also on July 17, 1922, in Winnipeg, Canada, 215-pound Harry Wills knocked out 177-pound Jeff Clark in the 3rd round.[931]

---

[930] *Elmira Star-Gazette*, July 15, 1922.

On the afternoon of July 18, in Cornwall, Ontario, 1,200 spectators, including women, saw Dempsey box Jack Renault for 4 rounds. Renault hit the air more often than he hit Dempsey, whose footwork and head movement helped him avoid many blows.

That evening, the athletic carnival was in Montreal at the Mount Royal Arena, performing for an estimated crowd of 4,000 to 5,000. Wearing 14-ounce gloves, showing cleverness of hand and foot, Jack boxed 6 rounds, 2 apiece with three men: provincial light-heavyweight amateur champion Paul Lahaye, heavyweight Jack Renault - a former Montreal policemen who had been a Dempsey sparring partner for the Carpentier fight, and 23-year-old, 6'4", 215-pound Elzear Rioux. Dempsey held back, but could have knocked out all three any time he wanted. He bloodied Rioux's nose.

On his tour, Jack typically would spar 4 rounds with either Jack Renault or Larry Williams. Also with him were welterweight "Bermondsey" Billy Wells, Jack Thomas, and various wrestlers and boxers.[932]

On the afternoon of July 19 at the Kingston, Canada Armories, Dempsey sparred 4 rounds with Larry Williams, and that evening in Ottawa, Ontario, before an estimated crowd of 3,500 - 4,000 at Dey's Arena, Jack boxed 4 rounds with the powerfully built Renault. A crowd of thousands were on hand just to greet him upon his arrival in town.

The *Ottawa Journal* said the champ made a big hit with his affable manner. "Dempsey strikes one as a good-natured big boy without a worry or care, and it was evident that he has an almost childlike respect for the judgment and opinion of Jack Kearns, his astute manager." The champ was very approachable. He did not expect to meet Wills for a year, and in the meantime, likely would have fights with Brennan and Willard.

When the tour was in Halifax the previous week, the champ was besieged by ladies, young and old, wanting his autograph. Youngsters loved him too, for Dempsey was like a big kid. He enjoyed playing baseball with them. He and Babe Ruth were friends. When in New York, Dempsey often worked out with the Yankees during their morning practices at the Polo Grounds. Dempsey also loved dogs. At his Los Angeles home, established for his parents, he had a large kennel of dogs. He had acquired a couple of shepherd dogs while in Europe.

The *Ottawa Citizen* agreed that Dempsey was a very likable fellow, unassuming and as full of fun as a kid. He did not like to sit still for too long.

Dempsey's boxing created a great impression. "Lithe, clean-cut, sinewy, almost bubbling over with vitality, he is a beautiful physical specimen. One's first impression of him is that he seems so small." He danced around Renault and landed an occasional blow, just toying with him. Dempsey clearly could stop him quickly if he chose. The pleased

---

[931] *Montreal Gazette, Winnipeg Evening Tribune*, July 18, 1922. Dempsey was faster than Wells, but just tapped his sparring partners. Giant Canadian Elzear Rioux boxed with Jack Renault.
[932] *Montreal Gazette*, July 19, 1922; *Buffalo Times*, October 22, 1922; *Ottawa Journal*, July 20, 1922. As a result of having boxed with Dempsey, the Quebec branch of the Amateur Athletic Union suspended Paul Lehaye's amateur status.

spectators could see that he was as fast as a featherweight, and could hit from any angle. It looked like he would be champion for a long time.[933]

On the 20th in Toronto, 4,000 saw Dempsey box with Jack Renault, welterweight Bermondsey Billy Wells, and "Tex" McEwen or McEwin, a promising young heavyweight.[934]

Jess Willard said he would not be ready to fight by September 29. So, despite his purported eagerness to fight Dempsey again, and two more months to train, he was in no hurry to do so.[935]

Leo Flynn, Bill Brennan's manager, said Dempsey would fight Brennan on Labor Day. Apparently, that fight still was on.[936]

On July 24, 1922, in Buffalo, New York, before a crowd of 5,000 that packed the Auditorium, Dempsey boxed 4 rounds with California's Jim Darcy, showing championship form, hitting him at will.

The *Buffalo Enquirer* said Dempsey had everything and more. He was a Corbett on his feet, a Jeffries with his power, and a Sullivan with the complete indifference with which he accepted Darcy's best efforts to the head and body. The way he stepped in and out, coming under and over leads, was poetry in motion. He gently tapped his partner multiple times, and played defense, rarely letting out with hard blows.[937]

Dempsey had planned to box two others as well, but the New York state athletic commission ridiculously flexed their muscles and took a hand in matters, saying Dempsey could box only one man within a 24-hour period, and the bout had to have a formal/official decision. Hence, technically, the Darcy bout was an official contest.

Nevertheless, Dempsey treated it as an exhibition, which is all it really was intended to be, carrying Darcy. The *Buffalo Express* said, "Even though he checked his punches against Darcy, he gave the smaller man a tough time of it, occasionally sending him tottering across the ring and into the ropes with short jolts or half hooks, none of which carried his full force. The four rounds were as pretty an exhibition as Buffalo has ever witnessed."

The *Buffalo Commercial* said Dempsey appeared to be a more finished, polished fighter than ever before. He gave a pretty display, feinting, moving, hitting, and boxing smartly. He didn't cut loose though, pulling his punches, for when he did nail Jimmy Darcy solidly on the jaw, he went spinning into the ropes. A couple times Darcy sagged and tottered, but Jack grabbed him and held him up. He did not want to damage him badly. Dempsey also demonstrated his stonewall defense.

The *Buffalo Evening News* said Dempsey looked as fit as a fiddle, buffeting Jimmy Darcy around with big gloves for 4 rounds "to a decision," as required by the commission, though no one ever heard an official verdict. Everyone knew Dempsey was better, though.

---

[933] *Ottawa Citizen*, July 19, 20, 1922; *Ottawa Journal*, July 20, 1922. Larry Williams often mixed it up with the champ, but Kearns gave him the night off. On the 20th, they would do an afternoon show in Kitchener and an evening show in Toronto.
[934] *Regina Leader-Post*, *Vancouver Province*, July 21, 1922.
[935] *New York Times*, July 22, 1922.
[936] *New York Daily News*, July 22, 1922.
[937] *Buffalo Enquirer*, July 25, 1922.

The commission forgot to bar the pillow gloves, so Dempsey hit him skillfully without mussing him up, though once or twice he nearly sent Jimmy into the crowd.

The ring announcer thanked the assemblage for its warm reception and said Jack was as good as matched to meet Bill Brennan at Michigan City, Indiana on Labor day.[938]

The commission later confirmed that Dempsey received the decision, and that his title was on the line, as far as they were concerned. Although Dempsey treated it as a good workout/exhibition, for those who want to get technical, ridiculously, the New York State athletic commission treated this as an official title defense: W4 Dempsey. Add that to your record books.[939]

Tex Rickard offered Willard a Dempsey fight for October 6, but Jess said he wanted October 31. Rickard eventually told Willard that it was October 9 or no match.[940]

On August 2, Dempsey was in Scranton, Pennsylvania with Kearns and Dan McKetrick, who was acting as their press agent.

That evening, at the Scranton Athletic Park, to a delighted crowd of 3,500 men, women, and children, using 16-ounce gloves, Dempsey again boxed 4 rounds with middleweight Jimmy Darcy. Although he mostly worked with him, Jack decked Darcy in the 2nd round with two lead rights and a stinging left hook. Dempsey lifted him to his feet, smiled and asked if he was hurt. The champ mostly worked the body thereafter. Neither man wore head gear.

Dempsey was a shifty fighter who moved well, with grace, speed, and science, in-and-out like a flash, with a lot of spring in his feet. His defense was good, making blows miss with a mere twist or movement of his head or body. A bunch of happy kids shook his "Iron Mike," or right hand.

Dempsey said he was ready and willing to fight Wills or anyone else. He wanted to give them all a chance. He believed Willard was stalling and afraid to fight him again. "Why, he's had more than six months to train and if a fighter can't get in shape in six months there is something the matter with him, and a fellow like that couldn't get fit in a year." Willard had been bluffing, and they called his bluff.[941]

Dempsey said he had signed to meet Brennan, "who has given me the toughest battle I ever had, and we will meet in Michigan City on Labor day." He expected to fight Wills after that. "I believe that Wills is one of the best heavyweights in the game and I expect to have a tough fight on my hands when I go into the ring against him." Regardless, he expected to beat him decisively.

---

[938] *Buffalo Express, Buffalo Commercial, Buffalo Evening News*, July 25, 1922. Jimmy Darcy's record included: 1919 D4 and W4 (twice) Jeff Clark, D4 Al Norton, and L10 Tommy Gibbons; 1921 W10 Eddie McGoorty, L10 (twice) Harry Greb, and L15 Jeff Smith; and 1922 LND8 and L12 Tommy Loughran, and W12 Billy Shade.
[939] *Pittsburgh Post-Gazette*, July 26, 1922. Dempsey, Brennan, and Fitzsimmons were required to post forfeits by August 7.
[940] *New York Tribune*, July 30, 1922; *New York Daily News*, August 9, 1922.
[941] *Scranton Republican, Scranton Times*, August 2, 3, 1922. Dempsey was booked for a Boston exhibition on Friday August 4. Larry Williams needed a break owing to the maiming he had been receiving from so much sparring with Dempsey.

On Friday afternoon, August 4, 1922, before 700 at the baseball grounds in Lawrence, Massachusetts, Dempsey boxed 4 rounds, 2 each with Tommy (Kloby) Corcoran and Charlestown's Dan O'Dowd, Corcoran's sparring partner.

Speaking of Wills, Dempsey told the local press,

> I wanted to get the match badly, as I know what I can do to him. …. The New York Boxing Commissioners thought I was trying to get away from it and finally agreed to let us meet in that State. They thought I would not come through. There had been a lot of kicking as to not giving a colored man a chance to box a white man. When I signed to box Wills, the commissioners acted as if they did not want the match to come off, but I am going through with it.[942]

ACTING MAYOR DAVID J. BRICKLEY COURAGEOUSLY PUTS UP HIS "DUKES" TO CHAMPION JACK DEMPSEY AT CITY HALL.
Councillor Ford is at Brickley's shoulder and Councillor Moriarty is directly at Dempsey's right shoulder.

Jack met Boston's mayor, David J. Brickley.

Unfortunately, there were ongoing concerns regarding whether Indiana's politicians would allow Dempsey vs. Brennan. Signs were not good. Indiana's governor Warren McCray had come out against it, saying that prize fighting in Indiana was illegal (even though several boxing cards took place there). Governor McCray asked the attorney general for a legal opinion regarding whether the go was a prize fight or a boxing contest. If it constituted a prize fight, it would be prohibited. The governor seemed determined to prevent it, though.[943]

195-pound Brennan was working out as if the Dempsey fight was on. He was sparring with Kid Norfolk and Panama Joe Gans, a former Dempsey sparring partner who in 1921 had twice knocked out Tiger Flowers (KO6, KO5). Dan McKetrick said the fight was on.

JACK DEMPSEY IN A STRONG-MAN ACT.
Champion Raised in His Arms 125-Pounder Shown in Photograph and Held Him Up in the Air for Five Minutes.

[942] Boston Globe, August 3, 5, 13, 1922.
[943] Binghamton Press, August 10, 1922; New York Herald, August 9, 10, 1922.

Dempsey had given exhibitions in several locations, including Bridgeport, Pawtucket, Secaucus, Hohokus, Troy, and other small towns, using the exhibition bouts as preparation while making money.[944]

On August 14, 1922 in Chicago, formal articles were signed for the Dempsey-Brennan 10-round championship rematch to be held on Labor Day in Michigan City, Indiana. Kearns and Leo Flynn each posted forfeits of $10,000 to guarantee their fighters' performances, and promoter Floyd Fitzsimmons posted $20,000 as his guarantee.[945]

Speaking of their last fight, Brennan said, "For ten rounds I looked like a sure champion. They alibied for Dempsey that he couldn't get going. That little thing is always done for champions, you know. But that is exactly right. He couldn't get going because I was doing all the going myself." Bill said a body blow in the 12th sank into his heart and he went down. He rose and the fight was stopped.

Kearns, Brennan, stakeholder Harry Moir, Dempsey, Leo P. Flynn, (not shown, sitting next to Flynn, was promoter Floyd Fitzsimmons)

[944] *New York Daily News*, August 12, 1922; *New York Herald*, August 13, 1922.
[945] *Chicago Tribune, Muncie Star Press, Moline Daily Dispatch*, August 15, 1922; *New York Daily News*, August 14, 1922. Kearns said Jack would run 6-8 miles per day, and spar with Jock Malone, Bermondsey Billy Wells, Jack Thompson, and Jack Taylor.

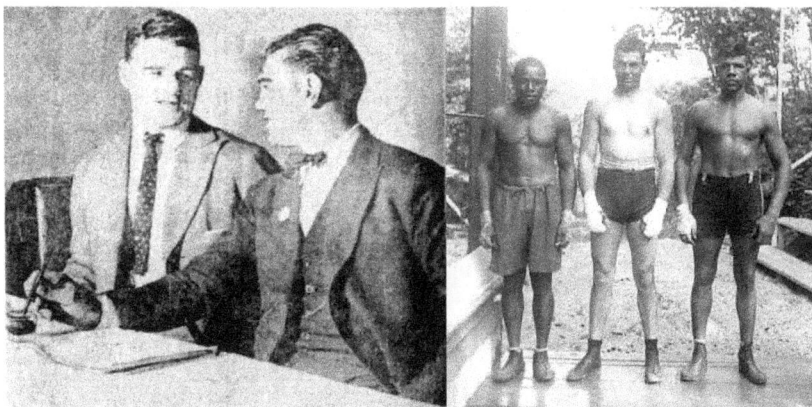

At left: Brennan and Dempsey sign. At right: Jack Taylor, Dempsey, and Jack Thompson

Dempsey headed to Michigan City to begin formal preparations, working with black sparring partners Jack Taylor and Jack Thompson (a former Wills opponent). On August 16 in Michigan City, Dempsey sparred 4 rounds, 2 each with Taylor and Thompson.[946]

Sadly though, also on August 16, via executive order, Indiana's governor formally prohibited the Dempsey-Brennan bout. He said the fight would violate the state law against prizefighting. "There will be no fight."

However, Floyd Fitzsimmons said the 10-round no-decision bout was not a violation of the law, and was just a boxing exhibition. He remained confident that the fight would occur. Fitz asserted that the governor's stand merely was a reiteration of the warnings given before all boxing bouts. Fitz had promoted several cards in Indiana.[947]

As often was the case, politicians got involved when it came to big fights. Boxing took place in Indiana all the time, with multiple cards all over the state. Although old-school "prizefighting" was illegal, modern boxing contests were not. Fitzsimmons recently had promoted Michigan City, Indiana boxing cards on July 4 and August 5, 1922. But politicians often had their own agendas when it came to

---

[946] Harry Wills' results against Jack Thompson included: 1916 KO9 and WND10; 1917 WND10; 1918 WND6 and DND8; 1920 W15 (though Thompson decked Wills); and 1921 WND8. A Denver bout in 1921 was declared a no contest in the 5th round when Thompson fell to the floor claiming a low blow. Thompson mostly had losses to Langford, though some draws as well: 1915 LKOby1; 1917 LND10; 1918 LND6; 1919 D15; 1920 L15 and L8; and 1921 D10. Thompson did have a 1916 WND10 victory over Sam McVey.

Jack Taylor's record included: 1914 D10 Kid Norfolk; 1918 LKOby3 Jack Thompson; 1921 W8 and D10 Bearcat Wright; 1922 D10 Kid Norfolk, and eventually, August 21, 1922 DND10 Sam Langford.

[947] *Buffalo Evening News, Belvidere Daily Republican, South Bend News-Times, Indianapolis News*, August 16, 17, 1922.

intervening to prevent major contests, particularly heavyweight championships. This was nothing new.

The governor's edict was exactly the type of nonsense that Rickard, Dempsey, and Kearns had wanted to avoid when it came to the Wills fight. Kearns and Dempsey wanted promoters to clear fights with the politicians before making them, and to post guarantee forfeits if they failed to bring off the contests for any reason. Rickard realized that one had to get fights approved behind the scenes with the politicians first. Even some white vs. white heavyweight championship fights were challenging to get approved, without the race angle being injected into the equation, so it can be understood why Rickard might be even more concerned when it came to mixed-race contests. The sport of boxing never had been looked upon with favor by politicians, who often buckled under to anti-boxing political pressure.[948]

Dempsey and Brennan kept training in Michigan City, Indiana, preparing for the scheduled September 4 contest as if it would happen.

The governor insisted that he would not allow the prize fight; while the promoters kept insisting that it was a legal boxing contest. Governor McCray said, "Either the affair is a prize fight or somebody is trying to fool the public." He also attacked the commercial features, which proved it would be a prizefight and not a boxing exhibition. "The charge for some seats, I understand, is $27.50. No one would pay that for any boxing contest." Why was that his business or concern? A delegation wanted to meet with the governor to convince him to allow the bout, but ultimately, the governor would not budge.[949]

On August 17, 1922 in Newark, New Jersey, 176-pound Gene Tunney won a 12-round no decision against 184-pound Charley Weinert (56-14-5). Weinert cut Gene's mouth in the 1st, and it bled throughout, though Tunney had Weinert groggy in the 4th and 9th rounds. Tunney fought a lot like Greb, and kept punching the face and body throughout, having Weinert's eye nearly closed at the end.[950]

Chicago's *Collyer's Eye* gave a scoop on the Indiana governor's potential reasons for preventing the Dempsey-Brennan contest. Back in late June, the Logansport American Legion Post had adopted a resolution protesting against the match. They simply could not get over Dempsey's lack of a war record. This paper had noted in late July that despite the

[948] *Buffalo Times*, August 17, 1922.
[949] *Muncie Morning Star, Lafayette Journal and Courier, Chicago Tribune*, August 18, 1922.
[950] *New York Daily News, Brooklyn Daily Times*, August 18, 1922.

activities and efforts of press agents, and articles promoting the fight, there was a "well defined feeling among officials in Indiana that the Dempsey-Brennan bout would not take place in that state." A lot of folks did not like the idea of a non-veteran earning huge sums of money. Hence, the governor's actions were no surprise to this newspaper.[951]

On August 19, after the local Michigan City, Indiana post of the American Legion pulled out as a sponsor, and Kearns had a long-distance telephone conversation with Governor McCray, he decided to pull out from the fight, convinced that it would not be allowed. Floyd Fitzsimmons could not give Kearns sufficient assurances that the bout would be allowed to be staged, and the governor insisted that it would not be permitted. Dempsey left town in disgust. Fitzsimmons had failed to clear the bout in advance with the politicians behind the scenes, something which Tex Rickard had learned was very important.

Dempsey said, "If the governor did not want us to box in Michigan City, I am glad he gave us enough warning. It would have been much worse had he waited until a few days before the contest. I believe in abiding by the law and when I heard he would not sanction it, I refused to be a party to any sort of agreement to evade the law."[952]

The New York Polo Grounds obtained Harry Wills' signature to fight Dempsey for 12.5% of the gate. Dempsey allegedly would be offered 37.5%, for a bout to be held on October 12.[953]

On August 21, 1922 in Newark, New Jersey, before a crowd of about 4,000, 215-pound Harry Wills scored a KO2 over 194-pound Buddy Jackson, defending his colored crown. Charles Mathison said, "Wills's condition and performance impressed the onlookers that he would make it very interesting for Jack Dempsey if he gets into the ring with the giant negro." Wills did not show whether he could assimilate the sort of punishment Dempsey could hand out, for Jackson could not land (and some said barely tried), but Wills was so powerful and so full of fight that it seemed that he could not fail to keep even the champion busy.

The New York Age noted that a mixed-race bout had been scheduled for that same card, but at the last minute, the New Jersey commission refused to allow it. Hence, signs were not good that Dempsey-Wills would be allowed there.[954]

A depressed Kearns told Jack Lawrence, "Jack's a great fighter, but he can't fight." They wouldn't let him fight Brennan in Michigan City, and it looked as though they would not let him fight Willard in New Jersey. "When Jack makes a match and really wants to fight, some governor or mayor pops up" and prevented it. Kearns said no tempting offer had been received for the Wills fight.[955]

[951] Collyer's Eye, August 19, 1922.
[952] Indianapolis Star, Muncie Star, Chicago Tribune, August 20, 1922.
[953] New York Daily News, August 18, 1922.
[954] New York Herald, Buffalo Times, August 22, 1922; New York Age, August 26, 1922.
[955] New York Tribune, August 24, 1922. Dempsey planned to box an exhibition on Labor Day in Michigan City with a sparring partner.

Cullen Cain for the *Philadelphia Public Ledger* said the upcoming Tunney vs. Loughran bout was one of the summer season's best matchups. "Loughran ought to outbox Tunney by a wide margin, and Tunney may be depended upon to force the pace. In all his past fights Loughran has shown great boxing skill, but has lacked aggressiveness."

Cain also said Jack Dempsey "may be caught in his own golden trap." By setting the price for his ring services so high, he was not fighting much. A year was a long lay-off, and now that the Indiana governor had stopped the Brennan bout, no doubt Jack would drift into his second year of idleness, with its corresponding rust and decline of his full powers and skill. Sooner or later, he would become "shelf-worn goods."[956]

On August 24, 1922 in Philadelphia, at the Phillies Ball Park, before a very large crowd of 20,000 - 22,000, 173-pound Gene Tunney won a close 8-round no decision against 163-pound local Philly-favorite 19-year-old Tommy Loughran (34-4-2).

The *Philadelphia Evening Public Ledger's* Louis Jaffe had it 4-3-2 for Tunney, who was entirely too big and strong for him, though Loughran rallied gamely at the end. Tunney decked Loughran in the 1st round with a right to the jaw, almost having him out. Gene crowded Tommy most of the time. Tunney's mouth bled from the first solid jab he received, having entered the ring with a previously damaged lip. Loughran showed speed and cleverness, and shook-up Gene momentarily in the 3rd. However, Tunney was the aggressor throughout.

Loughran said, "The weight was too much for me. I did not put up the bout of which I am capable, but I have no alibies." He was hurt in the 1st, and never felt like himself until late in the contest, near the end of the 7th. "I know I didn't put up my best fight. I can box a lot better."

The *Philadelphia Public Ledger's* Frank McCracken said Tunney's heavy guns conquered Loughran, who made a great finish despite being floored in the 1st round. The knockdown figured in the final reckoning. "He was sent down with a crashing right to the jaw," and was in a weak condition, rising at referee Rocap's count of nine. Loughran came back brilliantly, and it was only a hairline, but he lost. Tunney's 10 pounds greater weight was a big handicap, and he used his weight in the clinches. "Tommy lost, but not in popularity."

William Rocap, *Public Ledger* Sports Editor, who refereed the bout, said Tunney won, but Loughran's recovery after being decked stamped him as a big-timer. "To my mind it was only a question of that ten-pound advantage in weight enjoyed by Tunney that enabled him to come through the victor over Philadelphia's light-heavyweight hope." Showing that he had a hard punch, Tunney's right to the chin was "as true as a rifle bullet."

The *Philadelphia Evening Bulletin* also said Loughran put up a game fight, but lost. Even in the face of inevitable defeat, Loughran proved his staunch spirit. "Loughran proved conclusively that he is able to stand considerable punishment and still be able to come back fresh. But he also

[956] *Philadelphia Public Ledger*, August 23, 1922.

showed that his punch is not developed to the extent that it must be to take him to championship heights." Tommy landed a lot of clean blows, but none did any material damage, other than in the 2nd round, opening Gene's lip with a stiff left jab. A right in the 1st decked Loughran. After that, he fought much more cautiously, with better success, though Tunney's weight and power were evident throughout. "Tunney is a hard two-handed fighter but not the world's cleverest boxer." He missed several opportunities to land damaging blows. Loughran weakened perceptibly in the 6th and 7th rounds. Yet he finished strong in the 8th.

Loughran said, "Tunney is a hard man to beat, but I think I made more than a creditable showing."

Tunney said, "I thought it would be a much easier fight for me, but I wasn't over-confident. Loughran has many good points. … I think with more experience he will be able to go far."

In a minority opinion, the *Philadelphia Inquirer's* Perry Lewis gave it to Loughran on a hairline, for he rallied after being floored. This writer said Loughran landed the cleaner and sharper blows, and credited his superior ringcraft and masterful defense.

The *New York Evening Telegram* reported that the majority of newsmen gave Tunney the decision, though a few said Loughran did enough to earn a draw.[957]

Jack Kearns said demanding $500,000 guaranteed for Dempsey to box Wills was not too much, for the fight likely would generate well over a million dollars. They wanted half up front when the papers were signed, and the other half before the champion entered the ring. Kearns said Rickard was the only promoter with whom Dempsey would work on a percentage basis, for Tex was good for his word. Any other promoter would have to show them the money up front.[958]

On August 25, 1922 in St. Paul, Minnesota, Billy Miske knocked out Fred Fulton (75-8-3) in the 1st round, decking him twice, the first time with a left hook, and the second with a hook and overhand right. Fulton had been undefeated since his 1920 loss to Harry Wills, going 15-0-2.[959]

Some were mentioning a potential Dempsey bout with Luis Firpo. Dempsey said, "All I can say is that if Kearns says it's all right it goes. It's up to Kearns."[960]

The champion said he was not a big eater, and did not overeat. Regarding road work, Jack thought 5 miles was plenty, and he liked to change his pace throughout the run, inserting quick sprints for short distances. He judged by

[957] *Philadelphia Evening Public Ledger, Philadelphia Public Ledger, Philadelphia Evening Bulletin, Philadelphia Inquirer, New York Evening Telegram,* August 25, 1922.
[958] *New York Daily News, New York Herald,* August 25, 1922.
[959] *Minneapolis Morning Tribune, Minnesota Daily Star,* August 26, 1922. The fight drew $19,829.
[960] *Binghamton Press,* August 26, 1922.

his own feelings the pace he set, as well as when to stop, and how far to go.[961]

On August 29, 1922 at Ebbets Field in Brooklyn, before 17,000 spectators who generated over $60,000, 213 ½-pound Harry Wills scored a KO3 over 188 ½-pound Tut Jackson (35-1-3), another black fighter.

Despite the quick knockout victory, Thomas Rice said Wills failed to show that he deserved a bout with Dempsey. Nothing was proven by the contest; for Jackson was utterly incompetent, and either Wills was fighting under wraps and holding back, or he was not a fit opponent for Dempsey.

Rice admitted that he hoped Dempsey-Wills never would be held, "because of the disturbing influence it will have upon racial relations in many parts of the world." Regardless, Wills "displayed last night neither the science nor the punch to warrant any boxing fans paying more than $5 to see him tackle the white world's champion."

Nevertheless, newsmen agreed that Wills had dominated and won with ease, particularly with body blows, against an overmatched opponent who seemed afraid, barely tried, and never landed anything meaningful.

Rickard was negotiating for the possible use of Yankee stadium for a Dempsey-Wills fight. He also was discussing with Kearns the possibility of holding Dempsey-Brennan in October.[962]

Henry Farrell said Dempsey had nothing to worry about with Wills. "Dempsey can punch faster and hit harder than Wills. He is much faster on his feet, a better boxer, and he can take it 'downstairs' or on the chin." "Wills has won all his fights at close quarters. Many maintain he fights foul by holding and hitting." "Dempsey excels at the very kind of a fight that Wills would carry to him if the colored challenger followed his usual style against him. The champion is deadly at body punches at close quarters." Dempsey was at his best against big men, and would be perfectly comfortable with the "rough, wrestling-like tactics that Wills finds so effective." Farrell said Dempsey was faster, less hesitant, and more of a natural fighter than Wills. "Dempsey is not afraid of Wills. All this talk going on now that Kearns is dodging the colored challenger is but 'steam' to cook up the match and make it a popular card."[963]

Unfortunately, despite finishing a very close second to Wills in the *New York Daily News* poll regarding whom Dempsey should fight, the New York State Boxing Commission refused to sanction a Dempsey-Brennan fight, saying Bill had to prove his right to challenge Dempsey again. Commissioner William Muldoon said if Brennan first beat Miske, or some other suitable foe, he would authorize a Dempsey-Brennan bout. This was despite the fact that Brennan had put up a valorous effort against Dempsey in their last contest and had won 16 fights since then. Once again, politicians/administrators were getting in the way.[964]

[961] *New York Daily News*, August 28, 1922.
[962] *Brooklyn Daily Eagle, Brooklyn Standard Union, New York Times, New York Daily News, Brooklyn Citizen*, August 30, 1922.
[963] *Brooklyn Citizen*, August 31, 1922.
[964] *New York Herald*, August 31, 1922.

Kearns did not foresee a Wills match happening either, saying that too many governors were against the fight. Hence, the odds of it taking place were remote. Promoters had not even gotten a Brennan fight authorized, let alone Wills. Kearns said, "Let some promoter place $100,000 with the sporting editor of the *Tribune* to show faith he can go through with the match and Dempsey will fight Wills or anybody else tomorrow. If the promoter cannot go through with the contest then I will claim the forfeit." Meaning, don't make a match unless you have gotten it cleared first with the powers-that-be, and be certain enough about it that you are willing to post and forfeit significant money if you fail to make it happen.

Kearns said Wills should be matched with Miske, Brennan, or another top man to garner more momentum for the contest. "I am convinced [that] Wills, after the way he fought the other night, would not last 5 rounds with Dempsey."

Kearns was talking about taking Dempsey to Europe to fight Carpentier again. "Things don't look any too good in this country for a heavyweight match with Dempsey as one of the principals."

Indiana's governor did authorize Dempsey to perform in an actual sparring exhibition in Michigan City on Labor Day.[965]

Tom Sharkey said either Jeffries or Choynski would have beaten Dempsey. "Dempsey has to come to his opponent to be effective and that is just what Jeff liked. He slaughtered every one who did it." The only old-timer whom Sharkey believed Dempsey would have beaten was Corbett. "The trouble with boxers today is that they don't work hard enough when they reach the top. When they gain the championship they become actors and let their strength ebb away at some soft job."[966]

W. O. McGeehan said Harry Wills clearly was Dempsey's logical opponent. If the New York commission sanctioned any bout other than that one, then the commission "is incompetent − to say the least." Regardless, McGeehan was not saying that Dempsey would lose. "In fact, I am inclined to believe that Dempsey should be an easy victor." However, Wills was the most deserving of a title shot.[967]

Damon Runyon said Wills would prove to be a stout opponent for Dempsey. Some thought Harry should have disposed of Tut Jackson more handily and artistically, but Runyon said it should be remembered that Tut not only could not fight, but would not, and it was not an easy job to dispose of a man whose main idea was to pull and haul.

Runyon said Wills' style was criticized unjustly. Some thought it was foul because he had a trick of clamping his left under a foe's shoulder and yanking him to him while belting away with his right. It was doubtful that Dempsey would lodge any objection to that method, for he was a great body puncher, and "he could hardly ask anything better than to have an opponent pull him in. We should think the man apt to bother Dempsey

[965] *New York Daily News, Rochester Democrat and Chronicle, Chicago Tribune,* September 1, 1922; *South Bend Tribune,* September 3, 1922. Dempsey had been sparring in Chicago with Jimmy Darcy and Bermondsey Billy Wells.
[966] *Chicago Eagle,* September 2, 1922.
[967] *New York Herald,* September 3, 1922.

most is the fellow who keeps away from him." Wills liked the rabbit punch, but Dempsey liked that punch too. Both liked to hammer the kidneys as well. "In a state that stands for Harry Greb, however, we decline to admit that Wills' style is foul. And when the time comes, we do not believe that you will find Jack Dempsey offering the slightest criticism of it."

Runyon said Wills had changed his style materially in the last few years. "Seven or eight years ago he had a good left hand, and would slash away with it as he stepped and moved around. He had fine foot action. Now he seems to use his left more as an anchor and his footwork is largely a bound at his opponent to enable him to hook with the left." Such a style would suit Dempsey just fine. Regardless, Wills was big, strong, and experienced enough to give the champion a test.[968]

On Labor Day, September 4, 1922 in Michigan City, Indiana, which was about 50 - 60 miles from Chicago, using large gloves, Dempsey boxed 4 rounds of 2 minutes each, 2 apiece with black Jack Thompson and Andre Anderson. Despite the large gloves, it looked as if Jack could knock out either one if he wanted or really tried. Jack showed some compassion for Thompson, who would be his sparring partner for a contemplated theatrical tour, but he administered an awful lacing to Anderson.

On the same card, Joe Lynch successfully defended his world bantamweight championship title against Pal Moore in a 10-round no decision contest. Apparently, neither the law nor the governor cared about such a contest. That's politics for you.[969]

Hugh Fullerton said Dempsey was the fastest heavyweight he ever saw, and was a faster and harder hitter than Wills. He also had better footwork. Only Corbett was faster on his feet. Jack was very efficient, with no wasted motion. He bore in steadily, weaving and shifting, and driving in punches like a streak of light. "His blows travel much less distance than do those of Wills, travel straighter to the open spot and he seems to time them better." Wills was slower of hand and foot, had more wasted motion, did not shift as quickly, and took more time in launching his drives. Neither man was a long-range fighter, although at long range, Wills might have a shade because of his long reach and sharp-shooting left. "Wills at close quarters is wide open." Harry mostly used clinching for defense, holding with his left and hitting with his right.

Fullerton believed that Wills still had a chance with Dempsey, for he could punch and was strong. However, Dempsey had the edges in the areas of fighting spirit, speed, quickness in hitting, generalship, condition, legs, footwork, cleverness, defense, and stamina. Wills had the edges in sheer strength and experience.

[968] *Washington Times*, September 4, 1922.
[969] *Richmond Item, Chicago Tribune*, September 5, 1922.

Dempsey has all the advantage. At long range he has the better of the argument, his blows are straighter, cleaner, and applied with the least waste of effort.

Wills, in order to launch his knockout blows is compelled to draw back his arm and expose himself to a body attack. Dempsey, with his short arm drives, could land twice on Wills' body with his left while Wills is getting ready to sledge hammer downward with his right. In my opinion, after studying the two men, Dempsey will rip Wills's body and weaken him so much or force him to cover up so much that Wills's dangerous left and his deadly right will be worthless. The sole chance that I can see for Wills is for him to land his hooking, rasping left under Dempsey's heart early in the battle or to land one of his terrific right swings on Dempsey's jaw or near it.

The chances of such a blow landing with crippling effect I should figure at about one to three. Wills is wide open. ... In my opinion Dempsey has all the class and ought to win. But it is not a set up. ... The big colored man thinks he can whip Dempsey. When a colored man gets that idea he is dangerous.

Dempsey was hard to hit *effectively*. He tucked his jaw down, covered up by his shoulders, and kept his elbows close to his body, with arms held in front, and could weave as he advanced, swaying from side to side.

Big black 210-pound Jack Thompson, who sparred with Dempsey, remarked, "Mister, that man is the hardest man to hit in the world. I can hit him, but he aint never where you think he is. I miss him closer than any boxer I ever met. He just moves his jaw half an inch – and when you miss – wowie! – you get it."

Jack Taylor (who weighed around 185), another black sparring partner for Dempsey, said, "I hit more elbows and shoulders and tops of head boxing Jack, and fewer jaws and bodies than anyone in the world. He looks so easy to hit when he is coming at you, that it is a temptation to cut loose and bust him – but don't be tempted, mister – he is the fastest man with his eyes and hands you ever saw."

Fullerton did not believe Dempsey was dodging Wills. "He is willing to fight, even anxious to fight Wills." Kearns wanted to work up interest and secure a tremendous purse. Plus, there was uncertainty regarding whether the bout could be held.[970]

Len Wooster said, "There is no let up in the propaganda, agitation or whatever else you may wish to call it to sew up a Dempsey-Wills joust. All our best sport writers are on the job."[971]

---

[970] *Rochester Democrat and Chronicle*, September 4, 5, 8, 1922, *Chicago Tribune*, September 5, 1922.
[971] *Brooklyn Daily Times*, September 5, 1922.

CHAPTER 12

Politics of the Deep and Dark Kind

In early September 1922, New York State Boxing Commission chairman William Muldoon created rules and requirements that specifically would apply only to a Dempsey-Wills contest, which Ed Van Every said virtually would bar the bout in New York. The commission would require promoters to post a $250,000 bond, provide arrangements to seat at least 100,000, with 40,000 seats at just $2 each, with $15 as the top price. Such socialistic price-fixing/limits/controls would make the fight less economically feasible. Yet, that was what Muldoon was requiring, for this bout alone. Muldoon said the commission was not yet aware of any bona fide offer for the Dempsey-Wills fight.

The only sites that potentially had a seating capacity of 100,000 were the Polo Grounds and Yankee stadium, which still was under construction. Given the ticket price limits/requirements, many said Muldoon had "put the skids" under the proposed Dempsey-Wills match.

Essentially, Muldoon's financial restrictions were a way of showing that the fight was not wanted there, but he could not outright come out and say it, because the commission had pushed for the fight in its own way. The truth was that Muldoon historically had been a color line supporter, and many folks feared that a mixed-race heavyweight championship could result in the abolition of boxing in the state. Muldoon alluded to such, saying, "[I]f pugilism is given a black eye here and the game is killed in the leading state it will not live long elsewhere." Back in 1892, Muldoon had said, "There should be colored champions and white champions, and I would like to see the line drawn once and for all." But this way, the price controls could be spun as protecting the public, and since the impediments created were economic rather than racial, such would not offend certain constituencies. The commission could support the fight, but also thwart it.

With such price controls, Van Every estimated that the gross receipts would be only about $550,000, not likely to appeal to either the promoters or the managers; de facto killing New York as a possible Dempsey-Wills fight site. The gross receipts for the Carpentier fight the prior year in New Jersey were $1,626,580.

Responding to those critics who accused him of being prejudiced, Muldoon said, "They say I am opposed to the interests of the colored race in my capacity here, notwithstanding that I have given Harry Wills a chance to make more money in one bout than he has probably made in his entire career, and have forced the white champion to recognize his challenge." Muldoon insisted that Dempsey-Wills would be "handled in such a way as not to jeopardize the boxing game within the territory of this commission."[972]

Some reported that there was talk of the boxing law being repealed in New York, and banning the sport altogether. Governor Miller appeared amenable to such. "That is the talk on the inside. The much talked of Dempsey-Wills affair will never be staged in New York." Many politicians did not like the exorbitant financial demands that fighters were making, and wanted prices fixed.[973]

Jack Lawrence also said the New York commission mandate regarding Dempsey-Wills essentially barred the fight in New York. Lawrence noted Muldoon's hypocrisy. "It was Mr. Muldoon who insisted upon driving Dempsey into a match with the giant negro, Wills. Now, it would appear, he is anxious to drive the battle elsewhere, for Mr. Muldoon practically forbade the match in this state yesterday, when he announced the terms under which his commission would issue a license to promote a glove contest of such importance." No arena could hold 100,000 people. The Polo Grounds capacity was slightly over 80,000. The new Yankee Stadium, when completed, might fill the bill, but that would mean another year. Few promoters could afford the cost of a massive bond. Muldoon insisted emphatically that he had no prejudices against mixed bouts. Yet, he had created conditions for this bout alone which would thwart its occurrence.

New Jersey was not a viable alternative either, given the clear political animus towards a mixed-race championship. "[C]onditions are not ripe politically to go ahead with a big mixed bout over on the Jersey side right now."[974]

Harry Newman said a number of factors were preventing Dempsey-Wills. True, Dempsey/Kearns had exorbitant financial demands, but "politics is playing the most important part right now."[975]

In 1936, Mrs. Tex Rickard wrote a book called *Everything Happened to Him*, published by the Frederick A Stokes Company, New York. In it, she wrote that following the Carpentier fight, Tex tried to make Dempsey vs. Wills. He had promoted several mixed-race fights, including Gans-Nelson.

> At the height of the ballyhoo a very destructive bombshell in the form of the Boxing Commission blew Tex's plans higher than the statue of Diana on top of the Garden.
>
> "The State of New York," announced Chairman Muldoon of the Commission in sonorous tones, like Jehovah handing the tables to Moses, "will never permit a boxing contest between Mr. Dempsey and Mr. Wills."

[972] *New York Evening World*, September 6, 1922; *New York Daily News*, September 10, 1922. *National Police Gazette*, September 24, 1892.
[973] *Brooklyn Daily Times*, September 7, 1922.
[974] *New York Tribune, New York Evening World*, September 7, 1922.
[975] *New York Daily News*, September 9, 1922.

Tex knew, at that moment the word was relayed to him, that he might as well forget the match, since he had as much chance of changing the minds of the triumvirate of politicos who made up the Commission as a Russian peasant of pre-war days had of telling the Czar exactly what he thought of him. The masters of New York fisticuffs had spoken; the better part of valor, as far as he was concerned, was to hurry up and get a new contender for Dempsey's crown.

On September 9, 1922 in New York, at the annual police field-day games, which drew crowds of up to 50,000, Dempsey exhibited in a good-natured manner against featherweight Babe Herman and another sparring partner. Police commissioner Richard Enright refereed.[976]

The *Duluth News-Tribune* wrote that no one seemed to know just how good a fighter Harry Wills was. It had been a long time since he was extended in a bout. "Ever since there was a chance that he might get a match for the title he has met nothing but set-ups."

In recent years, Wills had changed his style. Back in 1915, he was clever, but not hard-hitting or tough enough to trade with Sam Langford, though he could outmaneuver him, using a left jab and nimble footwork to win popular decisions. Langford knocked him out a couple times.

Of late Wills has grown stronger and he has learned to hit harder, but it is a long time since he showed a trace of boxing skill. Now he wins all his battles by mauling with one arm free. At long range he is wild and does no great amount of damage, but at close quarters he has had no trouble battering down the third raters he has met.

Aside from whether Harry's style of fighting is foul, there is no question that it is unsightly and primitive in the extreme. He shows none of the skill of a trained boxer, but a world of strength and hitting ability.

Wills has won all his recent bouts by the simple method of holding his opponent fast in the hollow of his left arm and belaboring him with the right hand.

Sometimes his foes were foul and at fault, because they tried to hold him, and he hit them legally, like with Tut Jackson. Other times, he did the holding and hitting, as he did with Fulton.

[976] *Brooklyn Daily Eagle, New York Daily News,* September 10, 1922.

At all times Harry's style borders on the foul and very often it crosses the line. In any case it is far from pleasing to the crowd. Wills has indulged in it to such an extent that there now is a question of whether he can fight any other way. … By mauling in the clinches he escapes punishment himself and at the same time he can do damage enough to beat his man down.

Wills could get away with such a style against frightened set ups who held and did not fight back much. It was a question whether it would work against those who hit back.

It is said that he cannot stand a wallop on the jaw and that probably is true. Everyone who has hit him on the chin has knocked him down and some of them were not first-class men by any means.

As a boxer Wills is a long way behind Dempsey, judging by their work in recent bouts. The Wills of 1916 was a better boxer than Dempsey is today, but it is so long since Harry has shown anything in that line it is reasonable to suppose that he has forgotten how to hit and get away.[977]

On September 24, 1922 in Stade Buffalo, Montrouge, France, a southern Paris suburb, before a crowd of 50,000 or 60,000, in a huge upset, 174-pound black Battling Siki (49-9-3) of Senegal (a French colony) knocked out 173 ½-pound Georges Carpentier in the 6th round to win the world light heavyweight championship. The fight was filmed, and it was an exciting, competitive scrap, with a controversial ending.

On the films, in the 1st round, Carpentier decked Siki with a short right. Siki rose quickly and seemed to be okay. Carp moved subtly in and out, calmly pecking away and looking to land his right, while Siki had a crab-like, crouching, arms-crossed defense.

In the 3rd round, Carp's outstretched left stiff-arm was followed quickly by an explosive right that sent Siki down to the canvas for the second time in the fight.

Siki rose immediately and played defense very well, crouching down low, covering up, moving a bit, having sturdy balance. Yet, a Carp combination penetrated and staggered him. Carp chased him to the ropes, where another right decked Siki for the second time in the round, the third time in the fight.

Siki rose at about the count of 7 and fought back, countering Carp's attempts to finish him. Siki landed a jolting right uppercut. When Carp overthrew a right, Siki's counter right seemed to hurt him a bit, sending Georges backwards. Siki stepped in and belted away with a combination to the head, the final right decking Carpentier.

[977] *Duluth News-Tribune*, September 17, 1922.

Carp rose in a few seconds, moved in, and attempted to clinch, but Siki kept working, hitting the body and nailing his jaw with a right uppercut. Carp fired away with both hands, and Siki worked his right uppercut. They went at it, each trying to land a big blow. The exciting 3rd round ended, and at that point, it looked like anybody's fight. Both seemed able to hurt the other.

At the start of the 4th round, Siki was the aggressor, working away as Carp was more defensive, seeming either tired, a bit hurt, or pacing himself. However, eventually the game Carp exploded again with several combinations that made Siki cover up for a while. Yet, once Carp slowed down, Siki sensed it and began firing to the head and body, seeking to capitalize on his fatigue. Carp was defensive, and took several blows.

According to newsmen, Siki had split Carpentier's lips and started closing his right eye in the 4th round.

In the 5th round, Siki kept plugging away consistently on the inside, while Carp was defensive, leaning in with his arms crossed, seeming fatigued, rarely throwing. Siki lambasted him, though Carp nailed him with a left hook near the end of the round.

In the 6th round, Siki kept pelting Carpentier with a shower of blows to the body and head, including his right uppercut, and Carpentier went down and out. Yet, the referee did not count. Carp never received a count. He was down, frozen on the canvas. Newsmen said he was out of it for 30 seconds.

The reason Referee Henri Bernstein did not count was that he ruled that Carpentier had been fouled. The referee disqualified Siki, claiming he had tripped Carpentier. The fans booed vociferously. The press believed Carp had been whipped fairly. 20 minutes later, the judges overruled him, apparently an option in France. The referee was supposed to consult the judges before disqualifying a contestant, and since he did not, and the judges both believed Carpentier had been beaten, it was a Siki victory. At first glance, it seems as if Carpentier was fatiguing, hurt, and knocked out.

Yet, a review of the slow-motion version of the films reveals a foul, for Siki stuck out and swung his left leg in an unnatural sweeping manner to the right, not only tripping but jolting Carp's left leg, twisting his leg/ankle as a result and sending him down. Carp even kept his leg high up in the air, holding it with his left glove while on the canvas. So, quite interestingly, the referee's foul claim was justified. Siki indeed appeared to kick/trip him intentionally. What at first glance seemed to be a matter of bias actually had a basis in fact. But one might not notice it on a first, live viewing, in normal speed.

Afterwards, Carpentier said, "I made the mistake of trying to study Siki in the early rounds. He got over a lucky punch and took all my strength away. I hit him with everything I had. He has wonderful powers of recuperation. His race is not made like mine."[978]

---

[978] *Oklahoma News, London Daily Telegraph*, September 25, 1922. The *London Daily Telegraph's* B. Bennison said Siki was nicknamed "The Fighting Ape."

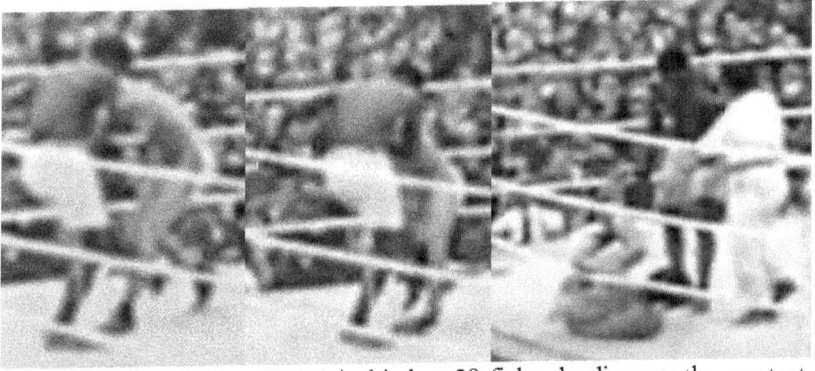

Siki, who had gone 28-0-1 in his last 29 fights leading up the contest, challenged Dempsey to fight.[979] Siki was the first black world champion in more than 7 years, since Jack Johnson lost the heavyweight title in 1915.

Jack Dempsey would embark on a vaudeville tour starting October 9 and continuing until December 24. The tour would start in Toronto and conclude in San Diego, California.[980]

On September 29, 1922 at New York's Madison Square Garden, 213 ¾-pound Harry Wills stopped 204-pound black Clem Johnson (10-13-2) in the 12th round, when the referee intervened while Johnson was helpless on the ropes.

Charles Mathison said although Wills outclassed him, the performance was less than impressive, given that it took Wills 12 rounds to stop a relative unknown. Johnson took a terrific beating, but survived by doing a lot of clinching. Wills was not a great puncher or finisher though, and his punches often were wild. The spectators "were of the opinion that Wills would not last very long in a contest with Jack Dempsey. Wills's boxing was mediocre, and as Johnson, while on the defensive, reached Wills's jaw a great many times, it would be an easy matter for a sharpshooter like Dempsey to land on the mark."

Ben Rosenberg said Wills was disappointing, for his blows lacked steam. "Slowly but surely the drawing power of a bout between Harry Wills and Jack Dempsey is waning." Many increasingly were feeling that Wills would be no match for the champ. "Dempsey undoubtedly could have finished Johnson in one round last night."

Jack Kearns, who was there, remarked, "Gosh, someone's going to knock that bird out before we get him."

Ed Van Every said if Wills gave a few more performances like that, the boxing board no longer would have to insist that the club staging the proposed Dempsey-Wills fight seat 100,000 people. Wills was "fed another set up," but despite being in there with a punching bag, he struggled to finish him off. Johnson rarely fought back, but, "Even at that he shook up Wills now and then with blows to the jaw."

979 *New York Daily News, Yonkers Herald, New York Herald*, September 25, 1922. Siki said he wanted a million dollars to fight Harry Wills. *Buffalo Express*, September 26, 1922.
980 *Yonkers Herald*, September 26, 1922. On a vacation hunting trip at St. John, N.F. Canada, Dempsey killed a 700-pound Canadian moose. *Glens Falls Post-Star*, September 28, 1922.

The *Brooklyn Citizen* said Wills failed to show real class, and was lacking a knockout punch.

The *Brooklyn Standard Union* said Wills' performance was poor, requiring 12 rounds to stop a prelim fighter. Even then, he never knocked Johnson off his feet. "The referee finally brought the agonizing thing to an end, after a thousand of Wills' punches failed to do it." Harry appeared to have forgotten his boxing skills. He was wide open, and drew his hands way back before punching. Johnson rarely threw, but when he did, he landed flush on the chin.

Thomas Rice said the bout was a wearisome joke. Wills displayed little punch, but beat up Johnson, who survived by clinching.

The *New York Times* said the "negro's chances of dethroning Dempsey took a downward trend in the opinion of the majority of those who witnessed his exhibition against Johnson." Wills failed to show any startling ability at long range, his attack was confused and uncertain, he missed many blows like a novice, and though he landed plenty of times, not once did his foe drop.

Even Harry Newman said the Black Panther's prestige suffered by letting his inexperienced, slow, plodding but willing opponent last so long. Wills hit him with everything, and was open to blows himself. The ringside comment was if he fought the same way against Dempsey, Wills would be knocked out quickly.

That same night, September 29, 1922 in Grand Rapids, Michigan, Harry Greb won a 10-round no decision over Bob Roper by outboxing him, significant because Roper was coming off a 12-round draw with Billy Miske earlier that month.[981]

FLOYD JOHNSON.

On the afternoon of October 2, 1922 at Stillman's gym in New York, Jack Dempsey sparred 3 rounds with Iowa's 195-pound Floyd Johnson (23-2-7). The champ rocked Johnson with a few rights, but did not try to land a finishing blow. Between each round, Dempsey gave the promising up-and-coming Johnson advice and tips, for Floyd was preparing for a bout with Bob Martin in four days. Jack Lawrence said Dempsey's stuff was "amazing," and he appeared to be just as good as he did a year ago. He still was quick and powerful.[982]

On October 6, 1922 at Madison Square Garden, 194-pound Floyd Johnson stopped 188-pound Bob Martin (43-9-1) in the 10th round.

Dempsey had attended World Series games (New York Yankees vs. New York Giants) on the 4th and the 6th, at the Polo Grounds.

---

[981] *New York Herald, Brooklyn Daily Times, New York Evening World, Brooklyn Citizen, New York Daily News, Brooklyn Standard Union, Brooklyn Daily Eagle, New York Times*, September 30, 1922.
[982] Dempsey and Johnson sparred 3 rounds again on the 3rd. *Brooklyn Citizen, Brooklyn Daily Times, New York Tribune*, October 3, 1922; *New York Evening World*, October 4, 1922.

Jack Dempsey (right), world's fistic champion, came out of the press stand at Polo Grounds before third game of World Series just long enough to pose with John McGraw, world's greatest ball club manager, and Cozy Dolan, Giant coach.

The complete Dempsey-Carpentier films were showing in Salt Lake City. An ad was posted in the local newspaper. Clearly, folks associated with the promotion/filming had utterly disregarded the federal law against the interstate transportation of fight films.[983]

Will "Babe" Philbrick declared that Dempsey-Wills never should take place, despite Dempsey's desire to take the fight that would make him the most money. He said Dempsey's decision not to draw the color line, brought on by the New York State Boxing Commission, was a big mistake, despite economics and the desire to have the best two boxers face one another. He wrote,

> The history of mixed bouts has shown that these things cannot be without bringing about race prejudice. No matter what the Constitution says about all men being equal, you cannot change the mind of the individual and white people cannot be legislated into believing that they are no more than equal to the colored races, whether they are black, brown, or yellow. … Is the public mind so short that it does not remember the search for a white hope to beat down Jack Johnson, an undeniably clever boxer whose claims that he was hounded are not without foundation. If Johnson had been white, many of his sins would have been overlooked. While the New York State Boxing Commission's ruling that champions, to keep their titles, should battle with logical contenders, is undoubtedly right in spirit, but for the good of the game, the color line should be drawn.[984]

The *Buffalo Commercial's* C. J. Murray said quite a few New York sportswriters liked to jab a harpoon into Harry Wills. "Maybe they draw the color line. But whatever the reason is, Wills gets more than his share of panning." Murray said he was not a Wills admirer, and would cheer if Dempsey knocked him out. "But the critic who closes his eyes to talent is a chump. Wills can fight. Anyone who thinks he can't doesn't know much about fighting." He was the "only man…with a chance to lick Dempsey."

However, writers like W. N. Jones of the *New York Globe* said,

---

[983] *Buffalo Commercial*, October 5, 1922. The champ was scheduled for another tour, which would include Buffalo, Toronto, and other Canadian towns, working west all the way to California.
[984] *Binghamton Press*, October 5, 1922.

[The Wills-Clem Johnson bout] proved conclusively what we have long contended – that Wills is a greatly overrated fighter, and hardly in a class with Jack Dempsey. Seven or eight years ago Wills was a pretty good scrapper, but he has slipped considerably, and for the last few years has been getting by on his reputation. …

Wills couldn't do a thing in two bouts with Bill Tate out on the Pacific coast last year and Tate was just a punching bag for Dempsey when he was a member of Jack's training corps.

Jack Thompson who is one of Dempsey's sparring mates now, and just as much a mark for the champ as was Tate, has held off Wills on several occasions.

Jones predicted that Wills would not last 3 rounds with Dempsey.[985]

Muscular Jack Thompson, Dempsey's sparring partner, who had fought Wills multiple times, said Wills would not last 2 rounds with Dempsey. Thompson proclaimed Dempsey as the most terrific hitter he ever met, while Wills was not even a fair puncher by comparison.

In 11 battles he never even stung me, yet with eight-ounce gloves Dempsey hit me on the arm and for two days I couldn't lift it. For hours it was paralyzed. If Jack just hooks his left into Wills' stomach the fight will be over. Neither he nor any other man can stand under the punishment that Jack can hand out with regulation gloves.[986]

On October 7, 1922 in Boston, at the Faneuil A.C. show in Mechanic's Building, Dempsey exhibited 4 rounds of two minutes each with "giant negro" Jack Thompson, his regular sparring partner. Dempsey liked Thompson because he was big and tough enough to take his blows, and attack and give back enough to make it interesting and make him work. Allegedly, Dempsey knocked out a couple of Thompson's teeth.[987]

Dempsey's theatrical tour would start in Toronto on October 9, 1922 and take him all the way to the West Coast.

Jack said he was waiting around for action. He was doing the stage stuff to earn money, for it was the only avenue open to him at present. "The stage is all right, but it's a tough grind and I'm not crazy about it. Fighting is my business, but for me there isn't any business."

Dempsey said he would fight Wills just as soon as soon as a legitimate offer was made, along with a guarantee of a location to host the fight. They had received no offers. Furthermore, "They're razzing Wills something awful for that last fight he put up in New York. I hope they don't pick him to pieces before I get a shot at him." "Jocko" Kearns chimed in, "If they give me a decent sum, I'll make the [Wills] match for

[985] *Buffalo Commercial*, October 6, 1922. Dempsey was advertised to be at the Buffalo auditorium on Monday October 9, stopping en route from New York to Toronto. *Buffalo Times*, October 7, 1922.
[986] *Boston Globe*, October 3, 1922.
[987] *Boston Globe*, October 7, 8, 1922.

July 4th or any date." Dempsey said he was willing to fight Battling Siki as well, "tonight, if I could."[988]

C. J. Murray said,

> Dempsey is really anxious to trade punches with the ebony-hued giant [Wills]. There are no ifs or ands about that. Some people believe the champion would like to sidestep Wills. That is not true. Dempsey would rather step in and fight Wills than dodge the issue. The champion is chockful of confidence on this particular match. He actually believes he can 'sock' (Dempsey's pet substitution for punch) Wills into dreamland in a few rounds. This writer doesn't share Dempsey's opinion. Wills is a fighter. You can't take that away from him. He is a wicked puncher. He would at least give Dempsey a grueling battle.

Dempsey said he rarely watched his opponents, which was unusual, for most fighters liked to utilize some advance preparation to get a line on their foes. Jack said if Wills knew he was watching, he might pull and not show his best stuff. Or he might fight one way when Jack was watching, and fight another in their actual contest. Jack prepared by expecting everything. He also feared overconfidence, for if he saw a fighter and was not impressed, he might not train as hard as he would if he didn't know what was coming. "Any man who fights when he's not in tiptop shape is crazy. I tried it once, with Fireman Jim Flynn and he knocked me out. Never again." Jack said he actually got more nervous watching fights than he did fighting himself. "And still I literally love to fight."

The champ said he was at Grupp's gym on Thursday October 5, and there was a big fellow, almost as big as Willard, with the most marvelous physique he ever saw. He had the strength of a bull. That fellow asked Jack to put on the gloves with him, and the champ obliged him.

> I wasn't mistaken about his strength. He could break steel bars with his hands. He had twice as much strength as yours truly. But just to prove to you that bull strength doesn't mean much in boxing, I fooled him around for a minute or so and gave him a little poke on the jaw. … Down he goes. His nose on the floor and he's out. … It's a queer game – this boxing. You must watch your step every second and keep the button covered up.[989]

On October 8, 1922 in Buenos Aires, Argentina, Luis Firpo knocked out Jim Tracey in the 4th round.

The *Brooklyn Standard Union* said the winner of the upcoming Miske vs. Gibbons fight likely would get a chance at the crown. It was an excellent matchup. "Both are fast, clever boxers, and each can punch hard enough to knock the other over." Miske had looked so good in recent bouts and in his training that he was the betting favorite. Gibbons the previous year had a string of about 19 knockouts in a row until he ran into Greb, but

[988] *Buffalo Commercial*, October 9, 1922.
[989] *Buffalo Commercial*, October 10, 1922.

many unfairly judged him based on that bout. He was stale, and Greb never did hurt him. "Mechanically, Gibbons is about as perfect as it is possible for a human to become. He boxes every bit as well as his brother Mike and has a lot of the speed and style of Jack Dempsey along with it. When he crouches and weaves his head from side to side he presents a mighty difficult target for anyone to shoot at." Gibbons had knockout power, and was a harder puncher than Miske, even though Billy weighed more. Still, both men could punch.[990]

Jack Lawrence said Miske in training "seemed to us yesterday to be the most formidable heavyweight we have looked upon since we watched Jack Dempsey preparing for his historic meeting with Georges Carpentier." Weighing 189 pounds, Billy seemed to be a revived and rejuvenated fighter. "Yesterday Miske appeared to us to be the nearest approach to a Jack Dempsey that we have seen."[991]

On October 13, 1922 at New York's Madison Square Garden, 176-pound Tommy Gibbons (79-2-4) clearly was winning his fight against 187-pound Billy Miske (72-12-15), but was disqualified controversially in the 10th round for a low blow, though many thought he should have won by knockout. The bout only raised Gibbons' stock, for he appeared to be en route to certain victory at the time, regardless of whether there was a low blow.

During that 10th round, some said a paralyzing right to the pit of the stomach decked Miske. Referee Kid McPartland, who did not see it, after consulting with one of the judges, ruled it was a foul blow, and disqualified Gibbons, but the spectators and much of the press insisted that it was a fair blow. Some insisted there was a low blow amongst the combination of punches, yet questioned whether it was the low blow that ended Miske. Others said the disqualification was fair, but the bout still proved that Gibbons was the better man.

Brooklyn Daily Times sportswriter Ben Rosenberg said the referee was incompetent, and deprived Gibbons of his rightful victory by 10th round knockout, disgusting thousands of fans. Afterwards, Miske was booed and Gibbons cheered.

Harry Newman of the *New York Daily News* said Miske was beaten, but made a fake cry of foul. "It looked like a deliberate quit on the part of Miske, who got the worst beating of his life up to the time of the alleged foul punch." Gibbons insisted it was fair and well above the belt line. Ringside spectators agreed.

The *Brooklyn Citizen*'s William Granger said the verdict of the majority of fans at ringside was that Miske quit. Gibbons had outclassed him by a wide margin in every round. Granger said Gibbons missed a left to the

[990] *Brooklyn Standard Union*, October 13, 1922.
[991] *New York Tribune*, October 10, 1922.

body and followed with a right that landed on the chest, sending Miske down. Yet, Judge Artie McGovern substantiated Miske's claim of foul. Gibbons had Miske hurt and befuddled. "Gibbons is easily his master."

The *New York Tribune's* Jack Lawrence said, "The blow appeared to be a right hook that landed squarely in the pit of the stomach." Gibbons urged Miske to continue, declaring that the blow was not low, and the biggest fight crowd that attended a Garden bout that year seemed to agree with Tommy. "The fight was the best that has been seen in Madison Square Garden this year, and Gibbons had a decisive lead when it ended." It had been an exciting, fast and furious contest.

However, the *New York Herald's* Charles Mathison said the blow was palpably low and the disqualification deserved. Yet, Mathison admitted that Gibbons had outboxed, outpunched, and outgeneraled Miske throughout. Miske was a thoroughly beaten man.

The *Brooklyn Daily Eagle's* W. C. Vreeland suggested that although the blows may have been foul, landing on the left side of the groin, the feeling was that Miske was not that hurt, for he was wearing an aluminum protective cup, and it was not dented, and he used a trick to obtain victory and get himself out of a fight he was losing. Gibbons "was a winner, on points, by a wide margin, until the fatal tenth session."

Robert Edgren said Gibbons, with a big lead, on the verge of a knockout victory, landed an accidental foul blow. It went just a few inches below the belt. It was a combination – a crack on the chin, hard left to the stomach, another that went below the belt, and the third punch landed in the pit of the stomach again, and Miske went down.

> From where I sat at the edge of the ring I saw the low blow clearly – even saw Tom's glove rumple Miske's silk fighting trunks where it landed. The referee could give no other decision. Still it is doubtful that the blow was low enough to hurt Miske as much as the two punches that struck him fairly in the solar plexus in almost the same instant, and that might easily have put him down for the count.

The *Brooklyn Standard Union* said Gibbons handed out a lacing, giving Miske one of the worst beatings administered to a high-class fighter in a long time, but was disqualified for a clearly low blow. Most thought Miske had faked rather than admit defeat. "But that isn't true. Billy Miske doesn't do things that way." He stood up under a terrible plastering for 9 rounds. "He's all heart." But he needed more, for "Tommy is the most perfect boxing machine among the big fellows." Gibbons outgeneraled him, and might have knocked him out in another round or two, while defensively he was a marvel, blocking, slipping, and eluding punches. On both defense and attack, Gibbons was graceful, smooth, and efficient. He constantly was in-and-out, landing and eluding. He hooked, stabbed, and crossed to the body and head, and was the complete master of the situation.

Ultimately, the press treated Gibbons as the better man, even if technically he had not won the fight.[992]

Gibbons' performance was significant, given that since losing to Dempsey in late 1920, Billy Miske had gone 17-0-1 if one counts newspaper decision victories, including a close 1921 WND10 Bill Brennan; and 1922 KO1 Willie Meehan and KO1 Fred Fulton. This garnered more momentum for a Gibbons title challenge.

The *New York Tribune*'s Grantland Rice said, "Jack Dempsey's opponent remains hidden somewhere in the future. The poor showing made by Harry Wills and the lack of bidding on this bout have taken away some of the early edge." Carpentier's recent defeat ruined a potential lucrative European rematch.[993]

W. O. McGeehan said any bout against Wills could not take place in winter, for only outdoor arenas were big enough to hold the necessary spectators. The New York commission would not let Dempsey fight Brennan.

Kearns lamented, "Every time we seem to be getting somebody built up for Jack some other bird comes along and unexpectedly knocks him kicking. And Mr. Muldoon won't let Jack take one more sock at Bill Brennan."[994]

Eddie Kane, Gibbons' manager, said Tom wanted to meet the champion. "Gibbons is now in the best form of his career and he believes he is entitled to a chance at the heavyweight title."[995]

There was talk of Madison Square Garden potentially hosting a tournament amongst the heavies, with the winner to fight Dempsey.[996]

On October 27, 1922 in Boston, 175 ½-pound Gene Tunney easily won a 10-round decision over 174-pound Chuck Wiggins (55-23-12), who mostly feinted and covered up, playing defense as Tunney attacked. Some said the bout was slow, with a great deal of clinching and neither man doing damage.[997]

Harry Wills and Jack Johnson agreed to fight in Newark. However, obstacles would need to be removed. "Johnson has been barred in New Jersey, as well as in every other state in the country," and unless the bar was lifted, he would not be allowed to fight.[998]

William Muldoon said he would consent to Dempsey being allowed to meet the winner of a Brennan vs. Gibbons fight.[999]

In late October, Tex Rickard said Tommy Gibbons was the only white man capable of giving Dempsey a real battle. "Gibbons is big enough to tackle any fighter in the ring today. I would be glad to stage a battle

---

[992] *Brooklyn Daily Times, New York Herald, New York Daily News, Brooklyn Daily Eagle, Brooklyn Citizen, New York Tribune, New York Evening World, Brooklyn Standard Union*, October 14, 1922. That same day, Gibbons' father died of stomach cancer, though Tom was not told until after the bout.
[993] *New York Tribune*, October 15, 1922.
[994] *New York Herald*, October 16, 1922.
[995] *Brooklyn Daily Times*, October 24, 1922.
[996] *Buffalo Times*, October 27, 1922.
[997] *Boston Globe, New Castle Herald*, October 28, 1922. Wiggins previously had fought Greb three times in 1921, most saying the fights were draws, though Greb clearly won their 1922 10-round no decision.
[998] *New York Daily News*, October 30, 1922.
[999] *New York Evening World*, October 31, 1922.

between Gibbons and the champion. If I can't get that match I would like to have Gibbons and Greb for a return bout, or Gibbons against Gene Tunney." Rickard did not think Brennan could be induced to fight Gibbons. "Gibbons, in my opinion, stands head and shoulders over every other contender for the world heavyweight championship, so far as white men are concerned. He is today, I believe, a better man than Carpentier ever was."[1000]

The *Yonkers Statesman and News* wrote that Tommy Gibbons might fight Dempsey next. "Gibbons is treated by some of the experts as the only fighter of the present era who has a chance to beat Jack and he may be given this opportunity very soon."[1001]

The Ontario Athletic Commission in Toronto frowned upon a potential Dempsey-Wills fight. Floyd Fitzsimmons had been trying to see if the fight could be held there.[1002]

Harry Newman believed Gibbons was big enough to tackle the champ. He could hit, was skillful, experienced, and bigger than Carpentier. "In the old days they never quibbled over the weight question. The only thought was when and where do we fight?"[1003]

The British Empire's Home Office forbade a proposed Joe Beckett vs. Battling Siki heavyweight contest, saying that "contests between white and black men are not compatible with the interests of the Empire."

The *London Daily Telegraph's* B. Bennison said, "The vetoing of the fight will surprise no one; it was inevitable." Such a fight "would have made for an entirely undesirable condition of things; the probability is that it would have killed professional boxing."

England's *Daily Mail* also noted, "Such contests, considering that there are a very large number of men of colour in the British Empire, are considered against the highest national interest, and they tend to arouse passions which it is inadvisable to stimulate. The Home Office relies upon the precedent made when the Johnson-Wells fight was contemplated in 1911." Just as the Home Office had prevented Jack Johnson vs. Billy Wells in 1911, it prevented Siki vs. Beckett in 1922. Many lamented that Carpentier-Siki had been allowed. The Home Office certainly was not going to allow Dempsey-Siki or Dempsey-Wills anywhere in the Empire.

In the *London Evening Standard*, Sir Arthur Conan Doyle, famous for his Sherlock Holmes novels, supported the Home Secretary in his decision to prohibit the Siki-Beckett fight.

> There is no good object in these colour matches. Sport has nothing to gain by them. Let black and white keep separate and fight straight among themselves. ... Nowadays a mixed fight gets beyond sport, and enters the region of inter-racial politics. There is no doubt that, whoever wins, bad feeling is created between the white races and the black.

[1000] *New York Daily News*, October 31, 1922; *Pittsburgh Post*, November 1, 1922.
[1001] *Yonkers Statesman and News*, November 2, 1922.
[1002] *Brooklyn Daily Eagle*, November 3, 1922.
[1003] *New York Daily News*, November 5, 1922.

Furthermore, Siki recently had struck another fighter's manager, and as a result of his actions, the French announced that they were stripping him of his French title and suspending him for 9 months. The proposal to suspend Siki for life was defeated narrowly by a vote of 8 to 6. Bennison wrote, "Boxing France has but shed her swaddling clothes, and there is cause for suspecting that she already regrets that the opportunity was given to Siki to fight Carpentier."

The *Liberte* in France said it was lucky for Siki that the incident took place in France. "If it had occurred in America, or even in England, spectators would have taken his punishment into their own hands, and they would have been right."

Bennison further noted, "In all my long experience I have known but very few negroes who, once they had beaten a white fighter of high degree, did not become insufferable. Peter Jackson and Joe Jeannette were the exception that proved the rule." Bennison said Siki, like Jack Johnson, was "given to strutting and posturing, and is generally obnoxious." At first, Johnson was modest, but after he won the title, "he was a menace not only to sport, but to law and order. The scandal of his fight with Jim Jeffries made it impossible for a white and black man ever to fight again for a world's title. Johnson as near as possible sounded the death-knell of boxing." Such was why Dempsey-Wills never would be allowed.

Bennison called Siki an "obtuse nigger," and regretted that after his defeat of Carpentier, "men of his colour grinned and leered into the faces of whites. The victory of Siki to them was not a victory for Siki the individual; it was the conquest of a black at the expense of a white." "[T]he gloating of the negro element in the multitude of folk who looked on was a sickening sight. ... There was scarcely a place on the sidewalk for the white."

Even the *San Francisco Examiner's* Bill Yeager wrote of Siki, "The big colored fellow would live a short life in this country if he started any of the rough stuff he pulls in France."[1004]

Clearly, concerns about mixed-race boxing contests were not limited to the United States. It was a world-wide issue.

On November 10, 1922 in Buffalo, New York, before a crowd of 7,000 to 8,000, 168-pound Harry Greb won a 12-round decision over 180-pound Bob Roper. The grueling fight featured a lot of head butting by both men, and both were cut as a result. The *Buffalo Commercial* wrote, "Speed is Greb's middle name. If the Pittsburgher had a knockout wallop he would be the greatest fighter of the age, but he sacrifices the old kayo sting for speed and must depend solely on this to carry him to victory."

The *Buffalo Enquirer* said Greb gave Roper a sweet lacing. "Yet, the loser was never in serious danger at any time of the contest simply because Greb doesn't carry a knockout punch, never did and, so it would seem, never will." "He is the same lunging, plunging battler." He threw with bewildering abandon and activity. He seemed wide open, winging,

[1004] *London Daily Telegraph, London Evening Standard, Daily Mail, San Francisco Examiner,* November 10, 1922.

flinging, and whaling away, yet his amazing awkwardness seemed to bewilder foes. He was like a bounding rubber ball, inside one second and outside the next. He had wonderful stamina, and could take a punch.

Bob Stedler for the *Buffalo Times* said Greb was too fast, aggressive, and busy for Roper. "Greb's punches, however, did not seem to carry the steam necessary for a heavyweight."

The *Buffalo Evening News* said Greb's whirlwind attack bewildered Roper. "Greb used his full bag of tricks in the early rounds. He swung and smashed and poked and banged and jabbed and uppercut and hammered and cuffed and poked and ripped and mugged and jumped in and out," having Roper battered and bleeding. Roper's smashes only stirred up Greb even more.[1005]

On November 13, 1922 in Detroit, Michigan, Tommy Gibbons knocked out 115-fight veteran George Ashe in the 1st round.

Tex Rickard said he would promote a Wills-Dempsey match if and when he was assured of the public demand for it and was certain there would be no legal/political objections or interference. He was concerned that there was prejudice against the idea of a mixed bout for the heavyweight championship. "As soon as they convince me that everything is O.K. I would be glad to put on the big bout."

Word was that the politicians, including New York Governor Nathan Miller, had been concerned that a mixed-race contest could impact their ability to secure re-election. Chances for the fight being allowed in 1923 were better, given that it would be after the 1922 elections. Or so it was hoped.[1006]

The *Nashville Tennessean* said Dempsey was the biggest attraction in boxing, but had no one marketable to fight. Wills was not a great option, for various reasons. "First of all, Wills is a negro and mixed bouts are not popular with the authorities. It is not even certain a fight between Jack and the black would be tremendously thrilling to the public at large. Not so thrilling at least, as to induce some ninety or a hundred thousand of the fans to pay big money to see the go." Many thought Wills was past his prime anyhow.[1007]

On November 19, 1922 at the Pantages theater in Memphis, as part of his theatrical tour, Dempsey knocked out with a straight right to the jaw his husky sparring partner Johnny Lee, who sank to the floor in a mass.[1008]

Frank Menke said that some of the same folks who said Carpentier was big and strong enough to beat Dempsey now were saying that Gibbons was too light to beat him.

> It may be that Gibbons can't whip Dempsey. But one thing is certain, and that is if the French False Alarm was deserving of a crack at a world's championship, Gibbons is worthy of ten of them. For Tom Gibbons has more real fighting blood in his ankles than

[1005] *Buffalo Commercial, Buffalo Enquirer, Buffalo Evening News* November 11, 1922.
[1006] *New York Daily News,* November 13, 14, 1922; *Buffalo Courier,* November 14, 1922.
[1007] *Nashville Tennessean,* November 19, 1922.
[1008] *Memphis Commercial Appeal,* November 20, 1922.

Carpentier has in his whole system. … Gibbons is a fighter infinitely superior to Carpentier and far worthier of a chance at the title.

Menke said Gibbons was taller, heavier, and had a longer reach than Carpentier. "And Gibbons can give boxing lessons to the Frenchman." He never had been knocked out or even knocked off his feet in his life, whereas Carpentier had been knocked out several times. Menke said Gibbons never quit or looked for a way out of a fight, or tried to win on a foul. Gibbons was deserving of a title challenge, particularly given that the public paid over a million dollars to see Dempsey against "the most overrated fighter of all time – a man smaller and inferior to Gibbons."[1009]

Harry Greb wanted to fight Dempsey as well. "I can't quite understand all this talk of a match between Harry Wills and Jack Dempsey. Neither can I understand why everybody should be so crazy about seeing a Tom Gibbons – Dempsey match. My record is sufficient proof that I have knocked over about every heavyweight in sight, barring Dempsey himself, and Harry Wills."

Greb had beaten Miske, Brennan, Gibbons, and Tunney. "I should think that the public by this time would be giving me a tumble as the one man able to give Jack Dempsey the fight of his career."[1010]

Edward Tranter was not keen on a Greb-Dempsey contest. "Those who have seen Harry in action may give him a chance of pure speed, but we believe that Dempsey is fast enough to catch Harry and give him a wallop that would knock him into the middle of next week."[1011]

On November 29, 1922 at New York's Madison Square Garden, 178 ½-pound Gene Tunney stopped 184 ¾-pound Charley Weinert (55-16-5) in the 4th round. Tunney decked him twice in the 3rd round with a fusillade of rights and lefts. Early in the 4th round, Weinert was so wobbly that his seconds tossed in the towel.[1012]

Tex Rickard offered Luis Firpo a fight with Bill Brennan. Rickard said if Firpo could knock out Brennan, then he would become the most logical opponent for Dempsey.[1013]

The *New York Daily News'* Harry Newman said that in the search to find an opponent for Dempsey, many had overlooked 178-pound Gene Tunney. Newman believed that Tunney was improving rapidly and growing into a heavyweight. His manager Doc Bagley thought the young Irish American would be ready for the champion in about a year. Tunney was 24 years old and getting heavier. He was very clever, with plenty of sting to his blows.[1014]

The *Brooklyn Daily Eagle's* W. C. Vreeland said concerns about riots and race hatred likely would prevent Dempsey-Wills from being staged anywhere in the U.S. Antipathy to a mixed championship was strong.

[1009] *Nashville Banner*, November 23, 1922.
[1010] *New York Tribune*, November 25, 1922.
[1011] *Buffalo Enquirer*, November 28, 1922
[1012] *New York Tribune, New York Times*, November 30, 1922.
[1013] *New York Daily News*, December 2, 1922.
[1014] *New York Daily News*, December 12, 1922.

"There is not the slightest doubt that if Jack Johnson, after his ring triumph over Jim Jeffries, had behaved himself and not aroused such unpleasant notoriety, that there would have been no objection to a bout between white and colored boxers since then."

Wills was the clear logical contender. Nevertheless, "I don't wish the readers of The Eagle to infer that I think Wills can whip Dempsey. I don't. I think that Dempsey would trounce him quite as easily as he did Willard and Carpentier." Dempsey was in a class by himself. Still, Wills was the best heavyweight other than Dempsey.[1015]

Jess Willard's name kept popping up as a potential foe, but the general feeling was that he needed to fight again in order to prove his readiness to compete with Dempsey.

Harry Greb announced that he was breaking away from his manager George Engel, and wanted to handle his own business and save himself the 33 1/3%. Greb said, "I want about four or five matches before taking on Gene Tunney in a championship bout, as I want to be in the best of shape when I meet him. I need a few bouts to put me on edge."

Writer Tom Andrews said Greb had better forget about fighting Dempsey, whom he had challenged, for he would "take a beating." "As a middle and light heavyweight Harry Greb is a great battler, but when it comes to Dempsey in the heavyweight division – well, just forget it."[1016]

Tommy Gibbons was coming off 1st round knockout victories over 173-pound George Ashe in November and 194 ½-pound Joe Burke on December 11. He was scheduled for another match with Miske just four days after the Burke contest. His manager Eddie Kane said Tom was the best bet of any heavyweight to get a crack at Dempsey.[1017]

Edward Walker said a decisive victory for Gibbons over Miske would go a long way towards getting him a bout with Dempsey.[1018]

In the follow-up to their recent controversial fight, on December 15, 1922 in St. Paul, Minnesota, before 7,000 to 8,000 fans which generated $18,669.10, 182 ½-pound Tom Gibbons won an official 10-round decision over 196-pound Billy Miske. Minnesota recently had authorized points decisions to be rendered.

The *St. Paul Pioneer Press'* L. S. McKenna said Gibbons earned a clear and easy victory in their fifth bout (and now was 3-1-1 against Miske), convincing the fans that he was Miske's master. Gibbons' slashing attack spoiled Miske's gameplan, and Billy was a badly beaten battler at the end. Tom had Miske groggy in the 10th round. Miske was game and showed courage to stand up under the terrible onslaught; as a result, losing none of his popularity. Gibbons was as shifty as ever, but punching harder and more accurately than ever before. He was bigger too than in the past. He was in the lead from start to finish, landing left hooks to the head and

[1015] *Brooklyn Daily Eagle*, December 12, 1922.
[1016] *Boxing Blade*, December 16, 1922.
[1017] *Buffalo Express*, December 11, 1922. Kane claimed that he had tried to get Greb to agree to another bout with Gibbons, but Harry had refused even a $40,000 offer.
[1018] *Minneapolis Journal*, December 15, 1922.

body, and a damaging right to the kidneys, wearing Miske down. Still, Gibbons had a shiner, proving that he was hit with some good ones too.

The *St. Paul Daily News'* Ed Shave said Gibbons won every round, but Miske put up a game, slashing battle. At the end, Miske was bruised and battered by the terrific bombardment of blows to the head and midsection. Gibbons was faster, the better boxer, used his left hook with deadly effect, a right to the head, and a right uppercut, and had Miske in a bad way many times. Miske took punishment that would have stopped practically anyone else, giving a great exhibition of gameness.

The *Minneapolis Morning Tribune's* Earl Arnold said that despite being the smaller man, Gibbons won a decisive victory, 9-0-1. He gave Miske a boxing lesson, hitting him almost at will. He settled beyond all doubt the question of supremacy. Twice Billy wobbled. Miske landed a hard left in the 5th round, which totally closed Tommy's left eye by the 6th. Nevertheless, Gibbons tore into Miske in the last three rounds, and Billy's face was a mass of blood, swollen and battered from the terrific hammering. Miske was game, always looking for a chance to land a knockout blow, but was beaten to the punch, outboxed, outgeneraled, and outslugged.

Two judges rendered the decision (with the referee acting as a potential tiebreaker if there was disagreement). "It was the first time in the history of legalized boxing in the state that a decision was called from the ring in a main event."

The *Minnesota Daily Star's* Charles Johnson said Gibbons gave Miske a smart boxing lesson, winning decisively. Eventually, he had to be given a heavyweight championship title fight. He showed so much clever boxing ability and an occasional hard stinging wallop such that "he must be considered among the best in the heavyweight ranks today." He stepped around quickly and boxed as smartly and cleverly as any heavyweight who ever appeared there. He peppered Miske's face, kidneys, and stomach with left uppercuts and right crosses. Billy held on in the 9th and 10th rounds, dazed, but with enough sense to clinch to prevent the knockout. "Gibbons was a master." He danced in and out, landing a wicked left jab all over. Miske tried, "but was no match for the fleet Gibbons." However, some wondered whether Gibbons had enough kick in his blows to bother Dempsey.

The *Minneapolis Journal's* Edward G. Walker said although Gibbons was considered by many as the logical man to fight Dempsey, if he was wise, he would wait until Dempsey got old. Although perhaps his power had improved over the years, he still did not hit hard enough to bother a man like Dempsey. Nevertheless, Gibbons outsmarted the larger Miske in an entertaining contest. "Boxers of such a caliber of Gibbons and Miske are a credit to the game."[1019]

[1019] *St. Paul Pioneer Press, St. Paul Daily News, Minneapolis Morning Tribune, Minnesota Daily Star, Minneapolis Journal*, December 16, 1922. Gibbons was guaranteed $5,000, while Miske worked on percentage, and would be paid nearly the same amount.

Gibbons said it would not be hard to sign him up for a fight with Dempsey; for he would not squabble over terms. Any date and reasonable terms would suffice.

The *Binghamton Press* said, "Gibbons is really by far the best white opponent for Dempsey." Gibbons was more skilled than Carpentier, and had power in both hands, not just one. Gibbons had much better defense than Georges, and proven resilience. He never had been knocked out or floored. "Gibbons is such a remarkably clever fellow that he would be sure to puzzle Dempsey, who never met a man just like him." Unlike Carpentier, Gibbons had an inside game as well as outside. "Gibbons is the most scientific infighter that has appeared in the last 25 years. When it comes to tying up an opponent at close quarters Gibbons is in a class by himself." As a result of his skill, two-fisted speed and power, defense, and ability to take a punch, he would be confident. His only weakness was that at times he seemed to lack the fighting spirit of a great fighter. "Tom showed that he lacked the right spirit when he let Harry Greb bull him out of a victory he should have won with plenty to spare."[1020]

On December 24 in San Diego, Dempsey completed his theatrical engagement. He said he was willing and eager to fight Gibbons.[1021]

De Witt Van Court said Gibbons' victory over Miske took him closer to a Dempsey fight. Miske had beaten Brennan, so Tom's clear victory over Miske was significant. "Gibbons's showing with Harry Greb should not count for so much. Greb is one of those freak boxers who seldom knock any good men out. Of the jumping-jack, slapping, wiggling style, they often made good men look foolish. It can hardly be said that Greb would be with the high-class boxers today were the contests of 20 rounds or more. He does not carry the punch." Gibbons landed harder and more effectively, and could hurt and deck his foes. "Tommy looks about the best of the bunch outside of Harry Wills and Jess Willard."[1022]

Some noted that inactivity was the worst enemy of a fighting man. It had been the prime cause of nearly every heavyweight champion's downfall since Sullivan's day. Dempsey had reached the same grave stage of idleness which contributed to many champions' defeats.[1023]

Dempsey at Danger Stage of Idleness - By Ed Hughes

The reason why Wills had not fought recently was he was resting up, nursing two broken hands suffered during his fight with Clem Johnson.

The *Binghamton Press* wrote, "How a Dempsey-Wills match would affect the welfare of boxing is a question that would take the judgement

[1020] *Rochester Democrat and Chronicle, Binghamton Press,* December 22, 1922.
[1021] *New York Daily News,* December 25, 1922.
[1022] *Los Angeles Times,* December 25, 1922.
[1023] *Buffalo Courier,* December 25, 1922.

of a Solomon to decide. Many persons believe that another mixed match for the championship would be fatal." In England, they did not allow a fight between Battling Siki and Joe Beckett "because of the race issue." Harry Wills was a well-behaved gentleman.

> However, it is a sure thing that Wills as champion could not help boxing. There is a grave danger that he might injure boxing. Men vitally interested in the sport see that there is nothing to be gained and a great deal to be risked as a result of the match. Those who depend on the sport for a livelihood are to a man against the taking the chance.[1024]

Yet, it was reported that newly-elected New York Governor Al Smith potentially might tolerate a Dempsey-Wills contest. It remained to be seen.[1025]

Luis Firpo informed Tex Rickard that he was willing to fight the winner of the upcoming Bill Brennan vs. Floyd Johnson contest. Tex said he hoped to match the winner of the elimination bouts against Dempsey. "Firpo surely looked pretty good last summer and I think that he and Dempsey would put up a great scrap."[1026]

Thomas Rice predicted that Dempsey still would be champion at the end of 1923. "There is no one on the horizon who could give him a battle except Harry Wills, and the odds are in favor of Dempsey winning if they ever meet, which is extremely doubtful." Battling Siki would be a "chopping block" for Dempsey. Floyd Johnson was being press-agented and nursed along with easy marks, gaining experience and confidence. "On appearances he may come through some day." A match with Brennan would give him his first real test.

Greb was the American light heavy champ, though Siki was the world champ. "Greb can be reached by an orthodox boxer who can move rapidly in following up a lead, and who has a proper one-two punch. Tunney and Tom Gibbons demonstrated that, but neither had the enterprise, or the stamina, or the nerve to continue that style of attack upon their bouncing adversary."[1027]

Harry Newman said it was about time that Dempsey fought someone. "The public pay the freight, and they want you to fight or quit the game. Harry Wills is still around waiting to take a crack at you any time you say the word. You can't keep dodging much longer. If you don't care for Wills, how about Tom Gibbons, or perhaps Floyd Johnson?"

Tex Rickard was trying to match Willard with Firpo as well. He told Jess that he needed a big win to justify another fight with Dempsey, given how long it had been since he last fought. The winner of that bout would be able to create demand for a Dempsey contest.[1028]

[1024] Binghamton Press, December 28, 1922.
[1025] Canandaigua Daily Messenger, December 29, 1922.
[1026] New York Daily News, December 30, 1922.
[1027] Brooklyn Daily Eagle, December 31, 1922.
[1028] New York Daily News, January 1, 1923.

On or about January 4, 1923, Rosewood, Florida was the scene of another racially motivated massacre of blacks and destruction of a black town. A mob of several hundred whites killed at least 20 - 27 blacks, though some report up to 150 were killed, filling mass graves. The mob burned down the predominantly black town. Members of the mob even kept body parts of a lynched man as souvenirs. The shootings, hangings, and burnings were precipitated by a white woman's claim that a black man had assaulted her, although domestic workers said she actually had been struck during an argument with the white lover she was seeing while her husband was at work. No arrests were made. The town was abandoned, and none of its black residents ever moved back.[1029]

Whites in Wait for Fleeing Negroes in Florida Race Riot

Dempsey and Kearns closed a real estate deal in Los Angeles for an apartment building for $250,000, which they would own jointly.[1030]

Damon Runyon said Dempsey's latest purchase proved he was far from being broke, contrary to rumors. He already owned a Los Angeles home that cost him over $100,000. He also had property in Salt Lake City. Not bad for a 27-year-old former hungry hobo.[1031]

Billy Miske supported Tom Gibbons' efforts to secure a title shot, saying he believed that Gibbons would give Dempsey "the fight of his life." Billy had fought Dempsey three times and Gibbons five times, so his opinion was respected. Miske said,

> Gibbons is like a shadow. It's almost impossible to land a solid punch on him. Dempsey never has been in the ring with such a fast and clever boxer as Gibbons, and I think Tommy would make the champion miss more punches in five or six rounds than Dempsey has missed in any ten of his fights. … Honest, trying to hit Gibbons squarely is pretty much like trying to hit a jackrabbit with a sponge.[1032]

[1029] In 1994, Florida became the first U.S. state to compensate survivors and their descendants for damages incurred because of racial violence, reacting to an investigation and report regarding the Rosewood massacre which revealed that law enforcement failed to help or protect the residents while the murders and arson in the town were occurring.

[1030] *Buffalo Times*, January 5, 1923.

[1031] *Buffalo Courier*, January 9, 1923.

[1032] *Brooklyn Citizen*, January 8, 1923; *Brooklyn Daily Eagle*, January 9, 1923.

The *Elmira Star-Gazette* said Gibbons was Dempsey's logical foe. He looked like the real thing. Although very few would wager against Dempsey if he fought anyone, "Gibbons looks just about as promising as any opponent in sight and a great deal more so than the majority." He was fast, clever, would lead the "Manassa Mauler" on a merry chase for several rounds, and prove more of a ring enigma than either Willard or Carpentier. His footwork was a "work of art." He was as shifty as a featherweight. He had a trained left, good defense, and plenty of knockouts on his record. He had been boxing since 1913, so he had plenty of experience, too.[1033]

On January 12, 1923 in New York at Madison Square Garden, before a crowd of 14,250, which generated a gate of $57,380, in an upset, 194-pound Iowa-native Floyd Johnson (27-2-7) won a clear 15-round decision over 200 ½-pound Bill Brennan (77-15-8). It was a furious fight. Johnson could not finish Brennan, but he came close to doing it, rocking Bill with lefts. "He outboxed, outfought and outgeneraled the more experienced Brennan." Some criticized Johnson's power, because he failed to stop Brennan, but the only man to have accomplished that in 100 fights was Jack Dempsey.

Present at the contest were Jess Willard, Jack Johnson, Jim Corbett, Tommy Gibbons, Harry Wills, and Gene Tunney. Willard and Johnson shook hands.[1034]

In Los Angeles, Dempsey's trainer Teddy Hayes lost a verdict for $250 in damages for assaulting and beating house painter Owen Bartlett. The court dismissed Jack Dempsey from the case on the ground that he was not present, and Joe Dempsey because he only was acting as a peacemaker.[1035]

On January 15, 1923 in Pittsburgh, 168 ¼-pound Harry Greb won a clear 10-round newspaper decision over 164 ½-pound Tommy Loughran (36-5-3). Harry Keck said,

> Greb crowded him throughout, never letting him get set to do any effective work. In fact, Harry literally mobbed Tommy from start to finish. It was a typical Greb fight, with Harry bouncing all around the ring, rushing and plunging in to close quarters and then working both arms like pistons to head and body. The local man did a lot of holding and hitting, and there were moments when he had Loughran fairly dizzy with his fast pace, but Tommy always

[1033] *Elmira Star-Gazette*, January 9, 1923.
[1034] *Brooklyn Daily Times, New York Daily News, Brooklyn Standard Union, Brooklyn Daily Eagle*, January 13, 1923. Floyd Johnson's prior record included: 1922 W4 Willie Meehan and TKO10 Bob Martin. Since losing to Dempsey, Brennan had been 17-1, the only loss a close newspaper decision to Miske.
[1035] *Illustrated Buffalo Express*, January 14, 1923.

straightened up and came back ready to mix at the slightest opportunity.

It was a rough fight. "Loughran was guilty of using his elbows repeatedly, while Greb butted and in other ways made the going rough." The gate was $10,717.[1036]

Jim Corbett discussed the various contenders. Willard "is probably as good as any of them." Regarding Harry Wills, Corbett said, "An in-and-outer, dangerous always. He might beat Dempsey easily and he might lose just as easily. But a good, dangerous man, let me tell you." Corbett said Jack Johnson might be old and through, but still could be depended upon to make a good showing against anyone, for he was a splendid boxer, timely hitter, and wonderful on defense.

Corbett ranked St. Paul's Tom Gibbons as the best man in sight to go against Dempsey. "Gibbons is clever, and with his agility could avoid a lot of punishment that the others would have to take. He is my best bet for Dempsey."

When asked about Gibbons' loss to Greb, Corbett responded, "Don't fool yourself about Greb. Harry might make a sucker out of Dempsey himself in a 10-round bout. He's a slapper and a mauler, and Jack would find it hard to get in on him effectively in a short-stop bout." The longer it went though, the better for Dempsey it would be.[1037]

Thomas Rice said the result of the National Boxing Association's meeting was confirmation of his prediction that Ontario would not countenance a mixed-race heavyweight championship. "Our dope was that the Canadian officials would not stand for a heavyweight championship bout between a negro and a white man because of the disturbing influence such a contest, no matter how it ended, would have upon racial relations wherever whites and non-whites were living side by side."

The chair of the Ontario Boxing Commission was a delegate to the N.B.A. meeting, and refused to discuss the matter, but "from other sources it was learned that there was not a chance of staging the battle in Canada." They would not think of licensing the bout, for the same reasons that the British Home Office forbade the proposed Siki vs. Beckett contest. Even if they did "go crazy" and sanction the fight, "they would be ousted by the Canadian Government, and the bout would be barred anyhow."[1038]

New York Governor Al Smith, when asked if he would authorize a Dempsey vs. Wills fight, initially responded by asking, "Who is Jack Dempsey?" He said all matters relating to boxing were up to the athletic commission. "I have nothing to do with boxing." "There is no law against mixed bouts in New York."[1039]

[1036] *Pittsburgh Post, Pittsburgh Press, Pittsburgh Gazette Times,* January 16, 1923.
[1037] *Buffalo Express,* January 16, 1923.
[1038] *Brooklyn Daily Eagle,* January 16, 1923. The N.B.A. meeting included a speech in which it was said that the commissions would work in close harmony, and a man barred by one would be barred by all.
[1039] *Brooklyn Standard Union,* January 17, 1923.

Tex Rickard said Gibbons would make a sturdy opponent for Dempsey. "I think that Tom Gibbons is a wonderful fighter."

The *New York Daily News* said Kearns probably would not allow Dempsey to fight for anything less than $500,000 guaranteed. Apparently, the New York Commission ruled that no guarantees would be allowed, and all boxers would have to work on a percentage basis. If the commission insisted on such terms, then Dempsey would demand 60%.

After Tom Gibbons attempted to post $2,500 for a formal challenge to Dempsey, the New York Commission/Muldoon rejected it, declaring that a Dempsey-Gibbons match would not be approved, for Gibbons was too small and would be outclassed (even though Tom weighed 182 ½ pounds in his last fight). Hence, in the past year, Muldoon had thwarted Dempsey fights with Brennan and Gibbons overtly, and Wills indirectly.[1040]

Jimmy De Forest, who at one time had trained Kid McCoy and Jack Dempsey, was known for being the world's best boxing teacher. He said that with a year of instruction, Luis Firpo would give Dempsey a tremendous battle. "He will not say that Luis could beat Jack because he regards the champion as the finest type of natural fighter the world has produced." Still, he believed that with Dempsey slipping as a result of his lengthy inactivity, Firpo possibly could wrest the title from him if he continued to develop. Firpo was scheduled to fight Brennan.[1041]

The *Brooklyn Daily Eagle's* Thomas Rice applauded the New York commission for rejecting Gibbons-Dempsey. "Those who saw Gibbons lose to Harry Greb, a smaller man and one notorious for lack of a stiff punch, will agree that the commission has acted rightly and deserves congratulations."

However, the *Brooklyn Daily Times'* Henry Farrell said Gibbons was one of the world's best heavyweights and would give the champ a good fight.

> If any of the contenders for the title has a real chance to beat Dempsey, it is Gibbons. He is fast on his feet, he can box, he has had experience and he can hit with either hand. He is a great infighter and he is as good at close quarters as Dempsey. Gibbons wants a fight with Dempsey next summer and he ought to get it. He is popular around New York and there is no doubt that it would be a good card for any promoter.[1042]

On January 22, 1923 in Jersey City, before a crowd of 6,000, 168 ½-pound Harry Greb won a clear 12-round newspaper decision over 166-pound Billy Shade (48-16-18). Greb dropped Shade in the 7th with a straight left to the mouth, en route to the newspaper decision.

However, Thomas Rice criticized that Greb displayed a "woeful lack of punch" in beating a man "who can't hit at all," making little impression on a smaller man. While admitting that he won every round, Rice called

[1040] *New York Daily News*, January 18 - 20, 1923; *Buffalo Courier, Brooklyn Standard Union*, January 21, 1923.
[1041] *Buffalo Courier*, January 21, 1923.
[1042] *Brooklyn Daily Eagle, Brooklyn Daily Times*, January 22, 1923.

Greb "a bigger disappointment than even the present writer has always conceded him to be."

Rice said Greb was not fit to fight Dempsey. "About the only point of interest to the dismal affair was to see if Greb would display signs of a punch, because writers of gullible dispositions and having space at their disposal are going to afflict the helpless boxing fans with many yammers that Greb be matched with Jack Dempsey." Rice said Greb was open defensively, missed as many as he landed, and left himself wide open when he missed. Furthermore, "If that was all Greb could accomplish offensively against such a feeble flailer as Shade, Greb could not hurt Dempsey if he were given a blackjack, and Dempsey were restrained by manacles."

> Tom Gibbons, a clever boxer of the orthodox school, could have beaten Greb a year ago if he had displayed the proper energy and nerve. Even Gene Tunney, who is not esteemed highly by the critics, but who has a fairly good straight left and right cross, could have beaten Greb...but like all the others Tunney allowed Greb to buffalo him by his bouncing footwork and windmill swinging until Tunney forgot all he ever knew about boxing, and plainly lost his nerve besides. When either Gibbons or Tunney went after Greb with the one-two punch they got him, but both were so lamentably shy on a proper will-to-win that they failed to stick to a winning policy.

> Dempsey does not shine at the one-two punch, but he would absorb, without blinking an eye, all of those light blows from Greb, would keep after him and would corner him often enough to beat him to a whisper. And if Tom Gibbons could not beat Greb...what chance would Gibbons have with Dempsey? Make your own book on that.[1043]

Dempsey said he would fight anybody - Wills, Willard, Gibbons, Floyd Johnson, Greb, or whomever a promoter wanted him to fight (if Kearns approved the offer and the bout could be held). "I want to fight the man who will draw the most money." "Bring them on. I have an old agreement to meet Harry Wills and this still holds good if some promoter thinks well enough of the match to stage it." He also said Willard should be given another chance, for former champions typically were given such opportunities. "Tom Gibbons can have the match if the promoters want it. So can Floyd Johnson, who recently defeated Bill Brennan. I am not sidestepping any of them." Jack said he and Gibbons would not have that much of a weight discrepancy, only about 10 pounds or so. "I don't care who they get for me. ... I want to fight."[1044]

George Underwood wrote that Dempsey affirmed that no one was barred. "I'll fight anyone, white, black or green!" "Show me the money,

[1043] *Brooklyn Daily Eagle*, *New York Daily News*, January 23, 1923.
[1044] *New York Daily News*, January 23, 24, 1923.

that's all. It doesn't make any difference who is in the opposite corner. Just let 'em get the man who will draw the biggest gate. I don't care what color he is or who he is. I'm not picking 'em nor never did."

Dan McKetrick interjected, "The promoters are the pulse of the public. Both Tex Rickard and Tom O'Rourke are after the Dempsey-Willard match. They represent the public." Underwood believed that they did not represent the public, but rather "commercialized sport gone mad."

Dempsey said it was not up to him to pick his opponents. "The promoters represent the public, inasmuch as they are not going to put on anything that the public will not attend. Through Jack Kearns, my manager, I do my business with the promoters. It is up to them to make their offers. I don't care who they name as long as I get paid for it." Jack said he signed an agreement to fight Wills, and was willing to go through with it. "But how am I going to fight Wills without any offer?" It was up to the promoters to make bona fide offers.

McKetrick said Dempsey was willing to fight Wills last year. Why didn't it happen? "Ask Muldoon." It was Muldoon who was thwarting the fight, possibly for political reasons, and placing obstacles against it, including limiting ticket prices. He was being unreasonable. Still, Underwood believed that Dempsey's advisers, if not himself, wanted anyone but Wills.[1045]

In other news, Gene Tunney had parted with his old manager, Frank Bagley, and signed up with Billy Gibson, who had been a guiding hand for Benny Leonard.

Kansas records proved that Jess Willard was 40 years old, and would be 41 the following month. He was born in February 1882. At the time of his birth, his father, Myron B. Willard, had died. A July 1896 school record signed by his stepfather, E. L. Stalker, listed him as age 14. Jess had an older brother, Robert O. Willard.[1046]

The *Buffalo Enquirer* reported that up to that point, there had been no real bona-fide offers for a Dempsey-Wills match (in terms of economics, legal assurances, and sufficient financial backing/guarantees/forfeit money).[1047]

Hugh Fullerton said,

> Every time you scratch deeply enough into a boxing match in New York you find Tammany Hall or the other gang. In this mess of politics and boxing in New York we find that there isn't a chance for a real fighter unless he is Jake with the politicians, and that the only 'out' they have is to slip across the river to Jersey, where conditions are rottener than they are in New York.[1048]

Rickard was proposing fights for Dempsey against Willard in New Jersey and then Firpo if Luis beat Brennan. Tex said, "No matter what the

[1045] *New York Evening Telegram*, January 24, 1923.
[1046] *New York Daily News*, January 24, 1923.
[1047] *Buffalo Enquirer*, January 25, 1923.
[1048] *New York Daily News*, January 27, 1923.

papers say, I still think that Willard is a formidable fighter. I'll bet money that there isn't a contender in the class that can beat him."

Rickard said Dempsey had agreed to work on a percentage basis.

> After his experience against Carpentier he does not want a guarantee. He demanded a guarantee of $300,000 and I gave it to him. When they figured up the receipts and their purse they found out they got less than 18%. I would not guarantee them $300,000 for another bout, but I am willing to go – say around 33%, and they will make plenty.[1049]

Harry Newman said Willard was too old, Gibbons and Greb too small, and Firpo not quite ready. The public would not stand for a soft mark. "You cannot fool the fight fan all the time." Wills was the real and logical opponent. He hoped "there would be some promoter game enough to go through with such a bout [Dempsey-Wills]."[1050]

Sparrow McGann said Dempsey planned to retire after one more year of ring activity. Jack said, "There is nothing to being a champion except worry. When I step out and the next champion comes along I am not going to envy him. He will have my sympathy. What I want to do this year is to clean up all the real contenders and then turn to some other business."

McGann said there never had been a fighter who had changed so completely in a few years as Dempsey. He dressed better and was more of a businessman. From fights, moving picture rights, and stage appearances, he and Kearns probably had or soon will have earned about $2 million.

Regarding a potential Wills contest, McGann said, "Tex Rickard's silence about Wills means only one thing and that is that Tex has been shooed off this bout because of the race question involved."[1051]

On January 29, 1923 in Philadelphia, Gene Tunney and Jack Renault were thrown out of the ring by referee Pop O'Brien in the 4th round for nonperformance; their contest was so tame.[1052]

Harry Greb and Tommy Loughran

[1049] *Brooklyn Citizen*, January 28, 1923.
[1050] *New York Daily News*, January 28, 1923.
[1051] *Buffalo Times*, January 29, 1923.
[1052] *Philadelphia Inquirer*, January 30, 1923.

On January 30, 1923 in New York at Madison Square Garden, before a crowd of 5,640 that paid $19,090, 166-pound Harry Greb won a 15-round decision over 166-pound Tommy Loughran.

William Granger said although he won, "Greb will have to be stronger than he was last night if he is to retain his crown when he tackles Gene Tunney." The crowd was with Loughran, "probably because of Greb's reputation of using unfair tactics to subdue opponents." Still, he mostly fought fairly on this occasion, only roughing Loughran when Tom tried to tie him up.

The *Brooklyn Standard Union* agreed with the decision, but noted that the fans booed Greb. "Fight fans like the sockers," which Greb was not. "In ring parlance, he couldn't dent a pane of glass with his punch." Over time, fans had shifted from initial appreciation for his novel style to having grown weary of it. They also did not like his tactics. "He held Loughran with one hand and hit him with the other, used his thumb and heel to jab and stab the Philadelphian in the eye and mouth and his head to butt Loughran under the chin." Still, Harry clearly won. "Greb, clawing, hooking and pushing, hacked his way to a victory." Loughran was too timid, failing to punch often enough, and defending and clinching too much.

W. C. Vreeland said Loughran was too slow to take advantage of the champ's wild boxing. The fight was neither interesting nor worthwhile. Vreeland said this version of Greb would lose to Gibbons or Tunney. He was as wild as a drunken man, not in the best shape, and looked fat even at 166 pounds, his weight taken at 2 p.m. on the day of the fight. Greb won by a wide margin, but was booed because of his penchant for using the heel of his glove, butting, and low blows. However, Loughran was just as foul.[1053]

Harry Newman said the New Jersey boxing bosses put the kibosh on a Dempsey-Willard fight. Commissioner Louis Messano simply said, "New Jersey is opposed to the bout." He did not view Willard as a fit foe. New York had barred Willard as well, saying he was too old and inactive.

New Jersey Commissioner Messano further held that a Dempsey-Wills contest might have disastrous effects upon racial relations; confirming

[1053] *Brooklyn Citizen, Brooklyn Daily Times, New York Daily News, Brooklyn Standard Union, Brooklyn Daily Eagle,* January 31, 1923.

that such a fight could not be held in New Jersey. It was possible that Dempsey-Wills "may be barred" in New York on racial grounds as well, although such had not yet been referenced explicitly or openly by the powers-that-be.

Newman said all of the promoters were ducking Wills. "They all admit that Harry Wills is the boy to meet the champion, but they all seem wary about putting up the necessary coin to bind such a match."

The *Brooklyn Daily Times* said neither Dempsey-Willard nor Dempsey-Wills would be authorized in either New Jersey or New York, which put such fights on the ropes. "Wills can't fight in New York for the title, because Albany does not think it would be a good thing for the sport or the State." Rickard never figured the authorities would allow Dempsey-Wills, so he was focused primarily on making other matches. With Wills and Willard out of the equation, Gibbons appeared to be the likely choice. Muldoon's mind regarding Gibbons possibly could be changed if he beat Floyd Johnson.[1054]

SELECTING AN OPPONENT FOR CHAMPION JACK DEMPSEY

JESS WILLARD.   FLOYD JOHNSON.   HARRY WILLS.   TOMMY GIBBONS.   HARRY GREB.

Tex Rickard was in a dilemma in terms of finding an acceptable and marketable opponent for Dempsey. Tex said,

> It is evident that opinion is divided as to the man capable of making the best showing against Dempsey. I have always had press and public with me in my big undertakings, and I won't attempt any match unless that condition prevails now. If any match that I propose should ever bring boxing as a sport into disfavor, I am always ready to withdraw.[1055]

Tom O'Rourke offered Dempsey $500,000 total for two fights, one with Joe Beckett and one with Harry Wills. Of course, O'Rourke's offer likely was not going to be acceptable, for the offer only averaged out to $250,000 per fight. The Carpentier fight generated over $1.6 million, and Jack earned $300,000, or only about 18.75% of the total gross. He and Kearns wanted their fair share of what would be the sport's biggest fight. There also was the question regarding whether the authorities would allow a Wills-Dempsey fight.

Thomas Rice said Wills was a "political problem – and a big one." Governor Al Smith was a Democrat, who hoped to become either a presidential candidate or an important power in the party. "If he permits

[1054] *New York Daily News, Brooklyn Daily Eagle, Brooklyn Daily Times,* February 1, 1923.
[1055] *New York Daily News,* February 2, 1923.

within New York State a white-black bout for a heavyweight world's championship, he will inevitably bring upon himself a huge bunch of trouble. If he forbids such a bout he will still bring upon himself a huge bunch of trouble." If he allowed the bout, "the Southern Democrats would never forgive him. Should he put up the bars against Wills – no matter how sound his reasons, and we believe they would be absolutely sound – he would offend Negro Democrats and be accused by many whites of showing race prejudice."

Rice noted how the French authorities had allowed Siki-Carpentier "in order to escape the charge of race prejudice, and what a nauseous mess resulted! The British authorities had the moral courage to forbid a Jack Johnson–'Bombardier' Wells bout, and later to forbid a Siki-Beckett bout – and saved themselves from serious complications."[1056]

It was suspected that Governor Smith might adroitly try to walk a tightrope and engage in various political methods to ensure that neither side was angered. The governor simply could abstain from the issue and allow the commission to be the bad guy, so to speak.

Lo and behold, William Muldoon openly came out and said that although he had no prejudices against Harry Wills personally (oh, of course not!), there could be no fight between Dempsey and Wills. But, he gave an odd statement to justify his decision, claiming that although Wills deserved a title shot, "the commercialism which had crept into the game was his reason for taking the step to halt all the heavyweight battles now in prospect." Whatever the heck that meant. Was he a socialist? Such nonsense! Essentially, he was stopping heavyweight boxing altogether. What was happening? Was this his way of avoiding using race as the reason? Muldoon said big purses were a threat to the game, using that, rather than race, as his reasoning.

> There won't be any Dempsey and Wills bout in this State while I am head of the State Athletic Commission. The opposition to such bouts is not because of the two boxers named. They are not to blame for the existing situation. It is the commercialized condition produced by crazy promoters and managers that is responsible for this opposition. Talk of millions and hundreds of thousands for heavyweight championship bouts is repulsive.

Muldoon said talk of such amounts was an attack on boxing, the managers/promoters were "insane," and if they did not "stop their silly talk about million dollar purses they will kill the game."[1057]

As Rickard accurately predicted long ago, something, some reason, commission, politician, or issue, always was going to arise to thwart Dempsey-Wills. Of course, it was not clear what fight the commissions would allow. Rickard said it was such a huge pain to make a Dempsey heavyweight championship fight at the moment that he was withdrawing

[1056] *Poughkeepsie Eagle-News, Brooklyn Daily Eagle,* February 2, 1923.
[1057] *New York Daily News,* February 3, 4, 1923.

his attempts to do so any time in the immediate future. The commissions would not allow Tex to make matches for Dempsey against Willard, Wills, or Gibbons. The thinking was that white contenders would have to fight amongst themselves and justify a title shot.

Rice said if politicians thought the Dempsey-Wills fight would benefit them, it would be allowed or facilitated. If they thought otherwise, then reasons would arise why it could not happen. "Muldoon was first to insist that Dempsey accept a challenge from Wills, but a change has come over his dreams." Muldoon's various rulings appeared "illogical" unless one knew about inside politics and things folks did not always reveal. "Muldoon does not want the white vs. black bout. By keeping Muldoon in office Governor Smith will have an alibi for a year, at least."

In the meantime, Senator James J. Walker could give a stump speech about how the Democratic party was a friend to the colored brother, and would not stand for race prejudice, claiming the boxing law would be repealed if there was any race prejudice. They could have their cake and eat it too. The governor would not be blamed for preventing the fight, and Muldoon would not be accused of race prejudice, because his purported reasons were not racial. Hence, those who were ready to shriek about race prejudice would be soothed, and the governor would not be getting into trouble with southern whites or those who did not like the idea of a mixed-race championship contest. It was a compromise in which both ends could be played. Welcome to politics.

Louis Messano was more direct and forthright regarding his inclination to refuse to allow Dempsey-Wills in New Jersey, saying his object was to protect the boxing game, and a match between a white man and black man might hurt the game and have disastrous results for boxing, not only in New Jersey but all over the country, even though there was nothing personally objectionable about the characters of either man. "Mr. Messano deserves credit for being one politician above the Mason and Dixon line frank enough to concede that under any circumstances whatever the color question might be considered." Technically though, Messano said no official decision had been made, since the matter had not formally come before the commission.[1058]

Sparrow McGann said,

> The writer has held throughout that a Dempsey-Wills fight was a bad project. In many communities the race question is a slumbering issue and a mixed battle would be an awakening influence not agreeable to contemplate. And assuming Wills should win – the writer does not believe there is a great chance of this; but he might – well, the country has had the experience of a negro champion and does not wish to repeat it. And in any event the incidental publicity

---

[1058] *Brooklyn Daily Eagle*, February 4, 1923.

to such a bout would bring pugilism acutely before the general public in an unfavorable way.[1059]

Governor Smith announced a hands-off policy, leaving it up to the athletic commission, saying, "The Dempsey-Wills fight is in the hands of the commission. I didn't appoint that commission. It was appointed by Gov. Miller." That was his way of saying, 'Not only is it not up to me, but if you wind up unhappy with their decision, blame the prior governor who appointed them.' That way, he was safe, politically.[1060]

Edward Tranter said, "Politics of the deep and dark kind undoubtedly have been injected into the matter. ... Politics is behind all this furor that has been created by proposed heavyweight boxing matches."[1061]

On February 3, 1923 in New York City, Gene Tunney won a 12-round decision over Chuck Wiggins (55-24-13). The *Brooklyn Daily Eagle* said that despite the victory, Tunney "made a poor showing."[1062]

Word was that Dempsey's father was ill. Jack would visit him in Salt Lake City, and likely take a movie contract in Los Angeles, given that there was no fight for him on the horizon.[1063]

Harry Newman said Dempsey's career was at a crossroads. He could not get a fight in the U.S. or overseas, and was forced to play the vaudeville circuit.

> The word is being whispered around that Dempsey could not then and never will be able to secure a fight in either France or England because of his war record in the ship yards. That same is said to hold good in Canada and in Australia. It will be remembered that Dempsey received a tremendous ovation in Berlin, but there is no money in the fight game in Berlin or anywhere else in Germany.

Therefore, Kearns had on his hands a "wonderful fighter" who was not able to earn except on the stage. "And his drawing power can be kept alive only by victories in the ring."

Kearns still hoped that Dempsey-Wills eventually would happen, for "the bout is too big to pass up."[1064]

Can Jack Dempsey make—   Harry Wills lose smile?

[1059] *Buffalo Courier*, February 5, 1923.
[1060] *New York Daily News*, February 5, 1923.
[1061] *Buffalo Enquirer*, February 6, 1923.
[1062] *Brooklyn Daily Eagle*, February 4, 1923. Before the month was over, Tunney and Greb would fight a rematch.
[1063] *Brooklyn Daily Eagle*, February 6, 1923; *Buffalo Courier*, February 15, 1923.
[1064] *New York Daily News*, February 7, 1923.

CHAPTER 13

Emerging

A Jess Willard vs. Floyd Johnson bout was arranged, set to be held in May 1923. Coming off a victory over Brennan, either Floyd Johnson could use Willard as an additional stepping-stone up the ladder, or Willard could use a victory over Floyd as a way of proving that he was not past-it.

Not long ago, while the champ was on the coast, "Sailor" Tom Sharkey boxed several short rounds with Dempsey in a gym. Sharkey called Dempsey a great fighter, and said,

> Dempsey would have been a great fighter at any period. He hits just as hard and just as solidly as any man I ever knew. He hits pretty much the same way as did Jeffries. He isn't so big as was Jeffries, of course, but he makes up for that by putting more snap into his punches. He and Bob Fitzsimmons would have made a great fight. I won't try to say which would have beaten the other. That would only be guesswork. Fitz, you know, could hit some himself. When he dug that bony fist into you nobody had to tell you that you got hit. There's one thing I'll say for Dempsey. He's more aggressive than was either Fitzsimmons or Jeffries. They used to pause and think a little between punches. Dempsey just runs in and slams and slams.[1065]

De Witt Van Court said Tom Gibbons was not too light to fight for the title, for he was skillful, experienced, tough, and known for being a hard hitter. Choynski was no bigger, but likewise could punch and box and had done well with many top heavyweights. Charlie Mitchell was the same.[1066]

When asked about the greatest and toughest fight of his career, Dempsey said, "My fight with Billy Miske, back in 1918, is the big event in my life as a fighter. Miske and I fought 10 rounds. ... Some of the writers gave Miske the edge, others favored me. At that time Miske was a commanding figure in the fight game. ... That bout convinced me that some day I would be champion."[1067]

The *New York American's* Ed Curley said Gene Tunney planned to do a little roughing himself in the upcoming rematch with Harry Greb. Last time, Greb beat him in a very "ungentlemanly manner." Gene realized that just being a clever boxer was not enough. "The A.E.F. champion can sock, but formerly made little use of his strength." In Greb's recent bouts, he "failed to make any tremendous hit with the fans." "All Tunney needs

[1065] *New York Evening Telegram*, February 12, 1923.
[1066] *Los Angeles Times*, February 12, 1923.
[1067] *Yonkers Statesman and News*, February 14, 1923.

is determination, for he is stronger, cleverer and hits much harder than the lad endowed with perpetual motion."[1068]

For the *New York Sun*, Fred Keats said Tunney had a good chance to regain his laurels from Greb, for he was improving. He showed gameness and courage in their first contest, but lacked the proper experience against top men. "In the first few seconds of the bout Tunney's nose was broken with a butt. A little later both eyes were cut by the same means, so that he was almost blinded by the flow of blood." The adrenaline used to stop the blood running from his nose went into his stomach and made him sick, and he vomited after the fight.

> Despite these handicaps, Tunney fought the full fifteen rounds at top speed. He made Greb either clinch or back away from every mixup. In fact, if the judges had paid any attention to the rules, which say that points must be detracted for fouls, Tunney would have received the decision. So far as the actual exchange of blows with the gloves were concerned, Tunney had the better of it despite his gory appearance.

This time, Greb would be minus the services of George Engel, who worse still would be with Tunney, who now was managed by Billy Gibson. Gene had paid Doc Bagley, his former manager, to release him from their contract.[1069]

Ed Curley noted that Tunney said Greb violated every known rule of fair play in their first fight. This time, Tunney was ready to treat Greb just as harshly as Greb handled him. "Tunney has shown so much improvement that he has a grand chance of winning back his crown." Still, Greb was an 8 to 5 favorite.[1070]

On February 20, three days before the fight, Tunney sparred 2 rounds each with Wolf Larsen and Larry Williams. Fred Keats said, "That Tunney is at the top of his form was shown in every move he made. His left hook was working to perfection and his right hand rip to the body carried a world of steam. Tunney means to pay a great deal of attention to Greb's body this time."

Billy Gibson wanted Chairman Muldoon to instruct the referee to make Greb observe the rules like any other boxer. "Greb has been getting by with much rough stuff that would not be permitted another fighter on the plea that he knows no other way to fight. That argument should not hold water because Greb has shown in bouts with easy marks that he can live up to the rules."

Regarding Dempsey-Wills, Keats noted that previously the commission had ordered Dempsey to fight Wills, but after he agreed, it put up the bars on the match. Since then, the commission had ceased making matches, for it was an idea that had not worked out too well.[1071]

[1068] *New York American*, February 19, 1923.
[1069] *New York Sun*, February 19, 1923.
[1070] *New York American*, February 20, 1923.
[1071] *New York Sun*, February 21, 1923.

So much Tunney money was being wagered that the odds were shifting to even, and it was anticipated that Tunney might be the slight 6 to 5 favorite over Greb.[1072]

Billy Gibson wrote the *Sun*, "It is a matter of public knowledge that Greb is a flagrantly foul boxer. Every person who saw him box Tunney last spring will recall that he continuously butted Tunney, held with one hand and hit with the other; wrestled and roughed Gene on the ropes and heeled him. All of these offences constitute fouls." Gibson wanted the commission to instruct the judges and referee regarding the official rules, Section III – Officials, which stated, "Points should be deducted for a foul even though it is unintentional and not of a serious enough nature to warrant disqualification." Gibson believed that Greb would box fairly if he knew that the rules would be enforced, and if he boxed fairly, Tunney would win.

Greb complained that there was a plan to intimidate him, and Gibson was trying to influence the referee to disqualify him by calling him a foul fighter. Chairman Muldoon responded to Greb,

> You have won all your fights, and I have never heard of you being disqualified for foul tactics... It is quite apparent that the referees do not regard you as a foul fighter, even if some of your opponents make the charge. The referee who will officiate at the bout to-morrow night will judge the bout on what is done in the ring and not by threats or accusations made by Tunney or his partisans.[1073]

The *Newark Star-Eagle's* Bert Dodge said it was hard to compare Greb and Tunney. "Gene is a remarkably hard hitter and a good all-around boxer. Usually he is in tip-top form and able to go the route at high speed. Greb depends on agility and speed for victory. He is hitting constantly and tries to keep an opponent so busy avoiding blows that the man opposed to him won't have an opportunity to hand out many wallops on his own account." It also was difficult to land effectively on Greb.[1074]

Luis Firpo had returned to the U.S. There were some alleged million-dollar offers for Dempsey to fight him in South America. Jimmy De Forest would train Luis for his upcoming fight with Bill Brennan. Tex Rickard said, "Why, that bird wanted to know who I would match him with after the Brennan fuss. He appears to be the most confident kid I have ever seen. ... I

[1072] *New York American*, February 22, 1923.
[1073] *New York Sun*, February 22, 1923.
[1074] *Newark Star-Eagle*, February 22, 1923.

583

honestly believe that inside of a year, if that bird lives up to my expectations, I will be arranging a match between him and the champion."

Firpo currently was weighing 235 pounds and stood 6'3½". He planned to weigh under 225 for the Brennan fight. Others said Firpo weighed 220 pounds. Through a translator, Firpo said, "I'm ready to fight anybody in the world." "I know Brennan will give me the hardest fight I've ever had, but I am sure I can whip him. Mr. Rickard has promised me a match with Dempsey if I defeat Brennan, but I am willing to fight other contenders before meeting the champion."

Rickard said if Firpo beat Brennan, he might match him with the winner of the scheduled May bout between Jess Willard and Floyd Johnson. Firpo and Floyd Johnson would spar with one another to prepare for their respective upcoming contests.[1075]

Luis Firpo, Argentine Heavyweight, Starts Training

Floyd Johnson and Luis Firpo

Heading into the Greb-Tunney rematch, the *New York Call* said,

> Being young and strong, a good boxer and fair hitter, and also very angry at Greb, Tunney is by all odds the most formidable fighter that Greb has met since he took the title away from Gene a year ago. Tunney has been annoyed all this time because Greb smashed his nose by butting him in the first round of their previous fight …

> Tunney would stand a good chance against almost any other light heavyweight in the world, but Greb's speed and erratic manner of slashing away with dozens of blows from unconventional angles completely baffled him in their previous fight.[1076]

Fred Keats said that in their prior bout, Greb was allowed to do as he pleased. "He butted, wrestled, held and hit, used the thumb of his glove as an eye gouge and brought his elbows into play at every opportunity, while Referee Kid McPartland looked on and did nothing." Keats said butts broke Tunney's nose and caused a cut over his eye. "McPartland recently called the writer on the phone to explain his action – or rather lack of action – that night. He said that he did not disqualify Greb because Tunney was strong and full of fight. He wanted to give the fans a run for their money." Keats responded, "The fans got a run for their money, but Greb's fouling cost Tunney his title. That was not fair to Tunney, neither was it helpful to the sport in general."

[1075] *New York Daily News, New York American, Newark Evening News,* February 23, 1923.
[1076] *New York Call,* February 23, 1923. To avoid any appearance of crookedness, the referee would not be named until ring time.

The Walker law listed fouls, which included holding or deliberately maintaining a clinch, holding with one hand and hitting with the other, butting with the head or shoulder, hitting with the inside or butt of the hand, the wrist, or elbow, and wrestling or roughing on the ropes.

FIGHTING POSES OF THE PRINCIPALS IN TO-NIGHT'S BOUT.

GENE TUNNEY HARRY GREB

It is true that Greb's natural style is unorthodox and that often he breaks the rules without deliberately intending to do so. He is a little fellow who generally has to give away many pounds of weight and suffer a handicap of many inches in height and reach. Even for a man of his weight he is a pitifully weak hitter. Because of these things he has developed an original style of fighting that wins bouts. The only thing wrong with it is that it does not conform to the rules of the ring.

Greb never boxes in the open for more than a few seconds at a time. His system of defence consists of rushing from one clinch right back into another with the least possible delay between embraces. As he rushes in he swings one or both hands from some uncouth angle that no one but a novice would attempt.

For that sort of thing Greb invariably receives credit for forcing the fight and being the aggressor. In reality he is retarding the action, for every clinch slows the bout and detracts something from the interest.

If the judges and fans understood this more clearly, Greb would lose many bouts that he gets credit for winning. A boxer who brings about a clinch is not truly aggressive and he does not deserve the credit that goes to the man who does the forcing.[1077]

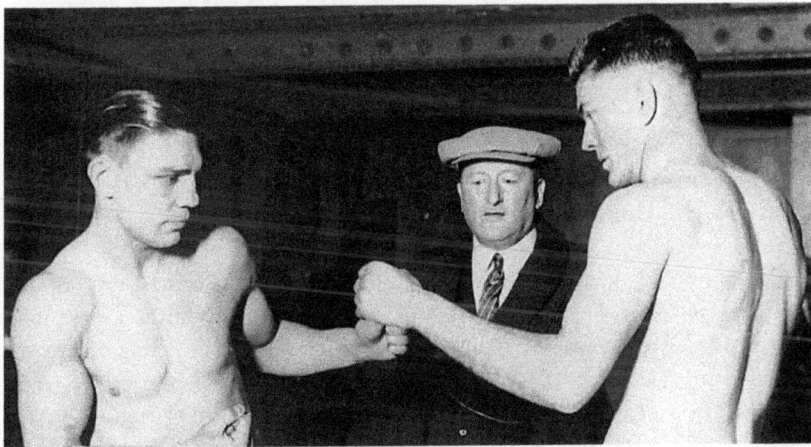

On February 23, 1923 at Madison Square Garden, New York City, 12,438 fans paid $47,396.45 or $49,891 to see 174-pound Gene Tunney win a very close and competitive but hotly debated and controversial 15-round split decision victory over 165 ½-pound Harry Greb to win back the American light heavyweight championship. Both had to weigh in at 175 pounds or less at 2 p.m. on the day of the fight.

Despite the reported numbers, George Underwood said, "The crowd seemed larger and the gate bigger, but those are the official figures, and that is all we know about it."

Harry Keck said the Garden was packed to the rafters, sold out, but what kept the gate revenues down was the fact that the top price for seats was only $7.70, including $.70 war tax, instead of the usual $16.50 for championship matches there. Greb received 37.5% and Tunney 12.5% of the gate. Greb took the fight in New York, challenger Tunney's home state, for financial reasons. He was guaranteed the lion's share, regardless of result. Greb earned $17,773.66, while Tunney earned $5,924.55. Tunney got the decision, but Greb got the money.

Reflecting how close and controversial the fight was, many thought Greb clearly won, many thought Tunney clearly won, while others insisted a draw would have been the proper result, or that Greb should have received no worse than a draw.

Those who supported the official decision said Tunney landed the cleaner, harder, more effective, properly thrown and legally landed blows, particularly to the body, while much of what Greb landed was set up by or the result of fouls, including holding, holding and hitting, and butting.

Those who supported a Greb victory said he outhustled Tunney, threw and landed more, and was the aggressor throughout. Any fouls were incidental and mutual as a result of the heavy combat, and both men fouled.

Many seemed to feel that Greb at least had earned a draw, when weighing all of the pros and cons for both in the balance.

Strong arguments were made for all three positions. It depended on one's scoring criteria. Ultimately, the official verdict was a split decision victory for Tunney, although initial reports incorrectly gave the impression that it was unanimous.

Scoring it for Tunney

George Underwood, *New York Evening Telegram*: Tunney, 11-3-1.
Henry Farrell, United Press: Tunney, 9-6.
Hype Igoe, *New York World*: "Tunney deserved the decision." "Greb's unsportsmanlike tactics probably went a long way toward bringing the title back to Gene Tunney." Greb generously used head butts. Those who wagered on Greb were not happy with the decision, "but it was a fair one. Discounting Greb's roughhousing, his eternal clinching, the butting and holding, the clean work, straight hitting, honest fighting was done by Tunney." "Greb used everything but Mexican spurs. On last night's showing Tunney can always lick Greb."

James Dawson, *New York Times*: "I thought Tunney won." "The majority of ringside critics approved the decision." "Tunney carried off 9 of the 15 rounds."

Ed Curley, *New York American*: "There is not the slightest doubt attached to Tunney's victory. He did the cleaner work, landed the most blows and his ring generalship overshadowed the effort of Greb."

Fred Keats, *New York Sun*: "Tunney deserved the decision because he scored more often and landed the only damaging wallops that connected." Greb was aggressive and led more, but also clinched a great deal and held and hit. Tunney landed solid body blows and hurt him in the 14th round.

Joe Vila, *New York Sun*: Tunney earned the decision by landing the greater number of clean blows, while Greb fouled throughout, and should have been disqualified.

Westbrook Pegler, *New York Call*: Tunney.

Dan Lyons, *New York Globe*: Tunney, 8-5-2. "The decision was a just one. … Tunney won cleanly… reckoning the disposition of points with strict regard to the rules laid down by the New York State Boxing Commission. … Scores of times…Referee Haley would have been fully justified in disqualifying Greb. … He was cautioned repeatedly, his transgressions, as of old, being holding and hitting with one hand, thumbing and heeling, clinching and wrestling…"

Fair Play: Tunney should have won by disqualification.

New York Evening Post: Tunney won by 2 rounds.

Scoring it for Greb

Charles Mathison, *New York Herald*: "Greb deserved the decision." "Tunney…made a radical change in his style of fighting and out-roughed even Greb. It is difficult to believe that the judges penalized Greb for his alleged rough work and thus found for the challenger."

W. C. Vreeland, *Brooklyn Daily Eagle*: Greb, 8-5-2.

Brooklyn Standard Union: Greb, 9-5-1.

Davis Walsh, International News Service: Greb close, 6-5-4.

Brooklyn Daily Times: Greb.

Grantland Rice, *New York Tribune*: "It was a poor decision. If anyone won, Greb did." "Greb did most of the fighting, most of the hitting and most of the holding. He used his head repeatedly, but, even considering the number of points he lost in this way, he still deserved the decision." "At the very worst Greb might have got a draw."

Sid Mercer, *New York Evening Journal*: "It was another one of those decisions. Greb should have been given the verdict."

James Sinnott, *New York Morning Telegraph*: Greb, 8-5-2. "I have never seen a decision that in my opinion was so unfair. If Harry Greb ever beat a fighter in his life, he beat Gene Tunney last evening."

Warren Brown, *New York Evening Mail*: "There are those today…who will say that the Pittsburgher was given the 'works,' and not without reason, for in this writer's opinion, the very worst Greb should have had was a draw. ... Greb's cry that he was 'jobbed' will find many sympathetic listeners."

Harry Keck, *Pittsburgh Gazette Times*, Greb, 7-4-4.

Jim Jab, *Pittsburgh Press*: Greb.

Regis Welsh, *Pittsburgh Post:* Greb in a landslide. Tunney won only 2 rounds.

Louis Jaffe, *Philadelphia Evening Ledger:* "I can't see how they gave Greb anything worse than a draw."

Newark Sunday Call: Tunney won only one round, the 14th. All the rest were Greb's. "Greb, who is a fighter every inch, battered the sedate Mr. Tunney from pillar to post."

Newark Evening News: Greb won decisively, just as clearly as he did in their first contest, so it was a terrible decision.

Newark Star Eagle: Tunney was lucky to get the decision.

Scoring it a Draw

Harry Newman, *New York Daily News:* "A draw would have been more like it."

William Granger, *Brooklyn Citizen*: Draw.

Walter Trumbull, *New York Herald:* "A draw would have been the fairer decision."

Jack Lawrence, *New York Tribune:* "A draw would have been just."

Ed Van Every, *Evening World*: Draw, 6-6-3. "Greb should have been credited with a draw." "The only reason for swaying the decision in favor of Tunney is Greb's known inability to box within the rules and regulations of the game. ... Otherwise, Tunney did not prove that he was the better man of the two in the fight last night."

Jersey Journal: Most of the newspaper critics asserted that Greb should have been given a draw at least, and should not have been uncrowned. The majority anti-Greb crowd greeted the decision with mingled acclaim and disapproval. Tunney raked and slashed at Greb's body, and the red marks shone on his torso. The 14th was Gene's big round, for he rocked Greb with a hard right to the jaw. Not once did Greb do as much damage to him. (It appears that this newspaper did not send a writer to the fight.)

The *New York Daily News'* Harry Newman noted that the decision was not a popular one. Most fans believed a draw would have been more appropriate. "It was drawing it very fine to wrest the championship title from a man when the battle seemed to be so close at the end."

The first six rounds of the fight were all Tunney, who plugged away at the body, and seemed to be more effective with his blows. But then Greb pitched into him with a fury in the 7th round and thereafter. Neither one was a puncher, but they slugged it out in a rough, unscientific manner throughout.

Once he appeared to have drawn even, Greb was accused of butting and fouling. He held in the clinches as well. Referee Patsy Haley cautioned him several times in the 12th round, and seemed on the verge of disqualifying Greb. "The famous rough tactics of Harry Greb were much in evidence as usual."

In the 14th round, Tunney staggered Greb with a straight right to the chin, and the follow-up attack forced him to the ropes. Greb recovered in the 15th, and his attack nearly closed Gene's right eye.

Newman concluded,

> Tunney grabbed a decision, but by a very scant margin. It might have just as well have been called a draw, and there were those who thought Greb was entitled to the verdict and the retention of his honors. ... No doubt the officials took into consideration the fact that Harry did considerable holding during the clinches and he was probably penalized when they reckoned the point score.

The *Brooklyn Citizen*'s William Granger said Tunney was lucky to get the decision, for Greb was the aggressor. Many believed it was nothing less than a robbery. The proper verdict should have been a draw.

Greb did the leading in 12 of the 15 rounds, but Tunney landed the cleaner and harder punches. Toward the end, Greb continually was in hot water with Referee Patsy Haley as a result of his holding around the neck with one arm and hitting with the other. Tunney never was in danger. In the 12th round, hard body smashes hurt Greb. That was when Harry started the holding and hitting tactics. A right to Greb's jaw in the 14th round sent Harry reeling back to the ropes. He clinched hard to survive. A powerful body shot made Harry grab again. That was the only time a decisive result seemed possible.

In typical fashion, Greb jumped around with his arms flailing in windmill fashion, while Tunney focused his attack on the body. Tunney landed harder, but he permitted his opponent to do so much of the leading that the fairness of the decision was open to question. Tunney started slowly, but Greb tired somewhat at the end, which made it easier for Tunney to hit him.

TUNNEY

GREB   GREB

The *Brooklyn Daily Eagle*'s W. C. Vreeland said the judges decided against Greb, who actually had a lead on points. Vreeland strongly disagreed, scoring it 8-5-2 for Greb. Everyone was surprised. Many reporters believed a draw should have been the worst that Greb received. It was 15 rounds of mauling and clawing.

The patrons were Tunney supporters for the most part. Whenever Greb used rough and foul tactics, and he did it often, he was booed and abused by the spectators. When Tunney struck Greb low and mauled him in the clinches, and he did it often, not a word was said.

Greb made the fight fast and furious with his aggressive work, but it smacked more of a street fight than a boxing match. Greb took a decided lead from the 7th to 10th rounds, staggering Tunney in the 7th. Greb liked to whirl swings from his waist, clinch, then let go and fire again. Sometimes he butted. He also did his usual dancing and flyaway leaps, but always was active and aggressive. His punches had more of a sting than force. Had his swings and uppercuts been as powerful as those of Tunney's, he would have done more damage. After the 8th round, Referee Patsy Haley cautioned Tunney for holding and using rough stuff in the clinches. In the 12th, Greb held and hit, and used his elbow to the face, which drew very stern warnings. Tunney's best round was the 14th, which may have influenced the judges. A right to the chin rocked Greb, the closest thing to a knockdown during the fight. Tunney's gloves and the ropes cut Greb's sides. Gene's lips were slightly cut. Tunney was the stronger and cleaner puncher, but only at times did he carry the battle to Greb. Still, Gene was more aggressive than in their first fight.

The *Brooklyn Daily Times* said Greb was the victim of a poor decision after outclassing his rival. It was one of the most unpopular verdicts for some time. Gene's own fans booed. Tunney's best round was the 14th, when a stiff right to the jaw sent Greb into the ropes. But Greb came back and was holding his own at the gong. The early rounds were fairly even, with Tunney having slightly the better of two rounds, but after the 6th round, Greb's tactics caused Gene to lose all semblance of form. Greb fought his usual whirlwind crowding battle, never allowing Gene to get set, beating him to the punch nearly every time. He leapt in with both hands flying. He clawed away, grabbed, and held with one hand while mauling with the other. Gene was tied in knots. Tunney suffered slight cuts under both eyes, but was strong at the finish. Greb had welts on his body from where he had been pulled along the ropes.

The *Brooklyn Standard Union* said Tunney won a rough and tumble bout, though the decision was a surprise to many who believed Greb deserved the honors. He didn't whip Greb, but the judges declared that he did, and their decision was official. Unbiased observers were shocked, and some thought rumors of a fix were true.

> It is an unwritten rule of the ring that a champion cannot be deprived of his titular possessions by a hairline verdict. And if ever there was a hairline verdict it was that of last night. At the very worst the Pittsburger should have been given a draw. A decision in his favor, while probably not a popular one, would have been more in line with what actually happened in the ring.

Tunney had no choice but to fight Greb's fight. They mauled and pushed and punched each other throughout, with Greb doing most of the leading. The crowd was with Tunney, a local product, and was hostile towards Greb, whom they booed and hissed at every provocation.

This writer gave Greb 9 rounds, Tunney 5 rounds, mostly early, as well as the 14th, with 1 even. A right in the 14th almost decked Greb, sending him across the ring and crashing into the ropes. It was the only punch that had Greb in serious trouble. Tunney mostly focused on the body. Greb really got going after the 5th round and won the rest of the way, except for the 14th round. Tunney complained to the referee continually, though he wasn't perfect either. The crowd roared with acclaim at the decision, but plenty disapproved.

Davis Walsh, International News Service Sports Editor, said the verdict was unjust to Greb, for he appeared to have won the majority of the rounds. This writer saw it close for Greb, 6-5-4.

Walsh said Greb was foul and rough, holding and hitting, but he was not disqualified, so it should have no bearing on the decision. Tunney fought a smarter and more strategic fight than last time. He feinted and rushed to close quarters, even outroughing Greb on occasion. Tunney scored best when slipping leads and countering to the body. It was his constant body attack that convinced some observers of his right to the decision. However, Walsh believed Greb landed the most punches, "although neither could have dented a charlotte russe." Greb also forced the pace throughout. Even when Tunney staggered him with an overhand right in the 14th round, his best punch of the night, Greb carried the honors in the furious exchange that followed.

Henry Farrell, United Press Staff Correspondent, agreed with the decision, saying Tunney had the edge in at least 9 rounds. New Yorkers approved of the decision, but it was not unanimously approved. Several competent critics thought Greb had won or it was a draw.

Most of the fight was a wrestling match, with very few clean blows landed. Greb fought foul throughout. He was warned at least two dozen times. "Even if Greb had been close to winning the decision, his foul work probably would have influenced the judges against him. Greb could not have gone much farther. In a 20-round bout he most certainly would have been knocked out."

George Underwood, for the *New York Evening Telegram*, said Tunney's concentrated, determined, prolonged body assault justly earned him the victory, for he administered grueling punishment there. He had Greb's body red, raw, bruised, and swollen, with angry welts.

> Tunney's body barrage slowed up Greb and robbed him of his effectiveness. Game as a bulldog, Harry kept flailing away, but his old bouncing, whirlwind attack was missing and he kept throwing his punches wide. On actual points, Tunney won by an unquestionable margin, taking eleven of the fifteen rounds. One of the rounds was even and three went to Greb. Harry would have taken a couple more stanzas were it not for the points which, as rendered imperative by the rules, had to be deducted for infractions of the rules.

Greb fought in his usual rough and tumble style, frequently holding and hitting. He also occasionally butted, though Tunney was almost as much at fault, for he ducked in a manner that Greb could not help sticking the top of his head into Tunney's face. Gene's leaning forward when Greb came rushing or jumping in made it inevitable that their heads would clash. Sometimes it seemed that referee Patsy Haley went a bit too far and annoyed Greb unnecessarily. Overall, though, the referee's work was beyond reproach, for he had a very tough job on his hands.

Underwood insisted, "Tunney won clearly, decisively, and by a margin that left no doubt of his superiority." He won convincingly by doing more real fighting than usual and keeping up a steady and merciless fire to the heart and wind. Greb's punches did not worry Tunney. "No other decision except 'Tunney wins' could honestly have been rendered. Despite this fact there were many who disagreed with it."

Underwood thought the complainers were disgruntled bettors, and those who sat far back from the ring and were not able to see the terrible body punishment Tunney administered. "But even in actual blows to the head Tunney landed more effective punches than Greb. And for every punch that Greb landed to the head Tunney poured a good half dozen to the body." Tunney was stronger too. Where Greb had the edge on Tunney was in his fighting instinct and raw stamina and endurance. He also was very tough. Some of the punches he took would have sent other men down.

The *New York Call's* Westbrook Pegler said Tunney whipped Greb from pillar to post, giving him a "thoroughgoing smashing" to win a slashing bout. Joe Humphries made the "obvious announcement that

Tunney was the winner and new champion." The fight was a "teamsters' brawl."

Tunney had improved power and science from their first fight. "This time Tunney had a useful knack of stepping forward or back a half stride as Greb came whaling in, which made Greb fall short or wrap his punches around Gene's shoulders. And as this flashing action occurred Tunney's solid knuckles would grind into Greb's body or pop him on the jaw." By the end, Greb's body was red and raw with welts. How he could accumulate all those punches was a mystery.

Tunney had the more distinct advantage in the first 8 - 10 rounds, avoiding the rushes or meeting them with a flurry of fists, but Greb improved in the later rounds, when Tunney faded. Greb often held with his left and landed a right uppercut to the face. His long smacking blows to the back did no harm.

Tunney seemed to have made a study of the things which bewildered him so badly the first time. He blocked the body blows with his arms, "and if he did catch many bursts of short right punches to the face or the side of his head they were trivial, mussy blows and not to be reckoned against the solid, well-directed smashes which he was always pouring into Greb's tropical zone." The nearest thing to a knockout was in the 12th, when Tunney caught him with a pair of body shots and a hard right on the chin, and Greb wobbled, but snapped back in a second. In the 13th, Greb doubled up from clouts to the head and body.

The crowd gave Tunney "a more than perfunctory hooray" at the decision, but many thought Greb was entitled to a draw.

The *New York Evening Post* said the fight was marked by much roughness and little real fighting. Greb was aggressive throughout, but marred his fighting by his "usual foul tactics, and to this more than any evident superiority of Tunney must he credit the loss of his title." The crowd was hostile towards Greb from the start.

Greb dashed in with arms flailing, but Tunney learned from the prior fight, blocked the blows, went in close and thumped Harry's ribs lustily with both hands. "This, in short, was the mode of the battle most of the fifteen rounds." Greb commenced his rough work early on, but the referee allowed it until the 12th round, when he was threatened with disqualification. "The contest was not up to championship standards, and Tunney didn't shine particularly." Tunney's body attack slowed up Greb late in the fight. Gene's best round was the 14th, when he almost floored Greb with a right to the jaw. "He had a lead of two rounds over Greb, but can thank the latter's roughness for his victory."

Jim Jab, for the *Pittsburgh Press*, said it was a coup, for Greb won, and should have received no worse than a draw. Tunney was an improved mixer, and fought Harry in a niftier fashion than half a century of glovemen who had been bamboozled by him. "Tunney shot a left for Greb's midsection and caught Harry coming in a score of times." He slowed up Harry and had his lips crimson. Greb often held with one fist around the neck and hit him with the other. Still, the aggressive Greb had thrown and landed more. "Tunney fought well but the best he should have was a draw. Even this plum could be questioned."

Regis Welsh, for the *Pittsburgh Post*, said Tunney received a gift, for he won only two rounds, and it was one of the worst robberies ever. Greb led and led, cut both of Tunney's eyes, hammered him at long range, and just kept fighting despite all the claims of foul. Tunney merely countered, and was beaten as badly as he was in their first match the previous May, winded and weak at the end.

Harry Keck, for the *Pittsburgh Gazette Times,* said it was a very questionable and unjust decision. The majority of fans cheered with joy, but most fair-minded spectators believed Greb had won. Keck scored it 7-4-4 for Greb.

Tunney primarily focused on the body. Greb set the pace and did the most leading, and was busier in the clinches. "The only possible excuse for the decision rendered tonight may be that the judges and the referee deprived Greb of points for his alleged fouling and the many warnings he received." Still, it was a hollow victory for Tunney. "Officially he is the winner, but to all other intents and purposes Greb came out of the scrap with a lion's share of the honors. The worst Greb should have been given was a draw and even that would have been a howling injustice, as we see it."

Writer Fair Play said Referee Haley overlooked Greb's holding, butting, and heeling methods, and could and should have disqualified Greb several times. Hence, the verdict for Tunney was "eminently just." "Greb started his holding with one hand and slamming with the other in the first round. He continued using this system with an occasional use of the top of his head against Tunney's chin and an intermittent flick of the heel of his glove. Referee Pat Haley cautioned him several times to no avail." At times, Haley literally had to pry Greb loose from Tunney. Haley should have disqualified Greb by the 5th round. "This would have been the technically legal way of giving the decision...and it would have been eminently fair."

Yet, ultimately, Fair Play harshly concluded, "Neither Greb nor Tunney showed real championship caliber."

The *Newark Evening News* said that fighting against physical odds of height, weight, and reach, and battling to overcome the reputation of being a foul scrapper, Greb rose to the acme of his career, but failed to win the decision. "The verdict was probably the most unsatisfactory one rendered in New York since the Walker law. ... Greb gave Tunney as bad a beating as he handed Gene when he took the light heavyweight championship from him." Rumors floated that it was "in" for Tunney to win if the contest was at all close, but not even those who thought they had an inside track figured Greb would get the worst of it, for "he made such a decisive job of the fight." Tunney landed but few real clean blows, the best one in the 14th, when a right made Greb's knees sag for a second.

"Outside of that Tunney never really landed a solid blow on Greb's head or chin, most of his attack being centered at Greb's body."

Tunney had much success in the first 8 rounds, countering every blow with body smashes. A right to the ribs landed almost every time, but after the 9th, Tunney couldn't connect as often, slowed up a great deal, and his defense weakened, other than his good moment in the 14th. Haley threatened to disqualify Greb in the 12th, when he had trouble separating them from the clinches. Again he cautioned him for holding and hitting.

All that said, Tunney fought differently than the first time, discarding the "timidity" which characterized his work in their prior bout.

The *Newark Star-Eagle's* Bert Dodge said Tunney was lucky to get the decision. Billy Gibson's propaganda about Greb's alleged foul work was a factor in Tunney's victory, but the new champ was just as rough as the Pittsburgher. "His change in style was successful, and he got the vote of the judges."

In the 14th round, Tunney landed a clean right to the jaw and followed it with a series of hard smashes which had Greb backing away, clearly dazed, which likely affected the decision. "Aside from that fourteenth round I fail to see how the officials could pick Tunney over Greb. The affair was fiercely fought and both men were doing a lot of clinching and holding. If there was any rough work Tunney was as guilty as Greb." Gene landed some low blows, but Greb made no complaint. Late in the contest, Greb was accused of twisting Tunney's neck in the clinches, and Haley warned him. "Greb went into the fight handicapped in that he had been accused of using illegal tactics in the former bout." Hence, much emphasis was laid on the necessity of clean fighting. "Looks very much as if Greb's reputation of being a foul scrapper had as much to do with causing the judges to decide against him last night as any other factor." "Most of the newspaper critics asserted that the champion should not have been uncrowned – that at least he should have been given a draw. The crowd, the majority anti-Greb, greeted the decision of the judges with mingled acclaim and disapproval."

Both men tried hard and fought fiercely throughout, but the constant holding marred the exhibition. "Tunney made use of his superior weight and forced Greb around the ring and against the ropes in the clinches. His style was much different than he usually employs. Gene shows better at clean, open work, where he has a chance to box, than he does in close fighting."

For the *New York Sun*, Fred Keats said Tunney regained the title in a bitter struggle. Just before they entered the ring, Greb was the 8 to 5 favorite, though earlier in the evening Tunney was the 6 to 5 choice.

> As a contest the bout was disappointing. It consisted mostly of clinching and arguments with the referee over the rules. At the finish little Patsey Haley was more exhausted than either of the fighters, as a result of his struggles to tear them apart. ...

Greb lost because for once he was forced to live up to the rules. In their previous battle Greb had defeated Tunney by fracturing his nose by rushing at him with head down and butting him squarely in the face. Deep gashes over both eyes caused by the same method killed Tunney's chances of winning.

Greb's tactics on that occasion aroused so much criticism that particular pains were taken last night to see that the rules were observed. ... Unable to practice his usual tricks Greb was harmless. He inflicted no wounds and he failed to land a dangerous wallop at any stage of the proceedings. For the first six rounds he stuck close to the rules and there was no trouble, but he did not have a chance. If he cannot fight in a bar room style Greb cannot fight at all.

Rendered desperate by the fact that he was losing Greb began to rough it in the seventh. From that point on he met with more success, but he was constantly in trouble with the referee. Twice in the twelfth round Greb got Tunney's head in chancery and pummeled him with his free hand. Haley stopped the fight to warn him and Greb talked back with much heat.

Tunney deserved the decision because he scored more often and landed the only damaging wallops that connected. He played for the body continually and at the close of the battle Greb's left side was covered with welts from the right handers that Tunney had driven home as Greb came rushing in. Tunney also showed the better defense, blocking, slipping and ducking Greb's wild leads in clever style.

Greb, however, did the major portion of the leading and it was on this account that many thought he deserved a draw at least. Greb played for the head, and the crowd always pays more attention to leads of that kind than body blows, which are less spectacular although really more damaging.

Greb's leading would have earned him far more points if he had not nullified everything he gained by clinching after every lead. The fact that he had to be warned constantly for fouling also detracted from his point score.

Although Tunney deserved the decision, he won more because Greb put up a poor fight than because of anything remarkable that he accomplished. ... As it happened, Greb had nothing at all and Tunney was only a trifle better.

Keats noted that in the 14th round, Tunney landed the fight's only staggering blow, a right hook on the chin. Greb staggered back a few paces, almost going to the floor. "This blow undoubtedly had a great deal of influence with the judges in making their decision."

Another article in the *Sun* said the battle was "either a robbery or a reward of merit. It all depends upon the point of view or the opinion of the individual. And opinion, be it said, was as divergent as the zenith and nadir." "Had the crowd been canvassed, however, a great diversity of opinion might have been recorded." Bantamweight champion Joe Lynch strongly denounced the decision. Others fully supported the decision.

Greb declared that he was jobbed out of his title. Harry said it was "one of those things."

> That was a pippin. If ever I beat a man, if ever I tamed a man, I tamed Tunney. ... I'll fight him any place, at any time, for any purse. I can lick him seven days a week. .... I never was hurt. He never stopped me for a second, but he whined and whimpered to the referee for help, and he got it. Haley was on me half a dozen times, until I lost my temper and argued with him. I'd like to battle him fifteen more rounds right now.

His manager, Red Mason, said a robbery can happen even in New York. "I am making no charges. I don't even insinuate, but there was a lot of talk about this battle. We heard rumblings and whispers, but they were all of the same thing. We were warned that this would be put over on us, and it surely was. In my judgment the bout was not even close."

Conversely, Tunney partisans declared that Gene won by a city block. Billy Gibson said, "Right and fair play were vindicated. ... Greb merited disqualification not once but half a dozen times. He transgressed every rule of the game. ... He was bad to-night, but worse when he beat Gene for the title."

Tunney said, "I feel fine. I came through almost without a scratch and at the end was full of fight and go. ... I don't care to discuss the methods pursued by Greb. He did not get away with the stuff that featured his previous fight with me, and therefore was not able to win. I am tickled to death over winning back my title."

Referee Patsy/Patsey Haley said Greb's foul tactics, including holding and butting, influenced his verdict for Tunney. "I warned Greb repeatedly after the 1st round, and threatened to disqualify him in the 12th after he had ignored my repeated admonitions." He also said, "Greb violated the rules frequently, and finally carried his work to a point where I had to threaten to throw him out of the ring. ... He held and hit many times. ... There was no other decision possible." Haley did not disqualify Greb because he wanted to give the fans a run for their money.

The *New York American's* Ed Curley said Greb had no excuse for losing, and his squawk about being jobbed was entirely out of place. The day after the fight, there were many torrid discussions. Many claimed Greb at least was entitled to a draw, but that just weakened their argument. Curley opined that there was no such thing as a draw, for a man either won or lost a fight. Oftentimes draws were rendered, but usually it was because both were putting up a corking close fight and it seemed cruel to one to declare the other a winner.

> There is not the slightest doubt attached to Tunney's victory. He did the cleaner work, landed the most blows and his ring generalship overshadowed the effort of Greb. The latter was persistent most of the time, but though he threw his gloves around steadily they missed more often than they landed. Several times he hooked Tunney with a light left and received a terrific body blow in return.

The referee was not alone in his contention that Greb broke the rules throughout. "There was no other recourse for the officials than to give the battle to Tunney."

Curley believed that Tunney needed to become more vicious and leave his manners outside the ring. He had a golden opportunity in the 14th round, but did not throw enough desperation into his blows as a Dempsey would have done. "Jack Dempsey is one of the most genial men one could meet socially. In the ring he's a rip rarin' wildcat."

There likely would be another match, for both would earn good money for it. "When they meet again it is next to certain that Tunney will win by a bigger margin."

The *New York Times* reported, "The majority of ringside critics approved the decision. However, they were not undivided. Like the spectators, the critics were not unanimous." The spectators booed Greb, while they cheered Tunney.

> A withering body fire with which he raked his rival throughout the bout won the title for Tunney. The new champion started his body attack with the opening gong, and did not cease fire until the final clang of the bell. In the closing four rounds Tunney, in a desperate attempt to score a knockout, pounded Greb unmercifully in the stomach, wind and ribs. He had Greb's left side bruised and sore. The red blotches which appeared upon Greb's skin spoke louder than did Greb's involuntary holding at every opportunity of the terrific punishment the Pittsburgh boxer assimilated from the wicked right and left hand drives of Tunney.

> Tunney carried off nine of the fifteen rounds. The Greenwich Village boxer won the first five and with his furious assault in the closing rounds carried off the twelfth, thirteenth, fourteenth and fifteenth. In the fourteenth session Tunney almost floored his rival with a terrific right to the jaw. Greb recovered quickly, however, and resumed his peculiar style of battling, plunging and tearing in wildly, his arms swinging incessantly but without any sense of direction. Tunney met Greb in one of the latter's rushes with a terrific right to the heart that almost doubled Greb in the centre of the ring. The failing champion dove in and held tenaciously until the effects of the blow passed.

These indications of distress on the part of Greb were the nearest things to a knockdown the bout produced. In the early rounds Greb was punished severely about the body and it seemed that he could not withstand the assault. Greb not only stood up under the battering but gave Tunney a worrisome spell for a time after fifth round.

Greb's best work was done in the sixth, seventh, eighth, ninth, tenth, and eleventh rounds. In these rounds Greb worried his rival with a relentless assault which completely baffled Tunney and had the Greenwich Village idol on the run. ... In these six rounds Greb was tireless. ... A left hook in the seventh cut Tunney's right eye and drew blood.

From the 6th through 8th rounds, Tunney seemed to be tiring, affected by the pace, harried by the rushing, plunging Greb's ceaseless fire.

Tunney unleashed a furious drive in the 9th, but Greb still outscored him in this as well as the next two rounds.

In the 12th, Greb was threatened with disqualification for holding as well as holding and hitting. "Tunney directed his fire throughout the round to Greb's body and hurt Greb noticeably." Tunney continued his assault until the end of the contest.

Tunney fought a much different battle than last time. He was less indecisive and timid, and sailed right in, meeting Greb's rushes with a barrage of his own. "The blows had the effect of diminishing Greb's resistance and made him seek the shelter of clinches early."[1078]

The next day, the New York Boxing Commission said there was nothing wrong with the decision. A great number of the gamblers who had wagered on Greb were upset. The *Brooklyn Citizen* said, "Opinion was widely divided on the justice of the decision, even in neutral circles, but it was unanimously agreed that Greb was a very poor loser and that he would not get very far in claiming that he did not lose on the level." In response to Greb's accusations and insinuations, Tunney said, "All I know is that the judges said I won and I thought I did win. If they had voted Greb the winner, I would have said nothing."[1079]

Despite all of the next-day newspapers giving the impression that the decision was unanimous, Charles Mathison announced that in fact, it was a split decision.

Charles E. Miles, one of the judges, wrote the name of Greb as the winner, while Charles J. Meegan, the other judge, registered that Tunney was the victor. With a division between the judges, it devolved on the referee, Patsy Haley, to cast the deciding vote.

[1078] *Buffalo Times*, February 23, 1923; *New York Daily News*, *Brooklyn Citizen*, *Brooklyn Daily Eagle*, *Brooklyn Daily Times*, *Brooklyn Standard Union*, *Buffalo Courier*, *New York Evening Telegram*, *New York Call*, *Syracuse Journal*, *New York Evening Post*, *Evening Star*, *Harrisburg Telegraph*, *Newark Evening News*, *Newark Star-Eagle*, *New York Sun*, *New York Times*, *Jersey Journal*, February 24, 1923; *New York American*, *Pittsburgh Press*, *Pittsburgh Post*, *Pittsburgh Gazette Times*, February 24, 25, 1923; Tunney had his manager, Billy Gibson, in his corner, while Greb had current manager James Mason and Tom Dolan.
[1079] *Brooklyn Citizen*, February 25, 1923.

Haley wrote the name of Tunney on his slip, which gave the decision to Tunney.[1080]

Regis Welsh said an appeal might be made to "William Muldoon, who by illness, was absent from the ring last night."

Despite his alleged absence, speaking unofficially, Muldoon said the decision was unjust, for Greb should have won. However, Muldoon only was offering his own private opinion. The commission's accredited representatives decided that Tunney was the victor. "That is the official decision. The commission will stand by it." Muldoon ridiculed reports of a conspiracy to deprive Greb of his title. The *Brooklyn Standard Union* said, "There will be no investigation, because the officials rendering the decision are regarded as being above suspicion." Did Muldoon even see the fight?

The *New York Times* said "opinion was divided as to the justification for the decision."[1081]

Regis Welsh favored Tommy Gibbons to knock out Tunney. "Gibbons can stop Tunney, having a punch, which Greb lacks."[1082]

Joe Vila said the New York State Athletic Commission was embarrassed by Chairman Muldoon's criticism of the officials' decision in Greb-Tunney. "Haley is considered the most competent referee in the East, if not in this country. Meegan is a former sporting editor and boxing critic of long experience. Haley and Meegan...decided that Tunney had won. They based their judgment on a strict interpretation of the rules prescribed by the Walker boxing law." In explaining their verdict, they noted that Greb's foul tactics counted against him, "in accordance with the rules as they are set forth in black and white." Miles cast his vote for Greb. It was true that there was a "wide difference of opinion" regarding the decision, but Vila felt it was just.

> If Referee Haley had exercised full authority with which he was clothed by the boxing law he would have disqualified Greb the moment the latter showed a disposition to ignore his words of warning, which were prompted by foul tactics. Such action by Haley might have disappointed some of the fans, yet it would have prevented the present unpleasant controversy.

> Greb is a 'roughhouse' fighter, not a boxer. ... Greb violated the rules against "holding and hitting," "butting," "roughing on the ropes" and "heeling with the gloves." ... Greb flagrantly broke the rules and, in view of that undeniable fact, he didn't deserve to win. Tunney earned the decision for two outstanding reasons – he landed the greater number of clean blows and honestly tried to observe the rules of fair play.

[1080] *Pittsburgh Post*, February 25, 1923; *Brooklyn Daily Eagle*, February 28, 1923.
[1081] *New York Times*, February 25, 1923; *Brooklyn Standard Union*, February 26, 1923.
[1082] *Pittsburgh Daily Post*, February 26, 1923.

Vila said both men would have been easy marks for Stanley Ketchel, who "would have stopped both the same night in a few rounds." He also harshly said, "Neither Greb nor Tunney is a first class ringman." Gibbons was not much better than Tunney. Bob Fitzsimmons would have stopped all of them – Greb, Tunney, Gibbons, Carpentier, and Siki.[1083]

Henry Farrell interviewed Jack McAuliffe, the old lightweight champion, who said,

> This Gene Tunney howling about Harry Greb's foul fighting makes me sick. A great big fellow like Tunney ought to be ashamed of himself to ask the referee to make a little fellow like Greb stop fouling him. If Tunney had been fighting in our day he would have fouled back and if he fouled back harder, he would have stopped Greb. With big gloves like they wear now it is ridiculous to howl about gouging and heeling. … No one ever heard Jack Dempsey or any of the real fighters talk about being fouled… A real fighter will make a foul fighter quit before he gets started.
>
> There are too many rules now. There should be no rule against holding and hitting because it is a part of real fighting. As long as either man can do anything in a clinch they ought not to be separated. Only when both are blocked completely is it a real clinch.
>
> America has been taking the lead among the world's nations in the production of real fighters so far, because the Americans were allowed to fight.[1084]

W. C. Vreeland said, "Every man who knows the least thing about boxing, who was unprejudiced and has no axe to grind in behalf of either Greb or Tunney, realized at the termination of the bout that there was no way, shape or manner that Tunney could be adjudged the winner on points." Vreeland believed both fighters were foul, and if Greb indeed was so foul, he should have been disqualified. But if he was not disqualified, the fight should have been decided on points, not fouls.[1085]

Gotham scribe Fred Keats said Greb lost because he committed so many minor fouls that his score was reduced to nothing. "He adds that the judge and referee who voted against Greb was simply applying one of the New York commission's rules, which says that 'points must be deducted for fouls of a minor character.'" He argued that Greb only scored when he held and hit, which was a violation of the rules, so he received no credit. Keats added, "The truth about Greb is that he does not belong in modern boxing. The methods he employs are those of the old days when London prize ring rules were in force. The Marquis of Queensberry rules were adopted to do away with wrestling, hugging and head in chancery work." Greb did not like open fighting at long range,

[1083] *New York Sun*, February 27, 1923. *New York Daily Standard Union*, February 28, 1923.
[1084] *Pittsburgh Press*, February 28, 1923.
[1085] *Brooklyn Daily Eagle*, February 28, 1923.

without clinching and mauling, because he was "utterly incompetent to do so."

> He never makes a lead that he does not follow with a clinch. His aim is so poor that nine out of ten of his leads miss the mark. ... It is only when Greb gets a firm grip with one hand that he does any real fighting. Prevent him from holding and hitting at the same time and he is lost. ... That is why he was constantly in hot water during Friday night's bout. ... But why call a man a champion who cannot get along without holding?[1086]

Most agreed that the best way to settle matters was for Greb and Tunney to fight again. As seen from the scoring and multiple and at times widely divergent, diametrically opposed viewpoints regarding this fight, it became abundantly clear that Tunney vs. Greb was a very close, competitive, interesting matchup, and scoring their fights could be challenging, depending on what one liked, disliked, and the scoring criteria being utilized.

Interestingly, in somewhat of a bombshell, shortly after the Greb-Tunney fight, it was reported that Harry Greb had paid $3,000 "publicity money" to New York writers to boost him and help him get a bout with Jack Dempsey. The problem with that though, is whether and to what degree such might have influenced writers in their opinions of his performances and in rendering their newspaper opinions. Greb subsequently made denials, but Charles J. Doyle, a Pittsburgh sport critic who first reported the story, declared that Greb made the admissions to him personally. "He said he received something like $15,000 for fighting (his first fight with Gene Tunney), but left New York shortly afterward with about $8,000. Three thousand of this amount, he said, was to be used for New York newspaper men for booming a fight with Dempsey." Apparently, he claimed to have made the payments "under protest," feeling that he should not have had to do so. However, his revelations backfired to some degree, and several writers called such actions unethical.

Ralph Davis said Greb must have forgotten to "sweeten" some of the newsmen, "or perhaps a few of them were too honest to take the money. At any rate, some of them are still camping on Harry's trail, telling the world all about the Pittsburgher, and a few things besides."[1087]

Headwork Couldn't Save Greb

Roughhouse Harry Greb used everything but Mexican spurs on Gene Tunney in an unsuccessful attempt to retain the light heavyweight championship in Madison Square Garden, New York. Greb is shown here butting Tunney in the twelfth round of the battle.

[1086] *Pittsburgh Press*, February 28, 1923.
[1087] *Pittsburgh Press*, February 28, 1923; Davis Walsh, *Akron Beacon Journal*, March 6, 1923.

William Muldoon said the commission would take no action on the report. It really was not relevant to him, because the writers technically had no formal role in the sport. It was between Greb and them.[1088]

Bert Dodge said ring experts had decided that Luis Firpo was no boob. The powerful giant was an impressive figure when in action, with a lot more speed than Willard ever had. He was a potential menace to Dempsey. "Luis can hit with his left, and he is able also to wallop with a mighty powerful right." He had unusual strength and a wonderful ability to resist hard blows. However, it was questionable whether he (or anyone else) could take the type of punches that Dempsey could hand out. His defense was his offense. If he landed his powerful sledgehammer blows on Brennan, Firpo likely would win their upcoming bout. Dodge said if his handlers were wise, they would hire (or keep) Jimmy De Forest as his trainer, the Newark veteran, who prepared Dempsey for Willard and knew about his methods.[1089]

In other news, the New York Commission granted Joe Jeannette a license to referee and judge, making him New York's first "colored" official.[1090]

Damon Runyon said Jack Dempsey and Babe Ruth were the kings of the two biggest sports, but were a contrast in personalities. Jack was quieter and more polished. Both were restless, liking to be on the go constantly. The Babe probably could sit still longer than Dempsey. Strange as it may seem, Dempsey was the gentler of the two, in talk and in general. He had a soft voice and shy manner. The Babe had a deep vocal tone and was bold, almost truculent in his approach. The Babe was a talker, while Jack was more of a listener. The Babe would talk baseball at length, while Jack talked little about any topic, and hardly at all about boxing. Jack was two years younger, but seemed to have an even greater quality of youthfulness; yet at the same time greater seriousness. He smiled more than Babe, but his smile struck one as politely perfunctory, rather than joyful. He seemed to have a deeper sense of responsibility toward life than King Babe. Both liked a tinge of roughness to their fun, and enjoyed practical jokes. Both started life with little advantage. Jack had acquired more polish, though Babe when he desired could glow with the shine of politeness and manners. Babe was a spendthrift, tossing his money around freely. Jack spent his money lavishly for his own living and in providing for his family, but was no sucker with it. Babe had bet as much as $20,000 on a horse race, while Jack "wouldn't bet you that much money that the sun will rise tomorrow." Both liked the good things – nice hotels, clothes, good food. They were sociable and enjoyed having company around them. Both liked children and outdoor life. They were well-aware of the public's fickleness. The Babe said the minute he stopped hitting home runs, he would be treated like a nobody. Jack said the instant

[1088] *Pittsburgh Post*, March 7, 1923.
[1089] *Newark Star-Eagle*, February 24, 1923.
[1090] *New York Morning Telegraph*, February 25, 1923.

some chap hit him on the jaw and knocked him out, the crowds would stop following him.[1091]

Jack Kearns said that once a challenger really hurt or decked Dempsey, those who were skeptical about his greatness would alter their views when he came back to win. Or so he believed. "In all the years that I have handled him I have never seen him on the floor; never really seen him hurt." The real test of a fighter was when he was hurt and the battle was going against him. He was stunned momentarily against Carpentier, but came back strong with brutal blows. "I know that he is game to the core and I know that he is a madman when hurt – that he is three times a better fighter when fury prompts him than when he is battling in cold, calculating fashion in an effort to bring down his man at the earliest possible moment." Kearns believed Dempsey hit harder than any man who ever lived.[1092]

A March 1, 1923 dispatch claimed that a Dempsey-Gibbons fight would take place in Shelby, Montana on July 4. Local sportsmen had arranged everything. An arena would be erected, as well as training quarters for Gibbons at Shelby, and Dempsey at Great Falls, Montana.[1093]

Montana's Attorney General, Wellington Rankin, said the Dempsey-Gibbons match would be legal if it was limited to 15 rounds.

Shelby promoters had raised money to make a $100,000 deposit, and they were prepared to guarantee $200,000 to Dempsey and $50,000 to Gibbons.[1094]

It was unclear whether the match really was on, or was one of many rumored Dempsey fights being negotiated.

On the afternoon of March 1 at Tommy McFarland's gym in Los Angeles, 199-pound Dempsey boxed 6 rounds, 2 each with three men – Jack Moore, George Lavine, and Morris Lux, and then he wrestled for 10 minutes with Johnny Meyers.

On March 2 at the same gym, Dempsey boxed 8 rounds, 2 each with Joe Benjamin, Lee Moore, Morris Lux, and an unknown.[1095]

Dempsey's mom currently lived in a Los Angeles residence at 2915 South Western avenue, which Jack had given to her. She was a small, dark, shy, 63-year-old woman. She was the mother of 11 children, 4 of whom were dead. Jack was the ninth child. She did not care much for society, but loved California, and was proud of her new home. His mother said,

> Jack always liked to fight, and I never tried to persuade him against it. I have always encouraged my children to follow the line of their liking, and Jack seems to have been blessed in his work. The danger of prize fighting never even occurred to me. He has never been injured but once, when he had two ribs broken, and then he fought on to a finish and won.

[1091] *Buffalo Courier*, February 25, 1923.
[1092] *Binghamton Press*, February 28, 1923.
[1093] *Los Angeles Times*, March 2, 1923.
[1094] *Buffalo Express*, March 4, 1923. Allegedly, an arena would be constructed large enough to seat 100,000 people.
[1095] *Los Angeles Times*, March 2, 3, 1923.

Early on, Jack fought in mining camps for meal tickets. He had come a long way.

Mrs. Dempsey was related to Senator Reed Smoot of Utah. Her father was John Smoot of Kentucky, the first cousin of Abram Smoot, the senator's father. Her father, who weighed more than 200 pounds, was known as the bully of Logan County, West Virginia, where she was born.

Mrs. Dempsey even discussed the color line. "Although like other Southerners, Mrs. Dempsey loves the colored folks, she believes her son was right when he drew the color line." She said, "If the public compels Jack to defend his title against a colored person, then the public should pay a million dollars for it."[1096]

On March 5, 1923 in Chicago, Tommy Gibbons knocked out Jim Tracey in the 2nd round, first decking him with a left hook, and then a second time with a right cross to the jaw.

The *Chicago Tribune* said, "Gibbons showed all the stuff he has been credited with. He boxed cleverly and nearly every punch hit the intended marks. He picked off most of Tracey's blows in the air and always beat his opponent to the counter. There was power in his punches and he made them all count. He made a decided impression on the fans."[1097]

Mike Collins was representing the Shelby promotional interests. He admitted that formal articles had not yet been signed, but claimed that Gibbons' manager Eddie Kane and Jack Kearns had told him the offer was satisfactory.[1098]

Some wondered where unfamiliar Shelby, Montana was located.

On March 7, 1923 in New York, Luis Firpo, who was preparing for his upcoming bout against Bill Brennan, sparred 9 rounds, 3 each with former champion Jack Johnson, Jamaica Kid, and Al Reich. Firpo appeared to advantage against Reich and the Jamaica Kid, but "with Johnson he was a sad spectacle. He couldn't lay a glove on the man who conquered Jim Jeffries." Another said, "Johnson enthused all hands with his fine defensive tactics. ... Jack allowed Firpo to get within striking distance of him, but when he got a little too fresh Jack assented him himself with a variety of left hooks and light right crosses." Johnson gave Firpo advice on how to improve. Trainer

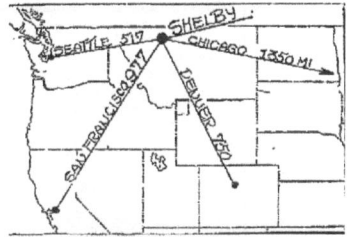

[1096] *Los Angeles Times*, March 4, 1923.
[1097] *Chicago Tribune*, March 6, 1923.
[1098] *Belvidere Daily Republican*, March 6, 1923.

Jimmy De Forest, who was handling Firpo, said Luis would knock out Brennan with a right cross.[1099]

Firpo was not the most skilled heavyweight, relying more on strength and power, but he was improving rapidly under De Forest's tutelage.

On March 9, Firpo's sparring with John Lester Johnson (a former Dempsey opponent) and Jamaica Kid resembled an actual fight.[1100]

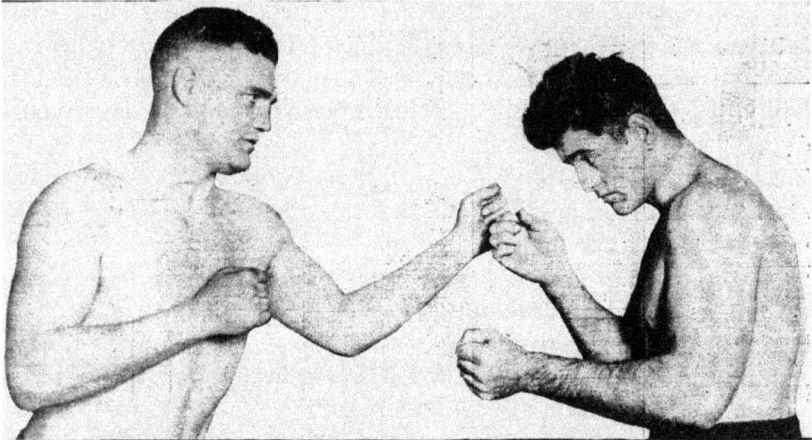

BRENNAN		FIRPO
Twenty-nine	Age	Twenty-six
198 pounds	Weight	223 pounds
6 feet 1 inch	Height	6 feet 2½ inches
17 inches	Neck	17 inches
79½ inches	Reach	79 inches
15½ inches	Biceps	13½ inches
41 inches	Chest, Normal	44 inches
45 inches	Chest, Expanded	48¼ inches
34 inches	Waist	36½ inches
9¼ inches	Wrist	8¼ inches
25 inches	Thigh	23¾ inches
19½ inches	Calf	15 inches
9¼ inches	Ankle	9½ inches

On March 12, 1923 in New York at Madison Square Garden, before 11,035 fans who generated $42,741, 220-pound 26-year-old Luis Firpo of Argentina knocked out 203-pound 29-year-old Bill Brennan (77-16-8) in the 12th round of a scheduled 15-round bout. Firpo was the first man other than Dempsey to stop Brennan. He had accomplished the feat in the same round that the champion had stopped Brennan.

The *Brooklyn Daily Eagle's* W. C. Vreeland called Firpo the Tarzan of the Ring. He wore down Bill with a shower of blows. Firpo had great strength and endurance. He stood up to all of Brennan's heavy blows, showing that he could take it too. His punches carried terrible force. He had the strength of a "man-ape." An avalanche of punches finally knocked out the very tough Brennan. "The marvel was that he stood up as long as he did under Firpo's sledgehammer blows." Many Spanish-Americans came to support Luis.

Vreeland said there was both good and bad to Firpo. He was as powerful as a "great ape." His right could fell an ox. He had courage, fighting spirit, and came back after being stung. He could take punches,

[1099] *Brooklyn Citizen, Pittsburgh Daily Post*, March 8, 1923.
[1100] *New York Daily News*, March 10, 1923.

and his lungs were wonderful. He showed no fatigue, despite his hard work and exertions in throwing Brennan away from him during the clinches. He was cool and unperturbed by anything Brennan did.

The bad was that Firpo's boxing was crude and undeveloped. He was wide open in his attack. Yet, he showed improvement over his last visit, against a superior world-class opponent to what he had fought previously. Still, "I wouldn't let him go up against men like Harry Wills or Jack Dempsey for at least another year." He was open to punches, and his left was puny in comparison with his right. He needed to improve upon his weaknesses. Despite all that, he had knocked out a world-class man.

The *Brooklyn Standard Union* said Firpo won with a looping overhead right to the back of the neck. It took several minutes to revive Brennan. Firpo was not particularly skillful, but he was big, strong, powerful, hard-punching, and game, aggressive, tough, and well-conditioned enough to knock out a highly respected contender late in the fight. Firpo was called a crude caveman, rough, strong, uncouth, with a terrible right wallop, and the fiercest fighting face ever seen, "almost maniacal in expression." He fought like an enraged bull. Brennan was outpointing him, but Firpo did not fight for points, but to score a knockout.

The *Brooklyn Citizen's* William Granger said there never had been a heavyweight battle in New York like it. There was no fancy boxing; no clinching to speak of – just a slam-bang fight from the start until Brennan was beaten to the floor, unconscious. Some said the final punch was a rabbit punch to the back of the neck (perfectly legal at that time), while others said it was a right to the jaw, which was set up by body blows and uppercuts. Firpo had improved in boxing knowledge, but his forte was brute strength – throwing every punch in the book, rights, hooks, uppercuts, to the body and head, with power.

The *Brooklyn Daily Times* said brute strength and determination beat superior experience and generalship. Brennan had forgotten more than Firpo ever knew, but nevertheless was battered to the canvas. Brennan gave his best, but Firpo was too strong. "He is a natural fighter, and what he lacks in science he makes up in brute power."

The *Daily News'* Harry Newman said Brennan was leading on points, outboxing Firpo, when in the 12th round, after a series of terrific right and left wallops had Brennan reeling and tottering about, until a heavy, crushing right-slam put him to sleep, out cold.

Firpo was too strong, and kept ripping and tearing in, swinging powerful blows throughout. When he landed, he shook up Brennan considerably. Brennan had a wonderful capacity to absorb punishment, or he would have been out cold long before he was under the terrible barrage. Still, Bill stung Firpo repeatedly with lefts to the face, though they did not hurt him. He cut Firpo's eye in the 5th round, and kept pecking away, outpointing him. Brennan was the better boxer, leading on points, but Firpo just pounded him down to defeat. Whenever Firpo landed, his blows had an awful effect.

One writer said there was no question as to Firpo's ability to stand up under punishment, for Brennan hit him plenty, and hard, but he took it and kept firing heavy blows. In the 5th round, Firpo was cut between his eyes, which split his nose, and he bled profusely. Defense was not his specialty. Still, "There is going to be some work for Jack [Dempsey] to do before long." Firpo had "arrived."

Based on the limited films in existence, Firpo had a brand of wild but effective awkwardness, combining aggression, impetuous sudden bursts of speedy and ferocious swings, but mixing it up well, with heavy overhand rights, wide hooking rights, left hooks, left and right uppercuts, and some lead set-up jabs and body blows. He could step in quickly, and had bull-like strength in the clinches. He was good at sensing when he landed a good one or hurt his foe, following up well, proving that he was a finisher. He seemed determined to impose his will on his Brennan.[1101]

Fight fans were excited and eager to see the big, strong, aggressive, hard-punching Firpo go against Dempsey. It likely would be a very entertaining war. Dempsey had the speed and skill, but Firpo had the superior size and overall brute strength. Both could hit very hard. Since visiting America for the first time, Firpo had scored all knockouts leading up to the Brennan bout: KO7 Tom Maxted, KO5 Joe McCann, TKO5 Italian Jack Herman, KO4 Jim Tracey (in Buenos Aires), and now KO12 Bill Brennan. Fight fans always have loved an aggressive puncher, and they knew a Dempsey-Firpo fight would yield explosive fireworks.

From Los Angeles, Dempsey said Firpo had to be a good fighter to stop Brennan, who was mighty tough. Jack was willing to fight him. "I am ready to fight any man any time a promoter can put the bout on in a satisfactory manner."[1102]

[1101] *Brooklyn Standard Union, Brooklyn Citizen, Brooklyn Daily Times, Brooklyn Daily Eagle, New York Daily News*, March 13, 1923.
[1102] *Los Angeles Times*, March 14, 1923.

Tex Rickard planned to match Firpo with the winner of the Willard vs. Floyd Johnson fight, which would earn that last man standing the right to fight Dempsey.[1103]

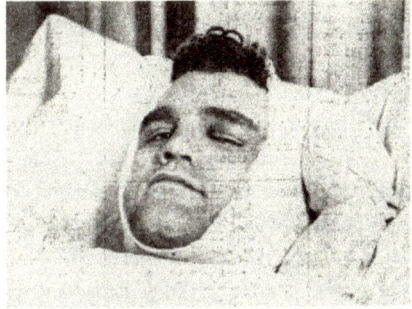

As a result of the Firpo contest, Bill Brennan was hospitalized for several days, having suffered a severe concussion. The left side of his head was quite inflamed.

Brennan admitted that it was the worst beating he ever received. "Firpo hurt me with every body blow he landed. Dempsey never hit me any harder than this fellow. ... I gave him the best I had but couldn't weather the storm."[1104]

As of the 17th, five days after the fight, Bill still was at the Jewish Memorial Hospital. Although he was resting comfortably, at times he was "mentally deranged." A doctor said he was improving, but still suffered from dizziness and fainting spells. He probably would leave the hospital within the next five or six days, but he might not be able to fight again.[1105]

The state of Montana was strong for the Dempsey-Gibbons bout. Sports enthusiasts of the little oil town of Shelby had pledged $200,000 for the July 4 fight. The American Legion would oversee the affair, and profits would be devoted to caring for the state's disabled soldiers.[1106]

Kearns noted that Dempsey was itching to fight, so they likely would fight Gibbons in Shelby.

On March 17, 1923 in Dublin, Ireland, former middleweight Mike McTigue (86-24-8) won the world light heavyweight championship by winning a 20-round decision over Battling Siki (50-9-3).

On March 19, 25-year-old Morris Reisler, son of John the Barber Reisler (who had sued Dempsey multiple times), pled guilty to 2nd degree murder for killing his aunt, Bertha Katz, his mother's sister. He had been indicted jointly with his mother, brother, and uncle in connection with the shooting, but charges against the other defendants were dismissed.

Morris Reisler's mother Minnie alleged that her sister Bertha had been having an affair with her husband John the Barber for about 12 years. In an attempt to protect her son, Mrs. Minnie Reisler had tried to take the blame for the killing, claiming that she fired the fatal shots. At his sentencing, Morris said as far as he was concerned, his father John was dead to him. Morris was sentenced to 20 years in prison.[1107]

Tex Rickard said Dempsey got $309,967 less on the Carpentier fight than he could have earned had he fought on percentage. Kearns asked for a $300,000 guarantee and got it, and they thought Rickard was foolish to

[1103] *Brooklyn Daily Eagle*, March 14, 1923.
[1104] *Binghamton Press, Yonkers Herald*, March 15, 1923.
[1105] *New York Daily News*, March 17, 1923; *Brooklyn Daily Eagle*, March 18, 1923.
[1106] *Los Angeles Times*, March 15, 1923.
[1107] *Los Angeles Times*, March 20, 1923.

give such a huge guarantee. "If he had asked me for percentage I would have given him 30%. Yes, I would have given him 37 ½ %. That bout drew $1,626,580. Dempsey's guarantee was about 18% of that. If he had insisted on getting 37 ½ he would have drawn down $609,967.50." Of course, the risk of working on percentage is if the fight did not do well, the fighter might come away with very little, or less than the guarantee. But this was Rickard's way of trying to sell the percentage.[1108]

On March 26, 1923 in Peoria, Illinois, Tom Gibbons knocked out Andy Schmader in the 1st round, decking him twice with blows to the head and body.

The Shelby promoters were planning to deposit $110,000 in cash to show the managers of Gibbons and Dempsey evidence of good faith, to prove that their offer was backed legitimately with coin. Shelby was a booming oil town. American Legion posts of Montana were working with the state department of the Legion to host the big scrap there. Dempsey had been offered a $200,000 guarantee, but the fight technically had not yet been signed.[1109]

"Al" of the *Binghamton Press* noted that Harry Wills had not fought since September, since he fought Clem Johnson. "Just previous to that affair Wills was making more money than at any time during his career. The publicity he received as Dempsey's challenger made him a big card and he was in demand." However, "he was not adding anything to his prestige by his performances. Most of them were distinctly disappointing. No doubt that is why he has turned down all offers of late. He must be very sure that he is going to get the Dempsey match or he would not pass up so much easy money." The fear or concern was that he might lose or not look good, and further diminish the big fight.

The hope was that Dempsey would fight Gibbons in July as a warmup after such a long spell of inactivity, and then fight Wills in September, if that match could be made.[1110]

Promoter Mike Collins claimed that $150,000 already was in a Montana bank. $50,000 would be turned over to Dempsey upon the signing of articles of agreement, and another $50,000 would be deposited in a Montana bank to be paid to him as a forfeit if the fight did not go through. He would be paid another $100,000 24 hours prior to the July 4 Gibbons contest. The methodical Kearns was thinking about the offer.[1111]

Harry Newman said the majority did not give Gibbons a look-in with Dempsey, and yet he was a very tough customer, hard to knock over, could sock, and was clever, so he had the attributes to make it difficult for the champion.[1112]

Dempsey was the president and investor in the Great Western Coal Mine Company in Salt Lake City, along with Kearns and Bernard

[1108] *Binghamton Press*, March 20, 1923. Rickard was discussing with Kearns potential fights with Firpo, Willard, and Wills. *Los Angeles Times*, March 26, 1923.
[1109] *Los Angeles Times*, March 27, 1923.
[1110] *Binghamton Press*, March 28, 1923.
[1111] Allegedly, Gibbons would receive $50,000 as his end. *Yonkers Statesman and News*, April 7, 1923; *New York Daily News*, April 8, 1923.
[1112] *New York Daily News*, April 15, 1923.

Dempsey. Harry Pollock, who was associated with him in the business, said Dempsey might quit the ring. Dempsey allegedly said, "I've got all the glory there is in the game and I've got the dough. So why keep on until I get soaked on the chin? If I could fight every few months, fine and dandy. But I have to wait a year or two between fights and in the meantime I have to keep on razor edge. Life is too short."[1113]

Well aware of Jack's frustration by his lack of ring activity, Kearns was determined to get Dempsey a fight by July 4.[1114]

Despite the fact that four Montana Legion posts had opposed Dempsey fighting there owing to his war record, State Commander Loy Molumby declared confidence that Kearns would sign up Dempsey to fight Gibbons in Shelby. The contest appeared to have official political approval.[1115]

On April 23, 1923 in Jersey City, 190-pound Floyd Johnson won a 12-round newspaper decision over 210-pound Fred Fulton (77-10-3).

Harry Wills said that so far as he and Dempsey were concerned, they would fight tomorrow, but Chairman Muldoon in New York was against the match, and "authorities in other states seem to have taken that same pattern." Jack Johnson was not allowed to fight anyone at all. "All Harry wants is one big fight."[1116]

The Montana folks flew out to see Kearns in Chicago to negotiate and finalize a contract. They were prepared to meet all of Kearns' demands, and would post a substantial forfeit. Tough negotiator Kearns had gotten them to raise their flat fee offer to Dempsey up to $300,000.[1117]

On April 30, 1923 in New Orleans, Louisiana, before a crowd of 6,000, 172-pound Tommy Gibbons stopped 178-pound Chuck Wiggins (58-26-13) in the 10th round of a scheduled 15-round bout. Gibbons scored knockdowns in the 5th, 6th, and 7th rounds, and three more in the 10th before Chuck's seconds threw in the towel.[1118]

Gibbons was the first man to stop Wiggins, who had gone the full 10- and 12-round distance in decision losses to Gene Tunney in 1922 and 1923, and also had fought multiple 10-round no decisions with Greb, several being called newspaper draws. Wiggins previously had gone the 10- and 12-round distance with Gibbons in newspaper decision losses. To that point, Tommy Gibbons was 85-3-4.

That same day, it was announced that the Dempsey-Gibbons fight in Shelby was a go, according to Loy Molumby, state commander of the

[1113] *Buffalo Commercial*, April 16, 1923.
[1114] *Brooklyn Daily Times*, April 20, 1923.
[1115] *New York Daily News*, April 21, 1923.
[1116] *Yonkers Herald*, April 25, 1923.
[1117] *Elmira Star-Gazette*, April 26, 1923; *Los Angeles Times*, April 26, 27, 1923.
[1118] *Brooklyn Daily Eagle*, May 1, 1923; *Shreveport Times*, May 2, 1923.

American Legion, who was the prime mover in the promotional scheme along with Mike Collins. Molumby declared that an agreement had been reached with Kearns via telephone in New York.[1119]

The next day, Kearns admitted that the Dempsey-Gibbons fight was on. They would sign a contract soon. It was understood that in addition to a $300,000 guarantee, the champ would receive liberal expense money, and the privilege of selecting the referee. The champ was at Dempsey city, Utah.

Tex Rickard had not wanted a Gibbons fight under guaranteed terms, but wanted Kearns to take it on a percentage basis. Kearns liked guarantees rather than taking the risk of a failed promotion.[1120]

The *Brooklyn Standard Union* thought the Dempsey-Gibbons deal was odd and inexplicable. The town only had a population of about 1,700. Generating enough ticket sales to cover $300,000 to Dempsey and an alleged $50,000 to Gibbons was a very speculative undertaking in a remote location like Shelby. An arena would need to be built, which also would cost a lot of money. It would be no easy task to get 50,000 people to take the time and pay for travel, lodging, and tickets at $10 (or more) a head, which was what was needed to cover all of the likely expenses. It seemed that Mr. Molumby was in the fight promotion business "just for the excitement" or "philanthropy" designed to boost Shelby. Apparently, the town was more interested in advertising than the fight itself.[1121]

The promoters believed they could generate the money by constructing a 40,000-seat arena and charging $20 to $50 per ticket, which would generate over a million dollars.[1122]

William Granger was upset that New York appeared to be losing out on the Dempsey-Gibbons match, which would have been held there had it not been for Muldoon erroneously concluding that Gibbons was too small. "There never has been any question but what Gibbons was the real class of the heavyweight challengers." His only bad performance was against Greb, who was a freak who could make anyone look bad, even Dempsey. "Gibbons is one of the most scientific heavyweights ever developed. There is nothing about ringcraft that he does not know. He is a good puncher and a wizard at tying up an opponent in the clinches." He was the smoothest heavyweight since the days of Jim Corbett. "Those who are figuring Dempsey to walk right in and brush aside Gibbons's defense may be disappointed." Tom had a left that would make things "mighty uncomfortable for the champion." Carpentier only had a right, but Gibbons had jabs and left hooks that carried a lot of kick, as well as a solid right hand, and he had decked many men with both hands. Gibbons had not had a long layoff like Dempsey, who had been thwarted by various commissions, which also would help Tom. He had been very active, with 20 bouts in the two years that Dempsey had none, since Jack's

[1119] *Los Angeles Times*, May 1, 1923.
[1120] *Los Angeles Times*, May 2, 1923.
[1121] *Brooklyn Standard Union*, May 2, 1923.
[1122] *Buffalo Express*, May 3, 1923.

last fight in July 1921. If both were at their best and fight sharp, Dempsey would be a heavy favorite, but with Dempsey having been idle for so long, he would not be as big a favorite.[1123]

On May 5, 1923 at Chicago's Morrison hotel, after weeks of dickering and three more days of quibbling and wrangling about minor details, the final articles of agreement for Dempsey-Gibbons were signed. Signing the contract were Kearns and Eddie Kane for the fighters, and Mike Collins and Loy J. Molumby, commander of the Montana American Legion Posts, representing the promoters.

(By Pacific & Atlantic)
Signing for the big fight.—Seated (l. to r.) Jack Kearns, Dempsey's manager; Michael Collins and L. J. Molumby, Legion promoters of scrap; Eddie Kane, Gibbons's manager.

Dempsey was guaranteed $300,000; but he also had a privilege of 45% of the gross receipts in lieu of the guarantee if such amount exceeded the guarantee, and a percentage of all concessions. Gibbons would get 50% of all receipts over $300,000 up until the $600,000 mark was reached. After that amount, Gibbons would get 25% of the moving picture rights. The fight would be held on July 4, 1921, and would be 15 rounds to a decision if the fight was not stopped prior to that.

$110,000 would be deposited as the first installment on the $300,000 guarantee, with $10,000 going to Dempsey for training expenses. The promoters had to advance and deposit another $100,000 on June 15, and on July 2, two days before the fight, the third installment of $100,000 had to be paid. If the promoters failed to make the second installment, Kearns would get to keep the original $110,000 as a forfeit and could call off the match. Kearns would post a like $110,000 bond to guarantee his fighter's appearance, but the promoters would pay the premiums.

Hence, Gibbons/Kane would not receive a cent of the money until the receipts had reached $300,000, and would be working on a percentage, not a guarantee.[1124]

The guarantee was the same amount that Dempsey had earned to fight Carpentier. The Montana promoters had conceded on everything, such that Kearns essentially had to sign, because the deal was so good. His tough negotiations appeared to have paid off.

[1123] *Brooklyn Citizen*, May 3, 1923.
[1124] *Los Angeles Times, Chicago Tribune*, May 5, 1923.

Gibbons' manager Eddie Kane said he did not care who refereed, as long as he had a reputation for being honest and competent. When James Dougherty was mentioned as the man Kearns wanted, Kane said, "Dougherty is a fine fellow personally and is noted for his honesty, but I don't think much of him as a referee."

An arena would be built, big enough to seat at least 40,000 people. Ticket prices would range from $20 up to $50. 40 miles of additional railroad siding would be laid. The 177 American Legion posts in the state were supporting the promotion. The money to support the fight allegedly was backed by Montana oil men and bankers.

Shelby was an oil town of less than 1,000 inhabitants, served only by the Great Northern railway. It was approximately 1,350 miles from Chicago, 977 miles from San Francisco, 517 from Seattle, and 750 from Denver. It was more than 60 miles north of Great Falls, where Dempsey would train. It was 40 miles from the Canadian border. Originally a cow town, it allegedly was in the midst of an oil boom.

Shelby, Mont., fight scene. Arrow indicates where stadium will be built.

Dempsey was training in Dempsey City, Utah (near Helper), a town named after him since he owned coal lands there.[1125]

Tom's brother Mike Gibbons was a recently retired top middleweight, so Tom had a great sparring partner.

The real question was how the Montana promotion was going to overcome a lot of obstacles and not suffer heavy losses. They needed to interest fight fans and get them to the scene of the battle-ground. Folks would have to be willing to pay train fares, travel a great distance, find and pay for lodging, and expensive tickets, then have to travel far to return from where they came, all of which would cost them a fair amount of time as well as money. There was not much of a population base in Montana, or anywhere nearby. So, they were taking a huge financial risk. There weren't even good telegraph wires there, and it would cost thousands of dollars to equip it. "How many are going to drag from 500 to 1,500 miles to see a few minutes of fighting?"[1126]

[1125] *Chicago Tribune*, May 6, 1923; *Brooklyn Standard Union*, May 5, 1923.
[1126] *Chicago Tribune*, May 9, 1923.

On May 7, 1923 in Salt Lake City, at a boxing show, Dempsey sparred 6 rounds, 2 each with three local lightweights: Midget Smith, Frankie Buffington, and Danny O'Brien. To the delight of the several hundred fans, Jack just played defense and dodged about the ring, allowing his sparring partners to throw everything they could at him.[1127]

That same day, May 7, 1923, in Detroit, Michigan, Gene Tunney scored an 8th round TKO over Jack Clifford, when a right opened up a big and bloody cut over Clifford's left eye, a cut under the eye having been opened earlier, and his cornerman retired him.[1128]

On May 8 in Provo, Utah, the armory was jammed from floor to ceiling to see the champ, who boxed exhibition rounds with Herman Auerbach (former manager A. J. Auerbach's son) and Abe Mishkind of Salt Lake. Jack primarily played defense. He also refereed the main event: Billy Murray W8 Eddie Douglas.

Dempsey was not much of a talker. When asked what he thought of Gibbons, and how many rounds the fight would go, Jack simply answered, "I don't know." His trainers were more talkative, and said Gibbons was a better man overall than Carpentier.[1129]

On May 12, 1923 at the new Yankee Stadium in the Bronx, New York, Tex Rickard hosted an important boxing card that drew a huge attendance of 65,000 to 70,000 people.

In the main event, former world heavyweight champion 6'6" 248-pound 41-year-old Jess Willard stopped highly touted up-and-comer 6'1" 195-pound 22-year-old Floyd Johnson (31-2-8) in the 11th round.

In the 9th round, Willard hurt Johnson with several right uppercuts. Finally, a right to the jaw decked the aggressive Johnson for the first time. In the 11th round, Willard decked him again, with a right uppercut. Soon after rising, another brutal right uppercut to the jaw almost knocked his head off and sent Floyd down so hard that the boom shook the ring. He was saved by the bell at the count of 8. Johnson was dragged back to his corner, but they were not able to revive him, and threw in the sponge as a token of defeat.

Johnson had not been able to hurt the iron-jawed yet overall cautious Willard, who at one point even allowed Johnson to hit him.

The limited films still in existence show that owing to Willard's height and reach, Johnson had to be more aggressive to get close enough to land,

[1127] *Salt Lake Tribune*, May 8, 1923, *Butte Miner*, May 9, 1923.
[1128] *Detroit Free Press*, May 8, 1923. Clifford's cut would require at least 6 stitches.
[1129] *Provo Daily Herald*, May 9, 1923.

but Willard was good at clinching and smothering his attack, or moving back a little. Both would lead and then clinch quite often. Jess used his long left jab and sneaky right uppercut fairly regularly.

The win was significant, given that Floyd Johnson had victories such as: 1922 KO10 Bob Martin; and 1923 W15 Bill Brennan and WND12 Fred Fulton. It was only Johnson's third loss in 41 fights, and the first time he had been stopped. Despite not having fought in nearly four years, since July 1919, Jess Willard showed that he still could fight.

Willard and Johnson were paid $25,000 apiece.

Thomas Rice said on points boxing, Johnson was ahead after 10 rounds, and should have been more cautious, but was too game for his own good. However, "On punishment Willard was distinctly the winner." When Jess landed it meant something. Johnson could not hurt the former champion.

Willard said, "I think I proved that I'm not so old, pugilistically, as they thought. Johnson fought as game a battle as any man I ever was up against, but I never was in danger. I purposely held back in the early rounds, waiting for my chance, for I knew I could finish him before the limit." "I'm ready to fight Firpo or any one else to prove that I'm entitled to a return match with Dempsey."

Floyd Johnson said, "I fought the best I could. He was too big for me, that's all."

JOHNSON   WILLARD

JOHNSON   WILLARD

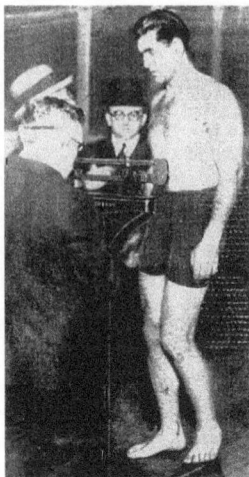

On the undercard, 210- or 212-pound Luis Firpo knocked out 200-pound Jack McAuliffe II (who held a 1922 W6 over Floyd Johnson) in the 3rd round, using his pile-driver blows. In the 2nd round, a right to the jaw like a rifle shot sent McAuliffe down. In the 3rd round, rights to the body and jaw decked him again, and then a whipping, pile-driver right to the chin sent him down and out like a log for nearly 30 seconds.

Firpo earned $15,000 and McAuliffe $10,000.

Thomas Rice called Firpo "by far the most logical candidate to tackle Jack Dempsey." Rice did not think Willard could survive 15 rounds with Firpo, who had improved wonderfully. Luis had more science than before, and his punch still was there.

The *Brooklyn Citizen* said McAuliffe was remarkably clever, but unable to hold off the South American cave-man, who had the more powerful wallop. "The knockout scored by the Argentine contender for Jack Dempsey's laurels was royally received by the crowd. He was cheered fully five minutes." The enthralled crowd enjoyed watching Firpo's crushing wallops.

James Crusinberry called Firpo the pampas wildcat. McAuliffe earned every penny. "It's worth a helluva good sized roll to face that Argentine roughneck for even one round." Firpo had a frightening enough scowl to send many men jumping out of the ring. "When he frowns, he means it and trouble is sure to follow." Firpo was "like a prehistoric being. A good boxer can't stop him. Nothing can stop him. He fights like a mad bull. He crushes his opponent to the floor." He was the type of man that the fans wanted to see go against the champion.

The *Brooklyn Daily Times* said Firpo was a sensation, who fought like a champion. "His attack was savage and irresistible." McAuliffe was confident, clever, and game, but Firpo broke him down with a lightning-like attack. His blows made the vast assemblage gasp, cheer, and shriek. Unless Dempsey fought Wills, "his next serious adversary will unquestionably be Firpo, who, it may be, will give the champion an even harder battle than would Wills." Wills was more skillful, but not as ferocious as Firpo.

Harry Newman said Firpo made a great hit with the massive crowd, "who voted him the man who might have a chance against Champion Dempsey." McAuliffe outboxed him in the 1st round. However, in the 2nd, Firpo got his range, and some rights coupled with a short left hook to the wind slowed up Jack, and he no longer could evade the fierce lunges, until a right decked him. In the 3rd, a wallop to the chin dropped him again. Another right chop sent him down and out. "Firpo looked like a champion." Although his boxing skill still was crude, "the fact remains that he does not require very much knowledge of the boxing game. His fierce punches seem to break down the guard of all his opponents and once he gets them on the run he slips over the old haymaker and the officials start counting all over the place." Even after the two men left the ring, the crowd was in a whirl of excitement for several minutes.

The show's profits were donated to the Milk Fund. Tex Rickard gave his services for free. Cols. Ruppert and Huston donated the use of Yankee Stadium. Rickard estimated the receipts at $390,000. Customers paid from $1 up to $15 or $20 per seat. The show's expenses were estimated to be $140,000 to $150,000.

Rickard announced that Willard vs. Firpo would be next.[1130]

[1130] *Brooklyn Standard Union, Brooklyn Daily Eagle, Brooklyn Citizen, New York Daily News, Brooklyn Standard Union, Brooklyn Daily Times,* May 13, 1923. The card also included: 218 ½-pound Jim "Babe" Herman KO6 206 ½-pound Al Reich; 185-pound Harry Drake W4 202-pound Joe McCann; and 190 ½-pound Jack Renault WDQ4 214-pound Fred Fulton (low blow).) Both Reich had McCann had sparred with Firpo in preparation. Firpo was said to be improving rapidly under Jimmy De Forest's tutelage. He was shortening his punches, hitting straighter, and was faster. *Brooklyn Standard Union,* May 5, 1923.

CHAPTER 14

Tom Gibbons

Eddie Kane said crafty Tom Gibbons would beat Jack Dempsey. "This bone crushing, slashing, bang-up champion of the world is about to lose his crown. And we will permit him to use his 'rabbit punch' or anything else, because he can't hit Gibbons with a whole glove factory."

In mid-May 1923, Promoter Mike Collins announced that the advance sale of the Dempsey-Gibbons tickets already had reached $275,000. Shelby Mayor James Johnson had been appointed the show's treasurer. 200 men began working on the huge arena.

Gibbons would open his training at Havre, Montana.[1131]

On May 15, Dempsey arrived in Great Falls, Montana, at the Great Northern railroad station. He was greeted warmly by a sea of humanity that formed a parade a mile long. Thousands greeted him at the station and throughout the town, including Senator Thomas Walker of Butte. Jack said, "I'll remember this welcome as long as I live." Asked about the upcoming fight, he said, "I expect one of the toughest battles of my ring career. Gibbons is a mighty good man."

Dempsey's sparring partners in Great Falls would include 170-pound Jack Burke and a giant black fighter named George Godfrey.[1132]

Tex Rickard announced that he had signed Jess Willard to fight Luis Firpo, with the winner to meet Dempsey. Kearns had agreed.[1133]

In an interview with Robert Edgren, Bill Tate said, "I'm going back to New York to give Wills a chance to fight me again and get back the colored heavyweight championship if he can. I beat Wills a couple years ago, Referee Griffin giving me the fight twice on fouls. ... They made Wills fight me at Portland, Ore. He fouled me so often he was disqualified." They fought again four days later.

> It sure was a rough fight. I beat Wills all the way. When he tried to hold my arm the way he did Fulton's and wallop me with his other hand I let him hold and hooked him with my left until he was glad

[1131] *Chicago Tribune, Chicago Herald and Examiner*, May 15, 1923.
[1132] *Great Falls Tribune*, May 16, 1923; *Salt Lake Tribune*, May 16, 18, 1923.
[1133] *Chicago Herald and Examiner*, May 16, 1923.

to let go. I was too big for him to use that trick, and I was stronger than he. ...

In the first couple of rounds he roughed me and lifted me around and I let him lift. It doesn't do any man any good to lift 229 pounds around on his arm. He soon gave that up and from that time on he did a lot of running around the ring. I caught him in the tenth and knocked him flat on his face and the bell saved him.

I got the decision [actually, a D10] and since that time Mr. Wills can't be induced to talk about fighting me.

Wills and I used to be good friends. One day we were up in Harlem, and Wills began kidding me about what Dempsey did to me in training and what he could do to Dempsey.

"Don't forget that Dempsey would hit you," I said. "That boy's sure fast!"

"Yeah!" says Wills, "I know all about Dempsey. He might slip one through, but he'd never lay another glove on me in a week!"

"'Harry,' I says, "If Dempsey hits you once he wouldn't need to hit you again in the same week!'"

After that Wills and I never did get along.

Tate believed, "Wills would be a soft mark for Dempsey." He said Harry was a great "down-hill fighter" when he had his own way, but if you stood up to him and came back smiling and wanting more, "Why that just about settles him."[1134]

On May 16, 1923 in Chicago, before a crowd of 5,000 - 6,000 which generated around $25,000, 175-pound Gene Tunney won a 10-round no decision over 174-pound Jimmy Delaney (26-1-3) of St. Paul, Minnesota, but fractured his right hand in the 2nd round and had to win with his left. During the fight, many were wondering why he did not use his right.

Afterwards, Dr. O'Connell confirmed that the small bones of Tunney's right hand indeed were fractured. The *Chicago Tribune* said, "Gene Tunney gave a remarkable exhibition considering the hand he broke in the second session." This paper gave Delaney only the 2nd round. "The third was about even, but Tunney scored enough points in the other rounds to win the popular verdict." "Tunney looked every part a fighter. He has a nice left hand, with which he won the fight. He jabbed, hooked and uppercutted with this member in such a manner as to pile up enough points to win. He was the aggressor most of the way and did most of the leading."

The *Chicago Daily News* said Tunney "proved to the satisfaction of Chicago boxing fans that he is a real champion." Gene was the aggressor all the way, defeating the highly touted Delaney, Mike Gibbons' protégé.

[1134] *Chicago Daily News*, May 16, 1923.

He fractured his right thumb in the 2nd round when landing on the top of Jimmy's head, rendering his right useless the rest of the way, but still won using one hand, a "remarkable" achievement.

The *Chicago Evening Post's* Harry Hochstadter said although handicapped by injury, Tunney "stabbed his way" to a 10-round victory.

> Seconded by the lightweight champion, Benny Leonard, Tunney had no trouble whatever in buffeting Mike Gibbons' protégé all around the ring for nine of the ten sessions. In only one round did Delaney excel, and that was the second session, when he drew blood and socked in a few timely left-handed wallops to the wind. After that, Tunney, who knows he can take care of Mike McTigue, took charge of Mr. Delaney and beat him all the way.

The Associated Press said newsmen at ringside agreed that Tunney had the shade the better of St. Paul's Delaney. Tunney drew blood from Delaney's mouth in the 1st, but Delaney outboxed Tunney in the 2nd through 4th rounds, countering well and drawing blood from Gene's nose. The 5th and 6th were fairly even, but Tunney had the edge from the 7th through 10th rounds.[1135]

Most newspapers reported Tunney as the winner, either clearly or by a shade. However, in a minority report, the Minneapolis-based *Boxing Blade* (which in December 1922 had a front-cover drawing of Minnesota's Delaney, comparing him with Jim Corbett in boxing skill) reported in its June issue that 22-year-old Delaney clearly outpointed Tunney, winning 6-2-2. Delaney looked so "sensational" that world light heavyweight champion Mike McTigue declined to fight him. "McTigue saw Delaney fight Tunney."[1136]

1.2 million feet of lumber would be required to build the Shelby arena, which would seat 40,208. A five-story hotel would be built to host the patrons. Railroads would have sleeping cars along the tracks as well. Huge tanks would be erected to hold 100,000 gallons of water.[1137]

Jim Corbett said Gibbons was the world's most skillful heavyweight, and possessed speed and power, a combination that gave him a chance with the champ.

Corbett said Dempsey did better with giants, for they simply gave him a bigger target, particularly with his superior speed and crashing attack. There was no doubt that Dempsey was a terrific puncher, but power did not matter if he could not land. The champ rarely had difficulty connecting against big men like Morris, Fulton, and Willard. But Gibbons was different. He was fast with both feet and hands. He was a splendid boxer, with defense, and had a two-fisted attack himself.

Dempsey usually was able to man-handle opponents in the clinches. "But, unless all signs are wrong, he isn't going to do much punishing in

[1135] *Chicago Tribune, Chicago Daily News, Chicago Evening Post, Minneapolis Morning Tribune,* May 17, 1923. Delaney's record included 1920 D10 and WDQ7 Johnny Sudenberg; 1922 TKO5 Sudenberg; and 1923 WND10 (twice) Ted Jamieson.
[1136] *Boxing Blade,* June 2, 1923, December 16, 1922.
[1137] *Great Falls Tribune,* May 18, 1923.

the clinches with Gibbons." Tom was a masterful infighter himself, and a great clincher.

Everyone knew that Dempsey could take it and continue his rushing, tearing tactics, seeming almost impervious. However, no one ever stopped Gibbons, who rarely was hurt, and even when stung, knew how to cover up in a shell and/or clinch. Hence, Dempsey figured to win, but Gibbons was a real test.[1138]

Robert Edgren said Gibbons was the type of boxer that Dempsey feared. "Gibbons has as much right to consideration as any of the heavyweight challengers. Tom is now at the peak of his fighting form, and … it's hardly likely he'll ever be better." He had knockouts over men like Al Reich, Willie Meehan, Clay Turner, and Porky Flynn. Although Greb had beaten him with a constant flurry of blows, Gibbons had come back to score several knockouts, and beat Miske soundly. He was very fast, and knew as much as anyone. "Dempsey has often said that a very fast man a little lighter than he is could give him more trouble than the giants, who were easy to hit." Gibbons was a very good smaller man, but Dempsey was the greatest heavyweight since Jeffries; hence he would rule a 3-1 favorite. The fight would provide a line on Dempsey's present condition, and whether his long ring absence had robbed him of the speed and perfect timing that made him unbeatable.

Jess Willard and Luis Firpo agreed to fight for Rickard in July.

Jack Kearns said he wanted Dempsey to fight Wills next, for Wills would draw better than Willard or Firpo. He and Dempsey wanted whomever would make them the most money.[1139]

Gibbons arrived in Montana on Sunday May 20, and he too was received by several thousand people. He planned an exhibition tour of the state (population c. 550,000), making money by allowing folks to pay to watch him train and spar. His tour would open in Helena on the 21st. Tom already was fight sharp, having just fought at the end of April.[1140]

On Monday afternoon, May 21, 1923 at the Great Falls, Montana pavilion, Dempsey did his first sparring there. A large crowd was present to watch, including a liberal sprinkling of women.

Dempsey boxed 2 rounds each (6 total) with middleweight Frank Powers, light heavy Jack Burke, and black heavyweight George Godfrey.

[1138] *Buffalo Times*, May 16, 1923.
[1139] *Great Falls Tribune*, May 20, 1923.
[1140] *Great Falls Tribune*, May 21, 1923.

In their first round, Dempsey decked Powers with a left body smash. A left to the jaw floored him again. Both times, Jack lifted him up to his feet. Dempsey could have stopped him if he so chose.

After the round, Jack Burke absorbed some stiff wallops for a round.

Wearing a headgear, 6'3" 212-pound George Godfrey moved with astonishing speed for his big frame. He obviously was pulling his punches, perhaps not wanting to rile the champ. His body was the best suited of all to absorb the Dempsey attack, and they boxed a fast round.

Powers came back in for his second round. Such was the pattern. Each partner did a round, then rotated in the next man, while Dempsey remained.

Dempsey's footwork appeared particularly fast, and his blocking and ducking a delight. He made his sparring partners look like "dubs."

Kearns admitted that Gibbons was perhaps the most knowledgeable and speediest boxer Dempsey ever had met, so the focus was on speed.[1141]

Dempsey and George Godfrey

Kearns allegedly was in negotiations with Rickard for a Dempsey-Wills fight on Labor Day in New York. Tom O'Rourke and Simon Flaherty both wanted to bid on such a fight as well.[1142]

Jess Willard declared that the claimed Dempsey-Wills bout simply was a Kearns yarn, and there would be no such fight. Jess said the government

[1141] *Great Falls Tribune, Los Angeles Times*, May 22, 1923.
    George Godfrey's record included: 1920 W10 Bill Tate and LKOby2 Sam Langford; 1921 LKOby4 Jack Thompson and LKOby1 Langford; 1922 TKO5 Jack Thompson; 1923 W12 Clem Johnson and LKOby11 Jack Renault.
    Jack Burke's record included: 1921 LKOby4 Bill Brennan and LTKOby3 Gene Tunney; and 1922 LTKOby9 Tunney.
[1142] *Los Angeles Times*, May 22, 1923.

would not allow a mixed-race heavyweight championship contest. "Believe me, there will be no more championship bouts between the whites and blacks. Those bouts are a thing of the past. The talk of such bouts are all bosh. Why, even if promoters succeeded in signing up such a match, the government would step in and stop it right away."[1143]

Responding to Willard, Dempsey said he would fight anyone. "I will fight any of them. ... Kearns does the arranging and I do the fighting, and if Kearns signs for Wills it will be Wills. They all look alike to me."[1144]

"Black Panther" Wills' manager, Paddy Mullins, asked the New York State Athletic Commission to state just where they stood in connection with the Wills title challenge. Simon Flaherty, manager of the Queensboro Stadium in Long Island City, allegedly was willing to guarantee Dempsey $500,000 as his end for a Wills fight on Labor Day. Mullins wanted to know one legitimate reason from the commission why Wills should not be permitted to fight for the championship there.[1145]

Tex Rickard also asked the New York State Athletic Commission to state its attitude regarding Dempsey-Wills, but his request was refused. The commission's silence spoke louder than words, and was not a good sign.[1146]

On Tuesday May 22, Dempsey sparred 7 rounds with his three sparring partners. Godfrey absorbed a heap of punishment. Neither one put their full force into the blows, but occasionally a hard punch was thrown. "Godfrey has something more than 20 pounds advantage over Dempsey, but it isn't enough when Dempsey gets rough." Godfrey was big, willing, and clever. Dempsey forced him to work at top speed, and their milling was fast and the most interesting. Jack demonstrated his effective infighting, his chin tucked down, his body leaning on his foe, and his fists flying into the body. He also shifted and weaved. Two left uppercuts snapped Godfrey's head back.

After their 3 rounds, Dempsey went against Jack Burke for 2 rounds. There was more speed and open fighting, and the champ did more damage.

For his 2 rounds against Frank Powers, Dempsey played defense and worked on his footwork, yet he decked him with a back-hand slap.[1147]

Kearns said Dempsey could beat anyone he could hit. The question was whether he could hit Gibbons, who was world's cleverest fighter, with the best defense. Kearns said it might be the hardest fight of Dempsey's career.[1148]

On Wednesday afternoon, May 23, Dempsey exhibited at the Grand theater for the benefit of St. Thomas orphans, raising $300. He boxed 4 rounds with English welter champ Bermondsey Billy Wells, primarily defending.[1149]

[1143] *Los Angeles Times*, May 22, 1923.
[1144] *Los Angeles Times*, May 25, 1923.
[1145] *New York Daily News*, May 22, 1923.
[1146] *Buffalo Courier*, May 23, 1923.
[1147] *Great Falls Tribune*, May 23, 1923. Jack ran 6 miles in the morning, accompanied by his sparring partners and trainer Jerry Luvadis.
[1148] *Great Falls Tribune, Rochester Democrat and Chronicle*, May 24, 1923.
[1149] *Great Falls Tribune*, May 24, 1923.

Jess Willard said that *he* would meet Dempsey on Labor Day, not Harry Wills. "There is nothing to a Dempsey-Wills fight anyway. I do not think Jack Kearns, Dempsey's manager, wants a Wills fight. However, I do not think Dempsey is afraid of Wills, but I do predict they will never fight."

On May 24, Dempsey sparred 6 rounds, 2 apiece with George Godfrey (who wore a headgear), Jack Burke, and 176-pound British heavyweight Harry Drake. In the 1st round with Drake, a left to the jaw stood Drake up to his heels, and a follow-up right cross to the heart sent him crashing to the floor. Drake rose, continued, and boxed well, for he was big, rangy, quick, and had a good defense.[1150]

The Pathe Moving Picture Company was going to be taking moving pictures of the site, training quarters, and the fight.[1151]

Dempsey with "Dinky" Dean Riesner

Dempsey was photographed with 5-year-old moving-picture star "Dinky" Dean Riesner, who appeared in Charlie Chaplin's 1923 film, *The Pilgrim.* Many years later, Riesner would be a screenwriter for several Clint Eastwood films, including *Dirty Harry, The Enforcer, Coogan's Bluff,* and *Play Misty for Me.*

On Saturday May 26 at his Great Falls training quarters, before a big crowd, a third of which were women, Dempsey sparred 6 fast rounds, 2 each with Godfrey, who covered up most of the way, Burke, landing more easily, drawing blood and jarring him, and Drake, who took the brunt of the heavy attack.[1152]

On Sunday May 27, a crowd of 2,000 watched Dempsey hammer, stagger, and rock his partners all over the ring; five of them for 2 rounds each, for 10 rounds total, including "giant negro" George Godfrey, light heavy Jack Burke, British heavy Harry Drake, New York middleweight Frank Powers, and British welterweight Billy Wells. The champ showed speed, agility, fast footwork, and effective blocking. He decked the skillful and plucky Wells with a flush right to the jaw.

At the conclusion of his 10 rounds of sparring, "The champion showed no evidence of exhaustion when he waved in response to the crowd's cheering and ran for his shower."[1153]

[1150] *Great Falls Tribune, Los Angeles Times,* May 25, 1923.
[1151] *Great Falls Tribune,* May 26, 1923.
[1152] *Great Falls Tribune,* May 27, 1923.
[1153] *Great Falls Tribune, Missoulian,* May 28, 1923.

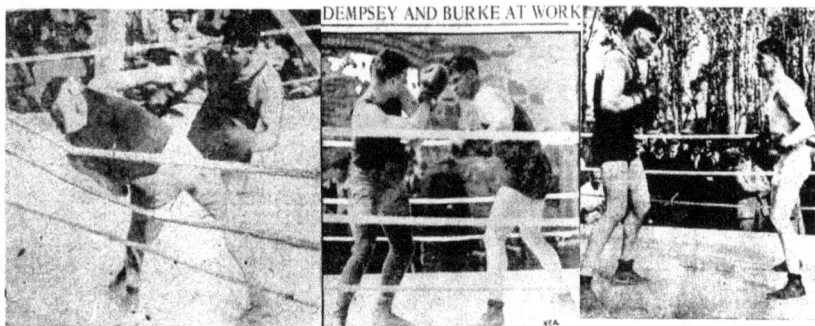

DEMPSEY AND BURKE AT WORK

Dempsey attacks Jack Burke   Sparring Bermondsey Billy Wells

Some reported that Godfrey cut Dempsey's lip. The next day, Jack wore a small plaster on his upper lip.

Jack Kearns said,

> I look for Dempsey to have trouble with Tommy Gibbons on July Fourth. ... If Gibbons weaves in and out the fight may go the limit. ... Dempsey is ready to go in there as he is now. I intend to lay him off part of the time. He'd burn himself out if I let him. ...
>
> The champ ducks and slips punches, judging them to a fraction of an inch. He hasn't fought for two years but his judge of distance seems as good as ever. A fellow who likes to fight as good as Dempsey never gets out of shape.
>
> I don't think Gibbons is going to hit Dempsey very often. If he does the best asset the champ has is that he can take it. I've seen him shaken from toe to head with a wallop but he always comes back with his ace in the hole – his punch. Dempsey is high strung – but not nervous. It isn't nerves. It's energy that burns him up and keeps him fidgety and jumpy. ...
>
> Dempsey's fists don't travel far. But there's a kick in them that would upset a building. Gibbons is a good hitter too. He may be able to make Dempsey miss. You can't tell.[1154]

Willie Meehan, who had fought both, was positive that Dempsey would win, for he hit harder and could take everything Gibbons had to offer. "Gibbons couldn't hurt me when I'm feeling right. But, well, when Dempsey hit me – I knew it!" Of course, Gibbons has stopped Meehan, and Dempsey had not, although the fights occurred at different stages of Meehan's career.[1155]

On May 28 in Great Falls, 183-pound Tommy Gibbons sparred 4 rounds, 2 each with local light heavy Marine Ranieri and 220-pound Bud Gorman, his regular sparring partner, who had been on tour with Gibbons throughout the state. Tom's boxing, feinting, shifting, and footwork were impressive.

[1154] *Butte Miner*, May 28, 1923.
[1155] *Helena Daily Independent*, May 28, 1923.

627

Gibbons said, "I have won thirty out of my last thirty-four fights by knockouts, and expect to win this fight. I have been trying two years to get the match – the one chance of my life."[1156]

Tommy decided to set up his training camp in Shelby, Montana.[1157]

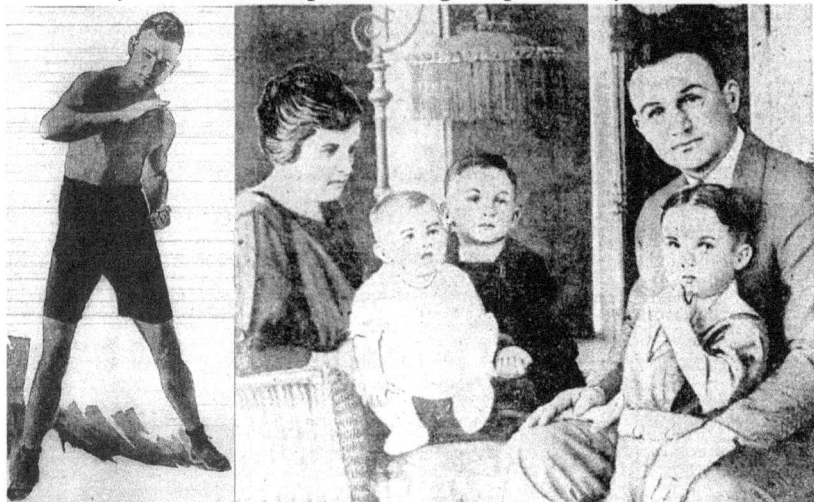

Tom Gibbons and family

Shelby, Montana

TOMMY GIBBONS
and His Sparring Partners Will Show at the
Liberty Theater, Tomorrow Night
FIRST AND LAST SHOWING IN MISSOULA

Prices		Prices
$1.00		$1.00
$2.00		$2.00
$3.00		$3.00
and		and
$4.00		$4.00

TOMMY GIBBONS

FEATURING THE MAN WHO WILL FIGHT
JACK DEMPSEY
For the World's Heavyweight Championship at Shelby, July 4
ALSO AN ALL STAR LINEUP
PRICES: $1.00, $2.00, $3.00 and $4.00
The Gibbons Show is Under the Auspices of the Disabled Vets

[1156] *Great Falls Tribune, Los Angeles Times, Chicago Tribune*, May 29, 1923.
    Bud Gorman's record included a LND10 and WND10 Eddie McGoorty.
[1157] *Great Falls Tribune*, May 30, 1923.

Gibbons arrives in Shelby with his family

According to the *Butte Miner*, 32-year-old Gibbons stood 6' tall (the *Great Falls Tribune* listed Gibbons as 6' ¾") and weighed about 180 pounds. He was clever and skillful, hit hard, and had good conditioning. Gibbons had been boxing since 1913. He had 88 fights; Dempsey about 60. Not only had Gibbons never been knocked out; he never had been knocked down. He had stopped 33 of his last 36 foes. He had been boxing regularly since 1921, 34 fights in that span, while Dempsey had only 1 fight, so many believed that Tom would have the superior fight sharpness.[1158]

Gibbons' sparring partners included three heavies - Jack Clifford, Bud Gorman, and Joe Burke, two light heavies - Jimmy Delaney and Harry Foley, one middle - Martin Moore, and two bantams – Sammy Mandell and Bud Taylor.

Jack and brother Bernard

The *San Francisco Chronicle* wanted to arrange for airplane delivery of photographs of the fight so that they could be printed on July 6, two days after the contest.

Harry Wills said he took Kearns at his word that Dempsey would fight him next. "The state boxing commission is understood to be preparing to give a decision on the proposal to hold the bout in this state [New York]."

Robert Edgren said Godfrey was a 6'4" giant, a sweet boxer, and could hit hard. He was Jack Johnson's choice to "bring the title back to the colored race." Allegedly, Wills refused to box him. He and Dempsey traded hard blows and tried to outmatch one another in speed and skill, as well as punch.[1159]

[1158] *Butte Miner, Great Falls Tribune,* June 1, 1923.
[1159] *Great Falls Tribune,* June 2, 1923.

Great Falls and Shelby both were greater than 3,000 feet above sea level. Dempsey was used to high altitude from his youth.

Jack's brother Bernard was going back to Utah to tend to his fast-ripening strawberries at American Fork. Father Hiram might visit when Bernard returned for Jack's 28th birthday on June 24.[1160]

James J. Jeffries planned to see the fight. Jeff said Gibbons had a chance to win, and should not be underestimated simply because of his size. If Dempsey was not in the best condition, Gibbons could whip him. "He'll know he's been in a fight, anyway!" Jeff knew from experience, because some smaller heavyweights had given him stiff challenges. Jeff predicted it would be a better fight than the one against Carpentier. Jeffries advised Dempsey not to retire or take a great deal of time off between fights. Such had cost him his athletic prowess.[1161]

Trainer Jerry Luvadis, English welter Bermondsey Billy Wells, Dempsey, California lightweight Joe Benjamin, English heavy Harry Drake, Jack's brother Johnny Dempsey, heavy Jack Burke, and George Godfrey

Luis Firpo was like Dempsey in that his desire was to win by knockout in the shortest time possible. He countered blows and put everything he had into his punches. He had long arms, and could hit hard at any range. He was fast, but not as fast as Dempsey, and he did not sway and weave the way Jack did. His 214 pounds was all muscle. Firpo's opponents said his blows were paralyzing. Against Willard, he could prove whether or not he could take it, because according to Floyd Johnson, Willard hit very hard too. Jess had the height, reach, and weight advantages.[1162]

Robert Edgren said Kearns had offered Harry Wills a good sum to spar with Dempsey for the Willard fight at Toledo. Wills replied that he was the one who ought to be fighting Willard. Kearns responded, "Knock out Jack and you can have the Willard fight."

[1160] *Great Falls Tribune*, June 3, 1923.
[1161] *Buffalo Times*, June 3, 1923. Jeff was picking Firpo to beat Willard.
[1162] *Great Falls Tribune*, June 3, 1923.

Brother Bernard said he had seen Jack tired only once in the last 10 years. Last spring, Jack rode 45 miles on horseback, loaded a wagon with coal all by himself, took it several miles, and then went on a 25-mile deer-trailing expedition. That night, he was really tired and glad to crawl into bed.[1163]

They started charging 50 cents per person to watch Dempsey's training, yet nearly 1,500 folks willingly paid daily, and kept coming.

Generally, in the morning, Dempsey ran, walked, hiked, jogged, and sprinted. He then rested and played pinochle, his favorite card game, and read and responded to letters written to him from all over the world. In the afternoon, he punched the bags, shadow boxed, and/or sparred. Evenings were devoted to music and storytelling. His quarters had two phonographs, a piano, and a music box.

When asked to describe his hardest battle, "giant killer" Dempsey said it was with Gunboat Smith.

> In that bout I thought I was knocked out. In one of the early rounds Gunboat cracked me one on the jaw. I never remembered what happened after that. When the bout was over I said to Jack Kearns, my manager, 'What round did he get me in?' 'Sh', answered Kearns. 'Don't say a word. You got the decision.' Well, I never knew that I had done fairly well after Gunboat hit me. I thought he had knocked me for the full count and I was almost crying when I came to and asked Kearns that question. Say that was sure my toughest fight.[1164]

On June 5, 1923, the champ sparred 5 rounds total with Frankie Grandetta, Terry Brown, and Lee Moore.[1165]

Frankie Grandetta, unknown in back, Rocco Stramaglia, Billy Wells, Kearns in back, Jack Burke, Dempsey, Harry Drake, Jerry Luvadis, George Godfrey

On Wednesday June 6, Dempsey sparred 6 rounds, 2 each with British welter "Bermondsey" Billy Wells, Los Angeles feather Lee Moore, and Portland light heavy Rocco Stramaglia, the latter of whom accidentally

[1163] *Great Falls Tribune*, June 4, 1923.
[1164] *Anaconda Standard*, June 6, 1923.
[1165] *Great Falls Tribune*, June 6, 1923.

butted the champion, opening an old scar over his left eye. It bled just a little.[1166]

Others reported that the cut required several stitches. Hence, Dempsey's eye was bandaged with plaster, cotton, and a dressing.[1167]

On June 8, the champ removed his eye bandage. The cut appeared to be healing nicely.

On June 9, Dempsey hit the heavy sand bag so hard that he opened a seam and the packing began to ooze out.

The *Chicago Tribune's* Frank Smith, who had arrived in Great Falls with three staff members, liked Gibbons' chances. The East was strong for the challenger. Dempsey never had met a man of his caliber of skill. Gibbons had elusive footwork and defense, and Dempsey would find it mighty hard to land on him. Tom was the world's best boxer amongst the big men, a master who also could punch with the wallop of a mule. A great fight was predicted. Many thought it was an even fight.[1168]

Dan Tracey, Montana hotel owner and mining operator, fooling around with Jack

Harry Newman, special writer for the *Tribune* and the *New York Daily News*, said he rolled into town to find out Dempsey was on a fishing trip. When Newman tried to ask him about the fight, Jack said, "I never care to talk about my coming fights. At any rate, I never care to predict the outcome of any battle. I know that Tom is a good man and I would be silly to venture how the fight will go."

In Shelby on June 11, Gibbons jarred his sparring mates during 4 fast rounds; 200+-pound Bud Gorman for 2, and 1 apiece with 175-pound Kid Sales and Kid Rocco Stramaglia, the latter of whom recently sparred with Dempsey.

Gibbons said there was nothing super about Dempsey's record. He looked great only against big, slow-moving giants. Carpentier had speed and skill, but also a "tin chin." Dempsey had been beaten by Meehan. Fulton had a glass jaw. Willard was too fat and inactive. Morris was too big and slow. Dempsey had two competitive, close fights with Miske prior to stopping him. He had real trouble with Brennan, who had some

[1166] *Great Falls Tribune*, June 7, 1923.
[1167] *Great Falls Tribune*, June 8, 1923.
[1168] *Great Falls Tribune*, June 9 - 11, 1923.

cleverness and could take it. Bill punched and chopped Dempsey into a sight for much of the fight. Hence, Tom was not intimidated.

Dempsey was humble. "I want to say that I look forward to the Gibbons battle with an idea that it will be the toughest of my career. ... I'm saying it because I mean it." It was a puzzle to him why some thought he was in soft. He noted that Gibbons never had been knocked down or out, was almost as tall, and did not weigh that much less. Tom was regarded as the fastest, cleverest heavy around, and had knocked out 30 of the last 34 men he had fought, so he could

JACK DEMPSEY, champion of the world, and his dog, "Jerry"

punch, too. "The record of Gibbons is so infinitely superior to that of the Frenchman that there's no comparison." Carpentier had been knocked out before, but nearly a hundred men had failed to stop or drop Gibbons. "It's rather odd to me that men who thought Carpentier might whip me now think Tom Gibbons is going to be easy for me."

Henry Farrell agreed that Gibbons was no cinch. "Gibbons is a dangerous fighter and a good fighter. He will be in condition because he has been fighting a lot in the last three years, and he always keeps himself in shape." Conversely, no fighter could afford to stay out of the ring for two years and be the same without a lot of hard work. In his training, Gibbons was looking better than ever. "He is hitting harder, boxing like a flash and his morale is perfect." Bud Gorman said Tom's timing and judgment of distance were the most perfect he ever faced.

Conversely, Dempsey "has been working and laying off so irregularly that odds on the champ are coming down substantially in this section."

170-pound local Italian Rocco Stramaglia, who opened Dempsey's eye in sparring and was given his release, now was working with Gibbons. After sparring 2 rounds with Tommy, Rocco said, "Dempsey hits harder, but Gibbons hits twice as often, and they hurt almost as much."

The second installment payment of $100,000 guaranteed to Jack Dempsey allegedly was deposited in the bank, and would be paid to the champion on June 15.[1169]

On June 12, Gibbons sparred with Mexican fighter Tillie "Kid" Herman, Bud Gorman, Kid Rocco Stramaglia, Ernie Kid Sales, and Dan Dorey, for 8 rounds total.

Dempsey closed his training quarters to the public and even newsmen. He wanted to be left alone. Some said he was loafing more than training. Others said he had become like Carpentier, who trained privately. He was not sparring, owing to his healing eye.

[1169] New York Daily News, Great Falls Tribune, Buffalo Courier, Brooklyn Daily Times, Helena Independent, June 12, 1923.

In Shelby, Gibbons was the town's idol. In Great Falls, Dempsey was almost as much a hero. "The happy Dempsey faculty of making everyone believe he is glad to meet them has not lost any of its kick."

Ed W. Smith said Dempsey recognized that it might be challenging to stop Gibbons, saying that Tom "is not going to be an easy man to hit by any means." Even when hit, Tom could take it.

Gibbons said Carpentier allowed Dempsey to rip and smash at his body, failing to cover up sufficiently. He staggered Dempsey in the 2nd round, but failed to follow up in the right way. That fight convinced Tom that he could beat Dempsey.[1170]

The *Los Angeles Times* reported that there were rumors floating about that Godfrey had knocked out Dempsey in one of their sparring sessions. Walter Miller, wrestling instructor at the Los Angeles Athletic Club, said that Jim Johnson, Shelby Mayor, told him that Dempsey was not training seriously, and Godfrey essentially had knocked him out. Miller said,

> I had a long talk with Johnson and Mike Collins. ... Johnson ... said that Kid Godfrey had actually knocked [Dempsey] out in a training bout. Godfrey put over an unexpected sock on the chin and Dempsey was falling when Godfrey realized what he had done and grabbed the champion and held him up until Jack's wits collected themselves.

Another quoted him as saying, "It was a full minute before they were able to get Dempsey to his feet so that he was able to stand unaided." Mayor Johnson said Dempsey was out of shape as a result of associating with "the worthless lot who hang around him in Los Angeles." "Dempsey has failed to take his training seriously and it is on this account that Montana sportsmen are almost to a unit in backing Gibbons to win." Allegedly, the odds had tumbled to even money in the northwest states.[1171]

However, this alleged incident/event was not reported in any of the Montana newspaper accounts of the Dempsey-Godfrey sparring sessions, so the claim seemed suspicious. It possibly was made for publicity purposes, to garner further interest in the bout by giving the impression that Dempsey was vulnerable, boosting the fight. Or it could have been the result of newsmen's frustration with Dempsey for not working out for them as often as they would like. Was it done to affect the odds? Or was it simply the typical false information and wild rumors that often surrounded contests? Had Godfrey indeed nailed him with a good one?

Dempsey denied the report that Godfrey had knocked him out. Jack said, "Our George is a nice man and a good boxer but he did not do

[1170] *Great Falls Tribune, Billings Gazette, Buffalo Times, Buffalo Enquirer, Buffalo Courier*, June 13, 1923.
[1171] *Los Angeles Times, Grand Rapids Press*, June 13, 1923.

anything like that. Someone must have misinformed Mayor Johnson because I know he would not say that if he did not believe it was so."

Still, that report and other stories claiming Dempsey was in poor form had been going around. Several newspapermen allegedly saw the bout. "The negro boxer roughed up Dempsey for several rounds and made him look bad." However, Dempsey's camp mates said he was letting Godfrey look good, and was taking all of Godfrey's stuff to harden himself to punishment, as he often did in training bouts. He did the same with Bill Tate prior to the Willard fight.[1172]

Apparently, in sparring with Rocco Stramaglia, Dempsey had cracked him hard, and Rocco got rough and mad. Dempsey's eye was cut. Like a hurt animal, Dempsey got rough and mad too, and floored Rocco, who leapt from the floor and soaked Dempsey again, until Kearns stopped the proceedings.

Rocco said Gibbons had the better defense, for he could not hit Gibbons squarely, but could hit Dempsey.

> I found Dempsey wide open. I didn't have any trouble in laying them in there. Gibbons is a lot harder to hit. He makes you miss, while he connects. Dempsey slugged me harder because he was trying to knock me out. But he didn't. I didn't mean to hurt his eye. … Dempsey stung me and I stung back. Kearns claimed I butted Dempsey. I don't think I did. We were at close range when I landed on his eye.

Rocco said Gibbons had a chance to win, for he landed more often than Dempsey did and was harder to hit.

> Gibbons had me dizzy from so many punches that I was weaker after a couple of rounds with him than I was with Dempsey. Gibbons keeps popping you with a left hand. He beats you to the punch so you can't start or get your balance. … My clash with Dempsey turned out to be a regular fight; with Gibbons it was boxing.[1173]

On June 13, Gibbons sparred with Herman, Gorman, Rocco, and Dorey.

That day, Dempsey, wearing a headguard to protect his cut eye, which had healed nicely, made Godfrey, Burke, and Drake suffer in heavy slugfests, 2 rounds each. Jack said the cut originally was caused by the Jamaica Kid at Toledo when he was training for Willard. Larry Williams reopened it when he was training in Atlantic City for Carpentier.

The *Great Falls Tribune* said Dempsey tore after Godfrey, knocking the grin off his face, slamming in real punches. Godfrey was hurt, but absorbed the punches. Burke landed some rights, but Dempsey's body blows slowed him down. Drake was cautious, but a right from the champ drew blood from his nose and sent him onto the ropes. He was groggy,

[1172] *Trenton Evening Times*, June 13, 1923.
[1173] *Billings Gazette*, June 13, 1923.

but Dempsey allowed the wobbly Drake to recover and mostly clinch thereafter.

The AP reported that Dempsey knocked down Godfrey with a left hook to the chin in the first 15 seconds of their 1st round, though he quickly rose and clinched. Burke was on the retreat to the ropes most of the time. In the 2nd round against Drake, Dempsey's smashes sent him sagging into the ropes, and he virtually was out on his feet. Jack carried him the rest of

Dempsey sparring Harry Drake

the way, but Drake left the ring dazed and bleeding from the mouth. Jack only rested for 30 seconds between rounds.

Henry Farrell's version said Dempsey was not the same fighter of previous days. He weighed about 200 pounds and seemed listless in his work, lacking pep, and was weaker in the clinches. His judgment of distance seemed poor. Against Godfrey and Burke, he missed quite often, and got hit a fair amount by Godfrey's straight right. His body punches in the clinches, which drove sparring partners out of his Atlantic City camp, seemed to lack the same steam. He still hit hard though, practically knocking out Harry Drake. But Godfrey had no great trouble smothering his body blows in close. He and Burke both pushed Dempsey around considerably, and Burke scored repeatedly with his snappy left hook. Gibbons looked to be much further advanced his preparation.

Farrell said Dempsey gave the impression of being older and much less boy-like than he used to be. Jack said, "It's 15 rounds and Gibbons is a real fighter. I don't know when it will be over."

Harry Newman said Dempsey socked his sparring partners, but showed a strange wildness. He was weak on defense with Godfrey. Still, he plastered his corps of partners good and plenty. In the 1st round, Dempsey landed a left hook and Godfrey went down onto his back. (Perhaps that was Jack's retort to those who claimed Godfrey previously had made him look bad.) Burke was mostly defensive. In their 2nd round, Harry Drake was knocked out standing against the ropes, bleeding at the mouth and staggering about.

Yet, despite the fact that Jack was socking good and hard, he was missing a whole lot and was too wild, his distance was off, and he got hit too much as well. Godfrey hit him often with his right. "Surely Dempsey was in a violent mood, but he did not look so good on the defense and was as wild as a hawk in aiming his blows."[1174]

[1174] *Great Falls Tribune, Butte Miner, Binghamton Press, New York Daily News,* June 14, 1923.

On June 14, using huge 18-ounce gloves, wearing a leather headguard to protect his healing cut, Dempsey again worked 2 rounds each with Godfrey, Burke, and Drake, and each one was spitting blood within 20 seconds of the opening bell with the champ. Godfrey was the only one who weathered the storm. Jack shook Burke in the 1st, and in the 2nd round, a left hook knocked him cold, flat on his back, with his neck hitting the lower rope with such force that the rebound nearly left him in a sitting posture. Burke had refused to wear a headguard, even though Jack asked them all to wear protective gear. A jarring right to the chin sent Drake halfway across the ring on his heels.

Dempsey and Godfrey sparring. Dempsey lifts up Jack Burke after knocking him out.

Observers opined that his sparring partners earned whatever they were getting. Dempsey could punish and knock out men even while wearing 18-ounce gloves and limiting his rests between rounds to 30 seconds. He would wear only 5-ounce gloves for the fight. The *Great Falls Tribune* said, "The champion looked better yesterday than at any time since he started training three weeks ago." Henry Farrell said Dempsey was improving. However, he still missed many punches and took several rights with his jaw.

In Shelby on the 14th, Gibbons sparred 8 rounds with four men: Rocco Stramaglia, Bud Gorman, local Dan Dorey, and Spokane lightweight Lakey Morrow. A Gibbons left hook decked Stramaglia. Tom helped him up, patted his shoulder, and went easy with him thereafter. Usually, Tom pulled his blows in sparring.[1175]

It turned out that the promoters had lied about their ability to pay the second of three $100,000 installments due. However, local businesspersons and bankers came to the rescue, pledging support. George H. Stanton, president of the Stanton Trust and Savings Bank, Dan Tracey, hotel owner and mining operator, and Shirley and Lee Ford, owners of the Great Falls National Bank, would pay the second installment. Bank

<hr>

[1175] *Great Falls Tribune, Binghamton Press,* June 15, 1923. Salt Lake lightweight Herman Auerbach joined Dempsey's staff. Auerbach's father was Dempsey's manager back in the early days.

President Stanton said there had been misrepresentation and mismanagement by certain individuals connected with the promotion. Mayor Johnson admitted that only $30,000 of the second $100,0000 due was immediately available. He had hoped that the balance would be made up from advance ticket sales.

Kearns refused to take over the promotion, and was threatening to walk away with the $100,000 forfeit. To save face for the state, rather than cancel the promotion, the bankers agreed to underwrite the affair. Dan Tracey took over and was placed in charge of the promotion, supplanting Loy Molumby and Shelby Mayor Jim Johnson.[1176]

Tom Gibbons said some believed that Dempsey could not be hurt, but his record proved the contrary. Johnny Sudenberg decked him. Meehan and John Lester Johnson hurt him. Jim Flynn knocked him out, though whether he did it by "accident" or whether he really was knocked cold was not certain. Miske hurt him a bit, so did Brennan, and Carpentier staggered him.

Dempsey said he would focus on speed to keep pace with Gibbons, and perhaps outstep him. He hit big men with relative ease. "But with the twisting, turning, agile Gibbons it will be different." He was a smaller target, and a moving one. Hence Jack was focusing on accuracy.[1177]

Godfrey, Frank Murray, Dempsey, Jack Burke

On the 15th, Dempsey eased up a bit on his sparring partners, Godfrey, Burke, and Drake, working 2 rounds with each, not throwing as often, playing defense, and not following up when he landed. He took some mercy on them, having lambasted them the previous day. It had been whispered about that unless he pulled his blows, he would lose the entire stable. The champ seemed content, amused even, to take punches from his sparring partners. Still, he gave Godfrey an awful drubbing on the inside.

Dempsey had a little black eye on the right side, while a bandage covered the old cut over his left eye.

Gibbons said if he wasn't supremely confident of winning, he would not have agreed to fight under the terms of this contest. "Dempsey gets

[1176] *Brooklyn Daily Eagle, Brooklyn Standard Union*, June 15, 1923.
[1177] *Buffalo Courier*, June 15, 1923.

$310,000. I get $2,500, which hardly covers my training expenses. Yes, I do get a percentage of all money taken in beyond Dempsey's purse, but that doesn't positively assure me that I will get more than $2,500." He could make ten times that fighting soft ones, but believed he would win the title and make even more. He wasn't fighting for a loser's end, because there was none. He was fighting for a chance at the title. He would have paid for the chance. "I've wanted this chance at Dempsey, wanted it more than anything I've ever wanted in my life." Dempsey was choosing the referee, but Tom planned to win so clearly, hopefully by knockout, that there could be no dispute.[1178]

Folks were saying that Gibbons' condition was top notch, better than Dempsey's. Jack Curley said Gibbons would stay the full 15 rounds, and likely win the decision.

> Throw out that fight Tom had with Harry Greb in New York and you have the strongest contender for Dempsey's laurels. Can Harry Wills beat Gibbons? I should say not. Wills cannot beat Gibbons nor can he beat Dempsey. The two best men in the heavyweight class will clash at Shelby... and I feel confident that Gibbons will be the winner.

Dempsey's crew said he was in the best condition of his career, that rumors to the contrary were false. Godfrey said Dempsey was hitting harder and faster than ever, from all angles. Still, many were skeptical of his condition, and particularly criticized his defense.

Jack rose at 7:30 a.m. He had a light breakfast of bran, rhubarb, toast, coffee, prunes, dried stewed peaches, and dried apples or grapefruit. Occasionally he had two eggs and bacon, two poached eggs on toast, or two soft boiled eggs. He never ate meat for breakfast. Usually, he just had toast and coffee. He took a morning hike or run. He ate a big lunch at 12 noon, usually his heartiest meal of the day. He had roast beef, roast pork, or roast lamb, with boiled potatoes and selections from many fruits and vegetables, including fresh apricots, cherries, and peaches, lettuce with dressing, cold raw carrots, turnips, spinach, and tomatoes. For dessert was an egg-custard or bread- or rice-pudding. Buttermilk and water were the drinks. He worked out in the afternoon, usually after 3 p.m. He ate a medium sized dinner at 6 p.m., generally consisting of a broiled steak, pork chops, or liver and onions, with vegetable salad, custard pudding and milk or tea. At 9:30 or 10 p.m. he had a late-night snack of fruit.[1179]

On the evening of June 16, one day late, the second $100,000 installment was paid to Kearns, who was threatening to leave and pull out of the fight.

Promoters in Cleveland and New York (Tom O'Rourke) were trying to lure the fight there, saying if for whatever reason the Shelby promotion was derailed, the fight could be transferred to their locales. Kearns still

[1178] *New York Daily News, Great Falls Tribune, Buffalo Courier,* June 16, 1923.
[1179] *Anaconda Standard,* June 17, 1923.

was owed the third $100,000 installment, to be paid two days before the fight. Various Montana businessmen were helping to raise the funds.

On the 16th, Dempsey sparred his usual 6 rounds. He and Godfrey went at it for 2 rounds, slugging and infighting. Dempsey had to protect himself from Godfrey's uppercuts, which George tried every time they came together. Dempsey effectively used left hooks and rips to the head and body, but "the negro" remained on his feet despite several solid smashes. Of course, Dempsey was wearing 18-ounce gloves. Burke and Drake went 2 rounds each as well. Drake left the ring with a bloody nose.

Some said Dempsey's boxing was slower than on previous days. Harry Newman said, "There isn't any use straddling the issue. Jack Dempsey does not look good." His defense and sense of distance were off, and he was not impressive. Though he did paste Godfrey good and hard, George took it and landed in return.[1180]

Noted was the fact that Gibbons, who never had been down, had lost only one formal decision in his career, to the nonstop-punching Greb, though reporters said Gibbons demonstrated more skill and power than Greb, who just outhustled him, as he did with everyone.

GIBBONS SHOWS BLOW HE EXPECTS TO USE AGAINST DEMPSEY. Challenger landing a right to the solar plexis on Bud Gorman of Kenosha, one of his sparring partners.

Dempsey called attention to the fact that this fight would be outdoors in the hot sun, and his training took that into account. One could burn up too quickly trying to fight the same way outdoors as for an indoor fight.

Jack said he weighed 195 pounds, which was good for this fight. He did not want to be much lighter. He did not need to train that hard, for he had been working for the past six months in anticipation of a potential fight (which never materialized), work which the general public may not have realized he was doing.[1181]

IF GIBBONS LANDS LIKE THIS DEMPSEY IS DONE FOR. Gibbons landing his left to the solar plexis on Bud Gorman of Kenosha, who appears rather complacent.

On Monday June 18, Dempsey sparred 6 rounds, 2 each with Bermondsey Billy Wells, Salt Lake junior welter Herman Auerbach, and heavy Harry Drake. Dempsey primarily worked on his defense, using speed, footwork, and dodging, rarely being hit, and almost never solidly. One or two counters drew blood from Auerbach's mouth.

[1180] *Brooklyn Daily Eagle, Butte Miner, New York Daily News*, June 17, 1923. Dempsey slipped and went down with Burke in a clinch (though earlier in the article Newman implied, perhaps to advertise the article, that Dempsey had been dropped, though admitting later on that such was not the case).
[1181] *Great Falls Tribune*, June 18, 1923.

DEMPSEY GETS A NEW MASCOT. Margaret Carter of Great Falls, Mont., presenting the champion with a white angora kitten.

[TRIBUNE Photo.]

Harry Drake landed a couple solid blows, but soon regretted it, for Dempsey landed a one-two that sent him staggering back on his heels half-way across the ring, being saved from a fall by the ropes, but then a left to the face decked him. He rose and clinched until his head cleared. Drake was so out of it in the final round that even after time was called, he kept hanging on. When he finally realized it was over, a blood-smeared smile appeared on Drake's face. His legs were wobbly. Wells said, "Poor Dryke. E stops more of 'em than hall of us."[1182]

James Dougherty was named to be the fight's referee. Dan Tracey, current head of the association promoting the bout, confirmed that Dougherty would be paid $5,000 plus expenses. Dempsey wanted him more than any other man. Dougherty had refereed Jack's fights with Levinsky in Philadelphia and Miske at Benton Harbor. Dougherty had been in boxing for 25 years and had been a referee, promoter, and manager.

The *Anaconda Standard* found the alleged stories of Dempsey being knocked groggy by Godfrey to be somewhat questionable and humorous, given that they came from Los Angeles and Denver, but not any local or semi-local paper. The allegation was that it was covered up, but the rumor got out and it was printed elsewhere. Still, Great Falls people on scene laughed at the idea of Godfrey doing that to Dempsey. "He's one of the punching bags at Great Falls park." "At any rate the 'knockout story,' true or only rumor, goes to build up the fight, mostly from the Gibbons side."

The *San Francisco Chronicle*'s Harry Smith said the fight had not produced much in the way of real news, but more in the way of gossip and discussion of the financial end, given the big financial risks.

Smith said Dempsey figured to win, and the best that Gibbons supporters could say was that they had a hunch. Smith believed there was no logic behind their hunch. The only thing that weighed against Dempsey was his two years of inactivity from fights.

[1182] *Great Falls Tribune, New York Daily News,* June 19, 1923. Godfrey and Burke were given the day off.

No man can lay off from his usual work without having his efficiency impaired, and it goes for fighters as well as the desk man. Dempsey in four years has had just two real fights, and that's hardly enough to keep him going. Yet I doubt whether that handicap is sufficient to give Gibbons more than a passing chance.[1183]

On June 19, the cold drizzling rain did not stop Dempsey from sparring 6 rounds with Wells, 218-pound Godfrey, and Burke in a fast and rough manner. The weather concerned Trainer Jerry Luvadis. Another worry was a slight cold which the champ picked up the previous day, which was apparent in his breathing. Although Dempsey was wearing a headgear, Burke landed a right that ripped away the plaster bandage over his healed cut, but luckily there was no blood.

All reports from Gibbons' camp said he was fast, in great shape, and displaying excellent form. Gibbons pounded on 210-pound Gorman, knocking him back on his heels. Jimmy Delaney, who was coming off a 10-round no decision loss to Tunney, was bleeding at the end of his 3 rounds. Welter Tillie Kid Herman also slugged with the challenger. Observers were convinced that Tom would give Dempsey a real test.[1184]

Gibbons was satisfied with the selection of Jimmy Dougherty as referee. "As a matter of fact, I might have chosen Jimmy myself, if the choice had been left to me."

Dempsey signed a $200,000 moving picture contract to star in a movie for the Amalgamated Exchanges of America.

On the 20th, Dempsey boxed Billy Wells and newly arrived light heavy Bill Wolpin, 2 rounds each. Dempsey quickly decked Wolpin twice. A left deposited him in the first row. Thereafter he showed a wholesome respect for the champ. Kearns was satisfied. "He's in good shape. Why should he come out here and work himself to death every afternoon?"

In his sparring with Rocco Stramaglia that day, Gibbons landed a lightning left hook, followed by a right to the body, and Rocco went down and out. Rocco left the camp.

1183 *Anaconda Standard*, June 20, 1923.
1184 *Great Falls Tribune, Brooklyn Daily Times*, June 20, 1923.

Dempsey laughingly denied the reports that Godfrey hurt or knocked him out, or that Burke floored him. "Just about now I am coming to the conclusion that I'm an awful has been. That's because I've been reading what some of the boys write about me." Newsmen were declaring that he had been decked and/or knocked out, had slowed up, was not hitting like he used to, and could not get out of his own way. "Poor little me. If Godfrey, my negro sparring partner, ever knocked me out, it must have been when I was asleep. He certainly never did it while I was awake. And never, at any time while he has been in my camp, has he ever shaken me up." Once, Jack let George step a little, permitting him to make a nice showing. "That was the day a negro musical show played Great Falls and all the dark chorus girls came out to see what George could do. I let George do it that afternoon so as to please his guests." One time, in a clinch, Burke stumbled, Jack fell against him, and they both fell to the floor. (Harry Newman verified this.) Others claimed that Dempsey had been taking it too easy in his training. "Every such story is a deliberate falsehood."

Gibbons decks Stramaglia

Confident Gibbons said he was a faster, cleaner, and more versatile hitter than Carpentier, and was going to win. "Never felt surer of anything in my life." "I have never felt quite so good in my life as I do at this moment." He was fighting for his family. He would make the real money as champion, which could ensure a real chance for his children. He wanted them to go to college and have some money to go into business. He wanted his mother to know the full comforts of life. He had a fine, sweet wife, and he wanted her to have nice things too. He was highly motivated.[1185]

Trainer Buck Pape, Ernie/Eddie Sales, Bud Gorman, Manager Eddie Kane, Tommy Gibbons, Rocco Stramaglia

[1185] *New York Daily News, Great Falls Tribune, Buffalo Courier,* July 21, 1923; *Great Falls Tribune,* June 22, 1923.

Gibbons with his kids at Glacier Park, MT   Gibbons on left with Tillie Kid Herman

Oklahoma giant 24-year-old Ben Wray wanted to spar with Dempsey. He stood 7'2" and weighed 250 pounds. He had an 87 ½" reach. He was 4-0 with 4 knockouts in his career, including a KO4 over Carl Morris, according to Wray. Kearns warned Tex McCarthy, his manager, that Dempsey hit pretty hard. McCarthy said Wray could take it and dish it.

On Friday June 22, a crowd of 1,500 watched Dempsey take on Big Ben Wray and knock him out in only 28 seconds, breaking his jaw with a left hook, even though he only used sparring gloves. Wray's jaw swelled badly, and a doctor said it was fractured.

Dempsey sparred 6 rounds total. He first worked with Godfrey. A left clip on the jaw caused George to spit blood. In the 2nd round, the champ shook him with right and left hooks. Wells was next. Jack played defense for the 1st round, but opened up with harder blows in the 2nd.

Wells said, "E's 'itting 'ard tiddye. Four beauties, 'e caught me."

Wray was next. Dempsey felt him out for a few seconds, then uncorked. Two lefts missed short, but the third landed and down toppled Wray. He was out, with a bleeding mouth. Afterwards, Wray said, "Man, how he can hit." He then watched the champ drive Bill Wolpin around the ring for a round.

[TRIBUNE Photo.]
DEMPSEY ROUNDS INTO CONDITION. Here the champion and Billy Wells of London are seen at Dempsey's Great Falls training camp.

[Pacific and Atlantic Photo.]
THIRD MAN IN RING
at Dempsey-Gibbons clash will be Jim Dougherty of Leiperville, Pa.

644

Dempsey and Johnny Kilbane lift Ben Wray

Cold sores on Gibbons' lower lip were opened in sparring with Jim Delaney, but Tom was not concerned. Against Delaney, Gibbons demonstrated his footwork, feinting, and strong, quick left, snapping Jim's head back several times with his left hook, and repeatedly driving a right to the body.

DEMPSEY'S CHALLENGER, Tom Gibbons, training at Great Falls for their world's championship fight at Shelby, Mont., on July 4. Gibbons is at the left, sparring with Bud Gorman, a Wisconsin boxer. As the day of battle nears, experts are taking Gibbons more and more seriously. He's a great boxer, for a big fellow, and some wise men of the ring sport begin to feel he has a chance to take the title from Dempsey by outpointing him for fifteen rounds.

Gibbons said, "If I didn't think I could whip Dempsey I wouldn't have taken the match." He had lost officially only once in 88 battles. Tom said he liked to look a man directly in the eye when receiving instructions. Nearly all of them looked away from his stare. "They say Dempsey never looks an opponent in the eye until the bell rings. ... I never fought a man yet who didn't look me in the eye that I couldn't lick ... He had better take a look at me when we shake hands, for he won't see much of me to hit at after the bell rings. He'll do lots of shadow boxing July 4."[1186]

On June 23, Dempsey sparred 6 rounds with George Godfrey, Jack Burke, and Harry Drake. Jack landed 4 to 1. He varied his style. He carried them along for a time, and then opened up with a fusillade which almost carried them off their feet. Then he would ease down again and dance around the ring with his wary partners in pursuit. He was considerably aggressive against Godfrey. Burke was bleeding. Dempsey's defense was good, and what solid blows did land, he merely shook off and went in for more.

Dempsey in headgear against Burke

[1186] *Great Falls Tribune*, June 23, 1923.

Dempsey spars Godfrey, with Kilbane refereeing

That same day in Shelby, Gibbons sparred 10 fast rounds with Bud Gorman, Jimmy Delaney, George Manley, Tillie "Kid" Herman, and Lakey Morrow. Many of those who initially thought Gibbons did not have a chance had changed their minds. The *Great Falls Tribune* said he was bigger and faster than the records showed, and in excellent shape.

Tom Andrews said Gibbons was listed as weighing over 180 pounds and standing 6" ¾". Andrews said in fact, Tom was 5' 9 ½" and about 178. Gibbons was cleverer than Dempsey, and had been very active, unlike Dempsey. Good, smaller heavyweights had beaten larger heavies, so victory was possible. (Corbett beat Sullivan; Fitz beat Corbett; Burns beat Hart, Dempsey beat Willard). However, Dempsey's power had a way of making a man forget all about his cleverness. Conversely, Gibbons did not hit hard enough to hurt the iron-jawed Dempsey, so if he won, it would have to be on cleverness alone.

Minnesota referee George Barton, who had seen Minnesota native Gibbons in action many times, as well as the champion, said Dempsey had a real fight on his hands. Tom was no set-up. At the prevailing 3 to 1 odds, Gibbons was one of the best short-enders ever. He had lost only one decision in 88 fights, to Greb. Gibbons was not fully recovered from the flu for that fight. He had victories over Miske, Greb twice, Meehan, Wiggins, Madden, Roper, etc. He was fast, clever, could punch with both hands, and could take it. (Of course, neither Willard, Miske, nor Brennan ever had been down or stopped prior to meeting Dempsey either.)

Gibbons was a wonderful ring general. He was an elusive target, hard to hit cleanly, and knew how to guard his jaw and body. He would make Dempsey miss, which would be a new experience for him. Conversely, Gibbons could land through the smallest openings with the skill of a sharpshooter. "It is my honest opinion that if Gibbons can keep Dempsey at bay for 6 or 7 rounds he stands an excellent chance of going the route." Dempsey's lengthy inactivity had to affect him adversely. Gibbons was not fighting for the money, but to win and cash in later. He did not weigh that much less than Dempsey, only was about an inch shorter, and actually had a longer reach than the champ. "I am convinced the champion will have to be in his best form to retain his title." Barton saw Gibbons spar 10 rounds on June 23, and he looked great, better than ever.[1187]

On June 24, Jack Dempsey celebrated his 28th birthday. He took on five of his mitt mates for 10 rounds of furious milling. He never looked better. He hit them all when and where he willed, keeping himself protected against all manner of blows. Burke and Drake were up first. 170-pound Bill Wolpin suffered the only knockdown. A right turned him around, and then another right to the jaw sent him down. The champ kept his power under wraps for the last 4 rounds, 2 with Herman Auerbach and 2 more with Connie Curry. It was a boxing, dodging, weaving Dempsey against the lighter men, showing such speedy defense that neither one could lay a glove on him.[1188]

In his sparring on the 25th, Gibbons buffeted middleweight Mark Moore all around the ring, easily defending blows. Moore said, "He is the fastest man I ever met. It is hard to get at him." Gibbons also sparred with Tillie "Kid" Herman, firing rapid blows that bloodied Herman's face.

Jack Burke spars Dempsey

Gibbons sparring Mark Moore

The week before the fight, Dempsey would work with the lighter men, before the drying-out process. Kearns said Dempsey was a finished fighter, hitting harder and boxing faster than ever before.

Big Ben Wray was in the hospital with a broken jaw. Godfrey was injured too, with splintered ribs, which kept him from sparring further. Dempsey literally was a rib cracker.[1189]

[1187] *Great Falls Tribune, Brooklyn Daily Eagle, Minneapolis Tribune,* June 24, 1923.
[1188] *Great Falls Tribune,* June 25, 1923.
[1189] *Great Falls Tribune,* June 26, 1923.

GLOVES THAT WILL DECIDE CHAMPIONSHIP.
The gloves that will be worn by Jack Dempsey and Tom Gibbons at Shelby, Mont., on July 4, were made in San Francisco.

Thomas Rice said in order to promote the fight, many were giving out false reports, saying Gibbons was heavier, taller, and younger than he was, and was showing prodigious prowess in sparring, while Dempsey was not.

Rice said Brennan's career showed how a victim of the champion might profit from defeat, especially if he was competitive and put up a good performance. Bill had earned a lot of money since the Dempsey fight. Rice wondered whether Gibbons miscalculated the fight's drawing power, or simply was hoping to do well enough to make him more marketable for future contests and exhibitions. Lasting 15 rounds and losing a decision "would be a great monetary gain for the defeated man. He would be pointed to with pride as the only person who had stuck a route with Dempsey since the champion began to champ."

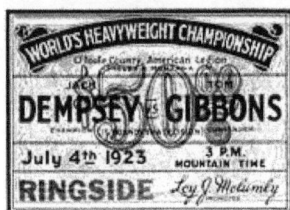

Henry Farrell noted that the third installment payment still had not been raised. It was unclear whether Dempsey would fight regardless (either because he wanted the work or because of public opinion), or stand on the contract, take the money paid thus far as a forfeit, and leave.

Gibbons stood to receive nothing if the receipts did not exceed $310,000, but Tommy said he did not mind. "I'll fight for a postage stamp. I'm after the title, and I didn't go into this contest for the money. If Dempsey and I are the only ones in the arena, I'll fight." Such statements made Gibbons even more beloved and admired in Montana, and by the boxing community.[1190]

Dempsey was due to be paid the third $100,000 installment on July 2. Great Falls bankers had advanced much of the money associated with the venture. Many businessmen financially interested included nine local lumber dealers and labor contractors who held a mortgage of $85,000 against the completed arena.

On Tuesday June 26, Dempsey boxed 3 rounds with Billy Wells, and single rounds with Connie Curry and Lee Moore in a fast workout, but tried to keep his punches in check as much as his natural hitting proclivities would permit. Jack's father had arrived to watch his son in action.[1191]

[1190] Brooklyn Daily Eagle, Buffalo Times, June 26, 1923.
[1191] Great Falls Tribune, June 27, 1923.

Dan Tracey resigned as manager for the promotion, saying he had been unable to collect the amount promised. Art Kelly, bookkeeper for the original promoters, filed an attachment, claiming a $1,005 commission on the sale of tickets.

Kearns said he had nothing to say until July 2, at which time the third installment payment was due. The promotion had kept its contract thus far. Privately though, he was threatening to pull out if not paid in full.

The International News Reel would film the fight. Kearns/Dempsey would receive 33 1/3%, Kane/Gibbons 25%, and 41 2/3% would be divided between Mayor Jim Johnson, Mike Collins, and Loy Molumby. Allegedly, more than $160,000 in tickets had been sold.

On Wednesday June 27, under the sweltering hot sun, Dempsey boxed 6 rounds total with welter Billy Wells, 126-pound feather Lee Moore, and bantam Connie Curry. Jack tried not to sock his light mates too hard, though he drew blood from all three. The normally stone-faced Dempsey laughed at Curry's efforts to hit him. Father Hiram Dempsey watched, while Brother Bernard Dempsey refereed the bouts.[1192]

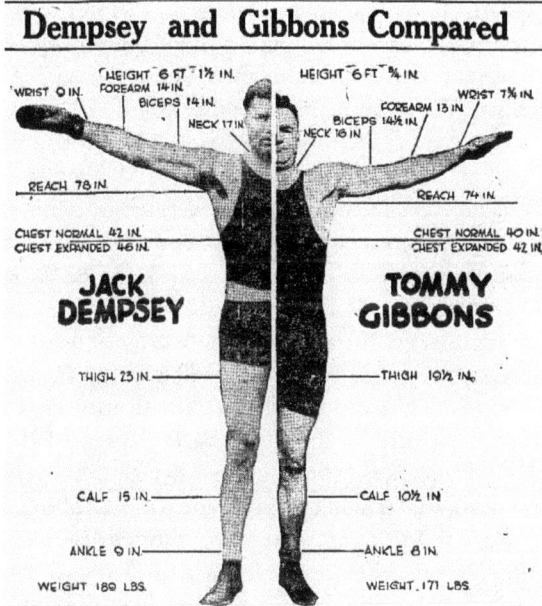

Dempsey and Gibbons Compared

JACK DEMPSEY — HEIGHT 6 FT 1½ IN. / WRIST 0 IN. / FOREARM 14 IN. / BICEPS 14 IN. / NECK 17 IN. / REACH 78 IN. / CHEST NORMAL 42 IN. / CHEST EXPANDED 46 IN. / THIGH 23 IN. / CALF 15 IN. / ANKLE 0 IN. / WEIGHT 180 LBS.

TOMMY GIBBONS — HEIGHT 6 FT ¾ IN. / WRIST 7¾ IN. / FOREARM 13 IN. / BICEPS 14½ IN. / NECK 16 IN. / REACH 74 IN. / CHEST NORMAL 40 IN. / CHEST EXPANDED 42 IN. / THIGH 19½ IN. / CALF 10½ IN. / ANKLE 8 IN. / WEIGHT 171 LBS.

On the 28th, Dempsey boxed another 6 rounds, 2 apiece with Jack Burke and Harry Drake, and 1 round each with Connie Curry and Herman Auerbach. Jack was so elusive; they could not lay a glove on him. A right uppercut in the 2nd round drew blood from Drake. He was wobbly when he left the ring, and he displayed a discolored right eye. Spectator Ben Wray had his jaw wired shut and a lump on the inside of his mouth.

Harry Newman said Dempsey was ready. A week ago he seemed slow and out of shape, but the way he blazed through his companions that day was worth the trip to see. "He never looked better in his life than he did today."[1193]

Thomas Rice said the general public had refused to bite on the bout, which looked like a big bloomer/financial bust. Although the fight would

---

[1192] *Great Falls Tribune, New York Daily News*, June 28, 1923. One report said featherweight Lee Moore had caught a right cross which split his eyelid, which required three stitches. An uppercut in the 2nd round clipped him under the chin and split the skin there too, which required a pair of stitches.
[1193] *Great Falls Tribune, New York Daily News*, June 29, 1923.

draw a large crowd, it still would be far below expectations and the financial requirements necessary to meet all of the expenses.

Henry Farrell said there was substantial debate about Dempsey's condition. It generally was believed that he did not look as good as he did before Carpentier. "The champion, however, has always been an erratic trainer and it is hard to get any accurate judgment on his real form." Gibbons, on the other hand, was in perfect shape, and all agreed that if Dempsey had neglected his preparation, he might come to regret it.

Gibbons had become the "Thunder Chief," adopted as a member of the local Blackfeet Indian tribe. This was somewhat ironic, given that Dempsey was the one who actually was part Native American.[1194]

On June 29, when Dempsey was hitting the big leather dummy, someone called out, "You won't have any dead man like that July 4 at Shelby. Tommy Gibbons isn't like any bag." The air was charged with silence. The champ smiled and responded, "I hope not."

On the 29th, Gibbons sparred 10 rounds, with Bud Gorman, Jimmy Delaney, Tillie Kid Herman, George Manley, and Tad Harrigan.

Allegedly, 20 businessmen throughout the state had raised the final $100,000, each pledging $5,000, so that it would be paid on July 2. George Stanton, president of the Stanton Trust & Savings bank, personally had advanced $50,000. Folks were appealing to the state's honor, not wanting the fight to fall through. The state did not want to be embarrassed.[1195]

Dempsey said his wallop still was there, and it was enough to beat Gibbons. "The old punch is still with me. That's the thing that lifted me from obscurity in those far back days of 1914 and 1915 to a world's championship, it's the thing that has kept me at the top since 1919 and it's the thing that will lift me over the Tom Gibbons hurdle on July 4th."

Jack did not care that some thought he had slowed a bit or was not showing the same old cleverness on defense. They could think what they wanted. "But they can't say that I have lost the power from my wallop. And, while that remains I'll continue as a world's champion." As long as he could punch, he was confident of victory against all comers.

> They can dance and prance away from me for a while. They can sock me if they wish. Other men have done it. But nothing will worry me…while I know this: I can still hit with crushing power and can still drop men and can still take away all the fighting will that is theirs when I land. Maybe I'm not hitting as frequently as I did. But I'm hitting as hard.[1196]

When asked what he thought of Gibbons, Dempsey said,

> Well, he can hit hard. Otherwise he wouldn't have knocked out 33 men in his last 37 fights, even though none of them were really tough opponents. But I won't fight him any different from the way

[1194] *Brooklyn Daily Eagle, Buffalo Times,* June 29, 1923.
[1195] *Great Falls Tribune,* June 30, 1923; *Minneapolis Journal,* July 1, 1923.
[1196] *Buffalo Courier,* June 30, 1923. Dempsey was sparring with 14-ounce gloves.

I have fought Willard or any of the other heavyweights I have met and defeated. A fight is a fight to me. ... I am not figuring that I'm going to have a cinch in this fight and I'm not predicting when I will win it, but I expect to keep my title. I want to say, however, right here that I expect to have a real scrap.

Gibbons said 1923 was the year of the upset. Several champions had lost their crowns. Kilbane lost to Criqui, Britton lost to Walker, Wilde lost to Villa, Greb lost to Tunney, Dundee lost to Bernstein, while Siki beat Carpentier but then lost to McTigue.

I cannot see Dempsey as the man-eating superman that some folks have pictured him to be. He can be gotten the same as all the rest of the champions. He can be knocked out. To my way of thinking he has fought only one real opponent in his entire career. That was Billy Miske, and Miske was far from being a well man when he tackled Dempsey. All the rest of Dempsey's victims have been setups. And I do not even except Jess Willard when I say this.

Gibbons noted that Dempsey had been fairly inactive as champion, and had not fought in 2 years. "And a fighter cannot keep in fighting trim if he fights only four rounds in two years. He is bound to slip under such circumstances. Dempsey is just human, the same as the rest of us, and this long period of ring idleness is bound to tell on him. It can't help but slow him up." Tom said he had fought 37 times in the last three years, taking on anyone who would fight him, scoring 33 knockouts in that span. "I am right now at the top of my fighting form."[1197]

Former featherweight champ Johnny Kilbane, who was on scene and had seen both men spar, said, "Dempsey fights primarily because he is a fighting animal. He's happiest when he's in the ring. The great vitality which distinguishes him from other men finds its greatest outlet in fighting." He had an abundance of stored-up energy, and ordinary amusements did not allow him to release it the way boxing did. "Dempsey enters the ring with the same feeling that a hungry man advances on his dinner." Dempsey loved fighting. His only plan was ceaseless attack. Jack's defense was instinctive, with his primary thought to hit his foe hard.

Conversely, Gibbons did not love fighting. It was his business, his trade, and he studied it accordingly. He was thorough, hardworking, analytical, mechanically perfect, and knew all the details of the game. He was cool and collected. Gibbons was more likely to have a game plan.

A man sued Dempsey and Kearns for $20,000, as a result of a dog biting his 7-year-old daughter at Dempsey's training camp. However, it was not their dog, and just was roaming around nearby at the time. The dog was euthanized.[1198]

All of the leading sportswriters who were in Great Falls were predicting a Dempsey victory, including Damon Runyon, Grantland Rice

[1197] *Helena Independent-Record*, June 30, 1923.
[1198] *Missoulian*, July 1, 1923.

- *New York Tribune*, Hype Igoe - *New York World*, Scoop Gleason – *San Francisco Call*, Fane Norton – *Los Angeles Herald*, William McGeehan – *New York Herald*, Sam Hall – *Los Angeles Examiner*, Ed Smith – *Chicago American*, Otto Floto – *Denver and Kansas City Post*, Harry Newman – *New York News*, George Barton – *Minneapolis Tribune*, and J. E. Wray – *St. Louis Post Dispatch*. Others picking Dempsey included Ed Walker, Bob Edgren, Hugh Fullerton, Charley Johnson, Charley Harvey, and Billy Miske. Most thought Dempsey would stop him within 4 - 6 rounds on average. George Barton thought Gibbons would go 12 rounds, which was the longest prediction.

On June 30, Gibbons sparred 7 fast rounds with Jim Delaney, Tillie Kid Herman, George Manley, and Tad Hannigan. Gibbons buckled Delaney with a left hook.

That same day, Dempsey boxed 2 rounds each with Burke and Wells, doing much infighting.

Dempsey sparring Billy Wells

Major J. E. Lane of Lewistown was the bout's new trustee, declaring that the final amount owed to Dempsey would be paid. 20 men had pledged the final $100,000. Those men allegedly received from Kearns his entire interest in the moving picture rights (which he later disputed). Another interest in the film rights was released to the guarantors by Loy Molumby and Mayor Jim Johnson, all of which got them to agree to finance the remaining payment. Or so it was claimed.

Hugh Fullerton said normally Dempsey seemed so super-charged with nervous vitality that it was impossible for him to remain still. He was restless, and liked to stay on the move. Yet, he seemed to have calmed down greatly over the last year. "He no longer shows extreme nervous activity." He was more poised, either the result of getting older, or because of extreme confidence in himself. He fought more calmly, threw fewer blows, but placed them with more deadly certainty.

Gibbons was the antithesis of Dempsey in nerves. He was calm, friendly, and pleasant, even in the ring. "Fighters say he is too good natured and kindly to be a great fighter. He is one of the most pleasant, obliging, and decent men in ring history." His calmness and poise were apt to be disturbing to an opponent. Dempsey was higher strung in nature and had the greatest excess of nervous energy. Gibbons only had one bad fight in his career, with Greb, though some said he was sick or stale. He was sluggish in that fight.

Robert Edgren said the champion had beaten the best men, with decisive victories over Fulton, Willard, Brennan, Miske, and Carpentier, all of which augured ill for Gibbons. Neither man had neglected his work. Gibbons had the advantage of being more active in the past couple years, and having more overall experience. Yet, Dempsey always kept active, particularly with his exhibitions and general training for fights that failed to materialize. "Dempsey is always delighted when he can find a sparring partner who will hit him and hit him hard, for that gives him a chance to cut loose with his own blows and enjoy a real combat."

Jack did not expect to have an easy time simply because Gibbons was smaller, for he thought it was easier to topple the giants. Gibbons was quick and elusive, and a little bigger than Carpentier. He had a good punch, but had not knocked out the caliber of men that Dempsey had. Dempsey was rugged and could take it. Harry Greb's fast pace had bewildered Gibbons. "And Dempsey can go as fast as Greb and hit about four times as hard." Hence, Gibbons' chance to win was very slight, and most likely he would be knocked out within 5 rounds.

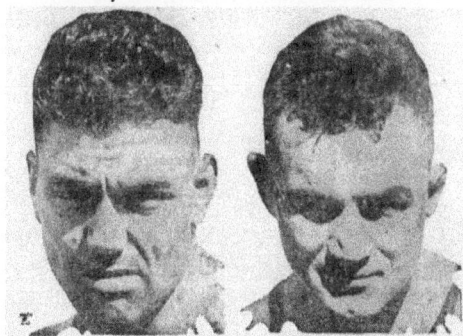

Edward Walker predicted a Dempsey victory within 8 rounds. Gibbons had speed and cleverness, but it would not be enough. He had a chin, but never had absorbed Dempsey's brand of power.

Billy Miske predicted that Gibbons would last 9 or 10 rounds. "He'll give the champion quite a fight. I've fought them both and ought to know. Tom can hurt with his punches and he'll give Dempsey plenty of trouble to land squarely."[1199]

On July 1, three days before the fight, Dempsey tugged, mauled, and wrestled with Burke, and only late in the 2nd round did he endeavor to punch him. One right cross to the chin caused Burke to see some stars.

A couple of jabs snapped Wells' head back, but both men were pulling their punches. The scar over Dempsey's eye appeared to be well healed.

[1199] *Great Falls Tribune, Chicago Tribune, Minneapolis Journal,* July 1, 1923.

Wells hits Dempsey in the nose

Gibbons facing camera in final sparring session

That day, Gibbons boxed 8 rounds total with Bud Gorman, Jimmy Delaney, Kid Herman, and George Manley/Manly. Delaney remarked that Gibbons was a terror and could lick anything on two feet.

Tommy said, "I am going in to win, and if I do not win, it will not be my fault." According to his manager, Eddie Kane, Gibbons weighed 178 pounds. Tom would enter the ring at that weight or slightly more.[1200]

Robert Edgren said the biggest betting point was how many rounds the fight would last. Little was wagered on the ultimate outcome, for most believed Dempsey would win, because he had too much tremendous strength and astonishing speed, mixed with great intensity. Both men were fit. "There is nothing to criticize in the condition of either man."

[1200] *Great Falls Tribune, Missoulian,* July 2, 1923.

Edward Walker said Gibbons was concentrating on his defense for the left hook. He looked better than ever in his sparring. "He slipped off punches by fractions of inches and made his sparring partners sit up and take notice by shaking them up with terrific left hooks." He also worked his right hand more often than usual.

Harry Newman said his first look at Dempsey a couple weeks ago did not impress, for he was slow and inaccurate. However, the last two weeks of work had done wonders, and now "he looks just as good as ever."

Regarding the money due to be paid, Kearns said, "Nothing at all to say until Monday. I'm keeping my contract, and the other people will have to if they want a fight."[1201]

Some newspapers reported that the fight had been called off owing to financial difficulties; for the promoters could not come up with the final $100,000. They had not deposited the money after all. Kearns refused to allow Dempsey to fight until the final installment was paid.

Others reported that Kearns said he would take $50,000 up front, plus the remaining $50,000 out of the first gate receipts. Apparently though, only $4,000 had been raised. Negotiations were ongoing. The fight was off again, on again. Many investors who had pledged money got cold feet. Kearns might have to wait for his final $100,000 to be paid with gate receipts.

Kearns said he had warned the promoters at the outset that he had doubts about the feasibility of the promotion, that very few men in the country were able to stage a world's heavyweight championship successfully. The promoters had lied to induce him to sign the contract, having promised that the money already was on hand. They chased him around the country via airplane, in Salt Lake City and Chicago, before he consented. "From the outset they have never been frank with me." Kearns said the promotion had been grossly mismanaged, and Gibbons likely would come away with no money.

Eventually, after some uncertainty regarding whether the fight would take place, Kearns agreed to have jurisdiction over the gate until the first $100,000 was paid in, which he would receive immediately. At minimum, Kearns and Dempsey would earn at least $200,000 for the fight, which already had been paid, and still was phenomenal money for the time.

Mrs. Gibbons said she would not attend the fight, for the nervous strain would be too much for her, and she also did not want to distract Tom. "But we are confident that he will win and he most of all."

Hugh Fullerton predicted a Dempsey victory within 4 rounds. Dempsey was better in every way. He hit harder and took it better. The champ roughed and pulled and hugged with Godfrey, a "giant Negro," who went to the hospital with broken ribs from the murderous body blows. Hence, Gibbons' best bet would be to keep away and use his jab and hook, to annoy and sting him, and hope Dempsey lost his head and got wild.

[1201] *Minneapolis Journal*, July 2, 1923.

Edward Walker said 90% of the fans would be pulling for Gibbons to win. "Gibbons has the distinction of being the most popular challenger the boxing game ever has seen." Tom likely would fight for free if the receipts did not exceed $300,000 and therefore would have to be content with what he could make from his 25% share of the motion picture profits, and what he could earn as champion if he won. He and his manager were banking on him winning the crown and earning big money thereafter. Dempsey was the 3 to 1 favorite.

Gibbons was willing to take a chance, for he was certain that he would win. "If confidence and coolness count for anything, Tom has the crown won now." His wife and three children distracted him from talking about the fight, but after they went to bed, Tom said, "I'll win. I've never been knocked down yet, and I'll not make the first trip to the canvas Wednesday. I trained carefully and earnestly, and will enter the ring believing that I am the champion's master."

They would fight in an 18-foot ring, as required by the state's boxing laws.

The undercard bouts would start at noon. The main fight was scheduled to start at 3 p.m. on July 4. The various sparring partners of each opposing camp were scheduled take on one another, including Jimmy Delaney vs. Jack Burke, and Bud Gorman vs. Harry Drake.

About 160 members of American Legion posts would act as ushers.

Although there were not many, those picking Gibbons to win included Doc Bagley, Harry Greb (by decision), Mike McTigue, Dan Morgan, Jack Britton, and Mike McNulty. Jethro Bezine humorously picked "Jack Kearns."[1202]

Edward Walker said a sportswriter's poll revealed that only 5 were picking Gibbons.

Another pre-fight prediction poll of 14 sportswriters had it 12-2 for Dempsey. The only two picking Gibbons were E. W. Dickerson of Grand Rapids and Frank Menke of the *New York Journal*, who predicted Gibbons by knockout in the 8th round.

The *New York Daily News* reported that Dempsey unofficially weighed around 190, while Gibbons was about 180.

On July 3, Dempsey said,

[1202] *Los Angeles Times, Chicago Tribune, New York Daily News, Anaconda Standard, Great Falls Tribune, Minneapolis Journal,* July 3, 1923.

I regard every challenger as dangerous. They are all dangerous until they are on the floor. I am not going to take any chances with Gibbons. … Anything is liable to happen to a champion any time he goes into the ring. So I am going to do my best, and if my best fails, I shall be the first to welcome Gibbons as the new champion. It is my confident feeling that I never was in better shape. I feel better than I have in many years on the day before I fought.

Gibbons said he was trained to perfection, and if he did not win, he was not meant to be champion.

A 10,000-person attendance was predicted, but 18,000 were needed for the promotion not to be a financial failure.

Harry Newman said Dempsey was bigger and stronger, the harder puncher, and although he might not be as clever, he had his own brand of cleverness, and was no sucker when it came to speed. The small ring would help him. "Gibbons will have an awful time keeping away from the plunging, tearing champion." Still, Gibbons had to be given a chance, because he was clever, more experienced, there was nothing he did not know, and he had a good sock in either hand.

From Atlantic City, Jack Johnson said, "Tom Gibbons has a wonderful chance to last 15 rounds, and if he does, mark my words, he will be the next heavyweight champion of the world. … Gibbons packs a punch in either hand, and, if it goes 15 rounds, he should have the decision. He's a lot more clever than Dempsey."[1203]

JACK DEMPSEY — TOM GIBBONS

	DEMPSEY	GIBBONS
HEIGHT	6' 1"	6' ¾"
WEIGHT	195 Lbs	176
REACH	73"	74"
NECK	17"	17"
CHEST	41"	41"
NORMAL	41"	41"
EXPANDED	44"	44½"
BICEPS	15"	14"
FOREARM	12½	12½
WRIST	8¼"	9"
WAIST	32½"	35"
THIGH	22"	22½
CALF	15"	14½
ANKLE	9"	9½
AGE	28 YEARS	34 YEARS

[1203] New York Daily News, Great Falls Tribune, Missoulian, July 4, 1923.

Shelby and the arena

On Wednesday July 4, 1923 in Shelby, Montana, an alleged 188-pound Jack Dempsey (55-4-9) defended his title for the first time in two years, against alleged 175 ½-pound Tom Gibbons (86-3-3).[1204] Most thought Dempsey was around 190-194, but he might have lost weight from drying out. Eddie Kane had said Gibbons would fight at 178 pounds or more.

The day of the fight, the *Great Falls Tribune* listed Dempsey as age 28 to Gibbons' 29, though some papers claimed Tom was 32 or 34. He actually was 32 years old.

The Associated Press reported that the local townspeople overwhelmingly were pulling for a Gibbons victory.

Dempsey arrived in Shelby at daybreak on a special train. He remained in his train car until it was time to enter the ring.

At 10 a.m., the state commission's physician examined the principals.

175 members of the American Legion acted as ushers.

Planes were ordered not to fly low over the arena.

Moving pictures would be allowed only by the official company.

Most of the choice seats had been given to the men who invested the money for the fight.

Four bands kept things lively on the main drag. The night before, the local dance halls had been crowded for the first time since Shelby became famous.

[1204] There was no official weigh-in. The following account is an amalgamation of multiple sources, including: *Anaconda Standard, Butte Miner, Chicago Tribune, Great Falls Tribune, Missoulian, St. Paul Dispatch, Los Angeles Times, Buffalo Times, Buffalo Enquirer, San Francisco Examiner, St. Louis Post-Dispatch, Minneapolis Morning Tribune, Minneapolis Journal*, all July 5, 1923.

Hotels raised their rates from $3.50 up to $5. Even the eating shops got a boost. Strawberry prices jumped from 25 cents up to 45 cents.

Folks could pay $2.50 for field glasses, which would make the combatants appear close up, even from a far-away seat. The cheapest price for seats was $20. Concession booths were present inside the arena.

A group of Native American fans were at ringside, wearing traditional garb, including head feathers. Oddly enough, despite Dempsey having Native American ancestry, they were there to support Gibbons, who had ingratiated himself to the locals by training in Shelby, touring throughout Montana giving exhibitions, and being friendly.

Also present were the former Mrs. Reggie Vanderbilt and Hollywood's Tom Mix.

Bill Henry said the betting was so light as to be negligible. Dempsey was the 3 to 1 favorite, with no Gibbons money in sight.

One man, in his attempt to avoid the street police, foolishly took an alcoholic drink into the Prohibition office.

The main bout would be held under straight Queensberry rules, which meant protecting oneself at all times, including on breaks. One report said the ring would be 21 feet square, though a prior report said it was 18 feet, perhaps inside the ropes.

Gibbons would be seconded by manager Eddie Kane, Bud Gorman, and Jim Delaney, as well as trainer Buck Pape.

Tommy would shadow box in his dressing room before the bout.

Tom's breakfast consisted of eggs and toast. He planned to eat nothing more until the fight. He was utterly confident of victory, saying he would have no excuses if he lost.

Burglars thought it was the perfect time to raid the Gibbons home at 1517 Goodrich avenue in St. Paul, Minnesota. A neighbor saw them break in and called the police.

Jack Kearns hired special police to protect the champion. Gibbons was so strongly favored by the Shelby contingent that Kearns feared violence upon Dempsey if he knocked him out.[1205]

The show, which was supposed to start at 12 noon, was an hour late in getting started. Likely the promoters were waiting for more folks to arrive.

The crowd endured a burning sun, as did the various principals. The arena was mammoth in size, but just a few thousand souls initially paid to enter, although more came later. The only section which had its full quota

[1205] *Minneapolis Journal,* July 4, 1923.

was the press. Clinking typewriters, telegraph keys, and rows crammed with perspiring scribes surrounded the ring. On towers high above, movie-camera machines filmed the proceedings. Ringside sections were well filled. But there also was great open space, as row upon row of pine boards were shining in their newness but pathetic in emptiness.

Many women wore yellow kerchiefs, and this, combined with the green eyeshades which found a liberal sale to ward off the blazing sun, added some color. Most of the patrons wore hats and caps to shield their heads from the sun.[1206]

Bide Dudley said the arena contained cowboys, Indians, gamblers, women, children, and all sorts. There was one woman present to every man.

Cigars and cigarettes were banned, owing to the fire concern.

A band played music. A couple of soloists, both soldiers in uniform, sang for a bit. One was a blind sergeant who lost his sight with the Canadian forces.

At 1:15 p.m., Hiram Dempsey, the champ's father, took a seat in the press section. He was stoic throughout.

Once the show started, many folks scrambled to get down closer for better seats.

In the opener, Jack McDonald scored a 2nd round knockout over Kid Ernie Sales/Sayles, a Gibbons sparring partner.

The show was held up again, for nearly another hour, until 2:10 p.m.

Apparently, the money to pay the preliminary fighters had been "mislaid," or never was there in the first place. The promoters failed to pay the referee his $5,000, or to produce money for the preliminaries. As a result, the prelim scrappers immediately became scarce.

Most of the crowd had been sitting in the hot, wooden bowl since noon. The crowd started singing, "Yes, We Have No Preliminaries."

[1206] Although all the reporters said it was very hot that day in Shelby, there is no available temperature data. The surrounding towns of Conrad, Cut Bank, and Valier reported high temperatures of 76, 74, and 73. Great Falls was 85. Chinook was 86. Havre was 79. It is possible that the large, newly-built wooden arena and the thousands of spectators captured or intensified the heat from the sun, particularly at an elevation of 3,297 feet. Thanks to Jesse Garrison, Iowa State University. https://mrcc.purdue.edu/CLIMATE/

As a result of the financial issues, only two preliminary bouts preceded the main go. It later was learned that Kearns eventually agreed to pay the prelim fighters who had fought, as well as the referee.

Gibbons' sparring partner Bud Gorman clearly won an 8-round decision over Dempsey's sparring partner Harry Drake of London. Gorman hit him with everything, winning every round, but the Englishman refused to drop.

To cut down on expenses, the Jimmy Delaney vs. Jack Burke bout was called off. There was another great delay.

The baking sun left the crowd impatient. "We want a fight." "Where are the fighters?" Rumors that there was no money to pay the preliminary fighters led to grumbles and audible remonstrances.

Several score of Blackfeet Indians followed a large American flag to a section reserved for them. Even the "squaws" were there. The Indian parade of "highly painted savages in costume" failed to excite the crowd. The *Great Falls Tribune* wrote, "Following the lead of their civilized brethren, the Indians were no sooner seated than a stampede sent bucks and squaws on the climb for better seats."

The big fight had been scheduled to start at 3 p.m., but neither fighter was seen at all until half-an-hour later, and it was almost 4 before the first bell rang to start the fight.

To stimulate more ticket sales,prices were cut in half. Eventually, they were cut down to only $5, and some folks even wound up crashing the gates while the championship fight was in progress.

At 3:30 p.m., Dempsey approached, walking down the aisle with his entourage, and stepped into the ring. Everyone stood up to get a glimpse of him. The *Anaconda Standard* said he was given an uproarious reception. He wore white silk trunks with a red, white, and blue ribbon-sash around his waist, and a closed/buttoned-up long-sleeve blue sweater. His hands were wrapped already. With him were Kearns, trainer Jerry Luvadis, British welter Billy Wells, lightweight Joe Benjamin, Jack Burke, feather Lee Moore, and Chicago detectives Mike Trant and Hugh McCarthy, acting as security.

Ray Rocene said that when he entered the ring, Dempsey appeared slightly drawn, with several days' growth of beard. Another said he had a shade of a frown on his face.

Dempsey went to his corner and took a seat on his small four-legged stool, over which a second had placed a small towel.

Trant and Luvadis alternated holding an umbrella over his head to shield Dempsey from the blazing sun. Two other Chicago detectives, Bayne and Tapscott, entered the ring and stood on either side of the champion.

Dempsey removed his sweater, and instead, a large towel was placed over his shoulders from behind his neck, covering his arms.

Mayor Jim Johnson climbed into Jack's corner and shook hands with him and Kearns.

Gibbons made Dempsey wait a bit, entering the ring either 5, 8, or 10 minutes later, depending on the source. He was greeted by a tremendous ovation of loud cheering for several minutes, showing that he was the crowd's favorite. One said he received twice the ovation that Dempsey did, for the crowd really let loose with a rousing reception as he approached and entered. Dempsey's reception, while warm, paled in comparison and seemed relatively tame.

Gibbons was clad in a closed, faded brown, patterned bathrobe. Tom crossed the ring, went over to Dempsey, and they shook hands. Tom carefully examined the champ's bandaged hands. He then returned to his corner, moved around a bit to warm up his legs, then sat down. He too had a black umbrella in his corner to shade him from the hot sun, held by Gorman, who had won his undercard bout.

Tom bandaged his hands while in the ring, taking his time about it.

The ropes were tested, and new resin was strewn.

Dempsey's sweater was placed back over him, with only one top button fastened.

Gibbons removed his robe and revealed that he was clad in dark green trunks. He briefly wore a dark sweater shirt to keep his upper body warm in the absence of the robe.

Their hands were taped, and a new pair of 6-ounce gloves was provided to each fighter. The managers tied on their gloves.

Tom's sweater shirt was removed. A trainer wiped the sweat from his body with a towel. He did not seem quite as finely trained down as did Dempsey.

Jerry Luvadis rubbed Dempsey's neck. Kearns was smearing the champ's face/eyebrows with Vaseline. A nurse in a khaki skirt climbed through the ropes and gave Jack an embrace.

At 4 p.m., they stood at ring center and posed for photographers, with Referee James Dougherty between them, and their handlers around them. Damon Runyon said Dempsey's brown skin contrasted strongly with Gibbons' white body.

The combatants returned to their corners.

The announcer then led Gibbons to ring center, and with his large megaphone introduced him as "Tommy Gibbons, of St. Paul, the contender for the title of the heavyweight championship of the world." Tom looked embarrassed or bashful. His weight was announced as 175 ½ pounds.

Writers noted that Tom wore his trunks higher than the proper waist level (which during the fight made some in the crowd holler that Dempsey's blows were low when they were not).

Dempsey, who had been dancing about in his corner with a white towel around his shoulders, was led out by the announcer and introduced simply as "Jack Dempsey, the world's heavyweight champion, 188 pounds, who will box Tom Gibbons 15 rounds to a decision." He certainly was sparing of speech. There was just a 12 ½-pound weight difference between them, if those weights were to be believed. Since there was no official weigh-in, no one knew for certain.

Referee James Dougherty called the fighters and seconds to ring center and gave them their perfunctory final instructions/orders. The ring was cleared, and the fighters returned to their corners to await the bell.

At 4:05 p.m., an hour late, with a light tinkling of the bell, the bout started and away they went.

1st round

According to the sportswriters, Dempsey fought like a fiend, closing in and pummeling Gibbons' body. They exchanged hard blows. Dempsey landed several lefts. Jack seemed to have made up his mind to crowd him from the jump.

Runyon said Dempsey was all over him, punching his body with short uppercuts. Gibbons landed just one good left, shaking the champ a bit.

Edward Walker said Dempsey hit the midsection until a right hook landed high on Tom's cheekbone and rendered him groggy. That nearly disastrous blow took a lot of the fight out of Gibbons.

The *Anaconda Standard* said Tom's mouth was bleeding.

Harry Newman said Dempsey had the better of the clinch fighting, but Gibbons had the better of the outside boxing.

The films show that Dempsey quickly got to the inside, and Gibbons was content to clinch and scuffle with him up close. Dempsey outworked Gibbons by far, constantly digging away with single shots in his usual metronome nonstop fashion, mostly uppercuts with both hands to the body and head, and occasional hooks to the head. Jack was good at working one arm at a time, doubling his left uppercut to the body, then bringing it up to the head, and then going back down to the body with a right uppercut, and/or up to the head or around in hooking fashion.

Gibbons mostly clinched, blocked, smothered, or ducked, and sometimes moved around a bit, but only occasionally fired back. The few times he did punch, his punches were fast and snappy. On the inside, Tom snuck in some hooks, short rights, and uppercuts. On the outside, Gibbons mostly fired jabs early on, a jab and solid right in the middle of the round, and later on, a solid left hook that sent Jack back for a moment, and each time, the crowd got excited, for he was good at landing cleanly, but overall, Dempsey seemed unphased, and kept attacking and plugging away up close. Tom played defense for long periods of time before punching again.

Dempsey's body blows were landing. A fast left hook and right to the head combination landed well. Jack moved in and followed up with left uppercuts to the body and a hook to the head, moving towards the retreating Gibbons. He again worked his left to the body and head, behind the ear, and double rights, down to the body and up to the head. Dempsey was relentless in his pace, as always. Jack's right uppercut jolted Tom's head up. Gibbons kept clinching and defending, only punching back with a couple sneaky rights either in desperation or when he thought there was a moment that he could land without getting countered. Sometimes they turned/spun one another on the inside. It was a clear Dempsey round.

2nd round

The writers said Dempsey was right on top of him again. They fought at close quarters, with Dempsey hooking to the body. Jack kept attacking with blows to the body and head, and Gibbons retaliated. Gibbons momentarily sent Jack back on his heels with a left hook to the chin and another chopping left hook under the champ's right eye, on the cheek, cutting it slightly.

Tom turned and ran a couple times, but Jack kept prancing after him, head bobbing, hands flying constantly. Gibbons was not fast enough to keep away. When they got close, Dempsey punished him fearfully about the body.

The champ kept attacking, and had all the better of the infighting. However, Tom again slightly jolted/staggered him momentarily with a left hook on the chin. Yet, as usual, Dempsey kept coming and working.

Toward the close of the round, Gibbons let go his right and nailed Dempsey on the jaw. Jack fell back and Tom followed with another punch to the same place. Dempsey opened his mouth and snarled something at Tom, unusual for him. As in other fights, Jack was not deterred.

On the films, the dipping Dempsey ducked a jab, moved in, and they clinched. Break. On the outside, Gibbons usually flicked his quick jab. When Jack got close, Tom grabbed his left arm. They scuffled on the inside with some short blows. Jack usually tried to sneak in a left hook on the breaks, as allowed under straight rules. He kept digging in short punches to the body and head throughout the round, but the pace had slowed a bit, in part because Gibbons was clinching more. Tom also used a cross-arm defense to block blows, and he moved in close to smother.

Jack moved about, then moved in with punches, but again was held. Jack landed a hook and right and Tom moved away. On occasion, Gibbons let go and fired a right or a left hook. Tom moved about, working his jab, but Jack got in, worked the body, and snuck in a right uppercut to the head. The champ moved, jabbed, moved in, then ducked Tom's attempted right and left hook combo. Jack dipped and rolled as Tom jabbed. Dempsey consistently punched on the way in on the retreating Gibbons, then kept working in the clinches. The alleged staggering punches the writers claimed Gibbons landed are not depicted, or at least Jack did not react to them in that way. Dempsey round.

3rd round

The sportswriters said Dempsey tore after him, landing hard body blows. Dempsey kept administering terrific body punishment throughout. When Gibbons clinched, Dempsey rapped away at Tom's ear. Jack also landed a nice right uppercut. On the outside, Gibbons landed some jabs. Jack hooked a hard left below the heart, and subsequently a vicious right below the heart.

Dempsey's furious infighting had Gibbons puffing hard. He looked tired from the snappy rights to the body. Jack hurt Tom with a straight right to the jaw and a fierce drive to the ribs over the heart. A distressed Gibbons wriggled in and grasped Jack's left arm, holding it with both hands and bending over to throw weight on the arm and get his head and neck out of range. Tom's legs seemed to be weakening under the pounding.

However, at the end of the round, Gibbons came to life a bit and jumped in with a hard one-two that landed on Jack's eye.

On the films, they clinched as usual. Dempsey fired his inside blows, mostly to the body, a few uppercuts and hooks to the head as well, and some lead jabs or rights on the way in. Gibbons fired back here and there, both to the body and head, but Dempsey was more of the aggressor and threw and landed more. Tom was good at grabbing, crossing his arms, or stepping away. Tom jabbed a couple times, then fired a 1-2 that Jack rolled. Tom clinched again. Jack kept trying to work free from the holds so he could dig in blows. He spun Tom around to get loose and fire. Dempsey particularly liked to use his wide right or right uppercut to the body, but he threw whatever he thought he could land. It primarily was a grinding inside contest, with only brief, intermittent exchanges from the outside. Dempsey round.

4th round

The writers said Dempsey kept chasing and attacking, punishing the body. When Gibbons held and smothered, Jack hit the back of his head with his right. After some wrestling and holding, Dempsey sunk a right into Tom's side.

Dempsey led a hard right to the face and followed with hook to the body. The champion was much stronger in the clinches. He turned Tom at will, smacking him as the latter raced away. Dougherty found it difficult to separate them from the clinches. Dempsey's rights to the ribs raised welts and caused Tom to weaken and break ground. Jack came dancing in on his toes.

Gibbons was getting all the worst of it on the inside, but still was landing some occasional clean blows to the body and head, mostly from the outside. Tom leaped in and drove the champ's head back with a hard left hook to the jaw, catching Dempsey off guard. Tom would cut loose with sudden unexpected punches that had a world of snap and power in them. Every time he landed; the crowd yelled with wild encouragement. Tom's left was working and bothering Dempsey a bit. Tom also feinted him out of position several times by stamping his foot. Dempsey would duck, expecting a left, but Tom fooled him by coming in with a left and right hook.

However, Dempsey simply renewed his attack and ripped a right into the body. He tried doggedly to force his way in and hit the body, though he often met with jarring left and right hooks.

The old cut over Jack's eyebrow, often cut in sparring, including during training camp for this fight, was slightly re-opened during one of the clinches, and some blood flowed from it.

Dempsey would gather Tom in a clinch, twist and turn him with his left, and batter him with his right to the body, varying it with the rabbit punch - a chop to the back of the neck.

On the films, Dempsey quickly stepped in and fired a hook to the body. Tom clinched. As usual, Dempsey advanced quickly and worked or tried to work up close, but Tom clinched, fired occasionally, and clinched some more. Gibbons also tried to move or bounce away a bit, but his movement did not last for long, preferring to clinch the relentlessly advancing Dempsey. When Tom grabbed Jack's left, the champ would fire away with rights to the body and head, sometimes behind the neck. Sometimes Jack would spin him around with his left and punch with his right. If Tom held the right, Jack worked his left. Tom was a bit more active than usual with his punches in this round, both on the inside and outside. He even nailed Dempsey with a right and left hook. But as always, Jack was more consistent, and never phased, advancing with a lead right or left jab, following underneath with uppercuts to the body, and then cuffing head blows. Jack fired a left hook to the head, and Tom countered with a hard right uppercut. In the next clinch, Tom did some work, but Jack kept working. It always was Gibbons who was first to stop punching, or grab, or move away. Another Dempsey round, but closer.

George Barton said the first four rounds were all Dempsey, carrying the milling to Gibbons in a savage manner. He tore in, getting to close quarters at every opportunity, shooting short but hard punches to the body and face. "Gibbons could not cope successfully with the champion at infighting, and tried to tie up Jack's arms. The champion, however, always managed to keep one fist free and slashed away viciously at every unprotected spot." By the end of the 4th, it looked like Gibbons would not last, for he had been on the receiving end of a terrible pasting.

Harry Newman was the most generous towards Gibbons. He believed that Gibbons was doing enough good work to hold Dempsey even in the 1st, 2nd, and 4th rounds, although Dempsey won the 3rd. Robert Edgren gave Dempsey the 1st and 3rd, scored the 2nd even, but said Gibbons won the 4th. Edward Walker said that after taking a terrific body pummeling for the first 3 rounds, Gibbons made a flash in the 4th, which won him the honors. Yet, he also said Tommy's punches lacked steam. Damon Runyon gave the 1st and 3rd to Dempsey and scored the 2nd and 4th even. The majority of reporters believed that Dempsey was winning, though Gibbons still flashed some good moments interspersed amongst Dempsey's overall superior work.

Based on the films, Dempsey was winning the rounds, being more consistent, outworking Gibbons, but he was not quite as ferocious or explosive as he had been in the past. He was calm and relaxed, plugging away methodically, but not with quite the same relentless intensity seen in other fights. This possibly was because of Tom's cautious style and ability to fire occasional well-timed quick blows but not leave himself open much, for he would block, duck, grab, smother, or move. It also might have been that Dempsey was using his poise and experience, and knew not to waste too much energy on a skillful, crafty, hard-to-hit, experienced man, pacing himself well while winning the rounds, hoping to break his man gradually, knowing he might have to go a potential 15 rounds while having to endure a hot July sun at an altitude of 3,297 feet above sea level. Or it is possible that the two-year layoff indeed had dimmed his passion just a bit. This isn't to say that Dempsey didn't keep a fast pace, because he did, and he kept working as much as he could, and that pace, power, and output was keeping Gibbons very cautious and mostly defensive, only opening up with intermittent flashes. Tom's cautiousness and defense-first style did not give the champion a lot of openings.

5th round

According to observers, Gibbons waited for the attack, turned to elude a left and then clinched. After much tugging and reeling about, Gibbons landed two left hooks that knocked Jack back on his heels, some saying he hit the ropes, and the crowd cheered loudly. Gibbons had become aggressive, grinning and talking to the champ. He was landing and making Jack miss. However, Dempsey rocked him with a right and left to the head and nailed him with a solid right to the jaw, forcing Tom to clinch. Tom later landed a left to the nose that knocked the champ's head back. More cheers.

Dempsey was fighting furiously. He ran at Gibbons and chased him around the ring, but could not catch him, for Tom turned, twisted and wriggled out of danger. Tom landed stinging jabs and counters with both hands. Jack sent Tom back with a hard right to the head, and Tom held. Gibbons kept hooking the head. The crowd cheered when he made Jack miss his left.

Gibbons would dance backward, spearing with his left and just ticking the champ's face. Dempsey snarled and kept crowding him about the ring, seeking an opening. Twice he nailed Tom with a right to the chin, but could not land with any force.

Dodging, swaying, and looking for an opening, Dempsey shot over one hard right to the ear and dug into Tom's body. Tom gave way, stopped, and suddenly cracked him on the nose. Jack slowed up and seemed bewildered. Tom was in like a flash with another hard left and then got away.

Suddenly Gibbons began rushing and had Dempsey trying to box him. Dempsey just dodged a stout right-hand swing. The crowd was in an uproar as the bell rang and Dougherty pulled them apart.

Robert Edgren said the round looked tough for Dempsey, for Tom outfought and outguessed him in streaks. Dempsey rushed but could not land, while Tom was landing. At that point, it looked like Gibbons had a chance, and he was confident. Gibbons had done his best work thus far.

Damon Runyon said Gibbons had been on the offensive in this round, boxing better than ever. If he had any round, it was this one.

George Barton said Gibbons electrified the crowd by staging a sensational rally in which he hooked his left repeatedly to Dempsey's body and face and drove him into the ropes with a hefty right cross. The crowd went wild as he made the champ miss and clipped Jack on the chin and side of his head with well-timed left hooks and right crosses.

Edward Walker said Gibbons was blocking nicely and scoring, one left hook catching Dempsey off balance and making him back into the ropes. Dempsey missed badly. Tom showed his boxing ability.

Harry Newman also said Gibbons won the round.

Although most observers had Dempsey winning up to this point, some had it close, and several had it an even fight through the 5th round. Hence, the writers thought it was close and competitive through the first third of the fight, with some doubts as to the ultimate outcome.

On the films, Dempsey circled, weaved, and stepped in with a lead hook to the body. Tom clinched. Break. Tom peppered with jabs, then fired a left hook that landed high on the head. The crowd applauded. Jack circled back momentarily, but then advanced again, got inside with his jab and right to the body. Tom held, but Jack worked his cuffing right to the side of the head, and his right uppercut. Break. Jack approached, Tom fired a hook, but Jack retreated away from it, and then circled around.

Tom started a right but leapt forward with a jolting hard left jab that knocked Dempsey's head back, and Jack took a step back, his back touching the ropes for a brief moment, but he immediately moved forward again, dipping. Tom moved about, then jabbed and clinched. After the break, Tom immediately landed a solid left jab. He ducked Jack's jab and fired a jab of his own to the body. They exchanged jabs.

Dempsey advanced with a 1-2 that landed, then a hook-right as well. Tom grabbed the rope with his right and feinted a blow, so Jack moved back, then advanced with a lead right. Tom moved away. Jack advanced with a jab and right uppercut to the body. Clinch and break. Tom flicked his quick jab and retreated and circled. He ducked a Dempsey jab and moved away. He stopped and advanced, and Jack backed away, as if to bait him, then dipped in preparation. Tom backed away, then advanced with a snappy head-jolting jab and clinched. Jack snuck in his right hook to the side of the head. Break.

Dempsey advanced with a right to the body and left to the head. After a brief clinch and break, he circled, and they jousted with some jabs that missed. Clinch and break. Tom snipered in a quick jab. Dempsey feinted a lead right, took a jab, but followed with a right uppercut and left hook. Tom counter hooked and moved away, then advanced with a hook to the head and right to the body. He was pretty quick. Inside clinching, scuffling, and short chops. Break. Tom peppered his jab.

Gibbons' round. He landed more of the cleanly landed blows. Dempsey's offense had slowed. However, the round was nowhere near as exciting as the writers implied, nor did Gibbons land as many effective blows as the writers said he did. His jab landed the most solidly. It still was a close and competitive round. But Gibbons fans had something to cheer about, with the sense that perhaps Tom was adjusting and improving.

6th round

The writers said Gibbons carefully side-stepped and boxed. Dempsey went after him with fresh determination and planted a heavy left to the stomach. There were a series of clinches. Jack pounded the body. He also fired in some hard rights to the face. Both landed some good blows in the clinches, but Dempsey was stronger.

Dempsey drove Gibbons through the ropes so far that his head was outside the ropes, and while he was there in that precarious position, Jack hit him, which led to the crowd hissing and booing Dempsey. However, there was nothing illegal about it; his actions were fair under the rules.

Gibbons was riled and he piled in, firing a volley of blows that forced Dempsey to break ground momentarily.

Dempsey hit the body time and again. Some landed on the belt line, but Tom had his trunks high, so the punches were fair. Toward the close of the round, Gibbons was talking to Dempsey, possibly telling him to get his punches up. Jack drove a right solidly to the head. At the bell, Tom cracked him with a left hook to the face.

Edgren said Gibbons was breathing hard and showed some signs of weakening under the constant battering in the clinches. Still, he covered well and held Jack's left arm to prevent punishment.

Walker said Dempsey got going and sped up again, winning the round. Newman also gave this round to Dempsey.

Runyon remarked to Bernie Dempsey, referring to Gibbons, "He's tough." Bernie responded, "He can take a few, at that."

However, in a minority view, Barton gave the round to Gibbons.

On the films, Dempsey got going again, moving in, not boxing from long range as much as he did in the prior round. Gibbons clinched often. Jack kept trying to work whatever punches he could in the clinches. His increased aggression made Gibbons more defensive.

Dempsey fired a jab to the chest, moved in, lead right, and then, as he was spinning Tom around with his right, a couple short lefts. Tom ducked down, and his head and body went under the top rope. Jack snuck in a left uppercut to the head. Jack put out his right glove and helped pull Tom back in from under the rope as the referee got between them. Tom clinched and the referee struggled to break them.

Gibbons jabbed, but Jack backed away, circled, then jabbed Tom's body. In the clinch, Jack worked his short right and right uppercut to the head. After breaking, they exchanged jabs. In the clinch, Jack worked his left hook several times, and then several rights. They leaned on one another. Break. Jack ducked Tom's left hook and moved away.

The champ advanced with his lead right, grabbed around Tom's body with his right, turned him, and worked in a short left uppercut and some rights to the back of the neck. Break. Jack hit the body with both hands, right uppercut to the jaw, back down to the body with the left, and just kept working short shots with both hands to the head and body, first right, then left, as Tom tried to clinch and smother. Break.

Jack jabbed and stepped around, then stepped in with a lead left hook and short right, and worked the inside again, rights and right uppercuts to the head, and left uppercuts to the body. Tom snuck in a few counter lefts.

Clear Dempsey round, for he got back to attacking and outworking Gibbons on the inside. Gibbons did not let his hands go as much as he did in the prior round.

7th round

The writers said the champ smashed a terrific right to the wind under the heart, several stiff lefts to the face, and in the clinch, battered Gibbons about the head. Dempsey was reaching out with his left and closing in behind it, trying for a right in close. Gibbons sent a couple left uppercuts to the mouth and a left to the ear.

Tom had one of his sudden, unexpected rallies, and caught the champ with a left and two crashing rights to the jaw. The last punch landed on the upper lip and drove it between Jack's teeth. The champ made faces, and after a moment, pulled his lip free.

The challenger's spurt roused Dempsey, and for the first time in the fight, he seemed to be hitting with all his strength, though Gibbons blocked most of the blows. Jack chased him until they clinched again.

Dempsey gave him quite a beating in the clinches. Tommy was bleeding from his mouth, and he spat blood.

Dempsey kept chasing, and forced Tom to the ropes, rapping him with savage rights to the body.

Runyon said it was hard to understand how Gibbons stood up under the body punishment, though he did not seem as strong as in previous rounds. He went to his corner bleeding from his nose and mouth.

Harry Newman said it was apparent that Tommy was weakening under the awful attack in the clinches; the punches clearly beginning to have their effect. Jack kept rapping the heart. Dempsey's round.

The *Anaconda Standard* said Dempsey's savage body attack appeared to be wearing on Gibbons.

Edgren said Gibbons seemed weak and weary when the bell rang.

George Barton said Dempsey still was as fresh as a daisy, pummeling Gibbons plentifully.

Edward Walker confirmed that it was all Dempsey.

The films show that Dempsey walked right in and led with a fast right to the head before being held. Break. Tom fired his left as Jack approached and they clinched. Tom snuck in a cuffing right and Jack dug in a left to the body. Break. Jack advanced with a left and right to the body, and while his left was being held, he snuck in right uppercuts to the jaw. Tom clinched more tightly. Break. Jack jabbed and hooked, working several short lefts. When Tom held his left arm, Jack worked his right, sometimes to the back of the head, in part because Tom turned away with his left shoulder in front. Jack followed with a right uppercut. Break.

Jack jabbed a couple times, moving in quickly on the retreating Gibbons, then followed with a fast right to the head before the inevitable clinch. The champ worked his short shots as best he could. Break. Jack advanced with another lead right. Clinch and short smothered blows again before the break. Jack advanced with a lead right and worked his left until Tom clinched.

Gibbons let go and landed a couple hard left hooks to the head and followed with a couple snappy rights to the head. Jack got free from Tom's grasp and landed a left to the body, and then short right to the head when Tom held his left again. Break. Jack moved in, clinch, and each worked some short shots. Break. Jack jabbed the head. Gibbons moved around, with Dempsey rapidly moving in with a lead right. More clinching, scuffling, and digging inside shots from both, though Dempsey was doing more of the work. Break.

Dempsey rapidly advanced with a fast lead left hook and followed with crisp lefts to the body. Tom broke away and moved but Jack was right back on top of him with a jab, rights to the body, then lefts to the body, then right, then up with short right hooks to the head. Jack fired whatever he could with whichever hand was free or he could get loose. Break. Jack fired a jab to the body. Tom moved, and missed a jab that Jack ducked. Dempsey dug a right uppercut to the body, then kept digging multiple single shots with both hands to the body until the bell. Clear Dempsey round, outworking Gibbons by far.

8th round

The writers said they both landed some good blows in this round. A Gibbons left to the jaw rocked Dempsey, but the champ retaliated with a pair of jolts. Tom again snapped his head back with a left, but Jack's infighting put him in the lead again. Dempsey shifted and nailed him with a right and left to the jaw, staggering Gibbons. He also punched his body.

There was a slight cut over Tom's right eye. He kept firing jabs and hooks from range, but Dempsey kept rushing into clinches, where he had the advantage.

Jack smashed behind the right ear and landed a left which appeared a bit low. He kept forcing. Tom landed a couple straight lefts to the face and a couple left hooks to the chin, but either they did not have a lot of force or Dempsey took them well and kept plunging in. He rushed Tom to the ropes. Jack kept pounding away on the inside. Tom landed a right smash to the chin, but Jack came right on in anyway. He gave Tommy an awful pasting inside, whipping in two hard uppercuts to the face, but Tom still was strong on his legs. Dougherty was perspiring from struggling with the two men.

The reporters again agreed that it was a Dempsey round.

On the films, Dempsey ducked Tom's jabs, stepped in with a hook to the head and then stepped away from a counter hook. When Jack got inside, this time Tom worked more than usual, firing a right uppercut, right to the body, and a counter left hook after Jack snuck in a short right. Break. Tom timed Dempsey on the way in with a couple fast left hooks. Dempsey approached with more caution, firing a jab, and then quickly stepping in off of Tom's jab with a right to the body and a couple left hooks to the head up close. Tom clinched and snuck in a left to the body. Break.

Dempsey advanced and threw a left jab, right, and left hook to the body, then back up with a left hook to the head. As usual, Tom was good at tucking his chin and putting his head down. Tom pushed off, and then flitted away. Jack approached, fired a stiff jab as Tom danced around and fired his own jab. Tom moved in and Jack worked his right. Break. Jack again moved in with his lead right and double left hook – head and body. Clinch and break.

Tom jabbed, and Jack again moved in with his lead right and left uppercuts. This time, Tom countered with a couple fast hooks, which got the crowd applauding. Jack stepped in with a lead hook and worked his right in the clinch. On the inside, Tom fired his left hook to the head a couple times, and right. Tom's punches had more of a fast, snappy quality to them. Jack worked his right to the side of the head. Break. Jack jabbed, Tom moved about, jabbed and moved in, grabbing Jack's left arm, as usual. Jack worked his right and turned him. Break. Dempsey jabbed and moved in with a hook on the ducking/covering Gibbons. Clinch and break. Tom fired a fast, wide, lead hook but Jack circled left, away from it.

Jack approached, Tom jabbed, stepped back, but then moved in. Jack hooked the body, perhaps a little low. He snuck in his usual short right hook to the head. Break. As Jack approached, Tom landed a fast right. Nevertheless, Jack jabbed and moved in with a combination - double jab – right - left uppercut. Inside clinching and scuffling, with both working in short shots. Break. Jack jabbed and moved in with a right to the body and left hook to the head. Closer round, but Dempsey probably edged it.

9th round

The sportswriters said both men indulged in a lot of clinching. The elusive Gibbons was a tough target for the champ, turning and moving away. Dempsey came after him, pecking away with a long left. Jack drove him to the ropes with a bombardment of blows. Gibbons clinched as usual.

Dempsey gave Tom his usual drubbing. He was the aggressor all the way. Both landed some hooks and rights. Jack hit the head and body. Tom mostly hit the head, with hooks, jabs, and rights. Coming out of a clinch, Dempsey hit him with a hard right to the face.

It was hard fighting with little rest for either man. Gibbons made another sudden rally, landing hard left hooks on the chin and body. However, Runyon said Dempsey slipped a number of punches by moving his head, although the crowd cheered, thinking they had landed. Gibbons was getting a fierce pummeling inside. Gibbons landed a stinging left hook to the mouth at the bell.

Most said Dempsey won the round, though Newman and Edgren said Gibbons held him even.

The film version showed Dempsey starting off moving a bit, then Gibbons moving. Tom moved in and Jack dipped and retreated. They both mutually moved in, and Dempsey dipped left and dug in a left uppercut to the body, another up to the face, and cuffing lefts to the neck in the clinch. Break. Dempsey used his peppering left jab as a rangefinder, not wanting to smother himself. Tom moved away. Jack pumped his jab, then came in with his right, then held with his right and worked his left uppercut to the head a couple times. When Tom grabbed his left, Jack worked his short right hook to the head. Break.

Jack fired a hook off the jab, but Tom landed his hook at the same time. Jack advanced, lightly bouncing, jabbing a couple times, then firing a short hook when he got close. Tom clinched and they scuffled. Break. Jack advanced, dipped, and jabbed, advanced some more, jabbed and followed with a right uppercut underneath. Tom clinched, bulled in and smothered, and each fighter tried to work in short shots, but Jack was more active, and Tom held more tightly. Break.

Jack immediately fired a left, worked in close with a jab and right uppercut to the body, but was held again, and snuck in his usual cuffing right. Break. Jack circled, dipped, and stepped back away from Tom's jab. He jabbed and moved in for another clinch and break. Tom jabbed but Jack moved off to the side away from it. Jack jabbed and hooked in, then came under with his left to the body, and as Tom smothered, Jack tried short, somewhat cuffing lefts to the side of the head. Break.

Jack dipped, and Tom came in with a left hook and right, but they appeared to be partially blocked or rolled. Jack worked in some short, smothered lefts and rights. Jack immediately jabbed on the break, jabbed the body, followed with a jab to the head and short left hook, then cuffing right and left as Tom held. Inside scuffling. Break.

Dempsey advanced with a lead right uppercut to the head, both men landed left hooks at the same time, and Jack followed with a right. Tom fired a couple inside rights, and a hard left hook to the body, and Dempsey moved off to the side, bouncing.

Overall, it seemed as if Dempsey was trying to figure out the best way to approach and hit Gibbons without being held or smothered so much, but also not get hit with long-range blows. He still was throwing and landing more.

10th round

According to the writers, at first, there was a bit of casual long-range boxing. Then the champ drove Tom to the ropes and pounded him with jarring lefts and rights. In a clinch, Jack socked the ribs with hard rights. He kept pummeling Tom with rights and lefts to the face in the clinches. He rocked Tom with two short rights to the face. Jack sunk two lefts into the body, forcing Tom around. Jack kept pegging and smashing lefts to the body but could not land a haymaker. Tom hit the champion on the breakaway, but immediately put out his gloves to apologize. Dempsey merely nodded. However, since they were using straight Queensberry rules, it was perfectly legal.

Newman and Runyon said it was Dempsey's round.

However, in a minority view, Barton said Gibbons boxed carefully, making the champ miss, getting an even break.

The films show both cautious early on. Gibbons fired a jab. Once inside, Dempsey worked multiple rights, up and down. He jabbed his way in before being held. He again worked his right, up and down. Dempsey worked the outside a bit more in this round, dipping and moving his head and circling before stepping in. The pattern in this round was Dempsey would move about a bit, jab, step in with a lead left or right, or hook off the jab, get held, and try to work one hand or the other free and fire multiple blows with that one hand. Overall in the fight, Gibbons seemed primarily interested in holding Jack's left, preferring to get hit with short, often smothered rights rather than lefts. Tom sometimes even used both hands to grab Jack's left arm. Still, Jack worked both hands. Gibbons rarely led or countered, content to move, block, clinch, or smother, tucking his chin and leaning his head down and/or turning away to the right as he moved in close, being very defensive. There was not much exciting action in the round, but Dempsey won by working consistently.

11th round

The sportswriters said Gibbons came on strong, boxing with more confidence in this round. He nailed Jack with a hard left hook to the chin, but received lefts to the body and head in return. Tom tried his old side-stepping and broke up an attack. Dempsey hooked and uppercut him with both hands. Gibbons again landed a dandy hook to the mouth that drove Jack's lip between his teeth, bothering him until he could get it clear. Tom also landed his nice jab, scoring points with it. Dempsey still was the aggressor.

Tom landed two lefts to the mouth. Jack tore in, forcing Tom to clinch. As usual, Jack pounded the ribs. One of Dempsey's low punches caused the crowd to murmur. Tom rapped him with a right to the back of the ear. When Dempsey wanted to bore in, Tom turned and walked away. Jack chased him around. Tom sent a hard right to the chin, and another right to the face. He was firing his right more in this round than before. Dempsey shook him with a left to the face. He missed a right and Tom crossed him hard with a right.

Newman said it was Gibbons' round.

Runyon said it was Gibbons' best round, and the crowd gave him a big cheer.

Walker said Gibbons had the champ bewildered, and it was his best round, the first ray of sunshine for him in many rounds.

However, Edgren and Barton both said it was an even round.

The film version shows Gibbons ducking a left and clinching tightly. Break. Tom fired a right but Dempsey moved back away from it to make it fall short. Jack moved in with a left jab and right uppercut to the body, then hook to the head. In close, Gibbons fired a counter right and a hook. Tom then fired left and right uppercuts to the body. Jack worked his cuffing right hook to the head. Jack moved in with left hooks to the head, body, and head, back and forth, up and down. Clinch and break. Another clinch and inside scuffling with some short, smothered shots.

Tom bounced about firing snappy jabs. Dempsey fired some very hard left hooks and uppercuts, doubling and tripling them up to the head and body. After breaking, Jack advanced with a short hook and missed a very hard left uppercut. He fired a lead right to the body and followed with a left hook. Clinch. Jack snuck in a couple rabbit shots with his right. Break.

Tom double jabbed and followed with a right that landed. Clinch. Gibbons came over the top with a hard overhand right that landed as Dempsey landed a counter left hook, and Tom moved away and feinted as Dempsey advanced. Tom changed direction and moved off to the right. Jack fired a jab and then landed a heavy head-jolting hook off of it. Clinch and break.

Tom missed his jab and retreated. Jack stepped in with a lead right and Tom held. Break. Jack stepped in with a lead right followed by a left uppercut to the head. Tom stepped back.

Jack again fired a hard straight right, but Tom responded with a fast counter right and then leaping left hook. Jack moved off to the side, dipped, then came in with a lead right and left underneath, while Gibbons responded with a right uppercut and clean left to the body. Dempsey worked his right uppercut to the chin and right hook to the side of the head. Break. Jack parried Tom's jab and circled away. He moved in dipping, leaned in, held around Tom's body with his right and worked his left several times, body and head, but mostly was smothered by Tom's leaning in, clinching and smothering. Break.

It was a fairly even round, but any advantage would be slightly towards Dempsey. Gibbons did better in this round than in prior rounds, but not as well as some writers indicated.

12th round

The writers said Dempsey found himself again and took the upper hand. Gibbons fiddled and danced. Dempsey made him break ground with a right to the face. He kept hammering the clinching Gibbons on the face, back of the ear, and back of the neck with his right. A sharp left to the jaw jarred the challenger. Dempsey swung hard lefts and forced the infighting. Dempsey was fighting viciously. Gibbons was troubled, and was content to play defense only, backing around and clinching at every opportunity. Jack rapped him with hard rights and lefts to the body. He pounded Tom at will on the inside, while the referee made little effort to separate them. In the clinch, Jack hit Tom behind the ear, and rabbit punches with his right. Dempsey struck him low a couple times too. The referee ignored the crowd's booing and hollering. Dempsey was punishing him, trying to finish him off. The champ sunk a hard right to the ribs. Tom landed a hard right to the face. Jack pummeled the body. Tom ripped a left to the head. Dempsey chased him. A right smash to Tom's left side made him grunt. He looked distressed at the bell.

The reporters all agreed that Dempsey won the round. Runyon said although Dempsey was fighting viciously, he did not seem to be hitting as hard as usual. At least, Gibbons apparently was not hurt. Barton said Gibbons was punished but weathered the storm, playing defense.

Edgren said Dempsey was pressing-in steadily, and his constant rights, pounding at the neck and back of the head, the only exposed spots while Tom was holding Jack's left arm, were getting him a bit dizzy. Tom could not match him at infighting. But he was no easy mark, either. He could hold and twist and turn out of trouble.

The films show Dempsey circling about at first. Tom's jab fell short. Jack moved in, only to be held. Jack worked rights and lefts to the body, and then his cuffing blows with both hands to the side or back of the head. Break. Jack immediately moved in with another barrage of hooks, rights, and uppercuts, body and head. Tom moved around. Dempsey advanced quickly, dipped, jabbed and uppercut with his left, landing well. Tom clinched, and Jack worked his usual cuffing blows and rabbit punches.

After breaking, Dempsey advanced with a hard lead right, and followed with lefts as he spun Tom around using his right around the waist as leverage. Jack moved in, and Tom held, but then let go with a short right to Jack's head. Dempsey hit the back of his head with his nonstop right.

After the break, Dempsey advanced, and Tom moved, walked, and side-stepped away. Jack led with a right, Tom held his right arm, and Jack whacked away with lefts uppercuts underneath to the head and body. Tom snuck in a short hook in the clinch. Break.

Jack again fired his lead right and left uppercut, broke free from Tom's grasp and jolted in a left hook and some cuffing rights, particularly rabbit shots. As soon as the referee broke them, Jack was right back on top of him, working hooks, rights, and his uppercut as Tom tried to clinch and smother, leaning in. Jack turned him to create an angle and punching room, and he kept working his body shots and uppercuts.

Dempsey stepped away but then stepped right back in with a hook and hard right to the body. Tom spun away, walked off, but then stopped and jabbed. Dempsey ducked, and in the clinch, he worked multiple lefts down and up. Break.

Gibbons moved, stopped, then moved away again. Jack missed a hook, and Tom jabbed him and held. Jack worked both hands, particularly to the body. Tom stepped away but Jack quickly was on top of him again with a left jab and right to the body, and right to the back of the head as his left arm was being held. Break. Jack immediately attacked and Tom was leaning in to smother, but Jack kept trying to work in short shots.

Tom fired a right, then right and a snappy hook, the latter punch nailing Dempsey well. Tom pushed and Jack spun away. Jack bounced and moved to the side, then reapproached with a jab as Tom retreated.

Overall, Dempsey was much more relentless in this round, throwing more, keeping a fast pace, not giving Tommy time or room to punch. He seemed much more determined to put it on him. Gibbons was so defensive-minded that it practically was a surprise when he did punch, which in part helped him land. Clear Dempsey round.

13th round

The reporters said Gibbons remained defensive, backing away and clinching often. Dempsey was unable to open him up for a telling smash. Jack struck him low one time. He held and hit. He tried anything he could to penetrate the defensive, clinching shell. Dempsey kept working, battering as much as he could. Tom countered only occasionally.

Edgren said Dempsey, finding him hard to hit, tried something new. He let Tom grab, and then he'd swing around in a circle, throwing Tom off balance and firing away with rights until he was forced to let go, and then Jack would bring a snappy left up to the chin. The crowd didn't like it, but it was perfectly fair. Once or twice, when Dougherty pried them apart, Dempsey leaped in suddenly to catch Tom off guard.

Runyon said Dempsey seized him, rolled him in a clinch backward and forward like a sack of meal, then pummeled him with both hands. Dempsey was lengthening out his punches and throwing his body behind them, trying to put over a haymaker finisher. He would follow in behind his right, which generally fell short, then grab Gibbons and maul his body. Yet, Tom did not seem quite as tired at the close of this round as he did the one prior.

Everyone agreed that it was Dempsey's round.

The films show that Dempsey moved in and Gibbons held his left arm tightly. Dougherty struggled to break Tom away. They exchanged lefts, but Jack doubled his up. Jack moved in with his jab and Tom hooked him and clinched. Jack worked his short rights to the head and neck. Break.

Dempsey moved in, jabbed, held with his right around Tom's body, turned him and fired lefts. Tom moved in close and held both arms more tightly. Jack struggled to get one arm or the other free so he could punch, but Tom was like a leech, so it was futile. Break.

Jack fired a lead hook and stepped away, off to the side, then moved in with a right to the body and left hook to the head before being held. Tom initially held Jack's left arm with both hands, but kept holding it with his left and fired in some rights to the body. Break.

Gibbons fired a leaping lead left hook that seemed to be blocked as Jack raised his right glove and danced away off to the side. Dempsey fired a right to the body, and Tom moved to the right, off to the side. Both jabbed, and as Jack snuck in a short hook off his jab, Tom held. Break.

Dempsey approached, but Gibbons gave him a little footwork, dipping, feinting, stepping off, and moving in. Jack missed a lead right, but followed with a left uppercut. Tom held his left arm, and Jack slapped away with his right to the back of the neck. Break.

Jack jabbed but Tom hooked at the same time and landed, then moved away. Jack advanced with a lead right uppercut to the jaw and followed with left uppercuts as well. Tom held and Jack worked his cuffing rights to the neck. Break.

The champion shot a straight lead right and Tom moved in to smother, while Jack tried to fire whatever he could, including a sneaky left uppercut, right to the body, and cuffing right to the head. Break. Another Dempsey lead right, missing, with follow-up short lefts in the clinch. Break. Tom jabbed and Jack stepped back. Tom feinted but then stepped away. Jack stepped in with a left, and Tom again held the left arm while Jack worked his right. Break. Dempsey eluded a left jab. Tom walked away. Jack stalked and stepped in with a lead hook.

The overall pattern was Dempsey would dip and set up a lead or two on the way in, get held, and then try to work in what he could. Gibbons occasionally lashed out with quick, snappy blows, but primarily was cautious and defensive. Dempsey's round.

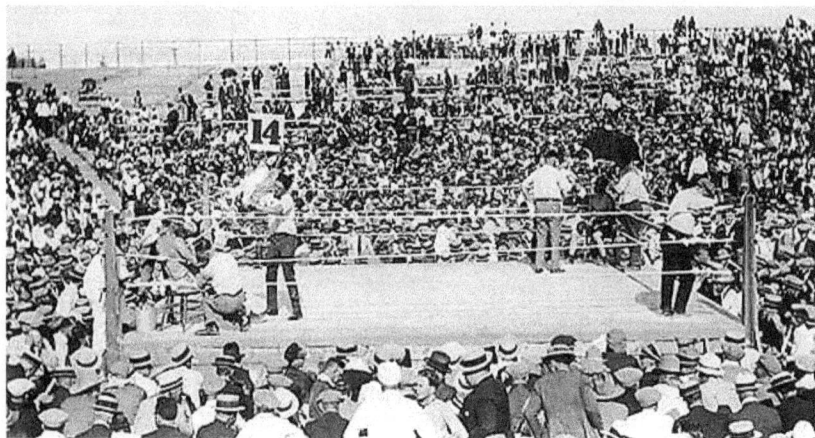

14th round

The press said Dempsey advanced with his crouch and they clinched. Jack turned him around with rights and lefts to the face and body. He chased Tom, then hooked sharply to the jaw. He kept forcing the fighting, even with Gibbons clinching at every opportunity. The referee found it difficult to break them.

Tom sent a strong left to the face and made Jack miss. Jack kept crowding him to the ropes. He ripped a hard right to the wind that the crowd thought was low. Tom sent a left to the ear but Jack sent a right to the kidney. In another clinch, Jack rapped his face with hard rights.

Gibbons landed a right hook and left to the head which caused Jack to back away momentarily, and Tom forced him into a neutral corner. Jack fought him away with a right to the head and came back again before being held.

George Barton said Gibbons astonished the multitude by making a game stand, boxing himself to an even break, keeping Jack at bay and pecking him with straight lefts to the face, varying occasionally with an overhand right to the jaw.

Harry Newman said the crowd cheered Gibbons, who fought to an even round.

Damon Runyon said Dempsey won the round, doing most of his execution in the clinches. Tom hit him just once, with a sharp left hook.

After the round concluded, some of the crowd began sailing cushions into the air and at the ring. Dougherty had to throw them out.

The films start as a repetition of the patten, with Dempsey moving in, Tom crossing his arms and smothering, or holding, with Jack trying to work, mostly rights, until the referee broke them. Tom moved away as Jack moved in with his jab. Jack lightly bounced, dipped, and moved in, only to be held. Both men worked inside rights. Break.

Repeat of Dempsey bouncing lightly and moving in, jabbing and getting held. The referee was struggling to break them. Dempsey moved in and fired a couple short hooks as Tom tucked his chin and tried to block and clinch. Break.

Gibbons jabbed and moved away, feinted, then circled to his right. Jack shot a short left followed by a right uppercut to the body before being held. Jack worked a couple rights. Dougherty struggled to break them. Tom threw a right before holding again, but was forced to break.

Tom jabbed and Dempsey hooked. Jack stuck out a measuring left and came underneath with a right to the body, and followed with more hooks and uppercuts to the head and body as Tom smothered and clinched. Break.

Jabs were exchanged, and Jack came in with hooks to the head and body and followed with his rapping right to the side of the head. Break. Dempsey moved in and fired more short left hooks followed by cuffing rights. Break.

Tom feinted, stepped off, fired a hard and fast jab that Jack ducked, right that landed high on the side of the head of the dipping Dempsey, and then left hook. Tom moved in, smothered, and held as Jack tried to work. Break. Tom backed away but then feinted and moved forward as Jack moved back. Tom flicked his jab, then retreated. Jack moved in with a jab and right to the head. Clinch with short inside shots by both.

Dempsey round, but closer than usual. The rounds were somewhat similar, monotonous, and lacking the dramatic. Gibbons primarily was defensive, throwing only intermittently, and mostly moving or grabbing.

15th round

The men shook hands at ring center. Dempsey ferociously attacked, wailing away, trying hard to finish off Gibbons, who was purely defensive. Tom kept moving, backing away, covering up, or hanging on as much as possible to deal with the onslaught. Tom was tiring quickly. Dempsey forced Gibbons around the ring and pounded away in the clinches. Gibbons was just trying to last the distance.

Newman said Gibbons seemed groggy as the bout ended. Dempsey's round.

Edgren said that in the last three rounds, it was evident that Gibbons' only goal was to stick it out. He no longer let go at the referee's order, but held on until Dougherty jammed between them, caught Tom's wrists and broke his hold.

Runyon said Gibbons seemed determined just to last. He began running and clinching from the jump. Dempsey followed him; his head crouched. He hammered Tom in the clinches, but Gibbons broke away, turned and trotted out of danger. Dempsey was jolting his head with rights and lefts, and Tom was so tired that he held on until Dougherty had to grab one arm and jerk him away.

Barton said Dempsey was determined to win by knockout, while Gibbons was determined to stay the limit. The champ staggered Tommy several times with terrific blows to the jaw, body, and back of the neck. Tom was too busy trying to save himself to do much fighting back. At times he held one of Dempsey's arms with both of his, and the referee had trouble prying him away. Every time they broke, Dempsey would resume his vicious attack. Tom was almost on the verge of a knockout when the gong finally sounded.

Barton said from the 12th round on, Dempsey made a desperate effort to finish him, and although Gibbons was punished severely, he weathered the storm, backing around or clinching at every opportunity, though he made a game stand in the 14th round, fighting evenly. Yet, Gibbons was on the verge of a knockout in the 15th, fighting only to survive.

Walker said the final round was hard on Gibbons. Dempsey dealt out a lot of punches, walloping away with both hands, and it looked as if Tom would go down, but he refused to waver.

Ray Rocene said from the 12th round on, Dempsey swung hard lefts and forced the infighting. Gibbons was troubled, content to play defense only. The last three rounds were uninteresting. Gibbons fell into clinches often. Dempsey was unable to open him up for a telling smash.

The films show them briefly touch gloves before starting the round. Dempsey circled and moved in with a sweeping left. Clinch, cuffing rights to the head, and break. Jack landed a lead hook to the body. Clinch and break. Jack immediately leapt in with a hook that missed the running-away Gibbons. Clinch and break. Gibbons walked away and then ducked forward while moving in, clinching. The referee struggled to break them.

Dempsey jabbed in and worked his right to the body and head in the clinch. Break. Tom moved a bit, and Dempsey doubled his left hook to the head and body. Clinch and even greater struggle for the referee to pry Gibbons loose and push him away.

Dempsey jabbed in and fired a right uppercut and left hook, then came under with body blows. Clinch and break. Dempsey fired a hook, right, and left uppercut to the body, and kept working his right to the head and left to the body as Tom held and bulled forward. Slight break.

Jack immediately hooked the head and kept cuffing away with it. Break. They both missed jabs.

Tom moved away, circling and walking rapidly to the right. Jack jabbed in and tried to work inside, particularly with his right as he was being held. Break. Jack quickly tracked down the moving Gibbons and fired away with a hard hook and long leaping right hook before Tom held and smothered, pushing in to crowd him. Referee Dougherty again struggled to pull Tom away, and Dempsey even had to lend an assist by pushing Tom with his right while Gibbons was grabbing Jack's left.

Dempsey led with a right to the head and followed with short lefts to the body and head as Tom bulled in and held. Partial break, but Tom just moved in again, and as he held Jack's left arm, Jack fired several rabbit shots with his right. The referee tried to break Tom free, but was only partially successful. As soon as there was just a bit of room, Jack landed a hard hook to the head. Tom moved away. Gibbons hooked Dempsey's head and leaned in and clinched, bulling forward. Break. Jack threw a lead right and followed with left uppercuts to the head. Clear Dempsey round.

At the bell, the crowd applauded, cheered, and stood up. Referee Dougherty immediately grabbed and raised Dempsey's right glove upward in the air, signifying that he had won and retained the title. As Dougherty dropped it, Gibbons grabbed the champion's glove and shook it firmly. Tom smiled. Dempsey returned to his corner, his retainers closed around him, and he left and forced a passage through the crowd.

Tom remained a little longer, and the crowd cheered him again and again. They were happy that he had gone the distance. The ring soon was packed with people, and it was a long time before it was cleared.

Based on what the existing films show, overall, for the most part, every round was similar. Gibbons was quite defensive, mostly fighting to survive and protect himself, only rarely firing blows. When he did punch, his punches were quick and snappy, fairly well-timed, and appeared to have a decent amount of pop, but he rarely threw, and was very inconsistent with his offensive output. Most of the time, Gibbons clinched, ducked, covered up, leaned in, and/or turned away, trying to smother Dempsey and hold one or both of his arms.

Intermittently, Gibbons moved a bit, but he only moved for short bursts, for Dempsey relentlessly advanced, and Gibbons apparently did not want to use too much energy moving around or punching very often or for too long. Perhaps he feared opening up either would leave him vulnerable to counter blows or cause fatigue.

Dempsey was on the attack, very consistent at plugging away, always trying to find an opening. As he advanced, he used his usual dipping, rolling, and weaving, and mostly ignored Tom's punches, whether they landed or missed, and kept attacking. He threw his consistent nonstop single shots, working the body and head with uppercuts, hooks, and lead rights, but found it difficult to get through Gibbons' defense on a consistent basis. Tom was too good at grabbing, tucking his chin and leaning in, covering, smothering, blocking with arms, turning, or ducking. Jack kept firing away, trying to find or create what openings he could, but found it difficult to penetrate Tom's defense, or get much momentum owing to Tom's tactics. It seemed like he often could not get full leverage and snap on his blows, in part because of Gibbons' clinching and smothering. Sometimes Jack held and hit, and even fired rabbit punches to the back of Tom's head. He was trying to get something going, but simply could not break him down despite his best efforts.

Through the first 4 rounds, Dempsey was the aggressor and completely outworked Gibbons. Tom was a pretty good inside defensive fighter, seeming comfortable attempting to tie up Jack or crowd him. Nevertheless, Dempsey still was able to maintain a good work rate, especially landing good hooks to the body.

Dempsey slowed his attack in the 5th round, enabling Gibbons to box on the outside a bit more, landing some good snapping jabs.

Dempsey reasserted himself from the 6th round on, being the aggressor, primarily fighting on the inside, doing most of the work. However, he was unable to hurt Gibbons, who was fairly effective at neutralizing him in the clinches. Gibbons fought to survive, being more interested in defense than punching. Because he did not fight to win, throwing very few punches, taking few risks, he did not wear himself out, and left few openings. His focus on defense, clinching, smothering, spinning on the inside, or moving about a bit on the outside made it challenging for Dempsey to land effectively very often.

As the fight progressed, increasingly it became obvious, at least from the films, that Gibbons' main objective was to stay in there and last the distance. Or he was hoping that eventually Dempsey would tire, so he could fire away and hurt him late in the contest. Often, the foe most difficult to hit is the one who rarely opens up or takes any risks, but primarily focuses on defense. Gibbons had so much respect for Dempsey's power that he clearly did not want to throw unless he was confident that he would land and not get hit in return.

Dempsey won the rounds with sheer effort and superior work rate and gameness, outhustling him, but could not achieve the spectacular finish owing to Tom's tactics. Overall, the fight had somewhat of a lackluster feel to it. The rounds had a certain sameness and monotony to them, the only question being whether Dempsey would be able to break him down, whether Tom would open up more and take more risks and try to win, and/or whether Dempsey would tire and make Gibbons more confident and willing to punch more.

Ultimately, all Gibbons proved was his defensive prowess and ability to take it, having never been down or out in his 92-fight career. Gibbons was defensively clever, and Dempsey probably was not at his sharpest after a two-year layoff, so the bout was not very exciting. Still, Dempsey proved that he could plug away at a good clip for 15 rounds. Dempsey clearly won the 15-round decision against an experienced, clever man.

Many gave Gibbons great credit for having gone the distance, something no other Dempsey challenger had done, and having lasted longer than any other Dempsey opponent in his career. He had proven his defense and ability to take it. But beyond that, his success in lasting, in part, was the result of the fact that he really did not make the same effort to win that other fighters had. Miske, Brennan, and Carpentier had tried their best to win, not simply survive, and in doing so got knocked out. Gibbons never was close to winning, but he also did not get knocked out. Of course, opening up too often or for too long against a man like Dempsey could be quite dangerous. To his credit, Dempsey's work-rate and power kept Gibbons defensive. Even when Tom landed solidly, Jack seemed impervious to his blows.

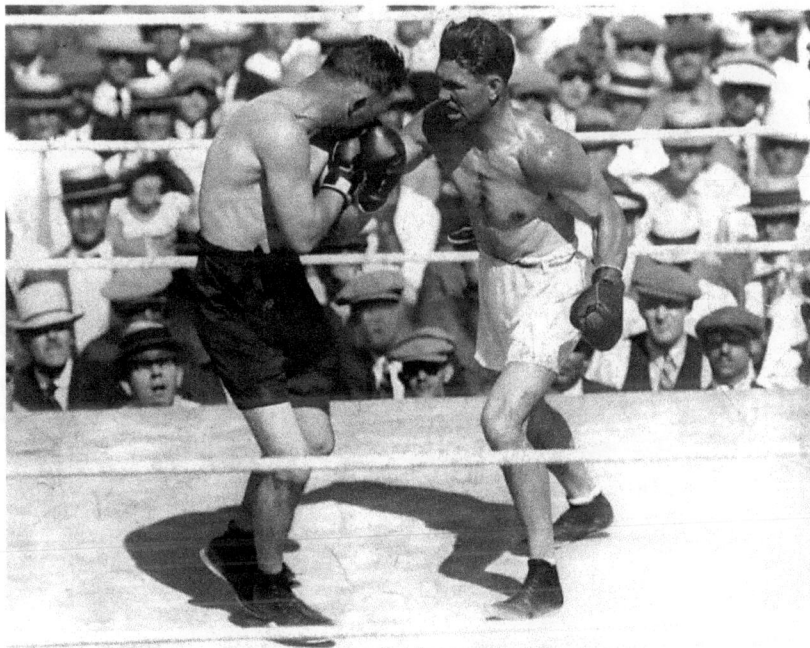

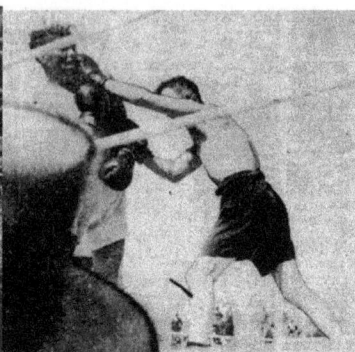

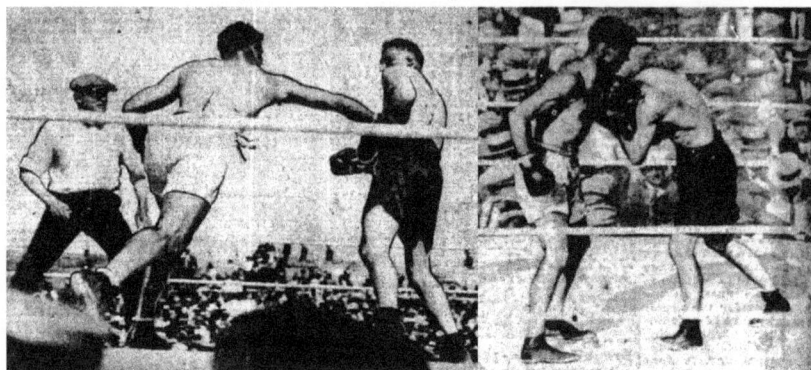

Gibbons treated like a hero by his St. Paul fans

Estimates of crowd size varied widely, in part because the size of the crowd increased as the day and main event progressed. The *Butte Miner* said estimates of attendance and receipts were "out of order." When the show started, less than 3,000 seats were occupied. Before the main event, the ticket prices were reduced in half, and the crowd doubled. Then there was another price reduction during the Dempsey fight, down to $10 and $5, which also increased the crowd size. Eventually, thousands crashed the gate and entered for free.

The Associated Press said the total number of tickets taken in at the gate was 7,202, according to Rasmussen. 2,300 tickets in the $20 section were sold at half price. 764 passes were given out, bringing the total recorded official attendance to 7,966. The government revenue collector admitted that at least 1,000 more crashed the gates. The discrepancy between the number of paid admissions and the number of those actually present was due to the fact that so many crashed the gate.

The *Anaconda Standard* said barely 8,000 people were in the arena at the start of the championship fight, though soon thereafter about 25,000 entered and crowded as near as they could to the ringside, when the prices were cut in half or more. Also, thousands crashed the gates, overwhelming the gatekeepers and police, swarming into the arena. One estimated the crowd at 15,000 to 20,000.

The *Great Falls Tribune* said huge gaps in the stands marked the missing fans. Few guests strolled in until the ticket prices were reduced.

Harry Newman said the attendance was about 15,000. Ticket prices had been cut down to half, and then almost down to nothing.

Hugh Fullerton said 20,000 were present for the main event. The initial cutting of ticket prices and throwing them onto the open market for almost any price swelled the crowd to 10,000. Then after cutting rates further, the crowd swarmed in, and by 4 p.m., the crowd was about 12,000. Another price cut, mixed with gate crashers, and more than 20,000 wound up being inside the arena. Still, it was only half filled, for it could have handled up to 40,000.

Damon Runyon said the crowd was 16,000, half of which got in for free. The crowd even included kids.

The *Chicago Tribune* reported the paid-in-full attendance at 7,200; cut-rate and free attendance at 8,000.

Henry Farrell reported 12,000 spectators.

Robert Edgren said that by the end of the fight, the arena was nearly filled. The guards at the barbed-wire fences and outer gates came in to see the fight, and with the gates open, folks entered for free. "Probably there were 25,000 people in the arena at the finish."

Richard Henry Little said at one point, Kearns started letting folks in for $5 apiece. In the mad scramble, many simply entered without paying. There must have been 18,000 inside.

Edward Walker said trains had failed to unload the expected crowds. When the first prelim was called, only about 5,000 were in the arena.

When the champ entered at 3:30 p.m., mountain time, about 30 minutes after the scheduled time, about 7,000 were there. While the main event was in progress, the promoters let in most of the town at $10 a head. Some said the tickets eventually went for $5. Financially, the fight was a bust for everyone but Dempsey/Kearns.

The Associated Press reported the total gate at $201,485, and federal tax at $22,448.50. This was according to Charles Rasmusson, Montana collector of internal revenue. Approximately 2,300 tickets in the $20 seat section were sold at half price. The government collected a 10% tax, even though the promoters did not get full price.

The *Great Falls Tribune* and *Chicago Tribune* also said the total bout revenue was $201,485.

The promoters said the official attendance by the government's check was only 7,202 and the receipts $225,000, of which the government took $22,500 in taxes.

The *Chicago Tribune* said the promotion's expenses were $358,000, and loss to the promoters $156,500.

The *Anaconda Standard* said the total loss to the promoters and businessmen of Shelby, Great Falls, and other Montana towns was estimated to be about $80,000. The *Examiner* echoed that number.

Heywood Broun said the fight's backers probably lost about $300,000, for the gross receipts only were $250,000. Likely, no more championship battles would be held outside of big cities. But Shelby could take pride from the fact that it did see it through.

The locals hated the newspapermen and fight experts, and were glad that the fight was better than all of them had expected. The visiting reporters had made fun of Shelby, calling it a dismal swamp.

George Barton said the show's uncertainty cost the promotion a lot of money. Many thought the fight would be called off, owing to the promoters' inability to make timely payments. The uncertainty caused thousands who had planned to attend to cancel their ticket reservations and travel plans.

Harry Newman said Mayor Jim Johnson, who staked his fortune to put on the fight only to have his associates show the white feather and quit, had the most expensive seat in the arena. It was estimated to have cost him $120,000 or $130,000 in losses. Johnson claimed that he lost $150,000 on the venture. Still, he had an interest in the motion pictures, which likely would prove to be valuable. Gibbons had a 25% interest. Kearns and Dempsey allegedly gave up their interest in the pictures, though the next day, Kearns said otherwise.

Bill Henry, at ringside for the *Los Angeles Times*, estimated that the financial fiasco cost the town of Shelby about $150,000.

Henry Farrell called it "Shelby's folly!" Experts figured Shelby lost about $150,000.

Financial difficulties were so great that Kearns agreed to pay the referee his $5,000, and personally guaranteed $3,000 to the preliminary fighters.

The *Anaconda Standard* reported that allegedly, Kearns received "almost all" of the remaining $100,000 owed, which he took out of the first gate receipts. Kearns said, "About $30,000 was obtained just before the fight, when we sold the remaining tickets for $10 each. The balance was taken in at the gate today and at fight headquarters yesterday."

Another paper quoted Kearns as saying, "We got about $75,000 out of it these last two days." Skeptics doubted that. Kearns also said, "I reduced the price of $20 tickets to $10 at the last hour rather than have the tickets go to waste entirely." The last big crowd crashed the gates and didn't pay anything. The sheriff and deputies tried to stop them, but there were too many.

Several reported that Kearns fell approximately $48,000 short of getting paid the third $100,000 guarantee. The Associated Press reported that Kearns got $52,000 from the receipts the day before and the day of the fight. This made the Dempsey/Kearns share $252,000, if those numbers were accurate, less various expenses and taxes. Kearns seemed to imply that he obtained more. Regardless, either way, it still was one of the biggest paydays in boxing's history...for Dempsey/Kearns. The promoters/financiers and Gibbons/Kane fared horribly. They would have to try to reduce their losses and earn money with the film revenues, which could be quite significant if the federal law was violated.

Writing for the *Missoulian*, which was another Montana newspaper, French Ferguson, who was at ringside, said there were many gate crashers, but the majority entered by paying $5 or $10 apiece. In this way, the management came up with $27,000 more for Kearns.

Henry Farrell said Gibbons earned nothing but honors and a chance at some motion picture money.

The *Chicago Tribune* said Gibbons only received $7,500 for training expenses, which had been advanced to him. Gibbons and Dempsey also would receive a percentage of the moving picture receipts.

Some noted that Gibbons made money from sparring exhibitions as a result of being matched for the championship, and he earned money in interim fights as a result of being a contender to Dempsey's crown. Plus, he could make more from the films, and in future fights and exhibitions as a result of the reputation of being the first man to take the champion 15 rounds, and the only one to last the distance with Dempsey in a title defense.

George Barton said Gibbons earned a $5,000 bonus for training in Shelby, about $5,000 from an exhibition tour, $2,500 for training expenses, and about $2,500 by charging the public to watch him train every day ($15,000). Because he lasted the full 15 rounds, the moving pictures would be worth a fortune to him. Just his 25% share could generate over $150,000 for him. Plus, he could earn more for future fights and exhibitions as the first man to go the championship distance with Dempsey. So, it wasn't as bad as some might think for Gibbons.

It seems that most writers by that point presumed that promoters would violate the federal law against interstate transport of fight films, particularly since most violators were receiving only fines for such violations.

Some said the moving pictures would be worth 20 times what they were prior to the fight. Collins, Molumby, and Kane allegedly had the rights, but that was unclear.

Tex Rickard announced that he would start negotiations to match Dempsey with the winner of the July 12 Firpo-Willard bout, hopefully for September or October, perhaps at Boyle's Thirty Acres in Jersey City.

Rickard said, "I have said all along that Gibbons is the best man of his weight in the country and his fight today proves it. He was under a heavy handicap in weight but battled gamely and cleverly. I don't think Dempsey has gone back. He simply had a hard man to beat."

Having heard about the fight's result, Luis Firpo said, "I always thought I could beat Dempsey, but now I'm sure that I can knock him out."

Previously, Tom O'Rourke had tried to make the Dempsey-Wills fight at the Polo Grounds, but his mere percentage offer rather than guarantee was not acceptable to Kearns because of the park's smaller seating capacity and the New York commission's ticket price limitations. Kearns wanted a guarantee, or a much higher percentage.

Kearns said they would accept 37.5% of the gate receipts for a Wills fight at Yankee stadium, which currently had a seating capacity of 75,000. Jimmy Johnston, matchmaker, said the fight was all but arranged for September 3. Wills would earn 12 1/8%. However, he admitted that Kearns had not yet signed on the dotted line.

Regardless, they still needed to overcome official/political hurdles. Regarding a potential fight with Wills, the *Anaconda Standard* noted that although Dempsey waived the color line, "the various boxing commissions seemed unwilling to."

In other news, that same day, July 4, 1923, in Kokomo, Indiana, the Ku Klux Klan held a massive rally, the largest in the organization's history. Attendance estimates ran from 75,000 to 150,000, and some later reported up to 200,000. Supposedly, Indiana's enrollment even exceeded Texas' Klan membership, which was 85,000. The Klan was on the rise everywhere.[1207]

Regarding Dempsey-Gibbons, Montana's *Anaconda Standard* said the St. Paul boxer held the record of 86 fights without a knockdown. Dempsey never was in danger throughout,

LECTURE

AMERICANISM
and
The Klu-Klux-Klan

By National Lecturer, Under Auspices of National
Organization of Knights of the Ku-Klux-Klan
and Protection Klan No. 34.
—AT NORTH PARK ON—

JULY 10, 1923

8:45 p. m.

Protection Post, Kansas,
July 5, 1923

[1207] *South Bend Tribune, Fort Wayne Journal-Gazette, Richmond Palladium and Sun-Telegram,* July 5, 1923.

winning 12 of the 15 rounds. Gibbons' masterful defense kept him on his feet, although he was tiring rapidly in the closing rounds. There was no debate regarding the decision.

This newspaper said Gibbons had a shade in the 5th, 11th, and 13th rounds, but those were the only rounds that arguably were his. The remaining 12 rounds clearly were Dempsey's.

Gibbons was the undoubted favorite with the crowd, but not a word of dissent was heard regarding referee Jim Dougherty's decision, which was given immediately and without any hesitation as soon as the final bell rang. Many had believed that Gibbons would outpoint Dempsey if there was no knockout, but they were wrong.

Gibbons' face was somewhat blood-smeared; his lips and nose bruised, but he smilingly shook Dempsey's hand afterwards. The crowd gave him an ovation for his cleverness in lasting. Everyone was good-natured. Mayor Jim Johnson's wife hugged Gibbons. Hundreds tried to shake hands with him. He smiled broadly.

Kearns was stunned after the first 5 or 6 rounds demonstrated that the champion was not able to hit Gibbons effectively. He had expected a knockout.

This writer said Gibbons played a hit and run game, putting forth a remarkable defensive performance throughout. In some rounds, he even attacked and outboxed the champ in spots.

Throughout, referee Dougherty was kept busy separating them from clinches. Dempsey fought furiously, pounding Gibbons about the head and midsection, but seemed unable to get over a blow that was effective or decisive. During most of the rounds, Gibbons appeared to be fighting entirely on the defensive, only occasionally landing a blow. When Jack threw, Tommy quickly would fall into a clinch. Much of the time he was backing away from the champ, who constantly was seeking an opening that was not there. Gibbons was in and out of the clinches, calm and collected throughout. He had equal or greater speed than the champ, but he rarely used it.

No matter what Dempsey hit him with, Gibbons did not seem to be affected. He never staggered. Sometimes he countered or fired blows at the advancing Dempsey, but never kept it up or really got going offensively.

Gibbons seemed somewhat groggy and fatigued in the 15th round, and it was a matter of conjecture regarding how much longer he could have lasted.

Gibbons said he wanted a rematch.

> This fight gave me an insight into his style of fighting and I know what I can do against him. Perhaps I did do a little holding. I had to. Toward the end I became weary. My body became tired. He is a bigger, stronger man than I am and he punches hard. Of course, I stopped a few hard ones, but I was not dazed. My mind remained clear and I knew what I wanted to do. If I fight Dempsey again, I

will fight him differently. In the first round I was watching his left too closely. He shot his right and before I realized my mistake I had taken some hard blows.

Gibbons said he had planned to make an effort in the 11th round to stop Dempsey, "but when the time came the stamina wasn't there. I couldn't bring over the punch. I had been wrestled and yanked around too much. One or two punches were low. Only one of them, in the left thigh, hurt me."

Eddie Kane said they had no kick about the decision, but they wanted a return bout.

Referee James Dougherty said,

> It was a tough assignment for the third man in the ring. Working out there in the sun trying to separate the men through 15 rounds was action enough for any one single day. But it was a great bout. I don't think anybody will question that. Nor do I think anybody will question the decision. There was no other decision possible. Dempsey was the aggressor all the way and accomplished the most damaging work the majority of the rounds. There were cries that the rules were not observed, but those who yelled at supposed violations did not know the rules which specify that the men should protect themselves at all times. As to the cries of low blows, I saw none struck, and I don't think anybody else did.

One writer said Gibbons fought gamely and well, giving and receiving some terrific wallops, showing nerve, endurance, speed, and science, and demonstrating a marvelous artistry as an artful dodger. Dempsey failed to prove himself an irresistible force at scoring a knockout. Gibbons stood up against his violence for 15 rounds, and though at the conclusion was a bit dazed in the head, he still was strong on his feet. Tom was credited with a "moral victory," which enhanced his reputation and market value.

Another said Dempsey got the coin and the victory, but Gibbons got the glory. The master boxer put up a fine defensive battle. The champ launched a furious attack in the final round, attempting to put over a knockout, but Gibbons managed to stave off a decisive blow.

Gibbons continually looked to land a big blow, dancing and hotstepping around the ring, occasionally slipping in a right or left to the face or body, then eluding danger by clinching or stepping back. Toward the end though, he seemed to be fading fast and repeatedly hung on in the clinches. Dempsey never was in any danger in any round. Gibbons cut and slightly blackened the champ's right eye in the opening round, and Dempsey brought blood once or twice from the challenger, but neither was marked to any appreciable extent.

The American Legion regretted that Gibbons had failed to knock Dempsey's block off, as they had hoped.

One reporter said the fight was paid for with Montana money, and the crowd was 90% Montanans. The crowd was pulling for Gibbons, and they admired his performance, but recognized that he had lost.

The *Butte Miner's* Jean Jordan said Gibbons fought on the defensive and stayed on his feet, despite a fierce battering. The challenger upset the fight dope by staying the distance when most thought he would be stopped in 6 or 7 rounds. Dempsey proved that he would be champion for years to come. Gibbons resorted to tactics that kept him further out of the running for the championship than ever; sprinting and holding to keep out of danger. This writer said Tom won the 5th round only. The 2nd and 11th were even. All the rest were Dempsey's by a wide margin. Hence, Jordan said Dempsey won 12-1-2.

At the start, many cheered Gibbons and booed the champ. Throughout, Dempsey landed from eight to ten blows to every one scored by Gibbons. Yet, the noisy Gibbons faction cut loose with deafening applause every time the contender swung. Four out of five of the challenger's attempts were picked off in midair or glanced across Dempsey's shoulders, but each and every one was cheered lustily.

Either to protect those who bet he would last, or to save his record of never having been knocked off his feet, or to make the pictures more valuable, Gibbons stayed within his shell. Other than keeping his feet, he failed to live up to what was expected of him. One hasty retreat after another gave him a few opportunities to whirl and jab. Even more than retreating, the holding counted the heaviest against Gibbons. He was ever-clinching, attempting to grab an arm with one or both of his own each time the champ rushed or drew near. Heralded as the cleverest boxer, he was beaten at his own game. Dempsey beat him all the way at infighting. Gibbons never showed his power. Whenever he appeared ready to open up, each time, his manager urged him to take cover. "Cover up, cover up, or he will get you." Gibbons complied.

Dempsey was the aggressor for 15 rounds and finished unmarked. Gibbons was beaten crimson from waist up and appeared winded much of the time during the last 8 rounds. His sides were beaten to a pulp, until the skin on both sides was broken. A light cut on his right cheek and one over his right eye was opened. A long cut was opened on his forehead and his lips were severely split.

Jordan's version is the most consistent with what the films show.

French Ferguson, at ringside for Montana's *Missoulian*, said the crowd was for Gibbons. The men who bet on Dempsey to win by knockout sporadically yelled encouragement to him. If Dempsey was worried by the crowd or Mr. Gibbons, he never showed it.

Ray Rocene said a 3rd round rally saved Gibbons. As Dempsey waged a formidable assault on him in that round, a woman yelled out, "Remember the kiddies at home, Tommy." That shout of encouragement inspired new life into the faltering Gibbons, distinctly on the short end up to that time. He fought back valiantly and gallantly, stopped the Dempsey attack in the 4th, and then charged forth on the offensive for the first time in the 5th, gaining a shade in that round. From that point on to the end, though outpointed, and forced to clinch and hold in the closing rounds, the challenger proved to be a fair foe for the champion.

Dempsey defended his crown, not spectacularly, but in such style that the shifting of the fight to Gibbons never was apparent. Dempsey relied on his ferocious infighting, constant pummeling at close quarters, trying to wear Gibbons down. Few killing or heavy-voltage blows landed on the clever and agile Gibbons. Whenever Jack became a real menace, Tommy skillfully clinched and hung on doggedly until the referee pried them apart.

Some thought that Dempsey had gone back. Others thought Gibbons' style simply did not give the champion many opportunities to land the knockout wallop. Tom clinched too often and took no chances. Trying harder might have landed the challenger on his back. Both used their lefts to a great extent, Gibbons almost exclusively so. Dempsey was much superior at infighting.

Gibbons occasionally spurted, snapped in a wallop or two to bounce Jack's head back, and momentarily assumed the offensive. But Tom inevitably went back into his shell.

The effects of the short, crushing punches to the ribs began to tell after the 12th round, when Tom ceased any serious offensive operations.

Neither was groggy or off his feet, though twice Gibbons looked like he had been hurt. The bloodshed was microscopic. Gibbons slashed a slight cut under Dempsey's right eye, while Jack brought blood from Gibbons' eyebrow, but in a small quantity.

Grantland Rice, an eastern writer, said, "Dempsey met a fine defensive fighter, who did not make a mistake." The champ showed that his long rest had done him no good. He needed to fight more often if he expected to keep his honors.

Ed Hughes, sports editor for the *New York Evening Mail*, called it a disappointing fight. "Dempsey was handicapped by Gibbons' safety-first tactics, which reflected much credit on Gibbons as a defensive fighter. Dempsey needs a few fights to perfect his punches and timing."

Bert Bates of the *Portland Telegram* said although Dempsey was not the man-killer of the Willard contest, he still was the world's best puncher. Meaning, if he was not hitting so hard, Gibbons would not have fought so defensively or have refused to open up more. Clearly, Dempsey's powerful and consistent offense kept Gibbons' offense in check.

Heywood Broun said, "Dempsey shows unmistakably the ill effect upon any fighter of two years of inactivity. I would not be greatly surprised to see him defeated by Firpo should they meet in the fall."

Gibbons showed why he never had been off his feet. He could take it and he had great defense. Dempsey said, "I just couldn't hit him." Gibbons was on the defensive throughout, except for a spurt in the 5th and 6th rounds. Particularly in the last two rounds, Gibbons clung desperately. He ignored orders to break, and literally had to be pried off his man.

Dempsey did not fight foul. This reporter saw only two low blows, which seemed unintentional, and moreover, Gibbons wore his belt very high. Jack did hold and hit a bit. There was much pulling and hauling. It was not a good fight. There was little open work. There was no question about the champ's superiority. Yet, "Dempsey is not invincible. He is no superman. Now that he is off the pedestal there will be a lot more fun in watching contenders swing at him."

The *Great Falls Tribune* said although the main sympathy was with Gibbons, most realized early on that it was the champion's fight. Most prayed for Gibbons to stay away. They were relieved when each round ended and he still was on his feet. Spectators also realized that Gibbons was a master of defense, and they praised his foiling of Dempsey's attempts to land knockout blows.

Shrieks of delight followed Tom's frequent jabs which he planted on the champ. Dempsey really went after him hammer and tongs in the last round. Tom had been slowed by the punishing body socks and rabbit punches. But feinting, clinching, hanging on, and retreating with all his skill, Gibbons survived.

Afterwards, Jack Kearns said, "[T]hey cannot say now that Dempsey is not a boxer. They've called him a slugger only, but he has outboxed Gibbons this afternoon." That was stretching it a bit, but the statement also contained much truth too. He indeed had outworked and outpointed Gibbons, who was known as a master boxer with speed and a punch.

Kearns said Dempsey should not be censured for failing to win by knockout. He tried his hardest, but Gibbons was a difficult target. Jack could not get him propped up for a solid, clean smash that would end the contest. Gibbons deserved credit for standing up under enough punishment that would have stopped most men. Dempsey proved he could go 15 rounds at a good pace without tiring. "Now let the others come – Willard, Firpo, Wills or anybody else. Dempsey will be ready. It is up to the promoters to provide reasonable inducements and a battleground."

An hour after the fight, Dempsey boarded his private rail car and started the trip back to his Great Falls training camp. Dempsey was disappointed by the result, for he had wanted and expected a knockout. He lauded the challenger, saying,

> In a way I am disappointed with the result. I think I won clearly enough to dispel any doubt on the decision, but I felt sure when I entered the ring I could knock Gibbons out. In this I failed and, while I am disappointed, I want to express my admiration for Gibbons and the bout he put up. I know I hit him often enough and hard enough to drop any ordinary heavyweight, but I guess everybody is convinced now that Gibbons is not an ordinary heavyweight. He certainly gave me a great fight. He is one of the

hardest men to hit cleanly or solidly than I ever boxed. I get a measure of satisfaction out of the bout, however. I have convinced myself and skeptics too, that I can travel the route. I felt fine at the finish and was strong. Gibbons never hurt me, and I felt fine all through the bout. While they are talking of my fight I hope they don't overlook Gibbons. He sure surprised me. He's a great boxer.

Another quoted Dempsey as saying, "Tommy Gibbons is a great boxer. He put up a fine fight today and I want to give him credit for a wonderful performance. As to my performance, I will say I am content and satisfied."

Dempsey changed clothes in a private car, and wore a black suit, silver striped. He also wore a straw hat pulled low over his forehead, partially hiding his right eye, which was blue. His old cut over his left eye was hit and slightly reopened. But Dempsey bore no other evidence of the bout. He was not tired.

Jack was friendly with the newspapermen in the adjoining car, saying, "Hello pardner. How goes it." He traveled in a private car attached to a special train. He arrived back in Great Falls at 11 p.m. Wednesday night, July 4. With him were his father Hiram, brother Bernard, Mike Trant, and his sparring partners. He planned to visit Salt Lake City.

Harry Newman of the *New York Daily News* was on scene. He said Gibbons made a game stand against the champion's onslaughts. He won at least two rounds. Dempsey won but did not prove to be such a "wonderman" after all. He was on the aggressive all the way but met an opponent who tested him. There were times when the smaller Gibbons rocked the champ with stinging rights and lefts.

In the 5th round, Gibbons sent the champ back on his heels with a left chop to the face and a right rip to the head. He again sent him back on his heels in the 11th round. Those were the only two rounds he won.

Newman scored it 8-2-5 for Dempsey, and that probably was being quite generous to Gibbons: 1 – Even, 2 – Even, 3 – Dempsey, 4 – Even, 5 – Gibbons, 6 – Dempsey, 7 - Dempsey, 8 – Dempsey, 9 – Even, 10 – Dempsey, 11 – Gibbons, 12 - Dempsey, 13 – Dempsey, 14 – Even, 15 – Dempsey.

Overall, Dempsey was too strong for him. Gibbons outboxed him at long range, but could not hold him off, and could not evade the body assaults. Dempsey's terrible heart punches took the steam out of the game Gibbons and slowed him down. He rallied every time the champ attempted to put over a finisher, but the terrible wallops below the heart had a damaging effect.

Gibbons could not keep Dempsey off of him. Jack got in his best work at close range. He hammered and battered at will in the clinches. He moved and turned him and pasted Tom. Jack held and kept him there while he plastered him all over the place.

It was a moral victory to weather the storm for 15 rounds. Dempsey's stock flopped, given that he was expected to annihilate Gibbons within 6 rounds. Many believed he had lost his old sting. Of course, Gibbons made him miss many blows. Dempsey was used to men he could hit. Gibbons was not slow, but could move, punch fast, duck, cover, and block. Dempsey could not land his haymakers. Still, there were times when the champ landed well, without disturbing Gibbons.

Regardless, there was no question about Dempsey's victory. He was the aggressor all the way, landed more blows, and inflicted more punishment. He won, but also knew that he had been in there with someone who knew the boxing game as well or better than he. If Gibbons were bigger and stronger, he might have done a whole lot better.

Kearns was surprised. He had not realized that Gibbons would be so formidable, or he might not have allowed Dempsey to fight at cut rates.

Gibbons said he was sorry that he had to hang on in the last few rounds. "I'd fight him a great deal differently if I met him again. He's a great big strong rough fighter, and he could rough me around a lot. Toward the last of the fight I began to get weak. I wasn't nervous, but I just couldn't get started right. I've got him figured out now. This was only the third time I had ever seen him fight."

Mayor Jim Johnson said, "Well, we saw a fight, didn't we? Slip me the price of a shave."

Bill Henry was at ringside for the *Los Angeles Times*. The defeated man was cheered as he left the ring, after a game exhibition of stamina and skill in the face of Dempsey's attacking onslaught. The Colorado killer missed his quarry, unable to stop the man who at first exhibited marvelous and then later desperate defense. It was a victory for Gibbons to last the 15 rounds. The huge Coloradan pumped in sickening rights and lefts to the midsection. It was a question of how long Tom could withstand the terrific mauling. Dempsey shoved and shook him in the clinches at will, ramming in piston-like rights and lefts.

Referee Daugherty did his best to break them, but from first to last it was a battle of clinches. Early on it was Dempsey who held, but in an offensive manner, hoping to keep Gibbons close, not allow him to escape, and to maneuver him into punches. Later, it was Gibbons who desperately clung to Jack's left arm, killing time as best as he could.

As a fight it was not much, but as a revelation of how to fight a defensive battle, and how little so-called experts knew, it was a wonder. It was Dempsey's fight from the start, although Gibbons rallied in the 5th, which gave him an edge in that round. The champ's terrific strength was almost unbelievable, and was matched against the challenger's gameness, stamina, and cleverness. Gibbons' ability to smother frightful attacks was marvelous. Round after round, Dempsey mauled and shoved him around. Gibbons chose to meet him at his own game, seeking the crushing embrace of the bear. His ability to withstand the terrific lunges was one of the greatest spectacles of the age.

Kearns said, "Well, we won didn't we? Gibbons is a tough boy, but Jack gave him an awful beating."

Hugh Fullerton, who also was there, said a prejudiced crowd frequently hooted Dempsey's rough tactics and applauded everything Gibbons did. The decision was fair and correct.

Dempsey retained his title in a great battle, while feathered Indians, kilted Scots, cowboys, and American sports cheered for Gibbons. Tom took everything that could be handed to him, and although he was groggy, hanging on and trying desperately to last, he was treated like the hero of the day.

The fight was preceded by scandal and financial failure but was great enough to justify everything. 20,000 fans sat under a glaring sun and stewed in the intense heat but witnessed a struggle worthy of it all. The crowd went wild when at frequent intervals the St. Paul boxer carried the fight to the champ and rocked him with repeated lefts. Had Gibbons possessed Dempsey's punching power he could have won. It wasn't until the end, in the final round, that Dempsey's murderous body blows finally sapped Gibbons' strength. The 5th, 11th, and possibly the 13th belonged to Gibbons. The 2nd and 4th were even, but Dempsey won all the other rounds. Hence, Fullerton had it 10-3-2 for Dempsey.

Although Dempsey drove his blows with murderous force to the body, Gibbons was not hurt. Tom blocked many blows with his arms and elbows. The darting speed of his head enabled him to avoid knockout blows. Never before did Dempsey miss so many hard drives. But he won decisively without a doubt. He was too strong.

The crowd jeered Dempsey's methods. Sometimes Jack's blows strayed low, but often that was because Tom blocked them down. Plus, the waistline of Tom's trunks was pulled up high, and frequently the crowd was deceived. The low punches did not hurt the challenger.

In frequent rallies, Gibbons outboxed the champ. But he did not have enough power to hurt Dempsey or keep him off. He was competitive in the first five rounds, but from that point to the finish, save for a minute flash in the 11th, Gibbons was not dangerous. Dempsey punched him in the stomach and kidneys until Tom's blows lacked sting. More and more it became a question of whether Gibbons could stave off a knockout. He moved into clinches, clung desperately to Jack's arms, and held on while the referee wrestled to tear them apart.

In the 15th round, Dempsey still tried to knock him out. A right to the heart almost finished it. Gibbons clung to him, hugging and holding on to his arm, while the referee worked hard to tear them apart. Tom was weary but alert, ducking inside blows. He took a shower of short body blows and clung blindly, hoping for the bell.

When the bell rang, Dempsey seemed disappointed, even when his glove was raised in the air. Then, smiling, he shook Tom's hand. The crowd cheered and applauded the smiling Gibbons. He had lost without a cent for his work, but won the crowd's admiration.

Some debated whether Dempsey had gone back or just met a really good boxer. Fullerton acknowledged, "Whether Dempsey has gone back or not is a problem. My opinion is that he met a master boxer and it was mighty fortunate he trained for 15 rounds. Had he not been in superb condition there would have been a different story."

Crowd outside *Los Angeles Times* building receiving fight returns

James Dawson for the *Chicago Tribune* said Dempsey won by a mile, but had a hard battle, for Gibbons was a brainy fighter with a masterful defense. Dempsey never came close to scoring a knockout, though he had Gibbons weary, tired, and sore about the body and mind at the final bell. Gibbons earned glory for withstanding Dempsey's blows for 15 rounds.

This author said Dempsey's form was disappointing. He was not the reliable, death-dealing hitter that was expected. He was the persistent aggressor, but his blows were not as lightning-like or bone-crushing as seen in the past. He pressed continually and shifted and weaved in and out in his own peculiar way, always ready to strike any opening, but he could not land solidly.

Gibbons proved to be a difficult, elusive target. He had speed, skill, cleverness, and a cool head. Plus, he was impervious to blows. Though weakened and weary at the end, he stood up to the champ and tried to fight him as best he could. He took a terrific beating nevertheless, particularly to the body. However, he never showed any outward indication that the blows hurt.

Regardless, Dempsey was the clear winner, without question. He won at least 13 of the 15 rounds. Gibbons won the 5th and possibly the 9th, which may have been even. "In every other round Dempsey had a decided margin."

Dawson believed that Dempsey should fight more often. A life of ease and luxury had taken something from him. Still, he fought with the same characteristic fury, tireless in his assault, unflinching in his fast pace, and never stopped trying to land a haymaker. His body assault was effective, but never did Gibbons lower his guard enough for a knockout punch to land.

Pat O'Malley, a Chicago veteran bookmaker and fight fan had laid down wagers that the fight would last 8 rounds and that it would last 10, and allegedly won $20,000. He had been strong for Gibbons for a long time.

According to Henry Farrell, Kearns said, "Dempsey hadn't fought for two years and this was a good workout for him. Gibbons was just in there to stay the limit and he was a hard, slippery man to fight."

Regarding their future, Kearns said, "Jack is going to Salt Lake City from Great Falls and I am going to New York to try to arrange a fight with Harry Wills."

Kearns said he had to pay the referee and prelim boys, the workers around the arena, and part of the police costs when the Great Falls bankers failed at the last minute to keep their promise to furnish $8,000 for such purposes.

Dempsey got the title and the money. Gibbons received admiration from the spectators who saw him stand up to and evade the tiger rushes. Tom had a "puffed face, a split lip, sore ribs that glared an angry red."

Gibbons said he had plans that would have won him the fight, "but I got several hard bumps on the head in the 1st round and my plans slipped." Still, he vindicated himself as a worthy challenger.

Tom claimed he got hit low in the 9th round and could not move after that. "I held on a lot in the last three rounds, and don't blame me for it."

The next day, Dempsey said he was tired of the training grind and would welcome a vacation. He admired Gibbons' ability as a boxer and gave him credit for a wonderful showing. "I hope that Gibbons was not hurt. He is a great boxer and put up a fast bout. I hope the crowd was pleased."

Jack had two slightly discolored eyes, a wound under the right eye, and an old cut opened up over the left as a result of Gibbons' left hooks and right crosses. That old cut eye had been opened up in training, and simply re-opened.

Dempsey always called Kearns "Doc." He said Doc had four Chicago detectives around them for security, fearing something might happen.

Hiram Dempsey saw his son box in a championship match for the first time. He was glad to see Gibbons stay the limit, for that was what the crowd wanted, and Tom strained every muscle in his body to be on his feet at the end.

Robert Edgren said, "All that Jack Dempsey needed to stop Tom Gibbons yesterday afternoon was a lasso and a pry bar, the first to catch Tom when he was running and dodging around the ring, the second to pry Tom loose from the two-handed death grip Gibbons held on Dempsey's left arm in hundreds of clinches." That summed it up.

Everyone agreed with the decision, even Gibbons. Dempsey tried to stop him in the last round, almost enraged, galloping after him at top speed, whaling away with all his strength at close quarters, rocking and shaking Gibbons with short blows, but could not land the wallop needed.

Gibbons made heroic efforts to stick it out, "and he did it by using every wile and trick known to the ancient game." Gibbons was slippery and hard to corner. When Dempsey did get in, Gibbons was great at holding the left arm and bearing down with all his weight while Jack ineffectually hit him in the back of the head with his right. "All through the 15th round Gibbons held persistently." Referee Jimmy Dougherty was red-faced because he could not make Tom break his grip, but did not want to disqualify him, particularly because the local rules did not mention either holding or rabbit punches as being foul. Dempsey punched as much as he could, and the groggy Gibbons could not be pried loose. No one objected to the decision, which was the only one possible.

Edgren scored it 10-2-3 for Dempsey. Gibbons did his best work in the 4th and 5th rounds, the only rounds he won in the fight, although he held Dempsey even in the 2nd, 9th, and 11th. All the rest were Dempsey's.

Afterwards, Gibbons laughed. He was delighted at having lasted. He had stayed longer than any other man, had outboxed Dempsey at times, and could make more money in other contests as a result. He was 13 pounds smaller, and inferior in strength. Tom was weary, but practically unhurt. He was no more bruised than the champ. It was a moral victory alone though.

It was only during the last 3 or 4 rounds that Gibbons was purely defensive. Dempsey must have been in fine condition, because he showed no signs of weariness or of feeling the hard smashes that Gibbons occasionally landed on his chin. At times, Gibbons had outtricked and outboxed him. Jack could not hit him squarely with his best punches. Tom was an elusive, turning, shifting shadow, and he blocked very well with arms and elbows. No one blamed Tom for holding. He was fighting for nothing, while Dempsey got well over $200,000. Nearly every man in the arena wanted to see him stick it out.

In conclusion, Edgren said Gibbons made a great defensive fight, while Dempsey did everything that he could offensively against a man who knew every trick of the game and was there to stay. That said, Dempsey's showing was not spectacular enough to think that the winner of Willard vs. Firpo would not have a chance with him. Dempsey proved that he could fight over a distance without losing speed, but his vaunted punch never appeared.[1208]

Ultimately, Edgren concluded that Dempsey was not as good as he once was. What Dempsey needed was more fighting. "Too much

---

[1208] Of course, his lack of punch might have been because Tom's defense was so good. Jack's punch was hard enough to keep Gibbons mostly defensive throughout, except for a few sudden bursts, not wanting to take the risks necessary to win, for that might have left him vulnerable to getting hit with knockout blows.

attention to the money and too little action in the ring may bring him to his finish. The combination is almost as deadly as the dissipation that ended the careers of so many great champions."

Edward Tranter said a happy consequence of the fight was that it would remove the handicap that Dempsey was superhuman, and therefore fill more challengers with hope of victory. It also could make the public and boxing commissioners believe that other potential fights were competitive.

Some said Dempsey had lost his punch. Others said no one was as fast, clever, or brainy as the elusive Gibbons. Dempsey did not inflict much punishment because he "faced a pastmaster of ring abilities."

Dempsey did whatever he could, including mauling, wrestling, hitting on the breaks, and firing rabbit punches. "In the east the rules would ban these tactics."

Davis Walsh, I.N.S. sports editor, said Gibbons fought a fine defensive battle, but that was another way of saying his activities were uninteresting. It would have been suicide to mix it up with the champ. Yet, it was the first time in five years that Dempsey had failed to finish a man before the prescribed number of rounds. Walsh concluded that Dempsey either was overrated or had slipped back. He was not the man-killer of the past, in part because Gibbons was an elusive target, and also because Dempsey's punches seemed to lack the downright sincerity of other contests.[1209]

Damon Runyon scored it 8-3-4 for Dempsey. Dempsey won his 8 rounds by a wide margin. Gibbons won the 5th, 11th, and 13th rounds. The 2nd, 4th, 12th, and 14th were even. All the others went to Dempsey – the 1st, 3rd, 6th, 7th, 8th, 9th, 10th, and 15th rounds.

Dempsey won the decision, but Gibbons got the glory. Gibbons was the coyote, wise, fast, and shifty, while Dempsey was the greyhound, strong, speedy, alert, and dangerous. Gibbons ran, and at the end of the chase, twisted, doubled, and covered up. By the end, he was panting and bleeding a little, but safe.

Folks expected a slaughter, but Gibbons surprised. He was older and smaller, and the sentimental favorite because he was the underdog and fighting for nothing. Tom was blocky-looking and white skinned, with a tin ear mangled into a blob of flesh and cartilage, the result of a career of getting hit there.

Gibbons stood up under a merciless hammering. The men were to protect themselves at all times, and could hit on breakaways, as allowed by straight Queensberry rules. Dempsey benefited by his superior strength. He mauled him around like a rag doll, smashed his body, and hammered the back of his neck.

Runyon said either Dempsey could not hit as hard as he used to or Gibbons had a body made of rubber. Once or twice, Tom looked a bit

---

[1209] However, if Dempsey hit harder, he might have wasted his energy hitting arms and gloves, and not been able to keep up the fast and consistent pace with solid blows that was keeping Gibbons so defensive-minded for most of the contest.

sick, but then he would make a quick twist and turn and recover, seeming as fresh as ever. His elbows diminished and broke down the force of a lot of blows. Tom usually was going away with the smashes, and often made Jack miss, allowing the champ to spend his energy.

For the first time ever, Dempsey made a remark to his foe during a fight, when Tom speared him with a good hard blow, and the champ muttered something.

Dempsey looked to be in perfect condition, but could not step as he used to step, or move as he used to do. The two years of idleness rusted the springs in his legs. Some said he was not the same fighter, but others said he was facing the craftiest and toughest ringman he ever met. Dempsey had no smile on his face at the end. He seemed chagrined. Kearns patted Gibbons on the back and told him he was a great fighter.

Each round was almost alike in many respects. Dempsey would crowd in, hold with one hand and belt him with the other about the body. Occasionally Jack would hit him under the chin with uppercuts.

Gibbons' best work was at long range. He pelted Jack with a sharp left, opened a small cut under the left eye, and once or twice let go with a right that would have been disastrous had it connected. It was a great fight because of the masterly, heady way Gibbons fought.

Afterwards, Eddie Kane, Tommy's manager, said, "The only reason Tom Gibbons isn't heavyweight champion of the world tonight is because he didn't study up enough on wrestling and because Dempsey was blessed by nature with greater strength." With a referee in the ring who did not allow Dempsey to "get away with everything," Gibbons could "take" Dempsey. Of course, he said nothing about a referee who might not allow Gibbons to get away with so much holding.

Gibbons wrote that he was satisfied with what he had proven.

> I can fight them all, regardless of size. ... I lost to a better wrestler, not a fighter. The rules under which the bout was staged permitted Dempsey to get away with everything short of actual murder, his superior size and strength telling heavily in the clinches. ... I may be wrong, but I think the majority of clean punches fell to my credit. But with Dempsey rushing me constantly in the hope of smothering me in a clinch, I hardly had a chance to show at my best.

> I was surprised at the lightness of his punches, having been led to believe that he was a real man killer. Jack Dempsey didn't hurt me at any time today. He merely tired me out just as a 15-round tussle with a grizzly bear would. ...

> Had Referee Dougherty broken us as many times in the first ten rounds today as he did in the last five, I fully believe that nothing could have kept me out of the championship. ... I didn't win a nickel at the box office this afternoon, but that doesn't make the slightest difference to me. I won lots of friends.

Jack Dempsey said,

Well, I'm still champion of the world. But what a fight it was. And what a marvel is Tommy Gibbons in the matter of taking punishment, in gameness, in cleverness. My hat is off to him, even if Tommy did decide in the last few rounds of the fight that the better thing for him to do would be to clinch and last the distance. It was about the toughest fight of my career. ...

Either Tommy is a wonder of wonders both in dodging and ducking and taking a pounding, or I'm not hitting quite so hard these days. Two years of idleness perhaps did a little of the harm.

But now that I've had a fight under my belt, and really been warmed up, I hope I'll get a little more action. I guess I will. Since Tommy was able to travel the fifteen rounds I suppose everybody will begin slinging challenges at me. That'll suit me fine. I've always wanted action, but I couldn't get much. They hung the 'super-man' thing on me and it scared off a lot of folks.

It gave the crowd a little joy when Tommy socked a few with his left hand, but they didn't do much more than tickle. Tommy is quite a wall of power, I hear, but he didn't do much to me. Maybe, if he had stepped out in the last few rounds and made it a slugging bee, I guess he might have shown all his stuff. And so could I.

I pounded Georges Carpentier to a pulp in the Jersey City clinches of 1921. I thought I could do the same with Gibbons. But Tommy showed that he certainly could take it. I hit him harder and oftener in the infighting than I've ever hit any man. But Tommy kept his feet and stepped right along.

I've met something close to sixty men in my ring career, some tough, some tougher, some really good, but I want to say that the best man I ever fought is the man I outpointed this afternoon – Tommy Gibbons of St. Paul.

Sports editor for the *St. Louis Post-Dispatch*, John Wray, was on scene. He said Dempsey's heaviest guns were spiked by Gibbons' clinch-and-run tactics. Aside from administering a body mauling in close, the champ did not land with full force with either hand.

Gibbons was sick from a cruel body mauling, tired out, gasping for air through blood-flecked lips, clinging to the champ's left arm with a desperate two-handed clutch that defied the referee's best efforts to break, but true to his bulldog purpose, Gibbons lasted. When the gong ended the 15th round, Dougherty was "in the act of prying Gibbons loose from his thousandth (or more) grip on Dempsey's wing."

The result was a moral victory for Gibbons. He was outweighed by 13 pounds, older, less powerful, and fighting for little or no money. This made him the man of the hour.

However, Gibbons did not fight to win. Dempsey won 12-2-1.

Gibbons made it plain from the beginning that he was there with the sole thought of remaining the 15 rounds. To this end he employed masterful knowledge of defense, and clung like ivy to the champion throughout the match except at such times as he was running away or ducking and dodging his dynamic foe. In the middle stages of the fight, when Dempsey, exasperated and puzzled by his inability to reach his foe let up in his aggressive efforts, Gibbons took the offensive for a few moments. He had a shade in the 5th and 11th rounds and a draw in the 9th. For the rest it was a case of Dempsey tearing in, pounding his foe in the clinches and trying to wear him down and at the end there was not the slightest doubt that the champion had gained the verdict. Even the crowd, strongly biased in favor of Gibbons, had not a boo for the $5,000 hand-picked referee, brought on by the titleholder, when he made his decision.

Dempsey smiled before the fight, the first time he had done so. Usually, he was scowling and sullen. By the close of the bout, he was not smiling at all.

Dempsey could not land with full force because Gibbons was great at ducking and running away. Jack crowded in hard throughout, turned and twisted him around as if he was a boy, and was in good condition at the end. Still, Dempsey had poor timing and judgment of distance. The crafty and clever work of Gibbons had plenty to do with this. Often, Jack was late or short. Whether Dempsey was not the same as he was in 1921 or merely was not the same against a clever, shifting opponent as he was against a slower, heavier, or more aggressive and open target it would remain for future fights to prove.

The fight could be divided into three phases, with the first and third distinctly Dempsey, and the second slightly Gibbons. In the first 4 rounds, the agile Dempsey was at his best and Gibbons at his worst. Jack pounded punches to the head and body in close, turning Gibbons and seeking places to inflict punishment. Gibbons was clinging desperately, trying to block Dempsey's infighting. At times he ran, turning now and then to shoot lefts to the head or body.

At long range, Gibbons showed great cleverness in making Dempsey miss. But inside, Dempsey pounded away at any exposed part of Tom's anatomy.

Dempsey's blows were low on several occasions, but the mistakes were inconsequential and properly ignored. Dougherty was fair in that he allowed Dempsey to linger longer in the clinches than was necessary before breaking them, but he also ignored the "unreasonable holding of the challenger." Breaking Tom loose from a clinch at times seemed to require a hydraulic crane rather than a referee.

When Gibbons scored, it was all in the open, and he received a great ovation every time he landed. Many blows that Dempsey blocked or smothered received the same reception from the crowd.

By the end of the 4th round, Tom's lips were bleeding slightly, and he suffered from the constant body mauling from which all his head-rolling, body-twisting, running, and dodging could not elude.

But then Gibbons surprisingly rallied and flared during the 5th, 9th, and 11th rounds. He outpointed Dempsey in the 5th, rallied well in the 9th, and shaded the champ in the 11th. However, at no time did he land a blow that the champion seemed to mind in the least.

Gibbons had a trick to prevent Dempsey from doing damage in close. He seized Jack's left arm with both gloves and turned with it and avoided presenting any vulnerable spot for the right to hit. On the outside, Gibbons made Dempsey miss often. Dempsey fired blows hard enough to knock down a cathedral, but he hit the air. Dempsey did nine-tenths of the leading, while Gibbons rarely attacked. Tom's pecks to the body with his left had about as much effect on the champ as slapping him with a strip of bacon. Dempsey shook him up occasionally, but "that jaw and stomach were hard to hit squarely." Whenever Dempsey did land hard to the body, the effect could be seen in Gibbons' boxing.

Despite occasional flashes from Gibbons, by the 11th round, the effects of the grueling were beginning to show, and Tom was wearing down fast. The third and final phase of the fight saw Gibbons doing nothing but holding on. In the 12th, he did not make one lead, and in the last three rounds his attack was just a feeble attempt to make Dempsey believe he still was there. The final round was pitiful. Tom clung on at every occasion with both hands. The referee had to tear him loose, only to see him grab again. Dempsey struggled and landed some telling punches, but still could not get through to a vital place.

For the *Minneapolis Morning Tribune*, referee George Barton scored the fight for Dempsey, 10-2-3. Although he lost clearly, Gibbons gained the honor of being the first man to stay the limit with the Utah "Tigerman" since he won the championship. Dempsey's margin was so wide that the decision could not be questioned. Gibbons was tired and in bad shape in the last round, but managed to weather the storm by clinching at every opportunity. He held on like a leech, but still took severe punishment in the last round.

Dempsey was the aggressor from first to last, ever forcing the pace and endeavoring to batter his foe into submission. He smothered Gibbons' attack for the greater part of the fight. He held Tom with one arm and hit the stomach, heart, jaw, and back of his neck with his free fist. The crowd was surprised that Tom was able to stand up under such a heavy barrage of blows, and loudly cheered him round after round for remaining on his feet.

It was moral victory, because Dempsey had toppled men such as Willard, Fulton, Morris, Smith, Miske, Flynn, Brennan, etc., but could not drop Gibbons, let alone stop him.

Continuing, Barton said that while it was true that Gibbons fought largely on the defensive during the last four rounds, overall, he stood up and fought. He tried to stop Dempsey with slashing left hooks to the body and right hooks and crosses to the jaw. Whenever it looked as if he must succumb to the punishment, he would stage rallies. It took rare courage to face a murderous puncher for little to no pay. Carpentier was paid $200,000, Willard earned $100,000, and even Brennan earned between $40,000 and $50,000.

Barton said Dempsey was a foul fighter. He hit low at least seven times, hit on the breaks, and even after the bell. Once, Jack shoved Tom's head and shoulders through the ropes, struck him a savage blow in the face, and again as he pushed his head back. The referee allowed Dempsey to hold Tom with one arm and whack away with the other. He mauled him throughout, using every conceivable punch. But Gibbons never complained. A less courageous fighter would have claimed foul at least a dozen times. A couple times, Gibbons claimed the blows were foul/low, but he addressed his remarks to Dempsey, not the referee.

Gibbons' best rounds were the 5th and 6th, which he won, making the champ miss and driving home many blows to the face and body. However, his spurt proved to be only a flash in the pan, for Dempsey's wonderful stamina stood him in good stead and he came back with a vengeance in the next few rounds, battering Tom all over the ring. "Gibbons stopped punches today that would have killed an ordinary man." Ringsiders winced as Dempsey's heavy fists crashed against the St. Paul boy's body and face. "It seemed unbelievable that a human could stand up under such a savage attack." Tom was weak and wobbly at the finish, but did not show many marks, though his lips were cut and there were red welts over his left kidney and under his heart. Dempsey escaped unscratched, and even the wound over his left eye, sustained in sparring, was not reopened.

Barton was impressed with the champion. "Dempsey proved today that he is a real champion and that he is in excellent condition despite his long layoff. A man has to be in the best physical shape to go through 15 fast rounds as Dempsey did today under the pitiless rays of a scorching hot sun." He forced the pace throughout and seemed almost as fresh at the end as at the start.

> He was Gibbons' master at fighting and almost proved his equal at boxing. It was the consensus of opinion among sports writers and spectators that if Gibbons had opened up and traded punches with the champion with reckless abandon he would have been knocked out. No one, however, criticized Gibbons for fighting on the defensive whenever he could, for it was worth a fortune for him to stay the limit.

Tom took no foolish chances. No one protested the referee's decision. Yet, the fans sung Tommy's praises for staying the limit.

Afterwards, Gibbons said,

Yes, I guess I held a little toward the end, but Dempsey is a bigger and stronger man than I, and I was a little tired. My mind, however, was always clear and I knew what I was doing every minute of the fight. I learned enough about the champion to convince myself that I can fight a winning fight against him next time. I want another chance. I made my last effort for victory in the 11th round. At that time I thought I could win if my plan went through, but I had lost the stamina necessary to carry on the necessary sustained effort. The decision was fair, but I believe it will be different next time. Yes, I'm feeling fine.

Eddie Kane said, "The champion roughed it all the way and did as he pleased in the clinches without any interruption from the referee. ... Gibbons can beat Dempsey and the latter knows it. We want another chance."

Richard Henry Little said, "Personally, I like Tommy Gibbons, and I wanted to see him win, but although he frequently landed on the Dempsey countenance, it seemed of no more effect than slapping a stone wall with a feather duster." Dempsey was cool and collected throughout, never ruffled or bothered by anything Tom did. To annoy Dempsey at all, Gibbons would need to swing on him with a pickax. Being unable to do anything effective, Tommy's "only chance was to cover up and try to stick out the 15 rounds." Tom's fans were happy their hero had lasted.

Some, rather than giving Gibbons credit, or criticizing his style and methods, believed that Dempsey had slipped.:

Henry Farrell: "His marksmanship is off and his blows seem to lack the old time power he displayed against Carpentier."

Hype Igoe, *New York World*: "The champion...was not quite up to the Dempsey brand. He was a trifle short with his punches."

Damon Runyon, *New York American*: "He had all his old time form, but he was not the fighter that beat down the giant Willard at Toledo."

Grantland Rice, *New York Tribune*: "The vital spark has not been killed, but its once mighty flame has been dimmed."

W. O. McGeehan, *New York Herald*: "The inference now must be that Dempsey is going back."

The *Minneapolis Journal's* Edward Walker said all eyes now were on Gibbons as the only man Dempsey had failed to floor. His success in staying the 15 rounds meant a future fortune. Walker believed the champion had gone back, and his terrific sock was missing. However, Walker also said that Gibbons had remarkable defense, which was the feature of his work.

The contest was just fair, and short of thrills. "Gibbons never had a chance to win and was exceedingly lucky to last the 45 minutes of fighting." Walker scored it 12-3 in rounds for Dempsey. The intrigue was the question of how long Gibbons could last.

Dempsey, with a murderous body attack in the first three sessions, took all the pep out of the St. Paul challenger and at the start of the fourth stanza it looked like the curtains for Tommy. Tom stood stock still at times gasping for breath, but for some unknown reason Dempsey did not tear in with the ferocious attack that has swept all other challengers before him.

The champion went along just about as he pleased and never was in danger of defeat. About the only solid punch that Tom landed was in the fifth round, when he caught Dempsey with a left hook on the chin that sent the kingpin of the heavyweight division back on his heels.

Although only 12 ½ pounds larger at an alleged 188 vs. 175 ½ pounds, Dempsey used his weight on his rival in the clinches, and it had a telling effect. Tommy, after his spurt in the 4th and 5th rounds, found that his punches had no effect, and thereafter was content to stay the limit.

He hung on in the clinches to Dempsey's left like a leech. He clutched with both hands at times, tucking his head back on his shoulder to ward off Dempsey's right. Gibbons also made Dempsey do all the leading, and the second the champion came in he grabbed and hung on.

Gibbons was helpless in close except when he got his deathlike grip on Jack's left. Dempsey spun him out of clinches with ease and landed many effective punches on the breakaway.

Dempsey has gone back, there is no doubt of that. He is far from the man who sent Jess Willard, Billy Miske, Bill Brennan and Georges Carpentier to slumberland. The terrific sock was missing yesterday. … It was the first time that Dempsey has been called on to meet a fast and shifty boxer, such a fast moving target. Even when Tom was dog weary his head-slipping of punches was wonderful. Dempsey missed badly and his footwork has slowed up. Tom fought a heady battle.

The champion had several opportunities to send home his hard wallops, but passed them up. Tom was fazed on several occasions, but his excellent condition was a decided factor in his ability to withstand the attack.

Gibbons did not receive over 10 solid punches on the chin during the whole fight. Dempsey concentrated on a body attack, and it was well he did. It worked to perfection, slowed Tom up and made it possible for the champion to win in a walk.

A remarkable defense was the feature of Gibbons' work. He seemed to have elbows and arms in the way of a majority of the champion's blows. He always had something in the way.

Gibbons did not box as well as he has in bouts in the twin cities. That is easily explained. The challenger was facing Jack Dempsey, and just that had a tendency to keep him from his best form.

Ultimately, Gibbons was a boxer, not a knockout king. None of his punches halted the champ. His best punch was a left hook, which landed at intervals, but the effect was "nil." Dempsey left without hardly a mark, while Tom was battered badly. Yet, Tom was cheered from start to finish.

In the 1st round, after pummeling his body, Dempsey hurt Gibbons with a right to the cheekbone, which took a lot of the fight out of him. Walker believed that punch robbed Gibbons of any real chance to win. After taking a terrific body pummeling over the first 3 rounds, Gibbons had a good 4th round, boxing and landing well and opening the cut over Jack's right eye. He kept doing well in the 5th, blocking and scoring well. However, Dempsey sped up again in the 6th, and had it all his own way until the 11th, when Gibbons made another rally. However, Dempsey took the upper hand thereafter, and especially punished Gibbons in the 15th round.

Walker suspected that Dempsey might have been carrying Gibbons to some degree, hoping for another bout in a bigger city, where they could make even more money. Possibly some sympathy was shown because Tom was fighting practically for nothing. Jack seemed content to do what he needed to win the rounds, but not more.

Bide Dudley said a grim, relentless July sun looked down on the inflated cow town. The arena, glistening in its newness, hurled the heat rays back as a crowd of nearly 20,000 watched the superman of the ring lambast the popular Gibbons for 15 rounds. "Jack couldn't knock Tommy out because Tommy held on." "Each blow that Tommy landed, and they were few, brought forth cheer after cheer. It was a Gibbons crowd by 8 to 1. Jack couldn't knock him out because Tommy loved him so." Gibbons fought to survive, rather than to win, and he accomplished his goal. Yet, the crowd was pleased.

> The fight itself narrowed down on the Gibbons side to a strenuous effort to last the limit. Dempsey sought to knock his man out and did practically all the fighting. Tommy's embrace, however, was something he couldn't escape. It might be said Dempsey had his hands full while Tommy had his arms full.

In subsequent days, Harry Newman said most experts thought Dempsey was going back and slipping.:

Harry Smith, *San Francisco Chronicle*: "I certainly do think that Jack Dempsey is going back. .... His wallops lack the old sting."
George Wheeler, *St. Paul Pioneer Press*: "I believe that Dempsey's long lay-off has affected the champion. His blows don't seem to have the old smack."

Ed Wray, *St. Louis Post-Dispatch*: "I don't think that Dempsey's showing against Gibbons was quite up to the champion's best standard. The next time out I think that he will be better."

Fred Digby, *New Orleans Item*: "The old snap was missing against Gibbons."

Ed Walker, *Minneapolis Journal*: "It was a rotten fight from a boxing standpoint. Gibbons was in there trying to stay. I think that Dempsey has gone back. His old sock is diminishing."

However, Tom McDonald, *Great Falls Tribune*, said, "It sure was a great fight. Dempsey is still a bruising fighter with many years left in him."[1210]

W. C. Vreeland said it takes two to make a fight, and it did not require Sherlock Holmes to figure out from the majority of news reports that there was just one man doing the fighting, and that was Dempsey. The vast majority said Gibbons spent all of his time grasping Dempsey's arms and holding him in a vice-like grip.

It was a fight in name only. Dempsey tried to stop him but could not do so simply because of Tom's holding tactics. Gibbons did not fight to win, but to survive and last the limit. That was his plan and goal and that's all he did. The same thing happened occasionally to John L. Sullivan, who was knocking them over regularly, but met some who fought just to survive and did. That did not mean he couldn't punch or no longer was the same puncher. The same applied to Dempsey.

Vreeland also said do not believe the bunk that Gibbons earned nothing. He got paid to train in Shelby, earned for exhibitions leading up to the fight, money he only earned because he was matched to fight the champ, earned $100 to $400 a day for allowing folks to watch him train in Shelby, and would earn a lot from the moving pictures. He also would have more drawing power in the future. "All in all, Gibbons made more money from this bout than he has made in any previous match this year. He was well paid for a moral victory."

Federal government agents were attempting to thwart any effort to smuggle copies of the films outside the state into Canada and elsewhere, and planned to seize any copies that were transported outside of the state. Of course, they had been thwarted before, and likely would be again.[1211]

On July 6, the Associated Press reported that Kearns said Harry Wills probably would be Dempsey's next opponent. He was headed to New York to close negotiations for a Labor Day bout with Wills. "We want to box Wills, if for nothing more than to convince the public that Dempsey does not draw the color line and has no fear of him. The match was red

[1210] *New York Daily News*, July 6, 1923.
[1211] *Brooklyn Daily Eagle, Brooklyn Daily Times*, July 6, 1923.

hot a few months ago but for some reason it was sidetracked. It is my opinion that it will draw better than a return match with Willard." Kearns wanted the fight that would earn them the most money.

Kearns revealed (or claimed) that he still retained a 33 1/3% interest in the motion picture rights from the Gibbons fight. Gibbons had 25%, while Loy Molumby and Mayor Jim Johnson had a 41 2/3% share. "Plans are being made to exhibit them throughout the country immediately." Apparently, they didn't think the federal law would be an issue. It seemed that law enforcement was slackening in its intensity against boxing, or so many thought or hoped. The pictures were declared to be perfect.

No more than 12,000 saw the contest, according to C. A. Rasmusson, a collector of internal revenue in Montana. About 2,000, including women and children, crashed the gate after cutting and breaking down the barbed wire entanglement.

> Women with children in their arms even poured through the opening in the wire, and we couldn't stop them. As soon as the wires were cut, the crowd scrambled though, many of the women catching their dresses on the barbs on the wire. They did not even stop to attempt to loosen their skirts from the wire, but kept right on going, leaving parts of their dresses behind.[1212]

Hugh Fullerton said Dempsey had not gone back physically, but simply needed more fighting. Fullerton believed that the version of Dempsey who fought Gibbons would be beaten by Firpo or Wills. His timing was off. That said, Gibbons survived by hanging on. Fullerton believed that Dempsey would look much better in his next fight, in part as a result of getting the 15 rounds of work with Gibbons. The fact that he was strong and fresh in the 15th round proved that he was in superb condition. He actually got stronger and was boxing better after the 11th round, which showed that he was working his way back into his old form.

Dempsey needed real fights to be at his best, not sparring exhibitions. "He has told me half a dozen times that he needed fights. Wednesday he proved that he was right. He was strong, fast, a better boxer than he ever was before, but he was not hitting. This was partly because of the extreme cleverness of Gibbons, partly because Dempsey was missing his punches."

Fullerton said Dempsey hurt Gibbons in the 1st, but in the 2nd, 4th, and 5th rounds he allowed his smaller foe to outbox him and make him look bad in spots. However, after the 5th round, Gibbons was not dangerous. He could not hurt the champ, and he was weakening, while Dempsey kept forcing at every stage and never allowed him to get set. Tom began holding and trying to stick it out to the limit.

Robert Edgren echoed Fullerton's sentiments, saying Dempsey needed fights to get back his timing. He believed Firpo would have stopped him within 6 rounds if they had fought on the 4th of July. Waiting around for

---

[1212] *Minneapolis Journal*, July 6, 1923. The government tax owed was $22,000.

big $300,000 purses was not good for a champion. He needed to keep fighting to keep his eye keen. "In the days when he fought every couple of weeks he hit naturally and instinctively, and his timing of punches was perfect." Edgren thought Dempsey should fight often, against guys like Greb, Fulton, Renault, or anyone else who could give him a fight, and demand no guarantee, but get the work and get back his punch.

Dempsey always was nervous before a fight, and Gibbons played upon that with his experience, delaying his entry into the ring, then taking a long time to tape his hands, while Dempsey's hands were taped already.

Now and then Dempsey would catch his timing by holding himself back deliberately, feinting and waiting before going in, and he hurt Gibbons. But the instant he started to press his advantage, he lost his timing again. Gibbons was good at holding and moving in close and leaning his weight onto Dempsey, keeping his chin tucked down. "But Dempsey did hit Gibbons around the head and neck a hundred times, while Tom was holding, and these punches wore Gibbons down gradually so that he was in danger of being knocked out if he had made a single mistake in the last three rounds." Yet, the careful Gibbons made no mistakes.

Once in a while, when the puzzled Dempsey stopped and stood straight up, Gibbons instantly would fire in a hard left hook, sometimes followed by a right, landing cleanly, but he never dazed Dempsey. Tom could land, but he never followed up, perhaps fearful of the return fire. The referee was fair, for although Dempsey was rough on the inside, Dougherty also allowed Gibbons to kill at least half of the time by hanging on.

Edgren thought Harry Wills might be losing his effectiveness too, for he had not fought since September 1922.

Edward Walker said Gibbons would make more money than ever before. The films would net him a tidy sum. Offers for his services were pouring in. He even had an offer for a vaudeville tour.

Gibbons came through the fight in much better condition than expected. He had two black eyes, a pair of mighty sore sides, and his left ear was mussed up.

Tommy said,

> I had been warned about Dempsey's left, and was watching for it, which gave him the opportunity to get in a good many licks with his right. ... Dempsey's strongest punch is his left. It was a right that wobbled me in the first round. It was high on the cheek bone and hurt. Dempsey can not jab with his left but hooks. He is a great puncher, but not the man killer he has been painted. I have been hit just as hard by Billy Miske. ... Jack's punches are hard but you can see them coming. If he had had speed he would have knocked me out of the ring.[1213]

[1213] *Minneapolis Journal*, July 6, 1923.

The bout's timekeeper, Richard T. Burke of New Orleans, said Dempsey fouled Gibbons with several low blows, though Burke did not believe it was intentional. During the fight, Dempsey never spoke, but Gibbons said in an early round, "Jack, get 'em up." Gibbons showed Burke the black-and-blue marks from the blows that landed low.

Dempsey's left eye was black. Having reached Salt Lake City on the 6th, he said, "I'm disappointed over not knocking out Tommy Gibbons, but I found him a pretty tough boxer. ... I didn't get hit real hard after the first two or three rounds." When asked why he missed so often, Jack replied, "I did miss quite a few of them I guess, but he was a clever little boxer, one of the hardest that I have gone against."

Regarding his future, Jack said, "I don't know what I will do next. Jack Kearns is making arrangements for a bout in the East, possibly with Harry Wills in New York." In the meantime, he would visit with his mother.[1214]

Herman Loewe, a Milwaukee salesman who claimed to have seen every heavyweight champion in action from Sullivan in 1882 to the present, was as enthusiastic about Dempsey as ever. He believed that Jack had gone forward, not backward. Loewe said Dempsey was the greatest fighter of all time, and could have beaten all of the past champions. "Of course it is difficult to make a comparison between Dempsey and the old-time fighters, because the rules of the game have changed so much. ... But Dempsey is the supreme, the superfighting man of all time."

Loewe said the only reason Dempsey was not able to knock out Gibbons was because Tom was able to race about the ring and then clinch throughout the bout, hanging on almost at will. Hence, Loewe did not believe the champion had lost his punch. He noted that Gibbons wore his trunks very high, giving the impression that the champ was hitting low when he was not. "Gibbons looked as though he was wearing a kimono when he entered the ring. He had his trunks way up over his stomach."

Dempsey fought under adverse circumstances, for he and Kearns both were extremely unpopular with the crowd. Loewe said it is possible that in view of that fact, the champ was content to joggle along with a comfortable lead, not trying for a kayo.

The bout enabled Dempsey to show the world that he could go the distance without getting tired and that he was a master boxer, beating a clever man like Gibbons. "We should be proud of a champion like Dempsey, for it is my guess we will never have another one like him. He is superb in the ring in every detail. His great stamina, his cleverness, his fighting head, his good hands, his fast feet, his perfect fighting body, his peculiar weave and his general performance between the ropes make him a champion who has never been duplicated." While he was champion, no one had him groggy, tired, or hanging on. Perhaps one day someone would, but even then, "I think Dempsey will be able to withstand

1214 *San Francisco Examiner*, July 7, 1923.

something he perhaps has never shown, severe punishment, and in the end will triumph."[1215]

On July 9, the Stanton Trust & Savings Bank closed its doors. Interestingly, George Stanton claimed that the financing of the fight had nothing to do with it. Stanton traced the bank's failure to conditions prevailing following the war and lack of confidence by depositors following the failure of two other banks in Great Falls. The bank entered into voluntary liquidation.[1216]

The First State Bank of Shelby, the second bank to collapse (supposedly) as a result of Dempsey-Gibbons, closed its doors on July 10. Mayor Jim Johnson, bank president, allegedly had sunk more than $150,000 into the fight. George Stanton had advanced $50,000. A state bank examiner took charge of the Stanton Trust and Saving Bank, which stopped payments on the 9th.

The *Great Falls Tribune* reported that the inability to get ready cash caused the banks to close. The institutions were indebted only to depositors, and the closures had nothing to do with the fight, so they declared.

So, at least two Montana banks associated with the fight closed within a week of the fight, both banks claimed the fight had nothing to do with it, but certainly the timing seemed odd.

Opinion was expressed that the real losers were the concessionaires, the guarantors who purchased large blocks of tickets and had to sell them at a loss, and individual businessmen who made "donations" to help meet the purse.

Jack Dempsey wanted to fight again soon. He said, "My bout with Tommy Gibbons taught me one thing, and that is that I must keep fighting. No more long layoffs for me. It makes no difference whether Kearns signs Harry Wills, Willard, or Firpo to box me. They all look alike to me. But I want to fight one of them on Labor Day."[1217]

[1215] *Great Falls Tribune*, July 9, 1923.
[1216] *Missoulian*, July 10, 1923.
[1217] *New York Daily News, Great Falls Tribune, Brooklyn Daily Times, Brooklyn Daily Eagle*, July 11, 1923.

CHAPTER 15

Luis Firpo

The next big fight on the horizon was Luis Firpo vs. Jess Willard, the battle of the giants. Willard was coming off the big comeback knockout win over Floyd Johnson. Since knocking out Bill Brennan in 12 rounds, Firpo had scored three more knockouts: KO3 Jack McAuliffe II, KO2 Italian Jack Herman, and KO2 Jim Hibbard. Willard was the well-respected former champion who had proven that he still had it, while Firpo was the exciting, impetuous, power-puncher who was mowing them down and enthralling the fans. At that point, Firpo had the best knockout percentage in boxing.

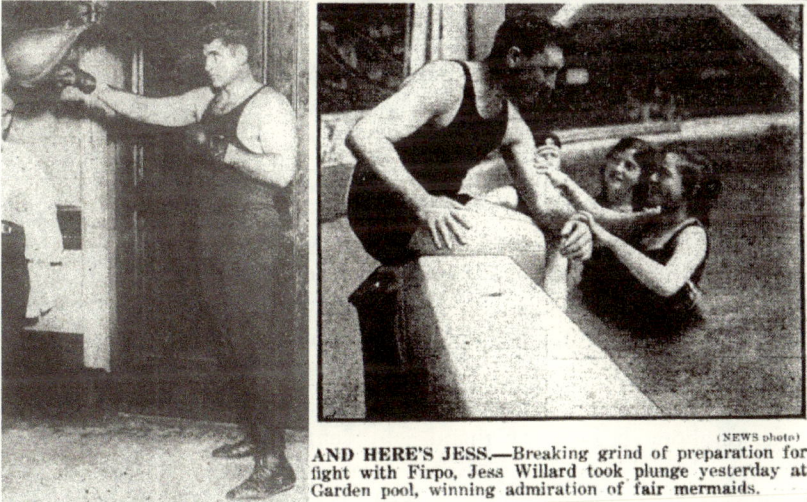

(NEWS photo)
AND HERE'S JESS.—Breaking grind of preparation for fight with Firpo, Jess Willard took plunge yesterday at Garden pool, winning admiration of fair mermaids.

Bill Tate, Firpo's current sparring partner, said Firpo packed a wicked wallop, as hard as Dempsey's.[1218]

[1218] *Binghamton Press,* July 7, 1923. *Brooklyn Standard Union,* July 10, 1923.

FIRPO   WILLARD

26, AGE, 41
214 WEIGHT 241
79 REACH 84
6'2½" HEIGHT 6'7"

17"NECK 18"
8¼" WRIST 8"
13½" BICEPS 16"
CHEST,
44"NORMAL 49"
48½"EXPANDED 53"
36½ WAIST 36"
23¾" THIGH 25"
15" CALF 15½"
9½" ANKLE 9½"

On Thursday July 12, 1923 at Boyle's Thirty Acres in New Jersey, before a massive world's record crowd of over 100,000, in what was labeled as the Battle of the Giants, in a scheduled 12-round no decision contest, 6'2 ½" 26-year-old 214-pound "Bull of the Pampas" Luis Firpo knocked out former champion 6'6 ½" 41-year-old 242-pound Jess Willard in the 8th round. Jess fought gallantly and competitively, but ultimately was unable to resist the powerful Firpo's charges and heavy onslaughts. Firpo was ahead throughout, winning nearly every round.

The press reported that in the 1st round, a Firpo right drew blood from Willard's ear. In the 4th round, Firpo stung Willard with a right the jaw, administering punishment, but Jess clinched and recovered. Firpo seemed surprised that Jess stood up to his blows. Willard kept fighting back, landing here and there, getting some respect, holding him even in the 5th, but the aggressive Firpo had been more effective overall up to that point. By the 6th round, Willard's body was red from the clubbing rights. In the 7th, a Willard left jab opened a small cut under Firpo's right eye or had it bruised, depending on the source. Firpo landed a big right to the body, dodged a right, and drove a right to the jaw that staggered Willard just before the bell.

The films show that in the 8th round, utilizing measuring lead lefts, a series of about six Firpo overhand rights sent Willard down. Interspersed amongst those blows, Firpo feinted some right uppercuts when Willard bent over, but instead followed with the overhand clubbing rights, pounding him down to the canvas. Willard got to a knee but was not able (or did not want) to beat the count.

The press said Firpo floored Willard with a succession of rights and lefts to the head and jaw, and Jess could not beat the ten-count. One reported that a Willard tooth had been knocked out.

WILLARD

FIRPO

WILLARD   FIRPO   WILLARD   FIRPO

WILLARD   FIRPO

WILLARD

FIRPO

The *Brooklyn Standard Union* said Firpo had a peculiar, clumsy manner of throwing blows. His overhand right was like a baseball pitcher's motion. Willard mostly used his left, while Firpo mostly used his right. There was a great deal of clinching. The mauling that Firpo administered in the 4th, 7th, and 8th rounds took the fight out of Willard.

The huge, record crowd was the greatest mob of fight fans ever assembled, certainly something of which promoter Tex Rickard took note. The fight generated just under half a million dollars (some said more), second only to record-holder Dempsey-Carpentier. The *New York Daily News* reported the gross receipts were $429,920.70. The only reason it did not generate as much or more than the Carpentier fight was because the ticket prices were lower, with ringside seats selling for $15, and the cheapest seats for $1 ($50 was the highest for Dempsey-Carpentier). Still, it was a *non-title fight* that generated more money than most of history's world heavyweight *championship* contests up to that point.

The *Daily News* said more than 100,000 people were present, but paid admissions were 75,712. Firpo's 20% or 22% share was $85,984 (some said $110,000), while Willard's 32% or 35% share was $150,472 (some said $180,000). Willard made more than he did for fighting Dempsey, and Firpo made more than Dempsey did for fighting Willard for the championship. The fight was a huge financial bonanza. Rickard would earn well over $100,000. Of course, taxes had to be paid, and there were additional expenses, but nevertheless, it was a huge payday for all.

Firpo, the Wild Bull of the Pampas, won with his usual scowling, almost sullen appearance. Luis said, "He gave me hell all right, but I was the better fighter." "I am ready to fight any man in the world."

Jack Kearns, who was present at the fight, said Dempsey would slaughter Firpo, and would be ready for him any time. He said Dempsey's next opponent probably would be Harry Wills.

From Los Angeles, Dempsey said, "I am anxious to meet Firpo or Harry Wills and it is up to my manager, Jack Kearns, to sign up one of them for a match for me on Labor Day."

The feeling among experts was that Firpo was very big, strong, powerful, tough, determined, and relentless, a natural-born fighter, with stamina and grit, and was developing rapidly. Yet, his skills still needed polishing, and he was hittable. Jimmy De Forest was improving him, but he needed further development to be ready for a man like Dempsey, who was a master. It remained to be seen whether he could handle Dempsey's terrific blows. Hence, the champ would be the favorite if they fought.

Thomas Rice said Firpo boxed with Willard and showed his skill, demonstrating knowledge of the tricks of the trade and how to take care of himself. But Rice wondered whether Firpo had learned too much, sparring with Willard too often and too long, feeling that he had lost some of the ferocity that made him so good. His battering-ram tactics and odd style were what made him so effective, not boxing orthodoxy.

Jack Britton, former welter champion agreed. "Why teach him to be clever? It would spoil him. He's a natural fighter and a dangerous one."

Henry Farrell echoed the sentiment, saying teaching Firpo was a waste, for he was a club-swinger and rock thrower, who rarely used his left, and in the heat of battle discarded De Forest's teachings about blocking and using his left hand.

William Granger said Firpo still was clumsy, but deadly. He relied on his right so much that he often led with it. "Dempsey may beat the South American but if he does he will know he has been in a fight before he has Luis Angel on the floor for the full count." Granger thought Firpo and Wills should fight, with the winner to meet Dempsey. However, both likely would want a Dempsey fight without such an interim match.

Tom Dugan said he always backs the jockey, and in Jimmie De Forest, Firpo the wild man had the world's best boxing adviser. De Forest told

Firpo to focus on the heart, and by heeding that advice, he weakened Willard with body blows. Jess was able to cavort around the ring until Firpo made his mad rush and caught him in the body. Firpo hit him hard in the head in the clinches, too, especially in the 4th round. Conversely, not once did Willard hurt Firpo.

Robert Edgren said Firpo "has the stuff in him to give even Dempsey a battle," but needed to work on his left. "Give him a left hand and Dempsey's crown won't be safe, for Firpo has shown that he can take everything that comes his way, and still have the strength and grit and speed too, and above all the punch to win."

Jess Willard said Firpo was a good, game, tough, hard-hitting young fellow who would make "a great match for the champion."

Clearly, based on the record-size crowd, fans were intrigued by Firpo, especially when pitted against a championship-caliber man. Firpo had sent both Brennan and Willard down for the full count, whereas Willard retired in the corner against Dempsey (though he had taken the count at the end of the 1st round), and the referee stopped the Dempsey-Brennan contest after Brennan rose from the knockdown (although he was counted out). Brennan ended the Firpo fight unconscious and wound up in the hospital for several days. Firpo had pulverizing power, and the fans paid to see him fight. Hence, Rickard likely would try to make Dempsey-Firpo, because from an economic standpoint, it would be a financial bonanza, and he did not have to worry about the racial/political issues or fallout associated with a Dempsey-Wills contest.[1219]

Several days after the fight, Jimmy De Forest said Firpo fought just as he instructed him to do. He was not supposed to go after Willard until told to do so, and he wasn't really told to go after him until the 7th round. "Firpo is improving every day, but is not quite ready for Dempsey. However, I look for Luis to take on the champion in about another year."

Tex Rickard was baffled by De Forest's statement that Firpo was not yet ready for Dempsey. Tex wanted to promote Firpo-Dempsey next. "I cannot understand it. Only yesterday De Forest told me Firpo was ready and able to meet any one in the world." In the wake of Firpo's impressive knockout over Willard, Tex thought a Firpo-Dempsey fight was ripe.

Harry Newman noted that Harry Wills had been waiting patiently for a crack at Dempsey, but promoters had been wary about trying to put it on.

Jack Dempsey had to pay $77,146 to the government in income taxes for the Gibbons fight. Kearns would be taxed $38,533.[1220]

Kearns said he wanted a fight with Firpo and then one with Wills. "I am anxious to have them in that order." They wanted 50% of the gate. Apparently, Kearns was in discussions for a Wills fight at Yankee Stadium with promoter Jimmy Johnston, who claimed to have some assurance that the commission would sanction it. Kearns also said, "Dempsey and I have decided to get a date for Labor Day, and we are going to get it. If New

[1219] New York Daily News, Brooklyn Daily Times, Brooklyn Standard Union, Brooklyn Citizen, Buffalo Times, Buffalo Courier, Passaic Daily Herald, July 13, 1923; New York Daily News, July 14, 1923.
[1220] New York Daily News, July 14, 15, 1923; Brooklyn Daily Eagle, July 15, 1923.

York promoters can't stir up something we'll go out to the Middle West and meet Gibbons or Greb." Tom O'Rourke also was bidding for the champ's services. However, Kearns said, "No one has shown us any dough." After Shelby, he wanted sufficient guarantees posted before he would sign any papers. Promoters could say any number, but that did not mean they actually had said amount. Kearns wanted to deal with promoters who already had the money to pay in full, and would post it, or at least had a proven track record of doing so, like Rickard.[1221]

The next day, Rickard said Dempsey-Firpo was close to being finalized, save a few details. "I have Firpo under contract to meet Dempsey this year and if I am unable to make the match I am no promoter." He believed the fight was so lucrative that it had to be made.[1222]

On July 18, the United States Department of Justice in Los Angeles seized copies of the Dempsey-Gibbons fight pictures. Just how they were brought into the state was a mystery. Harry Grossman, who was at Dempsey's home, said he had made the pictures, and surrendered them voluntarily. He claimed that the films would be developed in Los Angeles and then shown in Montana only. The government said the films were seized pursuant to a search warrant.

> They were in a local studio. We are going to try to find out who brought them into California. That act was a violation of the law. The rule is against transporting the pictures from the State in which they are made. Apparently the man who exhibits such pictures and who has no connection with their being brought in is not subject to punishment.[1223]

Of course, it could be challenging to prove exactly who brought the films across state lines. The person who had the films did not necessarily transport them, nor would he be inclined to name names, assuming he knew, and if subpoenaed, that person always could assert his 5th amendment right against self-incrimination. It seemed that once the films were transported across state lines, they could be successfully and legally exhibited.

On July 25, Tex Rickard announced that he had made the Dempsey-Firpo match, and articles had been signed by Kearns and Firpo. As usual, Tex had beaten out the competition. He knew how to offer the coin, provide guarantees, and come through. Harry Wills would have to wait longer, out in the cold yet again.[1224]

Just two weeks after Firpo-Willard, on July 27, 1923 in Grand Rapids, Michigan, 227-pound Luis Firpo knocked out a reported 200- or 201-pound (according to press reports) or 193-pound (according to the commission) Joe Burke (a former Gibbons sparring partner) in the 2nd

[1221] *Buffalo Courier, Brooklyn Citizen*, July 17, 1923.
[1222] *Brooklyn Daily Times*, July 18, 1923.
[1223] *New York Daily News*, July 19, 1923.
[1224] *Brooklyn Citizen, New York Daily News*, July 25, 26, 1923.

round with a right to the heart. Firpo had decked Burke in the 1ˢᵗ round as well, with a right to the neck.[1225]

It was announced that Dempsey-Firpo would be held on September 14 at the Polo Grounds in New York. It would be scheduled for 15 rounds to a decision. Ticket prices would range from $3 up to $25, the highest amount the commission would allow.

It was understood that Firpo would be paid $100,000 plus a cut of the motion pictures, while Dempsey's end "may run to $400,000." The arena would seat about 80,000.

Dempsey planned to train at Thomas C. Luther's White Sulphur Springs Hotel in Saratoga Lake, New York, starting in early August.

The combination of Dempsey's showing against the smaller Gibbons, and the larger-sized Firpo's showing against the even bigger Willard garnered a great deal of interest in the fight. Folks did not think Dempsey was impervious to defeat, and there was an aura of risk, given that Firpo was young, strong, taller, heavier, longer, very powerful, and had proven his stamina in a big fight. Others said Firpo hit hard with this right, but Dempsey hit hard with both hands, was faster, more experienced, and better skilled than Firpo.

Firpo noted, "I have done everything I have been asked to do. I have knocked out every opponent I faced."

Rickard also had arranged a world middleweight championship fight between champion Johnny Wilson and Harry Greb, set for August 31. Greb finally was going to get another middleweight title shot.

When asked to compare them, Jess Willard said, "Luis Firpo hits a heavier and more crushing blow than Dempsey, but it is not as snappy as Dempsey's punch. The hardest puncher I ever met was Jack Johnson, and he was the best all around fighting man I ever met." Yet, Johnson was even better at defense than offense. Willard also said Firpo could take it. Jess noticed that his blows had little effect on Luis.

Regarding the loaded gloves rumors, Willard said, "Yes, I have read the stories charging Dempsey with having had lead in his glove…but if he had I knew nothing of it then, and know nothing now except what I have read. It is true that his blows did seem to cut me out of proportion to their heft, but I have no kick coming."

Regarding his opposition to Dempsey-Wills, Willard said,

> I have nothing against Wills personally, and he is reported to be an exceptionally clean cut fellow, but the fact remains that whether he wins or loses with Dempsey, the bout will create race disorder in this country and elsewhere. … I am afraid the element opposed to boxing would use a Dempsey-Wills match as a means of killing the game sooner or later.

Hence, Jess did not think Dempsey-Wills would or should be made.[1226]

[1225] *Detroit Free Press, Brooklyn Daily Eagle, Akron Beacon Journal, Battle Creek Enquirer and Evening News*, July 28, 1923.
[1226] *Elmira Star-Gazette* July 28, 1923; *New York Daily News, Brooklyn Citizen, Brooklyn Daily Eagle*, July 29, 1923.

OUTALUCK.—Harry Wills and his manager, Paddy Mullins, yesterday protested to boxing board against Firpo getting Dempsey match, but plea fell on deaf ears.

Harry Wills and his manager Paddy Mullins were frustrated by the fact that fight promoters were ignoring them. They complained to the New York Commission. The commission responded that no promoter had applied for a license to conduct a Dempsey-Wills match, so there was nothing for them to do. Essentially, Wills was being told to "get a promoter," one ready, willing, and able to back financially a match with Dempsey. That was the commission's way of washing its hands of the matter, for now.

Tex Rickard said, "I think Firpo is a much better opponent for Dempsey than is Wills."

On July 31, 1923 at the Queensboro A.C. stadium in Long Island City, Queens, New York, before a crowd of more than 7,000, 174-pound Gene Tunney won a 12-round judges' decision over Boston's 175-pound Dan O'Dowd, retaining his American light heavyweight championship. Gene cuffed O'Dowd at will, while O'Dowd rarely landed.

Dan O'Dowd   Gene Tunney

However, the *Daily News* said Tunney's punches lacked power, and despite his efforts, he could not rock the Bostonian to sleep. Billy Gibson said Gene hurt his right hand in the 4th round, which affected him. The *Brooklyn Daily Times* reported that Tunney did not create much of an impression, failing to land a damaging punch on the defensive O'Dowd. The *Brooklyn Daily Eagle* said, "Tunney gave a decidedly poor exhibition." He missed often, and his punches lacked power. "Tunney was bad. O'Dowd was worse. Dan made few attempts to fight back, apparently being content to stay the limit."[1227]

Harry Wills was frustrated by his inability to obtain a championship match. He felt that he should have been considered before Firpo as Dempsey's next opponent. But since the commission was not willing to back him, he would have to wait. Some said he had not been fighting enough, having been inactive for the past year, and had turned down several matches, including one with George Godfrey. Harry replied,

[1227] *Moline Daily Dispatch, New York Daily News, Brooklyn Daily Times, Brooklyn Daily Eagle,* August 1, 1923. Tom Gibbons had stopped O'Dowd in 3 and 6 rounds.

We haven't turned down an offer without a good reason. I didn't want to go on in a preliminary bout of a big show because I felt I was better than some of the men in the main bouts. I never turned down any big offers with any of the contenders, because no such big offers were made. I haven't dodged fights. I have fought twenty-two fights while Dempsey has fought four. I am in condition all the time. They say I looked bad in my last big fight with Clem Johnson, but I haven't seen anyone do much better against Johnson. [Wills had stopped black Clem Johnson twice – 1921 KO6 and 1922 KO12.]

They said I want set-ups, but I never did have a list of set-ups handed me like Firpo got for his build up. I have nothing against Firpo, but sometimes I do get peeved when I think that a foreigner can come to this country and pick up over a quarter of a million dollars for fighting opponents that they wouldn't let me fight. I want to fight Dempsey because I think I can win the title. ... I'm ready for the fight if they'll let me fight.[1228]

The black-owned *New York Amsterdam News* wrote that a stiff rumor was going the rounds in Harlem that the reason why Wills had not been successful in getting a Dempsey fight was because his manager Paddy Mullins "is top tight with the dough. It is said by certain ones in a position to know that a few hundred dollars spent judiciously would have brought about the contest, but Paddy refuses to function like other managers..." This paper criticized that Mullins, as a white man, was not handling the top challenger to the throne in the manner that he should, for he should have doggedly trailed Dempsey and Kearns.

When Kearns realized that he was in bad on account of the Shelby fiasco, he announced that he was coming to New York to make Dempsey-Wills, but this paper called that a lot of bunk, though many fell for it. "We know better." "Wills lost his chance and if Dempsey wins from Firpo, which we expect him to do, the champion of the whites will be hitting the road, raking in the shekels from the stage and then going to the mountains to rest up until they discover another ham while Wills will be cooling his heels."

If Firpo won, he would return to Argentina and bask in his honors for a long while, so Wills still would be no better off. Hence, Harry might as well remain active and pick up purses where he could. The McMahons were ready to stage a Wills-Tate fight, which this paper supported.[1229]

Dempsey said he was anxious to be fighting Firpo, who was a dangerous and worthy rival, not afraid of anyone. "I'm not underestimating him. Anyone who can punch like he can is dangerous, and I won't take any chances with him." A puncher always had a chance.

[1228] *Brooklyn Citizen*, August 1, 1923.
[1229] *New York Amsterdam News*, August 1, 1923.

"That's what brought home the bacon." Nan Collins, casting director at the United Studios, is shown holding Jack Dempsey's million-dollar arm.

Still, Jack also said he would rather be fighting Wills first, for Harry had asked for a fight before anyone ever heard of Firpo. Regardless, "Fighting is my business and I'll fight anybody."

Dempsey thought Wills would be his next opponent after the Firpo bout. Jack attributed his performance in the Gibbons fight to his long layoff. "I'm as good as ever, but I was a little rusty." Still, he admitted that Gibbons was a great fighter. Jack was willing to rematch him.[1230]

Even with the Dempsey fight scheduled, Firpo kept fighting, earning money, gaining experience, and remaining fight sharp.

On August 3, 1923, in Omaha, Nebraska, 3,000 or 5,000 saw 214 ½-pound Luis Firpo win a 10-round decision over 188 ½-pound Homer Smith (45-22-7), who went down multiple times and fought purely to survive.

The *Omaha Daily News* said Smith was able to go the distance because of his ability to run, wrestle, box, stall, and clinch. He went to the floor 15 times, including 5 times in the 6th round. Sometimes he was knocked down, and at other times he dropped down intentionally in order to survive and get a 9-second rest. Firpo fired hard uppercuts, rights, and jabs.

The *Omaha Bee* said Smith took 9-counts 16 times, and was on his "bicycle" the rest of the time, in there to stay the limit.

Both of these local papers believed Firpo had carried him a bit.

Ed Hughes said, "Firpo, in my judgment, is as good a boxer now as he ever will be. And that isn't saying much." De Forest had tried, but Firpo just would not polish. He was by nature a pure slugger.

Sandy Griswold, while admitting that Firpo won every round, predicted that Dempsey would stop him in the 1st round.

Sid Sutherland said Smith went down 20 times. Firpo was a "marvelous specimen of pugilistic splendor. He has everything – the build, the strength, the willingness." He could hit like a "falling skyscraper" with his right, and he was trying to connect all the time. If he ever connected solidly to the chin or solar plexus "of any man on earth he will stop him dead in his tracks." Still, Firpo would be lucky to hear the bell for the 5th round with Dempsey, unless Jack had gone back and elected to indulge in right-hand slugging. "Anybody who slugs with Firpo without boxing, too, will be knocked out."[1231]

[1230] *Brooklyn Daily Eagle, Buffalo Times*, August 2, 1923.
[1231] *Omaha Daily News, Omaha Bee, Omaha Evening World-Herald*, August 4, 1923. Luis earned $5,000 plus 40% of the gate.

The *Daily News'* James Crusinberry noted that big fights were not made based on merit, but economics. Promoters had their eyes on the gate. Firpo had been knocking big fellows out, and the fans paid to see him, excited by his style and hard punch. A Dempsey-Firpo fight would be a big money maker, and Rickard could avoid all the difficulties he foresaw in making a black-white heavyweight championship contest, and all of the potential fallout even if it did take place. So Harry Wills once again was crowded into the background.[1232]

Firpo had another upcoming fight scheduled, with Charley Weinert. Certainly, Firpo was remaining fight sharp, and capitalizing financially upon the fact that he was the next man that Dempsey would face. This helped garner more interest in the big fight as well. The only risk was that he potentially could lose or get hurt.

Harry Wills said if Firpo lost, he would be happy to step in and take his place. "As to Firpo, I think that if Dempsey is half the man he was when he licked Carpentier and Willard he ought to beat that bird Firpo easily."[1233]

On August 13, 1923 in Philadelphia, before a crowd of about 28,000, 212-pound Luis Firpo stopped 188-pound Charley Weinert, (58-17-5), in the 2nd round, decking him three or four times in that round. Firpo earned $20,000. The Dempsey fight was one month away.

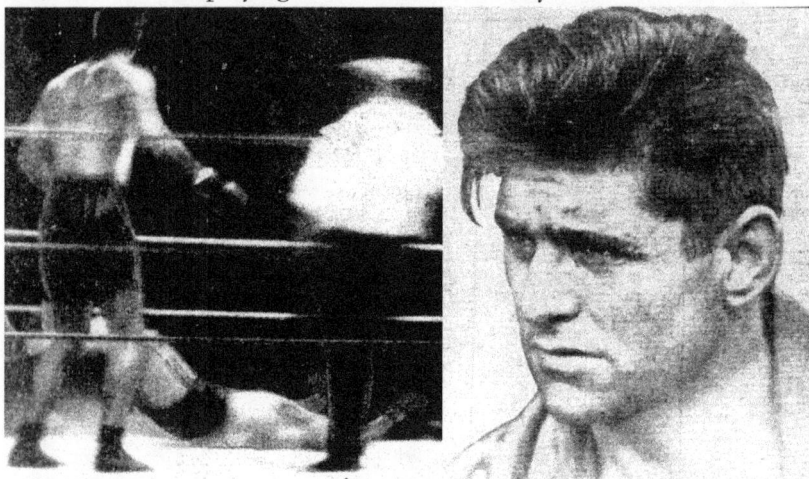

The local *Philadelphia Inquirer's* Gordon MacKay said, "Firpo again demonstrated that his crudity as a boxer is woeful, but that his right fist is a menace to anybody when it lands. Jack Kearns…was on hand to watch the mill and he evidently carried back a message that will instill wholesome respect for the Latin's right mauler to the champion."[1234]

1232 *New York Daily News*, August 5, 1923.
1233 *New York Daily News*, August 9, 1923.
1234 *Philadelphia Inquirer, Brooklyn Citizen*, August 14, 1923; *New York Daily News*, August 13, 14, 1923.
Weinert's record included victories over Gunboat Smith (1915 WND10), Porky Dan Flynn (1915 WND10), Willie Meehan (1920 WND12), and Battling Levinsky (1921 W15), but losses to Billy Miske (1917 LND10 twice and 1922 LND12), Fred Fulton (1917 LKOby2), Harry Greb (1921 L15), and Gene Tunney (1922 LND12 and LKOby4)).

Henry Farrell, for the United Press, said Firpo was dangerous because he had a tremendous punch combined with the heart to come back under punishment. He might be crude and rough, and did not particularly use his left, but he had the hardest right in the business. It was veritable dynamite.

Firpo's "desire to save a few dollars caused him to break relations with Jimmy De Forest, his trainer. If Dempsey has any weakness, there is no one who should know it better than De Forest, and if there is one man in the world who could train Firpo properly for such an important fight, that one man certainly is De Forest."[1235]

Jack with a leopard cub, a gift from an admirer

A report out of Oil City, Pennsylvania claimed that Dempsey allegedly had accepted an offer of $100,000 to fight Greb in Johnstown in early October, according to promoter Fred Kelly. Greb had accepted $25,000 for the match.

Another report several days later claimed that Dempsey would box Greb in a 10-round no decision at Forbes field, Pittsburgh, on September 28, although final arrangements had not yet been completed. Such claims seemed unlikely, given that Dempsey was scheduled to fight Firpo on September 14, and for a whole lot more money.[1236]

Road work with trainer Jerry Luvadis

Wrestling with Luvadis

Rowing on Saratoga Lake

Dempsey playing with his dog

[1235] *Plainfield Courier-News*, August 13, 1923.
[1236] *Pittsburgh Post, Brooklyn Standard Union*, August 14, 1923; *Buffalo Express*, August 18, 1923.

Every day at Saratoga Lake, hundreds came to see Dempsey train, even at $10 round trip by taxi and 50 cents admission.[1237]

Jimmy De Forest had been training Firpo for his U.S. fights, but for the Dempsey contest, he would not be working with him, and was dismissed. He had been working on Firpo's skill, but skill and defense were not his forte, but hard punching and strength. He was as strong as an ox, not a boxer, but a man who tried to beat down his foes. Folks said he was about as good as he ever was going to get.[1238]

Firpo's handler, Senor Felix Bunge, said Firpo had science and skill all his own, and North American methods were not necessary. Luis now was being trained by Horatio Lavalle, who with Firpo had made a careful study of Dempsey's technique and methods by watching motion pictures of his fights. Bunge said Firpo was not merely a wild bull. His science was sufficient, and the criticism of his style unwarranted. They were training Firpo how to beat Dempsey using "methods which we believe to be superior to North American methods."

> He will beat Dempsey because he is stronger, quicker and more scientific, and because we know Dempsey while Dempsey does not know us. … Firpo has been criticized for wasting blows on his opponents' arms. Anyone who has ever felt the paralyzing effect of Firpo's right on the biceps realizes that such a blow is not wasted. It is not true that Firpo does not know how to use his left, but he uses it in a different way than do the North American fighters, and in a manner that fits in effectively with his style.[1239]

Dempsey and fly champ Pancho Villa

Dempsey was training with world flyweight champion Pancho Villa of the Philippines, who also had an upcoming bout. Hence, the biggest and the smallest world champions were training together.[1240]

Robert Edgren said Harry Wills was good about five years ago, but had gone back so far that he had not done any fighting for the past year. "No doubt his manager thinks it foolish to send Wills in to show how much he has deteriorated, which might spoil all chance to induce people to pay big money to see a Wills-Dempsey match." Edgren said Wills was showing his age. "He used to box. Of late he has only roughed and wrestled and punched in clinches, where his bulk and the strength

[1237] New York Daily News, August 15, 1923.
[1238] Brooklyn Citizen, August 16, 1923.
[1239] Buffalo Times, August 18, 1923.
[1240] Binghamton Press, August 17, 1923. George Godfrey, Jack Burke, and Jules Rioux (also called Elzear or Eleazar R. Rioux) would arrive and act as Dempsey's sparring partners. Binghamton Press, Glens Falls Post-Star, August 16, 1923.

gained in working as a longshoreman has helped him. His early speed has disappeared." His recent fights were "merely exhibitions of holding and hitting in clinches." Tex Rickard made it clear that he did not want anything to do with a Dempsey-Wills match. "He thinks it might kill boxing in New York and perhaps in other states."[1241]

On August 16, Dempsey ran on the mountain road, swam in the lake, and played golf. In the afternoon, he sparred with George Godfrey and 6'4" 203-pound Eleazar Rioux, a French-Canadian woodsman who had a rough, awkward style of hitting, much like Firpo.[1242]

Frank Menke noted that although folks enjoyed watching him fight, Dempsey was not popular with the fans and general public, owing to his draft dodger reputation; even though he beat the charges. They still felt he should have joined up anyway. He was boyish, sincere, and likable, and ought to have been the greatest pugilistic idol of all time, yet was not so with the masses owing to the ugliest of charges – slacker. Others wanted him to lose because they did not like Jack Kearns, who they thought was greedy, and they saw Dempsey as his meal ticket and wanted him beaten as a result.

Fans generally rooted for his opponents more than they cheered for Dempsey. Such was the case with Miske, Brennan, Carpentier, and Gibbons. Carpentier was built up as the soldier hero, and the majority wanted to see the soldier win. Kearns' greed soured the Montana folks to Dempsey, and they cheered and rooted for Gibbons.

Some would root for Firpo too. But others would pull for Dempsey because they wanted the title to remain in North America and to be held by a U.S. citizen. They also believed that Firpo was greedy too, so they did not necessarily like him any better. Regardless, fans enjoyed watching both men fight, and would pay to see them in the ring.[1243]

Charley Weinert's manager, Babe Culnan, predicted that Dempsey would knock out Firpo in the 1st round. Firpo would try to fight him, and anyone who fought with Dempsey was going to get stopped quickly. He could not be outfought.

Jimmy De Forest said the Pampas prodder had great confidence and did not believe there was any man living who could out-maul him.

Bermondsey Billy Wells, who had been a Dempsey sparring partner in Great Falls, Montana, said Jack had not lost his punch. "I don't care what Dempsey showed in the ring at Shelby. You accept my word that Dempsey's wallop is as powerful as it ever was."[1244]

[1241] *Buffalo Times*, August 16, 1923.
[1242] *Buffalo Courier, Glens Falls Post-Star*, August 17, 1923. Rioux was called a real caveman.
[1243] *Hornell Evening Tribune-Times*, August 17, 1923.
[1244] *Elmira Star-Gazette*, August 17, 1923.

On August 17, 1923 in Indianapolis, Indiana, wearing 16-ounce gloves, Luis Firpo boxed Ohio heavyweight Joe Downey in a 10-round exhibition bout, each round lasting only 2 minutes. Firpo outpointed Downey clearly. The political powers-that-be threatened to stop the bout and arrest them if the contest became "rough" or if any participant was "floored" or "staggered." Firpo was warned to pull his punches and not to score a knockout, and he complied, to some degree.

However, by not stopping his man, ironically, he actually administered greater overall punishment. Unfortunately, shortly after the bout, Downey was so badly hurt that he fainted and collapsed in his dressing room. He was taken to a local hospital in a semi-conscious condition, suffering from severe head injuries.

Indiana Governor McCray had ordered them to use 16-ounce gloves, which ironically might have caused more damage, because instead of being stopped quickly, Downey absorbed more blows and took a terrific mauling. Sheriff Snider said Downey would have been knocked down had it not been for the fact that they boxed with 16-ounce gloves.

The locals were impressed with Firpo. "He made a good impression and acted like a fighter who would have at least a chance with Dempsey."[1245]

Dempsey was taking Firpo seriously. He said Firpo hit hard enough to stop world-class fighters like Gunboat Smith, Bill Brennan, and Jess Willard. Despite what many were saying, Firpo had to have some skill and defense or those men would have stopped or beaten him, because they all had skill, experience, and could punch.

Dempsey also said if someone was better than him, he did not want to be champion. "That's why I want to fight Wills, if I get by Firpo. Loads of people think he can lick me and I want to prove to them that they are wrong or that I am wrong."

Tex Rickard agreed that Firpo was going to give Dempsey the fight of his life, and possibly might stop him.

> Firpo is young, strong, fired with ambition, a murderous puncher and he has been fighting regularly, which helps his judgment of distance, whereas Dempsey has had but one fight in two years, has tasted of the high life and no longer has the championship goal to strive for. In a sense, Dempsey has reached the shore and is sitting pretty. It's a lot different when you are on top as compared to when you are climbing.

Firpo was going after the championship, "and he has that courageous spirit, characteristic of the Latin race." Tex said Firpo had the strength of a bull, could take a punch and a beating, and had great stamina, carrying his power late into fights. "Dempsey will have to knock him cold to win. I for one don't think Dempsey strikes a harder punch than Firpo." Tex said

[1245] *Buffalo Commercial, Indianapolis News, Indianapolis Star*, August 18, 1923. Joe Downey's 9-5-1 record included: 1921 LKOby9 and LKOby11 Martin Burke; D12 Dick O'Brien; 1922 LKOby10 Jack Burke; and 1923 LKOby1 Homer Smith.

Firpo was a much better puncher than Wills. Ultimately, Rickard said the fight was an even-money proposition.[1246]

On Saturday August 18, for hospital and church benefits, Dempsey gave 3-round exhibitions at both Schenectady and Saratoga. Pancho Villa also participated. Dempsey boxed with Charles Schwartz, the millionaire banker, race fan, and amateur boxer, and George Godfrey.[1247]

Folks wrote the black-owned *New York Age*, protesting the "raw deal given Harry Wills, the logical contender for Dempsey's crown." The New York Boxing Commission deserved no respect. "This is clearly a case of political graft and unless stopped right now, boxing in the future is destined to lose its dignity." Rickard deliberately had defied the wishes of the New York public, which by a large majority had asked for a Dempsey-Wills contest. Quite a few papers took a straw vote, and each time, Dempsey-Wills won out. Paying money to see the Firpo fight was a way to reward Rickard and Kearns for avoiding Wills. Hence this writer encouraged a boycott.[1248]

In an interview with Hype Igoe, Jimmy De Forest said he did not understand Firpo, who had told him that they never would part, and he wanted to be with him always. "It is the others want me-you part." Jimmy did not understand why the Firpo camp would discard him just when Luis needed him the most.

Speaking of Dempsey, De Forest fondly said Jack was a splendid, fine fellow. Mrs. De Forest said Jack "used to buy dolls for little Virginia" and would "sit on the floor with her and make and help make doll's clothes."

Speaking of the allegation that De Forest loaded Dempsey's wraps for the Willard fight, De Forest said,

> I am accused of saying that Dempsey had iron, horseshoes, window weights or some other fool thing in his gloves at Toledo. I never said such a thing, for it is a lie from the beginning to end. Ray Archer, Willard's manager, sat in our dressing room talking to Dempsey, Kearns and myself as Jack wound the soft bandages around his hands. To say that he used other than tape to help his hands is robbing the boy of the credit of a great victory. I still have the gloves and bandages.

De Forest further said that when Dempsey first came to him, he was a wild hitter, always hurting his hands, and did not know how to hit properly. He had him continually carry and run with a little dumbbell in his left hand, and shadow box with it. He did not hurt his hands after that.[1249]

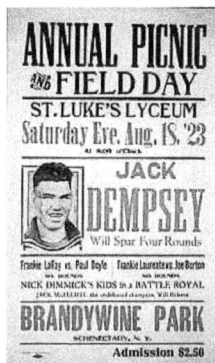

[1246] *Buffalo Commercial*, August 18, 1923.
[1247] *Glens Falls, Post-Star*, August 18, 1923; *Buffalo Morning Express, Rochester Democrat and Chronicle*, August 19, 1923; *Buffalo Commercial*, August 20, 1923.
[1248] *New York Age*, August 18, 1923.
[1249] *Detroit Free Press*, August 19, 1923.

On August 19 at White Sulphur Springs, Saratoga, New York, Dempsey sparred several rounds each with Godfrey and Joe Burke.[1250]

Luis Angel Firpo.

Firpo would train in Atlantic City.

Jess Willard said the upcoming fight was a toss-up. Both were tough, tearing fighters who ripped and slashed, "and it is merely a question of which one lands the first punch." Both hit very hard. "I consider Dempsey the greatest quick starter in the business, but I do believe that unless he cops in five rounds he will not cop at all. I honestly believe Dempsey is going to get the surprise of his life when he goes against Firpo."

On August 20, 195-pound Dempsey boxed 2 rounds each with Godfrey, Burke, and Rioux.[1251]

Luether's Hotel, White Sulphur Springs, where Dempsey stayed. An admirer asks for Jack's photograph.

On the 21st, during their 3 rounds, Dempsey showed his savage disposition against 240-pound Godfrey, pounding away and nearly having him out. Jack also boxed 3 rounds with lightweight Jack Bernstein.

C. J. Murray said there was not a mitt artist in the business who prepared more conscientiously for a fight than the champ. He trained willingly and in abundance. His danger was overtraining, not the opposite. "Dempsey is not kidding himself about Firpo. ... Firpo will not catch Dempsey napping." He was taking the fight seriously and looked marvelous in his workouts, up on his toes and moving quickly. He had his old fighting snarl and slashed his sparring partners unmercifully. The way he shot his punches was cruel. "He was as accurate as a bullet and hit with deadly force." Godfrey was the only one left who could lift an arm. Rioux and Jack Burke had been punched out of commission. Jack hit Godfrey with every conceivable punch. "Dempsey's wallops went straight to the mark with rare accuracy. He had Godfrey punch drunk in the third round and practically knocked out the 240-pounder."

[1250] *Glens Falls Post Star, Buffalo Commercial, Elmira Star-Gazette*, August 20, 1923. Bermondsey Billy Wells and Jack Britton, former welter champ, arrived in camp as well.
[1251] *Buffalo Commercial, Buffalo Courier*, August 21, 1923.

Against Jack Bernstein, the champ just worked speed and defense, and actually seemed faster than the lightweight.

Dempsey said he was hoping for a fight with either Gibbons or Wills next.[1252]

Jimmy De Forest, "the maker of champions," said, "Dempsey is up against a tougher fight than he realizes if he fails to take the coming match seriously. Firpo is not to be trifled with. He is a dangerous fighting man. However, I will repeat what I have said before, that Firpo is not yet quite ready for the champion." Jimmy said he was familiar with being let go. "I trained Dempsey into a champion and then was let out, so my experience with Firpo is nothing new."[1253]

Godfrey and Burke still were suffering from the grind against Dempsey from the Gibbons fight and could not withstand a daily battering. Few could. They needed off days to recover from Dempsey's bombardment. Godfrey complained of pain in his ribs, which still hurt from sparring with Dempsey prior to the Gibbons fight. Jack said he wanted sparring partners capable of fighting him back.[1254]

On the 22nd, Dempsey sparred 6 light rounds, 3 apiece with 130-pounders Jack Bernstein and Billy DeFoe, showing remarkable speed.

Philadelphia Jack O'Brien, who saw the champ in action, said Dempsey would have a tough time for a few rounds, but was too fast for Firpo and eventually would chop him down within 6 rounds.

Jack kidded folks that his baby leopard had escaped, but in fact he had it shipped to Los Angeles.[1255]

Kearns was anticipating a sellout. He said the fight could sell 200,000 tickets if that number of seats were available; the demand was so great.

A Dempsey friend came into camp and told Jack that Firpo was a real fighter, no soft thing, and could hit too. "He's tough and rough and he's a whole lot faster than most folks think he is." The champ responded,

> But can he take it – can he take? You ain't said anything about that, and that's the most important thing there is in the cute little game where men try to bust each other into twilight sleep. I never care about how hard guys can hit, how fast they are and stuff like that. That's not the test of a great fighter.

Jack said guys like Fulton, Willard, and Brennan could sock hard, but they couldn't take it from him. If Firpo couldn't take it, and take a lot of them, then he wouldn't win the championship, no matter how hard he hit.[1256]

On August 23, before a crowd of 400, Dempsey sparred 2 rounds each with Godfrey and Burke, battering them around. The champ almost decked 225-pound Godfrey in the 1st round with a right to the chin. Jack had no trouble in hooking solidly with his left as well.

[1252] *Buffalo Express, Brooklyn Daily Times, Buffalo Commercial, Rochester Democrat and Chronicle*, August 22, 1923.
[1253] *Brooklyn Standard Union*, August 22, 1923.
[1254] *Brooklyn Daily Eagle*, August 23, 1923. Wells had a hurt hand and might be heading home because of an ill child. Rioux returned to Montreal, satisfied that Dempsey hit too hard for him.
[1255] *Glens Falls Post-Star, Buffalo Commercial*, August 23, 1923.
[1256] *Brooklyn Standard Union*, August 24, 1923.

Burke mostly retreated, trying to escape punishment. Still, Dempsey finally cornered him in the 2nd round and had him groggy from a right cross to the chin. Burke clinched and held on until his head cleared.

The management of the resort where Dempsey was training had paid Kearns $4,000 to establish Dempsey's training camp there. As a result, they were increasing the price of admission to see his training sessions from 55 cents up to $1.10. The champ did not participate in the gate receipts, for Kearns had accepted the flat-fee fixed-sum instead.[1257]

JACK DEMPSEY IN OIL—THE PAINTING THAT STARTED A SQUABBLE

An oil painting of Dempsey by Alonzo Victor Lewis, which was hung in the Kansas City Art Institute, caused quite a stir and debate, for many in the art world did not believe a painting of a boxer belonged. "Alonzo Victor Lewis is perhaps the first artist who has had the temerity to paint a portrait of a prize fighter and then offer it as a work of art."[1258]

Paddy Mullins said under no circumstances would he allow Wills to fight Jack Johnson.

Although Dempsey was a tiger with no mercy in the ring, in everyday life, "Dempsey is just a big, good-natured, overgrown boy. Any time he can turn a helping hand to a pal he leaps at the chance."[1259]

Firpo's sparring partners included Natalio Anvela Para, Joe McCann, and Frank Koebele.

On August 24, owing to the furious pace Dempsey set, Godfrey found it next to impossible to land an effective blow. Jack drove him around the ring under a shower of heavy rights and lefts.

Jack Burke found Dempsey to be an easy target for solid rights, Firpo's most effective punch. Burke landed so well and often that the

[1257] *Buffalo Times, Buffalo Courier,* August 24, 1923.
[1258] *Evansville Press,* August 9, 1923; *Chicago Tribune,* August 12, 1923; *Fort Wayne News-Sentinel,* August 17, 1923; *Poughkeepsie Eagle-News,* August 24, 1923.
[1259] *Brooklyn Daily Eagle, Buffalo Commercial,* August 24, 1923. Word was that Jack Johnson had been matched with Billy Miske for September 10 in Newark.

champ's headgear was knocked about. He caused Dempsey to fight mad at the finish of their 2 slugging rounds. Burke left the ring bleeding from the mouth and nose as a result of stopping left hooks.

Against welterweight Terry Michell of Bayonne, Jack held his punches in restraint, yet still had Michell groggy and staggering. The champ was suffering from a slight cold.

Although the admission price had been doubled, 400 spectators had shown up and paid to watch Dempsey train.

The New York State athletic commission granted licenses for the Firpo-Dempsey contest.[1260]

The *New York Age* reported that Governor Alfred E. Smith had barred a meeting between Dempsey and Wills in New York. The fight most certainly would not be allowed there, at least not until after the 1924 Democratic National Convention, and possibly not ever. Supposedly, the governor had presidential aspirations, and such a fight would agitate and upset those who supported the color line in all aspects of life. Smith said the votes of the presidential delegates from the South meant more to him than the fight did to boxing fans. The *Age* criticized that the New York voters put him into office, and the voters wanted the fight, but he was putting his own political aspirations ahead of what the voters wanted. "Putting the Dempsey-Wills contest off until after next year's convention is putting it off for good as far as New York is concerned. Twice the match has been made red hot here and then allowed to cool. It can't be heated again."

Publicly though, the governor denied having anything to do with boxing, and denied that he had put a ban on Dempsey-Wills. He said the commission made all boxing-related decisions. However, those in the know, including politicians, said that behind the scenes, the governor was saying otherwise.

Paddy Mullins declared that Wills was the real champion, and they had been the victims of a huge hoax, stalled off for several years so that Dempsey could battle soft marks. He said Wills could take Firpo in one punch.[1261]

On August 25, Dempsey came dangerously near knocking out Burke and Godfrey in a rough workout, 2 rounds with each man. Clinching probably saved his sparring partners from hitting the floor. Junior lightweight Jack Bernstein went 2 more, for a total of 6 rounds. Jack still was affected by a cold, but his boxing improvement was marked, exhibiting good judgment of distance and impressive speed.[1262]

On Sunday the 26th, Dempsey battled 2 hard rounds with Godfrey, 2 speedy rounds with Burke, and 2 rounds with Bernstein, "world's junior lightweight champ."

Dempsey decided to take a few days off, for his stuffy cold had advanced. He also was a bit annoyed by all the people who constantly

[1260] *Glens Falls Post-Star*, August 25, 1923. Jeff Clark or Clarke, otherwise known at the Joplin Ghost, was set to join Firpo's camp as well.
[1261] *New York Age*, August 25, 1923.
[1262] *Buffalo Times*, August 26, 1923. Jack also tugged at the weights and did a round of shadow boxing.

wanted to meet him. He wanted more peace and seclusion. He was good-natured enough to indulge them, but he was mortal, and had his limits.[1263]

Gibbons and Firpo were said to be exact opposites. Gibbons was harder to hit, and was quicker and more skilled, but Firpo was a much bigger man, very powerful, gamer, and more determined to win, always trying to knock out his foe. Gibbons was more cautious and careful. Firpo would fight to win by knockout, and to do so would risk being knocked out, whereas if Gibbons did not think he could win, he would fight to survive. Hence, the upcoming fight likely would be exciting.

On August 27, wearing 16-ounce gloves, Firpo pummeled his trio of sparring partners, black Jeff Clark/Clarke, Frank Koebele, and Joe McCann. His punches made the sounds of dull thuds and cracks. Critics said his technique had improved. 210-pound Firpo kept pounding on his sparring partners, from 8 to 10 rounds daily.

Manager Horatio Lavelle said Firpo was 26 years old, lost his first fight on a knockout, but then won 26 in a row, 22 by knockout.

Firpo's sparring partners offered their thoughts. McCann said, "Firpo is faster than ever before." Koebele/Koble said, "He is not nearly so easy to reach, and has a far better eye than when he started training here." Clarke said, "Hitting Firpo is just like hitting a stone wall – no rebound."

Firpo and trainer Horatio Lavalle

Nevertheless, Dempsey was the 2 to 1 or 3 to 1 favorite.[1264]

Paddy Mullins complained that Wills was "the victim of rank discrimination." He had deposited $2,500 as a good faith challenge, but the commission had given him no justice, allowing Dempsey to fight Firpo.[1265]

Edward Tranter said the powers-that-be in the boxing game were inclined to frown upon a mixed-race heavyweight championship match. Whenever there was a black-white heavyweight championship discussion, "somebody raises a rumpus that can be heard way around the globe. This

[1263] *Buffalo Enquirer, Buffalo Commercial*, August 27, 1923. Jack was down to 194 pounds and expected to fight at 188.
[1264] *Buffalo Express, Buffalo Enquirer*, August 28, 1923. *Poughkeepsie Eagle-News*, August 29, 1923.
[1265] *New York Daily News*, August 29, 1923.

state athletic commission of ours, having the sport at heart, doesn't care to be identified with any contest which may leave in its wake rumblins that may eventually bring disaster to the situation." Tranter opined that those who wanted to make Wills-Dempsey cared more for the "golden shekels" than for the sport.[1266]

Dempsey admitted to feeling nervous before his fights. "I'm nervous when I climb into the ring and wait for the first bell. It seems that the second is about two hours long, but the moment I hear the gong all the nervousness disappears and then my whole mind is concentrated on the business in hand."[1267]

With camp chef William Mathes   Godfrey sparring Dempsey

A confident Firpo said any human being would be knocked out if he hit him in the proper place on the jaw with his right, including Dempsey. The champion was hittable, because everyone hit him. Hence, Luis believed that he would win by knockout.[1268]

On August 30, Dempsey sparred 201-pound heavyweight Jack McAuliffe II, who had to stop after 1 round, for his right eye was shut and left ear bleeding from a slight cut. Dempsey had him dangerously close to a knockout, and the champ even held him up once and refrained from hitting him.

McAuliffe, whom Firpo had stopped in the 3rd round of an actual fight, said, "Dempsey is a harder puncher than Firpo." He said Jack hit twice as hard and was a snappier puncher. He predicted a 1st round knockout victory for Dempsey. "Dempsey steps around so fast and shoots his punches with such speed and force that Firpo will be bewildered. Dempsey will hook him to pieces. Firpo's punch is a long right. He is made to order for one of Dempsey's left hooks. Firpo hasn't a chance unless he hits Dempsey by accident." The *Pittsburgh Post* quoted McAuliffe as saying that there was no comparison. "Dempsey is a 100% better hitter with either hand. He's the snappier puncher and can step around with such speed that Firpo won't know what it's all about."

[1266] *Binghamton Press, Buffalo Enquirer*, August 29, 1923. Promoters were looking at Stamford, Connecticut as a possible location for a Dempsey-Wills fight.
[1267] *Brooklyn Standard Union*, August 29, 1923. Jack Johnson was training to fight Miske. He wanted Wills next, to prove that he and not Wills was entitled to a fight with Dempsey. *Glens Falls Post-Star*, August 29, 1923.
[1268] *Elmira Star-Gazette*, August 30, 1923.

Dempsey also ripped into 6'2" 201-pound Jack Burke, sending him back on his heels half a dozen times with jolting right crosses. Burke fought back though and landed rights when he saw an opening.

The Associated Press said Dempsey and Firpo were two of the hardest-hitting heavyweights ever. Both were natural fighters, with their own unique style. Dempsey crouched low, but on his toes, and weaved around, ready to lash out at the body or head with both arms. He was deceiving, with precise, powerful punches. His jolts seldom traveled more than a foot. He appeared to be an open target, but was so fast of foot and head that only the cleverest and fastest punchers had been able to land on him effectively. Carpentier landed his lightning right, and Gibbons his fast left, but Jack was rugged enough to take it.

Firpo had a clubbing right and a savage style of attack. He seldom used his left other than to jab, measure or cover up. The "Wild Bull of the Pampas" drove his foes into retreat with the impetuousness of his rushes, and he battered them down. Defense was not his specialty, though he had improved in general ringmanship. He was game and able to take punishment. He was fast for his size, and like Dempsey, had a knack for anticipating his opponents' blows.

New Jersey barred Jack Johnson from boxing there, citing his criminal record (as if no other boxers had criminal records). Thomas Rice suspected that it really was a desire to avoid "almost certain interracial troubles" if Johnson were allowed to box white men.

Rice said Dempsey-Wills had been prevented in New York, New Jersey, Canada, and elsewhere because of the ultimate effects such a contest would have in the far corners of the world. Rice's predictions about the bout had come true. The British Empire was concerned about such a fight's implications throughout the world, especially since it owned so many colonies in which whites and nonwhites were living side by side. The U.S. had sway over the Philippines, Puerto Rico, and other places. Rice said anyone who depended on boxing for a living, who had any common sense, would not have anything to do with such a fight.[1269]

In a translated interview with George Trevor, Firpo said he wanted to refute false ideas about him. Americans called his right hand awkward, clumsy, and club-like. "Maybe it is not what you call graceful, but I have noticed that not one of my opponents has ever managed to evade it." Hence, it was effective, and perhaps not as awkward as it seemed. "Dempsey will not block it. You will see!"

Folks said he had no left, but Luis disagreed. He said his left actually was stronger and more damaging than his right. The first time he decked Weinert was with a left, as well as the second. "But you writers never mention those left-handed blows."

Luis said Americans were so easy to hit with his right that he simply went ahead and hit them with it, including as a lead. "You notice that my opponents do not counter successfully."

[1269] *Buffalo Commercial, Glens Falls Post-Star, Pittsburgh Post, Brooklyn Daily Eagle,* August 31, 1923.

Regarding his defense, despite claims that he fought wide open, "Why, then, are there no marks on my face?" The only scar he had was from a butt. Otherwise, he was unscathed. "That is strange, isn't it, since I have no defense?" He was speaking using a bitingly ironic tone. He disagreed that he had no defense or skill. He managed to block Willard's best punch, the uppercut, with his left hand.

Firpo had no fear of Dempsey or anyone else. "I will go in to get Dempsey just as I went in to finish the others. I have a firm belief that there is no man living who can hurt me more than I can hurt him."

Firpo said he had kept on fighting even after signing to fight Dempsey, because "I can learn more by actual fighting than by sparring."

Trevor said Firpo was the typical "killer," with a true fighting face. The "savage" in him was not far below the surface. Of one thing the writer was certain, "Luis Angel Firpo will not enter the ring with Jack Dempsey merely with the idea of collecting the loser's end. He thinks he is going to win."[1270]

On the 31st, the champ's sparring partners had a rough afternoon. Dempsey boxed 5 rounds total. The first 2 rounds were with 175-pound Ray Newman/Neuman. Jules/Elzear Rioux, the big French Canadian who worked with Dempsey about 10 days ago, gave it another try, but was knocked out in less than a round. The final 2 rounds were with Godfrey, who didn't risk getting too close to Dempsey.

Farmer Lodge had arrived in camp. He asked McAuliffe and Rioux how to avoid the champ's knockout punches, and their advice was, "Run a hundred yards in four seconds."[1271]

On Friday August 31, 1923 at the Polo Grounds in New York, 29-year-old 158-pound Harry Greb (208-12-16) won the world middleweight championship, defeating 158-pound champ Johnny Wilson (55-21-8) via clear 15-round unanimous decision. Their weights were taken at 2 p.m. on the day of the fight, each having to make 158 pounds. Greb was too fast, active, and aggressive, and the fight primarily was an inside clinching affair, where Greb did most of his damage. There were no knockdowns, but Wilson's eye was closed.

HARRY GREB.

Robert Edgren complained that Greb utilized his usual holding and hitting tactics, doing so about a hundred times, often holding around the neck with his left and hitting with his right, yet no referee since Charlie White had enforced the rules. Neither man did much effective damage. Edgren was not impressed with Greb, saying that greats like Bob Fitzsimmons, Tommy Ryan, or Stanley Ketchel would beat him with ease. "If the fight did nothing else, it made a joke of all that talk about

[1270] *Brooklyn Daily Eagle*, August 31, 1923.
[1271] *New York Daily News, Buffalo Enquirer*, September 1, 1923.

matching Greb against Jack Dempsey. Greb might last a few rounds with the heavyweight champion, but so would a punching bag."

The fight was considered a "financial bloomer," with 6,154 paid admissions generating $24,157, low for a world championship fight held in New York. One wrote, "The passing of Wilson is not greatly lamented, and the advent of Greb, not a very popular figure here, occasioned no particular stir." Wilson earned 37 ½% to Greb's 12 ½%.[1272]

On September 1, Dempsey sparred 8 rounds with only 30 seconds rest between rounds, 2 each with McAuliffe, Burke, Farmer Lodge, and Ray Newman.

A right in the 2nd round sent Burke bouncing off the ropes, and a short right when he bounded back dropped him to his knees. Burke rose and danced, and Dempsey tore after him, until another right to the chin sent him crashing to the floor. He was groggy and unable to rise. Jack picked him up and held him in a clinch for a while until his dizzy brain cleared.

Burke was his third victim in a week. McAuliffe was all but knocked out on Thursday, and Rioux had been dragged unconscious to the corner to be revived with a splash of cold water.

In order to escape a mauling, Big Farmer Lodge ran all over the ring, grabbed, and wrestled. Against McAuliffe, Jack held his punches in reserve, except in the 2nd round, when he cut loose with jolting left hooks and rights to the head.

The champ was nearly recovered from his cold.

On September 2, Dempsey boxed 6 relatively tame rounds, 2 each with Godfrey, Lodge, and McAuliffe, primarily working on defense. More than 2,500 people packed the canvas-walled outdoor arena.[1273]

Dempsey was a 3 ½ to 1 betting favorite. Many were betting that the fight would end inside of 4 rounds. Some wagered that Firpo would win by knockout. Few anticipated a long fight, because both liked to fight and win by knockout.[1274]

[1272] *Brooklyn Citizen, Brooklyn Standard Union, Brooklyn Daily Eagle, New York Daily News, Brooklyn Daily Times, Buffalo Express, Buffalo Times,* September 1, 1923. Federal tax was 10%.
[1273] *Brooklyn Daily Eagle,* September 2, 3, 1923.
[1274] *New York Daily News,* September 3, 1923.

On September 3, before a crowd of about 2,500, while motion picture operators filmed them, Dempsey boxed 6 snappy rounds, 2 each with Lodge, Godfrey, and McAuliffe. Dempsey worked on his defense, ducking or blocking as Godfrey attempted to hit him with the rabbit punch.

Trainer Jerry Luvadis said Jack was in better shape than he was for the Gibbons fight. "The match with Gibbons did Dempsey a world of good. He needed it after the layoff of two years." 193-pound Dempsey said he had not felt quite so fit and ready to fight in four years.[1275]

Trying to stop the Dempsey-Firpo fight, Paddy Mullins went to court and filed for an injunction, asking that it be prevented.[1276]

George Trevor said Firpo was attempting to fulfill the Latin race's dream for a champion. "Firpo's fists represent the consummation of a racial prayer. At last their vision of a champion who can beat the Gringo at his own game is on the verge of becoming an actuality." Firpo was fighting for all Latinos.

> Americans do not realize the intense racial hatred for the United States underlying the polite veneer which cloaks the secret thoughts of our Latin neighbors. This hostility is doubtless inspired by our own attitude to South Americans. It is an incontrovertible fact that we of the North look down contemptuously upon all peoples to the south of the Rio Grande. This contemptuous dislike is feverishly reciprocated.

Firpo realized the responsibility that rested upon him. He carried the hopes not only of his Argentinian countrymen, but the entire Latin race. He was "symbolic of the embattled Latin people." There was no love lost in the fight.

Perhaps to get under his skin, or to garner more support, Firpo was contemptuous of Dempsey's war record. Luis said of Dempsey, "He had a nice picture taken all dressed up in shipyard overalls. But I hear that it is that Kearns who is responsible for Dempsey's staying at home. I do not admire Kearns." Firpo's representative, Vegas, said, "[Kearns] thinks he is so clever, that one, but he will get the surprise of his life. He will lose his meal ticket next week. You will see."[1277]

On September 4, Firpo kept pounding away at Joe McCann, Jeff Clarke, Frank Koeble, and Natalio Pera, boxing 7 rounds. Luis suffered a slight cut at the corner of his right eye from a head butt in a clinch with McCann.

Grantland Rice said Firpo had improved greatly. He was in great shape, and at ease. He was no speed marvel, or master of science, but he handled himself well, and was not slow for a big man of 6'2 ½" and 214 pounds. Dempsey was faster. But there were moments when Firpo whipped himself into action in which his speed was almost astonishing.

[1275] *Brooklyn Daily Eagle, Buffalo Enquirer*, September 4, 1923.
[1276] *Middletown Daily Herald*, September 5, 1923.
[1277] *Brooklyn Daily Eagle*, September 5, 1923.

Outside the ring, Firpo had a dignified, poised, unhurried, stately manner about him, quiet, courteous, and considerate. In the ring, he could lash out with ferocity.

Firpo's friend said Luis had great stamina, strength, and vitality. He never smoked or drank. He had worked at heavy physical labor. He was much stronger than his size, even stronger than Willard ever was, and faster than folks realized. He was a master of his own method of fighting, had confidence, and was so much stronger than Dempsey that the result was quite uncertain. If Dempsey had an off day, he would be beaten for sure.[1278]

First Showing in America—OFFICIAL

DEMPSEY-GIBBONS FIGHT PICTURES

SHELBY, MONTANA

Not Booked in Any Other Theater

TO ACCOMMODATE THE CROWD, THEATER WILL BE OPEN TWENTY-FOUR HOURS DAILY

SHOW EVERY HOUR

ROSE THEATRE

Madison and Dearborn Streets

Not a Training Camp Picture—15 Rounds—Round by Round

In early September, the Rose Theatre in Chicago began showing the complete Dempsey vs. Gibbons fight films, advertising them in the *Chicago Tribune*. The films would be shown for 24 hours daily, with a show every hour. Clearly, someone had ignored the federal law and transported the films across state lines.

The local U.S. district attorney's office wanted to prevent the exhibitions, and impounded the films. However, Judge Fisher enjoined the police from interfering, because it was not a violation of Illinois law to show the motion pictures, and not an offense against public morals and decency. Hence, the film exhibitions could proceed, and did, for the next couple of months, along with advertisements for the showings at various theaters throughout Illinois. In this way, the promoters, fighters, and managers would earn plenty of money.

Fight films were big business, as were fights. The *Chicago Tribune* noted that whenever there was a big fight, about 100,000 extra *Tribunes* were sold the next morning above and beyond the norm. The paper made money with advertisements for the films as well. This paper wanted the "paternalistic U.S.A." to stay out of it, for boxing was perfectly legal, and boxing and the films were a matter for the states to regulate, not the federal government.

The *Tribune* noted that the real reason the federal law against interstate transport of fight films was passed was because black Jack Johnson beat white Jim Jeffries.

> That adds to the explanation revealing the real reason why American citizens try to pay as little respect to law as possible and why they succeed so well in doing so. If the Johnson-Jeffries pictures were about to undo the social structure of the United States, local authority was perfectly able to handle the situation. The federal government in a panic ran down all the rights of the states

---

[1278] *Buffalo Courier, Glens Falls Post-Star*, September 5, 1923.

and made an absurd use of the interstate commerce act to exercise local police powers. … Therefore a great many people know it is a joke. It is a law so misconceived and misconstructed that it is absurd in principle and administration.[1279]

ROSE MADISON AT DEARBORN

—5th Smashing Week—

DEMPSEY-GIBBONS FIGHT PICTURES

NORTH
JULIAN 918 BELMONT
DEMPSEY-GIBBONS
FIGHT PICTURES

DREXEL

CHATHAM
COTTAGE GROVE AT 75TH STREET
—MATINEE DAILY—
EXTRAORDINARY
SPECIAL ATTRACTION
"THE MIDNIGHT ALARM"
ALSO
DEMPSEY-GIBBONS
Fight Pictures
Round by Round—Blow by Blow

858 E. 63RD STREET
MATINEE DAILY
DEMPSEY-GIBBONS FIGHT

Of the Dempsey-Gibbons films, one man wrote, "I was a neighbor of Gibbons when I lived in St. Paul, so I suppose I should be a Gibbons enthusiast, but the picture of him rather disappoints me." Another said Firpo was an open fighter who would try to win, and would give Dempsey a greater opportunity to exert himself than Gibbons gave him.[1280]

On September 5, Dempsey boxed 6 fast rounds, displaying astonishing hand and foot speed. He was a wizard on defense, although 225-pound Godfrey landed several long left jabs as he danced away and tried to keep the champ at a distance. Jack paid no attention to them, and always tore or bore in relentlessly, weaving in a half crouch to find an opening for a left hook or short right to the body or head, forcing George to clinch.

Dempsey cut and bloodied 235-pound Farmer Lodge's right eye and drew blood from his nose, despite Lodge's frequent clinching.

Against Ray Newman, Jack primarily played defense.

Dempsey told Kearns that he did not want the fight stopped until he was down and out cold for the ten-count. Unless he was out cold on his back, he believed he always would have a chance to win. "I'm going out fighting."[1281]

Jack Kearns declared that Dempsey would lose one day if he fought long enough, but it would not be to Firpo. "When Dempsey loses it will be on a decision – not through a knockout." He might possibly be outboxed, but no one could outfight him, and Firpo was a fighter. If Firpo hurt him, it just would make Jack mad, and then Luis would see the ferocity of several tigers, lions, and panthers all rolled up into one.

New York Supreme Court Justice Edward Lazansky directed the state boxing commission to show cause why a peremptory writ of mandamus should not issue compelling it to perform certain acts in accordance with the petition of Harry Wills and his manager. Wills/Mullins' lawyer called attention to the commission's alleged actions in 1922 when it deprived or

[1279] *Chicago Tribune*, September 7, 1923.
[1280] *Chicago Tribune*, September 9, 1923.
[1281] *Buffalo Commercial, Poughkeepsie Eagle-News*, September 6, 1923.

threatened to deprive several title holders of their titles if they refused to fight logical contenders. The question was why the same should not happen with Dempsey and Wills.[1282]

Rickard informed Firpo and Dempsey that they were required to weigh in at 2 p.m. on the day of the fight, for an official weigh-in, to conform with the commission's new policy of having the principals in a championship fight conduct a public weigh-in in front of press representatives.

Dempsey purchased a $65,000 residence in Garden City, Long Island, New York.

Harry Newman said Firpo's victory over Brennan was more impressive than Dempsey's performance. However, others said Brennan was not the same man that he was when he fought Dempsey.

Grantland Rice said Firpo's long reach would astonish Dempsey. He could strike and land from much further away than folks realized.

Jack Britton said Firpo would not last 3 rounds with Dempsey. Firpo never had met a puncher like Dempsey, who hit with staggering, crushing force. Luis would try to knock out Dempsey, and in doing so, would leave himself open to Jack's big blows. Firpo hit hard, but Dempsey was a fast, shifting, ever-rushing fighter who would be a whole lot harder to hit and knock out than Brennan, Willard, and others. If Firpo lasted longer than 3 rounds, he likely would suffer a bigger beating than Willard did.[1283]

Jack was pickling his face and hands in a combination of beef brine and vinegar to toughen his skin.

On September 6, wearing a headgear, Dempsey ripped into Farmer Lodge and George Godfrey for 2 vicious rounds with each man. Everyone agreed that Jack looked better than he did going into the Gibbons fights. His skill had improved, and the snap and accuracy of his hitting was amazing. He tore in with characteristic aggressiveness; shooting blows with such speed that his foes were bewildered. He used a puzzling, swaying attack, crouching low and bobbing up and down to draw a lead, and then countering with a hook or right.

The legal action started by Paddy Mullins and Harry Wills truly angered Dempsey. By trying to get the Firpo fight stopped, they were trying to interfere with his ability to earn money. That crossed the line with Dempsey. Never mess with a man's ability to earn a living. "The titleholder declared he never would give Wills a 'shot' at the title as long as he was champion." Jack allegedly said,

> That means the end of Wills so far as I am concerned. If they have gone into the courts to stop the Firpo match, you can tell the world that I never will consent to give him a chance, not under any

[1282] *Brooklyn Standard Union*, September 6, 1923. In several cases, the New York commission had stripped its recognition of champions and awarded titles to contenders when the champions failed to defend against them, including Johnny Wilson, who lost/forfeited his title to Dave Rosenberg; Johnny Kilbane to Danny Frush; Joe Lynch – Joe Burman; and Mickey Walker – Dave Shade. However, the general public and other jurisdictions did not necessarily agree.

[1283] *New York Daily News, Glens Falls Post Star, Buffalo Courier,* September 7, 1923. Firpo added sparring partners to his retinue: John Lester Johnson and Young Bob Fitzsimmons. Dempsey added 170-pound black fighter Jamaica Kid, and St. Paul light heavy Jimmy Delaney. The Kid had worked with Dempsey for the Willard fight.

circumstances. I never had the slightest objections to fighting Wills. In fact, I was afraid I wouldn't get the chance to meet him. We intended to close this match after disposing of Firpo, provided I won. Both Mullins and Wills knew this. Now they are trying to gum up the works. I would just as soon have fought Wills as Firpo, but there wasn't a promoter in sight to stage it. But I'm not going to allow Mullins and Wills to make a chump out of me this way. This is his finish while I am holder of the championship. I never will give him a shot at the title.[1284]

Dempsey spars Alex Trambitas

Robert Edgren said Dempsey was in excellent condition. He had been sparring 250-pound Farmer Lodge, 210-pound Jack McAuliffe, 175-pound Jack Burke, 175-pound Ray Newman, 220-pound Rioux, 220-pound Godfrey, and 145-pound Alex Trambitas. They all were well marked up, but Dempsey did not have a scratch. When asked if he felt good to get a day of rest, Godfrey responded, "You bet your life."

The *Daily News* said Dempsey intimated that he intended to get married soon after the Firpo fight, and probably would retire, regardless of the fight's result.

Jack said this time, they were working on a percentage instead of a guarantee. The advance sale of seats already had reached $900,000.[1285]

On September 7, motion picture cameras filmed Firpo sparring John Lester Johnson - who once allegedly broke Dempsey's ribs, 185-pound Young Bob Fitzsimmons, Joe McCann, and Frank Koebele. Firpo was fast, found a way to land stinging blows on all of them, and was not bothered by the blows he took.[1286]

On the 7th, to work on his speed, Dempsey sparred 6 fast rounds with his lighter sparring partners; middleweight Alex Trambitas, featherweight Billy DeFoe, and 175-pound Ray Newman. When he did throw, Jack often led with his right and followed with a lightning-fast left hook. He took only 30 seconds of rest between rounds.

Billy De Foe

The champ said the only time a challenger was not dangerous was when he was on the floor. He would be ready for Mr. Firpo. He finally was through fighting off his cold.

[1284] *Brooklyn Daily Eagle, New York Daily News,* September 7, 1923.
[1285] *Buffalo Times, New York Daily News, Rochester Democrat and Chronicle,* September 7, 1923.
[1286] *Buffalo Courier,* September 8, 1923. Another black fighter, Buddy Jackson, arrived to work with Firpo. Jeff Clark still was resting.

Speaking of Dempsey, Farmer Lodge said, "Boy you might as well monkey with a bull as fight that man. He's simply awful. Oh, how he can sock."

Before the New York Supreme Court, Wills, through counsel, argued that the state athletic commission had been unjust in dealing with his challenge, and tyrannical in its attitude. Wills had challenged Dempsey formally more than a year ago but had been passed up for less dangerous foes.

The commission responded that Dempsey and Wills had made an agreement to fight, but the contract allowed them to take other fights until their fight could be arranged. No promoter had made the fight between them.

Rickard submitted an affidavit stating that he had invested $20,000 on the upcoming fight already, so an injunction would cost him that much and more in damages.

Dempsey denied the report which claimed that he said he never would box Wills. He also denied the rumor of an upcoming wedding. "What, again? Who's the girl this time?"

Walter Kelly said Firpo had deadly wallops, so just the possibility that he could land and hurt Dempsey made folks excited to see the fight, even though most believed that Dempsey's superior speed, skill, and two-fisted attack made him a strong favorite. It was an intriguing and likely entertaining matchup, for both men would come to win by knockout.[1287]

Most were saying that Firpo had a puncher's chance. He was big, strong, powerful, and tough. But he was hittable and could be outboxed. The champion had better defense, put his punches together better, and was a two-fisted fighter, whereas Firpo primarily relied on his heavy, long right. Firpo remained the 3 to 1 underdog.

John Lester Johnson was the only sparring partner capable of giving Firpo real work. He was strong and knew the game well. Still, when Firpo landed his right, even with 16-ounce gloves, it made Johnson retreat.[1288]

Sparrow McGann believed a knockout punch with his right was Firpo's lone chance for victory, which he would have a chance to land so long as he was on his feet. However, Dempsey was superior in every department.

> If you saw a gunman whom you knew to be a sharpshooter up against another gunman who was a poor shot, and yet was fearless and had a forty-four from which he could spray death-dealing shots, you would pick the sharpshooting gunman to win. Yet you would concede that the other guy had a chance of getting home one of his bullets. That is the only way you can dope out the result of this coming battle between Jack Dempsey and Luis Firpo.[1289]

[1287] *Buffalo Courier, Buffalo Commercial, Buffalo Enquirer, New York Daily News*, September 8, 1923.
[1288] *New York Daily News, Buffalo Express*, September 9, 1923. Firpo also worked with Young Bob Fitzsimmons and Joe McCann.
[1289] *Buffalo Courier*, September 9, 1923.

Firpo on horseback at the beach

Firpo lands right on Young Bob Fitzsimmons

HOW CHAMPION AND CHALLENGER SHAPE UP

Dempsey.		Firpo.
28 yrs.	Age	26 yrs.
6 ft. 1½ in.	Height	6 ft. 2½ in.
189 lbs.	Weight	214 lbs
73 in.	Reach	79 in.
17 in.	Neck	17 in
15 in.	Biceps	13½ in.
41 in.	Chest (normal)	44 in.
44¼ in.	Chest (expanded)	48½ in.
32½ in.	Waist	36½ in.
8¼ in.	Wrist	8¼ in.
22 in.	Thigh	23¾ in.
15 in.	Calf	16 in
9 in.	Ankle	9½ in.

Dempsey said he had wanted a real slugging match for a long time, to go against someone who really could fight him back. "This Firpo battle gives me the chance. I certainly will be glad when the old gong bangs, because then I can step right out and begin socking with everything I've got, and know the joy of mixing it toe to toe with somebody who is big enough and dangerous enough to hand it back." Jack said Firpo never had met a puncher like himself, and Jack was going to find out just how game Firpo really was.

YOUNGSTERS WATCH THEIR HERO
While giving his training quarters the once over Jack Dempsey met some real country kids. They asked their hero to honor them by riding on their bike and the champion did so. He proved to be as good a bike rider as he is a boxer.

Jimmy De Forest, who had trained both, said Dempsey would win quickly, within 3 rounds, for he was too fast and clever for Firpo.

Dempsey at left attacks Farmer Lodge

On September 9, the champ boxed 6 rounds, 2 each with 235-pound Farmer Lodge, 225-pound Godfrey, whom he shook up with hard blows to the head, though George kept pumping left jabs to the face, and Jack Geyer, whom he tore to pieces.

After he was through with his regular sparring, writer Paul Gallico, who weighed 200 pounds, wanted to know what it felt like to be hit by Dempsey, so he asked to spar with him. Gallico had been an all-around athlete during his college days, having played football and basketball. In response, Jack asked him, "Do you want to be killed?" Gallico said not killed. Jack replied that Gallico wanted to be only half killed, so when he recovered, he could write about it. Yes. He got the idea. Jack agreed to box him for 1 round. Gallico wore a headguard.

Gallico feinted a right, then Dempsey fired a left hook that landed beneath the eye, jarring him from stem to stern. Paul ducked, dodged, and moved. The champ was on top of him. A flash of an arm and he was hit again. Gallico poked his left to the face several times, and nothing happened. Dempsey shifted suddenly and fired away with both hands. Two tremendous thuds and his head was swimming.

As he was falling, Dempsey caught Gallico and held him up. Breaking, Gallico poked at him again, then Jack's right fired to the jaw, there was a bump, and he was on the floor. Gallico wrote, "We had experienced a knockdown. It's a good deal like having a building fall on you."

Gallico rose and rushed into a clinch. Jack pounded the back of his neck. Paul moved away, and then got chipped on the jaw again. The timekeeper called time, and it was over.

Jack shook his hand, and Gallico left the ring with a headache, cut lip, and satisfied curiosity. "Of course, Dempsey wasn't hitting us as hard as he can. Had he, this story would have been written a week or so after the fight, from the hospital. But we know that when he hits, light or hard, YOU FEEL IT."

Billy McCarney had predicted that Gibbons would go the distance, and that Firpo would stop Willard within 10 rounds. He had been right both times. This time, McCarney picked Firpo to be the next champion.[1290]

Grantland Rice noted that the experts were not always right. 38 out of 40 experts picked Dempsey to knock out Gibbons within 6 rounds. They said Tom was too small and Dempsey too strong. When he lasted 15 rounds, the shock was terrific. Gibbons was a far better boxer than Firpo, but Firpo was nearly 40 pounds bigger, taller, far stronger, and a much

---

[1290] *Buffalo Express, New York Daily News, Buffalo Times*, September 10, 1923.

harder hitter. So, it was a different matchup. In Gibbons, Dempsey had to deal with a cautious master of defense, who countered selectively, used speed, generalship, footwork, clinching, ducking, smothering, and caution, none of which Firpo would do. But Firpo would try his hardest to send Dempsey to sleep, so there was an aura of danger, whereas Gibbons never had Dempsey in any danger whatsoever.

Firpo was looking faster and more effective than ever in his sparring. His sparring partners, John Lester Johnson, Young Bob Fitzsimmons, and Joe McCann were showing the wear and tear.[1291]

Young Fitzsimmons and Firpo   Firpo wallops John Lester Johnson

Jess Willard, who had fought both, said Dempsey was a terrific fighting man, but there was no such thing as an unbeatable fighter. His greatest asset was his punching power. He had a distinctive style of swaying from side to side and making unusual use of both hands. He was a dangerous man, fast and strong. The fact that Dempsey had so few fights over the past four years would hurt him. "The best man I ever fought was Jack Johnson. ... His best was better than the best of either Dempsey or Firpo. My advice to Firpo is to be careful with Dempsey the first two or three rounds. Dempsey makes a lightning start, but I don't think he can go for a long grind."

Willard said the fight was a toss-up. "Firpo is far more dangerous than most fans give him credit for being." Despite his deficiencies, he was "more terrific in punching than Dempsey, on the whole a stronger man,

[1291] *Glens Falls Post-Star*, September 10, 1923.

and he is likely to stand up under Dempsey's attack in far better shape than a lot of the experts think he will."[1292]

New York Supreme Court Justice William Hagarty denied the requested Wills/Mullins writ of mandamus seeking an injunction which would prevent the Dempsey-Firpo championship fight and force Dempsey to fight Wills or forfeit the title. The judge believed the remedy requested was too drastic. So, the fight was on.

In issuing his ruling, Justice Hagarty noted the July 8, 1922 Dempsey-Wills contract which called for them to fight at a time and place mutually agreed upon. "But it does not appear that the relator, Wills, ever suggested a time and place for the holding of this contest either to the respondents or to the said Dempsey, nor does it appear that bids were ever solicited or received by either party." Only after the arrangements already had been made for Dempsey-Firpo did Wills secure a promoter who endeavored to talk business with Kearns.[1293]

Supposedly, Firpo was to receive $100,000, regardless of result, for the scheduled 15-round contest. Firpo had generated big money while in the U.S. He had earned $10,000 for Brennan, $25,000 for McAuliffe II, and $80,000 for Willard. He also earned money from exhibitions, motion picture rights, and other fights.

Angel Rodriguez, South American light heavyweight champion, who in 1918 had knocked out an overmatched, inexperienced Firpo in the 1st round, in what was only Firpo's second pro bout (his only KO loss), when Rodriguez was 25-2, gave his thoughts. He believed Firpo was sure to win, for the champ had been too inactive. Angel said that instead of being discouraged by the loss to him, Firpo was even more determined to improve and learn the sport. He had been boxing all the time since then, and had many matches, constantly improving. Since winning the title, Dempsey had fought only four times. From the point in time that Jack had won the title, Firpo had 22 fights at least, so he was sharp and hungry. "Boxing is like a woman – jealous when neglected, it requires constant attention. Dempsey is suffering from this neglect. Firpo will win." Firpo's only other loss was a 15-round decision to former Jack Johnson sparring partner Dave Mills, early in his career, in his ninth pro bout, which he twice avenged with two 1st-round knockouts, proving his ability to improve.

[1292] Brooklyn Citizen, September 10, 1923; Buffalo Express, September 11, 1923.
[1293] New York Age, September 15, 1923; Buffalo Commercial, September 11, 1923.

Dempsey planned to have at least three days growth of beard. He thought shaving irritated the skin too much.

On September 10, Jack boxed 5 spirited rounds with four different sparring partners: 1 round with British 157-pounder George West, 2 rounds with Jack Burke, 1 with welterweight Frank Laureate, and 1 with middleweight Alex Trambitas. The latter two men both hit the floor, but it was unintentional.[1294]

One report said Dempsey was to receive 37.5% of the gross receipts, and Firpo 12.5%. The commission would name the referee. Ticket prices went from $3 up to $25, plus tax.

Ticket speculators were selling front-row seats for $100 each. Ticket sales at the box office already had surpassed one million dollars.[1295]

Responding to questions from newspaper reporters asking him to predict what round he would stop Firpo, Dempsey said, "You guys are 'experts' and ought to know more about that than I do." Jack said both he and Firpo could knock out the other if they landed right. "I expect to take some rough punches, because Firpo is dangerous – more dangerous than you fellows think. He will continue to be dangerous until I have him on the floor."

Jack read aloud to the newspaper men several mash notes from women. He remarked that he never knew he was good looking until he read some of the letters. "Maybe the girls will not say I am so good looking next Saturday morning."

Jack was playful and liked to apply the headlock to newsmen and sock them with playful jolts that almost knocked them down.

Dempsey said he felt better than at any time since Toledo, and though he never would be quite that good and powerful again, he had learned some things that made up for it. Jack said Luis was a big, rough, tough fellow who could hit, and therefore it would be a tough contest.

When a lady reporter asked Dempsey in what round he would win, he responded, "I don't know." She asked, "When can you tell me?" "Saturday morning – if I can talk." The fight would be held on Friday.

Jack McAuliffe, former lightweight champion, who had watched both, insisted that Dempsey would lose to Firpo, who was awkwardly effective and had a lot of knockout power. Even with 16-ounce gloves and holding back, he put Downey in the hospital. McAuliffe believed that Firpo could take it too.

On September 11, three days before the fight, the champ sparred 4 rounds. He viciously pounded on Jack Burke with every punch for 2 rounds, and it resembled a real fight. Burke was bleeding from the mouth, groggy, and on the verge of collapse when Jack's brother Bernie called time. The champ then boxed English middleweight George West for 1 round, and smacked him all over, but had to pull back when West started acting like a man who had been punched silly, making figure eights. Jack

[1294] *Buffalo Commercial*, September 11, 1923. Scheduled undercard bouts included: Tunney vs. Leo Gates, and Jack Burke vs. Bill Reed.
[1295] *Brooklyn Standard Union*, September 11, 1923. Some noted that the income tax was progressive, so the more Dempsey made the greater his tax percentage. He would have to pay 60% tax on an income over 1 million dollars.

then went at Alex Trambitas for a round. Dempsey was fast on his feet and his punches were timed perfectly. All of his partners left the ring leg weary, with bleeding mouths.

Dempsey said that was his last sparring. He gave all of his sparring partners ringside tickets.

Harry Newman said Firpo had youth and strength on his side. He hit a mean blow. Skill and science were not his thing, and although he had improved in that respect, he probably was about as good as he was going to get. When stung, he often threw away his skill and tore in madly. It might be fatal for him to lose his head against a puncher like Dempsey. Given that he could hit with knockout force, for long as he could take it, he would have a chance to win.[1296]

Damon Runyon gave Firpo almost zero chance, even though the odds had dropped to 2 to 1. He thought Dempsey should be 10 to 1 or 100 to 1. Firpo's best chance would be if he could last 6 rounds. In Firpo's favor, "He is a big, powerful man, stronger than Dempsey, a tremendous hitter with his right hand. He seems able to take a hard punching. He has natural real pugilistic ability." He was more dangerous than some thought. If he could stand the punching he was bound to receive in the early rounds and could take Dempsey's slams, it would be a hard battle, and he had a shot. But on form, Dempsey ought to win as easily as he won against Jess Willard. He was too fast and experienced for Firpo.[1297]

Various folks weighed in with their picks. Jess Willard said it was a toss-up. "Dempsey can hit. So can Firpo. Dempsey is clever. Firpo is awkward. But Firpo's awkwardness is puzzling. Firpo is dangerous." William Wrigley, Jr., owner of the Chicago Cubs, picked Dempsey. Rocky Kansas, lightweight contender, said Dempsey was too fast, knew too much, and would win within 3 rounds. Many said Dempsey would win, but Firpo had a chance. Lew Shank, Indianapolis mayor, said if Dempsey did not win in 3 or 4 rounds, Firpo would knock him out. "Firpo is the most wonderful hitter I ever saw." Tad Dorgan said it was a pick 'em. Bill Brennan, who fought both, picked Dempsey. Firpo was dangerous and hit hard enough to wear Jack down, but Dempsey hit hard enough to score a clean knockout at any time. Referee Toby Irwin said, "Dempsey in the first or second round." Referee Eddie Graney said the rough Firpo might tire out Dempsey and win, owing to Dempsey's relative lack of activity since winning the championship. Lemuel Bolles, national adjutant of the American Legion, said Firpo looked like the best bet to win the championship in a long time.

Robert Edgren said Firpo was dangerous but did not have Dempsey's class. All respected fight experts were picking Dempsey. Jack had better offense and defense. He had the superior skills. The one punch that landed most on Dempsey was a jab, but Firpo didn't hardly jab. Firpo was hittable, though he had real fighting spirit and was game. He fought to

[1296] *New York Daily News, Buffalo Courier,* September 12, 1923.
[1297] *Buffalo Times, Buffalo Times, Buffalo Times, Brooklyn Citizen, Binghamton Press, Buffalo Courier,* September 12, 1923.

win by knockout. He had great fighting instincts. Ultimately, Edgren thought only an accident would cause Dempsey to lose, an accident in the form of Firpo's right to the jaw. He thought Dempsey likely would win in 6 - 8 rounds, though he probably would try to win in 2 - 3 rounds.[1298]

DEMPSEY

HEIGHT 6' 1½
NECK 17"
REACH 73"
BICEPS 15"
CHEST, NORMAL 41"
EXPANDED 44"
WAIST 32½
WRIST 8¼"
THIGH 22"
CALF 15"
WEIGHT 189 LBS
ANKLE 9"
AGE 28 YRS.

FIRPO

HEIGHT 6' 2½"
AGE 26 YEARS
NECK 17"
REACH 79"
WRIST 8¼"
BICEPS 13½"
FOREARM 13¾"
WAIST 36½
CHEST NORMAL 44"
EXPANDED 48½"
THIGH 23¾
CALF 15"
WEIGHT 214 lbs
ANKLE 9½"

(NEWS photo)
Firpo measures Lester Johnson for right swing

Firpo lands on McCann

Carpenters installed enough seats for 88,000 spectators. It was anticipated that the fight would be either the largest or at least the second largest grossing fight in history.

Six men were arrested, in possession of $50,000 in counterfeit tickets. They were selling tickets listed at $27.50 for $77.50.[1299]

[1298] *Buffalo Enquirer, Buffalo Times*, September 13, 1923.
[1299] *New York Daily News*, September 13, 1923.

Dempsey and Mike Trant open the champ's mail

Dempsey's sparring partners were glad that their work was done. They had earned their money the hard way. Godfrey said getting hit by a ten-ton truck would feel like a flea bite after what he had been through with Dempsey. When asked what a sparring partner thinks about when in there facing the champion, Godfrey responded, "You don't think about nothing. He don't give you time."

Bill Brennan said Firpo was a more punishing hitter. If Bill could fight either man again, he would prefer to fight Dempsey rather than Firpo. Dempsey's knockout blow was painless. Firpo was the type who wore you down steadily and knocked you to pieces. Bill had to go to the hospital after the Firpo fight. Dempsey did not do that to him. "Firpo is immune to punishment. I gave him all I had." Bill hit him as hard as he could but could not keep him off. It was like shooting BB shots on a hippopotamus. It was impossible to hurt him. Every punch Firpo landed hurt. It would be a war of attrition.

Jess Willard said Firpo managed to land somehow, and when he did, you felt it, particularly to the kidneys. He had a fearful right. Luis was awkward and hard to box against, using his unorthodox style to his advantage. Dempsey had to be very careful with him.

Tex Rickard said the gate would have exceeded the Carpentier fight had the State of New York allowed him to charge the same prices for seats as he did for that fight. The state regulation would cut down on the gate. The highest ticket price was $27.50, whereas two years ago it was $50. Regardless of the government price-fixing regulation, by the end of the fight, Jack Dempsey would be involved in the three highest grossing fights in boxing's history; Carpentier and Willard being the other two. Firpo-Willard would be in fourth place. The receipts likely would surpass $1.25 million, and the fight also would exceed the paid attendance record set by Firpo-Willard, which was 74,716.

Like Dempsey-Carpentier, the upcoming fight would be broadcast on the radio as well, via radio station WJZ, with Major James Andrew White, the pioneer radio announcer of championship boxing contests.[1300]

The forecast was for a clear and cool evening. Since it was an outdoor arena, if there was rain, the fight would be moved to the following night or the first clear night.

Dempsey said,

> I'm feeling fine – not a worry in the world, and am ready for battle. I have no battle plan, other than to keep my jaw out of range of Firpo's right and keep my back off the floor. I'll make my battle plans when the opening gong sounds. My only hope is that Firpo is feeling as fine as I do, then the public will see a real championship scrap.

Firpo said, "I feel fit to fight any man in the world, and I am confident I will be the winner. It is not my habit to say in what round I will win – but win I will. The longer the battle goes the better will be my chances."

Firpo also said, "I am in good shape. I feel like fighting as I never have before. ... I am confident. I am not afraid. If I am knocked down again and again, I will come up again and again. ... I don't think Jack Dempsey can beat me and I don't think that he can stand up under my punches."

[1300] *Buffalo Courier, Glens Falls Post-Star, Buffalo Commercial,* September 13, 1923. Most say Dempsey–Carpentier was the first live radio broadcast of a world title fight, via New York radio station WJY. Others say Dempsey–Miske at Benton Harbor in 1920 was the first boxing match broadcast on radio. Dempsey-Miske might have had more of a delay and reached a smaller audience.

The *Buffalo Commercial* noted that the Pampas Bull had advantages in height, reach, and weight over Dempsey the Man Mauler.

Kearns said Dempsey was too quick for Firpo and was the better puncher. He would stop him as quickly as possible. Jack was hitting faster, more accurately, and harder than he was before he fought Gibbons. That fight helped prepare him for this one. If Firpo was as good as they said, it would be a slashing fight.

Expert predictions included: Hype Igoe – Dempsey in the 1st round; Damon Runyon – Dempsey in 3 rounds; W. O. McGeehan – If Dempsey does not win in 5 rounds, Firpo will win; Vincent Treanor – Nothing to it but Dempsey; Harry Newman – Dempsey in 3.

Henry Farrell said Harry Wills likely would be Dempsey's next foe. Political obstacles which stood in the way of the fight would be removed next year, after the national conventions. "Dempsey is not afraid of Wills. Those who intimate that he is timid about fighting the big colored stevedore have reasons for saying so that have no connection with Dempsey. It is part of a ballyhoo."

Farrell said Firpo was no set-up, and if Dempsey knocked him out, it simply was because he was a great fighter. Dempsey had a chance to win public popularity if he won, something he had not possessed before.[1301]

On Friday September 14, 1923 at the Polo Grounds in New York, Jack Dempsey defended his world heavyweight championship for the fifth time, against Luis Angel Firpo (25-2) of Argentina. Firpo had been a professional fighter for nearly six years.

Dempsey and Firpo weighed in at different times. Jack showed up at the boxing commission's offices first, at 2 p.m., and weighed 192 ½ pounds. He waited 15 minutes, but when Firpo did not show up, he left.

Firpo showed up 30 minutes later, and weighed 216 ½ pounds, giving him a 24-pound weight advantage, more than what Dempsey had over Carpentier or Gibbons.

William Muldoon asked both fighters not to wear their flags around their waists. He did not want the patrons' patriotic passions to become overly inflamed. Firpo had planned to wear the Argentine flag as his belt, which was blue and white, while Dempsey typically wore an American flag belt.[1302]

Although the anticipated fight time temperature was less than 50 degrees, actually, the low that day was 55 degrees, and the high 69 degrees Fahrenheit. The championship fight would be taking place outdoors at night at about 9:30 p.m., so temperatures likely were closer to the lower end of that spectrum. The preliminary bouts would begin at 8 p.m.

Rickard said a throng of more than 90,000 would pay approximately $1,340,000 to witness the fight. Builders had erected temporary additions to the Polo Grounds field. Hence, there were a total of 90,374 seats.

[1301] *Brooklyn Standard Union, Buffalo Commercial, Buffalo Express, Brooklyn Daily Times, New York Daily News,* September 14, 1923. Gene Tunney and Leo Gates, the Mohawk Indian, were scheduled for the 12-round semifinal.
[1302] *Elmira Star-Gazette,* September 14, 1923; *New York Daily News,* September 15, 1923.

600 patrolmen, 3 captains, 10 lieutenants, 56 sergeants, and a mounted squad of 40 men would be on police duty at and inside the arena.

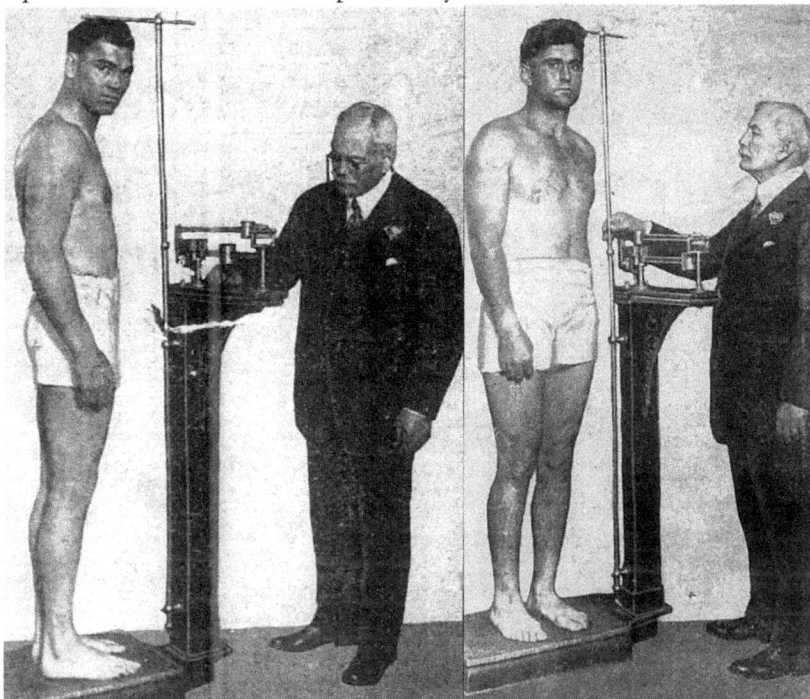

William Muldoon, New York State Athletic Commission chair, weighs Dempsey and Firpo.

The Polo Grounds arena

Dempsey was quoted as saying,

> I have trained hard for this match, because I expect it will be a tough one. I do not pay any attention to those who expect Firpo will be an easy opponent. I am not holding him lightly, but I do not fear him. Firpo is big and strong and dangerous. They are all dangerous until you have them on the floor. ... If I can end the fight in one round, I'll do it, because I can't take any chances with him. Perhaps the fight will go farther than many expect because Firpo probably can take a lot of punishment. I'll give him plenty of chances to demonstrate this, because I intend to sock as hard as I can from the start, but not take any early risks myself. He is too dangerous with his right hand.[1303]

[1303] *Poughkeepsie Eagle-News*, *Brooklyn Daily Eagle*, September 14, 1923.

That evening, traffic outside the arena was very heavy, and folks barely could move, either walking or via auto.

The "Hot Dog Boys" were selling frankfurters in the arena, calling them "Wild Bulls of the Pampas."

Press row was hard at work with typewriters and telegraph machines. A platform high in the air filmed the proceedings. A band played music to entertain the patrons.

William Muldoon was in attendance, as well as George M. Cohan and John Barrymore. Jim Corbett, former lightweight champ Jack McAuliffe, and other pugilistic celebrities were at ringside. Jess Willard sat in a chair close to the ring. Babe Ruth was near him, chewing on a cigar. Playing for the Yankees, Ruth would earn a $52,000 annual salary in 1923 and 1924.

There was not a vacant seat to be seen anywhere. At least 85,000 were present. It was a wonderful sight, with the stands packed, distant lights, and twinkling flags fluttering in the dusky sky.

Amongst the prelims, Jack Burke scored a TKO4 over Bill Reed. Because of a right-hand injury, Gene Tunney had to withdraw from the scheduled co-main event against Leo Gates. 182-pound Bartley Madden filled in and won a 12-round decision over 189-pound Gates.

At 9:50 p.m., while the last two rounds of the final preliminary were being fought, there was a sudden, great roar from the crowd as Firpo, wearing a black-and-gold checkerboard bathrobe/dressing gown, with royal purple trimming, which he wore for all of his U.S. fights, with a towel over his shoulders, made his way towards the ring, and sat down in a corner outside of the ring.

A few seconds later, a great roar went up from the crowd as Dempsey entered and took a seat in the press box in a corner.

When the semi-final ended, there was another great roar and clapping as Firpo climbed into the ring. He had a full set of Thursday's whiskers.

A moment later, Kearns jumped in, quickly followed by the champ. Dempsey wore his usual white silk trunks, with a white sweater over his shoulders. Like Firpo, he was not clean-shaven.

As soon as the men entered the ring, all of the spectators stood up, and they remained standing until the fight was over.

Dempsey walked over to Firpo to shake hands. They were photographed together. Jack returned to his corner and sat down, wrapped in an army blanket.

Kearns, Joe Benjamin, and Jerry Luvadis seconded Dempsey.

Dan Morgan and the Argentine handlers were behind Firpo.

Joe Humphries introduced "the champion of all champions, our own Jack Dempsey." Immense roar of cheers. "The pugilistic champion of all South America, Luis Angel Firpo." Cheering again. Weights were announced as Dempsey, 192 ½, Firpo 216 ½. The judges were Kid McPartland and George Partrich.

Referee Johnny Gallagher, appointed by the commission, met with the fighters at mid-ring for instructions. Dempsey's head was lowered. He gazed grimly at Firpo's stomach, or he looked away from him. Firpo seemed to tower over him.

When they returned to their corners, one writer said Dempsey seemed nervous and impatient for the gong to ring. Firpo showed no anxiety. Another said Dempsey did a little jig step while waiting for the gong.

Firpo imitated but was clumsy. Once he removed his robe, it could be seen that Firpo was wearing his favorite lavender/purple trunks.

1st round

On the films, at the bell, Dempsey immediately quickly charged across the ring and fired a lead left hook that was short, while Firpo stepped back and fired a counter right that landed, and as Dempsey's left arm reached out to grab behind Firpo's head, the combination of the Firpo punch and forward momentum caused Jack's left leg to go out from underneath him and he went down, his left knee touching the canvas, but he quickly rose and pulled himself back up, with his left arm behind Firpo's neck in a clinch, in less than a second. This first flash technical knockdown occurred within the first five seconds of the fight. There is a bit of a glitch/missing footage here, but it is clear that Jack's left knee touched the canvas.

Many writers failed to notice this first knockdown, but some did, calling it a flash. Davis Walsh said Jack fired a left hook, missed, lost his balance, and grabbed for Firpo's neck, but Firpo chopped his right on the jaw, and Dempsey went to his knees. He still held on to Firpo and was up on the rebound. Damon Runyon noted, "Dempsey did not go to the floor the first time Firpo clipped him solidly, although some reckon it a technical knockdown. His knees bent, he held himself partially erect by clinging to Firpo's big arm." The Associated Press called it a slip. Westbrook Pegler said, "At that first clinch, Dempsey slipped to his knees, grasping his opponent as he hauled himself up again." W. C. Vreeland said Dempsey rushed, practically running, shot over a left, but Firpo swung his right and caught him on the chin. Jim Corbett exclaimed, "My God, right on the button!" Dempsey half slid and half fell to his knees but jumped up quickly. Vreeland said Jack's momentum as much as the blow caused him to drop. He was off balance at the time the punch landed. Another version said Dempsey slipped, and Luis connected with a solid right high on the jaw that sent him to his knees.

From the start, the pace was very fast. Dempsey advanced quickly and Firpo fought ferociously in response, which continued throughout.

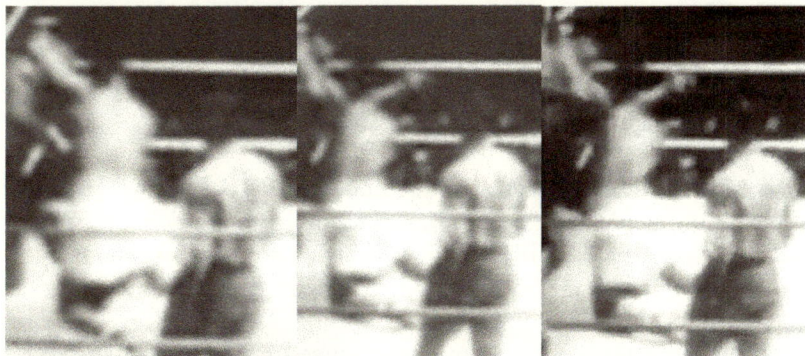

They clinched and scuffled up close. Firpo broke free and fired a right. He backed away and fired a 1-2 on the advancing, dipping Dempsey, and then in the clinch kept firing away with a couple high somewhat overhand rights, seeming to land on the back of Jack's head.

Freeing himself from the clinch, on or immediately after the break, Dempsey decked him, but the footage is truncated at this point (potentially edited intentionally, or so some later alleged), so it is difficult to see, but it looks like a left hook to the head may have been involved. It appears, and some reporters claimed, that when they broke, Firpo dropped his hands and looked at the referee, but Dempsey nailed him and he went down. The question is whether they were supposed to break clean at the referee's command, or protect themselves at all times, including on breaks (straight Queensberry rules). Most reporters did not mention anything odd at all, and simply noted that Dempsey decked Firpo.

William Granger said a left and right to the body, followed by a left hook to the chin put Firpo down. The AP said it was a right to the body and left to the jaw. Robert Edgren said it was a left hook to the jaw. W. C. Vreeland agreed it was a short left hook. Firpo seemed more bewildered than hurt. Sid Sutherland said Dempsey scored his first knockdown by hitting on the breakaway from a clinch, which he called a foul.

Dempsey walked over and hovered near a corner. Firpo rose relatively quickly, within a few seconds (Charles Murray said he rose at 3), and Jack was right back on him again, immediately rushing across the ring. Firpo fired a lead right, Dempsey ducked under it, and Luis clinched. The referee broke them.

Dempsey advanced aggressively. Firpo landed a well-timed lead right uppercut on the ducking Dempsey, and followed with a right to the body and head as they scuffled and clinched up close, with Dempsey turning/spinning them both around in a semi-circle, a move he used against Gibbons. Referee break.

Firpo moved away and Dempsey advanced rapidly. Firpo landed his overhand right and Dempsey landed his left hook. While Firpo's left and Dempsey's right arm were mutually clinched, Dempsey kept firing away with his left as they spun around - two hooks to the head, a couple to the body, followed by a short left uppercut to the jaw and a left hook high on the head of the forward-leaning Firpo, and Firpo went down for the second time, on one hand and knee. Dempsey quickly walked off to the side as the referee pointed him in the direction of a corner.

Firpo rose very quickly again, after only one or two seconds. Dempsey rapidly advanced with a jab to the body as Firpo fired a right to the head and clinched. Dempsey partially freed himself and punched with a couple right hooks to the head (as he did with Gibbons), and then he freed his left arm, fired four left uppercuts to the head in rapid succession, and Firpo went down for the third time. Dempsey immediately walked off, as if he was going to a corner to await the count.

Firpo quickly rose again (though there seems to be a cut or missing footage here). Some reports said he was right up, while others said he rose at 9. Knockdown counts for this fight were all over the map, in part because the action was so fast and frenetic, reporters hardly could agree on how many knockdowns there were, let alone how long the count was for each one, or even which punches led to the knockdowns.

Dempsey moved in immediately, and Firpo landed his overhand right to the head while Dempsey was landing his right uppercut to the body. Firpo followed with a close-in right to the head in the clinch. Dempsey responded with a short inside left uppercut to the jaw and a short left to the body. Referee break.

Again, Firpo landed a lead right on the advancing Dempsey and they clinched. Dempsey fired short lefts to the body and head, then shifted to firing rights to the body and head, and then a short, fast, snappy left to the body and Firpo went down. He rolled over onto his back, sprawled out, his fourth knockdown. Dempsey disappeared from view as he walked off to a corner.

Firpo appeared to be quite hurt, more than previously, laying outstretched on his back, then rolling over onto his belly at about the referee's count of 5, still down. He rose just after the count of 8, possibly 9 (which some said), though one said it was after 10, and the fight should have been over. W. C. Vreeland said he sat in the first row and had a splendid view. When Referee Gallagher counted 10, this author believed that Firpo's fingers still were on the mat, but the referee allowed it to continue.

As Luis was in the process of rising, Dempsey already was on his way towards him, and as soon as Firpo's left glove left the canvas, Jack fired an overhand right, landing immediately after he was upright, sending him right back down again, for the fifth time. There is a bit of missing footage here. Some said Dempsey's act was foul, but most ignored it. He seemed to have timed his advance perfectly such that his punch would be on its way to land as soon as Firpo was upright.

Firpo rose almost immediately, at the count of 1, after Dempsey had stepped back a pace and had turned to the side to walk away, so instead Jack quickly changed directions and stepped in to attack again, but this time Firpo caught him on the way in with a fast and powerful lead right that appeared to land on the back of the head as Dempsey was dipping to the right. It knocked him off balance towards the right, but then when Dempsey came back up towards the left, Firpo had another right on the way and it nailed Dempsey at the perfectly timed moment, and Jack's

773

gloves went forward and down onto the canvas, though his legs still were up. It was the second time Dempsey technically went down in the round.

Dempsey's hands were down for less than a second, possibly half a second (Edgren said he rose without a count), and he immediately pushed up off the canvas with his body in the bent over position. Firpo, who was right there, instantly landed a right uppercut and left hook, and, holding with his left, followed with a right to the head that sent Jack back a step, but then the undeterred Dempsey immediately advanced again as Firpo took a step back and fired his wild right wallop in hooking fashion, but Dempsey ducked under it and Firpo clinched. Dempsey dug three right uppercuts into the body. The referee broke them.

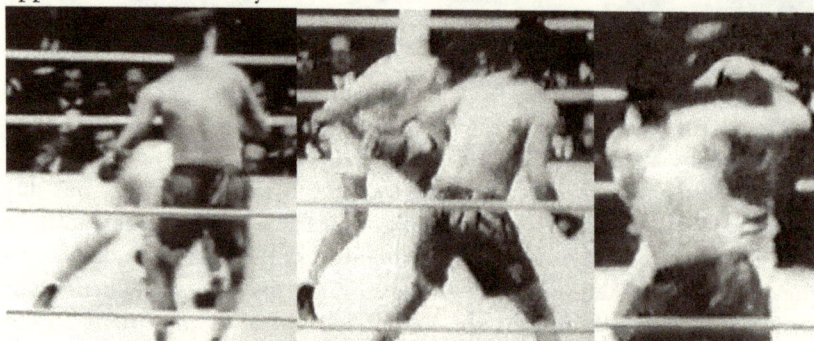

Dempsey quickly advanced with a lead hook that was more of a set-up punch, and immediately followed with a fast, powerful, pulverizing right that went over the top of Firpo's attempt at a left hook, landing on Firpo's head, sending Luis down for the sixth time.

This time, Dempsey did not go anywhere, but stood right next to, over, and slightly behind Firpo, who was down near a corner. The referee counted 1, and at what would be the count of 2, momentarily swiped his hand out to the side as if directing Dempsey to step back.

However, foolishly, Firpo rose quickly again, at about 2. Since there was no mandatory 8 count, when Firpo's gloves left the canvas, Dempsey was entitled to hit him again.

As soon as Firpo's hands left the canvas, with him still in a partially bent-over position, Dempsey stepped in and fired a lead left uppercut to the head and Firpo dropped down again, the seventh time he had been down in the round. This time, Dempsey stepped over him and went to a corner, though it was the one that was closest.

Firpo seemed to rise at 5 and wisely backed away as Dempsey advanced, eagerly looking to pounce on his prey. Firpo threw a couple rights and held. Dempsey dug his left into the body and head as Firpo pushed forward while holding. The referee broke them, and Firpo backed up. As Dempsey was advancing into range, Firpo landed a lead right on Jack's jaw just as Jack was firing a right uppercut to the body, which also landed. Firpo pushed him back. The relentless Dempsey advanced again as Firpo poised to meet him.

Firpo landed a heavy wide right to the body and followed with a jarring right to the head, but then kept throwing and landing nonstop rights to the head as Dempsey backed up from the fusillade, hitting the ropes. Firpo measured him with an outstretched left and fired an overhand right to the jaw, and in a nonstop furious combination kept firing hard rights off of measuring left leads and hooks, but the rights were landing, over and over again, despite Dempsey's efforts to block, duck, or hold. After about nine total rapid rights had been fired, most of them landing on Jack's head, the final overhand right ¾-decked and ¼-pushed Dempsey through the ropes and out of the ring, the third time Dempsey had been down in the round. However, this time it was not just a knee or his gloves that were down, but his entire body fell out of the ring, right into the laps of those at ringside. There was not much ring platform space between the ropes and the edge of the ring, and there were only three ropes, with no spacers holding them taut, so it was easy to fall through them and into the crowd. Dempsey's legs were over and then on the ring, so he did not fall that far.

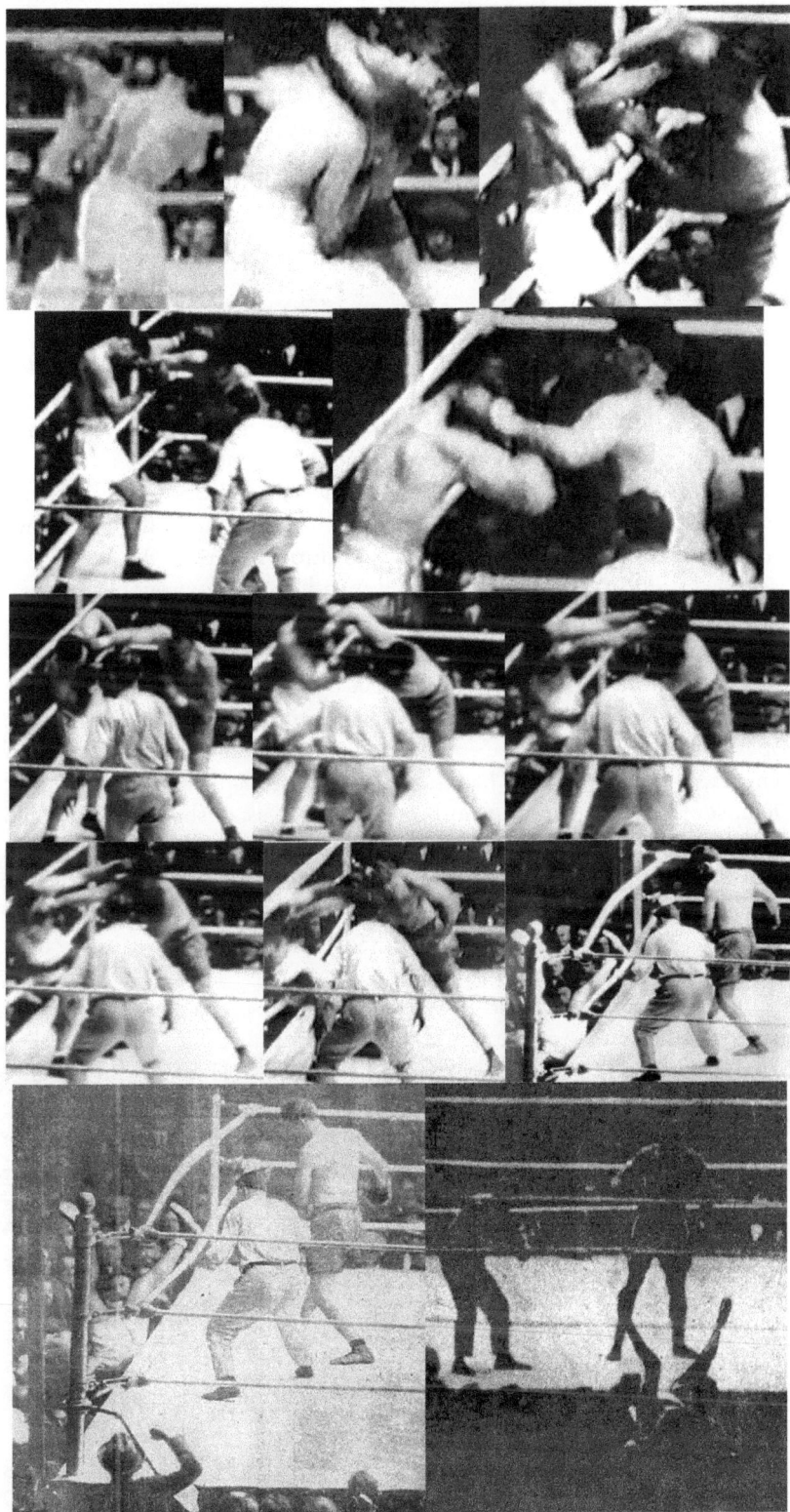

Dempsey quickly got back into the ring, seemingly between the referee's count of 3 and 4 (though some said it was longer, and there may be an edit/missing footage here), climbing over the lower rope, placing his hands on the canvas inside the ring, and then standing up.

In describing the events, Charles Murray said a hurricane of punches sent Dempsey clean through the ropes, the champ's heels flashing above the second rope as he plunged backward into press row. At six, he was back in the ring. Yet, Murray also said men in the press row pushed him back in.

Damon Runyon noted some slight controversy regarding Dempsey's re-entry back into the ring. "Some think he might not have gotten back into the ring as quickly as he did when Firpo punched him through the ropes if he had not had a couple of kindly hands pushing him from beneath, these hands the hands of friendly newspapermen. However, Dempsey was struggling upward, even as he was pushed, so he would probably have gotten there unaided just the same." At another point, Runyon said the timekeeper had counted three when Dempsey, hanging with his feet in the air, his head outside, hauled himself back into the ring.

W. C. Vreeland said Jack was pushed back into the ring, but started fighting at once, none the worse.

Davis Walsh initially said Dempsey went into the laps of reporters in the first row. As the referee was counting, Jack pulled himself to the edge of the ring and then climbed through the ropes. However, at another point in his article, Walsh said Dempsey's feet were hooked over the middle strand of the ropes and his head was in some typewriter in the press row. "Somehow, he righted himself, or obliging hands did it for him. Then he crawled about on hands and knees over the space outside the rope, and finally stepped back into the ring."

The Associated Press said Dempsey was back in the ring in an instant.

Robert Edgren said Dempsey scrambled back into the ring.

Ring Lardner said when Dempsey was knocked out of the ring, "Grantland Rice was there to receive him." "Even when he fell into Mr. Rice's lap he picked himself up without assistance and stepped right back to the place where all the shooting was going on."

Heywood Broun said Dempsey sprawled across the lap of a boxing expert who had written that the fight was ludicrous and Firpo had no chance, so the irony was noted. Jack was hurt. "But the fighting instinct of the champion was functioning. He crawled back and clinched before the clumsy Argentine could push him away."

On the films, Firpo had stepped back a few paces, but when Jack re-entered and was in the process of rising, Luis stepped towards him (just as Jack had done to him), and as soon as Jack stood up, Luis had a right on its way towards the body, which Jack rolled right, and Firpo followed with a right to the head off a lead left. Dempsey clinched, and Luis snuck in a short right. The referee broke them.

DEMPSEY CLIMBS BACK THROUGH THE ROPES.

Dempsey advanced and Firpo fired right that missed over top of a ducking Dempsey, but followed with a combination of nonstop lefts and rights, landing solidly, jolting Jack's head back, and sending him backwards into the ropes as the rapid fusillade continued. Dempsey fired a counter right off the ropes, ducked and smothered, and then in the clinch tried to sneak in his left to the body and head while Firpo was holding tightly. The referee broke them.

Dempsey advanced, Firpo missed a right uppercut as Jack backed away, but Firpo advanced and stepped in with 1-2, 1-2 that sent Dempsey back to the ropes. Dempsey tried to hold but Firpo kept firing rights high on the side and back of his head.

While eating a Firpo jab, Dempsey landed his own right in response that sent Firpo back into the ropes near the corner. Firpo missed a left over the top of the ducking Dempsey, who countered with a right uppercut to the body, and they clinched. Dempsey dug a left hook into the body. The referee broke them.

Firpo retreated and Dempsey advanced with a quick lead left hook. Firpo attempted to clinch, and the bell rang, because the referee raised his arms up in the air, indicating the round's conclusion, but as Firpo was heading towards his corner, Dempsey snuck in an extra left hook for good measure after the bell. Dempsey walked across the ring to his corner. Firpo was next to his own corner.

Most reporters noted that Dempsey had thrown after the bell. Walsh said he landed a left and right after the bell, and did not seem to know the round was over. The AP said Dempsey hit him after the bell, but the referee did not seem to notice it. Edgren said when the bell rang, few could hear it, the clamor from the crowd was so great and loud. Jack struck three more blows before he realized time had been called. Heywood Broun said when the bell rang, Dempsey kept punching away at Firpo, the referee tugged at his arm and slapped him on the back, and still he tried to hit the Argentine. "It was not until the crowd started to boo that Dempsey shook his head, blinked and woke."

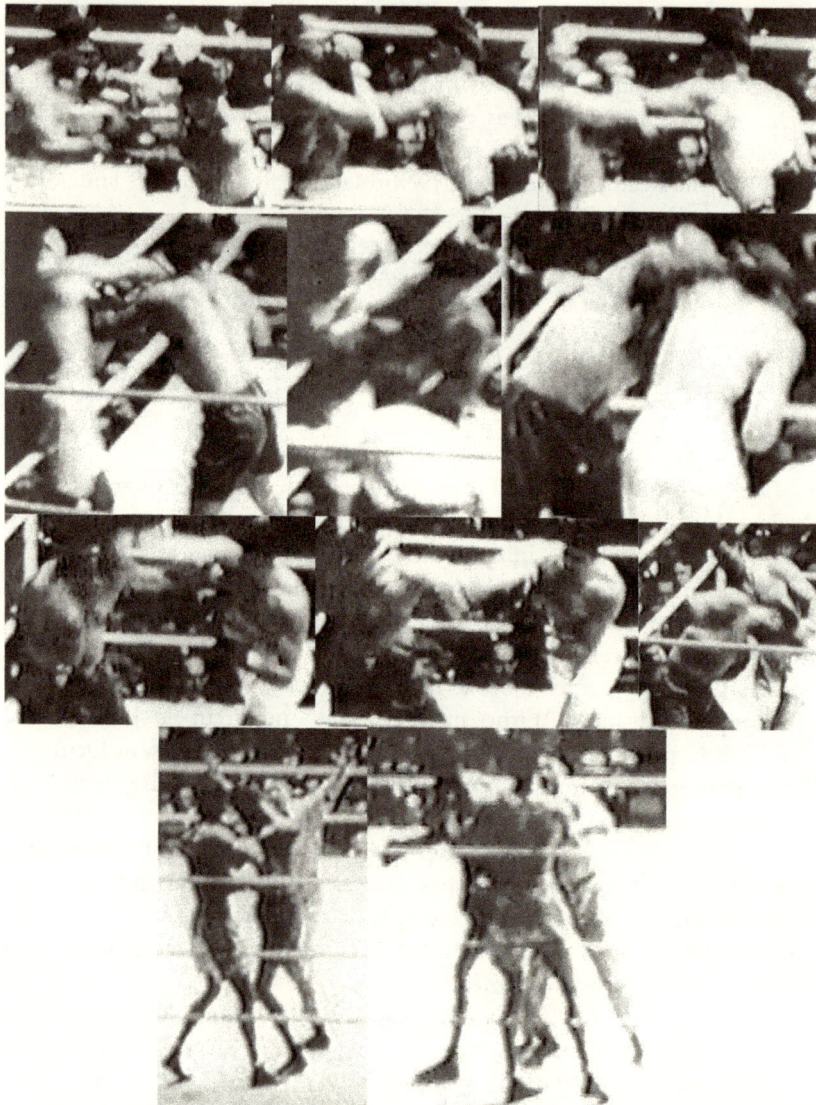

It had been the wildest, most exciting, brutal, fastest-paced, action-packed, frenetic 1st round ever, filled with 10 knockdowns total. Firpo was down 7 times, and Dempsey 3 times. First, Dempsey went down on a knee. Then Firpo went down five times. Dempsey went down again on his hands. Firpo went down twice more. Finally, Dempsey went through the ropes.

Both men had been hurt. It was a wild, nonstop, vicious brawl, the kind that makes fans stand on their feet and cheer and yell with delight. Both men were perfectly content to fight it out, bombs away, each believing that they had the power to stop the other, and believing that they could handle or recover from whatever the other landed. It was a legendary 1st round. One hardly could follow the flying fists. Dempsey and Firpo packed more furious fighting into one round than many do in 12 rounds. Dempsey was absolutely relentless, advancing quickly with no hesitation, punching away. Firpo was content to meet him on the way in and fire away with his pulverizing right, even attacking with nonstop series of blows when he sensed an advantage.

Charles Murray said Firpo was a man of enormous strength, with bone-crushing blows, and blessed with a bull-dog fighting instinct. He swung like an enraged bull. Dempsey's marvelous ring generalship came to his rescue after being knocked through the ropes. He had enough sense to duck the follow-up and survive the onslaught.

The AP said Firpo's mouth gushed blood. His sledgehammer right to the ribs created a thud that could have been heard a block away. He had stupendous, staggering rushes.

William Granger also said blood flowed from Firpo's mouth.

W. C. Vreeland said Luis' lips were bleeding. Blood trickled from Dempsey's mouth as well. Both were breathing heavily from the furious pace.

Westbrook Pegler noticed that Firpo's huge back was powdered gray with resin from the canvas.

Robert Edgren said Dempsey's blows decked Firpo as if he had been hit with an axe. The champion had terrific power. But Firpo fought with a rage, and tore in with redoubled fury, firing terrible rights to the head and body. Both hit furiously, with little or no defense.

After the round, Kearns talked and Dempsey nodded. Firpo's cornermen were working too hard to talk to him.

Davis Walsh said, "It was Dempsey's round, but any one's fight at this juncture." After the round, as he approached his chair, Kearns splashed cold water in Dempsey's face. After he sat, Kearns shoved smelling salts under his nostrils. He kept them there for the full minute rest, while the other attendants rubbed his neck and chest.

2nd round

Dempsey advanced very quickly and moved in to clinch as Firpo fired a right. As they were breaking, Dempsey landed a left hook to the head. Dempsey followed up with a lead right that landed and hook that missed as Firpo blocked and clinched with his back to the ropes. As the referee broke them, Dempsey landed another left hook on the break.

Firpo backpedaled away. Dempsey advanced, and both threw at nearly the same time, Firpo twice with his right and Dempsey with his right to the body and left hook to the head combination twice in rapid succession, both fighters landing. However, Firpo was the one who seemed affected, dipping down and clinching, while Dempsey kept trying to work, missing his left uppercut. Firpo kept bulling in and clinching, and Dempsey wrestled and pushed him off, but in doing so, pushed the clutching Firpo down to the canvas.

Yet, despite being pushed down, the referee called it a knockdown. In truth it was not. Certainly though, it showed Dempsey's strength and the fact that Firpo was weakening and affected by the blows. Regardless, the referee and nearly all of the reporters said Firpo had been hit and dropped. So, it is possible that there was a punch obscured by the camera angle, but it sure does not look that way. It might have been considered a delayed effect and knockdown as a result of the punches that caused Firpo to clinch tightly in the first place. Dempsey slowly walked to a corner; the referee possibly ordering him there.

Firpo remained down until the count of 5. Murray said it was 5. Some said he jumped right up, while others said it was 7, 8, or 9. Dempsey advanced, Firpo fired a lead right, but Dempsey ducked under it well, and Firpo clinched. Dempsey struggled to work his hands free, which he did, digging short shots, a left uppercut, left hook, left uppercut, and right hook. Firpo kept bulling in, smothering, and clinching. The referee moved in to help break them apart, but it was not a complete break.

Dempsey freed himself further and landed a short left hook to the chin and a wide, hooking, snappy right to the jaw, and Firpo collapsed straight down to his hands and knees, and then rolled over onto his back, arms outstretched, one leg straight out and the other bent.

At about the count of 7, Firpo slowly rolled over onto his stomach. At 10, he still was on his hands and knees, with torso close to the canvas, but pushing up slightly. Firpo was struggling against an unseen force, as if a ton of weight was on top of him holding him down. Dempsey walked over and picked him up off the canvas. Firpo clearly could not rise under his own power, and he barely could stand, his legs wobbly and unstable. His seconds assisted him to his corner and sat him down on his stool. He seemed not to understand entirely that the fight was over.

Walsh said Firpo's purple trunks, as well as his gloves, were covered with resin. His face was smeared with blood. Dempsey had a cut on his left cheek and his eye was swollen. While the count was concluding, Jack seemed calm and cool, smiling to the scribes in his corner, rubbing his nose with his left thumb. "It was the end of possibly the shortest and greatest heavyweight championship battle ever held."

The AP said Firpo, his purple trunks streaked with resin, was out, laying under the cluster of arc lights. Blood streamed from his mouth. He struggled to rise but could not.

Edgren said when Firpo went down for the final time, Dempsey ran to his corner, leaned on the ropes, and then turned to watch the count. He knew it was over. After the count, he caught Luis under the arms and dragged him up to his feet, helping him to his corner. Shortly thereafter, he came back to shake hands with Firpo, who stood up to meet him. Jack slapped his back, looking happy.

Vreeland said Dempsey had shown great recuperative power, coming out for the 2nd round looking refreshed. Firpo landed a right smash on the ribs that seemed powerful enough to cave them in. He landed another to the head, and Corbett yelled, "Keep your head down, Jack, keep it down!" But soon it was Firpo who was down twice and out. His efforts to rise were futile. After assistance, the dazed Firpo suddenly recovered his senses and wanted to fight again, but was held back.

The knockout—with Referee Gallagher just before start of fatal count eliminated Firpo's threat

The fight was over at 57 seconds of the 2nd round. Luis Firpo had been down officially 9 times in the contest (although one knockdown appeared to be a push). Dempsey had been down 3 times. 12 knockdowns in 1 1/3 rounds. Not a bad fight, eh?

Having won the "Battle of the Americas," Dempsey left the ring to "ear-splitting applause." The crowd had absolutely loved the frenetic fight.

Not only had it been a great fight, but it also was a great financial success. The huge crowd of 85,800 generated $1,250,000, making it the second greatest financial attraction in ring history.

Joe Humphries announces Jack as the winner

Dempsey-Carpentier, which did not have the same ticket-price restrictions, was first, at $1.6 million. It was estimated that 5,000 more were inside the park, including policemen, firemen, ushers, pop vendors, and other employees. Rickard said about 50,000 people were in the stands, while the rest were on the field.

Dempsey's share, 37 ½% of the $1.25 million, was $468,750, his greatest payday yet, by far. Some said Firpo's share was 12.5%, or $156,250. The fighters' total share was 50% of the total receipts. Others said Firpo fought for a $100,000 flat fee. Dempsey earned $2,100.70 for every second of actual fighting. Firpo earned $659.28 per second.

Dempsey said, "I won as I thought I would, but I can truthfully say that I never had such a fight in all my life. When he socked me on the chin in the first round, knocking me through the ropes after I had knocked him down I thought my finish had come." Jack said those who told him that Firpo would be easy did not know what they were talking about. Firpo was tough from the start.

> After he slammed me with that first right, I knew that I had a fight on my hands. Firpo is dangerous every second. I hit him with everything I had and certainly was surprised when he continued to crawl off the floor. He is game and the hardest puncher I ever faced. It was the first time I was knocked down since I became champion and I'll never forget it. I saw 8,000,000 stars.

Dempsey said Firpo was a "strong, game fighter with a natural style that science is no good against. I was forced to beat him with the same wild tactics that he employed against me. Yes, I was hurt several times, but I'm glad that I also had the chance to prove that I am game."

When asked why he hit Firpo after the bell rang ending the 1st round, Dempsey replied, "I do not remember hitting Firpo after the gong in the first round." He might have been so hurt and dazed, and the crowd so loud, that he did not hear the bell.

Another quoted him as saying,

> Firpo can fight. He's a dangerous man in the ring. What a right he has! When he knocked me through the ropes I knew something struck me, but wasn't sure just what. It was the first time I had been knocked down since I became champion. But I gave Firpo all I had. I did a little knocking down myself. I knew I was in a fight, but so did Firpo.

Dempsey said it was "my toughest fight," and Firpo was the hardest puncher he ever faced. "How that baby can hit with his right. I saw a million stars. I was a little careless when I had him licked in the first round. He got me. There is no denying that. But he didn't get me entirely, though I guess I had a close shave. He sure can hit."

Jack asked, "Did I look bad when he knocked me through the ropes?" The reporter said it looked like he was on the verge of a knockout. "It wasn't as bad as that. I was hurt, but I was all right. I knew what I was doing and while I probably looked foolish with my legs sticking through the ropes, believe me I was glad when the gong rang. That baby sure can hit."

Yet, another quoted him as saying, "Firpo is a big, strong and tough fellow and he can hit. When I went through the ropes I half slipped. I don't mean to say he didn't hit me. He did. I went in to finish the thing quickly and we started to swap punches. He beat me to it. But my head was clear when I climbed back into the ring."

Dempsey also told folks that he was not propelled out of the ring, but only fell out. "Say, I wasn't knocked through the ropes that time. I stepped back from a swing and stumbled. But this Firpo can hit. He hit me harder than anyone ever did before."

J. J. Wood quoted Dempsey as saying, "Firpo is a terrific hitter and the gamest fighter I have ever met. … In coming back repeatedly when knocked down by the hardest blows I could deliver, he left no room for doubt of his gameness."

Dempsey concluded, "Where's Harry Wills? Get him in here. I think I could lick him too, tonight."

Jack Kearns said,

> I knew Jack would win, but I didn't anticipate the terrific battle put up by Firpo. Dempsey's prime condition enabled him to withstand Firpo's powerful blows. Jack showed himself even a greater puncher than the Argentinian, who is the greatest hitter Jack ever met. The fact that Dempsey withstood all Firpo's blows and then knocked Firpo out, shows him to be the champion of champions, the greatest of all time.

Kearns admitted that he got the scare of his life when Dempsey went through the ropes. Still, his prediction of victory within 6 rounds was correct.

> Dempsey may have been dizzy, but was not badly hurt when he crawled back into the ring after being knocked through the ropes. At least he knew enough to take care of himself. Firpo certainly was a surprise to me. I never saw another heavyweight with the exception of Jack that can hit like he can. That right hand was murderous. I'll admit my heart nearly stopped beating when I saw the champion nearly knocked stiff. It was a great fight while it lasted.

Luis Firpo said, "Dempsey is a great fighter. He hit me plenty. I had my chance, too, when I put him through the ropes. It was anybody's fight for a while. I am disappointed at not winning, but I think I put up a creditable fight, and I want another chance at Dempsey, inside a year."

Another quoted Firpo as saying,

> Dempsey is a great fighter and a great champion. I do not understand how he was able to stand up under the blows that I landed on him. I still believe that I did not have enough experience to go into the fight. My friends tell me that I had Dempsey three times on the verge of a knockout. I thought I was the champion when I knocked him out of the ring. I would like to have a return bout and in another year I am certain that I can win the championship.

In another interview, Firpo said,

> I had him dizzy with the first punch I landed right at the start of the 1st round, but I couldn't keep him that way. My only complaint is that the referee did not make Dempsey observe the rules he laid

down before the fight. He told us if one of us was knocked down the other one should go to a neutral corner. Dempsey did not do that. Within a year I would like to fight Dempsey again after I have had more experience.

Westbrook Pegler said Firpo still was dazed 20 minutes after the fight. His speech was a bit wobbly too. Luis said, "As I said before the fight, I could beat Dempsey if given six months more experience. I thought I was about to get him when the gong sounded at the end of the 1st round."

Edgren quoted Firpo as saying, "I nearly had him."

Felix Bunge, Firpo's mentor, said, "The best man won. That is all I can say."

Referee John Gallagher said, "It was a thriller while it lasted. Dempsey showed that he is a real champion by taking the blows he did and then come back and put the big fellow away as neatly as he did. That boy Firpo can sock, and he can take it, too."

Gallagher said the champ showed wonderful recuperative powers, emerging for the 2nd round with the same spring and snap as in the 1st. A terrific left to the chin dropped Firpo. A snappy, short left, followed almost instantly by a right smash, and down and out went Firpo. The Andes Annihilator's body quivered, and he was unable to rise. Dempsey lifted Firpo's crumpled body erect.

Both had been practically out on their feet. Dempsey came back, and eventually Firpo could not. In the 1st round, the title swayed to and fro, from one to the other, and in the closing seconds, it was anybody's fight.

Firpo went down fighting and was dangerous to the end. Dempsey was catapulted out of the ring like a shell from the mouth of a Big Bertha. But he won, and Firpo made a showing far beyond what was expected of him. He proved his gameness and ability.

When informed of Firpo's comments about the referee's failure to enforce the neutral corner rule, Referee Gallagher said, "So Firpo thinks I didn't give him a square deal? All I have to say is that I stand on what I did in the ring. If there is any criticism due it will be made by the Boxing Commission."

The truth was that neither Firpo nor Dempsey consistently went to a neutral corner. Sometimes Dempsey did, and sometimes he did not. Firpo stepped back a bit, but was right there to hit Dempsey as soon as he rose, just as Dempsey did to him.

Tex Rickard said, "The thrill of my lifetime. A battle which will live forever in the recollection of those who saw it." "Firpo is one of the best fighters I ever have seen. ... He will be heard from again." "He is a big, strong young fellow and a terrific fighter."

Rickard said he wanted to arrange a bout between Wills and Firpo, and a potential rematch between Firpo and Dempsey the following summer, or with Wills, if such was possible.

The fight films would be shown throughout New York almost immediately, starting the day after the fight.

Jess Willard said, "Dempsey had a close call. That Firpo can hit." Jess said he now understood how Dempsey floored him seven times in the 1st round of their battle four years ago. Dempsey had done the same thing to him and Firpo both.

However, Firpo was younger and had been more active than Willard. He had fought more ferociously and faster than Jess had, and decked Dempsey, but wound up getting stopped sooner (although Willard was out cold at the end of the 1st round, saved by the bell, fighting on until retiring after the 3rd round).

Davis Walsh, International News Service Sport Editor, said Dempsey's powerful wallops were predominant in an epic of flying fists. Firpo was battered down seven times in the 1st round and twice in the 2nd, but the champ was close to a knockout in the 1st when he was slammed through the ropes. Both fought like it was a barroom brawl, swapping punch for punch. "As a battle of flying fists, the affair was epic." However, the skill was absent, for they simply brawled away.

Dempsey proceeded to charge in and mix it from the start, in a do-or-die manner, and Firpo was happy to oblige. Jack stepped out, led for the body with a left that was short, then took a powerful right to the side of the jaw. From then on, Jack abandoned all pretense of boxing skill. His strategy seemed almost suicidal. "Don't lose your head, Jack," Jim Corbett howled, but his excellent advice fell upon deaf ears. "Firpo never missed a punch for the remainder of the fight." The man who missed many swings at Brennan and Willard did not miss Dempsey, even though Jack reputedly was faster and better than those men. Dempsey simply met Firpo at his own game and exchanged punches until one or the other dropped. Sometimes it was one and sometimes the other, but mostly it was Firpo who went down.

The blows that dropped Firpo did not appear to be all that hard, although one time he fell with a convincing boom on the ring floor. Firpo's knocking of Dempsey through the ropes was quite another matter. The writer thought he never would come back, but somehow did. In the 2nd round, Dempsey decked him twice more and it was over.

Walsh called it the greatest fight ever. He concluded that Dempsey proved he could take a punch as well as give one. Yet, Walsh also harshly said Dempsey did not prove anything else, except that "he is quite probably over rated."

Afterwards, as he walked down the steps from the ring in his corner, a grinning Dempsey said, "Well boys, the Irish can still fight a little."

During the fight, several temporary benches throughout the arena went crashing to the ground. They were a broken mess and no doubt many people were injured. Every time Firpo went down, it seemed as though other sections went down as well.

Charles Murray for the *Buffalo Commercial* said Jack the Giant Killer's vicious, enraged-tiger attack saved his championship and annihilated Firpo. Sheer pluck linked with generalship never-equaled in the heat of a great ring battle rescued Dempsey from the depths of defeat and crushed the Argentinian hero like an eggshell under one's heel. He knocked Firpo stiff as a poker in the 2nd round. It was one of the fiercest and briefest battles ever fought between big men.

Dempsey had a narrow escape from being knocked out. In the 1st round, he was dropped by a terrific right swing to the chin, and though groggy, came up fighting.

Another fearful punch drove Dempsey through the ropes. "When Dempsey was pushed back into the ring by men in the press row, staggering as he advanced to trade blows with his foe, that old tigerish spirit magnified so that it stood out boldly in a thrilling spectacle, instantly blossomed and carried Dempsey on to victory."

The champ was endowed with unbreakable courage, and sent Firpo back by willpower. If he had any flaw in his gameness, Firpo would have exposed it, for he plunged in, slashing wickedly as he strove to floor the champion for the count. They fought punch for punch. Firpo the lion clawed with all his superhuman strength, trying to batter down the "greatest modern fighting man."

Firpo had withstood an unmerciful hammering, pounded to the floor no less than six times in the 1st round. After the bell, both men staggered and were unsteady. Pandemonium reigned, with throats roaring volcanically.

In the 2nd round, they tore into one another yet again like fiends, though Dempsey was a bit more cautious, crouching and ducking the rights. Firpo had fresh confidence, showing courage and ferocity. A Dempsey bone-crushing right into the ribs turned the tide, and Firpo hung on for dear life, until decked twice more and out. Firpo went down like a cow hit on the head with a mallet. He rolled over at the count of eight, but still was full length on the canvas at the count of ten.

They crowded 20 ordinary rounds of fighting into four minutes. "This writer never gazed at a more sensational struggle than Dempsey and Firpo put up. It was fierce from start to finish." No two experts could agree on the actual number of times Dempsey pounded Firpo to the canvas in the 1st round, so fast and furious the fighting was.

The *Binghamton Press,* reporting the Associated Press version, said it was 3 minutes 57 seconds of the most furious fighting ever recorded, packed full of action. The challenger was floored at least seven times. Dempsey was near defeat on two occasions. The champ was sent crashing through the ropes and was battered to his knees.

More action was crammed into the 2 rounds than most 15-round fights. The crowd witnessed an elemental, gripping, nerve-shaking battle between two great, lion-hearted fighting men to whom the word quit was unknown. They fought fast and hard, to win, and would not stop unless one or the other was out cold. The vast majority of the 85,000 fans believed Firpo when he said he would be back.

Retired lightweight champ Jack McAuliffe, who predicted a Firpo victory, said he was wrong by only one blow. He was so close to being right that his opinion was vindicated. Going through the ropes actually saved Dempsey, for if he simply had rebounded off of them and been hit again, he might have been knocked out. "Dempsey had a chance to revive while he was being pushed back into the ring and if he had been forced to do his reviving inside the ropes he would not have survived."

Firpo was a great fighter, with a great heart, and only his lack of experience cost him. He fought all the time, though. He came up fighting instead of covering up, and he fought savagely.

McAuliffe criticized that the referee allowed Dempsey to hover close to Firpo when he was down. "Once, I believe, the referee allowed Dempsey to remain too close to Firpo. The rules require a fighter after a knockdown to go to his corner or at least five paces away from his opponent, but once Dempsey cracked the South American before he had a chance to get himself in a fighting position."

McAuliffe admitted that Dempsey proved himself to be a great fighting machine, with a magnificent heart. "I do not believe that Dempsey knew what he was doing after the first punch of the fight, a right to the jaw, knocking him to one knee. He fought through the whole round on instinct and it was proven that he didn't know what he was doing when he hit Firpo twice after the gong rang." In conclusion, it was "one of the greatest fights I have ever seen."

For the *Brooklyn Citizen*, William Granger said it had been a thrilling slugfest. It was expected to be a Battle of the Ages, and it did not disappoint. It was a modern champion pitted against a warrior of the stone ages. However, Dempsey fought as much on the stone-age style as Firpo. It was an out-and-out battle between two prehistoric giants, the greatest thriller ever seen. The champ had plenty of anxious moments.

Instead of stepping around Firpo and avoiding his right, Dempsey plunged in headfirst, and more than once Firpo landed his right solidly. Jack fought as if he had no fear of the right, and as a result, there were seconds in the 1st round when Firpo looked like a winner.

Regarding fouls, Granger said Dempsey tore at Firpo when he was down and landed a blow on his arm as he was in the process of rising at four. Referee Gallagher took no notice of it. On more than one occasion, Dempsey hit on the break as well.

Though Dempsey decked Firpo multiple times in the 1st round, the biggest thrill was when Firpo's right sent Jack toppling out of the ring onto the heads of some of the scribes.

The count reached five by the time Dempsey got back into the ring. Firpo rushed and pinned him against the ropes, banging away at his head with his right. It looked like there was going to be a new champion.

But the terrific punching that Firpo had taken already in the stomach probably had taken some of the zip from his punches, and Dempsey, by rolling his head and putting up his left glove to his head, managed to break the force of Firpo's wallops. As Firpo stepped in, Jack landed his right under the heart and Firpo immediately clinched. They wrestled over to Firpo's corner, and Dempsey landed three left uppercuts to the chin as the bell rang to end the 1st round.

Although blows to the jaw sent Firpo to the floor several times in the 1st round, actually, the body punches made the knockdowns possible. They weakened the giant.

In the 2nd round, both came out surprisingly fresh. Dempsey worked to the side of Firpo instead of plunging in head on, and decked him with stomach and head blows. Firpo tried to clinch, but a left hook to the jaw sent him down and out. Firpo came to in a few minutes, and left the ring.

The fight proved that Dempsey was hitting just as hard as ever, and could take a lot of punishment, too. But it also was not hard to realize why a highly skilled veteran like Gibbons might be able to last 15 rounds with him. Dempsey's style was crude. He was quicker on his feet than Luis but did not show much more skill than Firpo, who showed almost none. Dempsey won because he could hit faster and harder, especially in close. Still, Firpo had him in more trouble than ever before.

The *New York Daily News'* James Crusinberry said it was the best fight of modern times. If ever there was a better fight, it was back in the dark ages when man was a beast. The crowd was all but in a state of bedlam. A left to the jaw ended the fight. Dempsey's fighting instinct nearly cost him his championship. If Firpo had landed his right once more, he possibly would have been champion. Firpo was down six times in the 1st round. Once, the giant barely was able to rise at nine. But he rose, grit his teeth, and fired his clubbing right.

The wild-bull moniker was no misnomer. Firpo was a mad man. He swung his mighty right, decked Dempsey, once clear through the ropes into the laps of newspaper men. It looked like the end, but he crawled back and re-entered the ring at about 7. He was distressed, held in desperation, weathered out the round and almost staggered to his corner.

The throng was in an uproar between rounds. Men called out and implored Jack to be careful. Firpo's friends smiled. They believed he had weathered the storm and was on his way to victory.

However, the bell for the 2nd round came, and in less than a minute Dempsey showed that he was a real champion. He had collected himself. Kearns was not excited, but acted as if nothing had happened. Dempsey had regained his composure and poise, and his head had cleared. He rushed and landed, and ducked nicely whenever Firpo fired his right. Dempsey's powerful left on the point of the chin ended matters.

Dempsey knew it was over, stepped over to a neutral corner, and waited until the count had concluded. He then helped carry the giant to his corner.

Luis had fooled the experts, for he was a much greater man than expected. He was game, took almost as much as Willard did, but got up and knocked the champ down and out of the ring.

Believing that he had the battle won, Dempsey had been a bit careless. Firpo's right wallops were ferocious and very powerful. Few could take one of his rights on the chin and survive. Those who saw the fight never would forget it, for it had been an epochal event.

Harry Newman of the *New York Daily News* said Dempsey still was the champion, "but oh, boy! What a tough time he had in retaining his title against the plunging, rip-tearing Bull of the Pampas." Nothing like this fight ever had been staged. It was one of the fastest fights ever. Luis showed all of his wonderful hitting ability and proved beyond any question that he could take a sock and come back. He showed no fear. He was down six times (actually, seven) in the 1st round, but up and after Dempsey like a mad bull. Dempsey still had his wallop. Firpo was not disgraced. When he left, he received as big an applause as the champ did. Few agreed on the number of knockdowns.

The *Brooklyn Daily Times*' J. J. Wood said the Argentine Mauler was no setup. He took a terrific lacing, rose from the canvas, and knocked Dempsey through the ropes. Dempsey proved his right to the heavyweight crown. It was the most sensational 1st round in history, with both down and nearly out. Dempsey's panther-like strides quickly carried him right to Firpo, and the action was almost too fast for the eye to follow. It was a real battle, and both were on the edge.

Former world welterweight champion Jack Britton said experience and condition enabled Dempsey to win. Dempsey proved that he could take it as well as dish it out. He took it all right – took it all and came back looking for more. Firpo's right could drop anyone, but his lack of boxing knowledge was a weakness against such a master as Dempsey. He failed to take the full benefit of the count on several occasions. Still, he was dangerous, and always would be.

Westbrook Pegler said the two fighters rushed from their corners, came together like two wild locomotives, and brawled, stumbled, fell, got up, and flung their huge mitts about until Firpo went down, powerless to arise again. Everyone was satisfied that they got their money's worth. The cold white lights illuminated it all.

Dempsey began the fight with a hurricane sweep as if the bell had released a spring. "Then the knockdowns came so fast that it was almost impossible to follow the swirl of the combat. The eye seemed too slow to receive the swift changes as first one man went down and then the other."

After receiving all of this punching and many jarring trips to the floor, Firpo tore back with the blind bravery of a jungle beast fighting to the death. He banged Dempsey out of the ring with a series of blows and a final smash on the chin which sent him hurtling backward over the second strand of the ropes clear out of the ring into press row.

Dempsey clambered back, reaching upward to his feet, "to grasp the lower rope and pull himself onto the floor." Kearns was in the corner on the top step, his face as white as snow. Firpo again rushed, and Jack went back to the ropes, but he survived.

In the 2nd round, Dempsey tore in and soon had Firpo on his back for a six-count. Luis drove a couple of rights to the body, but Dempsey was swifter and the cleaner hitter and landed a left and right to the chin that finished it.

Afterwards, the familiar black-and-gold checkered bathrobe, with royal purple trimming, was flung over Firpo's shoulders. Jack grabbed his victim's red glove to shake hands.

Robert Edgren said it was the most furious and terrific battle ever fought, replete with heavy hitting. The champion's crown was in danger when he was knocked out of the ring. It lasted only 1 round and 57 seconds, but there was more real fighting than the old-timer used to see in 40 rounds. Although Firpo was down many more times, Dempsey never before came so close to being whipped. Once he was on the floor from Firpo's terrific flailing right, and once he was knocked through the ropes and out of the ring into the lap of Kid McPartland, one of the judges.

Dempsey reeled under the mad bull's furious attack. Firpo threw right after right into the body and jaw. "It is lucky for Dempsey that he can take it." However, Dempsey showed the "fiercest, the fastest and most relentless attack ever let loose by a champion."

From the first bell, Dempsey leaped at Firpo like a flash. They fired blows back and forth, primarily Dempsey's left hook vs. Firpo's right. "There was no questioning Firpo's speed, but Dempsey was lightning unleashed." Dempsey threw away all his skill and relied upon the sudden fury of his attack. He matched punch for punch and found a man as strong, dangerous, and game as himself. Firpo went down multiple times, but fought back like an enraged wildcat, dropping Dempsey twice (actually thrice).

In the 2nd round, Dempsey hit the body and decked him with a right to the chin. They slugged some more, until a couple Dempsey lefts decked Firpo for the ten-count. Firpo was beaten, but "no man ever went down to defeat with more glory."

Damon Runyon said that each time Dempsey decked the Wild Bull of the Pampas, Firpo staggered to his feet, punch-drunk, glassy-eyed, reeling, and fought back. 85,000 men and women were on their feet screaming. It was the wildest, maddest flurry of fists ever seen, in a brawling, crazy, thrilling struggle. There was more thrill in the two times Firpo put Dempsey down than in all the times Dempsey put Firpo down. That was because when Firpo fell it was the expected, but when Dempsey fell, it was shocking.

They started the fight by brawling away, Firpo with his right and Dempsey with his left hook. A left hook sent Firpo to the floor. Firpo not only rose but met Dempsey's attack swinging. Luis tried to clinch, but Dempsey was as strong as a wolf, shook himself free, and ripped and tore. The knockdowns came so rapidly that it was difficult to keep track of them. The timekeeper was almost constantly out of his chair shrieking the count. Men and women were besides themselves with excitement and blood-lust. "Kill him, Jack! Kill him!" roared some. Others sent sympathy Firpo's way.

Firpo went down over and over again but kept getting up and fighting with grim determination. After every knockdown, Dempsey would walk behind the fallen man, and before getting up, Firpo would look around to locate Dempsey. Firpo rushed and hurled his fists blindly, desperately. His body reeled, shook, and slumped, absorbing great punishment.

After suffering a brutal beating and going down several times, just when he seemed to be punched silly, Firpo suddenly let go with a chopping right flush to the chin. Firpo blazed away with new strength, and the crowd started roaring for him. He clipped Dempsey on the chin with his right and the champ went down. At first there was gasping silence, and then a wolf-yell of humans scenting blood.

Firpo clubbed away with blind fury. One of the wild clubbing smashes hit Dempsey on the chin and he went back through the ropes, clear out of the ring. When Dempsey hauled himself back into the ring, he was the cool, experienced fighter who, finding himself in momentary trouble, steadied himself as Firpo tore in on a mad attack until the bell rang.

Dempsey looked dazed. He seemed unsteady as he walked to his corner. Kearns worked over him, babbling in his ear.

At the start of the 2nd round, Dempsey's head was clear. Firpo came tearing in, hands flying. Dempsey quietly moved around him, then clipped him with a hard left hook. A clinch, and grinding, Dempsey clipped him with a short, sharp left hook, and Firpo slumped down.

Firpo rose immediately and rushed in. Kearns and Benjamin shrieked, "Wipe off those gloves!" They wanted the resin dust to be wiped off, for it was considered dangerous. But referee Johnny Gallagher never had a chance to do it.

Dempsey moved in swiftly, head bobbing, like a rattlesnake about to strike. At close quarters, Dempsey cut him down. A left hook to the jaw, followed by a right chop to the jaw settled Firpo, who floundered to the canvas like a pole-axed bull, blood trickling in a tiny stream from his mouth and nose.

Firpo had made a gallant stand, while no champion ever demonstrated better ability to come back after fierce punishment than Dempsey. His title seemed about to be lost as he hung over the ropes in the 1st round. Firpo had a great chance to win at that point. Even while absorbing heavy blows, Dempsey would not be denied. He had the strength of mind and body that made him king. "No one who saw the fight tonight will ever look on Jack Dempsey again as other than a high class ring man, a real champion." Dempsey proved he could take them, and there never again would be any doubt about it. Few could have survived the smashes he received on the ropes; Firpo firing with all of his weight and strength with blows to the head and chin in his berserk-like fury.

General opinion was that Firpo proved he had courage, spirit, and power, and could whip anyone else other than Dempsey.

Ring Lardner said there were so many knockdowns that he lost count. Firpo proved he could take it. "He took it and took it plenty and come back for more, and got it." No living man could take what he took and keep going.

Dempsey proved he could take it too. "Jack was on the receiving end of four or five of the most murderous blows ever delivered in a prize ring, but he come back after each one and fought all the harder." Even after sent out of the ring, he quickly climbed back in without help.

Between the 1st and 2nd rounds, Kearns and Benjamin asked Dempsey "as a personal favor to not leave himself quite so exposed." Jack did so in the 2nd round. He kept his head low and covered up, but still flayed away with both hands, with the goal of getting Firpo as quickly as possible, and he accomplished it.

Heywood Broun said Dempsey saved his crown in the greatest heavyweight battle in history. The champ sailed into his man at the sound of the bell, and proceeded to knock Firpo down six times with blows so short and fast they hardly could be seen.

Then Firpo landed a right behind the ear and Dempsey went to his knees. He was up quickly and defiantly as if to indicate he only slipped. The next time, Firpo's great swinging right which moved in a circle like a scythe of death toppled Jack, sweeping him off his feet and tumbling heels over head across the middle rope. He hung horizontal for a split second, then "fell upon the heads of the front row of sporting writers."

Dempsey's recovery in the next round was remarkable. He came back, and Firpo did not. Dempsey was by no means gun-shy. He charged in close and whaled away with both hands. Firpo went down almost immediately. He rose, and Dempsey dropped him again, down and out.

Broun said the fight proved that Dempsey had not lost his punch, but that Gibbons lasted simply because he had waged a defensive fight, intent on staying the limit. Against a fighter ready to struggle toe to toe, Dempsey could give and take the mightiest of knockout punches and win.

Dempsey removed all concerns. He was the same old relentless man-killer that had smashed Willard to the canvas. And in defeat, Firpo gained glory and prestige as one of the most dangerous of all title challengers.

The *Brooklyn Daily Eagle*'s W. C. Vreeland agreed that it was the greatest ring battle ever; just a whirlwind of blows. Dempsey was a super fighter. Firpo carried a bludgeon in his right, while Dempsey had the hammer of Thor in both fists, fighting equally well with big power in both hands. They wore five-ounce padded gloves.

Dempsey was a ruthless and relentless destroyer. With his pile-driving blows, he put to shame those who said he had lost his punch after his merry-go-round with Gibbons.

Folks who saw it would remember the battle to their dying days. It was a tornado of crashing blows. They fought with the ferocity of animals garbed in the form of men. Jack fought fast, furiously, and mercilessly. They had the strength of gorillas, throwing blows of such force that any one of them could have ended the battle on the spot. It was a wonder that their bones did not snap under the strain of the shock. Each man for a time was able to stand up under the pounding, and both went down. It was no boxing match. It was a fight only. No time was wasted in sparring or feeling each other out. It was rip, tear, and smash from the start. Dempsey's blows were shorter, more compact, and had such destructive force that he dropped a strong 216 ½ -pound man with relative ease.

Firpo started the fight with a right on the chin as Dempsey rushed toward him and his knee hit the floor for a moment. After Luis had been dropped three times, Firpo keeled Dempsey over the second time. Then, after being all but counted out, Firpo knocked Dempsey through the ropes.

The bout was too fast and furious for any real boxing. Dempsey's ability to step in close and fight at short range gave him the advantage. Firpo could not cope with the short hooks. He only could fight at long range with his swinging right that curved in its flight like a boomerang.

In the 2nd round, two short hooks to the jaw, and a left and right in quick succession knocked Firpo out.

Dempsey had proven his merit and mettle. When he knocked out Carpentier, many said he simply was too big for him. Here, he was 24 pounds the smaller man, but still won quickly by knockout.

Afterwards, the crowd was pop-eyed, speechless, and spellbound with excitement. Corbett jumped into the ring and congratulated Dempsey.

Firpo said he would be ready to fight for the title again in another year. He noted that he was the first man to deck Dempsey since he had become champion, and he came close to winning the championship.

Charles Schweiger, official timekeeper, said Firpo was floored five times in the 1st round. He was wrong.

Jimmy De Forest said if he had trained Firpo, he would have won. "He has the stuff."

The *Port Chester Daily Item* said Dempsey was the greatest heavyweight champion ever. He showed his true fighting spirit as well as mental power when in peril. He was everything that a real champion should be. He not only showed his hitting ability but his true colors when in danger. Those who wondered how he would fare if forced to "take it" had their answer.

He was struck by terrible rights, delivered by a man who slashed out savagely, with killing instincts fully aroused. Dempsey showed his class and brain, thinking clearly when in danger. The efficient way he went to work in the 2nd round proved that he had recovered completely. He simply could not be denied. "Although it lasted but two rounds, consensus of opinion has it that it was one of the greatest fights in the history of the game."

This author opined that most likely, no one on Earth could beat Dempsey, including Harry Wills. "[U]nless Harry Wills springs a big surprise…Dempsey will remain king of the heavies for a while yet."[1304]

The next day, Carlos Vega insisted that Dempsey should have been disqualified when newspapermen helped him back into the ring.[1305]

Sid Sutherland also said Firpo was robbed and Dempsey should have been disqualified. He claimed that the films had been doctored. He indicted Dempsey on five counts: 1. Dempsey scored his first knockdown by hitting on the breakaway from a clinch, when Firpo turned to see what the referee had ordered. 2. Dempsey rarely stepped away from the downed man, which also was a violation of New York boxing rules. 3. He three times hit Firpo before he had arisen. 4. After being knocked into the press seats,

> Dempsey never could have reentered the ring unaided. I saw two men lift him to the edge of the platform outside the ropes. And the 'powers that prevail' in Gotham have scissored this shameful scene from the moving pictures. … Since no one, the rules command, must help a boxer back into the battle ground, Firpo should have won right there.

5. At the end of the 1st round, after the bell rang, after Firpo had dropped his hands and started for his corner, Dempsey deliberately hooked him on the chin with his left.

Sutherland said Dempsey was a marvelous fighter, but he also was a savage who engaged in reprehensible, disgraceful behavior in the ring.[1306]

In subsequent days, Davis Walsh reported that William Muldoon said Dempsey could have been disqualified *if* really helped back into the ring by those at ringside. A fighter had to return to the ring through his own power. "As soon as Dempsey went out of the ring, the referee should have rushed to the ropes and warned the men in the press row that they should not aid the fighter under pain of his disqualification."

Yet, Walsh said,

> The writer is not at all certain that Dempsey was intentionally aided, if at all, by those at the ringside. With 192 pounds of athlete tumbling suddenly down on you there is bound to be some confusion and the chances are that the natural movements of those trying to escape an unwelcome burden contributed to Dempsey's efforts to arise. Just a flurry of arms and legs and the next instant the champion was righting himself on the platform outside the ropes. A moment more and he crawled through.

[1304] *Brooklyn Standard Union, Buffalo Enquirer, Buffalo Commercial, Buffalo Times, Buffalo Courier, Binghamton Press, Yonkers Herald, Brooklyn Citizen, New York Daily News, Brooklyn Daily Times, Brooklyn Daily Eagle, Port Chester Daily Item,* September 15, 1923.
[1305] *New York Daily News, Chicago Tribune,* September 16, 1923.
[1306] *Rochester Democrat and Chronicle,* September 17, 1923.

All of this occurred within five seconds by the time-keeper's watch. Surely the champion could not have been hurt as badly as some accounts of the fight would have it.[1307]

The films do not show whether reporters pushed Dempsey back into the ring. Either way, it is irrelevant. He had no control over what they did. More likely, it was more a matter of them holding their hands up and out to block Dempsey as he fell in their laps, and they wanted him to get off of them (and their typewriters), putting their hands out to catch or push him off of them in a natural self-preservation reaction, and he was only too happy to oblige quite quickly. Clearly, though, the films show him re-enter the ring on his own, and he stood up on his own quite quickly.

Ultimately, even assuming they did anything, Dempsey was not and should not have been penalized for the acts of those over whom he had no power or control. It was not as if his own seconds helped him. He could not be charged with or responsible for the independent actions of ringside observers. On the films, Dempsey can be seen climbing back through the ropes and re-entering the ring under his own power almost immediately after being knocked out of the ring. So, it is questionable whether he had help at all. Several writers said he did not receive any help. Even if he did, it likely was of negligible assistance, given how quickly he re-entered the ring. Taking his time might have been wiser. But some love to make controversy when there is none because it makes for good copy.

Some later claimed that Dempsey took more than ten seconds to get back into the ring when he was punched/pushed out. However, most noted that it was well within 10 seconds. Some reporters said it was five or six seconds, which is consistent with what the films show.

Others criticized that the neutral corner rule was not observed. Neither fighter was consistent in returning to a neutral corner after knockdowns. Clearly, this rule was only loosely followed/observed in that era. According to some, the rule was in effect, but neither fighter obeyed it, and the referee almost never attempted to enforce it. The purpose of the rule was to ensure that a fighter could rise completely before being struck again, to help prevent him from being hit while still down. Even the original Queensberry rules required a fighter scoring a knockdown to return to his own corner. Over the years, referees have become stricter in the neutral corner rule's enforcement; but back then, not so much.

Dempsey did not hit Firpo while he was down, although he often hit him immediately after he rose.

Many overlooked what happened at the beginning of the bout. Dempsey began the fight by attacking with a long hook that missed and Firpo countered with a right that momentarily dropped Dempsey, his left knee touching the canvas. Jack instantly sprang back up into a clinch, and the referee did not count.

[1307] *Cedar Rapids Gazette, Buffalo Enquirer,* September 18, 1923.

There clearly is a fast edit at the point Dempsey dropped down to the canvas, for the next moment he is in a clinch. The edit to Dempsey in a clinch partially masks the knockdown. It is unclear whether this moment was intentionally edited out, or deteriorated over time due to the poor nitrate film quality, or there was a bright photo flash, or someone blocked the camera, etc. But Firpo actually scored the first knockdown.

There also is missing footage/a fast edit on the first knockdown scored by Dempsey, when he might have hit on a break, as some claimed. However, the notion of "Protect yourself at all times" most certainly prevailed in this era, and in this fight. But some argued that clean break rules, if in effect, meant that there should be no punching on breaks. Yet, Dempsey appeared to have hit Firpo immediately *after* the break, and if so, Firpo foolishly failed to protect himself.

Several reporters noticed when Dempsey went down to his hands for a brief moment later on in the round, after scoring several knockdowns. Some neglected to note that Dempsey scored a couple more knockdowns after that, prior to getting knocked out of the ring. There were no further knockdowns in the 1st round after Dempsey went out of the ring.

Dempsey clearly hit Firpo after the bell, though he might have been so dazed and the crowd so loud that he did not hear the bell. Yet, Firpo and the referee heard it.

Regardless of the controversies, the fight made Dempsey legendary. It had been one of the most brutal and entertaining championship bouts in history. Certainly, no other filmed heavyweight championship bout had been as entertaining. Dempsey clearly had been the superior fighter on the inside, where he did most of his damage.

Explaining his loss, writers cited one or more of several alleged Firpo deficiencies, including lack of: experience, left-hand development, overall boxing skill and generalship, defense, and/or inside game.

Harry Newman said the moving pictures were exhibited starting the very next day. The pictures showed a lot of things not noticed before, but by the same token, hid many things the fans knew happened but were not portrayed.

Some wondered whether Dempsey should have been disqualified for assistance in getting back into the ring. "The pictures show Dempsey going through the ropes, but for some reason they do not show him coming back. Now, why is it that there seems to be a cut in the pictures at that particular point?" There was a blank in the reel after he went into the arms of spectators. It was odd that the camera caught the rest of the round, but strange not to show how he got back into the ring. The pictures also did not show when Dempsey hit on the break at one point.

Newman said the pictures showed that Dempsey ignored the rules and neglected several times to go to a neutral corner when he knocked Firpo down. The referee paid no attention to the infractions. Dempsey was permitted to stand almost on top of Firpo. Once, it appeared that Dempsey stepped in and hit Firpo before he fully regained his feet.

In truth, the camera framing simply was not wide enough. The cameraman should have shifted to the left, to catch it all, but when he went out of the ring, Dempsey went out of the picture just off frame to the left, so it is hard to tell what happened, though Dempsey can be seen crawling back through the ropes unassisted. But there could have been an edit, too. It is interesting though that the first knockdown that Dempsey scored, potentially on or just after a break, was truncated. Such led to some suspicions about the editing.

William Kid McPartland, who was one of the judges for the fight, said nobody helped Dempsey back into the ring. Jack landed on top of him, so he ought to know. McPartland tried to swerve as the champ came through, but before he could get out of the way, the champ's right hand struck him on the nose. The rest of his body landed on the judge's ledge, breaking his fall. From that position, Dempsey grabbed the lower rope and swung himself back into the ring. McPartland insisted that no one helped Dempsey back into the ring, though he thought the champ was in bad shape as he scrambled back. Hence, from his perspective, the press was generating a false controversy.[1308]

Some writers claimed that the newsmen indeed pushed Dempsey up, in part in self-protection for themselves. Either way, that was not his fault, and he had no control over their actions. He is the one who climbed back in, and if there was any assistance, it simply would have been a mere push from seated ringside writers upon whom he fell, who were trying to get him off of them. The *Brooklyn Standard Union* wrote, "They shoved his shoulders upward, his gloved hands seized the top rope, his feet went over the one below, and he was in the ring again."

Firpo had been badly underrated. He almost won. Dempsey was "not invulnerable, but he was a faster, sharper, harder hitter than Fitzsimmons at his best." He could slay anyone he could hit. He was a marvel, with an "unprecedented constitutional combination of speed, heart, power, precision, fighting instinct, endurance, butcher-like surgical coolness, a hair-trigger thinker, the poetry of graceful execution, the impulse of the brute with the scientific technique of the artist." Dempsey was Firpo's master in every way. Yet, Firpo always would have a chance with everyone, because of his toughness, gameness, and hard punch.

Dempsey accepted the plaudits of a delirious public which thoroughly enjoyed the thriller. Fans cheered Firpo as well. Folks said Dempsey and Firpo had fought the greatest heavyweight battle in history.

The day after the fight, according to the *New York Daily News*, Firpo said he was defeated legally "by an adversary who is today invincible." In the 1st round, the fight was a toss-up. "I had Mr. Dempsey out on his feet, and I thought that I would win, but he is too great for me today. Later, perhaps…" He bore few marks. His lips were cut inside, his right cheek swollen, and blood still trickled from his nose from time to time. The Firpo team had no excuses to offer.

In another interview, according to the *Brooklyn Standard Union*, Luis said,

> I had a very square deal from the American public. It was a great surprise to me. Everyone treated me in the fairest manner, but I think the referee made a mistake. That was when I knocked Dempsey out of the ring and again when he hit me before I got to my feet in the first round. When we went to the center of the ring for instructions the referee said, "Look here, gentlemen, if any one is knocked down the man on his feet must go to a neutral corner." Dempsey did not do that.

Of course, Firpo did not go to a neutral corner either.

[1308] *New York Daily News*, September 16, 1923.

Firpo thought he was rushed into the Dempsey fight, and probably needed a bit more experience.[1309]

The *Daily News* reported that Dempsey would receive $475,000 and Firpo $100,000. There were 80,000 paid admissions for a gate close to $1,200,000.

Dempsey had a left eye blackened and puffed, but otherwise was all right. With his shiner, he was meeting with all comers at the Hotel Belmont. "Everybody loves a winner." Jack said,

> A big tough fellow, that Firpy, and don't you think he can't hit. We had a great fight, and while I might have been a little careless in that first round, when I thought that I had Luis on the run, there never was a time during the fight that I did not feel that I would get him. That right smack to the chin which Firpo laid in during the first round probably did not make me look so good, but we were both shooting with everything on the ball. It was a good sock, and while I was a little dazed the blow did not hurt me.

Jack said he had decided before the fight to go get the big fellow right away. There was no sense in waiting and laying back with a rough guy like that, figuring that getting it over with as soon as possible was the best course of action. "He proved to be a game fellow and never stopped coming, no matter how often I knocked him down."

When asked how he felt after being knocked through the ropes, Jack chuckled,

> Well, not so good. I was somewhat humiliated, but not hurt. The punch with which Luis sent me through the ropes was more of a shove. ... They tell me that I was pretty bad when I got back there after that flop, but I didn't think so. I mixed it with Firpo when I got back in and told Kearns when I went to my corner at the bell that I was going to go out and get Luis in the next round.

[1309] *Brooklyn Standard Union*, September 16, 1923.

Jack said he had nothing but admiration for Firpo. He was willing to give him another chance.[1310]

George Underwood criticized that Referee Gallagher had allowed Dempsey to stand over Firpo instead of retiring to the furthest corner as the rules required. The referee "should have ceased the count, ordered Dempsey to retire to the corner and not resumed the count until Dempsey obeyed the instructions." Underwood further criticized that despite being observed throughout the world, the rule "has been allowed to be ignored in contests in this city." Underwood wanted the commission to compel referees to follow the rules strictly.[1311]

However, Underwood said Dempsey's act of cuffing Firpo after the bell was excusable in that he did not hear it amid the din and bedlam. "That offense the referee rightly overlooked."

The *Brooklyn Daily Eagle* reported that Dempsey would have to pay $498,840 in taxes on the $800,000 in fight profits he earned that year. He likely earned even more than his fight purses, in view of his vaudeville, exhibitions, and motion picture contracts. New York State income tax was just 3%.[1312]

The day after the fight, on the 15th, at the Police Games, Dempsey, along with Kearns and Rickard, met New York Governor Al Smith. Governor Smith said, "It is my pleasure to greet you now and congratulate you on your victory." Dempsey replied, "On the contrary, it is my pleasure to congratulate the greatest Governor of New York." Smith said, "I am sorry I was not present to see you win." Police Commissioner Enright shook hands with Dempsey as well. Jack asked, "What should I do here?" The commissioner replied, "You can do anything you please. We won't deny you anything, especially after your exhibition last night. Will you be our guest and sit alongside the Governor?" Jack responded, "Fine. There's quite a crowd out here to-day."

The crowd cheered for the champion, who smiled and bowed with his blackened left eye. Motion picture men filmed him beside the governor. At Kearns' suggestion, Jack got into an open auto for a trip around the field to let the crowd "meet" him. He complied, sitting in the car with the Police Commissioner. The cheers that Jack encountered from the crowd actually drew tears from his eyes. After he returned to the guests' stand, when called upon for a speech, Jack said, "Hello everybody. I hope you are all as happy as I am." He received more applause.[1313]

Dempsey wrote about the fight. In an article published within a few days of the contest, he said,

> I came out of that fight with the South American slugger gladdened
> by the knowledge that no matter how hard I was hit, no man at this
> time can put me on the floor and keep me there. I took everything

[1310] *New York Daily News*, September 16, 1923.
[1311] *New York Evening Telegram*, September 16, 1923.
[1312] *Brooklyn Daily Eagle*, September 16, 1923.
[1313] *Brooklyn Citizen*, September 16, 1923.

that Firpo could hand out to the jaw and to the body – and that iron chin of mine and that concrete stomach stood up wonderfully against those sledge-hammer drives.

I shall always admit with positive and glad frankness that Firpo hit me harder than any man I have ever faced in the prize ring. The opening punch of the fight, which he landed – a right-hander flush to the point of my chin – came with the speed of a lightning flash and with the concentrated power of dynamite.

When I stood up under the impact I knew right then and there that Firpo could not hammer me into unconsciousness and that it would only be a question of time, if I were fairly careful, before I would put him down and out.

Later in that round, Firpo caught me in an unguarded moment with another right-hander, which landed under my heart. He was racing into me at the time, and every ounce of strength in his body was behind that blow. I thought for a second that his right fist had gone all the way through to my spinal column. But the punch, instead of dropping me, simply shook me up, made me wilder than ever and infinitely more anxious to revenge myself by putting him away in a hurry.

Those who were at the ringside insist that I threw boxing skill and everything else but slugging ability to the four winds, and that I fought very open and seemingly unafraid of any hurt which Firpo could cause with his pile-driving blows. That is probably true. ... Realizing that boxing him would merely prolong the struggle, I decided not to do any boxing, but to step right in and pit my 192 pounds against his 216 and make it the survival of the fittest slugger.

I'll say that Firpo gave [me] the toughest fight of my career, and the most cyclonic action. But I believe in dropping him something like nine times in four minutes, as newspaper reports have it, that I demonstrated I am his master. ...

As matters stand now, only two men loom up as real foemen. One is Harry Wills, the Negro, and the other is Tom Gibbons. I whipped Tommy at Shelby fairly and cleanly, but I whipped him on points alone. ... There are many persons who feel that I cannot put away Gibbons. I have a contrary viewpoint. ...

As far as Wills is concerned:

In all frankness I saw that I never could regard him as a man to be afraid of. Certainly Wills cannot hit with the fury of Firpo, and I don't think he could take the punishment that Firpo took on Friday night. There may be folks who think otherwise. If there is any promoter who has the same viewpoint, who is anxious to match me up, I shall be found ready and willing to meet this "Black Panther" anywhere, any time and over any distance.[1314]

Apparently, the omission in the films after Dempsey was sent out of the ring was not the result of some plot. Hank Olen, photographer for the *New York Daily News*, in his anxiety to get a snappy picture, got his head in the way of the movie camera by standing up in front of it. Hence, his head allegedly was the reason for the break in the films. Also, it appears that some of it was not captured off to the left side as a result of the framing of the camera, and the cameraman failed to shift the camera to the left (if such could have been done).[1315]

The *Daily News* said Dempsey certainly was no gentleman or diplomat in the ring. This writer, after having watched the fight three times, once live and twice on film, saw that after knocking Firpo down, at least twice Dempsey stood within striking distance and knocked him down again as soon as Firpo's knee barely was clear of the floor. "As we understand the rules, Mr. Dempsey should have migrated to a neutral corner and waited there politely until his opponent regained his feet or was counted out." Once, Dempsey socked Firpo on the jaw when Luis turned his head at a word from the referee. Apparently, that sock was not portrayed in the films either. The impetuous champion wanted to fight and punch at all times, on the breaks, as soon as possible after knockdowns, and even after the bell.

The *Daily News'* James Crusinberry said the films proved that Firpo landed 30 blows in the 1st round, about a half dozen on spots that hurt. Any other man probably would have been knocked out. Other wallops landed on the shoulders or were blocked by arms. The champ was hit on the side of the head with a right, and then played defense for ten or fifteen seconds as the giant swung his sledge-hammer right. He swung nine times in a row on the champ, who was backing away, dodging and covering up. The ninth landed with Dempsey backed against the ropes and it knocked or shoved him down into the laps of those at ringside.

Going out of the ring might have helped, because at that moment Firpo still was not done swinging. When he got back into the ring, Jack was able to clinch and hang on, and once more resume the offensive.

Some criticized Referee Johnny Gallagher for allowing Dempsey to strike at Firpo before he was off the floor, and for not making sure he went to a neutral corner. Some said his count, when Dempsey went through the ropes, was slow.[1316]

The next day, Crusinberry said that without knowing Johnny Gallagher's qualifications to referee a contest of such importance, "we believe that in some instances he neglected to enforce the rules to the letter. At the same time, we realize that the combat was most intense and exceptional, probably the most exciting ring battle ever staged, and it is

[1314] *Yonkers Herald*, September 17, 1923.
[1315] *New York Daily News*, September 17, 1923.
[1316] *New York Daily News*, September 17, 1923.

not at all impossible that Mr. Gallagher, like about 85,000 other folk who watched the struggle, was far from normal in mind during that intense period." Meaning, perhaps any referee would have done the same under the exciting, bedlam-like circumstances and frenetic activity. However, "There is no doubt that on at least two occasions Dempsey failed to go to a corner after knocking his opponent down. On one occasion he stood directly over Firpo and clipped him on the jaw the very instant both knees were off the floor."

Yet, Gallagher was consistent. When Firpo decked Dempsey, and knocked him out of the ring, Firpo was not made to go to his corner or step back much further either, attacking right away himself.

Despite Dempsey's written statement saying that he was willing to fight Wills, others quoted him as saying otherwise. Dempsey allegedly said, "When they went into the civil courts and tried to get an injunction preventing my match with Firpo it ended both Mullins and Wills with me." Kearns said they would have nothing to do with Wills or Mullins, owing to their attempt to stop the Firpo fight. When asked if he would fight Wills, Kearns said,

> No! I should say not. Give them a fight after they tried their best to stop Jack's bout with Luis Firpo? Nix. Never. They're through so far as we are concerned. They haven't got a chance. We tried to do business with Mullins and Wills before the Firpo match was made and both of them know it. We were willing enough to fight and it wasn't our fault that no promoter came forward to put it on. They know that too.

Kearns said if Wills was so anxious to fight, he should take on Firpo. He said if he could beat Firpo, "we might talk business with him." However, Kearns predicted that Firpo would beat Wills and knock his brains out. "Jack Dempsey feels about this matter exactly as Kearns does, but it was not discussed too deeply with him. … The champion declares that he won't fight Wills under any circumstances."[1317]

Tex Rickard said the fight films were not tampered with, calling such allegations silly and preposterous. He said that like everyone else, the cameraman was human, and became excited and did not focus on the machines properly when Dempsey fell out of the ring. He also understood that a photographer from a morning paper got in the way of the machine by standing up in front of it in his excitement at that moment, and got a right-hand poke in the nose for butting in. Leon D. Britton took the motion pictures.[1318]

Henry Farrell said, "Dempsey did commit a few minor infractions of the rules, it is true, but they were not serious enough to make him liable for disqualification and when he did transgress the rules it was done at a

[1317] *Binghamton Press*, September 17, 1923.
[1318] *Pittsburgh Daily Post*, September 18, 1923.

time when it was obvious that the champion was groggy and did not know exactly what he was doing."

Dempsey did hit him once before Firpo was entirely erect after a knockdown, once when he punched him after the bell, and Jack also was helped back into the ring by a little push/shove.

However, Farrell said Firpo got the best break when he was given a count of more than 12 seconds early in the 1st round. He was on the floor soon after the fight started, and both the referee and timekeeper each reached the count of ten. In the confusion, the referee thought it was the timekeeper's duty to declare out, and the timekeeper thought vice-versa, and while they were hesitating, Firpo got to his feet and continued, which happened before any of Dempsey's fouls. He easily could and should have been counted out right then and there, according to Farrell. Was this long count also missing or edited from the footage?

William Muldoon said Dempsey had not been given much assistance. He was given a little shove by a newspaperman who was actuated more by the motive to get 192 pounds off him than by the desire to help Dempsey back into the ring.

Farrell agreed that Dempsey fell in such a position that he had little difficulty in squirming around and pulling himself back into the ring *without* help. "Anyone who sat in the narrow seats in the press box would know that no one man or two men could get leverage enough to push close to 200 pounds up over their heads into the ring." The purported controversy was much ado about nothing. Dempsey climbed through the ropes without any functional assistance, as shown on the films.[1319]

In subsequent days, as usual, the final numbers changed and varied, depending on the source. The *Daily News* said 78,011 fans paid $1,070,380 to see the Firpo fight, $530,000 less than the Carpentier fight. More people saw this fight than Dempsey-Carpentier, but they paid less, owing to the restrictive New York laws. It was a record for number of paid admissions at any fight. The State deducted $53,518.40 as its share in taxes.

Many argued that Dempsey should have been disqualified for alleged rules infractions, including failing to go to the furthest corner after each knockdown, that he hit Firpo once before his knee had left the floor (not true), and that he struck him after the bell had rung at the end of the 1st round. Regardless, the New York boxing commission declined to take any action, holding that the referee was the sole arbiter of the contest.

The *Buffalo Courier* reported that Dempsey said he would not fight Wills until Harry beat Firpo and proved his worth.

The *Courier* said Dempsey was careless and overconfident, having decked Firpo so many times that he left himself wide open to his big blows. Dempsey was dazed, stunned, and battered by Firpo's clublike fist. It was a wonder that the champion came back to stand up under further pounding of the same kind, still finish the round fighting, and then to

[1319] *Lebanon Daily News*, September 18, 1923.

come back in the 2nd round and lick Firpo within the first minute of the round, "a thing almost incomprehensible. It makes one believe more and more that Dempsey is the greatest of the heavyweight champions."

This paper said official total paid attendance was 82,228 which generated $1,188,822.80. Another 5,000 were present. It was second to the Carpentier fight, which was $1.6 million. Federal tax of $180,074 was owed, and state tax was $57,197, leaving net receipts of $951,551. Using those numbers, Dempsey would earn $445,808.55.[1320]

Jess Willard said Harry Greb "is the only boxer who has a good chance to win a decision over Jack Dempsey today." He believed that Greb's peculiar style would baffle Dempsey, and he might be able to outpoint him.[1321]

Some reported that slow motion movies of the fight had been taken. Dempsey knocked Firpo down 7 times in the 1st round. Firpo shot eight consecutive punches to Dempsey's jaw, sending him through the ropes into the press benches, head first. The fighters, managers, and the promoter would earn a great deal of money from the films.[1322]

Dempsey and friend Babe Ruth, baseball's biggest name

The *New York Age's* William Clark said Dempsey's victory over Firpo had provoked fresh discussion of Harry Wills' chances with the champion, should he ever be lucky enough to get a fight with him. "The opinion seems to be growing that Wills would have very little chance." He was getting older, was in his 30s, and had brittle hands, breaking his right in his last fight. Harry's biggest asset would be the "killer's instinct." Outside the ring, Wills was gentle and easy-going, but inside, he fought with a will to win as speedily as possible. But Dempsey was the same type of fighter. "Wills is a better boxer than Dempsey and a better in-fighter, but there is no doubt that his chances with the champion are not so good now as they were a year ago."[1323]

Dempsey left New York and headed west.

When the champ stopped off in Salt Lake City, his mom, who greeted him, clapped her hands with glee and chuckled, "Jack, you are still my

[1320] *New York Daily News*, September 18, 1923; *Buffalo Courier*, *Spokane Spokesman-Review*, September 19, 1923.
[1321] *Reading Eagle*, September 20, 1923.
[1322] *Glens Falls Post-Star*, September 21, 1923.
[1323] *New York Age*, September 22, 1923.

boy. I used to lick you, and I bet I still can." With tears in his eyes, Jack assured his wee mother, "You bet you always can."

After his Utah visit, on September 27, Dempsey arrived back in Los Angeles. His arrival was treated like the homecoming of Spartacus or David. Those greeting him in Los Angeles included Teddy Hayes, Jack's brother Joe and sister Elsie, Chuck Riesner and son Dinky Dean, Bull Montana, and others. Jack's shiner was gone and totally healed.

JACK AND THE KID—One of the proudest young fellows at the train yesterday to meet Jack Dempsey was Dinky Dean, son of Chuck Reisner and protege of Charlie Chaplin. You would hardly say he was walking with the champion, although his dad is.

—Illustrated Daily News Photo

(By Pacific & Atlantic) HERO.—Jack Dempsey, conqueror of Firpo, was given great reception by his Los Angeles admirers, who carried him on shoulders from his train to a waiting auto.

Jack said he wanted the world to know, "Firpo's right-hand sock to my chin as the fight opened not only dropped me to my knees, but it had me dizzy and battling by instinct alone during the entire first round." Firpo had a "peculiar right hand." Luis threw his right like a man swinging a sledge-hammer, and "any time he lands you know you are hit."

Regarding that first right, it seemed as if Firpo started it, stopped, and then drove it the rest of the way and it landed. "I did not go down because of being over-balanced from missing him with my left but because of the terrific jar and mingled surprise of the blow." Thereafter, Jack fought on instinct and his mind was blank. "That first blow was not only the hardest Firpo hit me, but it was the hardest I was ever hit in my life. I guess I forgot everything I knew about boxing and began swinging along with Luis. The critics said we fought like a couple of longshoremen in that first round."

Regarding the time he went out of the ring, Dempsey did not know whether he was hit on the chin or the shoulder. "There was a peculiar sensation of flight as I was sailing through the air, but when I landed in the first row of seats I guess it sort of awakened me and I quickly clambered back through the ropes."

Between rounds, his head cleared up quickly, and he was himself again when he went out for the 2nd round.

Jack planned to undergo a minor surgical operation and take a long rest. The operation would be for a minor ailment, more aggravating than serious, though he did not say what it was. "I'm going to eat and drink and sleep for a few weeks. I figure I'm in cold storage until next summer and I'm out to gain all the weight I can." He might do some work at a moving picture studio if Kearns reached an agreement. He did not plan to fight again until 1924. "One thing you can say and that is – there will be no Dempsey-Wills bout."

Ed Frayne said that for the first time since he won the championship, Dempsey had captured the sympathy of the American boxing public. Up until the Firpo fight, the crowds at his fights always were for the challenger. Jack said sentiment changed when he climbed back into the ring, showing his heart.

> Away off, I could hear them shouting, "Come on, Jack!" And I've been hearing it ever since, and I like it. I'm human, just like everyone else. We all like to have others like us. It gets awkward sometimes when I'm hemmed in and can't move until cops rescue me, but I don't mind. I appreciate the good will behind the situation. Tell everybody that I'm grateful and that's right from the heart.

The champ's close friends said he needed a long rest. The strain of two fights within 3 months, and all the training associated with the bouts, had told on him.[1324]

Kearns said he expected a return match with Gibbons in 1924.[1325]

Dempsey-Firpo oil painting by George Bellows

The Firpo fight had been so exciting, one of the most exciting fights in history, that it helped make Jack Dempsey legendary. It was the type of fight that the fans loved, and it increased their admiration of him. It confirmed their feelings about him as an all-time great fighter. He was a devastating puncher, and once again proved that he could take a punch too, whether it was from a 245-pound, heavy, thudding puncher like Willard, a whipping, snapping, cracking puncher like Carpentier, or an explosive, clubbing, overhand puncher like Firpo.

Dempsey had proved that he could win in several different ways, in different kinds of fights, against different kinds of fighters and styles. He had danced around the huge, tall, and long Willard, ducking and rolling, before attacking explosively and relentlessly, and then consistently after the 1st round. He had boxed the clever and fast Miske, carefully selecting his punches before moving in aggressively to drop him with vicious, well-

---

[1324] *Los Angeles Record, Los Angeles Illustrated Daily News, Los Angeles Times, Brooklyn Daily Times,* September 28, 1923; *Los Angeles Express,* September 29, 1923.
[1325] *Los Angeles Express,* September 29, 1923.

placed blows. Against the frisky, power-boxing, tough Brennan, Jack had to use a more consistent, methodical style to wear him down gradually. Against Carpentier, he had been relentless, yet methodical, utilizing a fast pace and aggression with a lot of inside body punching to pressure and wear down his foe fairly quickly. In the Gibbons fight, he proved that he had the endurance to throw a lot of punches, clearly outwork and outgame a very defensively clever boxer who held a lot, and keep him very defensive except in short, very intermittent spurts. Against Firpo, he proved he could duke it out against a bigger, stronger, taller, longer, power-punching fighter. Gameness, heart, toughness, chin, speed, power, conditioning, mixed in with fast footwork and head movement, and the ability to maintain a rapid pace throughout fights all made Dempsey at his best nearly unbeatable as heavyweight champion during these years.

At this point, Jack Dempsey was more popular than ever.

The story continues: *In the Ring With Jack Dempsey - Part III.*

Dempsey and Babe Ruth

Acknowledgments

Thank you to all who have helped me in some way with this book, be it research, photographs, promotion, editing, or general support:

Gregory Speciale

Mike DeLisa

Kurt Noltimier

Jeremy Willett

Barry Deskins

John Ochs

Clay Moyle

Vincent Ciaramella

Lisa Sanchez, Cleveland Public Library

Thomas Hauser

Matt McGrain

Evan Grant

Anthony Reader

Gabriella Kent

Audrey Felderman

Bob Yalen

Sergei Yurchenko

University of Iowa / Interlibrary Loan

Boxrec.com

BoxingForum24.com

Cyberboxingzone.com

Trufanboxing.com

Index

815

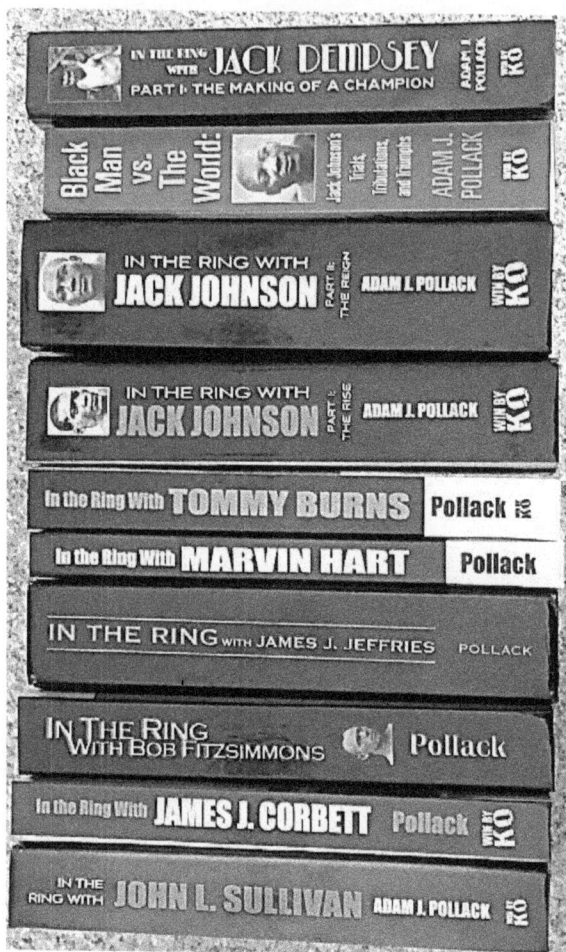

Adam J. Pollack is a professional boxing referee and judge, attorney, publisher, author of the *In the Ring With* series, and member of the Boxing Writers Association of America.

To learn about more boxing books, go to winbykopublications.com.